my Perspectives™

AMERICAN LITERATURE

SAVVAS
LEARNING COMPANY

ISBN-13: 978-0-13-333880-5
ISBN-10:   0-13-333880-0

22 21

Welcome!

*my*Perspectives™ *English Language Arts* is a student-centered learning environment where you will analyze text, cite evidence, and respond critically about your learning. You will take ownership of your learning through goal-setting, reflection, independent text selection, and activities that allow you to collaborate with your peers.

Each unit of study includes selections of different genres—including multimedia—all related to a relevant and meaningful Essential Question. As you read, you will engage in activities that inspire thoughtful discussion and debate with your peers allowing you to formulate, and defend, your own perspectives.

*my*Perspectives *ELA* offers a variety of ways to interact directly with the text. You can annotate by writing in your print consumable, or you can annotate in your digital Student Edition. In addition, exciting technology allows you to access multimedia directly from your mobile device and communicate using an online discussion board!

We hope you enjoy using *my*Perspectives *ELA* as you develop the skills required to be successful throughout college and career.

Authors' Perspectives

*my*Perspectives is informed by a team of respected experts whose experiences working with students and study of instructional best practices have positively impacted education. From the evolving role of the teacher to how students learn in a digital age, our authors bring new ideas, innovations, and strategies that transform teaching and learning in today's competitive and interconnected world.

> "The teaching of English needs to focus on engaging a new generation of learners. How do we get them excited about reading and writing? How do we help them to envision themselves as readers and writers? And, how can we make the teaching of English more culturally, socially, and technologically relevant? Throughout the curriculum, we've created spaces that enhance youth voice and participation and that connect the teaching of literature and writing to technological transformations of the digital age."

Ernest Morrell, Ph.D.

is the Macy professor of English Education at Teachers College, Columbia University, a class of 2014 Fellow of the American Educational Research Association, and the Past-President of the National Council of Teachers of English (NCTE). He is also the Director of Teachers College's Institute for Urban and Minority Education (IUME). He is an award-winning author and in his spare time he coaches youth sports and writes poems and plays. Dr. Morrell has influenced the development of *my*Perspectives in Assessment, Writing & Research, Student Engagement, and Collaborative Learning.

Elfrieda Hiebert, Ph.D.

is President and CEO of TextProject, a nonprofit that provides resources to support higher reading levels. She is also a research associate at the University of California, Santa Cruz. Dr. Hiebert has worked in the field of early reading acquisition for 45 years, first as a teacher's aide and teacher of primary-level students in California and, subsequently, as a teacher and researcher. Her research addresses how fluency, vocabulary, and knowledge can be fostered through appropriate texts. Dr. Hiebert has influenced the development of *my*Perspectives in Vocabulary, Text Complexity, and Assessment.

> " The signature of complex text is challenging vocabulary. In the systems of vocabulary, it's important to provide ways to show how concepts can be made more transparent to students. We provide lessons and activities that develop a strong vocabulary and concept foundation—a foundation that permits students to comprehend increasingly more complex text."

Kelly Gallagher, M.Ed.

teaches at Magnolia High School in Anaheim, California, where he is in his thirty-first year. He is the former co-director of the South Basin Writing Project at California State University, Long Beach. Mr. Gallagher has influenced the development of *my*Perspectives in Writing, Close Reading, and the Role of Teachers.

> " The *my*Perspectives classroom is dynamic. The teacher inspires, models, instructs, facilitates, and advises students as they evolve and grow. When teachers guide students through meaningful learning tasks and then pass them ownership of their own learning, students become engaged and work harder. This is how we make a difference in student achievement—by putting students at the center of their learning and giving them the opportunities to choose, explore, collaborate, and work independently."

> " It's critical to give students the opportunity to read a wide range of highly engaging texts and to immerse themselves in exploring powerful ideas and how these ideas are expressed. In *my*Perspectives, we focus on building up students' awareness of how academic language works, which is especially important for English language learners."

Jim Cummins, Ph.D.

is a Professor Emeritus in the Department of Curriculum, Teaching and Learning of the University of Toronto. His research focuses on literacy development in multilingual school contexts as well as on the potential roles of technology in promoting language and literacy development. In recent years, he has been working actively with teachers to identify ways of increasing the literacy engagement of learners in multilingual school contexts. Dr. Cummins has influenced the development of *my*Perspectives in English Language Learner and English Language Development support.

UNIT 1 Writing Freedom

Words That Shaped a Nation

COMPARE

INDEPENDENT LEARNING

These selections can be accessed via the
Interactive Student Edition.

 **PERFORMANCE-BASED
ASSESSMENT PREP**

 **PERFORMANCE-BASED
ASSESSMENT**

UNIT REFLECTION

 **DIGITAL
PERSPECTIVES**

SCAN FOR
MULTIMEDIA

Use the BouncePage app
whenever you see "Scan
for Multimedia" to access:

• Unit Introduction Videos
• Media Selections/Media Enrichment
• Modeling Videos
• Selection Audio Recordings

Additional digital resources can be found in:

• Interactive Student Edition
• *my*Perspectives+

INDEPENDENT LEARNING

These selections can be accessed via the Interactive Student Edition.

 PERFORMANCE-BASED
ASSESSMENT

UNIT REFLECTION

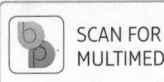

**DIGITAL
PERSPECTIVES**

SCAN FOR MULTIMEDIA

Use the BouncePage app whenever you see "Scan for Multimedia" to access:

- Unit Introduction Videos
- Media Selections/Media Enrichments
- Modeling Videos
- Selection Audio Recordings

Additional digital resources can be found in:

- Interactive Student Edition
- *my*Perspectives+

UNIT 3 Power, Protest, and Change

A Spirit of Reform

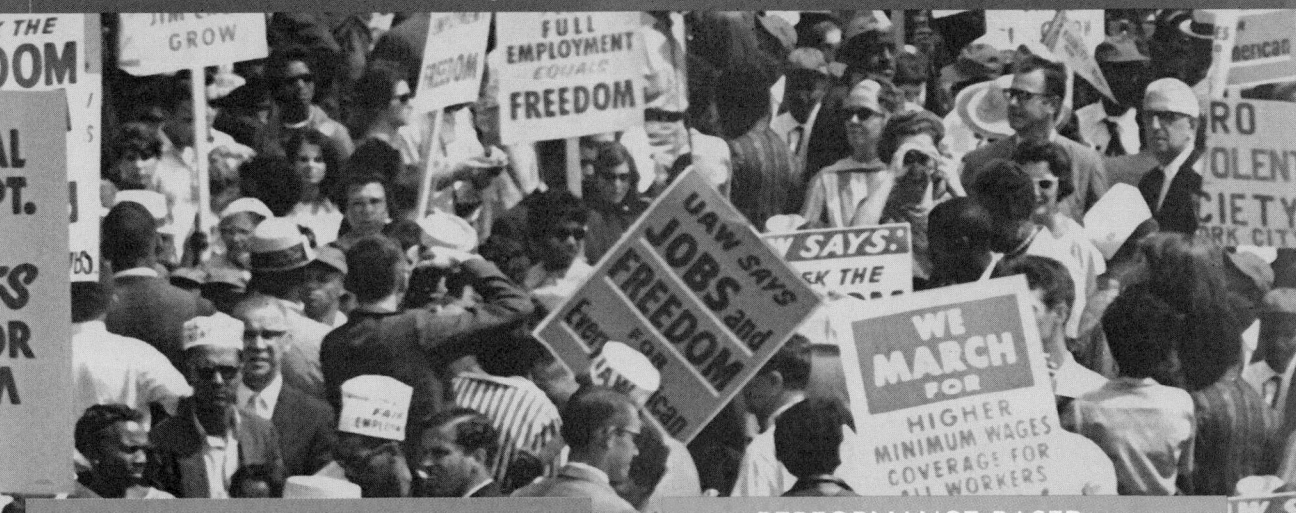

INDEPENDENT LEARNING

These selections can be accessed via the
Interactive Student Edition.

 **PERFORMANCE-BASED
ASSESSMENT PREP**

PERFORMANCE-BASED
ASSESSMENT

UNIT REFLECTION

DIGITAL
PERSPECTIVES

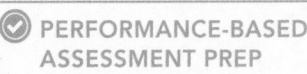 SCAN FOR
MULTIMEDIA

Use the BouncePage app
whenever you see "Scan
for Multimedia" to access:

• Unit Introduction Videos
• Media Selections/Media Enrichment
• Modeling Videos
• Selection Audio Recordings

Additional digital resources can be found in:

• Interactive Student Edition
• *my*Perspectives+

INDEPENDENT LEARNING

These selections can be accessed via the Interactive Student Edition.

 PERFORMANCE-BASED
ASSESSMENT

UNIT REFLECTION

DIGITAL
PERSPECTIVES

 SCAN FOR MULTIMEDIA

Use the BouncePage app whenever you see "Scan for Multimedia" to access:

- Unit Introduction Videos
- Media Selections/Media Enrichment
- Modeling Videos
- Selection Audio Recordings

Additional digital resources can be found in:

- Interactive Student Edition
- *my*Perspectives+

UNIT (5) Facing Our Fears

Victims and Victors

INDEPENDENT LEARNING

MAGAZINE WRITING

What You Don't Know Can Kill You

Jason Daley

POETRY

Runagate Runagate

Robert Hayden

POETRY COLLECTION

1-800-FEAR

Jody Gladding

Bears at Raspberry Time

Hayden Carruth

For Black Women Who Are Afraid

Toi Derricotte

ESSAY

What Are You So Afraid Of?

Akiko Busch

These selections can be accessed via the Interactive Student Edition.

PERFORMANCE-BASED ASSESSMENT PREP

PERFORMANCE-BASED ASSESSMENT

UNIT REFLECTION

DIGITAL PERSPECTIVES

SCAN FOR MULTIMEDIA

Use the BouncePage app whenever you see "Scan for Multimedia" to access:

- Unit Introduction Videos
- Media Selections/Media Enrichment
- Modeling Videos
- Selection Audio Recordings

Additional digital resources can be found in:

- Interactive Student Edition
- *my*Perspectives+

UNIT **6** Ordinary Lives, Extraordinary Tales
The American Short Story

DIGITAL
PERSPECTIVES

 SCAN FOR
MULTIMEDIA

Use the BouncePage app whenever you see "Scan for Multimedia" to access:

- Unit Introduction Videos
- Media Selections/Media Enrichment
- Modeling Videos
- Selection Audio Recordings

Additional digital resources can be found in:

- Interactive Student Edition
- *my*Perspectives+

Interactive Student Edition

myPerspectives is completely interactive because you can work directly in your digital or print Student Edition.

All activities that you complete in your Interactive Student Edition are saved automatically. You can access your notes quickly so that reviewing work to prepare for tests and projects is easy!

Enter answers to prompts right in your digital Notebook and "turn it in" to your teacher.

The in-line annotation tool allows you to practice close reading by highlighting and adding comments about the text.

Interactivities are available for you to complete and submit directly to your teacher.

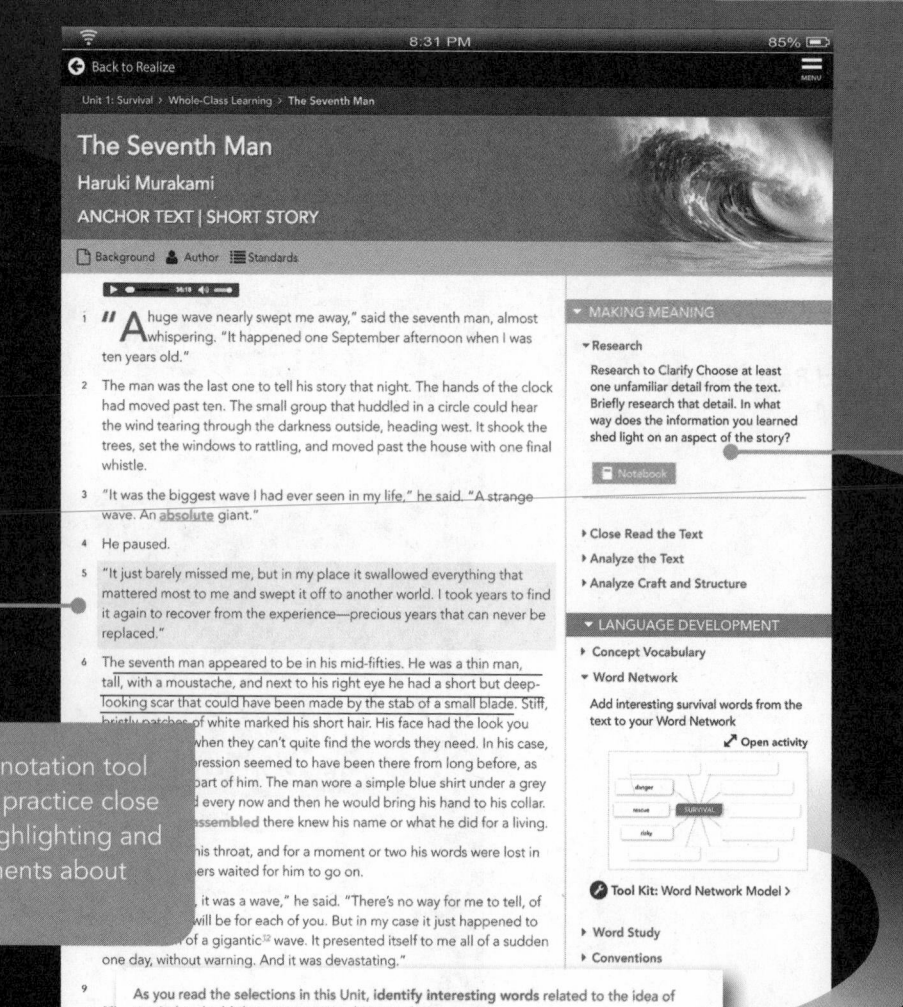

the shops in town lowered their shutters in preparation for the storm. Starting early in the morning, my father and brother went around the house nailing shut all the storm-doors, while my mother spent the day in the kitchen cooking emergency provisions. We filled bottles and canteens with water, and packed our most important possessions in rucksacks[2] for possible evacuation. To the adults, typhoons were an annoyance and a threat they had to face almost annually, but to the kids, removed as we were from such practical concerns, it was just a great big circus, a wonderful source of excitement.

12   Just after noon the color of the sky began to change all of a sudden. There was something strange and unreal about it. I stayed outside on the porch, watching the sky, until the wind began to howl and the rain began to beat against the house with a weird dry sound, like handfuls of sand. Then we closed the last storm-door and gathered together in one room of the darkened house, listening to the radio. This particular storm did not have a great deal of rain, it said, but the winds were doing a lot of damage, blowing roofs off houses and capsizing ships. Many people had been killed or injured by flying debris. Over and over again, they warned people against leaving their homes. Every once in a while, the house would creak and shudder as if a huge hand were shaking it, and sometimes there would be a great crash of some heavy-sounding object against a storm-door. My father guessed that these were tiles blowing off the neighbors' houses. For lunch we ate the rice and omelettes my mother had cooked, waiting for the typhoon to blow past.

13   But the typhoon gave no sign of blowing past. The radio said it had lost momentum[3] almost as soon as it came ashore at S. Province, and now it was moving north-east at the pace of a slow runner. The wind kept up its savage howling as it trie[...] stood on land.

14   Perhaps an hour had gone by with the [...] when a hush fell over everything. All of a [...] could hear a bird crying in the distance. M[...] door a crack and looked outside. The win[...] rain had ceased to fall. Thick, gray clouds [...]

NOTES

This sentence is leading up to an exciting story.

CLOSE READ

ANNOTATE: In paragraph 12, annotate at least four vivid details about the storm. Underline those that compare one thing to another.

QUESTION: What is being compared? What picture does each detail create in the reader's mind?

CONCLUDE: How do these descriptions help you visualize the typhoon?

Typhoons are powerful, scary storms that can do a lot of damage.

Use the close-read prompts to guide you through an analysis of the text. You can highlight, circle, and underline the text right in your print Student Edition.

Respond to questions and activities directly in your book!

THE SEVENTH MAN

WORD NETWORK

Add interesting survival words from the text to your Word Network.

LANGUAGE DEVELOPMENT

Concept Vocabulary

desperate	hallucination	profound
entranced	premonition	meditative

Why These Words? These concept words help to reveal the emotional state of the seventh man. For example, when the wave approaches, the seventh man is *entranced*, waiting for it to attack. After the wave hits, the seventh man believes he sees his friend K. in the wave and claims that this experience was no *hallucination*. Notice that both words relate to experiences that occur only in the mind of the seventh man.

1. How does the concept vocabulary sharpen the reader's understanding of the mental or emotional state of the seventh man?
   These words describe the scared feelings people feel during a storm.

2. What other words in the selection connect to this concept?
   ominous, overcome, swirling

Practice

⊙ Notebook The concept vocabulary words appear in "The Seventh Man."

1. Use each concept word in a sentence that demonstrates your understanding of the word's meaning.

2. Challenge yourself to replace the concept word with one or two synonyms. How does the word change affect the meaning of your sentence? For example, which sentence is stronger? Which has a more positive meaning?

Word Study

Latin suffix: -tion The Latin suffix *-tion* often indicates that a word is a noun. Sometimes this suffix is spelled *-ion* or *-ation*. These related suffixes mean "act, state, or condition of." In "The Seventh Man," the word *premonition* means "the state of being forewarned."

1. Record a definition of *hallucination* based on your understanding of its root word and the meaning of the suffix *-tion*.
   To see something that is not real

2. Look back at paragraphs 37–40 and find two other words that use the suffix *-tion*. Identify the root word that was combined with the suffix. Record a definition for each word.
   cooperation - working together
   direction - heading towards something

Digital Resources

You can access digital resources from your print Student Edition, or from Savvas Realize™.

To watch videos or listen to audio from your print Student Edition, all you need is a device with a camera and Pearson's BouncePages app!

ANCHOR TEXT | SHORT STORY

The
Seventh Man

Haruki Murakami

BACKGROUND
Hurricanes that originate in the northwest Pacific Ocean are called typhoons. They can stretch up to 500 miles in diameter and produce high winds, heavy rains, enormous waves, and severe flooding. On average, Japan is hit by three severe typhoons each year due to its location and climatic conditions.

SCAN FOR MULTIMEDIA

1   "A huge wave nearly swept me away," said the seventh man, almost whispering. "It happened one September afternoon when I was ten years old."

2   The man was the last one to tell his story that night. The hands of the clock had moved past ten. The small group that huddled in

NOTES

CLOSE READ
ANNOTATE: Mark details in paragraph 2 that

How to watch a video or listen to audio:

1. Download Pearson's BouncePages App from the Apple App or Google Play Store.

2. Open the app on your mobile device.

3. Aim your camera so the page from your Student Edition is viewable on your screen.

4. Tap the screen to scan the page.

5. Press the "Play" button on the page that appears on your device.

6. View the video or listen to the audio directly from your device!

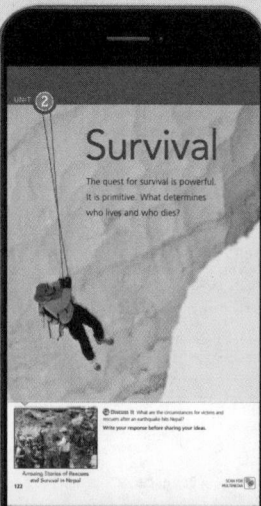

Unit 2

Survival

The quest for survival is powerful. It is primitive. What determines who lives and who dies?

Amazing Stories of Rescues and Survival in Nepal
122

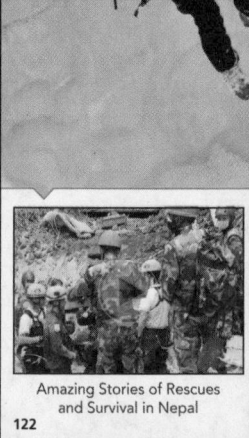

Amazing Stories of Rescues and Survival in Nepal
122

Digital resources, including audio and video, can be accessed in the Interactive Student Edition. Your teacher might also assign activities for you to complete online.

SAVVAS eText 2.0 for Schools

Unit 2: Survival

UNIT 2
Survival

UNIT INTRODUCTION

WHOLE-CLASS LEARNING

SMALL-GROUP LEARNING

INDEPENDENT LEARNING

PERFORMANCE-BASED ASSESSMENT

UNIT REFLECTION

The quest for survival is powerful. It is primitive. What determines who lives and who dies?

You will also find digital novels, interactive lessons, and games!

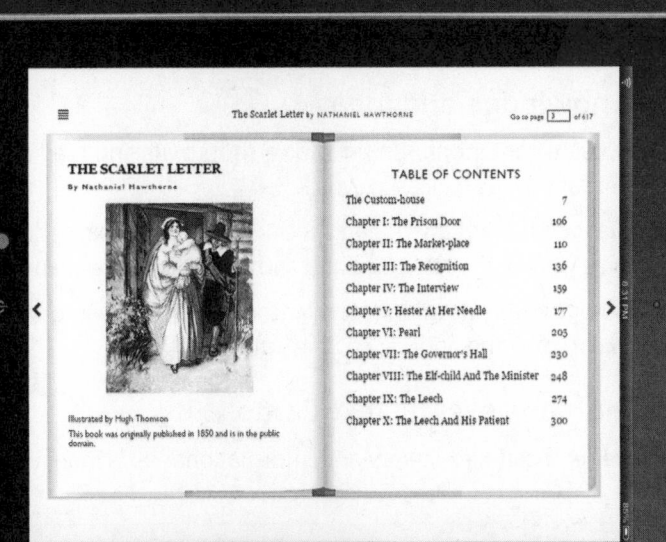

The Scarlet Letter by NATHANIEL HAWTHORNE — Go to page 3 of 617

THE SCARLET LETTER
By Nathaniel Hawthorne

Illustrated by Hugh Thomson
This book was originally published in 1850 and is in the public domain.

Standards Overview

The following English Language Arts standards will prepare you to succeed in college and your future career. The College and Career Readiness Anchor Standards define what you need to achieve by the end of high school, and the grade-specific Standards define what you need to know by the end of your current grade level.

The following provides an overview of the Standards.

Standards for Reading

College and Career Readiness Anchor Standards for Reading

Key Ideas and Details

1. Read closely to determine what the text says explicitly and to make logical inferences from it; cite specific textual evidence when writing or speaking to support conclusions drawn from the text.

2. Determine central ideas or themes of a text and analyze their development; summarize the key supporting details and ideas.

3. Analyze how and why individuals, events, and ideas develop and interact over the course of a text.

Craft and Structure

4. Interpret words and phrases as they are used in a text, including determining technical, connotative, and figurative meanings, and analyze how specific word choices shape meaning or tone.

5. Analyze the structure of texts, including how specific sentences, paragraphs, and larger portions of the text (e.g., a section, chapter, scene, or stanza) relate to each other and the whole.

6. Assess how point of view or purpose shapes the content and style of a text.

Integration of Knowledge and Ideas

7. Integrate and evaluate content presented in diverse formats and media, including visually and quantitatively, as well as in words.

8. Delineate and evaluate the argument and specific claims in a text, including the validity of the reasoning as well as the relevance and sufficiency of the evidence.

9. Analyze how two or more texts address similar themes or topics in order to build knowledge or to compare the approaches the authors take.

Range of Reading and Level of Text Complexity

10. Read and comprehend complex literary and informational texts independently and proficiently.

Grade 11 Reading Standards for Literature

Standard

Key Ideas and Details

Cite strong and thorough textual evidence to support analysis of what the text says explicitly as well as inferences drawn from the text, including determining where the text leaves matters uncertain.

Determine two or more themes or central ideas of a text and analyze their development over the course of the text, including how they interact and build on one another to produce a complex account; provide an objective summary of the text.

Analyze the impact of the author's choices regarding how to develop and relate elements of a story or drama (e.g., where a story is set, how the action is ordered, how the characters are introduced and developed).

Craft and Structure

Determine the meaning of words and phrases as they are used in the text, including figurative and connotative meanings; analyze the impact of specific word choices on meaning and tone, including words with multiple meanings or language that is particularly fresh, engaging, or beautiful. (Include Shakespeare as well as other authors.)

Analyze how an author's choices concerning how to structure specific parts of a text (e.g., the choice of where to begin or end a story, the choice to provide a comedic or tragic resolution) contribute to its overall structure and meaning as well as its aesthetic impact.

Analyze a case in which grasping a point of view requires distinguishing what is directly stated in a text from what is really meant (e.g., satire, sarcasm, irony, or understatement).

Integration of Knowledge and Ideas

Analyze multiple interpretations of a story, drama, or poem (e.g., recorded or live production of a play or recorded novel or poetry), evaluating how each version interprets the source text. (Include at least one play by Shakespeare and one play by an American dramatist.)

Demonstrate knowledge of eighteenth-, nineteenth- and early-twentieth-century foundational works of American literature, including how two or more texts from the same period treat similar themes or topics.

Range of Reading and Level of Text Complexity

By the end of grade 11, read and comprehend literature, including stories, dramas, and poems, in the grades 11–CCR text complexity band proficiently, with scaffolding as needed at the high end of the range.

Standards Overview

Grade 11 Reading Standards for Informational Text
Standard
Key Ideas and Details
Cite strong and thorough textual evidence to support analysis of what the text says explicitly as well as inferences drawn from the text, including determining where the text leaves matters uncertain.
Determine two or more central ideas of a text and analyze their development over the course of the text, including how they interact and build on one another to provide a complex analysis; provide an objective summary of the text.
Analyze a complex set of ideas or sequence of events and explain how specific individuals, ideas, or events interact and develop over the course of the text.
Craft and Structure
Determine the meaning of words and phrases as they are used in a text, including figurative, connotative, and technical meanings; analyze how an author uses and refines the meaning of a key term or terms over the course of a text (e.g., how Madison defines *faction* in *Federalist* No. 10).
Analyze and evaluate the effectiveness of the structure an author uses in his or her exposition or argument, including whether the structure makes points clear, convincing, and engaging.
Determine an author's point of view or purpose in a text in which the rhetoric is particularly effective, analyzing how style and content contribute to the power, persuasiveness or beauty of the text.
Integration of Knowledge and Ideas
Integrate and evaluate multiple sources of information presented in different media or formats (e.g., visually, quantitatively) as well as in words in order to address a question or solve a problem.
Delineate and evaluate the reasoning in seminal U.S. texts, including the application of constitutional principles and use of legal reasoning (e.g., in U.S. Supreme Court majority opinions and dissents) and the premises, purposes, and arguments in works of public advocacy (e.g., *The Federalist*, presidential addresses).
Analyze seventeenth-, eighteenth-, and nineteenth-century foundational U.S. documents of historical and literary significance (including The Declaration of Independence, the Preamble to the Constitution, the Bill of Rights, and Lincoln's Second Inaugural Address) for their themes, purposes, and rhetorical features.
Range of Reading and Level of Text Complexity
By the end of grade 11, read and comprehend literary nonfiction in the grades 11–CCR text complexity band proficiently, with scaffolding as needed at the high end of the range.

Standards for Writing

College and Career Readiness Anchor Standards for Writing

Text Types and Purposes

1. Write arguments to support claims in an analysis of substantive topics or texts, using valid reasoning and relevant and sufficient evidence.

2. Write informative/explanatory texts to examine and convey complex ideas and information clearly and accurately through the effective selection, organization, and analysis of content.

3. Write narratives to develop real or imagined experiences or events using effective technique, well-chosen details, and well-structured event sequences.

Production and Distribution of Writing

4. Produce clear and coherent writing in which the development, organization, and style are appropriate to task, purpose, and audience.

5. Develop and strengthen writing as needed by planning, revising, editing, rewriting, or trying a new approach.

6. Use technology, including the Internet, to produce and publish writing and to interact and collaborate with others.

Research to Build and Present Knowledge

7. Conduct short as well as more sustained research projects based on focused questions, demonstrating understanding of the subject under investigation.

8. Gather relevant information from multiple print and digital sources, assess the credibility and accuracy of each source, and integrate the information while avoiding plagiarism.

9. Draw evidence from literary or informational texts to support analysis, reflection, and research.

Range of Writing

10. Write routinely over extended time frames (time for research, reflection, and revision) and shorter time frames (a single sitting or a day or two) for a range of tasks, purposes, and audiences.

Grade 11 Writing Standards

Standard

Text Types and Purposes

Write arguments to support claims in an analysis of substantive topics or texts, using valid reasoning and relevant and sufficient evidence.

Introduce precise, knowledgeable claim(s), establish the significance of the claim(s), distinguish the claim(s) from alternate or opposing claims, and create an organization that logically sequences claim(s), counterclaims, reasons, and evidence.

Standards Overview

Grade 11 Writing Standards
Standard
Text Types and Purposes (continued)
Develop claim(s) and counterclaims fairly and thoroughly, supplying the most relevant evidence for each while pointing out the strengths and limitations of both in a manner that anticipates the audience's knowledge level, concerns, values, and possible biases.
Use words, phrases, and clauses as well as varied syntax to link the major sections of the text, create cohesion, and clarify the relationships between claim(s) and reasons, between reasons and evidence, and between claim(s) and counterclaims.
Establish and maintain a formal style and objective tone while attending to the norms and conventions of the discipline in which they are writing.
Provide a concluding statement or section that follows from and supports the argument presented.
Write informative/explanatory texts to examine and convey complex ideas, concepts, and information clearly and accurately through the effective selection, organization, and analysis of content.
Introduce a topic; organize complex ideas, concepts, and information so that each new element builds on that which precedes it to create a unified whole; include formatting (e.g., headings), graphics (e.g., figures, tables), and multimedia when useful to aiding comprehension.
Develop the topic thoroughly by selecting the most significant and relevant facts, extended definitions, concrete details, quotations, or other information and examples appropriate to the audience's knowledge of the topic.
Use appropriate and varied transitions and syntax to link the major sections of the text, create cohesion, and clarify the relationships among complex ideas and concepts.
Use precise language, domain-specific vocabulary, and techniques such as metaphor, simile, and analogy to manage the complexity of the topic.
Establish and maintain a formal style and objective tone while attending to the norms and conventions of the discipline in which they are writing.
Provide a concluding statement or section that follows from and supports the information or explanation presented (e.g., articulating implications or the significance of the topic).
Write narratives to develop real or imagined experiences or events using effective technique, well-chosen details, and well-structured event sequences.
Engage and orient the reader by setting out a problem, situation, or observation and its significance, establishing one or multiple point(s) of view, and introducing a narrator and/or characters; create a smooth progression of experiences or events.
Use narrative techniques, such as dialogue, pacing, description, reflection, and multiple plot lines, to develop experiences, events, and/or characters.

Grade 11 Writing Standards

Standard

Text Types and Purposes (continued)

Use a variety of techniques to sequence events so that they build on one another to create a coherent whole and build toward a particular tone and outcome (e.g., a sense of mystery, suspense, growth, or resolution).

Use precise words and phrases, telling details, and sensory language to convey a vivid picture of the experiences, events, setting, and/or characters.

Provide a conclusion that follows from and reflects on what is experienced, observed, or resolved over the course of the narrative.

Production and Distribution of Writing

Produce clear and coherent writing in which the development, organization, and style are appropriate to task, purpose, and audience. (Grade-specific expectations for writing types are defined in standards 1–3 above.)

Develop and strengthen writing as needed by planning, revising, editing, rewriting, or trying a new approach, focusing on addressing what is most significant for a specific purpose and audience. (Editing for conventions should demonstrate command of Language standards 1–3 up to and including grades 11–12)

Use technology, including the Internet, to produce, publish, and update individual or shared writing products in response to ongoing feedback, including new arguments or information.

Research to Build and Present Knowledge

Conduct short as well as more sustained research projects to answer a question (including a self-generated question) or solve a problem; narrow or broaden the inquiry when appropriate; synthesize multiple sources on the subject, demonstrating understanding of the subject under investigation.

Gather relevant information from multiple authoritative print and digital sources, using advanced searches effectively; assess the strengths and limitations of each source in terms of the task, purpose, and audience; integrate information into the text selectively to maintain the flow of ideas, avoiding plagiarism and overreliance on any one source and following a standard format for citation.

Draw evidence from literary or informational texts to support analysis, reflection, and research.

Apply *grades 11–12 Reading standards* to literature (e.g., "Demonstrate knowledge of eighteenth-, nineteenth- and early-twentieth-century foundational works of American literature, including how two or more texts from the same period treat similar themes or topics").

Apply *grades 11–12 Reading standards* to literary nonfiction (e.g., "Delineate and evaluate the reasoning in seminal U.S. texts, including the application of constitutional principles and use of legal reasoning [e.g., in U.S. Supreme Court Case majority opinions and dissents] and the premises, purposes, and arguments in works of public advocacy [e.g., *The Federalist*, presidential addresses]").

Range of Writing

Write routinely over extended time frames (time for research, reflection, and revision) and shorter time frames (a single sitting or a day or two) for a range of tasks, purposes, and audiences.

Standards Overview

Standards for Speaking and Listening

College and Career Readiness Anchor Standards for Speaking and Listening

Comprehension and Collaboration

1. Prepare for and participate effectively in a range of conversations and collaborations with diverse partners, building on others' ideas and expressing their own clearly and persuasively.

2. Integrate and evaluate information presented in diverse media and formats, including visually, quantitatively, and orally.

3. Evaluate a speaker's point of view, reasoning, and use of evidence and rhetoric.

Presentation of Knowledge and Ideas

4. Present information, findings, and supporting evidence such that listeners can follow the line of reasoning and the organization, development, and style are appropriate to task, purpose, and audience.

5. Make strategic use of digital media and visual displays of data to express information and enhance understanding of presentations.

6. Adapt speech to a variety of contexts and communicative tasks, demonstrating command of formal English when indicated or appropriate.

Grade 11 Standards for Speaking and Listening

Standard

Comprehension and Collaboration

Initiate and participate effectively in a range of collaborative discussions (one-on-one, in groups, and teacher-led) with diverse partners on *grades 11–12 topics, texts, and issues*, building on others' ideas and expressing their own clearly and persuasively.

Come to discussions prepared, having read and researched material under study; explicitly draw on that preparation by referring to evidence from texts and other research on the topic or issue to stimulate a thoughtful, well-reasoned exchange of ideas.

Work with peers to promote civil, democratic discussions and decision-making, set clear goals and deadlines, and establish individual roles as needed.

Propel conversations by posing and responding to questions that probe reasoning and evidence; ensure a hearing for a full range of positions on a topic or issue; clarify, verify, or challenge ideas and conclusions; and promote divergent and creative perspectives.

Respond thoughtfully to diverse perspectives; synthesize comments, claims, and evidence made on all sides of an issue; resolve contradictions when possible; and determine what additional information or research is required to deepen the investigation or complete the task.

Integrate multiple sources of information presented in diverse formats and media (e.g., visually, quantitatively, orally) in order to make informed decisions and solve problems, evaluating the credibility and accuracy of each source and noting any discrepancies among the data.

Evaluate a speaker's point of view, reasoning, and use of evidence and rhetoric, assessing the stance, premises, links among ideas, word choice, points of emphasis, and tone used.

Presentation of Knowledge and Ideas

Present information, findings, and supporting evidence, conveying a clear and distinct perspective, such that listeners can follow the line of reasoning, alternative or opposing perspectives are addressed, and the organization, development, substance, and style are appropriate to purpose, audience, and a range of formal and informal tasks.

Make strategic use of digital media (e.g., textual, graphical, audio, visual, and interactive elements) in presentations to enhance understanding of findings, reasoning, and evidence and to add interest.

Adapt speech to a variety of contexts and tasks, demonstrating a command of formal English when indicated or appropriate. (See grades 11–12 Language standards 1 and 3 for specific expectations.)

Standards Overview

Standards for Language

College and Career Readiness Anchor Standards for Language

Conventions of Standard English

1. Demonstrate command of the conventions of standard English grammar and usage when writing or speaking.

2. Demonstrate command of the conventions of standard English capitalization, punctuation, and spelling when writing.

Knowledge of Language

3. Apply knowledge of language to understand how language functions in different contexts, to make effective choices for meaning or style, and to comprehend more fully when reading or listening.

Vocabulary Acquisition and Use

4. Determine or clarify the meaning of unknown and multiple-meaning words and phrases by using context clues, analyzing meaningful word parts, and consulting general and specialized reference materials, as appropriate.

5. Demonstrate understanding of figurative language, word relationships, and nuances in word meanings.

6. Acquire and use accurately a range of general academic and domain-specific words and phrases sufficient for reading, writing, speaking, and listening at the college and career readiness level; demonstrate independence in gathering vocabulary knowledge when considering a word or phrase important to comprehension or expression.

Grade 11 Standards for Language

Standard

Conventions of Standard English

Demonstrate command of the conventions of standard English grammar and usage when writing or speaking.

Apply the understanding that usage is a matter of convention, can change over time, and is sometimes contested.

Resolve issues of complex or contested usage, consulting references (e.g., *Merriam-Webster's Dictionary of English Usage*, *Garner's Modern American Usage*) as needed.

Demonstrate command of the conventions of standard English capitalization, punctuation, and spelling when writing.

Observe hyphenation conventions.

Spell correctly.

Grade 11 Standards for Language

Standard

Knowledge of Language

Apply knowledge of language to understand how language functions in different contexts, to make effective choices for meaning or style, and to comprehend more fully when reading or listening.

Vary syntax for effect, consulting references (e.g., Tufte's *Artful Sentences*) for guidance as needed; apply an understanding of syntax to the study of complex texts when reading.

Vocabulary Acquisition and Use

Determine or clarify the meaning of unknown and multiple-meaning words and phrases based on *grades 11–12 reading and content*, choosing flexibly from a range of strategies.

Use context (e.g., the overall meaning of a sentence, paragraph, or text; a word's position or function in a sentence) as a clue to the meaning of a word or phrase.

Identify and correctly use patterns of word changes that indicate different meanings or parts of speech (e.g., *conceive, conception, conceivable*).

Consult general and specialized reference materials (e.g., dictionaries, glossaries, thesauruses), both print and digital, to find the pronunciation of a word or determine or clarify its precise meaning, its part of speech, its etymology, or its standard usage.

Verify the preliminary determination of the meaning of a word or phrase (e.g., by checking the inferred meaning in context or in a dictionary).

Demonstrate understanding of figurative language, word relationships, and nuances in word meanings.

Interpret figures of speech (e.g., hyperbole, paradox) in context and analyze their role in the text.

Analyze nuances in the meaning of words with similar denotations.

Acquire and use accurately general academic and domain-specific words and phrases, sufficient for reading, writing, speaking, and listening at the college and career readiness level; demonstrate independence in gathering vocabulary knowledge when considering a word or phrase important to comprehension or expression.

Writing Freedom

Words That Shaped a Nation

🗨 **Discuss It** In what ways is the concept of "no taxation without representation" central to America's identity as a nation?

Write your response before sharing your ideas.

Boston Tea Party

SCAN FOR
MULTIMEDIA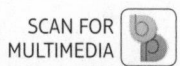

UNIT INTRODUCTION

ESSENTIAL QUESTION:

What is the meaning of freedom?

LAUNCH TEXT
ARGUMENT MODEL
Totally Free?

WHOLE-CLASS LEARNING

HISTORICAL PERSPECTIVES

Focus Period: 1750–1800

A New Nation

ANCHOR TEXT: FOUNDATIONAL DOCUMENT

Declaration of Independence
Thomas Jefferson

▶ MEDIA CONNECTION:
John F. Kennedy Reads the Declaration of Independence

ANCHOR TEXT: FOUNDATIONAL DOCUMENTS

Preamble to the Constitution
Gouverneur Morris

Bill of Rights
James Madison

ANCHOR TEXT: SPEECH

Speech in the Convention
Benjamin Franklin

▶ MEDIA CONNECTION:
The U. S. Constitution

MEDIA: IMAGE GALLERY

The American Revolution: Visual Propaganda

PERFORMANCE TASK

WRITING FOCUS:
Write an Argument

SMALL-GROUP LEARNING

COMPARE

EXPOSITORY NONFICTION

from America's Constitution: A Biography
Akhil Reed Amar

GRAPHIC NOVEL

from The United States Constitution: A Graphic Adaptation
Jonathan Hennessey and Aaron McConnell

AUTOBIOGRAPHY

from The Interesting Narrative of the Life of Olaudah Equiano
Olaudah Equiano

LETTER | BIOGRAPHY

Letter to John Adams
Abigail Adams

from Dear Abigail: The Intimate Lives and Revolutionary Ideas of Abigail Adams and Her Two Remarkable Sisters
Diane Jacobs

SPEECH

Gettysburg Address
Abraham Lincoln

PERFORMANCE TASK

SPEAKING AND LISTENING FOCUS:
Present an Argument

INDEPENDENT LEARNING

ESSAY

from Democracy Is Not a Spectator Sport
Arthur Blaustein with Helen Matatov

SPEECH

Reflections on the Bicentennial of the United States Constitution
Thurgood Marshall

POETRY

Speech to the Young Speech to the Progress-Toward
Gwendolyn Brooks

The Fish
Elizabeth Bishop

SHORT STORY

The Pedestrian
Ray Bradbury

POLITICAL DOCUMENT

from the Iroquois Constitution
Dekanawidah, translated by Arthur C. Parker

ARGUMENT

from Common Sense
Thomas Paine

PERFORMANCE-BASED ASSESSMENT PREP

Review Evidence for an Argument

PERFORMANCE-BASED ASSESSMENT

Argument: Essay and Video Commentary

PROMPT:

What are the most effective tools for establishing and preserving freedom?

Unit Goals

Throughout this unit, you will deepen your perspective of American freedoms by reading, writing, speaking, listening, and presenting. These goals will help you succeed on the Unit Performance-Based Assessment.

Rate how well you meet these goals right now. You will revisit your ratings later when you reflect on your growth during this unit.

SCALE	1	2	3	4	5
	NOT AT ALL WELL	NOT VERY WELL	SOMEWHAT WELL	VERY WELL	EXTREMELY WELL

READING GOALS

	1	2	3	4	5
• Read a variety of texts to gain the knowledge and insight needed to write about American freedoms.					
• Expand your knowledge and use of academic and concept vocabulary.					

WRITING AND RESEARCH GOALS

	1	2	3	4	5
• Write an argument that has a clear structure and that draws evidence from texts and original research to support a claim.					
• Conduct research projects of various lengths to explore a topic and clarify meaning.					

LANGUAGE GOALS

	1	2	3	4	5
• Note differences in language style over time and in various contexts.					
• Establish a writing "voice."					
• Correctly use parallelism and verb tenses to convey meaning and enrich your writing and presentations.					

SPEAKING AND LISTENING GOALS

	1	2	3	4	5
• Collaborate with your team to build on the ideas of others, develop consensus, and communicate.					
• Integrate audio, visuals, and text to present information.					

≡ STANDARDS

Language
Acquire and use accurately general academic and domain-specific words and phrases, sufficient for reading, writing, speaking, and listening at the college and career readiness level; demonstrate independence in gathering vocabulary knowledge when considering a word or phrase important to comprehension or expression.

SCAN FOR MULTIMEDIA

Academic Vocabulary: Argument

Understanding and using academic terms can help you to read, write, and speak with precision and clarity. Here are five academic words that will be useful to you in this unit as you analyze and write arguments.

Complete the chart.

1. Review each word, its root, and the mentor sentences.

2. Use the information and your own knowledge to predict the meaning of each word.

3. For each word, list at least two related words.

4. Refer to a dictionary or other resources if needed.

TIP

FOLLOW THROUGH
Study the words in this chart, and mark them or their forms wherever they appear in the unit.

WORD	MENTOR SENTENCES	PREDICT MEANING	RELATED WORDS
confirm ROOT: **-firm-** "strong"; "steadfast"	1. We could *confirm* the bird's species by its unusual song. 2. Please *confirm* your position on this topic; right now, I am unsure where you stand.		confirmation; unconfirmed
demonstrate ROOT: **-mon-** "show"; "point out"	1. In today's art class, Justin will *demonstrate* his use of pastels. 2. Like humans, some apes use facial expressions to *demonstrate* feelings.		
supplement ROOT: **-ple-** "fill"	1. Some people *supplement* their diet with a daily multivitamin. 2. Camila will *supplement* her income by taking a second, part-time job.		
establish ROOT: **-sta-** "stand"	1. That observant witness was able to *establish* the suspect's alibi. 2. Max reports that he is second in his class, but his grades *establish* that he is actually first.		
conviction ROOT: **-vict-/-vinc-** "conquer"	1. A speaker is far more effective if she speaks with confidence and *conviction*. 2. During the debate, the candidate's *conviction* about the rightness of his policies seemed to weaken.		

LAUNCH TEXT | ARGUMENT MODEL

This selection is an example of an **argument**, a type of writing in which the author presents a claim and organizes evidence and reasons to support that claim. This is the type of writing you will develop in the Performance-Based Assessment at the end of the unit.

As you read, look closely at the writer's argument, including the consideration of various viewpoints. Mark facts and examples that provide strong evidence to support the main claim.

Totally Free?

NOTES

1   If you ask a dozen high school students to define *freedom*, odds are that ten of them will answer, "Freedom means that I can do anything I want." For many people, freedom is an absolute. It implies the right to think, speak, or act however one wishes. Because we live in a civil society, however, we need to consider other people's rights as we exercise our own freedoms. A better world would combine essential human freedoms with the understanding that my freedoms should not conflict with your right to lead a safe and happy life.

2   Suppose that those ten high school students had the total freedom they describe. They might drive a car without a license, because they were free to do so. They might even drive *your* car, because total freedom means that they can have anything they want and do anything they like. They would be free to attend school or not, to run screaming down the hallways if they chose, or even to treat other people cruelly without fear of reprisal. Total freedom could result in lawless mayhem.

3   Despite their desperate desire to be free from England's rule, our nation's early leaders carefully defined freedoms in the Bill of Rights. They did not say, "Everyone is free to do as he or she chooses." They said, "Congress shall make no law respecting an establishment of religion, or prohibiting the free exercise thereof; or abridging the freedom of speech, or of the press; or the right of the people peaceably to assemble, and to petition the Government for a redress

SCAN FOR MULTIMEDIA

of grievances." They established a delicate line between the rights of individuals and the power of the government.

4   In his 1941 State of the Union address, President Franklin Roosevelt identified four key freedoms as being basic human rights: freedom of speech and expression, freedom of worship, freedom from want, and freedom from fear. Those are not freedoms that one finds in a dictatorship. Nor are they freedoms that we grant to each other without the oversight and protection of government institutions. With the government's help, and the writing of laws, my freedom from want does not allow me to steal your food, and your freedom of speech does not let you publish lies about me. We are free, but only up to the point at which our freedoms clash.

5   Is it even possible to be "totally free"? A person living "off the grid," far away from civilization, might achieve that kind of liberation. Such a person could live as he or she pleased without ever imposing on the freedoms of others.

6   Most of us, however, live in a community. We are bound by laws that both restrict and protect us. If we live in a dictatorship, we may be more restricted and less protected. If we live in a democracy, we may be more protected and less restricted. Human history is a balancing act between the desire for individual freedom and the need to protect everyone's freedoms.

7   *Freedom* implies a lack of restraint, but we are all better off if our freedoms are preserved and protected. At the same time, as members of a society, we must be sure that our freedoms do not conflict. "Life, liberty, and the pursuit of happiness" are powerful goals, but we must never allow one person's liberty to impose on another's happiness. ❧

NOTES

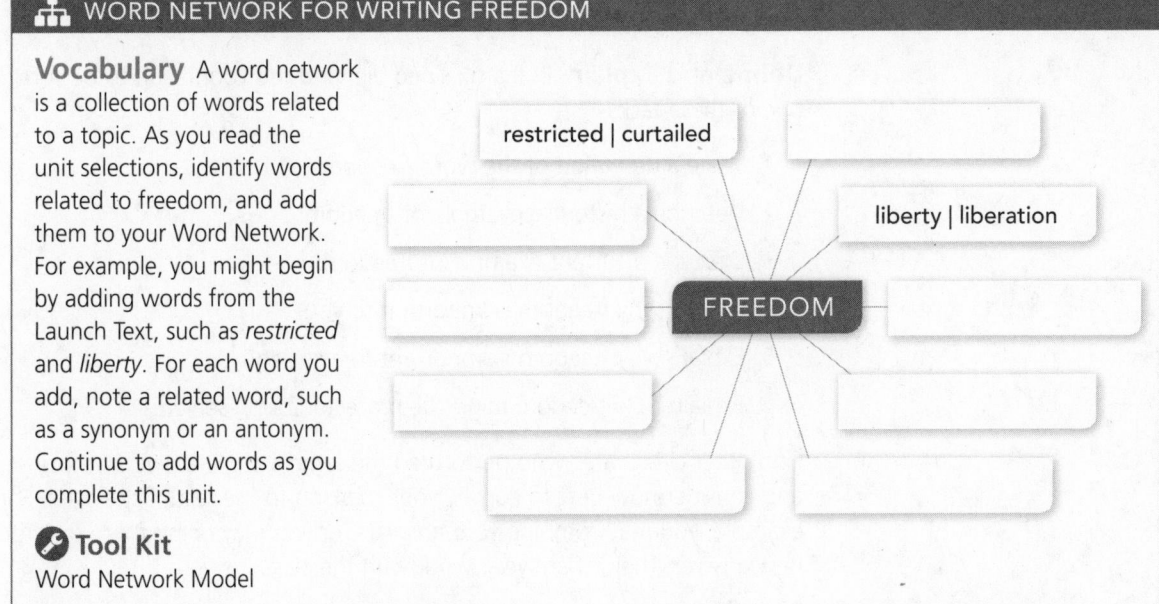

🔠 WORD NETWORK FOR WRITING FREEDOM

Vocabulary A word network is a collection of words related to a topic. As you read the unit selections, identify words related to freedom, and add them to your Word Network. For example, you might begin by adding words from the Launch Text, such as *restricted* and *liberty*. For each word you add, note a related word, such as a synonym or an antonym. Continue to add words as you complete this unit.

restricted | curtailed

liberty | liberation

FREEDOM

🔑 Tool Kit
Word Network Model

Summary

Write a summary of "Totally Free?" Remember that a **summary** is a concise, complete, and accurate overview of a text. It should not include a statement of your opinion or an analysis.

Launch Activity

Define and Explain Roll a six-sided die, and use your result to perform one of these tasks.

1. Write a definition of the word *freedom*.
2. Describe a historical example of freedom.
3. Describe a current example of freedom.
4. Explain why freedom is important to you.
5. Explain why freedom is important to a society.
6. Explain how freedom might be protected or preserved.

Find other classmates who performed the same task. Share your responses, and consider how best to convey your thinking to the rest of the class. For example, you may combine your answers, or you may revise them to write a new answer. Then, share your work with the class.

QuickWrite

Consider class discussions, the video, and the Launch Text as you think about the prompt. Record your first thoughts here.

PROMPT: **What are the most effective tools for establishing and preserving freedom?**

EVIDENCE LOG FOR WRITING FREEDOM

Review your QuickWrite. Summarize your initial position in one sentence to record in your Evidence Log. Then, record evidence from "Totally Free?" that supports your position.

After each selection, you will continue to use your Evidence Log to record the evidence you gather and the connections you make. The graphic shows what your Evidence Log looks like.

Tool Kit
Evidence Log Model

Title of Text:		Date:
CONNECTION TO PROMPT	TEXT EVIDENCE/DETAILS	ADDITIONAL NOTES/IDEAS

How does this text change or add to my thinking? Date:

 SCAN FOR MULTIMEDIA

ESSENTIAL QUESTION:

What is the meaning of freedom?

As you read these selections, work with your whole class to explore the meaning of freedom.

From Text to Topic For Thomas Jefferson and the other founders, freedom meant breaking away from Great Britain and establishing a nation based on democratic principles and individual liberties. Convincing the colonial majority of that idea would take persuasive words and images. For James Madison and Benjamin Franklin, after independence, freedom needed to be codified in a constitution—again, not an easy task. Issues relating to independence gripped Americans in the mid-eighteenth century. As you read, consider what the selections show about the meaning of American freedom during the country's formative years, and how they continue to shape our ideas about freedom today.

Whole-Class Learning Strategies

Throughout your life, in school, in your community, and in your career, you will continue to learn and work in large-group environments.

Review these strategies and the actions you can take to practice them as you work with your whole class. Add ideas of your own for each step. Get ready to use these strategies during Whole-Class Learning.

STRATEGY	ACTION PLAN
Listen actively	• Eliminate distractions. For example, put your cellphone away. • Jot down brief notes on main ideas and points of confusion. •
Clarify by asking questions	• If you're confused, other people probably are, too. Ask a question to help your whole class. • Ask follow-up questions as needed—for example, if you do not understand the clarification or if you want to make an additional connection. •
Monitor understanding	• Notice what information you already know and be ready to build on it. • Ask for help if you are struggling. •
Interact and share ideas	• Share your ideas and answer questions, even if you are unsure. • Build on the ideas of others by adding details or making a connection. •

SCAN FOR
MULTIMEDIA

CONTENTS

A New Nation

Voices of the Period

"Courage, then, my countrymen; our contest is not only whether we ourselves shall be free, but whether there shall be left to mankind an asylum on earth for civil and religious liberty."

—Samuel Adams,
advocate for colonial rights and
signer of the Declaration of Independence

"The Enemy have now landed on Long Island, and the hour is fast approaching, on which the Honor and Success of this army, and the safety of our bleeding Country depend. Remember officers and Soldiers, that you are Freemen, fighting for the blessings of Liberty—that slavery will be your portion, and that of your posterity, if you do not acquit yourselves like men."

—George Washington,
then- Commander-in-Chief
of the Continental Army

"Accordingly he signed the manumission that day; so that, before night, I who had been a slave in the morning, trembling at the will of another, . . . became my own master, and completely free. I thought this was the happiest day I had ever experienced. . . . "

—Olaudah Equiano,
abolitionist and formerly
enslaved African

History of the Period

Founded on Freedom The quest for freedom drove the establishment of the colonies. The Pilgrims and Puritans settled Massachusetts so that they could practice their religion freely. The Quakers, who settled Pennsylvania, and the Catholics, who settled Maryland, also brought their religious convictions with them as they fled from England's restrictions.

An "American" Society By the mid-eighteenth century, the thirteen disparate colonies had created a new society. Each colony was fiercely independent, but together they viewed themselves as different from societies across the Atlantic. "American" society generally valued equality and opportunity. It was much more homogenous than what was commonplace in Europe, without either nobility or a class of paupers who had no chance of bettering their lives. (Enslaved African Americans were the notable exception. Indentured servants also had limits on their freedom.) Furthermore, most of the colonial governments had two-house legislatures, elected by voters. The colonial governments may not have been fully democratic by modern standards, but colonists had—and expected—far more rights and freedoms than their counterparts in England did.

Tightening Controls By the mid-1700s, most Americans took pride in being in charge of their colonial governments, so the demands that Great Britain began to make after winning the French

TIMELINE

1754: The Albany Congress discusses Benjamin Franklin's Plan of Union for the Colonies.

1755: England Samuel Johnson's *Dictionary of the English Language* is published.

1765: The British Parliament taxes the Colonies with the Stamp Act.

1768: British troops occupy rebellious Boston.

1700

Integration of Knowledge and Ideas

Notebook How was each of the causes resolved as a result of the American Revolution? Which effect do you think may have been most on the minds of the Americans when they rebelled? Which may have been least?

Causes and Effects of the American Revolution

CAUSES

- Britain imposes taxes without providing for colonial representation in Parliament.
- Britain issues the Intolerable Acts to punish the American "rebels."
- A growing number of colonial leaders see themselves more as American than as British.

The American Revolution

EFFECTS

- The thirteen British colonies become the independent United States of America.
- The United States becomes an example for other peoples seeking freedom and self-government.
- American trade becomes free of British restrictions.
- Westward expansion becomes possible, extending to the Mississippi River.

and Indian War (known in Britain as the Seven Years' War) led inevitably to trouble. Colonists who were eager to move west were stymied by the Proclamation of 1763, which forbade settlement beyond the Appalachian Mountains. Furthermore, the taxes that Britain imposed to pay the cost of securing victory grew more and more onerous to the colonists. Quickly, "no taxation without representation" became a colonial rallying cry.

In response, England tightened its grip. In 1774, Parliament cracked down on American freedoms even more, with laws that the colonists called the Intolerable Acts. Then, in April 1775, the conflict turned from words and laws to bullets and deaths when the first shots were fired at Lexington and Concord in Massachusetts, the hotbed of rebellion.

Declaring Independence Six months before patriots and redcoats clashed in Massachusetts, colonial delegates had gathered to consider their complaints at the First Continental Congress. A few weeks after the events at Lexington and Concord, the Second Continental Congress convened in Philadelphia. By June, the colonies were on the road to a real break from Britain.

1770: Colonists and British soldiers clash in the Boston Massacre.

1773: Parliament's Tea Act prompts the Boston Tea Party.

1774: Colonial representatives meet for the First Continental Congress.

1775: The American Revolution begins.

1776: The Second Continental Congress adopts the Declaration of Independence.

1776

When the delegates officially declared the colonies' independence, they made freedom a central factor in their rationale. It is "self-evident," they stated, that all people have "unalienable rights, that among these are life, liberty, and the pursuit of happiness." In concluding, they pronounced the colonies to be "free and independent states."

Breaking the Bonds The new United States battled for independence for the next seven years. The British had a clear goal: to keep the rebellious colonies within the British Empire. The Americans were more divided, however. Although probably no more than 20 percent of the American people were loyal to Great Britain, many others were uncertain about this radical venture of independence. Undeterred, the patriots fought on.

The colonies had a population of about 2.5 million and no standing military forces. By contrast, Great Britain boasted a population of about 7.5 million as well as the world's most powerful army and navy. However, the colonists were fighting on home territory, whereas the British were 3,000 miles away from home and lacked easy access to supplies.

Then, in 1778, France entered the war on the side of the Americans. It was French aid that enabled the Americans to win the decisive battle at Yorktown. Tradition says that as the British surrendered, their band played "The World Turn'd Upside Down," a fitting tune for what had happened. The new nation that had demanded and won its independence would be unique in the world of its day: a self-governing democracy. In 1783, the Treaty of Paris officially brought the American Revolution to an end.

Defining Freedoms Having fought for freedom, the new nation had to structure a government that would preserve it. The Articles of Confederation, approved in 1777 and formally ratified in 1781, confirmed the union of the thirteen states as one nation. However, the agreement largely left each state free to function on its own—an arrangement that created an often dysfunctional union. Correcting the problems led to a complete re-creation of the governmental structure and triggered the writing of the Constitution of the United States.

Not satisfied with the guarantees of freedom embedded in the Constitution, however, many leaders urged the creation of what became the Bill of Rights. These first ten amendments to the Constitution focus on guarantees of individual liberties, including freedom of speech, freedom of the press, and the right to legal counsel and trial by jury.

These rights did not extend to all Americans, however. For all of the focus on freedom and individual rights in the founding of the United States, enslaved African Americans—about 20 percent of the population—were left out of this discussion. In addition, even though property requirements were abolished for male voters in the new nation, 125 years would pass before suffrage was extended to American women.

A Motivating Force Freedom has been a defining goal throughout American history. The literature in this unit explores how freedom has shaped the United States, and how authors of both the past and present have applied visions of freedom to an ever-changing world.

TIMELINE

1777: The thirteen original states adopt the Articles of Confederation.

 1777

1781: American forces defeat the British at Yorktown.

1783: The Treaty of Paris ends the American Revolution.

1787: Delegates meet in Philadelphia to create a new constitution.

1788: The United States Constitution is ratified.

Literature Selections

Literature of the Focus Period Several of the selections in this unit were written during the focus period and pertain to the establishment of a free United States and the rights granted to some, but not all, of its people:

Declaration of Independence, Thomas Jefferson

Preamble to the Constitution, Gouverneur Morris

Bill of Rights, James Madison

Speech in the Convention, Benjamin Franklin

from *The Interesting Narrative of the Life of Olaudah Equiano*, Olaudah Equiano

Letter to John Adams, Abigail Adams

from *Common Sense*, Thomas Paine

Connections Across Time A consideration of the importance of freedom both preceded and continued past the focus period. Indeed, it has influenced writers and commentators in many times and places.

from *America's Constitution: A Biography*, Akhil Reed Amar

from *Dear Abigail: The Intimate Lives and Revolutionary Ideas of Abigail Adams and Her Two Remarkable Sisters*, Diane Jacobs

Gettysburg Address, Abraham Lincoln

from *Democracy Is Not a Spectator Sport*, Arthur Blaustein with Helen Matatov

Reflections on the Bicentennial of the United States Constitution, Thurgood Marshall

"Speech to the Young | Speech to the Progress-Toward," Gwendolyn Brooks

"The Fish," Elizabeth Bishop

"The Pedestrian," Ray Bradbury

from the Iroquois Constitution, Dekanawidah, translated by Arthur C. Parker

1789: George Washington is elected the first President of the United States.

1791: Ten amendments— the Bill of Rights—are added to the Constitution.

1800: Thomas Jefferson is elected the third U.S. president.

1800

1789: France The French Revolution begins.

1796: John Adams is elected the second U.S. president.

Declaration of Independence

Concept Vocabulary

You will encounter the following words as you read the Declaration of Independence. Before reading, note how familiar you are with each word. Then, rank the words in order from most familiar (1) to least familiar (6).

WORD	YOUR RANKING
unalienable	
constrains	
tyranny	
assent	
acquiesce	
rectitude	

After completing the first read, come back to the concept vocabulary and review your rankings. Mark changes to your original rankings as needed.

First Read NONFICTION

Apply these strategies as you conduct your first read. You will have an opportunity to complete the close-read notes after your first read.

🔧 Tool Kit
First-Read Guide and
Model Annotation

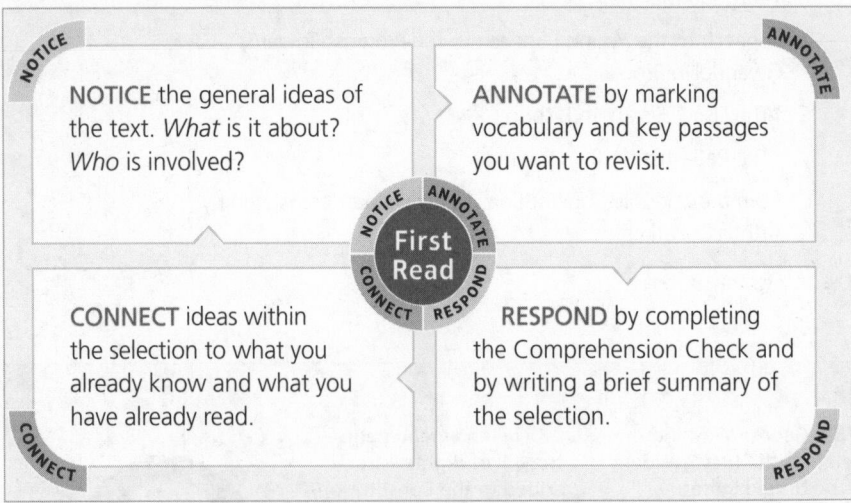

NOTICE the general ideas of the text. *What* is it about? *Who* is involved?

ANNOTATE by marking vocabulary and key passages you want to revisit.

CONNECT ideas within the selection to what you already know and what you have already read.

RESPOND by completing the Comprehension Check and by writing a brief summary of the selection.

First Read

⦂ STANDARDS
Reading Informational Text
By the end of grade 11, read and comprehend literary nonfiction in the grades 11–CCR text complexity band proficiently, with scaffolding as needed at the high end of the range.

About the Author

Thomas Jefferson (1743–1826)

Author of the Declaration of Independence

When you look at all of Thomas Jefferson's achievements, it seems almost nothing was beyond his reach. Not only did he help our nation win its independence and serve as its third president, but he also founded the University of Virginia, helped establish the public school system, designed his own home, invented a type of elevator for sending food from floor to floor, and created the decimal system for American money. He was a skilled violinist, an art enthusiast, and a brilliant writer.

Revolutionary Leader Born into a wealthy Virginia family, Jefferson attended the College of William and Mary and went on to earn a law degree. While serving in the Virginia House of Burgesses, he became an outspoken defender of American rights. When conflict between the colonists and the British erupted into revolution, Jefferson emerged as a leader in the effort to win independence.

Valued Statesman When the war ended, Jefferson served as the American minister to France for several years. He then served as the nation's first secretary of state and second vice president before becoming president in 1801.

Building the Nation While in office, Jefferson negotiated with France to buy a tract of land extending from the southern coast of Louisiana north into what is now Canada. This vast expanse of land included all of present-day Arkansas, Missouri, Iowa, Oklahoma, Kansas, and Nebraska. It also included most of North and South Dakota, northeastern New Mexico, northern

Texas, and portions of Minnesota, Colorado, Montana, and Wyoming. This enormous real-estate deal became known as the Louisiana Purchase, and it was one of the defining achievements of Jefferson's presidency. In a single treaty, Jefferson added more than 800,000 uncharted square miles to the holdings of the nation, effectively doubling its size.

The Lewis and Clark Expedition Jefferson had long wanted to pursue exploration of the Pacific Northwest. The completion of the Louisiana Purchase strengthened his resolve. He convinced Congress to allocate $2,500 to fund an expedition, writing:

> *The river Missouri, and Indians inhabiting it, are not as well known as rendered desirable by their connection with the Mississippi, and consequently with us. . . . An intelligent officer, with ten or twelve chosen men . . . might explore the whole line, even to the Western Ocean. . . .*

The "intelligent officer" he had in mind was his secretary, Captain Meriwether Lewis (1774–1809). Captain William Clark became co-leader of the group, which became known as the Corps of Discovery. Between 1804 and 1806, the team completed an 8,000-mile trek from St. Louis to the source of the Missouri River, across the Rocky Mountains to the Pacific coast, and back to Missouri.

A Patriotic Departure On the morning of July 4, 1826, the fiftieth anniversary of the Declaration of Independence, Jefferson died at the age of 83. John Adams, Jefferson's fellow contributor to the Declaration of Independence, died several hours later, after his longtime friend. Adams's last words were "Thomas Jefferson still survives."

Declaration of Independence

Thomas Jefferson

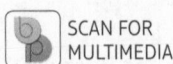

SCAN FOR
MULTIMEDIA

BACKGROUND

The Continental Congress was formed in 1774 by the American colonies to coordinate resistance to British laws considered by most colonists to be unfair. In the summer of 1776, after about a year of war against Britain, representatives met to consider an official break with Britain.

NOTES

IN CONGRESS, July 4, 1776.

1   *The unanimous declaration of the thirteen united states of America,*

2   When in the course of human events, it becomes necessary for one people to dissolve the political bands which have connected them with another, and to assume among the powers of the earth, the separate and equal station to which the laws of nature and of nature's God entitle them, a decent respect to the opinions of mankind requires that they should declare the causes which impel them to the separation.

3   We hold these truths to be self-evident: that all men are created equal; that they are endowed by their creator with certain **unalienable** rights, that among these are life, liberty and the pursuit of happiness; that to secure these rights, governments are instituted among men, deriving their just powers from the consent

unalienable (uhn AYL yuh nuh buhl) *adj.* impossible to take away or give up of the governed; that whenever any form of government becomes destructive of these ends, it is the right of the people to alter or to abolish it, and to institute new government, laying its foundation on such principles and organizing its powers in such form, as to them shall seem most likely to effect their safety and happiness. Prudence, indeed, will dictate that governments long established should not be changed for light and transient causes; and accordingly all experience hath shown, that mankind are more disposed to suffer, while evils are sufferable, than to right themselves by abolishing the forms to which they are accustomed. But when a long train of abuses and usurpations,[1] pursuing invariably the same object evinces a design to reduce them under absolute despotism, it is their right, it is their duty, to throw off such government, and to provide new guards for their future security. Such has been the patient sufferance of these colonies; and such is now the necessity which **constrains** them to alter their former systems of government. The history of the present King of Great Britain is a history of repeated injuries and usurpations,[1] all having in direct object the establishment of an absolute **tyranny** over these states. To prove this, let facts be submitted to a candid world.

4   He has refused his **assent** to laws the most wholesome and necessary for the public good.

5   He has forbidden his governors to pass laws of immediate and pressing importance, unless suspended in their operation till his assent should be obtained; and when so suspended, he has utterly neglected to attend to them.

6   He has refused to pass other laws for the accommodation of large districts of people, unless those people would relinquish the right of representation in the legislature, a right inestimable to them and formidable to tyrants only.

7   He has called together legislative bodies at places unusual, uncomfortable, and distant from the depository of their public records, for the sole purpose of fatiguing them into compliance with his measures.

8   He has dissolved representative houses repeatedly, for opposing with manly firmness his invasions on the rights of the people.

9   He has refused for a long time, after such dissolutions, to cause others to be elected, whereby the legislative powers, incapable of annihilation, have returned to the people at large for their exercise, the state remaining in the mean time exposed to all the dangers of invasion from without, and convulsions within.

10   He has endeavored to prevent the population of these states; for that purpose obstructing the laws for naturalization of foreigners, refusing to pass others to encourage their migrations hither, and raising the conditions of new appropriations of lands.

---

1. **usurpations** (yoo zuhr PAY shuhnz) *n.* unlawful or violent seizures of power or possessions.

11   He has obstructed the administration of justice, by refusing his assent to laws for establishing judiciary powers.

12   He has made judges dependent on his will alone, for the tenure of their offices, and the amount and payment of their salaries.

13   He has erected a multitude of new offices, and sent hither swarms of officers to harass our people, and eat out their substance.

14   He has kept among us in times of peace standing armies without the consent of our legislatures.

15   He has affected to render the military independent of, and superior to, the civil power.

16   He has combined with others to subject us to a jurisdiction foreign to our constitution, and unacknowledged by our laws; giving his assent to their acts of pretended legislation:

17   For quartering[2] large bodies of armed troops among us:

18   For protecting them, by a mock trial, from punishment for any murders which they should commit on the inhabitants of these states:

19   For cutting off our trade with all parts of the world:

20   For imposing taxes on us without our consent:

21   For depriving us in many cases, of the benefits of trial by jury:

22   For transporting us beyond seas to be tried for pretended offenses:

23   For abolishing the free system of English laws in a neighboring province, establishing therein an arbitrary government, and enlarging its boundaries so as to render it at once an example and fit instrument for introducing the same absolute rule into these colonies:

24   For taking away our charters, abolishing our most valuable laws, and altering fundamentally the forms of our governments:

25   For suspending our own legislatures, and declaring themselves invested with power to legislate for us in all cases whatsoever.

26   He has abdicated government here, by declaring us out of his protection and waging war against us.

27   He has plundered our seas, ravaged our coasts, burned our towns, and destroyed the lives of our people.

28   He is at this time transporting large armies of foreign mercenaries to complete the works of death, desolation and tyranny, already begun with circumstances of cruelty and perfidy scarcely paralleled in the most barbarous ages, and totally unworthy the head of a civilized nation.

29   He has constrained our fellow citizens taken captive on the high seas to bear arms against their country, to become the executioners of their friends and brethren, or to fall themselves by their hands.

30   He has excited domestic insurrections amongst us, and has endeavored to bring on the inhabitants of our frontiers, the merciless Indian savages, whose known rule of warfare, is an undistinguished destruction of all ages, sexes, and conditions.

31   In every stage of these oppressions we have petitioned for redress in the most humble terms: Our repeated petitions have been

CLOSE READ

ANNOTATE: Mark the verbs in paragraph 27 that describe what the king has done to the colonists.

QUESTION: Why do you think Jefferson chose these verbs?

CONCLUDE: What is the effect of this language?

---

2. **quartering** *v.* housing.

answered only by repeated injury. A prince whose character is thus marked by every act which may define a tyrant, is unfit to be the ruler of a free people.

32   Nor have we been wanting in attentions to our British brethren. We have warned them from time to time of attempts by their legislature to extend an unwarrantable jurisdiction over us. We have reminded them of the circumstances of our emigration and settlement here. We have appealed to their native justice and magnanimity, and we have conjured them by the ties of our common kindred to disavow these usurpations, which, would inevitably interrupt our connections and correspondence. They too have been deaf to the voice of justice and of consanguinity.[3] We must, therefore, **acquiesce** in the necessity, which denounces our separation, and hold them, as we hold the rest of mankind, enemies in war, in peace friends.

33   We, therefore, the representatives of the United States of America, in General Congress assembled appealing to the Supreme Judge of the world for the **rectitude** of our intentions, do in the name and by authority of the good people of these colonies, solemnly publish and declare that these united colonies are and of right ought to be free and independent states; that they are absolved from all allegiance to the British Crown, and that all political connection between them and the state of Great Britain is and ought to be totally dissolved; and that as free and independent states, they have full power to levy war,

NOTES

acquiesce (ak wee EHS) *v.* accept something reluctantly but without protest

rectitude (REHK tuh tood) *n.* morally correct behavior or thinking; uprightness

---

3. **consanguinity** (kon sang GWIHN uh tee) *n.* blood relationship.

Image of the final, signed version of the Declaration of Independence conclude peace, contract alliances, establish commerce, and to do all other acts and things which independent states may of right do. And for the support of this declaration, with a firm reliance on the protection of divine providence, we mutually pledge to each other our lives, our fortunes and our sacred honor.

The 56 signatures on the Declaration appear in the positions indicated:

Column 1

Georgia:
Button Gwinnett
Lyman Hall
George Walton

Column 2

North Carolina:
William Hooper
Joseph Hewes
John Penn

South Carolina:
Edward Rutledge
Thomas Heyward, Jr.
Thomas Lynch, Jr.
Arthur Middleton

Column 3

Massachusetts:
John Hancock

Maryland:
Samuel Chase
William Paca
Thomas Stone
Charles Carroll
  of Carrollton

Virginia:
George Wythe
Richard Henry Lee
Thomas Jefferson
Benjamin Harrison
Thomas Nelson, Jr.
Francis Lightfoot Lee
Carter Braxton

Column 4

Pennsylvania:
Robert Morris
Benjamin Rush
Benjamin Franklin
John Morton
George Clymer
James Smith
George Taylor
James Wilson
George Ross

Delaware:
Caesar Rodney
George Read
Thomas McKean

Column 5

New York:
William Floyd
Philip Livingston
Francis Lewis
Lewis Morris

New Jersey:
Richard Stockton
John Witherspoon
Francis Hopkinson
John Hart
Abraham Clark

Column 6

New Hampshire:
Josiah Bartlett
William Whipple

Massachusetts:
Samuel Adams
John Adams
Robert Treat Paine
Elbridge Gerry

Rhode Island:
Stephen Hopkins
William Ellery

Connecticut:
Roger Sherman
Samuel Huntington
William Williams
Oliver Wolcott

New Hampshire:
Matthew Thornton

Discuss It In 1957, then-Senator John F. Kennedy read the Declaration of Independence as part of an Independence Day radio broadcast. What do you think the reading would have meant to radio listeners?

Write your response before sharing your ideas.

John F. Kennedy Reads the Declaration of Independence

SCAN FOR MULTIMEDIA

Comprehension Check

Complete the following items after you finish your first read.

1. What does Jefferson state directly as the reason this declaration had to be written?

2. According to Jefferson, what is a people's duty when their government is abusive?

3. What new relationship between Great Britain and the United States is announced in this document?

4. **Notebook** Write a summary of the Declaration of Independence to confirm your understanding of the text.

- -

RESEARCH

Research to Clarify Choose at least one unfamiliar detail from the text. Briefly research that detail. In what way does the information you learned shed light on an aspect of the document?

Research to Explore Conduct research to find out how some signers of the Declaration of Independence expressed their convictions about the document.

Close Read the Text

1. This model, from paragraph 2 of the text, shows two sample annotations, along with questions and conclusions. Close read the passage, and find another detail to annotate. Then, write a question and your conclusion.

> **ANNOTATE:** This is very grand language, referring to all of human history.
>
> **QUESTION:** Why does Jefferson present this argument in the context of the entirety of human history?
>
> **CONCLUDE:** Jefferson is saying that the severing of political ties between nations is of momentous importance.

> When in the course of human events, it becomes **necessary** for one people to **dissolve** the political bands which have connected them with another, . . . a **decent** respect to the opinions of mankind requires that they should declare the causes which **impel** them to the **separation.**

> **ANNOTATE:** These words seem to be gentle.
>
> **QUESTION:** Why might Jefferson have chosen such language?
>
> **CONCLUDE:** Perhaps he wanted to make his argument sound reasoned and logical, and not angry.

Close Read — ANNOTATE · QUESTION · CONCLUDE

2. For more practice, go back into the text and complete the close-read notes.

3. Revisit a section of the text you found important during your first read. **Annotate** what you notice. Ask yourself **questions** such as "Why did the author make this choice?" What can you **conclude**?

Tool Kit
Close-Read Guide and Model Annotation

Analyze the Text

CITE TEXTUAL EVIDENCE
to support your answers.

Notebook Respond to these questions.

1. Make Inferences Why does Jefferson begin with points about human rights before discussing the colonists' specific grievances?

2. (a) Interpret What does Jefferson mean by saying that people do not change governments for "light reasons"? **(b) Speculate** Why might people be more inclined to put up with a government that is less than satisfactory rather than change it?

3. (a) Generalize According to Jefferson, what has been the king's attitude toward the laws of the colonies? **(b) Analyze** Why is that attitude an important factor in the decision to declare independence?

4. Historical Perspectives The signers of the Declaration of Independence knew that their announcement could mean war with powerful, well-equipped Britain. In your opinion, why isn't that idea more prominent in the document?

5. Essential Question: *What is the meaning of freedom?* What have you learned about American freedoms from reading this text? How does Jefferson connect the meaning of freedom to the idea of human rights?

STANDARDS

Reading Informational Text
• Cite strong and thorough textual evidence to support analysis of what the text says explicitly as well as inferences drawn from the text, including determining where the text leaves matters uncertain.
• Delineate and evaluate the reasoning in seminal U.S. texts, including the application of constitutional principles and use of legal reasoning and the premises, purposes, and arguments in works of public advocacy.
• Analyze seventeenth-, eighteenth-, and nineteenth-century foundational U.S. documents of historical and literary significance for their themes, purposes, and rhetorical features.

Analyze Craft and Structure

Author's Purpose: Argumentation An **argument** is writing that is meant to get readers to think in a certain way or take a particular action. In an effective argument, the writer presents reasons and supports them with convincing evidence. He or she also uses a variety of **persuasive appeals**, or ways of framing ideas for specific effect:

- **Appeals to Emotion:** ideas or language that attempts to influence readers' feelings; appeals to emotion may include **charged language**—strong words with powerful connotations—as well as references to the divine, references to concepts like justice or fairness, and stories or anecdotes.

- **Appeals to Logic:** ideas or language that connects to readers' rationality or reason; appeals to logic emphasize relationships between evidence, such as facts, and consequences or outcomes.

- **Appeals to Authority:** ideas or language that suggests the writer has special expertise or demonstrates character in a way that merits readers' attention on the subject.

Practice

CITE TEXTUAL EVIDENCE
to support your answers.

📓 **Notebook** Respond to these questions.

1. (a) What appeal to emotion does Jefferson use in paragraph 1?
(b) Why is this an important technique for him to use as he begins his argument?

2. (a) Mark examples of appeals to emotion in this excerpt from paragraph 2.

   But when a long train of abuses and usurpations, pursuing invariably the same object, evinces a design to reduce them under absolute despotism, it is their right, it is their duty, to throw off such government, and to provide new guards for their future security. Such has been the patient sufferance of these colonies; and such is now the necessity which constrains them to alter their former systems of government. The history of the present king of Great Britain is a history of repeated injuries and usurpations, all having in direct object the establishment of an absolute tyranny over these states.

   (b) How does the description of Great Britain and its king constitute charged language? Explain, citing specific words.

3. (a) Which kind of appeal is represented by Jefferson's organized list of grievances? (b) How does the evidence he provides add to his argument?

4. Jefferson wrote this document during the Age of Reason, an era characterized by logic and scientific methodology. How does the Declaration of Independence reflect Jefferson's faith in reason?

DECLARATION OF INDEPENDENCE

Concept Vocabulary

unalienable	tyranny	acquiesce
constrains	assent	rectitude

Why These Words? These concept vocabulary words convey ideas about power and rights. For example, Jefferson refers to life, liberty, and the pursuit of happiness as *unalienable* rights. He states that the king's actions established absolute *tyranny* over the colonies.

1. How does the concept vocabulary help readers grasp the issues leading to the Declaration of Independence?

2. What other words in the selection connect to these concepts?

WORD NETWORK

Add words related to freedom from the text to your Word Network.

Practice

Notebook **Complete these activities.**

1. Use each concept vocabulary word in a sentence that demonstrates your understanding of the word's meaning.

2. In two of your sentences, replace the concept vocabulary word with a synonym. What is the effect? For example, which sentence is stronger? Which one makes the sentence seem more positive or more negative?

Word Study

Latin Root: *-rect-* The Latin root *-rect-* means "right" or "straight." It is the basis for many English words, including such mathematical terms as *rectangular* (having right angles) and *rectilinear* (formed by straight lines).

1. Write a definition of *rectitude* that demonstrates your understanding of its Latin root.

2. Use a print or online college-level dictionary to find the meanings of *rectify* as the word relates to chemistry and as it relates to electronics.

STANDARDS

Language
• Apply the understanding that usage is a matter of convention, can change over time, and is sometimes contested.
• Resolve issues of complex or contested usage, consulting references as needed.
• Vary syntax for effect, consulting references for guidance as needed; apply an understanding of syntax to the study of complex texts when reading.
• Identify and correctly use patterns of word changes that indicate different meanings or parts of speech.
• Consult general and specialized reference materials, find the pronunciation of a word or determine or clarify its precise meaning, its part of speech, its etymology, or its standard usage.

Conventions and Style

Changes in Syntax and Usage Language changes over time. During the eighteenth century, when Jefferson wrote the Declaration of Independence, English spelling was almost identical to that of today's English. However, there are elements of Jefferson's style—the style of his era—that may seem old-fashioned to today's readers.

- **Syntax:** the structure of sentences. Some of Jefferson's sentences are very long by today's standards; in fact, the second paragraph of the Declaration is a lengthy single sentence.

- **Usage:** the way in which a word or phrase is used. Jefferson uses some words that would rarely be used—and might even be contested—today. For example, the word *consanguinity* in paragraph 32 is a term that few modern writers would use.

- **Formality:** the level of familiarity with which writers address the reader. While there are still ceremonial and public forums that require formal language, American culture is more casual now than it was in the eighteenth century. Both the purpose of the document and the style of the era are reflected in the Declaration's high level of formality.

Read It

1. Reread paragraphs 1–2 of the Declaration of Independence. Identify four words or phrases that represent an earlier style of English.

2. Locate Jefferson's use of *conjured* in paragraph 32. What does the word mean to Jefferson in this context? What does the word often mean today? Use an etymological dictionary or other source to explain how the two meanings are connected by word origin and word history.

3. **Connect to Style** What qualities of eighteenth-century style do you find in paragraphs 28–29? Consider syntax, usage, and level of formality.

Write It

📝 **Notebook** Rewrite this excerpt from the Declaration of Independence. Use modern English usage and syntax to express the same meaning. Then, compare the two versions and take note of ways in which each version would likely appeal to different audiences.

> He has refused his assent to laws, the most wholesome and necessary for the public good.
>
> He has forbidden his governors to pass laws of immediate and pressing importance, unless suspended in their operation till his assent should be obtained; and when so suspended, he has utterly neglected to attend to them.

DECLARATION OF INDEPENDENCE

Writing to Sources

The Declaration of Independence represents the position of one side in a conflict. There were numerous other colonial writings, including speeches, pamphlets, and essays, that centered on the same conflict. Together, these multiple writings are a record of the ongoing debate over the colonies' relationship with Britain. Today, debates over public issues often take place in the media—in newspaper articles and editorials.

Assignment

An editorial is a brief argumentative essay that appears in a newspaper or on a news site and expresses a position on an issue. Write an **editorial** for a local or school newspaper in which you argue your side of an issue that affects your school or community. Use modern syntax and usage, but apply some of Jefferson's persuasive techniques. For example, present a list of reasons just as Jefferson does in the Declaration of Independence.

Your editorial should include:

- a clear statement of your claim, or position
- a list of reasons that support and clarify your claim
- appeals to emotion, logic, and—if warranted—authority
- a concluding statement that follows from the argument

Vocabulary and Conventions Connection Consider including several of the concept vocabulary words. Also, remember to use appropriate word choices, grammar, syntax, and a style that makes your ideas clear.

unalienable	tyranny	acquiesce
constrains	assent	rectitude

- -

Reflect on Your Writing

After you have drafted your editorial, answer the following questions.

1. How did writing your editorial help you understand Jefferson's writing process?

2. Which of the reasons that you listed do you think offers the strongest evidence in support of your argument?

3. **Why These Words?** The words you choose can greatly increase the effect of your writing. Which words helped you create a clear and memorable argument?

Speaking and Listening

Assignment

You may have listened to the 1957 recording of Senator John F. Kennedy reading the Declaration of Independence. Listen to that recording again and think about his presentation. Then, participate in a **class discussion** about these questions:

- Would you find it meaningful to hear a modern politician of your choice reading this historical document today? Why or why not?

- Would it be just as meaningful to hear the document read by a classmate or a neighbor? Explain.

1. **Think About the Question** Before the discussion, consider the meaning of the Declaration of Independence.
   - Does Kennedy's reading enhance your understanding of the document?
   - Which aspects of the Declaration would a modern politician most likely consider important?

2. **Prepare Your Contribution** Make some notes for the discussion.
   - Which modern politician would you choose as a reader? Why?
   - In what ways would a reading from a classmate or a neighbor be more or less meaningful?

3. **Discuss the Questions** Keep these principles in mind.
   - Speak clearly so that your listeners can follow what you are saying.
   - Respond respectfully to the opinions of others.
   - Be prepared to answer questions that your teacher or classmates ask about your positions.

4. **Listen and Evaluate** As your classmates speak, listen attentively. Decide whether you agree or disagree with their ideas, and why. Contribute your responses with care, and support them with specific examples. In addition, take brief notes that will help as you complete a presentation evaluation guide.

PRESENTATION EVALUATION GUIDE

Rate each statement on a scale of 1 (not demonstrated) to 5 (demonstrated).

☐ Classmates made meaningful contributions to the discussion.

☐ All of the details in the assignment were discussed.

☐ Each person spoke clearly and in an appropriate tone of voice.

☐ Speakers supported their positions with specific examples.

✎ EVIDENCE LOG

Before moving on to a new selection, go to your Evidence Log and record what you learned from the Declaration of Independence.

About the Authors

Gouverneur Morris (1752–1816), a distinguished scholar, represented Pennsylvania at the Constitutional Convention. He made some 173 speeches during the proceedings of the Convention, many of them in opposition to slavery. His work on the Preamble to the Constitution earned him the title "Penman of the Constitution."

James Madison (1751–1836) grew up in Virginia and later served in the state's legislature. The youngest member of the Continental Congress, he was skilled at working with delegates who held opposing views. He is often called "Father of the Constitution" for his role in drafting that document and the Bill of Rights, which followed it. Madison later served as the United States's fourth president.

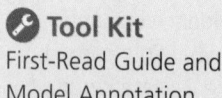 **Tool Kit**
First-Read Guide and
Model Annotation

STANDARDS

Reading Informational Text
By the end of grade 11, read and comprehend literary nonfiction in the grades 11–CCR text complexity band proficiently, with scaffolding as needed at the high end of the range.

Preamble to the Constitution
Bill of Rights

Concept Vocabulary

You will encounter the following words as you read the Preamble to the Constitution and the Bill of Rights. Before reading, note how familiar you are with each word. Then, rank the words in order from most familiar (1) to least familiar (6).

WORD	YOUR RANKING
exercise	
abridging	
petition	
redress	
infringed	
prescribed	

After completing the first read, come back to the concept vocabulary and review your ratings. Mark changes to your original rankings as needed.

First Read NONFICTION

Apply these strategies as you conduct your first read. You will have an opportunity to complete the close-read notes after your first read.

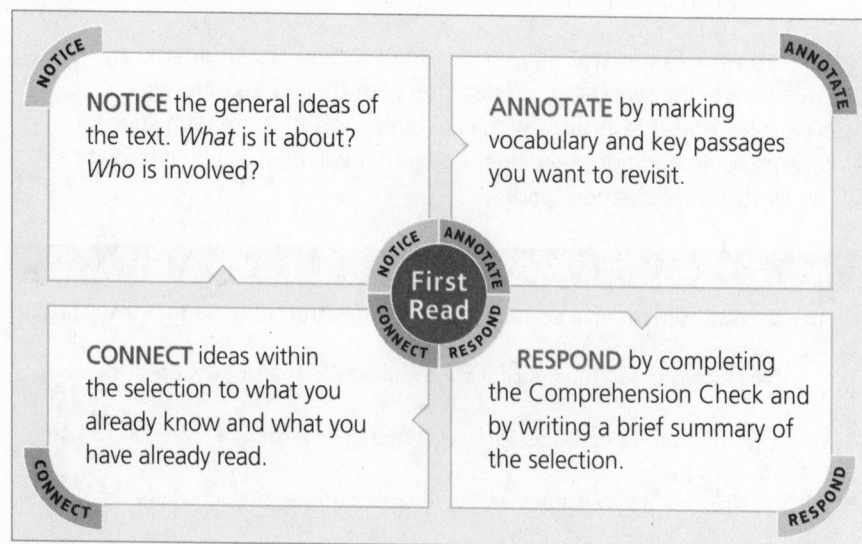

NOTICE the general ideas of the text. *What* is it about? *Who* is involved?

ANNOTATE by marking vocabulary and key passages you want to revisit.

CONNECT ideas within the selection to what you already know and what you have already read.

RESPOND by completing the Comprehension Check and by writing a brief summary of the selection.

First Read

Preamble to the Constitution

Gouverneur Morris

Bill of Rights

James Madison

BACKGROUND

After the Framers approved the Constitution, several of them called for the addition of more protections for individual liberties. James Madison wrote up a list of amendments. Congress passed them, and the states ratified ten of them. These ten amendments are now known as the Bill of Rights.

Preamble to the United States Constitution

1 We the people of the United States, in order to form a more perfect union, establish justice, insure domestic tranquility, provide for the common defense, promote the general welfare, and secure the blessings of liberty to ourselves and our posterity, do ordain and establish this Constitution for the United States of America.

※ ※ ※

Bill of Rights
Preamble

2 Congress of the United States begun and held at the City of New York, on Wednesday the fourth of March, one thousand seven hundred and eighty-nine.

3 THE Conventions of a number of the States, having at the time of their adopting the Constitution, expressed a desire, in order to prevent misconstruction or abuse of its powers, that further declaratory and restrictive clauses should be added: And as extending the ground of public confidence in the Government, will best ensure the beneficent ends of its institution.

4 RESOLVED by the Senate and House of Representatives of the United States of America, in Congress assembled, two thirds of both Houses concurring, that the following Articles be proposed to the Legislatures of the several States, as amendments to the Constitution of the United States, all, or any of which Articles, when ratified by three fourths of the said Legislatures, to be valid to all intents and purposes, as part of the said Constitution; viz.[1]

---

1. **viz** *abbr.* that is; namely.

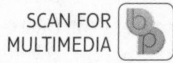

SCAN FOR
MULTIMEDIA

NOTES

CLOSE READ
ANNOTATE: Mark the nouns in paragraph 1, which is the Preamble to the Constitution.

QUESTION: Why does the author list this particular series of nouns?

CONCLUDE: What do these nouns establish as the purpose of this document?

exercise (EHK suhr syz) *n.* implementation; state of putting something into action

abridging (uh BRIHJ ihng) *adj.* limiting

petition (puh TIHSH uhn) *v.* formally request; seek help from

redress (rih DREHS) *n.* correction; setting right of some wrong

infringed (ihn FRIHNJD) *v.* violated

prescribed (prih SKRYBD) *v.* stated in writing; set down as a rule

5 ARTICLES in addition to, and Amendment of the Constitution of the United States of America, proposed by Congress, and ratified by the Legislatures of the several States, pursuant to the fifth Article of the original Constitution.

Amendment I

6 Congress shall make no law respecting an establishment of religion, or prohibiting the free **exercise** thereof; or **abridging** the freedom of speech, or of the press; or the right of the people peaceably to assemble, and to **petition** the Government for a **redress** of grievances.

Amendment II

7 A well regulated militia, being necessary to the security of a free State, the right of the people to keep and bear arms, shall not be **infringed**.

Amendment III

8 No soldier shall, in time of peace be quartered in any house, without the consent of the owner, nor in time of war, but in a manner to be **prescribed** by law.

Amendment IV

9 The right of the people to be secure in their persons, houses, papers, and effects, against unreasonable searches and seizures, shall not be violated, and no warrants shall issue, but upon probable cause, supported by oath or affirmation, and particularly describing the place to be searched, and the persons or things to be seized.

Amendment V

10 No person shall be held to answer for a capital,[2] or otherwise infamous crime, unless on a presentment or indictment of a Grand Jury, except in cases arising in the land or naval forces, or in the militia, when in actual service in time of war or public danger; nor shall any person be subject for the same offence to be twice put in jeopardy of life or limb; nor shall be compelled in any criminal case to be a witness against himself, nor be deprived of life, liberty, or property, without due process of law; nor shall private property be taken for public use, without just compensation.

Amendment VI

11 In all criminal prosecutions, the accused shall enjoy the right to a speedy and public trial, by an impartial jury of the State and district wherein the crime shall have been committed, which district shall have been previously ascertained by law, and to be informed of the nature and cause of the accusation; to be confronted with the witnesses against him; to have compulsory process for obtaining witnesses in his favor, and to have the Assistance of Counsel[3] for his defense.

---

2. **capital** *adj.* punishable by execution.
3. **Counsel** *n.* lawyer or group of lawyers giving advice about legal matters and representing clients in court.

CLOSE READ

ANNOTATE: Mark the adjectives that appear in Amendment VI.

QUESTION: Why are the few adjectives used in this section important?

CONCLUDE: What effect might this language have on someone accused of a crime?

Amendment VII

12 In suits[4] at common law, where the value in controversy shall exceed twenty dollars, the right of trial by jury shall be preserved, and no fact tried by a jury, shall be otherwise re-examined in any Court of the United States, than according to the rules of the common law.

Amendment VIII

13 Excessive bail[5] shall not be required, nor excessive fines imposed, nor cruel and unusual punishments inflicted.

Amendment IX

14 The enumeration in the Constitution, of certain rights, shall not be construed to deny or disparage others retained by the people.

Amendment X

15 The powers not delegated to the United States by the Constitution, nor prohibited by it to the States, are reserved to the States respectively, or to the people. ❧

---

4. **suits** *n.* lawsuits, or legal actions brought by one party against another.
5. **bail** *n.* property or money given to the court to ensure that an arrested person released from custody will return at a certain time.

Comprehension Check

Complete the following items after you finish your first read.

1. According to its Preamble, who is responsible for establishing the Constitution?

2. What laws are forbidden in Amendment I of the Bill of Rights?

3. Which amendments cover legal proceedings?

4. 🗐 **Notebook** Write a summary of the Preamble to the Constitution and a summary of the Bill of Rights to confirm your understanding of the texts.

- -

RESEARCH

Research to Clarify Choose at least one unfamiliar detail from these texts. Briefly research that detail. In what way does the information you learned shed light on an aspect of these documents?

Close Read the Text

1. This model—Amendment III of the Bill of Rights—shows two sample annotations, along with questions and conclusions. Close read the passage, and find another detail to annotate. Then, write a question and your conclusion.

Close Read
ANNOTATE · QUESTION · CONCLUDE

> **ANNOTATE:** These parallel phrases speak to both peace and wartime situations.
>
> **QUESTION:** What do these details say about early American attitudes toward the military?
>
> **CONCLUDE:** They suggest that early Americans wanted to limit military power unless it was needed.

> No soldier, shall in time of peace be quartered in any house, without the consent of the owner, nor in time of war, but in a manner to be prescribed by law.

> **ANNOTATE:** The paragraph presents contrasting ideas—"consent of the owner" and "prescribed by law."
>
> **QUESTION:** What balance of power do these terms suggest?
>
> **CONCLUDE:** In peacetime, personal choice overrides government concerns; the opposite may be true during wartime.

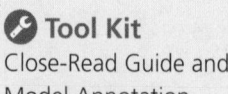 **Tool Kit**
Close-Read Guide and
Model Annotation

2. For more practice, go back into the text and complete the close-read notes.

3. Revisit a section of the text you found important during your first read. **Annotate** what you notice. Ask yourself **questions** such as "Why did the author make this choice?" What can you **conclude**?

Analyze the Text

CITE TEXTUAL EVIDENCE to support your answers.

Notebook Respond to these questions.

1. **Analyze** How can you tell from the Preamble that the Constitution is meant to do more than merely resolve the country's issues at that time?

2. **Connect** How does Amendment II of the Bill of Rights reinforce Amendment I?

3. (a) **Paraphrase** When you **paraphrase**, you restate a text in your own words. Paraphrase Amendment VIII. (b) **Analyze** How does this amendment relate to the theme of freedom? Explain.

4. **Historical Perspectives** Which Americans were not granted the freedoms and rights set forth in the Constitution and the Bill of Rights?

5. **Essential Question: *What is the meaning of freedom?*** What have you learned about American freedoms by reading these documents?

STANDARDS

Reading Informational Text
• Analyze and evaluate the effectiveness of the structure an author uses in his or her exposition or argument, including whether the structure makes points clear, convincing, and engaging.
• Analyze seventeenth-, eighteenth-, and nineteenth-century foundational U.S. documents of historical and literary significance for their themes, purposes, and rhetorical features.

Analyze Craft and Structure

Author's Choices: Structure Both the Constitution and the Bill of Rights are **resolutions**, or legal foundational statements that explain a set of decisions approved by a governing body. Likewise, both begin with a **preamble**, a statement that explains who is issuing the document and for what purpose. The text that follows the Preamble to the Bill of Rights illustrates a simple structure called **enumeration**, in which the major ideas (the first ten amendments) are listed in numerical order. Each of the amendments follows a regular structure, beginning with a **heading**, or label.

Practice

CITE TEXTUAL EVIDENCE to support your answers.

Answer these questions.

1. What does the preamble to the Bill of Rights tell readers about the reasons the document was created?

2. Why is "RESOLVED" used to begin the second paragraph of the Preamble?

3. Explain why enumeration is an effective organizational pattern for the Bill of Rights.

4. (a) In the chart, record the major idea of each amendment listed—specifically, what rights or related set of rights does each amendment protect? (b) How is Amendment IX different from the other amendments? Explain.

AMENDMENT	MAJOR IDEA
II	
III	
IV	
VI	
VII	
X	

Concept Vocabulary

exercise	petition	infringed
abridging	redress	prescribed

Why These Words? These concept vocabulary words suggest legal limitations or remedies. For example, the Bill of Rights was written to ensure that nothing *infringed* upon citizens' rights. The document outlines basic rights but does not explain certain points in detail—for example, exactly what *redress* will be available when a wrong is committed. Both *infringed* and *redress* refer to legal matters.

1. How does the concept vocabulary allow the writers to present ideas with both formality and precision?

2. What other words in these documents connect to the concept of legal limitations or remedies?

Practice

📓 **Notebook** **Complete these activities.**

1. Use each concept vocabulary word in a sentence that demonstrates your understanding of the word's meaning.

2. Replace each concept word with a synonym. Use a thesaurus, if you wish. Then, consider which word best expresses your meaning. Which is the clearer, more precise word?

Word Study

Multiple-Meaning Words The concept vocabulary word *exercise* has more than one meaning. As a noun, *exercise* can refer to physical exertion that maintains or improves health. It also can refer to an activity that tests or displays a particular skill. As a verb, it can refer to the action of physical training or the action of implementing one's right to do something.

1. Write four sentences using the word *exercise*. Each sentence should demonstrate one of the four meanings of the word noted above.

2. The concept words *abridging*, *petition*, and *prescribed* are also multiple-meaning words. For each word, write its meaning as it is used in the Bill of Rights. Then, write a second meaning for each word. Use a college-level dictionary to verify your work.

🗂 **WORD NETWORK**

Add words related to freedom from the text to your Word Network.

Conventions and Style

Punctuation for Enumeration Listing, or enumeration, is an important characteristic of the style used in these documents. When enumerating ideas, place a comma between each item in the series. The choice to use the **serial comma** in a list of three or more enumerated items is a matter of style. If it is used, the serial comma is placed immediately before the coordinating conjunction (usually *and, or,* or *nor*). In addition, enumerated text must demonstrate **parallel structure.** For instance, if two items in the list are prepositional phrases, then the remaining items should also be prepositional phrases.

TYPE OF ITEM	EXAMPLE OF PARALLEL STRUCTURE
single words	*nor be deprived of life, liberty, or property (nouns, from Amendment V)*
phrases	*in order to form a more perfect union, [to] establish justice, [to] insure domestic tranquility, [to] provide for the common defense, [to] promote the general welfare, and [to] secure the blessings of liberty to ourselves and our posterity (infinitive phrases, from the Preamble to the Constitution)*
clauses	*Excessive bail shall not be required, nor [shall] excessive fines [be] imposed, nor [shall] cruel and unusual punishments [be] inflicted (independent clauses, from Amendment VIII)*

Read It

1. Add commas to each sentence about these documents. Then, identify what type of item has been enumerated in each sentence.
   a. The Preamble to the Constitution secures "the blessings of liberty" to the American people to their descendants and to every generation.
   b. These brief historic and comprehensive amendments shape many aspects of American life.
   c. Today, Americans can read the text of the Bill of Rights online they can purchase printed copies or they can see one of the original documents on display.

2. **Notebook** **Connect to Style** Reread the Preamble to the Constitution. Explain how enumeration helps Madison convey a great deal of information in a compact space.

Write It

 Notebook Use enumeration to revise and expand upon these sentences. Use commas to make the enumeration clear.

> EXAMPLE
> **Original Sentence:** Amendment VI identifies rights of defendants.
> **Sentence with Enumeration:** According to Amendment VI, defendants **will have a speedy and public trial, will face witnesses,** and **will be represented by a lawyer.**

1. James Madison included several freedoms in Amendment I.
2. Today, the Bill of Rights does many things for Americans.

TIP

CLARIFICATION
Serial commas can increase the clarity of your writing. Consider this sentence without a serial comma: "The actress plays Marina, a mermaid and a comedian." Did the actress play one person, Marina, who is a mermaid and a comedian? Or did she play three separate characters? Use of the serial comma eliminates this ambiguity.

PREAMBLE TO THE
CONSTITUTION | BILL OF RIGHTS

Writing to Sources

The Preamble to the Constitution and the Bill of Rights are examples of informative writing. Like other kinds of informative writing, they were written primarily to convey facts. The facts are organized and presented in a way that best suits the writer's purpose and the audience's needs.

Assignment

An extended definition is an informative text—usually one or two paragraphs—that explains a key concept. Choose and reread one amendment from the Bill of Rights. Then, write an **extended definition** of a key word or concept presented in that amendment. Your extended definition should explain both the dictionary meaning of the word or concept and any shades of meaning reflected in the amendment. Use at least two of these techniques to clarify your information and engage readers.

- Compare and contrast the word or concept with more familiar words or concepts.
- Discuss what the word or concept does *not* mean.
- Identify meanings that people often assign to the word or concept.
- Provide examples of ways in which the word or concept is used today.
- Share a personal experience that helped you understand the word or concept.

Vocabulary and Conventions Connection Consider including several of the concept vocabulary words. Also, remember to use commas correctly if you include enumeration.

exercise	petition	infringed
abridging	redress	prescribed

Reflect on Your Writing

After you have drafted your extended definition, answer these questions.

1. Which techniques did you use to develop your extended definition?

2. In what ways did those techniques strengthen your writing?

3. Why These Words? The words you choose make a difference in your writing. Which words made your text more powerful or precise?

STANDARDS

Writing
Develop the topic thoroughly by selecting the most significant and relevant facts, extended definitions, concrete details, quotations, or other information and examples appropriate to the audience's knowledge of the topic.

Speaking and Listening
Present information, findings, and supporting evidence, conveying a clear and distinct perspective such that listeners can follow the line of reasoning, alternative or opposing perspectives are addressed, and the organization, development, substance, and style are appropriate to purpose, audience, and a range of formal and informal tasks.

Speaking and Listening

Assignment

Write and deliver a **speech** about the Bill of Rights, in which you explain how the document as a whole, or a particular amendment, applies to your life. If you wish, work as a class to share these speeches as part of a lecture series called "It's My Right!"

1. **Write the Speech** Think about the Bill of Rights. How does it relate to your life? Which amendments are especially significant to you? Why?

   - Have you had any experiences involving freedom of religion, freedom of speech, or freedom of the press? If so, think about the protections offered by Amendment I.

   - How do you expect the Bill of Rights to affect your life in the future?

   - Draft your speech, using facts and examples to illustrate your personal response to the document.

2. **Deliver the Speech** To prepare to deliver your speech, review your text and practice presenting it. Mark the words you will emphasize, points at which to pause or stop for effect, and so on.

   - As you deliver the speech, make eye contact with your audience. Don't stare; rather, look at audience members for a few seconds to make sure they understand your message.

   - Use appropriate volume so everyone can hear you, even in the back rows. Carry yourself proudly, and hold your head up so that your voice carries.

   - Avoid rushing. Remember that your audience has not heard your speech before. Give them time to absorb your words and meaning.

3. **Evaluate Your Presentation** After your speech, use the evaluation guide to assess how well you presented your ideas. Did you fulfill the assignment by showing how the Bill of Rights applies to your life? Were your ideas logical, clear, and appropriate to your audience and subject? Use your self-evaluation to establish several goals for your next oral presentation.

PRESENTATION EVALUATION GUIDE
Rate each statement on a scale of 1 (not demonstrated) to 5 (demonstrated).
☐ I conveyed a personal understanding of the Bill of Rights.
☐ I held the audience's attention.
☐ I used appropriate eye contact to convey meaning and sufficient volume to be heard.
☐ I did not rush and pronounced words correctly and clearly.

✐ EVIDENCE LOG

Before moving on to a new selection, go to your Evidence Log and record what you learned from the Preamble to the Constitution and from the Bill of Rights.

Speech in the Convention

Concept Vocabulary

You will encounter the following words as you read the speech Benjamin Franklin gave at the Constitutional Convention in 1787. Before reading, note how familiar you are with each word. Then, rank the words in order from most familiar (1) to least familiar (6).

WORD	YOUR RANKING
infallibility	
despotism	
corrupted	
prejudices	
salutary	
integrity	

After completing the first read, come back to the concept vocabulary and review your rankings. Mark changes to your original rankings as needed.

First Read NONFICTION

Apply these strategies as you conduct your first read. You will have an opportunity to complete the close-read notes after your first read.

Tool Kit
First-Read Guide and
Model Annotation

NOTICE the general ideas of the text. *What* is it about? *Who* is involved?

ANNOTATE by marking vocabulary and key passages you want to revisit.

First Read

CONNECT ideas within the selection to what you already know and what you have already read.

RESPOND by completing the Comprehension Check and by writing a brief summary of the selection.

STANDARDS

Reading Informational Text
By the end of grade 11, read and comprehend literary nonfiction in the grades 11–CCR text complexity band proficiently, with scaffolding as needed at the high end of the range.

About the Author

Benjamin Franklin

From his teen years until his retirement at age forty-two, Benjamin Franklin (1706–1790) worked as a printer. He got his start as an apprentice to his brother James Franklin, a Boston printer. By the time he was sixteen, Ben was not only printing, but writing parts of his brother's newspaper. Using the name "Silence Dogood," he wrote letters satirizing daily life and politics in Boston. When he was seventeen, Franklin moved to Philadelphia to open his own print shop. This move gave birth to one of his most enduring contributions to American culture, *Poor Richard's Almanack*. This annual publication, which was published from 1732 to 1752, contained information, observations, and advice and was a colonial bestseller.

The "Write" Reputation Just as he had signed "Silence Dogood" to the letters he wrote for his brother's paper, Franklin created a fictitious author/editor for the *Almanack*. The chatty Richard Saunders, or Poor Richard, first appeared as a dull and foolish astronomer. However, over the years his character developed, becoming more thoughtful, pious, and funny.

Like most almanacs, *Poor Richard's Almanack* contained practical information about the calendar, the sun and moon, and the weather. It also featured a wealth of homespun sayings and observations, or aphorisms, many of which are still quoted today. It was these aphorisms that made the *Almanack* so popular. Franklin included an aphorism at the top or bottom of most of the Almanack's pages. The wit and brevity of these sayings allowed him to weave in many moral messages, while also entertaining his readers.

Inventor and Scientist When Franklin was forty-two, he retired from the printing business to devote himself to science. He proved to be as successful a scientist as he had been a printer. Over the course of his life, Franklin was responsible for inventing the lightning rod, bifocals, and a new type of stove. He confirmed the laws of electricity, charted the Gulf Stream, and contributed to the scientific understanding of earthquakes and ocean currents. In spite of all these achievements, Franklin is best remembered for his career in politics.

Statesman and Diplomat Franklin played an important role in drafting the Declaration of Independence, enlisting French support during the Revolutionary War, negotiating a peace treaty with Britain, and drafting the United States Constitution. In his later years, he was the United States ambassador to England and then to France. Even before George Washington earned the title, Franklin was considered to be "the father of his country."

American Success Story Perhaps it is no surprise that a person of Franklin's accomplishments, longevity, and historic importance would write the story of his life. Franklin's *The Autobiography* remains a classic of the genre as well as a prototype for the American success story. Franklin wrote the first section of the work in 1771, when he was sixty-five years old. At the urging of friends, he wrote three more sections—the last shortly before his death—but succeeded in bringing the account of his life only to the year 1759. Though never completed, his autobiography, filled with his opinions and advice, provides not only a record of his achievements, but also an understanding of his extraordinary character.

Speech
in the
Convention

Benjamin Franklin

BACKGROUND

After the American Revolution, each of the newly independent states created its own constitution. While Congress was able to pass limited laws, it had no power to tax the states or regulate issues, such as trade, that were affected by state boundaries. These problems led to the Constitutional Convention in 1787. Representatives from twelve states met to approve a national constitution. The argument was lively and often contentious. At the age of eighty-one, Benjamin Franklin—representing Pennsylvania—brought his diplomatic skills to the debate.

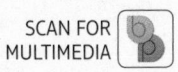

SCAN FOR
MULTIMEDIA

NOTES

Mr. President,

1   I confess, that I do not entirely approve of this Constitution at present; but, Sir, I am not sure I shall never approve it; for, having lived long, I have experienced many instances of being obliged, by better information or fuller consideration, to change my opinions even on important subjects, which I once thought right, but found to be otherwise. It is therefore that, the older I grow, the more apt I am to doubt my own judgment of others. Most men, indeed, as well as most sects in religion, think themselves in possession of all truth, and that wherever others differ from them, it is so far error. . . . Though many private persons think almost as highly of their own **infallibility** as of that of their sect, few express it so naturally as a certain French lady, who, in a little dispute with her sister, said, "But I meet with nobody but myself that is *always* in the right." "*Je ne trouve que moi qui aie toujours raison.*"

2   In these sentiments, Sir, I agree to this Constitution, with all its faults,—if they are such; because I think a general government necessary for us, and there is no form of government but what may be a blessing to the people, if well administered; and I believe, farther, that this is likely to be well administered for a course of years, and can only end in **despotism**, as other forms have done before it, when the people shall become so **corrupted** as to need despotic government, being incapable of any other. I doubt, too, whether any other convention we can obtain, may be able to make a better constitution; for, when you assemble a number of men, to have the advantage of their joint wisdom, you inevitably assemble with those men all their **prejudices**, their passions, their errors of opinion, their local interests, and their selfish views. From such an assembly can a *perfect* production be expected? It therefore astonishes me, Sir, to find this system approaching so near to perfection as it does; and I think it will astonish our enemies, who are waiting with confidence to hear, that our councils are confounded like those of the builders of Babel, and that our states are on the point of separation, only to meet hereafter for the purpose of cutting one another's throats. Thus I consent, Sir, to this Constitution, because I expect no better, and because I am not sure that it is not the best. The opinions I have had

infallibility (ihn fal uh BIHL uh tee) *n*. inability to be in error

CLOSE READ

ANNOTATE: Franklin refers humorously to "a certain French lady." Mark her words and their English translation in paragraph 1.

QUESTION: Why does Franklin choose to illustrate his point in this way?

CONCLUDE: What is the effect of this quotation?

despotism (DEHS puh tihz uhm) *n*. absolute rule; tyranny

corrupted (kuh RUHPT ihd) *adj*. dishonest

prejudices (PREHJ uh dihs ihz) *n*. unfavorable opinions or feelings formed beforehand or without factual support

salutary (SAL yuh tehr ee) *adj.* beneficial; promoting a positive purpose

integrity (ihn TEHG ruh tee) *n.* virtue; commitment to moral or ethical principles

of its *errors* I sacrifice to the public good. I have never whispered a syllable of them abroad. Within these walls they were born, and here they shall die. If every one of us, in returning to our constituents, were to report the objections he has had to it, and endeavor to gain partisans in support of them, we might prevent its being generally received, and thereby lose all the **salutary** effects and great advantages resulting naturally in our favor among foreign nations, as well as among ourselves, from our real or apparent unanimity. Much of the strength and efficiency of any government, in procuring and securing happiness to the people, depends on *opinion*, on the general opinion of the goodness of that government, as well as of the wisdom and **integrity** of its governors. I hope, therefore, for our own sakes, as a part of the people, and for the sake of our posterity, that we shall act heartily and unanimously in recommending this Constitution, wherever our influence may extend, and turn our future thoughts and endeavors to the means of having it *well administered*.

3   On the whole, Sir, I cannot help expressing a wish, that every member of the convention who may still have objections to it, would with me on this occasion doubt a little of his own infallibility, and, to make manifest our *unanimity*, put his name to this instrument. ❧

MEDIA CONNECTION

The U. S. Constitution

💬 **Discuss It** How does this video help you understand the challenges that Franklin faced in persuading the delegates to approve the Constitution?

Write your response before sharing your ideas.

SCAN FOR MULTIMEDIA

Comprehension Check

Complete the following items after you finish your first read.

1. What does Franklin admit has caused him to change his mind in the past?

2. Why does Franklin believe that any constitution the Convention approves will be an imperfect document?

3. Why does Franklin want the delegates to keep their divided opinions to themselves once the Constitution is approved?

4. Whose "opinion" does Franklin believe is key to a government's strength and efficiency?

5. 🗐 **Notebook** Write a summary of Franklin's speech to confirm your understanding of the text.

RESEARCH

Research to Clarify Choose at least one unfamiliar detail from the text. Briefly research that detail. In what way does the information you learned shed light on an aspect of the speech?

Research to Explore Conduct research on an aspect of the text you find interesting. For example, you might research why Franklin was one of the most popular authors and public figures of his time.

SPEECH IN THE CONVENTION

Close Read the Text

1. This model, from paragraph 1 of the speech, shows two sample annotations, along with questions and conclusions. Close read the passage, and find another detail to annotate. Then, write a question and your conclusion.

> **ANNOTATE:** The word "confess" is a startling beginning to a speech.
>
> **QUESTION:** Why does Franklin say this?
>
> **CONCLUDE:** By confessing to his own struggle, Franklin shows that compromise is not a sign of weakness.

> I confess, that I do not entirely approve of this Constitution at present; but, Sir, I am not sure I shall never approve it; for, having lived long, I have experienced many instances of being obliged, by better information or fuller consideration, to change my opinions. . . .

> **ANNOTATE:** Franklin reminds listeners of his old age.
>
> **QUESTION:** Why does he make this point?
>
> **CONCLUDE:** He is reminding them of his age and experience—he has authority his listeners lack.

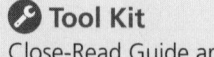 **Tool Kit**
Close-Read Guide and Model Annotation

2. For more practice, go back into the text and complete the close-read notes.

3. Revisit a section of the text you found important during your first read. Read this section closely, and **annotate** what you notice. Ask yourself **questions** such as "Why did the author make this choice?" What can you **conclude**?

Analyze the Text

CITE TEXTUAL EVIDENCE to support your answers.

📓 **Notebook** Respond to these questions.

1. **Draw Conclusions** Franklin addresses his remarks to "Mr. President"— George Washington, who led the proceedings. How can you tell that his remarks do not concern Washington alone?

2. (a) Early in the speech, what does Franklin admit that he sometimes doubts? (b) **Connect** How does this admission relate to his overall argument?

3. An **allusion** is a passing or unexplained reference to something from history or culture. (a) **Interpret** In paragraph 2, what is the purpose of Franklin's allusion to the builders of Babel? (b) **Criticize** Do you consider this allusion to be effective? Explain.

4. **Historical Perspectives** In what ways does Franklin fear the delegates may undermine the Constitution even after they sign it? Explain.

5. **Essential Question:** *What is the meaning of freedom?* What have you learned about the nature of freedom by reading this speech?

STANDARDS
Reading Informational Text
• Cite strong and thorough textual evidence to support analysis of what the text says explicitly as well as inferences drawn from the text, including determining where the text leaves matters uncertain.
• Determine an author's point of view or purpose in a text in which the rhetoric is particularly effective, analyzing how style and content contribute to the power, persuasiveness or beauty of the text.

Analyze Craft and Structure

Author's Purpose: Rhetoric Franklin's speech was successful: The Constitution was approved and sent to the states for ratification. Franklin's text provides examples of several **rhetorical devices**, or ways of using language for effect, that appeal to an audience and produce a successful oratory.

- **Paradox** is a statement or idea that seems contradictory but actually presents a truth. For example, in Shakespeare's *Hamlet*, the statement "I must be cruel to be kind" seems illogical. On reflection, however, it demonstrates a deeper truth: Sometimes, one must face a painful reality in order to rise above or learn from it.

- **Concession** is the acknowledgment of an opponent's arguments.

- **Rhetorical questions** are questions asked for effect—to make a point, or introduce a topic. The speaker does not expect the audience to answer, because the answer is obvious.

While not strictly an example of a rhetorical device, a speaker's **tone,** or attitude toward the subject and audience, can also sway listeners. Phrasing and word choice combine to convey tone, which may be ironic, serious, humorous, friendly, distant, cynical, earnest, and so on.

Practice

CITE TEXTUAL EVIDENCE to support your answers.

📓 **Notebook** Complete these activities.

1. Use the chart to identify examples from Franklin's speech of each rhetorical device noted. Explain how each device serves to strengthen Franklin's argument or influence his audience.

RHETORICAL DEVICE	EFFECT
paradox:	
concession:	
rhetorical question:	

2. (a) Choose the set of adjectives that best describes the tone of the first paragraph of this speech.

   ☐ slyly humorous and self-deprecating

   ☐ deeply earnest, concerned, and frustrated

   ☐ serious, witty, and informal

   (b) Explain your choice, citing specific words and phrases that support your answer.

3. During his long political career, Franklin had extensive experience as a diplomat. In what ways does this speech reflect a diplomatic approach to conflict? Explain.

SPEECH IN THE CONVENTION

Concept Vocabulary

infallibility	corrupted	salutary
despotism	prejudices	integrity

Why These Words? These concept vocabulary words are used to describe human vices and virtues, especially when it comes to the power governments can wield over citizens. Franklin believes any government can be *corrupted*, and that those in positions of leadership should have *integrity*.

1. How does the concept vocabulary suggest human goals—and the human failings that make the achievement of those goals difficult?

2. What other words in the speech connect to this concept?

Practice

🗐 **Notebook** Respond to these questions.

1. Why might it be difficult to deal with people who never doubt their own *infallibility*?

2. What are two negative effects that might result from a government ruled by *despotism*?

3. What safeguards could a constitution include to minimize the chance that a government will be *corrupted*?

4. Name two ways in which *prejudices* can affect human behavior.

5. What *salutary* effects can result from cooperation?

6. Would you vote for a candidate who displayed *integrity*? Why or why not?

Word Study

Latin Suffix: -ity The suffix *-ity* means "state or quality of." When this suffix is added to an adjective, the resulting word is a noun. For example, in the word *infallibility,* the suffix is added to the adjective *infallible,* which means "incapable of failing." The resulting noun means "the state of being incapable of failing."

1. Find and define two other words near the end of Franklin's speech that end with the suffix *-ity*. Check your definitions in a print or digital college-level dictionary.

2. Identify and define two other words that end with the suffix *-ity*. Use a dictionary to verify your definitions.

Conventions and Style

Syntax and Rhetoric **Parallelism** is the use of similar grammatical forms or patterns to express similar ideas. Effective use of parallelism adds rhythm and balance to writing and strengthens connections among ideas. Faulty parallelism presents equal ideas in a distracting and potentially confusing mix of grammatical forms.

> EXAMPLE
>
> **Nonparallel:** Franklin **was supportive of** the Constitution, **went to express** his feelings, and **was writing** emphatically about the document.
>
> **Parallel:** Franklin **supported** the Constitution, **expressed** his feelings to others, and **wrote** emphatically about the document.

The parallel sentence states three similar ideas as phrases that begin with an action verb in the simple past tense.

Read It

1. Underline the parallel elements in these sentences.

   a. The sensible, brilliant, and influential James Wilson was among the delegates from Pennsylvania.

   b. Franklin was too weak to deliver the speech himself—but was the weakness due to his unremitting pain, his unceasing work for compromise, or his exhaustion after days of argument?

   c. Wilson read the speech, which came at a critical moment in the proceedings, addressed the need for compromise, and swayed several delegates.

2. **Connect to Style** Reread paragraph 2 of Franklin's speech. Identify two examples of parallelism. Explain the ideas the parallel items express.

Write It

 Notebook Rewrite each sentence so that it uses parallelism. Be sure to place commas to separate the ideas or details.

> EXAMPLE
>
> **Incorrect:** *Fueled by love for liberty, eager to form an effective government,* and *with personal determination,* several political leaders founded the Society for Political Inquiries in 1787.
>
> **Correct:** *Fueled by love for liberty, eagerness to form an effective government,* and *personal determination*, several political leaders founded the Society for Political Inquiries in 1787.

1. The society's members considered issues of government, wrote essays on political topics, and there were discussions about how governments can serve people.

2. At the Constitutional Convention, throughout the fight for state ratification, and when Washington was president, this group continued to function.

TIP

USAGE

When you use correlative conjunctions (which appear in pairs) to achieve parallelism, make sure that the words are in the correct order.

Incorrect: Franklin **not only** wanted unanimity **but also** civility.

Correct: Franklin wanted **not only** unanimity **but also** civility.

SPEECH IN THE CONVENTION

Writing to Sources

When you evaluate a text—whether you do so in writing, in discussions with other readers, or just in your own thinking process—you consider what an author sought to achieve in a piece of writing and whether he or she was successful.

Assignment

Franklin's speech in the Convention has been called a masterpiece. Do you agree? Write an **evaluation** of the speech. Consider Franklin's goal and the techniques he used to accomplish it. Be sure to include these elements in your evaluation:

- an introduction that includes a statement of your position
- at least one reference to Franklin's goal
- valid reasoning, supported by textual evidence that clearly relates to each point
- specific references to the ideas Franklin conveyed and to his use of rhetorical devices
- original rhetorical devices that help you make your points
- a conclusion that reasserts your opinion in a memorable way

Vocabulary and Conventions Connection Consider including several of the concept vocabulary words in your evaluation. Also, remember to use parallelism to emphasize related ideas and create rhythm in your writing.

infallibility	corrupted	salutary
despotism	prejudices	integrity

Reflect on Your Writing

After you have drafted your evaluation, answer the following questions.

1. What evidence did you provide in your evaluation?

2. What rhetorical devices did you use in your evaluation?

3. Why These Words? The words you choose make a difference in your writing. Which words helped you express your ideas?

☷ STANDARDS

Writing
- Write arguments to support claims in an analysis of substantive topics or texts, using valid reasoning and relevant and sufficient evidence.
- Provide a concluding statement or section that follows from and supports the argument presented.

Speaking and Listening
- Evaluate a speaker's point of view, reasoning, and use of evidence and rhetoric, assessing the stance, premises, links among ideas, word choice, points of emphasis, and tone used.
- Make strategic use of digital media in presentations to enhance understanding of findings, reasoning, and evidence and to add interest.

Speaking and Listening

Assignment

As a class, prepare to make a **video recording** of a dramatic delivery of Franklin's speech. Follow these steps to complete the assignment.

1. **Discuss the Speech** Use a class discussion to clarify your thoughts about the speech. Be prepared to share notes you made while reading the text as you and your classmates respond to these questions.

   - What is Franklin's opinion of the Constitution in its draft form?

   - How does he use concession and paradox as he argues his position?

   - What is his tone? How does Franklin's tone appeal to his audience and help persuade them of the validity of his opinion?

   - What are some of the ways in which Franklin's tone could be expressed in a dramatic reading?

2. **Practice and Present** Work together to decide who will read various parts of the speech. Have classmates take a few minutes to practice their parts individually, using Franklin's punctuation to help with phrasing and checking the pronunciation of challenging words. Next, practice together so that the reading moves smoothly from one speaker to the next. Then, present the speech as your teacher makes a video recording. Remember these points:

   - Be quiet and attentive while others are presenting their parts.

   - Use the tone and emphasis that you think Franklin might have used if he had delivered the speech himself.

   - Use appropriate gestures to convey key points.

3. **Evaluate the Video** Schedule sufficient time to watch the video. Allow about ten minutes for the follow-up discussion. Then, use the evaluation guide to analyze what you saw and heard. Encourage everyone to contribute. If possible, add the video to the class website or digital portfolio.

EVALUATION GUIDE

Rate each statement on a scale of 1 (not demonstrated) to 5 (demonstrated). Be prepared to defend your rating, using examples.

☐ Speakers clearly conveyed the text's meaning.

☐ Speakers held the audience's attention.

☐ Speakers used the tone and emphasis that Franklin likely intended when he wrote the speech.

☐ Speakers used appropriate gestures and body language.

✎ EVIDENCE LOG

Before moving on to a new selection, go to your Evidence Log and record what you learned from Franklin's speech in the Convention.

About Visual Propaganda

Whether printed on posters or in newspapers, sewn into the design of a flag, broadcast in television commercials, or presented in other forms, **visual propaganda** uses striking images (and sometimes simple slogans) to convey a persuasive message, especially during times of turmoil, such as war. One of the earliest examples can be seen in Mesopotamian carvings announcing a military victory in 2250 B.C. The Bayeux Tapestry provided woven visual propaganda about the Norman Conquest in A.D. 1066. Visual propaganda was especially critical during the Russian Revolution in 1917, and during World War I, when the political poster was created to rouse patriotic fervor.

The American Revolution: Visual Propaganda

Media Vocabulary

These words or concepts will be useful to you as you analyze, discuss, and write about visual propaganda.

propaganda: information, ideas, or rumors spread widely and deliberately to help or harm a person, group, movement, cause, or nation	• Creators of propaganda attempt to persuade people by presenting images and words that strongly suggest a particular *slant*, or viewpoint. • Propaganda encourages people to react emotionally rather than logically—for example, to vote a certain way out of fear or to oppose a cause out of anger.
appeal: the ability to attract and engage an audience's mind or emotions	• A logical appeal (called *logos*) influences reason. • An emotional appeal (called *pathos*) targets or manipulates people's feelings. • Propaganda depends much more heavily upon pathos than upon logos.
symbolism: the use of images or objects to represent ideas or qualities	• Symbolism uses images and objects that many people associate with certain concepts, such as a flag to represent a country, a rose to represent love, or the color red to represent danger. • In propaganda, symbolism appears primarily in visuals because it provides a quick way to convey meaning. • An image or object can have more than one symbolic meaning. The meaning can vary from one culture to another.

First Review MEDIA: ART AND PHOTOGRAPHY

Apply these strategies as you conduct your first review.

LOOK at each image and determine *whom* or *what* it portrays.

NOTE elements in each image that you find interesting and want to revisit.

First Review

CONNECT details in the images to other media you've experienced, texts you've read, or images you've seen.

RESPOND by completing the Comprehension Check at the end.

STANDARDS

Reading Informational Text
By the end of grade 11, read and comprehend literary nonfiction in the grades 11–CCR text complexity band proficiently, with scaffolding as needed at the high end of the range.

The American Revolution:
Visual Propaganda

BACKGROUND

The practice of persuading people with paintings, drawings, and other kinds of images has a long history in the United States, dating back to the colonial period. The images that follow are examples of visual propaganda published by both the colonists and the British in support of their respective causes.

SCAN FOR
MULTIMEDIA

IMAGE 1: Join or Die This political cartoon was published by Benjamin Franklin in 1754. The segments of the snake are labeled with the initials of American colonies. The purpose of the cartoon was to urge the colonies to unite against the French in the French and Indian War. During the American Revolution, it took on new meaning as a symbol of colonial protest against Great Britain.

NOTES

IMAGE 2: The Boston Massacre

Paul Revere engraved this image in 1770 after the Boston Massacre, in which several colonists were shot to death by British soldiers. Revere's depiction does not show the events exactly as they happened. For example, the Americans had been rioting against the British authorities when the shots were fired. Also, the British did not have a clear firing line. Rather, they had been surrounded and were struggling with the crowd.

NOTES

IMAGE 3: The Bostonians in Distress This print was published in a London newspaper during the British blockade of Boston in 1774. In the image, colonists feed caged Bostonians as the British navy continues to keep Boston Harbor closed. The image may have amused the British—but it may have provoked very different feelings among Americans who saw it.

NOTES

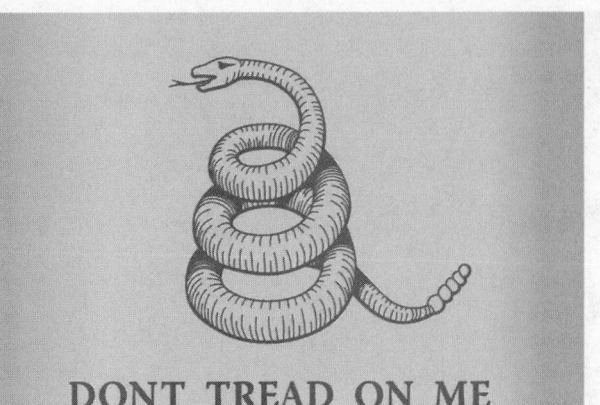

IMAGE 4: The Gadsden Flag Colonist Christopher Gadsden created this flag during the American Revolution. Referencing Franklin's "Join or Die" cartoon, the flag is expressly directed at the English, showing a whole snake ready to strike.

NOTES

IMAGE 5: Poor Old England The caption for this cartoon reads, "Poor Old England, Endeavoring to Reclaim His Wicked American Children." The scene represents efforts by King George III to harness and control the colonists, who show no signs of either respecting or submitting to the king's wishes. This cartoon was published in London in 1777, fourteen months after the signing of the Declaration of Independence.

NOTES

Comprehension Check

Use the chart to note details about each image. Identify the main people and/or objects in the image and the activity depicted. Use the captions where helpful. In the final column, express your idea about the overall purpose of the image as a piece of propaganda.

IMAGE	PEOPLE AND/OR OBJECTS	ACTIVITY IN THE IMAGE	PURPOSE OF THE IMAGE
IMAGE 1			
IMAGE 2			
IMAGE 3			
IMAGE 4			
IMAGE 5			

JOIN, or DIE.

THE AMERICAN REVOLUTION:
VISUAL PROPAGANDA

Close Review

Revisit the images and your first-review notes. Write down any new observations that seem important. What **questions** do you have? What can you **conclude**?

Close Review

REVIEW • QUESTION • CONCLUDE

Analyze the Media

CITE TEXTUAL EVIDENCE to support your answers.

📓 **Notebook** Respond to these questions.

1. (a) In Image 1, what does the snake represent? (b) **Connect** How does that representation shed light on the meaning of Image 4?

2. (a) **Compare and Contrast** From the colonial point of view, how do Images 2 and 3 have a similar slant? (b) **Analyze** Which details in the two images suggest that slant? Explain.

3. **Historical Perspectives** What do these images suggest about the colonists' growing sense of an American versus a British sense of identity? Explain.

4. **Essential Question:** *What is the meaning of freedom?* What have you learned about American freedoms from analyzing these images?

LANGUAGE DEVELOPMENT

Media Vocabulary

Use these words as you discuss and write about the images.

propaganda	appeal	symbolism

1. Which image most clearly presents the British as aggressors in the conflict with the colonies? Explain your choice, citing details from the image.

2. Which image most clearly expresses the colonists' resolve in their fight against Britain? Explain your choice, citing details from the image.

3. (a) In what ways does Image 2 distort facts in order to present a story that is favorable to one side? (b) What does this image suggest about propaganda as a source of reliable information? Explain.

📋 STANDARDS

Reading Informational Text
• Analyze and evaluate the effectiveness of the structure an author uses in his or her exposition or argument, including whether the structure makes points clear, convincing, and engaging.
• Integrate and evaluate multiple sources of information presented in different media or formats as well as in words in order to address a question or solve a problem.

Speaking and Listening

Assignment

With a partner, create an imaginary candidate who is campaigning for a major office, and develop a **political infomercial,** or extended, informative advertisement. Design and write the script for a presentation, including images that take a particular slant. Include a campaign slogan and a logo. As you work, take into account aspects of propaganda, appeal, and symbolism. Record and present the infomercial to the class.

1. Plan the Project To help you prepare your infomercial, consider these questions.

- What ideas does the candidate represent? What is his or her stance on issues such as education, the economy, and national defense?

- What facts from real life will you include? Which sources will you research for that information? Which visuals will best present that information in a way that helps the candidate's cause?

- How will you display your ideas and images? For example, you might create a video, use presentation software, or project on a whiteboard.

2. Consider Image Choices As you select or create images, consider the appeal that each one will have. For example, decide whether it adds emotional impact, symbolism, information, or serves another purpose.

ELEMENT	PURPOSE

3. Prepare the Script Once you have a final set of images and ideas, decide how you will weave them together to create your infomercial.

- Decide on the order of presentation. Add transitions to link related ideas.

- Create a pacing guide to determine the amount of time you will spend on each image.

- Choose which partner will narrate, and allow time to practice.

4. Present and Discuss Record the infomercial and share it with the class. After all of the infomercials have been presented, discuss how the types of techniques and images students used compare to that of American Revolutionary War propaganda.

TIP

PROCESS
Make sure that you and your partner agree to and understand the slant that your infomercial will present. Doing so will help you choose images and decide what to say about them.

EVIDENCE LOG

Before moving on to a new selection, go to your Evidence Log and record what you learned from "The American Revolution: Visual Propaganda."

STANDARDS
Speaking and Listening
Make strategic use of digital media in presentations to enhance understanding of findings, reasoning, and evidence and to add interest.

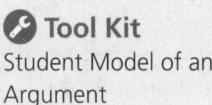 **Tool Kit**

Student Model of an Argument

ACADEMIC VOCABULARY

As you craft your argument, consider using some of the academic vocabulary you learned in the beginning of the unit.

confirm

demonstrate

supplement

establish

conviction

STANDARDS

Writing
• Write arguments to support claims in an analysis of substantive topics or texts, using valid reasoning and relevant and sufficient evidence.
• Write routinely over extended time frames and shorter time frames for a range of tasks, purposes, and audiences.

Write an Argument

You have just read a variety of documents from the early years of our nation. Each text reveals, in its own way, the principles that guided the nation's founders and other Americans of that era.

Assignment

Write a brief **argumentative essay** in which you address this question:

> **Which statement do you find most compelling for Americans today: the Preamble to the Constitution or the first sentence of paragraph three of the Declaration of Independence?**

Begin by choosing a position and stating a claim. Then, use specific details from the texts, historical examples, and your observations of our society today to support your claim. Make sure that your reasons link directly to your claim.

Elements of an Argument

In an **argument** a writer articulates a position, viewpoint, belief, or stand on an issue. Well-written arguments may convince readers to change their minds about an issue or to take a certain action.

An effective argument contains these elements:

- a precise claim
- consideration of counterclaims, or opposing positions, and a discussion of their strengths and weaknesses
- logical organization that makes clear connections among claim, counterclaims, reasons, and evidence
- word choices that are appropriate for a given audience
- clear reasoning and well-chosen evidence
- a concluding statement or section that logically completes the argument
- formal and objective language and tone
- error-free grammar, including correct and consistent use of verbs

Model Argument For a model of a well-crafted argument see the Launch Text, "Totally Free?" Review the Launch Text for examples of the elements of an effective argument. You will look more closely at these elements as you prepare to write your own argument.

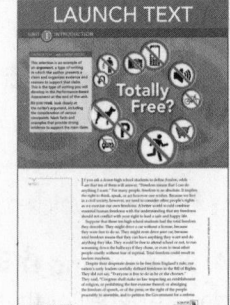

Prewriting / Planning

Break Down the Prompt Reading the prompt carefully and thoroughly can assist you in your planning. Complete these sentences to ensure that you understand the task that you are being asked to accomplish.

1. I am supposed to write a(n) _____.

2. In my own words, the question I must answer is _____.

3. My writing must include _____

and _____.

4. I need to use examples from _____ as evidence and

connect my ideas to _____.

Develop a Claim Start by deciding on a basic response to the question in the prompt. Then, develop your response into a claim. Use the sentence frame below to do so. Then, as you gather details and clarify your ideas, adjust your claim to reflect your new thinking.

I believe that _____

_____

because _____

_____.

Gather Evidence The assignment asks you to use a variety of evidence, including examples from history, to support your position. In what sorts of resources might you find the types of historical information you need? Write some possibilities here.

_____ _____ _____

_____ _____ _____

_____ _____ _____

Always confirm your evidence by using more than one source.

Connect Across Texts The prompt asks you to connect your ideas to the texts you have read. The Launch Text shows you two means of doing this:

- You may **paraphrase**, or restate ideas in your own words. The Launch Text presents a paraphrase in the discussion of Roosevelt's "Four Freedoms" speech (his 1941 State of the Union address).

- You may also use **direct quotations**, as happens when the Launch Text quotes from the Declaration of Independence.

✍ EVIDENCE LOG

Review your Evidence Log and identify key details you may want to cite in your argument.

≡ STANDARDS

Writing
- Introduce precise, knowledgeable claim(s), establish the significance of the claim(s), distinguish the claim(s) from alternate or opposing claims, and create an organization that logically sequences claim(s), counterclaims, reasons, and evidence.
- Develop claim(s) and counterclaims fairly and thoroughly, supplying the most relevant evidence for each while pointing out the strengths and limitations of both in a manner that anticipates the audience's knowledge level, concerns, values, and possible biases.

ENRICHING WRITING WITH RESEARCH

Using Research A strong argument is always based on sound evidence and thoughtful, logical support. You may find support for your ideas in online or library resources.

Read It

This excerpt from the Launch Text provides an example of the use of researched evidence. After doing some reading, the writer decided to use Franklin D. Roosevelt's "Four Freedoms" speech to support the contention that freedoms should not clash.

> LAUNCH TEXT EXCERPT
>
> In his 1941 State of the Union address, President Franklin Roosevelt identified four key freedoms as being basic human rights: freedom of speech and expression, freedom of worship, freedom from want, and freedom from fear. Those are not freedoms that one finds in a dictator. Nor are they freedoms that we grant to each other without the overs and protection of government institutions. With the government's h and the writing of laws, my freedom from want does not allow me to your food, and your freedom of speech does not let you publish lies me. We are free, but only up to the point at which our freedoms clash.

The writer located a specific speech from American history to support the claim that we need to consider other people's rights and needs as we exercise our own freedoms.

Using a Search Engine As you develop an argument, you may not have specific examples and reasons in mind. You may need to use a search engine wisely to develop your argument's support. The writer of the Launch Text may have used a path like this.

To narrow the search, the writer used a phrase rather than just the word *freedom*.

> Search: Freedom in American History

> Result: A website on different meanings of freedom over time in America

> Action: Skim article to locate interesting and relevant examples.
> 1. Civil War: A new birth of freedom
> 2. World War II: The Four Freedoms
> 3. Cold War: The Free World

> Search: The Four Freedoms

Notice how one search led to a second, more specific search, and so on until the writer found the best possible support for the claim.

> Result: An article about the "Four Freedoms" speech from the FDR Presidential Library

> Actions: Skim article to learn about the Four Freedoms.
> Decide whether they apply to the original argument—and, if so, how.

Write It

Review the facts and evidence that you have gathered. Use this flowchart to organize your materials.

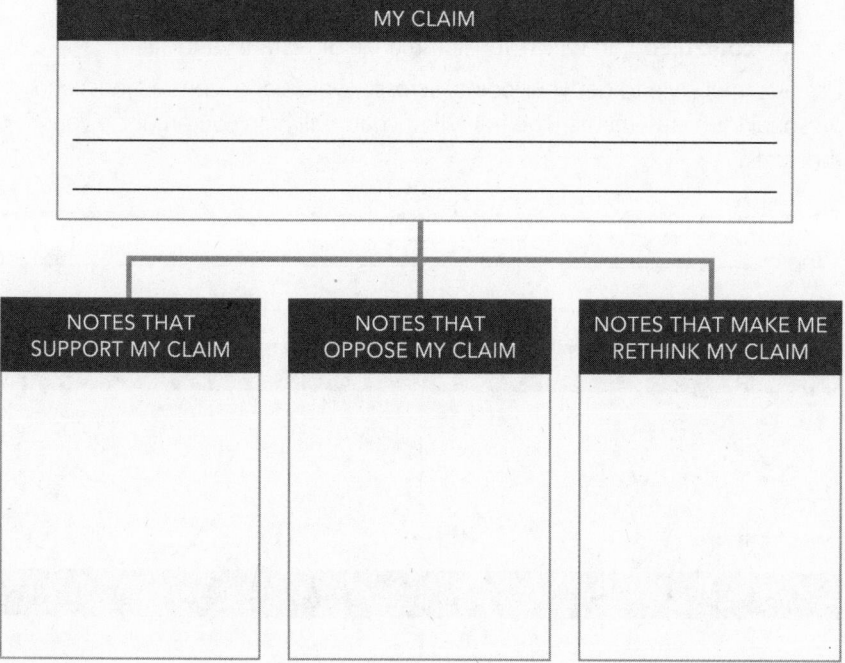

MY CLAIM

NOTES THAT SUPPORT MY CLAIM	NOTES THAT OPPOSE MY CLAIM	NOTES THAT MAKE ME RETHINK MY CLAIM

Notes That Support My Claim Some information you find may offer direct and fairly obvious support for your claim. Other information may require some interpretation or explanation on your part. For example, in the excerpt from the Launch Text, the writer analyzed the researched information about Roosevelt's speech and demonstrated how it supports the claim.

Notes That Oppose My Claim As you read and review sources, you may find some material that contradicts your claim. Consider working that material into the discussion of a counterclaim. You might start in one of these ways:

- Although [research source] states that _____, I believe that _____.
- [Research source] claims that _____. Nevertheless, it is clear that _____.
- Despite [research source]'s assertion that _____, it seems more likely that _____.

Remember to supply evidence that supports your rejection of any counterclaim that you mention.

Notes That Make Me Rethink My Claim Sometimes, your research will send you in a new direction. It may change your original ideas and make you rethink your claim. Do not be afraid to scrap your original plan if new evidence changes your mind. Just as architects or engineers do, good writers frequently discard a flawed plan and start over.

Drafting

Organize Your Text Your text should include three parts:

- the **introduction**, in which you state your claim
- the **body**, in which you provide analysis, supporting reasons, and evidence. Each paragraph of your body should focus on one idea and evidence that directly supports it.
- the **conclusion**, in which you summarize or restate your claim

Use a formal style to get your points across. Avoid slang, contractions, and personal ("I") statements. The following chart will help you organize your thoughts.

Topic: _____

Question: _____

CLAIM	COUNTERCLAIM

EVIDENCE	EVIDENCE
1. _____	1. _____
2. _____	2. _____
3. _____	3. _____

REASONS/SUPPORT FOR EVIDENCE	REASONS/SUPPORT FOR EVIDENCE
1. _____	1. _____
2. _____	2. _____
3. _____	3. _____

Write a First Draft Refer to your chart as you write your first draft. Make sure to include a precise claim and to address counterclaims where possible. Write a conclusion that follows logically from your argument, supports your claim, and adds interest to your writing.

Use Rhetorical Devices **Rhetorical devices** are patterns of language that create emphasis and build emotion. While they do not replace sound reasoning and evidence, they can help to present your ideas in a memorable way. Consider using one or more of the following rhetorical devices in your essay:

- **Repetition:** Repeat key words to focus your argument.
- **Parallelism:** Repeat related ideas in the same grammatical structures.
- **Analogy:** Use comparisons to help readers grasp ideas.

STANDARDS

Writing
• Introduce precise, knowledgeable claim(s), establish the significance of the claim(s), distinguish the claim(s) from alternate or opposing claims, and create an organization that logically sequences claim(s), counterclaims, reasons, and evidence.
• Provide a concluding statement or section that follows from and supports the argument presented.

LANGUAGE DEVELOPMENT: CONVENTIONS

Create Cohesion: Tense Sequence

A **sequence of tenses** means that there is agreement among the tenses of verbs in related sentences or clauses. In formal writing, it is important to maintain **consistency of tense** from one sentence to the next unless the time frame of the action changes.

Read It

The Launch Text uses verbs correctly to point to both past and current situations.

> *President Franklin Roosevelt **identified** four key freedoms… (past)*

> *These **are** not freedoms that one **finds** in a dictatorship. (present)*

Within a sentence, verbs are consistent in tense if the actions are consistent in time.

> *Because we **live** in a society, we **need** to consider other people's rights and needs as we **exercise** our own freedoms.*
> *(all present tense)*

When actions vary in time, the writer applies logic to sequence the verbs. In this example, the action of developing laws took place in the past but still applies today, and those laws restrict and protect us in the present.

> *Our government **has developed** laws that both **restrict** us and **protect** us. (present perfect; present; present)*

Write It

As you draft your essay, use logic to sequence verbs. Use the tense of the independent clause plus any key transitional words to determine the tense of dependent clauses. In most compound sentences, keep the tense consistent. Here are some examples.

present + past	I **am** eager to read the biography that you **recommended.**
present perfect + present	Now that she **has mastered** French, Alice **enjoys** Quebec.
present + future	Until the senator **returns,** I **will wait** patiently in her office.
present + present	Actors **recite** the Bill of Rights, and the audience **listens** raptly.
past perfect + past perfect	The colonists **had complained,** but the king **had ignored** them.
future + future	We **will follow** the law, or we **will face** the consequences.
past + past perfect	We **arrived** in plenty of time, but the tour guide **had left.**

 TIP

USAGE
Change tense only when the timing of an action changes. In general:

- Use the present tense when writing about your own ideas and opinions, factual topics that are widely known, or actions in a written work.
- Use the past tense when writing about past events or completed studies or analyses.

STANDARDS
Writing
Use words, phrases, and clauses as well as varied syntax to link the major sections of the text, create cohesion, and clarify the relationships between claim(s) and reasons, between reasons and evidence, and between claim(s) and counterclaims.

Language
Demonstrate command of the conventions of standard English grammar and usage when writing or speaking.

Revising

Evaluating Your Draft

Use this checklist to evaluate the effectiveness of your first draft. Then, use your evaluation and the instructions on this page to guide your revision.

FOCUS AND ORGANIZATION	EVIDENCE AND ELABORATION	CONVENTIONS
☐ Provides an introduction that establishes a precise claim.	☐ Develops the claim and responds to counterclaims by using facts and details that provide relevant evidence and reasons.	☐ Attends to the norms and conventions of the discipline, especially regarding sequence and consistency of verb tenses.
☐ Distinguishes the claim from opposing claims.		
☐ Provides a conclusion that follows from the argument.	☐ Provides adequate examples for each major idea.	
☐ Establishes a logical organization and develops a progression throughout the argument.	☐ Uses word choices and rhetorical devices effectively.	
☐ Uses words, phrases, and clauses to clarify the relationships between and among ideas.	☐ Establishes and maintains a formal style and an objective tone.	

⛓ WORD NETWORK

Include interesting words from your Word Network in your argument.

Revising for Focus and Organization

Strong, Logical Connections An argument should be built on sound logic that includes strong reasons, definitive evidence, and clear connections. Consider these strong and weak reasons for a pay increase. Connecting words that clarify relationships between ideas are underlined.

- Strong Reasoning: I deserve a raise, <u>as shown by the fact</u> that clients consistently ask to work with me.

- Strong Reasoning: I deserve a raise <u>because</u> my contract calls for an increase after six months.

- Weak Reasoning: <u>Since</u> my brother makes more than I do, I deserve a raise.

- Weak Reasoning: I deserve a raise <u>because</u> I want one.

Revising for Evidence and Elaboration

Word Choice and Style As you work to create an objective, formal tone, consider replacing informal words and phrases with more formal choices. Here are some examples of informal and formal transitional words and phrases.

INSTEAD OF . . .	USE . . .
also	in addition
anyway	nevertheless
basically	in summary
plus	furthermore
so	therefore

≣ STANDARDS

Writing
Establish and maintain a formal style and objective tone while attending to the norms and conventions of the discipline in which they are writing.

Exchange arguments with a classmate. Use the checklist to evaluate your classmate's argument and provide supportive feedback.

1. Is the claim clear?

☐ yes   ☐ no   If no, explain what confused you.

2. Do you find the argument convincing?

☐ yes   ☐ no   If no, tell what you think might be missing.

3. Does the essay conclude in a logical way?

☐ yes   ☐ no   If no, indicate what you might change.

4. What is the strongest part of your classmate's argument? Why?

_____

_____

_____

_____

Editing and Proofreading

Edit for Conventions Reread your draft for accuracy and consistency. Correct errors in grammar and word usage. Check for consistency of verb tense in related sentences and clauses.

Proofread for Accuracy Read your draft carefully, looking for errors in spelling and punctuation. Be sure to capitalize place names and names of documents correctly.

Publishing and Presenting

Post your claim and your strongest reason or piece of evidence on your class's online discussion board. Ask classmates to comment on your post. Review others' posts and point out what you like best about what you read.

Reflecting

Consider what you learned by writing your text. Did you use research effectively to find support for your claim? What did you find to be the most difficult part of this assignment? Why? Think about what you might do differently the next time you write an argument.

⊞ STANDARDS

Writing
Develop and strengthen writing as needed by planning, revising, editing, rewriting, or trying a new approach, focusing on addressing what is most significant for a specific purpose and audience.

ESSENTIAL QUESTION:

What is the meaning of freedom?

As you read these selections, work with your group to explore the meaning of freedom.

From Text to Topic The colonies had gained their independence and created a free nation, but freedom had not come to all. The Constitution had not settled the issue of slavery—and by 1790, when the first census in the United States was taken, approximately 700,000 African Americans were enslaved. The issue of slavery laid the foundation for the Civil War, arguably the most tragic time in the history of the United States. As you read, consider what these selections show about the nation's continuing efforts to define freedom.

Small-Group Learning Strategies

Throughout your life, in school, in your community, and in your career, you will continue to learn and work with others. Use these strategies during Small-Group Learning. Add ideas of your own at each step.

STRATEGY	ACTION PLAN
Prepare	• Complete your assignments so you are prepared for group work. • Take notes on your reading so you can contribute to your group's discussions. •
Participate fully	• Make eye contact to signal that you are listening and taking in what is being said. • Use text evidence when making a point. •
Support others	• Build on ideas from others in your group. • State the relationship of your points to those of others—whether you are supporting someone's point, refuting it, or taking the conversation in a new direction. •
Clarify	• Paraphrase the ideas of others to ensure that your understanding is correct. • Ask follow-up questions. •

SCAN FOR
MULTIMEDIA

CONTENTS

PERFORMANCE TASK

SPEAKING AND LISTENING FOCUS
Present an Argument

The Small-Group readings provide further glimpses into the concept of freedom. After reading, your group will present a panel discussion about the usefulness of narratives as evidence in arguments about freedom.

Working as a Team

1. **Take a Position** In your group, discuss the following question:

   Do you think teenagers today should have more freedom—or less—than they do now?

   As you take turns sharing your positions, be sure to provide reasons for your choice. After all group members have shared, discuss the convictions that students expressed and the arguments they proposed to support their views.

2. **List Your Rules** As a group, decide on the rules that you will follow as you work together. Two samples are provided. Add two more of your own. As you work together, you may add or revise rules based on your experience.

   • Everyone should have a chance to speak.

   • Group members should not interrupt each other.

   • _____

     _____

   • _____

     _____

3. **Apply the Rules** Share what you have learned about the meaning of freedom. Make sure each person in the group contributes. Take notes and be prepared to share with the class something you learned from another member of your group.

4. **Name Your Group** Choose a name that reflects the unit topic.

   Our group's name: _____

5. **Create a Communication Plan** Decide how you want to communicate with one another. For example, you might use email, an online bulletin board, or a collaborative annotation tool.

   Our group's decision: _____

   _____

Making a Schedule

First, find out the due dates for the small-group activities. Then, preview the texts and activities with your group, and make a schedule for completing the tasks.

SELECTION	ACTIVITIES	DUE DATE
from America's Constitution: A Biography		
from The United States Constitution: A Graphic Adaptation		
from The Interesting Narrative of the Life of Olaudah Equiano		
Letter to John Adams from Dear Abigail: The Intimate Lives and Revolutionary Ideas of Abigail Adams and Her Two Remarkable Sisters		
Gettysburg Address		

Working on Group Projects

As your group works together, you'll find it more effective if each person has a specific role. Different projects require different roles. Before beginning a project, discuss the necessary roles, and choose one for each group member. Some possible roles are listed here. Add your ideas to the list.

Project Manager: monitors the schedule and keeps everyone on task

Researcher: organizes research activities

Recorder: takes notes during group meetings

_____

_____

_____

SCAN FOR
MULTIMEDIA

AMERICA'S CONSTITUTION: A BIOGRAPHY

Comparing Text to Media

You will read and compare an excerpt from *America's Constitution: A Biography* and an excerpt from the graphic novel *The United States Constitution: A Graphic Adaptation*. First, complete the first-read and close-read activities for *America's Constitution: A Biography*.

THE UNITED STATES CONSTITUTION: A GRAPHIC ADAPTATION

About the Author

Akhil Reed Amar (b. 1958), an expert on constitutional law, has been called one of the nation's top legal thinkers. Amar graduated from Yale Law School, where he was an editor for the *Yale Law Journal.* He has written several books and articles about the law—works important enough to have been referenced in a number of Supreme Court cases.

from America's Constitution: A Biography

Concept Vocabulary

As you perform your first read, you will encounter these words.

conclave	eminent	populist

Context Clues An unfamiliar word may become clearer if you use **context clues**—that is, helpful words and phrases in the surrounding text. Here are two types of context clues.

> **Synonyms:** New Hampshire became the ninth state to **ratify** the Constitution, approving the document by a margin of 57 to 47.
>
> **Antonyms:** Opponents of the new Constitution were relatively **rigid**, but proponents such as Madison and Franklin were resourceful and flexible.

Apply your knowledge of context clues and other vocabulary strategies to determine the meanings of unfamiliar words you encounter during your first read.

First Read NONFICTION

Apply these strategies as you conduct your first read. You will have an opportunity to complete a close read after your first read.

NOTICE the general ideas of the text. *What* it is about? *Who* is involved?

ANNOTATE by marking vocabulary and key passages you want to revisit.

First Read

CONNECT ideas within the selection to what you already know and what you have already read.

RESPOND by completing the Comprehension Check and by writing a brief summary of the selection.

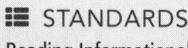 STANDARDS

Reading Informational Text
By the end of grade 11, read and comprehend literary nonfiction in the grades 11–CCR text complexity band proficiently, with scaffolding as needed at the high end of the range.

Language
Use context as a clue to the meaning of a word or phrase.

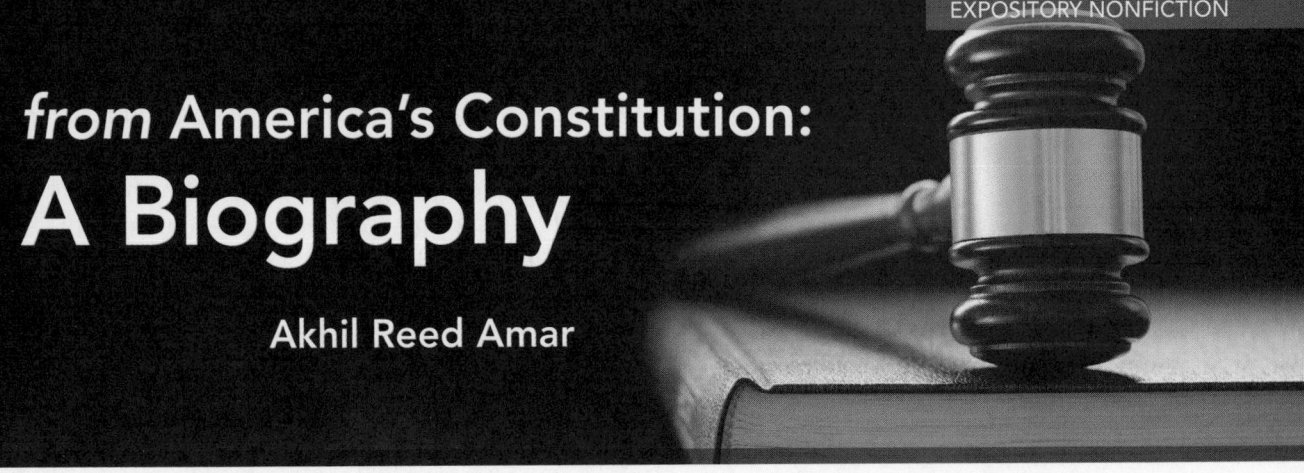

from America's Constitution:
A Biography

Akhil Reed Amar

BACKGROUND

Between 1777 and 1787, the United States used a constitution called the Articles of Confederation rather than the Constitution we use today. The Articles of Confederation created a very weak federal government. It soon became apparent that a document demonstrating more clarity would be helpful. There was great debate about whether to simply change the Articles of Confederation or replace them, as well as what this replacement might look like.

SCAN FOR
MULTIMEDIA

1   It started with a bang. Ordinary citizens would govern themselves across a continent and over the centuries, under rules that the populace would ratify and could revise. By uniting previously independent states into a vast and indivisible nation, New World republicans would keep Old World monarchs at a distance and thus make democracy work on a scale never before dreamed possible.

NOTES

"We . . . do"

With simple words placed in the document's most prominent location, the Preamble laid the foundation for all that followed. "We the People of the United States, . . . do ordain[1] and establish this Constitution . . ."

2   These words did more than promise popular self-government. They also embodied and enacted it. Like the phrases "I do" in an exchange of wedding vows and "I accept" in a contract, the Preamble's words actually performed the very thing they described. Thus the Founders' "Constitution" was not merely a text but a deed—a *constituting*. We the People *do* ordain. In the late 1780s, this was the most democratic deed the world had ever seen.

3   Behind this act of ordainment and establishment stood countless ordinary American voters who gave their consent to the Constitution via specially elected ratifying conventions held in the thirteen states beginning in late 1787. Until these ratifications took place, the Constitution's words were a mere proposal—the text of a contract yet to be accepted, the script of a wedding still to be performed.

4   The proposal itself had emerged from a special conclave held in Philadelphia during the summer of 1787. Twelve state governments— all except Rhode Island's—had tapped several dozen leading public

Mark context clues or indicate another strategy you used that helped you determine meaning.

conclave (KON klayv) *n.*

MEANING:

---

1. **ordain** *v.* officially order or decree.

Mark context clues or indicate another strategy you used that helped you determine meaning.

eminent (EHM uh nuhnt) *adj.*

MEANING:

servants and private citizens to meet in Philadelphia and ponder possible revisions of the Articles of Confederation, the interstate compact that Americans had formed during the Revolutionary War. After deliberating behind closed doors for months, the Philadelphia conferees unveiled their joint proposal in mid-September in a document signed by thirty-nine of the continent's most **eminent** men, including George Washington, Benjamin Franklin, James Wilson, Roger Sherman, James Madison, Alexander Hamilton, Gouverneur Morris, John Rutledge, and Nathaniel Gorham. When these notables put their names on the page, they put their reputations on the line.

5   An enormous task of political persuasion lay ahead. Several of the leaders who had come to Philadelphia had quit the conclave in disgust, and others who had stayed to the end had refused to endorse the final script. Such men—John Lansing, Robert Yates, Luther Martin, John Francis Mercer, Edmund Randolph, George Mason, and Elbridge Gerry—could be expected to oppose ratification and to urge their political allies to do the same. No one could be certain how the American people would ultimately respond to the competing appeals. Prior to 1787, only two states, Massachusetts and New Hampshire, had ever brought proposed state constitutions before the people to be voted up or down in some special way. The combined track record from this pair of states was sobering: two successful popular ratifications out of six total attempts.

6   In the end, the federal Constitution proposed by Washington and company would barely squeak through. By its own terms, the document would go into effect only if ratified by specially elected conventions in at least nine states, and even then only states that said yes would be bound. In late 1787 and early 1788, supporters of the Constitution won relatively easy ratifications in Delaware, Pennsylvania, New Jersey, Georgia, and Connecticut. Massachusetts joined their ranks in February 1788, saying "we do" only after weeks of debate and by a close vote, 187 to 168. Then came lopsided yes votes in Maryland and South Carolina, bringing the total to eight ratifications, one shy of the mark. Even so, in mid-June 1788, a full nine months after the publication of the Philadelphia proposal, the Constitution was still struggling to be born, and its fate remained uncertain. Organized opposition ran strong in all the places that had yet to say yes, which included three of America's largest and most influential states. At last, on June 21, tiny New Hampshire became the decisive ninth state by the margin of 57 to 47. A few days later, before news from the North had arrived, Virginia voted her approval, 89 to 79.

7   All eyes then turned to New York, where Anti-Federalists initially held a commanding lead inside the convention. Without the acquiescence of this key state, could the new Constitution really work as planned? On the other hand, was New York truly willing to say no and go it alone now that her neighbors had agreed to form a new, more perfect union among themselves? In late July, the state

ultimately said yes by a vote of 30 to 27. A switch of only a couple of votes would have reversed the outcome. Meanwhile, the last two states, North Carolina and Rhode Island, refused to ratify in 1788. They would ultimately join the new union in late 1789 and mid-1790, respectively—well after George Washington took office as president of the new (eleven!) United States.

8   Although the ratification votes in the several states did not occur by direct statewide referenda,[2] the various ratifying conventions did aim to represent "the People" in a particularly emphatic way— more directly than ordinary legislatures. Taking their cue from the Preamble's bold "We the People" language, several states waived standard voting restrictions and allowed a uniquely broad class of citizens to vote for ratification-convention delegates. For instance, New York temporarily set aside its usual property qualifications and, for the first time in its history, invited all free adult male citizens to vote. Also, states generally allowed an especially broad group of Americans to serve as ratifying-convention delegates. Among the many states that ordinarily required upper-house lawmakers to meet higher property qualifications than lower-house members, none held convention delegates to the higher standard, and most exempted delegates even from the lower. All told, eight states elected convention delegates under special rules that were more **populist** and less property-focused than normal, and two others followed standing rules that let virtually all taxpaying adult male citizens vote. No state employed special election rules that were more property-based or less populist than normal.

9   In the extraordinarily extended and inclusive ratification process envisioned by the Preamble, Americans regularly found themselves discussing the Preamble itself. At Philadelphia, the earliest draft of the Preamble had come from the quill of Pennsylvania's James Wilson, and it was Wilson who took the lead in explaining the Preamble's principles in a series of early and influential ratification speeches. Pennsylvania Anti-Federalists complained that the Philadelphia notables had overreached in proposing an entirely new Constitution rather than a mere modification of the existing Articles of Confederation. In response, Wilson—America's leading lawyer and one of only six men to have signed both the Declaration of Independence and the Constitution—stressed the significance of popular ratification. "This Constitution, proposed by [the Philadelphia draftsmen], claims no more than a production of the same nature would claim, flowing from a private pen. It is laid before the citizens of the United States, unfettered by restraint. . . . By their *fiat*,[3] it will become of value and authority; without it, it will never receive the character of authenticity and power." James Madison agreed, as he made clear in a mid-January 1788 New York newspaper essay today known as *The Federalist* No. 40—one of a long series

Mark context clues or indicate another strategy you used that helped you determine meaning.

populist (POP yuh lihst) *adj.*

MEANING:

---

2. **referenda** *n.* public votes on particular issues.
3. **fiat** (FEE uht) *n.* command that creates something.

of columns that he wrote in partnership with Alexander Hamilton and John Jay under the shared pen name "Publius." According to Madison/Publius, the Philadelphia draftsmen had merely "proposed a Constitution which is to be of no more consequence than the paper on which it is written, unless it be stamped with the approbation[4] of those to whom it is addressed. [The proposal] was to be submitted *to the people themselves*, [and] the disapprobation of this supreme authority would destroy it forever; its approbation blot out antecedent errors and irregularities." Leading Federalists across the continent reiterated the point in similar language.

10   With the word *fiat*, Wilson gently called to mind the opening lines of Genesis. In the beginning, God said, *fiat lux*, and—behold!—there was light. So, too, when the American people (Publius's "supreme authority") said, "We do ordain and establish," that very statement would do the deed. "Let there be a Constitution"—and there would be one. As the ultimate sovereign of all had once made man in his own image, so now the temporal sovereign of America, the people themselves, would make a constitution in their own image.

11   All this was breathtakingly novel. In 1787, democratic self-government existed almost nowhere on earth. Kings, emperors, czars, princes, sultans, moguls, feudal lords, and tribal chiefs held sway across the globe. Even England featured a limited monarchy and an entrenched aristocracy alongside a House of Commons that rested on a restricted and uneven electoral base. The vaunted English Constitution that American colonists had grown up admiring prior to the struggle for independence was an imprecise hodgepodge of institutions, enactments, cases, usages, maxims, procedures, and principles that had accreted[5] and evolved over many centuries. This Constitution had never been reduced to a single composite writing and voted on by the British people or even by Parliament.

12   The ancient world had seen small-scale democracies in various Greek city-states and pre-imperial Rome, but none of these had been founded in fully democratic fashion. In the most famous cases, one man—a celebrated lawgiver such as Athens's Solon or Sparta's Lycurgus—had unilaterally ordained his countrymen's constitution. Before the American Revolution, no people had ever explicitly voted on their own written constitution.

13   Nor did the Revolution itself immediately inaugurate popular ordainments and establishments. True, the 1776 Declaration of Independence proclaimed the "self-evident" truth that "Governments are instituted among Men, deriving their just Powers from the Consent of the Governed." The document went on to assert that "whenever any Form of Government becomes destructive of [its legitimate] Ends, it is the Right of the People to alter and abolish it, and to institute new Government." Yet the Declaration only

---

4. **approbation** *n.* praise or approval.
5. **accreted** *v.* grown or accumulated gradually.

imperfectly acted out its bold script. Its fifty-six acclaimed signers never put the document to any sort of popular vote.

14 Between April and July 1776, countless similar declarations issued from assorted towns, counties, parishes, informal assemblies, grand juries, militia units, and legislatures across America. By then, however, the colonies were already under military attack, and conditions often made it impossible to achieve inclusive deliberation or scrupulous tabulation. Many patriots saw Crown loyalists in their midst not as fellow citizens free to vote their honest judgment with impunity, but rather as traitors deserving tar and feathers, or worse. (Virtually no arch-loyalist went on to become a particularly noteworthy political leader in independent America. By contrast, many who would vigorously oppose the Constitution in 1787–88—such as Maryland's Samuel Chase and Luther Martin, Virginia's Patrick Henry and James Monroe, and New York's George Clinton and John Lansing—moved on to illustrious post-ratification careers.)

15 Shortly before and after the Declaration of Independence, new state governments began to take shape, filling the void created by the ouster of George III. None of the state constitutions ordained in the first months of the Revolution was voted on by the electorate or by a specially elected ratifying convention of the people. In many states, sitting legislatures or closely analogous Revolutionary entities declared themselves solons[6] and promulgated or revised constitutions on their own authority, sometimes without even waiting for new elections that might have given their constituents more say in the matter, or at least advance notice of their specific constitutional intentions.

16 In late 1777, patriot leaders in the Continental Congress proposed a set of Articles of Confederation to govern relations among the thirteen states. This document was then sent out to be ratified by the thirteen state legislatures, none of which asked the citizens themselves to vote in any special way on the matter.

17 Things began to change as the Revolution wore on. In 1780, Massachusetts enacted a new state constitution that had come directly before the voters assembled in their respective townships and won their approval. In 1784, New Hampshire did the same. These local dress rehearsals (for so they seem in retrospect) set the stage for the Preamble's great act of continental popular sovereignty in the late 1780s.

18 As Benjamin Franklin and other Americans had achieved famous advances in the natural sciences—in Franklin's case, the invention of bifocals, the lightning rod, and the Franklin stove—so with the Constitution America could boast a breakthrough in political science. Never before had so many ordinary people been invited to

NOTES

America could boast a breakthrough in political science.

---

6. **solons** (SOH luhnz) *n.* lawmakers, especially wise ones. Refers to Solon, the statesman who framed the democratic laws of Athens.

deliberate and vote on the supreme law under which they and their posterity would be governed. James Wilson fairly burst with pride in an oration delivered in Philadelphia to some twenty thousand merrymakers gathered for a grand parade on July 4, 1788. By that date, enough Americans had said "We do" so as to guarantee that the Constitution would go into effect (at least in ten states—the document was still pending in the other three). The "spectacle, which we are assembled to celebrate," Wilson declared, was "the most dignified one that has yet appeared on our globe," namely, a

> people free and enlightened, establishing and ratifying a system of government, which they have previously considered, examined, and approved! . . .
>
> . . . You have heard of Sparta, of Athens, and of Rome; you have heard of their admired constitutions, and of their high-prized freedom. . . . But did they, in all their pomp and pride of liberty, ever furnish, to the astonished world, an exhibition similar to that which we now contemplate? Were their constitutions framed by those, who were appointed for that purpose, by the people? After they were framed, were they submitted to the consideration of the people? Had the people an opportunity of expressing their sentiments concerning them? Were they to stand or fall by the people's approving or rejecting vote?

19   The great deed was done. The people had taken center stage and enacted their own supreme law. ❧

Comprehension Check

Complete the following items after you finish your first read. Review and clarify details with your group.

1. When and where was the Constitution drafted?

2. Once the Constitution was approved, what more had to happen before it could go into effect?

3. What was *The Federalist*, and who was "Publius"?

4. 📓 **Notebook** Confirm your understanding of the text by writing a summary.

- -

RESEARCH

Research to Explore Choose something that interested you from the text, and formulate a research question.

Close Read the Text

With your group, revisit sections of the text you marked during your first read. **Annotate** details that you notice. What **questions** do you have? What can you **conclude**?

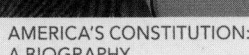

AMERICA'S CONSTITUTION:
A BIOGRAPHY

Analyze the Text

CITE TEXTUAL EVIDENCE
to support your answers.

 Notebook Complete the activities.

1. **Review and Clarify** With your group, reread paragraphs 4 and 5 of the selection. What kind of document was the Constitution in the summer of 1787? What does this fact indicate about the power of "We the People"?

2. **Present and Discuss** Now, work with your group to share the passages from the selection that you found especially important. Take turns presenting your passages. Discuss what you noticed in the selection, what questions you asked, and what conclusions you reached.

3. **Essential Question:** *What is the meaning of freedom?* What has this text taught you about American freedoms? Discuss with your group.

 TIP

GROUP DISCUSSION
Keep in mind that readers often have differing interpretations of a text. Use the varying perspectives to encourage group members to learn from one another and to clarify their own views.

LANGUAGE DEVELOPMENT

Concept Vocabulary

conclave	eminent	populist

Why These Words? The three concept vocabulary words from the text are related. With your group, determine what the words have in common. How do these word choices contribute to the meaning of the text?

 WORD NETWORK

Add words related to freedom from the text to your Word Network.

Practice

 Notebook Confirm your understanding of these words by writing a two- or three-sentence paragraph that includes all three words. Make their meaning clear from the context.

Word Study

 Notebook **Latin Suffix: *-ist*** The Latin suffix *-ist* identifies a word as an adjective or a noun. It often appears in words that relate to attitudes or philosophies. For example, the word *realist* means "a person who sees thing as they really are."

1. Write two definitions for the concept vocabulary word *populist*—one for the word's meaning as a noun and the other for the word's meaning as an adjective.

2. Use a dictionary to find definitions for *naturist, feminist,* and *idealist.* Then, choose one of the words and write two sentences—one using the word as a noun and the other using it as an adjective.

STANDARDS
Language
Consult general and specialized reference materials, both print and digital, to find the pronunciation of a word or determine or clarify its precise meaning, its part of speech, its etymology, or its standard usage.

AMERICA'S CONSTITUTION: A BIOGRAPHY

Analyze Craft and Structure

Author's Choices: Rhetoric An **analogy** is an extended comparison. It is based on the idea that the relationship between one pair of things is like the relationship between another pair. The use of an analogy can clarify complex ideas by explaining an unfamiliar notion in terms of a familiar one. For example, in paragraph 4, Amar introduces the idea that the Preamble to the Constitution is like the words "I accept" in a contract:

> Like the phrases "I do" in an exchange of wedding vows and "I accept" in a contract, the Preamble's words actually performed the very thing they described.

Using this analogy, Amar makes the point that the Constitution represented a binding commitment that affected how people live their lives.

Practice

CITE TEXTUAL EVIDENCE to support your answers.

Reread the passages noted in the chart. For each analogy, identify the two things being compared. Then, explain the idea the analogy helps to clarify. Work independently. Then, share your analysis with your group.

TEXTUAL DETAILS	TWO THINGS BEING COMPARED	MEANING
"I do" / "we do" (paragraphs 1, 2, 3, 6, 18)		
fiat lux (paragraph 10)		
invention of bifocals, the lightning rod, and the Franklin stove (paragraph 18)		

▦ STANDARDS

Reading Informational Text
Determine an author's point of view or purpose in a text in which the rhetoric is particularly effective, analyzing how style and content contribute to the power, persuasiveness, or beauty of the text.

Author's Style

Historical Narrative as Argument A **biography** is a type of narrative nonfiction that tells the story of someone's life. By calling his book a "biography" of the Constitution, Amar indicates that he is telling a story. However, it is not the story of a life, but of a document. Within that story, Amar presents his point of view or position on the Constitution's significance. The story he tells, then, is not just a historical narrative—it is also an argument. Amar states his main idea or principal claim at the end of paragraph 2:

> In the late 1780s, this [the drafting of the U. S. Constitution] was the most democratic deed the world had ever seen.

Amar goes on to present an in-depth description of the conflicts and drama that arose around the ratification of the Constitution, using varied techniques and evidence to tell the story and develop his claim.

- **Historical Details:** Amar is writing for an audience of general readers, not scholars. He includes historical details that provide important background information for such readers. For example, in paragraph 8, he shows how the rules of the ratifying conventions were based on groundbreaking democratic principles.
- **Numerical Data:** Amar presents numerical facts to support his interpretation of events.
- **Quotations:** Amar interweaves quotations from historical figures. These passages add drama to the story he is telling and reinforce the argument he is presenting.

Read It

Work on your own to identify examples of Amar's use of historical details, numerical data, and quotations. Explain how each example helps to tell the story of the Constitution and build Amar's argument. Share and discuss your responses with your group.

TYPE OF EVIDENCE	EFFECT
Historical Details	
Numerical Data	
Quotations	

Write It

📓 **Notebook** Choose a favorite song, graphic novel or comic book, movie, game, or other text. Write a "biography" of the work in which you both tell the story of its development and defend a claim about its importance. Weave in historical details, facts, and quotations.

✍ EVIDENCE LOG

Before moving on to a new selection, go to your Evidence Log and record what you have learned from the excerpt from *America's Constitution: A Biography*.

STANDARDS

Reading Informational Text
- Analyze a complex set of ideas or sequence of events and explain how specific individuals, ideas, or events interact and develop over the course of the text.
- Analyze and evaluate the effectiveness of the structure an author uses in his or her exposition or argument, including whether the structure makes points clear, convincing, and engaging.

AMERICA'S CONSTITUTION: A BIOGRAPHY

Comparing Text to Media

This graphic adaptation focuses on the ratification process of the Constitution and the creation of the Bill of Rights. After reviewing this selection, you will look for similarities and differences between the selections.

THE UNITED STATES CONSTITUTION: A GRAPHIC ADAPTATION

About the Author

As an adult, **Jonathan Hennessey** gained a new appreciation for his childhood in historic New England, and he notes that "I often find nothing more entertaining than some scrupulously researched historical account." *The United States Constitution: A Graphic Adaptation* is his first published work.

STANDARDS

Reading Informational Text
By the end of grade 11, read and comprehend literary nonfiction in the grades 11–CCR text complexity band proficiently, with scaffolding as needed at the high end of the range.

Language
Acquire and use accurately general academic and domain-specific words and phrases, sufficient for reading, writing, speaking, and listening at the college and career readiness level; demonstrate independence in gathering vocabulary knowledge when considering a word or phrase important to comprehension or expression.

from The United States Constitution: A Graphic Adaptation

Media Vocabulary

These words or concepts will be useful to you as you analyze, discuss, and write about graphic novels.

Layout: overall design and look of a graphic presentation	• Layout deals with the arrangement of graphic panels on a page and with the relationship of text and images within each panel.
Speech Balloon: shape used in graphic novels and comic books to show what a character says	• A "tail" points from the balloon to the person speaking. If the tail is a series of small bubbles, the balloon expresses a thought. • An artist may use a dotted balloon outline to indicate whispered words or jagged "spikes" in the outline to indicate shouting or screaming.
Caption: separate text that presents information that cannot be expressed quickly and easily in dialogue	• A caption may appear anywhere inside or outside a panel. It may be broken into several boxes for a panel.

First Review MEDIA: ART AND PHOTOGRAPHY

Apply these strategies as you conduct your first review.

LOOK at each panel and determine *whom* or *what* it portrays.

NOTE elements that you find interesting and want to revisit.

CONNECT details in the images to other media you've experienced, texts you've read, or images you've seen.

RESPOND by completing the Comprehension Check and writing a brief summary of the selection.

First Review
LOOK NOTE CONNECT RESPOND

📓 **Notebook** As you study the graphic novel, record your observations and questions, noting which panel they refer to for later reference.

WRITTEN BY
JONATHAN HENNESSEY
ART BY
AARON McCONNELL

THE UNITED STATES CONSTITUTION

A GRAPHIC ADAPTATION

BACKGROUND

While the Articles of Confederation created Congress, it did not create a capable national government. Individual states continued to conduct foreign diplomacy, and Georgia was threatening its own war with Spain. Furthermore, Congress failed to deal effectively with Shays's Rebellion in Massachusetts. These and other weaknesses convinced leaders that revisions to the Articles were necessary to form a stronger national government.

SCAN FOR
MULTIMEDIA

RATIFICATION: Federalists vs. Anti-Federalists

1 IN THE VOTE TO SEND DELEGATES TO RATIFY THE CONSTITUTION, MORE PEOPLE WOULD HAVE A SAY ON THEIR LAWS—AND THE SHAPE OF THEIR FUTURE—THAN EVER BEFORE.

AND FOR THIS VOTE, MOST STATES REDUCED OR ABOLISHED THEIR RULES ABOUT OWNING PROPERTY.

2 UP TO THAT TIME A *FEDERALIST* WAS SOMEONE WHO BELIEVED FIRST AND FOREMOST IN THE SOVEREIGNTY OF THE STATES, WHILE AN *ANTI-FEDERALIST* WANTED A STRONG, CENTRAL GOVERNMENT TO RULE OVER THEM, JUST AS THE CONSTITUTION WOULD ESTABLISH...

...BUT IN WHAT TODAY WOULD BE CALLED POLITICAL SPIN, THE ONES PUSHING HARDEST TO RATIFY THE CONSTITUTION TOOK THE FEDERALIST NAME FOR THEIR OWN PURPOSE, TO HELP WIN OVER THE COMMON PEOPLE.

3 UNDER THE PEN NAME PUBLIUS, HAMILTON, MADISON, AND JOHN JAY WROTE 85 ESSAYS NOW KNOWN AS *THE FEDERALIST PAPERS* TO EXPLAIN AND CHAMPION THEIR CAUSE.

To the people of the state of New York: you are called upon to deliberate on a new Constitution for the United States of America ...

4 NOW STUCK WITH THE ANTI-FEDERALIST NAME, OPPONENTS OF RATIFICATION—MANY PEOPLE, MANY DIFFERENT IDEAS—ATTACKED!

SOME THOUGHT THE CONSTITUTION, WHICH NEVER MENTIONS GOD, WAS ANTIRELIGIOUS.

WITH NO RELIGIOUS TEST FOR OFFICE, PAGANS, DEISTS, AND MAHOMETANS MIGHT OBTAIN OFFICE!

MANY RESENTED THAT THE FRAMERS HAD OVERSTEPPED THEIR JOB OF SIMPLY FIXING THE ARTICLES OF CONFEDERATION...

...WHAT RIGHT HAD THEY TO SAY, WE, THE PEOPLE...WHO AUTHORIZED THEM TO SPEAK THE LANGUAGE OF WE, THE PEOPLE, INSTEAD OF WE, THE STATES?

THE GREATNESS OF THE POWERS GIVEN... PRODUCE A COALITION OF MONARCHY MEN, MILITARY MEN, ARISTOCRATS AND DRONES. WHOSE NOISE, IMPUDENCE AND ZEAL EXCEEDS ALL BELIEF!

...AND HAD SET UP A POWERFUL NEW GOVERNMENT TO DOMINATE THE STATES.

THEY WERE SUSPICIOUS OF ALL POLITICAL POWER AND WANTED TO KEEP AMERICA A COUNTRY OF LANDOWNING FARMERS FOREVER.

85

5 "PUBLIUS" VIVIDLY POINTED OUT THE IMMINENT DANGER IF THE STATES FAILED TO JOIN IN A STRONG UNION.

ON THEIR OWN OR IN SMALL GROUPS, THE STATES COULD EASILY BE BROUGHT TO THEIR KNEES BY FOREIGN INVADERS...

...America, if not connected at all, or only by the feeble tie of a simple league... would... be gradually entangled in all the pernicious labyrinths of European politics and wars...

FROM *THE FEDERALIST*, NO. 7.

...OR, GIVEN ALL THE FIERCE COMPETITION BETWEEN THEM, BY EACH OTHER.

6 OVER TIME BLOODSHED BETWEEN THEM COULD BECOME AS COMMON AS AMONG EUROPE'S MANY COUNTRIES IN THEIR CENTURIES OF ARMED CONFLICTS.

...we shall be... an infinity of little jealous, clashing, tumultuous commonwealths, the wretched nurseries of unceasing discord...

FROM *THE FEDERALIST*, NO 9.

AND JUST AS IMPORTANT, "PUBLIUS" SET FORTH WHY THE STATES SHOULD FORM A UNION.

ONE PIVOTAL REASON...

7

THAT'S RIGHT, MEN! KEEP AT IT!

AS LONG AS YOU DO IT ALL TOGETHER—IN A UNION—THE MORE YOU PULL, THE MORE STABLE WE WILL ALL BE!

...THAT THE BIGGER THE COUNTRY—THE MORE DIVERSE ITS PEOPLE, THEIR PASSIONS AND IDEAS ABOUT WHAT THEY WANT FROM GOVERNMENT—THE BETTER.

FROM *THE FEDERALIST*, NO. 10: "THE SMALLER THE SOCIETY... THE FEWER THE DISTINCT PARTIES AND INTERESTS, THE MORE FREQUENTLY WILL A MAJORITY...EXECUTE...PLANS OF OPPRESSION. EXTEND THE SPHERE...TAKE IN A GREATER VARIETY OF PARTIES AND INTERESTS; YOU MAKE IT LESS PROBABLE THAT A MAJORITY... [WILL] INVADE THE RIGHTS OF OTHER CITIZENS..."

The Bill of Rights: AMENDMENTS 1-10

THE POWER OF A GOVERNMENT CAN BE ENORMOUS. IF LEFT UNCHECKED, DANGEROUS.

ARTICLES I-VII OF THE CONSTITUTION MOSTLY GIVE GOVERNMENT POWER. BUT WITH THE BILL OF RIGHTS...

...PROPOSED BY THE FIRST CONGRESS, DRAFTED BY MADISON, AND SWIFTLY RATIFIED IN 1791...

...GOVERNMENT VOLUNTARILY GIVES UP POWER. IT RESTRAINS ITSELF.

AFTER ALL, ONE OF THE CORNERSTONE IDEAS OF THE AMERICAN REVOLUTION ITSELF IS THAT PEOPLE HAVE CERTAIN RIGHTS *BY BIRTH.*

AND SO THE BILL OF RIGHTS CONFIRMS THIS. THUS, THE CONSTITUTION REASSERTS THAT IT IS THE PEOPLE – NOT THEIR GOVERNMENT – WHO RULE.

THE RIGHT TO TRIAL BY JURY?

THANKS... I ALREADY HAVE ONE.

THE BILL OF RIGHTS SPELLS OUT WHAT FREEDOMS THE GOVERNMENT MAY NOT TAKE AWAY. IT IS THERE TO PROTECT YOUR RIGHTS, NOT TO GIVE THEM TO YOU.

TODAY MOST THINK ABOUT THE BILL OF RIGHTS AS EXCLUSIVELY PROTECTING THE RIGHTS OF THE INDIVIDUAL AGAINST THE MAJORITY.

BUT THE ANTI-FEDERALISTS WERE EQUALLY CONCERNED ABOUT PROTECTING THE MAJORITY.

...THAT IS, THE PEOPLE, OR GROUPS OF PEOPLE—FROM GOVERNMENT.

FROM *THE FEDERALIST, NO. 51:* "IT IS OF GREAT IMPORTANCE IN A REPUBLIC...TO GUARD THE SOCIETY AGAINST THE OPPRESSION OF ITS RULERS."

Comprehension Check

Complete the following items after you finish your first review. Review and clarify details with your group.

1. As the fight for ratification began, how did the meaning of the word *federalist* change? Refer to panels 1–4.

2. How does the artist visually depict the three branches of government? Refer to panels 4 and 11.

3. Identify three reasons "Publius" gave in support of a strong federal government. Refer to panels 5–7.

4. According to the author, what assumption about human rights does the Bill of Rights reflect?

5. ▣ **Notebook** Write a summary to confirm your understanding of the ratification of the Constitution, as presented in the graphic adaptation.

- -

RESEARCH

Research to Clarify Choose at least one unfamiliar detail from the graphic adaptation. Briefly research that detail. In what way does the information you found shed light on your understanding of the Constitution or the Bill of Rights?

Research to Explore Choose something that interested you from the graphic adaptation, and formulate a research question about it.

Close Review

With your group, review your notes and, if necessary, revisit the graphic adaptation. Record any new observations that seem important. What **questions** do you have? What can you **conclude**?

Close Review — REVIEW · QUESTION · CONCLUDE

THE UNITED STATES CONSTITUTION: A GRAPHIC ADAPTATION

Analyze the Media

CITE TEXTUAL EVIDENCE to support your answers.

Complete the activities.

1. **Present and Discuss** Choose the part of the graphic adaptation you find most interesting or powerful. Share your choice with the group and discuss why you chose it. Explain what you noticed about that part, what questions it raised for you, and what conclusions you reached about it.

2. **Synthesize** With your group, review the entire graphic adaptation. How do the images, speech balloons, and captions work together to reveal the difficult moments in this part of the Constitution's "story"? Do they inform, entertain, or both? Explain.

3. 🗐 **Notebook** **Essential Question:** *What is the meaning of freedom?* How did the Constitution and the Bill of Rights clarify the meaning of freedom for Americans? Support your response with evidence from the graphic adaptation.

LANGUAGE DEVELOPMENT

Media Vocabulary

| layout | speech balloon | caption |

Use these vocabulary words in your responses to the following questions.

1. **(a)** Which panel presents a caption with no image? **(b)** What do readers learn from that panel? **(c)** How does the arrangement of the caption text reflect its content?

2. **(a)** Which appears more often in this excerpt—speech balloons or captions? **(b)** Why do you think that Hennessey and McConnell chose to present so much information in one way instead of the other?

3. Choose the series of panels that you think most clearly conveys a large amount of information. Explain the visual choices that make those panels effective.

⊞ STANDARDS

Reading Informational Text
• Analyze a complex set of ideas or sequence of events and explain how specific individuals, ideas, or events interact and develop over the course of the text.

• Analyze and evaluate the effectiveness of the structure an author uses in his or her exposition or argument, including whether the structure makes points clear, convincing, and engaging.

AMERICA'S CONSTITUTION:
A BIOGRAPHY

THE UNITED STATES
CONSTITUTION: A GRAPHIC
ADAPTATION

Writing to Compare

You have read two works that provide historical information about the ratification of the U.S. Constitution. Now, deepen your understanding by comparing and writing about the two works.

Assignment

An informative text explains how or why something is true. Write an **informative essay** in which you explain how reading both *America's Constitution: A Biography* and *The United States Constitution: A Graphic Adaptation* helps a person more fully understand the ratification of the U.S. Constitution. Your essay should address these questions:

- What are the strengths of each medium?
- What unique kinds of information does each text present, and how?

To support your central idea, cite evidence from both texts. Support may take the form of quotations, paraphrases, summaries, or descriptions.

Planning and Prewriting

Analyze the Texts With your group, discuss how each text presents different types of information about the Constitution. Use the chart to gather your notes. Generate your own topic for the last row.

TOPIC	AMERICA'S CONSTITUTION: A BIOGRAPHY	THE UNITED STATES CONSTITUTION: A GRAPHIC ADAPTATION
the need for a Constitution		
objections to the Constitution		
the ratification process		

Notebook Respond to these questions.

1. What strategies or techniques are used to communicate key ideas in each text?

2. Which gives a more thorough account of the Constitution's origins? How?

3. Which gives a more memorable account? How so?

STANDARDS

Reading Informational Text
Integrate and evaluate multiple sources of information presented in different media or formats as well as in words in order to address a question or solve a problem.

Writing
- Write informative/explanatory texts to examine and convey complex ideas, concepts, and information clearly and accurately through the effective selection, organization, and analysis of content.
- Apply *grades 11–12 Reading standards* to literary nonfiction.

Drafting

Develop a Main Idea Review your Prewriting notes. With your group, draw some conclusions about the main strengths of each text. Then, work independently to draft a main idea for your essay by completing the following frame.

> **Main Idea:** Reading both the historical narrative and the graphic novel can help a person better understand the origins of the Constitution. This is because the historical narrative _____, whereas the graphic novel _____.

Take turns sharing your completed main idea with the group. Discuss which versions are stronger, and why. Use group members' feedback to revise your main idea.

Choose Evidence Your main idea contains a general statement about each text. In your essay, you must support each general statement with evidence—quotations, descriptions, summaries, or paraphrases. One possible general statement and two pieces of supporting evidence are shown here.

> **EXAMPLE**
>
> **General Statement:** The graphic novel communicates key ideas in memorable ways.
>
> - **Evidence:** Panel 8 showing shaded stamps of states that had ratified the Constitution and unshaded stamps of those that had not
> - **Evidence:** vivid image in panel 5 of the U.S. flag being sliced like a cake

Work with your group to identify strong pieces of evidence for each of your general statements. Take notes in a chart like this one.

GENERAL STATEMENT	EVIDENCE	PAGE/PANEL NUMBER

Write a Draft Draft your essay independently. Include your main idea in the introduction. Include each general statement and your evidence for it in a separate body section. In your conclusion, make an observation about one or both texts that leaves your reader with some food for thought.

Review, Revise, and Edit

When you are finished drafting, exchange papers with a group member. Ask your peer to comment on both the content and organization of your essay. Use the feedback to guide your revisions. Finally, edit and proofread your work. Replace vague language with more specific words and phrases. Correct any errors in grammar, spelling, or punctuation that you discover.

✎ EVIDENCE LOG

Before moving on to a new selection, go to your Evidence Log and record what you learned from the excerpts from *America's Constitution: A Biography* and *The United States Constitution: A Graphic Adaptation.*

About the Author

The son of a West African tribal elder, **Olaudah Equiano** (1745–1797) might have followed in his father's footsteps had he not been sold into slavery. He was taken first to the West Indies and later brought to Virginia, where he was purchased by a British captain and employed at sea. Renamed Gustavus Vassa, Equiano was enslaved for nearly ten years. After managing his master's finances and making his own money in the process, he amassed enough to buy his own freedom. In later years, he settled in England and devoted himself to the abolition of slavery. In addition to writing his two-volume autobiography to publicize the plight of slaves, he lectured and rallied public sympathy against the cruelties of slavery.

STANDARDS

Reading Informational Text
By the end of grade 11, read and comprehend literary nonfiction in the grades 11–CCR text complexity band proficiently, with scaffolding as needed at the high end of the range.

Language
Determine or clarify the meaning of unknown and multiple-meaning words and phrases based on *grades 11–12 reading and content*, choosing flexibly from a range of strategies.

from The Interesting Narrative of the Life of Olaudah Equiano

Concept Vocabulary

As you perform your first read of this excerpt from *The Interesting Narrative of the Life of Olaudah Equiano*, you will encounter these words.

loathsome	wretched	dejected

Base Words Words that seem unfamiliar may actually contain words you know. Try looking for such familiar base words "inside" unfamiliar words. The word *insupportable*, for example, contains the base word *support*. You know that *support* means "to bear" or "to hold up." In this word, the prefix *in-* means "not," and the suffix *-able* means "capable of being." *Insupportable* means "not capable of being borne or held up."

Note how the addition of prefixes or suffixes affects the meaning of the base word in these words.

un**merci**fully	in a manner without mercy
heightened	made higher or more intense
mariners	sailors

Apply your knowledge of base words and other vocabulary strategies to determine the meanings of unfamiliar words you encounter during your first read.

First Read NONFICTION

Apply these strategies as you conduct your first read. You will have an opportunity to complete a close read after your first read.

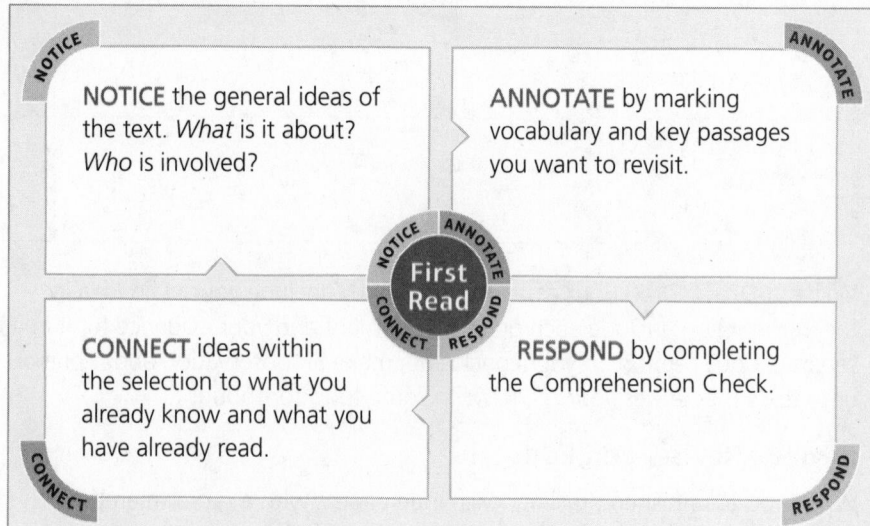

NOTICE the general ideas of the text. *What* is it about? *Who* is involved?

ANNOTATE by marking vocabulary and key passages you want to revisit.

CONNECT ideas within the selection to what you already know and what you have already read.

RESPOND by completing the Comprehension Check.

from
The Interesting Narrative of the Life of
Olaudah Equiano

Olaudah Equiano

BACKGROUND

In the first several chapters of his autobiography, Olaudah Equiano describes how slave traders kidnapped him and his sister from their home in West Africa and transported them to the African coast. During this six- or seven-month journey, Equiano was separated from his sister and held at a series of way stations. After reaching the coast, Equiano was shipped with other captives to North America. The following account describes this horrifying journey.

SCAN FOR
MULTIMEDIA

1   At last when the ship we were in, had got in all her cargo, they made ready with many fearful noises, and we were all put under deck, so that we could not see how they managed the vessel. But this disappointment was the least of my sorrow. The stench of the hold while we were on the coast was so intolerably loathsome, that it was dangerous to remain there for any time, and some of us had been permitted to stay on the deck for the fresh air; but now that the whole ship's cargo were confined together, it became absolutely pestilential. The closeness of the place, and the heat of the climate, added to the number in the ship, which was so crowded that each had scarcely room to turn himself, almost suffocated us.

NOTES

Mark base words or indicate another strategy you used that helped you determine meaning.

loathsome (LOHTH suhm) *adj.*

MEANING:

Mark base words or indicate another strategy you used that helped you determine meaning.

wretched (REHCH ihd) *adj.*

MEANING:

2   This produced copious perspirations, so that the air soon became unfit for respiration, from a variety of loathsome smells, and brought on a sickness among the slaves, of which many died—thus falling victims to the improvident avarice, as I may call it, of their purchasers. This **wretched** situation was again aggravated by the galling of the chains, now become insupportable, and the filth of the necessary tubs, into which the children often fell, and were almost suffocated. The shrieks of the women, and the groans of the dying, rendered the whole a scene of horror almost inconceivable. Happily perhaps, for myself, I was soon reduced so low here that it was thought necessary to keep me almost always on deck; and from my extreme youth I was not put in fetters.[1] In this situation I expected every hour to share the fate of my companions, some of whom were almost daily brought upon deck at the point of death, which I began to hope would soon put an end to my miseries. Often did I think many of the inhabitants of the deep much more happy than myself.

3   I envied them the freedom they enjoyed, and as often wished I could change my condition for theirs. Every circumstance I met with, served only to render my state more painful, and heightened my apprehensions, and my opinion of the cruelty of the whites.

4   One day they had taken a number of fishes; and when they had killed and satisfied themselves with as many as they thought fit, to our astonishment who were on deck, rather than give any of them to us to eat, as we expected, they tossed the remaining fish into the sea again, although we begged and prayed for some as well as we could, but in vain; and some of my countrymen, being pressed by hunger, took an opportunity, when they thought no one saw them, of trying to get a little privately; but they were discovered, and the attempt procured them some very severe floggings. One day, when we had a smooth sea and moderate wind, two of my wearied countrymen who were chained together (I was near them at the time), preferring death to such a life of misery, somehow made through the nettings and jumped into the sea; immediately, another quite **dejected** fellow, who, on account of his illness, was suffered to be out of irons, also followed their example; and I believe many more would very soon have done the same, if they had not been prevented by the ship's crew, who were instantly alarmed. Those of us that were the most active, were in a moment put down under the deck; and there was such a noise and confusion amongst the people of the ship as I never heard before, to stop her, and get the boat out to go after the slaves. However, two of the wretches were drowned, but they got the other, and afterwards flogged him unmercifully, for thus attempting to prefer death to slavery. In this manner we continued to undergo more hardships than I can now relate, hardships which are inseparable from this accursed trade. Many a time we were near suffocation from the want of fresh

Mark base words or indicate another strategy you used that helped you determine meaning.

dejected (dee JEHK tihd) *adj.*

MEANING:

---

1. **fetters** (FEHT uhrz) *n.* chains.

air, which we were often without for whole days together. This, and the stench of the necessary tubs, carried off many.

5 During our passage, I first saw flying fishes, which surprised me very much; they used frequently to fly across the ship, and many of them fell on the deck. I also now first saw the use of the quadrant;[2] I had often with astonishment seen the mariners make observations with it, and I could not think what it meant. They at last took notice of my surprise; and one of them, willing to increase it, as well as to gratify my curiosity, made me one day look through it. The clouds appeared to me to be land, which disappeared as they passed along. This heightened my wonder; and I was now more persuaded than ever, that I was in another world, and that every thing about me was magic. At last, we came in sight of the island of Barbados, at which the whites on board gave a great shout, and made many signs of joy to us. We did not know what to think of this; but as the vessel drew nearer, we plainly saw the harbor, and other ships of different kinds and sizes, and we soon anchored amongst them, off Bridgetown.[3] Many merchants and planters now came on board, though it was in the evening. They put us in separate parcels,[4] and examined us attentively. They also made us jump, and pointed to the land, signifying we were to go there.

---

2. **quadrant** (KWOD ruhnt) *n.* instrument used by navigators to determine the position of a ship.
3. **Bridgetown** capital of Barbados.
4. **parcels** (PAHR suhlz) *n.* groups.

This portion of a 1788 British abolitionist poster depicts the *Brookes*, a slave ship, and the maximum number of slaves that it could transport legally. Slave traders carried as many slaves as the law allowed, knowing that many would die during the journey.

6   We thought by this, we should be eaten by these ugly men, as they appeared to us; and, when soon after we were all put down under the deck again, there was much dread and trembling among us, and nothing but bitter cries to be heard all the night from these apprehensions, insomuch, that at last the white people got some old slaves from the land to pacify us. They told us we were not to be eaten, but to work, and were soon to go on land, where we should see many of our country people. This report eased us much. And sure enough, soon after we were landed, there came to us Africans of all languages.

7   We were conducted immediately to the merchant's yard, where we were all pent up together, like so many sheep in a fold, without regard to sex or age. . . . We were not many days in the merchant's custody, before we were sold after their usual manner, which is this: On a signal given (as the beat of a drum), the buyers rush at once into the yard where the slaves are confined, and make choice of that parcel they like best. . . . ❧

Comprehension Check

Complete the following items after you finish your first read. Review and clarify details with your group.

1. According to Equiano, what physical hardships do the captives suffer during their passage across the Atlantic Ocean?

2. What do some captives do to escape the misery of the Atlantic crossing?

3. Why does Equiano blame the illness aboard ship on the "improvident avarice" of the slave traders?

4. How does Equiano's youth affect his treatment during the voyage?

5. What happens to the captives when the ship reaches Barbados?

6. 📓 **Notebook** Confirm your understanding of the text by creating a timeline of the narrative's events.

- -

RESEARCH

Research to Clarify Choose at least one unfamiliar detail from the text. Briefly research that detail. In what way does the information you learned shed light on an aspect of the narrative?

Research to Explore This autobiographical account may spark your curiosity to learn more about the author, the era, or the topic. You may want to share what you discover with your group.

THE INTERESTING NARRATIVE OF
THE LIFE OF OLAUDAH EQUIANO

Close Read the Text

With your group, revisit sections of the text you marked
during your first read. **Annotate** details that you notice.
What **questions** do you have? What can you **conclude**?

Analyze the Text

> **CITE TEXTUAL EVIDENCE**
> to support your answers.

Complete the activities.

1. **Review and Clarify** With your group, reread paragraph 1 of the
selection. Discuss the conditions that the African captives endured aboard
the ship. Why were so many people crowded below deck?

2. **Present and Discuss** Now, work with your group to share the passages
from the selection that you found especially important. Take turns
presenting your passages. Discuss what you noticed in the selection, what
questions you asked, and what conclusions you reached.

3. **Essential Question:** *What is the meaning of freedom?* What have
you learned about American freedoms from reading this text? Discuss
with your group.

Concept Vocabulary

loathsome	wretched	dejected

Why These Words? The three concept vocabulary words from the text are
related. With your group, discuss the words and determine what they have in
common. How do these word choices enhance the impact of the text?

Practice

Notebook Confirm your understanding of these words from the text
by using them in sentences. Be sure to include context clues that hint at each
word's meaning.

Word Study

Notebook **Latin Root: *-ject-*** The Latin root *-ject-* means "to throw."
It contributes to the meaning of the concept vocabulary word *dejected*, as
well as many other words in English.

1. Explain how the meaning of the root *-ject-* is evident in the meaning of
the word *dejected*.

2. Look up each of these words in a dictionary: *conjecture, trajectory,* and
projection. Explain how the root *-ject-* contributes to the meaning of each
of the words.

Analyze Craft and Structure

Literary Nonfiction: Persuasive Purpose *The Interesting Narrative of the Life of Olaudah Equiano* is an example of a **slave narrative**, or an autobiographical account of a person's life as a slave. Most slave narratives, written when slavery was a legal practice, have an implicit, or unstated, persuasive purpose: to expose the evils of slavery and, in so doing, turn the public against the practice. Equiano's account combines factual details and personal reflections with powerful descriptive language that constitute **emotional appeals** to his readers. Notice, for example, how words such as *shrieks* and *groans* evoke readers' sympathy and outrage in this depiction of the ship that brought Equiano from Africa:

> The shrieks of the women, and the groans of the dying, rendered the whole a scene of horror almost inconceivable.

The abolitionist movement in the United States owed much to the revelations of former slaves. Only the hardest of hearts could fail to be moved by Equiano's narrative.

Practice

CITE TEXTUAL EVIDENCE to support your answers.

As a group, complete this chart. Identify passages from the autobiography that give factual details, passages that convey personal reflections, and passages that feature strong descriptive language. Then, explain the persuasive impact of each passage.

ELEMENT OF SLAVE NARRATIVE	EXAMPLES FROM TEXT	PERSUASIVE IMPACT
Factual details		
Personal reflections		
Strong descriptive language		

THE INTERESTING NARRATIVE OF
THE LIFE OF OLAUDAH EQUIANO

Conventions and Style

Eighteenth-Century Narrative Style Equiano's account is an example of eighteenth-century narrative style. The formal language of the period has several characteristics that distinguish it from modern style.

CHARACTERISTIC	EIGHTEENTH-CENTURY STYLE	MODERN STYLE
Sentence Length: the number of words, phrases, and clauses in a sentence	Sentences are long and contain multiple clauses and phrases.	Sentences vary in length, and most have fewer than three clauses.
Usage: the ways in which words are commonly used	Word meanings change over time, as do word forms, including formation of singular and plural nouns. Modern readers may contest usage or need to confirm archaic meanings.	Word meanings and forms continue to change over time. In addition, new words continue to enter the English language from other languages or are coined to refer to new situations, ideas, or objects.
Mechanics: punctuation and spelling	Eighteenth-century writers punctuated text however they chose.	Punctuation marks are used according to established conventions.

Read It

🗒 **Notebook** Work individually. Read the passage from Equiano's narrative carefully, and then answer the questions that follow.

One day they had taken a number of fishes; and when they had killed and satisfied themselves with as many as they thought fit, to our astonishment who were on deck, rather than give any of them to us to eat, as we expected, they tossed the remaining fish into the sea again, although we begged and prayed for some as well as we could, but in vain; and some of my countrymen, being pressed by hunger, took an opportunity, when they thought no one saw them, of trying to get a little privately; but they were discovered, and the attempt procured them some very severe floggings.

- How many sentences does the passage contain?
- Identify an example of eighteenth-century usage.
- What punctuation marks does the author use to separate details regarding the plight of the captives?

Write It

🗒 **Notebook** Rewrite the passage in modern style. Then, share passages with your group and discuss whether or not the change in style lessened the persuasive impact of the original passage.

Writing to Sources

Assignment

With your group, prepare an **argument** related to the abolitionist cause. Choose from the following options.

☐ a **literary review** of Equiano's autobiography, arguing that the events he describes, and the manner in which he describes them, provide powerful support for the abolitionist movement

☐ a **letter** to the British Parliament, using evidence from the selection to urge its members to abolish the slave trade

☐ an **advertisement** for the British abolitionist movement that uses graphics and text, inspired by specific details from the autobiography, to make a strong point about the need for change

Project Plan Work with your group to divide the option that you chose into manageable sections or parts. Discuss your ideas and consider the types of supporting evidence you will use, including those that appeal to readers' emotions. Then, assign each member one part of the writing.

Working Title: _____

SECTION OR PART	ASSIGNED GROUP MEMBER
Claim	
Reason 1	
Supporting details from the selection	
Reason 2	
Supporting details from the selection	
Reason 3	
Supporting details from the selection	

Tying It Together Work together to draft an introduction that touches on all the sections that you plan to write. Once everyone has written his or her section, work together to draft a logical and memorable conclusion.

TIP

COLLABORATION
Group members responsible for preparing the reasons that support the claim should work together to decide the order in which to list the reasons.

✎ EVIDENCE LOG

Before moving on to a new selection, go to your Evidence Log and record what you learned from *The Interesting Narrative of the Life of Olaudah Equiano.*

LETTER | BIOGRAPHY

Letter to John Adams

from Dear Abigail: The Intimate Lives and Revolutionary Ideas of Abigail Adams and Her Two Remarkable Sisters

Concept Vocabulary

As you perform your first read of these two texts, you will encounter the following words.

> vassals   foment   dissented

Context Clues When you come to an unfamiliar word in a text, you can often determine its meaning by using **context clues**—nearby words and phrases that provide hints to a word's meaning. Such hints may come in the form of descriptions.

> **Description as Context Clue:**
> **Passage:** "Others have committed abominable **ravages** . . . both the house and furniture of the Solicitor General have <u>fallen prey to their own merciless party</u>."
>
> **Explanation:** The description of a person's house and furniture as "prey" to a "merciless party" suggests that ravages means something like "destruction."

Apply your knowledge of context clues and other vocabulary strategies to determine the meanings of unfamiliar words you encounter during your first read.

First Read NONFICTION

Apply these strategies as you conduct your first read. You will have an opportunity to complete a close read after your first read.

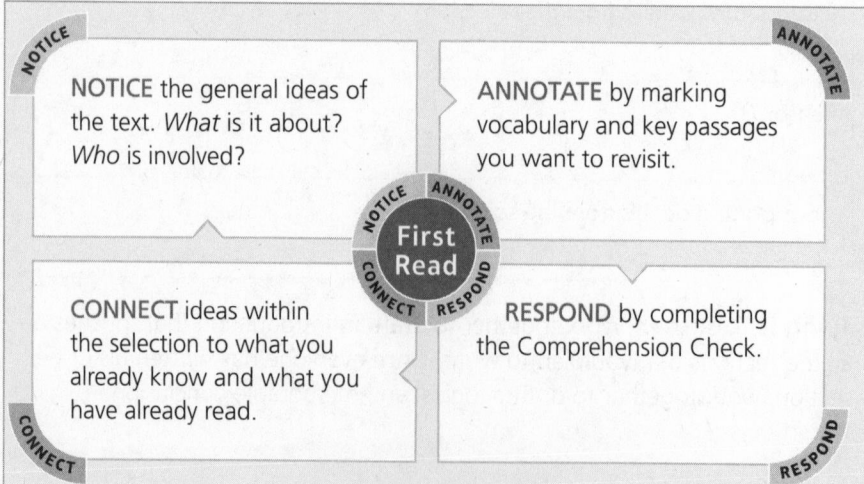

NOTICE the general ideas of the text. *What* is it about? *Who* is involved?

ANNOTATE by marking vocabulary and key passages you want to revisit.

CONNECT ideas within the selection to what you already know and what you have already read.

RESPOND by completing the Comprehension Check.

First Read

STANDARDS

Reading Informational Text
By the end of grade 11, read and comprehend literary nonfiction in the grades 11–CCR text complexity band proficiently, with scaffolding as needed at the high end of the range.

Language
Use context as a clue to the meaning of a word or phrase.

About the Authors

 Abigail Adams (1744–1818) was the wife of John Adams, the second president of the United States, and the mother of John Quincy Adams, the sixth president. She was also one of the most important and influential women of her time. A dedicated supporter of women's rights and the American Revolutionary movement, Adams wrote many letters to her husband and others expressing her opinions. In these letters, she included vivid descriptions that capture the essence of life in early America.

Adams was born Abigail Smith in Weymouth, Massachusetts. At the age of nineteen, she married John Adams. The couple had three sons and two daugthers. Abigail, who had not been educated as a child, made sure all of her children—including a daughter—received a thorough education. This was something few American girls enjoyed at the time.

Abigail died in 1818, after spending the last seventeen years of her life at the Adams family home in Massachusetts. In 1840, a first volume of her letters was published. In the ensuing decades, other collections, biographies, and histories have followed. Today, Abigail Adams is widely recognized as a writer and a pioneer of the American women's movement.

Diane Jacobs, who lives in New York City, is the author of several acclaimed biographies. In addition to *Dear Abigail*, Jacobs has written about the contemporary filmmaker Woody Allen and about Mary Wollstonecraft, the eighteenth-century British author of *A Vindication of the Rights of Woman*.

Backgrounds

Letter to John Adams

Throughout their courtship and marriage, John and Abigail Adams wrote more than one thousand letters to one another. Although their letters are often affectionate and even playful, they also reflect the couple's underlying awareness that they were key players in the unfolding of history. Abigail wrote this and several other letters to her husband while he attended the Second Continental Congress in Philadelphia.

From Dear Abigail: The Intimate Lives and Revolutionary Ideas of Abigail Adams and Her Two Remarkable Sisters

The correspondence between Abigail and John Adams sheds light on Revolutionary-era America. This selection by a modern historian sets their letters within the context of the work of the Continental Congress and the adoption of the Declaration of Independence.

Letter to
John Adams

Abigail Adams

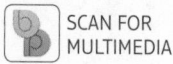

SCAN FOR
MULTIMEDIA

Mark context clues or indicate another strategy you used that helped you determine meaning.

vassals (VAS uhlz) *n.*

MEANING:

Braintree[1] *March 31, 1776*

1   I wish you would ever write me a letter half as long as I write you; and tell me if you may where your fleet are gone? What sort of defense Virginia can make against our common enemy? Whether it is so situated as to make an able defense? Are not the gentry[2] lords and the common people **vassals**, are they not like the uncivilized natives Britain represents us to be? I hope their rifle men who have shown themselves very savage and even blood thirsty; are not a specimen of the generality of the people.

2   I am willing to allow the Colony great merit for having produced a Washington but they have been shamefully duped by a Dunmore.[3]

3   I have sometimes been ready to think that the passion for liberty cannot be equally strong in the breasts of those who have been accustomed to deprive their fellow creatures of theirs. Of this I am certain that it is not founded upon that generous and Christian principal of doing to others as we would that others should do unto us.

4   Do not you want to see Boston; I am fearful of the small pox, or I should have been in before this time. I got Mr. Crane to go to our

---

1. **Braintree** town in eastern Massachusetts that was the home of John and Abigail Adams.
2. **gentry** (JEHN tree) *n.* people of high social standing.
3. **Dunmore** John Murray, 4th earl of Dunmore, was the British colonial governor of Virginia. He provoked strong feelings among Virginians when he dissolved the legislature and later used troops loyal to the British throne to attack the colony's troops in late 1775 and early 1776.

house and see what state it was in. I find it has been occupied by one of the doctors of a regiment, very dirty, but no other damage has been done to it. The few things which were left in it are all gone. Cranch has the key which he never delivered up. I have wrote to him for it and am determined to get it cleaned as soon as possible and shut it up. I look upon it a new acquisition of property, a property which one month ago I did not value at a single shilling,[4] and could with pleasure have seen it in flames.

5   The town in general is left in a better state than we expected, more owing to a percipitate[5] flight than any regard to the inhabitants, though some individuals discovered a sense of honor and justice and have left the rent of the houses in which they were, for the owners and the furniture unhurt, or if damaged sufficient to make it good.

6   Others have committed abominable ravages. The mansion house of your President [John Hancock] is safe and the furniture unhurt whilst both the house and furniture of the Solicitor General [Samuel Quincy] have fallen a prey to their own merciless party. Surely the very fiends feel a reverential awe for virtue and patriotism, whilst they detest the paricide[6] and traitor.

7   I feel very differently at the approach of spring to what I did a month ago. We knew not then whether we could plant or sow with safety, whether when we had toiled we could reap the fruits of our own industry, whether we could rest in our own cottages, or whether we should not be driven from the sea coasts to seek shelter in the wilderness, but now we feel as if we might sit under our own vine and eat the good of the land.

8   I feel a gaieti de Coar[7] to which before I was a stranger. I think the sun looks brighter, the birds sing more melodiously, and nature puts on a more cheerful countenance. We feel a temporary peace, and the poor fugitives are returning to their deserted habitations.

9   Though we felicitate[8] ourselves, we sympathize with those who are trembling least the lot of Boston should be theirs. But they cannot be in similar circumstances unless pusillanimity and cowardice should take possession of them. They have time and warning given them to see the evil and shun it.—I long to hear that you have declared an independency—and by the way in the new code of laws which I suppose it will be necessary for you to make I desire you would remember the ladies, and be more generous and favorable to them than your ancestors. Do not put such unlimited power into the hands of the husbands. Remember all men would be tyrants if they could. If particuliar care and attention is not paid

I desire you would remember the ladies, and be more generous and favourable to them than your ancestors.

NOTES

4. **shilling** *n.* former British coin worth one twentieth of a pound.
5. **percipitate** *adj.* precipitate; done very hastily or rashly.
6. **paricide** *n.* parricide; person who kills a parent or other relative.
7. **gaieti de Coar** *gaieté de coeur;* French for "joy of heart."
8. **felicitate** *v.* wish happiness; to congratulate.

NOTES

Mark context clues or indicate another strategy that you used helped you determine meaning.

foment (foh MEHNT) *v.*

MEANING:

to the ladies we are determined to **foment** a rebellion, and will not hold ourselves bound by any laws in which we have no voice, or representation.

10   That your sex are naturally tyrannical is a truth so thoroughly established as to admit of no dispute, but such of you as wish to be happy willingly give up the harsh title of master for the more tender and endearing one of friend. Why then, not put it out of the power of the vicious and the lawless to use us with cruelty and indignity with impunity. Men of sense in all ages abhor those customs which treat us only as the vassals of your sex. Regard us then as beings placed by providence under your protection and in imitation of the supreme being make use of that power only for our happiness.

April 5

11   Not having an opportunity of sending this I shall add a few lines more; though not with a heart so gay. I have been attending the sick chamber of our neighbor Trot whose affliction I most sensibly feel but cannot describe, stripped of two lovely children in one week. George the eldest died on Wednesday and Billy the youngest on Friday, with the canker fever, a terrible disorder so much like the throat distemper, that it differs but little from it. Betsy Cranch has been very bad, but upon the recovery. Becky Peck they do not expect will live out the day. Many grown persons are now sick with it, in this street. It rages much in other towns. The mumps too are very frequent. Isaac is now confined with it. Our own little flock are yet well. My heart trembles with anxiety for them. God preserve them.

12   I want to hear much oftener from you than I do. March 8 was the last date of any that I have yet had.—You inquire of whether I am making salt peter.[9] I have not yet attempted it, but after soap making believe I shall make the experiment. I find as much as I can do to manufacture clothing for my family which would otherwise be naked. I know of but one person in this part of the town who has made any, that is Mr. Tertias Bass as he is called who has got very near a hundred weight which has been found to be very good. I have heard of some others in the other parishes. Mr. Reed of Weymouth has been applied to, to go to Andover to the mills which are now at work, and has gone. I have lately seen a small manuscript describing the proportions for the various sorts of powder, fit for cannon, small arms and pistols. If it would be of any service your way I will get it transcribed and send it to you.—Every one of your friends send their regards, and all the little ones. Your brother's youngest child lies bad with convulsion fits. Adieu. I need not say how much I am your ever faithful friend.

---

9. **salt peter** *n.* saltpeter; a form of potassium nitrate used to make gunpowder.

from
Dear Abigail

The Intimate Lives and Revolutionary Ideas of Abigail Adams and Her Two Remarkable Sisters

Diane Jacobs

SCAN FOR MULTIMEDIA

NOTES

1   Writing to Abigail about the fierce effort it took him to compose *Thoughts on Government*[1] at the same time that he was working day and night at Congress, John lamented that none of his present endeavors would bring them an easier life. "I shall get nothing [for writing this pamphlet], I believe, because I never get any thing by any thing that I do," he complained, while assuring her he was not above commiserating her lack of help on the farm or writing paper for all his preoccupation with posterity and the greater good. Strawberries and an early spring in the dirty city did little to console him. He longed, he said, to walk in their garden and to the cornfields, the orchards, and the Common.[2] "Instead of domestic felicity, I am destined to public contentions," he brooded. "Instead of rural felicity, I must reconcile myself to the smoke and noise of a city."

2   So he wished to be home. And yet his overriding desire at the moment was for Congress to make a declaration of independence

---

1. ***Thoughts on Government*** document written by John Adams in 1776, notable for proposing the three branches of American government, including a system of checks and balances.
2. **the Common** large public park in Boston, Massachusetts.

from Great Britain. It had to be sooner rather than later because without it there was no hope for the foreign assistance—from France in particular—which was crucial to winning the war. On June 7, the Virginia delegate Richard Henry Lee of Virginia raised a motion for independence in Congress; it was supported by Massachusetts and six other colonies, while another six—Pennsylvania, Delaware, Maryland, South Carolina, New Jersey, and New York—remained unsure.

3   With everyone hoping for a unanimous verdict, the vote was set three weeks in the future, while a committee to consider the tone and nature of the prospective document immediately convened. It consisted of five members: the most prominent being John, Benjamin Franklin, and the redheaded Virginian who shared Thomas Paine's[3] veneration for the passions: Thomas Jefferson. Considered to be even more eloquent than the far better-known authors of *Poor Richard* and *Thoughts on Government*, 33-year-old Jefferson was chosen to write the text.

4   Like Franklin, Jefferson was a scientist and inventor. He had created a retractable bed and a tilt-top table as well as an indoor weather vane and his own Palladian estate, Monticello. Educated at William and Mary, he was as steeped in history and philosophy as Adams and also adored his wife, a wealthy widow, who was currently pregnant and in poor health. He was a slaveholder who professed to dislike slavery, a statesman ambitious to succeed on the large stage who hated leaving home. As he began drafting the American declaration—in the middle state of Pennsylvania, on a desk of his own design—he longed for southern Monticello as Adams longed for northern Braintree. Though Jefferson was a deist, rejecting Christ and original sin, he shared Adams's obsession with goodness. "Everything is useful which contributes to fix in the mind principles and practices of virtue," he believed.

5   Jefferson was gangly, fidgety, six-foot-two-and-a-half, and as quiet as Franklin in Congress. But he rode his horse elegantly, spoke up regularly in committees, and, despite his aversion to arguing, proved impregnable to opposing views. For better and for worse, no one and nothing swayed him. He had little use for either the vagaries[4] of individuals or venerated ideals.

6   "We are hastening rapidly to great events," John had written Abigail at the end of April, adding that "It requires . . . serenity of temper, a deep . . . understanding and . . . courage . . . to ride in this whirlwind" of Congressional discord. By the end of May, he was telling her that affairs were in a critical state. Then, in the middle of June, exultant after Henry Lee raised a motion for separation from England, he wrote, "These throes will usher in the birth of a fine boy."

---

3. **Thomas Paine's** Thomas Paine was a highly influential writer who argued passionately for American independence from England.
4. **vagaries** (VAY guh reez) *n.* unpredictable actions or ideas.

7   On July 1, twenty days after that initial motion, Congress resumed its debate on independence with John Dickinson of Pennsylvania arguing against and John Adams for an immediate break from both Parliament and King George III. John spoke fervidly for two hours to a rapt audience. A clear majority of nine colonies sided with him, but in a preliminary vote the delegates from Pennsylvania (out of respect for Dickinson, though most of its citizens favored independence), South Carolina, and Delaware **dissented**, while New York, with its high percentage of loyalists, abstained. Still hoping for unanimity, Congress agreed to delay the formal vote until the following morning.

8   That night word arrived that a flotilla of British boats had sailed into New York Harbor, panicking George Washington's unprepared Army and adding pressure for some buoying news. The next day John Dickinson, for the sake of unity, announced he would abstain from the voting, throwing Pennsylvania to the majority. South Carolina and Delaware joined Pennsylvania, while New York continued to abstain. The motion was called to the floor and carried.

9   July 3 was spent amending Jefferson's declaration—much to the proprietary writer's chagrin. The most significant change, insisted on by South Carolina and Georgia, was the elimination of a passage implicitly condemning slavery. Jefferson had accused the King of waging "cruel war against human nature" by capturing and transporting innocent Africans "into slavery in another hemisphere, or to incur miserable death in their transportation thither." This was a daring, if bewildering, opinion from a southern slaveholder. Jefferson claimed to be proud of it and to rue its loss. Other of his favorite passages were also cut or tightened during the nearly twelve-hour debate over wording, but Jefferson's voice remained, and on the afternoon of July 4, all of Congress endorsed it.

"We are hastening rapidly to great events"

10   John Adams could hardly contain his exuberance. "Yesterday the greatest question was decided, which ever was debated in America, and a greater, perhaps, never was or will be decided among men," he wrote Abigail. What felt hopelessly slow just a month ago now seemed remarkably expeditious. Looking back to the first arguments with England in the early 1760s, "and recollect[ing] the series of political events, the chain of causes and effects, I am surprised at the suddenness as well as the greatness of this Revolution," he exulted. And, of course, "calamities" and "distresses" might lie in the future; surely the threat of tyranny by the majority, which he had warned against in *Thoughts on Government*, would pose a threat in the coming years. And, yes, it would be far better for the war if independence had been declared seven months before and foreign alliances were set in place. And yet: "July [of] 1776, will be the most memorable

Drafting the Declaration of Independence in 1776 This 1859 painting by Alonzo Chappel depicts the work of the "Committee of Five": (*right to left*) Roger Sherman, Robert Livingston, John Adams, Thomas Jefferson, and Benjamin Franklin.

epocha,[5] in the history of America.—I am apt to believe that it will be celebrated, by succeeding generations, as the great anniversary." It ought, John declared, to be commemorated and "solemnized with pomp and parade, with shews,[6] sports, guns, bells, bonfires and illuminations from one end of this continent to the other from this time forward forever."

11   On July 18, a week after they were inoculated for smallpox, and with no one yet showing symptoms of the disease, Mary and Richard, Abigail, and Betsy joined masses of patriots lining King Street in front of the Boston State House, the seat of the first elected legislature in the New World. The ragtag troops who had chased the British out of Boston four months earlier stood before them, respectably armed at least for the moment. An officer, Colonel Crafts, appeared on the balcony and began to read:

---

5. **epocha** (EHP uh kuh) *n.* archaic form of "epoch," a distinct and significant era in history.
6. **shews** *n.* archaic form of "shows."

12   When in the course of human events, it becomes necessary for one people to dissolve the political bands which have connected them with another, and to assume among the powers of the earth a separate and equal station to which the Laws of Nature and of Nature's God entitle them, a decent respect to the opinions of mankind requires that they should declare the causes which impel them to the separation.

13   The Smith sisters'[7] lives spoke volumes on the causes for separation, and the spirit of the declaration was familiar, for they had avidly read the great thinkers of the Enlightenment[8] who so informed Jefferson's view. Yet, if his concepts were not original, the occasion was a first in history, and Richard Cranch as well as Mary, Abigail, and Betsy stood spellbound at the beautiful expression of what they felt and knew. "We hold these truths to be self-evident, that all men are created equal, that they are endowed by their Creator with certain unalienable Rights, that among these are Life, Liberty, and the pursuit of Happiness." And on it went.

14   "God Save the King" was already a memory. When Colonel Crafts finished reading the Declaration of Independence, he shouted, "God Save our American States." The people picked up this chant and ran with it, as Richard Cranch reported to John in a letter the following week. There were three cheers that "rended the air," Abigail wrote in her own description, and they were followed by an elated ringing of bells; the cannons roared, and rifles' shots rang in the air. "After dinner the king's arms were taken down from the State House and every vestige of him from every place in which it appeared and burnt in King Street. Thus ends royal authority in this State," she concluded, "and all the people shall say Amen."

15   By July 22, Abigail was ill with the "excruciating pain in my head and every limb" that was said to "portend[9] a speedy eruption," which occurred a few days later, and though she produced only one pox, her symptoms were sufficiently grueling for the doctor to declare her immune. John Quincy's case too was mild but conclusive, while Mary's eldest daughter, Betsy Cranch, the frailest of them all, fainted and lay listless in bed. Her mother and brothers, on the other hand, produced no symptoms. By the end of July, Mary had been inoculated four times and was still healthy as the day she left Braintree, as were Charles and Tommy Adams, who had been inoculated twice. It seemed fitting when Nabby, the calmest of them all, came through with almost no suffering. The doctor, however, insisted that she be inoculated a second time, on the odd chance that her symptoms were "false."

16   Even after her single pox dissipated, Abigail felt light-headed from the disease. "The smallpox is a great confuser of the mind, I am really

---

7. **Smith sisters** Abigail Adams and her sisters; Smith was their family surname.
8. **the Enlightenment** European intellectual movement in the seventeenth and eighteenth centuries that emphasized the power of reason.
9. **portend** (pawr TEHND) *v.* foreshadow; indicate.

put to it to spell the commonest word," she told John. Yet when John gave her an opening, she had no trouble expounding on her favorite topic of women in the new nation. "If you complain of neglect of education in sons, What shall I say with regard to daughters, who every day experience the want of it," she began. And continued:

17   I most sincerely wish that some more liberal plan might be laid and executed for the benefit of the rising generation, and that our new constitution may be distinguished for learning and virtue. If we mean to have heroes, statesmen, and philosophers, we should have learned women. The world perhaps will laugh at me, and accuse me of vanity, but you know I have a mind too enlarged and liberal [to be vain]. If much depends as is allowed upon the early education of youth and the first principals which are instilled take deepest root, great benefit must arise from literary accomplishments in women.

18   This time John assured Abigail "Your sentiments of the importance of education in women are exactly agreeable to my own," though women who displayed their wits were contemptible, he felt impelled to add. ✺

Comprehension Check

Complete the following items after you finish your first read. Review and clarify details with your group.

LETTER TO JOHN ADAMS

1. In her letter of March 31, 1776, what does Abigail Adams ask that John provide?

2. What does Abigail report to John about the state of homes in Boston?

3. What advice does Abigail Adams give her husband regarding women's rights?

4. 📓 **Notebook** Confirm your understanding of the text by writing a summary.

from DEAR ABIGAIL

1. Cite two reasons for John Adams's unhappiness in the late spring of 1776.

2. Name two contradictions regarding Thomas Jefferson that the text explores.

3. What document does Colonel Crafts, an army officer, read to a crowd assembled in front of the Boston State House?

4. 📓 **Notebook** Confirm your understanding of the text by drawing a storyboard of events.

RESEARCH

Research to Clarify Choose at least one unfamiliar detail from one of the texts. Briefly research that detail. In what way does the information you found shed light on an aspect of that text?

LETTER TO JOHN ADAMS
from DEAR ABIGAIL

Close Read the Text

With your group, revisit sections of the text you marked during your first read. **Annotate** details that you notice. What **questions** do you have? What can you **conclude**?

Analyze the Text

> **CITE TEXTUAL EVIDENCE**
> to support your answers.

Complete the activities.

1. **Review and Clarify** With your group, reread paragraph 14 from *Dear Abigail*, in which the author discusses the public reading of the Declaration of Independence. Why do you think the Bostonians reacted as they did?

2. **Present and Discuss** Now, work with your group to share the passages from the two selections that you found especially important. Take turns presenting your passages. Discuss what you noticed in the selections, what questions you asked, and what conclusions you reached.

3. **Essential Question:** *What is the meaning of freedom?* What have you learned about American freedoms from reading these texts? Discuss with your group.

Concept Vocabulary

vassals	foment	dissented

Why These Words? The three concept words from the texts are related. With your group, discuss the words and determine what they have in common. How do these word choices enhance the impact of the texts?

Practice

📓 **Notebook** Confirm your understanding of these words by using each one in a sentence. Include context clues that help readers figure out what each word means.

Word Study

📓 **Notebook Word Families** Groups of words that share a common base but have different prefixes, suffixes, or both, are called **word families**. The concept word *dissented*, for instance, is built upon the base word *dissent*.

Complete the following activities.

1. Use an online dictionary or other source to identify other members of the word family that includes *dissented*. Write three of those related words, and identify their parts of speech.

2. Choose a word from one of these texts that you think is part of a word family. Research the word and verify your choice. Write the original word and two related words. Identify each word's part of speech.

Analyze Craft and Structure

Primary and Secondary Sources Research sources can be classified into one of two categories—primary sources or secondary sources.

- **Primary sources**, created by people who directly participated in or observed an event, give readers first-hand information about a topic. They include diaries, journals, letters, newspaper articles, and speeches. They may also include functional texts, such as government forms, schedules, or blueprints.

- **Secondary sources**, written by people with indirect knowledge, rely on primary sources or other secondary sources for information. Secondary sources include biographies, encyclopedias, and book reviews.

These classifications into primary and secondary categories are not absolutely set, but depend largely on how a text is used by a researcher.

TIP

CLARIFICATION
Original drawings, paintings, news footage, pottery, and photographs are some non-text items that are categorized as primary sources. These can be excellent research sources, and they should be documented with citations.

Practice

Analyze and evaluate how Jacobs uses primary sources to add interest, clarity, and legitimacy to the points she is making. For example, ask: "What does this quotation from a primary source do? Does it make the point clearer?" Work individually to gather your notes in this chart. Then, share your observations with your group.

CITE TEXTUAL EVIDENCE to support your answers.

DEAR ABIGAIL	PRIMARY SOURCE INFORMATION	EFFECT
Paragraph 1		
Paragraph 6		
Paragraph 10		
Paragraph 17		

📓 **Notebook** Respond to these questions.

1. Which use of a primary source in the excerpt from *Dear Abigail* did you find most effective? Why?

2. Review or scan the two secondary sources related to Abigail Adams in this text—the brief biography and the excerpt from *Dear Abigail*. Identify one trait each secondary source attributes to Abigail Adams. Then, cite a passage from Adams's letter that either supports that interpretation of her character or challenges it. Explain your choices.

LETTER TO JOHN ADAMS
from DEAR ABIGAIL

Author's Style

Voice A writer's **voice** is the way in which his or her personality is revealed on the page. It is the sense the reader gains of the person behind the words. Voice is created through a combination of elements:

- **diction:** the types of words a writer uses
- **syntax:** the types of sentences a writer uses, including structure, length, and variety
- **tone:** the writer's attitude toward the topic or audience

Voice is also influenced by the writer's consideration of his or her **audience**, or readers, and **purpose**, or reason for writing. Since writers adapt their diction, syntax, and tone to suit specific audiences and purposes, a writer's voice can vary from one text to another. For example, John Adams's voice is warm and personal in letters to his wife, but impersonal and formal in public documents.

Read It

Work individually. Use this chart to explore aspects of Abigail Adams's voice as a writer. Cite examples from both texts, and briefly explain how her combination of diction, syntax, and tone creates a sense of her personal qualities. Discuss your findings with your group.

PASSAGES FROM LETTER TO JOHN ADAMS	TYPE(S) OF DICTION, SYNTAX, AND TONE	PERSONALITY TRAIT(S) OF ADAMS
PASSAGES QUOTED IN *DEAR ABIGAIL*		

STANDARDS

Reading Informational Text
Determine an author's point of view or purpose in a text in which the rhetoric is particularly effective, analyzing how style and content contribute to the power, persuasiveness or beauty of the text.

Write It

Notebook Review your notes from the chart. Then, write a paragraph in which you describe Abigail Adams's voice as a writer. Use textual examples to support your view. Share your paragraph with your group, and discuss.

Speaking and Listening

Assignment

Create an **oral presentation** based on the selections and present it to the whole class. Choose from the following options.

☐ **Dialogue** Write and present a dramatization of a conversation between John and Abigail Adams in which the two discuss the colonies' struggle for freedom from Great Britain. Base the conversation on the information provided in the texts. Strive to capture each speaker's unique opinions and point of view.

☐ **Dramatic Reading** Present a reading of the March 31st portion of Abigail Adams's letter to John Adams. Decide how you will divide the text among members of your group so that everyone participates. Then, discuss your interpretation of the text, and consider how you will use your voices and gestures to capture its distinct qualities.

☐ **Public Announcement** Both Abigail Adams's letter and the excerpt from *Dear Abigail* mention the threat that smallpox posed in Revolutionary-era America. Research the symptoms of smallpox; the types of people who are especially vulnerable; its progression, treatment, and potential outcomes. Then, write and deliver the announcement that might have been read to citizens of Boston in 1776 warning them of the presence of the disease in their community. Refer to Adams's letter for ideas about diction and tone.

Project Plan First, identify the information, details, or passages you will use from the texts. Use the chart to determine which details you will include, why they are important, and how you will use them in the presentation. If you feel that you need additional material, decide which group members will do the research.

Detail from Text(s)	Reason to Use Detail	How Group Will Present Detail

Presentation Plan Decide which members of the group will produce the writing required for the assignment, and which members will deliver the presentation. Make sure that all members have an equal role, and allow all members to contribute their ideas before finalizing the presentation.

EVIDENCE LOG
Before moving on to the next selection, go to your Evidence Log and record what you learned from Abigail Adams's letter to John Adams and the excerpt from *Dear Abigail*.

STANDARDS
Speaking and Listening
Present information, findings, and supporting evidence, conveying a clear and distinct perspective and a logical argument, such that listeners can follow the line of reasoning, alternative or opposing perspectives are addressed, and the organization, development, substance, and style are appropriate to purpose, audience, and a range of formal and informal tasks.

Gettysburg Address

Concept Vocabulary

As you perform your first read of the Gettysburg Address, you will encounter these words.

> dedicated   consecrate   hallow

Familiar Word Parts When determining the meaning of an unfamiliar word, look for word parts, such as roots or affixes, that you know. Doing so may help you unlock word meanings.

> **Unfamiliar Word:** *prologue*
>
> **Familiar Word Parts:** You may recognize the prefix *pro-*, which means "forward" or "forth." Likewise, you may recognize the root *-log-*, which means "word" or "reason" and appears in the words *dialogue*, *logic*, and *eulogy*.
>
> **Possible Meaning:** When you combine your knowledge of the two word parts, you can figure out that *prologue* means something like "words that come first."
>
> **Confirm Meaning:** Use a dictionary or other language resource to check your analysis of a word's meaning. One dictionary definition of *prologue* is "an introductory part of a text; a preface."

Apply your knowledge of familiar word parts and other vocabulary strategies to determine the meanings of unfamiliar words you encounter during your first read.

First Read NONFICTION

Apply these strategies as you conduct your first read. You will have an opportunity to complete a close read after your first read.

STANDARDS

Reading Informational Text
By the end of grade 11, read and comprehend literary nonfiction in the grades 11–CCR text complexity band proficiently, with scaffolding as needed at the high end of the range.

Language
• Determine or clarify the meaning of unknown and multiple meaning words and phrases based on *grades 11–12 reading and content*, choosing flexibly from a range of strategies.

• Verify the preliminary determination of the meaning of a word or phrase.

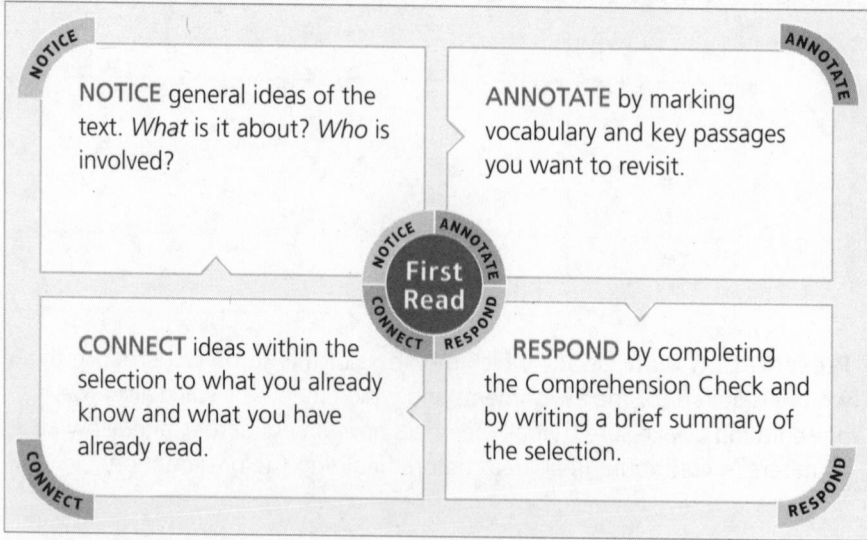

NOTICE general ideas of the text. *What* is it about? *Who* is involved?

ANNOTATE by marking vocabulary and key passages you want to revisit.

CONNECT ideas within the selection to what you already know and what you have already read.

RESPOND by completing the Comprehension Check and by writing a brief summary of the selection.

First Read

About the Author

Abraham Lincoln

Serving as president during one of the most tragic periods in American history, Abraham Lincoln (1809–1865) fought to reunite a nation torn apart by war. His courage, strength, and dedication in the face of an overwhelming national crisis made him one of the most admired and respected American presidents.

Lincoln was born into a family of humble means. As a child, his duties on his parents' farm limited his opportunities to receive a formal education. Still, he was an avid reader and developed an early interest in politics. He served in the Illinois state legislature and ran for the United States Senate against Stephen Douglas. Lincoln lost the election, but his heated debates with Douglas brought him national recognition and helped him win the presidency in 1860.

Troubled Times Shortly after his election, the Civil War erupted. Throughout the war, Lincoln showed great strength and courage. He also demonstrated his gift for oratory. He was invited to make "a few appropriate remarks" in November 1863 for a dedication of the Gettysburg battlefield as a national cemetery. The world has long remembered what he said there.

Lincoln's great care as a writer shows in the Gettysburg Address, as it does in many of his other speeches. He worked diligently and thoughtfully to prepare messages that would have the effect he desired. Two important aspects of the Gettysburg speech are its brevity—just 272 words—and its reaffirmation of the democratic principles at the heart of American government.

Stories abound regarding Lincoln's drafting of the speech: He wrote it the week before; he wrote it the night before; he wrote it on the train while traveling to the event; he wrote it on a scrap of paper. Certainly, he was still revising as he spoke, adding key words, such as "under God," that he knew would stir his listeners.

A Life Cut Short While the Civil War continued to rage, Lincoln was elected to a second term as President. He was killed by an assassin's bullet in 1865 while attending the theater with his wife.

Gettysburg Address

Abraham Lincoln

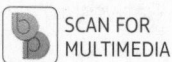
BACKGROUND

Abraham Lincoln gave this speech to 15,000 people at the consecration of a new military cemetery in the town of Gettysburg, Pennsylvania—the site of the bloodiest battle ever fought on American soil, and the turning point of the Civil War. At the time of this speech, the war had been raging for more than two years. Lincoln needed to gain continuing support for a bloody conflict that was far from over.

NOTES

Mark familiar word parts or indicate another strategy you used that helped you determine meaning.

dedicated (DEHD uh kayt ihd) *adj.*

MEANING:

consecrate (KON suh krayt) *v.*

MEANING:

hallow (HAL oh) *v.*

MEANING:

November 19, 1863

1   Four score and seven years ago our fathers brought forth on this continent a new nation, conceived in Liberty, and **dedicated** to the proposition that all men are created equal.

2   Now we are engaged in a great civil war, testing whether that nation, or any nation so conceived and so dedicated, can long endure. We are met on a great battle-field of that war. We have come to dedicate a portion of that field, as a final resting place for those who here gave their lives that that nation might live. It is altogether fitting and proper that we should do this.

3   But, in a larger sense, we cannot dedicate—we cannot **consecrate**— we cannot **hallow**—this ground. The brave men, living and dead, who struggled here, have consecrated it, far above our poor power to add or detract. The world will little note, nor long remember what we say here, but it can never forget what they did here. It is for us the living, rather, to be dedicated here to the unfinished work which they who fought here have thus far so nobly advanced. It is rather for us to be here dedicated to the great task remaining before us—that from these honored dead we take increased devotion to that cause for which they gave the last full measure of devotion—that we here highly resolve that these dead shall not have died in vain—that this nation, under God, shall have a new birth of freedom—and that government of the people, by the people, for the people, shall not perish from the earth.

Comprehension Check

Complete the following items after you finish your first read. Review and clarify details with your group.

1. According to Lincoln, what did "our fathers" create eighty-seven years ago?

2. According to Lincoln, the Civil War is a test of what idea?

3. Why have the speaker and the audience met on the battlefield at Gettysburg?

4. According to Lincoln, why are they unable to "dedicate," "consecrate," or "hallow" the battlefield?

5. At the end of the speech, how does Lincoln characterize the American system of government?

6. 🗐 **Notebook** Confirm your understanding of the text by writing a summary.

RESEARCH

Research to Clarify Choose at least one unfamiliar detail from the text. Briefly research that detail. In what way does the information you learned shed light on an aspect of the speech?

Research to Explore Ask one focused question you would like answered about the Battle of Gettysburg. Then, do some research to find the answer.

GETTYSBURG ADDRESS

Close Read the Text

With your group, revisit sections of the text you marked during your first read. **Annotate** details that you notice. What **questions** do you have? What can you **conclude**?

Analyze the Text

CITE TEXTUAL EVIDENCE to support your answers.

Complete the activities.

1. **Review and Clarify** With your group, reread paragraph 2. How does Lincoln build upon his introduction and prepare the audience for his main points in paragraph 3?

2. **Present and Discuss** Now, work with your group to share the passages from the selection that you found especially important. Take turns presenting your passages. Discuss what you noticed in the selection, what questions you asked, and what conclusions you reached.

3. **Essential Question:** *What is the meaning of freedom?* What has this text revealed about American freedoms? Discuss with your group.

Concept Vocabulary

dedicate	consecrate	hallow

Why These Words? The three concept vocabulary words are related. With your group, discuss the words and determine what they have in common. How do these word choices enhance the impact of the text?

Practice

⬛ **Notebook** Confirm your understanding of the vocabulary words by using them in sentences. Use context clues that hint at each word's meaning.

Word Study

⬛ **Notebook Denotation and Connotation** In his address, Lincoln says that he cannot *dedicate, consecrate,* or *hallow* the battlefield ground. The three concept vocabulary words have similar **denotations**, or definitions, but different **connotations**, or nuances in meaning.

1. Write the denotations of the three words. Then, explain the connotations each one conveys. Note that connotations may involve slightly different meanings, or simply intensity of meaning.

2. Use a thesaurus to find two other words that share denotations with *dedicate*. Then, explain how their connotations differ.

Sidebar

TIP

CLARIFICATION

The Gettysburg Address is short, but it is by no means a group of random comments. As a group, discuss the purpose of each paragraph and the main idea it expresses. How would an outline of the speech look?

WORD NETWORK

Add words related to freedom from the text to your Word Network.

STANDARDS

Reading Informational Text
• Determine an author's point of view or purpose in a text in which the rhetoric is particularly effective, analyzing how style and content contribute to the power, persuasiveness, or beauty of the text.

• Analyze seventeenth-, eighteenth-, and nineteenth-century foundational U.S. documents of historical and literary significance for their themes, purposes, and rhetorical features.

Language
Analyze nuances in the meaning of words with similar denotations.

Analyze Craft and Structure

Author's Choices: Diction A writer's choice and arrangement of words, known as **diction**, helps to express the writer's ideas clearly and precisely and to give the writing a unique quality. Diction may be formal or informal, technical or plain, elevated or simple. A speaker's choice of diction is intimately connected to his or her purpose for writing, as well as to considerations of the audience and the occasion.

Consider the solemn, serious formality of Lincoln's diction at the beginning of his address at Gettysburg—and imagine how he might have expressed the same ideas more informally.

> **FORMAL:** Four score and seven years ago, our fathers brought forth on this continent a new nation. . . .

> **INFORMAL:** Eighty-seven years ago, our early leaders created a new nation, right here. . . .

Practice

CITE TEXTUAL EVIDENCE to support your answers.

Identify passages in the Gettysburg Address that include diction you find powerful or beautiful. Consider how the passage might sound with less formality by rewriting it. Then, explain the impact of Lincoln's diction. One example has been done for you. Complete the chart independently, and then share with your group.

PASSAGE WITH POWERFUL DICTION	REWRITTEN PASSAGE	IMPACT OF LINCOLN'S DICTION
Four score and seven years ago, our fathers brought forth on this continent a new nation.	Eighty-seven years ago, our early leaders created a new nation, right here.	adds power, grandeur to the speech

GETTYSBURG ADDRESS

Author's Style

Rhetorical Devices: Antithesis Lincoln was both a master writer and a master orator. In the Gettysburg Address, he makes insightful use of **contrast,** or the juxtaposition of opposing ideas. In some cases, he uses the rhetorical device of **antithesis,** which is a type of parallelism. Antithesis presents contrasting ideas in similar grammatical structures, such as the same types of phrases or clauses. Thus, antithesis allows a speaker to make use of the rhythmic effects of parallelism, while drawing readers' or listeners' attention to powerful oppositions.

EXAMPLES

Parallelism: I stand here today <u>humbled by the task before us</u>, <u>grateful for the trust you have bestowed</u>, <u>mindful of the sacrifices borne by our ancestors</u>. —Barack Obama

Antithesis: My fellow Americans, <u>ask not what your country can do for you</u>, <u>ask what you can do for your country</u>. —John F. Kennedy

---

Read It

Mark the contrasting or opposing elements in each passage from the address. Then, note whether or not each is an example of formal antithesis. Share your work with your group, and discuss and clarify any points of confusion.

1. We have come to dedicate a portion of that field, as a final resting place for those who here gave their lives that the nation might live.

2. The brave men, living and dead, who struggled here…

3. The world will little note, nor long remember what we say here, but it can never forget what they did here.

4. …we here highly resolve that these dead shall not have died in vain—that this nation, under God, shall have a new birth of freedom…

Write It

Write a paragraph in which you describe a speech, performance, artwork, concert, or other cultural work that you saw live, on television, or online. Use at least two examples of antithesis in your paragraph.

STANDARDS

Reading Informational Text
Determine an author's point of view or purpose in a text in which the rhetoric is particularly effective, analyzing how style and content contribute to the power, persuasiveness, or beauty of the text.

Speaking and Listening
Evaluate a speaker's point of view, reasoning, and use of evidence and rhetoric, assessing the stance, premises, links among ideas, word choice, points of emphasis, and tone used.

Research

Assignment

With your group, prepare a **research report** that focuses on an aspect of Lincoln's speech. Choose from the following options.

☐ a **comparison-and-contrast presentation** about the five different known versions of the Gettysburg Address, showing the changes that Lincoln made each time and evaluating their effectiveness

☐ a **review** of three eyewitness accounts of the ceremony at Gettysburg that day, summarizing each account and noting details that shed light upon the address itself

☐ an **analysis of the historical context** of the address, sharing information about the Battle of Gettysburg (July 1863) and considering how that context shaped the content of Lincoln's address

Project Plan Before you begin, identify the tasks you will need to accomplish in order to complete your report. Start with the tasks noted in the chart, and add others that you consider important. Then, assign individual group members to each task. Finally, determine how you will present the report. For example, will you include historical images—and, if so, where will you find them, and how will you show them?

Working Title: _____

TASK	ASSIGNED TO
researching texts for factual information	
researching images (if used)	

Tying It Together Work together to organize the information all group members collect. Write paragraphs incorporating this information. Then, write an introduction and a conclusion for the report. Read the report aloud within the group, and decide together on revisions. Then, share your finished product with the whole class.

 EVIDENCE LOG

Before moving on to a new selection, go to your Evidence Log and record what you learned from the Gettysburg Address.

▤ STANDARDS

Writing
• Write informative/explanatory texts to examine and convey complex ideas, concepts, and information clearly and accurately through the effective selection, organization, and analysis of content.

• Conduct short as well as more sustained research projects to answer a question or solve a problem; narrow or broaden the inquiry when appropriate; synthesize multiple sources on the subject, demonstrating understanding of the subject under investigation.

SOURCES

- *from* AMERICA'S CONSTITUTION: A BIOGRAPHY

- *from* THE UNITED STATES CONSTITUTION: A GRAPHIC ADAPTATION

- *from* THE INTERESTING NARRATIVE OF THE LIFE OF OLAUDAH EQUIANO

- LETTER TO JOHN ADAMS

- *from* DEAR ABIGAIL: THE INTIMATE LIVES AND REVOLUTIONARY IDEAS OF ABIGAIL ADAMS AND HER TWO REMARKABLE SISTERS

- GETTYSBURG ADDRESS

Present an Argument

Assignment

You have read a variety of texts, both historic and contemporary, in a range of different genres. Several of these texts are narratives that the writers use to support or imply positions on questions of American freedom. Work with your group to present a **panel discussion** that addresses this question:

> **Do narratives provide strong evidence to support arguments about American freedoms?**

Use examples from the texts in this section to support your positions.

Plan With Your Group

Analyze the Texts With your group, identify the texts in this section that are either fully narratives or include narrative elements. Consider the arguments about freedom that are either directly stated or that readers can infer from the narrative details. Use the chart to gather your observations.

NARRATIVE DETAILS	RELATED ARGUMENT

Make a Generalization Using your analysis, write a generalization about the use of narrative as evidence to support an argument.

Generalization: Narratives do/do not provide strong evidence to support an argument because _____

_____

Gather Evidence Prepare for the discussion by identifying additional examples from the texts that you might use to illustrate your ideas during the panel discussion.

▤ STANDARDS

Speaking and Listening
Work with peers to promote civil, democratic discussions and decision-making, set clear goals and deadlines, and establish individual roles as needed.

Organize Your Discussion Assign roles, including a role for a moderator who will keep panelists on point and ask questions if there is a lull in the conversation. Have each person in your group use the evidence you gathered to write his or her own talking points for the presentation. Then, meet to decide how you will begin the discussion, the amount of time each speaker will talk, how you will deal with follow-up questions, and how you will end the discussion.

Rehearse With Your Group

Practice With Your Group Once you have established the rules for your discussion, try a run-through. Use this checklist to evaluate how well your process works and whether your ideas and evidence are sound. Then, use your evaluation and these instructions to make changes before you present your discussion to the class.

CONTENT	COLLABORATION	PRESENTATION TECHNIQUES
☐ The discussion responds to the question in the assignment.	☐ The discussion flows smoothly and seems well-planned.	☐ Panelists have equal opportunities to speak, and respond appropriately to one another's insights or questions.
☐ Speakers present a position and supporting evidence.	☐ Speakers interact with each other naturally.	☐ Speakers speak clearly and at an appropriate volume.
☐ Speakers support their observations with evidence from the texts.	☐ The moderator introduces the speakers and keeps the conversation on track.	☐ Speakers use gestures and eye contact effectively.

Fine-Tune the Content Does one panelist dominate the conversation? Make sure that every group member has a chance to present his or her views. If necessary, go back to the texts to gather additional details that will help balance the presentation.

Brush Up on Your Presentation Techniques Remember that you are holding a conversation that is also, to some extent, a performance. Modify your tone and volume so that your audience understands your ideas and evidence. Explain your observations clearly, using language that is appropriate for an academic setting.

Present and Evaluate

As you present your panel discussion, consider your audience's response. Do listeners seem convinced by your argument? Are they interested in the ideas? Watch the presentations by other groups and discuss how yours is similar to or different from theirs.

▦ STANDARDS

Speaking and Listening
Present information, findings, and supporting evidence, conveying a clear and distinct perspective, such that listeners can follow the line of reasoning, alternative or opposing perspectives are addressed, and the organization, development, substance, and style are appropriate to purpose, audience, and a range of formal and informal tasks.

ESSENTIAL QUESTION:

What is the meaning of freedom?

Ideas about what freedom means, and who is or is not free, may depend on time, place, and the person telling the story. In this section, you will complete your study of writings about American freedom by exploring an additional selection related to the topic. You'll then share what you learn with classmates. To choose a text, follow these steps.

Look Back Think about the selections you have already studied. Which aspects of the meaning of freedom do you wish to explore further?

Look Ahead Preview the texts by reading the descriptions. Which one seems most interesting and appealing to you?

Look Inside Take a few minutes to scan the text you chose. Choose a different one if this text doesn't meet your needs.

Independent Learning Strategies

Throughout your life, in school, in your community, and in your career, you will need to rely on yourself to learn and work on your own. Review these strategies and the actions you can take to practice them during Independent Learning. Add ideas of your own for each category.

STRATEGY	ACTION PLAN
Create a schedule	• Understand your goals and deadlines. • Make a plan for what to do each day. •
Practice what you have learned	• Use first-read and close-read strategies to deepen your understanding. • After reading, evaluate the usefulness of the evidence to help you understand the topic. • After reading, consult reference sources for background information that can help you clarify meaning. •
Take notes	• Record important ideas and information. • Review your notes before preparing to share with a group. •

SCAN FOR
MULTIMEDIA

CONTENTS

Choose one selection. Selections are available online only.

SCAN FOR MULTIMEDIA

First-Read Guide

Use this page to record your first-read ideas.

🔧 **Tool Kit**
First-Read Guide and
Model Annotation

Selection Title: _____

NOTICE

NOTICE new information or ideas you learned about the unit topic as you first read this text.

ANNOTATE

ANNOTATE by marking vocabulary and key passages you want to revisit.

First Read

NOTICE · ANNOTATE · CONNECT · RESPOND

CONNECT ideas within the selection to other knowledge and the selections you have read.

CONNECT

RESPOND by writing a brief summary of the selection.

RESPOND

STANDARD

Reading Read and comprehend complex literary and informational texts independently and proficiently.

Close-Read Guide

Use this page to record your close-read ideas.

Selection Title: _____

Close Read the Text

Revisit sections of the text you marked during your first read. Read these sections closely and **annotate** what you notice. Ask yourself **questions** about the text. What can you **conclude**? Write down your ideas.

Analyze the Text

Think about the author's choices of patterns, structure, techniques, and ideas included in the text. Select one and record your thoughts about what this choice conveys.

QuickWrite

Pick a paragraph from the text that grabbed your interest. Explain the power of this passage.

▤ STANDARD
Reading Read and comprehend complex literary and informational texts independently and proficiently.

EVIDENCE LOG
Go to your Evidence Log and record what you learned from the text you read.

Share Your Independent Learning

Prepare to Share

What is the meaning of freedom?

Even when you read something independently, your understanding continues to grow when you share what you have learned with others. Reflect on the text you explored independently and write notes about its connection to the unit. In your notes, consider why this text belongs in this unit.

Learn From Your Classmates

Discuss It Share your ideas about the text you explored on your own. As you talk with your classmates, jot down ideas that you learn from them.

Reflect

Review your notes, and mark the most important insight you gained from these writing and discussion activities. Explain how this idea adds to your understanding of the meaning of freedom.

STANDARDS
Speaking and Listening
Initiate and participate effectively in a range of collaborative discussions (one-on-one, in groups, and teacher-led) with diverse partners on *grades 11–12 topics, texts, and issues,* building on others' ideas and expressing their own clearly and persuasively.

Review Evidence for an Argument

At the beginning of this unit, you took a position on the following question:

> What are the most effective tools for establishing and preserving freedom?

EVIDENCE LOG

Review your Evidence Log and your QuickWrite from the beginning of the unit. Have your ideas changed?

☐ YES	☐ NO
Identify at least three pieces of evidence that have caused you to reevaluate your ideas. 1. 2. 3.	Identify at least three pieces of evidence that have reinforced your initial position. 1. 2. 3.

State your position now: _____

_____

_____

Identify a possible counterclaim: _____

_____

_____

Evaluate the Strength of Your Evidence Consider your argument. Do you have enough evidence to support your claim? Do you have enough evidence to refute a counterclaim? If not, make a plan.

☐ Do online research.   ☐ Skim a textbook.

☐ Reread a selection.   ☐ Speak with an expert.

☐ Other:_____

STANDARDS

Writing
Introduce precise, knowledgeable claim(s), establish the significance of the claim(s), distinguish the claim(s) from alternate or opposing claims, and create an organization that logically sequences claim(s), counterclaims, reasons, and evidence.

SOURCES

- WHOLE-CLASS SELECTIONS

- SMALL-GROUP SELECTIONS

- INDEPENDENT-LEARNING SELECTION

PART 1

Writing to Sources: Argument

In this unit, you read a variety of texts that considered the meaning of American freedom. You saw the Founders' concerns about how to establish a nation that offered freedom to at least some of its citizens, and you read other texts that demonstrated how a nation "conceived in liberty" was tested over time.

Assignment

Write an **argumentative essay** in which you respond to this question:

> **What are the most effective tools for establishing and preserving freedom?**

Use the Anchor Texts to identify some of the most successful tools (processes, government institutions, value systems, documents, and so on) that the Founders established. Use other texts from the unit to demonstrate how well those tools have stood the test of time. Supplement your ideas with examples from your own research that confirm your argument. Consider and address possible counterclaims.

Reread the Assignment Review the assignment to be sure you fully understand it. The task may reference some of the academic words presented at the beginning of the unit. Be sure you understand each of the words given below in order to complete the assignment correctly.

Academic Vocabulary

confirm	supplement	conviction
demonstrate	establish	

Review the Elements of Effective Argument Before you begin writing, read the Argument Rubric. Once you have completed your first draft, check it against the rubric. If one or more of the elements are missing or not as strong as they could be, revise your essay to add or strengthen those components.

WORD NETWORK

As you write and revise your argument, use your Word Network to help vary your word choices.

STANDARDS

Writing
• Write arguments to support claims in an analysis of substantive topics or texts, using valid reasoning and relevant and sufficient evidence.
• Write routinely over extended time frames and shorter time frames for a range of tasks, purposes, and audiences.

Argument Rubric

	Focus and Organization	Evidence and Elaboration	Language Conventions
4	The introduction is engaging and establishes the claim in a compelling way.	The sources of evidence are comprehensive and specific and contain relevant information.	The argument consistently uses standard English conventions of usage and mechanics.
	Valid reasons and evidence address and support the claim. Counterclaims are clearly acknowledged.	The tone of the argument is formal and objective.	
	The ideas progress logically, connected by a variety of sentence transitions.	Vocabulary is used strategically and appropriately for the audience and purpose.	
	The conclusion offers fresh insight into the claim.		
3	The introduction is engaging and establishes the claim in a way that grabs readers' attention.	The sources of evidence contain relevant information.	The argument demonstrates accuracy in standard English conventions of usage and mechanics.
	Reasons and evidence address and support the claim. Counterclaims are acknowledged.	The tone of the argument is mostly formal and objective.	
	The ideas progress logically, and sentence transitions connect readers to the argument.	Vocabulary is generally appropriate for the audience and purpose.	
	The conclusion restates important information.		
2	The introduction establishes the claim.	The sources of evidence contain some relevant information.	The argument demonstrates some accuracy in standard English conventions of usage and mechanics.
	Some reasons and evidence address and support the claim. Counterclaims are briefly acknowledged.	The tone of the argument is occasionally formal and objective.	
	The ideas progress somewhat logically. A few sentence transitions connect readers to the argument.	Vocabulary is somewhat appropriate for the audience and purpose.	
	The conclusion offers some insight into the claim and restates information.		
1	The claim is not clearly stated.	No reliable or relevant evidence is included.	The argument contains mistakes in standard English conventions of usage and mechanics.
	No reasons or evidence for the claim are included, and counterclaims are not acknowledged.	The tone of the argument is informal.	
	The ideas do not progress logically. The sentences are often short and choppy and do not connect readers to the argument.	The vocabulary is limited or ineffective.	
	The conclusion does not restate any information that is important.		

PART 2

Speaking and Listening: Video Commentary

> **Assignment**
>
> Imagine that representatives of a television station have called on you to be their expert on the concept of freedom. Present a **video commentary,** based on the final draft of your argument, to be used during coverage of a presidential debate.

Follow these steps to make your presentation lively and engaging.

- Read your text aloud, keeping the television audience in mind. Highlight the material you most want to emphasize for that audience.
- Practice your delivery. Remember to look up at the camera regularly instead of staring down at your paper.
- Have a classmate operate the camera as you deliver your commentary.

Review the Rubric The criteria by which your commentary will be evaluated appear in the rubric below. Review the criteria before delivering your commentary to ensure that you are prepared.

	Content	Use of Media	Presentation Techniques
3	The content and delivery are appropriate for a television audience. The commentary is clearly organized and easy to follow.	The voice on the recording is consistent and audible. The camera holds steady, and facial expressions are clearly visible.	Speech is clear and at an appropriate volume. Tone and pace vary to maintain interest. The speaker looks regularly at the camera to engage the audience.
2	The content and delivery are consistent, although some content may not be clearly meant for a television audience. The commentary is organized and fairly easy to follow.	The voice on the recording may vary but is mostly audible. The camera generally holds steady, so most facial expressions are visible.	Speech is clear most of the time and usually has an appropriate volume. Tone and pace are inconsistent. The speaker looks occasionally at the camera.
1	The content and delivery are generic, with no specific audience in mind. The commentary is disorganized and may be difficult to follow.	The voice on the recording sometimes fades in and out. The camera does not hold steady or is not focused on the face, so the expressions are rarely visible.	The speaker mumbles occasionally, speaks too quickly, and/or does not speak loudly enough. The speaker fails to look at the camera.

Reflect on the Unit

Now that you've completed the unit, take a few moments to reflect on your learning.

Reflect on the Unit Goals

Look back at the goals at the beginning of the unit. Use a different colored pen to rate yourself again. Think about readings and activities that contributed the most to the growth of your understanding. Record your thoughts.

Reflect on the Learning Strategies

Discuss It Write a reflection on whether you were able to improve your learning based on your Action Plans. Think about what worked, what didn't, and what you might do to keep working on these strategies. Record your ideas before joining a class discussion.

Reflect on the Text

Choose a selection that you found challenging, and explain what made it difficult.

Explain something that surprised you about a text in the unit.

Which activity taught you the most about the meaning of American freedoms? What did you learn?

SCAN FOR
MULTIMEDIA

The Individual and Society

Fitting In, or Standing Out?

Richard Blanco Reads
"One Today"

Discuss It This poem, read by its author at President Barack Obama's 2013 inaugural, praises America as a society of individuals. How do the details of the poem present individual Americans? What connections among individuals does Blanco see?

Write your response before sharing your ideas.

SCAN FOR
MULTIMEDIA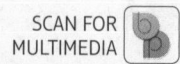

UNIT INTRODUCTION

ESSENTIAL QUESTION: **What role does individualism play in American society?**

LAUNCH TEXT
NARRATIVE MODEL
from Up from Slavery
Booker T. Washington

WHOLE-CLASS LEARNING

HISTORICAL PERSPECTIVES

Focus Period: 1800–1870
An American Identity

ANCHOR TEXT: ESSAY | POETRY

The Writing of Walt Whitman
Walt Whitman

ANCHOR TEXT: POETRY COLLECTION

The Poetry of Emily Dickinson
Emily Dickinson

MEDIA: RADIO BROADCAST

from Emily Dickinson
from **Great Lives**
BBC Radio 4

COMPARE

SMALL-GROUP LEARNING

PHILOSOPHICAL WRITING

from Nature

from Self-Reliance
Ralph Waldo Emerson

PHILOSOPHICAL WRITING

from Walden

from Civil Disobedience
Henry David Thoreau

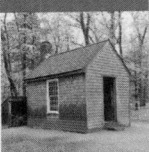

MEDIA: PUBLIC DOCUMENTS

Innovators and Their Inventions

POETRY

The Love Song of J. Alfred Prufrock
T. S. Eliot

SHORT STORY

A Wagner Matinée
Willa Cather

INDEPENDENT LEARNING

NEWS ARTICLE

Sweet Land of . . . Conformity?
Claude Fischer

LITERARY CRITICISM

Reckless Genius
Galway Kinnell

SHORT STORY

Hamadi
Naomi Shihab Nye

SHORT STORY

Young Goodman Brown
Nathaniel Hawthorne

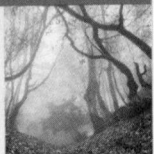

PERFORMANCE TASK

WRITING FOCUS:
Write a Personal Narrative

PERFORMANCE TASK

SPEAKING AND LISTENING FOCUS:
Present a Personal Narrative

PERFORMANCE-BASED ASSESSMENT PREP

Review Evidence for a Personal Narrative

PERFORMANCE-BASED ASSESSMENT

Narrative: Personal Narrative and Storytelling Session

PROMPT:
What significant incident helped me realize that I am a unique individual?

Unit Goals

Throughout this unit, you will deepen your perspective on the concept of individualism by reading, writing, speaking, listening, and presenting. These goals will help you succeed on the Unit Performance-Based Assessment.

Rate how well you meet these goals right now. You will revisit your ratings later when you reflect on your growth during this unit.

SCALE	1	2	3	4	5
	NOT AT ALL WELL	NOT VERY WELL	SOMEWHAT WELL	VERY WELL	EXTREMELY WELL

READING GOALS

1 2 3 4 5

- Read a variety of texts to gain the knowledge and insight needed to write about individualism.

- Expand your knowledge and use of academic and concept vocabulary.

WRITING AND RESEARCH GOALS

1 2 3 4 5

- Write a personal narrative that establishes a clear point of view and uses a variety of narrative techniques to develop a personal experience.

- Conduct research projects of various lengths to explore a topic and clarify meaning.

LANGUAGE GOALS

1 2 3 4 5

- Make effective style choices regarding diction and sentence variety.
- Correctly use concrete, abstract, and compound nouns.

SPEAKING AND LISTENING GOALS

1 2 3 4 5

- Collaborate with your team to build on the ideas of others, develop consensus, and communicate.

- Integrate audio, visuals, and text to present information.

STANDARDS

Language
Acquire and use accurately general academic and domain-specific words and phrases, sufficient for reading, writing, speaking, and listening at the college and career readiness level; demonstrate independence in gathering vocabulary knowledge when considering a word or phrase important to comprehension or expression.

SCAN FOR MULTIMEDIA

Academic Vocabulary: Personal Narrative

Academic terms appear in all subjects and can help you read, write, and discuss with more precision. Here are five academic words that will be useful to you in this unit as you analyze and write personal narratives.

Complete the chart.

1. Review each word, its root, and the mentor sentences.

2. Use the information and your own knowledge to predict the meaning of each word.

3. For each word, list at least two related words.

4. Refer to a dictionary or other resources if needed.

 TIP

FOLLOW THROUGH

Study the words in this chart, and mark them or their forms wherever they appear in the unit.

WORD	MENTOR SENTENCES	PREDICT MEANING	RELATED WORDS
significant ROOT: **-sign-** "sign"	1. The fire was a *significant* event in our town's history. 2. Ms. Barnes made no *significant* changes to my report.		signify; significance
incident ROOT: **-cid-** "fall"	1. Myron described the *incident* in great detail to the reporter. 2. We avoided an embarrassing *incident* by leaving the room.		
unique ROOT: **-uni-** "one"	1. Each of these tables is a *unique*, handmade item. 2. My hairstyle is *unique*; no one would dare to copy it.		
sequence ROOT: **-sequ-** "follow"	1. A first-grader should be able to recite numbers in *sequence* to 100. 2. Follow the *sequence* of directions, and the recipe will turn out well.		
impact ROOT: **-pact-** "press"; "fasten"	1. His books had a strong *impact* on my beliefs and interests. 2. The *impact* of vaccines on public health has been considerable, and has lead to a healthier population.		

LAUNCH TEXT | NARRATIVE MODEL

This selection is an example of a **narrative text**. It is a **personal narrative**—the author tells a story about himself, using a first-person point of view. This is the type of writing you will develop in the Performance-Based Assessment at the end of the unit.

As you read, notice the author's use of specific details. Mark words and phrases that convey his experiences and feelings with vividness and clarity.

About the Author

Booker T. Washington (1856–1915) was born into slavery and overcame enormous obstacles to become a noted author, educator, and advisor to two American presidents. This excerpt is from chapter 3 of his autobiography *Up From Slavery*, in which Washington describes his experiences at Hampton Institute in the early 1870s.

from

Up From Slavery

Booker T. Washington

NOTES

1. When I had saved what I considered enough money with which to reach Hampton, I thanked the captain of the vessel for his kindness, and started again. Without any unusual occurrence I reached Hampton, with a surplus of exactly fifty cents with which to begin my education. To me it had been a long, eventful journey; but the first sight of the large, three-story, brick school building seemed to have rewarded me for all that I had undergone in order to reach the place. . . .

2. As soon as possible after reaching the grounds of the Hampton Institute, I presented myself before the head teacher for assignment to a class. Having been so long without proper food, a bath, and change of clothing, I did not, of course, make a very favorable impression upon her, and I could see at once that there were doubts in her mind about the wisdom of admitting me as a student. I felt that I could hardly blame her if she got the idea that I was a worthless loafer or tramp. For some time she did not refuse to admit me, neither did she decide in my favor, and I continued to linger about her, and

SCAN FOR
MULTIMEDIA

to impress her in all the ways I could with my worthiness. In the meantime I saw her admitting other students, and that added greatly to my discomfort, for I felt, deep down in my heart, that I could do as well as they, if I could only get a chance to show what was in me.

3   After some hours had passed, the head teacher said to me: "The adjoining recitation-room needs sweeping. Take the broom and sweep it."

4   It occurred to me at once that here was my chance. Never did I receive an order with more delight. I knew that I could sweep, for Mrs. Ruffner had thoroughly taught me how to do that when I lived with her.

5   I swept the recitation-room three times. Then I got a dusting-cloth and I dusted it four times. All the woodwork around the walls, every bench, table, and desk, I went over four times with my dusting-cloth. Besides, every piece of furniture had been moved and every closet and corner in the room had been thoroughly cleaned. I had the feeling that in a large measure my future depended upon the impression I made upon the teacher in the cleaning of that room. When I was through, I reported to the head teacher. She was a "Yankee" woman who knew just where to look for dirt. She went into the room and inspected the floor and closets; then she took her handkerchief and rubbed it on the woodwork about the walls, and over the table and benches. When she was unable to find one bit of dirt on the floor, or a particle of dust on any of the furniture, she quietly remarked, "I guess you will do to enter this institution."

6   I was one of the happiest souls on earth. The sweeping of that room was my college examination, and never did any youth pass an examination for entrance into Harvard or Yale that gave him more genuine satisfaction. I have passed several examinations since then, but I have always felt that this was the best one I ever passed.

NOTES

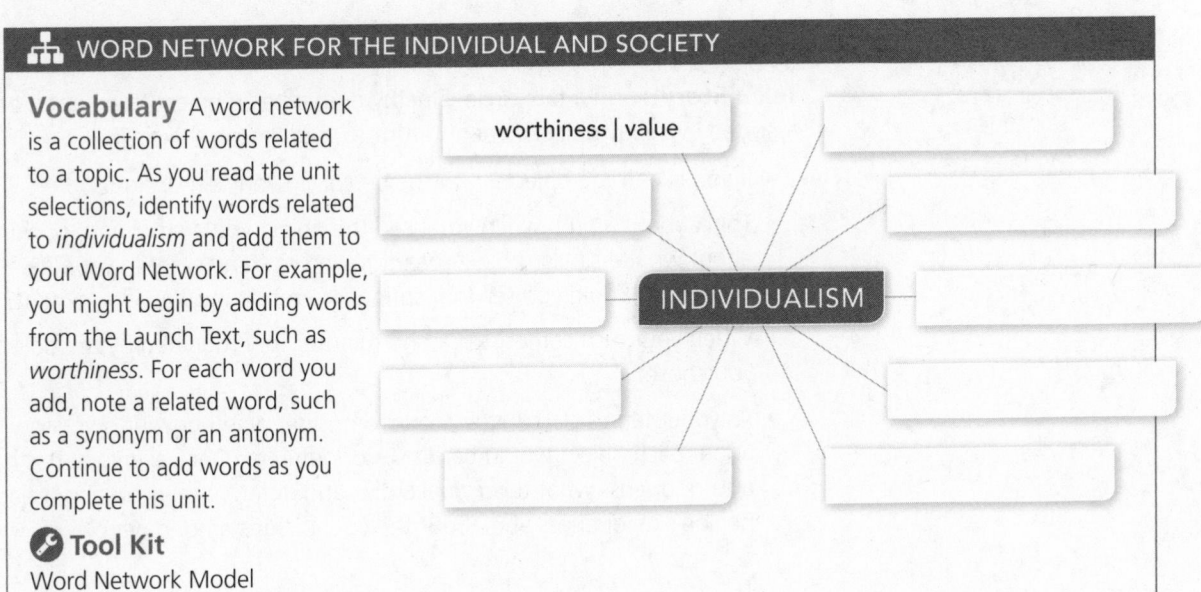

⬡ WORD NETWORK FOR THE INDIVIDUAL AND SOCIETY

Vocabulary A word network is a collection of words related to a topic. As you read the unit selections, identify words related to *individualism* and add them to your Word Network. For example, you might begin by adding words from the Launch Text, such as *worthiness*. For each word you add, note a related word, such as a synonym or an antonym. Continue to add words as you complete this unit.

🔧 Tool Kit
Word Network Model

worthiness | value

INDIVIDUALISM

Summary

Write a summary of the excerpt from *Up From Slavery*. A **summary** is a concise, complete, and accurate overview of a text. It should not include a statement of your opinion or an analysis.

Launch Activity

Tell a Story Form a talk circle. One by one, take an object from a bag of assorted everyday objects. Then, return to your seat in the circle.

- If you like, trade objects with the person to your left or right.

- Think about a time when you used the object you are holding, or think about what a similar object meant to you at some point in your life. What story could you tell that springs from that incident or moment?

- When your turn comes, tell a one-minute story triggered by the object you chose.

- As you listen to classmates' stories, consider whether your own story about each object would be similar or different. Once everyone has had a turn, discuss what those similarities and differences mean about each person's uniqueness and about the connections among people.

QuickWrite

Consider class discussions, the video, and the Launch Text as you think about the prompt. Record your first thoughts here.

PROMPT: **What significant incident helped me realize that I am a unique individual?**

EVIDENCE LOG FOR THE INDIVIDUAL AND SOCIETY

Review your QuickWrite and summarize your initial idea in one sentence to record in your Evidence Log. Then, record evidence from the excerpt from *Up From Slavery* that connects to your idea.

After each selection, you will continue to use your Evidence Log to record the evidence you gather and the connections you make. The graphic shows what your Evidence Log looks like.

🔧 Tool Kit
Evidence Log Model

Title of Text: _____ Date: _____

CONNECTION TO PROMPT	TEXT EVIDENCE/DETAILS	ADDITIONAL NOTES/IDEAS

How does this text change or add to my thinking? _____ Date: _____

SCAN FOR MULTIMEDIA

ESSENTIAL QUESTION:

What role does individualism play in American society?

As you read these selections, work with your whole class to explore the meaning of individualism.

From Text to Topic For Walt Whitman, individualism formed the cornerstone of life in America. His writing celebrates the promise of America, in which all people can make an impact by developing their unique abilities. For Emily Dickinson, individualism meant looking inward to express the deepest musings of the soul. As you read, consider what the selections show about perceptions of individualism in American society in the nineteenth century. Also, consider how these works influence American attitudes toward individualism today.

Whole-Class Learning Strategies

Throughout your life, in school, in your community, and in your career, you will continue to learn and work in large-group environments.

Review these strategies and the actions you can take to practice them. Add ideas of your own for each step. Get ready to use these strategies during Whole-Class Learning.

STRATEGY	ACTION PLAN
Listen actively	• Eliminate distractions. For example, put your cellphone away. • Record brief notes on main ideas and points of confusion. •
Clarify by asking questions	• If you're confused, other people probably are, too. Ask a question to help your whole class. • Ask follow-up questions as needed—for example, if you do not understand the clarification or if you want to make an additional connection. •
Monitor understanding	• Notice what information you already know and be ready to build on it. • Ask for help if you are struggling. •
Interact and share ideas	• Share your ideas and answer questions, even if you are unsure. • Build on the ideas of others by adding details or making a connection. •

SCAN FOR
MULTIMEDIA

CONTENTS

COMPARE

PERFORMANCE TASK

WRITING FOCUS
Write a Personal Narrative

The Whole-Class readings were written during a time when American literature celebrated the individual. After reading, you will write a personal narrative that shows how a life experience has shaped your understanding of individuality.

An American Identity

Voices of the Period

"I have always supported measures and principles and not men. I have acted fearless and independent and I never will regret my course."

—Davy Crockett,
frontiersman, folk hero, and statesman

"I have an almost complete disregard of precedent, and a faith in the possibility of something better. It irritates me to be told how things have always been done. I defy the tyranny of precedent. I go for anything new that might improve the past."

—Clara Barton,
founder of the American Red Cross

"There will never be a really free and enlightened State until the State comes to recognize the individual as a higher and independent power, from which all its own power and authority are derived, and treats him accordingly."

—Henry David Thoreau,
author of "Civil Disobedience" and *Walden*

History of the Period

What Is an American? French writer Alexis de Tocqueville came to America in the early 1830s with a colleague to study and write about American prisons. Instead, they ended up traveling extensively and studying American democracy. In his book *Democracy in America,* de Tocqueville coined the word *individualism* as a way of describing the attitudes he found in America, where people are "always considering themselves as standing alone, [imagining] that their whole destiny is in their own hands."

Jefferson's Bargain In 1803, President Thomas Jefferson purchased from France 828,000 square miles of North America for $15 million—about three cents per acre—and in the process, more than doubled the size of the United States. Jefferson sent explorers Meriwether Lewis and William Clark, with their Corps of Discovery, to investigate the land, people, and plants and animals of the new territory. They crossed the continent, reached the Pacific Ocean, and led the way for decades of westward-bound settlers.

The War of 1812 In the War of 1812, the United States once again defeated Great Britain, asserting its independence from European control. However, the most important effect of the war may have been the sense of solidarity it fostered within the young nation.

The People's President The 1828 election of Andrew Jackson, "the People's President," ushered in the era of the "common man." The center of power began to shift west, even as a two-party system was emerging.

TIMELINE

1803: The Louisiana Purchase nearly doubles the size of the United States.

1804: France Napoleon Bonaparte declares himself emperor.

1808–1833: Latin America Independence movements result in wars and the creation of new governments.

1800

1804–1806: Lewis and Clark lead an exploration of the Louisiana Purchase, reaching the Pacific Ocean.

1807: Robert Fulton's steamboat makes its first trip, from New York City to Albany.

Integration of Knowledge and Ideas

📓 **Notebook** From which countries did the United States acquire land during this era? How do you think these acquisitions influenced the way that Americans viewed themselves and their nation's future by the 1850s?

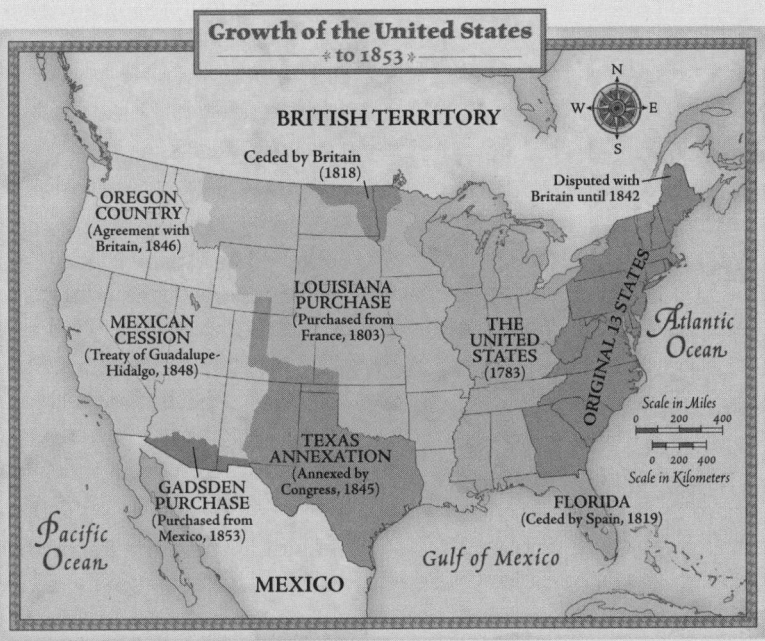

Growth of the United States
to 1853

BRITISH TERRITORY

Ceded by Britain (1818)

Disputed with Britain until 1842

OREGON COUNTRY (Agreement with Britain, 1846)

MEXICAN CESSION (Treaty of Guadalupe-Hidalgo, 1848)

LOUISIANA PURCHASE (Purchased from France, 1803)

THE UNITED STATES (1783)

ORIGINAL 13 STATES

Atlantic Ocean

Scale in Miles
0 200 400

Scale in Kilometers
0 200 400

TEXAS ANNEXATION (Annexed by Congress, 1845)

GADSDEN PURCHASE (Purchased from Mexico, 1853)

FLORIDA (Ceded by Spain, 1819)

Pacific Ocean

MEXICO

Gulf of Mexico

Manifest Destiny Many Americans believed in Manifest Destiny, the idea that it was their right to settle America's lands across the continent. By 1840, about 40 percent of the U.S. population lived west of the Appalachian Mountains. By 1860, following the great pioneer migrations to Oregon, California, and Texas, only about half of the population lived in the eastern part of the United States. Westward expansion inspired an upsurge of national pride and self-awareness.

Trail of Tears The tragic policy of "Indian removal," a result of westward expansion, resulted in the confiscation of tribal lands and the relocation of more than 100,000 Native Americans. On the 1838 Trail of Tears, for example, thousands of Cherokee perished on the trek from Georgia to Oklahoma, where the promise of freedom from white settlement would last for only about 15 years.

1812: The United States declares war on Great Britain; a treaty ends the war in 1814.

1831: Cyrus McCormick invents the mechanical reaper.

1840

1813: England Jane Austen's *Pride and Prejudice* is published.

1825: The Erie Canal is completed, spurring canal building across the nation.

1838: Cherokees are forced from Georgia to Oklahoma Territory on the "Trail of Tears."

On the Move Travel was transformed in the nineteenth century by new methods and routes of transportation. The National Road, begun in 1811, reached St. Louis and the Mississippi River by mid-century. In 1860, nearly 1,000 steamboats were plying the Mississippi, and some 30,000 miles of railroad track had been spread across the nation. The lure of the West motivated this revolution in transportation, which created a bond between existing and new states.

Coming to America In the first half of the nineteenth century, hundreds of thousands of immigrants—mostly European—were arriving on American shores. By the 1850s, the number was in the millions. Pushed from home by hardships and revolutions, these people were lured by a land of opportunity.

The Industrial Revolution A machine called the cotton gin, which separated cotton fibers from seeds, invented in 1793, revolutionized American industry. By 1860, more than 1,000 factories, mainly in New England, were turning more than 400 million pounds of Southern cotton into cloth, which was then sold around the world. However, while factories boomed in the North, enlarging the job market for women and immigrants, slavery grew stronger in the South.

A Flood of New Ideas Buoyed by a sense of their power to improve society, Americans set out to reform what they saw as problems or failures. Voters demanded better schools and public education slowly began to expand. Reform movements sprang up in religion, in temperance, and in women's rights. All brought important changes, but the most revolutionary movement was the drive to end slavery.

Slavery and the Civil War States in the North had declared slavery illegal by 1804 and had begun the gradual emancipation of enslaved African Americans within their borders. By 1860, however, slavery was more entrenched than ever in the South. Out of a population of 31.5 million, there were four million enslaved African Americans and about 500,000 free blacks. In six states in the Deep South, the slave population accounted for approximately half of the total population.

Abolitionists—people who worked to end slavery—were black and white, Northern and sometimes Southern. They organized, preached, spoke, published newspapers, and wrote books. They also helped fugitives flee slavery via a network of secret escape routes into the North and into Canada, known as the Underground Railroad. As their actions intensified, they helped push the nation to the breaking point—the eruption of the Civil War. The war lasted for four years and remains to date the deadliest conflict in American history.

Individualism in the Reconstruction Era
America emerged from the Civil War with many questions unresolved. Chief among these was how to guarantee the rights of millions whom law and tradition had previously treated as property rather than people. The Reconstruction Era that followed the war was a tumultuous period in which former slaves capitalized on their newfound freedoms, including sending a record number of African Americans into government. The period did not last long, however, as a backlash ensued that included widespread violence. Freedoms for African Americans were rolled back and the rights of individuals were quashed, as the gains of Reconstruction evaporated and the Jim Crow system became firmly established throughout the South.

TIMELINE

1837: Samuel F. B. Morse patents the telegraph.

1849: The Gold Rush begins in California.

1851: Herman Melville's *Moby-Dick* is published.

1836

1845: Ireland Potato famine begins, leading to massive immigration to North America.

1850: Nathaniel Hawthorne's *The Scarlet Letter* is published.

Literature Selections

Literature of the Focus Period A number of the selections in this unit were written during the Focus Period and pertain to the expansion of the United States, the reforms of American society, and the actions of individuals who influenced its history and culture:

The Writing of Walt Whitman

The Poetry of Emily Dickinson

from "Nature" • from "Self-Reliance," Ralph Waldo Emerson

from *Walden* • from "Civil Disobedience," Henry David Thoreau

"Young Goodman Brown," Nathaniel Hawthorne

Connections Across Time A consideration of the importance of American individualism both preceded and continued past the Focus Period. Indeed, it has influenced writers and commentators in many times and places.

"The Love Song of J. Alfred Prufrock," T. S. Eliot

"A Wagner Matinée," Willa Cather

"Sweet Land of . . . Conformity?" Claude Fischer

"Reckless Genius," Galway Kinnell

"Hamadi," Naomi Shihab Nye

ADDITIONAL FOCUS PERIOD LITERATURE

UNIT 1
The Gettysburg Address, Abraham Lincoln

UNIT 3
"What to the Slave Is the Fourth of July?," Frederick Douglass

Second Inaugural Address, Abraham Lincoln

"Ain't I a Woman?," Sojourner Truth

Declaration of Sentiments, Elizabeth Cady Stanton

UNIT 4
"The Notorious Jumping Frog of Calaveras County," Mark Twain

UNIT 6
"The Tell-Tale Heart," Edgar Allan Poe

1854: Japan The Treaty of Kanagawa opens Japan to trade with the United States.

1861–1865: The Union and the Confederacy fight the Civil War.

1865: The Reconstruction Era begins in the South.

1870

1860: Abraham Lincoln is elected the sixteenth U.S. President.

ESSAY | POETRY COLLECTION

The Writing of Walt Whitman

- *from* the Preface to the 1855 Edition of *Leaves of Grass*
- *from* Song of Myself
- I Hear America Singing
- On the Beach at Night Alone
- America

Concept Vocabulary

You will encounter the following words as you read part of an essay and a number of poems by Walt Whitman. Before reading, note how familiar you are with each word. Then, rank the words in order from most familiar (1) to least familiar (6).

WORD	YOUR RANKING
ampler	
teeming	
vast	
breadth	
prolific	
multitudes	

After completing the first read, come back to the concept vocabulary and review your rankings. Mark changes to your original rankings as needed.

First Read NONFICTION and POETRY

Apply these strategies as you conduct your first read. You will have an opportunity to complete the close-read notes after your first read.

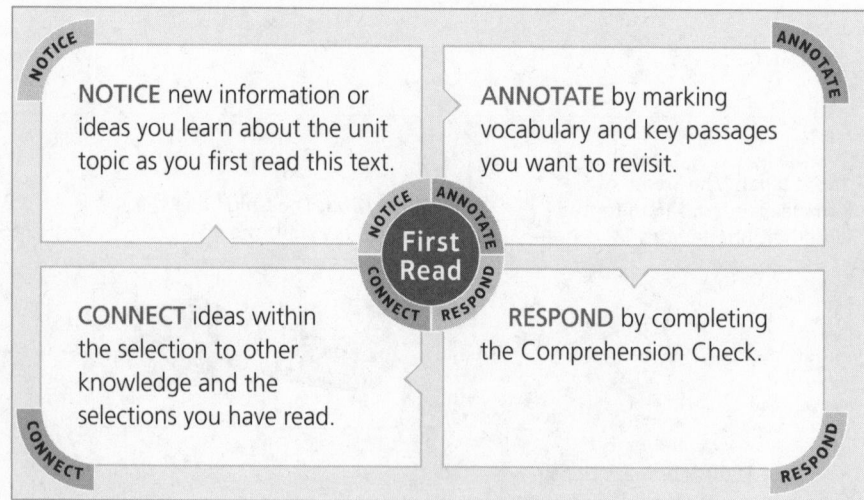

NOTICE new information or ideas you learn about the unit topic as you first read this text.

ANNOTATE by marking vocabulary and key passages you want to revisit.

CONNECT ideas within the selection to other knowledge and the selections you have read.

RESPOND by completing the Comprehension Check.

First Read

🔧 Tool Kit
First-Read Guide and Model Annotation

≡ STANDARDS

Reading Literature
By the end of grade 11, read and comprehend literature, including stories, dramas, and poems, in the grades 11–CCR text complexity band proficiently, with scaffolding as needed at the high end of the range.

Reading Informational Text
By the end of grade 11, read and comprehend literary nonfiction in the grades 11–CCR text complexity band proficiently, with scaffolding as needed at the high end of the range.

About the Author
Walt Whitman

Walt Whitman (1819–1892) was born on Long Island and raised in Brooklyn, New York. His education was not formal, but he read widely, including the works of Sir Walter Scott, Shakespeare, Homer, and Dante. Trained to be a printer, Whitman spent his early years working at times as a printer and at other times as a journalist. When he was twenty-seven, he became the editor of the *Brooklyn Eagle*, a respected newspaper, but the paper fired him in 1848 because of his opposition to slavery. After accepting a job at a newspaper in New Orleans, Whitman traveled across the country for the first time, observing the diversity of America's landscapes and people.

A New Vocation Whitman soon returned to New York City, however, and in 1850, he quit journalism to devote his energy to writing poetry. Impressed by Ralph Waldo Emerson's prophetic description of a new kind of American poet, Whitman had been jotting down ideas and fragments of verse in a notebook for years. His work broke every poetic tradition of rhyme and meter as it celebrated America and the common person. When the first edition of *Leaves of Grass* was published in 1855, critics attacked Whitman's subject matter and abandonment of traditional poetic devices and forms. Noted poet John Greenleaf Whittier hated Whitman's poems so much that he hurled his copy of *Leaves of Grass* into the fireplace. Emerson, on the other hand, responded with great enthusiasm, remarking that the collection was "the most extraordinary piece of wit and wisdom that America has yet contributed."

His Life's Work Though Whitman did publish other works in the course of his career, his life's work proved to be *Leaves of Grass*, which he continually revised, reshaped, and expanded until his death in 1892. The poems in later editions became less confusing, repetitious, and raucous, and more symbolic, expressive, and universal. He viewed the volume as a single long poem that expressed his evolving vision of the world, and in its poems he captured the diversity of the American people and conveyed the energy and intensity of all forms of life. Today, *Leaves of Grass* is regarded as one of the most important and influential collections of poetry ever written.

Background

The Writing of Walt Whitman

During the nineteenth century, American writers found their own voices and began to produce literature that no longer looked to Europe. Emerson, Thoreau, Poe, Dickinson—each contributed to a recognizably American style, but no one sounded as utterly American as Whitman. His style incorporates the plain and the elegant, the high and the low, the foreign and the native. It mixes grand opera, political oratory, journalistic punch, everyday conversation, and biblical cadences. Whitman's sound is the American sound. From its first appearance as twelve unsigned and untitled poems, *Leaves of Grass* grew to include 383 poems in its final, "death-bed" edition (1892). In the preface to the 1855 edition, Whitman wrote: "The proof of a poet is that his country absorbs him as affectionately as he absorbed it." There is little doubt that, according to his own definition, Whitman proved himself a poet.

from the
Preface to the 1855 Edition of

Leaves of Grass

Walt Whitman

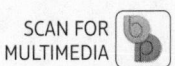

1   America does not repel the past or what it has produced under its forms or amid other politics or the idea of castes or the old religions . . . accepts the lesson with calmness . . . is not so impatient as has been supposed that the slough still sticks to opinions and manners and literature while the life which served its requirements has passed into the new life of the new forms . . . perceives that the corpse is slowly borne from the eating and sleeping rooms of the house . . . perceives that it waits a little while in the door . . . that it was fittest for its days . . . that its action has descended to the stalwart and well-shaped heir who approaches . . . and that he shall be fittest for his days.

2   The Americans of all nations at any time upon the earth have probably the fullest poetical nature. The United States themselves are essentially the greatest poem. In the history of the earth hitherto the largest and most stirring appear tame and orderly to their **ampler** largeness and stir. Here at last is something in the doings of man that corresponds with the broadcast doings of the day and night. Here is not merely a nation but a **teeming** nation of nations. Here is action untied from strings necessarily blind to particulars and details magnificently moving in **vast** masses. Here is the hospitality that forever indicates heroes. . . . Here are the roughs and beards and space and ruggedness and nonchalance that the soul loves. Here the performance disdaining the trivial unapproached in the tremendous audacity of its crowds and groupings and the push of its perspective spreads with crampless and flowing **breadth** and showers its **prolific** and splendid extravagance. One sees it must indeed own the riches of the summer and winter, and need never be bankrupt while corn grows from the ground or the orchards drop apples or the bays contain fish or men beget children upon women. . . . ❧

NOTES

CLOSE READ
ANNOTATE: Mark details in paragraph 1 that relate to death and other details that relate to new life or rebirth.

QUESTION: Why does Whitman include these details? What is dying and what is being born?

CONCLUDE: What impression of America do these references create?

ampler (AM pluhr) *adj.* more abundant

teeming (TEE mihng) *adj.* full

vast (vast) *adj.* very great in size

breadth (brehdth) *n.* wide range; expansive extent

prolific (pruh LIHF ihk) *adj.* fruitful; abundant

from
Song of
Myself

Walt Whitman

1

I celebrate myself, and sing myself,
And what I assume you shall assume,
For every atom belonging to me as good belongs to you.

I loaf and invite my soul,
5   I lean and loaf at my ease observing a spear of summer grass.

My tongue, every atom of my blood, formed from this soil, this air.
Born here of parents born here from parents the same, and
      their parents the same,
I, now thirty-seven years old in perfect health begin,
Hoping to cease not till death.

10 Creeds and schools in abeyance,[1]
Retiring back a while sufficed at what they are, but never forgotten,
I harbor for good or bad, I permit to speak at every hazard,
Nature without check with original energy.

6

A child said *What is the grass?* fetching it to me with full hands,
How could I answer the child? I do not know what it is any
      more than he.

I guess it must be the flag of my disposition, out of hopeful
      green stuff woven.

Or I guess it is the handkerchief of the Lord,
5   A scented gift and remembrancer[2] designedly dropped,
Bearing the owner's name someway in the corners, that we may see
      and remark, and say *Whose?*

. . .

What do you think has become of the young and old men?
And what do you think has become of the women and children?

They are alive and well somewhere,
10 The smallest sprout shows there is really no death,
And if ever there was it led forward life, and does not wait at the
      end to arrest it,
And ceas'd the moment life appear'd.

All goes onward and outward, nothing collapses,
And to die is different from what anyone supposed, and luckier.

1. **abeyance** (uh BAY uhns) *n.* temporary suspension.
2. **remembrancer** *n.* reminder.

CLOSE READ
ANNOTATE: In Section 6, mark the questions.

QUESTION: Why does Whitman choose to present these ideas as questions?

CONCLUDE: What is the effect of these questions?

9

The big doors of the country barn stand open and ready,
The dried grass of the harvest-time loads the slow-drawn wagon.
The clear light plays on the brown gray and green intertinged,
The armfuls are pack'd to the sagging mow.

5   I am there, I help, I came stretch'd atop of the load,
I felt its soft jolts, one leg reclined on the other,
I jump from the crossbeams and seize the clover and timothy,
And roll head over heels and tangle my hair full of wisps.

14

The wild gander leads his flock through the cool night,
Ya-honk he says, and sounds it down to me like an invitation,
The pert may suppose it meaningless, but I listening close,
Find its purpose and place up there toward the wintry sky.

5   The sharp-hoof'd moose of the north, the cat on the house-sill,
    the chickadee, the prairie dog,
The litter of the grunting sow as they tug at her teats,
The brood of the turkey hen and she with her half-spread wings,
I see in them and myself the same old law.

The press of my foot to the earth springs a hundred affections,
10 They scorn the best I can do to relate them.

I am enamor'd of growing outdoors,
Of men that live among cattle or taste of the ocean or woods,
Of the builders and steerers of ships and the wielders of axes and
    mauls, and the drivers of horses,
I can eat and sleep with them week in and week out.

15 What is commonest, cheapest, nearest, easiest, is Me,
Me going in for my chances, spending for vast returns,
Adorning myself to bestow myself on the first that will take me,
Not asking the sky to come down to my good will,
Scattering it freely forever.

17

These are really the thoughts of all men in all ages and lands,
    they are not original with me,
If they are not yours as much as mine they are nothing, or next
    to nothing,
If they are not the riddle and the untying of the riddle they are nothing,
If they are not just as close as they are distant they are nothing.

5   This is the grass that grows wherever the land is and the water is,
This is the common air that bathes the globe.

51

The past and present wilt—I have fill'd them, emptied them,
And proceed to fill my next fold of the future.

Listener up there! what have you to confide to me?
Look in my face while I snuff the sidle of evening,[3]
5 (Talk honestly, no one else hears you, and I stay only a minute longer.)

Do I contradict myself?
Very well then I contradict myself,
(I am large, I contain **multitudes**.)

I concentrate toward them that are nigh,[4] I wait on the door-slab.

10 Who has done his day's work? who will soonest be through with
    his supper?
Who wishes to walk with me?

Will you speak before I am gone? will you prove already too late?

52

The spotted hawk swoops by and accuses me, he complains of
    my gab and my loitering.

I too am not a bit tamed, I too am untranslatable,
I sound my barbaric yawp[5] over the roofs of the world.

The last scud[6] of day holds back for me,
5 It flings my likeness after the rest and true as any on the shadow'd wilds,
It coaxes me to the vapor and the dusk.

I depart as air, I shake my white locks at the runaway sun,
I effuse[7] my flesh in eddies, and drift it in lacy jags.

I bequeath[8] myself to the dirt to grow from the grass I love,
10 If you want me again look for me under your boot soles.

You will hardly know who I am or what I mean,
But I shall be good health to you nevertheless,
And filter and fiber your blood.

Failing to fetch me at first keep encouraged,
15 Missing me one place search another,
I stop somewhere waiting for you. 🙚

3. **snuff . . . evening** put out the last light of day, which moves sideways across the sky.
4. **nigh** *adj.* near.
5. **yawp** *n.* hoarse cry or shout.
6. **scud** *n.* low, dark, wind-driven clouds.
7. **effuse** (ih FYOOZ) *v.* pour out.
8. **bequeath** (bih KWEETH) *v.* hand down or pass on.

CLOSE READ
ANNOTATE: In Section 51, mark details that suggest the speaker is talking to a specific person or group of people.

QUESTION: Why does the speaker include these references? Whom is the speaker addressing?

CONCLUDE: What is the effect of this approach?

multitudes (MUHL tuh toodz) *n.* large number of people or things; masses

I Hear America Singing

Walt Whitman

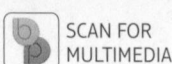 SCAN FOR MULTIMEDIA

NOTES

CLOSE READ

ANNOTATE: Mark the various kinds of workers mentioned in lines 2–8.

QUESTION: Why does the speaker name so many kinds of workers?

CONCLUDE: What is the effect of these references?

I hear America singing, the varied carols I hear,
Those of mechanics, each one singing his as it should be blithe
    and strong,
The carpenter singing his as he measures his plank or beam,
The mason singing his as he makes ready for work, or leaves
    off work.
5 The boatman singing what belongs to him in his boat, the
    deckhand singing on the steamboat deck,
The shoemaker singing as he sits on his bench, the hatter[1]
    singing as he stands,
The woodcutter's song, the plowboy's on his way in the
    morning, or at noon intermission or at sundown,
The delicious singing of the mother, or of the young wife at work,
    or of the girl sewing or washing,
Each singing what belongs to him or her and to none else,
10 The day what belongs to the day—at night the party of young
    fellows, robust, friendly,
Singing with open mouths their strong melodious songs.

---

1. **hatter** *n.* person who makes, sells, or cleans hats.

On the Beach at Night Alone

Walt Whitman

SCAN FOR MULTIMEDIA

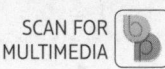

On the beach at night alone,
As the old mother sways her to and fro singing her husky song,
As I watch the bright stars shining, I think a thought of the clef[1]
    of the universes and of the future.

A vast similitude[2] interlocks all,
5 All spheres, grown, ungrown, small, large, suns, moons, planets,
All distances of place however wide,
All distances of time, all inanimate forms,
All souls, all living bodies though they be ever so different, or in
    different worlds,
All gaseous, watery, vegetable, mineral processes, the fishes, the
    brutes,
10 All nations, colors, barbarisms, civilizations, languages,
All identities that have existed or may exist on this globe, or any
    globe,
All lives and deaths, all of the past, present, future,
This vast similitude spans them, and always has spann'd,
And shall forever span them and compactly hold and enclose them.

NOTES

---

1. **clef** *n.* symbol that is placed at the beginning of a line of written music to indicate the pitch of the notes.
2. **similitude** (suh MIHL uh tood) *n.* similarity or likeness.

America

Walt Whitman

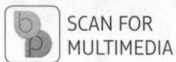

SCAN FOR
MULTIMEDIA

NOTES

Center of equal daughters, equal sons,
All, all alike endear'd, grown, ungrown, young or old,
Strong, ample, fair, enduring, capable, rich,
Perennial[1] with the Earth, with Freedom, Law and Love,
5 A grand, sane, towering, seated Mother,
Chair'd in the adamant[2] of Time.

---

1. **perennial** *adj.* enduring; consistently recurring or returning.
2. **adamant** *n.* legendary rock of impenetrable hardness.

Comprehension Check

Complete the following items after you finish your first read.

1. In his Preface to *Leaves of Grass*, how does Whitman define America's attitude toward the past?

2. In Section 1 of "Song of Myself," what does the speaker celebrate and sing?

3. In Section 52 of "Song of Myself," what does the speaker "bequeath" to the dirt?

4. Cite three types of songs the speaker hears in "I Hear America Singing."

5. According to the speaker in "On the Beach at Night Alone," what connects all things?

6. In the opening line of "America," how does the speaker describe the nation?

RESEARCH

Research to Clarify Choose at least one unfamiliar detail from the text. Briefly research that detail. In what way does the information you learned shed light on an aspect of Walt Whitman's work?

Research to Explore Conduct research to find out why Whitman was regarded as a revolutionary writer in his time.

THE WRITING OF WALT WHITMAN

Close Read the Text

1. This model, from paragraph 2 of the Preface to *Leaves of Grass*, shows two sample annotations, along with questions and conclusions. Close read the passage and find another detail to annotate. Then, write a question and your conclusion.

Close Read
ANNOTATE · QUESTION · CONCLUDE

> ANNOTATE: The passage contains some repeated words.
>
> QUESTION: What idea does the repetition emphasize?
>
> CONCLUDE: Whitman emphasizes a "right now" picture of America.

ANNOTATE: This list juxtaposes concrete and abstract nouns.

QUESTION: Why does Whitman include these particular nouns?

CONCLUDE: He is painting a diverse and exuberant picture of America.

> Here at last is something in the doings of man that corresponds with the broadcast doings of the day and night. Here is not merely a nation but a teeming nation of nations. . . . Here are the roughs and beards and space and ruggedness and nonchalance that the soul loves.

2. For more practice, go back into the text and complete the close-read notes.

3. Revisit a section of the text you found important during your first read. Read this section closely and **annotate** what you notice. Ask yourself **questions** such as "Why did the author make this choice?" What can you **conclude**?

🔧 **Tool Kit**
Close-Read Guide and Model Annotation

Analyze the Text

CITE TEXTUAL EVIDENCE to support your answers.

📝 **Notebook** Respond to these questions.

1. (a) **Interpret** In the Preface to *Leaves of Grass*, what does Whitman mean when he calls America a "nation of nations"? (b) **Connect** How does he develop that idea in "I Hear America Singing"?

2. (a) In Section 51 of "Song of Myself," what attitude toward time does the speaker express? Cite time-related details to support your answer. (b) **Analyze** What does the speaker seem to want of the listener? Explain.

3. **Summarize** What main idea does the speaker express in lines 2–3 of Section 52 of "Song of Myself"?

4. **Interpret** In "On the Beach at Night Alone," how does the second stanza state and develop the "thought" the speaker has in the third line of the poem? Explain.

5. **Historical Perspectives** The French political thinker Alexis de Tocqueville wrote that Americans are "always considering themselves as standing alone, [imagining] that their whole destiny is in their own hands." To what extent do you think Walt Whitman's writing illustrates that idea?

6. **Essential Question:** *What role does individualism play in American society?* What have you learned about American individualism from reading Whitman's writings?

📋 **STANDARDS**
Reading Literature
• Cite strong and thorough textual evidence to support analysis of what the text says explicitly as well as inferences drawn from the text, including determining where the text leaves matters uncertain.
• Analyze how an author's choices concerning how to structure specific parts of a text contribute to its overall structure and meaning as well as its aesthetic impact.
• Demonstrate knowledge of eighteenth-, nineteenth-, and early-twentieth-century foundational works of American literature, including how two or more texts from the same period treat similar themes or topics.

Analyze Craft and Structure

Poetic Structures Traditional epic poetry tells a long story about a hero whose adventures embody the values of a nation. Today, many readers consider *Leaves of Grass* an American epic because it expresses national ideals. Underlying the poem's diverse subjects is the constant echo of an **epic theme**—that all people are inherently equal and connected by the shared experience of being alive. Whitman uses specific poetic structures to establish a sense of epic sweep suitable for this theme.

- **Free Verse:** Unlike formal verse, which has strict rules, free verse has irregular meter, no rhyme scheme, and varying line lengths. It simulates natural speech. Free verse allows Whitman to shape every line and stanza to suit his meaning, rather than fitting his message to a form:

  Do I contradict myself?

  Very well then I contradict myself, . . .

- **Anaphora:** A type of rhetorical device, anaphora is the repetition of a word or group of words at the beginnings of successive sentences or sections of text. It creates a majestic tone and rhythm.

  If they are not yours as much as mine . . .

  If they are not the riddle and the untying of the riddle . . .

  If they are not just as close as they are distant . . .

- **Catalogue:** Whitman's use of catalogues, or lists, of people, objects, or situations evokes the infinite range of elements that make up human experience. "I am enamor'd," he writes,

  Of the builders and steerers of ships and the wielders of axes and mauls, and the drivers of horses . . .

Practice

CITE TEXTUAL EVIDENCE to support your answers.

📓 **Notebook** **Answer the questions, and complete the activity.**

1. **(a)** How does line 1 of Section 17 of "Song of Myself" express Whitman's epic theme? **(b)** How does "On the Beach at Night Alone" relate to this theme?

2. **(a)** Cite specific lines from Section 51 of "Song of Myself" that sound like natural speech. Explain your choices. **(b)** What does this speech-like quality suggest about the speaker's attitudes toward the listener and the topic?

3. **(a)** Identify at least one example of each poetic structure as it appears in the Preface or poems. **(b)** For each example, explain how it contributes to the expansive, epic-like quality of the work.

POETIC STRUCTURE	EFFECT
free verse:	
anaphora:	
catalogues:	

THE WRITING OF WALT WHITMAN

Concept Vocabulary

ampler	vast	prolific
teeming	breadth	multitudes

Why These Words? These concept words are used to describe abundance, even overabundance. Whitman believes that all people of all times are connected. As he writes in "On the Beach at Night Alone," a "*vast* similitude interlocks all." America is a "*teeming* nation of nations," Whitman declares, that "showers its *prolific* and splendid extravagance."

1. How does the concept vocabulary clarify the reader's understanding of Whitman's worldview?

2. What other words in these selections connect to this concept?

Practice

Notebook **Answer these questions.**

1. Which is the *ampler* unit of measure: a pint or a cup? Explain.

2. Why might life in a *teeming* urban area be challenging?

3. How would you feel if you were set adrift on a raft in a *vast* ocean? Why?

4. Why might a job candidate emphasize his or her *breadth* of experience?

5. What would a songwriter need to do to be considered *prolific*?

6. Why do *multitudes* of people sometimes gather in sports stadiums?

Word Study

Latin Combining Form: *multi-* A **combining form** is a word part that can be added to a word or to another word part—such as a root or an affix—to create a new word. The Latin combining form *multi-* means "many" or "much." In the word *multitudes*, it combines with *-tude*, another word-forming element that means "state or quality of." *Multitudes*, thus, means "the state or quality of being multiple or many."

1. *Multi-* is part of some words that relate to math or science. Write a definition of *multiply* that demonstrates your understanding of the combining form *multi-*. Check your answer in a college-level dictionary.

2. Identify and define two other words that include *multi-* and relate to math or science. Consult etymological references in a dictionary to verify your choices.

⬡ WORD NETWORK

Add words related to individualism from the text to your Word Network.

☰ STANDARDS

Reading Literature
Determine the meaning of words and phrases as they are used in the text, including figurative and connotative meanings; analyze the impact of specific word choices on meaning and tone, including words with multiple meanings or language that is particularly fresh, engaging, or beautiful.

Language
• Identify and correctly use patterns of word changes that indicate different meanings or parts of speech.
• Verify the preliminary determination of the meaning of a word or phrase.

Conventions and Style

Author's Choices: Diction Whitman's style is as individual and as revolutionary as his use of poetic structure. His **diction,** or word choice, features the following elements:

- **Variety of Types of Words:** Whitman's poetry features an exuberant blend of different types of diction.

Simple: *wherever the land is and the water is*	Intellectual: *Creeds and schools in abeyance*
Sensory: *I shake my white locks at the runaway sun.*	Abstract: *Nature without check with original energy.*
Specific: *I loaf and invite my soul*	General: *I am large, I contain multitudes*

- **Onomatopoeia:** Whitman sometimes uses sensory words that mimic the sounds they name.
  EXAMPLE: *I sound my barbaric <u>yawp</u> over the roofs of the world.*

- **Words in Pairs:** One of Whitman's favorite tactics is to use words in pairs joined by *and.* These pairings create a biblical cadence, assert the sacred quality of everyday things, and suggest a higher unity behind the diversity of life Whitman describes.
  EXAMPLE: *If they are not <u>the riddle and the untying of the riddle</u> they are nothing*

In the end, even Whitman's simple and specific words, such as *grass,* come to represent larger ideas, while his more intellectual or abstract words, such as *atom* and *multitudes,* come to take on an almost sensory weight.

Read It

1. In these lines of Whitman's, mark specific or sensory words. Then, mark abstract or general words. Finally, identify words paired by *and.*

   a. All goes onward and outward, nothing collapses.

   b. The old mother sways while she sings her husky song.

   c. I roll head over heels and tangle my hair full of wisps.

2. Reread Section 14 of "Song of Myself." Identify two instances of onomatopoeia, two sensory words or phrases, and two abstract or general words.

3. 📖 Notebook **Connect to Style** In a brief paragraph, explain how Whitman's diction in "I Hear America Singing" makes his portrait of America seem comprehensive and fundamental, like a passage in scripture or an epic. Then, identify the shift in diction in the final line and explain its effect.

Write It

📖 Notebook Write three sentences in which you imitate Whitman's style of pairing words, using pairs of words from the list.

sneakers	ocean	malls	stream	expand	data
sky	laboratories	pixels	laces	farms	channel surf

THE WRITING OF WALT WHITMAN

Writing to Sources

In "I Hear America Singing," Walt Whitman vividly describes the work that various Americans do. His descriptions are full of **sensory language**—words and phrases that appeal to one or more of the five senses. Sight and hearing are the chief senses engaged in "I Hear America Singing." However, Whitman also appeals to touch, as when he refers to the carpenter who is measuring "his plank or beam."

Assignment

Using Section 9 of "Song of Myself" as a model, write a brief **narrative account** about something that happened to you while you were working. You may narrate an event related to household chores, homework, or an after-school job. Use precise details and sensory language to make your account vivid and interesting for readers. Be sure to include your reactions to the event and also your reflections on what the event revealed to you about yourself.

Vocabulary Connection Consider using several of the concept vocabulary words in your narrative account.

ampler	vast	prolific
teeming	breadth	multitudes

Reflect on Your Writing

After you have drafted your narrative account, answer the following questions.

1. Does your narrative account both tell a story and share a reflection?

2. What sensory language did you use?

3. How much did you vary your diction?

4. Why These Words? The words you choose make a difference in your writing. Which words helped you make your narrative vivid and engaging?

≔ STANDARDS

Writing
• Write narratives to develop real or imagined experiences or events using effective technique, well-chosen details, and well-structured event sequences.
• Use precise words and phrases, telling details, and sensory language to convey a vivid picture of the experiences, events, setting, and/or characters.
• Provide a conclusion that follows from and reflects on what is experienced, observed, or resolved over the course of the narrative.

Speaking and Listening
Adapt speech to a variety of contexts and tasks, demonstrating a command of formal English when indicated or appropriate.

Speaking and Listening

Assignment

With a partner, prepare and deliver an **oral interpretation** of one of the poems by Whitman. As you prepare, discuss how to read the poem to preserve the flow of the lines and the excitement and expansiveness of the verse. Then, deliver your oral interpretation to the class as a whole.

1. **Choose a Poem** Together, review the poems by Walt Whitman in this section. Choose the one that appeals to you the most, whether for its themes or language.

2. **Analyze the Poem** Once you and your partner have chosen a poem, reread it carefully to analyze its structure and meaning. Decide whether you will present the text together in a choral reading or will divide it into parts for individual interpretation. Take a few minutes to discuss the level of formality and tone, or emotional attitude, you want to convey. In addition, consider how you will use your voices and gestures to emphasize meaning and demonstrate your interpretation of the poem. Together, mark up the text with notes that you can follow as you read for the class. Keep in mind that you should work together to build a single overall impression of the poem.

3. **Rehearse Your Presentation** Read the poem aloud, following the notes and presentation cues you have drawn up together. Pay special attention to the ways in which your reading can enhance Whitman's meaning. Consider how body language, including gestures, can contribute to the impact of your reading. Likewise, vary your volume and pace to make your reading as expressive as possible.

4. **Evaluate Partner Readings** After you have presented your oral interpretation and listened to those of your classmates, use a presentation evaluation guide like the one shown to assess what you heard.

PRESENTATION EVALUATION GUIDE

Rate each statement on a scale of 1 (not demonstrated) to 5 (demonstrated). Be prepared to defend your ratings, using examples.

☐ The speakers held the audience's attention.

☐ The speakers clearly conveyed the poem's main idea.

☐ The speakers used effective pacing and employed suitable volume, emphasis, and tone.

☐ The speakers used appropriate gestures and body language to emphasize aspects of the poem.

✎ EVIDENCE LOG

Before moving on to a new selection, go to your Evidence Log and record what you learned from the writing of Walt Whitman.

POETRY COLLECTION

The Poetry of Emily Dickinson

- The Soul selects her own Society –
- The Soul unto itself
- Fame is a fickle food

- They shut me up in Prose –
- There is a solitude of space
- I heard a Fly buzz – when I died –
- I'm Nobody! Who are you?

Concept Vocabulary

You will encounter the following words as you read these poems by Emily Dickinson. Before reading, note how familiar you are with each word. Then, rank the words in order, from most familiar (1) to least familiar (5).

WORD	YOUR RANKING
emperor	
imperial	
treason	
sovereign	
captivity	

After completing the first read, come back to the concept vocabulary and review your rankings. Mark changes to your original rankings as needed.

First Read POETRY

Apply these strategies as you conduct your first read. You will have an opportunity to complete the close-read notes after your first read.

🔧 Tool Kit
First-Read Guide and Model Annotation

NOTICE who or what is "speaking" the poem and whether the poem tells a story or describes a single moment.

ANNOTATE by marking vocabulary and key passages you want to revisit.

CONNECT ideas within the selections to what you already know and what you have already read.

RESPOND by completing the Comprehension Check.

First Read

≡ STANDARDS
Reading Literature
By the end of grade 11, read and comprehend literature, including stories, dramas, and poems, in the grades 11–CCR text complexity band proficiently, with scaffolding as needed at the high end of the range.

About the Poet
Emily Dickinson

 Emily Dickinson (1830–1886) wrote nearly two thousand poems with a unique voice of lyrical intensity. Dickinson is invariably named as one of our nation's greatest poets. Yet in her own lifetime, only a small circle of friends and relatives knew of Dickinson's poetic genius.

A Life Apart Born into a prominent family in Amherst, Massachusetts, Dickinson attended Amherst Academy and nearby Mount Holyoke Female Seminary. As a teenager she had an active social life, but over time she became increasingly reclusive, rarely venturing from her home after she was thirty. Devoting most of her time to writing poetry, she saw only the occasional visitor and communicated with friends and family mainly through letters.

Insecure Genius Uncertain about her abilities, in 1862 Dickinson sent four poems to the influential literary critic Thomas Wentworth Higginson. With the poems she enclosed a card in which she asked, "Are you too deeply occupied to say if my verse is alive?" Higginson recognized her talent and encouraged her to keep writing.

Dickinson's Legacy Although she sometimes enclosed poetry in letters, Dickinson published only a handful of her poems in her lifetime. When she died, her sister Lavinia found more than one thousand poems in the drawers of Dickinson's dresser, neatly tied in bundles known as fascicles. Dickinson left instructions that the poems be destroyed, but her family overrode that wish, recognizing that such a valuable legacy should be shared.

The Belle of Amherst In the years since the publication of her work, Dickinson has become the subject of plays, novels, and poems that have romanticized her life and celebrated her genius with varying levels of sentimentality and accuracy. In these works, Dickinson has been given a public personality that may or may not resemble the truth of who she was. However, in her poems, the writers who have followed her find no peer.

Background

The Poetry of Emily Dickinson

Unfortunately, Dickinson's early editors, including Thomas Wentworth Higginson, diminished the power of Dickinson's verse by changing it to be more conventional in language and style. Higginson was especially concerned by Dickinson's unorthodox use of dashes and capitalization. He failed to recognize that Dickinson crafted her poems with great precision and that eccentric capitalization and punctuation were important elements in her poetry.

When Thomas H. Johnson came out with his edition of Emily Dickinson's poetry in 1955, he restored original elements, including the dashes and capital letters, so that today we can read the poems as Dickinson meant them to be read. With the appearance of the Johnson edition, appreciation for Dickinson's poetic genius blossomed, and she is now acknowledged as a visionary who was far ahead of her time.

The Soul selects her own Society –

Emily Dickinson

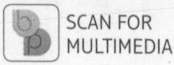

NOTES

emperor (EHM puhr uhr) *n.* ruler of highest rank and authority, especially of an empire

The Soul selects her own Society –
Then – shuts the Door –
To her divine Majority –
Present no more –

5 Unmoved – she notes the Chariots – pausing –
At her low Gate –
Unmoved – an **Emperor** be kneeling
Upon her Mat –

I've known her – from an ample nation –
10 Choose One –
Then – close the Valves of her attention –
Like Stone –

The Soul unto itself

Emily Dickinson

SCAN FOR
MULTIMEDIA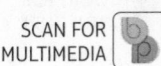

The Soul unto itself
Is an imperial friend –
Or the most agonizing Spy –
An Enemy – could send –

5 Secure against its own –
No treason it can fear –
Itself – its Sovereign – Of itself
The Soul should stand in Awe –

NOTES

imperial (ihm PEER ee uhl) *adj.*
like something associated
with an empire; magnificent
or majestic

treason (TREE zuhn) *n.*
betrayal of trust or faith,
especially against one's
country

sovereign (SOV ruhn) *n.*
monarch or ruler

Fame
is a
fickle food

Emily Dickinson

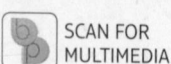 SCAN FOR
MULTIMEDIA

Fame is a fickle food
Upon a shifting plate
Whose table once a
Guest but not
5   The second time is set
Whose crumbs the crows inspect
And with ironic caw*
Flap past it to the
Farmer's corn
Men eat of it and die

---

*   **caw** *n.* piercing cry of a crow or raven.

They shut me up in Prose –

Emily Dickinson

SCAN FOR MULTIMEDIA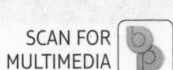

They shut me up in Prose –
As when a little Girl
They put me in the Closet –
Because they liked me "still" –

5 Still! Could themself have peeped –
And seen my Brain – go round –
They might as wise have lodged a Bird
For Treason – in the Pound –

Himself has but to will
10 And easy as a Star
Look down upon **Captivity** –
And laugh – No more have I –

NOTES

captivity (kap TIHV ih tee)
n. condition of being held prisoner

There is a
solitude of space

Emily Dickinson

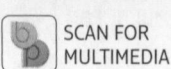

SCAN FOR
MULTIMEDIA

NOTES

CLOSE READ
ANNOTATE: Mark the types of solitude the speaker identifies in the first three lines.

QUESTION: Why does the speaker make a point of identifying different types of solitude?

CONCLUDE: What is the effect of these details?

There is a solitude of space
A solitude of sea
A solitude of Death, but these
Society shall be
5 Compared with that profounder site
That polar privacy
A soul admitted to itself –
Finite Infinity.

I heard a **Fly buzz –** when I died —

Emily Dickinson

SCAN FOR MULTIMEDIA
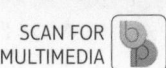

I heard a Fly buzz – when I died –
The Stillness in the Room
Was like the Stillness in the Air –
Between the Heaves of Storm –

5 The Eyes around – had wrung them dry –
And Breaths were gathering firm
For that last Onset – when the King
Be witnessed – in the Room –

I willed my Keepsakes – Signed away
10 What portion of me be
Assignable – and then it was
There interposed a Fly –

With Blue – uncertain – stumbling Buzz –
Between the light – and me –
15 And then the Windows failed – and then
I could not see to see –

NOTES

I'm Nobody! Who are you?

Emily Dickinson

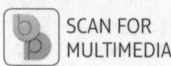
SCAN FOR MULTIMEDIA

NOTES

I'm Nobody! Who are you?
Are you – Nobody – too?
Then there's a pair of us!
Don't tell! they'd advertise – you know!

5 How dreary – to be – Somebody!
How public – like a Frog –
To tell one's name – the livelong June –
To an admiring Bog!

Comprehension Check

Complete the following items after you finish your first read.

1. In "The Soul selects her own Society –," what leaves the soul "unmoved"?

2. In "The Soul unto itself," of what does the speaker say the Soul should stand in awe?

3. In "Fame is a fickle food," what food do the crows prefer to the crumbs left by fame?

4. In "They shut me up in Prose –," why do "they" put the little girl in the closet?

5. According to the speaker in "There is a solitude of space," is death the deepest type of solitude?

6. In "I heard a Fly buzz – when I died –," what do the speaker and those in attendance expect to experience when "the last Onset" occurs?

7. According to the speaker in "I'm Nobody! Who are you?," what would be "dreary"?

- -

RESEARCH

Research to Clarify Choose at least one unfamiliar detail from the poems. Briefly research that detail. In what way does the information you learned shed light on an aspect of Emily Dickinson's poetry?

Research to Explore Conduct research to find out what happened to Dickinson's writing after her death.

THE POETRY OF EMILY DICKINSON

Close Read the Text

1. This model, from lines 1-4 of "I heard a Fly buzz – when I died –," shows two sample annotations, along with questions and conclusions. Close read the passage, and find another detail to annotate. Then, write a question and your conclusion.

ANNOTATE: The speaker repeats the word *Stillness*.

QUESTION: Why is this word important enough to repeat?

CONCLUDE: The word suggests the intensity of the atmosphere and the sense of waiting.

Close Read
ANNOTATE · QUESTION · CONCLUDE

ANNOTATE: Both *Stillness* and *Storm* begin with *s*.

QUESTION: Why does the poet use words with this sound pattern?

CONCLUDE: The sound connects *Stillness* and *Storm*, and suggests that the room only seems still; dramatic events are taking place under the surface.

> I heard a Fly buzz – when I died –
> The Stillness in the Room
> Was like the Stillness in the Air –
> Between the Heaves of Storm –

2. For more practice, go back into the poems and complete the close-read notes.

3. Revisit a section of a poem you found important during your first read. **Annotate** what you notice. Ask yourself **questions** such as "Why did the poet make this choice?" What can you **conclude?**

🔧 Tool Kit
Close-Read Guide and Model Annotation

Analyze the Text

> **CITE TEXTUAL EVIDENCE** to support your answers.

📓 **Notebook** Respond to these questions.

1. (a) In "The Soul selects her own Society –," what choice does the Soul make? (b) **Interpret** What happens after the soul makes her choice? (c) **Generalize** What is the soul's attitude toward the world's attractions?

2. **Compare and Contrast** How are the souls in "The Soul selects her own Society –" and "The Soul unto itself" alike and different? Explain.

3. (a) In the final stanza of "I heard a Fly buzz – when I died –," what adjectives does the speaker use to describe the buzzing of the fly? (b) **Draw Conclusions** What statement about dying is Dickinson making in this poem?

4. (a) **Interpret** In "I'm Nobody! Who are you?," how does the speaker feel about receiving attention? (b) **Connect** Identify two other poems in this grouping that express a similar tension between the private self and a social, or public, self. Explain your choices.

5. **Essential Question: *What role does individualism play in American society?*** What have you learned about the nature of individualism from reading these poems?

STANDARDS

Reading Literature
• Determine the meaning of words and phrases as they are used in the text, including figurative and connotative meanings; analyze the impact of specific word choices on meaning and tone, including words with multiple meanings or language that is particularly fresh, engaging, or beautiful.
• Analyze how an author's choices concerning how to structure specific parts of a text contribute to its overall structure and meaning as well as its aesthetic impact.

Analyze Craft and Structure

Poetic Structure and Style Poets use rhyme to emphasize ideas, convey mood, and unify groups of lines. With **exact rhyme,** two or more words have identical sounds in their final stressed syllables, as in *one/begun.* With **slant rhyme,** the final sounds are similar but not identical, as in *one/stone* or *firm/room.* Dickinson's frequent use of slant rhyme where readers expect exact rhyme makes her poetry surprising and thought-provoking.

> *I've known her – from an ample nation –*
> *Choose One –*
> *Then – close the Valves of her attention –*
> *Like Stone –*

Another hallmark of Dickinson's style is her fondness for paradox. A **paradox** is a statement that seems contradictory but actually presents a truth. For example, the statement "You must sometimes be cruel to be kind" is a paradox. It sounds contradictory, but it makes sense when you consider that there are times when seemingly unkind words or actions may actually help someone. Dickinson often explores paradoxes about the nature of solitude, selfhood, society, the mind, nature, and many other abstract concepts.

Practice

CITE TEXTUAL EVIDENCE to support your answers.

📝 **Notebook** Respond to these questions.

1. (a) Examine the use of slant and exact rhyme in "I heard a Fly buzz – when I died –."
   Use the chart to identify rhyming words, and note the lines on which they appear.
   (b) What is the effect of the exact rhyme after so many slant rhymes?

LINES	RHYMING WORDS	TYPE OF RHYME

2. (a) Which two words create a slant rhyme in the second stanza of "The Soul selects her own Society –"? (b) How does Dickinson's avoidance of exact rhyme in this poem fit with her characterization of the "Soul"?
3. (a) Explain how the first line of "I heard a Fly buzz – when I died –" is a paradox.
   (b) A two-word paradox, such as *cruel kindness*, is called an *oxymoron*. Identify an oxymoron in "There is a solitude of space," and explain the apparent contradiction.
   (c) For both poems, what explanation makes the situation possible, even though it seems impossible?
4. (a) Which of these poems present human understanding as something boundless or unlimited? (b) Which present it as something small and limited? (c) How would you define Dickinson's view of the individual self?

THE POETRY OF EMILY DICKINSON

Concept Vocabulary

emperor	treason	captivity
imperial	sovereign	

Why These Words? These concept words are used to discuss the power of nations. An *emperor* is a supreme ruler who oversees an *imperial* state. *Treason* is a crime against a nation, and *captivity* is a punishment a state can impose.

1. How does the concept vocabulary emphasize Dickinson's ideas about the supreme power of the soul?

2. What other words in the poems connect to this concept?

WORD NETWORK

Add words related to individualism from the text to your Word Network.

Practice

📓 **Notebook** Respond to the following.

1. Use each concept word in a sentence that demonstrates your understanding of the word's meaning.

2. Identify as many antonyms for each concept word as you can. Then, ask classmates about each antonym—for example, "True or false: *Monarch* is an antonym for *emperor*."

Word Study

Word Derivations In "The Soul selects her own Society –," Dickinson uses the word *emperor*. In "The Soul unto itself," she uses the word *imperial*. These words have similar derivations. *Emperor* is derived from the Latin noun *imperator*. *Imperial* is derived from the Latin adjective *imperialis*. Both Latin words can ultimately be traced back to the same root word, the Latin verb *imperare*, meaning "to command." As you would expect, the English words *emperor* and *imperial* have related meanings.

1. Find, define, and identify the parts of speech of two other words that have the same derivation as *imperial* and *emperor*.

2. Use a dictionary or online source to compare the precise meanings and derivations of these related words: *czar, kaiser, caesar.*

STANDARDS

Language
• Identify and correctly use patterns of word changes that indicate different meanings or parts of speech.

• Consult general and specialized reference materials, both print and digital, to find the pronunciation of a word or determine or clarify its precise meaning, its part of speech, its etymology, or its standard usage.

• Demonstrate understanding of figurative language, word relationships, and nuances in word meanings.

Conventions and Style

Parts of Speech Every English word, depending on its meaning and its use in a sentence, can be identified as one of the eight parts of speech: noun, pronoun, verb, adjective, adverb, preposition, conjunction, or interjection. A **noun** names any one of a class of people, places, things, or ideas.

- An **abstract noun** refers to an idea, quality, or concept rather than to a specific object.
- A **concrete noun** names something that you can experience through your five senses.

TIP

USAGE
There is no grammatical difference between concrete and abstract nouns. Both can be subjects, direct objects, or objects of prepositions. The difference is solely in the nature of the things they name.

ABSTRACT NOUNS		CONCRETE NOUNS	
individualism	requirement	door	chariot
eloquence	outrage	stone	windowsill
discovery	loneliness	sea	sky

Emily Dickinson uses concrete nouns to describe abstract concepts. This approach allows her to explore large abstract ideas—such as death, individuality, or fame—in ways that make them tangible and immediate.

Read It

1. Identify each underlined word as an abstract noun or a concrete noun.

   a. Fame is a fickle food / Upon a shifting plate

   b. They shut me up in Prose – / As when a little Girl

   c. A solitude of Death, but these / Society shall be

2. **Connect to Style** Reread the first stanza of "I heard a Fly buzz – when I died –." Identify two concrete nouns. How do those nouns suggest the speaker's view of death?

3. Notebook Choose another poem from this collection, and explain how Dickinson uses a concrete noun to describe an abstract idea.

Write It

Notebook Choose one of these abstract nouns. Then, write a passage in which you use concrete nouns and images to describe the abstract noun.

| charity | compassion | courage | determination |
| enthusiasm | fear | generosity | hope |

THE POETRY OF EMILY DICKINSON

Writing to Sources

A blog, short for *web log*, is a site on which a writer presents separate entries, or posts, in reverse chronological order. Blogs can focus on any topic and can be written for many different purposes. Perhaps you have read blog posts that recount events in the writer's life, revealing his or her personality and worldview. In some respects, Emily Dickinson's poems are like blog posts: They are serial expressions of her observations on fundamental aspects of life, including identity, love, nature, death, and immortality.

Assignment

Write a **blog post** as if you were the first-person speaker in Dickinson's poems. Give an account of a day in your life, using your interpretation of words, lines, and images from at least two of Dickinson's poems to describe your experiences and observations. Consider what the poetic details suggest about the speaker's character. Include elements such as these:

- precise words and sensory language
- words and phrases that suggest a specific tone, or emotional attitude, such as excitement, tranquility, or reflectiveness.
- a conclusion that sums up the speaker's worldview or opinion

Vocabulary and Conventions Connection Consider including several of the concept vocabulary words. Also, try to use concrete nouns to characterize abstract ideas and make them tangible and vivid for readers.

emperor	treason	captivity
imperial	sovereign	

Reflect on Your Writing

After you have drafted your blog post, answer the following questions.

1. Which poems contributed the most details to your blog post? Why did you choose those poems?

2. How would you describe the speaker that you created?

3. **Why These Words?** The words you choose make a difference in your writing. Which words helped you make your account descriptive and interesting?

STANDARDS

Reading Literature
Analyze multiple interpretations of a story, drama, or poem, evaluating how each version interprets the source text.

Writing
• Write narratives to develop real or imagined experiences or events using effective technique, well-chosen details, and well-structured event sequences.
• Use precise words and phrases, telling details, and sensory language to convey a vivid picture of the experiences, events, setting, and/or characters.

Speaking and Listening
• Propel conversations by posing and responding to questions that probe reasoning and evidence; ensure a hearing for a full range of positions on a topic or issue; clarify, verify, or challenge ideas and conclusions; and promote divergent and creative perspectives.
• Adapt speech to a variety of contexts and tasks, demonstrating a command of formal English when indicated or appropriate

Speaking and Listening

Assignment

Participate in a **class discussion** about "The Soul selects her own Society –." Either volunteer to read the poem aloud or simply listen as others do so. As you listen, consider how each reader's choices to emphasize certain words or phrases, indicate line breaks, and reflect the poem's distinctive punctuation affect how you hear and understand the poem. Then, discuss your observations.

1. **Listen to the Readings** Focus on the interpretive choices each reader makes.

   - As you listen, read along in the text.

   - Jot down points at which the reader's pace or emphasis surprises you. Consider whether this surprise illuminates an aspect of the poem, or—perhaps—misrepresents the poem in some way.

   - Share your responses, citing specific examples.

2. **Analyze the Readings** Now, take time to think more deeply about the effects of each reader's interpretive choices.

   - What words or phrases did different readings emphasize? Did these choices clarify or obscure the poem's meaning?

   - What emotional tone or attitude did different readers bring to the poem? Were some choices of tone more appropriate than others? Did some tonal choices reveal nuances in the poem's meaning?

   - Did the reader deliver his or her reading with conviction, speaking at an effective rate and volume? How did the speaker's delivery affect what you heard and appreciated in the poem?

   - Summarize your analysis in two or three sentences. Then, continue to participate in the discussion. As you share ideas and observations with classmates, ask questions and strive to understand one another's ideas and observations.

3. **Evaluate the Readings** Use a presentation evaluation guide like the one shown to assess each speaker's reading.

PRESENTATION EVALUATION GUIDE

Rate each statement on a scale of 1 (not demonstrated) to 5 (demonstrated). Be prepared to defend your rating, using examples.

☐ The reader's interpretation effectively communicated the poem's point of view, meaning, and tone.

☐ The reader's speaking rate and volume reflected the thoughts, feelings, and ideas expressed in the poem in an appropriate way.

☐ The reading held the audience's attention.

📝 EVIDENCE LOG

Before moving on to a new selection, go to your Evidence Log and record what you learned from the poetry of Emily Dickinson.

THE POETRY OF EMILY DICKINSON

Comparing Text to Media

The radio broadcast presented here offers another view of Emily Dickinson and her poetry. In this section, you will compare the ways in which a written text and a radio broadcast can provide information.

from EMILY DICKINSON

About the Poet

Gwyneth Lewis (b. 1959), the poet interviewed in this broadcast, was born and raised in Wales and grew up speaking both Welsh and English. After earning degrees from both Cambridge and Oxford, she moved to the United States, where she studied creative writing at Columbia and Harvard. Lewis returned to Wales to work as a producer and director of documentaries at BBC Wales. In 2005, she became the first National Poet of Wales, a post similar to that of Poet Laureate in the United States.

from Emily Dickinson

Media Vocabulary

These words will be useful to you as you analyze, discuss, and write about radio broadcasts.

Host: master of ceremonies, moderator, or interviewer on a broadcast	• An effective host puts the guests at ease so that the broadcast flows smoothly. • The host guides the conversation so that the guests stay on topic and provide useful or interesting information to the audience.
Interview: conversation in which a host asks questions of one or more guests	• Formal interviews are often prepared in advance with a script and rehearsal. • Informal interviews are unrehearsed and have a more free-flowing format.
Commentary: remarks that illustrate a point, prompt a realization, or explain something	• Commentary can come not only from guests but also from the host. • Authorities on a topic provide *expert commentary*.

First Review MEDIA: AUDIO

Apply these strategies as you conduct your first review. You will have an opportunity to complete a close review after your first review.

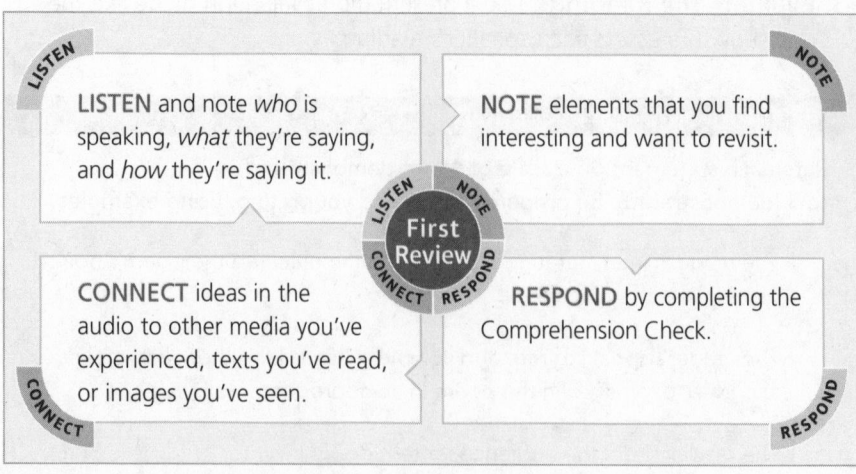

LISTEN

LISTEN and note *who* is speaking, *what* they're saying, and *how* they're saying it.

NOTE

NOTE elements that you find interesting and want to revisit.

First Review

CONNECT

CONNECT ideas in the audio to other media you've experienced, texts you've read, or images you've seen.

RESPOND

RESPOND by completing the Comprehension Check.

STANDARDS

Reading Informational Text
By the end of grade 11, read and comprehend literary nonfiction in the grades 11–CCR text complexity band proficiently, with scaffolding as needed at the high end of the range.

Notebook As you listen, record your observations and questions, making sure to note time codes for later reference.

from Emily Dickinson

from Great Lives

BBC Radio 4

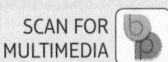

BACKGROUND

Emily Dickinson's poems are generally quite short and filled with everyday words. Those characteristics do not make them "easy," however. They are open to interpretation—indeed, much literary criticism over the years has been devoted to analyzing them and their author. In this 2011 episode of *Great Lives*, a biographical series produced by the British Broadcasting Company's Radio 4, Welsh poet Gwyneth Lewis is asked for her assessment of Dickinson's work.

SCAN FOR
MULTIMEDIA

NOTES

Comprehension Check

Complete the following items after you finish your first review.

1. Which poem does Gwyneth Lewis read at the beginning of the radio broadcast?

2. According to Lewis, what was Dickinson "adept" at doing?

3. What phrase does Lewis use to describe her relationship to Dickinson?

4. What type of pioneer does Lewis call Dickinson?

5. How does Lewis describe Dickinson's life?

6. What ability of Dickinson's does Lewis find encouraging?

Close Review

Review your notes and, if necessary, listen to the broadcast again. Record any new observations that seem important. What **questions** do you have? What can you **conclude?**

from EMILY DICKINSON

Analyze the Media

> **CITE TEXTUAL EVIDENCE**
> to support your answers.

📓 **Notebook** Respond to these questions.

1. **(a)** What did you notice about Gwyneth Lewis's reading of "I'm Nobody! Who Are You?" **(b) Connect** In what ways does her reading resemble or differ from the way you would read the poem?

2. **(a) Analyze** Lewis thinks that Dickinson speaks through her poetry about her vocation. What does she mean? **(b) Assess** Do you agree with Lewis's statement? Why or why not?

3. **Synthesize** Does Lewis's commentary change your own perception of Dickinson's work? Why or why not?

4. **Historical Perspectives** Lewis mentions that Dickinson was "able to live a life undistracted by many of the things that distract us." How do you think American life in the nineteenth century enabled Dickinson to live a less distracted life?

5. **Essential Question:** *What role does individualism play in American society?* What have you learned about American individualism from listening to this broadcast?

LANGUAGE DEVELOPMENT

Media Vocabulary

> host   interview   commentary

Use the vocabulary words in your responses to the questions.

1. What role does Matthew Parris play in the broadcast? How can you tell?

2. What does Matthew Parris add to the information that listeners get from Gwyneth Lewis?

3. Explain why you think the broadcast begins with Lewis's reading of "I'm Nobody! Who Are You?"

 WORD NETWORK

Add words related to individualism from the broadcast to your Word Network.

STANDARDS

Reading Literature
Analyze multiple interpretations of a story, drama, or poem, evaluating how each version interprets the source text.

Speaking and Listening
Evaluate a speaker's point of view, reasoning, and use of evidence and rhetoric, assessing the stance, premises, links among ideas, word choice, points of emphasis, and tone used.

THE POETRY OF EMILY DICKINSON

from EMILY DICKINSON

STANDARDS

Reading Literature
Analyze multiple interpretations of a story, drama, or poem, evaluating how each version interprets the source text.

Writing
• Apply *grades 11–12 Reading standards* to literature.
• Draw evidence from literary or informational texts to support analysis, reflection, and research.

Speaking and Listening
Evaluate a speaker's point of view, reasoning, and use of evidence and rhetoric, assessing the stance, premises, links among ideas, word choice, points of emphasis, and tone used.

Writing to Compare

You have read several of Emily Dickinson's poems, including "I'm Nobody! Who are you?" You have also listened to a radio broadcast in which the Welsh poet Gwenyth Lewis gives both a reading and an analysis of "I'm Nobody! Who are you?" Now, deepen your understanding of the poem by comparing Lewis's interpretation of it with your own, in writing.

> **Assignment**
> Write a **compare-and-contrast essay** in which you describe Lewis's interpretations of "I'm Nobody! Who are you?" and then present your own interpretation. How are your interpretations similar? How are they different? Support your ideas with details from Dickinson's poem, from the BBC broadcast, and from your own prior knowledge.

Prewriting

Analyze the Texts An **interpretation** can be a new version of a text, such as an oral reading, or a commentary on a text's meaning or importance. Listen again to the broadcast. Use the chart to record your observations and evaluation.

• First, record notes about Lewis's reading of "I'm Nobody! Who are you?" What is her tone of voice? What pace and volume does she use? What words does she emphasize? How would you describe the personality of the speaker she creates?

• Next, record notes about Lewis's understanding of both the poem and Dickinson. Include key quotations from both poets.

• Finally, decide whether you agree with each point you noted in the first column. Would you have made similar choices in an oral reading of the poem? Do you share Lewis's understanding of the poem and poet, or do you have different ideas?

LEWIS'S INTERPRETATION	AGREE OR DISAGREE? WHY?
Her reading of "I'm Nobody! Who are you?" • • • •	• • • •
Her understanding of the poem and poet • • • •	• • • •

Notebook Respond to these questions.

1. Where does your interpretation of Dickinson align with Lewis's?

2. Where does your interpretation of Dickinson depart from Lewis's?

Drafting

Draw Conclusions Review your Prewriting notes. Use one color to mark points of agreement between Lewis's interpretation(s) of Dickinson and your own. Use a second color to mark points of difference. Are your interpretations mostly similar, or mostly different? How so? Express your conclusions in the form of a thesis statement.

Thesis Statement: _____

_____

_____

Organize Ideas In this essay, you will compare and contrast Lewis's interpretation of Dickinson and your own. Consider using one of the following two formats.

Block Organization

I. Lewis's interpretations
   A. her oral reading of the poem
   B. her understanding of the poem
   C. her understanding of Dickinson

II. My interpretation
   A. how I would read the poem
   B. how I understand the poem
   C. my understanding of Dickinson

Point-by-Point Organization

I. Oral readings of the poem
   A. Lewis's choices
   B. what I would do similarly or differently

II. Understandings of the poem
   A. Lewis's
   B. my own

III. Understandings of Dickinson herself
   A. Lewis's
   B. my own

Express an Evaluation As you draft your essay, do the following:

- Include your thesis statement in the introduction.
- Write one paragraph for each major heading or subheading in your outline. Include evidence from both Dickinson's poem and the broadcast to support your ideas.
- Develop a conclusion in which you evaluate Lewis's interpretations of Dickinson in general terms. In your view, does she capture the spirit of both the poem and the poet? Does she help readers understand this poet in a new way? Or are her interpretations in some way "off the mark"?

Review, Revise, and Edit

When you are done drafting, reread your essay. Bracket your thesis statement. Mark sections about Lewis's interpretation in one color and sections about your own interpretation in another color. Are they generally balanced? If not, revise to emphasize both equally. After revising, edit for word choice and sentence structure. Proofread to eliminate errors in spelling, grammar, and punctuation.

✎ EVIDENCE LOG

Before moving on to a new selection, go to your Evidence Log and record what you've learned from the BBC radio broadcast featuring Gwenyth Lewis.

WRITING TO SOURCES

• THE WRITING OF
  WALT WHITMAN

• THE POETRY OF
  EMILY DICKINSON

• *from* EMILY DICKINSON

 Tool Kit

Student Model of a
Personal Narrative

**ACADEMIC
VOCABULARY**

As you craft your
personal narrative,
consider using some of
the academic vocabulary
you learned in the
beginning of the unit.

significant

incident

unique

sequence

impact

STANDARDS
Writing
• Write narratives to develop real or
imagined experiences or events using
effective technique, well-chosen
details, and well–structured event
sequences.
• Write routinely over extended
time frames and shorter time frames
for a range of tasks, purposes, and
audiences.

Write a Personal Narrative

Individualism usually refers to a belief in the value of self-reliance and
personal independence. You have just read several poems by writers who
embrace the importance of the individual as a unique soul or as a critical
part of a community.

> **Assignment**
>
> Write a brief **personal narrative** in which you address this question:
>
> > How has my personal experience shaped my view of
> > individualism? Do I see it as a guiding principle, something
> > to be avoided, or a combination of both?
>
> Begin by choosing an incident from your life that has shaped your view of
> individualism. Develop that memory into a narrative, sequencing events so
> that they reveal how you acquired the view you now hold. Connect your
> ideas to details from the texts you have just read.

Elements of a Personal Narrative

A **personal narrative** is a first-person story about a real-life experience.
In a personal narrative, the author is the narrator. In additional, a well-written
personal narrative contains these elements:

- a clear and consistent point of view
- a smooth sequence of events or experiences
- effective use of dialogue and/or description to develop the events and
  characterize the people in the narrative
- precise words and sensory language to clarify experiences
- a conclusion that follows from and reflects on the events presented in
  the narrative
- error-free grammar and spelling

Analyze the Writing Model

Model Personal Narrative For a model of a
well-crafted personal narrative, see the Launch Text
excerpt from *Up From Slavery*. Review the Launch
Text for examples of the elements of a well-crafted
personal narrative. You will look more closely at these
elements as you prepare to write your own personal
narrative.

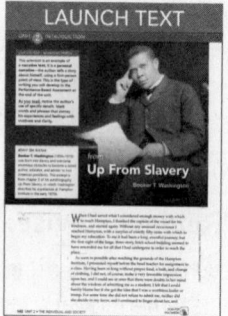

Prewriting / Planning

Establish the Situation Reread the questions in the prompt and think about the poems you have read and your own experiences. Then, think about a situation that influenced your views on individualism, whether in a positive or a negative way. Break down the situation into consecutive events, and tell how you felt then—and how you feel now. Remember that individualism involves how you weigh the needs of an individual against the sometimes competing needs of a larger group.

EVENT	HOW I FELT THEN	HOW I FEEL NOW
First,		
Next,		
Then,		
Finally,		

Gather Evidence Your evidence for a personal narrative often springs from your own memories. However, many things can spur those memories. Return to the reading selections in Whole-Class Learning, and find examples of the writers' views on individualism. Think about how their experiences reflect or contradict your own.

TITLE OF SELECTION	INDIVIDUALISM MEANS . . .

Connect Across Texts The prompt asks you to connect details from poems by Whitman or Dickinson to your own experience. Begin by skimming the texts and considering which of your chart entries might provide evidence. Note which text or texts come closest to your own views on individualism. Choose a comment from the text that you might quote within your narrative.

📝 EVIDENCE LOG

Review your Evidence Log and identify key details you may want to use in your personal narrative.

≡ STANDARDS

Writing
Engage and orient the reader by setting out a problem, situation, or observation and its significance, establishing one or multiple point(s) of view, and introducing a narrator and/or characters; create a smooth progression of experiences or events.

Drafting

Developing Conflict All narratives are driven by a **conflict**—a struggle between opposing forces. The conflict may be **internal**, or occurring within the thoughts and feelings of a narrator or person in the story. Alternatively, the struggle may be **external**, or occurring between two people, or between a person and an outside force. A story is more engaging for readers when the conflict is clearly developed using precise, exciting language.

Following Story Structure All narratives follow a basic progression in which the conflict is introduced, developed, and resolved. As you write, decide which details of your narrative belong in each section of the plot.

- In the **exposition,** set the scene and introduce the conflict. For this assignment, you may also choose to begin the discussion about individualism.
- In the **rising action, climax,** and **falling action,** present events in chronological order, build the conflict to its point of greatest tension, and then resolve it.
- In the **conclusion,** reflect on the events described in the narrative. For this assignment, you may choose to summarize how the events shaped your views of individualism.

STANDARDS

Writing

• Engage and orient the reader by setting out a problem, situation, or observation and its significance, establishing one or multiple point(s) of view, and introducing a narrator and/or characters; create a smooth progression of experiences or events.

• Use a variety of techniques to sequence events so that they build on one another to create a coherent whole and build toward a particular tone and outcome.

• Provide a conclusion that follows from and reflects on what is experienced, observed, or resolved over the course of the narrative.

LAUNCH TEXT EXAMPLE

Model: *from* Up From Slavery

EXPOSITION
Narrator arrives at Hampton, looking shabby after his travels. Head teacher fails to see him as an individual worthy of Hampton, her school.

MAIN PART OF NARRATIVE
Rising Action: Head teacher orders narrator to sweep. He cleans the room thoroughly.
Climax: Teacher evaluates the room.
Falling Action: Teacher accepts the narrator.

CONCLUSION
Adult narrator reflects on the incident and explains its importance.

Personal Narrative Organizer

EXPOSITION

MAIN PART OF NARRATIVE
Rising Action:
Climax:
Falling Action:

CONCLUSION

LANGUAGE DEVELOPMENT: STYLE

Add Variety: Precise Words and Phrases

The English language contains more than one million words. Nevertheless, as you write, you may find that only one word best fits your meaning for a certain detail. Narrowing down language to choose precise words and phrases means finding the word or words that say exactly what you mean.

Read It

Consider these examples from the Launch Text. Booker T. Washington chose precise words and phrases to help his readers understand his experience.

- *To me it had been a long, eventful journey; but the first sight of the large, three-story, brick school building seemed to have rewarded me for all that I had* <u>undergone</u> *in order to reach the place.* (*Undergone* means "experienced," but it has a connotation of suffering. It suggests that the author had a journey that was long and difficult.)

- *I felt that I could hardly blame her if she got the idea that I was a* <u>worthless</u> <u>loafer</u> *or* <u>tramp</u>. (The precise nouns *loafer* and *tramp*, combined with the adjective *worthless*, reveal Washington's fears about how the head teacher sees him.)

Write It

As you draft your personal narrative, carefully choose words that exactly express your feelings, actions, and observations. Here are a few examples that show the power of precise language.

INSTEAD OF...	TRY THIS...
The meal was **good.**	The meal was *mouthwatering, well-seasoned, substantial...*
I wore a red **top.**	I wore a *beet-colored polo,* a *burgundy turtleneck,* a *ruby t-shirt...*
We all felt **sad.**	We all felt *somber, regretful, sick at heart...*
They **walked** up the road.	They *sauntered, staggered, toddled like children...*
"Be careful," I **said.**	"Be careful," I *warned, whispered, muttered to myself...*

USAGE
Some words share denotations, or dictionary meanings, but have subtly different connotations. Some connotations are positive, whereas others are negative. For example, *clever* has a positive connotation, but *wily* has a negative one. Likewise, *cozy* has a positive connotation, but *cramped* has a negative one. Be careful to choose words that fit your meaning exactly.

STANDARDS
Writing
Use precise words and phrases, telling details, and sensory language to convey a vivid picture of the experiences, events, setting, and/or characters.

MAKING WRITING SOPHISTICATED

Reflecting on Events The difference between a compelling personal narrative and a simple anecdote is that in a personal narrative, the narrator usually reflects on and comments on events from the past. Nonfiction narrative writers relate events in sequence—but they also describe their feelings about those events and explain why and how those events were painful, instructive, or inspiring.

Read It

These examples from the Launch Text show how the writer moves back and forth between actions and thoughts, feelings and reflections.

> LAUNCH TEXT EXCERPT
>
> After some hours had passed, the head teacher said to me: "The adjoining recitation-room needs sweeping. Take the broom and sweep it."
>
> It occurred to me at once that here was my chance. Never did I receive an order with more delight. I knew that I could sweep, for Mrs. Ruffner had thoroughly taught me how to do that when I live with her.
>
> I swept the recitation-room three times.
>
> …
>
> When she was unable to find one bit of dirt on the floor, or a partic of dust on any of the furniture, she quietly remarked, "I guess you will do to enter this institution."
>
> I was one of the happiest souls on earth. The sweeping of that room was my college examination, and never did any youth pass examination for entrance into Harvard or Yale that gave him more genuine satisfaction. I have passed several examinations since ther but I have always felt that this was the best one I ever passed.

The writer turns from the head teacher's command to his own thoughts and feelings at the time. This detail helps the reader understand how the incident affected him.

Again, the writer turns from narrating the events to sharing his thoughts about the experience.

Here, the writer records a reflection from his present vantage point—the time in which he is actually writing, as opposed to the time he is writing about.

Connecting the Past to the Present Writers of strong personal narratives reflect on the importance of the stories they tell by connecting the past to the present. In any personal narrative, a reader must understand the importance of the memory being recalled.

Booker T. Washington connects his present self to his past self. He points out that although he has passed many exams in his life, the sweeping test was the most important because it allowed him to start his education at Hampton. This led, in turn, to his life as a teacher, an author, and an orator. If Washington had omitted the sentence that connects the past to the present, the reader might not understand why he recounted this incident in his autobiography.

Write It

Return to the "How I Felt Then/How I Feel Now" chart you completed in Prewriting. Use the following steps to integrate your feelings into your narrative.

- Find each event from the chart in your narrative.

- Have you mentioned your "then" feeling from the chart in your essay? If not, decide how you might work it into the narrative. Here are some basic examples:

    [Event happened], making me feel _____

    _____.

    I was never more [feeling] than when [event happened]. _____

    _____

- Remember that you may also show how you felt through dialogue, or by describing actions or appearance. Here are some more sophisticated examples:

    "I can't believe my luck," I moaned as [event happened]. _____

    _____

    As [event happened], my face got hot, and my hands felt sweaty.

    _____

- Consider how to include your "now" feeling. This might appear near the event in question, or it might appear in your conclusion. Here are examples of both:

    I felt _____ when [event happened], although now it just seems funny. _____.

    Although the [events] were traumatic at the time, looking back, I realize that they taught me a valuable lesson: _____

    _____

Use Precise Words Readers will better understand your feelings and ideas if you use powerful, precise words. Use this graphic to replace some of your "feelings" words with stronger, more precise choices. Write a feeling word from your text in the first box in each pair. Then, write a more precise word in the second box.

scared →

STANDARDS
Writing
• Use narrative techniques, such as dialogue, pacing, description, reflection, and multiple plot lines, to develop experiences, events, and/or characters.

• Provide a conclusion that follows from and reflects on what is experienced, observed, or resolved over the course of the narrative.

Revising

Evaluating Your Draft

Use this checklist to evaluate the effectiveness of your first draft. Then, use your evaluation and the instruction on this page to guide your revision.

FOCUS AND ORGANIZATION	EVIDENCE AND ELABORATION	CONVENTIONS
☐ Provides an exposition that sets the scene, introduces the conflict, and establishes a point of view.	☐ Uses techniques such as dialogue, description, and reflection to develop the experience being narrated.	☐ Attends to the norms and conventions of the discipline, especially regarding sequence of events and appropriate attention to connotative meanings.
☐ Establishes a sequence of events that unfolds smoothly and logically.	☐ Uses precise words and phrases, specific details, and sensory language to clarify events for the reader.	
☐ Includes a conclusion that resolves the narrative in a satisfying way.	☐ Uses vocabulary and word choice that is appropriate for the audience and purpose.	

Revising for Focus and Organization

First-Person Narration As the narrator of your own story, you can describe what you saw, experienced, thought, and felt. You can also describe what others did or said, as well as what you imagine they may have thought or felt. However, you cannot with authority say exactly what others felt or thought. Reread your narrative and make sure you have presented a first-person point of view consistently, and that you have not included information that steps outside the limits of that perspective.

Conclusion A satisfying, effective conclusion connects to the story being told and explores the significance of those events. Review your conclusion, and make sure it succeeds in doing both.

Revising for Evidence and Elaboration

Sensory Language Return to your narrative, and imagine that you are a stranger encountering your story for the first time. Decide whether any sections feel flat or uninteresting. Then, consider adding sensory details to show what you as the narrator saw, heard, smelled, tasted, and felt. This might involve simple additions or changes to certain words. Consider these examples:

Lacking Sensory Details: I *walked slowly* along the path.
Using Sensory Details: I *scuffed my way* along the *gravel* path.

Lacking Sensory Details: A *bird called* from a tree.
Using Sensory Details: An *owl screeched* from a *shadowy tree.*

⊹ WORD NETWORK

Include interesting words from your Word Network in your personal narrative.

▤ STANDARDS

Writing
Use precise words and phrases, telling details, and sensory language to convey a vivid picture of the experiences, events, setting, and/or characters.

Language
Demonstrate command of the conventions of standard English grammar and usage when writing or speaking.

Exchange narratives with a classmate. Use the checklist to evaluate your classmate's personal narrative and provide supportive feedback.

1. Did the narrative explain how the experience shaped the writer's views about individualism?

☐ yes   ☐ no   If no, explain what might be added.

2. Did the sequence of events lead naturally to the writer's views on individualism?

☐ yes   ☐ no   If no, tell what needs clarifying.

3. Are the writer's views on individualism clear to you now?

☐ yes   ☐ no   If no, suggest what you might change.

4. What is the strongest part of your classmate's narrative? Why?

_____

_____

_____

_____

Editing and Proofreading

Edit for Conventions Reread your draft for accuracy and consistency. Correct errors in grammar and word usage. Be sure that any shifts in time between past and present are clear.

Proofread for Accuracy Reread your draft carefully, looking for errors in spelling and punctuation. Be sure to punctuate dialogue correctly.

Publishing and Presenting

Use an app of your choice to save your personal narrative as an ebook. Depending on the app, you may include illustrations, and you may have a choice of preserving it in print or as a vocal recording. Share your ebook with others in your class. Ask your classmates to leave comments on a comment sheet that you provide. As you read classmates' ebooks, remember to keep your comments positive and helpful.

Reflecting

Consider what you learned by writing your personal narrative. Would a different incident from your life have provided a stronger response to the prompt? Does your narrative accurately reflect what happened to you and explain its importance in shaping your view about individualism? Think about what you might do differently the next time you write a personal narrative.

STANDARDS

Writing
• Develop and strengthen writing as needed by planning, revising, editing, rewriting, or trying a new approach, focusing on addressing what is most significant for a specific purpose and audience.
• Use technology, including the Internet, to produce, publish, and update individual or shared writing products in response to ongoing feedback, including new arguments or information.

ESSENTIAL QUESTION:

What role does individualism play in American society?

As you read these selections, work with your group to explore the meaning of individualism.

From Text to Topic In the nineteenth century, America's spirit of individualism was evident in every sphere of activity, from the arts to exploration to the development of new technologies. For instance, the completion of the Erie Canal in 1825—the first transportation system between New York City and the Great Lakes that did not require carrying cargo over land—helped open the West to settlers. In 1844, Samuel Morse sent the first telegraph message, pioneering the first near-instant means of communication between cities. As you read, consider how these selections show individualism in all realms of American life.

Small-Group Learning Strategies

Throughout your life, in school, in your community, and in your career, you will continue to develop strategies when you work in teams. Use these strategies during Small-Group Learning. Add ideas of your own for each step.

STRATEGY	ACTION PLAN
Prepare	• Complete your assignment so that you are prepared for group work. • Organize your thinking so you can contribute to your group's discussions.
Participate fully	• Make eye contact to signal that you are listening and taking in what is being said. • Use text evidence when making a point.
Support others	• Build on ideas from others in your group. • Invite others who have not yet spoken to join the discussion.
Clarify	• Paraphrase the ideas of others to ensure that your understanding is correct. • Ask follow-up questions.

SCAN FOR
MULTIMEDIA

CONTENTS

Working as a Team

1. **Take a Position** In your group, discuss the following question:

   Do you think American teenagers today would rather fit in than stand out? Explain.

   As you take turns sharing your positions, provide reasons for your choice. After all group members have shared, discuss connections among the ideas that were presented.

2. **List Your Rules** As a group, decide on the rules that you will follow as you work together. Two samples are provided. Add two more of your own. As you work together, you may add or revise rules based on your experience together.

   • Be open to multiple perspectives and creative responses.

   • Give reasons for your opinions and encourage others to do so as well.

   • _____

   _____

   • _____

   _____

3. **Apply the Rules** Share what you have learned about individualism in America. Make sure each person in the group contributes. Take notes as you listen to others and be prepared to share with the class one thing that you heard from another member of your group.

4. **Name Your Group** Choose a name that reflects the unit topic.

   Our group's name: _____

5. **Create a Communication Plan** Decide how you want to communicate with one another. For example, you might text, set up an online chat, or use the private messaging feature on a social media website.

   Our group's decision: _____

   _____

Making a Schedule

First, find out the due dates for the Small-Group activities. Then, preview the texts and activities with your group and make a schedule for completing the tasks.

SELECTION	ACTIVITIES	DUE DATE
from Nature *from* Self-Reliance		
from Walden *from* Civil Disobedience		
Innovators and Their Inventions		
The Love Song of J. Alfred Prufrock		
A Wagner Matinée		

Working on Group Projects

As your group works together, you'll find it more effective if each person has a specific role. Different projects require different roles. Before beginning a project, discuss the necessary roles and choose one for each group member. Some possible roles are listed here. Add your ideas to the list.

Project Manager: monitors the schedule and keeps everyone on task

Researcher: organizes research activities

Recorder: takes notes during group meetings

_____

_____

_____

_____

About the Author

Ralph Waldo Emerson
(1803–1882) was born
in Boston, the son of a
Unitarian minister. He
entered Harvard at the age of
fourteen. After postgraduate
studies at Harvard Divinity
School, he became pastor
of the Second Church of
Boston. Emerson's career as a
minister, however, was short-
lived. Grief-stricken at his
wife's death, and dissatisfied
with his faith, Emerson
resigned after three years
and went to Europe. There,
he met many of the leading
thinkers of the day. Upon
his return to the United
States, Emerson settled in
Concord, Massachusetts,
and began to write seriously.
His ideas helped forge the
Transcendentalist movement,
which celebrated the
individual and the power
of the human mind. Using
material from his lectures
and journals, Emerson
published *Essays* in 1841.
The collection brought him
international fame. Even
today, Emerson is one of
the most quoted writers in
American literature.

☰ STANDARDS

Reading Informational Text
By the end of grade 11, read and
comprehend literary nonfiction in
the grades 11–CCR text complexity
band proficiently, with scaffolding as
needed at the high end of the range.
Language
Use context as a clue to the meaning
of a word or phrase.

from Nature
from Self-Reliance

Concept Vocabulary

As you perform your first read of these excerpts from "Nature" and "Self-Reliance," you will encounter these words:

> sanctity   transcendent   redeemers

Context Clues To find the meaning of an unfamiliar word, look for **context clues.** Words and phrases that appear in the same sentence or in nearby sentences may help you determine the meaning of the unfamiliar word.

> **Example:** At all times she acts with respectful *decorum*, even when others try to anger her.
>
> **Context clues:** According to the sentence, *decorum* is a respectful way to behave—something that would be difficult for most people to maintain when angered.
>
> **Possible meaning:** *Decorum* means "dignity or control appropriate to an occasion."

Apply your knowledge of context clues and other vocabulary strategies to determine the meanings of unfamiliar words you encounter during your first read.

First Read NONFICTION

Apply these strategies as you conduct your first read. You will have an opportunity to complete a close read after your first read.

NOTICE the general ideas of the text. *What* is it about? *Who* is involved?

ANNOTATE by marking vocabulary and key passages you want to revisit.

First Read

CONNECT ideas within the selection to what you already know and what you have already read.

RESPOND by completing the Comprehension Check and by writing a brief summary of the selection.

from Nature

Ralph Waldo Emerson

BACKGROUND

During the 1830s and 1840s, Emerson and a small group of like-minded friends gathered regularly in his study to discuss philosophy, religion, and literature. The Transcendental Club developed a philosophical system that stressed intuition, individuality, and self-reliance. In 1836, Emerson published "Nature," the Transcendental Club's unofficial statement of belief.

SCAN FOR MULTIMEDIA

1   Nature is a setting that fits equally well a comic or a mourning piece. In good health, the air is a cordial[1] of incredible virtue. Crossing a bare common,[2] in snow puddles, at twilight, under a clouded sky, without having in my thoughts any occurrence of special good fortune, I have enjoyed a perfect exhilaration. I am glad to the brink of fear. In the woods, too, a man casts off his years, as the snake his slough, and at what period soever of life is always a child. In the woods is perpetual youth. Within these plantations of God, a decorum and **sanctity** reign, a perennial festival is dressed, and the guest sees not how he should tire of them in a thousand years. In

NOTES

Mark context clues or indicate another strategy you used that helped you determine meaning.

sanctity (SANGK tuh tee) *n.*

MEANING:

---

1. **cordial** (KAWR juhl) *n.* a strong, sweet liquor.
2. **common** *n.* piece of open public land.

the woods, we return to reason and faith. There I feel that nothing can befall me in life—no disgrace, no calamity (leaving me my eyes), which nature cannot repair. Standing on the bare ground—my head bathed by the blithe air and uplifted into infinite space—all mean egotism vanishes. I become a transparent eyeball; I am nothing; I see all; the currents of the Universal Being circulate through me; I am part or parcel of God. The name of the nearest friend sounds then foreign and accidental: to be brothers, to be acquaintances, master or servant, is then a trifle and a disturbance. I am the lover of uncontained and immortal beauty. In the wilderness, I find something more dear and connate[3] than in the streets or villages. In the tranquil landscape, and especially in the distant line of the horizon, man beholds somewhat as beautiful as his own nature.

2   The greatest delight which the fields and woods minister is the suggestion of an occult relation between man and the vegetable. I am not alone and unacknowledged. They nod to me, and I to them. The waving of the boughs in the storm is new to me and old. It takes me by surprise, and yet is not unknown. Its effect is like that of a higher thought or a better emotion coming over me, when I deemed I was thinking justly or doing right.

3   Yet it is certain that the power to produce this delight does not reside in nature, but in man, or in a harmony of both. It is necessary to use these pleasures with great temperance. For nature is not always tricked[4] in holiday attire, but the same scene which yesterday breathed perfume and glittered as for the frolic of the nymphs is overspread with melancholy today. Nature always wears the colors of the spirit. To a man laboring under calamity, the heat of his own fire hath sadness in it. Then there is a kind of contempt of the landscape felt by him who has just lost by death a dear friend. The sky is less grand as it shuts down over less worth in the population. ঌ

---

3. **connate** (KON ayt) *adj.* existing within someone since birth; inborn.
4. **tricked** *v.* dressed.

from Self-Reliance

Ralph Waldo Emerson

BACKGROUND

Individuality, independence, and an appreciation for the wonders of nature are just a few of the principles that Ralph Waldo Emerson helped to instill in our nation's identity. His essay "Self-Reliance" grew out of a series of lectures that he conducted in the 1830s.

SCAN FOR MULTIMEDIA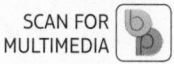

NOTES

1   There is a time in every man's education when he arrives at the conviction that envy is ignorance; that imitation is suicide; that he must take himself for better, for worse, as his portion; that though the wide universe is full of good, no kernel of nourishing corn can come to him but through his toil bestowed on that plot of ground which is given to him to till. The power which resides in him is new in nature, and none but he knows what that is which he can do, nor does he know until he has tried. Not for nothing one face, one character, one fact makes much impression on him, and another none. This sculpture in the memory is not without preestablished harmony. The eye was placed where one ray should fall, that it might testify of that particular ray. We but half express ourselves, and are ashamed of that divine idea which each of us represents. It may be safely trusted as proportionate and of good issues, so it be faithfully imparted, but God will not have his work made manifest by cowards. A man is relieved and gay when he has put his heart into his work and done his best; but what he has said or done otherwise, shall give him no peace. It is a deliverance which does not deliver. In the attempt his genius deserts him; no muse befriends; no invention, no hope.

NOTES

Mark context clues or indicate another strategy you used that helped you determine meaning.

transcendent (tran SEHN duhnt) *adj.*

MEANING:

redeemers (rih DEE muhrz) *n.*

MEANING:

2   Trust thyself: every heart vibrates to that iron string. Accept the place the divine providence has found for you; the society of your contemporaries, the connection of events. Great men have always done so and confided themselves childlike to the genius of their age, betraying their perception that the absolutely trustworthy was stirring at their heart, working through their hands, predominating in all their being. And we are now men, and must accept in the highest mind the same **transcendent** destiny; and not minors and invalids in a protected corner, but guides, **redeemers**, and benefactors. Obeying the Almighty effort and advancing on chaos and the Dark. . . .

3   Society everywhere is in conspiracy against the manhood of every one of its members. Society is a joint-stock company[1] in which the members agree for the better securing of his bread to each shareholder, to surrender the liberty and culture of the eater. The virtue in most request is conformity. Self-reliance is its aversion. It loves not realities and creators, but names and customs.

4   Whoso[2] would be a man must be a nonconformist. He who would gather immortal palms must not be hindered by the name of goodness, but must explore if it be goodness. Nothing is at last sacred but the integrity of your own mind. Absolve you to yourself, and you shall have the suffrage of the world. . . .

5   A foolish consistency is the hobgoblin of little minds, adored by little statesmen and philosophers and divines. With consistency a great soul has simply nothing to do. He may as well concern himself with his shadow on the wall. Speak what you think now in hard words and tomorrow speak what tomorrow thinks in hard words again, though it contradict everything you said today. "Ah, so you shall be sure to be misunderstood?"—is it so bad, then, to be misunderstood? Pythagoras was misunderstood, and Socrates, and Jesus, and Luther, and Copernicus, and Galileo, and Newton,[3] and every pure and wise spirit that ever took flesh. To be great is to be misunderstood. . . . ❧

---

1. **joint-stock company** similar to a publicly owned corporation, in which risk is spread among numerous investors.
2. **Whoso** *pr.* archaic term for "whoever."
3. **Pythagoras … Newton** individuals who made major contributions to scientific, philosophical, or religious thinking.

Comprehension Check

Complete the following items after you finish your first read. Review and clarify details with your group.

1. Under what circumstances, according to Emerson, does "mean egotism" vanish?

2. What does Emerson say is "the greatest delight" of being in contact with nature?

3. Under what circumstances, according to Emerson, does nature appear to be melancholy and sad?

4. **Notebook** Confirm your understanding of the text by writing a summary.

from SELF-RELIANCE

1. According to Emerson, what idea makes "every heart" vibrate?

2. What virtue does society demand, and what does Emerson recommend in its place?

3. According to Emerson, what is the "hobgoblin of little minds"?

4. **Notebook** Confirm your understanding of the excerpt by writing two sentences that summarize its key content.

RESEARCH

Research to Clarify Choose at least one unfamiliar detail from one of these texts. Briefly research that detail. In what way does the information you learned shed light on an aspect of the text?

Research to Explore Conduct research on an aspect of the text you find interesting. For example, you may want to learn more about Emerson's abolitionist politics. Share what you discover with your group.

from NATURE
from SELF-RELIANCE

 WORD NETWORK

Add words related to individualism from the texts to your Word Network.

Close Read the Text

With your group, revisit sections of the texts you marked during your first read. **Annotate** details that you notice. What **questions** do you have? What can you **conclude**?

Analyze the Text

CITE TEXTUAL EVIDENCE to support your answers.

Notebook Complete the activities.

1. **Review and Clarify** With your group, reread paragraph 1 of the excerpt from "Nature." Describe how Emerson is affected by nature. Is his experience in nature universal to all people, or is it unique to him?

2. **Present and Discuss** Now, work with your group to share the passages from the selections that you found especially important. Take turns presenting your passages. Discuss what you noticed in the selection, what questions you asked, and what conclusions you reached.

3. **Essential Question:** *What role does individualism play in American society?* What have these texts taught you about the individual and society? Discuss with your group.

Concept Vocabulary

sanctity	transcendent	redeemers

Why These Words? The three concept vocabulary words are related. With your group, determine what the words have in common. How do these word choices enhance the impact of the essays?

Practice

Notebook Confirm your understanding of these words by answering the questions. Use the vocabulary word in your answer.

1. What might people do to preserve the *sanctity* of a special place?

2. When might a person experience a *transcendent* moment?

3. How might *redeemers* help other people?

Word Study

Notebook Latin Root: -sanct- The word *sanctity* contains the Latin root *-sanct-*, which means "holy," and the suffix *-ity*, which turns adjectives into abstract nouns. Write several other words that you suspect contain the Latin root *-sanct-*. Use etymological information in a college-level dictionary to verify your choices. Record the words and their meanings.

Analyze Craft and Structure

Development of Ideas An **essay** is a short work of nonfiction in which an author presents ideas on a specific topic. Often, an essay involves an open-ended exploration of ideas. Reading Emerson's essays, you may feel as if you are walking beside him as he converses, continually discovering new connections. Through his explorations, Emerson elaborates a **philosophical vision,** or interpretation of humanity's situation in the world. To help readers see life from his perspective, he employs strategies such as these:

- **Setting the Scene:** Emerson grounds his discussion in a shared experience—a walk in the woods, or a moment when one takes charge of one's life.

- **Re-envisioning the Ordinary:** Starting from shared experience, Emerson transforms it, showing its larger implications. In "Nature," for example, he finds that a walk in the woods restores youth and connects him more deeply to the world. He re-envisions this walk as a journey into the infinite.

- **Re-defining Words:** Emerson develops specific associations for key terms. In "Nature," for example, the term *nature* grows from a reference to fields and woods to include associations with the spirit.

- **Finding Limits:** Emerson may reflect on how far his vision should extend. In "Nature," for example, he concludes that the power of nature to delight is not unlimited.

Practice

CITE TEXTUAL EVIDENCE to support your answers.

🗐 **Notebook** Work on your own to analyze Emerson's presentation of his vision in these two essays. Complete a chart like this one. Then, share and discuss your findings with your group.

from NATURE	from SELF-RELIANCE
Summary of Vision humanity's relationship to nature:	Summary of Vision significance of being an individual:
References to Shared Experience	References to Shared Experience
How the Shared Experience Reflects the Vision	How the Shared Experience Reflects the Vision
Meanings and Associations of Key Terms nature: harmony:	Meanings and Associations of Key Terms self-reliance: great men: manhood: society: conformity: consistency:
Limits/Lack of Limits	Limits/Lack of Limits

from NATURE
from SELF-RELIANCE

Conventions and Style

Sentence Variety One way in which writers hold the attention of their readers is by varying the types of sentences they use. There are four kinds of sentences, categorized by the number and types of clauses they contain. **Independent clauses** have a subject and verb and can stand alone as complete thoughts. **Subordinate** (or **dependent**) **clauses** also have a subject and verb but cannot stand alone as complete thoughts. This chart shows the components of the four kinds of sentences. (Independent clauses are underlined once; dependent clauses are underlined twice.)

KIND OF SENTENCE	COMPONENTS	EXAMPLES
simple	a single independent clause	I have enjoyed a perfect exhilaration. In the woods is perpetual youth.
compound	two or more independent clauses	They nod to me, and I [nod] to them. It takes me by surprise, and yet [it] is not unknown.
complex	one independent clause + at least one subordinate clause	The sky is less grand as it shuts down over less worth in the population.
compound-complex	two or more independent clauses + at least one subordinate clause	Within these plantations of God, a decorum and sanctity reign, a perennial festival is dressed, and the guest sees not how he should tire of them in a thousand years.

Emerson often uses the complex, compound, and compound-complex sentences typical of formal nineteenth-century prose. However, he also includes shorter, simple sentences to vary the flow of the text. The result is a text that is more conversational—and, therefore, more engaging.

Read It

📑 **Notebook** Identify each sentence in this paragraph as simple, compound, complex, or compound-complex. Explain each choice.

(1) Although society thrives on conformity, progress depends on individuality. (2) Emerson may celebrate individuality, but he does not address progress, and we should not ignore it. (3) While we need strong leaders, those leaders would be ineffective without loyal followers. (4) Every person must assume both roles. (5) No one can lead all the time, so we should become leaders in our areas of strength and follow others when they have greater experience and knowledge.

Write It

📑 **Notebook** Write a paragraph consisting of at least four sentences. Include at least one example of each kind of sentence: simple, compound, complex, and compound-complex.

▤ STANDARDS

Writing
Write narratives to develop real or imagined experiences or events using effective technique, well-chosen details, and well-structured event sequences.

Language
• Apply knowledge of language to understand how language functions in different contexts, to make effective choices for meaning or style, and to comprehend more fully when reading or listening.
• Vary syntax for effect, consulting references for guidance as needed; apply an understanding of syntax to the study of complex texts when reading.

Writing to Sources

Assignment

Respond to one of Emerson's essays by writing a **story element** for a first-person narrative related to Emerson's ideas. Work initially with other group members to use them as a sounding board for your ideas, but then write individually. The narrative can be either fiction or nonfiction. Choose from the following options. Check the box of the one you chose.

☐ **Setting:** Write a vivid description of a place in which a character feels the "perpetual youth" that Emerson describes in "Nature." For your narrative, choose a setting that is different from the forest that Emerson describes.

☐ **Character:** Create a personality profile of someone who fits Emerson's idea of a nonconformist in today's society. Describe in detail the types of things he or she eats, loves, writes, listens to, says, and so on. Make explicit connections to ideas in Emerson's essays where you can.

☐ **Dialogue:** Write a dialogue for a scene including two or more characters in which you capture what it means to "speak what you think now in hard words." Include a brief introduction explaining who the characters are and what the situation is.

Narrative Plan Work with your group to plan the narrative element that you chose. Discuss how your story element connects to Emerson's ideas, and consider integrating some quotations from his essays into your writing.

Working Title: _____

📝 EVIDENCE LOG

Before moving on to a new selection, go to your Evidence Log and record what you learned from the excerpts from "Nature" and "Self-Reliance."

NARRATIVE ELEMENT
Details to include:
Ideas to express:
Quotation(s) from Emerson's writing to use:

Tying It Together Work individually to draft your writing. Then, read your work aloud to a partner or your group and discuss revisions. Look for ways to make your writing stronger. Also, consider additional ideas or quotations from Emerson's essays that support the idea you are developing.

About the Author

Henry David Thoreau
(1817–1862) was born in
Concord, Massachusetts,
where he spent most of his
life. After graduating from
Harvard, he became a teacher.
In 1841, Thoreau moved into
the home of another famous
Concord resident, Ralph Waldo
Emerson, where he lived for two
years. Fascinated by Emerson's
Transcendentalist ideas, Thoreau
became Emerson's friend and
disciple. Rather than return to
teaching, he decided to devote
his energies to living by his
beliefs. The literary results of that
decision include his masterwork,
Walden (1854). When Thoreau
died at the age of forty-four, he
had published little and received
no public recognition. Emerson,
however, knew that future
generations would cherish his
friend. Speaking at Thoreau's
funeral, Emerson said: "The
country knows not yet, or in
the least part, how great a son
it has lost. . . . [W]herever there
is knowledge, wherever there is
virtue, wherever there is beauty,
he will find a home."

STANDARDS

Reading Informational Text
By the end of grade 11, read and
comprehend literary nonfiction in
the grades 11–CCR text complexity
band proficiently, with scaffolding as
needed at the high end of the range.

Language
Identify and correctly use patterns of
word changes that indicate different
meanings or parts of speech.

from Walden
from Civil Disobedience

Concept Vocabulary

As you perform your first read of the excerpts from *Walden* and "Civil
Disobedience," you will encounter these words.

sufficed	superfluous	vital

Familiar Word Parts Words that seem unfamiliar may contain **familiar
word parts,** such as roots, prefixes, or suffixes, that you already know.
When you encounter an unfamiliar word, identify any familiar word parts,
and consider how they might contribute to the meaning of the unfamiliar
word. Then, draw a conclusion about the word's likely meaning.

> **Unfamiliar Word:** *insensibly*
>
> **Word in Context:** It is remarkable how easily and *insensibly* we fall
> into a particular route, . . .
>
> **Familiar Word Parts:** the prefix *in-*, which often means "not"; the
> root *-sens-*, which means "sense"; and the suffix *-ly*, which often
> appears in adverbs that tell how something is done
>
> **Conclusion:** *Insensibly* has a meaning related to *sense*. The word
> probably means "in a way that is not connected to the senses" or
> possibly "in a way that does not make sense."

Apply your knowledge of familiar word parts and other vocabulary strategies
to determine the meanings of unfamiliar words you encounter during your
first read.

First Read NONFICTION

Apply these strategies as you conduct your first read. You will have an
opportunity to complete a close read after your first read.

NOTICE the general ideas of
the text. *What* is it about?
Who is involved?

ANNOTATE by marking
vocabulary and key passages
you want to revisit.

First Read

CONNECT ideas within
the selection to what you
already know and what
you've already read.

RESPOND by completing the
Comprehension Check and by
writing a brief summary of the
selection.

from Walden

Henry David Thoreau

BACKGROUND

From 1845 to 1847, Henry David Thoreau lived alone in a one-room cabin he built at Walden Pond near Concord, Massachusetts. This experience led him to write *Walden*, a blend of natural observation, social criticism, and philosophical insight. It remains one of the greatest examples of nature writing in American literature.

SCAN FOR
MULTIMEDIA

from Where I Lived, and What I Lived For

1   At a certain season of our life we are accustomed to consider every spot as the possible site of a house. I have thus surveyed the country on every side within a dozen miles of where I live. In imagination I have bought all the farms in succession, for all were to be bought, and I knew their price. I walked over each farmer's premises, tasted his wild apples, discoursed on husbandry[1] with him, took his farm at his price, at any price, mortgaging it to him in my mind; even put a higher price on it—took everything but a deed of it—took his word for his deed, for I dearly love to talk—cultivated it, and him too to some extent, I trust, and withdrew when I had enjoyed it long enough, leaving him to carry it on. This experience entitled me to be regarded as a sort of real-estate broker by my friends. Wherever I sat, there I might live, and the landscape radiated

NOTES

---

1. **husbandry** (HUHZ buhn dree) *n.* farming.

Mark familiar word parts or indicate another strategy you used that helped you determine meaning.

sufficed (suh FYST) *v.*

MEANING:

from me accordingly. What is a house but a *sedes*, a seat?—better if a country seat. I discovered many a site for a house not likely to be soon improved, which some might have thought too far from the village, but to my eyes the village was too far from it. Well, there might I live, I said; and there I did live, for an hour, a summer and a winter life; saw how I could let the years run off, buffet the winter through, and see the spring come in. The future inhabitants of this region, wherever they may place their houses, may be sure that they have been anticipated. An afternoon **sufficed** to lay out the land into orchard woodlot and pasture, and to decide what fine oaks or pines should be left to stand before the door, and whence each blasted tree could be seen to the best advantage; and then I let it lie, fallow² perchance, for a man is rich in proportion to the number of things which he can afford to let alone.

2   My imagination carried me so far that I even had the refusal of several farms—the refusal was all I wanted—but I never got my fingers burned by actual possession. The nearest that I came to actual possession was when I bought the Hollowell Place, and had begun to sort my seeds, and collected materials with which to make a wheelbarrow to carry it on or off with; but before the owner gave me a deed of it, his wife—every man has such a wife—changed her mind and wished to keep it, and he offered me ten dollars to release him. Now, to speak the truth, I had but ten cents in the world, and it surpassed my arithmetic to tell, if I was that man who had ten cents, or who had a farm, or ten dollars, or all together. However, I let him keep the ten dollars and the farm too, for I had carried it far enough; or rather, to be generous, I sold him the farm for just what I gave for it, and, as he was not a rich man, made him a present of ten dollars, and still had my ten cents, and seeds, and materials for a wheelbarrow left. I found thus that I had been a rich man without any damage to my poverty. But I retained the landscape, and I have since annually carried off what it yielded without a wheelbarrow. With respect to landscapes:

3   "I am monarch of all I *survey*,

My right there is none to dispute."³

4   I have frequently seen a poet withdraw, having enjoyed the most valuable part of a farm, while the crusty farmer supposed that he had got a few wild apples only. Why, the owner does not know it for many years when a poet has put his farm in rhyme, the most admirable kind of invisible fence, has fairly impounded it, milked it, skimmed it, and got all the cream, and left the farmer only the skimmed milk.

5   The real attractions of the Hollowell farm, to me, were: its complete retirement, being about two miles from the village, half a mile from the nearest neighbor, and separated from the highway by a broad field; its bounding on the river, which the owner said protected

---

2. **fallow** (FAL oh) *adj.* left uncultivated or unplanted.
3. **"I … dispute"** from William Cowper's *Verses Supposed to Be Written by Alexander Selkirk.*

it by its fogs from frosts in the spring, though that was nothing to me; the gray color and ruinous state of the house and barn, and the dilapidated fences, which put such an interval between me and the last occupant; the hollow and lichen-covered apple trees, gnawed by rabbits, showing what kind of neighbors I should have; but above all, the recollection I had of it from my earliest voyages up the river, when the house was concealed behind a dense grove of red maples, through which I heard the house-dog bark. I was in haste to buy it, before the proprietor finished getting out some rocks, cutting down the hollow apple trees, and grubbing up some young birches which had sprung up in the pasture, or, in short, had made any more of his improvements. To enjoy these advantages I was ready to carry it on; like Atlas,[4] to take the world on my shoulders—I never heard what compensation he received for that—and do all those things which had no other motive or excuse but that I might pay for it and be unmolested in my possession of it; for I knew all the while that it would yield the most abundant crop of the kind I wanted if I could only afford to let it alone. But it turned out as I have said.

6   All that I could say, then, with respect to farming on a large scale (I have always cultivated a garden) was that I had had my seeds ready. Many think that seeds improve with age. I have no doubt that time discriminates between the good and the bad; and when at last I shall plant, I shall be less likely to be disappointed. But I would say to my fellows, once for all, As long as possible live free and uncommitted. It makes but little difference whether you are committed to a farm or the county jail.

7   Old Cato,[5] whose "De Re Rustica" is my "Cultivator," says, and the only translation I have seen makes sheer nonsense of the passage, "When you think of getting a farm, turn it thus in your mind, not to buy greedily; nor spare your pains to look at it, and do not think it enough to go round it once. The oftener you go there the more it will please you, if it is good." I think I shall not buy greedily, but go round and round it as long as I live, and be buried in it first, that it may please me the more at last. . . .

8   I do not propose to write an ode to dejection, but to brag as lustily as chanticleer[6] in the morning, standing on his roost, if only to wake my neighbors up.

9   When first I took up my abode in the woods, that is, began to spend my nights as well as days there, which, by accident, was on Independence Day, or the fourth of July, 1845, my house was not finished for winter, but was merely a defense against the rain, without plastering or chimney, the walls being of rough weatherstained boards, with wide chinks, which made it cool at night. The upright white hewn studs and freshly planed door

---

4. **Atlas** (AT luhs) from Greek mythology, a Titan who supported the heavens on his shoulders.
5. **Old Cato** (KAY toh) Roman statesman (234–149 B.C.). "De Re Rustica" is Latin for "Of Things Rustic."
6. **chanticleer** (CHAN tuh klihr) *n.* rooster.

and window casings gave it a clean and airy look, especially in the morning, when its timbers were saturated with dew, so that I fancied that by noon some sweet gum would exude from them. To my imagination it retained throughout the day more or less of this auroral[7] character, reminding me of a certain house on a mountain which I had visited the year before. This was an airy and unplastered cabin, fit to entertain a traveling god, and where a goddess might trail her garments. The winds which passed over my dwelling were such as sweep over the ridges of mountains, bearing the broken strains, or celestial parts only, of terrestrial music. The morning wind forever blows, the poem of creation is uninterrupted; but few are the ears that hear it. Olympus is but the outside of the earth everywhere. . . .

10   I went to the woods because I wished to live deliberately, to front only the essential facts of life, and see if I could not learn what it had to teach, and not, when I came to die, discover that I had not lived. I did not wish to live what was not life, living is so dear; nor did I wish to practice resignation, unless it was quite necessary. I wanted to live deep and suck out all the marrow of life, to live so sturdily and Spartanlike[8] as to put to rout all that was not life, to cut a broad swath and shave close, to drive life into a corner, and reduce it to its lowest terms, and, if it proved to be mean, why then to get the whole and genuine meanness of it, and publish its meanness to the world; or if it were sublime, to know it by experience, and be able to give a true account of it in my next excursion. For most men, it appears to me, are in a strange uncertainty about it, whether it is of the devil or of God, and have *somewhat hastily* concluded that it is the chief end of man here to "glorify God and enjoy him forever."[9]

11   Still we live meanly, like ants; though the fable tells us that we were long ago changed into men; like pygmies we fight with cranes:[10] it is error upon error, and clout upon clout, and our best virtue has for its occasion a **superfluous** and evitable wretchedness. Our life is frittered away by detail. An honest man has hardly need to count more than his ten fingers, or in extreme cases he may add his ten toes, and lump the rest. Simplicity, simplicity, simplicity! I say, let your affairs be as two or three, and not a hundred or a thousand; instead of a million count half a dozen, and keep your accounts on your thumbnail. In the midst of this chopping sea of civilized life, such are the clouds and storms and quicksands and thousand-and-one items to be allowed for, that a man has to live, if he would not founder and go to the bottom and not make his port at all, by dead reckoning,[11] and he must be a great calculator indeed who succeeds. Simplify, simplify. Instead of three meals

Mark familiar word parts or indicate another strategy you used that helped you determine meaning.

superfluous (suh PUR floo uhs) *adj.*

MEANING:

---

7. **auroral** (aw RAWR uhl) *adj.* resembling the dawn.
8. **Spartanlike** *adj.* like the people of Sparta, an ancient Greek state whose citizens were known to be hardy, stoical, simple, and highly disciplined.
9. **"glorify ... forever"** the answer to the question "What is the chief end of man?" in the Westminster catechism.
10. **like ... cranes** In the *Iliad*, the Trojans are compared to cranes fighting against pygmies.
11. **dead reckoning** navigating without the assistance of stars.

a day, if it be necessary eat but one; instead of a hundred dishes, five; and reduce other things in proportion. Our life is like a German Confederacy,[12] made up of petty states, with its boundary forever fluctuating, so that even a German cannot tell you how it is bounded at any moment. The nation itself, with all its so-called internal improvements, which, by the way, are all external and superficial, is just such an unwieldy and overgrown establishment, cluttered with furniture and tripped up by its own traps, ruined by luxury and heedless expense, by want of calculation and a worthy aim, as the million households in the land; and the only cure for it as for them is in a rigid economy, a stern and more than Spartan simplicity of life and elevation of purpose. It lives too fast. Men think that it is essential that the *Nation* have commerce, and export ice, and talk through a telegraph, and ride thirty miles an hour, without a doubt, whether *they* do or not; but whether we should live like baboons or like men, is a little uncertain. If we do not get out sleepers,[13] and forge rails, and devote days and nights to the work, but go to tinkering upon our *lives* to improve *them*, who will build railroads? And if railroads are not built, how shall we get to heaven in season? But if we stay at home and mind our business, who will want railroads? We do not ride on the railroad; it rides upon us. . . .

> I have always been regretting that I was not as wise as the day I was born.

12   Time is but the stream I go a-fishing in. I drink at it; but while I drink I see the sandy bottom and detect how shallow it is. Its thin current slides away, but eternity remains. I would drink deeper; fish in the sky, whose bottom is pebbly with stars. I cannot count one. I know not the first letter of the alphabet. I have always been regretting that I was not as wise as the day I was born. The intellect is a cleaver; it discerns and rifts its way into the secret of things. I do not wish to be any more busy with my hands than is necessary. My head is hands and feet. I feel all my best faculties concentrated in it. My instinct tells me that my head is an organ for burrowing, as some creatures use their snout and forepaws, and with it I would mine and burrow my way through these hills. I think that the richest vein is somewhere here-abouts; so by the divining rod[14] and thin rising vapors I judge; and here I will begin to mine. . . .

from The Conclusion

13   I left the woods for as good a reason as I went there. Perhaps it seemed to me that I had several more lives to live, and could not spare any more time for that one. It is remarkable how easily and

---

12. **German Confederacy** At the time, Germany was a loose union of thirty-nine independent states with no common government.
13. **sleepers** *n.* ties supporting railroad tracks.
14. **divining rod** a forked branch or stick alleged to reveal underground water or minerals.

insensibly we fall into a particular route, and make a beaten track for ourselves. I had not lived there a week before my feet wore a path from my door to the pondside; and though it is five or six years since I trod it, it is still quite distinct. It is true, I fear that others may have fallen into it, and so helped to keep it open. The surface of the earth is soft and impressible by the feet of men; and so with the paths which the mind travels. How worn and dusty, then, must be the highways of the world, how deep the ruts of tradition and conformity! I did not wish to take a cabin passage, but rather to go before the mast and on the deck of the world, for there I could best see the moonlight amid the mountains. I do not wish to go below now.

14   I learned this, at least, by my experiment; that if one advances confidently in the direction of his dreams, and endeavors to live the life which he has imagined, he will meet with a success unexpected in common hours. He will put some things behind, will pass an invisible boundary; new, universal, and more liberal laws will begin to establish themselves around and within him; or the old laws be expanded, and interpreted in his favor in a more liberal sense, and he will live with the license of a higher order of beings. In proportion as he simplifies his life, the laws of the universe will appear less complex, and solitude will not be solitude, nor poverty poverty, nor weakness weakness. If you have built castles in the air, your

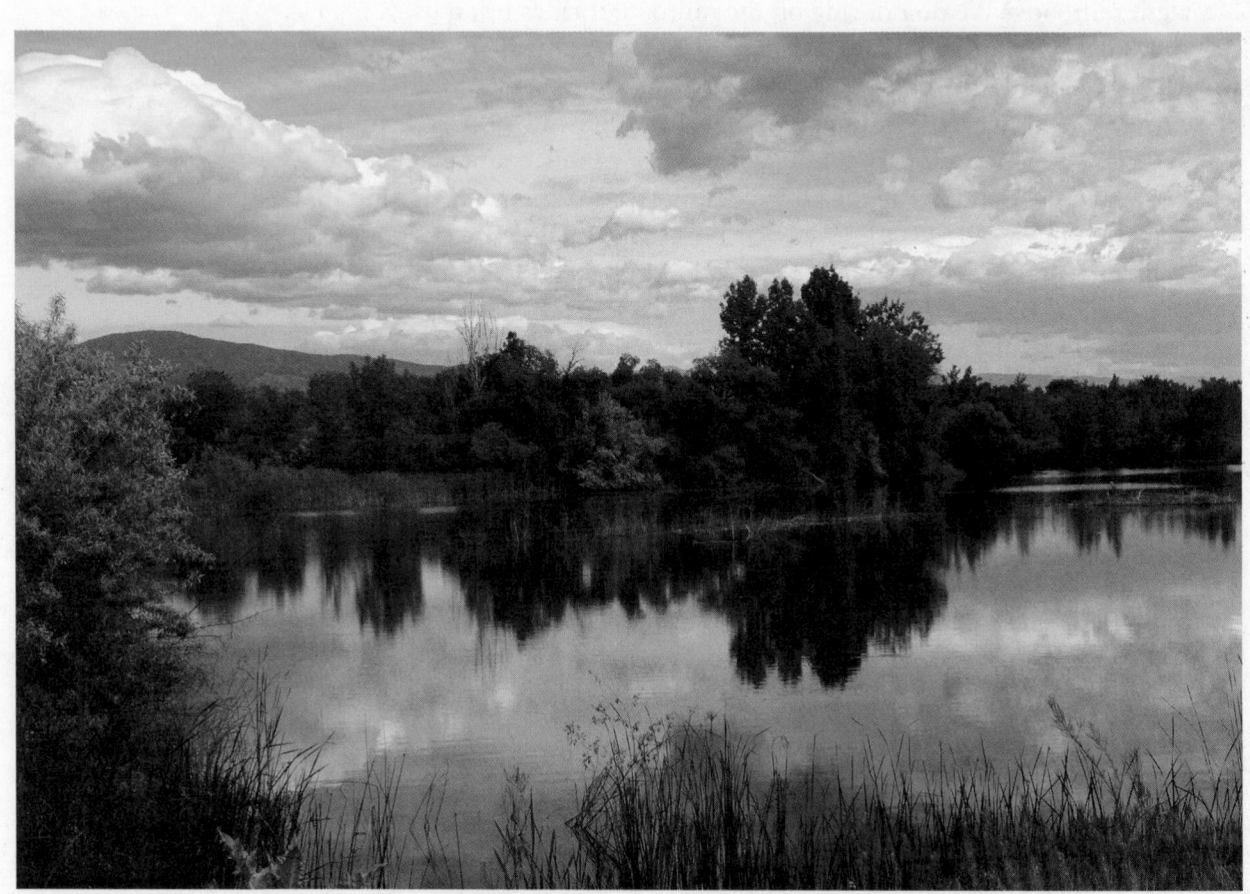

work need not be lost; that is where they should be. Now put the foundations under them. . . .

15   Why should we be in such desperate haste to succeed, and in such desperate enterprises? If a man does not keep pace with his companions, perhaps it is because he hears a different drummer. Let him step to the music which he hears, however measured or far away. It is not important that he should mature as soon as an apple tree or an oak. Shall he turn his spring into summer? If the condition of things which we were made for is not yet, what were any reality which we can substitute? We will not be shipwrecked on a vain reality. Shall we with pains erect a heaven of blue glass over ourselves, though when it is done we shall be sure to gaze still at the true ethereal heaven far above, as if the former were not? . . .

16   However mean your life is, meet it and live it; do not shun it and call it hard names. It is not so bad as you are. It looks poorest when you are richest. The faultfinder will find faults even in paradise. Love your life, poor as it is. You may perhaps have some pleasant, thrilling, glorious hours, even in a poorhouse. The setting sun is reflected from the windows of the almshouse[15] as brightly as from the rich man's abode; the snow melts before its door as early in the spring. I do not see but a quiet mind may live as contentedly there, and have as cheering thoughts, as in a palace. The town's poor seem to me often to live the most independent lives of any. Maybe they are simply great enough to receive without misgiving. Most think that they are above being supported by the town; but it oftener happens that they are not above supporting themselves by dishonest means, which should be more disreputable. Cultivate poverty like a garden herb, like sage. Do not trouble yourself much to get new things, whether clothes or friends. Turn the old; return to them. Things do not change; we change. Sell your clothes and keep your thoughts. God will see that you do not want society. If I were confined to a corner of a garret[16] all my days, like a spider, the world would be just as large to me while I had my thoughts about me. The philosopher said: "From an army of three divisions one can take away its general, and put it in disorder; from the man the most abject and vulgar one cannot take away his thought." Do not seek so anxiously to be developed, to subject yourself to many influences to be played on; it is all dissipation. Humility like darkness reveals the heavenly lights. The shadows of poverty and meanness gather around us, "and lo! creation widens to our view."[17] We are often reminded that if there were bestowed on us the wealth of Croesus,[18] our aims must still be the same, and our means essentially the same. Moreover, if you are restricted in your range by poverty, if you cannot buy books and

---

15. **almshouse** (OMZ hows) *n.* government-run home for people too poor to support themselves.
16. **garret** (GAR iht) *n.* attic.
17. **"and ... view"** from the sonnet "To Night" by the British poet Joseph Blanco White (1775–1841).
18. **Croesus** (KREE suhs) King of Lydia (d. 546 B.C.), believed to be the wealthiest person of his time.

NOTES

Mark familiar word parts or indicate another strategy you used that helped you determine meaning.

vital (VY tuhl) *adj.*

newspapers, for instance, you are but confined to the most significant and **vital** experiences; you are compelled to deal with the material which yields the most sugar and the most starch. It is life near the bone where it is sweetest. You are defended from being a trifler. No man loses ever on a lower level by magnanimity[19] on a higher. Superfluous wealth can buy superfluities only. Money is not required to buy one necessary of the soul. . . .

17   The life in us is like the water in the river. It may rise this year higher than man has ever known it, and flood the parched uplands; even this may be the eventful year, which will drown out all our muskrats. It was not always dry land where we dwell. I see far inland the banks which the stream anciently washed, before science began to record its freshets.[20] Everyone has heard the story which has gone the rounds of New England, of a strong and beautiful bug which came out of the dry leaf of an old table of apple-tree wood, which had stood in a farmer's kitchen for sixty years, first in Connecticut, and afterward in Massachusetts—from an egg deposited in the living tree many years earlier still, as appeared by counting the annual layers beyond it; which was heard gnawing out for several weeks, hatched perchance by the heat of an urn. Who does not feel his faith in a resurrection and immortality strengthened by hearing of this? Who knows what beautiful and winged life, whose egg has been buried for ages under many concentric layers of woodenness in the dead dry life of society, deposited at first in the alburnum[21] of the green and living tree, which has been gradually converted into the semblance of its well-seasoned tomb—heard perchance gnawing out now for years by the astonished family of man, as they sat round the festive board— may unexpectedly come forth from amidst society's most trivial and handselled furniture, to enjoy its perfect summer life at last!

18   I do not say that John or Jonathan[22] will realize all this; but such is the character of that morrow[23] which mere lapse of time can never make to dawn. The light which puts out our eyes is darkness to us. Only that day dawns to which we are awake. There is more day to dawn. The sun is but a morning star. ❧

---

19. **magnanimity** (mag nuh NIHM uh tee) *n.* generosity.
20. **freshets** (FREHSH its) *n.* river floods resulting from heavy rain or melted snow.
21. **alburnum** (al BUR nuhm) *n.* soft wood between the bark and the heartwood, where water is conducted.
22. **John or Jonathan** average person.
23. **morrow** *n.* literary term for "tomorrow;" archaic term for "morning."

from Civil Disobedience

Henry David Thoreau

BACKGROUND

The Mexican War was a conflict between Mexico and the United States that took place from 1846 to 1848. The war was caused by a dispute over the boundary between Texas and Mexico, as well as by Mexico's refusal to discuss selling California and New Mexico to the United States. Believing that President Polk had intentionally provoked the conflict before gaining congressional approval, Thoreau and many other Americans strongly objected to the war. In protest, Thoreau refused to pay his taxes and was forced to spend a night in jail. Afterward, he wrote "Civil Disobedience," urging people to resist governmental policies with which they disagree.

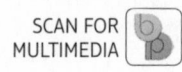

SCAN FOR
MULTIMEDIA

1   I heartily accept the motto, "That government is best which governs least";[1] and I should like to see it acted up to more rapidly and systematically. Carried out, it finally amounts to this, which also I believe: "That government is best which governs not at all"; and when men are prepared for it, that will be the kind of government which they will have. Government is at best but an expedient; but most governments are usually, and all governments are sometimes, inexpedient. The objections which have been brought against a standing army, and they are many and weighty, and deserve to prevail, may also at last be brought against a standing government.

NOTES

---

1. **"That ... least"** the motto of the *United States Magazine and Democratic Review,* a literary-political journal.

The standing army is only an arm of the standing government. The government itself, which is only the mode which the people have chosen to execute their will, is equally liable to be abused and perverted before the people can act through it. Witness the present Mexican war, the work of comparatively a few individuals using the standing government as their tool; for in the outset, the people would not have consented to this measure.

2   This American government—what is it but a tradition, though a recent one, endeavoring to transmit itself unimpaired to posterity, but each instant losing some of its integrity? It has not the vitality and force of a single living man; for a single man can bend it to his will. It is a sort of wooden gun to the people themselves; and, if ever they should use it in earnest as a real one against each other, it will surely split. But it is not the less necessary for this; for the people must have some complicated machinery or other, and hear its din, to satisfy that idea of government which they have. Governments show thus how successfully men can be imposed on, even impose on themselves, for their own advantage. It is excellent, we must all allow; yet this government never of itself furthered any enterprise, but by the alacrity with which it got out of its way. *It* does not keep the country free. *It* does not settle the West. *It* does not educate. The character inherent in the American people has done all that has been accomplished; and it would have done somewhat more, if the government had not sometimes got in its way. For government is an expedient by which men would fain[2] succeed in letting one another alone; and, as has been said, when it is most expedient, the governed are most let alone by it. Trade and commerce, if they were not made of India rubber,[3] would never manage to bounce over the obstacles which legislators are continually putting in their way; and, if one were to judge these men wholly by the effects of their actions, and not partly by their intentions, they would deserve to be classed and punished with those mischievous persons who put obstructions on the railroads.

3   But, to speak practically and as a citizen, unlike those who call themselves no government men, I ask for, not at once no government, but *at once* a better government. Let every man make known what kind of government would command his respect, and that will be one step toward obtaining it. . . . ❧

---

2. **fain** *adv.* gladly.
3. **India rubber** form of crude rubber.

Comprehension Check

Complete the following items after you finish your first read. Review and clarify details with your group.

from WALDEN

1. What advice does Thoreau offer to his "fellows" about ownership of land or property?

2. What did Thoreau hope to discover by living in the woods?

3. What advice does Thoreau give to those living in poverty?

4. 📓 **Notebook** Confirm your understanding of the text by writing a summary.

from CIVIL DISOBEDIENCE

1. What motto does Thoreau endorse at the beginning of this selection?

2. How does Thoreau define the best possible kind of government?

3. At the end of the text, what does Thoreau ask his readers to do?

4. 📓 **Notebook** Confirm your understanding of the text by writing two sentences that summarize its key content.

RESEARCH

Research to Clarify Choose at least one unfamiliar detail from one of the texts. Briefly research that detail. In what way does the information you learned shed light on an aspect of the text?

Research to Explore The excerpt from *Walden* may have sparked your curiosity to learn more. For example, you may want to know what Walden Pond is like today. Share what you discover with your group.

from WALDEN
from CIVIL DISOBEDIENCE

WORD NETWORK
Add words related to individualism from the texts to your Word Network.

Close Read the Text

With your group, revisit sections of the texts you marked during your first read. **Annotate** what you notice. What **questions** do you have? What can you **conclude?**

Analyze the Text

> **CITE TEXTUAL EVIDENCE**
> to support your answers.

Notebook Complete the activities.

1. **Review and Clarify** With your group, reread paragraph 1 of the excerpt from *Walden*. Describe Thoreau's attitude toward home ownership. How does this outlook relate to his experience in the woods and to his overall view of how life should be lived?

2. **Present and Discuss** Now, work with your group to share the passages from the selections that you found especially important. Take turns presenting your passages. Discuss what you noticed in the selections, what questions you asked, and what conclusions you reached.

3. **Essential Question:** *What role does individualism play in American society?* What have these texts taught you about the relationship between the individual and society? Discuss with your group.

Concept Vocabulary

| sufficed | superfluous | vital |

Why These Words? The concept vocabulary words from these texts are related. With your group, determine what the words have in common. How do these word choices enhance the impact of the texts?

Practice

Notebook Confirm your understanding of these words by answering these questions. Use the vocabulary word from each question in your answer.

1. If everything in someone's life *sufficed*, would he or she most likely be content? Explain.

2. How would refusing to purchase *superfluous* items help your budget?

3. In the modern world, is technology *vital* to survival?

Word Study

Notebook Latin Prefix: *super-* The Latin prefix *super-* means "above" or "over." Explain how the meaning of the prefix contributes to the meaning of *superfluous*. Then, find four other words that have this same prefix. Record the words and their meanings.

Analyze Craft and Structure

Author's Point of View An author's **point of view** is the perspective the writer adopts toward a situation or set of issues. In both *Walden* and "Civil Disobedience," Thoreau presents arguments that build on **philosophical assumptions,** or principles and beliefs that he takes for granted and that form a foundation for his ideas. Some assumptions are **explicit,** or directly stated. Other assumptions, however, are **implicit,** or not stated outright.

For example, a writer might hold certain beliefs about human nature, divine or spiritual matters, the nature of society, or another aspect of life. A writer may not explain these fundamental beliefs; nevertheless, they may be the basis for his or her ideas. In order to identify and consider these implicit assumptions, the reader must tease them out from details the writer does supply. Then, the reader must consider how these assumptions contribute to the author's overall position or ideas.

Practice

CITE TEXTUAL EVIDENCE to support your answers.

Notebook Respond to these questions.

1. (a) What implicit assumption does Thoreau rely on when he discusses the relationship of money and the soul in *Walden*? (b) Do you believe Thoreau's assumption is valid? Why or why not?

2. (a) Identify the explicit assumption with which Thoreau begins his discussion in "Civil Disobedience." (b) What counterarguments, or opposing views, to this assumption might someone present?

3. (a) In *Walden*, how does Thoreau support his point that "It makes but little difference whether you are committed to a farm or the county jail"? (b) What implicit assumption does this statement suggest? (c) Do you agree? Explain.

4. Record Thoreau's implicit assumptions on a variety of issues as they are revealed in *Walden*. List specific details that allow you to identify each assumption.

ISSUE	IMPLICIT ASSUMPTION	DETAILS
Desire for freedom		
Simplicity of life		
Nonconformity		

from WALDEN
from CIVIL DISOBEDIENCE

Conventions and Style

Author's Style A writer's **style** is the unique manner in which he or she puts thoughts into words. In his philosophical writing, Thoreau uses a broad range of devices to establish a **conversational style,** as if he were talking informally to a friend.

- Typically, Thoreau's **diction,** or **word choice,** is simple and direct:
  I went to the woods because I wished to live deliberately . . .

- Thoreau often combines plain statements with **figures of speech**—imaginative comparisons that engage the thinking of his readers:
  In the midst of this chopping sea of civilized life, such are the clouds and storms and quicksands . . .

- By using **analogy,** or extended comparison, Thoreau highlights related ideas or explains the unfamiliar in terms of the familiar:
  Our life is like a German Confederacy, made up of petty states, with its boundary forever fluctuating . . .

Other devices that contribute to Thoreau's conversational style include **direct address of the reader** (*Let your affairs be as two or three*), **brief anecdotes** (short, illustrative stories, like that of the Hollowell Place), and **pithy statements** (wise and concise statements—*we do not ride upon the railroad; it rides upon us*).

Read It

1. Work individually. In a sentence or two, explain how each underlined part of this passage from *Walden* contributes to Thoreau's conversational style and to his overall point. Then, meet with your group to compare your responses.

> Moreover, <u>if you are restricted in your range by poverty,</u> if you cannot buy books and newspapers, for instance, you are but confined to the most significant and vital experiences; you are compelled to deal with the material <u>which yields the most sugar and the most starch</u>. <u>It is life near the bone where it is sweetest</u>.

2. **Connect to Style** Reread paragraph 13 of the excerpt from *Walden*. Mark and then label two words or phrases that contribute to Thoreau's conversational style.

3. 📓 **Notebook** In a sentence or two, explain why a conversational style might be especially useful for a philosophical writer such as Thoreau.

Write It

📓 **Notebook** Write a paragraph-long review of the excerpt from "Civil Disobedience." Create a conversational style in your review by using some of the techniques discussed above.

▤ STANDARDS

Reading Informational Text
Determine an author's point of view or purpose in a text in which the rhetoric is particularly effective, analyzing how style and content contribute to the power, persuasiveness, or beauty of the text.

Speaking and Listening

Assignment

With your group, hold a **discussion** in which you respond to these excerpts from Thoreau's philosophical writings. Choose from the following options:

☐ Brainstorm for a **list** of current or past events in which citizens have followed Thoreau's advice in "Civil Disobedience" to stand up and *make known what kind of government would command [their] respect.* Explain your reasons for including each example.

☐ Prepare a **response** to this statement adapted from Thoreau: *It is always better to march to the beat of one's own drummer.* Take turns offering and supporting your opinions.

☐ Formulate a **prosecution** or a **defense** of Thoreau's decision to withhold payment of his taxes. Marshal evidence and reasons to support your perspective, making sure that you deal directly with Thoreau's rationale for civil disobedience.

Finding Evidence Most of the evidence you will use during this discussion should come from Thoreau's writings. However, you may need additional information to have a lively conversation. This decision will depend on the topic you have chosen to discuss. For example, you may need to conduct some research about American or world history, or U.S. tax laws.

Holding the Discussion Make sure that everyone has a chance to speak and to express opinions that are supported with evidence from the text or from related research. If questions emerge from your discussion, decide together how you will locate the answers.

Considering All Responses Philosophical ideas can generate a wide variety of responses—and that can make a discussion exciting. Be open to the idea that many interpretations can be valid.

Asking Questions Get in the habit of asking questions to clarify your understanding of another reader's ideas. You can also use questions to call attention to areas of confusion, debatable points, or errors. In addition, offer elaboration on the points that others make by providing examples. To move a discussion forward, summarize and evaluate tentative conclusions reached by the group members.

Notes:

✎ EVIDENCE LOG

Before moving on to a new selection, go to your Evidence Log and record what you learned from the excerpts from *Walden* and "Civil Disobedience."

≣ STANDARDS

Speaking and Listening
• Work with peers to promote civil and democratic discussions and decision-making, set clear goals and deadlines, and establish individual roles as needed.
• Propel conversations by posing and responding to questions that probe reasoning and evidence; ensure a hearing for a full range of positions on a topic or issue; clarify, verify, or challenge ideas and conclusions; and promote divergent and creative perspectives.
• Respond thoughtfully to diverse perspectives; synthesize comments, claims, and evidence made on all sides of an issue; resolve contradictions when possible; and determine what additional information or research is required to deepen the investigation or complete the task.

About Technical Drawings

Some public documents include **technical drawings,** which are scale diagrams that show how something is constructed or how it functions. Individual inventors often create technical drawings to explain their innovations to a wider audience. Multiple views, including close-up details of key parts, are usually required to fully illustrate a new invention. When applying for a **patent**—the exclusive right to sell a product—inventors include technical drawings that show each important part in detail.

Innovators and Their Inventions

Media Vocabulary

These words will be useful to you as you analyze, discuss, and write about visual public documents and the text features that they contain.

Specifications: section of a patent application in which the inventor fully describes the invention	• Specifications include both verbal descriptions and detailed diagrams that illustrate the invention's parts and functions. • Patent specifications come before the claims, in which the applicant defines the scope of protection being requested (such as the right to prevent others from selling the invention).
Cross-section: view of a three-dimensional object that shows the interior as if a cut has been made across the object	• A cross-section shows the parts inside a solid shape, revealing details that are not visible from the outside. • Labels or callouts may identify parts revealed within. • Details are shown using an exact scale, or ratio that compares the size of the illustration with the actual size of the invention.
Figure: one of a set of drawings or illustrations	• Figures are usually given consecutive numbers or letters so they can be referred to in accompanying text. • The term is often abbreviated as *fig.*

First Review MEDIA: PUBLIC DOCUMENT

Apply these strategies as you conduct your first review. You will have an opportunity to complete a close review after your first review.

LOOK at each image and determine *whom* or *what* it portrays.

NOTE elements in each image that you find interesting and want to revisit.

CONNECT details in the images to other media you've experienced, texts you've read, or images you've seen.

RESPOND by completing the Comprehension Check.

First Review

Innovators and Their Inventions

BACKGROUND

A patent documents the government's recognition that a person has invented something. Nobody else is allowed to make, use, or sell that invention without the inventor's permission until the patent expires. The federal government has been issuing patents, including those for the inventions discussed here, since George Washington signed the Patent Act of 1790.

SCAN FOR MULTIMEDIA

IMAGE 1: Diagram of Telephone Components Alexander Graham Bell was born in Scotland, but he did his most famous work as a scientist and inventor in the United States. After many years of experimenting with sound—specifically, how sound could be transmitted electrically—Bell filed a patent for the telephone on February 14, 1876. On the same day, another inventor, Elisha Gray, also submitted a claim that he had invented the telephone. The controversy was settled when Bell received the patent for the telephone, now considered one of the most valuable patents in the world.

NOTES

IMAGE 2: Mary Anderson's Window-Cleaning Device Patent applications often include detailed images to clarify the design and use of the device in the application. This image is a diagram of the first windshield wiper, patented by Mary Anderson. It is operated by pulling a lever inside of the vehicle. Before her invention, drivers would reach out and wipe down windshields by hand— sometimes stopping the vehicle to do so, and sometimes doing so while driving.

NOTES

Comprehension Check

Complete the following items after you finish your first review. Review and clarify details with your group.

1. In the technical drawings of Bell's telephone, which components are labeled 2 and 3?

2. In Figure 4 of the telephone components, what do the labels lettered *a* to *e* name?

3. According to information included on the diagrams of the window-cleaning device, when did Anderson apply for this patent, and when was it awarded?

4. In Figure 2 of the diagrams for the window-cleaning device, what is part A?

- -

RESEARCH

Research to Clarify Choose at least one unfamiliar element in the technical drawings. Briefly research that element. In what way does the information you learned shed light on an aspect of the drawings or on the work of inventing a new technology?

Research to Explore These technical drawings might make you curious about the patent application process. Find out what a patent application includes, where it is filed, who determines whether the patent is granted, and how that decision is made. You may want to share what you discover with your group.

INNOVATORS AND THEIR
INVENTIONS

Close Review

With your group, revisit the technical drawings and your first-review notes. Write down any new observations that seem important. What **questions** do you have? What can you **conclude**?

Analyze the Media

CITE TEXTUAL EVIDENCE
to support your answers.

📝 **Notebook** Complete the activities.

1. **Present and Discuss** Choose the drawing you find more interesting or informative. Share your choice with the group and discuss why you chose it. Explain what you noticed in the drawing, what questions it raised for you, and what conclusions you reached about it.

2. **Review and Synthesize** With your group, review both technical drawings. How do they provide information about the inventions they illustrate? What do the drawings alone tell you about how these inventions work? What information might accompanying text provide that would help you understand each device's function?

3. **Essential Question:** *What role does individualism play in American society?* What have these public documents taught you about the role that innovative individuals play in society? Discuss with your group.

Media Vocabulary

specifications	cross-section	figure

Use these words as you discuss and write about the technical drawings.

1. Why is it useful to have more than one technical drawing of an early telephone to understand the parts of this invention, as well as its origins?

2. In addition to the drawings shown here, what information did Anderson probably include in her patent application for a window-cleaning device? Explain.

3. Both drawings include multiple views of the invention. Why are multiple views needed to show how something works?

TIP

GROUP DISCUSSION
Begin your discussion of the technical drawings by reviewing all titles, captions, and labels as a group. Refer to the labels to make sure each group member is looking at the same image or part during the discussion.

≣ STANDARDS

Speaking and Listening
Present information, findings, and supporting evidence, conveying a clear and distinct perspective, such that listeners can follow the line of reasoning, alternative or opposing perspectives are addressed, and the organization, development, substance, and style are appropriate to purpose, audience, and a range of formal and informal tasks.

Speaking and Listening

Assignment

Consider this question with your group: How have each of the two inventions pictured in these public documents affected people's lives in different ways? Then, discuss other inventions that have changed people's lives. Consider surprising inventions, such as sticky notes, as well as more obvious ones. Decide which invention of all the ones you discussed has had the greatest impact on society. Then, write a one-minute **speech** in which you state and support your position. Deliver your speech to the class.

Choose a Position Begin to answer the question by considering as many impacts as possible. Ask yourselves how life would be different without each invention. Collect your thoughts in a chart.

	INVENTION	INVENTION	INVENTION
Use and function			
Importance			

Plan Your Argument After you have determined your position, plan your speech. Begin with a strong statement of your claim about the impact of the invention you chose, and then provide support. Aim to include at least three ideas that support your position. Finally, end your speech with a conclusion that restates your claim.

PLAN YOUR ARGUMENT
Claim:
Support: 1. 2. 3.
Conclusion:

Present Your Speech and Debate Deliver your speeches, and have your classmates score them. After the initial speeches, allow time for discussion, in which students compare their positions and make some generalizations about the impact of technical innovation on society.

EVIDENCE LOG

Before moving on to a new selection, go to your Evidence Log and record what you learned from "Innovators and Their Inventions."

The Love Song of J. Alfred Prufrock

Concept Vocabulary

As you perform your first read of "The Love Song of J. Alfred Prufrock," you will encounter these words.

tedious	indecisions	digress

Context Clues Use **context clues** to find the meanings of unfamiliar words in a text. Context clues include the words, punctuation, and images that surround an unknown word.

> **Example:** "the evening, sleeps so peacefully! / Smoothed by long, fingers. / Asleep . . . tired . . . or it *malingers,* / Stretched on the floor, here beside you and me."
>
> **Context clues:** The word *malingers* appears to be related to "asleep," "tired," and "stretched on the floor," but the word *or* suggests that it's not quite sleep.
>
> **Possible meaning:** *Malinger*s may mean "lazes about, sleepily."

Apply your knowledge of context clues and other vocabulary strategies to determine the meanings of unfamiliar words you encounter during your first read.

First Read POETRY

Apply these strategies as you conduct your first read. You will have an opportunity to complete a close read after your first read.

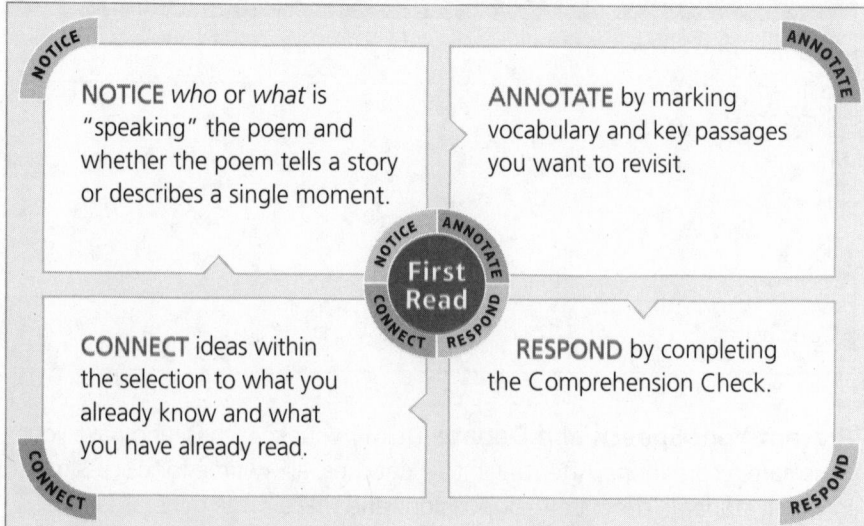

NOTICE *who* or *what* is "speaking" the poem and whether the poem tells a story or describes a single moment.

ANNOTATE by marking vocabulary and key passages you want to revisit.

CONNECT ideas within the selection to what you already know and what you have already read.

RESPOND by completing the Comprehension Check.

First Read

:::: STANDARDS

Reading Literature
By the end of grade 11, read and comprehend literature, including stories, dramas, and poems, in the grades 11–CCR text complexity band proficiently, with scaffolding as needed at the high end of the range.

Language
Use context as a clue to the meaning of a word or phrase.

About the Poet

T. S. Eliot

T. S. Eliot (1888–1965) was born into a wealthy family in St. Louis and grew up in an environment that promoted intellectual development. He attended Harvard University, where he published a number of poems in the school's literary magazine. In 1910, the year Eliot received his master's degree in philosophy, he completed "The Love Song of J. Alfred Prufrock."

A Literary Sensation Just before the outbreak of World War I, Eliot moved to England, where he became acquainted with Ezra Pound, another young American poet. Pound convinced Harriet Monroe, the editor of *Poetry* magazine, to publish "Prufrock." Shortly thereafter, Eliot published a collection entitled *Prufrock and Other Observations* (1917). Eliot's use of innovative poetic techniques and his focus on the despair of modern urban life caused a sensation in the literary world.

Facing a New World Eliot made his literary mark against the backdrop of a rapidly changing society. Disillusioned with the ideologies that produced the devastation of World War I, many people were searching for new ideas and values. Eliot was among a group of such writers and visual artists who called themselves Modernists. Modernist poets believed that poetry had to reflect the genuine, fractured experience of life in the twentieth century, not a romanticized idea of what life was once like.

In 1922, Eliot published *The Waste Land*, a profound critique of the spiritual barrenness of the modern world. Filled with allusions to classics of world literature and to Eastern culture and religion, it was widely read and greatly affected writers and critics.

A Return to Tradition In his search for something beyond the "waste land" of modern society, Eliot became a member of the Church of England in 1927. He began to explore religious themes in poems such as "Ash Wednesday" (1930) and *Four Quartets* (1943)— works that suggest a belief that religion can heal the wounds inflicted by society. In later years, Eliot wrote several plays and a sizable body of literary criticism. In 1948, he received the Nobel Prize in Literature.

Background

The Love Song of J. Alfred Prufrock

In this poem, J. Alfred Prufrock, a stuffy and inhibited man who is pained by his own passivity, invites the reader, or some unnamed visitor, to join him on a journey. Where Prufrock is and where he is going are open to debate. The most important part of this journey takes place within the inner landscape of Prufrock's emotions, memory, and intellect as he meditates on his life.

The Love Song
of J. Alfred Prufrock

T. S. Eliot

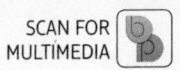
S'io credessi che mia risposta fosse
a persona che mai tornasse al mondo,
questa fiamma staria senza più scosse.
Ma per ciò che giammai di questo fondo
non tornò vivo alcun, s'i'odo il vero,
senza tema d'infamia ti rispondo.[1]

NOTES

Let us go then, you and I,
When the evening is spread out against the sky
Like a patient etherized[2] upon a table;
Let us go, through certain half-deserted streets,
5 The muttering retreats
Of restless nights in one-night cheap hotels
And sawdust restaurants with oyster-shells:
Streets that follow like a **tedious** argument
Of insidious intent
10 To lead you to an overwhelming question . . .
Oh, do not ask, "What is it?"
Let us go and make our visit.

In the room the women come and go
Talking of Michelangelo.[3]

15 The yellow fog that rubs its back upon the window-panes,
The yellow smoke that rubs its muzzle on the window-panes,
Licked its tongue into the corners of the evening,
Lingered upon the pools that stand in drains,
Let fall upon its back the soot that falls from chimneys,
20 Slipped by the terrace, made a sudden leap,
And seeing that it was a soft October night,
Curled once about the house, and fell asleep.

And indeed there will be time[4]
For the yellow smoke that slides along the street
25 Rubbing its back upon the window-panes;
There will be time, there will be time
To prepare a face to meet the faces that you meet;
There will be time to murder and create,
And time for all the works and days[5] of hands

> Mark context clues or indicate another strategy you used that helped you determine meaning.
>
> **tedious** (TEE dee uhs) *adj.*
>
> MEANING:

1. ***S'io credessi . . . ti rispondo*** This epigraph is a passage from Dante's *Inferno*, in which one of the damned, upon being asked to tell his story, says, "If I believed my answer were being given to someone who could ever return to the world, this flame [his voice] would shake no more. But since no one has ever returned alive from this depth, if what I hear is true, I will answer you without fear of disgrace."
2. **etherized** (EE thuh ryzd) *adj.* anesthetized with ether.
3. **Michelangelo** (my kuhl AN juh loh) famous Italian artist and sculptor (1475–1564).
4. **there will be time** These words echo the speaker's plea in the English poet Andrew Marvell's "To His Coy Mistress": "Had we but world enough and time . . . "
5. **works and days** The ancient Greek poet Hesiod wrote a poem about farming called "Works and Days."

Mark context clues or indicate another strategy you used that helped you determine meaning.

indecisions (ihn dee SIHZH uhnz) *n.*

MEANING:

30 That lift and drop a question on your plate;
Time for you and time for me,
And time yet for a hundred **indecisions**,
And for a hundred visions and revisions.
Before the taking of a toast and tea.

35 In the room the women come and go
Talking of Michelangelo.

And indeed there will be time
To wonder, "Do I dare?" and, "Do I dare?"
Time to turn back and descend the stair,
40 With a bald spot in the middle of my hair—
(They will say: "How his hair is growing thin!")
My morning coat, my collar mounting firmly to the chin,
My necktie rich and modest, but asserted by a simple pin—
(They will say: "But how his arms and legs are thin!")
45 Do I dare
Disturb the universe?
In a minute there is time
For decisions and revisions which a minute will reverse.

For I have known them all already, known them all—
50 Have known the evenings, mornings, afternoons,
I have measured out my life with coffee spoons;
I know the voices dying with a dying fall
Beneath the music from a farther room.
So how should I presume?

55 And I have known the eyes already, known them all—
The eyes that fix you in a formulated phrase,
And when I am formulated, sprawling on a pin,
When I am pinned and wriggling on the wall,
Then how should I begin
60 To spit out all the butt-ends of my days and ways?
And how should I presume?

And I have known the arms already, known them all—
Arms that are braceleted and white and bare
(But in the lamplight, downed with light brown hair!)
65 Is it perfume from a dress
That makes me so **digress**?
Arms that lie along a table, or wrap about a shawl.
And should I then presume?
And how should I begin?

Mark context clues or indicate another strategy you used that helped you determine meaning.

digress (dih GREHS) *v.*

MEANING:

⌘ ⌘ ⌘

70 Shall I say, I have gone at dusk through narrow streets
And watched the smoke that rises from the pipes
Of lonely men in shirt-sleeves, leaning out of windows? . . .

I should have been a pair of ragged claws
Scuttling across the floors of silent seas.[6]

✥ ✥ ✥

75 And the afternoon, the evening, sleeps so peacefully!
Smoothed by long fingers,
Asleep . . . tired . . . or it malingers,
Stretched on the floor, here beside you and me.
Should I, after tea and cakes and ices,
80 Have the strength to force the moment to its crisis?
But though I have wept and fasted, wept and prayed,
Though I have seen my head (grown slightly bald) brought in
        upon a platter,[7]
I am no prophet—and here's no great matter;
I have seen the moment of my greatness flicker,
85 And I have seen the eternal Footman[8] hold my coat, and snicker.
And in short, I was afraid.

And would it have been worth it, after all,
After the cups, the marmalade, the tea,
Among the porcelain, among some talk of you and me,
90 Would it have been worth while,
To have bitten off the matter with a smile,
To have squeezed the universe into a ball
To roll it towards some overwhelming question.
To say: "I am Lazarus,[9] come from the dead,
95 Come back to tell you all. I shall tell you all"—
If one, settling a pillow by her head,
        Should say: "That is not what I meant at all.
        That is not it, at all."

And would it have been worth it, after all,
100 Would it have been worth while,
After the sunsets and the dooryards and the sprinkled streets,
After the novels, after the teacups, after the skirts that trail
        along the floor—
And this, and so much more?—

---

6. **I should . . . seas** In Shakespeare's *Hamlet,* the hero, Hamlet, mocks the aging Lord
   Chamberlain, Polonius, saying, "You yourself, sir, should be old as I am, if like a crab you
   could go backward" (II. ii. 205–206).
7. **head . . . platter** a reference to the prophet John the Baptist, whose head was delivered
   on a platter to Salome as a reward for her dancing (Matthew 14:1–11).
8. **eternal Footman** death.
9. **Lazarus** (LAZ uh ruhs) Lazarus is resurrected from the dead by Jesus in John 11:1–44.

It is impossible to say just what I mean!
105 But as if a magic lantern[10] threw the nerves in patterns
    on a screen:
Would it have been worth while
If one, settling a pillow or throwing off a shawl,
And turning toward the window, should say:
    "That is not it at all,
110 That is not what I meant, at all."

⌘ ⌘ ⌘

No! I am not Prince Hamlet, nor was meant to be;
Am an attendant lord, one that will do
To swell a progress,[11] start a scene or two,
Advise the prince; no doubt, an easy tool,
115 Deferential, glad to be of use,
Politic, cautious, and meticulous;
Full of high sentence,[12] but a bit obtuse;
At times, indeed, almost ridiculous—
Almost, at times, the Fool.

120 I grow old . . . I grow old . . .
I shall wear the bottoms of my trousers rolled.

Shall I part my hair behind? Do I dare to eat a peach?
I shall wear white flannel trousers, and walk upon the beach.
I have heard the mermaids singing, each to each.

125 I do not think that they will sing to me.

I have seen them riding seaward on the waves
Combing the white hair of the waves blown back
When the wind blows the water white and black.

We have lingered in the chambers of the sea
130 By sea-girls wreathed with seaweed red and brown
Till human voices wake us, and we drown.

---

10. **magic lantern** early device used to project images on a screen.
11. **To swell a progress** to add to the number of people in a parade or scene from a play.
12. **Full of high sentence** speaking in a very ornate manner, often offering advice.

Comprehension Check

Complete the following items after you finish your first read. Review and clarify details with your group.

1. At what time of day are the opening lines of the poem set?

2. In the opening stanza, Prufrock invites someone to go with him. Describe the place he plans to visit.

3. What atmospheric condition does Prufrock describe in lines 15–25?

4. Name three questions that Prufrock asks himself.

5. Whom does Prufrock say he has heard singing "each to each"?

6. 📓 **Notebook** Confirm your understanding by drawing an illustration of one or more key moments from the poem.

- -

RESEARCH

Research to Clarify Choose at least one unfamiliar detail from the text. Briefly research that detail. In what way does the information you learned shed light on an aspect of the poem?

Research to Explore Find out more about Modernism, the artistic movement embraced by Eliot and other early-twentieth-century writers and artists. Find out how this movement broke with the past—and how the work of its pioneers was received at the time.

THE LOVE SONG OF
J. ALFRED PRUFROCK

Close Read the Text

With your group, revisit sections of the text you marked during your first read. **Annotate** details that you notice. What **questions** do you have? What can you **conclude?**

Analyze the Text

CITE TEXTUAL EVIDENCE
to support your answers.

Complete the activities.

1. **Review and Clarify** With your group, reread lines 1–12 of the poem. The speaker of the poem, J. Alfred Prufrock, invites someone to join him on a journey. What is unusual about his invitation? Is it likely to be accepted? Why or why not?

2. **Present and Discuss** Now, work with your group to share the passages from the poem that you found especially important. Take turns presenting your passages. Discuss what you noticed in the selection, what questions you asked, and what conclusions you reached.

3. **Essential Question:** *What role does individualism play in American society?* What has this poem taught you about the individual and society? Discuss with your group.

Concept Vocabulary

tedious	indecisions	digress

Why These Words? The three concept vocabulary words from the text are related. With your group, discuss the words and determine what they have in common. How do these word choices enhance the impact of the poem?

Practice

⬛ **Notebook** Confirm your understanding of the concept vocabulary words by answering these questions. Use the vocabulary word in your answer.

1. Would you like to have a *tedious* conversation? Explain.

2. How can *indecisions* affect someone's efficiency?

3. What are some signs that a speaker is beginning to *digress*?

Word Study

Latin Prefix: *di-* / *dis-* The Latin prefix *di-* or *dis-* means "not" or "away." This prefix (not to be confused with the Greek prefix *di-*, meaning "two") occurs in many common English words, as well as in some mathematical and scientific terms.

1. Write the meaning of the mathematical term *diverge*.

2. Write the meaning of the scientific term *dilate*.

Use a dictionary to confirm your definitions for both words.

TIP

GROUP DISCUSSION

When discussing poetry, begin by reading a passage for sense. Follow the sentence structure and identify the subject and verb, if necessary. After your group understands the basic meaning, continue your analysis by looking at the poetic techniques, such as rhythm and rhyme, imagery, and figurative language.

⬡ WORD NETWORK

Add words related to individualism from the text to your Word Network.

⬚ STANDARDS

Reading Literature
• Analyze how an author's choices concerning how to structure specific parts of a text contribute to its overall structure and meaning as well as its aesthetic impact.
• Analyze a case in which grasping point of view requires distinguishing what is directly stated in a text from what is really meant.

Language
Identify and correctly use patterns of word changes that indicate different meanings or parts of speech.

Analyze Craft and Structure

Poetic Structure A troubled J. Alfred Prufrock invites an unidentified companion, perhaps a part of his own personality, to walk with him as he considers how life and love are passing him by. His so-called love song is a **dramatic monologue,** a poem or speech in which a character addresses a silent listener. Images, dialogue, and other details reveal Prufrock's inner conflicts as he continues through his evening.

Prufrock is the **speaker,** or voice of the poem. Details reflect his **point of view,** the perspective or vantage point from which the monologue is told. To understand the speaker's point of view, consider details that describe the following elements:

- *Physical Traits:* What words does Prufrock use to describe his own appearance? How do others perceive him—or how does Prufrock feel he is perceived?

- *Emotional Traits:* What is Prufrock's overall mood? Which details reveal that mood?

- *Verbal Traits:* What is the speaker's unique way of talking? When Prufrock repeats himself, what kinds of things does he say? How does this reflect his values or preoccupations?

Practice

CITE TEXTUAL EVIDENCE to support your answers.

1. **(a)** Work together to complete the chart. Identify details that reveal Prufrock's personal qualities. **(b)** What do these details suggest about Prufrock's view of himself and life as a whole?

PHYSICAL TRAITS	EMOTIONAL TRAITS	VERBAL TRAITS

2. **(a)** How can the first line of the poem be interpreted to suggest that Prufrock sees himself as divided, both seeking and fearing action? **(b)** At what other points does he express a deeply conflicted sense of self?

3. **(a)** In lines 49–54, what image does Prufrock use to describe how he has "measured out" his life? **(b)** In your own words, explain how Prufrock has lived.

THE LOVE SONG OF
J. ALFRED PRUFROCK

Conventions and Style

Compound Nouns Eliot uses many compound nouns in "The Love Song of J. Alfred Prufrock," including some that he invented just for use in this poem. A **compound noun** is a noun that is made with two or more words. In a **closed compound,** there is no space between the words. In a **hyphenated compound,** a hyphen separates the words.

CLOSED COMPOUNDS	HYPHENATED COMPOUNDS
From "Prufrock":	**From "Prufrock":**
necktie	oyster-shells
afternoons	window-panes
lamplight	shirt-sleeves
Other examples:	**Other examples:**
basketball	brother-in-law
sunrise	house-builder
keyboard	six-year-old

Closed compounds are words that have been long accepted as single nouns. Hyphenated compounds often are newer forms, or words that are used less frequently.

Hyphens may be used to join words and avoid ambiguity. In some cases, hyphens are not required but are a matter of style. For example, Prufrock describes mermaids as "sea-girls." Eliot could have presented the phrase without a hyphen: "sea girls." By creating an original, hyphenated noun, Eliot may be suggesting Prufrock's skill with words, his need to categorize and classify, or his precise nature.

Read It

Mark the compound nouns in these sentences. Identify each one as closed or hyphenated.

1. Prufrock hears a conversation among women who seem to be partygoers.

2. He worries that he has spent his lifetime focused on trivial, unimportant matters.

3. The speaker's walk-through at nighttime seems to take place in isolation, without passers-by or companions other than the unnamed listener.

4. Prufrock's digressions might suggest daydreaming or woolgathering, but the precise way he presents his word-pictures makes that unlikely.

Write It

⊟ **Notebook** Write four sentences that include compound nouns. Include at least one compound noun that is not commonly used. Decide whether your new compound noun will be closed or hyphenated, and explain your reasoning.

☷ STANDARDS

Speaking and Listening
Make strategic use of digital media in presentations to enhance understanding of findings, reasoning, and evidence and to add interest.

Language
• Demonstrate command of the conventions of standard English grammar and usage when writing or speaking.
• Observe hyphenation conventions.

Writing to Sources

Assignment

With your group, create a **digital presentation** that explains, amplifies, or extends key ideas about J. Alfred Prufrock's worldview. Choose from these options:

- [ ] a **slide show** that presents images reflecting phrases from the poem or your mental picture of Prufrock, accompanied by appropriate music

- [ ] an **oral recitation and discussion** in which readers recite important lines from the poem and then discuss how those lines reflect Prufrock's character and concerns

- [ ] a **filmed oral response** in which group members share their reactions to the poem by citing specific lines and explaining their meaning and effect

Project Plan Work with your group to plan your digital presentation. Use this chart to determine how you will integrate content and media elements, including audio and visual materials. Also, consider how you will organize your presentation to include a strong introduction, a complete body, and an effective conclusion. Choose transitions that will make the organization of your presentation clear.

EVIDENCE LOG

Before moving on to a new selection, go to your Evidence Log and record what you learned from "The Love Song of J. Alfred Prufrock."

PART	CONTENT		MEDIA	
	Ideas	Related lines from Eliot's poem	Visual	Audio
Introduction				
Transition				
Body				
Transition				
Conclusion				

About the Author

As a child, **Willa Cather** (1873–1947) moved from her birthplace in Virginia to the Nebraska frontier, where many of her neighbors were immigrant farmers. Cather went on to receive a college degree, work as an editor at a Pittsburgh newspaper, and become a full-time writer in New York City. Still, it was prairie life that inspired many of her best-known works, including *O! Pioneers, My Ántonia,* and *One of Ours,* which won the Pulitzer Prize in 1923.

A Wagner Matinée

Concept Vocabulary

As you perform your first read of "A Wagner Matinée," you will encounter these words.

> overture   motifs   prelude

Familiar Word Parts When you come to an unfamiliar word in a text, see whether the word contains any familiar word parts you can use to determine the word's meaning. A familiar word part may be a prefix, a suffix, a base word, or a root. Consider this example of the strategy:

> **Unfamiliar Word:** *physiognomy*
>
> **Word in Context:** The most striking thing about her *physiognomy,* however, was an incessant twitching of the mouth and eyebrows, . . .
>
> **Familiar Word Part:** the root -*phys-,* which appears in words such as *physical* and *physician*
>
> **Conclusion:** *Physiognomy* has a meaning related to a person's body. Context clues, such as "incessant twitching," support that assumption. You can then verify the meaning in a reliable dictionary.

Apply your knowledge of familiar word parts and other vocabulary strategies to determine the meanings of unfamiliar words you encounter during your first read.

First Read FICTION

Apply these strategies as you conduct your first read. You will have an opportunity to complete a close read after your first read.

NOTICE *whom* the story is about, *what* happens, *where* and *when* it happens, and *why* those involved react as they do.

ANNOTATE by marking vocabulary and key passages you want to revisit.

First Read

CONNECT ideas within the selection to what you already know and what you have already read.

RESPOND by completing the Comprehension Check and by writing a brief summary of the selection.

STANDARDS

Reading Literature
By the end of grade 11, read and comprehend literature, including stories, dramas, and poems, in the grades 11–CCR text complexity band proficiently, with scaffolding as needed at the high end of the range.

Language
Identify and correctly use patterns of word changes that indicate different meanings or parts of speech.

A Wagner Matinée

Willa Cather

BACKGROUND

Richard Wagner was one of the nineteenth century's great composers. His operas are characterized by adventurous harmonies and an innovative blend of music and drama. To many, Wagner's music represents the idea of high culture. In this story, Cather contrasts the stark realities of frontier life with life in a more cultured world.

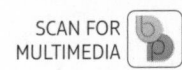

SCAN FOR MULTIMEDIA

NOTES

1   I received one morning a letter written in pale ink, on glassy, blue-lined notepaper, and bearing the postmark of a little Nebraska village. This communication, worn and rubbed, looking as though it had been carried for some days in a coat pocket that was none too clean, was from my Uncle Howard. It informed me that his wife had been left a small legacy by a bachelor relative who had recently died, and that it had become necessary for her to come to Boston to attend to the settling of the estate. He requested me to meet her at the station, and render her whatever services might prove necessary. On examining the date indicated as that of her arrival, I found it no later than tomorrow. He had characteristically delayed writing until, had I been away from home for a day, I must have missed the good woman altogether.

2   The name of my Aunt Georgiana called up not alone her own figure, at once pathetic and grotesque, but opened before my feet a gulf of recollections so wide and deep that, as the letter dropped from my hand, I felt suddenly a stranger to all the present conditions of my existence, wholly ill at ease and out of place amid the surroundings of my study. I became, in short, the gangling farmer boy my aunt had known, scourged with chilblains and bashfulness, my hands cracked and raw from the corn husking. I felt the knuckles of my thumb tentatively, as though they were raw again. I sat again before her parlor organ, thumbing the scales with my stiff, red hands, while she beside me made canvas mittens for the huskers.

3   The next morning, after preparing my landlady somewhat, I set out for the station. When the train arrived I had some difficulty in finding my aunt. She was the last of the passengers to alight, and when I got her into the carriage she looked not unlike one of those charred, smoked bodies that firemen lift from the *débris* of a burned building. She had come all the way in a day coach; her linen duster[1] had become black with soot and her black bonnet gray with dust during the journey. When we arrived at my boardinghouse the landlady put her to bed at once, and I did not see her again until the next morning.

4   Whatever shock Mrs. Springer experienced at my aunt's appearance she considerately concealed. Myself, I saw my aunt's misshapen figure with that feeling of awe and respect with which we behold explorers who have left their ears and fingers north of Franz Josef Land,[2] or their health somewhere along the upper Congo.[3] My Aunt Georgiana had been a music teacher at the Boston Conservatory, somewhere back in the latter sixties. One summer, which she had spent in the little village in the Green Mountains[4] where her ancestors had dwelt for generations, she had kindled the callow[5] fancy of the most idle and shiftless of all the village lads, and had conceived for this Howard Carpenter one of those absurd and extravagant passions which a handsome country boy of twenty-one sometimes inspires in a plain, angular, spectacled woman of thirty. When she returned to her duties in Boston, Howard followed her; and the upshot of this inexplicable infatuation was that she eloped with him, eluding the reproaches of her family and the criticism of her friends by going with him to the Nebraska frontier. Carpenter, who of course had no money, took a homestead in Red Willow County,[6] fifty miles from the railroad. There they measured off their eighty acres by driving across the prairie in a wagon, to the wheel of which they had tied a red cotton handkerchief, and counting its revolutions. They built a dugout in the red hillside, one of those

---

1. **duster** *n.* short, loose smock worn while traveling to protect clothing from dust.
2. **Franz Josef Land** group of islands in the Arctic Ocean.
3. **Congo** river in central Africa.
4. **Green Mountains** mountains in Vermont.
5. **callow** (KAL oh) *adj.* immature; inexperienced.
6. **Red Willow County** county in southwestern Nebraska that borders on Kansas.

cave dwellings whose inmates usually reverted to the conditions of primitive savagery. Their water they got from the lagoons where the buffalo drank, and their slender stock of provisions was always at the mercy of bands of roving Indians. For thirty years my aunt had not been farther than fifty miles from the homestead.

5   But Mrs. Springer knew nothing of all this, and must have been considerably shocked at what was left of my kinswoman. Beneath the soiled linen duster, which on her arrival was the most conspicuous feature of her costume, she wore a black stuff dress whose ornamentation showed that she had surrendered herself unquestioningly into the hands of a country dressmaker. My poor aunt's figure, however, would have presented astonishing difficulties to any dressmaker. Her skin was yellow from constant exposure to a pitiless wind, and to the alkaline water which transforms the most transparent cuticle into a sort of flexible leather. She wore ill-fitting false teeth. The most striking thing about her physiognomy, however, was an incessant twitching of the mouth and eyebrows, a form of nervous disorder resulting from isolation and monotony, and from frequent physical suffering.

6   In my boyhood this affliction had possessed a sort of horrible fascination for me, of which I was secretly very much ashamed, for in those days I owed to this woman most of the good that ever came my way, and had a reverential affection for her. During the three winters when I was riding herd for my uncle, my aunt, after cooking three meals for half a dozen farmhands, and putting the six children to bed, would often stand until midnight at her ironing board, hearing me at the kitchen table beside her recite Latin declensions and conjugations, and gently shaking me when my drowsy head sank down over a page of irregular verbs. It was to her, at her ironing or mending, that I read my first Shakespeare; and her old textbook of mythology was the first that ever came into my empty hands. She taught me my scales and exercises, too, on the little parlor organ which her husband had bought her after fifteen years, during which she had not so much as seen any instrument except an accordion, that belonged to one of the Norwegian farmhands. She would sit beside me by the hour, darning and counting, while I struggled with the "Harmonious Blacksmith"; but she seldom talked to me about music, and I understood why. She was a pious woman; she had the consolation of religion; and to her at least her martyrdom was not wholly sordid. Once when I had been doggedly beating out some passages from an old score of "Euryanthe" I had found among her music books, she came up to me and, putting her hands over my eyes, gently drew my head back upon her shoulder, saying tremulously, "Don't love it so well, Clark, or it may be taken from you. Oh! dear boy, pray that whatever your sacrifice be it is not that."

7   When my aunt appeared on the morning after her arrival, she was still in a semi-somnambulant[7] state. She seemed not to realize that

---

7. **semi-somnambulant** (SEHM ee som NAM byuh luhnt) *adj.* resembling a sleepwalker.

she was in the city where she had spent her youth, the place longed for hungrily for half a lifetime. She had been so wretchedly trainsick throughout the journey that she had no recollection of anything but her discomfort, and, to all intents and purposes, there were but a few hours of nightmare between the farm in Red Willow County and my study on Newbury Street. I had planned a little pleasure for her that afternoon, to repay her for some of the glorious moments she had given me when we used to milk together in the straw-thatched cowshed, and she, because I was more than usually tired, or because her husband had spoken sharply to me, would tell me of the splendid performance of Meyerbeer's *Les Huguenots*[8] she had seen in Paris in her youth. At two o'clock the Boston Symphony Orchestra was to give a Wagner program, and I intended to take my aunt, though as I conversed with her I grew doubtful about her enjoyment of it. Indeed, for her own sake, I could only wish her taste for such things quite dead, and the long struggle mercifully ended at last. I suggested our visiting the Conservatory and the Common[9] before lunch, but she seemed altogether too timid to wish to venture out. She questioned me absently about various changes in the city, but she was chiefly concerned that she had forgotten to leave instructions about feeding half-skimmed milk to a certain weakling calf, "Old Maggie's calf, you know, Clark," she explained, evidently having forgotten how long I had been away. She was further troubled because she had neglected to tell her daughter about the freshly opened kit of mackerel in the cellar, that would spoil if it were not used directly.

8   I asked her whether she had ever heard any of the Wagnerian operas, and found that she had not, though she was perfectly familiar with their respective situations and had once possessed the piano score of *The Flying Dutchman*. I began to think it would have been best to get her back to Red Willow County without waking her, and regretted having suggested the concert.

9   From the time we entered the concert hall, however, she was a trifle less passive and inert, and seemed to begin to perceive her surroundings. I had felt some trepidation[10] lest one might become aware of the absurdities of her attire, or might experience some painful embarrassment at stepping suddenly into the world to which she had been dead for a quarter of a century. But again I found how superficially I had judged her. She sat looking about her with eyes as impersonal, almost as stony, as those with which the granite Ramses[11] in a museum watches the froth and fret that ebbs and flows about his pedestal, separated from it by the lonely stretch of centuries. I have seen this same aloofness in old miners who drift into the Brown Hotel at Denver, their pockets full of bullion, their linen soiled, their

---

8. **Les Huguenots** (lay oo guh NOH) opera written in 1836 by Giacomo Meyerbeer (1791–1864).
9. **Common** Boston Common, a small park in Boston.
10. **trepidation** (trehp uh DAY shuhn) *n.* fearful anxiety; apprehension.
11. **Ramses** (RAM seez) one of the eleven Egyptian kings by that name who ruled from c. 1292 B.C. to 1075 B.C.

haggard faces unshorn, and who stand in the thronged corridors as solitary as though they were still in a frozen camp on the Yukon, or in the yellow blaze of the Arizona desert, conscious that certain experiences have isolated them from their fellows by a gulf no haberdasher could conceal.

10   The audience was made up chiefly of women. One lost the contour of faces and figures, indeed any effect of line whatever, and there was only the color contrast of bodices past counting, the shimmer and shading of fabrics soft and firm, silky and sheer, resisting and yielding: red, mauve, pink, blue, lilac, purple, ecru, rose, yellow, cream, and white, all the colors that an impressionist finds in a sunlit landscape, with here and there the dead black shadow of a frock coat. My Aunt Georgiana regarded them as though they had been so many daubs of tube paint on a palette.

11   When the musicians came out and took their places, she gave a little stir of anticipation, and looked with quickening interest down over the rail at that invariable grouping; perhaps the first wholly familiar thing that had greeted her eye since she had left old Maggie and her weakling calf. I could feel how all those details sank into her soul, for I had not forgotten how they had sunk into mine when I came fresh from plowing forever and forever between green aisles of corn, where, as in a treadmill, one might walk from daybreak to dusk without perceiving a shadow of change in one's environment. I reminded myself of the impression made on me by the clean profiles of the musicians, the gloss of their linen; the dull black of their coats, the beloved shapes of the instruments, the patches of yellow light thrown by the green-shaded stand-lamps on the smooth, varnished bellies of the cellos and the bass viols in the rear, the restless, wind-tossed forest of fiddle necks and bows; I recalled how, in the first orchestra I had ever heard, those long bow strokes seemed to draw the soul out of me, as a conjuror's stick reels out paper ribbon from a hat.

> I could feel how all those details sank into her soul, . . .

12   The first number was the Tannhäuser **overture**. When the violins drew out the first strain of the Pilgrims' chorus, my Aunt Georgiana clutched my coat sleeve. Then it was that I first realized that for her this singing of basses and stinging frenzy of lighter strings broke a silence of thirty years, the inconceivable silence of the plains. With the battle between the two **motifs**, with the bitter frenzy of the Venusberg[12] theme and its ripping of strings, came to me an overwhelming sense of the waste and wear we are so powerless to combat. I saw again the tall, naked house on the prairie, black and grim as a wooden fortress; the black pond where I had learned to swim, the rain-gullied clay about the naked house; the four dwarf ash seedlings on which the dishcloths were always hung to dry before

NOTES

Mark familiar word parts or indicate another strategy you used that helped you determine meaning.

overture (OH vuhr chuhr) *n.*

MEANING:

motifs (moh TEEFS) *n.*

MEANING:

---

12. **Venusberg** (VEE nuhs buhrg) legendary mountain in Germany where Venus, the Roman goddess of love, held court.

the kitchen door. The world there is the flat world of the ancients; to the east, a cornfield that stretched to daybreak; to the west, a corral that stretched to sunset; between, the sordid conquests of peace, more merciless than those of war.

13   The overture closed. My aunt released my coat sleeve, but she said nothing. She sat staring at the orchestra through a dullness of thirty years, through the films made, little by little, by each of the three hundred and sixty-five days in every one of them. What, I wondered, did she get from it? She had been a good pianist in her day, I knew, and her musical education had been broader than that of most music teachers of a quarter of a century ago. She had often told me of Mozart's operas and Meyerbeer's, and I could remember hearing her sing, years ago, certain melodies of Verdi. When I had fallen ill with a fever she used to sit by my cot in the evening, while the cool night wind blew in through the faded mosquito netting tacked over the window, and I lay watching a bright star that burned red above the cornfield, and sing "Home to our mountains, oh, let us return!" In a way fit to break the heart of a Vermont boy near dead of homesickness already.

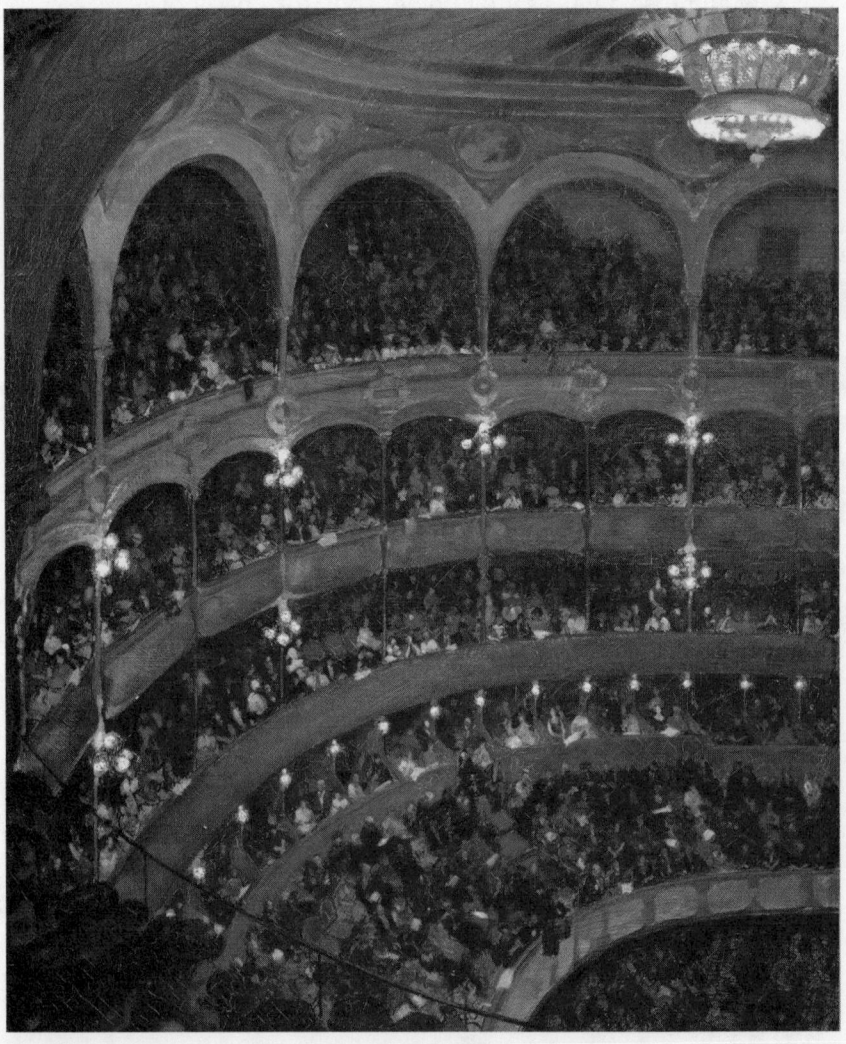

14 I watched her closely through the **prelude** to *Tristan and Isolde*, trying vainly to conjecture what that warfare of motifs, that seething turmoil of strings and winds, might mean to her. Had this music any message for her? Did or did not a new planet swim into her ken? Wagner had been a sealed book to Americans before the sixties. Had she anything left with which to comprehend this glory that had flashed around the world since she had gone from it? I was in a fever of curiosity, but Aunt Georgiana sat silent upon her peak in Darien.[13] She preserved this utter immobility throughout the numbers from the *Flying Dutchman*, though her fingers worked mechanically upon her black dress, as though of themselves they were recalling the piano score they had once played. Poor old hands! They were stretched and pulled and twisted into mere tentacles to hold, and lift, and knead with; the palms unduly swollen, the fingers bent and knotted, on one of them a thin worn band that had once been a wedding ring. As I pressed and gently quieted one of those groping hands, I remembered, with quivering eyelids, their services for me in other days.

15 Soon after the tenor began the "Prize Song," I heard a quick-drawn breath, and turned to my aunt. Her eyes were closed, but the tears were glistening on her cheeks, and I think in a moment more they were in my eyes as well. It never really dies, then, the soul? It withers to the outward eye only, like that strange moss which can lie on a dusty shelf half a century and yet, if placed in water, grows green again. My aunt wept gently throughout the development and elaboration of the melody.

16 During the intermission before the second half of the concert, I questioned my aunt and found that the "Prize Song" was not new to her. Some years before there had drifted to the farm in Red Willow County a young German, a tramp cow puncher who had sung in the chorus at Bayreuth,[14] when he was a boy, along with the other peasant boys and girls. On a Sunday morning he used to sit on his blue gingham-sheeted bed in the hands' bedroom, which opened off the kitchen, cleaning the leather of his boots and saddle, and singing the "Prize Song," while my aunt went about her work in the kitchen. She had hovered about him until she had prevailed upon him to join the country church, though his sole fitness for this step, so far as I could gather, lay in his boyish face and his possession of this divine melody. Shortly afterward he had gone to town on the Fourth of July, lost his money at a faro[15] table, ridden a saddled Texas steer on a bet, and disappeared with a fractured collarbone.

17 "Well, we have come to better things than the old *Trovatore* at any rate. Aunt Georgie?" I queried, with well-meant jocularity.

---

13. **peak in Darien** mountain on the Isthmus of Panama; from "On First Looking Into Chapman's Homer," by English poet John Keats (1795–1821).
14. **Bayreuth** (by ROYT) city in Germany known for its annual festivals of Wagner's music.
15. **faro** (FAR oh) *n.* gambling game in which players bet on the cards to be turned up from the top of the dealer's deck.

NOTES

Mark familiar word parts or indicate another strategy you used that helped you determine meaning.

prelude (PRAY lood) *n.*

MEANING:

18   Her lip quivered and she hastily put her handkerchief up to her mouth. From behind it she murmured, "And you've been hearing this ever since you left me, Clark?" Her question was the gentlest and saddest of reproaches.

19   "But do you get it, Aunt Georgiana, the astonishing structure of it all?" I persisted.

20   "Who could?" she said, absently; "why should one?"

21   The second half of the program consisted of four numbers from the *Ring*. This was followed by the forest music from *Siegfried*[16] and the program closed with Siegfried's funeral march. My aunt wept quietly, but almost continuously. I was perplexed as to what measure of musical comprehension was left to her, to her who had heard nothing for so many years but the singing of gospel hymns in Methodist services at the square frame schoolhouse on Section Thirteen. I was unable to gauge how much of it had been dissolved in soapsuds, or worked into bread, or milked into the bottom of a pail.

22   The deluge of sound poured on and on; I never knew what she found in the shining current of it; I never knew how far it bore her, or past what happy islands, or under what skies. From the trembling of her face I could well believe that the *Siegfried* march, at least, carried her out where the myriad graves are, out into the gray, burying grounds of the sea; or into some world of death vaster yet, where, from the beginning of the world, hope has lain down with hope, and dream with dream and, renouncing, slept.

23   The concert was over; the people filed out of the hall chattering and laughing, glad to relax and find the living level again, but my kinswoman made no effort to rise. I spoke gently to her. She burst into tears and sobbed pleadingly, "I don't want to go, Clark, I don't want to go!"

24   I understood. For her, just outside the door of the concert hall, lay the black pond with the cattle-tracked bluffs, the tall, unpainted house, naked as a tower, with weather-curled boards; the crookbacked ash seedlings where the dishcloths hung to dry, the gaunt, moulting turkeys picking up refuse about the kitchen door. ✦

16. ***Siegfried*** (SEEG freed) opera based on the adventures of Siegfried, a legendary hero in medieval German literature.

Comprehension Check

Complete the following items after you finish your first read. Review and clarify details with your group.

1. Why does Aunt Georgiana travel to Boston?

2. When Clark was a boy, what subjects did he learn from Aunt Georgiana?

3. What is Clark's initial feeling about being in public with his aunt?

4. What does Aunt Georgiana do when the violins start playing the Pilgrims' chorus?

5. What does Aunt Georgiana do and say at the end of the concert?

6. 🗒 **Notebook** Confirm your understanding of the story by writing a summary.

- -

RESEARCH

Research to Clarify Choose at least one unfamiliar detail from the text. Briefly research that detail. In what way does the information you learned shed light on an aspect of the story?

Research to Explore Conduct research on an aspect of the text you find interesting. For example, you may want to learn more about the operas by Richard Wagner that Cather mentions in the story. You may want to share what you discover with your group.

A WAGNER MATINÉE

Close Read the Text

With your group, revisit sections of the text you marked during your first read. **Annotate** details that you notice. What **questions** do you have? What can you **conclude**?

Analyze the Text

Complete the activities.

1. **Review and Clarify** With your group, reread paragraph 22. In what sense might Siegfried's funeral march be thought of as Georgiana's funeral march, too? Discuss with your group.

2. **Present and Discuss** Now, work with your group to share the passages from the selection that you found especially significant. Take turns presenting your passages. Discuss what you noticed in the selection, what questions you asked, and what conclusions you reached.

3. **Essential Question:** *What role does individualism play in American society?* What has this text taught you about individualism? Discuss with your group.

LANGUAGE DEVELOPMENT

Concept Vocabulary

overture	motifs	prelude

Why These Words? The three concept vocabulary words are related. With your group, discuss the words and determine which concept they share. How do these words contribute to your understanding of the text?

WORD NETWORK

Add words related to individualism from the text to your Word Network.

Practice

📓 **Notebook** Confirm your understanding of the concept vocabulary words by using them in sentences. Consult reference materials, such as print or online dictionaries, to check the accuracy of your work.

Word Study

📓 **Notebook** **Word Derivations** In "A Wagner Matinée," Clark refers to the *motifs* in an opera. The word *motif* descended from the Latin word *motivus*, meaning "moving; impelling."

1. Explain how the meaning of the Latin root word *motivus* contributes to the meaning of *motifs*.

2. Identify two other words that descend from *motivus*. Write their definitions.

STANDARDS

Reading Literature
Analyze the impact of the author's choices regarding how to develop and relate elements of a story or drama.

Language
Consult general and specialized reference materials, both print and digital, to find the pronunciation of a word or determine or clarify its precise meaning, its part of speech, its etymology, or its standard usage.

Analyze Craft and Structure

Author's Choices: Character Development The term **characterization** refers to the art of revealing characters' personalities. In **direct characterization,** a writer simply states what a character is like, as in "She was a pious woman." In **indirect characterization,** a writer uses one or more of the following methods to provide clues about a character:

- describing a character's appearance and mannerisms
- presenting a character's words, thoughts, and actions
- showing ways in which other characters react to a character
- including comments that other characters make about a character

The point of view in which a story is told also affects how readers learn about characters. For example, this story uses **first-person point of view**—Clark, the narrator, is part of the action and uses the pronouns *I, me,* and *we.* As a result, readers' impressions filter through Clark's eyes.

Practice

CITE TEXTUAL EVIDENCE
to support your answers.

1. Complete this chart independently to analyze Cather's use of Clark to characterize Aunt Georgiana indirectly. Record one example for each method. Then, share with your group.

METHOD OF CHARACTERIZATION	EXAMPLES FROM TEXT
physical description given by Clark	
other comments made by Clark	
Aunt Georgiana's words and actions	

📓 **Notebook** Answer the questions.

2. What do Clark's thoughts and feelings about his aunt indirectly reveal about his personality? Explain.

3. **(a)** How do Clark's feelings toward his aunt change during the story? **(b)** How do his feelings affect your response to Georgiana? **(c)** How do Clark's feelings about his aunt affect your attitude toward him as a character?

A WAGNER MATINÉE

STANDARDS

Reading Literature
Determine the meaning of words and phrases as they are used in the text, including figurative and connotative meanings; analyze the impact of specific word choices on meaning and tone, including words with multiple meanings or language that is particularly fresh, engaging, or beautiful.

Language
Interpret figures of speech in context and analyze their role in the text.

Conventions and Style

Figurative Language Language that is used imaginatively rather than literally is called **figurative language.** Most fiction writers and poets—and many nonfiction writers, as well—use figurative language to convey ideas and emotions in a more nuanced and expressive way than plain statements would allow. Simile, metaphor, and hyperbole are three common types of figurative language.

- A **simile** is a comparison between two dissimilar things using an explicit word of comparison, such as *like, as,* or *resemble.* (Note that some writers may use the expression "not unlike," which actually means "like.") For example, Cather compares the soul to moss in this simile: "It withers to the outward eye only, <u>like</u> that strange moss which can lie on a dusty shelf half a century and yet, if placed in water, grows green again."
- A **metaphor** is a comparison that does not use an explicit word of comparison. Instead, the comparison is either implied or directly stated, often using a form of the verb *to be*, as in this example: "Wagner <u>had been</u> a sealed book to Americans before the sixties." Wagner is a composer, not a book. Cather's metaphor shows that no orchestra played Wagner's music before the 1860s.
- **Hyperbole** is exaggeration for effect. For example, Cather uses hyperbole when Clark comments, "there were but a few hours of nightmare between the farm in Red Willow County and my study on Newbury Street." Georgiana had traveled from Nebraska to Boston, so clearly more than "a few hours" had passed.

Read It

Work individually. Identify each example as a simile, a metaphor, or hyperbole, and explain your response. Then, share and discuss your responses with your group.

EXAMPLE	TYPE OF FIGURATIVE LANGUAGE	EXPLANATION
The deluge of sound poured on and on; I never knew what she found in the shining current of it . . .		
. . . when I came fresh from ploughing forever and forever between green aisles of corn . . .		
. . . she looked not unlike one of those charred, smoked bodies that firemen lift from the *débris* of a burned building		

Write It

📓 **Notebook** Write a simile, a metaphor, and an example of hyperbole to describe Aunt Georgiana. Label each type of figurative language you use.

Writing to Sources

Assignment

Prepare an informative **research report** that will help readers understand the historical context of Cather's story. Choose from the following project options:

☐ a **comparison and contrast** of rural Nebraska and Boston in the early 1900s, in which you include information about population density, living situations, transportation, jobs, clothing, and culture

☐ a **how-to essay** with a diagram that explains in detail how cornhuskers in the early twentieth century husked corn, including what parts of the process were difficult or laborious

☐ a **problem-solution letter** that gives helpful information to someone considering moving far away to a very different locale in the late 1800s, and that includes topics such as ways to maintain communication with friends and relatives, ways to make a living, and possible lifestyle changes

Project Plan As a group, discuss the types of information you will need to find. Then, develop a research plan that assigns responsibilities to individual group members and establishes deadlines for everyone to meet. Consult a variety of sources, including primary, secondary, print, and digital. Use the chart to organize your efforts.

TYPE OF INFORMATION	PRIMARY SOURCES	SECONDARY SOURCES	ASSIGNED TO	DEADLINE

Tying It Together Your research goal is to gather information that will allow you to create a complete picture of the topic. Once you have gathered information, review it as a group. Make sure that the sources are reliable and that all of the information is sufficient, credible, and relevant. Then, organize the writing tasks and complete your report.

EVIDENCE LOG

Before moving on to the next selection, go to your Evidence Log and record what you learned from "A Wagner Matinée."

STANDARDS

Writing
• Write informative/explanatory texts to examine and convey complex ideas, concepts, and information clearly and accurately through the effective selection, organization, and analysis of content.
• Conduct short as well as more sustained research projects to answer a question or solve a problem; narrow or broaden the inquiry when appropriate; synthesize multiple sources on the subject, demonstrating understanding of the subject under investigation.

SOURCES

- *from* NATURE
- *from* SELF-RELIANCE
- *from* WALDEN
- *from* CIVIL DISOBEDIENCE
- INNOVATORS AND THEIR INVENTIONS
- THE LOVE SONG OF J. ALFRED PRUFROCK
- A WAGNER MATINÉE

Present a Personal Narrative

Assignment

Plan and deliver a **group speech** that uses evidence from the texts in Small-Group Learning, as well as your own experiences and observations, to explore the challenges of nonconformity. Use the following prompt to guide your work:

> When is it difficult to march to the beat of a "different drummer" and stand on your own as an individual? What are the risks and rewards of nonconformity?

Draw on both Emerson's and Thoreau's ideas about nonconformity as starting points. Use precise language and quotations from the texts, as well as individual experiences and observations to support your ideas.

Plan With Your Group

Analyze the Texts Discuss the ways in which the texts you have read approach the topic of nonconformity. For example, consider Emerson's experiences in nature, the creativity of inventors who find new solutions to old problems, or Aunt Georgiana's bravery and independence in setting a different course for her life, regardless of the results. Use the chart to record your group's ideas about nonconformity as expressed in these selections.

TEXT	WHAT IT SHOWS ABOUT NONCONFORMITY
from Nature / *from* Self-Reliance	
from Walden / *from* Civil Disobedience	
Innovators and Their Inventions	
The Love Song of J. Alfred Prufrock	
A Wagner Matinée	

Connect Evidence to Experiences Combine textual evidence with your own real-life examples and experiences that support your group's views. Then, complete this statement:

Nonconformity is difficult when _____. Nonconformity

is risky because _____. It can be rewarding when

_____.

:≡ STANDARDS
Speaking and Listening
Work with peers to promote civil, democratic discussions and decision-making, set clear goals and deadlines, and establish individual roles as needed.

Organize Your Presentation Work individually to write a three-minute informal speech. Remember to include references to the texts, quotations from the texts, and your own experiences to support your ideas. Then, review each group member's speech. Decide how you will introduce the speeches, provide transitions between them, and conclude your presentation.

Rehearse With Your Group

Practice With Your Group Use this checklist to evaluate the effectiveness of your group's first run-through. Then, use your evaluation and these instructions to guide your revision.

CONTENT	PRESENTATION TECHNIQUES
☐ The speeches respond to the prompt thoroughly and coherently.	☐ Speakers enunciate clearly and use gestures and eye contact effectively.
☐ The speeches are presented in a logical sequence.	☐ Speakers vary pitch and volume to add interest to their words.
☐ Speakers draw on evidence from both the texts and individual experiences and observations.	☐ Speakers speak fluently, without hesitations or repetitions.

Fine-Tune the Content If a speech is too long, too short, off-topic, or incomplete, work together to revise it.

Brush Up on Your Presentation Techniques Although an informal speech may be relaxed and friendly in tone, it should not be sloppy. Make sure that your speech is expressive and articulate, both in its content and in your presentation. Your words should help your audience to understand your ideas and to appreciate the textual evidence and personal experiences you use to support them.

Present and Evaluate

As you present your series of speeches, consider your audience's response. Use questions such as these to evaluate the presentation:

- Does the speech offer clear reasoning and provide enough evidence to support the group's overall position on nonconformity?
- Does the speech bring together real-life experiences with examples from the texts in this section?

Once all the speeches have been delivered, you may wish to select two or three favorite parts. Be ready to explain what you like about each one.

▤ STANDARDS

Speaking and Listening
• Evaluate a speaker's point of view, reasoning, and use of evidence and rhetoric, assessing the stance, premises, links among ideas, word choice, points of emphasis, and tone used.
• Present information, findings, and supporting evidence, conveying a clear and distinct perspective, such that listeners can follow the line of reasoning, alternative or opposing perspectives are addressed, and the organization, development, substance, and style are appropriate to purpose, audience, and a range of formal and informal tasks.

ESSENTIAL QUESTION:

What role does individualism play in American society?

In this section, you will complete your study of the role of individualism in American life by exploring an additional selection related to the topic. You'll then share what you learn with classmates. To choose a text, follow these steps.

Look Back Think about the selections you have already studied. Which aspects of individualism do you wish to explore further? Which time period interests you the most?

Look Ahead Preview the texts by reading the descriptions. Which one seems most interesting and appealing to you?

Look Inside Take a few minutes to scan the text you chose. Choose a different one if this text doesn't meet your needs.

Independent Learning Strategies

Throughout your life, in school, in your community, and in your career, you will need to rely on yourself to learn and work on your own. Review these strategies and the actions you can take to practice them during Independent Learning. Add ideas of your own for each category.

STRATEGY	ACTION PLAN
Create a schedule	• Understand your goals and deadlines. • Make a plan for what to do each day. •
Practice what you have learned	• Use first-read and close-read strategies to deepen your understanding. • After you read, evaluate the usefulness of the evidence to help you understand the topic. • Consider the quality and reliability of the source. •
Take notes	• Record important ideas and information. • Review your notes before preparing to share with a group. •

SCAN FOR
MULTIMEDIA

CONTENTS

Choose one selection. Selections are available online only.

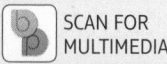

First-Read Guide

Use this page to record your first-read ideas.

Selection Title: _____

Tool Kit
First-Read Guide and
Model Annotation

NOTICE new information or ideas you learn about the unit topic as you first read this text.

ANNOTATE by marking vocabulary and key passages you want to revisit.

First Read

NOTICE ANNOTATE CONNECT RESPOND

CONNECT ideas within the selection to other knowledge and the selections you have read.

RESPOND by writing a brief summary of the selection.

STANDARD

Reading Read and comprehend complex literary and informational texts independently and proficiently.

Close-Read Guide

Use this page to record your close-read ideas.

Selection Title: _____

Close Read the Text

Revisit sections of the text you marked during your first read. Read these sections closely and **annotate** what you notice. Ask yourself **questions** about the text. What can you **conclude?** Write down your ideas.

Analyze the Text

Think about the author's choices of patterns, structure, techniques, and ideas included in the text. Select one, and record your thoughts about what this choice conveys.

QuickWrite

Pick a paragraph from the text that grabbed your interest. Explain the power of this passage.

_____
_____
_____
_____
_____
_____
_____
_____
_____

⋮≣ STANDARD
Reading Read and comprehend complex literary and informational texts independently and proficiently.

Share Your Independent Learning

Prepare to Share

What role does individualism play in American society?

Even when you read something independently, your understanding continues to grow when you share what you have learned with others. Reflect on the text you explored independently and write notes about its connection to the unit. In your notes, consider why this text belongs in this unit.

Learn From Your Classmates

Discuss It Share your ideas about the text you explored on your own. As you talk with your classmates, jot down a few ideas that you learn from them.

Reflect

Review your notes, and mark the most important insight you gained from these writing and discussion activities. Explain how this idea adds to your understanding of the concept of individualism.

STANDARDS

Speaking and Listening
Initiate and participate effectively in a range of collaborative discussions with diverse partners on grades 11–12 topics, texts, and issues, building on others' ideas and expressing their own clearly and persuasively.

Review Evidence for a Personal Narrative

At the beginning of this unit, you responded to the following question:

> **What significant incident helped me realize that I am a unique individual?**

✐ EVIDENCE LOG

Review your Evidence Log and your QuickWrite from the beginning of the unit. Have the texts you read altered your original thoughts about the incident?

☐ YES	☐ NO
Identify at least three ideas from the texts that have caused you to reevaluate your original idea.	Identify at least three ideas from the texts that reinforced your original idea.
1.	1.
2.	2.
3.	3.

Develop your thoughts into a topic sentence: *I first became aware of myself as a unique human being when:*

_____

_____

_____

The incident took place:

WHEN	WHERE	WITH WHOM

STANDARDS

Writing
Engage and orient the reader by setting out a problem, situation, or observation and its significance, establishing one or multiple point(s) of view, and introducing a narrator and/or characters; create a smooth progression of experiences or events.

PERFORMANCE-BASED ASSESSMENT

- WHOLE-CLASS SELECTIONS

- SMALL-GROUP SELECTIONS

- INDEPENDENT-LEARNING SELECTION

🔗 **WORD NETWORK**

As you write and revise your personal narrative, use your Word Network to help vary your word choices.

PART 1
Writing to Sources: Personal Narrative

In this unit, you read a variety of texts that explore ideas about individuality. Each text, in its own way, sings the praises of nonconformity, independence, and a life of awareness and contemplation.

> **Assignment**
>
> Write a **personal narrative** in which you describe an event from your life that answers this question:
>
> > What significant incident helped me realize that I am a unique individual?
>
> Choose an incident that you are comfortable describing and sharing with others. Connect your personal experience to ideas expressed in the texts from this unit. Show how your experience illustrates or departs from the ideas these texts express. End with a conclusion about the ways in which the understanding you gained from the incident affects your life today.

Reread the Assignment Review the writing prompt to be sure you fully understand it. The assignment may reference some of the academic words presented at the beginning of the unit. Be sure you understand each of the words in order to complete the assignment correctly.

Academic Vocabulary

significant	unique	impact
incident	sequence	

Review the Elements of a Personal Narrative Before you begin writing, read the Narrative Rubric. Once you have completed your first draft, check it against the rubric. If one or more of the elements is missing or is not as strong as it could be, revise your narrative to add to or strengthen that component.

Narrative Rubric

	Focus and Organization	Evidence and Elaboration	Language Conventions
4	The introduction engages the reader and sets the scene for a specific situation. A unique point of view is clearly established and maintained. The events appear in a clear sequence and build toward a particular outcome. The conclusion follows from and reflects on the rest of the narrative.	Dialogue, pacing, reflection, and description adeptly move the narrative forward. Precise details and vivid sensory language give readers a clear picture of events.	The text employs standard English conventions of usage and mechanics consistently and accurately.
3	The introduction is somewhat engaging and sets the scene for a specific situation. A clear point of view is established and maintained. The events appear in a clear sequence and mostly combine to build toward a particular outcome. The conclusion follows from the rest of the narrative.	Dialogue, reflection, and description move the narrative forward. Precise details and some sensory language give readers a clear picture of events.	The text generally employs standard English conventions of usage and mechanics.
2	The introduction sets the scene for a specific situation. A point of view is established and maintained, with occasional lapses. The events appear mostly in sequence, although some events may not belong, and some events that would clarify the narrative do not appear. The conclusion follows from the narrative.	Some dialogue, reflection, or description is used in the narrative. Some details and one or two examples of sensory language are included.	The text inconsistently employs standard English conventions of usage and mechanics.
1	The introduction fails to set a scene or is omitted altogether. The point of view is not always clear. The events do not appear in a clear sequence, and events that would clarify the narrative may not appear. The conclusion does not follow from the narrative or is omitted altogether.	Appropriate narrative techniques such as dialogue, pacing, or reflection, are not used. Details are vague or missing. No sensory language is included.	The text does not employ standard English conventions of usage and mechanics.

PART 2
Speaking and Listening: Storytelling Session

Assignment
Even if you have never seen a professional storyteller, you have probably witnessed great storytelling. Stand-up comedians, lecturers, teachers, and other public speakers tell stories that engage, amuse, and instruct listeners. Use the personal narrative you wrote as the basis for an oral **storytelling session.**

Follow these steps to make your storytelling presentation active and interesting.

- Read your personal narrative aloud, and consider ways to make it stronger as an oral piece. You may want to shorten some sections, or add dramatic detail to others. Make those revisions, and then memorize the story.
- Practice your delivery in front of a mirror. Modulate your voice, adding highs and lows, and use gestures that add meaningful emphasis. If you find yourself stumbling over some words, change them. You do not need to stick to the story exactly as it appears on the page.
- As you deliver your story, relax, avoid rushing, and speak with expression.

Review the Rubric The criteria by which your storytelling will be evaluated appear in the rubric below. Review the criteria before telling your story to ensure that you are prepared.

STANDARDS

Speaking and Listening
• Present information, findings, and supporting evidence, conveying a clear and distinct perspective, such that listeners can follow the line of reasoning, alternative or opposing perspectives are addressed, and the organization, development, substance, and style are appropriate to purpose, audience, and a range of formal and informal tasks.
• Adapt speech to a variety of contexts and tasks, demonstrating a command of formal English when indicated or appropriate.

	Content	Presentation Techniques
3	The story has a clear beginning, middle, and end, and the sequence is easy to follow.	The speaker enunciates clearly and uses an appropriate volume throughout the story.
	The story expresses a significant insight in an engaging, entertaining way.	The speaker varies the tone and pace to maintain interest.
		The speaker uses movement and expression to enliven the performance.
2	The story has a beginning, middle, and end, and the sequence is mostly easy to follow.	The speaker enunciates clearly most of the time and usually uses appropriate volume.
	The story expresses an insight and is somewhat entertaining or engaging.	The speaker varies the tone and pace to some extent.
		The speaker uses some movement and expression.
1	The story does not have a clear beginning, middle, and end, and the sequence is hard to follow.	The speaker does not enunciate clearly and does not use an appropriate volume.
	The story does not express an insight and is not engaging.	The speaker does not vary tone and pace at all.
		The speaker does not use movement or expression.

Reflect on the Unit

Now that you've completed the unit, take a few moments to reflect on your learning.

Reflect on the Unit Goals

Look back at the goals at the beginning of the unit. Use a different colored pen to rate yourself again. Think about readings and activities that contributed the most to the growth of your understanding. Record your thoughts.

Reflect on the Learning Strategies

💬 **Discuss It** Write a reflection on whether you were able to improve your learning based on your Action Plans. Think about what worked, what didn't, and what you might do to keep working on these strategies. Record your ideas before a class discussion.

Reflect on the Text

Choose a selection that you found challenging and explain what made it difficult.

Explain something that surprised you about a text in the unit.

Which activity taught you the most about the concept of individualism? What did you learn?

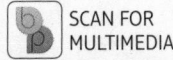
SCAN FOR
MULTIMEDIA

Power, Protest, and Change

A Spirit of Reform

Civil Rights Marches

Discuss It Perhaps more than any other country, the United States was founded on dreams people had of shaping the society in which they lived. What were some of those dreams?

Write your response before sharing your ideas.

SCAN FOR
MULTIMEDIA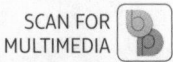

UNIT INTRODUCTION

ESSENTIAL QUESTION: In what ways does the struggle for freedom change with history?

LAUNCH TEXT
INFORMATIVE MODEL
The Zigzag Road to Rights

 WHOLE-CLASS LEARNING

HISTORICAL PERSPECTIVES

Focus Period: 1850–1890
Civil War and Social Change

ANCHOR TEXT: SPEECH

from What to the Slave Is the Fourth of July?
Frederick Douglass

ANCHOR TEXT: SPEECH

Second Inaugural Address
Abraham Lincoln

MEDIA: IMAGE GALLERY

Perspectives on Lincoln

PERFORMANCE TASK

WRITING FOCUS:
Write an Informative Essay

SMALL-GROUP LEARNING

SPEECH

Ain't I a Woman?
Sojourner Truth

PUBLIC DOCUMENT

Declaration of Sentiments
Elizabeth Cady Stanton

COMPARE

MEDIA: PODCAST

Giving Women the Vote
Sandra Sleight-Brennan

SHORT STORY

The Story of an Hour
Kate Chopin

LEGAL OPINION

Brown v. Board of Education: Opinion of the Court
Earl Warren

PERFORMANCE TASKS

SPEAKING AND LISTENING/RESEARCH FOCUS:
Panel Discussion/Research Presentation

 INDEPENDENT LEARNING

POETRY COLLECTION 1

The Poetry of Langston Hughes
Langston Hughes

POETRY COLLECTION 2

Douglass
Paul Laurence Dunbar

The Fifth Fact
Sarah Browning

Who Burns for the Perfection of Paper *Martín Espada*

HISTORY

from The Warmth of Other Suns
Isabel Wilkerson

ESSAY

What a Factory Can Teach a Housewife
Ida Tarbell

PERSUASIVE ESSAY

from Books as Bombs
Louis Menand

MEDIA: PODCAST

A Balance Between Nature and Nurture
Gloria Steinem

PERFORMANCE-BASED ASSESSMENT PREP

Review Evidence for an Informative Essay

PERFORMANCE-BASED ASSESSMENT

Informative Text: Essay and Podcast

PROMPT:
What motivates people to struggle for change?

Unit Goals

Throughout this unit, you will deepen your perspective on power, protest, and change by reading, writing, speaking, listening, and presenting. These goals will help you succeed on the Unit Performance-Based Assessment.

Rate how well you meet these goals right now. You will revisit your ratings later when you reflect on your growth during this unit.

SCALE	1 NOT AT ALL WELL	2 NOT VERY WELL	3 SOMEWHAT WELL	4 VERY WELL	5 EXTREMELY WELL

READING GOALS

	1	2	3	4	5
• Read and analyze a variety of texts to gain the knowledge and insight needed to write about the struggle for freedom.	○	○	○	○	○
• Expand your knowledge and use of academic and concept vocabulary.	○	○	○	○	○

WRITING AND RESEARCH GOALS

	1	2	3	4	5
• Write an informative essay that has a clear structure and that draws evidence from texts and original research.	○	○	○	○	○
• Conduct research projects of various lengths to explore a topic and clarify meaning.	○	○	○	○	○

LANGUAGE GOAL

	1	2	3	4	5
• Use appropriate and varied sentence structures to create cohesion and clarify relationships.	○	○	○	○	○

SPEAKING AND LISTENING GOALS

	1	2	3	4	5
• Collaborate with your team to build on the ideas of others, develop consensus, and communicate.	○	○	○	○	○
• Integrate audio, visuals, and text to present information.	○	○	○	○	○

≣ STANDARDS

Language
Acquire and use accurately general academic and domain-specific words and phrases, sufficient for reading, writing, speaking, and listening at the college and career readiness level; demonstrate independence in gathering vocabulary knowledge when considering a word or phrase important to comprehension or expression.

SCAN FOR MULTIMEDIA

Academic Vocabulary: Informative Text

Academic terms appear in all subjects and can help you read, write, and discuss with precision and clarity. Here are five academic words that will be useful to you in this unit as you analyze and write informative texts.

Complete the chart.

1. Review each word, its root, and the mentor sentences.

2. Use the information and your own knowledge to predict the meaning of each word.

3. For each word, list at least two related words.

4. Refer to a dictionary or other resources if needed.

TIP

FOLLOW THROUGH
Study the words in this chart, and mark them or their forms wherever they appear in the unit.

WORD	MENTOR SENTENCES	PREDICT MEANING	RELATED WORDS
informational ROOT: **-form-** "shape"; "image"	**1.** This *informational* pamphlet tells about the history of the village. **2.** The students found the remarks both *informational* and inspirational.		inform; informative; uninformed; misinformed
inquire ROOT: **-quir-/-quer-** "ask"	**1.** If you want to find out why your application was denied, you must *inquire*. **2.** In my research, I *inquire* about the reasons for certain social customs.		
verbatim ROOT: **-verb-** "word"	**1.** The actor knew the script so well that he could quote it *verbatim*. **2.** The witness's ability to give a *verbatim* account persuaded the jury that her memory was reliable.		
deduction ROOT: **-duc-** "lead"	**1.** The astronomer's *deduction* was based on years of observation. **2.** The writer presented the objective facts and then shared his *deduction* from them.		
specific ROOT: **-spec-** "sort"; "kind"	**1.** Your report topic is too broad; find one that is more *specific*. **2.** Was there one *specific* event that caused the war, or were there many?		

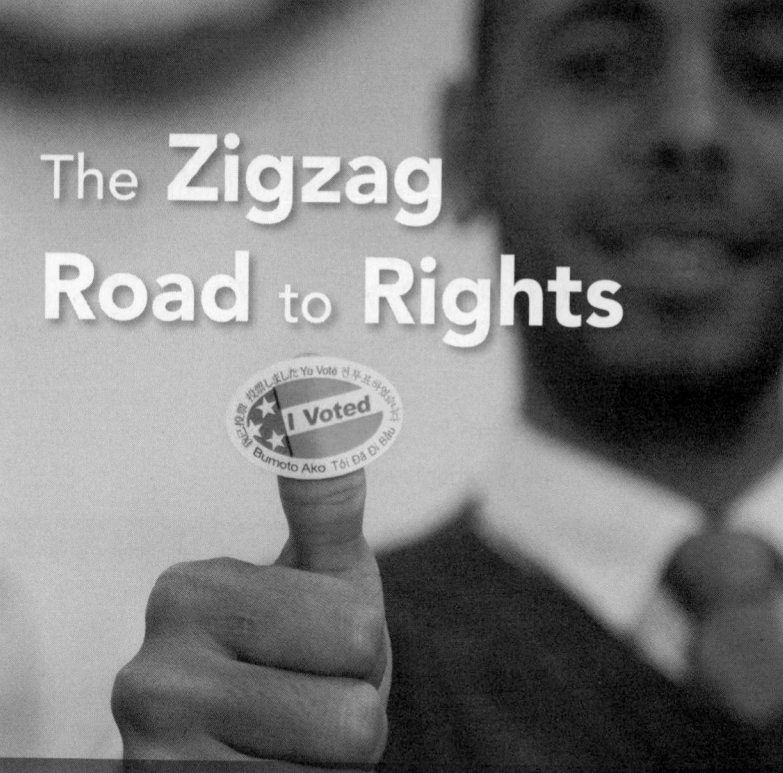

LAUNCH TEXT | INFORMATIVE MODEL

The **Zigzag Road** to **Rights**

This selection is an example of an **informative text,** a type of writing in which an author examines concepts through the careful selection, organization, and analysis of information. This is the type of writing you will develop in the Performance-Based Assessment at the end of the unit.

As you read, think about how the information is shared. Mark the text to help you answer this question: How does the writer help readers understand the main point of the essay?

NOTES

1   When we look back at history, we often like to identify trends. Viewing the big picture, we may see a steady push toward progress. However, every fight for rights involves a series of advances and setbacks. The struggle for equal recognition of African Americans demonstrates a zigzag road to rights.

2   The push-and-pull of this struggle was evident at the birth of the nation. In his original draft of the Declaration of Independence, Thomas Jefferson included a strong condemnation of slavery, protesting this "cruel war against human nature." Jefferson wanted the Declaration of Independence to grant freedom to all men. However, at the Continental Congress in 1776, both northern and southern slaveholders objected to any mention of African American rights. Powerful indeed was their pressure. Any mention of slavery was deleted from the Declaration.

3   Although the removal of Jefferson's antislavery paragraph was a severe setback, reformers did not give up hope. With the ratification of the Constitution, they gained an important tool for change. Article V describes the conditions required for amending the Constitution. Laws can be changed, and rights can be gained.

4   The struggle took another crucial step forward in 1863, when President Abraham Lincoln issued the Emancipation Proclamation. It asserted that "all persons held as slaves" within states that had seceded from the Union "are, and henceforward shall be, free." Still, freedom for slaves depended upon a Union victory. Slavery remained legal in border states loyal to the Union, as well as in Confederate areas under Northern control.

SCAN FOR MULTIMEDIA

5   The hope of change promised by Article V paid off in 1865. Congress passed the Thirteenth Amendment, abolishing slavery in the United States. "Neither slavery nor involuntary servitude . . . shall exist within the United States, or any place subject to their jurisdiction." The next two amendments, adopted in 1868 and 1870, made African Americans citizens and gave them the right to vote. The expanded Constitution reflects a nation willing to change.

6   Yet these significant advances did not guarantee full rights for black Americans, as evidenced by a landmark decision by the Supreme Court in 1896. In the case of *Plessy v. Ferguson*, seven of eight Supreme Court justices voted in support of Louisiana's Separate Car Act, which made it illegal for blacks to travel in trains reserved for white passengers. This decision set an important legal precedent: "Separate, but equal" facilities were constitutional.

7   That decision was eventually reversed in 1954, when the Supreme Court issued a unanimous decision in the case of *Brown v. Board of Education*. Finding that "separate educational facilities are inherently unequal," the decision promised an end to segregation. Once again, progress toward equal rights surged forward.

8   Nonetheless, no single case, law, or amendment could instantly erase the long tradition of prejudice and inequality. For example, even though the Fifteenth Amendment guaranteed African Americans the right to vote, state and local laws and policies often kept black Americans from voting through tactics such as poll taxes, voter registration exams, and intimidation. These strategies were outlawed by the Voting Rights Act of 1965.

9   The history of African American rights features many crucial victories, from the Emancipation Proclamation through the Voting Rights Act. However, the record of the struggle also includes the difficult stumbling blocks that have had to be overcome. While the path to progress is not smooth, one thing is certain: The zigzag will continue into the future. History teaches us that rights gained can be lost, curtailed, or ignored—and perhaps gained once more. ❧

NOTES

🔲 WORD NETWORK FOR POWER, PROTEST, AND CHANGE

Vocabulary A Word Network is a collection of words related to a topic. As you read the unit selections, identify words related to the idea of struggle, and add them to your Word Network. You might begin with words from the Launch Text, such as *setbacks*. For each word you identify, add a related word. Continue to add words as you complete this unit.

🔧 **Tool Kit**
Word Network Model

setbacks | impediments

STRUGGLE

Summary

Write a summary of "The Zigzag Road to Rights." Remember that a **summary** is a concise, complete, and accurate overview of a text. It should contain neither opinion nor analysis.

Launch Activity

Draft a Focus Statement Complete this focus statement: **The struggle for freedom is** _____, _____, and _____.

- Working individually, choose three words or phrases to complete the statement. Write each one on a separate sticky note.

- Place everyone's sticky notes on a board where they can be seen. Then, work together to group words or phrases that are synonyms or that are otherwise closely related.

- Again working individually, decide which three words or phrases you think best complete the focus statement. Place a tally mark on each sticky note that lists one of your choices.

- As a class, use the tally results to create a single focus statement. Identify the words or phrases that received the most votes. Then, discuss whether those three words or phrases create the strongest statement.

- Once the class has selected three words or phrases, discuss how the order in which they are placed affects the meaning of the focus statement. Choose the best order, and finish the statement.

QuickWrite

Consider class discussions, the video, and the Launch Text as you think about the prompt. Record your first thoughts here.

PROMPT: **What motivates people to struggle for change?**

✎ EVIDENCE LOG FOR POWER, PROTEST, AND CHANGE

Review your QuickWrite. Summarize your initial position in one sentence in your Evidence Log. Then, record evidence from "The Zigzag Road to Rights" that supports your position.

After each selection, you will continue to use your Evidence Log to record the evidence you gather and the connections you make. The graphic shows what your Evidence Log looks like.

🔧 **Tool Kit**
Evidence Log Model

Title of Text: _____ Date: _____

CONNECTION TO PROMPT	TEXT EVIDENCE/DETAILS	ADDITIONAL NOTES/IDEAS

How does this text change or add to my thinking? Date: _____

SCAN FOR
MULTIMEDIA

ESSENTIAL QUESTION:

In what ways does the struggle for freedom change with history?

As you read these selections, work with your whole class to explore the struggle for freedom.

From Text to Topic For Frederick Douglass, the struggle for freedom meant a perilous escape from slavery. For Abraham Lincoln, it meant waging war against his fellow citizens. The issue of slavery polarized the country before the Civil War. As you read, consider what the selections show about the struggle for freedom during the Focus Period—and its relationship to our ideas of freedom today.

Whole-Class Learning Strategies

Throughout your life, in school, in your community, and in your career, you will continue to learn and work in large-group environments.

Review these strategies and the actions you can take to practice them as you work with your whole class. Add ideas of your own for each step. Get ready to use these strategies during Whole-Class Learning.

STRATEGY	ACTION PLAN
Listen actively	• Eliminate distractions. For example, put your cellphone away. • Record brief notes on main ideas and points of confusion. •
Clarify by asking questions	• If you're confused, other people probably are, too. Ask a question to help your whole class. • Ask follow-up questions as needed; for example, if you do not understand the clarification or if you want to make an additional connection. •
Monitor understanding	• Notice what information you already know and be ready to build on it. • Ask for help if you are struggling. •
Interact and share ideas	• Share your ideas and offer answers, even if you are unsure of them. • Build on the ideas of others by adding details or making a connection. •

SCAN FOR
MULTIMEDIA

CONTENTS

Civil War and Social Change

Voices of the Period

" . . . I would write something that would make this whole nation feel what an accursed thing slavery is."

—Harriet Beecher Stowe,
author of *Uncle Tom's Cabin*

" In your hands, my dissatisfied fellow countrymen, and not in mine, is the momentous issue of civil war. The government will not assail you. . . . You have no oath registered in heaven to destroy the government, while I shall have the most solemn one to 'preserve, protect, and defend' it."

—Abraham Lincoln,
President of the United States
from 1861 to 1865

" Those who profess to favor freedom, and yet deprecate agitation, are men who want crops without plowing up the ground. They want rain without thunder and lightning. They want the ocean without the awful roar of its many waters. This struggle may be a moral one, or it may be a physical one, or it may be both moral and physical, but it must be a struggle. Power concedes nothing without a demand. It never did and it never will."

—Frederick Douglass,
abolitionist

History of the Period

Dreams of Shaping Society More than any other nation, the United States was founded on dreams people had of shaping the society in which they lived. The Puritans who colonized New England came to build a new society, a society in which they could freely practice their religion. Some 150 years later, the American revolutionaries wrote a constitution that gave citizens powerful tools to continue reshaping society—tools such as freedom of speech and an elected, representative government. With these tools, citizens could change the course of the country.

The Crisis of Slavery By 1850, though, the question of whether those tools were enough became grave. About 88 percent of the African Americans in the country—approximately 14 percent of the nation's total population—were enslaved: treated as property, forced to work for others, torn in many cases from their own families, and subject to various other abuses and cruelties. Many in the nation cried out for change, but the economy of the South depended on the use of enslaved African Americans for labor. When challenged, many in the South rallied to the defense of the institution.

In the North, industry was replacing agriculture as the motor of the economy. Northern states had begun passing antislavery laws in the eighteenth century, and by 1850 slavery had all but vanished in the North. Critics of slavery were becoming

TIMELINE

1850: China Taiping Rebellion begins.

1857: In the *Dred Scott* decision, the U.S. Supreme Court rules that people of African descent cannot become U.S. citizens.

1860: Abraham Lincoln is elected president.

1850

1852: Harriet Beecher Stowe's *Uncle Tom's Cabin* is published.

1859: John Brown, an abolitionist, leads a raid on the federal arsenal at Harpers Ferry, Virginia.

1861: The Civil War begins with Confederate forces firing on Fort Sumter, South Carolina.

Integration of Knowledge and Ideas

Notebook What does the information shown in these charts help you understand about differences between the North and South in their economies, population densities, and overall lifestyles? How do you think these differences affected the outcome of the Civil War?

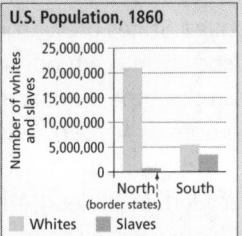

U.S. Population, 1860

Number of whites and slaves

25,000,000
20,000,000
15,000,000
10,000,000
5,000,000
0

North (border states)   South

■ Whites   ■ Slaves

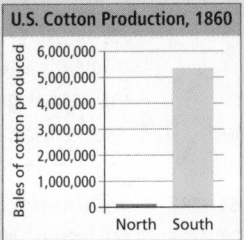

U.S. Cotton Production, 1860

Bales of cotton produced

6,000,000
5,000,000
4,000,000
3,000,000
2,000,000
1,000,000
0

North   South

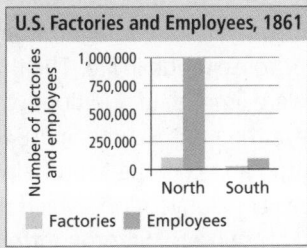

U.S. Factories and Employees, 1861

Number of factories and employees

1,000,000
750,000
500,000
250,000
0

North   South

■ Factories   ■ Employees

vocal in their opposition, with abolitionists campaigning against slavery and assisting runaway slaves.

Civil War When Abraham Lincoln was elected president in 1860, the divisions between North and South only sharpened. Beginning with South Carolina in 1860, 11 Southern states seceded (separated) from the United States. In 1861, the Civil War began, pitting North against South. After years of suffering and devastation, the North won the war in 1865. This victory set the nation's future course, for it decided the issue of slavery: No longer would anyone be enslaved in the United States. In addition, it made clear the fact that the centers of economic influence in the country had shifted from the agricultural South to the industrial North. Finally, it confirmed the strength of the country's central government in relation to the states.

Expansion and Progress Before the Civil War, the country had been busily expanding, adding new territories and states as settlers pushed west, seeking land. After the war, the country continued to grow at a furious pace. Settlers continued to move west, forcing Native Americans from their lands. Immigrants flooded the nation's cities, providing labor. For the first time, electricity was being used on a large scale for everything from city lights to factory machines. The nation began linking frontiers to cities with railway tracks and telegraph wires.

Reform Movements While forces such as westward expansion and immigration were reshaping the nation, reformers were attempting to transform society. Pioneers such as Horace

1862: France Louis Pasteur proposes the modern germ theory of disease.

1865: The Thirteenth Amendment, outlawing slavery, is added to the U.S. Constitution.

1867: The United States buys Alaska from Russia.

1870

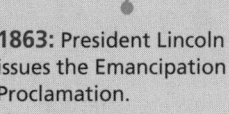

1863: President Lincoln issues the Emancipation Proclamation.

1865: President Lincoln is assassinated by John Wilkes Booth.

1869: Russia Leo Tolstoy's *War and Peace* is published.

Mann championed public education. Other activists pushed forward reforms of the justice system, leading to the development of the modern prison. During this period, women also began pursuing political and economic rights equal to men's.

A Historic Convention In the years around 1850, women were discouraged from playing most major roles in public life. Their rights to property were limited. In addition, women did not yet have the right to vote. In 1848, Elizabeth Cady Stanton and Lucretia Mott helped organize the Seneca Falls Convention, which met to discuss women's rights. There, Stanton introduced a resolution to pursue the right to vote for women. With the support of Frederick Douglass, a former slave and an active abolitionist, the resolution passed.

The Movement for Women's Rights Reformers such as Stanton, Mott, and Susan B. Anthony campaigned vigorously for women's rights. Their tactics included lobbying politicians, holding public lectures, publishing newspapers, picketing, and marching.

Social Progress Some reforms were seen at the time. Even before the Seneca Falls Convention, some states had passed laws giving women the right to their own property, although their husbands still had the right to manage shared property.

Some states, including ones newly added to the Union, passed laws allowing women to vote. The right to vote was not granted to women nationwide, however, until the ratification of the Nineteenth Amendment to the Constitution in 1920.

A Nation Comes of Age In the decades from 1850 to 1914, the United States grew from a largely agricultural society into a modern industrial giant. During this time, important issues such as the freedom of African Americans, the rights of women, and the rights of workers were discussed and argued. In the end, the society of the United States was reshaped, not just by reformers, but by forces such as war, technological progress, and economic development. These forces laid the foundations of the nation we know today.

A Legacy of Protest The issues of power and change raised during the period were not resolved once and for all, however. Even though slavery had been abolished, injustices against African Americans continued. New eras of protest were born in the effort to end racial discrimination. Women's lives had generally improved but voting equality was still an unachieved goal, and other forms of inequality continued to reign. Protests continued. The literature in this unit tells of the ongoing struggle for social justice.

TIMELINE

1872: Susan B. Anthony is arrested for trying to vote in a presidential election.

1876: Baseball's National League is founded.

1877: The Reconstruction Era ends in the South.

1870

1874: France Claude Monet gathers Impressionist painters for their first exhibit.

1876: Alexander Graham Bell patents the telephone.

1879: Thomas Edison invents a practical electric light.

Literature Selections

Literature of the Focus Period Several of the selections in this unit were written during the Focus Period and pertain to the deep conflicts of the era over power and change:

from "What to the Slave Is the Fourth of July?" Frederick Douglass

Second Inaugural Address, Abraham Lincoln

"Ain't I a Woman?" Sojourner Truth

Declaration of Sentiments, Elizabeth Cady Stanton

"The Story of an Hour," Kate Chopin

"Douglass," Paul Laurence Dunbar

Connections Across Time The struggle against social injustice and for the expansion of rights continued past the Focus Period. In addition, the struggles of the Focus Period have influenced contemporary writers and commentators.

Brown v. Board of Education: Opinion of the Court, Earl Warren

"Was *Brown v. Board* a Failure?" Sarah Garland

"The Fifth Fact," Sarah Browning

"Who Burns for the Perfection of Paper," Martín Espada

from *The Warmth of Other Suns,* Isabel Wilkerson

"What a Factory Can Teach a Housewife," Ida Tarbell

from *Books as Bombs*, Louis Menand

"A Balance Between Nature and Nurture," Gloria Steinem

ADDITIONAL FOCUS PERIOD LITERATURE

Student Edition

UNIT 2
The Writing of Walt Whitman

- *from* The Preface to the 1885 edition of *Leaves of Grass*
- *from* Song of Myself
- "I Hear America Singing"
- "On the Beach at Night Alone"
- "America"

The Poetry of Emily Dickinson

- "The Soul selects her own Society —"
- "The Soul unto itself"
- "Fame is a fickle food"
- "They shut me up in Prose —"
- "There is a solitude of space"
- "I heard a fly buzz — when I died —"
- "I'm Nobody! Who are you?"

1882: Europe The Triple Alliance (Germany, Austria-Hungary, and Italy) is formed.

1882: The Standard Oil trust becomes the first industrial monopoly.

1883: The Brooklyn Bridge is opened.

1884: Mark Twain's *The Adventures of Huckleberry Finn* is published.

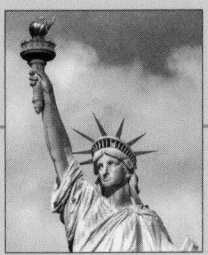

1886: The Statue of Liberty is dedicated in New York Harbor.

1890

1890: The U.S. Census Bureau declares the frontier closed.

About the Speaker

Frederick Douglass
(1818–1895) was born
into slavery in Maryland.
He nevertheless learned to
read and write, and at the
age of 21 he escaped to
Massachusetts. There, he
joined the abolitionist cause
and quickly became one
of its most powerful public
speakers, lecturing against
slavery and campaigning for
civil rights for all people. He
published his autobiography,
established a newspaper
for African Americans, and
went on to hold several
governmental positions.

🔧 **Tool Kit**
First-Read Guide and
Model Annotation

from What to the Slave Is the Fourth of July?

Concept Vocabulary

You will encounter the following words as you read this excerpt from "What to the Slave Is the Fourth of July?" Before reading, note how familiar you are with each word. Then, rank the words in order from most familiar (1) to least familiar (6).

WORD	YOUR RANKING
obdurate	
stolid	
disparity	
denounce	
equivocate	
conceded	

After completing the first read, come back to the concept vocabulary and review your rankings. Mark changes to your original rankings as needed.

First Read NONFICTION

Apply these these strategies as you conduct your first read. You will have an opportunity to complete the close-read notes after your first read.

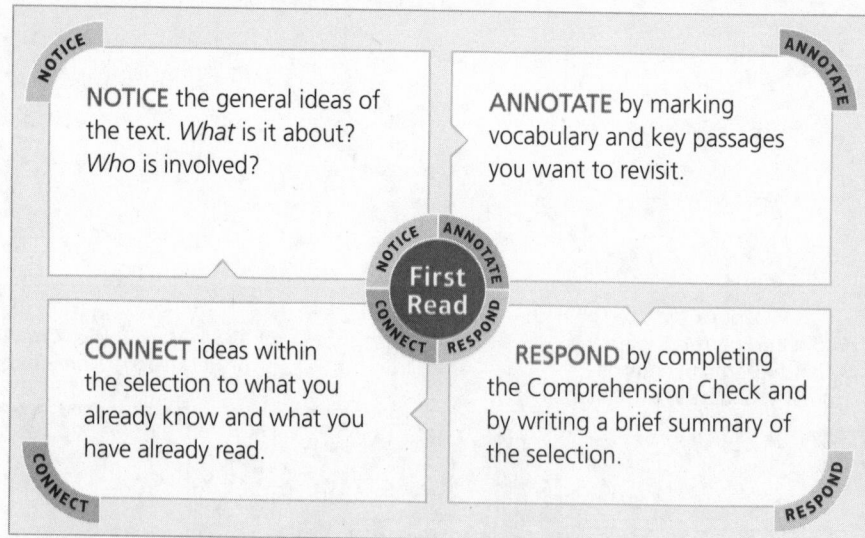

NOTICE the general ideas of the text. *What* is it about? *Who* is involved?

ANNOTATE by marking vocabulary and key passages you want to revisit.

First Read

CONNECT ideas within the selection to what you already know and what you have already read.

RESPOND by completing the Comprehension Check and by writing a brief summary of the selection.

📋 STANDARDS

Reading Informational Text
By the end of grade 11, read and
comprehend literary nonfiction in
the grades 11–CCR text complexity
band proficiently, with scaffolding as
needed at the high end of the range.

from
What to the Slave
Is the Fourth of July?

Frederick Douglass

BACKGROUND

On July 5, 1852, Frederick Douglass addressed an audience at the Rochester (New York) Ladies' Anti-Slavery Society. At a time when many people—some who were against slavery in principle—viewed the total abolition of slavery as a radical cause, Douglass pulled no punches in pleading his case.

SCAN FOR
MULTIMEDIA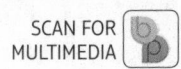

1   Fellow citizens, pardon me, allow me to ask, why am I called upon to speak here today? What have I, or those I represent, to do with your national independence? Are the great principles of political freedom and of natural justice, embodied in that Declaration of Independence, extended to us? And am I, therefore, called upon to bring our humble offering to the national altar, and to confess the benefits and express devout gratitude for the blessings resulting from your independence to us?

2   Would to God, both for your sakes and ours, that an affirmative answer could be truthfully returned to these questions! Then would my task be light, and my burden easy and delightful. For who is there so cold that a nation's sympathy could not warm him? Who so **obdurate** and dead to the claims of gratitude that would not thankfully acknowledge such priceless benefits? Who so **stolid** and selfish that would not give his voice to swell the hallelujahs of a nation's jubilee,[1] when the chains of servitude had been torn from

NOTES

obdurate (OB dur iht) *adj.*
resistant to persuasion

stolid (STOL ihd) *adj.*
feeling little or no emotion

---

1. **hallelujahs of a nation's jubilee** praises to God at the time of celebrating a national anniversary.

his limbs? I am not that man. In a case like that, the dumb might eloquently speak, and the "lame man leap as an hart."[2]

3 But such is not the state of the case. I say it with a sad sense of the **disparity** between us. I am not included within the pale of glorious anniversary! Your high independence only reveals the immeasurable distance between us. The blessings in which you, this day, rejoice are not enjoyed in common. The rich inheritance of justice, liberty, prosperity, and independence, bequeathed[3] by your fathers, is shared by you, not by me. The sunlight that brought light and healing to you has brought stripes and death to me. This Fourth of July is yours, not mine. You may rejoice; I must mourn. To drag a man in fetters[4] into the grand illuminated temple of liberty, and call upon him to join you in joyous anthems, were inhuman mockery and sacrilegious irony. Do you mean, citizens, to mock me, by asking me to speak today? . . .

4 Fellow citizens, above your national, tumultuous joy, I hear the mournful wail of millions! whose chains, heavy and grievous yesterday, are, today, rendered more intolerable by the jubilee shouts that reach them. If I do forget, if I do not faithfully remember those bleeding children of sorrow this day, "may my right hand forget her cunning, and may my tongue cleave to the roof of my mouth!"[5] To forget them, to pass lightly over their wrongs, and to chime in with the popular theme would be treason most scandalous and shocking, and would make me a reproach before God and the world. My subject, then, fellow citizens, is American slavery. I shall see this day and its popular characteristics from the slave's point of view. Standing there identified with the American bondman, making his wrongs mine, I do not hesitate to declare, with all my soul, that the character and conduct of this nation never looked blacker to me than on this Fourth of July! Whether we turn to the declarations of the past or to the professions of the present, the conduct of the nation seems equally hideous and revolting. America is false to the past, false to the present, and solemnly binds herself to be false to the future. Standing with God and the crushed and bleeding slave on this occasion, I will, in the name of humanity which is outraged, in the name of liberty which is fettered, in the name of the Constitution and the Bible, which are disregarded and trampled upon, dare to call into question and to **denounce**, with all the emphasis I can command, everything that serves to perpetuate slavery—the great sin and shame of America! "I will not **equivocate**; I will not excuse;" I will use the severest language I can command; and yet not one word shall escape me that any man, whose judgment is not blinded by prejudice, or who is not at heart a slaveholder, shall not confess to be right and just.

CLOSE READ
ANNOTATE: Parallelism is the repetition of words or phrases that have similar grammatical structures. In the last two sentences of paragraph 4, mark two examples of parallelism.

QUESTION: What ideas do these examples of parallelism connect?

CONCLUDE: How does the use of parallelism add to the power and meaning of this section of the speech?

---

2. **"lame man leap as an hart"** reference to the biblical passage Isaiah 35:6, promising God's rescue of the weak and fearful. (A *hart* is a male deer.)
3. **bequeathed** (bih KWEETHT) *adj.* handed down.
4. **fetters** *n.* chains.
5. **"may . . . mouth"** reference to the biblical passage Psalm 137, referencing the grief of Jews who had been taken as captives to Babylon (c. 600 B.C.).

5   But I fancy I hear some one of my audience say, "It is just in this circumstance that you and your brother abolitionists fail to make a favorable impression on the public mind. Would you argue more, and denounce less; would you persuade more, and rebuke[6] less; your cause would be much more likely to succeed." But, I submit, where all is plain, there is nothing to be argued. What point in the antislavery creed would you have me argue? On what branch of the subject do the people of this country need light? Must I undertake to prove that the slave is a man? That point is **conceded** already. Nobody doubts it. The slaveholders themselves acknowledge it in the enactment of laws for their government. They acknowledge it when they punish disobedience on the part of the slave. There are seventy-two crimes in the State of Virginia which, if committed by a black man (no matter how ignorant he be), subject him to the punishment of death; while only two of the same crimes will subject a white man to the like punishment. What is this but the acknowledgment that the slave is a moral, intellectual, and responsible being? The manhood of the slave is conceded. It is admitted in the fact that Southern statute books are covered with enactments forbidding, under severe fines and penalties, the teaching of the slave to read or to write. When you can point to any such laws in reference to the beasts of the field, then I may consent to argue the manhood of the slave. When the dogs in your streets, when the fowls of the air, when the cattle on your hills, when the fish of the sea, and the reptiles that crawl, shall be unable to distinguish the slave from a brute, then will I argue with you that the slave is a man!

NOTES

conceded (kuhn SEED ihd)
v. admitted

> Must I undertake to prove that the slave is a man?

6   For the present, it is enough to affirm the equal manhood of the Negro race. Is it not astonishing that, while we are plowing, planting, and reaping, using all kinds of mechanical tools, erecting houses, constructing bridges, building ships, working in metals of brass, iron, copper, silver and gold; that, while we are reading, writing and ciphering,[7] acting as clerks, merchants, and secretaries, having among us lawyers, doctors, ministers, poets, authors, editors, orators, and teachers; that, while we are engaged in all manner of enterprises common to other men, digging gold in California, capturing the whale in the Pacific, feeding sheep and cattle on the hillside, living, moving, acting, thinking, planning, living in families as husbands, wives, and children, and, above all, confessing and worshipping the Christian's God, and looking hopefully for life and immortality beyond the grave, we are called upon to prove that we are men!

7   Would you have me argue that man is entitled to liberty? That he is the rightful owner of his own body? You have already declared it. Must I argue the wrongfulness of slavery? Is that a question for Republicans? Is it to be settled by the rules of logic and

6. **rebuke** (rih BYOOK) *v.* criticize.
7. **ciphering** (SY fuhr ihng) *v.* computing using arithmetic.

argumentation, as a matter beset with great difficulty, involving a doubtful application of the principle of justice, hard to be understood? How should I look today, in the presence of Americans, dividing and subdividing a discourse, to show that men have a natural right to freedom—speaking of it relatively and positively, negatively and affirmatively? To do so would be to make myself ridiculous, and to offer an insult to your understanding. There is not a man beneath the canopy of heaven that does not know that slavery is wrong for him.

8   What, am I to argue that it is wrong to make men brutes, to rob them of their liberty, to work them without wages, to keep them ignorant of their relations to their fellow men, to beat them with sticks, to flay their flesh with the lash, to load their limbs with irons, to hunt them with dogs, to sell them at auction, to sunder their families, to knock out their teeth, to burn their flesh, to starve them into obedience and submission to their masters? Must I argue that a system thus marked with blood, and stained with pollution, is wrong? No! I will not. I have better employment for my time and strength than such arguments would imply.

9   What, then, remains to be argued? Is it that slavery is not divine; that God did not establish it; that our doctors of divinity are mistaken? There is blasphemy in the thought. That which is inhuman cannot be divine! Who can reason on such a proposition? They that can, may; I cannot. The time for such argument is passed.

10   At a time like this, scorching irony, not convincing argument, is needed. O! had I the ability, and could I reach the nation's ear, I would, today, pour out a fiery stream of biting ridicule, blasting reproach, withering sarcasm, and stern rebuke. For it is not light that is needed, but fire; it is not the gentle shower, but thunder. We need the storm, the whirlwind, and the earthquake. The feeling of the nation must be quickened; the conscience of the nation must be roused; the propriety[8] of the nation must be startled; the hypocrisy of the nation must be exposed; and its crimes against God and man must be proclaimed and denounced.

11   What, to the American slave, is your Fourth of July? I answer: a day that reveals to him, more than all other days of the year, the gross injustice and cruelty to which he is the constant victim. To him, your celebration is a sham; your boasted liberty, an unholy license; your national greatness, swelling vanity; your sounds of rejoicing are empty and heartless; your denunciation of tyrants, brass-fronted impudence; your shouts of liberty and equality, hollow mockery; your prayers and hymns, your sermons and thanksgivings, with all your religious parade and solemnity, are, to Him, mere bombast, fraud, deception, impiety,[9] and hypocrisy—a thin veil to cover up crimes which would disgrace a nation of savages. There is not a nation on the earth guilty of practices more shocking and bloody than are the people of these United States, at this very hour. . . .

CLOSE READ

ANNOTATE: In paragraph 10, mark words that suggest how strongly Douglass feels. Mark adjectives, nouns that name forms of expression, and nouns that name natural phenomena.

QUESTION: Why does Douglass compare certain forms of expression to natural phenomena?

CONCLUDE: What is the effect of this language?

---

8. **propriety** (pruh PRY uh tee) *n.* behavior that is accepted as socially correct or proper.
9. **impiety** (ihm PY uh tee) *n.* lack of respect for God.

12   Allow me to say, in conclusion, notwithstanding the dark picture I have this day presented, of the state of the nation, I do not despair of this country. There are forces in operation which must inevitably work the downfall of slavery. "The arm of the Lord is not shortened,"[10] and the doom of slavery is certain. I, therefore, leave off where I began, with hope. While drawing encouragement from the Declaration of Independence, the great principles it contains, and the genius of American institutions, my spirit is also cheered by the obvious tendencies of the age. ⇜

---

10. **"The arm of the Lord is not shortened"** reference to the biblical passage Isaiah 59:1, assuring that God is able to hear and rescue those who call on him.

Comprehension Check

Complete the following items after you finish your first read.

1. What kind of "easy and delightful" speech does Douglass wish he could present?

2. What is the "mournful wail" that gives Douglass the topic for his speech?

3. According to Douglass, how do laws in the South prove that slaves are human beings?

4. At the end of this excerpt, what encouraging signs does Douglass find?

5. 📝 **Notebook** Write a summary of this excerpt from "What to the Slave Is the Fourth of July?" to confirm your understanding of the speech.

- -

RESEARCH

Research to Clarify Choose at least one unfamiliar detail from the text. Briefly research that detail. In what way does the information you learned shed light on an aspect of the speech?

Research to Explore Choose something that interests you from the text, and formulate a research question about it.

from WHAT TO THE SLAVE IS
THE FOURTH OF JULY?

Close Read the Text

1. This model, from paragraph 3 of the text, shows two sample annotations, along with questions and conclusions. Close read the passage, and find another detail to annotate. Then, write a question and your conclusion.

> **ANNOTATE:** These terms are similar.
>
> **QUESTION:** What do these words show about Douglass's feelings toward American ideals?
>
> **CONCLUDE:** They show his reverence. The legacy of freedom is both sacred ("blessings") and a part of every American's identity ("rich inheritance").

> **ANNOTATE:** Here, Douglass is providing contrasts.
>
> **QUESTION:** What point is Douglass making by this series of contrasts?
>
> **CONCLUDE:** He is emphasizing the idea that enslaved Americans are denied freedom.

The blessings in which you, this day, rejoice are not enjoyed in common. The rich inheritance of justice, liberty, prosperity, and independence, bequeathed by your fathers, is shared by you, not by me. The sunlight that brought light and healing to you, has brought stripes and death to me. This Fourth of July is yours, not mine.

Close Read · ANNOTATE · QUESTION · CONCLUDE

2. For more practice, go back into the text, and complete the close-read notes.

3. Revisit a section of the text you found important during your first read. Read this section closely, and **annotate** what you notice. Ask yourself **questions** such as "Why did the author make this choice?" What can you **conclude**?

 Tool Kit
Close-Read Guide and
Model Annotation

Analyze the Text

CITE TEXTUAL EVIDENCE
to support your answers.

Notebook Respond to these questions.

1. **Analyze** How does Douglass's opening reference to the Declaration of Independence reinforce his message?

2. **Interpret** Identify two biblical allusions Douglass makes, and then explain how each contributes to Douglass's overall argument.

3. (a) **Analyze** In what ways is Douglass's word choice suited to his audience? (b) **Evaluate** How effective would it be for a modern audience? Explain.

4. **Historical Perspectives** Douglass presented this speech to an antislavery society—an audience that was already on his side. Why, then, did Douglass speak as harshly as he did? Whom was he trying to reach?

5. **Essential Question:** *How does the struggle for freedom change with history?* What have you learned about the struggle for freedom from reading this speech?

Analyze Craft and Structure

Argumentative Structure Frederick Douglass's famous speech "What to the Slave Is the Fourth of July?" is an **argument**, a discussion of a controversial or debatable issue. In an argument, a writer or speaker uses valid reasoning and evidence to support a **claim**—a particular belief, conclusion, or point of view. The person who presents the argument also may anticipate objections and challenges, or **counterclaims**, and then refute them.

In general, an argument addresses at least one of these purposes:

- to change the audience's mind about an issue
- to persuade the audience to accept an idea
- to motivate the audience to take a specific action

Douglass structures his speech to address all three purposes, either directly or by implication.

Practice

CITE TEXTUAL EVIDENCE to support your answers.

Notebook Respond to these questions.

1. (a) What main claim shapes Douglass's speech? (b) How early in the speech does he introduce this claim?

2. In paragraph 10, Douglass states that "scorching irony, not convincing argument, is needed." Nevertheless, his speech does make an argument. (a) In one sentence, state Douglass's argument. (b) Up to that point, what evidence has he presented to support his claim?

3. (a) In paragraph 5, what does Douglass acknowledge as a counterclaim to his position? (b) How does he refute that counterclaim?

4. Reread the three purposes that most arguments address. (a) In the left-hand column of the chart, record those purposes in the order in which you think Douglass was effective in addressing them, from most successful to least successful. (b) Use the right-hand column to explain your choices.

PURPOSE	EXPLANATION
addressed **most** effectively:	
addressed **fairly** effectively:	
addressed **least** effectively:	

from WHAT TO THE SLAVE IS THE
FOURTH OF JULY?

Concept Vocabulary

obdurate	disparity	equivocate
stolid	denounce	conceded

Why These Words? These concept vocabulary words help reveal the nature of the debate over slavery. For example, although many people *conceded* that slavery was profoundly wrong, few were willing to campaign against it. On the other hand, some Americans whose economic success depended on slave labor were *obdurate,* insisting that the institution continue. One word suggests an acknowledgement of another point of view, whereas the other suggests a rejection of it.

1. How does the concept vocabulary sharpen the reader's understanding of the debate over slavery?

2. What other words in the speech connect to this concept?

WORD NETWORK

Add words related to struggle from the text to your Word Network.

Practice

📓 **Notebook** **Respond to these questions.**

1. How would you expect *obdurate* people to respond to advertisements?

2. Would you want to have *stolid* friends? Why, or why not?

3. Give an example of a *disparity* that you have noticed between two groups of people.

4. How might a group of people *denounce* a government policy?

5. Suppose that you are trying to get information from people who *equivocate*. What would you ask them to do?

6. If someone *conceded* a point, did he or she continue to argue against it? Explain.

Word Study

📓 **Notebook** **Latin Prefix: *ob-*** The Latin prefix *ob-* often means "against." It combines with the root *-dur-*, which means "hard," to form *obdurate*, which means "hardened against." The word suggests a lack of sympathy toward someone else's difficulty or need and is a good synonym for *hard-hearted*.

1. Write a definition of *obstruction* based on your understanding of the prefix *ob-*. Check your answer in a print or an online college-level dictionary.

2. Identify and define two other words in which the prefix *ob-* means "against." Use etymological information in a dictionary to verify your choices.

STANDARDS

Language
• Demonstrate command of the conventions of standard English grammar and usage when writing or speaking.
• Apply knowledge of language to understand how language functions in different contexts, to make effective choices for meaning or style, and to comprehend more fully when reading or listening.
• Consult general and specialized reference materials, both print and digital, to find the pronunciation of a word or determine or clarify its precise meaning, its part of speech, its etymology, or its standard usage.

Conventions and Style

Types of Phrases A **noun phrase** consists of a noun and all of its modifiers. It functions just as a one-word noun does—as a subject, a direct or indirect object, a predicate nominative, an appositive, or the object of a preposition. A **verb phrase** consists of a main verb and all of its helping, or auxiliary, verbs.

Writers use noun phrases and verb phrases to add precision to their writing. A noun phrase can be quite specific and richly detailed. A verb phrase can indicate the exact tense, mood, and voice of the main verb.

This chart shows examples of noun phrases and verb phrases in the excerpt from "What to the Slave Is the Fourth of July?"

TIP

CLARIFICATION

Refer to the Grammar Handbook to learn more about verb tense, verb mood, and active and passive voice.

TYPE OF PHRASE	COMPOSITION	EXAMPLES
noun phrase	a noun and its modifiers, including articles, adjectives, and adjective phrases	*I am not* <u>*that man*</u>. (predicate nominative) <u>*Your high independence*</u> *only reveals* <u>*the immeasurable distance between us*</u>. (subject; direct object) *To drag . . . into* <u>*the grand illuminated temple of liberty*</u> *. . .* (object of a preposition)
verb phrase	a main verb and its helping verbs, but not any interrupting adverbs, such as *not*	*. . . when the chains of servitude* <u>*had been torn*</u> *from his limbs?* *In a case like that, the dumb* <u>*might*</u> *eloquently* <u>*speak*</u>. *. . .* *. . . I* <u>*do*</u> *not* <u>*despair*</u> *of this country.*

Read It

1. Each of these sentences contains at least one noun phrase or verb phrase—or both. Mark and label those phrases.

   a. Douglass spoke to the Rochester Ladies Anti-Slavery Society.

   b. He felt that listeners had not supported abolitionism strongly enough, and that he could stir them into action.

   c. His powerful words and his urgent tone shocked many and are still resonating with readers today.

2. **Connect to Style** Reread paragraph 4 of the excerpt from "What to the Slave Is the Fourth of July?" Mark and label two noun phrases and two verb phrases. Explain how the use of the phrases you identified shapes Douglass's style—how the reader "hears" the speaker's voice.

Write It

📝 **Notebook** Replace each of these nouns with a noun phrase: *crowd, message, shame.* Replace each of these verbs with a verb phrase: *feel, participate, work.* Then, use each phrase in an original sentence that relates to Douglass's speech.

from WHAT TO THE SLAVE IS THE FOURTH OF JULY?

Writing to Sources

As Douglass's speech demonstrates, you can strengthen an argument by addressing counterclaims. A similar technique can strengthen informative writing as well: By addressing misconceptions or disproven ideas, you can guide readers to a clearer understanding of the information that you present. For example, if you were writing to explain why explorer Christopher Columbus had difficulty gaining support for his first Atlantic voyage, you might correct the following misconception by stating the fact:

Misconception: People thought that the world was flat and that Columbus would sail off the edge.

Fact: People thought that Columbus had underestimated the distance and that the crew would die when supplies ran out.

Assignment

In this speech, Douglass mentions Southern laws that made it a criminal offense to teach a slave to read and write. Briefly research how some slaves, including Douglass himself, learned to read. Then, write an **informative paragraph** in which you draw connections between your research and Douglass's speech. Include these elements in your paragraph:

- a clear introduction to the topic
- a misconception that you correct with a fact
- a formal, objective tone

Vocabulary and Conventions Connection Consider using several of the concept vocabulary words. Also, remember to use noun phrases and verb phrases to make your sentences precise and informative.

obdurate	disparity	equivocate
stolid	denounce	conceded

Reflect on Your Writing

After you have drafted your informative paragraph, answer the following questions.

1. How do you think that refuting a misconception strengthened your presentation?

2. **Why These Words?** The words you choose make a difference in your writing. Which words helped you convey information precisely?

≡ STANDARDS

Writing
• Write informative/explanatory texts to examine and convey complex ideas, concepts, and information clearly and accurately through the effective selection, organization, and analysis of content.
• Establish and maintain a formal style and objective tone while attending to the norms and conventions of the discipline in which they are writing.

Speaking and Listening
Evaluate a speaker's point of view, reasoning, and use of evidence and rhetoric, assessing the stance, premises, links among ideas, word choice, points of emphasis, and tone used.

Speaking and Listening

Assignment

Tone is the attitude a speaker expresses toward the subject or audience. A speaker's tone may convey any emotion; for instance, it may be loving, angry, scornful, or amused. In this speech, Douglass changes his tone for a variety of reasons. With a partner, identify two passages from the excerpt that convey different tones. Then, take turns giving a **dramatic reading** of each example.

1. **Choose Examples** Together, look for examples of passages in which Douglass emphasizes each of these ideas.

   - He expresses confusion about his purpose for speaking at this occasion.
   - He seeks common ground with his audience.
   - He reaches a turning point.
   - He introduces a counterclaim.
   - He expresses outrage.

2. **Listen to Dramatic Readings** Before you present your dramatic readings, review your examples. Decide which example you will present and which one your partner will present. Then, follow these steps.

   - Practice reciting the passages. Try to convey the tone you feel Douglass wanted to express. Use your voice and body language to emphasize that tone.
   - Introduce each passage by stating the idea that Douglass wanted to present; then, deliver your dramatic reading.
   - After you have both recited, briefly summarize your thoughts about Douglass's use of tone in each passage.

3. **Evaluate the Examples** Use a presentation evaluation guide like the one shown to assess your classmates' readings. Then, as a class, discuss how Douglass's use of tone contributes to his argument.

PRESENTATION EVALUATION GUIDE
Rate each statement on a scale of 1 (not demonstrated) to 5 (demonstrated).
☐ The speaker clearly introduced the passage.
☐ The speaker communicated expressively.
☐ The speaker used body language, including gestures, to emphasize the tone of the passage.
☐ The speaker accurately interpreted the tone of the passage.
☐ The speaker showed a good understanding of the text.

✒ EVIDENCE LOG

Before moving on to a new selection, go to your Evidence Log and record what you learned from "What to the Slave Is the Fourth of July?"

Abraham Lincoln
(1809–1865) took office
as president on March 4,
1861—just six weeks before
the Civil War began. The war
shaped his presidency, as he
sought to reunify the nation.
Lincoln took a keen interest
in the operations of the war,
appointing senior officers,
following the war's progress
through telegraph updates,
and even visiting Union
encampments. His belief
that slavery was morally
wrong drove him to issue
a preliminary Emancipation
Proclamation in 1862 and a
final version on January 1,
1863. From that point on,
the Civil War was viewed as
a fight to end slavery, as well
as to restore the Union.

🔧 **Tool Kit**
First-Read Guide and
Model Annotation

Second Inaugural Address

Concept Vocabulary

You will encounter the following words as you read Lincoln's second inaugural address. Before reading, note how familiar you are with each word. Then, rank the words in order from most familiar (1) to least familiar (6).

WORD	YOUR RANKING
insurgent	
perish	
rend	
scourge	
unrequited	
malice	

After completing the first read, come back to the concept vocabulary and review your rankings. Mark changes to your original rankings as needed.

First Read NONFICTION

Apply these strategies as you conduct your first read. You will have an opportunity to complete the close-read notes after your first read.

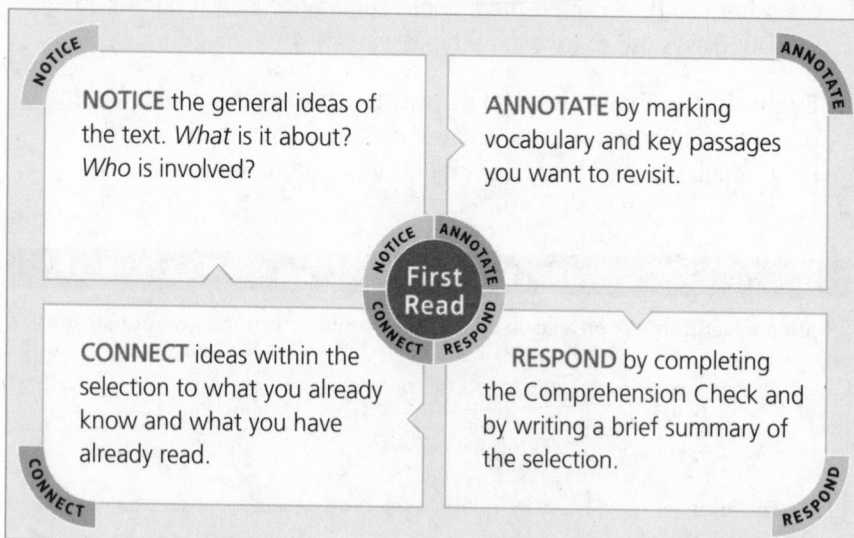

NOTICE the general ideas of the text. *What* is it about? *Who* is involved?

ANNOTATE by marking vocabulary and key passages you want to revisit.

CONNECT ideas within the selection to what you already know and what you have already read.

RESPOND by completing the Comprehension Check and by writing a brief summary of the selection.

≡ **STANDARDS**

Reading Informational Text
• By the end of grade 11, read and comprehend literary nonfiction in the grades 11–CCR text complexity band proficiently, with scaffolding as needed at the high end of the range.

Second Inaugural Address

Abraham Lincoln

SCAN FOR MULTIMEDIA

BACKGROUND

On March 4, 1865, a crowd of perhaps as many as 40,000 people gathered on the muddy grounds of the United States Capitol to see Abraham Lincoln sworn in for his second term. Despite rain earlier in the morning, the sun broke through the clouds as Lincoln came forward. He gave the following speech to hopeful listeners, who (as one of his bodyguards later said) "seemed to hang on his words as though they were meat and drink." Indeed, Frederick Douglass told Lincoln that the speech had been "a sacred effort." Following the speech, Chief Justice Salmon P. Chase administered the oath of office. Ironically, Lincoln would die a little more than a month later at the hands of John Wilkes Booth, who stood in the crowd on the Capitol steps that day and listened to Lincoln give the speech.

NOTES

Fellow-Countrymen:

1 At this second appearing to take the oath of the presidential office, there is less occasion for an extended address than there was at the first. Then a statement somewhat in detail of a course to be pursued seemed fitting and proper. Now, at the expiration of four years, during which public declarations have been constantly called

forth on every point and phase of the great contest which still absorbs the attention and engrosses the energies of the nation, little that is new could be presented. The progress of our arms, upon which all else chiefly depends, is as well known to the public as to myself, and it is, I trust, reasonably satisfactory and encouraging to all. With high hope for the future, no prediction in regard to it is ventured.

2   On the occasion corresponding to this four years ago, all thoughts were anxiously directed to an impending civil war. All dreaded it; all sought to avert it. While the inaugural address was being delivered from this place, devoted altogether to saving the Union without war, **insurgent** agents were in the city seeking to destroy it without war— seeking to dissolve the Union and divide effects by negotiation. Both parties deprecated war, but one of them would make war rather than let the nation survive, and the other would accept war rather than let it **perish**, and the war came.

3   One-eighth of the whole population were colored slaves, not distributed generally over the Union, but localized in the southern part of it. These slaves constituted a peculiar and powerful interest. All knew that this interest was somehow the cause of the war. To strengthen, perpetuate, and extend this interest was the object for which the insurgents would **rend** the Union even by war, while the government claimed no right to do more than to restrict the territorial enlargement of it. Neither party expected for the war the magnitude or the duration which it has already attained. Neither anticipated that the cause of the conflict might cease with or even before the conflict itself should cease. Each looked for an easier triumph, and a result less fundamental and astounding. Both read the same Bible and pray to the same God, and each invokes his aid against the other. It may seem strange that any men should dare to ask a just God's assistance in wringing their bread from the sweat of other men's faces, but "let us judge not, that we be not judged."[1] The prayers of both could not be answered. That of neither has been answered fully. The Almighty has his own purposes. "Woe unto the world because of offenses; for it must needs be that offenses come, but woe to that man by whom the offense cometh."[2] If we shall suppose that American slavery is one of those offenses which, in the providence of God, must needs come, but which, having continued through his appointed time, he now wills to remove, and that he gives to both North and South this terrible war as the woe due to those by whom the offense came, shall we discern therein any departure from those divine attributes which the believers in a living God always ascribe to him? Fondly do we hope, fervently do we pray, that this mighty **scourge** of war may speedily pass away. Yet, if God wills that it continue until all the wealth piled by the bondsman's two hundred and fifty years of **unrequited** toil

---

1. **"let us judge not, that we be not judged"** reference to the words of Jesus in the biblical passage Matthew 7:1.
2. **"Woe unto the world . . . the offense cometh."** reference to the biblical passage Matthew 18:7, in which Jesus warns about allowing sin into one's life.

insurgent (ihn SUR juhnt) *adj.* rebellious or in revolt against a government in power

perish (PEH rish) *v.* die

rend (rehnd) *v.* tear apart with violent force

CLOSE READ

ANNOTATE: Mark the sentence in paragraph 3 that states the government's policy regarding the expansion of slavery.

QUESTION: Why does the president include this information?

CONCLUDE: What effect does this information have, particularly in shaping the audience's view of the Confederacy?

scourge (SKURJ) *n.* cause of serious trouble or suffering

unrequited (uhn rih KWY tihd) *adj.* not repaid or avenged shall be sunk, and until every drop of blood drawn with the lash shall be paid by another drawn with the sword, as was said three thousand years ago, so still it must be said "the judgments of the Lord are true and righteous altogether."[3]

With **malice** toward none, with charity for all, with firmness in the right as God gives us to see the right, let us strive on to finish the work we are in, to bind up the nation's wounds, to care for him who shall have borne the battle and for his widow and his orphan, to do all which may achieve and cherish a just and lasting peace among ourselves and with all nations. ❧

3. **"the judgments of the Lord are true and righteous altogether"** reference to the biblical Psalm 19:9, praising the rightness of God's ways.

malice (MAL ihs) *n.* desire to harm or inflict injury

Comprehension Check

Complete the following items after you finish your first read.

1. To what event is Lincoln referring when he says, "On the occasion corresponding to this four years ago. . ."?

2. What was on people's minds at the time of the occasion you identified in item 1?

3. What is the "peculiar and powerful interest" that Lincoln says was "somehow the cause of the war?"

4. What does Lincoln intend to do to heal the nation, after the war?

5. 🗒 **Notebook** Write a summary of Lincoln's second inaugural address to confirm your understanding of the speech.

- -

RESEARCH

Research to Clarify Choose at least one unfamiliar detail from the text. Briefly research that detail. In what way does the information you learned shed light on an aspect of the speech?

Research to Explore Choose something that interests you from the text, and formulate a research question about it.

SECOND INAUGURAL ADDRESS

Close Read the Text

1. This model, from paragraph 2 of the text, shows two sample annotations, along with questions and conclusions. Close read the passage, and find another detail to annotate. Then, write a question and your conclusion.

Close Read

ANNOTATE QUESTION CONCLUDE

ANNOTATE: Lincoln is comparing and contrasting reasons the North and South went to war.

QUESTION: For what purpose might Lincoln do this?

CONCLUDE: By showing insight about the war's causes, Lincoln might be indicating his ability to reunite the nation.

ANNOTATE: The final words are very dramatic.

QUESTION: What is the effect of these words?

CONCLUDE: Appearing at the end of a long, complex sentence, the simple words emphasize the horror of war.

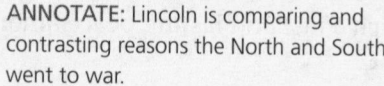

Both parties deprecated war, but one of them would make war rather than let the nation survive, and the other would accept war rather than let it perish, and the war came.

🔧 **Tool Kit**

Close-Read Guide and Model Annotation

2. For more practice, go back into the text, and complete the close-read notes.

3. Revisit a section of the text you found important during your first read. Read this section closely, and **annotate** what you notice. Ask yourself **questions** such as "Why did the author make this choice?" What can you **conclude**?

STANDARDS

Reading Informational Text
• Determine two or more central ideas of a text and analyze their development over the course of the text, including how they interact and build on one another to provide a complex analysis; provide an objective summary of the text.
• Analyze and evaluate the effectiveness of the structure an author uses in his or her exposition or argument, including whether the structure makes points clear, convincing, and engaging.
• Determine an author's point of view or purpose in a text in which the rhetoric is particularly effective, analyzing how style and content contribute to the power, persuasiveness, or beauty of the text.
• Analyze seventeenth-, eighteenth-, and nineteenth-century foundational U.S. documents of historical and literary significance for their themes, purposes, and rhetorical features.

Analyze the Text

CITE TEXTUAL EVIDENCE to support your answers.

📓 **Notebook** Respond to these questions.

1. (a) **Paraphrase**, or state in your own words, Lincoln's comment that "all else chiefly depends" upon "the progress of our arms." (b) **Interpret** To what is Lincoln referring with the words "all else"?

2. **Connect** How do Lincoln's statements in paragraph 2 connect to the rest of the speech?

3. (a) **Make Inferences** The term **irony** refers to a discrepancy between appearances and reality. Think about the irony in paragraph 3. In what way does Lincoln see irony in the abolition of slavery in the United States? (b) **Interpret** What does Lincoln find ironic about the prayers of both sides?

4. **Historical Perspectives** In what ways is this speech a commentary on the issue of slavery?

5. **Essential Question** *How does the struggle for freedom change with history?* What have you learned about the struggle for freedom from reading this speech?

Analyze Craft and Structure

Structure Writers often use a **chronological structure,** or time order, as a framework for their ideas. You may be used to seeing chronological order in the plot of a novel or play, but this kind of structure is also effective in nonfiction. For example, listeners can more easily follow the logic of a speech when ideas are presented within a chronological structure.

- The speaker establishes the chronological structure by discussing the events or actions that led to the present situation—which is often the occasion for the speech.
- The present situation is examined. At this point, the audience understands the central idea of the speech and contemplates the author's reasoning.
- The chronological framework is completed by a discussion of the future. This part can be a persuasive call to action or an explanation of a final step. It is always a clear statement of the speaker's central idea.

In his second inaugural address, Lincoln recalls the past, discusses the present, and looks to the future.

Practice

CITE TEXTUAL EVIDENCE to support your answers.

📓 **Notebook Respond to these questions.**

1. (a) What does Lincoln say about the nature of the speech he made when he first took office, four years earlier? (b) How does he contrast that information with the speech that he is making in the present, at his second inauguration?
2. In this chart, briefly record the content of each part of the chronological framework of Lincoln's speech.

LINCOLN'S SECOND INAUGURAL ADDRESS: CHRONOLOGICAL CONTENT	
Past	
Present	
Future	

3. What does the content of the speech tell you about Lincoln's intended policy for his second term?
4. (a) What national issue does Lincoln discuss in paragraph 3? (b) What might have been the effect of the speech if Lincoln had developed it to discuss only this issue? Explain.
5. How does Lincoln's use of chronological structure contribute to the effectiveness of the speech? Explain.

SECOND INAUGURAL ADDRESS

Concept Vocabulary

insurgent	rend	unrequited
perish	scourge	malice

Why These Words? These concept vocabulary words remind the audience of the terrible nature of the conflict that the nation was enduring at the moment. Lincoln says that the *insurgents* would *rend* the nation. He speaks of the *scourge* of war—and, indeed, the war took many American lives and destroyed much of the nation's property.

1. How does the concept vocabulary convey the nature of the conflict?

2. What other words in the speech connect to this concept?

Practice

📓 **Notebook** **Complete these activities.**

1. Use each concept vocabulary word in a sentence that demonstrates your understanding of the word's meaning.

2. In two of your sentences, replace the concept word with a synonym. What is the effect of your word change? For example, which sentence seems more powerful? Which one seems more positive or more negative?

Word Study

Synonyms and Nuances In this speech, Lincoln refers to the "scourge" of war. *Scourge* is a very strong word, an example of charged language. Lincoln might have chosen another word with a similar denotation, such as *blight* or *curse*. These words are synonyms because they have similar general meanings. They are also all examples of charged, or emotionally laden language. However, each word has its own **nuance,** or shade of meaning. For example, *blight* suggests disease or withering, whereas *curse* suggests a supernatural source of suffering.

1. Write two sentences, using a synonym for *scourge* in each sentence. Make sure that each sentence demonstrates the shade of meaning of the synonym you choose.

2. Reread the second inaugural address. Which synonym for *scourge* most closely reflects Lincoln's use of the word? Explain.

🔗 WORD NETWORK

Add words related to struggle from the text to your Word Network.

☰ STANDARDS

Language
• Demonstrate command of the conventions of standard English grammar and usage when writing or speaking.
• Apply knowledge of language to understand how language functions in different contexts, to make effective choices for meaning or style, and to comprehend more fully when reading or listening.
• Analyze nuances in the meaning of words with similar denotations.
• Acquire and use accurately general academic and domain-specific words and phrases, sufficient for reading, writing, speaking, and listening at the college and career readiness level; demonstrate independence in gathering vocabulary knowledge when considering a word or phrase important to comprehension or expression.

Conventions and Style

Types of Phrases A **prepositional phrase** is a group of words that begins with a preposition. Some prepositions are listed here.

about	across	at	beneath	by
concerning	despite	except	for	from
in	into	near	of	on
regarding	than	to	toward	with

A prepositional phrase also includes an object and any modifiers of that object. The object of the preposition may be a noun, a pronoun, a gerund (a verb form that acts as a noun), or, occasionally, a clause. Prepositional phrases function in sentences as either adverbs or adjectives. They help writers and speakers express their ideas with greater clarity and precision.

TYPE OF PHRASE	DEFINITION	EXAMPLES
adverb phrase	a prepositional phrase that modifies a verb, an adjective, or another adverb, by telling *how, where, when,* or *to what degree*	Lincoln was assassinated <u>at Ford's Theatre</u>. (tells *where*) John Wilkes Booth shot him <u>during a play</u>. (tells *when*)
adjective phrase	a prepositional phrase that modifies a noun or pronoun, by telling *what kind, how many,* or *which one*	The president <u>from Illinois</u> died soon after. (tells *which one*) Crowds <u>beyond number</u> mourned his loss. (tells *how many*)

Read It

1. Mark the prepositional phrase in each sentence. Then, label each one as an adverb phrase or an adjective phrase.

   a. Lincoln delivered his address at the White House.

   b. The East Portico of the White House was a historic place.

   c. Lincoln spoke in a clear, strong voice.

2. **Connect to Style** Reread paragraph 3 of Lincoln's speech. Mark and then label two adjective phrases and two adverb phrases. Explain how the use of prepositional phrases contributes to Lincoln's style and helps clarify his ideas.

Write It

📓 **Notebook** Expand the numbered sentences by adding one or more adverb phrases or adjective phrases. Label each phrase in parentheses.

> EXAMPLE
> The sun began shining.
> The sun began shining ***through the clouds*** (adverb phrase) ***at the moment*** (adverb phrase) ***of Lincoln's speech*** (adjective phrase).

1. Lincoln spoke, and everyone paid rapt attention.

2. Most listeners applauded when the words touched their minds and hearts.

SECOND INAUGURAL ADDRESS

Writing to Sources

Eyewitness accounts are important sources of historical information. Historians look for as many such accounts as are available in order to compare what each eyewitness has recorded. In addition to each person's unique insights, historians look for corroboration of descriptions and sequences of events.

Assignment

Imagine that you had been present when Abraham Lincoln delivered this inaugural address. Write an **informative eyewitness account** in the form of a letter or journal entry. Include details such as these:

- personal details, such as where you were standing
- an estimate of how many people were present
- Lincoln's appearance and delivery
- the effect of the speech on the crowd
- your opinion of the speech

Report narrative details in an orderly sequence. You might want to remark, for example, on your difficulties as you looked for a place to stand and observe the occasion. Then, describe the scene from the vantage point you eventually found.

Vocabulary and Conventions Connection Consider including several of the concept vocabulary words. Also, remember to use prepositional phrases to add precision to your account.

insurgent	rend	unrequited
perish	scourge	malice

Reflect on Your Writing

After you have drafted your informative eyewitness account, answer these questions.

1. Did you write as if you had been actually present?

2. What kinds of details did you add to make your account realistic?

3. Why These Words? The words you choose can greatly increase the effect of your writing. Which words do you think are most helpful in conveying the sense that "you had been there"?

STANDARDS

Writing
• Write informative/explanatory texts to examine and convey complex ideas, concepts, and information clearly and accurately through the effective selection, organization, and analysis of content.
• Write narratives to develop real or imagined experiences or events using effective technique, well-chosen details, and well-structured event sequences.

Speaking and Listening
Evaluate a speaker's point of view, reasoning, and use of evidence and rhetoric, assessing the stance, premises, links among ideas, word choice, points of emphasis, and tone used.

Speaking and Listening

Assignment

With a partner, prepare a brief **reading and discussion** of key passages from Lincoln's speech.

1. **Choose the Passages** Work together to choose two passages that you feel express key ideas with particular force or clarity.

   - Read the sentences or passages aloud, pausing to restate, or paraphrase, Lincoln's words.

   - Work together to develop a clear statement about the reasons you chose the two passages: What qualities in the language or ideas make these two passages especially powerful?

2. **Prepare Your Delivery** Read through the passages, and note natural breaks. These may be indicated by punctuation marks, but you also can choose places where you will want to pause for emphasis.

3. **Deliver Your Reading and Analysis** Follow these tips as you read your passages aloud and discuss your choices.

   - Speak slowly so that listeners can follow any challenging language or ideas.

   - Use gestures and body language carefully to emphasize meaning without causing distraction. In addition, vary the volume of your voice and the speed with which you speak to accurately reflect the ideas you are expressing.

   - Remember that the language of Lincoln's speech is formal. In addition, some word choices are different from those in modern speech. Make sure your interpretation reflects the meanings of such words accurately.

   - Pause after you complete your readings of the passages. Then, present your interpretations of the passages in your own words.

4. **Evaluate Presentations** As your classmates deliver their presentations, listen attentively. Use the evaluation guide to analyze their presentations.

PRESENTATION EVALUATION GUIDE

Rate each statement on a scale of 1 (not demonstrated) to 5 (demonstrated).

- [ ] The speaker read the text with proper emphasis on meaning.

- [ ] The speaker used appropriate gestures and body language.

- [ ] The speaker's pace and volume were varied and appropriate for the thoughts and feelings expressed in the text.

- [ ] The speaker's interpretations and evaluations were accurate and well expressed.

✎ EVIDENCE LOG

Before moving on to a new selection, go to your Evidence Log and record what you learned from Lincoln's second inaugural address.

About Political Cartoons and Photojournalism

Many **political cartoons**, especially in the nineteenth century, were published anonymously; in fact, of the three cartoons in this gallery, only the pro-Lincoln caricature of the President's height is attributable (to Frank Billew). The others, expressing the dissatisfaction with Lincoln's leadership that seethed in the North among the Democrats and those Republicans unsatisfied with Lincoln's leadership in the war, were published anonymously in various newspapers.

Photojournalism—capturing news in photographs—emerged in the 1840s. The new technology of photography found a use in revealing events and preserving images for history, including battlefield photographs of the Civil War.

Perspectives on Lincoln

Media Vocabulary

The following words will be useful to you as you analyze, discuss, and write about political cartoons and photojournalism.

Composition: arrangement of the parts of an image, whether drawn or recorded in some other visual format	• The composition may emphasize one part of an image more than another. • The composition may offer clues to the political purpose of the image.
Caricature: exaggeration of details relating to people and events, often for humorous effect, in a cartoon or other created image	• In political cartoons, caricature often shows how the cartoonist (or the publication that hired the cartoonist) feels about a particular person, group, or situation. • Sometimes, elements of a public figure's appearance become commonly caricatured, making that person easy to identify.
Labeling and Captions: written labels and other text that often accompany politically charged images to clarify their meanings	• In political cartoons, key details are often labeled to help readers recognize their meaning. • Photographs are more likely to use captions or annotations that present the context in which the photograph was taken.

First Review MEDIA: ART AND PHOTOGRAPHY

Apply these strategies as you conduct your first review. You will have an opportunity to conduct a close review after your first review.

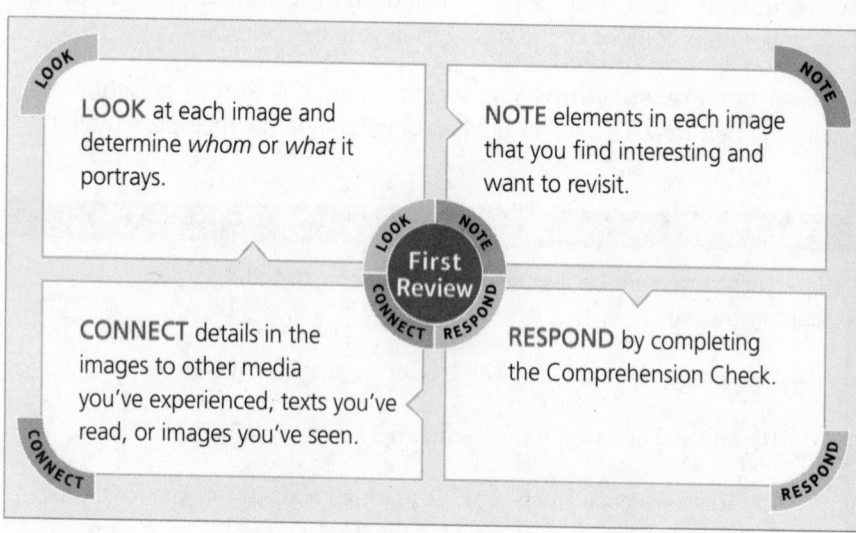

LOOK at each image and determine *whom* or *what* it portrays.

NOTE elements in each image that you find interesting and want to revisit.

CONNECT details in the images to other media you've experienced, texts you've read, or images you've seen.

RESPOND by completing the Comprehension Check.

Perspectives on Lincoln

BACKGROUND

As Lincoln's second election campaign approached, he was faced with a Republican party threatening to splinter, a bloody Civil War in its final stages, and a Democratic party ready to capitalize on his apparent vulnerability. However, Lincoln overcame these obstacles by combining the political heft of an impending Union victory, the support of the soldier vote, and political deals brokered within the Republican party. His campaign's slogan was "Don't change horses in the middle of a stream." As you study these images, ask yourself these questions: What opinions did people have of Lincoln in his own time? How is he thought of today?

SCAN FOR
MULTIMEDIA

IMAGE 1: The Union Must Be Preserved at All Hazards This 1864 cartoon depicts Democratic presidential candidate George Brinton McClellan trying to keep a map of the United States from being pulled apart by President Abraham Lincoln and the Confederate president Jefferson Davis. The cartoon depicts both Lincoln and Davis as short-sightedly putting their own political goals (abolition for Lincoln, secession for Davis) ahead of the country's well-being.

NOTES

IMAGE 2: Columbia Demands Her Children! "Columbia," a personification of America, is condemning Abraham Lincoln for the Union casualties of the Civil War. Lincoln's reply refers to a false report that Lincoln had told a joke on the battlefield of Antietam.

IMAGE 3: Long Abe a Little Longer In this celebration of Lincoln's reelection, Lincoln is caricatured as being president "even longer"—a play on words regarding his height and his length of time in office, as well as a reference to his "stature," or importance, as president.

IMAGE 4: The Body of the Martyr President, Abraham Lincoln, Lying in State Further increasing his stature in the eyes of the nation, Lincoln's assassination made him a martyr, as the North was united in grief. Many historians have called Lincoln's funeral the greatest in the history of the United States.

NOTES

NOTES

IMAGE 5: Funeral Procession in New York City Millions turned out to see Lincoln's funeral train pass on its way to his burial in Springfield, Illinois—and, in some cities, to attend a ceremony in his honor. In this photograph of a funeral procession held during a stop in New York City, a young Theodore Roosevelt (later President Roosevelt) and his brother watch the scene from a window (in the upper left-hand corner of the image).

IMAGE 6: Civil Rights Activists at the Lincoln Memorial Almost a century after Lincoln's death, leaders of the Civil Rights movement, including Dr. Martin Luther King, Jr., (seated, farthest right) gather in front of the Lincoln Memorial during the 1963 March on Washington. The Civil Rights movement often looked to Abraham Lincoln, "the Great Emancipator," for inspiration.

NOTES

Comprehension Check

Use the chart to note details about the subject of each image. Identify people and/or symbols, objects, the setting (if there is one), and activities or events depicted.

IMAGE	PEOPLE AND/OR SYMBOLS	OBJECTS	SETTING	ACTIVITIES AND/OR EVENTS
IMAGE 1				
IMAGE 2				
IMAGE 3				
IMAGE 4				
IMAGE 5				
IMAGE 6				
NOTES				

PERSPECTIVES ON LINCOLN

Close Review

Revisit the images and your first-review notes. Write down any new observations that seem important. What **questions** do you have? What can you **conclude?**

Analyze the Media

📄 **Notebook** Complete the activities.

1. **Present and Discuss** Choose the image you find most interesting or persuasive. Share your choice with the class, and discuss why you chose it. Explain what you noticed in the image, the questions it raised for you, and the conclusions you reached about it.

2. **Review and Synthesize** Review all the images. What perspectives do they present? What argument are they making? Are they examples of journalism, art, both, or neither? Explain.

3. **Essential Question:** *In what ways does the struggle for freedom change with history?* What have you learned about the struggle for freedom from these cartoons and photographs?

Media Vocabulary

| composition | caricature | labeling and captions |

Use these vocabulary words in your responses to the following questions.

1. (a) In Image 1, what are the positions of the three people in relation to one another? To the map of the United States? (b) What might the artist have intended to convey through this depiction?

2. (a) In Image 2, what visual details clarify the identity of the woman on the left? (b) On what visual details does Image 3 rely to convey its message?

3. (a) In what sense does Image 6 express a political idea? (b) How does that idea reflect the ideas expressed in Images 4 and 5?

STANDARDS

Reading Informational Text
Integrate and evaluate multiple sources of information presented in different media or formats as well as in words in order to address a question or solve a problem.

Speaking and Listening
• Integrate multiple sources of information presented in diverse formats and media in order to make informed decisions and solve problems, evaluating the credibility and accuracy of each source and noting any discrepancies among the data.
• Make strategic use of digital media in presentations to enhance understanding of findings, reasoning, and evidence and to add interest.

Speaking and Listening

Assignment

Create and present an **image gallery.** Choose a person about whom or an event about which Americans had or have varying perspectives. Conduct research, using print and online sources, to find relevant political cartoons and photographs. Create a slide show of your image gallery, and write an informative script to accompany your presentation.

EVIDENCE LOG

Before moving on to a new selection, go to your Evidence Log and record what you learned from "Perspectives on Lincoln."

Plan the Project To help you prepare your image gallery, consider these questions.

- Why is or was the person or event important? What are you trying to show your audience about the perspectives that people had or have of the person or event?
- What sources will you use to conduct your research?
- What technology will you need to present your image slide show?

When choosing photographs, consider how the images reflect attitudes, not just how they preserve a moment in time. When you have chosen your images, make a storyboard.

STORYBOARD TEMPLATE

Prepare the Informative Script Think about the relationships among the images. Consider how you might use the script to point out those relationships.

- Choose a logical sequence of images. Decide how to use transitions in your script to show that sequence.
- Decide how much time to spend on presenting each image. Tailor the length of each section of your script accordingly.
- Once you have written your script, practice reading it aloud.

Present and Discuss Present a slide show of your image gallery to the class, using your script to narrate each image as you show it. Afterward, discuss how well the various perspectives were captured in the images.

WRITING TO SOURCES

- *from* WHAT TO THE SLAVE IS THE FOURTH OF JULY?

- SECOND INAUGURAL ADDRESS

- PERSPECTIVES ON LINCOLN

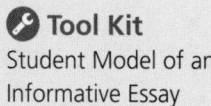 **Tool Kit**

Student Model of an Informative Essay

ACADEMIC VOCABULARY

As you write your essay, consider using some of the academic vocabulary you learned in the beginning of the unit.

informational

deduction

verbatim

inquire

specific

≣ STANDARDS

Writing

- Write informative/explanatory texts to examine and convey complex ideas, concepts, and information clearly and accurately through the effective selection, organization, and analysis of content.
- Conduct short as well as more sustained research projects to answer a question or solve a problem; narrow or broaden the inquiry when appropriate; synthesize multiple sources on the subject, demonstrating understanding of the subject under investigation.
- Write routinely over extended time frames and shorter time frames for a range of tasks, purposes, and audiences.

Write an Informative Essay

You've just read two important nineteenth-century speeches. In the first, Frederick Douglass looks forward to the liberation of people from slavery. In the second, Abraham Lincoln looks forward to the end of a war and to a just and lasting peace. You've also examined political cartoons and other images from the period that portray differing attitudes about Abraham Lincoln.

> **Assignment**
>
> Write an **informative essay** that looks at American history after the Civil War and that answers this question:
>
> > **Did the nation achieve the goals that Douglass and Lincoln desired?**
>
> Begin by doing some library or online research. Investigate the period following the Civil War by looking up "Reconstruction" and taking notes on your findings. Include facts, details, and definitions that clarify your response. Connect your findings to specific details from the selections in Whole-Class Learning.

Elements of an Informative Essay

An **informative essay** uses facts, details, data, and other kinds of evidence to present information about a topic. Readers turn to informative texts when they wish to learn about a specific idea, concept, or subject area.

An effective informative essay contains these elements:

- a thesis statement that introduces the concept or subject
- relevant facts and concrete details that expand upon the topic
- extended definitions, quotations, and other examples that support the information presented
- use of varied sentence structures to clarify the relationships among ideas
- precise language and technical vocabulary where appropriate
- a formal style and an objective tone
- a conclusion that follows from and supports the information presented

Model Informative Essay For a model of a well-crafted informative essay, see the Launch Text, "The Zigzag Road to Rights." Review the Launch Text for examples of the elements described above. You will look more closely at these elements as you prepare to write your own informative essay.

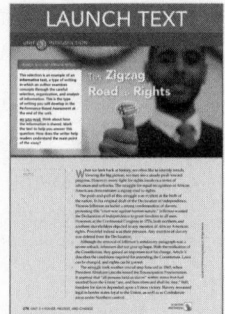

Prewriting / Planning

Write a Working Thesis Reread the assignment. Based on the work you have done so far in this unit, think about what you want to say in response to the question that the assignment asks. Write a draft of your **thesis statement** (or **thesis**)—the sentence that presents the controlling idea of your text.

_____

_____ .

Compare and Contrast Douglass and Lincoln had different goals, but some of their concerns were similar. Record some areas of comparison and contrast that you might use to support your thesis statement.

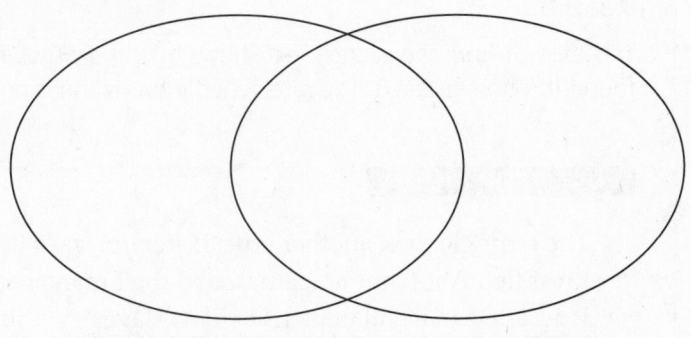

Douglass's Goals   Common Goals   Lincoln's Goals

Gather Evidence Several kinds of information support the thesis developed in the Launch Text. Think about ways in which you can effectively support your thesis. Consider these types of evidence:

- **facts:** relevant statements that can be proved true

- **statistics:** facts presented in the form of numerical data

- **definitions:** explanations of key terms that may be unfamiliar to readers

- **quotations:** statements from authoritative sources (such as historical documents)

- **examples:** specific circumstances that illustrate a general idea

Always confirm your evidence by using more than one source.

Connect Across Texts The prompt asks you to connect your findings to specific details from the speeches by Douglass and Lincoln. Also include details from the political cartoons and other images of Lincoln in your response. Return to those texts, and on note cards record **direct quotations** from the speeches that you might use to support your ideas. Look back at the Launch Text to see how the writer weaves direct quotations from court cases, proclamations, and amendments into the informative essay.

EVIDENCE LOG

Review your Evidence Log and identify key details you may want to cite in your informative essay.

STANDARDS
Writing
• Introduce a topic; organize complex ideas, concepts, and information so that each new element builds on that which precedes it to create a unified whole; include formatting, graphics, and multimedia when useful to aiding comprehension.
• Develop the topic thoroughly by selecting the most significant and relevant facts, extended definitions, concrete details, quotations, or other information and examples appropriate to the audience's knowledge of the topic.

ENRICHING WRITING WITH RESEARCH

Conducting Research Most informative writing requires some research. Find relevant information from reputable sources, and then weave it into your essay.

Assessing Strengths and Limitations of Information Some information is reliable and useful, whereas other information may be suspect or simply not helpful. Evaluate the quality of the information you find by answering these questions:

- Will this information help me develop my topic or thesis?
- Will my audience understand this information, or will I need to provide more background or detail?
- Is this information current, or is it outdated?

Read It

This excerpt from the Launch Text shows how the writer integrates details found through research. The researched information is underlined.

> The writer quotes directly from the researched text to illustrate one of the "zigzag" steps to rights for African Americans.

LAUNCH TEXT EXCERPT

The struggle took another crucial step forward in 1863, when President Abraham Lincoln issued the Emancipation Proclamation. It asserted that "all persons held as slaves" within states that had seceded from the Union "are, and henceforward, shall be free." Still, freedom for slaves depended upon a Union victory. Slavery remained legal in border states loyal to the Union, as well as in Confederate areas under Northern control.

Avoiding Plagiarism *Plagiarism* means taking someone's ideas and words and passing them off as your own. Nobody expects you to be an expert in every subject. However, when you rely on other experts, you must credit them. Follow these steps to avoid plagiarism.

1. **Quote.** If the source uses wording that you find especially strong or apt, quote it directly. Make sure the reader can tell whom you are quoting.

   Example: *In his original draft of the Declaration of Independence, Thomas Jefferson included a strong condemnation of slavery, protesting this "cruel war against human nature."*

2. **Paraphrase.** When an author's ideas are important but the wording is less critical, restate the information in your own words.

   Example:
   Original: *The struggle took another crucial step forward in 1863, when President Abraham Lincoln issued the Emancipation Proclamation.*

   Paraphrase: Lincoln's Emancipation Proclamation of 1863 would prove to be a benchmark in the fight for civil rights.

3. **Cite.** Follow the format your teacher prefers to cite sources for any information you use that is not common public knowledge.

STANDARDS

Writing
Gather relevant information from multiple authoritative print and digital sources, using advanced searches effectively; assess the strengths and limitations of each source in terms of the task, purpose, and audience; integrate information into the text selectively to maintain the flow of ideas, avoiding plagiarism and overreliance on any one source and following a standard format for citation.

ESSENTIAL QUESTION: In what ways does the struggle for freedom change with history?

College and Career Readiness

Write It

Organize your notes in a way that will best help you support your thesis statement.

Taking and Organizing Notes Develop a system for organizing your notes so that you know which are paraphrased and which are directly quoted. Try using this format for one of your notes to see whether it works well for you. Then, copy it or revise it to use for each of your sources.

> TITLE: _____ PAGE _____
>
> AUTHOR: _____
>
> SUMMARY, QUOTATION, OR PARAPHASE? (Circle one)
>
> NOTES:

Evaluating Sources Review your notes, and look for conflicting information. If you find substantial differences, consider the reliability and credibility of the sources: web sites ending with .edu or .gov generally provide more accurate information than sites ending with .com. When two sources conflict, look for a third source to confirm facts.

Weaving Research Into Text As you draft your essay, work to integrate quotations and other information from your sources. Clearly introduce each reference and note its relevance, as in this model.

INTEGRATING QUOTATIONS

> Lincoln's proclamation was not guaranteed to have the effects he wanted. In his Lincoln Prize–winning book, *Lincoln's Emancipation Proclamation*, Gettysburg College professor Allen Guelzo called it "one of the biggest political gambles in American history" (7). It might easily have backfired.

The writer clearly introduces the quotation, identifying its author and integrating it with surrounding text, and then links it to a main point: *The proclamation might have made a situation worse instead of better.*

TIP

CITATIONS
When citing sources, use a consistent style, such as the one established by the Modern Language Association (MLA):

- Sources are cited following the quotation or reference. The citation appears in parentheses with a page reference, as applicable.

- If the parenthetical citation appears at the end of a sentence, the period follows the final parenthesis.

Drafting

Organize Your Essay Your essay should include an introduction, a body, and a conclusion. Each section of the essay should build on what has come before.

This outline shows the key sections of the Launch Text. In an informative essay, you have the option of adding headings to separate sections that belong together. Whether or not you use headings, each section of the text should have a specific purpose.

Consider the Launch Text outline as you organize information for your draft.

Model: "The Zigzag Road to Rights" Outline

INTRODUCTION
Paragraph 1 states the thesis: *The struggle for equal recognition of African Americans demonstrates a zigzag road to rights.*

BODY
Paragraph 2 (failure): revisions to the Declaration of Independence

Paragraph 3 (improvement): Article V of the Constitution

Paragraph 4 (improvement): the Emancipation Proclamation

Paragraph 5 (improvement): the Thirteenth *Amendment*

Paragraph 6 (failure): *Plessy v. Ferguson*

Paragraph 7 (improvement): *Brown v. Board of Education*

Paragraph 8 (improvement): the Voting Rights Act of 1965

CONCLUSION
Paragraph 9 recalls the thesis: *History teaches us that rights gained can be lost, curtailed, or ignored— and perhaps gained once more.*

Informative Essay Outline

INTRODUCTION

BODY

CONCLUSION

☰ STANDARDS

Writing
• Develop the topic thoroughly by selecting the most significant and relevant facts, extended definitions, concrete details, quotations, or other information and examples appropriate to the audience's knowledge of the topic.
• Provide a concluding statement or section that follows from and supports the information or explanation presented.

Write a First Draft Use your outline to write your first draft. Include a variety of evidence, and make clear connections among ideas. Be sure that each paragraph has a purpose and follows logically from the paragraphs that come before it. Keep your readers in mind as you craft your text. Consider what they might already know and what might be unfamiliar. Work at making your writing engaging and logical. Include headings if they might clarify things for your readers. Write a conclusion that follows from your thesis and supports the information you presented.

LANGUAGE DEVELOPMENT: CONVENTIONS

Syntax: Sentence Patterns

Sentences come in a variety of patterns. Some sentence patterns are best suited for simple ideas; some patterns better convey complex, related ideas.

Read It

These sentences from the Launch Text demonstrate a variety of sentence patterns. Subjects are underlined once, and verbs are underlined twice.

- Simple Sentence (one independent clause): *In his original draft of the Declaration of Independence, Thomas Jefferson included a strong condemnation of slavery.*

- Inverted Sentence (verb precedes subject): *Powerful indeed was their pressure.*

- Compound Sentence (two or more independent clauses): *Laws can be changed, and rights can be gained.*

- Complex Sentence (one independent clause and one or more dependent clauses): *The struggle took another crucial step forward in 1863, when President Abraham Lincoln issued the Emancipation Proclamation.*

- Compound-Complex Sentence (two or more independent clauses and one or more dependent clauses): *While the path to progress is not smooth, one thing is certain: The zigzag will continue into the future.*

Write It

As you draft, choose sentence patterns that best match the ideas you want to convey. Here are some strategies and examples.

STRATEGY	EXAMPLES
To convey two closely related ideas, combine simple sentences to make compound sentences.	Today, all adult citizens can vote. Many hold higher office. *Today, all adult citizens can vote, and many hold higher office.*
Invert simple sentences to add interest.	Voting rights are among an American's most important privileges. *Among an American's most important privileges are voting rights.*
Add subordinate clauses to provide detail.	Eighteen-year-olds rarely vote. *Eighteen-year-olds who are not informed rarely vote. Even when the polls are nearby, eighteen-year-olds rarely vote.*

PUNCTUATION
Punctuate compound and complex sentences correctly.

- Use a comma before the coordinating conjunction in a compound sentence.

- Use a semicolon between independent clauses in a compound sentence with no coordinating conjunction.

- Use a comma after a subordinate clause that begins a complex sentence.

STANDARDS

Writing
Use appropriate and varied transitions and syntax to link the major sections of the text, create cohesion, and clarify the relationships among complex ideas and concepts.

Language
Vary syntax for effect, consulting references for guidance as needed; apply an understanding of syntax to the study of complex texts when reading.

Revising

Evaluating Your Draft

Use this checklist to evaluate the effectiveness of your first draft. Then, use your evaluation and the revising instructions on this page to guide your revision.

FOCUS AND ORGANIZATION	EVIDENCE AND ELABORATION	CONVENTIONS
☐ Provides an introduction that establishes the topic and thesis statement.	☐ Develops the topic using relevant facts, definitions, details, quotations, examples, and/or other evidence.	☐ Attends to the norms and conventions of the discipline, especially the correct use and punctuation of compound and complex sentences.
☐ Presents main points in a logical order.	☐ Uses vocabulary and word choices that are appropriate for the purpose and audience, including precise words and technical vocabulary where appropriate.	☐ Uses appropriate and varied sentence structures to create cohesion and clarify relationships.
☐ Uses words, phrases, and clauses to clarify relationships among ideas.		
☐ Provides a conclusion that follows logically from the preceding information.		

⬚ WORD NETWORK

Include interesting words from your Word Network in your informative essay.

Revising for Focus and Organization

Strong Conclusion Your conclusion should reflect the information that precedes it, but it also should suggest the topic's importance or somehow connect the topic to a broader view. Notice how the Launch Text writer draws a conclusion about the topic's connection to the past and the future in the conclusion of "The Zigzag Road to Rights."

> **LAUNCH TEXT EXCERPT**
>
> The history of African American rights features many crucial victories, from the Emancipation Proclamation through the Voting Rights Act. However, the record of the struggle also includes the difficult stumbling blocks that have had to be overcome. While the path to progress is not smooth, one thing is certain: The zigzag will continue into the future. History teaches us that rights gained can be lost, curtailed, or ignored—and perhaps gained once more.

Revising for Evidence and Elaboration

Technical Vocabulary If you use topic-specific words, consider how you might define them for your audience. Be sure to spell and use those words correctly.

☰ STANDARDS

Writing
• Use precise language, domain-specific vocabulary and techniques such as metaphor, simile, and analogy to manage the complexity of the topic.
• Provide a concluding statement or section that follows from and supports the information or explanation presented.

PEER REVIEW

Exchange essays with a classmate. Use the checklist to evaluate your classmate's essay and provide supportive feedback.

1. Is the thesis clear?

☐ yes ☐ no If no, explain what confused you.

2. Are there sufficient examples and details to support the thesis?

☐ yes ☐ no If no, tell what you think might be missing.

3. Does the text conclude in a logical, satisfying way?

☐ yes ☐ no If no, indicate what you might change.

4. What is the strongest part of your classmate's essay? Why?

_____

_____

_____

Editing and Proofreading

Edit for Conventions Reread your draft for accuracy and consistency. Correct errors in grammar and word usage. Make sure that you have quoted your sources accurately and indicated your sources.

Proofread for Accuracy Read your draft carefully, looking for errors in spelling and punctuation. If you are including technical vocabulary, use a dictionary to check your spelling.

Publishing and Presenting

Create a final version of your text. Pair up with a classmate (not your peer reviewer), and read each other's work. Discuss ways in which your two essays are alike and different. Are your thesis statements similar? Did you incorporate some of the same details? Even if the content is similar, do your styles differ? Share your findings with the class, and talk about what comparing the texts has taught you about developing a topic and supporting a thesis.

Reflecting

Consider what you learned by writing your text. Was your research sufficient to respond to the prompt, or would you have preferred to spend more time researching the topic? Think about what you will do differently the next time you write an informative essay.

≡ STANDARDS

Writing
Develop and strengthen writing as needed by planning, revising, editing, rewriting, or trying a new approach, focusing on addressing what is most significant for a specific purpose and audience.

ESSENTIAL QUESTION:

In what ways does the struggle for freedom change with history?

As you read these selections, work with your group to explore the various ways in which the struggle for freedom has changed over time.

From Text to Topic During the Civil War era, opponents of slavery argued that the nation had not fully lived up to its founding promise of liberty. In the selections in this section, others add their voices to the chorus, clamoring for liberty, justice, and equal rights. As you read, consider what the selections show about how the struggle for freedom has changed and grown over time.

Small-Group Learning Strategies

Throughout your life, in school, in your community, and in your career, you will continue to develop strategies when you work in teams. Use these strategies during Small-Group Learning. Add ideas of your own for each step.

STRATEGY	ACTION PLAN
Prepare	• Complete your assignments so that you are prepared for group work. • Organize your thinking so you can contribute to your group's discussions. •
Participate fully	• Make eye contact to signal that you are listening and taking in what is being said. • Use text evidence when making a point. •
Support others	• Build off ideas from others in your group. • Invite others who have not yet spoken to join the discussion. •
Clarify	• Paraphrase the ideas of others to ensure that your understanding is correct. • Ask follow-up questions. •

SCAN FOR
MULTIMEDIA

CONTENTS

PERFORMANCE TASKS

SPEAKING AND LISTENING FOCUS
Panel Discussion

RESEARCH FOCUS:
Research Presentation

Working as a Team

1. **Take a Position** In your group, discuss the following question:

   What issue today might persuade you to join a movement for social change?

   As you take turns sharing your positions, be sure to provide reasons for your response. After all group members have shared, discuss some of the connections among the issues that were presented.

2. **List Your Rules** As a group, decide on the rules that you will follow as you work together. Two samples are provided. Add two more of your own. As you work together, you may add or revise rules based on your experience together.

   • People should respect each other's opinions.
   • No one should dominate the discussion.

   • _____
     _____

   • _____
     _____

3. **Apply the Rules** Share what you have learned about power, protest, and change. Make sure each person in the group contributes. Take notes on and be prepared to share with the class one thing that you heard from another member of your group.

4. **Name Your Group** Choose a name that reflects the unit topic.

   Our group's name: _____

5. **Create a Communication Plan** Decide how you want to communicate with one another. For example, you might use online platforms, collaboration apps, video conferencing, email, or group texts.

   Our group's decision: _____

   _____

Making a Schedule

First, find out the due dates for the Small-Group activities. Then, preview the texts and activities with your group, and make a schedule for completing the tasks.

SELECTION	ACTIVITIES	DUE DATE
Ain't I a Woman?		
Declaration of Sentiments		
Giving Women the Vote		
The Story of an Hour		
Brown v. Board of Education: Opinion of the Court		
Was *Brown v. Board* a Failure?		

Working on Group Projects

As your group works together, you'll find it more effective if each person has a specific role. Different projects require different roles. Before beginning a project, discuss the necessary roles, and choose one for each group member. Here are some possible roles; add your own ideas.

Project Manager: monitors the schedule and keeps everyone on task

Researcher: organizes research activities

Recorder: takes notes during group meetings

_____

_____

_____

_____

_____

SCAN FOR
MULTIMEDIA

About the Author

Sojourner Truth (c. 1797–1883) was born into slavery in Swartekill, New York, as Isabella Baumfree. In 1826, when one of her owners refused to honor his promise to free her, Baumfree fled with Sophia, her infant daughter. In 1843, she changed her name to Sojourner Truth and began her career as an abolitionist. Her memoirs were published in 1850, and she toured the country to promote not only abolitionism but also equal civil rights for women.

Ain't I a Woman?

Concept Vocabulary

As you perform your first read of "Ain't I a Woman?" you will encounter these words.

racket	fix	obliged

Context Clues When you come across unfamiliar words in a text, you can often determine their meanings by using **context clues**—words and phrases Punishment was harsh; many were subjected to the lash, which tore the skin and caused lasting physical and emotional scars that appear in nearby text. There are various kinds of context clues. Some provide information from which you can draw inferences, or reasonable guesses, about a word's meaning.

> **Example Sentence:** Punishment was harsh: Many were subjected to the **lash**, which tore the skin and caused deep physical and emotional scars.
>
> **Inference:** Because it causes the skin to tear and leaves scars, a *lash* must be a whip or cane.
>
> You can verify your preliminary definition by consulting a reliable print or online dictionary.

Apply your knowledge of context clues and other vocabulary strategies to determine the meanings of unfamiliar words you encounter during your first read.

First Read NONFICTION

Apply these these strategies as you conduct your first read. You will have an opportunity to complete a close read after your first read.

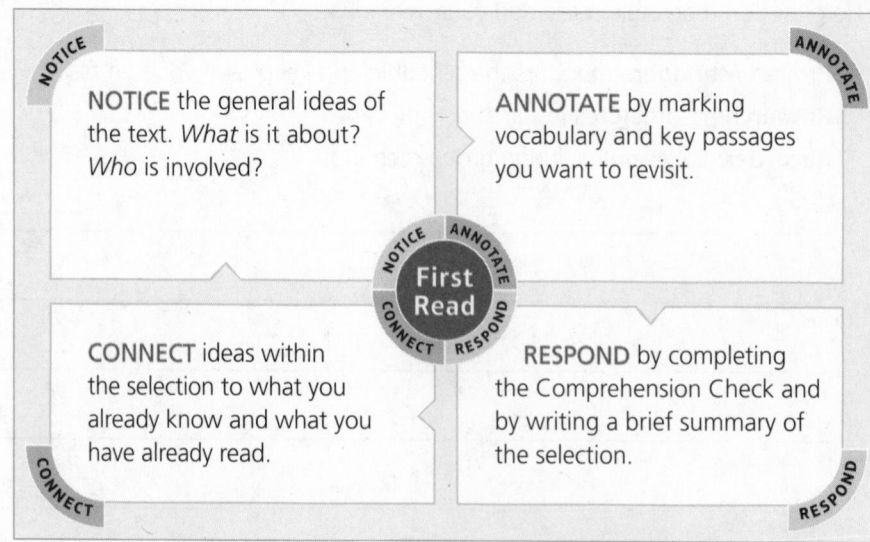

NOTICE the general ideas of the text. *What* is it about? *Who* is involved?

ANNOTATE by marking vocabulary and key passages you want to revisit.

CONNECT ideas within the selection to what you already know and what you have already read.

RESPOND by completing the Comprehension Check and by writing a brief summary of the selection.

≡ STANDARDS

Reading Informational Text
By the end of grade 11, read and comprehend literary nonfiction in the grades 11–CCR Text complexity band proficiently, with scaffolding as needed at the high end of the range.

Language
• Use context as a clue to the meaning of a word or phrase.
• Verify the preliminary determination of the meaning of a word or phrase.

Ain't I a Woman?

Sojourner Truth

BACKGROUND

Sojourner Truth delivered this speech at the Women's Rights Convention in Akron, Ohio, in 1851. It was never transcribed or recorded, but a woman in attendance, Frances Gage, committed it to paper from memory many years later. The words may not be entirely accurate, but the power of Truth's speech remains intact.

SCAN FOR MULTIMEDIA

W ell, children, where there is so much **racket** there must be something out of kilter.[1] I think that 'twixt[2] the Negroes of the South and the women at the North, all talking about rights, the white men will be in a **fix** pretty soon. But what's all this here talking about?

That man over there says that women need to be helped into carriages, and lifted over ditches, and to have the best place everywhere. Nobody ever helps me into carriages, or over mudpuddles, or gives me any best place! And ain't I a woman? Look at me! Look at my arm! I have ploughed and planted, and gathered into barns, and no man could head me! And ain't I a woman? I could work as much and eat as much as a man—when I could get it—and bear the lash as well! And ain't I a woman? I have borne thirteen children, and seen them most all sold off to slavery, and when I cried

> **NOTES**
>
> Mark context clues or indicate another strategy you used that helped you determine meaning.
>
> **racket** (RAK iht) *n.*
>
> MEANING:
>
> **fix** (fihks) *n.*
>
> MEANING:

1. **kilter** *n.* proper state or condition.
2. **'twixt** *prep.* between.

NOTES

Mark context clues or indicate another strategy you used that helped you determine meaning.

obliged (uh BLYJD) *adj.*

MEANING:

out with my mother's grief, none but Jesus heard me! And ain't I a woman? Then they talk about this thing in the head; what's this they call it? [A member of the audience whispers, "Intellect."] That's it, honey. What's that got to do with women's rights or Negroes' rights? If my cup won't hold but a pint, and yours holds a quart, wouldn't you be mean not to let me have my little half measure full? Then that little man in black there, he says women can't have as much rights as men, 'cause Christ wasn't a woman! Where did your Christ come from? Where did your Christ come from? From God and a woman! Man had nothing to do with him.[3] If the first woman God ever made[4] was strong enough to turn the world upside down all alone, these women together ought to be able to turn it back, and get it right side up again! And now they is asking to do it, the men better let them.

3 **Obliged** to you for hearing me, and now old Sojourner ain't got nothing more to say. ❧

---

3. **Man had nothing to do with him** reference to the biblical teaching of the virgin birth of Jesus.
4. **the first woman God ever made** the biblical Eve.

Comprehension Check

Complete the following items after you finish your first read. Review and clarify details with your group.

1. What two reform movements does Sojourner Truth connect?

2. According to Truth, what privileges do many people think women should enjoy?

3. Identify two hardships that Sojourner Truth says she has suffered.

4. What warning does Truth give just before concluding the speech?

5. 📓 **Notebook** Confirm your understanding of the text by writing a summary.

- -

RESEARCH

Research to Clarify Choose at least one unfamiliar detail from the text. Briefly research that detail. In what way does the information you learned shed light on an aspect of the speech?

Research to Explore This speech may spark your curiosity to learn more about the author, the era, or the topic. Briefly research a topic that interests you. You may want to share what you discover with your group.

AIN'T I A WOMAN?

WORD NETWORK

Add words related to struggle from the text to your Word Network.

Close Read the Text

With your group, revisit sections of the text you marked during your first read. **Annotate** details that you notice. What **questions** do you have? What can you **conclude**?

Analyze the Text

CITE TEXTUAL EVIDENCE
to support your answers.

Complete the activities.

1. **Review and Clarify** With your group, reread paragraph 2 of the selection. Discuss the figurative meanings of "pints" and "cups." What do they have to do with the overall argument in this speech?

2. **Present and Discuss** Now, work with your group to share the passages from the selection that you found especially important. Take turns presenting your passages. Discuss what you noticed in the selection, the questions you asked, and the conclusions you reached.

3. **Essential Question:** *In what ways does the struggle for freedom change with history?* What has this text taught you about power, protest, and change? Discuss with your group.

LANGUAGE DEVELOPMENT

Concept Vocabulary

racket	fix	obliged

Why These Words? The three concept vocabulary words are related. With your group, determine what the words have in common. How do these word choices enhance the impact of the text?

Practice

Notebook Confirm your understanding of the concept vocabulary words by using them in sentences. Be sure to use context clues that hint at each word's meaning.

Word Study

Latin Root: -lig- At the end of this speech, Sojourner Truth thanks her audience for listening by saying, "Obliged to you for hearing me. . . ." The English word *obliged* is built from the Latin root *-lig-,* which means "to bind." Find several other words that have this same root. Then, write the words and their meanings.

Analyze Craft and Structure

Effective Rhetoric "Ain't I a Woman?" is a speech that makes an **argument**; its message is meant to persuade an audience. Sojourner Truth connects her ideas and builds the argument to its climax by using a **refrain**, or repeated chorus. This refrain, "And ain't I a woman?" urgently restates Truth's main idea as she challenges listeners to rethink their ideas about equality.

Practice

CITE TEXTUAL EVIDENCE to support your answers.

Work on your own to fill in the chart. Track the ways in which Sojourner Truth uses refrain to build her argument. Find each use of the repeated question, "Ain't I a woman?" Then, list the textual details that lead up to each repetition. Finally, consider how each set of details adds meaning to Truth's question. After you have completed the chart, share and discuss your responses with your group.

TEXTUAL DETAILS THAT LEAD TO . . .	ADDED MEANING
first statement of the refrain:	
first repetition of the refrain:	
second repetition of the refrain:	
third repetition of the refrain:	
fourth repetition of the refrain:	

AIN'T I A WOMAN?

Author's Style

Use of Words and Phrases A writer or speaker's **diction** is his or her choice of words and phrases. Diction is a key element of a speaker's style—his or her distinct way of using language.

- Diction may be formal, informal, elevated, simple, technical, poetic, or have many other qualities.
- Diction may change to reflect the **audience**—the listeners a speaker is attempting to reach.
- A speaker's diction reflects both the occasion and purpose of a speech.

This example from President Lincoln's second inaugural address fits the formality of the occasion.

Formal Diction: At this second appearing to take the oath of the presidential office, there is less occasion for an extended address than there was at the first.

Sojourner Truth was born into slavery and received no formal education. This example of her colloquial, or informal, diction reflects those circumstances.

Colloquial Diction: Obliged to you for hearing me, and now old Sojourner ain't got nothing more to say.

However, Truth's diction also demonstrates other aspects of her personality, as well as her purpose for speaking at the Women's Rights Convention.

Read It

Work individually. For each example of formal diction, find the colloquial original in "Ain't I a Woman?" When you have completed the chart, meet with your group to discuss how the colloquial diction may have helped Truth connect with her audience.

FORMAL DICTION	ORIGINAL DICTION FROM "AIN'T I A WOMAN?"
Ladies and gentlemen, where one hears such pandemonium, one suspects that something has gone awry.	
If I have but a little, and you have a great deal, would it not be fair for you to share?	
Now that women are clamoring for change, it is incumbent on men to permit it.	

Write It

⊟ **Notebook** Write a paragraph that suggests the impact that Sojourner Truth may have had on her audience in 1851. Try to use a mix of formal and colloquial diction in your paragraph.

Writing to Sources

Assignment

With your group, prepare an **informative text** that presents facts about a topic. Choose from the following options:

☐ a **biographical sketch** about Sojourner Truth that expands upon the brief biography that accompanies this selection and that sheds light upon some of the references in "Ain't I a Woman?"

☐ an **extended definition** of *woman* as it would have been seen by many in Sojourner Truth's audience, focusing on the daily life of an ordinary woman in 1850s America

☐ a **cause-and-effect article** about the results of antislavery speeches by abolitionists in the 1850s

Project Plan Work with your group to divide the informative writing option that you chose into manageable sections or parts. Outline your ideas, and assign each member one part of the writing.

Working Title: _____

SECTION OR PART	ASSIGNED PERSON
Introduction	
Part I	
Part II	
Part III	
Part IV	
Part V	
Conclusion	

Tying It Together Work together to draft an introduction that touches on all the sections or parts that you plan to write. Once everyone has written his or her part of the project, get together again to read the parts aloud, suggest revisions, and draft a conclusion that follows from those parts.

✒ EVIDENCE LOG

Before moving on to a new selection, go to your Evidence Log and record what you learned from "Ain't I a Woman?"

⚏ STANDARDS

Writing
Write informative/explanatory texts to examine and convey complex ideas, concepts, and information clearly and accurately through the effective selection, organization, and analysis of content.

DECLARATION OF
SENTIMENTS

Comparing Text to Media

In this lesson, you will compare the Declaration of Sentiments, a public document related to the campaign for women's suffrage, and a podcast called "Giving Women the Vote." First, you will complete the first-read and close-read activities for the Declaration of Sentiments.

GIVING WOMEN THE VOTE

About the Author

Elizabeth Cady Stanton
(1815–1902) became interested in reform movements through a cousin, who introduced her to Henry Brewster Stanton, an abolitionist. Cady and Stanton married in 1840—agreeing that the bride's promise to obey her husband would be omitted from their vows. Stanton was the primary writer of the Declaration of Sentiments, adopted at the 1848 Seneca Falls Convention. Later, Stanton and Susan B. Anthony founded the National Woman Suffrage Association.

STANDARDS

Reading Informational Text
By the end of grade 11, read and comprehend literary nonfiction in the grades 11–CCR text complexity band proficiently, with scaffolding as needed at the high end of the range.

Language
• Use context as a clue to the meaning of a word or phrase.
• Verify the preliminary determination of the meaning of a word or phrase.

Declaration of Sentiments

Concept Vocabulary

As you perform your first read, you will encounter these words.

| degraded | oppressed | subordinate |

Context Clues If these words are unfamiliar to you, try using **context clues**—other words and phrases that appear in a text—to help you determine their meanings. There are various kinds of context clues. Some provide details that help you infer the word's meaning. You can then use a dictionary to confirm your inference.

Elaborating Details: Even when the terrifying storm was at its worst, my cousin maintained her usual <u>calm and cheerful</u> **demeanor**.

Inference: *Calm* and *cheerful* relate to a person's behavior. *Demeanor* must mean "how someone behaves."

Dictionary Meaning: "outward behavior or bearing"

Apply your knowledge of context clues and other vocabulary strategies to determine the meanings of unfamiliar words you encounter during your first read.

First Read NONFICTION

Apply these strategies as you conduct your first read. You will have an opportunity to complete a close read after your first read.

NOTICE the general ideas of the text. *What* is it about? *Who* is involved?

ANNOTATE by marking vocabulary and key passages you want to revisit.

First
Read

NOTICE · ANNOTATE · CONNECT · RESPOND

CONNECT ideas within the selection to what you already know and what you have already read.

RESPOND by completing the Comprehension Check and by writing a brief summary of the selection.

Declaration of Sentiments

Elizabeth Cady Stanton

For decades after the Declaration of Sentiments, American suffragists continued to campaign for the right to vote.

BACKGROUND

In 1848, Elizabeth Cady Stanton and Lucretia Mott convened the first women's rights conference to demand that women be given basic human rights, including the right to vote, to own property, and to have equal status under the law. Of those who attended the conference in Seneca Falls, New York, about a third—32 men and 68 women—signed the Declaration of Sentiments. The document was highly controversial. An article published shortly after the convention described it as "the most shocking and unnatural event ever recorded in the history of womanity."

SCAN FOR MULTIMEDIA

1   When, in the course of human events, it becomes necessary for one portion of the family of man to assume among the people of the earth a position different from that which they have hitherto occupied, but one to which the laws of nature and of nature's God entitle them, a decent respect to the opinions of mankind requires that they should declare the causes that impel them to such a course.

2   We hold these truths to be self-evident: that all men and women are created equal; that they are endowed by their Creator with certain inalienable[1] rights; that among these are life, liberty, and the pursuit of happiness; that to secure these rights governments are instituted, deriving their just powers from the consent of the governed. Whenever any form of government becomes destructive of these ends, it is the right of those who suffer from it to refuse allegiance to it, and to insist upon the institution of a new government, laying its foundation on such principles, and organizing its powers in such

NOTES

---

1. **inalienable** (ihn AYL yuh nuh buhl) *adj.* absolute; not able to be taken or given away.

form, as to them shall seem most likely to effect their safety and happiness. Prudence, indeed, will dictate that governments long established should not be changed for light and transient[2] causes; and accordingly all experience hath shown that mankind are more disposed to suffer, while evils are sufferable, than to right themselves by abolishing the forms to which they are accustomed. But when a long train of abuses and usurpations[3] pursuing invariably the same object, evinces a design to reduce them under absolute despotism,[4] it is their duty to throw off such government, and to provide new guards for their future security. Such has been the patient sufferance of the women under this government, and such is now the necessity which constrains them to demand the equal station to which they are entitled. The history of mankind is a history of repeated injuries and usurpations on the part of man toward woman, having in direct object the establishment of an absolute tyranny over her. To prove this, let facts be submitted to a candid world.

3   He has never permitted her to exercise her inalienable right to the elective franchise.[5]

4   He has compelled her to submit to laws, in the formation of which she had no voice.

5   He has withheld from her rights which are given to the most ignorant and degraded men—both natives and foreigners.

6   Having deprived her of this first right of a citizen, the elective franchise, thereby leaving her without representation in the halls of legislation, he has oppressed her on all sides.

7   He has made her, if married, in the eye of the law, civilly dead.

8   He has taken from her all right in property, even to the wages she earns.

9   He has made her, morally, an irresponsible being, as she can commit many crimes with impunity,[6] provided they be done in the presence of her husband. In the covenant of marriage, she is compelled to promise obedience to her husband, he becoming, to all intents and purposes, her master—the law giving him power to deprive her of her liberty, and to administer chastisement.[7]

10   He has so framed the laws of divorce, as to what shall be the proper causes, and in case of separation, to whom the guardianship of the children shall be given, as to be wholly regardless of the happiness of women—the law, in all cases, going upon a false supposition of the supremacy of man, and giving all power into his hands.

11   After depriving her of all rights as a married woman, if single, and the owner of property, he has taxed her to support a government which recognizes her only when her property can be made profitable to it.

---

2. **transient** (TRAN see uhnt) *adj.* not lasting.
3. **usurpations** (yoo suhr PAY shuhnz) *n.* illegal seizures.
4. **evinces a design . . . despotism** shows an intent to submit women to a situation of total control.
5. **elective franchise** right to vote.
6. **impunity** (ihm PYOO nih tee) *n.* total freedom from punishment.
7. **chastisement** (CHAS tyz muhnt) *n.* strong, punishing criticism.

The demands of suffragist leaders aroused intense passions. In this artist's interpretation of a real event, suffragist Lucretia Mott is attacked by a mob when she appears in public.

NOTES

12   He has monopolized nearly all the profitable employments, and from those she is permitted to follow, she receives but a scanty remuneration. He closes against her all the avenues to wealth and distinction which he considers most honorable to himself. As a teacher of theology, medicine, or law, she is not known.

13   He has denied her the facilities for obtaining a thorough education, all colleges being closed against her.

14   He allows her in church, as well as state, but a **subordinate** position, claiming apostolic[8] authority for her exclusion from the ministry, and, with some exceptions, from any public participation in the affairs of the church.

15   He has created a false public sentiment by giving to the world a different code of morals for men and women, by which moral delinquencies which exclude women from society, are not only tolerated, but deemed of little account in man.

16   He has usurped the prerogative of Jehovah himself, claiming it as his right to assign for her a sphere of action, when that belongs to her conscience and to her God.

17   He has endeavored, in every way that he could, to destroy her confidence in her own powers, to lessen her self-respect, and to make her willing to lead a dependent and abject life.

Mark context clues or indicate another strategy you used that helped you determine meaning.

subordinate (suh BAWR duh niht) *adj.*

MEANING:

---

8. **apostolic** (ap uh STOL ihk) *adj.* derived from the Bible (specifically, from the apostles appointed by Jesus to spread the gospel).

18   Now, in view of this entire disfranchisement of one-half the people of this country, their social and religious degradation—in view of the unjust laws above mentioned, and because women do feel themselves aggrieved, oppressed, and fraudulently deprived of their most sacred rights, we insist that they have immediate admission to all the rights and privileges which belong to them as citizens of the United States.

19   In entering upon the great work before us, we anticipate no small amount of misconception, misrepresentation, and ridicule; but we shall use every instrumentality within our power to effect our object. We shall employ agents, circulate tracts, petition the state and national legislatures, and endeavor to enlist the pulpit and the press in our behalf. We hope this convention will be followed by a series of conventions, embracing every part of the country.

20   Firmly relying upon the final triumph of the right and the true, we do this day affix our signatures to this declaration. ✍

Comprehension Check

Complete the following items after you finish your first read. Review and clarify details with your group.

1. According to this document, which truths are self-evident?

2. According to Stanton, why do women have a duty to throw off the government?

3. What does Stanton say is the result of denying women the right to vote?

4. What governmental action does the Declaration of Sentiments demand?

5. 📖 **Notebook** Confirm your understanding of the text by writing a summary.

- -

RESEARCH

Research to Explore This public document may spark your curiosity to learn more about this topic, author, or era. Briefly research a topic that interests you. You may wish to share what you discover with your group.

Close Read the Text

With your group, revisit sections of the text you marked during your first read. **Annotate** details that you notice. What **questions** do you have? What can you **conclude**?

DECLARATION OF SENTIMENTS

Analyze the Text

> **CITE TEXTUAL EVIDENCE**
> to support your answers.

Complete the activities.

1. **Review and Clarify** With your group, discuss the "long train of abuses and usurpations" that are listed in the document. If you were to categorize them, what headings would you use? Explain.

2. **Present and Discuss** Now, work with your group to share the passages from the selection that you found especially important. Take turns presenting your passages. Discuss what you noticed in the selection, the questions you asked, and the conclusions you reached.

3. **Essential Question:** *In what ways does the struggle for freedom change with history?* What have you learned about the struggle for freedom from reading this text?

TIP

GROUP DISCUSSION
Give everyone a chance to contribute to the discussion. If you notice that someone is not participating, encourage him or her to join in.

LANGUAGE DEVELOPMENT

Concept Vocabulary

degraded	oppressed	subordinate

Why These Words? The three concept vocabulary words are related. With your group, discuss the words, and determine a concept that the words, have in common. How do these word choices enhance the text's impact?

 WORD NETWORK

Add words related to struggle from the text to your Word Network.

Practice

📝 **Notebook** Confirm your understanding of the concept vocabulary words by using them in sentences. Be sure to use context clues that hint at each word's meaning.

Word Study

Latin Prefix: *sub-* According to the Declaration of Sentiments, the document should tell the world that American women are in a *subordinate* position. The word *subordinate* begins with the Latin prefix *sub-*, which means "under." Find several other words that begin with this prefix. Use etymological information from the dictionary to verify your choices. Then, write the words and their meanings.

STANDARDS
Language
Consult general and specialized reference materials, both print and digital, to find the pronunciation of a word or determine or clarify its precise meaning, its part of speech, its etymology, or its standard usage.

Declaration of Sentiments **343**

Analyze Craft and Structure

Author's Choices: Allusions An **allusion** is an unexplained reference within a literary work to a well-known person, place, event, text, or work of art. An allusion adds meaning to a text by offering a point of similarity or comparison to the ideas the author is presenting. Authors assume that readers understand both the reference and the layer of meaning it adds.

Although most allusions are conveyed in a word or a phrase, some provide structure for an entire piece of writing. In the Declaration of Sentiments, Elizabeth Cady Stanton creates an extended allusion by modeling her argument after the Declaration of Independence.

Practice

CITE TEXTUAL EVIDENCE to support your answers.

Use this chart to analyze how the extended allusion to the Declaration of Independence helps introduce, develop, and conclude the argument made in the Declaration of Sentiments. A first example has been done for you. Gather your notes, and then share your responses with your group.

DECLARATION OF SENTIMENTS	ALLUSION TO THE DECLARATION OF INDEPENDENCE	DEVELOPMENT OF IDEAS
Paragraphs 1–2	The Declaration of Independence reads: "We hold these truths to be self-evident: that all men are created equal. . . . " Stanton revises this to read:". . . all men and women are created equal."	The allusion suggests that the Declaration of Sentiments is equal in importance to—and perhaps even goes beyond— the Declaration of Independence.
Paragraphs 3–17		
Paragraphs 18–20		

Conventions and Style

Types of Clauses A **clause** is a group of words that has a subject and a predicate. An **independent clause** can stand on its own as a complete sentence. A **subordinate** (also called **dependent**) **clause** is unable to stand alone because it does not express a complete thought. Writers use a variety of subordinate clauses to add information, to clarify meaning, and to link related ideas.

DECLARATION OF SENTIMENTS

TYPE OF CLAUSE	COMPOSITION	EXAMPLES
Independent	subject, predicate; expresses a complete thought	*We hold these truths to be self-evident . . . (paragraph 2)* *. . . it is their duty to throw off such government . . . (paragraph 2)*
Subordinate	subject, predicate; does not express a complete thought; begins with a word such as *which, who, that, since, when, if, as, although,* or *because*	*. . . that they should declare the causes . . . (paragraph 1)* *. . . as she can commit many crimes with impunity . . . (paragraph 9)*

Read It

1. Each example contains one independent clause and one subordinate clause. Mark independent clauses once and subordinate clauses twice.

   a. Although some proponents of women's rights supported the Declaration of Sentiments, others considered it too radical.

   b. It was no secret that the work entailed danger and public censure.

   c. Because suffrage is such a precious right, Americans should vote in all elections.

2. **Connect to Style** Reread this excerpt from Declaration of Sentiments. Mark independent clauses once and subordinate clauses twice.

   We hold these truths to be self-evident: that all men and women are created equal; that they are endowed by their Creator with certain inalienable rights. . . .

Notebook Explain how the use of these clauses helps the writer show a main idea and the details that support it.

Write It

Notebook Complete this paragraph by adding a clause to each sentence as directed.

   If I had been working alongside Elizabeth Cady Stanton, [independent clause]. I also would have marched for female suffrage, [subordinate clause]. Many people fought against giving women the vote [subordinate clause]. The work was important, however, so [independent clause].

📝 EVIDENCE LOG

Before moving on to a new selection, go to your Evidence Log and record what you learned from "Declaration of Sentiments."

⬛ STANDARDS

Reading Informational Text
Analyze seventeenth-, eighteenth-, and nineteenth-century foundational U.S. documents of historical and literary significance for their themes, purposes, and rhetorical features.

Language
Demonstrate command of the conventions of standard English grammar and usage when writing or speaking.

DECLARATION OF SENTIMENTS

Comparing Text to Media

This podcast discusses the final steps that made women's suffrage a reality. After listening to it, you will compare how broadcast media can provide information in a way that differs from the way information is conveyed in a text.

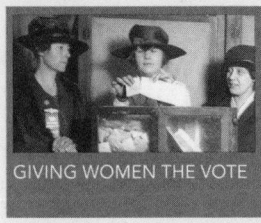

GIVING WOMEN THE VOTE

About the Producer

Sandra Sleight-Brennan (b. 1951) is an award-winning scriptwriter and media producer. She is the driving force behind many audio and video projects, Web-based documentaries, and a variety of multimedia efforts. Although she has covered a wide range of topics, she has a special interest in projects that show societal change and that reflect the struggles of minorities. Sleight-Brennan's work has been broadcast on radio stations across the country.

Giving Women the Vote

Media Vocabulary

These words or concepts will be useful to you as you analyze, discuss, and write about podcasts.

Frame: main spoken narrative of a production	• A frame has a clear beginning, middle, and end. • Usually, one narrator or host presents the frame.
Special Elements: features that provide points of emphasis in a production	• Sound effects can add realism. Background music can highlight the emotion connected with an event. Either element can set a mood. • Interview segments can add information and insights. Dramatic reenactments can bring events to life.
Tone: production's attitude toward a subject or audience	• In a podcast, tone is created through the narrator or host's word choice and vocal qualities, as well as the use of special elements.

First Review MEDIA: AUDIO

Apply these strategies as you listen to the podcast.

LISTEN and note *who* is speaking, *what* they're saying, and *how* they're saying it.

NOTE elements that you find interesting and want to revisit.

CONNECT ideas in the audio to other media you've experienced, texts you've read, or images you've seen.

RESPOND by completing the Comprehension Check.

First Review

Listening Strategy: Take Notes

Notebook As you listen, record your observations and questions, making sure to note time codes for later reference.

STANDARDS

Reading Informational Text
By the end of grade 11, read and comprehend literary nonfiction in the grades 11–CCR text complexity band proficiently, with scaffolding as needed at the high end of the range.

Giving Women the Vote

Sandra Sleight-Brennan

BACKGROUND

The campaign to give the vote to all American women faced many disappointments in the decades following the Seneca Falls Convention. Finally, however, in June 1919, Congress passed a women's suffrage amendment to the United States Constitution and sent it to the states for ratification. Nine months later, 35 states had ratified the amendment. Only one more state's ratification was needed, but the deadline for ratification was drawing near. "Giving Women the Vote," which Sandra Sleight-Brennan produced in 2010 to commemorate the ninetieth anniversary of the Nineteenth Amendment, tells the story of that final state's ratification—and the surprising way in which it happened.

SCAN FOR MULTIMEDIA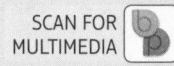

NOTES

Comprehension Check

Complete the following items after you finish your first review. Review and clarify details with your group.

1. According to the interview with the reporter from the Cleveland *Plain Dealer*, what was the result of the campaign for women's suffrage in the years just prior to 1920?

2. Which state became the final battleground for making the Nineteenth Amendment the law of the land?

3. What was the significance of the red or yellow roses worn by people on the scene?

4. According to the dramatic reenactment, why did Harry Burn change his vote?

5. 📝 **Notebook** Write a summary to confirm your understanding of the ratification of the Nineteenth Amendment, as presented in the podcast.

- -

RESEARCH

Research to Clarify Choose at least one unfamiliar detail from the podcast. Briefly research that detail. In what way does the information you learned shed light upon an aspect of the podcast? Share your findings with your group.

MAKING MEANING

Close Review

With your group, review your notes. If necessary, listen to the podcast again. Record any new observations that seem important. What **questions** do you have? What can you **conclude**?

GIVING WOMEN THE VOTE

Analyze the Media

> **CITE TEXTUAL EVIDENCE**
> to support your answers.

Complete the activities.

1. **Present and Discuss** Choose the part of the podcast you find most interesting or powerful. Share your choice with your group, and discuss why you chose it. Explain what you noticed about that section, what questions it raised for you, and what conclusions you reached about it.

2. **Synthesize** With your group, review the entire podcast. Do the frame and the special elements work together to inform listeners? Are they examples of information, of entertainment, or of both? Explain.

3. **Essential Question:** *In what ways does the struggle for freedom change with history?* What have you learned about the struggle for freedom from listening to this podcast? Discuss with your group.

LANGUAGE DEVELOPMENT

Media Vocabulary

frame	special elements	tone

Use these vocabulary words in your responses to the following questions.

1. **(a)** What do listeners learn from the narrator about the ratification process? **(b)** Why might Sleight-Brennan have wanted to include this information?

2. How do the comments dramatized by the characters of Harry Burn and his mother help to show the tensions surrounding this final vote for ratification?

3. This podcast was produced in recognition of the ninetieth anniversary of the Nineteenth Amendment. What attitude toward the event do you think it was meant to encourage in listeners? Explain.

STANDARDS

Speaking and Listening
Evaluate a speaker's point of view, reasoning, and use of evidence and rhetoric, assessing the stance, premises, links among ideas, word choice, points of emphasis, and tone used.

DECLARATION OF SENTIMENTS

GIVING WOMEN THE VOTE

≡ STANDARDS

Reading Informational Text
• Analyze and evaluate the effectiveness of the structure an author uses in his or her exposition or argument, including whether the structure makes points clear, convincing, and engaging.
• Determine an author's point of view or purpose in a text in which the rhetoric is particularly effective, analyzing how style and content contribute to the power, persuasiveness or beauty of the text.
• Integrate and evaluate multiple sources of information presented in different media or formats as well as in words in order to address a question or solve a problem.

Writing to Compare

You have read a document that launched the women's suffrage movement— Elizabeth Cady Stanton's Declaration of Sentiments. You have also listened to a podcast about the ratification of the nineteenth amendment in 1920. Now, deepen your understanding of the issue of women's suffrage by comparing and contrasting elements of the two selections and putting your ideas in writing.

Assignment

Both the document and the podcast illustrate the methods suffragists and politicians used to convince people that granting women the vote was the right course of action. Write a **compare-and-contrast essay** in which you analyze how each selection shows persuasion at work. Focus on the arguments and rhetorical strategies used by the people involved in the campaign. How did they seek to communicate key ideas in powerful, convincing ways?

Prewriting

Analyze the Texts Persuasion involves communicating a point of view and convincing others to adopt it. Persuasion is accomplished through effective **rhetoric,** or the use of stylistic elements to build meaning in a powerful way. The elements of rhetoric include:

- strong arguments—clearly stated claims supported by compelling evidence
- a lofty or passionate tone
- the repetition of words, phrases, or ideas
- the use of striking images
- allusions to established or respected ideas or texts
- the use of analogies, or comparisons.

Notebook Complete the activity, and answer the questions.

1. Analyze elements of rhetoric used by suffragists and their supporters in each selection. Assign each group member one element to look for in either one or both selections. Then, discuss and analyze your findings.

Rhetorical Element	Declaration of Sentiments	Giving Women the Vote
Argument		
Tone		
Repetition		
Imagery		
Allusion		
Analogy		

2. Which elements of persuasion are showcased in both selections?
3. These two selections focus on events 70 years apart. How did the suffragists' arguments or strategies change over time?

Drafting

Draw Conclusions As a group, review and discuss your Prewriting notes. Based on those notes, what can you conclude about the use of rhetoric in the suffrage movement, as illustrated by these two selections? Which elements carried the movement to its successful conclusion?

Thesis/central idea: _____

_____

_____

Develop a Project Plan Work with your group to outline the body of your essay and divide the writing task into manageable parts. Use a chart like this one to assign parts. Write a description of each part in the left column, and the name of the person assigned to it in the right. Discuss and note key pieces of evidence to use in each section.

SECTIONS OR PARTS	PERSON ASSIGNED
Part I: Evidence:	
Part II: Evidence:	
Part III: Evidence:	
Part IV: Evidence:	
Part V: Evidence:	

Write a Draft Work as a group to draft an introduction that includes your working thesis and touches on all the sections or parts the body of the essay will include. Then, work independently to draft the body sections. When everyone is finished, share your drafts aloud. Discuss revisions that will make each section stronger. Tie the parts of your essay together with effective transitions. Finally, draft a conclusion that follows logically from all sections of the essay.

Reviewing, Revising, and Editing

Have each group member edit and proofread the text independently. Apply all your changes to the draft. Then, have one person read the finished essay aloud. What last small changes need to be made to finalize your work?

> ✎ EVIDENCE LOG
>
> Before moving on to a new selection, go to your Evidence Log and record what you've learned from the Declaration of Sentiments and "Giving Women the Vote."

About the Author

Kate Chopin (1850–1904) was born Kate O'Flaherty in St. Louis, Missouri. At the age of 20, she married Louisiana cotton trader Oscar Chopin. The couple lived in New Orleans before moving to a rural Louisiana plantation. Chopin briefly ran the plantation after her husband's death but then returned to St. Louis with their six children. There, she began writing fiction. In the portraits of Louisiana that she created from that point forward, Chopin often addressed women's rights and racial prejudice.

The Story of an Hour

Concept Vocabulary

As you perform your first read of "The Story of an Hour," you will encounter these words.

persistence	imploring	importunities

Familiar Word Parts Separating a word into its parts can often help you identify its meaning. Those parts might include familiar prefixes.

Some prefixes, such as *im-*, have more than one meaning. When you come across an unfamiliar word, consider all the meanings of the prefix.

- For example, in the word *immobile*, *im-* means "not." Added to the base word *mobile*, which means "in motion," *im-* creates a new word that means "not mobile," or "still."

- In the word *immigrate*, *im-* means "into" or "toward." Added to the base word *migrate*, which means "move from one region to another," *im-* creates a new word that means "move into a new place."

When you read an unfamiliar word that has a prefix, think about other words with the same prefix. Consider which meaning makes the most sense with the base word. If a prefix has more than one meaning, try out both to determine the meaning of the unfamiliar word.

Apply your knowledge of familiar word parts and other vocabulary strategies to determine the meanings of unfamiliar words you encounter during your first read.

First Read FICTION

Apply these strategies as you conduct your first read. You will have an opportunity to complete a close read after your first read.

NOTICE *whom* the story is about, *what* happened, *where* and *when* it happened, and *why* those involved reacted as they did.

ANNOTATE by marking vocabulary and key passages you want to revisit.

First Read

CONNECT ideas within the selection to what you already know and what you have already read.

RESPOND by completing the Comprehension Check and by writing a summary of the selection.

⬛ STANDARDS

Reading Literature
By the end of grade 11, read and comprehend literature, including stories, dramas, and poems, in the grades 11–CCR text complexity band proficiently, with scaffolding as needed at the high end of the range.

Language
Identify and correctly use patterns of word changes that indicate different meanings or parts of speech.

The Story of an Hour

Kate Chopin

BACKGROUND

"The Story of an Hour" was considered daring in its time. The editors of at least two magazines refused the story, calling it immoral. They wanted Chopin to soften her female character and to make her less independent and less unhappy in her marriage. Undaunted, Chopin continued to deal with issues of women's growth and emancipation in her writing, advancing ideas that are widely accepted today.

SCAN FOR MULTIMEDIA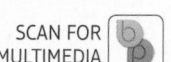

NOTES

1   Knowing that Mrs. Mallard was afflicted with a heart trouble, great care was taken to break to her as gently as possible the news of her husband's death.

2   It was her sister Josephine who told her, in broken sentences; veiled hints that revealed in half concealing. Her husband's friend Richards was there, too, near her. It was he who had been in the newspaper office when intelligence of the railroad disaster was received, with Brently Mallard's name leading the list of "killed." He had only taken the time to assure himself of its truth by a second telegram, and had hastened to forestall any less careful, less tender friend in bearing the sad message.

3   She did not hear the story as many women have heard the same, with a paralyzed inability to accept its significance. She wept at once, with sudden, wild abandonment, in her sister's arms. When the storm of grief had spent itself she went away to her room alone. She would have no one follow her.

4   There stood, facing the open window, a comfortable, roomy armchair. Into this she sank, pressed down by a physical exhaustion that haunted her body and seemed to reach into her soul.

5   She could see in the open square before her house the tops of trees that were all aquiver with the new spring life. The delicious breath of rain was in the air. In the street below a peddler was crying his wares. The notes of a distant song which someone was singing reached her faintly, and countless sparrows were twittering in the eaves.

6   There were patches of blue sky showing here and there through the clouds that had met and piled one above the other in the west facing her window.

7   She sat with her head thrown back upon the cushion of the chair, quite motionless, except when a sob came up into her throat and shook her, as a child who has cried itself to sleep continues to sob in its dreams.

8   She was young, with a fair, calm face, whose lines bespoke repression and even a certain strength. But now there was a dull stare in her eyes, whose gaze was fixed away off yonder on one of those patches of blue sky. It was not a glance of reflection, but rather indicated a suspension of intelligent thought.

9   There was something coming to her and she was waiting for it, fearfully. What was it? She did not know; it was too subtle and elusive to name. But she felt it, creeping out of the sky, reaching toward her through the sounds, the scents, the color that filled the air.

10   Now her bosom rose and fell tumultuously. She was beginning to recognize this thing that was approaching to possess her, and she was striving to beat it back with her will—as powerless as her two white slender hands would have been. When she abandoned herself a little whispered word escaped her slightly parted lips. She said it over and over under her breath: "free, free, free!" The vacant stare and the look of terror that had followed it went from her eyes. They stayed keen and bright. Her pulses beat fast, and the coursing blood warmed and relaxed every inch of her body.

11   She did not stop to ask if it were or were not a monstrous joy that held her. A clear and exalted perception enabled her to dismiss the suggestion as trivial. She knew that she would weep again when she saw the kind, tender hands folded in death; the face that had never looked save with love upon her, fixed and gray and dead. But she saw beyond that bitter moment a long procession of years to come that would belong to her absolutely. And she opened and spread her arms out to them in welcome.

12   There would be no one to live for during those coming years; she would live for herself. There would be no powerful will bending hers in that blind **persistence** with which men and women believe they have a right to impose a private will upon a fellow creature. A kind intention or a cruel intention made the act seem no less a crime as she looked upon it in that brief moment of illumination.

13   And yet she had loved him—sometimes. Often she had not. What did it matter! What could love, the unsolved mystery, count for in the face of this possession of self-assertion which she suddenly recognized as the strongest impulse of her being!

14   "Free! Body and soul free!" she kept whispering.

15   Josephine was kneeling before the closed door with her lips to the keyhole, **imploring** for admission. "Louise, open the door! I beg; open the door—you will make yourself ill. What are you doing, Louise? For heaven's sake open the door."

Mark familiar word parts or indicate another strategy you used that helped you determine meaning.

persistence (puhr SIHS tuhns) *n.*

MEANING:

imploring (ihm PLAWR ihng) *v.*

MEANING:

16   "Go away. I am not making myself ill." No; she was drinking in a very elixir of life[1] through that open window.

17   Her fancy was running riot along those days ahead of her. Spring days, and summer days, and all sorts of days that would be her own. She breathed a quick prayer that life might be long. It was only yesterday she had thought with a shudder that life might be long.

18   She arose at length and opened the door to her sister's **importunities**. There was a feverish triumph in her eyes, and she carried herself unwittingly like a goddess of Victory. She clasped her sister's waist, and together they descended the stairs. Richards stood waiting for them at the bottom.

19   Someone was opening the front door with a latchkey. It was Brently Mallard who entered, a little travel-stained, composedly carrying his gripsack[2] and umbrella. He had been far from the scene of the accident, and did not even know there had been one. He stood amazed at Josephine's piercing cry; at Richards' quick motion to screen him from the view of his wife.

20   But Richards was too late.

21   When the doctors came they said she had died of heart disease—of the joy that kills. ❧

---

1. **elixir of life** mythical liquid believed to prolong a person's life indefinitely.
2. **gripsack** small bag for holding clothes; suitcase.

NOTES

Mark familiar word parts or indicate another strategy you used that helped you determine meaning.

importunities (ihm pawr TOO nuh teez) *n.*

MEANING:

Comprehension Check

Complete the following items after you finish your first read. Review and clarify details with your group.

1. What medical problem afflicts Mrs. Mallard?

2. What news does Mrs. Mallard receive as the story opens?

3. As Mrs. Mallard sits alone in her room, what word does she keep whispering to herself?

4. What happens when Brently Mallard turns up, alive?

5. 📓 **Notebook** Write a summary of the story to confirm your understanding.

RESEARCH

Research to Explore This story may spark your curiosity to learn more. Briefly research a relevant topic that interests you. You may want to share what you discover with your group.

THE STORY OF AN HOUR

Close Read the Text

With your group, revisit sections of the text you marked during your first read. **Annotate** details that you notice. What **questions** do you have? What can you **conclude**?

Analyze the Text

> **CITE TEXTUAL EVIDENCE** to support your answers.

Notebook Complete the activities.

1. **Review and Clarify** With your group, discuss the ending of the story. Do you agree with the doctors' evaluation? Why, or why not?

2. **Present and Discuss** Now, work with your group to share the passages from the selection that you found especially important. Take turns presenting your passages. Discuss what you noticed in the selection, the questions you asked, and the conclusions you reached.

3. **Essential Question:** *In what ways does the struggle for freedom change with history?* What has this text taught you about the struggle for freedom? Discuss with your group.

LANGUAGE DEVELOPMENT

Concept Vocabulary

persistence	imploring	importunities

Why These Words? The three concept vocabulary words from the text are related. With your group, discuss the words, and determine what the words have in common. How do these word choices enhance the text?

Practice

Notebook Use a dictionary or thesaurus to find and record two synonyms for each of the concept vocabulary words. Then, write a sentence that explains how you think Chopin's word choices affect readers' understanding of the story. Share your sentences with your group.

Word Study

Notebook **Denotation and Connotation** The **denotation** of a word is its dictionary meaning. **Connotation** refers to the shades of meaning a word conveys. As Mrs. Mallard sits in her room, she hears Josephine's *importunities* for her to open the door. The denotation of the word is "instances of persistent begging." The connotation, however, suggests that such begging is especially annoying. Use a thesaurus to find four other words that mean "to beg," and think about their connotations. Then, list the words in order—from least to most forceful, or from most negative to most positive.

Analyze Craft and Structure

Development of Theme In this story, the author develops a central idea, or **theme**, about the ways in which the society of her time constrains women. To develop that thematic insight, Chopin focuses on the contrast between Mrs. Mallard's **internal monologue**—her main character's thoughts and conversation with herself—and the external situation in which Mrs. Mallard finds herself.

CITE TEXTUAL EVIDENCE to support your answers.

Practice

Use the chart to track Mrs. Mallard's actions and the emotional journey she undergoes. Then, explain how Mrs. Mallard's actions and feelings suggest Chopin's theme about the status of women in the society of her era. Note that there may be more than one theme. Complete this chart independently, and then share your responses with your group.

PARAGRAPH	WHAT MRS. MALLARD DOES	WHAT MRS. MALLARD FEELS	THEMATIC MEANING
3			
9			
10			
17			

THE STORY OF AN HOUR

Conventions and Style

Author's Choices: Irony "The Story of an Hour" is an ironic tale. **Irony** is a contradiction between appearance and reality, between expectation and outcome, or between meaning and intention. In literature, readers frequently encounter three types of irony.

Situational Irony: Something happens that contradicts readers' expectations.
Example: In the story "The Necklace," a couple must replace a diamond necklace that the wife borrowed from a friend and lost. Years later, after falling into poverty in order to pay for the replacement necklace, the couple discover the original was a fake.

Dramatic Irony: Readers or viewers are aware of something that a character does not know.
Example: In *Romeo and Juliet*, characters believe that Juliet is dead, but the audience knows that she is simply in a drugged sleep.

Verbal Irony: Someone says something that deliberately contradicts what that person actually means.
Example: In *Julius Caesar*, Marc Antony refers to Brutus as "an honorable man" when he means to prove that Brutus, Caesar's killer, is extremely dishonorable.

Read It

Work individually. Complete each situation below, and write your response to it based on the story. Then, reconvene with your group to compare and contrast your responses.

PARAGRAPHS	SITUATION	WHY IS THIS IRONIC?
5–6	Mrs. Mallard has just learned about her husband's death, but now she notices . . .	
20–21	Mrs. Mallard has reconciled herself to her newfound freedom, but now she discovers . . .	

Write It

📓 **Notebook** Choose a favorite movie with a classic, expected ending. Write a paragraph that changes the ending so that it becomes ironic. Explain how your new ending is an example of situational irony.

≣ STANDARDS

Reading Literature
Analyze a case in which grasping point of view requires distinguishing what is directly stated in a text from what is really meant.

Speaking and Listening
• Propel conversations by posing and responding to questions that probe reasoning and evidence; ensure a hearing for a full range of positions on a topic or issue; clarify, verify, or challenge ideas and conclusions; and promote divergent and creative perspectives.
• Respond thoughtfully to diverse perspectives; synthesize comments, claims, and evidence made on all sides of an issue; resolve contradictions when possible; and determine what additional information or research is required to deepen the investigation or complete the task.

Speaking and Listening

Assignment

Hold a **group discussion** to consider how readers of Chopin's time might have responded to "The Story of an Hour." Use what you know about the history of the era. Choose one of these social groups as the focus for your discussion.

☐ How might women in various social roles have responded to the story?

☐ How might other writers or artists have responded to the story?

☐ How might social critics or activists have responded to the story?

Preparing for the Discussion Locate areas of the text that support your ideas about how the social group you selected might respond to the story. Record your best examples here. Then, join up with others who chose the same perspective, and compare notes as a group.

Perspective: _____

SECTION OF TEXT	POSSIBLE RESPONSE / EXPLANATION

Holding the Discussion Decide as a group whether you want to go through the story section by section and have each person respond from his or her chosen perspective, or whether you prefer to look at the whole text through one perspective at a time. Either way, make sure that everyone has a chance to speak and to express opinions that are supported with evidence from the text and knowledge about 1890s America. If questions emerge from your discussion, decide together how you will locate the answers.

📝 EVIDENCE LOG

Before moving on to a new selection, go to your Evidence Log and record what you learned from "The Story of an Hour."

BROWN v. BOARD OF
EDUCATION: OPINION OF
THE COURT

Comparing Texts

In this lesson, you will read and compare the decision
of the Supreme Court in the case *Brown v. Board of
Education* and the magazine article "Was *Brown v.
Board* a Failure?" First, you will complete the first-
read and close-read activities for the Supreme Court
decision. The work you do with your group on this
title will help prepare you for your final comparison.

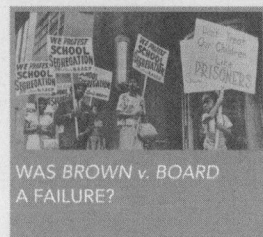

WAS *BROWN v. BOARD*
A FAILURE?

About the Author

Earl Warren (1891–1974),
a lawyer and three-time
governor of California,
served as the fourteenth
Chief Justice of the United
States, from 1953 to 1969.
Warren's time on the
Court was an active one,
with landmark decisions
in race relations, criminal
procedure, and legislative
apportionment. After the
assassination of President
John F. Kennedy in 1963,
Warren headed a federal
commission that investigated
the murder.

Brown v. Board of Education: Opinion of the Court

Concept Vocabulary

As you read the Supreme Court's opinion in *Brown v. Board of Education*,
you will encounter these words.

plaintiffs	jurisdiction	disposition

Familiar Word Parts In your reading, you may encounter words that are
a bit unfamiliar but that seem to have word parts that you recognize. As this
example shows, the word part that you recognize can help you determine
the meaning of the unfamiliar word.

Sentence: A sense of possibilities can **embolden** children to learn.

Familiar Word Part: *bold,* which means "without fear" or
"courageous"

Conclusion: Since *bold* involves a lack of fear, *embolden* must have
something to do with instilling fearlessness in someone.

First Read NONFICTION

Apply these strategies as you conduct your first read. You will have an
opportunity to complete a close read after your first read.

NOTICE the general ideas of
the text. *What* is it about?
Who is involved?

ANNOTATE by marking
vocabulary and key passages
you want to revisit.

First
Read

CONNECT ideas within the
selection to what you already
know and what you have
already read.

RESPOND by completing
the Comprehension Check and
by writing a brief summary of
the selection.

STANDARDS

Reading Informational Text
By the end of grade 11, read and
comprehend literary nonfiction in
the grades 11–CCR text complexity
band proficiently, with scaffolding as
needed at the high end of the range.

Language
Identify and correctly use patterns of
word changes that indicate different
meanings or parts of speech.

Brown v. Board of Education:
Opinion of the Court Earl Warren

BACKGROUND

In 1951, when 17 states required schools to be segregated by race, 13 parents brought a lawsuit against the Board of Education of Topeka, Kansas. At the forefront of the case was the Brown family. Linda Brown, an African American third-grader, was not allowed to attend the elementary school seven blocks from her house. Instead, she was required to take a bus to a school across town. Since the United States Supreme Court decision in the 1896 case *Plessy v. Ferguson*, racial segregation of schools had been allowed so long as the schools were "separate but equal." In the landmark case of *Brown v. Board of Education*, the Supreme Court ruled unanimously (9–0) to overrule *Plessy*.

SCAN FOR
MULTIMEDIA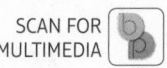

SUPREME COURT OF THE UNITED STATES

Brown v. Board of Education,
347 U.S. 483 (1954) (USSC+)
347 U.S. 483
Argued December 9, 1952
Reargued December 8, 1953
Decided May 17, 1954

APPEAL FROM THE UNITED STATES DISTRICT COURT
FOR THE DISTRICT OF KANSAS*

NOTES

Syllabus

1   Segregation of white and Negro children in the public schools of a State solely on the basis of race, pursuant to[1] state laws permitting or requiring such segregation, denies to Negro children the equal protection of the laws guaranteed by the Fourteenth Amendment— even though the physical facilities and other "tangible" factors of white and Negro schools may be equal.

1. **pursuant to** in a way that agrees with or follows.

2   (a) The history of the Fourteenth Amendment is inconclusive[2] as to its intended effect on public education.

3   (b) The question presented in these cases must be determined not on the basis of conditions existing when the Fourteenth Amendment was adopted, but in the light of the full development of public education and its present place in American life throughout the Nation.

4   (c) Where a State has undertaken to provide an opportunity for an education in its public schools, such an opportunity is a right which must be made available to all on equal terms.

5   (d) Segregation of children in public schools solely on the basis of race deprives children of the minority group of equal educational opportunities, even though the physical facilities and other "tangible" factors may be equal.

6   (e) The "separate but equal" doctrine adopted in *Plessy v. Ferguson*, 163 U.S. 537, has no place in the field of public education.

7   (f) The cases are restored to the docket[3] for further argument on specified questions relating to the forms of the decrees.

Opinion

8   MR. CHIEF JUSTICE WARREN delivered the opinion of the Court.

9   These cases come to us from the States of Kansas, South Carolina, Virginia, and Delaware. They are premised on[4] different facts and different local conditions, but a common legal question justifies their consideration together in this consolidated opinion.

10   In each of the cases, minors of the Negro race, through their legal representatives, seek the aid of the courts in obtaining admission to the public schools of their community on a nonsegregated basis. In each instance, they had been denied admission to schools attended by white children under laws requiring or permitting segregation according to race. This segregation was alleged to deprive the **plaintiffs** of the equal protection of the laws under the Fourteenth Amendment. In each of the cases other than the Delaware case, a three-judge federal district court denied relief to the plaintiffs on the so-called "separate but equal" doctrine announced by this Court in *Plessy v. Fergson*, 163 U.S. 537. Under that doctrine, equality of treatment is accorded when the races are provided substantially equal facilities, even though these facilities be separate. In the Delaware case, the Supreme Court of Delaware adhered to that doctrine, but ordered that the plaintiffs be admitted to the white schools because of their superiority to the Negro schools.

11   The plaintiffs contend that segregated public schools are not "equal" and cannot be made "equal," and that hence they are deprived of the equal protection of the laws. Because of the obvious importance of the question presented, the Court took **jurisdiction**.

Mark familiar word parts or indicate another strategy you used that helped you determine meaning.

plaintiffs (PLAYN tihfs) *n.*

MEANING:

Mark familiar word parts or indicate another strategy you used that helped you determine meaning.

jurisdiction (jur ihs DIHK shuhn) *n.*

MEANING:

---

2. **inconclusive** *adj.* not fully resolving all doubts or questions.
3. **docket** *n.* list of the legal cases that will be tried in a court of law.
4. **premised on** based on.

Argument was heard in the 1952 Term, and reargument was heard this Term on certain questions propounded[5] by the Court.

12 Reargument was largely devoted to the circumstances surrounding the adoption of the Fourteenth Amendment in 1868. It covered exhaustively consideration of the Amendment in Congress, ratification[6] by the states, then-existing practices in racial segregation, and the views of proponents and opponents of the Amendment. This discussion and our own investigation convince us that, although these sources cast some light, it is not enough to resolve the problem with which we are faced. At best, they are inconclusive. The most avid proponents of the post-War Amendments undoubtedly intended them to remove all legal distinctions among "all persons born or naturalized in the United States." Their opponents, just as certainly, were antagonistic to both the letter and the spirit of the Amendments and wished them to have the most limited effect. What others in Congress and the state legislatures had in mind cannot be determined with any degree of certainty.

13 An additional reason for the inconclusive nature of the Amendment's history with respect to segregated schools is the status of public education at that time. In the South, the movement toward free common schools, supported by general taxation, had not yet taken hold. Education of white children was largely in the hands of private groups. Education of Negroes was almost nonexistent, and practically all of the race were illiterate. In fact, any education of Negroes was forbidden by law in some states. Today, in contrast, many Negroes have achieved outstanding success in the arts and sciences, as well as in the business and professional world. It is true that public school education at the time of the Amendment had advanced further in the North, but the effect of the Amendment on Northern States was generally ignored in the congressional debates. Even in the North, the conditions of public education did not approximate those existing today. The curriculum was usually rudimentary; ungraded schools were common in rural areas; the school term was but three months a year in many states, and compulsory school attendance was virtually unknown. As a consequence, it is not surprising that there should be so little in the history of the Fourteenth Amendment relating to its intended effect on public education.

14 In the first cases in this Court construing the Fourteenth Amendment, decided shortly after its adoption, the Court interpreted it as proscribing all state-imposed discriminations against the Negro race. The doctrine of "separate but equal" did not make its appearance in this Court until 1896 in the case of *Plessy v. Ferguson*, supra,[7] involving not education but transportation. American courts have since labored with the doctrine for over half a century. In this

5. **propounded** *v.* suggested for consideration.
6. **ratification** *n.* process of officially approving and accepting an agreement.
7. **supra** mentioned earlier in this writing.

Court, there have been six cases involving the "separate but equal" doctrine in the field of public education. In *Cumming v. County Board of Education,* 175 U.S. 528, and *Gong Lum v. Rice,* 275 U.S. 78, the validity of the doctrine itself was not challenged. In more recent cases, all on the graduate school level, inequality was found in that specific benefits enjoyed by white students were denied to Negro students of the same educational qualifications. *Missouri ex rel. Gaines v. Canada,* 305 U.S. 337; *Sipuel v. Oklahoma,* 332 U.S. 631; *Sweatt v. Painter,* 339 U.S. 629; *McLaurin v. Oklahoma State Regents,* 339 U.S. 637. In none of these cases was it necessary to reexamine the doctrine to grant relief to the Negro plaintiff. And in *Sweatt v. Painter,* supra, the Court expressly reserved decision on the question whether *Plessy v. Ferguson* should be held inapplicable to public education.

15   In the instant cases, that question is directly presented. Here, unlike *Sweatt v. Painter,* there are findings below that the Negro and white schools involved have been equalized, or are being equalized, with respect to buildings, curricula, qualifications and salaries of teachers, and other "tangible" factors. Our decision, therefore, cannot turn on merely a comparison of these tangible factors in the Negro and white schools involved in each of the cases. We must look instead to the effect of segregation itself on public education.

16   In approaching this problem, we cannot turn the clock back to 1868, when the Amendment was adopted, or even to 1896, when *Plessy v. Ferguson* was written. We must consider public education in the light of its full development and its present place in American life throughout the Nation. Only in this way can it be determined if segregation in public schools deprives these plaintiffs of the equal protection of the laws.

17   Today, education is perhaps the most important function of state and local governments. Compulsory school attendance laws and the great expenditures for education both demonstrate our recognition of the importance of education to our democratic society. It is required in the performance of our most basic public responsibilities, even service in the armed forces. It is the very foundation of good citizenship. Today it is a principal instrument in awakening the child to cultural values, in preparing him for later professional training, and in helping him to adjust normally to his environment. In these days, it is doubtful that any child may reasonably be expected to succeed in life if he is denied the opportunity of an education. Such an opportunity, where the state has undertaken to provide it, is a right which must be made available to all on equal terms.

18   We come then to the question presented: Does segregation of children in public schools solely on the basis of race, even though the physical facilities and other "tangible" factors may be equal, deprive the children of the minority group of equal educational opportunities? We believe that it does.

19   In *Sweatt v. Painter,* supra, in finding that a segregated law school for Negroes could not provide them equal educational opportunities,

this Court relied in large part on "those qualities which are incapable of objective measurement but which make for greatness in a law school." In *McLaurin v. Oklahoma State Regents*, supra, the Court, in requiring that a Negro admitted to a white graduate school be treated like all other students, again resorted to intangible considerations: ". . . his ability to study, to engage in discussions and exchange views with other students, and, in general, to learn his profession." Such considerations apply with added force to children in grade and high schools. To separate them from others of similar age and qualifications solely because of their race generates a feeling of inferiority as to their status in the community that may affect their hearts and minds in a way unlikely ever to be undone. The effect of this separation on their educational opportunities was well stated by a finding in the Kansas case by a court which nevertheless felt compelled to rule against the Negro plaintiffs:

> Segregation of white and colored children in public schools has a detrimental effect upon the colored children. The impact is greater when it has the sanction[8] of the law, for the policy of separating the races is usually interpreted as denoting the inferiority of the negro group. A sense of inferiority affects the motivation of a child to learn. Segregation with the sanction of law, therefore, has a tendency to [retard] the educational and mental development of negro children and to deprive them of some of the benefits they would receive in a racial[ly] integrated school system.

20   Whatever may have been the extent of psychological knowledge at the time of *Plessy v. Ferguson*, this finding is amply supported by modern authority. Any language in *Plessy v. Ferguson* contrary to this finding is rejected.

21   We conclude that, in the field of public education, the doctrine of "separate but equal" has no place. Separate educational facilities are inherently unequal. Therefore, we hold that the plaintiffs and others similarly situated for whom the actions have been brought are, by reason of the segregation complained of, deprived of the equal protection of the laws guaranteed by the Fourteenth Amendment. This **disposition** makes unnecessary any discussion whether such segregation also violates the Due Process Clause of the Fourteenth Amendment.

22   Because these are class actions, because of the wide applicability of this decision, and because of the great variety of local conditions, the formulation of decrees in these cases presents problems of considerable complexity. On reargument, the consideration of appropriate relief was necessarily subordinated to the primary question—the constitutionality of segregation in public education. We have now announced that such segregation is a denial of the equal

NOTES

Mark familiar word parts or indicate another strategy you used that helped you determine meaning.

disposition (dihs puh ZIHSH uhn) *n.*

MEANING:

---

8. **sanction** *n.* official permission or approval.

protection of the laws. In order that we may have the full assistance of the parties in formulating decrees, the cases will be restored to the docket, and the parties are requested to present further argument on Questions 4 and 5 previously propounded by the Court for the reargument this Term. The Attorney General of the United States is again invited to participate. The Attorneys General of the states requiring or permitting segregation in public education will also be permitted to appear as amici curiae upon request to do so by September 15, 1954, and submission of briefs by October 1, 1954.

23   *It is so ordered.* ⁊

Comprehension Check

Complete the following items after you finish your first read. Review and clarify details with your group.

1. What change are the plaintiffs in this case seeking?

2. What standard had been set earlier by the *Plessy v. Ferguson* decision?

3. According to the opinion of the Court, what fundamental conflict exists between segregation and the Fourteenth Amendment?

4. 🗐 **Notebook** Write a summary of *Brown v. Board of Education*.

- -

RESEARCH

Research to Clarify Choose at least one unfamiliar detail from the text. Briefly research that detail. In what way does the information you learned shed light on an aspect of the Supreme Court's opinion? Share your findings with your group.

Close Read the Text

With your group, revisit sections of the text you marked during your first read. **Annotate** details that you notice. What **questions** do you have? What can you **conclude?**

BROWN v. BOARD OF EDUCATION: OPINION OF THE COURT

Analyze the Text

> **CITE TEXTUAL EVIDENCE** to support your answers.

Complete the activities.

1. **Review and Clarify** With your group, review paragraphs 15–19. Then, discuss the justices' argument about why "separate but equal" is inherently unequal.

2. **Present and Discuss** Share with your group the passages from the text that you found especially significant, taking turns with others. Discuss what you noticed in the text, what questions you asked, and what conclusions you reached.

3. **Essential Question:** *In what ways does the struggle for freedom change with history?* What has this text taught you about the struggle for freedom? Discuss with your group.

TIP

GROUP DISCUSSION
If you do not fully understand a classmate's comment, ask for clarification. Using a respectful tone, state exactly what you don't understand.

WORD NETWORK
Add words related to struggle from the text to your Word Network.

LANGUAGE DEVELOPMENT

Concept Vocabulary

> plaintiffs   jurisdiction   disposition

Why These Words? The three concept vocabulary words from the text are related. With your group, discuss the words, and determine what the words have in common. How do these word choices enhance the text?

Practice Use each concept vocabulary word in a sentence. Make sure to include context clues that hint at the word's meaning.

Word Study

Technical Words Most professions, including such fields as medicine and law, have their own technical language, often called **jargon**. In writing the Court's opinion in *Brown v. Board of Education*, Chief Justice Earl Warren uses technical legal words such as *plaintiffs*, *jurisdiction*, and *disposition*. Find four other words in the selection that could be classified as legal jargon. Write the words and their meanings.

STANDARDS

Reading Informational Text
Determine the meaning of words and phrases as they are used in a text, including figurative, connotative, and technical meanings; analyze how an author uses and refines the meaning of a key term or terms over the course of a text.

Language
Acquire and use accurately general academic and domain-specific words and phrases, sufficient for reading, writing, speaking, and listening at the college and career readiness level; demonstrate independence in gathering vocabulary knowledge when considering a word or phrase important to comprehension or expression.

BROWN v. BOARD OF EDUCATION:
OPINION OF THE COURT

Analyze Craft and Structure

Author's Choices: Structure In *Brown v. Board of Education*, Chief Justice Earl Warren delivers the **opinion**, or legal judgment, of the Court. He defends the Court's position in the form of an analytical argument. In an **analytical argument**, a writer or speaker uses logical reasoning and persuasive evidence to examine an issue and to support a particular conclusion, called a **claim**. In legal opinions, the writer presenting the argument anticipates and considers objections and challenges, or **counterclaims**.

Practice

CITE TEXTUAL EVIDENCE
to support your answers.

Work with your group to analyze the structure of the Court's opinion. Review the text, and complete the chart. Notice the order of topics: Warren proceeds from historical to legal to social considerations before arriving at a conclusion. Identify specific details from each section of the opinion, and explain the main idea they develop. Then, explain how each section adds to the line of reasoning that results in the Court's decision.

TOPIC	DETAILS IN THE TEXT	MAIN IDEA
Fourteenth Amendment (historical considerations)		
Plessy v. Ferguson (legal considerations)		
Importance of education (social considerations)		
Conclusions reached by the Court		

Conventions and Style

Coordinating Conjunctions A **coordinating conjunction** connects words, phrases, or clauses of equal rank. You can improve your sentence variety by using coordinating conjunctions to combine short, simple sentences into compound sentences.

> **Original:** These cases are premised on different facts. A common legal question justifies their consideration together.
>
> **Revision:** These cases are premised on different facts, *but* a common legal question justifies their consideration together.

Coordinating conjunctions show different relationships between the words or ideas that they connect. Study this chart.

COORDINATING CONJUNCTION	RELATIONSHIP
and	addition or similarity
but, yet	contrast
so	result or effect
for	reason or cause
or, nor	choice

Read It

In each item from or about the Supreme Court's opinion in *Brown v. Board of Education*, mark the coordinating conjunction and the words or groups of words that it connects.

1. Compulsory attendance laws and the great expenditures for education demonstrate our recognition of its importance.

2. Education is a principal instrument in awakening the child to cultural values, but success in life without the opportunity of an education is doubtful.

3. The state undertakes to make education available, yet it must be available to all on equal terms.

4. Education is a key function of government, for it is the very foundation of good citizenship.

Write It

📓 **Notebook** Use a coordinating conjunction to combine each pair of sentences. Write the new sentence.

1. According to the plaintiffs, public schools are not "equal." The schools cannot be made "equal."

2. Schools may have equal physical facilities. That fact doesn't guarantee equal educational opportunities.

3. Minority children in segregated schools may lack motivation to learn. By their very nature, such schools tend to instill a sense of inferiority.

4. The Court agreed. Segregation in public schools was struck down.

TIP

PUNCTUATION
If you use a coordinating conjunction to join two independent clauses, place a comma before the coordinating conjunction.

📝 **EVIDENCE LOG**

Before moving on to a new selection, go to your Evidence Log and record what you learned from the Supreme Court's opinion in *Brown v. Board of Education*.

STANDARDS

Reading Informational Text
Analyze and evaluate the effectiveness of the structure an author uses in his or her exposition or argument, including whether the structure makes points clear, convincing, and engaging.

Language
• Demonstrate command of the conventions of standard English grammar and usage when writing or speaking.

• Apply knowledge of language to understand how language functions in different contexts, to make effective choices for meaning or style, and to comprehend more fully when reading or listening.

BROWN V BOARD OF EDUCATION:
OPINION OF THE COURT

Writing to Sources

News articles inform the public about major events taking place in the world. They often summarize and explain complex happenings in a way that is easily understood.

Assignment

With your group, analyze the Supreme Court's opinion in *Brown v. Board of Education*. Then, write a **news article** in which you summarize and explain the Court's historic decision.

- Outline the essay, and take note of the key ideas you will include in your article.
- Provide an accurate summarization of the opinion.
- Use precise words to ensure your reporting is factual.
- Avoid injecting your own group's opinions or commentary.
- Title your article and list its contributors.

Vocabulary and Conventions Connection Consider including some of the concept vocabulary words. Also, consider using coordinating conjunctions to link ideas and to combine short sentences.

plaintiffs	jurisdiction	disposition

Reflect on Your Writing

After you have drafted your news article answer these questions.

1. In what ways is your writing suited to a general audience?

2. Are your summarizations and explanations an accurate reflection of the original text?

3. Why These Words? The words you choose can greatly increase the effect of your writing. To what extent are your word choices precise and clear?

Speaking and Listening

> ### Assignment
> Chief Justice Warren's Court tried several cases concerning civil rights. Choose one of the following cases to research. Then, hold a **group discussion** in which you share your findings.
>
> ☐ *Bolling v. Sharpe*
>
> ☐ *Cooper v. Aaron*
>
> ☐ *Lucy v. Adams*
>
> ☐ *Loving v. Virginia*

1. **Perform Research** As a group, decide which case to research, and then, working individually, find 2-3 reputable sources to consult. Keep the following in mind as you conduct research:

   • Internet sources that contain *.gov* or *.edu* are generally more reliable than sites containing *.com* or *.org*.

   • Be sure to verify evidence by cross-checking with another source.

2. **Take Notes** As you research, take careful, accurate notes and be sure to indicate which sources you used. At the end of your notes document, create a set of "talking points" to bring up during your group's discussion.

3. **Hold the Discussion** When all group members have completed their research, come together to discuss your findings.

   • Appoint a facilitator, who will lead the discussion and ensure that the group stays on topic and follows ground rules for discussion.

   • When it is your turn to share your research, refer to your talking points. Be brief and to the point, but try to make your research findings interesting to listeners. When you have finished presenting, invite questions from listeners.

   • When you are listening to others present, be respectful and attentive. When invited to do so, ask questions that are relevant to the topic.

4. **Summarize Findings** At the conclusion of your group discussion, work with your group's facilitator to summarize the work of Earl Warren's Court as it relates to civil rights. Share your findings with other groups, and invite questions from your audience.

✐ EVIDENCE LOG

Before moving on to a new selection, go to your Evidence Log and record what you learned from the Supreme Court's opinion in *Brown v. Board of Education*.

Panel Discussion

Assignment

You have read a variety of texts by people who sought to protest social ills and encourage change. Work with your group to hold an informative **panel discussion** that addresses these questions:

> **What were the goals of these reformers?**
>
> **Why did they want to achieve those goals?**

Make a video recording of your discussion to share with others.

Plan With Your Group

Analyze the Texts There are four texts in the chart. If there are four members in your group, have each member choose one text as his or her area of expertise. If there are more than four members, form partnerships to choose texts. Use the chart headings to formulate key ideas about the particular text you or your partnership has chosen.

TITLE	GOAL OF REFORMER	REASONS FOR GOAL
Ain't I a Woman?		
Declaration of Sentiments		
Giving Women the Vote		
The Story of an Hour		
Brown v. Board of Education: Opinion of the Court		

Gather Evidence Find specific details from your text to support your ideas. Take notes or use note cards to list quotations from the text that support your understanding of the reformer's goal. If necessary, conduct research to locate evidence that supports your understanding of why that goal was important to the reformer.

☰ STANDARDS

Speaking and Listening
Come to discussions prepared, having read and researched material under study; explicitly draw on that preparation by referring to evidence from texts and other research on the topic or issue to stimulate a thoughtful, well-reasoned exchange of ideas.

Organize Your Presentation Choose a moderator to present the assignment questions, which each panel member will answer in turn. The moderator should also make sure that each speaker keeps to agreed-upon time limits and doesn't speak out of turn. Decide on the order in which presenters will speak. Ask a classmate from another group to make a video recording of your discussion.

Rehearse With Your Group

Practice With Your Group Use this checklist to evaluate the effectiveness of your group's first run-through. Then, use your evaluation and these instructions to guide your revision.

CONTENT	USE OF MEDIA	PRESENTATION TECHNIQUES
☐ Each speaker clearly answers the questions asked. ☐ Each speaker supports ideas with evidence from the texts or additional research.	☐ The equipment functions properly. ☐ The focus moves smoothly from speaker to speaker.	☐ The speakers use formal language appropriately. ☐ The speakers make eye contact and speak clearly. ☐ Interactions between speakers and the moderator are civil and smooth.

Fine-Tune the Content If necessary, find additional examples from your chosen text to support your ideas. Make sure that you have incorporated all of the outside research you did as you respond to the moderator's questions.

Improve Your Use of Media Watch a playback of your recording, and give feedback to your recorder. In particular, make sure that the sound is audible so that viewers can easily hear what is being asked and answered.

Brush-Up on Your Presentation Techniques Listen for places where you may revert to language that is more informal or less polished. Try to speak as though you are educating an audience that is eager to learn about these reformers.

Present and Evaluate

As you record your final panel discussion, give all speakers equal time to share their ideas. As you watch the videos made by other groups, evaluate the presentations based on the evaluation checklist.

:≡ STANDARDS

Speaking and Listening
• Present information, findings, and supporting evidence, conveying a clear and distinct perspective, such that listeners can follow the line of reasoning, alternative or opposing perspectives are addressed, and the organization, development, substance, and style are appropriate to purpose, audience, and a range of formal and informal tasks.
• Adapt speech to a variety of contexts and tasks, demonstrating a command of formal English when indicated or appropriate.

PRIMARY SOURCES

- MARY CHESNUT'S CIVIL WAR
- BOMBARDMENT OF SUMTER (ART)
- RECOLLECTIONS OF A PRIVATE
- CIVIL WAR SOLDIER (ART)

Research Presentation

Assignment

You have explored ways in which people across history have struggled for freedom. Now, expand your knowledge by researching how individuals in the Civil War period dealt with realities of war. With your group, read the primary sources that have been provided. Then, form additional research questions based on your reading and locate another source to explore. Synthesize your learning to answer this question:

> What can we learn from ordinary people about extraordinary wartime events?

Share your learning in a **research presentation.**

Plan With Your Group

Analyze the Texts As a group, analyze and discuss each primary source listed here. Remember that a primary source is a document, image, or artifact that provides information about a historical topic. As you study each source, note what information it conveys and also note what further questions the source raises. Perform additional research as needed to find additional information on events, authors, or artists.

TITLE	WHAT WE LEARNED	QUESTIONS WE HAVE
Mary Chesnut's Civil War		
Bombardment of Sumter (art)		
Recollections of a Private		
Civil War Soldier (art)		

Formulate a Research Question Once you have studied the sources that have been provided, formulate a research question that arises from your reading. With your group, locate and analyze a source that will provide the information you seek, and take notes on your learning.

Synthesize Your Findings Review what you've learned from the primary sources you consulted. Then, with your group, answer the question posed in the assignment.

from Mary Chesnut's
Civil War

Mary Chesnut

BACKGROUND
The excerpts are from the diary of Mary Chestnut, who provides an eyewitness account of events leading to and following an attack on Fort Sumter.

APRIL 7, 1861. Today things seem to have settled down a little.

One can but hope still. Lincoln or Seward have made such silly advances and then far sillier drawings back. There may be a chance for peace, after all.

Things are happening so fast.

My husband has been made an aide-de-camp of General Beauregard.

Three hours ago we were quietly packing to go home. The convention has adjourned.

Now he tells me the attack upon Fort Sumter may begin tonight. Depends upon Anderson and the fleet outside. The Herald says that this show of war outside of the bar is intended for Texas.

John Manning came in with his sword and red sash. Pleased as a boy to be on Beauregard's staff while the row goes on. He has gone with Wigfall to Captain Hartstene with instructions.

Mr. Chesnut is finishing a report he had to make to the convention.

Mrs. Hayne called. She had, she said, "but one feeling, pity for those who are not here."

Jack Preston, Willie Alston—"the take-life-easys," as they are called—with John Green, "the big brave," have gone down to the island—volunteered as privates.

Seven hundred men were sent over. Ammunition wagons rumbling along the streets all night. Anderson burning blue lights— signs and signals for the fleet outside, I suppose.

Today at dinner there was no allusion to things as they stand in Charleston Harbor. There was an undercurrent of intense excitement. There could not have been a more brilliant circle. In addition to our usual quartet (Judge Withers, Langdon Cheves, and Trescot) our two governors dined with us, Means and Manning.

Primary Sources
Diaries and Journals What details of style and form tell you that you are reading a diary or journal entry?

Primary Sources
Diaries and Journals Judging from her list of dinner guests, what can you infer about Mary Chesnut's social circumstances?

> **Primary Source: Art**
Describe the spectators'
differing reactions to the
attack on Fort Sumter as
shown in this illustration.

Bombardment of Sumter, Harper's Weekly, 1861

These men all talked so delightfully. For once in my life I listened. That over, business began. In earnest, Governor Means rummaged a sword and red sash from somewhere and brought it for Colonel Chesnut, who has gone to demand the surrender of Fort Sumter.

And now, patience—we must wait.

Why did that green goose Anderson go into Fort Sumter? Then everything began to go wrong.

Now they have intercepted a letter from him, urging them to let him surrender. He paints the horrors likely to ensue if they will not.

He ought to have thought of all that before he put his head in the hole.

APRIL 12, 1861. Anderson will not capitulate.

Yesterday was the merriest, maddest dinner we have had yet. Men were more audaciously wise and witty. We had an unspoken foreboding it was to be our last pleasant meeting. Mr. Miles dined with us today. Mrs. Henry King rushed in: "The news, I come for the latest news—all of the men of the King family are on the island"—of which fact she seemed proud.

While she was here, our peace negotiator—or envoy—came in. That is, Mr. Chesnut returned—his interview with Colonel Anderson had been deeply interesting—but was not inclined to be communicative, wanted his dinner. Felt for Anderson. Had telegraphed to President Davis for instructions. . . .

I do not pretend to go to sleep. How can I? If Anderson does not accept terms—at four—the orders are—he shall be fired upon.

I count four—St. Michael chimes. I begin to hope. At half-past four, the heavy booming of a cannon.

I sprang out of bed. And on my knees—prostrate—I prayed as I never prayed before.

There was a sound of stir all over the house—pattering of feet in the corridor—all seemed hurrying one way. I put on my double gown and a shawl and went, too. It was to the housetop.

The shells were bursting. In the dark I heard a man say "waste of ammunition."

I knew my husband was rowing about in a boat somewhere in that dark bay. And that the shells were roofing it over—bursting toward the fort. If Anderson was obstinate—he was to order the forts on our side to open fire. Certainly fire had begun. The regular roar of the cannon—there it was. And who could tell what each volley accomplished of death and destruction.

The women were wild, there on the housetop. Prayers from the women and imprecations from the men, and then a shell would light up the scene. Tonight, they say, the forces are to attempt to land.

The *Harriet Lane* had her wheelhouse smashed and put back to sea.

We watched up there—everybody wondered. Fort Sumter did not fire a shot.

Today Miles and Manning, colonels now—aides to Beauregard—dined with us. The latter hoped I would keep the peace. I give him only good words, for he was to be under fire all day and night, in the bay carrying orders, etc.

Last night—or this morning truly—up on the housetop I was so weak and weary I sat down on something that looked like a black stool.

Primary Sources
Diaries and Journals
What seems to be Chesnut's emotional state as she writes this entry? What clues in the text support your analysis?

"Get up, you foolish woman—your dress is on fire," cried a man. And he put me out.

It was a chimney, and the sparks caught my clothes. Susan Preston and Mr. Venable then came up. But my fire had been extinguished before it broke out into a regular blaze. . . .

APRIL 13, 1861. Nobody hurt, after all. How gay we were last night.

Reaction after the dread of all the slaughter we thought those dreadful cannons were making such a noise in doing.

Not even a battery the worse for wear.

Fort Sumter has been on fire. He has not yet silenced any of our guns. So the aides—still with swords and red sashes by way of uniform—tell us.

But the sound of those guns makes regular meals impossible. None of us go to table. But tea trays pervade the corridors, going everywhere.

Some of the anxious hearts lie on their beds and moan in solitary misery. Mrs. Wigfall and I solace ourselves with tea in my room.

These women have all a satisfying faith.

APRIL 15, 1861. I did not know that one could live such days of excitement.

They called, "Come out—there is a crowd coming."

A mob indeed, but it was headed by Colonels Chesnut and Manning.

The crowd was shouting and showing these two as messengers of good news. They were escorted to Beauregard's headquarters. Fort Sumter had surrendered.

Those up on the housetop shouted to us, "The fort is on fire." That had been the story once or twice before.

When we had calmed down, Colonel Chesnut, who had taken it all quietly enough—if anything, more unruffled than usual in his serenity—told us how the surrender came about.

Wigfall was with them on Morris Island when he saw the fire in the fort, jumped in a little boat and, with his handkerchief as a white flag, rowed over to Fort Sumter. Wigfall went in through a porthole.

When Colonel Chesnut arrived shortly after and was received by the regular entrance, Colonel Anderson told him he had need to pick his way warily, for it was all mined.

As far as I can make out, the fort surrendered to Wigfall.

But it is all confusion. Our flag is flying there. Fire engines have been sent to put out the fire.

Everybody tells you half of something and then rushes off to tell something else or to hear the last news. . . . ❧

Primary Sources
Diaries and Journals
What do you learn from the entry of April 13, 1861, that you would probably not learn from a textbook?

Recollections of a Private

Warren Lee Goss

In the weeks that followed the attack on Fort Sumter, thousands of men on both sides volunteered to fight. Among the early enlistees was Warren Lee Goss of Massachusetts.

"Cold chills" ran up and down my back as I got out of bed after the sleepless night, and shaved preparatory to other desperate deeds of valor. I was twenty years of age, and when anything unusual was to be done, like fighting or courting, I shaved.

With a nervous tremor convulsing my system, and my heart thumping like muffled drumbeats, I stood before the door of the recruiting office, and before turning the knob to enter read and reread the advertisement for recruits posted thereon, until I knew all its peculiarities. The promised chances for "travel and promotion" seemed good, and I thought I might have made a mistake in considering war so serious after all. "Chances for travel!" I must confess now, after four years of soldiering, that the "chances for travel" were no myth; but "promotion" was a little uncertain and slow.

I was in no hurry to open the door. Though determined to enlist, I was half inclined to put it off awhile; I had a fluctuation of desires; I was fainthearted and brave; I wanted to enlist, and yet—Here I turned the knob, and was relieved. . . .

My first uniform was a bad fit: My trousers were too long by three or four inches; the flannel shirt was coarse and unpleasant, too large at the neck and too short elsewhere. The forage cap was an ungainly bag with pasteboard top and leather visor; the blouse was the only part which seemed decent; while the overcoat made me feel like a little nubbin of corn in a large preponderance of husk. Nothing except "Virginia mud" ever took down my ideas of military pomp quite so low.

∧ **Primary Source: Art**
What attitude toward war does this 1861 painting of a young Civil War soldier convey? Explain.

Primary Sources
Diaries and Journals
What does this account reveal about experiences of new soldiers?

After enlisting I did not seem of so much consequence as I had expected. There was not so much excitement on account of my military appearance as I deemed justly my due. I was taught my facings, and at the time I thought the drillmaster needlessly fussy about shouldering, ordering, and presenting arms. At this time men were often drilled in company and regimental evolutions long before they learned the manual of arms, because of the difficulty of obtaining muskets. These we obtained at an early day, but we would willingly have resigned them after carrying them a few hours. The musket, after an hour's drill, seemed heavier and less ornamental than it had looked to be.

The first day I went out to drill, getting tired of doing the same things over and over, I said to the drill sergeant: "Let's stop this fooling and go over to the grocery." His only reply was addressed to a corporal: "Corporal, take this man out and drill him"; and the corporal did! I found that suggestions were not so well appreciated in the army as in private life, and that no wisdom was equal to a drillmaster's "Right face," "Left wheel," and "Right, oblique, march." It takes a raw recruit some time to learn that he is not to think or suggest, but obey. Some never do learn. I acquired it at last, in humility and mud, but it was tough. Yet I doubt if my patriotism, during my first three weeks' drill, was quite knee high. Drilling looks easy to a spectator, but it isn't. After a time I had cut down my uniform so that I could see out of it, and had conquered the drill sufficiently to see through it. Then the word came: on to Washington! . . . ❧

Develop Your Script

Plan Your Presentation Now that you have gathered information, create an outline and script for your group to follow during your research presentation.

- Be sure your presentation provides a response to the Assignment prompt: *What can we learn from ordinary people about extraordinary wartime events?*

- Develop a working script in which you decide which group member will deliver what information. For example, you may want each group member to discuss findings from one particular primary source.

- Be sure to include information about your additional research question and how you went about finding answers to it.

- Conclude with a summary of your findings.

Rehearse With Your Group

Practice With Your Group Rehearse your presentation with your group. Use this checklist to evaluate the effectiveness of your group's first run-through. Then, use your evaluation and these instructions to guide your revision.

CONTENT	PRESENTATION TECHNIQUES
☐ Each speaker clearly identifies the topic of his or her portion of the presentation. ☐ Each speaker supports ideas with evidence from the texts or additional research.	☐ The focus moves smoothly from speaker to speaker. ☐ The speakers use formal language appropriately. ☐ The speakers make eye contact and speak clearly.

Fine-Tune the Content If necessary, find additional examples from your source materials to support your ideas. Consider switching the order of presenters, if necessary, for flow and logic. You may also want to include visuals to add interest to your presentation.

Brush-Up on Your Presentation Techniques Adapt your word choice if you find your presentation seems too informal. Make eye contact with your audience when it is your turn to speak. When others in your group are presenting, keep your focus on them.

Present and Evaluate

Once you have finished your presentation, invite comments and feedback from your audience. As you watch and listen to presentations of other groups, take notes and offer feedback based on the evaluation checklist.

ESSENTIAL QUESTION:

In what ways does the struggle for freedom change with history?

Freedom is a concept that means so many things, including the right to choose your path in life and to follow your ambitions wherever they may take you. In this section, you will complete your study of the struggle for freedom by exploring an additional selection related to the topic. You'll then share what you learn with classmates. To choose a text, follow these steps.

Look Back Think about the selections you have already studied. What more do you want to know about the topic of the struggle for freedom?

Look Ahead Preview the texts by reading the descriptions. Which one seems most interesting and appealing to you?

Look Inside Take a few minutes to scan the text you chose. Choose a different one if this text doesn't meet your needs.

Independent Learning Strategies

Throughout your life, in school, in your community, and in your career, you will need to rely on yourself to learn and work on your own. Review these strategies and the actions you can take to practice them during Independent Learning. Add ideas of your own for each category.

STRATEGY	ACTION PLAN
Create a schedule	• Understand your goals and deadlines. • Make a plan for what to do each day. •
Practice what you have learned	• Use first-read and close-read strategies to deepen your understanding. • After you read, evaluate the usefulness of the evidence to help you understand the topic. • After reading, consult reference sources for background information that can help you clarify meaning. •
Take notes	• Record important ideas and information. • Review your notes before preparing to share with a group. •

SCAN FOR
MULTIMEDIA

CONTENTS

Choose one selection. Selections are available online only.

SCAN FOR
MULTIMEDIA

First-Read Guide

Use this page to record your first-read ideas.

🔧 **Tool Kit**
First-Read Guide and
Model Annotation

Selection Title: _____

NOTICE new information or ideas you learn about the unit topic as you first read this text.

ANNOTATE by marking vocabulary and key passages you want to revisit.

First Read — NOTICE · ANNOTATE · CONNECT · RESPOND

CONNECT ideas within the selection to other knowledge and the selections you have read.

RESPOND by writing a brief summary of the selection.

NOTICE

ANNOTATE

CONNECT

RESPOND

▣ STANDARD

Reading Read and comprehend complex literary and informational texts independently and proficiently.

Close-Read Guide

Use this page to record your close-read ideas.

Selection Title: _____

Close Read the Text

Revisit sections of the text you marked during your first read. Read these sections closely and **annotate** what you notice. Ask yourself **questions** about the text. What can you **conclude**? Write down your ideas.

Analyze the Text

Think about the author's choices of patterns, structure, techniques, and ideas included in the text. Select one and record your thoughts about what this choice conveys.

QuickWrite

Pick a paragraph from the text that grabbed your interest. Explain the power of this passage.

_____

_____

_____

_____

_____

_____

_____

_____

▤ STANDARD
Reading Read and comprehend complex literary and informational texts independently and proficiently.

Share Your Independent Learning

Prepare to Share

In what ways does the struggle for freedom change with history?

Even when you read or learn something independently, your understanding continues to grow when you share what you have learned with others. Reflect on the text you explored independently, and write notes about its connection to the unit. In your notes, consider why this text belongs in this unit.

Learn From Your Classmates

💬 **Discuss It** Share your ideas about the text you explored on your own. As you talk with your classmates, jot down ideas that you learn from them.

Reflect

Review your notes, and mark the most important insight you gained from these writing and discussion activities. Explain how this idea adds to your understanding of the meaning of freedom.

📑 STANDARDS

Speaking and Listening
Initiate and participate effectively in a range of collaborative discussions with diverse partners on *grades 11–12 topics, texts, and issues,* building on others' ideas and expressing their own clearly and persuasively.

Review Evidence for an Informative Essay

At the beginning of this unit, you took a position on the following question:

What motivates people to struggle for change?

✎ EVIDENCE LOG

Review your Evidence Log and your QuickWrite from the beginning of the unit. Have your ideas changed?

☐ YES	☐ NO
Identify at least three pieces of evidence that have caused you to reevaluate your ideas.	Identify at least three pieces of evidence that reinforced your original ideas.
1.	1.
2.	2.
3.	3.

Develop your thoughts into a topic sentence: *One significant motivation that may inspire people to struggle for change is:* _____

_____

_____

Identify a historical example of the motivation you identified: _____

_____

_____

Evaluate the Strength of Your Evidence Which two texts that you read in this unit offer the strongest support for your topic sentence?

1. _____

2. _____

What are some other resources you might use to locate information about the topic?

1. _____   2. _____

☷ STANDARDS

Writing
Introduce a topic; organize complex ideas, concepts, and information so that each new element builds on that which precedes it to create a unified whole; include formatting, graphics, and multimedia when useful to aiding comprehension.

SOURCES

- WHOLE-CLASS SELECTIONS
- SMALL-GROUP SELECTIONS
- INDEPENDENT-LEARNING SELECTION

PART 1

Writing to Sources: Informative Essay

In this unit, you read a variety of texts by reformers whose goal was to initiate change. Not all struggles were alike: The writers faced various obstacles in their quests for reform.

Assignment

Write an **informative essay** in which you explore this question:

What motivates people to struggle for change?

Begin by defining the various reasons people decide to fight for change. Identify two or three texts from this unit that you feel most clearly show the connections between motivation and action. Use specific examples from each text to support your analysis and deductions.

Reread the Assignment Review the assignment to be sure you fully understand it. The assignment may reference some of the academic words presented at the beginning of the unit. Be sure you understand each of the words given below in order to complete the assignment correctly.

Academic Vocabulary

informational	verbatim	specific
inquire	deduction	

Review the Elements of an Informative Essay Before you begin writing, read the Informative Text Rubric. Once you have completed your first draft, check it against the rubric. If one or more of the elements are missing or not as strong as they could be, revise your text to add or strengthen those components.

⬥ WORD NETWORK

As you write and revise your text, use your Word Network to help vary your word choices.

▤ STANDARDS

Writing
- Write informative/explanatory texts to examine and convey complex ideas, concepts, and information clearly and accurately through the effective selection, organization, and analysis of content.
- Draw evidence from literary or informational texts to support analysis, reflection, and research.
- Write routinely over extended time frames and shorter time frames for a range of tasks, purposes, and audiences.

Informative Text Rubric

	Focus and Organization	Evidence and Elaboration	Language Conventions
4	The introduction is engaging and reveals the topic in a way that appeals to a reader. Facts, details, and examples progress logically, and transition words and phrases link and separate ideas. The conclusion leaves a strong impression on the reader.	Ideas are supported with specific and relevant examples from research and the texts. The style of the essay is formal, and the tone is objective. Vocabulary is used strategically and appropriately for the audience and purpose.	The essay demonstrates a clear command of standard English conventions of usage and mechanics.
3	The introduction is engaging and clearly reveals the topic. Facts, details, and examples progress logically, and transition words appear frequently. The conclusion follows from the rest of the essay.	Ideas are supported with relevant examples from research and the texts. The style of the essay is mostly formal, and the tone tends to be objective. Vocabulary is generally appropriate for the audience and purpose.	The essay demonstrates accuracy in standard English conventions of usage and mechanics.
2	The introduction states the topic. Facts; details and examples progress somewhat logically, and transition words may be used. The conclusion restates the main ideas.	Many ideas are supported with examples from research and the texts. The style of the essay is occasionally formal, and the tone is at times objective. Vocabulary is somewhat appropriate for the audience and purpose.	The essay demonstrates some accuracy in standard English conventions of usage and mechanics.
1	The introduction does not clearly state the topic, or there is no introduction. Facts, details, and examples do not progress logically, and sentences seem disconnected. The conclusion does not follow from the essay, or there is no conclusion.	Ideas are not supported with examples from research and the texts, or examples are irrelevant. The style of the essay is informal, and the tone frequently reveals biases. Vocabulary is limited, ineffective, or inappropriate.	The essay contains mistakes in standard English conventions of usage and mechanics.

PART 2
Speaking and Listening: Podcast

Assignment

After completing the final draft of your informative essay, make a **podcast** or audio recording that could be uploaded for listeners. Then, share your recording, so that your classmates can listen to your work.

Follow these steps to make your podcast both informative and interesting.

- Give your podcast a title, and provide your name.
- Mark key examples in your informative essay that answer this question: *How does the motivator I analyzed encourage people to struggle for change?* These are the key points you will want to emphasize in your delivery.
- Practice your delivery, keeping in mind that you will be heard but not seen. You will need to vary your voice accordingly. Also, take care to eliminate distracting background noises.
- Deliver your podcast, being sure to maintain an even distance from the recording device. Focus on speaking clearly, and build in pauses so that listeners can follow and digest your ideas.

Review the Rubric The criteria by which your podcast will be evaluated appear in the rubric below. Review the criteria before recording to ensure that you are prepared.

	Content	Use of Media	Presentation Technique
3	The podcast focuses on the question. The flow of ideas is logical, clear, and easy to follow.	The voice on the recording is consistent and audible. The podcast file has a title that clearly illustrates the focus.	The speaker's voice is consistently clear and appropriately loud for the recording. The speaker varies tone and pace consistently and effectively.
2	The podcast mostly focuses on the question. The flow of ideas is fairly logical and mostly easy to follow.	The voice on the recording may vary but is mostly audible. The podcast file has a logical title.	The speaker's voice is mostly clear and sufficiently loud for the recording. The speaker varies tone and pace to some extent.
1	The podcast has no clear focus. The flow of ideas is illogical and difficult to follow.	The voice on the recording sometimes fades in and out. The podcast file lacks a meaningful title.	The speaker mumbles or speaks too quickly or quietly. The speaker does not vary tone and pace.

Reflect on the Unit

Now that you've completed the unit, take a few moments to reflect on your learning. Use the questions below to think about where you succeeded, what skills and strategies helped you, and where you can continue to grow in the future.

Reflect on the Unit Goals

Look back at the goals at the beginning of the unit. Use a different colored pen to rate yourself again. Think about readings and activities that contributed the most to the growth of your understanding. Record your thoughts.

Reflect on the Learning Strategies

Discuss It Write a reflection on whether you were able to improve your learning based on your Action Plans. Think about what worked, what didn't, and what you might do to keep working on these strategies. Record your ideas before a class discussion.

Reflect on the Text

Choose a selection that you found challenging, and explain what made it difficult.

Explain something that surprised you about a text in the unit.

Which activity taught you the most about power, protest, and change? What did you learn?

STANDARDS

Speaking and Listening
Come to discussions prepared, having read and researched material under study; explicitly draw on that preparation by referring to evidence from texts and other research on the topic or issue to stimulate a thoughtful, well-reasoned exchange of ideas.

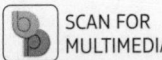
SCAN FOR MULTIMEDIA

RESOURCES

CONTENTS

Marking the Text: Strategies and Tips for Annotation

When you close read a text, you read for comprehension and then reread to unlock layers of meaning and to analyze a writer's style and techniques. Marking a text as you read it enables you to participate more fully in the close-reading process.

Following are some strategies for text mark-ups, along with samples of how the strategies can be applied. These mark-ups are suggestions; you and your teacher may want to use other mark-up strategies.

✳	Key Idea
!	I love it!
?	I have questions
◯	Unfamiliar or important word
----	Context Clues

Suggested Mark-Up Notations

WHAT I NOTICE	HOW TO MARK UP	QUESTIONS TO ASK
Key Ideas and Details	• Highlight key ideas or claims. • Underline supporting details or evidence.	• What does the text say? What does it leave unsaid? • What inferences do you need to make? • What details lead you to make your inferences?
Word Choice	• Circle unfamiliar words. • Put a dotted line under context clues, if any exist. • Put an exclamation point beside especially rich or poetic passages.	• What inferences about word meaning can you make? • What tone and mood are created by word choice? • What alternate word choices might the author have made?
Text Structure	• Highlight passages that show key details supporting the main idea. • Use arrows to indicate how sentences and paragraphs work together to build ideas. • Use a right-facing arrow to indicate foreshadowing. • Use a left-facing arrow to indicate flashback.	• Is the text logically structured? • What emotional impact do the structural choices create?
Author's Craft	• Circle or highlight instances of repetition, either of words, phrases, consonants, or vowel sounds. • Mark rhythmic beats in poetry using checkmarks and slashes. • Underline instances of symbolism or figurative language.	• Does the author's style enrich or detract from the reading experience? • What levels of meaning are created by the author's techniques?

CLOSE READING

First Read

NOTICE · ANNOTATE · CONNECT · RESPOND

* Key Idea
! I love it!
? I have questions
◯ Unfamiliar or important word
---- Context Clues

NOTES

In a first read, work to get a sense of the main idea of a text. Look for key details and ideas that help you understand what the author conveys to you. Mark passages which prompt a strong response from you.

Here is how one reader marked up this text.

MODEL

INFORMATIONAL TEXT

from Classifying the Stars

Cecilia H. Payne

1   Sunlight and starlight are composed of waves of various lengths, which the eye, even aided by a telescope, is unable to separate. We must use more than a telescope. In order to sort out the component colors, the light must be dispersed by a prism, or split up by some other means. For instance, sunbeams passing through rain drops, are transformed into the myriad-tinted rainbow. The familiar rainbow spanning the sky is Nature's most glorious demonstration that light is composed of many colors.

2   The very beginning of our knowledge of the nature of a star dates back to 1672, when Isaac Newton gave to the world the results of his experiments on passing sunlight through a prism. To describe the beautiful band of rainbow tints, produced when sunlight was dispersed by his three-cornered piece of glass, he took from the Latin the word *spectrum*, meaning an appearance. The rainbow is the spectrum of the Sun. . . .

3   In 1814, more than a century after Newton, the spectrum of the Sun was obtained in such purity that an amazing detail was seen and studied by the German optician, Fraunhofer. He saw that the multiple spectral tints, ranging from delicate violet to deep red, were crossed by hundreds of fine dark lines. In other words, there were narrow gaps in the spectrum where certain shades were wholly blotted out. We must remember that the word spectrum is applied not only to sunlight, but also to the light of any glowing substance when its rays are sorted out by a prism or a grating.

First-Read Guide

Use this page to record your first-read ideas.

Selection Title: _____ Classifying the Stars _____

You may want to use a guide like this to organize your thoughts after you read. Here is how a reader completed a First-Read Guide.

NOTICE

NOTICE new information or ideas you learned about the unit topic as you first read this text.

Light = different waves of colors. (Spectrum)

Newton - the first person to observe these waves using a prism.

Faunhofer saw gaps in the spectrum.

ANNOTATE

ANNOTATE by marking vocabulary and key passages you want to revisit.

Vocabulary
    myriad
    grating
    component colors

Different light types = different lengths

Isaac Newton also worked theories of gravity.

<u>Multiple spectral tints?</u> "colors of various appearance"

Key Passage:
Paragraph 3 shows that Fraunhofer discovered more about the nature of light spectrums: he saw the spaces in between the tints.

First Read
NOTICE · ANNOTATE · CONNECT · RESPOND

CONNECT

CONNECT ideas within the selection to other knowledge and the selections you have read.

I remember learning about prisms in science class.

Double rainbows! My favorite. How are they made?

RESPOND

RESPOND by writing a brief summary of the selection.

Science allows us to see things not visible to the naked eye. What we see as sunlight is really a spectrum of colors. By using tools, such as prisms, we can see the components of sunlight and other light. They appear as single colors or as multiple colors separated by gaps of no color. White light contains a rainbow of colors.

TOOL KIT: CLOSE READING

CLOSE READING

* **Key Idea**
! **I love it!**
? **I have questions**
◯ **Unfamiliar or important word**
---- **Context Clues**

In a close read, go back into the text to study it in greater detail. Take the time to analyze not only the author's ideas but the way that those ideas are conveyed. Consider the genre of the text, the author's word choice, the writer's unique style, and the message of the text.

Here is how one reader close read this text.

NOTES

MODEL

INFORMATIONAL TEXT

from Classifying the Stars

Cecilia H. Payne

explanation of sunlight and starlight

1 Sunlight and starlight are **composed of waves of various lengths**, which the eye, even aided by a telescope, is unable to separate. We must use more than a telescope. In order to sort out the **component colors**, the light must be dispersed by a prism, or split up by some other means. For instance, sunbeams passing through rain drops, are transformed into the myriad-tinted rainbow. **The familiar rainbow spanning the sky is Nature's most glorious demonstration that light is composed of many colors.**

What is light and where do the colors come from?

This paragraph is about Newton and the prism.

2 **The very beginning of our knowledge of the nature of a star** dates back to 1672, when **Isaac Newton** gave to the world the results of his experiments on passing sunlight through a prism. To describe the beautiful band of rainbow tints, produced when sunlight was dispersed by his three-cornered piece of glass, he took from the Latin the word *spectrum*, meaning an **appearance**. The rainbow is the spectrum of the Sun. . . .

What discoveries helped us understand light?

3 In 1814, more than a century after Newton, the spectrum of the Sun was obtained in such purity that an **amazing detail was seen and studied by the German optician, Fraunhofer**. He saw that the **multiple spectral tints, ranging from delicate violet to deep red, were crossed by hundreds of fine dark lines**. In other words, there were narrow gaps in the spectrum where certain shades were wholly blotted out. We must remember that the word spectrum is applied not only to sunlight, but also to the light of any glowing substance when its rays are sorted out by a prism or a grating.

Fraunhofer and gaps in spectrum

Close-Read Guide

Use this page to record your close-read ideas.

You can use the Close-Read Guide to help you dig deeper into the text. Here is how a reader completed a Close-Read Guide.

Selection Title: _Classifying the Stars_

Close Read the Text

Revisit sections of the text you marked during your first read. Read these sections closely and **annotate** what you notice. Ask yourself **questions** about the text. What can you **conclude?** Write down your ideas.

Paragraph 3: Light is composed of waves of various lengths. Prisms let us see different colors in light. This is called the spectrum. Fraunhofer proved that there are gaps in the spectrum, where certain shades are blotted out.

More than one researcher studied this and each built off the ideas that were already discovered.

Analyze the Text

Think about the author's choices of patterns, structure, techniques, and ideas included in the text. Select one, and record your thoughts about what this choice conveys.

The author showed the development of human knowledge of the spectrum chronologically. Helped me see how ideas were built upon earlier understandings. Used dates and "more than a century after Newton" to show time.

QuickWrite

Pick a paragraph from the text that grabbed your interest. Explain the power of this passage.

The first paragraph grabbed my attention, specifically the sentence "The familiar rainbow spanning the sky is Nature's most glorious demonstration that light is composed of many colors." The paragraph began as a straightforward scientific explanation. When I read the word "glorious," I had to stop and deeply consider what was being said. It is a word loaded with personal feelings. With that one word, the author let the reader know what was important to her.

Analyzing Legal Meanings and Reasoning

Reading historical and legal texts requires careful analysis of both the vocabulary and the logical flow of ideas that support a conclusion.

Understanding Legal Meanings

The language of historical and legal documents is formal, precise, and technical. Many words in these texts have specific meanings that you need to understand in order to follow the flow of ideas. For example, the second amendment to the U.S. Constitution states that "A well regulated Militia being necessary to the security of a free State, the right of the people to keep and bear Arms shall not be infringed." To understand this amendment, it is important to know that in this context *militia* means "armed forces," *bear* means "carry," and *infringed* means "denied." To understand legal meanings:

- Use your knowledge of word roots to help you understand unfamiliar words. Many legal terms use familiar Greek or Latin roots, prefixes, or suffixes.

- Do not assume that you know a word's legal meaning: Use a dictionary to check the meanings of key words to be certain that you are applying the correct meaning.

- Paraphrase the text to aid comprehension. Replace difficult words with synonyms to make sure you follow the logic of the argument.

Delineating Legal Reasoning

Works of public advocacy, such as court decisions, political proclamations, proposed laws, or constitutional amendments, use careful reasoning to support conclusions. These strategies can help you understand the legal reasoning in an argument:

- State the **purpose** of the document in your own words to help you focus on the writer's primary goal.

- Look for the line of reasoning that supports the **arguments** presented. To be valid and persuasive, key arguments should be backed up by clearly stated logical analysis. Be aware of persuasive techniques, such as citing facts and statistics, referring to expert testimonials, and using emotional language with strong connotations.

- Identify the **premises,** or evidence, upon which a decision rests. In legal texts, premises often include **precedents,** which are earlier examples that must be followed or specifically overturned. Legal reasoning is usually based on the decisions of earlier trials. Be sure you understand precedents in order to identify how the court arrived at the current decision.

NOTES

Note the strategies used to evaluate legal meanings and reasoning in this Supreme Court decision from 1954 regarding the legality of segregated, "separate but equal" schools for students of different races.

LEGAL TEXT

from *Brown v. Board of Education of Topeka*, Opinion of the Supreme Court by Chief Justice Earl Warren

We come then to the question presented: Does segregation of children in public schools solely on the basis of race, even though the physical facilities and other "tangible" factors may be equal, deprive the children of the minority group of equal educational opportunities? We believe that it does.

In *Sweatt v. Painter*, in finding that a segregated law school for Negroes could not provide them equal educational opportunities, this Court relied in large part on "those qualities which are incapable of objective measurement but which make for greatness in a law school." In *McLaurin v. Oklahoma State Regents*, the Court, in requiring that a Negro admitted to a white graduate school be treated like all other students, again resorted to intangible considerations: ". . . his ability to study, to engage in discussions and exchange views with other students, and, in general, to learn his profession." Such considerations apply with added force to children in grade and high schools. To separate them from others of similar age and qualifications solely because of their race generates a feeling of inferiority as to their status in the community that may affect their hearts and minds in a way unlikely ever to be undone. The effect of this separation on their educational opportunities was well stated by a finding in the Kansas case by a court which nevertheless felt compelled to rule against the Negro plaintiffs: Segregation of white and colored children in public schools has a detrimental effect upon the colored children. The impact is greater when it has the sanction of the law, for the policy of separating the races is usually interpreted as denoting the inferiority of the negro group. A sense of inferiority affects the motivation of a child to learn. Segregation with the sanction of law, therefore, has a tendency to [retard] the educational and mental development of negro children and to deprive them of some of the benefits they would receive in a racially integrated school system. Whatever may have been the extent of psychological knowledge at the time of *Plessy v. Ferguson*, this finding is amply supported by modern authority. Any language in *Plessy v. Ferguson* contrary to this finding is rejected.

We conclude that, in the field of public education, the doctrine of "separate but equal" has no place. Separate educational facilities are inherently unequal.

Use Word Roots The word *tangible* comes from the Latin root meaning "to touch." In this decision, the court contrasts tangible, measurable features with intangible features that are difficult to measure.

Identify the Premises The court cites two precedents: earlier cases relating to unequal education opportunities for black students.

Paraphrase the Text Here's one way you might break down the ideas in this sentence when you paraphrase: Segregating students just because of their race makes them feel as if they are less valued by our society. This separation can have a permanent negative influence on their character.

Line of Reasoning The conclusion makes the **purpose** of the decision clear: to overturn the precedent established by *Plessy v.* Ferguson. The **argument** describes the reasons the Court no longer considers the reasoning in that earlier case to be valid.

WRITING

Argument

When you think of the word *argument*, you might think of a disagreement between two people, but an argument is more than that. An argument is a logical way of presenting a belief, conclusion, or stance. A good argument is supported with reasoning and evidence.

Argument writing can be used for many purposes, such as to change a reader's point of view or opinion or to bring about an action or a response from a reader.

Elements of an Argumentative Text

An **argument** is a logical way of presenting a viewpoint, belief, or stand on an issue. A well-written argument may convince the reader, change the reader's mind, or motivate the reader to take a certain action.

An effective argument contains these elements:

- a precise claim
- consideration of counterclaims, or opposing positions, and a discussion of their strengths and weaknesses
- logical organization that makes clear connections among claim, counterclaim, reasons, and evidence
- valid reasoning and evidence
- a concluding statement or section that logically completes the argument
- formal and objective language and tone
- error-free grammar, including accurate use of transitions

ARGUMENT: SCORE 1

Community Service Should be a Requirement for High School Graduation

Volunteering is a great idea for high school students. Those who don't volunteer are missing out.

> The claim is not clearly stated in the introduction.

You can learn a lot at your volunteer job. It might not seem like a big deal at the time, but the things you learn and do can be useful. You might volunteer somewhere with a spreadsheet. Everyone needs to know how to use a spreadsheet! That's going to be a useful again really soon.

Their lots of reasons to get involved. One of them is to become a better student in school. Also, to feel better about yourself and not act out so much.

> The argument contains mistakes in standard English conventions of usage and mechanics.

So, volunteering helps you learn and get better at lots of things, not just what you are doing at your volunteer job. It's good not just to learn reading and writing and math and science all the time—the usual stuff we study in school. That's how volunteering can help you out.

> The vocabulary used is limited and ineffective, and the tone is informal.

Students today are really busy and they can't add anything more to they're busy schedules. But I think they can add a little more if it doesn't take too much time. Especially if it is important like volunteering.

> The writer does not acknowledge counterclaims.

High school students who volunteer get involved with the real world outside school, and that means a lot. They have a chance to do something that can make a difference in the world. This helps them learn things that maybe they can't learn in school, like, how to be kind and jenerous and care about making the world a better place.

Volunteering in high school is a great idea. Everybody should do it. There are lots of different ways to volunteer. You can even do it on weekends with your friends.

MODEL

ARGUMENT: SCORE 2

Community Service Should be a Requirement for High School Graduation

High school students should have to volunteer before they can graduate. It makes sense because it is helpful to them and others. Some students would volunteer anyway even if it wasn't required, but some wouldn't. If they have to do it for graduation then they won't miss out.

Their lots of reasons to get involved. One is to be a better student in school. Researchers have done studies to see the connection between community service and doing well in school. One study showed that most schools with programs said grades went up most of the time for kids that volunteered. Another study said elementary and middle school kids got better at problem-solving and were more interested in school. One study said students showed more responsibility. Another researcher discovered that kids who been volunteering have better self-esteem. They also have fewer problems.

Volunteering helps you learn and improve at lots of things, not just what you are doing at your volunteer job. One thing you might get better at is being a nicer person, like having more patience and listening well to others. Because you might need those skills when you are volunteering at a senior center or a preschool.

Some people say that volunteering in high school should NOT be required for graduation. They say students already have too much to do and they can't add anything more to they're schedules. But they can add a little more if it doesn't take too much time. Especially if it is important like volunteering.

Why should students be forced to do something, even if it is good? Well, that's just the way it is. When you force students to do something that is good, you are doing them a favor. Like forcing them to eat their vegetables or do their homework. The kids might not like it at first but what do you want to bet they are happy about it later on. That's the point.

Volunteering should be required for all high school students before they graduate. That's not just because they can do a lot of good in the world, but also because doing community service will help them in lots of ways.

The introduction establishes the claim.

The tone of the argument is occasionally formal and objective.

The writer briefly acknowledges and refutes counterclaims.

The writers relies too much on weak anecdotal evidence.

The conclusion offers some insight into the claim and restates some information.

ARGUMENT: SCORE 3

Community Service Should be a Requirement for High School Graduation

Requiring community service for high school graduation is an excellent idea that offers benefits not only to the community but to the student as well. Making it a requirement ensures that all students will be able to get in on the act.

Volunteering is a great way to build skills. It might not seem like a big deal at the time, but the experience you gain is very likely to be useful in the future. For example, while tracking, sorting, and distributing donations at an afterschool program, a volunteer might learn how to use a spreadsheet. That's going to come in handy very quickly, both in and out of school.

Participating in service learning can help you do better in school. ("Service learning" is when community service is part of a class curriculum.) For example, one study found that most schools with service learning programs reported grade point averages of participating students improved 76 percent of the time. Another study showed improved problem-solving skills and increased interest in academics among elementary and middle school students.

A study showed that middle and high school students who participated in quality service learning projects showed more personal and social responsibility. Another study found that students were more likely to help each other and be kind to each other, and care about doing their best. Studies also show better self-esteem and fewer behavioral problems in students who have been involved with service learning.

Despite all this, many people say that volunteering in high school should NOT be a requirement for graduation. They point out that students today are already over-stressed and over-scheduled. There simply isn't room for anything more.

True! But community service doesn't have to take up a lot of time. It might be possible for a group of time-stressed students to use class-time to organize a fundraiser, or to squeeze their service into a single "marathon" weekend. It's all a question of priorities.

In short, volunteering is a great way for students to help others, and reap benefits for themselves as well. Making it a requirement ensures that all students have the chance to grow through involvement with their communities. Volunteering opens doors and offers life-long benefits, and high school is the perfect time to get started!

The claim is established in the introduction but is not as clear as it could be.

The tone of the argument is mostly formal and objective.

The writer does not transition very well into new topics.

The writer uses some transitional phrases.

The writer gives a reason for the counterclaim, but does not provide firm examples.

The conclusion restates the claim and provides additional detail.

TOOL KIT: WRITING

WRITING

ARGUMENT: SCORE 4

Community Service Should be a Requirement for High School Graduation

Every high school student should be required to do community service in order to graduate. Volunteering offers life-long benefits that will prepare all students for adulthood.

First and foremost, studies show that participating in service learning —when community service is part of a class curriculum—often helps students do better in school. For example, a study conducted by Leeward County found that 83 percent of schools with service learning programs reported grade point averages of participating students improved 76 percent of the time. Another study, conducted by Hilliard Research, showed improved problem-solving skills and increased interest in academics among elementary and middle school students who participated in service learning.

But it's not just academic performance that can improve through volunteering: There are social and psychological benefits as well. For example, a student survey showed that students who participated in quality service learning projects showed more personal and social responsibility. Another survey found that students involved in service learning were more likely to be kind to each other, and care about doing their best. Studies also show better self-esteem and fewer behavioral problems in students who have been involved with service learning.

Despite all this, there are still many who say that volunteering in high school should NOT be a requirement for graduation. They point out that students today are already over-stressed and over-scheduled. What's more, requiring community service for graduation would be particularly hard on athletes and low-income students who work after school to help their families make ends meet.

Good points, but community service does not have to take up vast quantities of time. It might be possible for a group of time-stressed students to use class-time to organize a fundraiser, or to compress their service into a single "marathon" weekend. Showing students that helping others is something to make time for is an important lesson.

In short, volunteering encourages engagement: It shows students that their actions matter, and that they have the power—and responsibility—to make the world a better place. What could be a more important lesson than that?

The introduction establishes the writer's claim in a clear and compelling way.

The writer uses a variety of sentence transitions.

Sources of evidence are comprehensive and contain relevant information.

Counterclaims are clearly acknowledged and refuted.

The conclusion offers fresh insight into the claim.

Argument Rubric

	Focus and Organization	Evidence and Elaboration	Conventions
4	The introduction engages the reader and establishes a claim in a compelling way. The argument includes valid reasons and evidence that address and support the claim while clearly acknowledging counterclaims. The ideas progress logically, and transitions make connections among ideas clear. The conclusion offers fresh insight into the claim.	The sources of evidence are comprehensive and specific and contain relevant information. The tone of the argument is always formal and objective. The vocabulary is always appropriate for the audience and purpose.	The argument intentionally uses standard English conventions of usage and mechanics.
3	The introduction engages the reader and establishes the claim. The argument includes reasons and evidence that address and support my claim while acknowledging counterclaims. The ideas progress logically, and some transitions are used to help make connections among ideas clear. The conclusion restates the claim and important information.	The sources of evidence contain relevant information. The tone of the argument is mostly formal and objective. The vocabulary is generally appropriate for the audience and purpose.	The argument demonstrates general accuracy in standard English conventions of usage and mechanics.
2	The introduction establishes a claim. The argument includes some reasons and evidence that address and support the claim while briefly acknowledging counterclaims. The ideas progress somewhat logically. A few sentence transitions are used that connect readers to the argument. The conclusion offers some insight into the claim and restates information.	The sources of evidence contain some relevant information. The tone of the argument is occasionally formal and objective. The vocabulary is somewhat appropriate for the audience and purpose.	The argument demonstrates some accuracy in standard English conventions of usage and mechanics.
1	The introduction does not clearly state the claim. The argument does not include reasons or evidence for the claim. No counterclaims are acknowledged. The ideas do not progress logically. Transitions are not included to connect ideas. The conclusion does not restate any information that is important.	Reliable and relevant evidence is not included. The vocabulary used is limited or ineffective. The tone of the argument is not objective or formal.	The argument contains mistakes in standard English conventions of usage and mechanics.

Informative/Explanatory Texts

Informative and explanatory writing should rely on facts to inform or explain. Informative writing serves several purposes: to increase readers' knowledge of a subject, to help readers better understand a procedure or process, or to provide readers with an enhanced comprehension of a concept. It should also feature a clear introduction, body, and conclusion.

Elements of Informative/Explanatory Texts

Informative/explanatory texts present facts, details, data, and other kinds of evidence to give information about a topic. Readers turn to informational and explanatory texts when they wish to learn about a specific idea, concept, or subject area, or if they want to learn how to do something.

An effective informative/explanatory text contains these elements:

- a topic sentence or thesis statement that introduces the concept or subject
- relevant facts, examples, and details that expand upon a topic
- definitions, quotations, and/or graphics that support the information given
- headings (if desired) to separate sections of the essay
- a structure that presents information in a direct, clear manner
- clear transitions that link sections of the essay
- precise words and technical vocabulary where appropriate
- formal and object language and tone
- a conclusion that supports the information given and provides fresh insights

INFORMATIVE: SCORE 1

How Technology is Changing the Way We Work

Lot's of people work on computers. So, technology is everywhere. If you feel comfortable using computers and all kinds of other technology, your going to be a head at work, for sure.

They're new Devices and Apps out there every day. Each different job has its own gadgets and programs and apps that you have to learn. Every day their more new apps and devices, they can do all kinds of things.

In the past, people only worked at the office. They didn't get to work at home. Now, if you have a smart phone, you can check your email wherever. You can work at home on a computer. You can work in cafés or wherever. Also on a tablet. If you wanted to, you can be working all the time. But that will be a drag!

Technology is now an important part of almost every job. You also have to have a website. You have to have a social media page. Maybe if your business is doing really well you could afford to hire someone to take care of all that stuff—but it would be better if you knew how to do it yourself.

Technology brings people together and helps them work. It could be someone next to you or someone even on the other side of the world. You can connect with them using email. You can send a text. You could have a conference or video call.

Working from home is cheaper for the worker and boss. They can get stuff done during the day like going to the post office or the library, or picking up their kids at school. This is all thanks to technology.

Lots of jobs today are in technology. Way more than before! That's why it's a good idea to take classes and learn about something in technology, because then you will be able to find a job.

There are apps to find houses for sale, find restaurants, learn new recipes, keep track of how much you exercise, and all kinds of other things, like playing games and tuning your guitar. And there are apps to help you work. It's hard to imagine how people would manage to work now without this kind of technology to help them.

The writer's opening statement does not adequately introduce the thesis, and there are numerous spelling mistakes.

The writer's word choice often does not support the proper tone the essay ought to have.

The essay's sentences are often not purposeful, varied, or well-controlled.

The writer does not include a concluding statement.

WRITING

INFORMATIVE: SCORE 2

How Technology is Changing the Way We Work

Technology affects the way we work, in every kind of job and industry. Each different job has its own gadgets and programs and apps that you have to learn. Every day there are more new apps and devices that can do all kinds of things.

> The writer's opening does not clearly introduce the thesis.

In the past, people went to the office to work. That's not always true today. Now if you have a smart phone, you can check your email wherever you are. You can work at home on a desktop computer. You can work on a laptop in a café or wherever. Or a tablet. Technology makes it so people can work all the time.

It doesn't matter whether the person is on the other side of the world— technology brings you together. Theirs email. Theirs text messaging. You have conference calls. You've got video calling. All these things let people work together wherever they are. And don't forget, today people can access files from the cloud. That helps them work from whatever device they want. More than one person can work on the same file.

> The essay is somewhat lacking in organizational structure.

Different kinds of work places and schedules are becoming more common and normal. Working from home has benefits businesses. It means cost savings. It means higher productivity. It means higher job satisfaction. They can get stuff done during the day like going to the post office or the bank, or picking up their kids at school. That is very convenient.

> The essay has many interesting details, but some do not relate specifically to the topic.

It's also true that lots and lots of jobs today are in technology, or related to technology in some way. Way more than before! That's why it's a good idea to get a degree or take classes and learn about something in technology, because it seems like that's where all the new jobs are. Software designers make a really good salary, and so do other tech-related jobs.

> The writer's word choice is overly informal.

Technology is now an important part of almost every job. It's no longer enough to be just a photographer or whatever. You have to get a social media page. You have to be able to use the latest tech gadgets. You can't just take pictures.

> The writer's sentences are disjointed and ineffective.

In todays world, technology is changing how we work. You have to be able to feel comfortable with technology in order to survive at work. Even if you really don't like technology, you don't really have a choice. So, get used to it!

> The conclusion follow logically but is not mature and is overly informal.

How Technology Is Changing the Way We Work

Technology has been changing how we work for a long time, but the pace of change has gotten dramatically faster. No industry or job is exempt. Powerful computing technology and Internet connectivity affects all sectors of the economy. It doesn't matter what job you're talking about: Technology is transforming the way people work. It's an exciting time to be entering the workforce!

The Office Is Everywhere

Technology is rapidly changing not just *how* but *where, when,* and *with whom* we work. It used to be that work was something that happened only at the office. All kinds of different work places and schedules are becoming much more common and normal. According to a study, telecommuting (working from home) rose 79 percent between 2005 and 2012. Working from home has benefits for both the employee and employer. It means cost savings for both, increased productivity, and higher job satisfaction.

The Cloud

Cloud and other data storage and sharing options mean that workers have access to information whenever they want, wherever they are. Whether it's one person who wants the convenience of being able to work on a file from several devices (and locations), or several people who are working on something together, the ability to store data in the cloud and access it from anywhere is a huge change in the way we work. It's almost like all being in the same office, working on the same computer.

Tech Industries and Jobs

Technology is changing the way we work in part by making technology itself such an important element in almost every profession. Therefore, you can see it's no longer good enough to be just a photographer or contractor. You have to know something about technology to do your job, market yourself, and track your performance. No matter what jobs someone does they have to be tech-savvy to be able to use their devices to connect and interact with each other across the globe.

Conclusion

In todays world, technology is quickly and continuously changing how we work, what we do, where and when we do it. In order to do well and thrive, everyone has to be a little bit of a tech geek. So, get used to technology being a part of your work life. And get used to change. Because, in a constantly changing technological world, change is going to be one of the few things that stays the same!

The thesis is introduced but is buried in the introduction.

The writer uses headings to help make the organization of ideas clear.

Statistics support the writer's claim.

The writer uses some transitions and sentence connections, but more would be helpful.

There are a few errors in spelling and punctuation but they do not detract from the effectiveness of the essay.

The conclusion sums up the main ideas of the essay and links to the opening statements.

TOOL KIT: WRITING

WRITING

MODEL

INFORMATIVE: SCORE 4

How Technology Is Changing the Way We Work

While advances in technology have been changing how we work for hundreds of years, the pace of change has accelerated dramatically in the past two decades. With powerful computing technology and Internet connectivity affecting all sectors of the economy, no industry or profession is exempt. It doesn't matter whether you're talking about financial advisors, architects, or farmers: Technology is transforming the way people work.

The Office Is Everywhere

Technology is rapidly revolutionizing not just *how* but *where, when,* and *with whom* we work. It used to be that work was something that happened strictly at the office. In fact, non-traditional work places are becoming much more common. According to one study, telecommuting rose 79 percent between 2005 and 2012. Working from home has proven benefits for both the employee and employer, including cost savings for both, increased productivity, and job satisfaction.

Working with the Cloud

Another important technological advancement that is impacting how we work is the development of cloud computing. Whether it's one person who wants the convenience of being able to work from several devices, or several people who are working together from different locations, the ability to store data in the cloud and access it from anywhere is a huge change in the way we work. Over long distances, coworkers can not only *communicate* with each other, they can *collaborate*, in real time, by sharing and accessing files through the. Only five years ago, this kind of instant access was impossible.

Tech Industries and Jobs

Technology is changing the way we work is by making technology itself an important element in almost every job. It's no longer good enough to be just a photographer or contractor: you have to know something about technology to perform, market, and track your work. No matter what job someone is doing, he or she has to be tech-savvy to be able to use their devices to connect and interact.

Conclusion

In today's world, technology is quickly and continuously changing what work we do, and how, where, when, and with whom we do it. Comfort with new technology—and with rapid technological change—is a prerequisite for success, no matter where your interests lie, or what kind of job you are looking to find. It's a brave new technological world of work, and it's changing every day!

The opening paragraph ends with a thesis, which is strong and clear.

The writer makes an effort to be thoughtful and engage the reader.

Headings help ensure that the organizing structure of the essay is clear and effective.

The sentences in the essay are purposeful and varied.

The progression of ideas in the essay is logical and well-controlled.

The writer's word choice contributes to the clarity of the essay and shows awareness of the essay's purpose and tone.

Informative/Explanatory Rubric

	Focus and Organization	Evidence and Elaboration	Conventions
4	The introduction engages the reader and states a thesis in a compelling way. The essay includes a clear introduction, body, and conclusion. The conclusion summarizes ideas and offers fresh insight into the thesis.	The essay includes specific reasons, details, facts, and quotations from selections and outside resources to support the thesis. The tone of the essay is always formal and objective. The language is always precise and appropriate for the audience and purpose.	The essay uses standard English conventions of usage and mechanics. The essay contains no spelling errors.
3	The introduction engages the reader and sets forth the thesis. The essay includes an introduction, body, and conclusion. The conclusion summarizes ideas and supports the thesis.	The essay includes some specific reasons, details, facts, and quotations from selections and outside resources to support the thesis. The tone of the essay is mostly formal and objective. The language is generally precise and appropriate for the audience and purpose.	The essay demonstrates general accuracy in standard English conventions of usage and mechanics. The essay contains few spelling errors.
2	The introduction sets forth the thesis. The essay includes an introduction, body, and conclusion, but one or more parts are weak. The conclusion partially summarizes ideas but may not provide strong support of the thesis.	The essay includes a few reasons, details, facts, and quotations from selections and outside resources to support the thesis. The tone of the essay is occasionally formal and objective. The language is somewhat precise and appropriate for the audience and purpose.	The essay demonstrates some accuracy in standard English conventions of usage and mechanics. The essay contains some spelling errors.
1	The introduction does not state the thesis clearly. The essay does not include an introduction, body, and conclusion. The conclusion does not summarize ideas and may not relate to the thesis.	Reliable and relevant evidence is not included. The tone of the essay is not objective or formal. The language used is imprecise and not appropriate for the audience and purpose.	The essay contains mistakes in standard English conventions of usage and mechanics. The essay contains many spelling errors.

WRITING

Narration

Narrative writing conveys experience, either real or imaginary, and uses time to provide structure. It can be used to inform, instruct, persuade, or entertain. Whenever writers tell a story, they are using narrative writing. Most types of narrative writing share certain elements, such as characters, setting, a sequence of events, and, often, a theme.

Elements of a Narrative Text

A **narrative** is any type of writing that tells a story, whether it is fiction, nonfiction, poetry, or drama.

An effective nonfiction narrative usually contains these elements:

- an engaging beginning in which characters and setting are established
- characters who participate in the story events
- a well-structured, logical sequence of events
- details that show time and place
- effective story elements such as dialogue, description, and reflection
- the narrator's thoughts, feelings, or views about the significance of events
- use of language that brings the characters and setting to life

An effective fictional narrative usually contains these elements:

- an engaging beginning in which characters, setting, or a main conflict is introduced
- a main character and supporting characters who participate in the story events
- a narrator who relates the events of the plot from a particular point of view
- details that show time and place
- conflict that is resolved in the course of the narrative
- narrative techniques such as dialogue, description, and suspense
- use of language that vividly brings to life characters and events

NARRATIVE: SCORE 1

Getting Away With It

That night, Luanne made two mistakes.

She ran in the house.

The McTweedys were rich and had a huge place and there was an expensive rug.

She was sad in her room remembering what happened:

She was carrying a tray of glasses back to the kitchen and spilled on the carpet. She tried to put furniture over it. Then she ran in the rain.

Luanne should have come clean. She would of said I'm sorry, Mrs. Mc Tweedy, I spilled punch on ur carpet.

She knew getting away with it felt crummy for some reason. it was wrong and she also didn't want to get in trouble.

The phone rings.

"Oh, hello?"

"It's Mrs. Tweedy's!" said her mom. "You forgot to get paid!"

Luanne felt relieve. She was going to do the right thing.

> The introduction is interesting but is not built upon.

> The chronology and situation are unclear.

> The narrative contains mistakes in standard English conventions of usage and mechanics.

> The name of the character does not remain consistent.

> The conclusion reveals what will happen but is not interesting.

TOOL KIT: WRITING

WRITING

MODEL

NARRATIVE: SCORE 2

Getting Away With It

That night, Luanne made two fatal mistakes: ruining a rug, and thinking she could get away with it.

She ran in the house.

The McTweedys hired her to be a waiter at their party. They were rich and had a huge place and there was an expensive rug.

She was sad in her room remembering what happened:

Luanne was wearing black pants and a white shirt. She was carrying a tray of glasses back to the kitchen. One spilled on the carpet. She tried to put furniture to cover up the stain. She ran away in the rain.

Luanne should have come clean right away. But what would she have said? I'm sorry, Mrs. McTweedy, but I spilled punch all over your expensive carpet.

Luanne imagined getting away with it. But getting away with it felt crummy for some reason. She knew it was wrong somehow, but she also didn't want to get in trouble.

The phone rang.

"Oh, hello, how was the party?"

Luanne felt like throwing up.

"Mrs. McTweedy's on the phone!" her mom sang out. "She said you forgot your check!"

Luanne felt relieved. But she already made up her mind to do the right thing.

> The introduction establishes a clear context.

> The writer has made some mistakes in spelling, grammar, and punctuation.

> The chronology is sometimes unclear.

> Narrative techniques, such as the use of dialogue, are used at times.

> The conclusion tells what will happen but is not interesting.

Getting Away With It

That night, Luanne made two fatal mistakes: (1) ruining a priceless Persian rug, and (2) thinking she could get away with it.

She bursted in the front door breathless.

"How was it?" called her mom.

The McTweedys had hired her to serve drinks at their fundraiser. Henry and Estelle McTweedy loved having parties. They were rich and had a huge apartment filled with rare books, art, and tapestries from all over the world.

"Luanne? Are you alright?"

"Just tired, Mom."

Actually she was face-planted on her bed, replaying the scene over and over just in case she could change it.

It was like a movie: A girl in black trousers and a crisp white shirt carrying a tray of empty glasses back to the kitchen. Then the girl's horrified expression as she realizes that one of the glasses was not quite as empty as she'd thought and was dripping onto the carpet. The girl frantically moving furniture to cover up the stain. The girl running out of the apartment into the hard rain.

Luanne kicked herself. She should have come clean right away. But what would she have said? I'm sorry, Mrs. McTweedy, but I spilled punch all over your expensive carpet.

Luanne imagined getting away with it. But getting away with it felt crummy for some reason. She knew it was wrong somehow, but she also didn't want to get in trouble.

The phone was ringing. Luanne froze.

"Oh, hello there, Mrs. McTweedy! How was the party?"

Luanne felt felt like throwing up.

"Mrs. McTweedy's on the phone!" her mom sang out. "She said you forgot your check!"

Luanne felt relief. It was nothing at all! Although she'd already made up her mind to come clean. Because she had to do the right thing.

She walked into the kitchen. And then she explained the whole thing to both her mom and Mrs. McTweedy.

The story's introduction establishes a clear context and point of view.

Descriptive details, sensory language, and precise words and phrases help to bring the narrative to life.

The writer mostly attends to the norms and conventions of usage and punctuation, but sometimes makes mistakes.

The writer has effectively used dialogue in her story.

The conclusion follows logically but is not memorable.

TOOL KIT: WRITING

WRITING

MODEL

NARRATIVE: SCORE 4

Getting Away With It

That night, Luanne made two fatal mistakes: (1) ruining a priceless Persian rug, and (2) thinking she could get away with it.

She'd burst in the front door breathless.

"How was it?" called her mother from the kitchen.

The McTweedys had hired Luanne to serve drinks at their fundraiser. Henry and Estelle McTweedy loved entertaining. They loved traveling, and the opera, and the finer things in life. They had a huge apartment filled with rare books, art, and tapestries from all over the world.

"Luanne? Are you alright?"

"Just tired, Mom."

Actually she was face-down on her bed, replaying the humiliating scene over and over just in case she could make it come out differently.

It was like a movie: A girl in black trousers and a crisp white shirt carrying a tray of empty glasses back to the kitchen. Cut to the girl's horrified expression as she realizes that one of the glasses —not quite as empty as she'd thought—was dripping its lurid contents onto the carpet. Close in on the girl's frantic attempts to move furniture over the stain. Montage of images showing the girl running out of the apartment into the pounding rain. Fade to Black.

Luanne could kick herself. She should have come clean right away. But what would she have said? *I'm sorry, Mrs. McTweedy, but I spilled punch all over your irreplaceable carpet.*

Luanne imagined getting away with it. If she got away with it, she'd be a person who got away with things. For the rest of her life, no matter what, she'd be a person who got away with things. And if something good happened to her, she'd feel like she didn't deserve it.

Somewhere in the house, a phone was ringing. Luanne froze and listened in.

"Oh, hello there, Estelle! How was the party?" Luanne felt cold, then hot. Her skin prickled. She was sweating. She felt like throwing up.

"Mrs. McTweedy's on the phone!" Luanne's mother sang out. "She wants to tell you that you forgot your check!"

Luanne felt a surge a relief wash over her—it was nothing, nothing at all!—but she'd already made up her mind to come clean. Not because owning up to it was so Right, but because getting away with it was so wrong. Which made it right.

Luanne padded into the kitchen. "Don't hang up," she told her mother.

The writer provides an introduction that establishes a clear context and point of view.

The writer has used descriptive details, sensory language, and precise words and phrases.

The writer's use of movie terminology is clever and memorable.

The narrative presents a clear chronological sequence of events.

The writer effectively uses narrative techniques, such as dialogue.

The story's conclusion is abrupt but fitting. It reveals a critical decision that resolves the conflict.

Narrative Rubric

	Focus and Organization	Development of Ideas/ Elaboration	Conventions
4	The introduction establishes a clear context and point of view. Events are presented in a clear sequence, building to a climax, then moving toward the conclusion. The conclusion follows from and reflects on the events and experiences in the narrative.	Narrative techniques such as dialogue, pacing, and description are used effectively to develop characters, events, and setting. Descriptive details, sensory language, and precise words and phrases are used to convey the experiences in the narrative and to help the reader imagine the characters and setting. Voice is established through word choice, sentence structure, and tone.	The narrative uses standard English conventions of usage and mechanics. Deviations from standard English are intentional and serve the purpose of the narrative. Rules of spelling and punctuation are followed.
3	The introduction gives the reader some context and sets the point of view. Events are presented logically, though there are some jumps in time. The conclusion logically ends the story, but provides only some reflection on the experiences related in the story.	Narrative techniques such as dialogue, pacing, and description are used occasionally. Descriptive details, sensory language, and precise words and phrases are used occasionally. Voice is established through word choice, sentence structure, and tone occasionally, though not evenly.	The narrative mostly uses standard English conventions of usage and mechanics, though there are some errors. There are few errors in spelling and punctuation.
2	The introduction provides some description of a place. The point of view can be unclear at times. Transitions between events are occasionally unclear. The conclusion comes abruptly and provides only a small amount of reflection on the experiences related in the narrative.	Narrative techniques such as dialogue, pacing, and description are used sparingly. The story contains few examples of descriptive details and sensory language. Voice is not established for characters, so that it becomes difficult to determine who is speaking.	The narrative contains some errors in standard English conventions of usage and mechanics. There are many errors in spelling and punctuation.
1	The introduction fails to set a scene or is omitted altogether. The point of view is not always clear. The events are not in a clear sequence, and events that would clarify the narrative may not appear. The conclusion does not follow from the narrative or is omitted altogether.	Narrative techniques such as dialogue, pacing, and description are not used. Descriptive details are vague or missing. No sensory language is included. Voice has not been developed.	The text contains mistakes in standard English conventions of usage and mechanics. Rules of spelling and punctuation have not been followed.

▶ RESEARCH

Conducting Research

We are lucky to live in an age when information is accessible and plentiful. However, not all information is equally useful, or even accurate. Strong research skills will help you locate and evaluate information.

Narrowing or Broadening a Topic

The first step of any research project is determining your topic. Consider the scope of your project and choose a topic that is narrow enough to address completely and effectively. If you can name your topic in just one or two words, it is probably too broad. Topics such as Shakespeare, jazz, or science fiction are too broad to cover in a single report. Narrow a broad topic into smaller subcategories.

Science fiction

↓

Early science fiction

↓

Nineteenth-century science fiction

↓

Nineteenth-century science fiction that predicted the future accurately

When you begin to research a topic, pay attention to the amount of information available. If you feel overwhelmed by the number of relevant sources, you may need to narrow your topic further.

If there isn't enough information available as your research, you might need to broaden your topic. A topic is too narrow when it can be thoroughly presented in less space than the required size of your assignment. It might also be too narrow if you can find little or no information in library and media sources, so consider broadening your topic to include other related ideas.

Generating Research Questions

Use research questions to focus your research. Specific questions can help you avoid time-wasting digressions. For example, instead of simply hunting for information about Mark Twain, you might ask, "What jobs did Mark Twain have, other than being a writer?" or "Which of Twain's books was most popular during his lifetime?"

In a research report, your research question often becomes your thesis statement, or may lead up to it. The question will also help you focus your research into a comprehensive but flexible search plan, as well as prevent you from gathering unnecessary details. As your research teaches you more about your topic, you may find it necessary to refocus your original question.

Consulting Print and Digital Sources

Effective research combines information from several sources, and does not rely too heavily on a single source. The creativity and originality of your research depends on how you combine ideas from multiple sources. Plan to consult a variety of resources, such as the following:

- **Primary and Secondary Sources:** To get a thorough view of your topic, use primary sources (firsthand or original accounts, such as interview transcripts, eyewitness reports, and newspaper articles) and secondary sources (accounts, created after an event occurred, such as encyclopedia entries).

- **Print and Digital Resources:** The Internet allows fast access to data, but print resources are often edited more carefully. Use both print and digital resources in order to guarantee the accuracy of your findings.

- **Media Resources:** You can find valuable information in media resources such as documentaries, television programs, podcasts, and museum exhibitions. Consider attending public lectures given by experts to gain an even more in-depth view of your topic.

- **Original Research:** Depending on your topic, you may wish to conduct original research to include among your sources. For example, you might interview experts or eyewitnesses, or conduct a survey of people in your community.

Using Online Encyclopedias

Online encyclopedias are often written by anonymous contributors who are not required to fact-check information. These sites can be very useful as a launching point for research, but should not be considered accurate. Look for footnotes, endnotes, or hyperlinks that support facts with reliable sources that have been carefully checked by editors.

Evaluating Sources It is important to evaluate the credibility, validity, and accuracy of any information you find, as well as its appropriateness for your purpose and audience. You may find the information you need to answer your research question in specialized and authoritative sources, such as almanacs (for social, cultural, and natural statistics), government publications (for law, government programs, and subjects such as agriculture), and information services. Also, consider consumer, workplace, and public documents.

Ask yourself questions such as these to evaluate these additional sources:

- **Authority:** Is the author well known? What are the author's credentials? Does the source include references to other reliable sources? Does the author's tone win your confidence? Why or why not?

- **Bias:** Does the author have any obvious biases? What is the author's purpose for writing? Who is the target audience?

- **Currency:** When was the work created? Has it been revised? Is there more current information available?

Using Search Terms

Finding information on the Internet can be both easy and challenging. Type a word or phrase into a general search engine and you will probably get hundreds—or thousands—of results. However, those results are not guaranteed to be relevant or accurate.

These strategies can help you find information from the Internet:

- Create a list of keywords that apply to your topic before you begin using a search engine. Consult a thesaurus to expand your list.

- Enter six to eight keywords.

- Choose precise nouns. Most search engines ignore articles and prepositions. Verbs may be used in multiple contexts, leading to sources that are not relevant. Use modifiers, such as adjectives, when necessary to specify a category.

- Use quotation marks to focus a search. Place a phrase in quotation marks to find pages that include exactly that phrase. Add several phrases in quotation marks to narrow your results.

- Spell carefully. Many search engines autocorrect spelling, but they cannot produce accurate results for all spelling errors.

- Scan search results before you click them. The first result isn't always the most relevant. Read the text and consider the domain before make a choice.

- Utilize more than one search engine.

Evaluating Internet Domains

Not everything you read on the Internet is true, so you have to evaluate sources carefully. The last three letters of an Internet URL identify the Website's domain, which can help you evaluate the information of the site.

- **.gov**—Government sites are sponsored by a branch of the United States federal government, such as the Census Bureau, Supreme Court, or Congress. These sites are considered reliable.

- **.edu**—Education domains include schools from kindergartens to universities. Information from an educational research center or department is likely to be carefully checked. However, education domains can also include student pages that are not edited or monitored.

- **.org**—Organizations are nonprofit groups and usually maintain a high level of credibility. Keep in mind that some organizations may express strong biases.

- **.com** and **.net**—Commercial sites exist to make a profit. Information may be biased to show a product or service in a good light. The company may be providing information to encourage sales or promote a positive image.

Taking Notes

Take notes as you locate and connect useful information from multiple sources, and keep a reference list of every source you use. This will help you make distinctions between the relative value and significance of specific data, facts, and ideas.

For long-term research projects, create source cards and notecards to keep track of information gathered from multiple resources.

Source Cards
Create a card that identifies each source.

- For print materials, list the author, title, publisher, date of publication, and relevant page numbers.
- For Internet sources, record the name and Web address of the site, and the date you accessed the information.
- For media sources, list the title, person, or group credited with creating the media, and the year of production.

Notecards
Create a separate notecard for each item of information.

- Include the fact or idea, the letter of the related source card, and the specific page(s) on which the fact or idea appears.
- Use quotation marks around words and phrases taken directly from print or media resources.
- Mark particularly useful or relevant details using your own annotation method, such as stars, underlining, or colored highlighting.

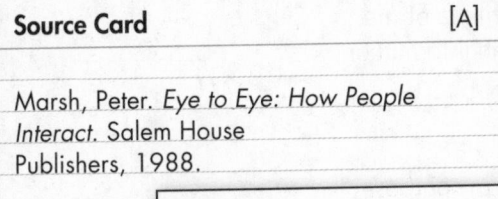

Source Card   [A]

Marsh, Peter. *Eye to Eye: How People Interact.* Salem House Publishers, 1988.

Notecard

Gestures vary from culture to culture. The American "OK" symbol (thumb and forefinger) is considered insulting in Greece and Turkey.

Source Card: A, p. 54.

Quote Accurately Responsible research begins with the first note you take. Be sure to quote and paraphrase your sources accurately so you can identify these sources later. In your notes, circle all quotations and paraphrases to distinguish them from your own comments. When photocopying from a source, include the copyright information. When printing out information from an online source, include the Web address.

Reviewing Research Findings

While conducting research, you will need to review your findings, checking that you have collected enough accurate and appropriate information.

Considering Audience and Purpose

Always keep your audience in mind as you gather information, since different audiences may have very different needs. For example, if you are writing an in-depth analysis of a text that your entire class has read together and you are writing for your audience, you will not need to gather background information that has been thoroughly discussed in class. However, if you are writing the same analysis for a national student magazine, you cannot assume that all of your readers have the same background information. You will need to provide facts from reliable sources to help orient these readers to your subject. When considering whether or not your research will satisfy your audience, ask yourself:

- Who am I writing for?
- Have I collected enough information to explain my topic to this audience?
- Are there details in my research that I can omit because they are already familiar to my audience?

Your purpose for writing will also influence your review of research. If you are researching a question to satisfy your own curiosity, you can stop researching when you feel you understand the answer completely. If you are writing a research report that will be graded, you need to consider the criteria of the assignment. When considering whether or not you have enough information, ask yourself:

- What is my purpose for writing?
- Will the information I have gathered be enough to achieve my purpose?
- If I need more information, where might I find it?

Synthesizing Sources

Effective research writing does not merely present facts and details; it synthesizes—gathers, orders, and interprets—them. These strategies will help you synthesize information effectively:

- Review your notes and look for connections and patterns among the details you have collected.
- Arrange notes or notecards in different ways to help you decide how to best combine related details and present them in a logical way.
- Pay close attention to details that support one other, emphasizing the same main idea.
- Also look for details that challenge each other, highlighting ideas about which there is no single, or consensus, opinion. You might decide to conduct additional research to help you decide which side of the issue has more support.

Types of Evidence

When reviewing your research, also consider the kinds of evidence you have collected. The strongest writing contains a variety of evidence effectively. This chart describes three of the most common types of evidence: statistical, testimonial, and anecdotal.

TYPE OF EVIDENCE	DESCRIPTION	EXAMPLE
Statistical evidence includes facts and other numerical data used to support a claim or explain a topic.	Examples of statistical evidence include historical dates and information, quantitative analyses, poll results, and quantitative descriptions.	"Although it went on to become a hugely popular novel, the first edition of William Goldman's book sold fewer than 3,000 copies."
Testimonial evidence includes any ideas or opinions presented by others, especially experts in a field.	Firsthand testimonies present ideas from eyewitnesses to events or subjects being discussed.	"The ground rose and fell like an ocean at ebb tide." —Fred J. Hewitt, eyewitness to the 1906 San Francisco earthquake
	Secondary testimonies include commentaries on events by people who were not involved. You might quote a well-known literary critic when discussing a writer's most famous novel, or a prominent historian when discussing the effects of an important event	Gladys Hansen insists that "there was plenty of water in hydrants throughout [San Francisco] . . . The problem was this fire got away."
Anecdotal evidence presents one person's view of the world, often by describing specific events or incidents.	Compelling research should not rely solely on this form of evidence, but it can be very useful for adding personal insights and refuting inaccurate generalizations. An individual's experience can be used with other forms of evidence to present complete and persuasive support.	Although many critics claim the novel is universally beloved, at least one reader "threw the book against a wall because it made me so angry."

Incorporating Research Into Writing

Avoiding Plagiarism

Plagiarism is the unethical presentation of someone else's ideas as your own. You must cite sources for direct quotations, paraphrased information, or facts that are specific to a single source. When you are drafting and revising, circle any words or ideas that are not your own. Follow the instructions on pages R34 and R35 to correctly cite those passages.

Review for Plagiarism Always take time to review your writing for unintentional plagiarism. Read what you have written and take note of any phrases or sentences that do not have your personal writing voice. Compare those passages with your resource materials. You might have copied them without remembering the exact source. Add a correct citation to give credit to the original author. If you cannot find the questionable phrase in your notes, revise it to ensure that your final report reflects your own thinking and not someone else's work.

Quoting and Paraphrasing

When including ideas from research into your writing, you will decide to quote directly or paraphrase.

Direct Quotation Use the author's exact words when they are interesting or persuasive. You might decide to include direct quotations for these reasons:

- to share an especially clear and relevant statement
- to reference a historically significant passage
- to show that an expert agrees with your position
- to present an argument that you will counter in your writing.

Include complete quotations, without deleting or changing words. If you need to omit words for space or clarity, use ellipsis points to indicate the omission. Enclose direct quotations in quotation marks and indicate the author's name.

Paraphrase A paraphrase restates an author's ideas in your own words. Be careful to paraphrase accurately. Beware of making sweeping generalizations in a paraphrase that were not made by the original author. You may use some words from the original source, but a legitimate paraphrase does more than simply rearrange an author's phrases, or replace a few words with synonyms.

Original Text	"*The Tempest* was written as a farewell to art and the artist's life, just before the completion of his forty-ninth year, and everything in the play bespeaks the touch of autumn." Brandes, Georg. "Analogies Between *The Tempest* and *A Midsummer Night's Dream*." *The Tempest*, by William Shakespeare, William Heinemann, 1904, p. 668.
Patchwork Plagiarism phrases from the original are rearranged, but too closely follows the original text.	A farewell to art, Shakespeare's play, *The Tempest*, was finished just before the completion of his forty-ninth year. The artist's life was to end within three years. The touch of autumn is apparent in nearly everything in the play.
Good Paraphrase	Images of autumn occur throughout *The Tempest*, which Shakespeare wrote as a way of saying goodbye to both his craft and his own life.

Maintaining the Flow of Ideas

Effective research writing is much more that just a list of facts. Be sure to maintain the flow of ideas by connecting research information to your own ideas. Instead of simply stating a piece of evidence, use transition words and phrases to explain the connection between information you found from outside resources and your own ideas and purpose for writing. The following transitions can be used to introduce, compare, contrast, and clarify.

Useful Transitions

When providing examples:

for example   for instance   to illustrate   in [name of resource], [author]

When comparing and contrasting ideas or information:

in the same way   similarly   however   on the other hand

When clarifying ideas or opinions:

in other words   that is   to explain   to put it another way

Choosing an effective organizational structure for your writing will help you create a logical flow of ideas. Once you have established a clear organizational structure, insert facts and details from your research in appropriate places to provide evidence and support for your writing.

ORGANIZATIONAL STRUCTURE	USES
Chronological order presents information in the sequence in which it happens.	historical topics; science experiments; analysis of narratives
Part-to-whole order examines how several categories affect a larger subject.	analysis of social issues; historical topics
Order of importance presents information in order of increasing or decreasing importance.	persuasive arguments; supporting a bold or challenging thesis
Comparison-and-contrast organization outlines the similarities and differences of a given topic.	addressing two or more subjects

RESEARCH

Formats for Citing Sources

In research writing, cite your sources. In the body of your paper, provide a footnote, an endnote, or a parenthetical citation, identifying the sources of facts, opinions, or quotations. At the end of your paper, provide a bibliography or a Works Cited list, a list of all the sources referred to in your research. Follow an established format, such as Modern Language Association (MLA) style.

Parenthetical Citations (MLA Style)

A parenthetical citation briefly identifies the source from which you have taken a specific quotation, factual claim, or opinion. It refers readers to one of the entries on your Works Cited list. A parenthetical citation has the following features:

- It appears in parentheses.
- It identifies the source by the last name of the author, editor, or translator, or by the title (for a lengthy title, list the first word only).
- It provides a page reference, the page(s) of the source on which the information cited can be found.

A parenthetical citation generally falls outside a closing quotation mark but within the final punctuation of a clause or sentence. For a long quotation set off from the rest of your text, place the citation at the end of the excerpt without any punctuation following.

Sample Parenthetical Citations

It makes sense that baleen whales such as the blue whale, the bowhead whale, the humpback whale, and the sei whale (to name just a few) grow to immense sizes (Carwardine et al. 19–21). The blue whale has grooves running from under its chin to partway along the length of its underbelly. As in some other whales, these grooves expand and allow even more food and water to be taken in (Ellis 18–21).

Authors' last names

Page numbers where information can be found

Works Cited List (MLA Style)

A Works Cited list must contain accurate information to enable a reader to locate each source you cite. The basic components of an entry are as follows:

- name of the author, editor, translator, and/or group responsible for the work
- title of the work
- publisher
- date of publication

For print materials, the information for a citation generally appears on the copyright and title pages. For the format of a Works Cited list, consult the examples on this page and in the MLA Style for Listing Sources chart.

Sample Works Cited List (MLA 8th Edition)

Carwardine, Mark, et al. *The Nature Company Guides: Whales, Dolphins, and Porpoises.* Time-Life, 1998.

"Discovering Whales." *Whales on the Net.* Whales in Danger, 1998, www.whales.org.au/discover/index.html. Accessed 11 Apr. 2017.

Neruda, Pablo. "Ode to Spring." *Odes to Opposites,* translated by Ken Krabbenhoft, edited and illustrated by Ferris Cook, Little, 1995, p. 16.

The Saga of the Volsungs. Translated by Jesse L. Byock, Penguin, 1990.

List an anonymous work by title.

List both the title of the work and the collection in which it is found.

Works Cited List or Bibliography?

A Works Cited list includes only those sources you paraphrased or quoted directly in your research paper. By contrast, a bibliography lists all the sources you consulted during research—even those you did not cite.

MLA (8th Edition) Style for Listing Sources

Book with one author	Pyles, Thomas. *The Origins and Development of the English Language.* 2nd ed., Harcourt Brace Jovanovich, 1971. [Indicate the edition or version number when relevant.]
Book with two authors	Pyles, Thomas, and John Algeo. *The Origins and Development of the English Language.* 5th ed., Cengage Learning, 2004.
Book with three or more authors	Donald, Robert B., et al. *Writing Clear Essays.* Prentice Hall, 1983.
Book with an editor	Truth, Sojourner. *Narrative of Sojourner Truth.* Edited by Margaret Washington, Vintage Books, 1993.
Introduction to a work in a published edition	Washington, Margaret. Introduction. *Narrative of Sojourner Truth,* by Sojourner Truth, edited by Washington, Vintage Books, 1993, pp. v–xi.
Single work in an anthology	Hawthorne, Nathaniel. "Young Goodman Brown." *Literature: An Introduction to Reading and Writing,* edited by Edgar V. Roberts and Henry E. Jacobs, 5th ed., Prentice Hall, 1998, pp. 376–385. [Indicate pages for the entire selection.]
Signed article from an encyclopedia	Askeland, Donald R. "Welding." *World Book Encyclopedia,* vol. 21, World Book, 1991, p. 58.
Signed article in a weekly magazine	Wallace, Charles. "A Vodacious Deal." *Time,* 14 Feb. 2000, p. 63.
Signed article in a monthly magazine	Gustaitis, Joseph. "The Sticky History of Chewing Gum." *American History,* Oct. 1998, pp. 30–38.
Newspaper article	Thurow, Roger. "South Africans Who Fought for Sanctions Now Scrap for Investors." *Wall Street Journal,* 11 Feb. 2000, pp. A1+. [For a multipage article that does not appear on consecutive pages, write only the first page number on which it appears, followed by the plus sign.]
Unsigned editorial or story	"Selective Silence." Editorial. *Wall Street Journal,* 11 Feb. 2000, p. A14. [If the editorial or story is signed, begin with the author's name.]
Signed pamphlet or brochure	[Treat the pamphlet as though it were a book.]
Work from a library subscription service	Ertman, Earl L. "Nefertiti's Eyes." *Archaeology,* Mar.–Apr. 2008, pp. 28–32. *Kids Search,* EBSCO, New York Public Library. Accessed 7 Jan. 2017. [Indicating the date you accessed the information is optional but recommended.]
Filmstrips, slide programs, videocassettes, DVDs, and other audiovisual media	*The Diary of Anne Frank.* 1959. Directed by George Stevens, performances by Millie Perkins, Shelley Winters, Joseph Schildkraut, Lou Jacobi, and Richard Beymer, Twentieth Century Fox, 2004. [Indicating the original release date after the title is optional but recommended.]
CD-ROM (with multiple publishers)	Simms, James, editor. *Romeo and Juliet.* By William Shakespeare, Attica Cybernetics / BBC Education / Harper, 1995.
Radio or television program transcript	"Washington's Crossing of the Delaware." *Weekend Edition Sunday,* National Public Radio, 23 Dec. 2013. Transcript.
Web page	"Fun Facts About Gum." ICGA, 2005–2017, www.gumassociation.org/index.cfm/facts-figures/fun-facts-about-gum. Accessed 19 Feb. 2017. [Indicating the date you accessed the information is optional but recommended.]
Personal interview	Smith, Jane. Personal interview, 10 Feb. 2017.

All examples follow the style given in the MLA Handbook, 8th edition, published in 2016.

MODEL

Evidence Log

Unit Title: Discovery

Perfomance-Based Assessment Prompt:
Do all discoveries benefit humanity?

My initial thoughts:
Yes - all knowledge moves us forward.

As you read multiple texts about a topic, your thinking may change. Use an Evidence Log like this one to record your thoughts, to track details you might use in later writing or discussion, and to make further connections.

Here is a sample to show how one reader's ideas deepened as she read two texts.

Title of Text: Classifying the Stars   Date: Sept. 17

CONNECTION TO THE PROMPT	TEXT EVIDENCE/DETAILS	ADDITIONAL NOTES/IDEAS
Newton shared his discoveries and then other scientists built on his discoveries.	Paragraph 2: "Isaac Newton gave to the world the results of his experiments on passing sunlight through a prism." Paragraph 3: "In 1814 . . . the German optician, Fraunhofer . . . saw that the multiple spectral tints . . . were crossed by hundreds of fine dark lines."	It's not always clear how a discovery might benefit humanity in the future.

How does this text change or add to my thinking? This confirms what I think.   Date: Sept. 20

Title of Text: Cell Phone Mania   Date: Sept. 21

CONNECTION TO THE PROMPT	TEXT EVIDENCE/DETAILS	ADDITIONAL NOTES/IDEAS
Cell phones have made some forms of communication easier, but people don't talk to each other as much as they did in the past.	Paragraph 7: "Over 80% of young adults state that texting is their primary method of communicating with friends. This contrasts with older adults who state that they prefer a phone call."	Is it good that we don't talk to each other as much? Look for article about social media to learn more about this question.

How does this text change or add to my thinking?   Date: Sept. 25
Maybe there are some downsides to discoveries. I still think that knowledge moves us forward, but there are sometimes unintended negative effects.

Word Network

A word network is a collection of words related to a topic. As you read the selections in a unit, identify interesting theme-related words and build your vocabulary by adding them to your Word Network.

Use your Word Network as a resource for your discussions and writings. Here is an example:

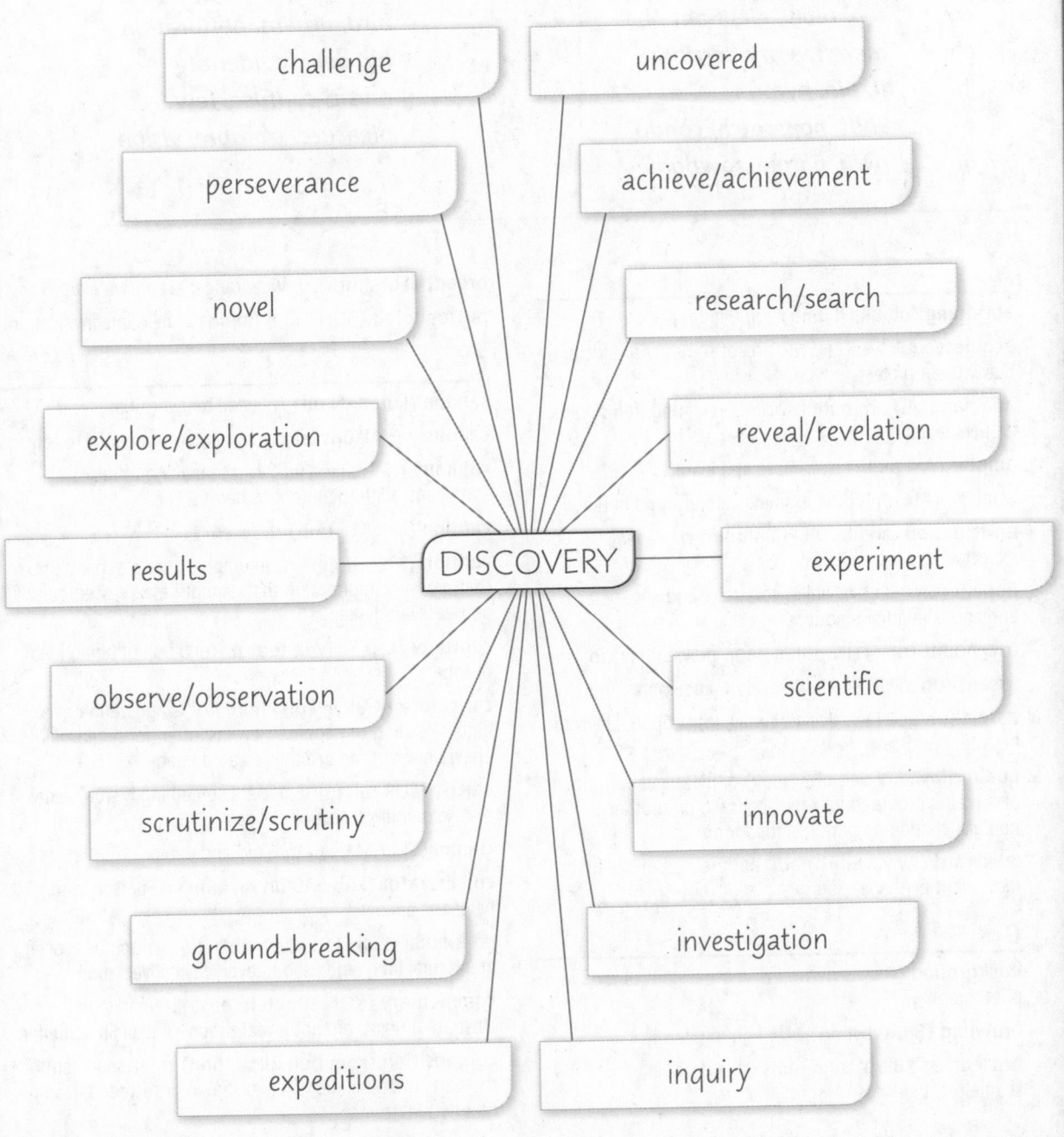

TOOL KIT: PROGRAM RESOURCES

ACADEMIC / CONCEPT VOCABULARY

Academic vocabulary appears in **blue type**.

Pronunciation Key

Symbol	Sample Words	Symbol	Sample Words
a	*at, catapult, Alabama*	oo	*boot, soup, crucial*
ah	*father, charms, argue*	ow	*now, stout, flounder*
ai	*care, various, hair*	oy	*boy, toil, oyster*
aw	*law, maraud, caution*	s	*say, nice, press*
awr	*pour, organism, forewarn*	sh	*she, abolition, motion*
ay	*ape, sails, implication*	u	*full, put, book*
ee	*even, teeth, really*	uh	*ago, focus, contemplation*
eh	*ten, repel, elephant*	ur	*bird, urgent. perforation*
ehr	*merry, verify, terribly*	y	*by, delight, identify*
ih	*it, pin, hymn*	yoo	*music, confuse, few*
o	*shot, hopscotch, condo*	zh	*pleasure, treasure, vision*
oh	*own, parole, rowboat*		

GLOSSARY: ACADEMIC / CONCEPT VOCABULARY

A

abridging (uh BRIHJ ihng) *adj.* limiting

acquiesce (ak wee EHS) *v.* accept something reluctantly but without protest

adamant (AD uh muhnt) *adj.* unrelenting; refusing to be persuaded

ampler (AM pluhr) *adj.* more abundant

analyze (AN uh lyz) *v.* examine carefully and in detail

anticipation (an tihs uh PAY shuhn) *n.* eager expectation

appeal (uh PEEL) *n.* ability to attract and engage an audience's mind or emotions

ascendant (uh SEHN duhnt) *adj.* moving upward; rising

assent (uh SEHNT) *n.* approval or agreement

assert (uh SURT) *v.* declare firmly; insist upon; claim to be true

audio play (AW dee oh) (play) *n.* theatrical performance of a drama produced for radio, podcast, or another non-visual and non-print recorded form

awkward (AWK wuhrd) *adj.* not graceful or skillful in movement or shape; clumsy

B

background (BAK grownd) *n.* more distant objects in a photograph

brawling (BRAWL ihng) *adj.* fighting noisily

brazenness (BRAY zuhn nuhs) *n.* act of being shameless; boldness

breadth (brehdth) *n.* wide range; expansive extent

buttonholed (BUHT uhn hohld) *v.* held in conversation

C

cabana (kuh BAN uh) *n.* small tent or cabin

callously (KAL uhs lee) *adv.* without sympathy; coldly

calumny (KAL uhm nee) *n.* the making of false statements with the intent to harm

cantina (kan TEE nuh) *n.* tavern

caption (KAP shuhn) *n.* in graphic novels, separate text that presents information that cannot be expressed quickly and easily in dialogue

captivity (kap TIHV ih tee) *n.* condition of being held prisoner

caricature (KAIR ih kuh chuhr) *n.* exaggeration of details relating to people or events, often for humorous effect, in a cartoon or other created image

certify (SUR tuh fy) *v.* declare something is true; verify that something is true

clammy (KLAM ee) *adj.* cold and damp

collaborator (kuh LAB uh ray tuhr) *n.* person who helps the enemy

colloquial (kuh LOH kwee uhl) *adj.* written or spoken in informal language used in everyday conversation

commentary (KOM uhn tehr ee) *n.* remarks that illustrate a point, prompt a realization, or explain something

composition (kom puh ZIH shuhn) *n.* arrangement of the parts of an image, whether drawn or recorded in some other visual format

conceded (kuhn SEED ihd) *v.* admitted

conciliatory (kuhn SIHL ee uh tawr ee) *adj.* in a manner intended to make peace and bring about agreement

conclave (KON klayv) *n.* private meeting

condemnation (kon dehm NAY shuhn) *n.* very strong disapproval

confirm (kuhn FURM) *v.* prove the truth of; verify

consecrate (KON sih krayt) *v.* set apart as holy; dedicate

conspirators (kuhn SPIHR uh tuhrz) *n.* people who join in a secret plan

constrains (kuhn STRAYNZ) *v.* requires or forces

constricting (kuhn STRIHKT ihng) *adj.* limiting; tightening

conviction (kuhn VIHK shuhn) *n.* strong belief; certainty

corrupted (kuh RUHPT ihd) *adj.* dishonest

cowering (KOW uhr ihng) *adj.* crouching or drawing back in fear or shame

cross-section (KRAWS sehk shuhn) *n.* view of a three-dimensional object that shows the interior as if a cut has been made across the object

cunning (KUHN ihng) *adj.* done with skill or cleverness

D

dedicated (DEHD uh kayt ihd) *adj.* committed; devoted

deduction (dih DUHK shuhn) *n.* the process of using reason or logic to come to a conclusion or form an opinion

defamation (dehf uh MAY shuhn) *n.* unjust injury to someone's good reputation through the making of false statements

deference (DEHF uhr uhns) *n.* great respect

definitive (dih FIHN uh tihv) *adj.* deciding or settling a question; final

degraded (dih GRAYD ihd) *adj.* reduced in respectablility; disgraced

deicide (DEE uh syd) *n.* killing of a god

dejected (dee JEHK tihd) *adj.* depressed; sad

demonstrate (DEHM uhn strayt) *v.* show how to do something

denounce (dih NOWNS) *v.* criticize harshly

depth of field (dehpth) (uhv) (feeld) n. distance between the closest and most distant objects that are in focus

despotism (DEHS puh tihz uhm) *n.* absolute rule; tyranny

determine (dih TUR muhn) *v.* decide; find out, as the exact cause or reason

dictum (DIHK tuhm) *n.* short statement that expresses a general truth; saying or proverb

digress (dih GREHS) *v.* go off topic in speaking or writing

dilatory (dihl uh TAWR ee) *adj.* inclined to delay; slow

discern (dih SURN) *v.* recognize as different

disparity (dihs PAR uh tee) *n.* great difference or inequality

disposition (DIHS puh ZIHSH uhn) *n.* act of settling a case or argument; decision

disputation (dihs pyu TAY shuhn) *n.* debate or argument

dissented (dih SENT ihd) *v.* rejected an official opinion; disagreed

documentary (dok yuh MEHN tuhr ee) *n.* program or film that provides a factual record or report of real events

dyspepsia (dihs PEHP see uh) *n.* indigestion

E

effrontery (ih FRUHN tuh ree) *n.* shameless boldness

eminence (EHM uh nuhns) *n.* position of great importance or superiority

eminent (EHM uh nuhnt) *adj.* distinguished; famous; noteworthy

emperor (EHM puhr uhr) *n.* ruler of highest rank and authority, especially of an empire

encroaching (ehn KROHCH ihng) *adj.* intruding; steadily advancing

epiphany (ih PIHF uh nee) *n.* flash of insight and understanding

equivocate (ih KWIHV uh kayt) *v.* use unclear language to avoid committing oneself to something

espionage (EHS pee uh nozh) *n.* use of spies to obtain secret information

establish (ehs TAB lihsh) *v.* set up; prove; demonstrate

etiquette (EHT uh kiht) *n.* proper manners

exalted (ehg ZAWLT ihd) *adj.* of high rank

exasperating (ehg ZAS puh rayt ihng) *adj.* annoying

exercise (EHK suhr syz) *n.* implementation; state of putting something into action

expression (ehk SPREHSH uhn) *n.* tone of voice that indicates specific emotion

eyewitness account (Y WIHT nihs) (uh KOWNT) n. description given by someone who was present at an event

F

figure (FIHG yuhr) *n.* one of a set of drawings or illustrations

fix (fihks) *n.* difficult or awkward situation

focal point (FOH kuhl) (poynt) *n.* center of activity or attention in a photograph

foment (foh MEHNT) *v.* stir up; agitate

foreground (FAWR grownd) *n.* nearer or closer objects in a photograph

forward (FAWR wuhrd) *adj.* bold; brazen; shameless

frame (fraym) *n.* main spoken narrative of a production

framing (FRAYM ihng) *n.* composing a visual so that an enclosing border surrounds the image in the foreground

furtive (FUR tihv) *adj.* done or acting in a stealthy way to avoid being noticed; secret

G

garrulous (GAR uh luhs) *adj.* very talkative

gilded (GIHLD ihd) *adj.* covered with a thin layer of gold

grandeur (GRAN juhr) *n.* state of being impressive; magnificence

H

hallow (HAL oh) *v.* make sacred; consecrate

hangdog (HANG dawg) *adj.* sad; ashamed; guilty

hermitage (HUR muh tihj) *n.* secluded retreat

hospitality (hos puh TAL uh tee) *n.* warm, welcoming attitude toward guests

host (hohst) *n.* master of ceremonies, moderator, or interviewer on a broadcast

hypodermic (hy puh DUR mihk) *n.* injection of medicine

I

immutable (ih MYOO tuh buhl) *adj.* never changing; not changeable

impact (IHM pakt) *n.* collision; powerful or lasting effect

imperial (ihm PEER ee uhl) *adj.* like something associated with an empire; magnificent or majestic

imploring (ihm PLAWR ihng) *v.* asking or begging someone for something

importunities (ihm pawr TOO nuh teez) *n.* annoyingly urgent requests

impressionism (ihm PREHSH uh nihz uhm) *n.* style of art where mood, color, and light matter more than details

incident (IHN suh duhnt) *n.* event; occurrence

indecisions (ihn dih SIHZH uhnz) *n.* things not decided or finalized

infallibility (ihn fal uh BIHL uh tee) *n.* inability to be in error

inflection (ihn FLEHK shuhn) *n.* rise and fall of pitch and tone in a person's voice

informational (ihn fuhr MAY shuh nuhl) *adj.* giving knowledge and facts

infringed (ihn FRIHNJD) *v.* violated

inquire (ihn KWYR) *v.* ask for information

instantaneously (ihn stuhn TAY nee uhs lee) *adv.* immediately

insurgent (ihn SUR juhnt) *adj.* rebellious or in revolt against a government in power

integrity (in TEHG rih tee) *n.* virtue of following moral or ethical principles

interminable (ihn TUR muh nuh buhl) *adj.* seemingly unending

interview (IHN tuhr vyoo) *n.* conversation in which a host asks questions of one or more guests

J

jurisdiction (juhr ihs DIHK shuhn) *n.* legal power to hear and decide cases

L

labeling and **captions** (LAY buhl ihng) (KAP shuhnz) *n.* written labels and other text that often accompany politically charged images to clarify their meanings

layout (LAY owt) *n.* overall design and look of a graphic presentation

legacy (LEHG uh see) *n.* anything handed down from someone

letterhead (LEHT uhr hehd) *n.* personalized stationery

literal (LIHT uhr uhl) *adj.* true to fact; not exaggerated

loathsome (LOHTH suhm) *adj.* causing disgust

loitered (LOY tuhrd) *v.* lingered; moved slowly

M

machetes (muh SHEHT eez) *n.* knives

magistrates (MAJ uh strayts) *n.* officials who have some of the powers of a judge

malice (MAL ihs) *n.* desire to harm or inflict injury

mission (MIHSH uhn) *n.* goal or ambition

monotonous (muh NOT uh nuhs) *adj.* boring due to a lack of variety

motifs (moh TEEFS) *n.* major themes, features, or elements

multitudes (MUHL tuh toodz) *n.* large number of people or things; masses

O

obdurate (OB duhr iht) *adj.* resistant to persuasion

obliged (uh BLYJD) *adj.* grateful

oppressed (uh PREHST) *v.* deprived of rights or power

ornamented (AWR nuh mehnt ihd) *adj.* decorated; adorned

overcast (OH vuhr kast) *adj.* covered with clouds, as a gray sky

overture (OH vuhr chuhr) *n.* musical introduction to an opera or symphony

P

palette (PAL iht) *n.* range of colors used in a particular work

perish (PEH rihsh) *v.* die

perpetually (puhr PEHCH oo uh lee) *adv.* happening all the time

persistence (puhr SIHS tuhns) *n.* act of not giving up

perspective (puhr SPEHK tihv) *n.* method of giving a sense of depth on a flat or shallow surface

petition (puh TIHSH uhn) *v.* formally request; seek help from

picturesquely (pihk chuh REHSK lee) *adv.* in a way that resembles a picture; in a way that is striking or interesting

plaintiffs (PLAYN tihfs) *n.* people who bring a lawsuit to court

policy (POL uh see) *n.* particular course of action by a person, government, organization

populist (POP yuh lihst) *adj.* related to serving the needs of common people

prejudices (PREHJ uh dihs ihz) *n.* unfavorable opinions or feelings formed beforehand or without factual support

prelude (PRAY lood) *n.* introduction to a musical work; overture

prescribed (prih SKRYBD) *v.* stated in writing; set down as a rule

proceedings (pruh SEE dihngz) *n.* events in a court of law

prolific (pruh LIHF ihk) *adj.* fruitful; abundant

propaganda (prop uh GAN duh) *n.* information, ideas, or rumors spread widely and deliberately to help or harm a person, group, movement, cause, or nation

protagonist (proh TAG uh nihst) *n.* main character in a play, story, or novel

Q

quaint (kwaynt) *adj.* unusual; curious; singular

R

racket (RAK iht) *n.* noisy confusion; uproar

realism (REE uh lihz uhm) *n.* style of art closely resembling reality

rectitude (REHK tuh tood) *n.* morally correct behavior or thinking; uprightness

redeemers (rih DEE muhrz) *n.* people who pay for the wrongdoing of others

redress (rih DREHS) *n.* correction; setting right of some wrong

relevant (REHL uh vuhnt) *adj.* puposeful; meaningful

remorseless (rih MAWRS lihs) *adj.* relentless; cruel

renaissance (REHN uh sons) *n.* revival; period of cultural importance

rend (rehnd) *v.* tear apart with violent force

resolution (rehz uh LOO shuhn) *n.* act of coming to a decision; the part of a story in which the plot is made clear

reverence (REHV uhr uhns) *n.* feeling of deep respect

rites (ryts) *n.* ceremonies

romanticism (roh MAN tuh sihz uhm) *n.* style of art evoking emotion by idealizing subjects

S

salutary (SAL yuh tehr ee) *adj.* beneficial; promoting a positive purpose

sanctity (SANGK tuh tee) *n.* fact of being sacred; holiness

scourge (skurj) *n.* cause of serious trouble or suffering

self-assurance (sehlf uh SHUR uhns) *n.* self-confidence

sequence (SEE kwuhns) *n.* particular order

shotgun (SHOT guhn) *n.* gun with a long, smooth barrel, that is often used to fire "shot," or small, pellet-like ammunition

shuffle (SHUHF uhl) *n.* dragging movement of the feet over the ground or floor without lifting them

sidle (SY duhl) *v.* move sideways, as in an unobtrusive, stealthy, or shy manner

significant (sihg NIHF uh kuhnt) *adj.* full of meaning; important

sinister (SIHN uh stuhr) *adj.* evil; threatening

sovereign (SOV ruhn) *n.* monarch or ruler

spatial (SPAY shuhl) *adj.* existing in space

special elements (SPEHSH uhl) (EHL uh muhnts) *n.* features that provide points of emphasis in a production

specific (spih SIHF ihk) *adj.* definite; precise; particular

specifications (spehs uh fuh KAY shuhnz) *n.* section of a patent application in which the inventor fully describes the invention

speech balloon (speech) (buh LOON) *n.* shape used in graphic novels and comic books to show what a character says

squalor (SKWOL uhr) *n.* filth; wretchedness

stolid (STOL ihd) *adj.* feeling little or no emotion

strife (stryf) *n.* act of fighting

subordinate (suh BAWR duh niht) *adj.* having less importance

sufficed (suh FYST) *v.* was adequate

superannuated (soo puhr AN yu ayt uhd) *adj.* too old to be usable; obsolete

superfluous (suh PUR floo uhs) *adj.* more than is needed or wanted; unnecessary

supplanted (suh PLANT ihd) *v.* took the place of; removed

supplement (SUHP luh muhnt) *n.* something added; *v.* add to

symbolism (SIHM buh lihz uhm) *n.* use of images or objects to represent ideas or qualities

T

tedious (TEE dee uhs) *adj.* boring; dull

teeming (TEE mihng) *adj.* full

temporal (TEHM puhr uhl) *adj.* not eternal; limited by time

tension (TEHN shuhn) *n.* mental or nervous stress; uneasiness; state of strained relations

tone (tohn) *n.* production's attitude toward a subject or audience

transcendent (tran SEHN duhnt) *adj.* beyond the limits of possible experience

treason (TREE zuhn) *n.* betrayal of trust or faith, especially against one's country

trivialize (TRIHV ee uhl yz) *v.* treat as not important; make trivial

tyranny (TIHR uh nee) *n.* oppressive power

U

unalienable (un AYL yuh nuh buhl) *adj.* impossible to take away or give up

unique (yoo NEEK) *adj.* being the only one of its kind

unrequited (uhn rih KWY tihd) *adj.* not repaid or avenged

V

vassals (VAS uhlz) *n.* subjects of a kingdom; servants

vast (vast) *adj.* very great in size

verbatim (vuhr BAY tihm) *adv.* in exactly the same words; *adj.* repeating the original word for word

vigilant (VIHJ uh luhnt) *adj.* on the alert; watchful

vindictive (vihn DIHK tihv) *adj.* characterized by an intense, unreasoning desire for revenge

vital (VY tuhl) *adj.* necessary or important

W

wanton (WON tuhn) *adj.* unrestrained; wild

waterfowl (WAWT uhr fowl) *n.* birds that live in or near water

wretched (REHCH ihd) *adj.* very unhappy; miserable

VOCABULARIO ACADÉMICO/ VOCABULARIO DE CONCEPTOS

abridging: abreviar *v.* limitar

acquiesce: consentir *v.* aceptar algo con pocas ganas pero sin protestar

adamant: terco/a *adj.* que no se deja convencer; inflexible

ampler: más copioso/a *adj.* más abundante

analyze: analizar *v.* examinar detalladamente y en profundidad

anticipation: anticipación *s.* expectación; espera ansiosa

appeal: cautivar *v.* capacidad de atraer e involucrar al público, sus pensamientos o emociones

ascendant: ascendente *adj.* que se mueve hacia arriba; que se eleva

assent: consentimiento *s.* aprobación o acuerdo

assert: aseverar *v.* afirmar; insistir

audio play: radioteatro *s.* obra de teatro producida para la radio, para un *podcast* o para otro tipo de grabación no visual ni impresa

awkward: torpe *adj.* desmañado/a; sin gracia, patoso

B

backdrop: fondo *s.* escena o decorado detrás de fotografías y retratos

background: fondo *s.* objetos lejanos en una fotografía

brawling: pendenciero/a *adj.* que se pelea ruidosamente; alborotador/a

brazenness: descaro *s.* no tener vergüenza; atrevimiento

breadth: anchura *s.* amplitud

buttonholed: acorraló *v.* detuvo a alguien en una conversación

C

cabana: cabaña *s.* tienda pequeña, choza

callously: despiadadamente *adv.* sin compasión; fríamente

calumny: calumnia *s.* afirmación falsa que intenta herir o dañar

cantina: cantina *s.* taberna

caption: leyenda *s.* en las novelas gráficas, texto en un recuadro que presenta información que no puede expresarse rápida y fácilmente en el diálogo

captivity: cautividad *s.* estado de privación de libertad; ser prisionero

caricature: caricatura *s.* exageración, generalmente con efecto humorístico, de detalles relacionados con personas o sucesos en una tira cómica u otra imagen creada

certify: certificar *v.* declarar que algo es cierto

clammy: sudado/a *adj.* frío y húmedo

collaborator: colaboracionista *s.* persona que colabora con o ayuda al enemigo

colloquial: coloquial *adj.* lenguaje informal que se usa en las conversaciones diarias

commentary: comentario *s.* observación o ejemplo que ilustra una idea, una opinión o explica algo

composition: composición *s.* disposición de las partes de una imagen, ya sea de un dibujo o de cualquier otro formato visual

conceded: concedió *v.* admitió

conciliatory: conciliador/a *adj.* que tiene la intención de hacer las paces y llegar a un acuerdo

conclave: cónclave *s.* reunión privada

condemnation: condena *s.* fuerte desaprobación; repulsa

confirm: confirmar *v.* probar la certeza de algo; verificar

consecrate: consagrar *v.* declarar algo como sagrado; dedicar

conspirators: conspiradores *s.* personas que se unen a un plan secreto

constrains: constriñe *v.* requiere, obliga

constricting: estrecho/a *adj.* limitado/a

conviction: condena *s.* acto de dar a alguien un veredicto de culpabilidad

conviction: convicción *s.* creencia firme

correlate: correlacionar *v.* mostrar la conexión entre dos elementos

corrupted: corrupto/a *adj.* deshonesto/a

cowering: achicarse *v.* encogerse de miedo

cross-section: sección transversal *s.* imagen de un objeto tridimensional que muestra su interior como si se hubiera hecho un corte transversal del objeto

cunning: astuto/a *adj.* con ingenio y astucia

D

dedicate: dedicar *v.* apartar para un objetivo especial

deduction: deducción *s.* el proceso de usar la razón o la lógica para llegar a una conclusión o formar una opinion

defamation: difamación *s.* dañar la reputación de alguien injustamente mediante afirmaciones falsas

deference: deferencia *s.* gran respeto

defining: definir *v.* aclarar el significado; explicar

definitive: definitivo *adj.* que decide y resuelve una cuestión

degraded: degradado *adj.* con respetabilidad reducida; desgraciado

deicide: deicidio *s.* matar a un dios

dejected: abatido/a *adj.* deprimido/a; triste

demonstrate: demostrar *v.* enseñar cómo hacer algo

denounce: denunciar *v.* criticar duramente

depth of field: profundidad de campo *s.* la distancia entre los objetos más cercanos y los más lejanos que enfoca una cámara

despotism: despotismo *s.* ejercicio de autoridad absoluta

determine: determinar *v.* decidir; buscar la causa o la razón exacta

dictum: dicho *s.* un enunciado corto que expresa una verdad general; un refrán o proverbio

digress: divagar *v.* desviarse del tema al hablar o escribir

dilatory: dilatorio/a *adj.* inclinado a retrasarse; lento/a

discern: discernir *v.* reconocer como diferente

disparity: disparidad *s.* gran diferencia o desigualdad

disposition: disposición *s.* el acto de llegar a un acuerdo en un caso o discusión; predisposición

disputation: disputa *s.* debate o discusión

dissented: disintió *v.* rechazó una opinion oficial; estuvo en desacuerdo

documentary: documental *s.* programa o película que ofrece datos o un informe sobre hechos reales

dyspepsia: dispepsia *s.* indigestión

E

effrontery: desfachatez *s.* descaro; desvergüenza

eminence: eminencia *s.* persona con un cargo de gran importancia o superioridad

eminent: eminente *adj.* distinguido; famoso; notorio

emperor: emperador *s.* gobernante supremo de un imperio

encroaching: traspasar *v.* infringir; meterse; avanzar continuamente

epiphany: epifanía *s.* sensación súbita de comprensión o entendimiento

equivocate: usar equívocos *v.* usar un lenguaje ambiguo para evitar comprometerse a algo

espionage: espionaje *s.* uso de espías para obtener información secreta

establish: establecer *v.* instituir, crear, montar

etiquette: etiqueta *s.* buenos modales

exalted: elevado/a *adj.* de alto rango

exasperating: exasperante *adj.* molesto

exercise: ejercicio *s.* implementación; puesta en práctica

expression: expresión *s.* tono de voz que indica una emoción específica

eyewitness account: declaración de un testigo *s.* descripción hecha por alguien que estuvo presente en un suceso

F

faultfinder: criticón/a *adj.* persona que critica con frecuencia; un quejica

figure: figura *s.* grupo de dibujos o ilustraciones

fix: momento difícil *s.* una situación complicada

focal point: punto de enfoque *s.* el centro de actividad o de atención de una fotografía

foment: fomentar *v.* suscitar, promover; agitar

foreground: primer plano *s.* objetos más cercanos en una fotografía

forward: atrevido/a *adj.* audaz; descarado/a

frame: prototipo *s.* la narrativa oral principal de una producción

framing: composición *s.* creación visual de forma que el marco rodee la imagen del primer plano

furtive: furtivo/a *adj.* hecho de forma sigilosa, a escondidas, para evitar ser descubierto: secreto/a

G

garrulous: charlatán/a *adj.* que habla mucho; parlanchín/a

gilded: bañado en oro *adj.* cubierto con una capa fina de oro

grandeur: esplendor *s.* magnificencia; grandeza; majestuosidad

H

hallow: santificar *v.* hacer sagrado; consagrar

hangdog: abatido/a *adj.* avergonzado/a; triste; culpable

heedless: ignorando *adj.* sin escuchar el consejo; imprudente

hermitage: retiro *s.* lugar apartado, solitario

hospitality: hospitalidad *s.* actitud cálida de bienvenida hacia los invitados

host: anfitrión *s.* maestro de ceremonia, moderador o presentador de un programa

hypodermic: inyección hipodérmica *s.* inyección de un medicamento

I

immutable: inmutable *adj.* que no cambia nunca

impact: colisión *s.* choque; *v.* colisionar, chocar

imperial: imperial *adj.* de calidad superior

imploring: implorar *v.* pedir algo a alguien o suplicar

importunities: importunidades *s.* peticiones urgentes molestas

impressionism: impresionismo *s.* estilo artístico en el que el estado de ánimo, el color y la luz importan más que los detalles

incident: incidente *s.* suceso

indecisions: indecisiones *s.* cosas que no están decididas o finalizadas

infallibility: infalibilidad *s.* imposibilidad de equivocarse

inflection: inflexión *s.* subidas y bajadas en el tono de voz de una persona

informational: informativo/a *adj.* que proporciona conocimientos y hechos

infringed: infringió *v.* violó la ley

instantaneously: instantáneamente *adv.* inmediatamente

insurgent: insurgente *adj.* rebelde o que se rebela contra el gobierno en el poder

integrity: integridad *s.* la virtud de seguir principios morales o éticos

interminable: interminable *adj.* que parece que no tiene fin

interview: entrevista *s.* conversación en la que un presentador hace preguntas a uno o más invitados

inquire: inquirir *v.* solicitar información; indagar

investigate: investigar *v.* indagar a fondo

J

jurisdiction: jurisdicción *s.* poder legal para escuchar una causa y dictar sentencia

L

labeling and **captions: rótulos** y **leyendas** *s.* etiquetas y texto que suelen acompañar las imágenes de contenido político para clarificar su significado

layout: diseño *s.* la disposición gráfica de una presentación

legacy: legado *s.* algo heredado, que se traspasa

letterhead: membrete *s.* papelería personalizada

literal: literal *adj.* acorde a los hechos; sin exagerar

loathsome: repugnante *adj.* que causa gran desagrado

loitered: deambuló *v.* holgazaneó; que se movió despacio

M

machetes: machetes *s.* cuchillos

magistrates: magistrados *s.* cargos públicos que tienen el poder de un juez

majority: mayoría *s.* más de la mitad

malice: malicia *s.* deseo de herir a alguien

mission: misión *s.* objetivo o ambición

monotonous: monótono/a *adj.* aburrido/a debido a la falta de variación

motifs: motivos *s.* temas, características o elementos principales

multitudes: multitudes *s.* gran número de personas

O

obdurate: obstinado/a *adj.* resistente a la persuasión

obliged: agradecido/a *adj.* que da las gracias

oppressed: oprimidos/as *s.* personas cuyo derechos son pisoteados por otros

ornamented: ornamentado *adj.* decorado; adornado

overcast: nublado *adj.* cubierto de nubes

overture: obertura *s.* introducción musical de un ópera o sinfonía

P

palette: paleta *s.* rango de colores usados en una obra determinada

perish: perecer *v.* morir; ser matado

perpetually: perpetuamente *adv.* que sucede todo el tiempo

persistence: persistencia *s.* acción de no darse por vencido

perspective: perspectiva *s.* método mediante el cual se le da sentido de profundidad a una superficie plana

petition: petición *s.* hacer una solicitud formal; buscar la ayuda de alguien

picturesquely: de modo pintoresco *adv.* de manera que parece un cuadro; de manera sorprendente o interesante

plaintiffs: demandantes *s.* las personas que interponen una demanda en un juicio

policy: política *s.* acciones específicas de una persona, gobierno u organización

populist: populista *adj.* persona que cree servir las necesidades del pueblo

prejudices: prejuicios *s.* sentimientos u opiniones desfavorables formados con anterioridad o sin apoyarse en los hechos

prelude: preludio *s.* introducción de una obra musical; obertura

prescribed: prescrito *v.* manifestado por escrito; mandado

proceedings: pleito *s.* proceso judicial, los sucesos de un juzgado

prolific: prolífico *adj.* fructífero

propaganda: propaganda *s.* información, ideas o rumores que se divulgan amplia y deliberadamente para hacerle daño a una persona, grupo, movimiento, causa o nación

protagonist: protagonista *s.* el personaje principal de una obra de teatro, cuento o novela

Q

quaint: singular *adj.* inusual; curioso

R

racket: barullo *s.* confusión ruidosa; jaleo

realism: realismo *s.* estilo artístico que se parece mucho a la realidad

rectitude: rectitud *s.* comportamiento o pensamiento moralmente correcto; integridad

redeemers: redentores *s.* personas que pagan por las malas acciones de otros

redress: rectificación *s.* corrección reparación de un daño

relevant: relevante *adj.* pertinente

remorseless: despiadado/a *adj.* que no tiene remordimientos; cruel

renaissance: renacimiento *s.* resurgimiento; periodo de importancia cultural

rend: rasgar *v.* hacer pedazos con fuerza

resolution: resolución *s.* acción de resolver o decidir; expresión formal de una opinión

reverence: reverencia *s.* sentimiento de profundo respeto

rites: ritos *s.* ceremonias

romanticism: romanticismo *s.* estilo artístico que evoca la emoción idealizando los sujetos

S

salutary: saludable *adj.* beneficioso/a

sanctity: santidad *s.* hecho de ser sagrado

scourge: azote *s.* causa de serios problemas o sufrimiento

self-assurance: autoconfianza *s.* seguridad en uno mismo

sequence: secuencia *s.* en un orden particular; *v.* (secuenciar) poner en orden

sequence photography: secuencia fotográfica *n.* una serie de imágenes en las que se ve el sujeto en instantes sucesivos

shotgun: escopeta *s.* arma de cañón largo, con frecuencia usada para disparar perdigones

shuffle: arrastrar los pies *v.* caminar sin levantar los pies

sidle: caminar de lado *v.* moverse de costado furtiva o tímidamente

significant: significativo/a *adj.* lleno/a de significado; importante

sinister: siniestro *adj.* malvado; amenazador

sovereign: soberano *s.* un monarca o gobernante

spatial: espacial *adj.* que existe en el espacio

special elements: elementos especiales *s.* características que dan puntos de énfasis en una producción

specific: específico/a *adj.* definido/a; preciso/a; particular

specifications: especificaciones *s.* apartado de una patente en que el inventor describe con detalle el invento

speech balloon: bocadillo *s.* el modo en que se representa lo que dice cada personaje en las novelas gráficas

squalor: mugre *s.* suciedad; estado lamentable

stolid: impasible *adj.* imperturbable; que no siente emoción alguna

strife: lucha *s.* acción de luchar; conflicto

subordinate: subordinado/a *adj.* que tiene menos importancia

subordinate: subordinado/a *s.* una persona de menor rango o clase

superannuated: viejo/a *adj.* demasiado viejo/a para usarse; obsoleto/a

superfluous: superfluo/a *adj.* más de lo necesario o deseado; innecesario/a

supplanted: suplantó *v.* tomó el lugar de; quitó a

supplement: suplemento *s.* algo añadido

surrealism: surrealismo *s.* uso intencional de detalles imaginativos y hasta extraños en el arte

symbolism: simbolismo *s.* uso de imágenes u objetos para representar ideas o cualidades

T

tedious: tedioso/a *adj.* aburrido/a, soso/a

teeming: repleto/a *adj.* lleno/a

temporal: temporal *adj.* no eterno, limitado por el tiempo

tension: tensión *s.* estrés causado al tirar

tone: tono *s.* la actitud de una producción hacia un tema o el público

transcendent: trascendente *adj.* más allá de los límites de la experiencia posible

treason: traición *s.* deslealtad hacia la confianza o la fe

trivialize: trivializar *v.* quitar importancia; hacer trivial

tyranny: tiranía *s.* poder opresivo

U

unalienable: inalienable *adj.* imposible de quitar o de abandonar

unique: único/a *adj.* que es el único de su especie o tipo

unrequited: no correspondido *adj.* que no se ha liquidado o vengado

V

vassals: vasallos *s.* sujetos de un reino; siervos

vast: vasto/a *adj.* de gran tamaño

verbatim: textualmente *adv.* palabra por palabra

vigilant: vigilante *adj.* en alerta, atento/a

vindictive: vengativo/a *adj.* lleno/a de un deseo intenso e irracional de venganza

W

wanton: excesivo/a *adj.* descontrolado/a; sin ley

waterfowl: ave acuática *s.* relativo a las aves acuáticas

wretched: desdichado/a *adj.* muy infeliz; desgraciado/a

LITERARY TERMS HANDBOOK

ALLEGORY An *allegory* is a story or tale with two or more levels of meaning—a literal level and one or more symbolic levels. The events, setting, and characters in an allegory are symbols for ideas and qualities.

ALLUSION An *allusion* is a reference to a well-known person, place, event, literary work, or work of art. Writers often make allusions to stories from the Bible, to Greek and Roman myths, to plays by Shakespeare, to political and historical events, and to other materials with which they can expect their readers to be familiar.

ANALOGY An *analogy* is an extended comparison of relationships. It is based on the idea that the relationship between one pair of things is like the relationship between another pair. Unlike a metaphor, an analogy involves an explicit comparison, often using the words *like* or *as*.

ANAPHORA Anaphora is a type of parallel structure in which a word or phrase is repeated at the beginning of successive clauses for emphasis.

ANECDOTE An *anecdote* is a brief story about an interesting, amusing, or strange event. An anecdote is told to entertain or to make a point.

APPEAL An *appeal* is a rhetorical device used in argumentative writing to persuade an audience.

An appeal to ethics (Ethos) shows that an argument is just or fair.

An appeal to logic (Logos) shows that an argument is well reasoned.

An appeal to authority shows that a higher power supports the ideas.

An appeal to emotion (Pathos) is designed to influence readers' feelings.

ARGUMENT An *argument* is writing or speech that attempts to convince a reader to think or act in a particular way. An argument is a logical way of presenting a belief, conclusion, or stance. A good argument is supported with reasoning and evidence.

AUTOBIOGRAPHY An *autobiography* is a form of nonfiction in which a person tells his or her own life story. *Memoirs*, first-person accounts of personally or historically significant events in which the writer was a participant or an eyewitness, are a form of autobiographical writing.

BIOGRAPHY A *biography* is a form of nonfiction in which a writer tells the life story of another person.

CATALOGUE A *catalogue* in poetry is a list of people, objects, or situations, used to evoke a range of experience and/or emotion.

CHARACTER A *character* is a person or an animal that takes part in the action of a literary work. The following are some terms used to describe various types of characters:

The *main character* in a literary work is the one on whom the work focuses. *Major characters* in a literary work include the main character and any other characters who play significant roles. A *minor character* is one who does not play a significant role. A *round character* is one who is complex and multifaceted, like a real person. A *flat character* is one who is one-dimensional. A *dynamic character* is one who changes in the course of a work. A *static character* is one who does not change in the course of a work.

CHARACTERIZATION *Characterization* is the act of creating and developing a character. In **direct characterization,** a writer simply states a character's traits. In **indirect characterization,** character is revealed through one of the following means:

1. words, thoughts, or actions of the character
2. descriptions of the character's appearance or background
3. what other characters say about the character
4. the ways in which other characters react to the character

CLAIM A *claim* is a particular belief, conclusion, or point of view that a writer presents in an *argument.*

CONCESSION *Concession* is a rhetorical device that acknowledges the opposition's arguments.

CONFLICT A *conflict* is a struggle between opposing forces. Sometimes this struggle is internal, or within a character. At other times, this struggle is external, or between a character and an outside force. Conflict is one of the primary elements of narrative literature because most plots develop from conflicts.

CONNOTATION The *connotation* is an association that a word calls to mind in addition to the dictionary meaning of the word. Many words that are similar in their dictionary meanings, or denotations, are quite different in their connotations. Poets and other writers choose their words carefully so that the connotations of those words will be appropriate.

COUNTERCLAIM A *counterclaim* is an objection or challange to the *claim*—or particular belief, conclusion, or point of view—that a writer presents in an *argument.* Counterclaims are often brought up by the writer of the argument in anticipation of challenges.

DENOTATION The *denotation* of a word is its objective meaning, independent of other associations that the word brings to mind.

DESCRIPTION A *description* is a portrayal, in words, of something that can be perceived by the senses. Writers create descriptions by using images.

DIALECT A *dialect* is the form of a language spoken by people in a particular region or group. Writers often use dialect to make their characters seem realistic and to create local color.

DIALOGUE A *dialogue* is a conversation between characters. Writers use dialogue to reveal character, to present events, to add variety to narratives, and to arouse their readers' interest.

DICTION *Diction* is a writer's or speaker's word choice. Diction is part of a writer's style and may be described as formal or informal, plain or ornate, common or technical, abstract or concrete.

DRAMA A *drama* is a story written to be performed by actors. The playwright supplies dialogue for the characters to speak, as well as *stage directions* that give information about costumes, lighting, scenery, properties, the setting, and the characters' movements and ways of speaking. Dramatic conventions include soliloquies, asides, or the passage of time between acts or scenes. *Dramatic exposition* is a brief essay, or prose commentary, inserted by the writer to help readers and producers understand the characters and past conflicts. *Background knowledge* includes information about the period during which the action takes place.

DRAMATIC MONOLOGUE A *dramatic monologue* is a poem or speech in which an imaginary character speaks to a silent listener.

DRAMATIC POEM A *dramatic poem* is one that makes use of the conventions of drama. Such poems may be monologues or dialogues or may present the speech of many characters. Robert Frost's "The Death of the Hired Man" is a famous example of a dramatic poem.

See also *Dramatic Monologue.*

EPIC THEME An *epic theme* is an underlying message that all people of all times are connected by their shared experiences.

EDITORIAL An *editorial* is a form of persuasive writing or argument. Editorials must have a clear position, be supported by reasons, and include an appeal to ethics, logic, authority, and/or emotion.

ELLIPTICAL PHRASING *Elliptical phrasing* is a style of poetry in which the poet omits words that are expected to be understood by the reader.

ENUMERATION *Enumeration* is a document style in which the major ideas are listed in numerical order.

ESSAY An *essay* is a short nonfiction work about a particular subject. Essays can be classified as *formal* or *informal, personal,* or *impersonal*. They can also

be classified according to purpose, such as *cause-and-effect, satirical,* or *reflective.* Modes of discourse, such as *expository, descriptive, persuasive,* or *narrative,* are other means of classifying essays.

EXPLANATORY ESSAY An *explanatory essay* describes and summarizes information gathered from a number of sources on a concept.

FICTION *Fiction* is prose writing that tells about imaginary characters and events. Short stories and novels are works of fiction.

FIGURATIVE LANGUAGE *Figurative language* is writing or speech not meant to be taken literally. Writers use figurative language to express ideas in vivid and imaginative ways.

FIGURE OF SPEECH A *figure of speech* is an expression or a word used imaginatively rather than literally.

FLASHBACK A *flashback* is a section of a literary work that interrupts the chronological presentation of events to relate an event from an earlier time. A writer may present a flashback as a character's memory or recollection, as part of an account or story told by a character, as a dream or a daydream, or simply by having the narrator switch to a time in the past.

FORESHADOWING *Foreshadowing* in a literary work is the use of clues to suggest events that have yet to occur.

FRAME STORY A *frame story* is a story that brackets—or frames—another story or group of stories. This device creates a story-within-a-story narrative structure.

FREE VERSE *Free verse* is poetry that lacks a regular rhythmical pattern, or meter. A writer of free verse is at liberty to use any rhythms that are appropriate to what he or she is saying.

GENRE A *genre* is a division, or type, of literature. Literature is commonly divided into three major genres: poetry, prose, and drama. Each major genre can in turn be divided into smaller genres. Poetry can be divided into lyric, concrete, dramatic, narrative, and epic poetry. Prose can be divided into fiction and nonfiction. Drama can be divided into serious drama, tragedy, comic drama, melodrama, and farce.

HUMOR *Humor*, used in an argument, can be an effective rhetorical device. Humorous language and details make characters and situations seem funny.

HYPERBOLE A *hyperbole* is a deliberate exaggeration or overstatement, often used for comic effect.

IDIOMATIC EXPRESSION *Idiomatic expressions* are figures of speech that cannot be understood literally. For example, a rainstorm might be described as "raining cats and dogs."

IN MEDIA RES *In media res*, which is Latin for "in the middle of things," is a plot device writers use to grab reader's attention.

IMAGE An *image* is a word or phrase that appeals to one or more of the five senses—sight, hearing, touch, taste, or smell.

IMAGERY *Imagery* is the descriptive or figurative language used in literature to create word pictures for the reader. These pictures, or images, are created by details of sight, sound, taste, touch, smell, or movement.

INCONGRUITY *Incongruity* is a technique writers use to create humor and occurs when two or more ideas relate to one another in a way that is contrary to the readers' expectations.

IRONY *Irony* is a contrast between what is stated and what is meant, or between what is expected to happen and what actually happens. In *verbal irony*, a word or a phrase is used to suggest the opposite of its usual meaning. In *dramatic irony*, there is a contradiction between what a character thinks and what the reader or audience knows. In *irony of situation*, an event occurs that contradicts the expectations of the characters, of the reader, or of the audience.

LETTER A *letter* is a written message or communication addressed to a reader or readers and is generally sent by mail. Letters may be *private* or *public*, depending on their intended audience. A public letter, also called a *literary letter* or *epistle*, is a work of literature written in the form of a personal letter but created for publication.

MEMOIR A *memoir* is a type of nonfiction autobiographical writing that tells about a person's own life, usually focusing on the writer's involvement in historically or culturally significant events—either as a participant or an eyewitness.

METAPHOR A *metaphor* is a figure of speech in which one thing is spoken of as though it were something else. The identification suggests a comparison between the two things that are identified, as in "death is a long sleep."

A *mixed metaphor* occurs when two metaphors are jumbled together. For example, thorns and rain are illogically mixed in "the thorns of life rained down on him." A *dead metaphor* is one that has been overused and has become a common expression, such as "the arm of the chair" or "nightfall."

MONOLOGUE A *monologue* is a speech delivered entirely by one person or character.

MOTIF A *motif* is a recurrent, or repeated, object or idea in a literary work.

NARRATION *Narration* is writing that tells a story. The act of telling a story is also called *narration*. The *narrative,* or story, is told by a storyteller called the *narrator.* A story is usually told chronologically, in the order in which events take place in time, though it may include flashbacks and foreshadowing. Narratives may be true or fictional. Narration is one of the forms of discourse and is used in novels, short stories, plays, narrative poems, anecdotes, autobiographies, biographies, and reports.

NARRATIVE A *narrative* is a story told in fiction, nonfiction, poetry, or drama. Narratives are often classified by their content or purpose. An *exploration narrative* is a firsthand account of an explorer's travels in a new land. "The Interesting Narrative of the Life of Olaudah Equiano" is a *slave narrative*, an account of the experiences of an enslaved person. A *historical narrative* is a narrative account of significant historical events.

A *personal narrative* is a first-person story about a real-life experience. In a *reflective narrative* the author describes describes his or her feelings about a scene, incident, memory, or event. A *nonlinear narrative* does not follow chronological order. It may contain flashbacks, dream sequences, or other devices that interrupt the chronological order of events.

NARRATOR A *narrator* is a speaker or character who tells a story. A story or novel may be narrated by a main character, by a minor character, or by someone uninvolved in the story. The narrator may speak in the first person or in the third person. An *omniscient narrator* is all-knowing, while a limited narrator knows only what one character does.

NONFICTION *Nonfiction* is prose writing that presents and explains ideas or that tells about real people, places, objects, or events. Two of the main types of literary nonfiction are historical writing and reflective writing. Essays, biographies, autobiographies, journals, and reports are all examples of nonfiction.

NOVEL A *novel* is a long work of fiction. A novel often has a complicated plot, many major and minor characters, a significant theme, and several varied settings. Novels can be classified in many ways, based on the historical periods in which they are written, the subjects and themes that they treat, the techniques that are used in them, and the literary movements that inspired them. A *novella* is not as long as a novel but is longer than a short story.

ONOMATOPOEIA *Onomatopoeia* is the use of words that imitate sounds. Examples of such words are *buzz, hiss, murmur,* and *rustle.*

ORATORY *Oratory* is public speaking that is formal, persuasive, and emotionally appealing. Patrick Henry's "Speech in the Virginia Convention" (p. 100) is an example of oratory.

OXYMORON An *oxymoron* is a figure of speech that combines two opposing or contradictory ideas. An oxymoron, such as "freezing fire," suggests a paradox in just a few words.

PACING *Pacing* is the speed or rhythm of writing. Writers use different paces to achieve different effects, such as suspense.

PARADOX A *paradox* is a statement that seems to be contradictory but that actually presents a truth.

PARALLELISM *Parallelism* is the presentation of similar ideas, in sequence, using the same grammatical structure.

PARALLEL STRUCTURE In a list, each item should use *parallel structure* in which the part of speech and grammatical phrasing is the same for all items.

PERSONIFICATION *Personification* is a form of figurative language in which a nonhuman subject is given human characteristics. Effective personification of things or ideas makes them seem vital and alive, as if they were human.

PHILOSOPHICAL ASSUMPTIONS Beliefs that are taken for granted are *philosophical assumptions*. Some assumptions are *explicit*, or directly stated. Other assumptions are *implicit*, meaning the reader must make inferences to understand.

PLOT *Plot* is the sequence of events in a literary work. In most fiction, the plot involves both characters and a central conflict. The plot usually begins with an *exposition* that introduces the setting, the characters, and the basic situation. This is followed by the *inciting incident,* which introduces the central conflict. The conflict then increases during the *development* until it reaches a high point of interest or suspense, the *climax*. The climax is followed by the end, or resolution, of the central conflict. Any events that occur after the *resolution* make up the *denouement*. The events that lead up to the climax make up the *rising action*. The events that follow the climax make up the *falling action*.

POETRY *Poetry* is one of the three major types of literature. In poetry, form and content are closely connected, like the two faces of a single coin. Poems are often divided into lines and stanzas and often employ regular rhythmical patterns, or meters. Most poems use highly concise, musical, and emotionally charged language. Many also make use of imagery, figurative language, and special devices such as rhyme.

POETIC STRUCTURE The basic structures of poetry are lines and stanzas. A *line* is a group of words arranged in a row. A line of poetry may break, or end, in different ways. Varied *line lengths* can create unpredictable rhythms.

An *end-stopped line* is one in which both the grammatical structure and sense are complete at the end of the line.

A *run-on, or enjambed*, line is one in which both the grammatical structure and sense continue past the end of the line.

POINT OF VIEW *Point of view* is the perspective, or vantage point, from which a story is told. Three commonly used points of view are first person, omniscient third person, and limited third person.

In the *first-person point of view*, the narrator is a character in the story and refers to himself or herself with the first-person pronoun "I."

The two kinds of third-person point of view, limited and omniscient, are called "third person" because the narrator uses third-person pronouns such as "he" and "she" to refer to the characters. There is no "I" telling the story.

In stories told from the omniscient third-person point of view, the narrator knows and tells about what each character feels and thinks.

In stories told from the *limited third-person point of view,* the narrator relates the inner thoughts and feelings of only one character, and everything is viewed from this character's perspective.

PREAMBLE A *preamble* is a statement that explains who is issuing the document and for what purpose.

PRIMARY SOURCE A *primary source* is one created by someone who directly participated in or observed the event being described.

PROSE *Prose* is the ordinary form of written language. Most writing that is not poetry, drama, or song is considered prose. Prose is one of the major genres of literature. It occurs in two forms: fiction and nonfiction.

PROTAGONIST The protagonist is the main character in a literary work.

REFRAIN A *refrain* is a repeated line or group of lines in a poem or song. Most refrains end stanzas. Although some refrains are nonsense lines, many increase suspense or emphasize character and theme.

REGIONALISM *Regionalism* in literature is the tendency among certain authors to write about specific geographical areas. Regional writers present the distinct culture of an area, including its speech, customs, beliefs, and history.

RHETORICAL DEVICES Rhetorical devices are special patterns of words and ideas that create emphasis and stir emotion, especially in speeches or other oral presentations. *Parallelism*, for example, is the repetition of a grammatical structure in order to create a rhythm and make words more memorable. Other common rhetorical devices include: *analogy, drawing comparisons between two unlike things;* *charged language,* words that appeal to the emotions; *concession*, an acknowledgement of the opposition's argument; *humor,* using language and details that make characters or situations funny; *paradox,* statements that seem to contradict but present a truth; *restatement,* expressing the same idea in different words, *rhetorical questions,* questions with obvious answers, ***tone, the author's attitude toward the audience***

RHYME *Rhyme* is the repetition of sounds at the ends of words. Rhyming words have identical vowel sounds in their final accented syllables. The consonants before the vowels may be different, but any consonants occurring after these vowels are the same, as in *frog* and *bog* or *willow* and *pillow*. ***End rhyme*** occurs when rhyming words are repeated at the ends of lines. ***Internal rhyme*** occurs when rhyming words fall within a line. ***Approximate,*** or ***slant, rhyme*** occurs when the rhyming sounds are similar, but not exact, as in *prove* and *glove*.

REPETITION *Repetition* of words and phrases is a literary device used in prose and poetry to emphasize important ideas.

RHYTHM *Rhythm* is the pattern of beats, or stresses, in spoken or written language. Prose and free verse are written in the irregular rhythmical patterns of everyday speech.

RHETORICAL QUESTIONS Rhetorical questions call attention to an issue by implying obvious answers.

ROMANTICISM *Romanticism* was a literary and artistic movement of the nineteenth century that arose in reaction to eighteenth-century Neoclassicism and placed a premium on imagination, emotion, nature, individuality, and exotica. Romanticism is particularly evident in the works of the Transcendentalists.

SECONDARY SOURCE A *secondary source* is one created by someone with indirect knowledge of the event being described. Secondary sources rely on ***primary sources,*** or firsthand descriptions.

SENSORY LANGUAGE *Sensory language* is writing or speech that appeals to one or more of the five senses.

SEQUENCE OF EVENTS Authors often use ***sequence of events***, or the order in which things happened, to structure nonfiction pieces that describe historical events or explain a change over time. Authors frequently describe important events in ***chronological order,*** or time order.

SETTING The ***setting*** of a literary work is the time and place of the action. A setting may serve any of a number of functions. It may provide a background for the action. It may be a crucial element in the plot or central conflict. It may also create a certain emotional atmosphere, or mood.

SHORT STORY A ***short story*** is a brief work of fiction. The short story resembles the novel but generally has a simpler plot and setting. In addition, the short story tends to reveal character at a crucial moment rather than developing it through many incidents. For example, Thomas Wolfe's "The Far and the Near" concentrates on what happens to a train engineer when he visits people who had waved to him every day.

SERIAL COMMA A ***serial comma*** is a comma placed after each item in a list except for the final item.

SIMILE A ***simile*** is a figure of speech that makes a direct comparison between two subjects, using either *like* or as.

SLANT RHYME In ***slant rhyme,*** the final sounds in two lines of a poem are similar, but not identical.

SOCIAL COMMENTARY In works of ***social commentary,*** an author seeks to highlight, usually in a critical way, an aspect of society.

SPEAKER The ***speaker*** is the voice of a poem. Although the speaker is often the poet, the speaker may also be a fictional character or even an inanimate object or another type of nonhuman entity. Interpreting a poem often depends upon recognizing who the speaker is, whom the speaker is addressing, and what the speaker's attitude, or tone, is.

STANZA A ***stanza*** is a group of lines in a poem that are considered to be a unit. Many poems are divided into stanzas that are separated by spaces. Stanzas often function just like paragraphs in prose. Each stanza states and develops a single main idea.

Stanzas are commonly named according to the number of lines found in them, as follows:

1. Couplet: a two-line stanza
2. Tercet: a three-line stanza
3. Quatrain: a four-line stanza
4. Cinquain: a five-line stanza
5. Sestet: a six-line stanza
6. Heptastich: a seven-line stanza
7. Octave: an eight-line stanza

STREAM OF CONSCIOUSNESS *Stream of consciousness* is a narrative technique that presents thoughts as if they were coming directly from a character's mind. Instead of being arranged in chronological order, the events are presented from the character's point of view, mixed in with the character's thoughts just as they might spontaneously occur.

STYLE A writer's ***style*** includes word choice, tone, degree of formality, figurative language, rhythm, grammatical structure, sentence length, organization—in short, every feature of a writer's use of language.

SUSPENSE *Suspense* is a feeling of growing uncertainty about the outcome of events. Writers create suspense by raising questions in the minds of their readers. Suspense builds until the climax of the plot, at which point the suspense reaches its peak.

SYMBOL A ***symbol*** is anything that stands for or represents something else. A ***conventional symbol*** is one that is widely known and accepted, such as a voyage symbolizing life or a skull symbolizing death. A ***personal***

symbol is one developed for a particular work by a particular author.

SYMBOLISM *Symbolism* refers to an author's use of people, places, or objects to represent abstract qualities or ideas.

SYNTAX *Syntax* is the structure of sentences.

THEME A *theme* is a central message or insight into life revealed by a literary work. In most works of fiction, the theme is only indirectly stated: A story, poem, or play most often has an *implied theme*.

TONE The tone of a literary work is the writer's attitude toward his or her subject, characters, or audience. A writer's tone may be formal or informal, friendly or distant, personal or pompous. The tone of a work can also be described as technical, conversational, or colloquial.

TRANSCENDENTALISM *Transcendentalism* was an American literary and philosophical movement of the nineteenth century. The Transcendentalists, who were based in New England, believed that intuition and the individual conscience "transcend" experience and thus are better guides to truth than the senses and logical reason. Influenced by Romanticism, the Transcendentalists respected the individual spirit and the natural world, believing that divinity was present everywhere, in nature and in each person.

USAGE *Usage* is the way in which a word or phrase is used. The meaning, pronunciation, and spelling of some words have changed over time.

VOICE A writer's voice is the way in which the writer's personality is revealed in his or her writing. Elements that influence a writer's style are diction, the types of words used, syntax, the types of sentences used, and tone, the writer's attitude toward the topic or audience.

LITERARY TERMS HANDBOOK

ALLEGORY / ALEGORÍA Una *alegoría* es un relato o cuento con dos niveles de significado: un nivel literal y uno o más niveles simbólicos. Los hechos, ambientación y personajes de una alegoría son símbolos de ideas o cualidades.

ALLUSION / ALUSIÓN Una *alusión* es una referencia a una persona, lugar, hecho, obra literaria u obra de arte muy conocida. Los escritores a menudo hacen alusiones a relatos de la Biblia, a los mitos griegos y romanos, a las obras de Shakespeare, a hechos políticos e históricos y a otros materiales con los que suponen que sus lectores estén familiarizados.

ANALOGY / ANALOGÍA Una *analogía* establece una comparación extensa de relaciones. Se basa en la idea de que la relación entre un par de cosas es como la relación entre otro par. A diferencia de la metáfora, una analogía requiere una comparación explícita, a menudo usando las palabras *como* o *semejante*.

ANAPHORA / ANÁFORA Una *anáfora* es un tipo de estructura paralela en la que una palabra o frase se repite al principio de cláusulas consecutivas para dar énfasis.

ANECDOTE / ANÉCDOTA Una *anécdota* es un relato breve sobre un hecho interesante, divertido o extraño, que se narra con el fin de entretener o decir algo importante.

APPEAL / APELACIÓN Una *apelación* es un recurso retórico que se usa en los escritos de argumentación para persuadir al público.

Una apelación a la ética (Ethos) muestra que un argumento es justo.

Una apelación a la lógica (Logos) muestra que un argumento está bien razonado.

Una apelación a la autoridad muestra que alguien importante respalda las ideas.

Una apelación a las emociones (Pathos) tiene como fin influenciar los sentimientos de los lectores.

ARGUMENT / ARGUMENTO Un *argumento* es un escrito o discurso que trata de convencer al lector para que siga una acción o adopte una opinión en particular. Un argumento es una manera lógica de presentar una creencia, una conclusión o una postura. Un buen argumento se respalda con razonamientos y pruebas.

AUTOBIOGRAPHY / AUTOBIOGRAFÍA Una *autobiografía* es una forma de no-ficción en la que una persona narra su propia vida. Las *memorias* son relatos en primera persona de hechos personal o históricamente significativos en los que el escritor participó o de los cuales fue testigo directo. Las memorias son una forma de escrito autobiográfico.

BIOGRAPHY / BIOGRAFÍA Una *biografía* es una forma de no-ficción en la que un escritor cuenta la vida de otra persona.

CATALOGUE / CATÁLOGO Un *catálogo* en poesía es una lista de gente, objetos o situaciones que se usan para evocar un abanico de experiencias o emociones.

CHARACTER / PERSONAJE Un *personaje* es una persona o animal que participa de la acción en una obra literaria. A continuación hay algunos términos que se usan para describir varios tipos de personajes:

El *protagonista*, o *personaje principal*, en una obra literaria es aquel en el que se centra la obra. Los *personajes importantes* en una obra literaria incluyen el personaje principal y otros personajes que tienen papeles significativos. Un *personaje menor* es aquel que no tiene un papel importante. Un *personaje complejo* es aquel que muestra muchos rasgos diferentes. Un *personaje plano* muestra solo un rasgo. Un *personaje dinámico* se desarrolla y crece en el curso del relato. Un *personaje estático* no cambia a lo largo de la obra.

CHARACTERIZATION / CARACTERIZACIÓN La *caracterización* es el acto de crear y desarrollar un personaje. En una *caracterización directa*, el autor expresa explícitamente los rasgos de un personaje. En una *caracterización indirecta*, el personaje se revela a partir de una de estas maneras:

1. palabras, pensamientos o acciones del personaje
2. descripciones de la apariencia física del personaje o de su procedencia
3. lo que otros personajes dicen sobre el personaje
4. la forma en la que otros personajes reaccionan al personaje

CLAIM / AFIRMACIÓN Una *afirmación* es una opinión, conclusión o punto de vista determinado que el escritor presenta mediante un *argumento*.

CONCESSION / CONCESIÓN La *concesión* es un recurso retórico que reconoce los argumentos de la oposición.

CONFLICT / CONFLICTO Un *conflicto* es una lucha entre fuerzas opuestas. A veces la lucha es interna, o dentro de un personaje. Otras veces la lucha es externa, o entre un personaje y una fuerza exterior. El conflicto es uno de los elementos principales de la literatura narrativa porque la mayoría de tramas se desarrollan a partir de conflictos.

CONNOTATION / CONNOTACIÓN La *connotación* es la asociación que una palabra trae a la mente, además de su definición del diccionario. Muchas palabras que son similares en sus significados del diccionario, o denotaciones, son muy diferentes en sus connotaciones. Los poetas y otros escritores escogen sus palabras cuidadosamente para que las connotaciones de esas palabras sean apropiadas.

COUNTERCLAIM / CONTRAARGUMENTO

Un **contraargumento** es una objeción o desafío a la **afirmación**—u opinión, conclusión o punto de vista determinado—que el escritor presenta en un **argumento**. El escritor suele incluir contraargumentos para anticiparse a los desafíos.

DENOTATION / DENOTACIÓN

La **denotación** de una palabra es su significado objetivo, independientemente de otras asociaciones que esa palabra traiga a la mente.

DESCRIPTION / DESCRIPCIÓN

Una **descripción** es un retrato en palabras de algo que se puede percibir con los sentidos. Los escritores crean descripciones usando imágenes.

DIALECT / DIALECTO

El **dialecto** es la forma de un lenguaje hablado por la gente en una región o grupo particular. Los escritores a menudo usan dialecto para hacer que sus personajes parezcan más reales y para reflejar el habla de una zona determinada.

DIALOGUE / DIÁLOGO

Un **diálogo** es una conversación entre personajes. Los escritores usan el diálogo para revelar personajes, para presentar hechos, para añadir variedad a la narración o para despertar el interés de los lectores.

DICTION / DICCIÓN

La **dicción** comprende la elección de palabras que hace un autor o hablante. La dicción es parte del estilo de un escritor y se puede describir como formal o informal, sencilla u ornamentada, común o técnica, abstracta o concreta.

DRAMA / DRAMA

Un **drama** es una historia escrita para ser representada por actores. El guión de un drama proporciona el diálogo para que los personajes hablen, así como las **acotaciones** que dan información sobre el vestuario, la iluminación, la ambientación, los objetos y la manera en la que los personajes se mueven o hablan. Las convenciones dramáticas incluyen soliloquios, apartes, o el paso del tiempo entre actos o escenas. La **exposición dramática** es un ensayo breve o comentario en prosa del escritor y que tiene como objetivo que los lectores y productores entiendan a los personajes y sus conflictos. El **conocimiento previo** incluye información sobre el período en el cual tiene lugar la acción.

DRAMATIC MONOLOGUE / MONÓLOGO DRAMÁTICO

Un **monólogo dramático** es un poema o discurso en el que un personaje imaginario le habla a un oyente silencioso.

DRAMATIC POEM / POEMA DRAMÁTICO

Un **poema dramático** es aquel que usa las reglas del drama. Estos poemas pueden ser monólogos o diálogos o pueden presentar el parlamento de varios personajes. "The Death of the Hired Man" de Robert Frost es un ejemplo muy famoso de poema dramático.

Ver también **monólogo dramático**.

EPIC THEME / TEMA ÉPICO

Un **tema épico** es el mensaje subyacente de que todas las personas de todas las épocas están conectadas por experiencias compartidas.

EDITORIAL / EDITORIAL

Un **editorial** es una forma de escritura persuasiva o argumento. Los editoriales deben tener una postura clara, respaldarse con razonamientos e incluir una apelación a la ética, a la lógica, a la autoridad o a la emoción.

ELLIPTICAL PHRASING / FRASEO ELÍPTICO

El **fraseo elíptico** es un estilo de poesía en el que el poeta omite palabras que se espera que sean comprendidas por el lector.

ENUMERATION / ENUMERACIÓN

Una **enumeración** es un estilo de documento en el que las ideas principales se listan en orden numérico.

ESSAY / ENSAYO

Un **ensayo** es una obra breve de no-ficción sobre un tema en particular. Los ensayos pueden clasificarse como **formal** o **informal**, **personal** o **impersonal**. También se pueden clasificar de acuerdo a su propósito, como por ejemplo **de causa y efecto**, **satírico** o **reflexivo**. Otras maneras de clasificar ensayos es por el modo de discurso, como por ejemplo **expositivo**, **descriptivo**, **persuasivo** o **narrativo**.

EXPLANATORY ESSAY / ENSAYO EXPLICATIVO

Un **ensayo explicativo** describe y resume información sobre un concepto recogida a partir de varias fuentes.

FICTION / FICCIÓN

La **ficción** es un escrito en prosa que cuenta algo sobre personajes y hechos imaginarios. Los cuentos y las novelas son obras de ficción.

FIGURATIVE LANGUAGE / LENGUAJE FIGURADO

El **lenguaje figurado** es un escrito o discurso que no se debe interpretar literalmente. Los escritores usan lenguaje figurado para expresar ideas de forma vívida e imaginativa.

FIGURE OF SPEECH / FIGURA RETÓRICA

Una **figura retória** es una expresión o palabra usada de forma imaginativa en vez de literal.

FLASHBACK / FLASHBACK

Un **flashback** o **escena retrospectiva** es una sección de una obra literaria que interrumpe la presentación cronológica de los hechos para relatar un hecho de un tiempo anterior. Un escritor puede presentar un flashback como el recuerdo de un personaje, como parte de lo que cuenta un personaje, como un sueño o simplemente haciendo que el narrador cambie a un tiempo en el pasado.

FORESHADOWING / PREFIGURACIÓN

La **prefiguración** es el uso, en una obra literaria, de claves que sugieren hechos que van a suceder.

FRAME STORY / CUENTO DE ENMARQUE

Un **cuento de enmarque** es un relato dentro del cual se incluye otro relato o relatos. Este recurso permite crear una estructura narrativa del tipo "cuento dentro del cuento".

FREE VERSE / VERSO LIBRE

El **verso libre** es una forma poética en la que no se sigue un patrón regular de metro ni de rima. Un escritor de verso libre tiene la libertad de usar cualquier ritmo que sea apropiado a lo que está diciendo.

GENRE / GÉNERO

Un **género** es una categoría o tipo de literatura. La literatura se divide por lo general en tres géneros principales: poesía, prosa y drama. Cada uno de estos géneros principales se dividen a su vez en géneros más pequeños. La poesía se puede dividir en lírica, concreta, dramática, narrativa y épica. La prosa se puede dividir en ficción y no ficción. El drama se puede dividir en drama serio, tragedia, drama cómico, melodrama y farsa.

HUMOR / HUMOR El *humor*, usado en un argumento, puede ser un recurso retórico efectivo. El lenguaje y los detalles humorísticos pueden hacer que los personajes y las situaciones parezcan divertidos.

HYPERBOLE / HIPÉRBOLE Una *hipérbole* es una exageración o magnificación deliberada que a menudo se usa para producir un efecto cómico.

IDIOMATIC EXPRESSION / EXPRESIÓN IDIOMÁTICA Las *expresiones idiomáticas* son figuras retóricas que no se pueden entender literalmente. Por ejemplo, una tormenta se puede describir como "llover a cántaros".

IMAGE / IMAGEN Una *imagen* es una palabra o frase que apela a uno o más de los cinco sentidos: la vista, el oído, el tacto, el gusto o el olfato.

IMAGERY / IMÁGENES Las *imágenes* son el lenguaje figurado o descriptivo que se usa en la literatura para crear una descripción verbal para los lectores. Estas descripciones verbales, o imágenes, se crean incluyendo detalles visuales, auditivos, gustativos, táctiles, olfativos o de movimiento.

IN MEDIA RES / IN MEDIA RES *In media res*, que quiere decir "en el medio de las cosas" en latín, es un resurso que usan los escritores para captar la atención del lector.

INCONGRUITY / INCONGRUENCIA La *incongruencia* es una técnica que usan los escritores para crear humor y ocurre cuando dos o más ideas se relacionan entre sí de una manera que no es de la esperada por el lector.

IRONY / IRONÍA *Ironía* es un contraste entre lo que se dice y lo que se quiere decir, o entre lo que se espera que ocurra y lo que pasa en realidad. En una *ironía verbal*, las palabras se usan para sugerir lo opuesto a lo que se dice. En la *ironía dramática* hay una contradicción entre lo que el personaje piensa y lo que el lector o la audiencia sabe que es verdad. En una *ironía situacional*, ocurre un suceso que contradice directamente las expectativas de los personajes, del lector o de la audiencia.

LETTER / CARTA Una *carta* es un mensaje escrito dirigido a un lector o lectores y generalmente se envía por correo. Las cartas pueden ser *privadas* o *públicas*, dependiendo de la audiencia a la que van dirigidas. Una *carta pública*, también llamada *carta literaria* o *epístola*, es una obra literara escrita en forma de carta personal pero creada para ser publicada.

MEMOIR / MEMORIAS Unas *memorias* son un tipo de escrito de no ficción autobiográfica en el que el autor cuenta algo de su propia vida, generalmente centrándose

en la participación del autor en hechos significativos históricos o culturales, ya sea como participante directo o como testigo.

METAPHOR / METÁFORA Una *metáfora* es una figura literaria en la que algo se describe como si fuera otra cosa. La identificación sugiere una comparación entre las dos cosas que se identifican, como "la muerte es un largo sueño".

Una *metáfora mixta* ocurre cuando dos metáforas se unen. Por ejemplo, las espinas y la lluvia se mezclan ilógicamente en "le llovieron encima las espinas de la vida". Una *metáfora muerta* es aquella que se ha sobreutilizado mucho y se ha convertido en una expresión común, como "el brazo del sillón" o "la noche que cae".

MONOLOGUE / MONÓLOGO Un *monólogo* es un discurso narrado por completo por una sola persona o personaje.

MOTIF / MOTIVO El *motivo* es un objeto o idea que se repite de forma recurrente en una obra literaria.

NARRATION / NARRACIÓN Una *narración* es un escrito que cuenta una historia. El acto de contar una historia de forma oral también se llama *narración*. La *narrativa*, o relato, la cuenta el *narrador*. Un relato generalmente se cuenta en orden cronológico, en el orden en el que suceden los hechos, aunque puede incluir flashbacks y prefiguración. Las narrativas pueden ser verdaderas o inventadas. La narración es una de las muchas formas de discurso que existen y se usa en novelas, cuentos, obras de teatro, poemas narrativos, anécdotas, autobiografías, biografías e informes.

NARRATIVE / RELATO Se llama *relato* a la historia que se narra en una obra de ficción, de no-ficción, en un poema o en un drama. Los relatos a menudo se clasifican por su contenido o propósito. Un *relato de exploración* es una narración en primera persona de los viajes de un explorador en una tierra desconocida. "The Interesting Narrative of the Life of Olaudah Equiano" es un *relato de esclavos*, la narración de las experiencias de una persona esclavizada. Un *relato histórico* es la narración de hechos históricos significativos. Un *relato personal* es una narración en primera persona sobre una experiencia real. En un *relato de reflexión* el autor describe sus sentimientos sobre una escena, incidente, recuerdo o hecho. Un *relato no lineal* no sigue el orden cronológico. Puede contener flashbacks, secuencias de sueño u otros recursos que interrumpen el orden cronológico de los hechos.

NARRATOR / NARRADOR Un *narrador* es el hablante o el personaje que cuenta una historia. El cuento o novela lo puede narrar un personaje principal, un personaje menor o alguien que no está involucrado en la trama. El narrador puede hablar en primera persona o en tercera persona. Un *narrador omnisciente* lo sabe todo, mientras que un *narrador limitado* sólo sabe lo que hace un personaje.

NONFICTION / NO-FICCIÓN La *no-ficción* es un escrito en prosa que presenta y explica ideas o cuenta algo acerca de personas, lugares, ideas o hechos reales. Dos de los tipos principales de literatura de no-ficción son los escritos históricos y los escritos de reflexión. Los ensayos, las biografías, las autobiografías, los diarios y los reportajes son todos ejemplos de no-ficción.

NOVEL / NOVELA Una *novela* es una obra extensa de ficción. A menudo tiene una trama complicada, con personajes principales y secundarios, con un tema significativo y una ambientación variada. Las novelas pueden clasificarse de muchas maneras, basadas en los periodos históricos en los que se escribieron, en los temas que tratan, en las técnicas que se usan en ellas y en los movimientos literarios que las inspiraron. Una *novela corta* no es tan extensa como una novela, pero es más larga que un cuento.

ONOMATOPOEIA / ONOMATOPEYA La *onomatopeya* es el uso de palabras que imitan sonidos, tales como *zum, pío-pío, tic-tac* o *susurro*.

ORATORY / ORATORIA La *oratoria* es hablar en público de manera formal, persuasiva y emocionalmente atractiva. El "Discurso en la Convención de Virginia" es un ejemplo de oratoria.

OXYMORON / OXÍMORON Un *oxímoron* es una figura literaria que combina dos ideas opuestas o contradictorias. Un oxímoron, como "fuego helado", sugiere una paradoja en solo unas palabras.

PACING / RITMO LITERARIO El *ritmo literario* es la velocidad o el paso de la escritura. Los escritores usan diferentes ritmos literarios para lograr distintos efectos, como el suspenso.

PARADOX / PARADOJA Una *paradoja* es un enunciado que parece contradictorio pero que sin embargo presenta una verdad.

PARALLELISM / PARALELISMO El *paralelismo* es la presentación de ideas similares, en secuencia, usando la misma estructura gramatical.

PARALLEL STRUCTURE / ESTRUCTURA PARALELA En una lista, cada objeto listado debe usar *estructura paralela* en la cual la morfología y frase gramatical sea igual para todos los objetos.

PERSONIFICATION / PERSONIFICACIÓN La *personificación* es una forma de lenguaje figurado en la que se da rasgos y actitudes humanas a un sujeto no humano. La personificación efectiva de cosas o ideas hace que se vean llenas de vida, como si fueran humanas.

PHILOSOPHICAL ASSUMPTIONS / SUPOSICIONES FILOSÓFICAS Las creencias que se dan por sentadas son *suposiciones filosóficas*. Algunas suposiciones son *explícitas*, o enunciadas directamente. Otras suposiciones son *implícitas*, que quiere decir que el lector debe hacer inferencias para comprenderlas.

PLOT / TRAMA o ARGUMENTO La *trama* o *argumento* es la secuencia de los eventos que suceden en una obra literaria. En la mayoría de las obras de ficción, la trama implica tanto a los personajes como al conflicto central. La trama por lo general empieza con una *exposición* que introduce la ambientación, los personajes y la situación básica. A ello le sigue el *suceso desencadenante*, que introduce el conflicto central. Este conflicto aumenta durante el *desarrollo* hasta que alcanza el punto más alto de interés o suspenso, llamado *clímax*. Al clímax le sigue el final o resolución del conflicto central. Todos los hechos que ocurren después de la *resolución*, forman el *desenlace*. Todos los sucesos que conducen al clímax constituyen la *acción dramática creciente*. Los sucesos que siguen al clímax forman la *acción dramática decreciente*.

POETIC STRUCTURE / ESTRUCTURA POÉTICA Las *estructuras poéticas* básicas son los versos y las estrofas. Un *verso* es un grupo de palabras ordenadas en un mismo renglón. Un verso puede terminar, o cortarse, de distintas maneras. La variedad en la *extensión de los versos* crea ritmos inesperados.

En un *verso no encabalgado* la estructura gramatical y el sentido se completan al final de esa línea.

En un *verso encabalgado* tanto la estructura gramatical como el sentido de una línea continúa en el verso que sigue.

POETRY / POESÍA La *poesía* es uno de los tres géneros literarios más importantes. En poesía, la forma y el contenido están íntimamente relacionados, como dos caras de la misma moneda. Los poemas a menudo se dividen en versos y estrofas y emplean patrones rítmicos regulares, llamados metros. La mayoría de los poemas están escritos en un lenguaje altamente conciso, musical y emocionalmente rico. Muchos también hacen uso de imágenes, de figuras retóricas y de sonoros, tales como la rima.

POINT OF VIEW / PUNTO DE VISTA El *punto de vista* es la perspectiva desde la cual se narran o describen los hechos de un relato. Tres puntos de vista que se usan frecuentemente son: primera persona, tercera persona omnisciente y tercera persona limitada.

En el *punto de vista de primera persona*, el narrador es un personaje del relato y se refiere a sí mismo con el pronombre de primera persona "yo".

Los dos tipos de punto de vista de tercera persona, limitado y omnisciente, se llaman "tercera persona" porque el narrador usa pronombres de tercera persona como "él o "ella" para referirse a los personajes. No hay "yo" que narre la historia.

En los relatos contados desde el *punto de vista de tercera persona omnisciente*, el narrador conoce y cuenta cosas sobre lo que cada personaje piensa y siente.

En los relatos contados desde el *punto de vista de tercera persona limitada*, el narrador relata los pensamientos internos y sentimientos de sólo un personaje y todo se ve desde el punto de vista de ese personaje.

PREAMBLE / PREÁMBULO El *preámbulo* es un enunciado que explica quién expide un documento y con qué propósito.

PRIMARY SOURCE / FUENTE PRIMARIA Una *fuente primaria* es la que ha sido creada por alguien que participó u observó directamente el suceso que se describe.

PROSE / PROSA La *prosa* es la forma común del lenguaje escrito. La mayoría de los escritos que no son poesía, ni drama, ni canciones, se consideran prosa. La prosa es uno de los géneros literarios más importantes y puede ser de dos formas: de ficción y de no-ficción.

PROTAGONIST / PROTAGONISTA El o la *protagonista* es el personaje principal de una obra literaria.

REFRAIN / REFRÁN Un *refrán* es un verso o grupo de versos que se repite en un poema o canción. Muchos refranes terminan estrofas. Si bien es cierto que algunos refranes no tienen sentido, la mayoría sirve para aumentar el suspenso o para realzar un personaje o enfatizar un tema.

REGIONALISM / REGIONALISMO El *regionalismo* en literatura es la tendencia entre ciertos autores a escribir sobre áreas geográficas específicas. Los escritores regionales presentan la cultura específica de un área, incluyendo su dialecto, costumbres, creencias e historia.

REPETITION / REPETICIÓN La *repetición* de palabras y frases es un recurso literario que se usa en prosa y poesía para dar énfasis a ideas importantes.

RHETORICAL DEVICES / FIGURAS RETÓRICAS Las *figuras retóricas* son patrones especiales de palabras e ideas que dan énfasis y producen emoción, especialmente en discursos y otras presentaciones orales. El *paralelismo*, por ejemplo, es la repetición de una estructura gramatical con el propósito de crear un ritmo y hacer que las palabras resulten más memorables.

Otras figuras retóricas muy frecuentes son: la *analogía*, que establece una comparación entre dos cosas diferentes; el *lenguaje emocionalmente cargado*, en el que las palabras apelan a las emociones; la *concesión*, mediante la que se acepta el argumento del oponente; el *humor*, que usa el lenguaje y los detalles para hacer que los personajes o las situaciones resulten cómicas; la *paradoja*, enunciados que parecen contradecirse pero que presentan una verdad; la *reafirmación*, en la que se expresa la misma idea con distintas palabras; las *preguntas retóricas*, que son interrogaciones cuyas respuestas son obvias; el *tono*, la actitud del autor hacia la audiencia.

RHETORICAL QUESTIONS / PREGUNTAS RETÓRICAS Las *preguntas retóricas* llaman la atención a un hecho al insinuar respuestas obvias.

RIMA La *rima* es la repetición de los sonidos finales de las palabras. Las palabras que riman tienen sonidos vocálicos iguales en las sílabas finales acentuadas. Las consonantes que están antes de esas vocales acentuadas pueden ser diferentes, pero las consonantes que estén después de esas vocales deben ser iguales, como en *frog* y *bog* o en *willow* y *pillow*. La *rima de final de verso* tiene lugar cuando se repiten las palabras que riman al final de dos o más versos. La *rima interna* se produce cuando las palabras que riman están en el mismo verso. La *rima aproximada* tiene lugar cuando los sonidos son parecidos pero no exactos, como en *prove* y *glove*.

RITMO El *ritmo* es el patrón de cadencia o acentuación en la lengua hablada o escrita. La prosa y el verso libre se escriben en los patrones rítmicos irregulares del lenguaje hablado cotidiano.

ROMANTICISM / ROMANTICISMO El *romanticismo* fue un movimiento literario y artístico del siglo. XIX que surgió como reacción contra el neoclasicismo del siglo. XVII y que daba énfasis a la imaginación, la emoción, la naturaleza, la individualidad y lo exótico. El romanticismo es particularmente evidente en las obras de los transcendentalistas.

SECONDARY SOURCE / FUENTE SECUNDARIA Una *fuente secundaria* es la que ha sido creada por alguien con información indirecta del suceso que se describe. Las fuentes secundarias dependen de las *fuentes primarias*, o descripciones de primera mano.

SENSORY LANGUAGE / LENGUAJE SENSORIAL El *lenguaje sensorial* es un escrito o discurso que incluye detalles que apelan a uno o más de los sentidos.

SEQUENCE OF EVENTS / SECUENCIA DE SUCESOS Los autores a menudo usan la *secuencia de sucesos*, o el orden en que sucenden las cosas, para estructurar piezas de no ficción que describen hechos históricos o que explican cambios a lo largo del tiempo. Los autores frecuentemente describen hechos importantes en *orden cronológico*, u orden de tiempo.

SETTING / AMBIENTACIÓN La *ambientación* de una obra literaria es la época y el lugar en el que se desarrolla la acción. La ambientación puede servir varias funciones. Puede proporcionar el telón de fondo para la acción. Puede ser un elemento crucial en la trama o conflicto central. También puede crear una atmósfera emotiva.

SHORT STORY / CUENTO Un *cuento* es una obra breve de ficción. El cuento se parece a la novela, pero suele tener una trama y ambientación más sencillas. Además, el cuento tiende a revelar el carácter de los personajes en un momento particular en lugar de irlo desarrollando a lo largo de numerosos acontecimientos. Por ejemplo, el cuento "The Far and the Near" de Thomas Wolfe se centra en lo que le sucede a un maquinista cuando visita a la gente que lo ha saludado diariamente.

SERIAL COMMA / COMA EN SERIE En inglés, se pone una *coma en serie* después de cada objeto en una lista, excepto en el objeto final.

SIMILE / SÍMIL Un *símil* es una figura retórica en la que se usa la palabra *como* para establecer una comparación directa entre dos cosas.

SLANT RHYME / RIMA ASONANTE En una *rima asonante* los sonidos finales de dos versos del poema son similares, pero no idénticos.

SOCIAL COMMENTARY / COMENTARIO SOCIAL En obras de *comentario social,* el autor tiene como objetivo resaltar, de forma crítica, un aspecto de la sociedad.

SPEAKER / HABLANTE El *hablante* es la voz de un poema. Aunque a menudo el hablante es el poeta, el hablante puede ser también un personaje imaginario o incluso un objeto inanimado o cualquier otro tipo de sujeto no humano. Interpretar un poema a menudo depende de reconocer quién es el hablante, a quién se dirige el hablante y cuál es la actitud o tono del hablante.

STANZA / ESTROFA Una *estrofa* es un grupo de versos en un poema que se consideran una unidad. Muchos poemas se dividen en estrofas que están separadas por espacios. Las estrofas a menudo funcionan como los párrafos en la prosa. Cada estrofa enuncia y desarrolla una sola idea principal.

Las estrofas a menudo reciben su nombre del número de versos que las componen, como siguen:

1. Pareado o dístico: estrofa de dos versos
2. terceta: estrofa de tres versos
3. cuarteta: estrofa de cuatro versos
4. quintilla: estrofa de cinco versos
5. sextilla: estrofa de seis versos
6. septeto: estrofa de siete versos
7. octavilla: estrofa de ocho versos

STREAM OF CONSCIOUSNESS / MONÓLOGO INTERIOR El *monólogo interior* es una técnica narrativa que presenta los pensamientos como si vinieran directamente de la mente de un personaje. En vez de ordenarse cronológicamente, los hechos se presentan desde el punto de vista del personaje, mezclados con los pensamientos como si ocurrieran espontáneamente.

STYLE / ESTILO El *estilo* de un escritor incluye su dicción, tono, grado de formalidad, lenguaje figurado, ritmo, estructura gramatical, tamaño de las oraciones, organización, etc. En resumen, cada rasgo del uso del lenguaje de un escritor.

SUSPENSE / SUSPENSO El *suspenso* es la sensación creciente de incertidumbre sobre el resultado de los hechos.

Los escritores crean suspenso poniendo preguntas en la mente de sus lectores. El suspenso crece hasta el clímax de la trama, punto en el que alcanza su momento álgido.

SYMBOL / SÍMBOLO Un *símbolo* es algo que representa otra cosa. Un *símbolo convencional* es uno ampliamente conocido y aceptado, como un viaje como símbolo de la vida o una calavera como símbolo de la muerte. Un *símbolo personal* es el que desarrolla un autor en concreto para una obra en particular.

SYMBOLISM / SIMBOLISMO El *simbolismo* hace referencia al uso de personas, lugares u objetos que usa un autor para representar cualidades o ideas abstractas.

SYNTAX / SINTAXIS La *sintaxis* es la estructura de las oraciones.

THEME / TEMA Un *tema* es el mensaje central o la concepción de la vida que revela una obra literaria. El tema de un ensayo a menudo se menciona directamente en la tesis. En la mayoría de obras de ficción el tema se enuncia sólo indirectamente: un cuento, poema u obra de teatro a menudo tienen un *tema implícito*.

TONE / TONO El *tono* de una obra literaria es la actitud del escritor hacia su tema, sus personajes o su audiencia. El tono de un escritor puede ser formal o informal, amistoso o distante, personal o pretencioso. El tono de una obra también se puede describir como técnico, conversacional o coloquial.

TRANSCENDENTALISM /TRANSCENDENTALISMO El *transcendentalismo* fue un movimiento estadounidense literario y filosófico del siglo. XIX. Los transcendentalistas, que estaban radicados en Nueva Inglaterra, creían que la intuición y consciencia individual "transcendían" la experiencia y por tanto eran mejores guías a la verdad que los sentidos y la razón lógica. Influidos por el Romanticismo, los transcendentalistas respetaban el espíritu individual y el mundo natural, creyendo que lo divino estaba presente en todas partes, en la naturaleza y en cada persona.

USAGE / USO El *uso* es la manera en la que una palabra o frase se usa. El significado, pronunciación y ortografía de algunas de las palabras ha cambiado con el tiempo.

VOICE / VOZ La *voz* es el "sonido" distintivo de un escritor, o la manera en que "habla" en la página. Se relaciona a elementos tales como la dicción, los tipos de palabras, la sintaxis, el tipo de oraciones empleadas y el tono, que es la actitud del autor hacia el tema o la audiencia.

PARTS OF SPEECH

Every English word, depending on its meaning and its use in a sentence, can be identified as one of the eight parts of speech. These are nouns, pronouns, verbs, adjectives, adverbs, prepositions, conjunctions, and interjections. Understanding the parts of speech will help you learn the rules of English grammar and usage.

Nouns A **noun** names a person, place, or thing. A **common noun** names any one of a class of persons, places, or things. A **proper noun** names a specific person, place, or thing.

Common Noun	Proper Noun
writer, country, novel	Charles Dickens, Great Britain, *Hard Times*

Pronouns A **pronoun** is a word that stands for one or more nouns. The word to which a pronoun refers (whose place it takes) is the **antecedent** of the pronoun.

A **personal pronoun** refers to the person speaking (first person); the person spoken to (second person); or the person, place, or thing spoken about (third person).

	Singular	Plural
First Person	I, me, my, mine	we, us, our, ours
Second Person	you, your, yours	you, your, yours
Third Person	he, him, his, she, her, hers, it, its	they, them, their, theirs

A **reflexive pronoun** reflects the action of a verb back on its subject. It indicates that the person or thing performing the action also is receiving the action.

I keep *myself* fit by taking a walk every day.

An **intensive pronoun** adds emphasis to a noun or pronoun.

It took the work of the president *himself* to pass the law.

A **demonstrative** pronoun points out a specific person(s), place(s), or thing(s).

this, that, these, those

A **relative pronoun** begins a subordinate clause and connects it to another idea in the sentence.

that, which, who, whom, whose

An **interrogative pronoun** begins a question.

what, which, who, whom, whose

An **indefinite pronoun** refers to a person, place, or thing that may or may not be specifically named.

all, another, any, both, each, everyone, few, most, none, no one, somebody

Verbs A **verb** expresses action or the existence of a state or condition.

An **action verb** tells what action someone or something is performing.

gather, read, work, jump, imagine, analyze, conclude

A **linking verb** connects the subject with another word that identifies or describes the subject. The most common linking verb is *be*.

appear, be, become, feel, look, remain, seem, smell, sound, stay, taste

A **helping verb,** or **auxiliary verb,** is added to a main verb to make a verb phrase.

be, do, have, should, can, could, may, might, must, will, would

Adjectives An **adjective** modifies a noun or pronoun by describing it or giving it a more specific meaning. An adjective answers the questions:

What kind?	*purple* hat, *happy* face, *loud* sound
Which one?	*this* bowl
How many?	*three* cars
How much?	*enough* food

The articles *the, a,* and *an* are adjectives.

A **proper adjective** is an adjective derived from a proper noun.

French, Shakespearean

Adverbs An **adverb** modifies a verb, an adjective, or another adverb by telling *where, when, how,* or *to what extent.*

will answer *soon, extremely* sad, calls *more* often

Prepositions A **preposition** relates a noun or pronoun that appears with it to another word in the sentence.

Dad made a meal *for* us. We talked *till* dusk. Bo missed school *because of* his illness.

Conjunctions A **conjunction** connects words or groups of words. A **coordinating conjunction** joins words or groups of words of equal rank.

bread *and* cheese, brief *but* powerful

Correlative conjunctions are used in pairs to connect words or groups of words of equal importance.

both Luis *and* Rosa, *neither* you *nor I*

Subordinating conjunctions indicate the connection between two ideas by placing one below the other in rank or importance. A subordinating conjunction introduces a subordinate, or dependent, clause.

> We will miss her *if* she leaves. Hank shrieked *when* he slipped on the ice.

Interjections An **interjection** expresses feeling or emotion. It is not related to other words in the sentence.

> ah, hey, ouch, well, yippee

PHRASES AND CLAUSES

Phrases A **phrase** is a group of words that does not have both a subject and a verb and that functions as one part of speech. A phrase expresses an idea but cannot stand alone.

Prepositional Phrases A **prepositional phrase** is a group of words that begins with a preposition and ends with a noun or pronoun that is the **object of the preposition.**

> before dawn   as a result of the rain

An **adjective phrase** is a prepositional phrase that modifies a noun or pronoun.

> Eliza appreciates the beauty **of a well-crafted poem.**

An **adverb phrase** is a prepositional phrase that modifies a verb, an adjective, or an adverb.

> She reads Spenser's sonnets **with great pleasure.**

Appositive Phrases An **appositive** is a noun or pronoun placed next to another noun or pronoun to add information about it. An **appositive phrase** consists of an appositive and its modifiers.

> Mr. Roth, **my music teacher**, is sick.

Verbal Phrases A **verbal** is a verb form that functions as a different part of speech (not as a verb) in a sentence. **Participles, gerunds,** and **infinitives** are verbals.

A **verbal phrase** includes a verbal and any modifiers or complements it may have. Verbal phrases may function as nouns, as adjectives, or as adverbs.

A **participle** is a verb form that can act as an adjective. Present participles end in *-ing;* past participles of regular verbs end in *-ed.*

A **participial phrase** consists of a participle and its modifiers or complements. The entire phrase acts as an adjective.

> Jenna's backpack, **loaded with equipment,** was heavy.
> **Barking incessantly,** the dogs chased the squirrels out of sight.

A **gerund** is a verb form that ends in *-ing* and is used as a noun.

A **gerund phrase** consists of a gerund with any modifiers or complements, all acting together as a noun.

> **Taking photographs of wildlife** is her main hobby. [acts as subject]
> We always enjoy **listening to live music.** [acts as object]

An **infinitive** is a verb form, usually preceded by *to,* that can act as a noun, an adjective, or an adverb.

An **infinitive phrase** consists of an infinitive and its modifiers or complements, and sometimes its subject, all acting together as a single part of speech.

> She tries **to get out into the wilderness often.** [acts as a noun; direct object of *tries*]
> The Tigers are the team **to beat.** [acts as an adjective; describes *team*]
> I drove twenty miles **to witness the event.** [acts as an adverb; tells why I drove]

Clauses A **clause** is a group of words with its own subject and verb.

Independent Clauses An independent clause can stand by itself as a complete sentence.

> George Orwell wrote with extraordinary insight.

Subordinate Clauses A subordinate clause, also called a dependent clause, cannot stand by itself as a complete sentence. Subordinate clauses always appear connected in some way with one or more independent clauses.

> George Orwell, **who wrote with extraordinary insight,** produced many politically relevant works.

An **adjective clause** is a subordinate clause that acts as an adjective. It modifies a noun or a pronoun by telling *what kind* or *which one.* Also called relative clauses, adjective clauses usually begin with a **relative pronoun:** *who, which, that, whom,* or *whose.*

> "The Lamb" is the poem **that I memorized for class.**

An **adverb clause** is a subordinate clause that, like an adverb, modifies a verb, an adjective, or an adverb. An adverb clause tells *where, when, in what way, to what extent, under what condition,* or *why.*

The students will read another poetry collection **if their schedule allows.**

When I recited the poem, Mr. Lopez was impressed.

A **noun clause** is a subordinate clause that acts as a noun.

William Blake survived on **whatever he made as an engraver.**

SENTENCE STRUCTURE

Subject and Predicate A **sentence** is a group of words that expresses a complete thought. A sentence has two main parts: a *subject* and a *predicate*.

A **fragment** is a group of words that does not express a complete thought. It lacks an independent clause.

The **subject** tells *whom* or *what* the sentence is about. The **predicate** tells what the subject of the sentence does or is.

A subject or a predicate can consist of a single word or of many words. All the words in the subject make up the **complete subject.** All the words in the predicate make up the **complete predicate.**

Complete Subject   Complete Predicate
Both of those girls | have already read *Macbeth*.

The **simple subject** is the essential noun, pronoun, or group of words acting as a noun that cannot be left out of the complete subject. The **simple predicate** is the essential verb or verb phrase that cannot be left out of the complete predicate.

Both of those girls | **have** already **read** *Macbeth*.
[Simple subject: *Both;* simple predicate: *have read*]

A **compound subject** is two or more subjects that have the same verb and are joined by a conjunction.

Neither the horse nor the driver looked tired.

A **compound predicate** is two or more verbs that have the same subject and are joined by a conjunction.

She **sneezed and coughed** throughout the trip.

Complements A **complement** is a word or word group that completes the meaning of the subject or verb in a sentence. There are four kinds of complements: *direct objects, indirect objects, objective complements,* and *subject complements.*

A **direct object** is a noun, a pronoun, or a group of words acting as a noun that receives the action of a transitive verb.

We watched the **liftoff**.
She drove **Zach** to the launch site.

An **indirect object** is a noun or pronoun that appears with a direct object and names the person or thing to which or for which something is done.

He sold the **family** a mirror. [The direct object is *mirror.*]

An **objective complement** is an adjective or noun that appears with a direct object and describes or renames it.

The decision made her **unhappy**.
[The direct object is *her.*]
Many consider Shakespeare the greatest **playwright.** [The direct object is *Shakespeare.*]

A **subject complement** follows a linking verb and tells something about the subject. There are two kinds: *predicate nominatives* and *predicate adjectives.*

A **predicate nominative** is a noun or pronoun that follows a linking verb and identifies or renames the subject.

"A Modest Proposal" is a **pamphlet.**

A **predicate adjective** is an adjective that follows a linking verb and describes the subject of the sentence.

"A Modest Proposal" is **satirical.**

Classifying Sentences by Structure

Sentences can be classified according to the kind and number of clauses they contain. The four basic sentence structures are *simple, compound, complex,* and *compound-complex.*

A **simple sentence** consists of one independent clause.

Terrence enjoys modern British literature.

A **compound sentence** consists of two or more independent clauses. The clauses are joined by a conjunction or a semicolon.

Terrence enjoys modern British literature, but his brother prefers the classics.

A **complex sentence** consists of one independent clause and one or more subordinate clauses.

Terrence, who reads voraciously, enjoys modern British literature.

A **compound-complex sentence** consists of two or more independent clauses and one or more subordinate clauses.

Terrence, who reads voraciously, enjoys modern British literature, but his brother prefers the classics.

Classifying Sentences by Function

Sentences can be classified according to their function or purpose. The four types are *declarative, interrogative, imperative,* and *exclamatory.*

A **declarative sentence** states an idea and ends with a period.

An **interrogative sentence** asks a question and ends with a question mark.

An **imperative sentence** gives an order or a direction and ends with either a period or an exclamation mark.

An **exclamatory sentence** conveys a strong emotion and ends with an exclamation mark.

PARAGRAPH STRUCTURE

An effective paragraph is organized around one **main idea,** which is often stated in a **topic sentence.** The other sentences support the main idea. To give the paragraph **unity,** make sure the connection between each sentence and the main idea is clear.

Unnecessary Shift in Person

Do not change needlessly from one grammatical person to another. Keep the person consistent in your sentences.

> **Max** went to the bakery, but **you** can't buy mints there. [shift from third person to second person]

> **Max** went to the bakery, but **he** can't buy mints there. [consistent]

Unnecessary Shift in Voice

Do not change needlessly from active voice to passive voice in your use of verbs.

> Elena and I **searched** the trail for evidence, but no clues **were found.** [shift from active voice to passive voice]

> Elena and I **searched** the trail for evidence, but we **found** no clues. [consistent]

AGREEMENT

Subject and Verb Agreement

A singular subject must have a singular verb. A plural subject must have a plural verb.

> **Dr. Boone uses** a telescope to view the night sky.
> The **students use** a telescope to view the night sky.

A verb always agrees with its subject, not its object.

> *Incorrect:* The best part of the show were the jugglers.
> *Correct:* The best part of the show was the jugglers.

A phrase or clause that comes between a subject and verb does not affect subject-verb agreement.

> His **theory**, as well as his claims, **lacks** support.

Two subjects joined by *and* usually take a plural verb.

> The **dog** and the **cat are** healthy.

Two singular subjects joined by *or* or *nor* take a singular verb.

> The **dog** or the **cat is** hiding.

Two plural subjects joined by *or* or *nor* take a plural verb.

> The **dogs** or the **cats are** coming home with us.

When a singular and a plural subject are joined by *or* or *nor,* the verb agrees with the closer subject.

> Either the **dogs** or the **cat is** behind the door.
> Either the **cat** or the **dogs are** behind the door.

Pronoun and Antecedent Agreement

Pronouns must agree with their antecedents in number and gender. Use singular pronouns with singular antecedents and plural pronouns with plural antecedents.

> **Doris Lessing** uses **her** writing to challenge ideas about women's roles.

> **Writers** often use **their** skills to promote social change.

Use a singular pronoun when the antecedent is a singular indefinite pronoun such as *anybody, each, either, everybody, neither, no one, one,* or *someone.*

> Judge **each** of the articles on **its** merits.

Use a plural pronoun when the antecedent is a plural indefinite pronoun such as *both, few, many,* or *several.*

> **Both** of the articles have **their** flaws.

The indefinite pronouns *all, any, more, most, none,* and *some* can be singular or plural depending on the number of the word to which they refer.

> **Most** of the *books* are in **their** proper places.
> **Most** of the *book* has been torn from **its** binding.

Principal Parts of Regular and Irregular Verbs

A verb has four principal parts:

Present	Present Participle	Past	Past Participle
learn	learning	learned	learned
discuss	discussing	discussed	discussed
stand	standing	stood	stood
begin	beginning	began	begun

Regular verbs such as *learn* and *discuss* form the past and past participle by adding *-ed* to the present form. **Irregular verbs** such as *stand* and *begin* form the past and past participle in other ways. If you are in doubt about the principal parts of an irregular verb, check a dictionary.

The Tenses of Verbs

The different tenses of verbs indicate the time an action or condition occurs.

The **present tense** expresses an action that happens regularly or states a current condition or a general truth.

> Tourists **flock** to the site yearly.

> Daily exercise **is** good for your heallth.

The **past tense** expresses a completed action or a condition that is no longer true.

> The squirrel **dropped** the nut and **ran** up the tree.
> I **was** very tired last night by 9:00.

The **future tense** indicates an action that will happen in the future or a condition that will be true.

> The Glazers **will visit** us tomorrow.
> They **will be** glad to arrive from their long journey.

The **present perfect tense** expresses an action that happened at an indefinite time in the past or an action that began in the past and continues into the present.

> Someone **has cleaned** the trash from the park.
> The puppy **has been** under the bed all day.

The **past perfect tense** shows an action that was completed before another action in the past.

> Gerard **had revised** his essay before he turned it in.

The **future perfect tense** indicates an action that will have been completed before another action takes place.

> Mimi **will have painted** the kitchen by the time we finish the shutters.

Degrees of Comparison

Adjectives and adverbs take different forms to show the three degrees of comparison: the *positive*, the *comparative*, and the *superlative*.

Positive	Comparative	Superlative
fast	faster	fastest
crafty	craftier	craftiest
abruptly	more abruptly	most abruptly
badly	worse	worst

Using Comparative and Superlative Adjectives and Adverbs

Use comparative adjectives and adverbs to compare two things. Use superlative adjectives and adverbs to compare three or more things.

> This season's weather was **drier** than last year's.
> This season has been one of the **driest** on record.
> Jake practices **more often** than Jamal.
> Of everyone in the band, Jake practices **most often.**

Pronoun Case

The **case** of a pronoun is the form it takes to show its function in a sentence. There are three pronoun cases: *nominative*, *objective*, and *possessive*.

Nominative	Objective	Possessive
I, you, he, she, it, we, you, they	me, you, him, her, it, us, you, them	my, your, yours, his, her, hers, its, our, ours, their, theirs

Use the **nominative case** when a pronoun functions as a *subject* or as a *predicate nominative.*

> **They** are going to the movies. [subject]
> The biggest movie fan is **she.** [predicate nominative]

Use the **objective case** for a pronoun acting as a *direct object,* an *indirect object,* or the *object of a preposition.*

> The ending of the play surprised **me.** [direct object]
> Mary gave **us** two tickets to the play. [indirect object]
> The audience cheered for **him.** [object of preposition]

Use the **possessive case** to show ownership.

> The red suitcase is **hers.**

Diction The words you choose contribute to the overall effectiveness of your writing. **Diction** refers to word choice and to the clearness and correctness of those words. You can improve one aspect of your diction by choosing carefully between commonly confused words, such as the pairs listed below.

accept, except

Accept is a verb that means "to receive" or "to agree to." *Except* is a preposition that means "other than" or "leaving out."

> Please **accept** my offer to buy you lunch this weekend.
>
> He is busy every day **except** the weekends.

affect, effect

Affect is normally a verb meaning "to influence" or "to bring about a change in." *Effect* is usually a noun meaning "result."

> The distractions outside **affect** Steven's ability to concentrate.
>
> The teacher's remedies had a positive **effect** on Steven's ability to concentrate.

among, between

Among is usually used with three or more items, and it emphasizes collective relationships or indicates distribution. *Between* is generally used with only two items, but it can be used with more than two if the emphasis is on individual (one-to-one) relationships within the group.

> I had to choose a snack **among** the various vegetables.
>
> He handed out the booklets **among** the conference participants.
>
> Our school is **between** a park and an old barn.
>
> The tournament included matches **between** France, Spain, Mexico, and the United States.

amount, number

Amount refers to overall quantity and is mainly used with mass nouns (those that can't be counted). *Number* refers to individual items that can be counted.

> The **amount** of attention that great writers have paid to Shakespeare is remarkable.
>
> A **number** of important English writers have been fascinated by the legend of King Arthur.

assure, ensure, insure

Assure means "to convince [someone of something]; to guarantee." *Ensure* means "to make certain [that something happens]." *Insure* means "to arrange for payment in case of loss."

> The attorney **assured** us we'd win the case.
>
> The rules **ensure** that no one gets treated unfairly.
>
> Many professional musicians **insure** their valuable instruments.

bad, badly

Use the adjective *bad* before a noun or after linking verbs such as *feel, look,* and *seem*. Use *badly* whenever an adverb is required.

> The situation may seem **bad**, but it will improve over time.
>
> Though our team played **badly** today, we will focus on practicing for the next match.

beside, besides

Beside means "at the side of" or "close to." *Besides* means "in addition to."

> The stapler sits **beside** the pencil sharpener in our classroom.
>
> **Besides** being very clean, the classroom is also very organized.

can, may

The helping verb *can* generally refers to the ability to do something. The helping verb *may* generally refers to permission to do something.

> I **can** run one mile in six minutes.
>
> **May** we have a race during recess?

complement, compliment

The verb *complement* means "to enhance"; the verb *compliment* means "to praise."

> Online exercises **complement** the textbook lessons.
>
> Ms. Lewis **complimented** our team on our excellent debate.

compose, comprise

Compose means "to make up; constitute." *Comprise* means "to include or contain." Remember that the whole comprises its parts or is composed of its parts, and the parts compose the whole.

> The assignment **comprises** three different tasks.
>
> The assignment is **composed** of three different tasks.
>
> Three different tasks **compose** the assignment.

different from, different than

Different from is generally preferred over *different than*, but *different than* can be used before a clause. Always use *different from* before a noun or pronoun.

> Your point of view is so **different from** mine.
>
> His idea was so **different from** [or **different than**] what we had expected.

farther, further

Use *farther* to refer to distance. Use *further* to mean "to a greater degree or extent" or "additional."

> Chiang has traveled **farther** than anybody else in the class.
>
> If I want **further** details about his travels, I can read his blog.

fewer, less

Use *fewer* for things that can be counted. Use *less* for amounts or quantities that cannot be counted. *Fewer* must be followed by a plural noun.

Fewer students drive to school since the weather improved.

There is **less** noise outside in the mornings.

good, well

Use the adjective *good* before a noun or after a linking verb. Use *well* whenever an adverb is required, such as when modifying a verb.

I feel **good** after sleeping for eight hours.

I did **well** on my test, and my soccer team played **well** in that afternoon's game. It was a **good** day!

its, it's

The word *its* with no apostrophe is a possessive pronoun. The word *it's* is a contraction of "it is."

Angelica will try to fix the computer and **its** keyboard.

It's a difficult job, but she can do it.

lay, lie

Lay is a transitive verb meaning "to set or put something down." Its principal parts are *lay, laying, laid, laid*. *Lie* is an intransitive verb meaning "to recline" or "to exist in a certain place." Its principal parts are *lie, lying, lay, lain*.

Please **lay** that box down and help me with the sofa.

When we are done moving, I am going to **lie** down.

My hometown **lies** sixty miles north of here.

like, as

Like is a preposition that usually means "similar to" and precedes a noun or pronoun. The conjunction *as* means "in the way that" and usually precedes a clause.

Like the other students, I was prepared for a quiz.

As I said yesterday, we expect to finish before noon.

Use **such as,** not **like,** before a series of examples.

Foods **such as** apples, nuts, and pretzels make good snacks.

of, have

Do not use *of* in place of *have* after auxiliary verbs such as *would, could, should, may, might,* or *must*. The contraction of *have* is formed by adding *-ve* after these verbs.

I **would have** stayed after school today, but I had to help cook at home.

Mom **must've** called while I was still in the gym.

principal, principle

Principal can be an adjective meaning "main; most important." It can also be a noun meaning "chief officer of a school." *Principle* is a noun meaning "moral rule" or "fundamental truth."

His strange behavior was the **principal** reason for our concern.

Democratic **principles** form the basis of our country's laws.

raise, rise

Raise is a transitive verb that usually takes a direct object. *Rise* is intransitive and never takes a direct object.

Iliana and Josef **raise** the flag every morning.

They **rise** from their seats and volunteer immediately whenever help is needed.

than, then

The conjunction *than* is used to connect the two parts of a comparison. The adverb *then* usually refers to time.

My backpack is heavier **than** hers.

I will finish my homework and **then** meet my friends at the park.

that, which, who

Use the relative pronoun *that* to refer to things or people. Use *which* only for things and *who* only for people.

That introduces a restrictive phrase or clause, that is, one that is essential to the meaning of the sentence. *Which* introduces a nonrestrictive phrase or clause—one that adds information but could be deleted from the sentence—and is preceded by a comma.

Ben ran to the park **that** just reopened.

The park, **which** just reopened, has many attractions.

The man **who** built the park loves to see people smiling.

when, where, why

Do not use *when, where,* or *why* directly after a linking verb, such as *is*. Reword the sentence.

Incorrect: The morning is when he left for the beach.

Correct: He left for the beach in the morning.

who, whom

In formal writing, use *who* only as a subject in clauses and sentences. Use *whom* only as the object of a verb or of a preposition.

Who paid for the tickets?

Whom should I pay for the tickets?

I can't recall to **whom** I gave the money for the tickets.

your, you're

Your is a possessive pronoun expressing ownership. *You're* is the contraction of "you are."

Have you finished writing **your** informative essay?

You're supposed to turn it in tomorrow. If **you're** late, **your** grade will be affected.

Capitalization

First Words

Capitalize the first word of a sentence.

Stories about knights and their deeds interest me.

Capitalize the first word of direct speech.

Sharon asked, "**D**o you like stories about knights?"

Capitalize the first word of a quotation that is a complete sentence.

Einstein said, "**A**nyone who has never made a mistake has never tried anything new."

Proper Nouns and Proper Adjectives

Capitalize all proper nouns, including geographical names, historical events and periods, and names of organizations.

Thames **R**iver	**J**ohn **K**eats	the **R**enaissance
United **N**ations	**W**orld **W**ar II	**S**ierra **N**evada

Capitalize all proper adjectives.

Shakespearean play	**B**ritish invaision
American citizen	**L**atin **A**merican literature

Academic Course Names

Capitalize course names only if they are language courses, are followed by a number, or are preceded by a proper noun or adjective.

Spanish	**H**onors **C**hemistry	**H**istory 101
geology	**a**lgebra	**s**ocial **s**tudies

Titles

Capitalize personal titles when followed by the person's name.

Ms. Hughes   **D**r. Perez   **K**ing George

Capitalize titles showing family relationships when they are followed by a specific person's name, unless they are preceded by a possessive noun or pronoun.

Uncle Oscar   Mangan's **s**ister   his **a**unt Tessa

Capitalize the first word and all other key words in the titles of books, stories, songs, and other works of art.

Frankenstein   "**S**hooting an **E**lephant"

Punctuation

End Marks

Use a **period** to end a declarative sentence or an imperative sentence.

We are studying the structure of sonnets.

Read the biography of Mary Shelley.

Use periods with initials and abbreviations.

D. H. Lawrence	Mrs. Browning
Mt. Everest	Maple St.

Use a **question mark** to end an interrogative sentence.

What is Macbeth's fatal flaw?

Use an **exclamation mark** after an exclamatory sentence or a forceful imperative sentence.

That's a beautiful painting!   Let me go now!

Commas

Use a **comma** before a coordinating conjunction to separate two independent clauses in a compound sentence.

The game was very close, but we were victorious.

Use commas to separate three or more words, phrases, or clauses in a series.

William Blake was a writer, artist, and printer.

Use commas to separate coordinate adjectives.

It was a witty, amusing novel.

Use a comma after an introductory word, phrase, or clause.

When the novelist finished his book, he celebrated with his family.

Use commas to set off nonessential expressions.

Old English, of course, requires translation.

Use commas with places and dates.

Coventry, England   September 1, 1939

Semicolons

Use a **semicolon** to join closely related independent clauses that are not already joined by a conjunction.

Tanya likes to write poetry; Heather prefers prose.

Use semicolons to avoid confusion when items in a series contain commas.

They traveled to London, England; Madrid, Spain; and Rome, Italy.

Colons

Use a **colon** before a list of items following an independent clause.

Notable Victorian poets include the following: Tennyson, Arnold, Housman, and Hopkins.

Use a colon to introduce information that summarizes or explains the independent clause before it.

She just wanted to do one thing: rest.

Malcolm loves volunteering: He reads to sick children every Saturday afternoon.

Quotation Marks

Use **quotation marks** to enclose a direct quotation.

"Short stories," Ms. Hildebrand said, "should have rich, well-developed characters."

An **indirect quotation** does not require quotation marks.

Ms. Hildebrand said that short stories should have well-developed characters.

Use quotation marks around the titles of short written works, episodes in a series, songs, and works mentioned as parts of collections.

"The Lagoon"   "Boswell Meets Johnson"

Italics

Italicize the titles of long written works, movies, television and radio shows, lengthy works of music, paintings, and sculptures.

Howards End   *60 Minutes*   *Guernica*

For handwritten material, you can use underlining instead of italics.

<u>The Princess Bride</u>   <u>Mona Lisa</u>

Dashes

Use **dashes** to indicate an abrupt change of thought, a dramatic interrupting idea, or a summary statement.

I read the entire first act of *Macbeth*—you won't believe what happens next.

The director—what's her name again?—attended the movie premiere.

Hyphens

Use a **hyphen** with certain numbers, after certain prefixes, with two or more words used as one word, and with a compound modifier that comes before a noun.

seventy-two

self-esteem

president-elect

five-year contract

Parentheses

Use **parentheses** to set off asides and explanations when the material is not essential or when it consists of one or more sentences. When the sentence in parentheses interrupts the larger sentence, it does not have a capital letter or a period.

He listened intently (it was too dark to see who was speaking) to try to identify the voices.

When a sentence in parentheses falls between two other complete sentences, it should start with a capital letter and end with a period.

The quarterback threw three touchdown passes. (We knew he could do it.) Our team won the game by two points.

Apostrophes

Add an **apostrophe** and an *s* to show the possessive case of most singular nouns and of plural nouns that do not end in *-s* or *-es*.

Blake's poems   the mice's whiskers

Names ending in *s* form their possessives in the same way, except for classical and biblical names, which add only an apostrophe to form the possessive.

Dickens's   Hercules'

Add an apostrophe to show the possessive case of plural nouns ending in *-s* and *-es*.

the girls' songs   the Ortizes' car

Use an apostrophe in a contraction to indicate the position of the missing letter or letters.

She's never read a Coleridge poem she didn't like.

Brackets

Use **brackets** to enclose clarifying information inserted within a quotation.

Columbus's journal entry from October 21, 1492, begins as follows: "At 10 o'clock, we arrived at a cape of the island [San Salvador], and anchored, the other vessels in company."

Ellipses

Use three ellipsis points, also known as an **ellipsis,** to indicate where you have omitted words from quoted material.

Wollestonecraft wrote, "The education of women has of late been more attended to than formerly; yet they are still . . . ridiculed or pitied. . . ."

In the example above, the four dots at the end of the sentence are the three ellipsis points plus the period from the original sentence.

Use an ellipsis to indicate a pause or interruption in speech.

"When he told me the news," said the coach, "I was . . . I was shocked . . . completely shocked."

Spelling

Spelling Rules

Learning the rules of English spelling will help you make **generalizations** about how to spell words.

Word Parts

The three word parts that can combine to form a word are roots, prefixes, and suffixes. Many of these word parts come from the Greek, Latin, and Anglo-Saxon languages.

The **root word** carries a word's basic meaning.

Root and Origin	Meaning	Examples
-leg- (-log-) [Gr.]	to say, speak	*legal, logic*
-pon- (-pos-) [L.]	to put, place	*postpone, deposit*

A **prefix** is one or more syllables added to the beginning of a word that alter the meaning of the root.

Prefix and Origin	Meaning	Example
anti- [Gr.]	against	*antipathy*
inter- [L.]	between	*international*
mis- [A.S.]	wrong	*misplace*

A **suffix** is a letter or group of letters added to the end of a root word that changes the word's meaning or part of speech.

Suffix and Origin	Meaning and Example	Part of Speech
-ful [A.S.]	full of: *scornful*	adjective
-ity [L.]	state of being: *adversity*	noun
-ize (-ise) [Gr.]	to make: *idolize*	verb
-ly [A.S.]	in a manner: *calmly*	adverb

Rules for Adding Suffixes to Root Words

When adding a suffix to a root word ending in *y* preceded by a consonant, change *y* to *i* unless the suffix begins with *i*.

ply + -able = pliable   happy + -ness = happiness

defy + -ing = defying   cry + -ing = crying

For a root word ending in *e*, drop the *e* when adding a suffix beginning with a vowel.

drive + -ing = driving   move + -able = movable

SOME EXCEPTIONS: traceable, seeing, dyeing

For root words ending with a consonant + vowel + consonant in a stressed syllable, double the final consonant when adding a suffix that begins with a vowel.

mud + -y = muddy   submit + -ed = submitted

SOME EXCEPTIONS: mixing, fixed

Rules for Adding Prefixes to Root Words

When a prefix is added to a root word, the spelling of the root remains the same.

un- + certain = uncertain   mis- + spell = misspell

With some prefixes, the spelling of the prefix changes when joined to the root to make the pronunciation easier.

in- + mortal = immortal   ad- + vert = avert

Orthographic Patterns

Certain letter combinations in English make certain sounds. For instance, *ph* sounds like *f*, *eigh* usually makes a long *a* sound, and the *k* before an *n* is often silent.

pharmacy   n**eigh**bor   **k**nowledge

Understanding **orthographic patterns** such as these can help you improve your spelling.

Forming Plurals

The plural form of most nouns is formed by adding -*s* to the singular.

computer**s**   gadget**s**   Washington**s**

For words ending in *s, ss, x, z, sh,* or *ch,* add -*es.*

circus**es**   tax**es**   wish**es**   bench**es**

For words ending in *y* or *o* preceded by a vowel, add -*s.*

key**s**   patio**s**

For words ending in *y* preceded by a consonant, change the *y* to an *i* and add -*es.*

cit**ies**   enem**ies**   troph**ies**

For most words ending in *o* preceded by a consonant, add -*es.*

echo**es**   tomato**es**

Some words form the plural in irregular ways.

women   oxen   children   teeth   deer

Foreign Words Used in English

Some words used in English are actually foreign words that have been adopted. Learning to spell these words requires memorization. When in doubt, check a dictionary.

sushi   enchilada   au pair   fiancé

laissez faire   croissant

INDEX OF SKILLS

Analyzing Text

Allegory, 681
Allusion, 46, 294, 344
American regional art, 472, 473
Analytical argument, 368
Analyze, 24, 34, 58, 165, 180, 414, 657, 680, 689, 802
  essential question, 79, 98, 114, 122, 210, 226, 234, 244, 258, 334, 343, 356, 367, 375, 469, 477, 488, 499, 507, 517, 527, 713, 734, 824, 839, 853
  media, 58, 89, 234, 349, 689
    essential question, 477, 719
    present and discuss, 477, 719
    review and synthesize, 477, 719
  prepare to compare, 856
  present and discuss, 79, 98, 114, 122, 210, 226, 234, 244, 258, 334, 343, 356, 367, 375, 469, 477, 488, 499, 507, 517, 527, 713, 734, 824, 839, 853
  review and clarify, 79, 98, 114, 122, 210, 226, 234, 244, 258, 334, 343, 356, 367, 375, 469, 488, 499, 517, 527, 713, 734, 824, 839, 853
  review and synthesize, 477, 507
Anecdotes, 415
Argument, 6
  analytical, 368
  claim, 295
  counterclaims, 295
  development of ideas, 211
  historical narrative as, 81
  persuasive appeals, 25
  rhetoric, 335
  structure, 295
Argumentative text, 548
Art and photography, 310, 472, 502
Assess, 189
Audience, 116
Audio, 186, 346, 686
Audio performance, 687
Author's style
  audience, 336
  author's choices, 659, 855
  author's point of view, 715
  diction, 336, 417
    colloquial language, 336, 417
    conversational tone, 417
    formal, 336

    technical language, 417
  enumeration, 37
  figurative language, 855
    metaphors, 855
    similes, 855
  formality, 27
  historical narrative as argument, 81
  irony, 358
    dramatic, 358
    situational, 358
    verbal, 358
  Irony, 659
    dramatic irony, 659
    verbal irony, 659
  mixed diction, 167
  onomatopoeia, 167
  parallelism, 49
  realism, 683
  rhetorical devices
    antithesis, 124
    parallelsim, 124
  syntax, 27
  tone, 417
  usage, 27, 336
  voice, 116
  word choice, 429
    dialect, 429
    idiomatic expressions, 429
  word pairing, 167
  words and phrases, 336
Autobiography, 93, 99, 481, 489, 704, 705
Biography, 72, 102, 107
Cite textual evidence, 24, 25, 34, 35, 46, 47, 58, 79, 80, 99, 114, 115, 122, 123, 164, 180, 181, 189, 210, 211, 226, 234, 244, 245, 258, 259, 294, 295, 304, 305, 334, 343, 344, 356, 357, 367, 368, 414, 415, 426, 427, 444, 445, 469, 470, 488, 499, 500, 507, 517, 518, 527, 528, 597, 598, 625, 626, 657, 658, 680, 681, 682, 689, 713, 714, 734, 735, 774, 775, 788, 789, 802, 803, 824, 825, 839, 840, 853, 854
Close read, 19, 20, 24, 31, 32, 34, 43, 46, 89, 157, 158, 160, 174, 176, 178, 290, 292, 302, 409, 411, 412, 421, 422, 424, 433, 434, 436, 439, 442, 564, 567, 570, 572, 575, 578, 582, 587, 588, 595, 597, 604, 606, 608, 613, 615, 619, 623, 625, 631, 635, 639, 643, 644, 648, 653, 655, 657,

662, 664, 667, 670, 672, 674, 677, 680, 765, 767, 768, 771, 772, 783, 784, 786, 795, 797, 798, 800
  annotate, 24, 34, 46, 79, 98, 114, 122, 164, 180, 210, 244, 258, 294, 304, 334, 343, 356, 367, 414, 426, 444, 469, 488, 559, 774, 788, 802, 824, 839, 853
  close-read guide, 131, 267, 385, 537, 743, 863
  conclude, 24, 34, 46, 79, 98, 114, 122, 164, 180, 210, 226, 244, 258, 294, 304, 343, 414, 426, 444, 469, 488, 499, 517, 527, 559, 713, 734, 774, 788, 802, 824, 839, 853
  notice, 517
  questions, 24, 34, 46, 79, 98, 114, 122, 164, 180, 210, 226, 244, 258, 294, 304, 334, 343, 356, 367, 375, 414, 426, 444, 469, 488, 499, 517, 527, 559, 713, 734, 774, 788, 802, 824, 839, 853
Close review, 58
  conclude, 58, 89, 189, 234, 316, 349, 477, 507, 689, 719
  questions, 58, 89, 189, 234, 316, 349, 477, 507, 689, 719
Compare and contrast, 58, 180, 774
Comparing texts, 72
  humor, 418
  legal opinion and magazine article, 360, 370, 378
  memoir and poems, 420, 510
  memoir and short story, 406
  narrative choices, 856
  short stories, 828, 842
Comparing text to media
  American regional art, 472
  artwork, 478
  audio performance of drama, 686, 690
  autobiography and video interview, 704
  fine art gallery, 462
  graphic adaptation, 82, 90
  interview, 716
  photographs, 502, 508
  podcast, 190
  podcast and public document, 338
  podcast and written text, 346, 350
  poem and radio episode, 186
  poems and photo gallery, 492
  video interview, 720

Index of Skills **R69**

Assessment

Speaking and Listening

Argument, 738
  planning, 738
  present and evaluate, 739
  rehearsing, 739
Assessment
  oral presentation, 542
  podcast, 390
  speech, 748
  storytelling, 272, 868
  videorecorded commentary, 136
Class discussion
  discuss the questions, 29
  listen and evaluate, 29
  prepare your contribution, 29
  think about the question, 29
Compare-and-contrast chart, 59
Debate, 449
  establish rules, 449
  evaluate, 449
  explore and evaluate claims, 449
Dialogue, 793
  analyze characters, 793
  evaluate, 793
  plan, 793
  prepare delivery, 793
Discussion, 229
  defense, 229
  finding evidence, 229
  list, 229
  project plan, 229
  response, 229
Dramatic reading, 299
  choose examples, 299
  evaluate examples, 299
  listen to readings, 299
Explanatory talk, 532
  planning, 532
  present and evaluate, 533
  rehearsing, 533
Group discussion
  holding the discussion, 359
  preparation, 359
Image gallery, 317
  plan the project, 317
  prepare the script, 317
  present and discuss, 317
Media connection, 23, 44, 96
Multimedia presentation, 59
Narrative presentation, 858
  planning, 858
  rehearsing, 859
Note taking, 186, 346
Oral interpretation

analyze readings, 185
evaluate reading, 185
listen to readings, 185
Oral presentation, 117, 169
  analyze selection, 169
  choose a text, 169
  compare-and-contrast discussion, 491
  discussion plan, 491
  evaluate partner readings, 169
  informative talk, 491
  interview, 491
  presentation plan, 117
  public service announcement, 117
  Reader's Theater, 117
  rehearse presentation, 169
  research plan, 117
  role-play, 117
Oral response to literature, 807
Panel discussion, 380
  planning, 380
  presenting and evaluating, 381
  rehearsing, 381
Partner discussion, 779
Personal narrative
  gather evidence, 262
  plan with your group, 262
  present and evaluate, 263
  rehearse with your group, 263
Political infomercial, 59
Present an argument, 126
  plan with your group, 126
  present and evaluate, 127
  rehearse with your group, 127
Reading and discussion
  choose the passages, 309
  deliver reading and analysis, 309
  evaluation presentation, 309
  prepare delivery, 309
Small-group learning
  making a schedule, 71, 203, 329, 461, 703, 819
  strategies for, 68, 200
    clarify, 68, 200, 326, 458, 700, 816
    participate fully, 68, 200, 326, 458, 700, 816
    prepare, 68, 200, 326, 458, 700, 816
    support others, 68, 200, 326, 458, 700, 816
  working as a team, 70, 202, 460, 818
    apply the rules, 70, 202, 328, 460, 702, 818
    create a communication plan, 70, 202, 328, 460, 702, 818

    list your rules, 70, 202, 328, 460, 702, 818
    name your group, 70, 202, 328, 460, 702, 818
    roles for group projects, 71, 203, 329, 461, 703, 819
    take a position, 70, 202, 328, 460, 702, 818
Speeches, 39
  choose a position, 235
  deliver the speech, 39
  discussing the speech, 51
  evaluate the video, 51
  evaluate your presentation, 39
  plan your argument, 235
  practice and present, 51
  present and debate, 235
  tone, 299
  video recording of, 51
  write the speech, 39
Storytelling, 144
Thematic analysis, 685
Tone, 299
Videorecorded commentary, 136
Visual propaganda
  consider image choices, 59
  plan the project, 59
  prepare the script, 59
  present and discuss, 59
Whole-class discussion, 627
Whole-class learning strategies, 10
  clarify by asking questions, 10, 146, 282, 400, 552, 758
  interact and share ideas, 10, 146, 282, 400, 552, 758
  listen actively, 10, 146, 282, 400, 552, 758
  monitor understanding, 10, 146, 282, 400, 552, 758

Vocabulary

Academic vocabulary, 5
  analyze, 395, 450, 540
  assert, 547, 692, 746
  certify, 547, 692, 746
  colloquial, 753, 866
  confirm, 5, 60, 134
  conviction, 5, 60, 134
  deduction, 277, 388
  definitive, 547, 692, 746
  demonstrate, 5, 60, 134
  determine, 395, 450, 540
  epiphany, 753, 866
  establish, 5, 60, 134
  immutable, 547, 692, 746
  impact, 141, 192, 270

INDEX OF AUTHORS AND TITLES

The following authors and titles appear in the print and online versions of *my*Perspectives.

ADDITIONAL SELECTIONS: AUTHOR AND TITLE INDEX

The following authors and titles appear in the Online Literature Library.

ACKNOWLEDGMENTS AND CREDITS

Acknowledgments

The following selections appear in Grade 11 of *my*Perspectives. Some selections appear online only.

Arte Publico Press. "The Latin Deli" from *America's Review* by Judith Ortiz Cofer (©1992 Arte Publico Press—University of Houston).

Audible Inc. "How to Tell a True War Story" from *The Things They Carried* by Tim O'Brien. Copyright ©1990 by Tim O'Brien.

BBC Worldwide Americas, Inc. Boston Tea Party ©BBC Worldwide Learning; The U. S. Constitution ©BBC Worldwide Learning; Great Lives: Emily Dickinson—BBC Worldwide Learning; Civil Rights Marches ©BBC Worldwide Learning; CBS Sunday Morning segment "Mark Twain and Tom Sawyer" ©BBC Worldwide Learning.

Bloomsbury Publishing Plc. "Antojos," Copyright ©1991 by Julia Alvarez. Later published in slightly different form in *How the Garcia Girls Lost Their Accents*. Used with permission of Bloomsbury Publishing Plc.

Brooks Permissions. "Speech to the Young, Speech to the Progress-Toward," reprinted By Consent of Brooks Permissions.

Browning, Sarah. "The Fifth Fact," from *Whisky in the Garden of Eden* (The Word Words, Washington, DC, 2007). Used with permission.

Chopin, Kate. "The Story of An Hour" by Kate Chopin, originally appeared in *Vogue*, 1894.

CNN. The Hollywood Blacklist: 1947–1960 ©CNN.

Contently. Why Do Stories Matter? That's Like Asking Why You Should Eat ©Contently 2015

Copper Canyon Press. Hayden Carruth, "Bears at Raspberry Time" from *Collected Shorter Poems 1946–1991*. Copyright ©1983 by Hayden Carruth. Reprinted with the permission of The Permissions Company, Inc., on behalf of Copper Canyon Press, www.coppercanyonpress.org.

Daily Signal. "Rugged Individualism Fades from National Character" by Marion Smith, from *Daily Signal*, June 11, 2012; http://dailysignal.com/print/?post_id=99695. Used with permission.

Don Congdon Associates. "The Pedestrian," reprinted by permission of Don Congdon Associates, Inc. Copyright ©1951 by the Fortnightly Publishing Company, renewed 1979 by Ray Bradbury.

Douglass, Frederick. "What to the Slave is the 4th of July?" by Frederick Douglass (1818–1895).

Dunbar, Paul Laurence. "Douglass" by Paul Laurence Dunbar (1872–1906).

Espada, Martin. "Who Burns for the Perfection of Paper," from *city of coughing and dead radiators* by Martin Espada. Copyright ©1993 by Martin Espada. Used by permission of the author.

Estate of Galway Kinnell. "Reckless Genius" by Galway Kinnell, from Salon.com. Used with permission of the Estate of Galway Kinnell.

Faber & Faber, Ltd. (UK). "The Love Song of J. Alfred Prufrock" from *Collected Poems*, 1909–1062 by T.S. Eliot. Reprinted by permission of the publisher, Faber and Faber, Ltd.

Farrar, Straus and Giroux. Jacket design and excerpts from *The United States Constitution: A Graphic Adaptation* by Jonathan Hennessey, artwork by Aaron McConnell. Text copyright ©2008 by Jonathan Hennessey. Artwork Copyright ©2008 by Aaron McConnell. Reprinted by permission of Hill and Wang, a division of Farrar, Straus and Giroux, LLC.; "The Fish" from *The Complete Poems 1927–1979* by Elizabeth Bishop. Copyright ©1979, 1983 by Alice Helen Methfessel. Reprinted by permission of Farrar, Straus and Giroux, LLC.

Fischer, Claude. "Sweet Land of...Conformity?," *Boston Globe*, June 6, 2010, as adapted from the blog, Made in America.

Harold Ober Associates. "Dream Variations," reprinted by permission of Harold Ober Associates Incorporated. Copyright ©1994 by The Estate Of Langston Hughes; "I, Too," reprinted by permission of Harold Ober Associates Incorporated. Copyright ©1994 by The Estate Of Langston Hughes; "The Negro Speaks of Rivers," reprinted by permission of Harold Ober Associates Incorporated. Copyright ©1994 by The Estate Of Langston Hughes; "Refugee in America," reprinted by permission of Harold Ober Associates Incorporated. Copyright ©1994 by The Estate Of Langston Hughes.

Harper's Magazine. "The Leap," Copyright ©1990 Harper's Magazine. All rights reserved. Reproduced from the March issue by special permission.

HarperCollins Publishers. Pages 33–40 from *Dust Tracks on a Road* by Zora Neale Hurston. Copyright 1942 by Zora Neale Hurston; renewed ©1970 by John C. Hurston. Reprinted by permission of HarperCollins Publishers; "Untying the Knot" from *Pilgrim at Tinker Creek* by Annie Dillard. Copyright ©1974 by Annie Dillard. Reprinted by permission of HarperCollins Publishers.

HarperCollins Publishers Ltd. (UK). "Storyteller," "How to Tell a True War Story" from T*he Things They Carried* by Tim O'Brien. Copyright ©1990 by Tim O'Brien. Reprinted by permission of HarperCollins Publishers Ltd.

Harvard Law Review. "Reflections on the Bicentennial of the United States Constitution," republished with permission of *Harvard Law Review*, from Harvard Law Review, 101, November 1987; permission conveyed through Copyright Clearance Center, Inc.

Harvard University Press. "They shut me up in Prose," *The Poems of Emily Dickinson: Reading Edition*, edited by Ralph W. Franklin, Cambridge, Mass.: The Belknap Press of Harvard University Press, Copyright ©1998, 1999 by the President and Fellows of Harvard College. Copyright ©1951, 1955 by the President and Fellows of Harvard College. Copyright © renewed 1979, 1983 by the President and Fellows of Harvard College. Copyright ©1914, 1918, 1919, 1924, 1929, 1930, 1932, 1935, 1937, 1942 by Martha Dickinson Bianchi. Copyright ©1952, 1957, 1958, 1963, 1965 by Mary L. Hampson; "I'm Nobody," *The Poems of Emily Dickinson*, edited by Thomas H. Johnson, Cambridge, Mass.: The Belknap Press of Harvard University Press, Copyright ©1951, 1955 by the President and Fellows of Harvard College. Copyright ©renewed 1979, 1983 by the President and Fellows of Harvard College. Copyright ©1914, 1918, 1919, 1924, 1929, 1930, 1932, 1935, 1937, 1942 by Martha Dickinson Bianchi. Copyright ©1952, 1957, 1958, 1963, 1965 by Mary L. Hampson.

Henry Holt & Co. "A Balance Between Nature and Nurture" by Gloria Steinem. Copyright ©2005 by Gloria Steinem. From the audio book collection THIS I BELIEVE: The Personal Philosophies of Remarkable Men and Women edited by Jay Allison and Dan Gedimen. Copyright ©2006 by This I Believe, Inc. Used by permission of Henry Holt and Company, LLC. All rights reserved; "A Balance Between

material, outside of this publication, is prohibited. Interested parties must apply directly to Penguin Random House LLC for permission; "Mother to Son," "Dream Variation," "I, Too," "The Negro Speaks of Rivers," and "Refugee in America" from *The Collected Poems of Langston Hughes* by Langston Hughes, edited by Arnold Rampersad with David Roessel, Associate Editor, copyright ©1994 by the Estate of Langston Hughes. Used by permission of Alfred A. Knopf, an imprint of the Knopf Doubleday Publishing Group, a division of Penguin Random House LLC. All rights reserved. Any third party use of this material, outside of this publication, is prohibited. Interested parties must apply directly to Penguin Random House LLC for permission.

Recorded Books, LLC. Excerpts from *Farewell to Manzanar* by Jeanne W. Houston and James D. Houston. Copyright ©1973 by James D. Houston, renewed 2001 by Jeanne Wakatsuki Houston and James D. Houston. Used with permission of Recorded Books.

Russell & Volkening, Inc. "Untying the Knot," reprinted by the permission of Russell & Volkening as agents for the author. Copyright ©1974 by Annie Dillard, renewed in 2002 by Annie Dillard.

Seymour Agency LLC. "A Brief History of the Short Story" by D. F. McCourt, from AE Sci Fi, http://aescifi.ca/index.php/non-fiction/37-editorials/792-a-brief-history-of-the-short-story?tmpl=component&print=1&layout=default&page=. Used with permission of the author and Seymour Agency.

Shihab Nye, Naomi. "Hamadi," by permission of the author, Naomi Shihab Nye, 2015. First appeared in *America Street*.

Simon & Schuster, Inc. "Old Man at the Bridge," reprinted with the permission of Scribner, a division of Simon & Schuster, Inc. from *The Short Stories of Earnest Hemingway* by Ernest Hemingway. Copyright ©1938 by Ernest Hemingway. Copyright renewed 1966 by Mary Hemingway. All rights reserved.

Skyhorse Publishing. Excerpted from *Democracy is Not a Spectator Sport* by Arthur Blaustein with the permission of Skyhorse Publishing, Inc.

Sleight Brennan, Sandra. Giving Women the Vote by Sandra Sleight-Brennan ©Sandra Sleight-Brennan.

Sterling Lord Literistic, Inc. "A Literature of Place," reprinted by permission of SLL/Sterling Lord Literistic, Inc. Copyright by Barry Holstun Lopez.

Susan Bergholz Literary Services. "Antojos," Copyright ©1991 by Julia Alvarez. Later published in slightly different form in *How the Garcia Girls Lost Their Accents* by Algonquin Books of Chapel Hill. By permission of Susan Bergholz Literary Services, New York, NY and Lamy, NM. All rights reserved.

Symphony Space. "Everyday Use" by Alice Walker, as performed by Carmen de Lavallade at Symphony Space on January 19, 1994. Courtesy of Symphony Space.

Syracuse University Press. *Arthur C. Parker on the Iroquois: Iroquois Uses of Maize and Other Food Plants, The Code of Handsome Lake; The Seneca Prophet, The Constitution of the Five Nations* by Arthur Parker. Copyright ©1981. Used with permission of Syracuse University Press.

Tarbell, Ida. "What a Factory Can Teach a Housewife" by Ida Tarbell, *The Association Monthly*, Volume X (February 1916–February 1917).

Television Academy Foundation. George Takei on the Japanese internment camps during WWII ©Television Academy Foundation.

The White House Photo Office. Richard Blanco reading 2013 inaugural poem courtesy of The White House.

U.S. Supreme Court. "Supreme Court Decision / Chief Justice Earl Warren's opinion, Brown v. Board of Education, 347 U.S. 483 (1954).

University of New Mexico Press (Rights). From *The Way to Rainy Mountain* by N. Scott Momaday. Copyright ©1969 University of New Mexico Press, 1969.

University of Pittsburgh Press. "For Black Women Who Are Afraid" from *Tender*, by Toi Derricotte, ©1997. Reprinted by permission of the University of Pittsburgh Press.

Venture Literary. From *The United States Constitution: A Graphic Adaptation* by Jonathan Hennessey, illustrated by Aaron McConnell. Copyright 2008. Used with permission of Venture Literary, Inc.

W. W. Norton & Co. "Who Burns for the Perfection of Paper," from *city of coughing and dead radiators* by Martin Espada. Copyright ©1993 by Martin Espada. Used by permission of W. W. Norton & Company, Inc.

Writers' Representatives, Inc. From *America's Constitution: A Biography* by Akhil Amar. Copyright ©2005. Used by permission of Akhil Amar c/o Writers Representatives LLC, New York, NY 10011. All rights reserved.

Wylie Agency. Excerpt from "Books as Bombs: Why the women's movement needed 'The Feminine Mystique'" by Louis Menand, originally published in *The New Yorker*. Copyright ©2011 by Louis Menand, used by permission of The Wylie Agency LLC.; *The Crucible* by Arthur Miller. Copyright ©1952, 1953, 1954 by Arthur Miller, copyright renewed © 1980, 1981, 1982 by Arthur Miller, used by permission of The Wylie Agency LLC.; "Everything Stuck to Him" by Raymond Carver, collected in *What We Talk About When We Talk About Love*. Copyright ©1974, 1976, 1977, 1978, 1980, 1981 by Raymond Carver; 1989 by Tess Gallagher, used by her permission; "The Man to Send Rain Clouds" from *Storyteller* by Leslie Marmon Silko. Copyright ©1981, 2012 by Leslie Marmon Silko, used by permission of The Wylie Agency LLC.; "Housepainting" by Lan Samantha Chang. Copyright ©1995 by Lan Samantha Chang, used by permission of The Wylie Agency LLC.

Yale University Press. From "Mary Chesnut's Civil War" by Mary Chesnut edited by C. Vann Woodward. Copyright © 1981 by C. Vann Woodward, Sally Bland Metts, Barbara G. Carpenter, Sally Bland Johnson, and Katherine W. Herbert. All rights reserved. Used by permission of the publisher, Yale University Press.

Credits

Photo locators denoted as follows Top (T), Center (C), Bottom (B), Left (L), Right (R), Background (Bkgd)

Cover ©niroworld/Fotolia, (Bkgd) Brandon Bourdages/ 123RF GB Ltd.

vi (C) David Smart/Shutterstock, (Bkgd) Ja-images/Shutterstock; **viii** Hidesy/Shutterstock; **x** Corbis; **xii** Spaces Images/Blend Images/Getty Images; **xiv** Fred de Noyelle/Godong/Corbis; **xvi** Sergey Nivens/Fotolia; **2** (C) David Smart/Shutterstock, (Bkgd) Ja-images/Shutterstock; **3** (B) Ken Schulze/Shutterstock, (BCL) Fine Art Premium/Corbis, (BCR) Zack Frank/Shutterstock, (BL) Prints & Photographs Division, Library of Congress, LC-USZC4-5315.,(BR) Louis S. Glanzman/National Geographic/Getty Images, (C) DEA/G. Dagli Orti/Getty Images, (CBR) Ramn Cami/EyeEm/Getty Images, (CL) 2/Craig Brewer/Ocean/Corbis, (CR) Jacek Chabraszewski/Shuterstock, (CT) Sergign/Shutterstock, (T) LDDesign/Shutterstock, (TCL) GL Archive/Alamy, (TCR) J. Helgason/Shutterstock, (TL) SuperStock/Glow Images, (TR) Rawpixel/Shutterstock; **6** LDDesign/Shutterstock; **11** (B) Prints & Photographs Division, Library of Congress, LC-USZC4-5315., (BR) Fine Art Premium/Corbis, (C) 2/Craig Brewer/Ocean/Corbis, (T) SuperStock/Glow Images, (TR) GL Archive/ Alamy; **12** (L) World History Archive/Alamy, (R) SuperStock/Glow Images; **13** (C) Lvy Close Images/Alamy, (L) The Gallery Collection/ Corbis, (R) Larryhw/123RF; **14** North Wind Picture Archives/Alamy; **15** (C) People and Politics/Alamy, (L) Bettmann/Corbis, (R) Dbimages/Alamy; **16, 18, 24, 26, 28** GL Archive/Alamy; **17** Painting/Alamy; **21** Susan Law Cain/Shutterstock; **23** Hank Walker/The LIFE Picture Collection/Getty Images; **30** (B) People and Politics/Alamy, (T) Everett Historical/ Shutterstock; **31, 34, 36, 38** 2/Craig Brewer/Ocean/Corbis; **40, 42, 46, 48, 50** Fine Art Premium/Corbis; **41** Akademie/Alamy; **50** Fine Art Premium/Corbis; **53** Prints & Photographs Division, Library of Congress, LC-USZC4-5315.; **54** North Wind Picture Archives/Alamy; **55** Prints and Photographs Division, Library of Congress, cph.3a13536.; **56** (B) Fotosearch/Stringer/Getty,(T) Universal Images Group Limited/Alamy; **57** (BL) Universal Images Group Limited/Alamy, (C) Prints and Photographs Division, Library of Congress, cph.3a13536.; **57** (T) Prints & Photographs Division, Library of Congress, LC-USZC4-5315.; (TL) North Wind Picture Archives/Alamy; **58** Prints & Photographs Division, Library of Congress, LC-USZC4-5315.; **60** LDDesign/Shutterstock; **69** (B) Ken Schulze/ Shutterstock, (C) DEA/G. Dagli Orti/Getty Images, (T) Sergign/ Shutterstock; **72** (BL) Akhil Reed Amar,(TL) Sergign/Shutterstock; **73, 79, 80** Sergign/Shutterstock; **82** (BL) David Shoenfelt, (TL) Sergign/ Shutterstock; **90** Sergign/Shutterstock; **92** World History Archive/Alamy; **93, 98** DEA/G. Dagli Orti/Getty Images; **95** ClassicStock/Alamy; **103, 119** Everett Historical/Shutterstock; **110** Glasshouse Images/Alamy; **118, 120, 122, 124** Ken Schulze/Shutterstock; **129** (T): Rawpixel/ Shutterstock, (TC): J. Helgason/Shutterstock, (B): Louis S. Glanzman/ National Geographic/Getty Images, (BC): Zack Frank/Shutterstock, (C): Jacek Chabraszewski/Shuterstock, (CB): Ramn Cami/EyeEm/Getty Images; **138** Hidesy/Shutterstock; **139** (BC) Nebraska State Historical Society, [Digital ID, e.g., nbhips 12036], (BCR) Babayuka/Shutterstock, (BR) Denis Belitsky/Shutterstock, (C) Mansell/The LIFE Picture Collection/ Getty Images, (BC) Eugene Ivanov/Shutterstock, (B(CL)) Atomic/Alamy, (BCR) adoc-photos/Corbis, (CL) Win Nondakowit/123RF, (CR) Pictorial Press Ltd/Alamy, (TC) Zack Frank/Shutterstock, (T) Everett Historical/ Shutterstock, (TC) Richard Cavalleri/Shutterstock, (CL) Solarseven/ Shutterstock, (TL) Ralf Hettler/Getty Images, (TR) Pogonici/Shutterstock; **142** Everett Historical/Shutterstock; **147** (B) Atomic/Alamy, (BL) Win Nondakowit/123RF, (T) Ralf Hettler/Getty Images, (TL) Solarseven/ Shutterstock; **148** (L) Gianni Dagli Orti/The Art Archive at Art Resource, New York, (R) Bettmann/Corbis; **149** (L) Bettmann/Corbis, (R) Ralf Hettler/Getty Images; **150** (L) Everett Historical/Shutterstock, (R) De Agostini Picture Library/Getty Images; **151** Joe_Potato/Getty Images; **152,154,164,166,168** Solarseven/Shutterstock; **153** History Archives/ Alamy; **156** (B) Pictorial Press Ltd/Alamy, (T) Ase/Shutterstock; **160** Strelka/Shutterstock; **161** Sarun T/Shutterstock; **162** Alex Pix/ Shutterstock; **170, 172, 180, 182, 184** Win Nondakowit/123RF; **171** Atomic/Alamy; **173** Victor Tongdee/Shutterstock; **174** Liveshot/ Shutterstock; **176** Poprotskiy Alexey/Shutterstock; **177** Edward Bruns/ Shutterstock; **178** GlebStock/Shutterstock; **186** (TL) Win Nondakowit/123RF, (TR) Atomic/Alamy; **187** Atomic/Alamy; **189** (B) Atomic/Alamy, (T) Win Nondakowit/123RF; **190** (B) Atomic/Alamy, (T) Win Nondakowit/123RF; **192** Everett Historical/Shutterstock; **201** (B) Solomon D. Butcher/Nebraska State Historical Society, (BR) Eugene Ivanov/Shutterstock, (C) Mansell/The LIFE Picture Collection/Getty Images, (T) Richard Cavalleri/Shutterstock, (TR) Zack Frank/Shutterstock; **204** Everett Historical/Shutterstock; **205 ,201 ,212** Richard Cavalleri/ Shutterstock; **207** W2 Photography/Corbis; **214** Everett Collection/ Alamy; **215, 226, 228** Zack Frank/Shutterstock; **220** Nelson Sirlin/ Shutterstock; **223** Nobeastsofierce/Shutterstock; **231** Mansell/The LIFE Picture Collection/Getty Images; **232** The National Archives Records of the Patent and Trademark Office, 1836–1978; **234** Mansell/The LIFE Picture Collection/Getty Images; **236, 238, 244, 246** Eugene Ivanov/ Shutterstock; **237** Lebrecht Music and Arts Photo Library/Alamy; **248** E.O. Hoppe/Corbis; **249, 258, 260** Solomon D. Butcher/Nebraska State Historical Society; **254** Erich Lessing/Art Resource, New York; **265** (T): Pogonici/Shutterstock, (B): Denis Belitsky/Shutterstock, (BR): Babayuka/ Shutterstock, (C): adoc-photos/Corbis, (TR): Pictorial Press Ltd/Alamy; **274** (C) Corbis, (Bkgd) BBC Worldwide Learning; **275** (B) National Archives/Getty Images, (BC) fstockfoto/Shutterstock, (BCR) Harold M. Lambert/Lambert/Getty Images, (BL) National Photo Company Collection/Library of Congress, (BR) Bettmann/Corbis, (C) Library of Congress Prints and Photographs Division [LC-USZ62-75334], (BC) Heritage Image Partnership Ltd/Alamy, (CBL) Corbis, (CBR) Three Lions/ Getty Images, (CT) GL Archive/Alamy, (CTR) Jack Delano Farm Security Administration/Office of War Information Black-and-White Negatives collection, Prints & Photographs Division, Library of Congress, LC-USF34-040837-D, (T) Hill Street Studios/Getty Images, (TC) Corbis, (TCL) Kutay Tanir/Digital Vision/Getty Images, (TCR) Bettmann/Corbis, (TL) Everett Historical/Shutterstock, (TR) Herber W. Pelton/Corbis; **278** Hill Street Studios/Getty Images; **283** (B) Corbis, (BC) National Photo Company Collection/Library of Congress, (T) Everett Historical/ Shutterstock, (TC) Kutay Tanir/Digital Vision/Getty Images; **284** Everett Historical/Shutterstock; **285** (L) Bob Pardue-SC/Alamy, (R) Randy Raszler/ Fotolia; **286** (C) World History Archive/Alamy, (L, R) Everett Historical/ Shutterstock; **287** (L) Everett Historical/Shutterstock, (R) Jorisvo/ Shutterstock; **288** Library of Congress Prints and Photographs Division [LC-3a18122u]; 289,294,296,298 Kutay Tanir/Digital Vision/Getty Images; 300 Library of Congress Prints and Photographs Division [LC-3a32145u]; **301, 304, 306, 308** National Photo Company Collection/Library of Congress; **311, 312, 314, 316** Corbis; **313** (B) Corbis, (T) Everett Collection/AGE Fotostock; **315** Corbis, (BC) Everett Collection/AGE Fotostock; **327** (B) National Archives/Getty Images, (BC) fstockfoto/Shutterstock, (C) Library of Congress Prints and Photographs Division [LC-USZ62-75334]; **327** (BC) Heritage Image Partnership Ltd/ Alamy, (T) Corbis, (TC) GL Archive/Alamy; 330 Library of Congress Prints and Photographs Division [LC-3c19343u]; **331, 334, 336** Corbis; **338** (CL) Everett Collection Historical/Alamy, (TL) GL Archive/Alamy; **338** (TR) Library of Congress Prints and Photographs Division [LC-USZ62-75334]; **339, 343, 345** GL Archive/Alamy; **346** (CL) Sandra Sleight Brennan; **346, 350** GL Archive/Alamy; **346** (TR), **347, 349, 350** (CL) Library of Congress Prints and Photographs Division [LC-USZ62-75334]; **352** Missouri History Museum, St. Louis.; **353, 356, 358** Heritage Image Partnership Ltd/Alamy; **360** (CL) New York Times Co/Getty Images, (TL) fstockfoto/Shutterstock, (TR) National Archives/Getty Images; **361, 367, 369** fstockfoto/Shutterstock; **370** (CL) Jackie Mader/The Hechinger Report, (TL) fstockfoto/Shutterstock, (TR) National Archives/Getty Images; **379** Young Soldier: Separate Study of a Soldier Giving Water to a Wounded Companion, (detail) 1861, Winslow Homer, Oil, gouache, black crayon on canvas, 36 x 17.5 cm., United States, 1836–1910, Cooper-Hewitt, National Museum of Design; **383** (T) Herber W. Pelton/ Corbis; **383** (B) Bettmann/Corbis; 383 (BC) Harold M. Lambert/Lambert/ Getty Images; **383** (C): Jack Delano Farm Security Administration/Office of War Information Black-and-White Negatives collection, Prints & Photographs Division, Library of Congress, LC-USF34-040837-D, (BC): Three Lions/Getty Images, (TC): Bettmann/Corbis; **392** Spaces Images/ Blend Images/Getty Images; **393** (B) George Burba/123RF, (BC) Marilyn Angel Wynn/Nativestock/Getty Images, (BCL) Pictorial Press Ltd/Alamy, (BCR) Ekaterina Fribus/Fotolia, (BL) Herbert Kratky/123RF, (BR) Anna Baburkina/Shutterstock, (T) Library of Congress, (C) Lake County

*my*Perspectives™

AMERICAN LITERATURE

SAVVAS
LEARNING COMPANY

ISBN-13: 978-0-13-333882-9
ISBN-10:   0-13-333882-7

22   21

Welcome!

*my*Perspectives™ *English Language Arts* is a student-centered learning environment where you will analyze text, cite evidence, and respond critically about your learning. You will take ownership of your learning through goal-setting, reflection, independent text selection, and activities that allow you to collaborate with your peers.

Each unit of study includes selections of different genres—including multimedia—all related to a relevant and meaningful Essential Question. As you read, you will engage in activities that inspire thoughtful discussion and debate with your peers allowing you to formulate, and defend, your own perspectives.

*my*Perspectives *ELA* offers a variety of ways to interact directly with the text. You can annotate by writing in your print consumable, or you can annotate in your digital Student Edition. In addition, exciting technology allows you to access multimedia directly from your mobile device and communicate using an online discussion board!

We hope you enjoy using *my*Perspectives *ELA* as you develop the skills required to be successful throughout college and career.

Authors' Perspectives

*my*Perspectives is informed by a team of respected experts whose experiences working with students and study of instructional best practices have positively impacted education. From the evolving role of the teacher to how students learn in a digital age, our authors bring new ideas, innovations, and strategies that transform teaching and learning in today's competitive and interconnected world.

> " The teaching of English needs to focus on engaging a new generation of learners. How do we get them excited about reading and writing? How do we help them to envision themselves as readers and writers? And, how can we make the teaching of English more culturally, socially, and technologically relevant? Throughout the curriculum, we've created spaces that enhance youth voice and participation and that connect the teaching of literature and writing to technological transformations of the digital age."

Ernest Morrell, Ph.D.

is the Macy professor of English Education at Teachers College, Columbia University, a class of 2014 Fellow of the American Educational Research Association, and the Past-President of the National Council of Teachers of English (NCTE). He is also the Director of Teachers College's Institute for Urban and Minority Education (IUME). He is an award-winning author and in his spare time he coaches youth sports and writes poems and plays. Dr. Morrell has influenced the development of *my*Perspectives in Assessment, Writing & Research, Student Engagement, and Collaborative Learning.

Elfrieda Hiebert, Ph.D.

is President and CEO of TextProject, a nonprofit that provides resources to support higher reading levels. She is also a research associate at the University of California, Santa Cruz. Dr. Hiebert has worked in the field of early reading acquisition for 45 years, first as a teacher's aide and teacher of primary-level students in California and, subsequently, as a teacher and researcher. Her research addresses how fluency, vocabulary, and knowledge can be fostered through appropriate texts. Dr. Hiebert has influenced the development of *my*Perspectives in Vocabulary, Text Complexity, and Assessment.

> " The signature of complex text is challenging vocabulary. In the systems of vocabulary, it's important to provide ways to show how concepts can be made more transparent to students. We provide lessons and activities that develop a strong vocabulary and concept foundation—a foundation that permits students to comprehend increasingly more complex text."

Kelly Gallagher, M.Ed.

teaches at Magnolia High School in Anaheim, California, where he is in his thirty-first year. He is the former co-director of the South Basin Writing Project at California State University, Long Beach. Mr. Gallagher has influenced the development of *my*Perspectives in Writing, Close Reading, and the Role of Teachers.

> " The *my*Perspectives classroom is dynamic. The teacher inspires, models, instructs, facilitates, and advises students as they evolve and grow. When teachers guide students through meaningful learning tasks and then pass them ownership of their own learning, students become engaged and work harder. This is how we make a difference in student achievement—by putting students at the center of their learning and giving them the opportunities to choose, explore, collaborate, and work independently."

> " It's critical to give students the opportunity to read a wide range of highly engaging texts and to immerse themselves in exploring powerful ideas and how these ideas are expressed. In *my*Perspectives, we focus on building up students' awareness of how academic language works, which is especially important for English language learners."

Jim Cummins, Ph.D.

is a Professor Emeritus in the Department of Curriculum, Teaching and Learning of the University of Toronto. His research focuses on literacy development in multilingual school contexts as well as on the potential roles of technology in promoting language and literacy development. In recent years, he has been working actively with teachers to identify ways of increasing the literacy engagement of learners in multilingual school contexts. Dr. Cummins has influenced the development of *my*Perspectives in English Language Learner and English Language Development support.

UNIT 1 Writing Freedom
Words That Shaped a Nation

DIGITAL
PERSPECTIVES

SCAN FOR MULTIMEDIA — Use the BouncePage app
whenever you see "Scan
for Multimedia" to access:

- Unit Introduction Videos
- Media Selections/Media Enrichment
- Modeling Videos
- Selection Audio Recordings

Additional digital resources can be found in:

- Interactive Student Edition
- *my*Perspectives+

UNIT 2 The Individual and Society

Fitting In, or Standing Out?

COMPARE

These selections can be accessed via the Interactive Student Edition.

DIGITAL PERSPECTIVES

 SCAN FOR MULTIMEDIA

Use the BouncePage app whenever you see "Scan for Multimedia" to access:

- Unit Introduction Videos
- Media Selections/Media Enrichments
- Modeling Videos
- Selection Audio Recordings

Additional digital resources can be found in:

- Interactive Student Edition
- *my*Perspectives+

UNIT ③ Power, Protest, and Change

A Spirit of Reform

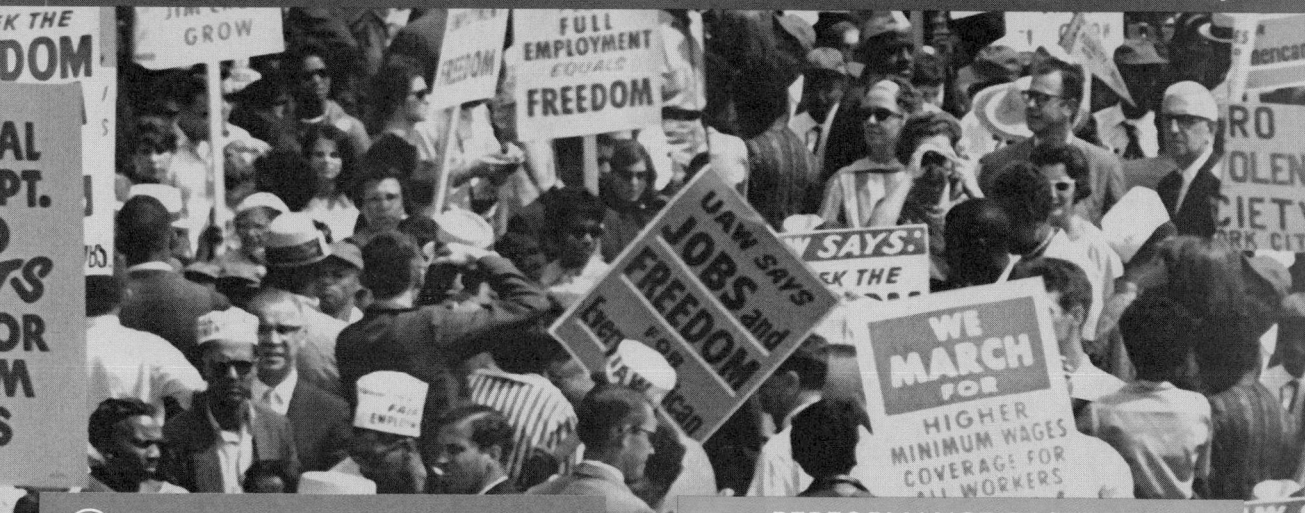

INDEPENDENT LEARNING

These selections can be accessed via the
Interactive Student Edition.

⊘ PERFORMANCE-BASED ASSESSMENT

UNIT REFLECTION

DIGITAL ⬀ PERSPECTIVES

 SCAN FOR MULTIMEDIA

Use the BouncePage app
whenever you see "Scan
for Multimedia" to access:

• Unit Introduction Videos
• Media Selections/Media Enrichment
• Modeling Videos
• Selection Audio Recordings

Additional digital resources can be found in:

• Interactive Student Edition
• *my*Perspectives+

UNIT 4 Grit and Grandeur

The Importance of Place

DIGITAL
PERSPECTIVES

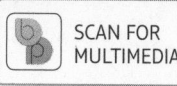 SCAN FOR MULTIMEDIA

Use the BouncePage app whenever you see "Scan for Multimedia" to access:

- Unit Introduction Videos
- Media Selections/Media Enrichment
- Modeling Videos
- Selection Audio Recordings

Additional digital resources can be found in:

- Interactive Student Edition
- *my*Perspectives+

UNIT **5** Facing Our Fears

Victims and Victors

INDEPENDENT LEARNING

These selections can be accessed via the Interactive Student Edition.

PERFORMANCE-BASED ASSESSMENT

UNIT REFLECTION

DIGITAL PERSPECTIVES

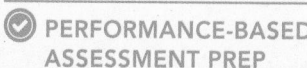

Use the BouncePage app whenever you see "Scan for Multimedia" to access:

- Unit Introduction Videos
- Media Selections/Media Enrichment
- Modeling Videos
- Selection Audio Recordings

Additional digital resources can be found in:

- Interactive Student Edition
- *my*Perspectives+

DIGITAL
PERSPECTIVES

SCAN FOR MULTIMEDIA

Use the BouncePage app whenever you see "Scan for Multimedia" to access:

• Unit Introduction Videos

• Media Selections/Media Enrichment

• Modeling Videos

• Selection Audio Recordings

Additional digital resources can be found in:

• Interactive Student Edition

• *my*Perspectives+

Interactive Student Edition

*my*Perspectives is completely interactive because you can work directly in your digital or print Student Edition.

All activities that you complete in your Interactive Student Edition are saved automatically. You can access your notes quickly so that reviewing work to prepare for tests and projects is easy!

Enter answers to prompts right in your digital Notebook and "turn it in" to your teacher.

The in-line annotation tool allows you to practice close reading by highlighting and adding comments about the text.

Interactivities are available for you to complete and submit directly to your teacher.

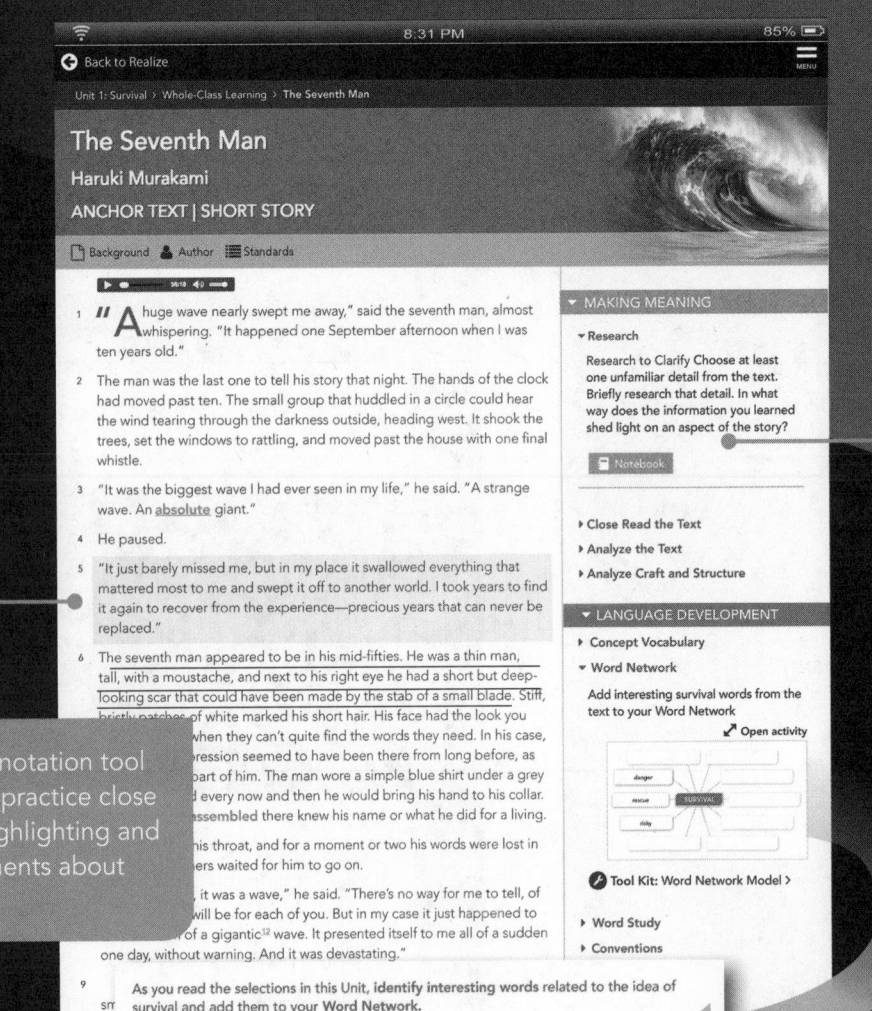

the shops in town lowered their shutters in preparation for the storm. Starting early in the morning, my father and brother went around the house nailing shut all the storm-doors, while my mother spent the day in the kitchen cooking emergency provisions. We filled bottles and canteens with water, and packed our most important possessions in rucksacks[2] for possible evacuation. To the adults, typhoons were an annoyance and a threat they had to face almost annually, but to the kids, removed as we were from such practical concerns, it was just a great big circus, a wonderful source of excitement.

12   Just after noon the color of the sky began to change all of a sudden. There was something strange and unreal about it. I stayed outside on the porch, watching the sky, until the wind began to howl and the rain began to beat against the house with a weird dry sound, like handfuls of sand. Then we closed the last storm-door and gathered together in one room of the darkened house, listening to the radio. This particular storm did not have a great deal of rain, it said, but the winds were doing a lot of damage, blowing roofs off houses and capsizing ships. Many people had been killed or injured by flying debris. Over and over again, they warned people against leaving their homes. Every once in a while, the house would creak and shudder as if a huge hand were shaking it, and sometimes there would be a great crash of some heavy-sounding object against a storm-door. My father guessed that these were tiles blowing off the neighbors' houses. For lunch we ate the rice and omelettes my mother had cooked, waiting for the typhoon to blow past.

13   But the typhoon gave no sign of blowing past. The radio said it had lost momentum[3] almost as soon as it came ashore at S. Province, and now it was moving north-east at the pace of a slow runner. The wind kept up its savage howling as it trie[...] [...]ood on land.

14   Perhaps an hour had gone by with the [...] when a hush fell over everything. All of a [...] could hear a bird crying in the distance. M[...] door a crack and looked outside. The win[...] rain had ceased to fall. Thick, gray clouds [...]

NOTES

This sentence is leading up to an exciting story.

CLOSE READ

ANNOTATE: In paragraph 12, annotate at least four vivid details about the storm. Underline those that compare one thing to another.

QUESTION: What is being compared? What picture does each detail create in the reader's mind?

CONCLUDE: How do these descriptions help you visualize the typhoon?

Typhoons are powerful, scary storms that can do a lot of damage.

Use the close-read prompts to guide you through an analysis of the text. You can highlight, circle, and underline the text right in your print Student Edition.

THE SEVENTH MAN

⛓ WORD NETWORK

Add interesting words related to survival from the text to your Word Network.

Respond to questions and activities directly in your book!

🗣 LANGUAGE DEVELOPMENT

Concept Vocabulary

| desperate | hallucination | profound |
| entranced | premonition | meditative |

Why These Words? These concept words help to reveal the emotional state of the seventh man. For example, when the wave approaches, the seventh man is *entranced*, waiting for it to attack. After the wave hits, the seventh man believes he sees his friend K. in the wave and claims that this experience was no *hallucination*. Notice that both words relate to experiences that occur only in the mind of the seventh man.

1. How does the concept vocabulary sharpen the reader's understanding of the mental or emotional state of the seventh man?
   These words are descriptive and precise.

2. What other words in the selection connect to this concept?
   ominous, overcome, nightmares

Practice

📓 **Notebook** The concept vocabulary words appear in "The Seventh Man."

1. Use each concept word in a sentence that demonstrates your understanding of the word's meaning.

2. Challenge yourself to replace the concept word with one or two synonyms. How does the word change affect the meaning of your sentence? For example, which sentence is stronger? Which has a more positive meaning?

Word Study

Latin Suffix: -tion The Latin suffix -tion often indicates that a word is a noun. Sometimes this suffix is spelled -ion or -ation. In any of its forms, it means "act, state, or condition of." In "The Seventh Man," the word *premonition* means "the state of being forewarned."

1. Record a definition of *hallucination* based on your understanding of its root word and the meaning of the suffix -tion.
   The condition of seeing something that is not real

2. Look back at paragraphs 37–40 and find two other words that end with the suffix -tion. In each case, identify the root word that has been combined with the suffix. Record a definition for each word.
   cooperate + -tion—the state of working together
   direct + -tion—the state of being guided

Digital Resources

You can access digital resources from your print Student Edition, or from Savvas Realize™.

To watch videos or listen to audio from your print Student Edition, all you need is a device with a camera and Pearson's BouncePages app!

ANCHOR TEXT | SHORT STORY

The Seventh Man

Haruki Murakami

BACKGROUND

Hurricanes that originate in the northwest Pacific Ocean are called typhoons. They can stretch up to 500 miles in diameter and produce high winds, heavy rains, enormous waves, and severe flooding. On average, Japan is hit by three severe typhoons each year due to its location and climatic conditions.

SCAN FOR MULTIMEDIA

1   "A huge wave nearly swept me away," said the seventh man, almost whispering. "It happened one September afternoon when I was ten years old."

2   The man was the last one to tell his story that night. The hands of the clock had moved past ten. The small group that huddled in

NOTES

CLOSE READ
ANNOTATE: Mark details in paragraph 2 that

How to watch a video or listen to audio:

1. Download Pearson's BouncePages App from the Apple App or Google Play Store.

2. Open the app on your mobile device.

3. Aim your camera so the page from your Student Edition is viewable on your screen.

4. Tap the screen to scan the page.

5. Press the "Play" button on the page that appears on your device.

6. View the video or listen to the audio directly from your device!

Amazing Stories of Rescues and Survival in Nepal
122

Digital resources, including audio and video, can be accessed in the Interactive Student Edition. Your teacher might also assign activities for you to complete online.

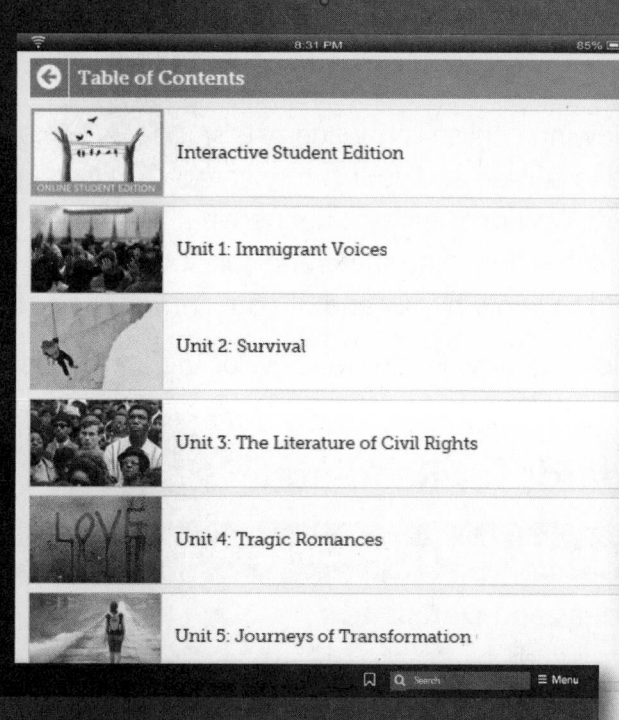

Table of Contents

Interactive Student Edition

Unit 1: Immigrant Voices

Unit 2: Survival

Unit 3: The Literature of Civil Rights

Unit 4: Tragic Romances

Unit 5: Journeys of Transformation

8:31 PM   85%

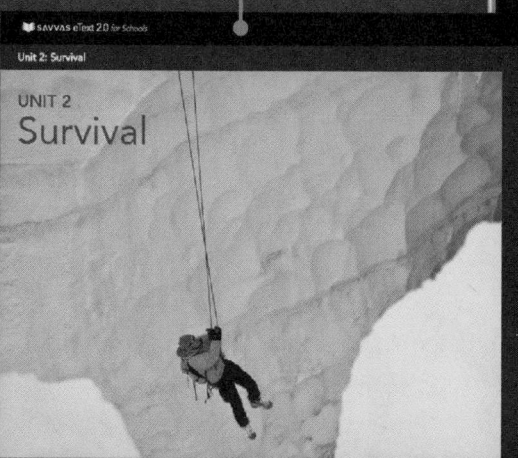

SAVVAS eText 2.0 for Schools

Unit 2: Survival

UNIT 2
Survival

UNIT INTRODUCTION

WHOLE-CLASS LEARNING

SMALL-GROUP LEARNING

INDEPENDENT LEARNING

PERFORMANCE-BASED ASSESSMENT

UNIT REFLECTION

The quest for survival is powerful. It is primitive. What determines who lives and who dies?

You will also find digital novels, interactive lessons, and games!

The Scarlet Letter by NATHANIEL HAWTHORNE   Go to page [3] of 617

THE SCARLET LETTER
By Nathaniel Hawthorne

Illustrated by Hugh Thomson
This book was originally published in 1850 and is in the public domain.

Standards Overview

The following English Language Arts standards will prepare you to succeed in college and your future career. The College and Career Readiness Anchor Standards define what you need to achieve by the end of high school, and the grade-specific Standards define what you need to know by the end of your current grade level.

The following provides an overview of the Standards.

Standards for Reading

College and Career Readiness Anchor Standards for Reading
Key Ideas and Details
1. Read closely to determine what the text says explicitly and to make logical inferences from it; cite specific textual evidence when writing or speaking to support conclusions drawn from the text.
2. Determine central ideas or themes of a text and analyze their development; summarize the key supporting details and ideas.
3. Analyze how and why individuals, events, and ideas develop and interact over the course of a text.
Craft and Structure
4. Interpret words and phrases as they are used in a text, including determining technical, connotative, and figurative meanings, and analyze how specific word choices shape meaning or tone.
5. Analyze the structure of texts, including how specific sentences, paragraphs, and larger portions of the text (e.g., a section, chapter, scene, or stanza) relate to each other and the whole.
6. Assess how point of view or purpose shapes the content and style of a text.
Integration of Knowledge and Ideas
7. Integrate and evaluate content presented in diverse formats and media, including visually and quantitatively, as well as in words.
8. Delineate and evaluate the argument and specific claims in a text, including the validity of the reasoning as well as the relevance and sufficiency of the evidence.
9. Analyze how two or more texts address similar themes or topics in order to build knowledge or to compare the approaches the authors take.
Range of Reading and Level of Text Complexity
10. Read and comprehend complex literary and informational texts independently and proficiently.

Grade 11 Reading Standards for Literature

Standard

Key Ideas and Details

Cite strong and thorough textual evidence to support analysis of what the text says explicitly as well as inferences drawn from the text, including determining where the text leaves matters uncertain.

Determine two or more themes or central ideas of a text and analyze their development over the course of the text, including how they interact and build on one another to produce a complex account; provide an objective summary of the text.

Analyze the impact of the author's choices regarding how to develop and relate elements of a story or drama (e.g., where a story is set, how the action is ordered, how the characters are introduced and developed).

Craft and Structure

Determine the meaning of words and phrases as they are used in the text, including figurative and connotative meanings; analyze the impact of specific word choices on meaning and tone, including words with multiple meanings or language that is particularly fresh, engaging, or beautiful. (Include Shakespeare as well as other authors.)

Analyze how an author's choices concerning how to structure specific parts of a text (e.g., the choice of where to begin or end a story, the choice to provide a comedic or tragic resolution) contribute to its overall structure and meaning as well as its aesthetic impact.

Analyze a case in which grasping a point of view requires distinguishing what is directly stated in a text from what is really meant (e.g., satire, sarcasm, irony, or understatement).

Integration of Knowledge and Ideas

Analyze multiple interpretations of a story, drama, or poem (e.g., recorded or live production of a play or recorded novel or poetry), evaluating how each version interprets the source text. (Include at least one play by Shakespeare and one play by an American dramatist.)

Demonstrate knowledge of eighteenth-, nineteenth- and early-twentieth-century foundational works of American literature, including how two or more texts from the same period treat similar themes or topics.

Range of Reading and Level of Text Complexity

By the end of grade 11, read and comprehend literature, including stories, dramas, and poems, in the grades 11–CCR text complexity band proficiently, with scaffolding as needed at the high end of the range.

Standards Overview

Grade 11 Reading Standards for Informational Text
Standard
Key Ideas and Details
Cite strong and thorough textual evidence to support analysis of what the text says explicitly as well as inferences drawn from the text, including determining where the text leaves matters uncertain.
Determine two or more central ideas of a text and analyze their development over the course of the text, including how they interact and build on one another to provide a complex analysis; provide an objective summary of the text.
Analyze a complex set of ideas or sequence of events and explain how specific individuals, ideas, or events interact and develop over the course of the text.
Craft and Structure
Determine the meaning of words and phrases as they are used in a text, including figurative, connotative, and technical meanings; analyze how an author uses and refines the meaning of a key term or terms over the course of a text (e.g., how Madison defines *faction* in *Federalist* No. 10).
Analyze and evaluate the effectiveness of the structure an author uses in his or her exposition or argument, including whether the structure makes points clear, convincing, and engaging.
Determine an author's point of view or purpose in a text in which the rhetoric is particularly effective, analyzing how style and content contribute to the power, persuasiveness or beauty of the text.
Integration of Knowledge and Ideas
Integrate and evaluate multiple sources of information presented in different media or formats (e.g., visually, quantitatively) as well as in words in order to address a question or solve a problem.
Delineate and evaluate the reasoning in seminal U.S. texts, including the application of constitutional principles and use of legal reasoning (e.g., in U.S. Supreme Court majority opinions and dissents) and the premises, purposes, and arguments in works of public advocacy (e.g., *The Federalist*, presidential addresses).
Analyze seventeenth-, eighteenth-, and nineteenth-century foundational U.S. documents of historical and literary significance (including The Declaration of Independence, the Preamble to the Constitution, the Bill of Rights, and Lincoln's Second Inaugural Address) for their themes, purposes, and rhetorical features.
Range of Reading and Level of Text Complexity
By the end of grade 11, read and comprehend literary nonfiction in the grades 11–CCR text complexity band proficiently, with scaffolding as needed at the high end of the range.

Standards for Writing

College and Career Readiness Anchor Standards for Writing

Text Types and Purposes

1. Write arguments to support claims in an analysis of substantive topics or texts, using valid reasoning and relevant and sufficient evidence.

2. Write informative/explanatory texts to examine and convey complex ideas and information clearly and accurately through the effective selection, organization, and analysis of content.

3. Write narratives to develop real or imagined experiences or events using effective technique, well-chosen details, and well-structured event sequences.

Production and Distribution of Writing

4. Produce clear and coherent writing in which the development, organization, and style are appropriate to task, purpose, and audience.

5. Develop and strengthen writing as needed by planning, revising, editing, rewriting, or trying a new approach.

6. Use technology, including the Internet, to produce and publish writing and to interact and collaborate with others.

Research to Build and Present Knowledge

7. Conduct short as well as more sustained research projects based on focused questions, demonstrating understanding of the subject under investigation.

8. Gather relevant information from multiple print and digital sources, assess the credibility and accuracy of each source, and integrate the information while avoiding plagiarism.

9. Draw evidence from literary or informational texts to support analysis, reflection, and research.

Range of Writing

10. Write routinely over extended time frames (time for research, reflection, and revision) and shorter time frames (a single sitting or a day or two) for a range of tasks, purposes, and audiences.

Grade 11 Writing Standards

Standard

Text Types and Purposes

Write arguments to support claims in an analysis of substantive topics or texts, using valid reasoning and relevant and sufficient evidence.

Introduce precise, knowledgeable claim(s), establish the significance of the claim(s), distinguish the claim(s) from alternate or opposing claims, and create an organization that logically sequences claim(s), counterclaims, reasons, and evidence.

Standards Overview

Grade 11 Writing Standards
Standard
Text Types and Purposes (continued)
Develop claim(s) and counterclaims fairly and thoroughly, supplying the most relevant evidence for each while pointing out the strengths and limitations of both in a manner that anticipates the audience's knowledge level, concerns, values, and possible biases.
Use words, phrases, and clauses as well as varied syntax to link the major sections of the text, create cohesion, and clarify the relationships between claim(s) and reasons, between reasons and evidence, and between claim(s) and counterclaims.
Establish and maintain a formal style and objective tone while attending to the norms and conventions of the discipline in which they are writing.
Provide a concluding statement or section that follows from and supports the argument presented.
Write informative/explanatory texts to examine and convey complex ideas, concepts, and information clearly and accurately through the effective selection, organization, and analysis of content.
Introduce a topic; organize complex ideas, concepts, and information so that each new element builds on that which precedes it to create a unified whole; include formatting (e.g., headings), graphics (e.g., figures, tables), and multimedia when useful to aiding comprehension.
Develop the topic thoroughly by selecting the most significant and relevant facts, extended definitions, concrete details, quotations, or other information and examples appropriate to the audience's knowledge of the topic.
Use appropriate and varied transitions and syntax to link the major sections of the text, create cohesion, and clarify the relationships among complex ideas and concepts.
Use precise language, domain-specific vocabulary, and techniques such as metaphor, simile, and analogy to manage the complexity of the topic.
Establish and maintain a formal style and objective tone while attending to the norms and conventions of the discipline in which they are writing.
Provide a concluding statement or section that follows from and supports the information or explanation presented (e.g., articulating implications or the significance of the topic).
Write narratives to develop real or imagined experiences or events using effective technique, well-chosen details, and well-structured event sequences.
Engage and orient the reader by setting out a problem, situation, or observation and its significance, establishing one or multiple point(s) of view, and introducing a narrator and/or characters; create a smooth progression of experiences or events.
Use narrative techniques, such as dialogue, pacing, description, reflection, and multiple plot lines, to develop experiences, events, and/or characters.

Grade 11 Writing Standards

Standard

Text Types and Purposes (continued)

Use a variety of techniques to sequence events so that they build on one another to create a coherent whole and build toward a particular tone and outcome (e.g., a sense of mystery, suspense, growth, or resolution).

Use precise words and phrases, telling details, and sensory language to convey a vivid picture of the experiences, events, setting, and/or characters.

Provide a conclusion that follows from and reflects on what is experienced, observed, or resolved over the course of the narrative.

Production and Distribution of Writing

Produce clear and coherent writing in which the development, organization, and style are appropriate to task, purpose, and audience. (Grade-specific expectations for writing types are defined in standards 1–3 above.)

Develop and strengthen writing as needed by planning, revising, editing, rewriting, or trying a new approach, focusing on addressing what is most significant for a specific purpose and audience. (Editing for conventions should demonstrate command of Language standards 1–3 up to and including grades 11–12)

Use technology, including the Internet, to produce, publish, and update individual or shared writing products in response to ongoing feedback, including new arguments or information.

Research to Build and Present Knowledge

Conduct short as well as more sustained research projects to answer a question (including a self-generated question) or solve a problem; narrow or broaden the inquiry when appropriate; synthesize multiple sources on the subject, demonstrating understanding of the subject under investigation.

Gather relevant information from multiple authoritative print and digital sources, using advanced searches effectively; assess the strengths and limitations of each source in terms of the task, purpose, and audience; integrate information into the text selectively to maintain the flow of ideas, avoiding plagiarism and overreliance on any one source and following a standard format for citation.

Draw evidence from literary or informational texts to support analysis, reflection, and research.

Apply *grades 11–12 Reading standards* to literature (e.g., "Demonstrate knowledge of eighteenth-, nineteenth- and early-twentieth-century foundational works of American literature, including how two or more texts from the same period treat similar themes or topics").

Apply *grades 11–12 Reading standards* to literary nonfiction (e.g., "Delineate and evaluate the reasoning in seminal U.S. texts, including the application of constitutional principles and use of legal reasoning [e.g., in U.S. Supreme Court Case majority opinions and dissents] and the premises, purposes, and arguments in works of public advocacy [e.g., *The Federalist*, presidential addresses]").

Range of Writing

Write routinely over extended time frames (time for research, reflection, and revision) and shorter time frames (a single sitting or a day or two) for a range of tasks, purposes, and audiences.

Standards Overview

Standards for Speaking and Listening

Grade 11 Standards for Speaking and Listening

Standard

Comprehension and Collaboration

Initiate and participate effectively in a range of collaborative discussions (one-on-one, in groups, and teacher-led) with diverse partners on *grades 11–12 topics, texts, and issues*, building on others' ideas and expressing their own clearly and persuasively.

Come to discussions prepared, having read and researched material under study; explicitly draw on that preparation by referring to evidence from texts and other research on the topic or issue to stimulate a thoughtful, well-reasoned exchange of ideas.

Work with peers to promote civil, democratic discussions and decision-making, set clear goals and deadlines, and establish individual roles as needed.

Propel conversations by posing and responding to questions that probe reasoning and evidence; ensure a hearing for a full range of positions on a topic or issue; clarify, verify, or challenge ideas and conclusions; and promote divergent and creative perspectives.

Respond thoughtfully to diverse perspectives; synthesize comments, claims, and evidence made on all sides of an issue; resolve contradictions when possible; and determine what additional information or research is required to deepen the investigation or complete the task.

Integrate multiple sources of information presented in diverse formats and media (e.g., visually, quantitatively, orally) in order to make informed decisions and solve problems, evaluating the credibility and accuracy of each source and noting any discrepancies among the data.

Evaluate a speaker's point of view, reasoning, and use of evidence and rhetoric, assessing the stance, premises, links among ideas, word choice, points of emphasis, and tone used.

Presentation of Knowledge and Ideas

Present information, findings, and supporting evidence, conveying a clear and distinct perspective, such that listeners can follow the line of reasoning, alternative or opposing perspectives are addressed, and the organization, development, substance, and style are appropriate to purpose, audience, and a range of formal and informal tasks.

Make strategic use of digital media (e.g., textual, graphical, audio, visual, and interactive elements) in presentations to enhance understanding of findings, reasoning, and evidence and to add interest.

Adapt speech to a variety of contexts and tasks, demonstrating a command of formal English when indicated or appropriate. (See grades 11–12 Language standards 1 and 3 for specific expectations.)

Standards Overview

Standards for Language

College and Career Readiness Anchor Standards for Language
Conventions of Standard English
1. Demonstrate command of the conventions of standard English grammar and usage when writing or speaking.
2. Demonstrate command of the conventions of standard English capitalization, punctuation, and spelling when writing.
Knowledge of Language
3. Apply knowledge of language to understand how language functions in different contexts, to make effective choices for meaning or style, and to comprehend more fully when reading or listening.
Vocabulary Acquisition and Use
4. Determine or clarify the meaning of unknown and multiple-meaning words and phrases by using context clues, analyzing meaningful word parts, and consulting general and specialized reference materials, as appropriate.
5. Demonstrate understanding of figurative language, word relationships, and nuances in word meanings.
6. Acquire and use accurately a range of general academic and domain-specific words and phrases sufficient for reading, writing, speaking, and listening at the college and career readiness level; demonstrate independence in gathering vocabulary knowledge when considering a word or phrase important to comprehension or expression.

Grade 11 Standards for Language
Standard
Conventions of Standard English
Demonstrate command of the conventions of standard English grammar and usage when writing or speaking.
Apply the understanding that usage is a matter of convention, can change over time, and is sometimes contested.
Resolve issues of complex or contested usage, consulting references (e.g., *Merriam-Webster's Dictionary of English Usage*, *Garner's Modern American Usage*) as needed.
Demonstrate command of the conventions of standard English capitalization, punctuation, and spelling when writing.
Observe hyphenation conventions.
Spell correctly.

Grade 11 Standards for Language

Standard

Knowledge of Language

Apply knowledge of language to understand how language functions in different contexts, to make effective choices for meaning or style, and to comprehend more fully when reading or listening.

Vary syntax for effect, consulting references (e.g., Tufte's *Artful Sentences*) for guidance as needed; apply an understanding of syntax to the study of complex texts when reading.

Vocabulary Acquisition and Use

Determine or clarify the meaning of unknown and multiple-meaning words and phrases based on *grades 11–12 reading and content*, choosing flexibly from a range of strategies.

Use context (e.g., the overall meaning of a sentence, paragraph, or text; a word's position or function in a sentence) as a clue to the meaning of a word or phrase.

Identify and correctly use patterns of word changes that indicate different meanings or parts of speech (e.g., *conceive, conception, conceivable*).

Consult general and specialized reference materials (e.g., dictionaries, glossaries, thesauruses), both print and digital, to find the pronunciation of a word or determine or clarify its precise meaning, its part of speech, its etymology, or its standard usage.

Verify the preliminary determination of the meaning of a word or phrase (e.g., by checking the inferred meaning in context or in a dictionary).

Demonstrate understanding of figurative language, word relationships, and nuances in word meanings.

Interpret figures of speech (e.g., hyperbole, paradox) in context and analyze their role in the text.

Analyze nuances in the meaning of words with similar denotations.

Acquire and use accurately general academic and domain-specific words and phrases, sufficient for reading, writing, speaking, and listening at the college and career readiness level; demonstrate independence in gathering vocabulary knowledge when considering a word or phrase important to comprehension or expression.

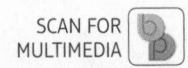

Grit and Grandeur

The Importance of Place

Ken Burns: Secrets of
Yellowstone National Park

② Discuss It Have you ever experienced a feeling of being changed by a place you visited? Describe what triggered the feeling.

Write your response before sharing your ideas.

UNIT 4

UNIT INTRODUCTION

ESSENTIAL QUESTION: **What is the relationship between literature and place?**

LAUNCH TEXT
EXPLANATORY MODEL
Planning Your Trip to Gold Country

 WHOLE-CLASS LEARNING

HISTORICAL PERSPECTIVES

Focus Period: 1880–1920
Bright Horizons, Challenging Realities

ANCHOR TEXT: MEMOIR
from Life on the Mississippi
Mark Twain
▸ MEDIA CONNECTION: Mark Twain and Tom Sawyer

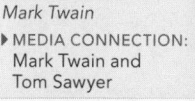

ANCHOR TEXT: SHORT STORY
The Notorious Jumping Frog of Calaveras County
Mark Twain

ANCHOR TEXT: SHORT STORY
A White Heron
Sarah Orne Jewett

PERFORMANCE TASK
WRITING FOCUS:
Write an Explanatory Essay

 SMALL-GROUP LEARNING

LITERARY CRITICISM
A Literature of Place
Barry Lopez

MEDIA: FINE ART GALLERY
American Regional Art

AUTOBIOGRAPHY
from Dust Tracks on a Road
Zora Neale Hurston

POETRY COLLECTION 1
Chicago

Wilderness
Carl Sandburg
▸ MEDIA CONNECTION: Carl Sandburg Reads "Wilderness"

MEDIA: PHOTO GALLERY
Sandburg's Chicago

POETRY COLLECTION 2
In the Longhouse, Oneida Museum
Roberta Hill

Cloudy Day
Jimmy Santiago Baca

MEMOIR
Introduction *from* The Way to Rainy Mountain
N. Scott Momaday

PERFORMANCE TASK
SPEAKING AND LISTENING FOCUS:
Give an Explanatory Talk

 INDEPENDENT LEARNING

SHORT STORY
The Rockpile
James Baldwin

POETRY
The Latin Deli: An Ars Poetica
Judith Ortiz Cofer

ESSAY
Untying the Knot
Annie Dillard

POETRY COLLECTION 3
The Wood-Pile

Birches
Robert Frost

PERFORMANCE-BASED ASSESSMENT PREP
Review Evidence for an Explanatory Essay

PERFORMANCE-BASED ASSESSMENT

Explanatory Text: Essay and Oral Presentation
PROMPT: **What makes certain places live on in our memory?**

Unit Goals

Throughout this unit, you will deepen your perspective on the importance of place by reading, writing, speaking, listening, and presenting. These goals will help you succeed on the Unit Performance-Based Assessment.

Rate how well you meet these goals right now. You will revisit your ratings later when you reflect on your growth during this unit.

SCALE				
1	2	3	4	5
NOT AT ALL WELL	NOT VERY WELL	SOMEWHAT WELL	VERY WELL	EXTREMELY WELL

READING GOALS

	1	2	3	4	5

- Read a variety of texts to gain the knowledge and insight needed to write about the importance of place.

- Expand your knowledge and use of academic and concept vocabulary.

WRITING AND RESEARCH GOALS

	1	2	3	4	5

- Write an explanatory text that develops a topic thoroughly and includes evidence from research.

- Conduct research projects of various lengths to explore a topic and clarify meaning.

LANGUAGE GOALS

	1	2	3	4	5

- Make effective style choices, including those regarding sentence variety, figurative language, and diction.

- Correctly use dashes and hyphens.

SPEAKING AND LISTENING GOALS

	1	2	3	4	5

- Collaborate with your team to build on the ideas of others, develop consensus, and communicate.

- Integrate audio, visuals, and text to present information.

≡ STANDARDS

Language
Acquire and use accurately general academic and domain-specific words and phrases, sufficient for reading, writing, speaking, and listening at the college and career readiness level; demonstrate independence in gathering vocabulary knowledge when considering a word or phrase important to comprehension or expression.

SCAN FOR MULTIMEDIA

Academic Vocabulary: Explanatory Text

Understanding and using academic terms can help you read, write, and speak with precision and clarity. Here are five academic words that will be useful in this unit as you analyze and write explanatory texts.

Complete the chart.

1. Review each word, its root, and the mentor sentences.

2. Use the information and your own knowledge to predict the meaning of each word.

3. For each word, list at least two related words.

4. Refer to a dictionary or other resources if needed.

 TIP

FOLLOW THROUGH
Study the words in this chart, and mark them or their forms wherever they appear in the unit.

WORD	MENTOR SENTENCES	PREDICT MEANING	RELATED WORDS
analyze ROOT: **-lys-** "break down"	1. The investigators will *analyze* the scene for signs of arson. 2. To *analyze* a poem, start by examining its words and phrasing.		analysis; analytical
subordinate ROOT: **-ord-** "order"	1. It's important to show how *subordinate* ideas relate to the main idea. 2. In her first job, she was in a *subordinate* role, but she later became chief executive of the company.		
literal ROOT: **-liter-** "letter"	1. The original, *literal* meaning of "awful" is "full of awe," but now it means "terrible." 2. In her essay, she explains both the *literal* and symbolic meanings of the movie.		
determine ROOT: **-term-** "end"	1. The choices you make now could *determine* your future options. 2. We must do more than treat the symptoms; we must *determine* the cause of the illness.		
trivialize ROOT: **-via-** "way"; "path"	1. Politicians tend to *trivialize* issues that they do not consider important. 2. Asher laughed at Maya's error, but he didn't mean to *trivialize* her struggle.		

Planning Your Trip to Gold Country

LAUNCH TEXT | EXPLANATORY TEXT

This selection is an example of an **explanatory text**, a type of writing in which the author explores the complexities of a topic, describes how to accomplish a task, or details how a process works. This is the type of writing you will develop in the Performance-Based Assessment at the end of the unit.

As you read, consider how each paragraph connects to the ideas presented in the introduction. Mark examples that the author provides to show the different types of trips a reader might undertake.

NOTES

1 Before you set off to explore California's Gold Country, you must make two key decisions: Choose the length of your trip, and determine the sort of explorer you are. First, decide the length of your trip, because that will tell you how much exploring you will be able to do. A map of the Sierra Nevada foothills will show you at a glance that Gold Country, the area where most of the California Gold Rush took place, extends from the Tahoe National Forest to the area around Lake Isabella, nearly 400 miles south. Second, decide what kind of explorer you are. Do you prefer museum-hopping and sightseeing, or do you want to get your hands dirty and find out what it was like to be a gold-seeker in the 1840s? Would you like to see history reenacted, or do you want to see the natural beauty of this special region?

2 If you have just a short time to spend in Gold Country, consider visiting the historic highlights. California's capital city, Sacramento, was founded in 1848 by John Sutter, Jr., a major Gold Rush figure. You may still visit the fort he built there and take a walking tour through streets lined with restored nineteenth-century buildings, departing on your tour from the excellent and informative Sacramento History Museum. From Sacramento, it's just an hour's drive north to Coloma, a tiny village along the sparkling American River. Coloma is home to Marshall Gold Discovery Park, which offers visitors dozens of activities that allow them to explore the history of the Gold Rush. Coloma is a must-see, because it is the very first place where gold was found in the Sierra Nevada foothills.

SCAN FOR MULTIMEDIA

3   If you have more time to spend and are eager for adventure, consider the trip my brother and I made last year. We drove from Coloma south to Jamestown along historic Highway 49. Stunned by the beautiful views, we enjoyed every mile. As we wound through hills and valleys dotted with wildflower meadows and piñon pines, we could imagine would-be miners on horses and in wagons making their way through the same landscape 165 years ago.

4   Jamestown boasts a number of businesses that allow you to take pans, trowels, and boots into the American River and test your ability to find gold. Sam and I found nothing but iron pyrite, the "fool's gold" that deceived many a Forty-Niner, but we had a thrilling time in the chilly water under a stark, blue sky. Searching Jamestown sites on the Internet will turn up a variety of tours and gold-prospecting adventures, and you can choose the one that best matches your needs.

5   Nature lovers should not pass up the opportunity to visit Yosemite, the world's first national park. The history of the region is a sad one; the spectacular Yosemite Valley was home to the native Ahwahnechee people before the influx of miners displaced them in the 1850s. Miners tore holes in the stately mountains and despoiled the clear water of the rivers until Abraham Lincoln signed a grant to preserve this territory for all time. Since that time, Yosemite's soaring cliffs and turbulent waterfalls have remained unique among American landscapes.

6   Start with a map and a schedule, and plan to spend at least a day at each major stop. Use the Internet to build your trip step by step, choosing the activities that suit your interests and fit into your timetable. There is plenty to do in Gold Country, no matter what kind of traveler you happen to be. Every acre of the region offers magnificent vistas and living tableaus of a significant era in American history. ❧

NOTES

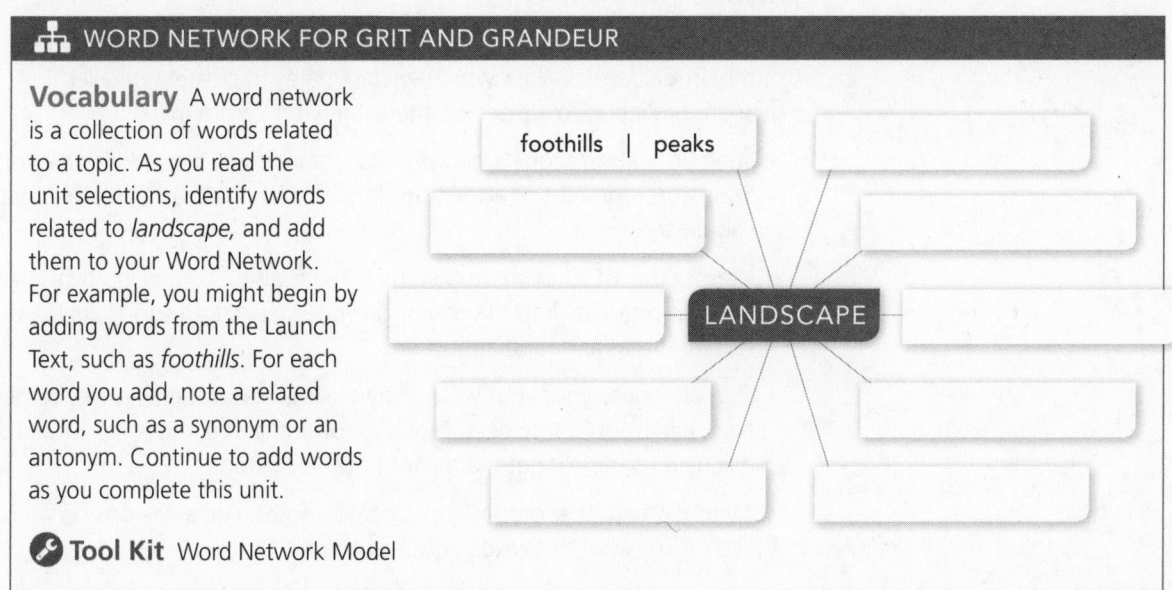

⬡ WORD NETWORK FOR GRIT AND GRANDEUR

Vocabulary A word network is a collection of words related to a topic. As you read the unit selections, identify words related to *landscape*, and add them to your Word Network. For example, you might begin by adding words from the Launch Text, such as *foothills*. For each word you add, note a related word, such as a synonym or an antonym. Continue to add words as you complete this unit.

foothills | peaks

LANDSCAPE

🔧 **Tool Kit** Word Network Model

Summary

Write a summary of "Planning Your Trip to Gold Country." A **summary** is a concise, complete, and accurate overview of a text. It should not include a statement of your opinion or an analysis.

Launch Activity

"How-to" Local Tourism The Launch Text explains how to tour Gold Country in California. Work with 4–6 classmates to create a parallel explanation relating to a place of interest in your community.

- Imagine that someone who lives in a distant place is coming for a visit. Brainstorm for a list of attractions in your area that you think the visitor should see.

- Narrow the list to three "top stops." They can be connected by a theme (such as historical importance) or be varied (such as a sports venue, a restaurant, a farm, and a museum).

- Plan an itinerary for your visitor. Share ideas about the best way to get from each stop to the next. More important, share "how-to" ideas that will help the visitor get the most out of each stop.

- Meet with another group, and compare notes. Are any stops on both lists? If so, what "how-tos" do they share?

QuickWrite

Consider class discussions, the video, and the Launch Text as you think about the prompt. Record your first thoughts here.

PROMPT: **What makes certain places live on in our memory?**

Review your QuickWrite. Summarize your thoughts in one sentence to record in your Evidence Log. Then, record evidence from "Planning Your Trip to Gold Country" that supports your thesis.

After each selection, you will continue to use your Evidence Log to record the evidence you gather and the connections you make. The graphic shows what your Evidence Log looks like.

🔧 **Tool Kit**
Evidence Log Model

Title of Text: _____ Date: _____

CONNECTION TO PROMPT	TEXT EVIDENCE/DETAILS	ADDITIONAL NOTES/IDEAS

How does this text change or add to my thinking? Date: _____

SCAN FOR MULTIMEDIA

ESSENTIAL QUESTION:

What is the relationship between literature and place?

As you read these selections, work with your whole class to explore the meaning and importance of the concept of "place."

From Text to Topic For Mark Twain, the majestic Mississippi River was a spiritual home that inspired his youthful daydreams of becoming a steamboat pilot. His writing celebrates the river's boats and bustling port towns—and the ambitions of all who were shaped by this busy place that linked America's East and West. For Sarah Orne Jewett, the Maine woods become the place where a lonely young girl learns what is most valuable to her. As you read, consider what the selections show about the importance of a sense of place in both literature and the lives of real-life Americans.

Whole-Class Learning Strategies

Throughout your life, in school, in your community, and in your career, you will continue to learn and work in large-group environments.

Review these strategies and the actions you can take to practice them. Add ideas of your own for each step. Get ready to use these strategies during Whole-Class Learning.

STRATEGY	ACTION PLAN
Listen actively	• Eliminate distractions. For example, put your cellphone away. • Record brief notes on main ideas and points of confusion. •
Clarify by asking questions	• If you're confused, other people probably are, too. Ask a question to help your whole class. • Ask follow-up questions as needed—for example, if you do not understand the clarification or if you want to make an additional connection. •
Monitor understanding	• Notice what information you already know, and be ready to build on it. • Ask for help if you are struggling. •
Interact and share ideas	• Share your ideas and offer answers, even if you are unsure. • Build on the ideas of others by adding details or making a connection. •

SCAN FOR
MULTIMEDIA

CONTENTS

Bright Horizons, Challenging Realities

Voices of the Period

"A wee child toddling in a wonder world, I prefer to their dogma my excursions into the natural gardens where the voice of the Great Spirit is heard in the twittering of birds, the rippling of mighty waters, and the sweet breathing of flowers."

—Zitkala-Ša, author and Native American activist

"The great city can teach something that no university by itself can altogether impart: a vivid sense of the largeness of human brotherhood; a vivid sense of man's increasing obligation to man; a vivid sense of our absolute dependence on one another."

—Seth Low, educator and politician

"A person may encircle the globe with mind open only to bodily comfort. Another may live his life on a sixty-foot lot and listen to the voices of the universe."

—Bess Streeter Aldrich, author

History of the Period

The Frontier Disappears Even as pioneers moved to the West, the vast plains at the center of the nation remained a frontier with huge unsettled tracts of land. By 1890, however, due in large part to the explosion of railroads carrying Americans across the continent, the Census Bureau declared the frontier officially gone. Replacing the open range were farms and small towns, plowed fields, grazing lands, and miles of fences. By 1900, what once had been frontier land had become 14 new states.

Tracks Across the Nation At the start of the twentieth century, almost 200,000 miles of train tracks crossed the continent, turning many small towns into cities. The federal government became involved, subsidizing railroad building and granting railroad companies western land to sell. As railroad networks increased and their wealthy owners grew in power, state governments and then the federal government tried to regulate the railroad monopolies. The federal government issued the Interstate Commerce Act of 1887, the first major government regulation of private business for the benefit of public interest.

Enclosing Native Americans As the frontier disappeared, the Native American peoples living there were displaced by settlers, fences, and towns. These new settlements often interfered with the ways in which the Native Americans had lived for centuries. The cultures clashed and the conflicts turned into battles, sometimes referred

TIMELINE

1882: Congress passes the first Chinese Exclusion Act (and later renews it).

1883: American railroads adopt standard time zones.

1880

1889: France The Eiffel Tower is completed in Paris, becoming the world's tallest structure.

1890: Congress establishes Yosemite National Park.

1890: Federal troops and Native Americans fight their last major battle at Wounded Knee, South Dakota.

Integration of Knowledge and Ideas

Notebook Overall, in which two census years was the immigrant population of these cities at its height? Review the events in the photographic timeline. Which event might account for the decline in the immigrant population of San Francisco?

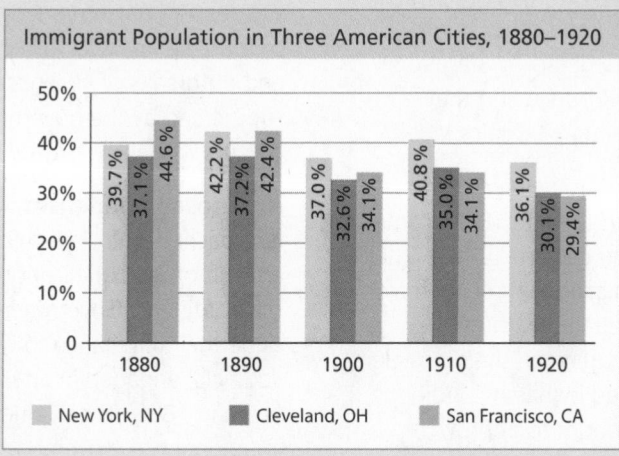

Immigrant Population in Three American Cities, 1880–1920

Year	New York, NY	Cleveland, OH	San Francisco, CA
1880	39.7%	37.1%	44.6%
1890	42.2%	37.2%	42.4%
1900	37.0%	32.6%	34.1%
1910	40.8%	35.0%	34.1%
1920	36.1%	30.1%	29.4%

Source: U.S. Bureau of the Census

to as the Indian Wars. Against their will, whole Native American nations—totaling about 250,000 people—were moved to reservations, often far from their traditional homelands.

The Second Industrial Revolution The introduction of electricity in the 1880s launched a second Industrial Revolution. Americans began to enjoy electric lights, telephones, automobiles, motion pictures, and skyscrapers. Urban populations exploded as millions of immigrants arrived and people moved away from rural areas, providing cheap labor. Low wages, child labor, and disease were the norm for the working class.

The Gilded Age Along with the growth of industry came the accumulation of enormous fortunes in the hands of a few "robber barons"—men such as banker John Pierpont Morgan, oil magnate John D. Rockefeller, and steel titan Andrew Carnegie. Author Mark Twain coined the term "the Gilded Age," characterizing this era as having a golden and shiny surface that covered a base of corruption and greed. The energy of the nation led to change, however, as the power of monopolies inspired government regulation such as the Sherman Anti-Trust Act and political movements such as the Populist Party.

1892: Ellis Island opens as a receiving center for immigrants.

1892: A steelworkers' strike at Pennsylvania's Homestead steel mill is brutally suppressed.

1895: The first professional football game is played in Latrobe, Pennsylvania.

1896: *The Country of the Pointed Firs,* Sarah Orne Jewett's masterpiece, is published.

1898: France Marie and Pierre Curie discover radium and polonium.

1900

Rise of Jim Crow Reconstruction was meant to rebuild the South after the Civil War. However, instead of freedom and opportunity, African Americans in the South soon faced a wall of systematically enforced discrimination that came to be known as Jim Crow laws. Poll taxes and other restrictions prevented African Americans from voting, while schools and other public facilities were strictly segregated—a situation reinforced by a Supreme Court ruling that declared "separate but equal" facilities legal.

Immigration—or Not The "new immigrants" who arrived in America in the late 1800s came mainly from southern and eastern Europe. They flocked to New York, Chicago, and other major cities, where they congregated with others from their homelands. In general, their crowded communities were marked by harsh conditions, which some reformers sought to improve. At the same time, political bosses lobbied for immigrants' votes. A backlash of opinion grew because many native-born Americans felt threatened by the flood of cheap immigrant labor. By 1882, Congress began to pass legislation restricting the entrance of certain groups of immigrants, including a complete prohibition of immigrants from China.

From Farm to City By 1900, four out of ten Americans lived in urban environments. Inventions such as the elevator encouraged the building of skyscrapers, which made it possible for many more people to inhabit and work in the ever-growing metropolises of the East Coast and Midwest. Increasing urban density spawned slums, where disease and poverty were rampant.

Reformers such as activist and Nobel Prize winner Jane Addams and photojournalist Jacob Riis worked to improve living conditions for the poor.

Workers Unite After the Civil War, American workers began to form labor unions. The new unions led workers in strikes to protest low salaries and harsh working conditions. The history of these strikes was full of setbacks and advances and outbreaks of violence. Many strikes were suppressed by the government or by business owners who hired private security firms.

American Imperialism As the twentieth century approached, the United States was growing as a result of industrialization and expansion across the continent. Governmental leaders, putting aside their reluctance to get involved in foreign conflicts, engaged in an international war with Spain in 1898, largely due to sympathy for an independence movement in nearby Cuba. The United States took control of the Philippines and Puerto Rico, freed Cuba from Spanish control, and annexed Hawaii. In 1901, a treaty that gave the United States the right to build a canal across the Isthmus of Panama was signed.

The Great War In 1914, the European Allies (the United Kingdom, France, and Russia) fought a war against the Central Powers (Germany and Austria-Hungary). Eventually Italy, Japan, the Ottoman Empire, and other nations were drawn into World War I, "the war to end all wars." The United States resisted involvement in the conflict until German attacks at sea precipitated a declaration of war in April 1917. By the war's end in November 1918, some 16 million people were dead, including more than 50,000 Americans.

TIMELINE

1901: Italy Guglielmo Marconi sends the first transatlantic radio telegraph message.

1903: The Wright brothers fly 852 feet in their airplane at Kitty Hawk, North Carolina.

1905: Germany Albert Einstein proposes his relativity theory.

1906: The Bureau of Immigration and Naturalization is established.

1908: The first Model T automobile is produced.

1900

Literature Selections

Literature of the Focus Period A number of the selections in this unit were written during the Focus Period and pertain to the sense of place expressed by Americans in different regions and of various cultural backgrounds:

from *Life on the Mississippi,* Mark Twain

"The Notorious Jumping Frog of Calaveras County," Mark Twain

"A White Heron," Sarah Orne Jewett

"Chicago," Carl Sandburg

"Wilderness," Carl Sandburg

"The Wood-Pile," Robert Frost

"Birches," Robert Frost

Connections Across Time A consideration of the importance of place both preceded and continued past the Focus Period. Indeed, it has influenced writers and commentators in many times and places.

"A Literature of Place," Barry Lopez

from *Dust Tracks on a Road*, Zora Neale Hurston

"In the Longhouse, Oneida Museum," Roberta Hill

"Cloudy Day," Jimmy Santiago Baca

Introduction from *The Way to Rainy Mountain*, N. Scott Momaday

"The Rockpile," James Baldwin

"Untying the Knot," Annie Dillard

"The Latin Deli: An Ars Poetica," Judith Ortiz Cofer

ADDITIONAL FOCUS PERIOD LITERATURE

Student Edition

UNIT 1
The Gettysburg Address, Abraham Lincoln

UNIT 2
The Writing of Walt Whitman

from "Nature," Ralph Waldo Emerson

from *Walden*, Henry David Thoreau

"The Love Song of J. Alfred Prufrock," T. S. Eliot

"A Wagner Matinée," Willa Cather

UNIT 3
The Poetry of Langston Hughes

from *The Warmth of Other Suns*, Isabel Wilkerson

UNIT 5
The Crucible, Arthur Miller

from *Farewell to Manzanar*, Jeanne Wakatsuki Houston and James D. Houston

"Antojos," Julia Alvarez

"Bears at Raspberry Time," Hayden Carruth

UNIT 6
"An Occurrence at Owl Creek Bridge," Ambrose Bierce

"The Man to Send Rain Clouds," Leslie Marmon Silko

1909: A multiracial group of activists founds the National Association for the Advancement of Colored People.

1913: Willa Cather's *O Pioneers!* is published.

1914–1918: World War I rages across Europe.

1916: Carl Sandburg's *Chicago Poems* is published.

1917: Russia Bolsheviks seize control of Russia in the October Revolution.

1920

1920: The Nineteenth Amendment to the Constitution gives American women the right to vote.

from LIFE ON THE MISSISSIPPI

Comparing Texts

You will read and compare an excerpt from Mark Twain's memoir with one of his short stories. First, you will complete the first-read and close-read activities for the excerpt from *Life on the Mississippi*. The work you do on this title will prepare you for the comparing task.

THE NOTORIOUS JUMPING FROG OF CALAVERAS COUNTY

from Life on the Mississippi

Concept Vocabulary

You will encounter the following words as you read this excerpt from *Life on the Mississippi*. Before reading, note how familiar you are with each word. Then, rank the words in order from most familiar (1) to least familiar (6).

WORD	YOUR RANKING
gilded	
ornamented	
grandeur	
picturesquely	
exalted	
eminence	

After completing your first read, come back to the concept vocabulary and review your rankings. Mark changes to your original rankings as needed.

First Read NONFICTION

Apply these strategies as you conduct your first read. You will have an opportunity to complete the close-read notes after your first read.

🛠 Tool Kit
First-Read Guide and Model Annotation

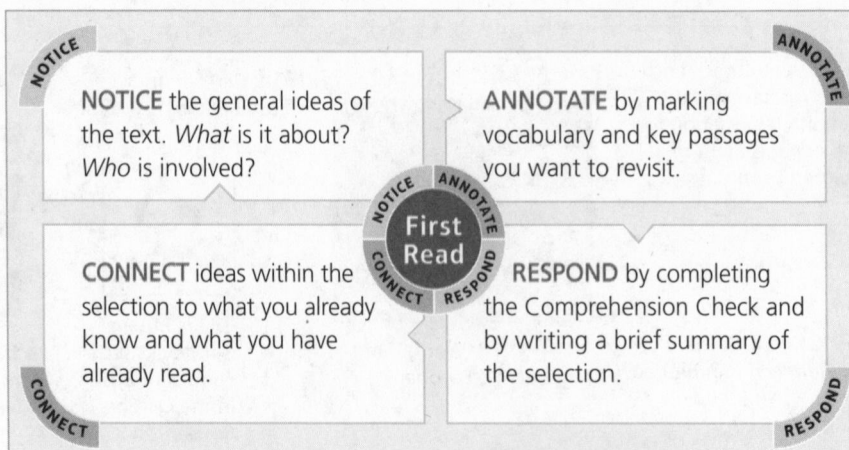

NOTICE the general ideas of the text. *What* is it about? *Who* is involved?

ANNOTATE by marking vocabulary and key passages you want to revisit.

CONNECT ideas within the selection to what you already know and what you have already read.

RESPOND by completing the Comprehension Check and by writing a brief summary of the selection.

First Read

☰ STANDARDS
Reading Informational Text
By the end of grade 11, read and comprehend literary nonfiction in the grades 11–CCR text complexity band proficiently, with scaffolding as needed at the high end of the range.

Mark Twain (1835–1910)

At a time when most American writers were copying European novelists, Twain wrote about American themes.

In the late 1800s, readers might have known him as Thomas Jefferson Snodgrass, W. Epaminondas Adrastus Blab, or simply Josh. Today we know Samuel Langhorne Clemens as Mark Twain, his most famous literary pseudonym. Whichever name he used, Twain pulled off a rare literary feat—he created stories, novels, and essays that were wildly popular in his own day and remain models of wit and skill more than a century later. Twain was so influential that fifty years after his death Ernest Hemingway said that "all modern American literature begins" with Twain's novel *The Adventures of Huckleberry Finn*.

Life on the Mississippi Born in 1835, Samuel Clemens grew up in the small river town of Hannibal, Missouri. Steamboat men, religious revivalists, circus performers, minstrel companies, showboat actors, and every other kind of traveler imaginable made appearances in Hannibal. As a boy, Clemens met many of the characters that he would later write about.

After his father's death in 1847, Clemens was forced to leave school and became a printer's apprentice. During the 1850s, he published a few stories and traveled the country. A boat trip down the Mississippi brought back childhood memories, and he decided to become a riverboat pilot. He served as a pilot until 1861, when the Civil War closed the Mississippi to boat traffic.

"Mark Twain" Finds His Voice In 1862, Clemens took a job as a reporter on a Virginia City, Nevada, newspaper, where he found his calling as a humorist under the byline Mark Twain. The new name, which is actually a signal yelled out by riverboat pilots, freed him to develop a new style. Before becoming "Twain," his work was typical of the low humor of the time, filled with bad puns and intentional misspellings. But in 1865, Twain published a short story entitled "The Notorious Jumping Frog of Calaveras County." The story won the author fame and financial success, and it marked the first appearance of his distinctive comic style.

Ordinary American Speech The targets of Twain's jokes were not new. He distrusted technology and railed against political figures, calling them swindlers and con men. What was new was Twain's feel for ordinary American people and their language. He wrote using the American English that people actually spoke. In that source, he found rich and comic poetry.

Twain's novels, such as *The Adventures of Tom Sawyer* and *The Adventures of Huckleberry Finn*, were unlike any books the world had ever seen. At a time when most American writers were copying European novelists, Twain wrote about American themes. His heroes were often poor and plain-spoken people, but in Twain's hands, their moral choices had as much drama as those of any tormented aristocrat in a European novel.

Not everyone appreciated Twain's humor. The author fled Virginia City when a rival journalist, offended by a story, challenged him to a pistol duel. He was chased out of San Francisco by policemen angered by critical articles. Even as his fame grew, some critics dismissed him as little more than a jokester. Yet the American public loved Twain. He made a fortune from his writings and eventually settled with his family into a Hartford, Connecticut, mansion that was decorated in cutting-edge style.

The Old Man in a White Suit In the late 1800s, Twain faced troubling challenges. He founded a publishing house that had moderate success but then went bankrupt. Other business ventures also failed. Although he presented a friendly face to the public, and despite the many awards that continued to come his way, Twain grew pessimistic. His mood darkened to bitterness and cynicism following the deaths of his wife and two of his daughters. Twain became reclusive—so much so that a newspaper reported he was dead. Twain immediately wired the editors, "Reports of my death have been greatly exaggerated." History has not exaggerated Twain's legacy. He was the first, and possibly the greatest, authentically American writer.

from Life on the Mississippi

Mark Twain

BACKGROUND

Mark Twain was an eyewitness to the nineteenth-century expansion of the western frontier. He traveled throughout the nation, working first on the Mississippi and then in the West, before settling in Connecticut. However, as this excerpt shows, the Mississippi River held a special place in his memory.

NOTES

The Boy's Ambition

1   When I was a boy, there was but one permanent ambition among my comrades in our village[1] on the west bank of the Mississippi River. That was, to be a steamboatman. We had transient ambitions of other sorts, but they were only transient.

2   When a circus came and went, it left us all burning to become clowns; the first Negro minstrel show that came to our section left us all suffering to try that kind of life; now and then we had a hope

---

1. **our village** Hannibal, Missouri.

that if we lived and were good, God would permit us to be pirates. These ambitions faded out, each in its turn; but the ambition to be a steamboatman always remained.

3   Once a day a cheap, gaudy packet² arrived upward from St. Louis, and another downward from Keokuk.³ Before these events, the day was glorious with expectancy; after them, the day was a dead and empty thing. Not only the boys, but the whole village, felt this. After all these years I can picture that old time to myself now, just as it was then; the white town drowsing in the sunshine of a summer's morning; the streets empty, or pretty nearly so; one or two clerks sitting in front of the Water Street stores, with their splint-bottomed chairs tilted back against the wall, chins on breasts, hats slouched over their faces, asleep—with shingle shavings enough around to show what broke them down; a sow and a litter of pigs loafing along the sidewalk, doing a good business in watermelon rinds and seeds;

---

2. **packet** *n.* boat that travels a regular route, carrying passengers, freight, and mail.
3. **Keokuk** (KEE uh kuhk) town in southeastern Iowa.

CLOSE READ

ANNOTATE: In paragraph 3, mark descriptive details that suggest sleepiness or languor. Mark other descriptive details that refer to noise and activity.

QUESTION: Why does the author create the steamboat scene in this way?

CONCLUDE: What is the effect of these descriptive details?

two or three lonely little freight piles scattered about the levee;[4] a pile of skids[5] on the slope of the stone-paved wharf, and the fragrant town drunkard asleep in the shadow of them; two or three wood flats[6] at the head of the wharf, but nobody to listen to the peaceful lapping of the wavelets against them; the great Mississippi, the majestic, the magnificent Mississippi, rolling its mile-wide tide a long, shining in the sun; the dense forest away on the other side; the point above the town, and the point below, bounding the river-glimpse and turning it into a sort of sea, and withal a very still and brilliant and lonely one. Presently a film of dark smoke appears above one of those remote points; instantly a Negro drayman,[7] famous for his quick eye and prodigious voice, lifts up the cry, "S-t-e-a-m-boat a-comin'!" and the scene changes! The town drunkard stirs, the clerks wake up, a furious clatter of drays follows, every house and store pours out a human contribution, and all in a twinkling the dead town is alive and moving. Drays, carts, men, boys, all go hurrying from many quarters to a common center, the wharf. Assembled there, the people fasten their eyes upon the coming boat as upon a wonder they are seeing for the first time. And the boat is rather a handsome sight, too. She is long and sharp and trim and pretty; she has two tall, fancy-topped chimneys, with a **gilded** device of some kind swung between them; a fanciful pilothouse, all glass and gingerbread,[8] perched on top of the texas deck[9] behind them; the paddleboxes are gorgeous with a picture or with gilded rays above the boat's name; the boiler deck, the hurricane deck, and the texas deck are fenced and **ornamented** with clean white railings; there is a flag gallantly flying from the jackstaff;[10] the furnace doors are open and the fires glaring bravely; the upper decks are black with passengers; the captain stands by the big bell, calm, imposing, the envy of all; great volumes of the blackest smoke are rolling and tumbling out of the chimneys—a husbanded **grandeur** created with a bit of pitch pine just before arriving at a town; the crew are grouped on the forecastle;[11] the broad stage is run far out over the port bow, and an envied deckhand stands **picturesquely** on the end of it with a coil of rope in his hand; the pent steam is screaming through the gauge cocks; the captain lifts his hand, a bell rings, the wheels stop; then they turn back, churning the water to foam, and the steamer is at rest. Then such a scramble as there is to get aboard, and to get ashore, and to take in freight and to discharge freight, all at one and the same time; and such a yelling and cursing as the mates facilitate it all with! Ten minutes later the steamer is under way again, with no flag on the jackstaff and no black

gilded (GIHLD ihd) *adj.* covered with a thin layer of gold

ornamented (AWR nuh mehnt ihd) *adj.* decorated; adorned

grandeur (GRAN juhr) *n.* state of being impressive; magnificence

picturesquely (pihk chuh REHSK lee) *adv.* in a way that resembles a picture; in a way that is striking or interesting

---

4. **levee** (LEHV ee) *n.* landing place along the bank of a river.
5. **skids** *n.* low, movable wooden platforms.
6. **flats** *n.* small, flat-bottomed boats.
7. **drayman** (DRAY muhn) *n.* driver of a dray, a low cart with detachable sides.
8. **gingerbread** *n.* showy ornamentation; fancy carving.
9. **texas deck** *n.* deck adjoining the officers' cabins, the largest cabins on the ship.
10. **jackstaff** *n.* small staff at the bow of a ship for flying flags.
11. **forecastle** (FOHK suhl) *n.* front part of the upper deck.

smoke issuing from the chimneys. After ten more minutes the town is dead again, and the town drunkard asleep by the skids once more.

4   My father was a justice of the peace, and I supposed he possessed the power of life and death over all men and could hang anybody that offended him. This was distinction enough for me as a general thing; but the desire to be a steamboatman kept intruding, nevertheless. I first wanted to be a cabin boy, so that I could come out with a white apron on and shake a tablecloth over the side, where all my old comrades could see me; later I thought I would rather be the deckhand who stood on the end of the stage plank with the coil of rope in his hand, because he was particularly conspicuous. But these were only daydreams—they were too heavenly to be contemplated as real possibilities. By and by one of our boys went away. He was not heard of for a long time. At last he turned up as apprentice engineer or striker on a steamboat. This thing shook the bottom out of all my Sunday school teachings. That boy had been notoriously worldly, and I just the reverse; yet he was **exalted** to this **eminence**, and I left in obscurity and misery. There was nothing generous about this fellow in his greatness. He would always manage to have a rusty bolt to scrub while his boat tarried at our town, and he would sit on the inside guard and scrub it, where we could all see him and envy him and loathe him. And whenever his boat was laid up he would come home and swell around the town in his blackest and greasiest clothes, so that nobody could help remembering that he was a steamboatman; and he used all sorts of steamboat technicalities in his talk, as if he were so used to them that he forgot common people could not understand them. He would speak of the labboard[12] side of a horse in an easy, natural way that would make one wish he was dead. And he was always talking about "St. Looey" like an old citizen; he would refer casually to occasions when he "was coming down Fourth Street," or when he was "passing by the Planter's House," or when there was a fire and he took a turn on the brakes of "the old Big Missouri"; and then he would go on and lie about how many towns the size of ours were burned down there that day. Two or three of the boys had long been persons of consideration among us because they had been to St. Louis once and had a vague general knowledge of its wonders, but the day of their glory was over now. They lapsed into a humble silence, and learned to disappear when the ruthless cub engineer approached. This fellow had money, too, and hair oil. Also an ignorant silver watch and a showy brass watch chain. He wore a leather belt and used no suspenders. If ever a youth was cordially admired and hated by his comrades. this one was. No girl could withstand his charms. He cut out every boy in the village. When his boat blew up at last, it diffused a tranquil contentment among us such as we had not known for months. But when he came home the next week, alive, renowned, and appeared in church all

---

NOTES

CLOSE READ

ANNOTATE: In the first few sentences of paragraph 4, mark the jobs that young Twain wanted to have someday.

QUESTION: Why does the author mention several jobs?

CONCLUDE: What is the effect of his including these details?

exalted (ehg ZAWLT ihd) *adj.* of high rank

eminence (EHM uh nuhns) *n.* position of great importance or superiority

CLOSE READ

ANNOTATE: In paragraph 5, mark the adjectives that describe the position and salary of a steamboat pilot.

QUESTION: Why does the author choose these adjectives to describe a pilot's status?

CONCLUDE: What is the effect of these adjectives?

battered up and bandaged, a shining hero, stared at and wondered over by everybody, it seemed to us that the partiality of Providence for an undeserving reptile had reached a point where it was open to criticism.

5   This creature's career could produce but one result, and it speedily followed. Boy after boy managed to get on the river. The minister's son became an engineer. The doctor's and the postmaster's sons became mud clerks; the wholesale liquor dealer's son became a barkeeper on a boat; four sons of the chief merchant, and two sons of the county judge, became pilots. Pilot was the grandest position of all. The pilot, even in those days of trivial wages, had a princely salary—from a hundred and fifty to two hundred and fifty dollars a month, and no board to pay. Two months of his wages would pay a preacher's salary for a year. Now some of us were left disconsolate. We could not get on the river—at least our parents would not let us.

6   So by and by I ran away. I said I never would come home again till I was a pilot and could come in glory. But somehow I could not manage it. I went meekly aboard a few of the boats that lay packed together like sardines at the long St. Louis wharf, and very humbly inquired for the pilots, but got only a cold shoulder and short words from mates and clerks. I had to make the best of this sort of treatment for the time being, but I had comforting daydreams of a future when I should be a great and honored pilot, with plenty of money, and could kill some of these mates and clerks and pay for them. ❧

MEDIA CONNECTION

Mark Twain and Tom Sawyer

💬 **Discuss It** From what you see in this video, what connection can you make between the way that Mark Twain depicts his hometown in *The Adventures of Tom Sawyer* and the way that he depicts it in *Life on the Mississippi*?

Write your response before sharing your ideas.

SCAN FOR MULTIMEDIA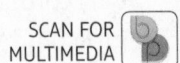

Comprehension Check

Complete the following items after you finish your first read.

1. What does Twain say is the one permanent ambition he and his boyhood friends shared?

2. According to Twain, how do the people of Hannibal respond to the arrival of the steamboat?

3. What kinds of activities impress young Twain during the steamboat's brief stop in Hannibal?

4. What happens when the boy who survived an explosion aboard a steamboat returns to town?

5. Under what condition does young Twain say he would return to Hannibal?

6. 🗒 **Notebook** Write a summary of this excerpt from *Life on the Mississippi*.

RESEARCH

Research to Clarify Choose at least one unfamiliar detail from the text. Briefly research that detail. In what way does the information you learned shed light on an aspect of the memoir?

Research to Explore Conduct research to find out why the Mississippi steamboats were essential to the economy of late-nineteenth-century America.

from LIFE ON THE MISSISSIPPI

Close Read the Text

1. This model, from paragraph 3 of the text, shows two sample annotations, along with questions and conclusions. Close read the passage, and find another detail to annotate. Then, write a question and your conclusion.

> **ANNOTATE:** Twain uses many synonyms for *beautiful*.
>
> **QUESTION:** Why does Twain describe the steamboat with these words?
>
> **CONCLUDE:** Twain wants readers to understand the awe and admiration he felt.

Close Read
ANNOTATE · QUESTION · CONCLUDE

> **ANNOTATE:** Twain creates a long sentence with semicolons.
>
> **QUESTION:** Why does Twain use this sentence structure?
>
> **CONCLUDE:** The complex structure conveys how large the boat looms over the town and in his imagination.

> She is long and sharp and trim and pretty; she has two tall, fancy-topped chimneys, with a gilded device of some kind swung between them; a fanciful pilothouse, all glass and gingerbread, perched on top of the texas deck behind them; the paddleboxes are gorgeous. . . .

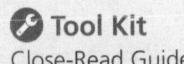 **Tool Kit**
Close-Read Guide and
Model Annotation

2. For more practice, go back into the text, and complete the close-read notes.

3. Revisit a section of the text you found important during your first read. Read this section closely, and **annotate** what you notice. Ask yourself **questions** such as "Why did the author make this choice?" What can you **conclude?**

Analyze the Text

CITE TEXTUAL EVIDENCE to support your answers.

Notebook Respond to these questions.

1. (a) **Analyze** What does a job working on the steamboats represent to the boys of Twain's hometown? (b) **Connect** How does this childhood ambition reflect the American spirit that gave rise to the settlement of the frontier?

2. (a) **Analyze** Why do the boys feel as they do about the young apprentice engineer? (b) **Draw Conclusions** Would they feel the same if another boy from town found a position on a steamboat? Explain.

3. **Evaluate** Is the desire for glory a reasonable motivation in life? Explain.

4. **Historical Perspectives** What careers other than steamboat pilot did the boys in Hannibal consider? Explain where these ideas came from.

5. **Essential Question:** *What is the relationship between literature and place?* What have you learned about the relationship between literature and place by reading this memoir?

STANDARDS

Reading Informational Text
• Cite strong and thorough textual evidence to support analysis of what the text says explicitly as well as inferences drawn from the text, including determining where the text leaves matters uncertain.
• Determine an author's point of view or purpose in a text in which the rhetoric is particularly effective, analyzing how style and content contribute to the power, persuasiveness, or beauty of the text.

Analyze Craft and Structure

Author's Purpose Every author has a purpose—or multiple purposes—for writing. For example, an author may write to inform, to persuade, to describe, or to entertain. One of Twain's purposes for writing *Life on the Mississippi* is to entertain readers, which he does by using anecdotes and humorous descriptions.

- **Anecdotes** are brief stories about interesting, amusing, or strange events. Writers include anecdotes to entertain and to make a point. For example, Twain entertains readers by sharing an anecdote about how he ran away and tried to join a steamboat crew. He explains that he got only "a cold shoulder and short words from mates and clerks." At the same time, Twain is making a point about his burning ambition to become a steamboat man.

- **Humorous descriptions** present details that appeal to the senses even as they amuse readers. Humorous details in this example from paragraph 4 of the story appeal to the senses of sight and touch:

  He would always manage to have a rusty bolt to scrub while his boat tarried at our town, and he would sit on the inside guard and scrub it, where we could all see him and envy him and loathe him.

In addition to being funny, Twain's writing has an undercurrent of **social commentary**—that is, a discerning examination of society. Twain shares his keen observations of human weakness, which he usually describes with affection. In *Life on the Mississippi*, Twain looks back on his friends and neighbors fondly, but he also points out their flaws.

Practice

CITE TEXTUAL EVIDENCE to support your answers.

Reread paragraphs 1–4 of *Life on the Mississippi*.

📓 **Notebook** Respond to these questions.

1. (a) In paragraph 3, are the town and steamboat described using humorous or nonhumorous details, or a mixture of both? Explain. (b) What purpose or purposes does Twain address by presenting these details?

2. What social commentary about the values of the town's boys does Twain offer in paragraph 4?

3. (a) In paragraph 4, why does Twain call the apprentice "an undeserving reptile"? (b) What comment is Twain making about the boys by using this phrase?

4. In a chart like this one, record examples of humorous description from the text. Explain why each example is humorous. Then, explain what social comment Twain is making with the description.

EXAMPLE OF HUMOROUS DESCRIPTION	EXPLANATION	SOCIAL COMMENTARY

from LIFE ON THE MISSISSIPPI

Concept Vocabulary

gilded	grandeur	exalted
ornamented	picturesquely	eminence

Why These Words? These concept vocabulary words are used to describe splendid objects or impressive people. For example, the *gilded* and *ornamented* devices on the steamboats added to their *grandeur*.

1. How does the concept vocabulary help readers understand how young Twain felt about the steamboat?

2. What other words in the selection connect to the idea of splendor?

Practice

🖪 **Notebook** Respond to these questions.

1. How might a building be *ornamented*? Give examples.

2. What object might you expect to be *gilded*?

3. How would you feel if you met an *exalted* person? Why?

4. How might a tourist react to the *grandeur* of the Rocky Mountains?

5. What is the proper way to address a person of *eminence*?

6. Where might you pose *picturesquely* for a photo?

Word Study

Suffix: -*esque* The suffix -*esque* is an adjective-forming suffix that means "having a certain style, manner, resemblance, or distinctive character." Thus, *picturesquely* means "in a way that resembles a picture."

The suffix has an interesting history. English borrowed it from French, which had previously borrowed it from Italian. It's ultimate source is unknown but was likely Germanic—that is, a language closely related to German and to English itself. Indeed, it is cognate with, or derives from the same source as, the English suffix -*ish* , and their meanings are still related.

1. Write a definition of *statuesque* based on your understanding of the suffix -*esque*. Check your answer in a print or digital college-level dictionary.

2. Identify and define two other words that end with the suffix -*esque*. Use a print or digital college-level dictionary to check your work.

WORD NETWORK

Add words related to a sense of place from the text to your Word Network.

STANDARDS

Reading Informational Text
Determine the meaning of words and phrases as they are used in a text, including figurative, connotative, and technical meanings; analyze how an author uses and refines the meaning of a key term or terms over the course of a text.

Language
• Identify and correctly use patterns of word changes that indicate different meanings or parts of speech.

• Verify the preliminary determination of the meaning of a word or phrase.

Author's Style

Words and Phrases Two of the key elements of Twain's distinctive style are his **diction**, or choice of words and phrases, and his **tone,** or attitude toward his subject. This chart identifies the types of diction and tone Twain uses in *Life on the Mississippi*.

TYPE OF DICTION OR TONE	DEFINITION	EXAMPLE
technical terms	words and phrases used in a specific technical or scientific field, such as nautical terms related to ships	*. . . the crew are grouped on the forecastle; the broad stage is run far out over the port bow. . . .* (paragraph 3)
colloquial language	informal words and phrases, including slang, that are used in speech but not in formal writing	*And he was always talking about "St. Looey" like an old citizen. . . .* (paragraph 4)
conversational tone	the effect created by the use of natural language spoken casually as in everyday life	*By and by one of our boys went away. He was not heard of for a long time.* (paragraph 4)

Twain's use of both technical and colloquial diction in *Life on the Mississippi* creates a mixture of formality and informality in the memoir. As a result, readers get a multidimensional sense of the busy place, its people, and what they value.

Read It

1. Mark the technical language in this passage from paragraph 3 of the excerpt from *Life on the Mississippi*. Then, explain how the diction helps establish a particular tone.

   . . . the boiler deck, the hurricane deck, and the texas deck are fenced and ornamented with clean white railings; there is a flag gallantly flying from the jackstaff. . . .

2. **Connect to Style** Mark two examples of colloquial language in paragraphs 4–6. Then, explain how Twain's diction helps create his humorous style.

3. 📓 **Notebook** Reread paragraph 6. How would you describe the diction in that paragraph? What tone does the diction help develop? Support your answer with textual evidence.

Write It

📓 **Notebook** Mimicking Twain's voice, write a paragraph about a minor argument between friends that uses the following examples of colloquial language. Create a relaxed, conversational tone.

ornery	reckon	rile	ruckus

from LIFE ON THE MISSISSIPPI

Comparing Texts

Read "The Notorious Jumping Frog of Calaveras County," and complete the first-read and close-read activities. Then, compare Twain's approach to humor in this story with his approach in the excerpt from *Life on the Mississippi*.

THE NOTORIOUS JUMPING FROG OF CALAVERAS COUNTY

About the Author

When the Civil War closed traffic on the Mississippi, **Mark Twain** (1835–1910) went west to Nevada. There, he supported himself as a journalist and lecturer, developing the entertaining writing style that made him famous. In 1865, Twain published "The Notorious Jumping Frog of Calaveras County," his version of a tall tale he had heard in a mining camp in California while working as a gold prospector. The story launched Twain's career as a humorist widely regarded as one of the greatest of American writers.

The Notorious Jumping Frog of Calaveras County

Concept Vocabulary

You will encounter the following words in "The Notorious Jumping Frog of Calaveras County." Before reading, note how familiar you are with each word. Then, rank the words from most familiar (1) to least familiar (6).

WORD	YOUR RANKING
garrulous	
exasperating	
tedious	
monotonous	
interminable	
buttonholed	

After completing your first read, come back to the concept vocabulary and review your rankings. Mark changes to your original rankings as needed.

First Read FICTION

Apply these strategies as you conduct your first read. You will have an opportunity to complete the close-read notes after your first read.

STANDARDS

Reading Literature
By the end of grade 11, read and comprehend literature, including stories, dramas, and poems, in the grades 11–CCR text complexity band proficiently, with scaffolding as needed at the high end of the range.

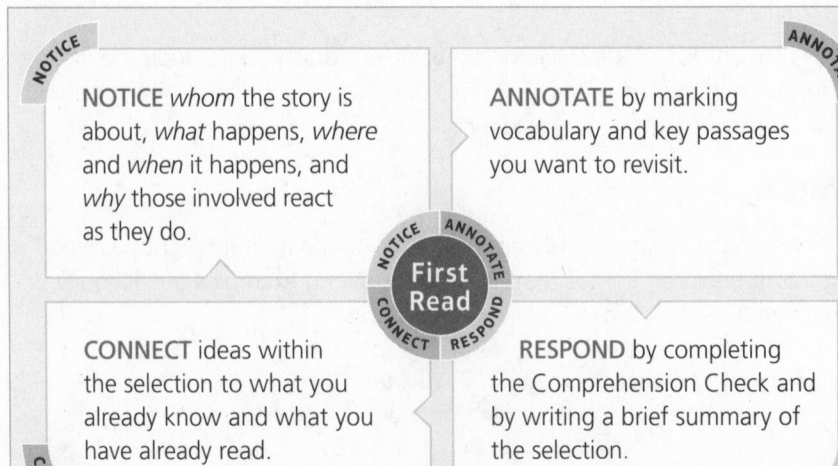

NOTICE *whom* the story is about, *what* happens, *where* and *when* it happens, and *why* those involved react as they do.

ANNOTATE by marking vocabulary and key passages you want to revisit.

CONNECT ideas within the selection to what you already know and what you have already read.

RESPOND by completing the Comprehension Check and by writing a brief summary of the selection.

First Read

The **Notorious Jumping Frog** of Calaveras County

Mark Twain

BACKGROUND

This story was Mark Twain's first successful fiction publication and exemplifies the author's sense of humor. It is framed as a story heard secondhand, and the narrator is himself a character. Published in 1865 under the title "Jim Smiley and His Jumping Frog," the story brought Twain national attention.

SCAN FOR MULTIMEDIA

1 In compliance with the request of a friend of mine, who wrote me from the East, I called on good-natured, **garrulous** old Simon Wheeler, and inquired after my friend's friend, Leonidas W. Smiley, as requested to do, and I hereunto append the result. I have a lurking suspicion that *Leonidas W.* Smiley is a myth; that my friend never knew such a personage: and that he only conjectured that if I asked old Wheeler about him, it would remind him of his infamous *Jim* Smiley, and he would go to work and bore me to death with some **exasperating** reminiscence of him as long and as **tedious** as it should be useless to me. If that was the design, it succeeded.

2 I found Simon Wheeler dozing comfortably by the barroom stove of the dilapidated tavern in the decayed mining camp of Angel's, and I noticed that he was fat and baldheaded, and had an expression of winning gentleness and simplicity upon his tranquil countenance.

NOTES

garrulous (GAR uh luhs) *adj.* very talkative

exasperating (ehg ZAS puh rayt ihng) *adj.* annoying

tedious (TEE dee uhs) *adj.* boring; dull

He roused up, and gave me good day. I told him a friend of mine had commissioned me to make some inquiries about a cherished companion of his boyhood named *Leonidas W.* Smiley—*Rev. Leonidas W.* Smiley, a young minister of the Gospel, who he had heard was at one time a resident of Angel's Camp. I added that if Mr. Wheeler could tell me anything about this Rev. Leonidas W. Smiley, I would feel under many obligations to him.

3   Simon Wheeler backed me into a corner and blockaded me there with his chair, and then sat down and reeled off the monotonous narrative which follows this paragraph. He never smiled, he never frowned, he never changed his voice from the gentle-flowing key to which he tuned his initial sentence, he never betrayed the slightest suspicion of enthusiasm; but all through the interminable narrative there ran a vein of impressive earnestness and sincerity, which showed me plainly that, so far from his imagining that there was anything ridiculous or funny about his story, he regarded it as a really important matter, and admired its two heroes as men of transcendent genius in *finesse*. I let him go on in his own way, and never interrupted him once.

4   "Rev. Leonidas W. H'm, Reverend Le—well, there was a feller here once by the name of *Jim* Smiley, in the winter of '49—or maybe it was the spring of '50—I don't recollect exactly, somehow, though what makes me think it was one or the other is because I remember the big flume[1] warn't finished when he first come to the camp; but anyway, he was the curiousest man about always betting on anything that turned up you ever see, if he could get anybody to bet on the other side; and if he couldn't he'd change sides. Any way that suited the other man would suit *him*—any way just so's he got a bet, *he* was satisfied. But still he was lucky, uncommon lucky; he most always come out winner. He was always ready and laying for a chance; there couldn't be no solit'ry thing mentioned but that feller'd offer to bet on it, and take any side you please, as I was just telling you. If there was a horse race, you'd find him flush or you'd find him busted at the end of it; if there was a dogfight, he'd bet on it; if there was a cat fight, he'd bet on it; if there was a chicken fight, he'd bet on it; why, if there was two birds setting on a fence, he would bet you which one would fly first; or if there was a camp meeting,[2] he would be there reg'lar to bet on Parson Walker, which he judged to be the best exhorter about here and so he was too, and a good man. If he even see a straddle bug[3] start to go anywheres, he would bet you how long it would take him to get to—to wherever he was going to, and if you took him up, he would foller that straddle bug to Mexico but what he would find out where he was bound for and how long he was on the road. Lots of the boys here has seen that Smiley, and can tell you about him. Why, it never made no difference to *him*—he'd bet on *any*

---

1. **flume** (floom) *n.* artificial channel for carrying water to provide power and transport objects.
2. **camp meeting** religious gathering at the mining camp.
3. **straddle bug** insect with long legs.

thing—the dangdest feller. Parson Walker's wife laid very sick once, for a good while, and it seemed as if they warn't going to save her; but one morning he come in, and Smiley up and asked him how she was, and he said she was considable better—thank the Lord for his inf'nite mercy—and coming on so smart that with the blessing of Prov'dence she'd get well yet; and Smiley, before he thought, says, 'Well, I'll resk two-and-a-half she don't anyway.'

5   "Thish-yer Smiley had a mare—the boys called her the fifteen-minute nag, but that was only in fun, you know, because of course she was faster than that—and he used to win money on that horse, for all she was so slow and always had the asthma, or the distemper, or the consumption, or something of that kind. They used to give her two or three hundred yards start, and then pass her under way; but always at the fag end[4] of the race she'd get excited and desperate like, and come cavorting and straddling up, and scattering her legs around limber, sometimes in the air, and sometimes out to one side among the fences, and kicking up m-o-r-e dust and raising m-o-r-e racket with her coughing and sneezing and blowing her nose—and *always* fetch up at the stand just about a neck ahead, as near as you could cipher it down.

6   "And he had a little small bull-pup, that to look at him you'd think he warn't worth a cent but to set around and look ornery and lay for a chance to steal something. But as soon as money was up on him he was a different dog; his under-jaw'd begin to stick out like the fo'castle[5] of a steamboat, and his teeth would uncover and shine like the furnaces. And a dog might tackle him and bullyrag him, and bite him, and throw him over his shoulder two or three times, and Andrew Jackson—which was the name of the pup—Andrew Jackson would never let on but what *he* was satisfied, and hadn't expected nothing else—and the bets being doubled and doubled on the other side all the time, till the money was all up; and then all of a sudden he would grab that other dog jest by the j'int of his hind leg and freeze to it—not chaw, you understand, but only just grip and hang on till they throwed up the sponge, if it was a year. Smiley always come out winner on that pup, till he harnessed a dog once that didn't have no hind legs, because they'd been sawed off in a circular saw, and when the thing had gone along far enough, and the money was all up, and he come to make a snatch for his pet holt,[6] he see in a minute how he'd been imposed on, and how the other dog had him in the door, so to speak, and he 'peared surprised, and then he looked sorter discouraged-like, and

> "... kicking up m-o-r-e dust and raising m-o-r-e racket with her coughing and sneezing and blowing her nose— and *always* fetch up at the stand just about a neck ahead, ..."

CLOSE READ
ANNOTATE: Mark details in paragraph 5 that describe the mare and the way that she acts.

QUESTION: Why does the narrator describe the mare in this way?

CONCLUDE: What is the effect of this description?

---

4. **fag end** last part.
5. **fo'castle** (FOHK suhl) *n.* forward part of the upper deck.
6. **holt** hold.

NOTES

CLOSE READ

ANNOTATE: In paragraph 7, mark the two skills that Smiley teaches Dan'l Webster.

QUESTION: Why might these details be important?

CONCLUDE: What is the effect of these details on readers?

didn't try no more to win the fight, and so he got shucked out bad. He give Smiley a look, as much as to say his heart was broke, and it was his fault, for putting up a dog that hadn't no hind legs for him to take holt of, which was his main dependence in a fight, and then he limped off a piece and laid down and died. It was a good pup, was that Andrew Jackson, and would have made a name for hisself if he'd lived, for the stuff was in him and he had genius—I know it, because he hadn't no opportunities to speak of, and it don't stand to reason that a dog could make such a fight as he could under them circumstances if he hadn't no talent. It always makes me feel sorry when I think of that last fight of his'n, and the way it turned out.

7   "Well, thish-yer Smiley had rat terriers,[7] and chicken cocks,[8] and tomcats and all them kind of things, till you couldn't rest, and you couldn't fetch nothing for him to bet on but he'd match you. He ketched a frog one day, and took him home, and said he cal'lated to educate him; and so he never done nothing for three months but set in his back yard and learn that frog to jump. And you bet you he *did* learn him, too. He'd give him a little punch behind, and the next minute you'd see that frog whirling in the air like a doughnut—see him turn one summerset, or maybe a couple, if he got a good start, and come down flatfooted and all right, like a cat. He got him up so in the matter of ketching flies, and kep' him in practice so constant, that he'd nail a fly every time as fur as he could see him. Smiley said all a frog wanted was education, and he could do 'most anything—and I believe him. Why, I've seen him set Dan'l Webster down here on this floor—Dan'l Webster was the name of the frog—and sing out, 'Flies, Dan'l, flies!' and quicker'n you could wink he'd spring straight up and snake a fly off'n the counter there, and flop down on the floor ag'in as solid as a gob of mud, and fall to scratching the side of his head with his hind foot as indifferent as if he hadn't no idea he'd been doin' any more'n any frog might do. You never see a frog so modest and straightfor'ard as he was, for all he was so gifted. And when it come to fair and square jumping on a dead level, he could get over more ground at one straddle than any animal of his breed you ever see. Jumping on a dead level was his strong suit, you understand; and when it come to that, Smiley would ante up money on him as long as he had a red.[9] Smiley was monstrous proud of his frog, and well he might be, for fellers that had traveled and been everywheres all said he laid over any frog that ever *they* see.

8   "Well, Smiley kep' the beast in a little lattice box, and he used to fetch him downtown sometimes and lay for a bet. One day a feller—a stranger in the camp, he was—come across him with his box, and says:

9   "'What might it be that you've got in the box?'

10   "And Smiley says, sorter indifferent-like, 'It might be a parrot, or it might be a canary, maybe, but it ain't—it's only just a frog.'

---

7. **rat terriers** dogs skilled in catching rats.
8. **chicken cocks** roosters trained to fight.
9. **a red** red cent; colloquial expression for "any money at all."

11   "And the feller took it, and looked at it careful, and turned it round this way and that, and says, 'H'm—so 'tis. Well, what's *he* good for?'

12   "'Well,' Smiley says, easy and careless, 'he's good enough for *one* thing, I should judge—he can outjump any frog in Calaveras county.'

13   "The feller took the box again, and took another long, particular look, and give it back to Smiley, and says, very deliberate, 'Well,' he says, 'I don't see no p'ints about that frog that's any better'n any other frog.'

14   "'Maybe you don't,' Smiley says. 'Maybe you understand frogs and maybe you don't understand 'em; maybe you've had experience, and maybe you ain't only a amature, as it were. Anyways, I've got *my* opinion, and I'll resk forty dollars that he can outjump any frog in Calaveras county.'

15   "And the feller studied a minute, and then says, kinder sad like, 'Well, I'm only a stranger here, and I ain't got no frog; but if I had a frog. I'd bet you.'

16   "And then Smiley says, 'That's all right—that's all right—if you'll hold my box a minute, I'll go and get you a frog.' And so the feller took the box, and put up his forty dollars along with Smiley's, and set down to wait.

17   "So he set there a good while thinking and thinking to hisself, and then he got the frog out and prized his mouth open and took a teaspoon and filled him full of quailshot[10]—filled him pretty near up to his chin—and set him on the floor. Smiley he went to the swamp and slopped around in the mud for a long time, and finally

---

10. **quailshot** *n.* small lead pellets used for shooting quail, a small wild game bird.

he ketched a frog, and fetched him in, and give him to this feller, and says:

18   "'Now, if you're ready, set him alongside of Dan'l, with his forepaws just even with Dan'ls, and I'll give the word.' Then he says, 'One—two—three—*git!*' and him and the feller touched up the frogs from behind, and the new frog hopped off lively, but Dan'l give a heave, and hysted up his shoulders—so—like a Frenchman, but it warn't no use—he couldn't budge; he was planted as solid as a church, and he couldn't no more stir than if he was anchored out. Smiley was a good deal surprised, and he was disgusted too, but he didn't have no idea what the matter was, of course.

19   "The feller took the money and started away; and when he was going out at the door, he sorter jerked his thumb over his shoulder—so—at Dan'l, and says again, very deliberate, 'Well,' he says, 'I don't see no p'ints about that frog that's any better'n any other frog.'

20   "Smiley he stood scratching his head and looking down at Dan'l a long time, and at last he says, 'I do wonder what in the nation that frog throw'd off for—I wonder if there ain't something the matter with him—he 'pears to look mighty baggy, somehow.' And he ketched Dan'l by the nap of the neck, and hefted him, and says, 'Why blame my cats if he don't weigh five pound!' and turned him upside down and he belched out a double handful of shot. And then he see how it was, and he was the maddest man—he set the frog down and took out after that feller, but he never ketched him. And—"

21   Here Simon Wheeler heard his name called from the front yard, and got up to see what was wanted. And turning to me as he moved away, he said: "Just set where you are, stranger, and rest easy—I ain't going to be gone a second."

22   But, by your leave, I did not think that a continuation of the history of the enterprising vagabond *Jim* Smiley would be likely to afford me much information concerning the Rev. *Leonidas W.* Smiley, and so I started away.

23   At the door I met the sociable Wheeler returning, and he **buttonholed** me and recommenced:

24   "Well, thish-yer Smiley had a yaller one-eyed cow that didn't have no tail, only just a short stump like a bannanner, and—"

25   However, lacking both time and inclination, I did not wait to hear about the afflicted cow, but took my leave. ❧

CLOSE READ

ANNOTATE: Mark the places in paragraph 20 where a dash (—) appears.

QUESTION: Why does the author use dashes instead of more ordinary punctuation and sentence structure?

CONCLUDE: What is the effect of this punctuation?

buttonholed (BUHT uhn hohld) *v.* held in conversation

Comprehension Check

Complete the following items after you finish your first read.

1. What prompts Simon Wheeler to tell the story of Jim Smiley?

2. What is Simon Wheeler's manner as he tells the story of Jim Smiley?

3. According to Simon Wheeler, how does Jim Smiley react to any event?

4. How does Andrew Jackson, the dog, win fights?

5. What does Jim Smiley teach Dan'l Webster to do?

6. How does the stranger prevent Dan'l Webster from jumping?

7. 📓 **Notebook** Write a summary of "The Notorious Jumping Frog of Calaveras County."

RESEARCH

Research to Clarify Choose at least one unfamiliar detail from the text. Briefly research that detail. In what way does the information you learned shed light on an aspect of the story?

Research to Explore Conduct research to learn more about life in the nineteenth-century mining camps of the American West.

THE NOTORIOUS JUMPING FROG
OF CALAVERAS COUNTY

Close Read the Text

1. This model, from paragraph 4 of the text, shows two sample annotations, along with questions and conclusions. Close read the passage, and find another detail to annotate. Then, write a question and your conclusion.

> **ANNOTATE:** Smiley bets on these things.
>
> **QUESTION:** Why does Twain include so many examples of Smiley's bets?
>
> **CONCLUDE:** Twain creates humor through repetition and exaggeration.

> **ANNOTATE:** These words don't sound like standard English.
>
> **QUESTION:** Why does Twain use this kind of language?
>
> **CONCLUDE:** He wants to convey Wheeler's informal personality.

If there was a horse race, you'd find him flush or you'd find him busted at the end of it; if there was a dogfight, he'd bet on it; if there was a cat fight, he'd bet on it; if there was a chicken fight, he'd bet on it; . . . or if there was a camp meeting, he would be there reg'lar, to bet on Parson Walker. . . .

2. For more practice, go back into the text, and complete the close-read notes.

3. Revisit a section of the text you found important during your first read. Read this section closely, and **annotate** what you notice. Ask yourself **questions** such as "Why did the author make this choice?" What can you **conclude**?

🔧 Tool Kit
Close-Read Guide and Model Annotation

Analyze the Text

CITE TEXTUAL EVIDENCE
to support your answers.

📓 **Notebook** Respond to these questions.

1. (a) **Draw Conclusions** Why does the narrator's friend suggest that the narrator ask Wheeler about Leonidas W. Smiley? (b) **Support** Which sentences support your conclusion?

2. (a) What punchline does Twain build to in paragraph 4?
   (b) **Analyze** What does this punchline reveal about Jim Smiley's character?

3. (a) **Analyze** What is humorous about the story of Andrew Jackson in paragraph 6? (b) **Evaluate** Do you find it amusing? Explain your position, citing textual evidence.

4. **Historical Perspectives** What insights do you gain about life in nineteenth-century miners' camps from the story?

5. **Essential Question:** *What is the relationship between literature and place?* What have you learned about the relationship between literature and place by reading this story?

☰ STANDARDS

Reading Literature
• Cite strong and thorough textual evidence to support analysis of what the text says explicitly as well as inferences drawn from the text, including determining where the text leaves matters uncertain.
• Analyze a case in which grasping point of view requires distinguishing what is directly stated in a text from what is really meant.

Language
Interpret figures of speech in context and analyze their role in the text.

Analyze Craft and Structure

Point of View In literature, the term **point of view** can refer to the type of narrator an author uses to tell a story. For example, a story might use a first- or third-person narrative point of view. Point of view can also refer to the attitudes a narrator expresses. In some cases, the narrator may spell out those attitudes. In other cases, readers need to tease them out by analyzing story details. "The Notorious Jumping Frog of Calaveras County" is a **frame story,** or a story that brackets another story, so it has two narrators—the unnamed narrator of the frame, and Simon Wheeler, the long-winded narrator of the interior story. To appreciate the two narrators' very different points of view, consider Twain's use of incongruity and hyperbole.

- **Incongruity** occurs when two or more opposing or contradictory ideas are connected. For example, incongruity results when a speaker uses a serious tone to describe ridiculous events.

- **Hyperbole** is exaggeration for effect. For example, it would be hyperbolic if someone were to come inside from a thunderstorm and exclaim, "It's like the end of the world out there!"

Practice

CITE TEXTUAL EVIDENCE to support your answers.

📓 **Notebook** Respond to these questions.

1. In a chart like this one, record and explain four examples of hyperbole in "The Notorious Jumping Frog of Calaveras County."

HYPERBOLE	WHAT IS EXAGGERATED	WHY IS IT HUMOROUS

2. (a) What happens at the beginning and the end of the frame story? (b) How does Twain use the frame story to create humor?

3. (a) What basic incongruity exists between the frame story's narrator and Simon Wheeler? (b) How does this incongruity emphasize each narrator's point of view? Explain.

4. (a) What is incongruous about Smiley's betting on the health of Parson Walker's wife? (b) Why is this incongruity humorous?

THE NOTORIOUS JUMPING FROG
OF CALAVERAS COUNTY

Concept Vocabulary

garrulous	tedious	interminable
exasperating	monotonous	buttonholed

Why These Words? These concept words are used to describe an experience with a boring, clueless person. For example, the *garrulous* Simon Wheeler tells the narrator a seemingly *interminable* story about Jim Smiley. At the end, the narrator is almost *buttonholed* by Wheeler for a second tale.

1. How does the concept vocabulary help readers understand how the narrator feels about Simon Wheeler?

2. What other words in the selection connect to this concept?

Practice

◉ **Notebook** Indicate whether each sentence is true or false. Explain your answers.

1. A *tedious* story is likely to fascinate an audience from start to finish.

2. If someone has been *buttonholed*, he or she is unable to get out of a conversation.

3. Listening to a *monotonous* speaker is a fun way to spend an evening.

4. An *interminable* wait goes by so quickly you hardly even notice that time has passed.

5. Most people enjoy *exasperating* tasks because they are filled with exciting surprises.

6. Someone who is naturally *garrulous* is likely to be very uncomfortable speaking in front of a crowd of attentive listeners.

Word Study

Denotation and Connotation A word's **denotation** is its literal dictionary definition. Every word has at least one denotation. Many words also have **connotations**, subtle shades of meaning that a word evokes. A word's connotations may be neutral, negative, or positive. The concept vocabulary words *tedious, monotonous,* and *interminable* all have negative connotations.

1. Of the three words noted—*tedious, monotonous,* and *interminable*—which is the most intensely negative? Explain.

2. Add two words to that list. Choose one that is less intense in its negativity, and one that is more intense. Sort your five words on a scale from least to most negative.

⬚ **WORD NETWORK**

Add words related to a sense of place from the text to your Word Network.

≡ **STANDARDS**

Reading Literature
Determine the meaning of words and phrases as they are used in the text, including figurative and connotative meanings; analyze the impact of specific word choices on meaning and tone, including words with multiple meanings or language that is particularly fresh, engaging, or beautiful.

Language
• Demonstrate understanding of figurative language, word relationships, and nuances in word meanings.
• Analyze nuances in the meaning of words with similar denotations.

Author's Style

Word Choice Mark Twain was among the first authors to use the American vernacular, or language as it is spoken by ordinary people. His diction includes both standard American English and variations that reflect a story's setting and characters' personalities. These variations include dialect and idiomatic expressions.

- **Dialect** is a way of speaking that is specific to a particular area or group of people. Twain spells passages of dialect as they would be pronounced.

  Dialect: *There couldn't be no solit'ry thing mentioned but that feller'd offer to bet on it, and take ary side you please. . . .*

  Standard English: You couldn't mention anything without having that fellow offer to bet on it, choosing either side.

- **Idiomatic expressions** are figures of speech that cannot be understood literally. For example, the idiom "it's raining cats and dogs" means that there is heavy rain, not that animals are falling from the sky.

  Idiomatic Expression: *If there was a horse race, you'd find him <u>flush</u>, or you'd find him <u>busted</u> at the end of it.*

  Actual Meaning: If there was a horse race, you would find him at the end either <u>with plenty of money</u> or <u>none</u>.

Read It

1. Rewrite each example of dialect from Twain's story into standard English.

DIALECT	STANDARD ENGLISH
I don't recollect exactly.	
Thish-yer Smiley had a mare.	
He would grab that other dog jest by the j'int of his hind leg.	
He never done nothing for three months but set in his back yard and learn that frog to jump.	

2. **Connect to Style** Reread paragraph 20 of the story. Identify an idiom in the paragraph, explain its literal meaning, and consider how it helps to develop Simon Wheeler's character.

3. 🗐 **Notebook** Explain how Twain's use of dialect and idioms helps him portray his characters vividly and create humor.

Write It

🗐 **Notebook** Use at least two of the following idioms in a paragraph. Use context clues to suggest their meaning.

a hot potato	**worth writing home about**
an arm and a leg	**barking up the wrong tree**

from LIFE ON THE MISSISSIPPI

THE NOTORIOUS JUMPING FROG
OF CALAVERAS COUNTY

Writing to Compare

You have read two works by Mark Twain—an excerpt from *Life on the Mississippi* and the short story "The Notorious Jumping Frog of Calaveras County." Now, deepen your understanding of Twain's humor by comparing the two works and expressing your ideas in writing.

Assignment

In an essay entitled "How to Tell a Story," Twain wrote: "The humorous story may be spun out to great length, and may wander around as much as it pleases, and arrive nowhere in particular. . . . it is told gravely; the teller does his best to conceal the fact that he even dimly suspects there is anything funny about it."

Write an **explanatory text** in which you explore whether Twain follows his own rules for telling a funny story in *Life on the Mississippi* and "The Notorious Jumping Frog of Calaveras County." Consider similarities and differences in the humor displayed in the two narratives.

Prewriting

Analyze the Texts First, analyze the quotation from Twain's essay. Rephrase it in your own words to make sure you understand it.

Paraphrase: _____

_____

Next, review the definitions of *diction, tone, dialect,* and *idiomatic expressions.* Then, choose several passages from both selections that are relevant to Twain's characterization of a humorous story. Use the chart to take notes.

☰ STANDARDS

Writing
• Write informative/explanatory texts to examine and convey complex ideas, concepts, and information clearly and accurately through the effective selection, organization, and analysis of content.
• Introduce a topic; organize complex ideas, concepts, and information so that each new element builds on that which precedes it to create a unified whole; include formatting, graphics, and multimedia when useful to aiding comprehension.
• Develop the topic thoroughly by selecting the most significant and relevant facts, extended definitions, concrete details, quotations, or other information and examples appropriate to the audience's knowledge of the topic.
• Develop and strengthen writing as needed by planning, revising, editing, rewriting, or trying a new approach, focusing on addressing what is most significant for a specific purpose and audience.

A HUMOROUS STORY . . .	LIFE ON THE MISSISSIPPI	THE NOTORIOUS JUMPING FROG . . .
"may be spun out to great length"		
"may . . . arrive nowhere in particular"		
"is told gravely"		
conceals humor		

📓 **Notebook** Respond to these questions.

1. Which narrative most closely aligns with Twain's characterization of humorous writing?

2. Do you find that selection the funnier of the two? Why, or why not?

Drafting

Formulate Your Thesis, or Central Idea In your essay, you will explain how the humor in the two narratives is similar and how it is different, with reference to the quotation from Twain. Clarify the focus of your essay by summarizing the similarities and differences you observe in the ways Twain makes each narrative funny. Then, write a working, or draft, thesis statement. You may always refine your thesis statement as you continue to work through your ideas.

I. **Main similarity:** _____
_____

II. **Main difference:** _____
_____

III. **Working Thesis Statement:** _____
_____
_____

Draft Your Essay Your essay should introduce and develop a unified, coherent set of ideas that you can trace from the introduction through the body paragraphs to the conclusion. As you draft your essay, follow these guidelines for each section:

Introduction:

- Identify which parts of Twain's quotation you will address.
- State your thesis or central idea.

Body Paragraphs:

- Develop your thesis with explanations and reasons.
- Include passages from both narratives to support your ideas. Introduce short passages with a comma. Introduce longer passages with a colon, and set them off by indenting them from both margins. Include a parenthetical page reference after each quotation.
- Explain how the passages you chose relate to Twain's quotation. Strengthen your analysis by including your own insights about how Twain builds humor.

Conclusion:

- Reintroduce Twain's quotation.
- Summarize or restate your thesis.
- End with a memorable statement, quotation, or insight.

Review, Revise, and Edit

Once you are done drafting, reread and revise your essay. Review Twain's quotation to make sure you establish a connection between his rules for telling a humorous story and each passage you discuss. Edit for diction, choosing words and phrases that create a formal tone. Finalize your essay by proofreading it carefully.

✏ EVIDENCE LOG

Before moving on to a new selection, go to your Evidence Log and record what you learned from *Life on the Mississippi* and "The Notorious Jumping Frog of Calaveras County."

About the Author

"A White Heron" is the most popular story **Sarah Orne Jewett** (1849–1909) wrote. As a young girl, she often accompanied her father, a physician, as he made house calls through rural Maine. Later, she would fold her keen recollections of the region's people and wildlife into her stories, novels, and poems. She sold her first story to the *Atlantic Monthly* when she was nineteen, and she soon became well-known for her precise descriptions and sharp observations of the women and men who lived near the Atlantic Ocean in southern Maine.

🔧 **Tool Kit**
First-Read Guide and Model Annotation

A White Heron

Concept Vocabulary

You will encounter the following words as you read "A White Heron." Before reading, note how familiar you are with each word. Then, rank the words in order from most familiar (1) to least familiar (6).

WORD	YOUR RANKING
dilatory	
loitered	
hospitality	
squalor	
hermitage	
quaint	

After completing your first read, come back to the concept vocabulary and review your ratings. Mark changes to your original rankings as needed.

First Read FICTION

Apply these strategies as you conduct your first read. You will have an opportunity to complete the close-read notes after your first read.

NOTICE *whom* the story is about, *what* happens, *where* and *when* it happens, and *why* those involved react as they do.

ANNOTATE by marking vocabulary and key passages you want to revisit.

First Read

CONNECT ideas within the selection to what you already know and what you have already read.

RESPOND by completing the Comprehension Check and by writing a brief summary of the selection.

A White Heron

Sarah Orne Jewett

BACKGROUND

The white heron in this story is another name for the snowy egret, a bird that nests near water and in swamps. At the time this story was written, the snowy egret was hunted for its feathers, and the species almost became extinct. However, the efforts of conservationists have since helped the snowy egret population to recover, and the bird is no longer considered endangered.

SCAN FOR
MULTIMEDIA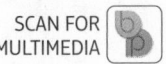

I.

1   The woods were already filled with shadows one June evening, just before eight o'clock, though a bright sunset still glimmered faintly among the trunks of the trees. A little girl was driving home her cow, a plodding, **dilatory**, provoking creature in her behavior, but a valued companion for all that. They were going away from whatever light there was, and striking deep into the woods, but their feet were familiar with the path, and it was no matter whether their eyes could see it or not.

2   There was hardly a night the summer through when the old cow could be found waiting at the pasture bars; on the contrary, it was her greatest pleasure to hide herself away among the huckleberry bushes, and though she wore a loud bell she had made the discovery that if one stood perfectly still it would not ring. So Sylvia had to hunt for her until she found her, and call Co'! Co'! with never an answering Moo, until her childish patience was quite spent. If the creature had not given good milk and plenty of it, the case would have seemed very different to her owners. Besides, Sylvia had all the time there

> **NOTES**
>
> **dilatory** (DIHL uh tawr ee) *adj.* inclined to delay; slow
>
> **CLOSE READ**
> **ANNOTATE:** In paragraph 1, mark four adjectives that describe the cow.
>
> **QUESTION:** Why does the author use these adjectives?
>
> **CONCLUDE:** What is the effect of this opening description?

was, and very little use to make of it. Sometimes in pleasant weather it was a consolation to look upon the cow's pranks as an intelligent attempt to play hide and seek, and as the child had no playmates she lent herself to this amusement with a good deal of zest. Though this chase had been so long that the wary animal herself had given an unusual signal of her whereabouts, Sylvia had only laughed when she came upon Mistress Moolly at the swamp-side, and urged her affectionately homeward with a twig of birch leaves. The old cow was not inclined to wander farther, she even turned in the right direction for once as they left the pasture, and stepped along the road at a good pace. She was quite ready to be milked now, and seldom stopped to browse. Sylvia wondered what her grandmother would say because they were so late. It was a great while since she had left home at half-past five o'clock, but everybody knew the difficulty of making this errand a short one. Mrs. Tilley had chased the hornéd torment too many summer evenings herself to blame any one else for lingering, and was only thankful as she waited that she had Sylvia, nowadays, to give such valuable assistance. The good woman suspected that Sylvia **loitered** occasionally on her own account; there never was such a child for straying about out-of-doors since the world was made! Everybody said that it was a good change for a little maid who had tried to grow for eight years in a crowded manufacturing town, but, as for Sylvia herself, it seemed as if she never had been alive at all before she came to live at the farm. She thought often with wistful compassion of a wretched geranium that belonged to a town neighbor.

3   "'Afraid of folks,'" old Mrs. Tilley said to herself, with a smile, after she had made the unlikely choice of Sylvia from her daughter's houseful of children, and was returning to the farm. "'Afraid of folks,' they said! I guess she won't be troubled no great with 'em up to the old place!" When they reached the door of the lonely house and stopped to unlock it, and the cat came to purr loudly, and rub against them, a deserted pussy, indeed, but fat with young robins, Sylvia whispered that this was a beautiful place to live in, and she never should wish to go home.

CLOSE READ

ANNOTATE: In paragraph 4, mark two references to shade or shadows.

QUESTION: Why does the author include these details in an otherwise pleasant scene?

CONCLUDE: What purpose do these details serve?

4   The companions followed the shady wood-road, the cow taking slow steps and the child very fast ones. The cow stopped long at the brook to drink, as if the pasture were not half a swamp, and Sylvia stood still and waited, letting her bare feet cool themselves in the shoal water, while the great twilight moths struck softly against her. She waded on through the brook as the cow moved away, and listened to the thrushes with a heart that beat fast with pleasure. There was a stirring in the great boughs overhead. They were full of little birds and beasts that seemed to be wide awake, and going about their world, or else saying good-night to each other in sleepy twitters. Sylvia herself felt sleepy as she walked along. However, it was not much farther to the house, and the air was soft and sweet. She was not often in the woods so late as this, and it made her feel as if she

were a part of the gray shadows and the moving leaves. She was just thinking how long it seemed since she first came to the farm a year ago, and wondering if everything went on in the noisy town just the same as when she was there; the thought of the great red-faced boy who used to chase and frighten her made her hurry along the path to escape from the shadow of the trees.

5   Suddenly this little woods-girl is horror-stricken to hear a clear whistle not very far away. Not a bird's-whistle, which would have a sort of friendliness, but a boy's whistle, determined, and somewhat aggressive. Sylvia left the cow to whatever sad fate might await her, and stepped discreetly aside into the bushes, but she was just too late. The enemy had discovered her, and called out in a very cheerful and persuasive tone, "Halloa, little girl, how far is it to the road?" And trembling Sylvia answered almost inaudibly, "A good ways."

6   She did not dare to look boldly at the tall young man, who carried a gun over his shoulder, but she came out of her bush and again followed the cow, while he walked alongside.

7   "I have been hunting for some birds," the stranger said kindly, "and I have lost my way, and need a friend very much. Don't be afraid," he added gallantly. "Speak up and tell me what your name is, and whether you think I can spend the night at your house, and go out gunning early in the morning."

8   Sylvia was more alarmed than before. Would not her grandmother consider her much to blame? But who could have foreseen such an accident as this? It did not seem to be her fault, and she hung her head as if the stem of it were broken, but managed to answer "Sylvy," with much effort when her companion again asked her name.

9   Mrs. Tilley was standing in the doorway when the trio came into view. The cow gave a loud moo by way of explanation.

10   "Yes, you'd better speak up for yourself, you old trial! Where'd she tucked herself away this time, Sylvy?" But Sylvia kept an awed silence; she knew by instinct that her grandmother did not comprehend the gravity of the situation. She must be mistaking the stranger for one of the farmer-lads of the region.

11   The young man stood his gun beside the door, and dropped a lumpy game-bag beside it; then he bade Mrs. Tilley good-evening, and repeated his wayfarer's story, and asked if be could have a night's lodging.

12   "Put me anywhere you like," he said. "I must be off early in the morning, before day; but I am very hungry, indeed. Yon can give me some milk at any rate, that's plain."

13   "Dear sakes, yes," responded the hostess, whose long slumbering hospitality seemed to be easily awakened. "You might fare better if you went out to the main road a mile or so, but you're welcome to what we've got. I'll milk right off, and you make yourself at home. You can sleep on husks[1] or feathers," she proffered graciously. "I

hospitality (hos puh TAL uh tee) n. warm, welcoming attitude toward guests

---

1. **husks** n. corn husks, used to stuff a mattress.

CLOSE READ

ANNOTATE: Colloquial language is informal and may not observe the conventions of standard English. In paragraph 16, mark four examples of colloquial language in Mrs. Tilley's words.

QUESTION: Why does the author choose to have Mrs. Tilley speak in this way?

CONCLUDE: What effect does this use of colloquial language have?

raised them all myself. There's a good pasturing for geese just below here towards the ma'sh. Now step round and set a plate for the gentleman, Sylvy!" And Sylvia promptly stepped. She was glad to have something to do, and she was hungry herself.

14   It was a surprise to find as clean and comfortable a little dwelling in this New England wilderness. The young man had known the horrors of its most primitive housekeeping, and the dreary **squalor** of that level of society which does not rebel at the companionship of hens. This was the best thrift of an old-fashioned farmstead, though on such a small scale that it seemed like a **hermitage**. He listened eagerly to the old woman's **quaint** talk, he watched Sylvia's pale face and shining gray eyes with ever growing enthusiasm, and insisted that this was the best supper he had eaten for a month, and afterward the new-made friends sat down in the door-way together while the moon came up.

15   Soon it would be berry-time, and Sylvia was a great help at picking. The cow was a good milker, though a plaguy thing to keep track of, the hostess gossiped frankly, adding presently that she had buried four children, so Sylvia's mother, and a son (who might be dead) in California were all the children she had left. "Dan, my boy, was a great hand to go gunning," she explained sadly. "I never wanted for pa'tridges or gray squer'ls while he was to home. He's been a great wand'rer, I expect, and he's no hand to write letters. There, I don't blame him, I'd ha' seen the world myself if it had been so I could."

16   "Sylvy takes after him," the grandmother continued affectionately, after a minute's pause. "There ain't a foot o' ground she don't know her way over, and the wild creaturs counts her one o' themselves. Squer'ls she'll tame to come an' feed right out o' her hands, and all sorts o' birds. Last winter she got the jaybirds to bangeing[2] here, and I believe she'd a' scanted herself of her own meals to have plenty to throw out amongst 'em, if I hadn't kep' watch. Anything but crows, I tell her, I'm willin' to help support—though Dan he had a tamed one o' them that did seem to have reason same as folks. It was round here a good spell after he went away. Dan an' his father they didn't hitch,—but he never held up his head ag'in after Dan had dared him an' gone off."

17   The guest did not notice this hint of family sorrows in his eager interest in something else.

18   "So Sylvy knows all about birds, does she?" he exclaimed, as he looked round at the little girl who sat, very demure but increasingly sleepy, in the moonlight. "I am making a collection of birds myself. I have been at it ever since I was a boy." (Mrs. Tilley smiled.) "There are two or three very rare ones I have been hunting for these five years. I mean to get them on my own ground if they can be found."

_____

2. **bangeing** lounging or hanging around.

19   "Do you cage 'em up?" asked Mrs. Tilley doubtfully, in response to this enthusiastic announcement.

20   "Oh no, they're stuffed and preserved, dozens and dozens of them," said the ornithologist,[3] "and I have shot or snared every one myself. I caught a glimpse of a white heron a few miles from here on Saturday, and I have followed it in this direction. They have never been found in this district at all. The little white heron, it is," and he turned again to look at Sylvia with the hope of discovering that the rare bird was one of her acquaintances.

21   But Sylvia was watching a hop-toad in the narrow footpath.

22   "You would know the heron if you saw it," the stranger continued eagerly. "A queer tall white bird with soft feathers and long thin legs. And it would have a nest perhaps in the top of a high tree, made of sticks, something like a hawk's nest."

23   Sylvia's heart gave a wild beat; she knew that strange white bird, and had once stolen softly near where it stood in some bright green swamp grass, away over at the other side of the woods. There was an open place where the sunshine always seemed strangely yellow and hot, where tall, nodding rushes grew, and her grandmother had warned her that she might sink in the soft black mud underneath and never be heard of more. Not far beyond were the salt marshes just this side of the sea itself, which Sylvia wondered and dreamed much about, but never had seen, whose great voice could sometimes be heard above the noise of the woods on stormy nights.

24   "I can't think of anything I should like so much as to find that heron's nest," the handsome stranger was saying. "I would give ten dollars to anybody who could show it to me," he added desperately, "and I mean to spend my whole vacation hunting for it if need be. Perhaps it was only migrating, or had been chased out of its own region by some bird of prey."

25   Mrs. Tilley gave amazed attention to all this, but Sylvia still watched the toad, not divining, as she might have done at some calmer time, that the creature wished to get to its hole under the door-step, and was much hindered by the unusual spectators at that hour of the evening. No amount of thought, that night, could decide how many wished-for treasures the ten dollars, so lightly spoken of, would buy.

26   The next day the young sportsman hovered about the woods, and Sylvia kept him company, having lost her first fear of the friendly lad, who proved to be most kind and sympathetic. He told her many things about the birds and what they knew and where they lived and what they did with themselves. And he gave her a jack-knife, which she thought as great a treasure as if she were a desert-islander. All day long he did not once make her troubled or afraid except when he brought down some unsuspecting singing creature from its bough. Sylvia would have liked him vastly better without his gun; she could not understand why he killed the very birds he

---

3. **ornithologist** (awr nih THOL uh jihst) *n.* one who practices the study of birds.

seemed to like so much. But as the day waned, Sylvia still watched the young man with loving admiration. She had never seen anybody so charming and delightful; the woman's heart, asleep in the child, was vaguely thrilled by a dream of love. Some premonition of that great power stirred and swayed these young creatures who traversed the solemn woodlands with soft-footed silent care. They stopped to listen to a bird's song; they pressed forward again eagerly, parting the branches—speaking to each other rarely and in whispers; the young man going first and Sylvia following, fascinated, a few steps behind, with her gray eyes dark with excitement.

27　She grieved because the longed-for white heron was elusive, but she did not lead the guest, she only followed, and there was no such thing as speaking first. The sound of her own unquestioned voice would have terrified her—it was hard enough to answer yes or no when there was need of that. At last evening began to fall, and they drove the cow home together, and Sylvia smiled with pleasure when they came to the place where she heard the whistle and was afraid only the night before.

II.

28　Half a mile from home, at the farther edge of the woods, where the land was highest, a great pine-tree stood, the last of its generation. Whether it was left for a boundary mark, or for what reason, no one could say; the woodchoppers who had felled its mates were dead and gone long ago, and a whole forest of sturdy trees, pines and oaks and maples, had grown again. But the stately head of this old pine towered above them all and made a landmark for sea and shore miles and miles away. Sylvia knew it well. She had always believed that whoever climbed to the top of it could see the ocean; and the little girl had often laid her hand on the great rough trunk and looked up wistfully at those dark boughs that the wind always stirred, no matter how hot and still the air might be below. Now she thought of the tree with a new excitement, for why, if one climbed it at break of day could not one see all the world, and easily discover from whence the white heron flew, and mark the place, and find the hidden nest?

29　What a spirit of adventure, what wild ambition! What fancied triumph and delight and glory for the later morning when she could make known the secret! It was almost too real and too great for the childish heart to bear.

30　All night the door of the little house stood open and the whippoorwills came and sang upon the very step. The young sportsman and his old hostess were sound asleep, but Sylvia's great design kept her broad awake and watching. She forgot to think of sleep. The short summer night seemed as long as the winter darkness, and at last when the whippoorwills ceased, and she was afraid the morning would after all come too soon, she stole out of the house and followed the pasture path through the woods, hastening toward the open ground beyond, listening with a sense of comfort and companionship to the drowsy twitter of a half-awakened bird, whose perch she had jarred in passing. Alas, if the great wave of human interest which flooded for the first time this dull little life should sweep away the satisfactions of an existence heart to heart with nature and the dumb life of the forest!

31   There was the huge tree asleep yet in the paling moonlight, and small and silly Sylvia began with utmost bravery to mount to the top of it, with tingling, eager blood coursing the channels of her whole frame, with her bare feet and fingers, that pinched and held like bird's claws to the monstrous ladder reaching up, up, almost to the sky itself. First she must mount the white oak tree that grew alongside, where she was almost lost among the dark branches and the green leaves heavy and wet with dew; a bird fluttered off its nest, and a red squirrel ran to and fro and scolded pettishly at the harmless housebreaker. Sylvia felt her way easily. She had often climbed there, and knew that higher still one of the oak's upper branches chafed against the pine trunk, just where its lowest boughs were set close together. There, when she made the dangerous pass from one tree to the other, the great enterprise would really begin.

NOTES

CLOSE READ

ANNOTATE: In the first sentence of paragraph 31, mark two adjectives that describe Sylvia and two adjectives that describe the pine tree.

QUESTION: Why does the author use these adjectives?

CONCLUDE: What is the effect of these word choices?

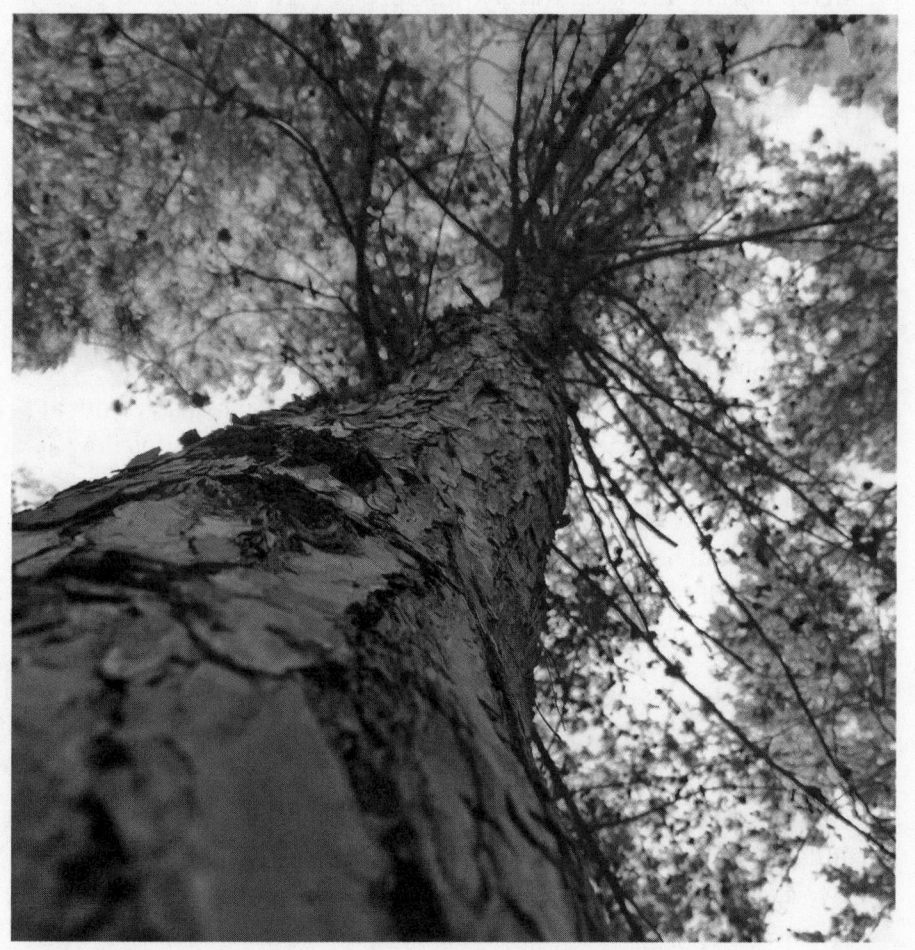

32   She crept out along the swaying oak limb at last, and took the daring step across into the old pine-tree. The way was harder than she thought; she must reach far and hold fast, the sharp dry twigs caught and held her and scratched her like angry talons, the pitch made her thin little fingers clumsy and stiff as she went round and round the tree's great stem, higher and higher upward. The sparrows and robins in the woods below were beginning to wake and twitter to the dawn, yet it seemed much lighter there aloft in the pine-tree, and the child knew she must hurry if her project were to be of any use.

33   The tree seemed to lengthen itself out as she went up, and to reach farther and farther upward. It was like a great main-mast to the voyaging earth; it must truly have been amazed that morning through all its ponderous frame as it felt this determined spark of human spirit wending its way from higher branch to branch. Who knows how steadily the least twigs held themselves to advantage this light, weak creature on her way! The old pine must have loved his new dependent. More than all the hawks, and bats, and moths, and even the sweet voiced thrushes, was the brave, beating heart of the solitary gray-eyed child. And the tree stood still and frowned away the winds that June morning while the dawn grew bright in the east.

34   Sylvia's face was like a pale star, if one had seen it from the ground, when the last thorny bough was past, and she stood trembling and tired but wholly triumphant, high in the tree-top. Yes, there was the sea with the dawning sun making a golden dazzle over it, and toward that glorious east flew two hawks with slow-moving pinions. How low they looked in the air from that height when one had only seen them before far up, and dark against the blue sky. Their gray feathers were as soft as moths; they seemed only a little way from the tree, and Sylvia felt as if she too could go flying away among the clouds. Westward, the woodlands and farms reached miles and miles into the distance; here and there were church steeples, and white villages, truly it was a vast and awesome world!

35   The birds sang louder and louder. At last the sun came up bewilderingly bright. Sylvia could see the white sails of ships out at sea, and the clouds that were purple and rose-colored and yellow at first began to fade away. Where was the white heron's nest in the sea of green branches, and was this wonderful sight and pageant of the world the only reward for having climbed to such a giddy height? Now look down again, Sylvia, where the green marsh is set among the shining birches and dark hemlocks; there where you saw the white heron once you will see him again; look, look! a white spot of him like a single floating feather comes up from the dead hemlock and grows larger, and rises, and comes close at last, and goes by the landmark pine with steady sweep of wing and outstretched slender neck and crested head. And wait! wait! do not move a foot or a finger, little girl, do not send an arrow of light and consciousness from your two eager eyes, for the heron has perched on a pine bough not far

beyond yours, and cries back to his mate on the nest and plumes his feathers for the new day!

36   The child gives a long sigh a minute later when a company of shouting cat-birds comes also to the tree, and vexed by their fluttering and lawlessness the solemn heron goes away. She knows his secret now, the wild, light, slender bird that floats and wavers, and goes back like an arrow presently to his home in the green world beneath. Then Sylvia, well satisfied, makes her perilous way down again, not daring to look far below the branch she stands on, ready to cry sometimes because her fingers ache and her lamed feet slip. Wondering over and over again what the stranger would say to her, and what he would think when she told him how to find his way straight to the heron's nest.

37   "Sylvy, Sylvy!" called the busy old grandmother again and again, but nobody answered, and the small husk bed was empty and Sylvia had disappeared.

38   The guest waked from a dream, and remembering his day's pleasure hurried to dress himself that might it sooner begin. He was sure from the way the shy little girl looked once or twice yesterday that she had at least seen the white heron, and now she must really be made to tell. Here she comes now, paler than ever, and her worn old frock is torn and tattered, and smeared with pine pitch. The grandmother and the sportsman stand in the door together and

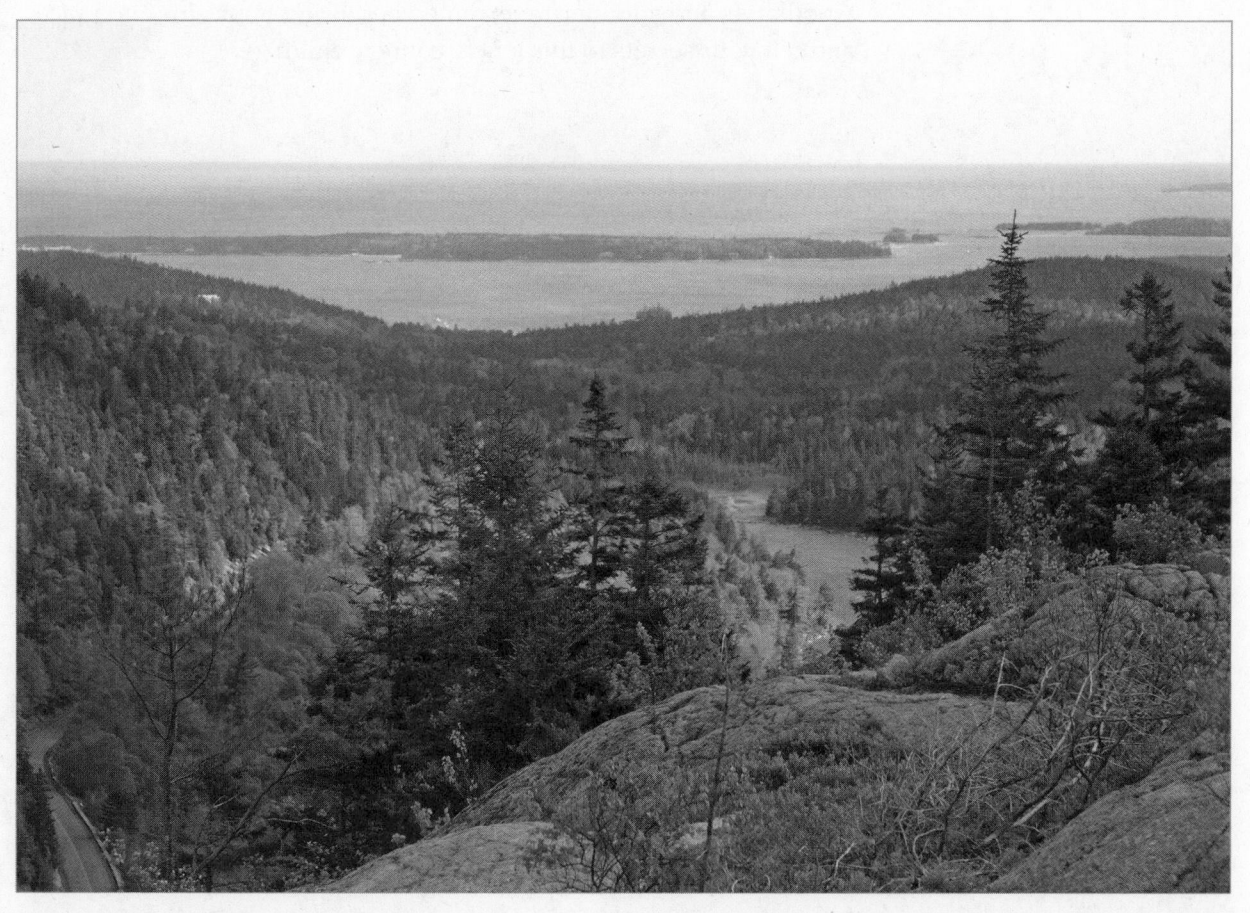

CLOSE READ

ANNOTATE: Mark the exclamation and the questions in paragraph 40.

QUESTION: Why does the author choose to use an exclamation and questions rather than statements?

CONCLUDE: What is the effect of these sentence variations?

question her, and the splendid moment has come to speak of the dead hemlock tree by the green marsh.

39   But Sylvia does not speak after all, though the old grandmother fretfully rebukes her, and the young man's kind, appealing eyes are looking straight in her own. He can make them rich with money; he has promised it, and they are poor now. He is so well worth making happy, and he waits to hear the story she can tell.

40   No, she must keep silence! What is it that suddenly forbids her and makes her dumb? Has she been nine years growing and now, when the great world for the first time puts out a hand to her, must she thrust it aside for a bird's sake? The murmur of the pine's green branches is in her ears, she remembers how the white heron came flying through the golden air and how they watched the sea and the morning together, and Sylvia cannot speak; she cannot tell the heron's secret and give its life away.

41   Dear loyalty, that suffered a sharp pang as the guest went away disappointed later in the day, that could have served and followed him and loved him as a dog loves! Many a night Sylvia heard the echo of his whistle haunting the pasture path as she came home with the loitering cow. She forgot even her sorrow at the sharp report of his gun and the sight of thrushes and sparrows dropping silent to the ground, their songs hushed and their pretty feathers stained and wet with blood. Were the birds better friends than their hunter might have been,—who can tell? Whatever treasures were lost to her, woodlands and summer-time, remember! Bring your gifts and graces and tell your secrets to this lonely country child! ❧

Comprehension Check

Complete the following items after you finish your first read.

1. Where had Sylvia lived before she came to stay at her grandmother's house?

2. What does the young stranger hope to find in the wilderness?

3. What does the stranger offer to give anyone who helps him achieve his goal?

4. Why does Sylvia climb the great pine tree?

5. What information does Sylvia refuse to share after her expedition to the pine tree?

6. 📓 **Notebook** Write a summary of "A White Heron" in order to confirm your understanding of the story.

- -

RESEARCH

Research to Clarify Choose at least one unfamiliar detail from the text. Briefly research that detail. In what way does the information you learned shed light on an aspect of the story?

Research to Explore Conduct research to learn more about Sarah Orne Jewett's life in the Maine woods.

A WHITE HERON

Close Read the Text

1. This model, from paragraph 33 of the text, shows two sample annotations, along with questions and conclusions. Close read the passage and find another detail to annotate. Then, write a question and your conclusion.

ANNOTATE: Jewett uses contradictory terms to describe Sylvia.

QUESTION: What idea about Sylvia is Jewett expressing?

CONCLUDE: Sylvia's spirit is stronger than her small body reveals.

Close Read
ANNOTATE · QUESTION · CONCLUDE

ANNOTATE: The pine tree is given human emotions.

QUESTION: Why does Jewett personify the tree?

CONCLUDE: If the grand tree loves Sylvia, then she must truly be exceptional.

> [The tree] must truly have been amazed that morning through all its ponderous frame as it felt this determined spark of human spirit wending its way from higher branch to branch. Who knows how steadily the least twigs held themselves to advantage this light, weak creature on her way! The old pine must have loved his new dependent.

2. For more practice, go back into the text, and complete the close-read notes.

3. Revisit a section of the text you found important during your first read. Read this section closely, and **annotate** what you notice. Ask yourself **questions** such as "Why did the author make this choice?" What can you **conclude**?

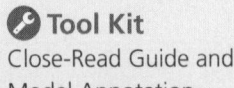 **Tool Kit**
Close-Read Guide and Model Annotation

Analyze the Text

CITE TEXTUAL EVIDENCE to support your answers.

📓 **Notebook** Respond to these questions.

1. (a) What is Sylvia's reaction when she first hears the stranger's whistle? (b) **Analyze** What later events in the story does this reaction foreshadow, or predict?

2. (a) **Interpret** On the second day, how does Sylvia feel about the stranger? (b) **Evaluate** What motivates Sylvia to climb the pine tree?

3. **Synthesize** Jewett ends the story by invoking "Dear loyalty." To whom or what does Sylvia remain loyal by not telling the heron's secret? Explain your answer.

4. **Historical Perspectives** How would Sylvia's and her grandmother's lives have changed if they had the ten dollars from the stranger? What does that tell you about their time period and circumstances? Explain.

5. **Essential Question:** *What is the relationship between literature and place?* What have you learned about the relationship between literature and place by reading this story?

STANDARDS
Reading Literature
• Cite strong and thorough textual evidence to support analysis of what the text says explicitly as well as inferences drawn from the text, including determining where the text leaves matters uncertain.
• Determine two or more themes or central ideas of a text and analyze their development over the course of the text, including how they interact and build on one another to produce a complex account; provide an objective summary of the text.

Analyze Craft and Structure

Thematic Development The **theme** of a literary text is its central message or insight about human life or behavior. Sometimes, the theme is explicitly stated. More often, however, readers must piece together related ideas from the text to infer the theme. Theme should be expressed in a statement, not a single word. An author may develop more than one theme in a single work.

To help determine theme, readers can examine the imagery and symbolism in the text.

- **Imagery** is language that uses sensory details—words related to sight, hearing, touch, taste, or smell—to create word pictures in readers' minds. More broadly, imagery can include figurative language, or language that presents surprising comparisons to help readers understand ideas in a new way. "A White Heron" begins with vivid imagery that helps readers picture the rural Maine setting.

- A **symbol** is something—an object, a character, an animal, or a place— that represents something else. In "A White Heron," the great pine tree and the white heron are two powerful symbols that represent more than simply a tree and a bird. The deeper meanings of these symbols are clues to the larger ideas or themes of the story.

Practice

CITE TEXTUAL EVIDENCE to support your answers.

📓 **Notebook** Respond to these questions.

1. Reread the description of the great pine tree in paragraph 33. (a) What imagery does Jewett use in her description of the tree? (b) Based on these images, what might the pine tree represent?

2. (a) Trace Sylvia's attitude toward the stranger from the beginning of the story to the end. How do her feelings about him change? (b) Is the stranger a symbolic figure? Why, or why not?

3. (a) What does Sylvia have to gain by revealing the white heron's location? What does she gain by remaining silent? (b) What does the white heron represent?

4. Use a chart like this one to analyze imagery, symbols, and themes. For each topic listed in the left-hand column, record images, symbols, and other details from the story that help to reveal the author's central messages or insights. Then, write a theme statement for each topic.

TOPIC	IMAGES, SYMBOLS, DETAILS	THEME STATEMENT
relationship of humans to nature and society		
self-discovery		
loyalty		

A WHITE HERON

Concept Vocabulary

dilatory	hospitality	hermitage
loitered	squalor	quaint

Why These Words? These concept vocabulary words help describe the pace and character of rural life. In contrast to life in a city, the pace of life in nineteenth-century rural Maine is unhurried. People often accept a *dilatory* speed, and it is not uncommon to *loiter*. The endurance of traditional values is evident in Mrs. Tilley's *hospitality* to the stranger.

1. How does the concept vocabulary clarify the reader's understanding of the story's setting?

2. What other words in the selection connect to this concept?

Practice

📓 **Notebook** The six concept words appear in "A White Heron."

1. Use each concept word in a sentence that demonstrates your understanding of the word's meaning.

2. In two of your sentences, replace the concept word with a synonym. How does the sentence change? For example, which word is stronger? Which one makes the sentence seem more positive or negative?

Word Study

Latin Root Word: *hospes* The concept vocabulary word *hospitality* comes from the Latin root word *hospes*, meaning both "host" and "guest." Thus, *hospitality* means "a warm, welcoming attitude toward guests."

1. Write a definition of the word *hospice* based on your understanding of the Latin root word *hospes*. Check your answer in a print or online college-level dictionary.

2. Identify and define two other words that are derived from the Latin root word *hospes*. Use a specialized reference such as an etymological dictionary to verify your choices.

Conventions and Style

Sentence Variety There are four types of sentences: declarative, interrogative, exclamatory, and imperative. In "A White Heron," Jewett varies declarative sentences with occasional **interrogative sentences**, or questions, and **exclamations** to develop Sylvia's character—especially the way in which Sylvia processes her thoughts and feelings.

FOLLOW THROUGH
Refer to the Grammar Handbook to learn more about these terms.

SENTENCE TYPE	FUNCTION	EXAMPLE
Declarative	makes a statement	*Besides, Sylvia had all the time there was, and very little use to make of it.* (paragraph 2)
Interrogative	asks a question	*What is it that suddenly forbids her and makes her dumb?* (paragraph 40)
Exclamatory	expresses strong feeling	*. . . there never was such a child for straying about out-of-doors since the world was made!* (paragraph 2)
Imperative	gives a command or makes a request	*Bring your gifts and graces and tell your secrets to this lonely country child!* (paragraph 41)

Read It

1. Reread paragraph 8 and identify the interrogative sentences. What do the questions reveal about Sylvia's feelings and state of mind?

2. Reread paragraphs 28 and 29. Mark the interrogative sentence and the exclamations. How does the progression of these sentences convey a steadily mounting sense of excitement in Sylvia?

3. **Connect to Style** Reread the last paragraph of "A White Heron." In a few sentences, explain how Jewett employs various types of sentences in this paragraph to create an effective conclusion to the story.

Write It

Notebook Write a brief sketch, or descriptive paragraph, of Sylvia, Mrs. Tilley, or the stranger. Use at least one interrogative sentence and one exclamatory sentence in your paragraph.

A WHITE HERON

Writing to Sources

In a critical analysis, you carefully examine the parts of a literary text. You identify the author's key techniques, and then evaluate their interaction and effectiveness. Your analysis should clarify important elements in the work and always be supported with textual evidence.

Assignment

Write a **critical analysis** of "A White Heron." Analyze the ways in which Jewett structures events and uses dialogue and description to keep readers uncertain about Sylvia's intentions until the end of the story. Include these elements in your writing:

- a clear discussion of Sylvia's character at the beginning and end of the story
- a commentary on the role that dialogue plays in the story
- an analysis of the effects of description and imagery
- an evaluation of the story's overall structure

Vocabulary Connection Consider including several of the concept vocabulary words in your critical analysis.

dilatory	hospitality	hermitage
loitered	squalor	quaint

Reflect on Your Writing

After you have drafted your critical analysis, answer the following questions.

1. How do you think that analyzing the related elements of plot, dialogue, and description improves your understanding and appreciation of the story?

2. What advice would you give another student writing a critical analysis?

3. **Why These Words?** The words you choose make a difference in your writing. Which words helped you to convey important elements of Jewett's story?

STANDARDS

Reading Literature
Analyze how an author's choices concerning how to structure specific parts of a text contribute to its overall structure and meaning as well as its aesthetic impact.

Speaking and Listening
Propel conversations by posing and responding to questions that probe reasoning and evidence; ensure a hearing for a full range of positions on a topic or issue; clarify, verify, or challenge ideas and conclusions; and promote divergent and creative perspectives.

Speaking and Listening

Assignment

Form two teams and hold a **debate** about the question that Jewett poses in the final paragraph of "A White Heron":

> *Were the birds better friends than their hunter might have been,—who can tell?*

Each team should adopt a clear point of view and formulate a claim to answer the question.

1. **Establish the Rules** Decide who will speak for each team. Assign roles to other team members—for example, note-taker, textual evidence finder, and argument evaluator. Discuss issues such as time limits and an alternating order of speakers, and then come to an agreement. Decide whether you will include time for rebuttals to refute the opposing side's arguments. Finally, determine who will judge the debate: your teacher or a student panel.

2. **Explore and Evaluate Claims** As you develop and assess a claim for your side of the issue, keep these factors in mind:

   - the characters' personalities
   - what Sylvia and the stranger know and don't know about each other
   - the characters' values, as revealed in the story
   - the characters' relationships to each other, as portrayed in the story

   Encourage everyone on your team to express opinions about these factors.

3. **Evaluate the Debate** As the other team presents their argument, listen attentively. Use an evaluation guide like the one shown to analyze their claims and evidence.

EVALUATION GUIDE

Rank each statement on a scale of **1** (not demonstrated) to **5** (demonstrated).

- ☐ Team members demonstrated that they were following orderly, practical rules.

- ☐ Team members explored and evaluated arguments on each side of the issue.

- ☐ Team members presented their arguments logically and effectively.

- ☐ Team members supported their arguments with relevant textual evidence from the story.

✎ EVIDENCE LOG

Before moving on to a new selection, go to your Evidence Log and record what you learned from "A White Heron."

WRITING TO SOURCES

- *from* LIFE ON THE MISSISSIPPI

- THE NOTORIOUS JUMPING FROG OF CALAVERAS COUNTY

- A WHITE HERON

 Tool Kit
Student Model of an Explanatory Text

Write an Explanatory Essay

You have read an excerpt from a memoir and two short stories in which setting plays an essential role. In the memoir *Life on the Mississippi,* the location of Hannibal, Missouri, on the Mississippi River is the driving force behind all the events described, and in Twain's short story, the setting is important enough to appear in the title. "A White Heron" depends on setting for character development, plot, and conflict.

Assignment

Write a five-paragraph explanatory essay in which you address this question:

> How do American authors use regional details to make the events and themes of a narrative come to life for readers?

Think about the role that specific geographic details play in the selections you have read. Use examples from each text to explain how authors use setting to create a desired impact on readers. In addition, briefly research American Regionalism, a literary movement that focused on the use of "local color" and celebrated the unique and varied landscapes of the country.

Elements of an Explanatory Essay

An **explanatory essay** is a brief work of nonfiction in which the writer explains a topic. The explanation may focus on how to do a task, the reasons for a particular situation, or how something is put together or works in a certain way. The main purpose for explanatory texts is to instruct and inform the reader.

A well-written explanatory essay contains these elements:

- a clear thesis statement that presents the writer's main idea
- relevant facts, details, and examples that develop the topic
- accurate and relevant facts and details
- appropriate and accurate vocabulary, including definitions of unfamiliar terms
- a conclusion that supports and reaffirms the explanation

ACADEMIC VOCABULARY

As you craft your explanatory essay, consider using some of the academic vocabulary you learned in the beginning of the unit.

analyze
subordinate
literal
determine
trivialize

Model Explanatory Text For a model of a well-crafted explanatory text, see the Launch Text, "Planning Your Trip to Gold Country." Review the Launch Text for examples of the elements of an effective explanatory text. You will look more closely at these elements as you prepare to write your own explanatory essay.

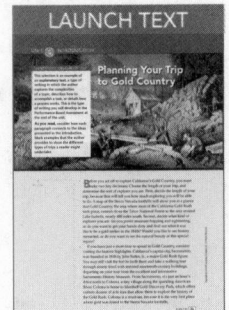

STANDARDS
Writing
- Write informative/explanatory texts to examine and convey complex ideas, concepts, and information clearly and accurately through the effective selection, organization, and analysis of content.
- Write routinely over extended time frames and shorter time frames for a range of tasks, purposes, and audiences.

Prewriting / Planning

Formulate a Thesis Statement Go back and reread or skim the selections in Whole-Group Learning to answer questions 1 and 2. Then, use your answers to develop a thesis statement.

1. Which of the three regional settings sticks in your mind the most? Why? How does that setting help to develop the plot and theme(s) of the memoir or story?

   _____

   _____

2. What techniques do the authors use to depict the regions in which their narratives take place?

   _____

   _____

3. Write a thesis statement to respond to the prompt. You will defend this thesis using examples from the texts and research about American literary history.

   _____

   _____

Notebook Gather Evidence Your evidence for this essay should come from Twain's and Jewett's narratives. Return to the texts to find specific examples in which the regional setting helps make the events and themes of the narrative seem realistic. Consider literary elements that the authors employ, such as imagery, diction, and tone.

TITLE	EXAMPLES
from Life on the Mississippi	
The Notorious Jumping Frog of Calaveras County	
A White Heron	

Evaluate Evidence Use the following strategies to evaluate the evidence you collect:

- Mark details that provide the strongest support for your thesis so you will be sure to include them in your essay.

- Look for connections between ideas and techniques in order to build a unified explanation. For example, you might consider how imagery and figurative language work together to bring a setting to life.

- Identify details that might contradict your thesis. You can include them as counterexamples and explain why they do not invalidate your thesis.

EVIDENCE LOG

Review your Evidence Log and identify key details you may want to use in your essay.

STANDARDS

Writing
Introduce a topic; organize complex ideas, concepts, and information so that each new element builds on that which precedes it to create a unified whole; include formatting, graphics, and multimedia when useful to aiding comprehension.

ENRICHING WRITING WITH RESEARCH

Gathering and Using Research Your goal in this essay is to inform your readers, but you are not expected to know everything about your subject. Thoughtful research can help you clarify or expand upon your ideas about the importance of setting in American literature.

Finding Information in Print and Digital Sources Look for information in sources that are reliable, using multiple resources to verify any details that are not common knowledge. Plan to consult the following resources:

- **Primary and Secondary Sources:** Primary sources—including news accounts, autobiographies, documentary footage, and journals—are texts created during the time period you are studying. In this case, you will use Twain's and Jewett's stories themselves as primary sources about regional writing. Secondary sources, such as textbooks or literary reviews, can help inform you about others' ideas. Be sure to credit ideas that are not your own.

- **Print and Digital Resources:** The Internet allows fast access to data, but print resources are often edited more carefully. Whenever possible, confirm information you find in one source by checking a second course.

- **Media Resources:** Documentaries, television programs, podcasts, and museum exhibitions are rich sources of information.

Conducting Digital Searches Careful strategies can help you locate reliable information on the Internet. In many search engines, using quotation marks can help you focus a search. Place a phrase in quotation marks to find pages that include exactly that phrase. To limit your search to .edu, .org, or .gov sites, which are generally more reliable than .com sites, use the search command "site:" followed by the extension. For example, enter "site:.edu" and "Lewis and Clark" and you will get a list of .edu (education) sites that include that exact phrase.

Using Research Effectively Thoughtful use of research can help you explain a subject to your readers. As you collect evidence, think about how each detail you find can support your thesis.

- **Precise Definitions:** Your readers may not recognize certain literary terms that you want to use. Researched information can help you define terms accurately.

- **Background and Context:** Your readers may need additional background information in order to understand elements of your analysis.

- **Additional Details:** You may need to go outside the texts or topic you are analyzing to add details that inform or engage your reader. Consider concepts in your writing that you might expand with interesting, relevant information you obtain from research.

≣ STANDARDS

Writing
• Develop the topic thoroughly by selecting the most significant and relevant facts, extended definitions, concrete details, quotations, or other information and examples appropriate to the audience's knowledge of the topic.
• Gather relevant information from multiple authoritative print and digital sources, using advanced searches effectively; assess the strengths and limitations of each source in terms of the task, purpose, and audience; integrate information into the text selectively to maintain the flow of ideas, avoiding plagiarism and overreliance on any one source and following a standard format for citation.

ESSENTIAL QUESTION: What is the relationship between literature and place?

College and Career Readiness

Read It

1. This excerpt shows how the Launch Text uses research to define a term.

> **LAUNCH TEXT EXCERPT**
>
> A map of the Sierra Nevada foothills will show you at a glance that Gold Country, <u>the area where most of the California Gold Rush took place</u>, extends from the Tahoe National Forest to the area named Lake Isabella, nearly 400 miles south.

The writer uses a resource to provide a detailed and thorough definition for the highlighted term.

2. Note two examples of information the Launch Text writer found through research. Explain how each detail provides necessary information.

3. Identify types of research sources the writer might have consulted.

Write It

Review your thesis statement and the examples you found in each text. Then, consider your audience and what they already know about your topic. Will you need to define any literary terms? What specific information does the prompt ask you to include to provide context for your explanation? How can interesting details from research strengthen your writing?

Use the chart below to organize and complete your research.

	WHERE COULD I FIND THIS INFORMATION?	INFORMATION FROM MY RESEARCH
Terms to Define (literary terms, unfamiliar terms from textual evidence or research)		
Background and Context (information readers need to understand the analysis or ideas)		
Additional Details (about settings, authors, history, and so on)		

 TIP

CONVENTIONS
If you include a definition or explanation that is a restrictive appositive, set it off with a comma, as in these examples:

- He writes about the Mississippi, North America's largest drainage system.
- Huckleberries, dark blue berries that grow on low shrubs, are key to this passage.

Organize Your Essay Here is a basic five-paragraph outline commonly used for explanatory essays. Note than an introduction can be more than a single paragraph, as can a conclusion. This outline provides the most basic scaffolding for your ideas. Adapt it to suit your purposes.

Introduction (1 paragraph)
Present and explain your thesis statement.
Body (3 paragraphs)
Support your thesis with facts, definitions, details, and examples. Each paragraph should have a specific topic, such as an author, a text, or a literary strategy.
Conclusion (1 paragraph)
Summarize and reaffirm your explanation.

Review your evidence before you begin to draft. If, after gathering evidence, your original thesis no longer works well, revise it to better fit the details and examples you will use. Plan the order in which you will write about the way American authors use regional details. Decide where you will include information about American literary regionalism you found during research.

Drafting

Write a First Draft Follow your outline to write your first draft. Start with your introduction and add examples from the three texts in a logical order. Well-developed body paragraphs put details and examples in context by using transitions and explaining how each example supports the thesis statement. Remember to add definitions and details from research that can help your readers understand your explanation. Include information about American literary regionalism, or local color, to provide context for your explanation. Finish with a conclusion that reaffirms your thesis.

Incorporate Anecdote You might choose to include a personal anecdote that strongly supports your explanation. Look closely at paragraph 4 of the Launch Text, "Planning Your Trip to Gold Country." It seamlessly combines an anecdote about the author's experience with facts and details related to planning a trip.

Jamestown boasts a number of businesses that allow you to take pans, trowels, and boots into the American River and test your ability to find gold. Sam and I found nothing but iron pyrite, the "fool's gold" that deceived many a Forty-Niner, but we had a thrilling time in the chilly water under a stark, blue sky. Searching Jamestown sites on the Internet will turn up a variety of tours and gold-prospecting adventures, and you can choose the one that best matches your needs.

STANDARDS
Writing
• Introduce a topic; organize complex ideas, concepts, and information so that each new element builds on that which precedes it to create a unified whole; include formatting, graphics, and multimedia when useful to aiding comprehension.
• Provide a concluding statement or section that follows from and supports the information or explanation presented.

LANGUAGE DEVELOPMENT: STYLE

Add Variety: Vary Syntax

Syntax is the way in which words and phrases are arranged in sentences. Effective writers vary syntax to keep their writing lively.

Read It

These examples from the Launch Text show some of the ways in which writers vary syntax.

VARY SENTENCE LENGTHS	
short	*We drove from Coloma south to Jamestown along historic Highway 49.*
long	*As we wound through hills and valleys dotted with wildflower meadows and piñon pines, we could imagine would-be miners on horses and in wagons making their way through the same landscape 165 years ago.*
VARY SENTENCE TYPES	
declarative	*California's capital city, Sacramento, was founded in 1848 by John Sutter, Jr., a major Gold Rush figure.*
interrogative	*Would you like to see history re-enacted, or do you want to see the natural beauty of this special region?*
imperative	*Start with a map and a schedule, and plan to spend at least a day at each major stop.*
VARY SENTENCE STRUCTURE	
Begin with an adverbial phrase	*Since that time, Yosemite's soaring cliffs and turbulent waterfalls remain unique among American landscapes.*
Begin with a participial phrase	*Stunned by the beautiful views, we enjoyed every mile.*
Begin with a subordinate clause	*If you have just a short time to spend in Gold Country, consider visiting the historic highlights.*

TIP

PUNCTUATION
Punctuate introductory phrases and clauses correctly.

- Use a comma after a subordinate clause that begins a sentence.
- Use a comma after an introductory participial phrase.
- Use a comma after a series of introductory prepositional phrases.

Write It

As you write, consider using a reference resource for ideas on how to vary your sentences. Here are a few titles that you might find useful:

- *Spellbinding Sentences* by Barbara Baig
- *It Was the Best of Sentences, It Was the Worst of Sentences* by June Casagrande
- *How to Write a Sentence: and How to Read One* by Stanley Fish
- *Artful Sentences: Syntax as Style* by Virginia Tufte

STANDARDS

Writing
Use appropriate and varied transitions and syntax to link the major sections of the text, create cohesion, and clarify the relationships among complex ideas and concepts.

Language
Vary syntax for effect, consulting references for guidance as needed; apply an understanding of syntax to the study of complex texts when reading.

Revising

Evaluating Your Draft

Use this checklist to evaluate the effectiveness of your first draft. Then, use your evaluation and the instruction on this page to guide your revision.

FOCUS AND ORGANIZATION	EVIDENCE AND ELABORATION	CONVENTIONS
☐ Provides an introduction that establishes the topic and thesis statement.	☐ Develops the topic using relevant facts, definitions, details, quotations, examples, and/or other evidence.	☐ Attends to the norms and conventions of the discipline, especially in the use of phrases and clauses to vary sentences.
☐ Presents main points in a logical order.	☐ Includes accurate and relevant information from research to support ideas.	
☐ Uses words, phrases, and clauses to clarify the relationships among ideas.	☐ Uses vocabulary and word choices that are appropriate for the purpose and audience, including precise words and technical vocabulary where appropriate.	
☐ Ends with a conclusion that follows logically from the preceding information.	☐ Establishes and maintains a formal style and objective tone.	

Revising for Focus and Organization

Focus Does your thesis answer the question in the assignment? Reread your essay and make sure that all of your evidence clearly relates to the question of how writers use setting to bring a story to life.

Organization Review your essay to make sure you have clearly referred to each text you are analyzing. If your draft seems choppy, consider adding transition words, phrases, and clauses to clarify the connections you are making between texts and ideas.

Revising for Evidence and Elaboration

Tone Although most of your explanation will be objective and formal, your tone may vary a bit if you include evidence from your own life—a personal anecdote that supports your explanation. Reread paragraphs 3 and 4 of the Launch Text to see how to blend anecdote with facts to keep your explanation seamless and consistent.

Definitions Make sure that you have defined any difficult vocabulary or special terms for your reader. You can define words without being too obvious about it if you use appositive phrases, as in these examples:

The characters' patois, <u>or regional slang</u>, adds to the reader's sense of place.

Small flats, <u>flat-bottomed wooden boats</u>, rock gently along the wharf.

⊞ WORD NETWORK

Include interesting words from your Word Network in your explanatory essay.

☰ STANDARDS

Writing
Establish and maintain a formal style and objective tone while attending to the norms and conventions of the discipline in which they are writing.

ESSENTIAL QUESTION: What is the relationship between literature and place?

PEER REVIEW

Exchange essays with a classmate. Use the checklist to evaluate your classmate's explanatory essay and provide supportive feedback.

1. Is the topic of the essay clear?

☐ yes   ☐ no   If no, explain what confused you.

2. Did the writer use relevant examples from the texts?

☐ yes   ☐ no   If no, tell what you think might work better.

3. Did the essay include relevant and interesting information from research?

☐ yes   ☐ no   If no, identify one place where details from research would make the essay more effective.

4. Did the text conclude in a logical way?

☐ yes   ☐ no   If no, suggest what you might change.

5. What is the strongest part of your classmate's essay? Why?

_____

_____

_____

_____

Editing and Proofreading

Edit for Conventions Reread your draft for accuracy and consistency. Correct errors in grammar and word usage. Make sure that you have used a variety of sentence lengths, types, and structures.

Proofread for Accuracy Read your draft carefully, looking for errors in spelling and punctuation. Use commas correctly with appositives and with introductory phrases and clauses.

Publishing and Presenting

Meet with a group of three other students and share your work. Discuss which examples from texts you used and why, and compare your selections to those of your classmates. What did you learn about how American writers use regional settings in their writing?

Reflecting

Reflect on what you learned by writing your explanatory essay. Was it difficult to find examples to support your thesis? How did researching American regional literature help you understand the texts and authors more deeply? Think about what you might do differently the next time you write an explanatory essay.

☰ STANDARDS

Writing
Develop and strengthen writing as needed by planning, revising, editing, rewriting, or trying a new approach, focusing on addressing what is most significant for a specific purpose and audience.

ESSENTIAL QUESTION:

What is the relationship between literature and place?

As you read these selections, work with a small group to explore the meaning and importance of the concept of "place."

From Text to Topic From 1880 to 1920, the United States experienced drastic changes. The frontier was continually settled until it was no longer considered a frontier. At the same time, cities boomed as their businesses attracted both new generations of Americans and immigrants who hoped for a better life in the United States. As you read the selections in this section, consider how the authors bring to life urban settings as well as rural ones, and how they continue to reveal the influence of place.

Small-Group Learning Strategies

Throughout your life, in school, in your community, and in your career, you will continue to develop strategies when you work in teams. Use these strategies during Small-Group Learning. Add ideas of your own for each step.

STRATEGY	ACTION PLAN
Prepare	• Complete your assignments so that you are prepared for group work. • Take notes on your reading so you can contribute to your group's discussions. •
Participate fully	• Make eye contact to signal that you are listening and taking in what is being said. • Use text evidence when making a point. •
Support others	• Build off ideas from others in your group. • State the relationship of your points to the points of others—whether you are supporting someone's point, refuting it, or taking the conversation in a new direction. •
Clarify	• Paraphrase the ideas of others to ensure that your understanding is correct. • Ask follow-up questions. •

SCAN FOR
MULTIMEDIA

CONTENTS

PERFORMANCE TASK

SPEAKING AND LISTENING FOCUS

Give an Explanatory Talk

The Small-Group readings are by authors who explore and celebrate the power of "place" in American life. After reading, your group will prepare and deliver a talk in which you explain the sense of place created by the authors in this section.

Working as a Team

1. **Take a Position** In your group, discuss the following question:

   Which do you think is a better way to record a person's sense of place: a writing journal or a camera/video recorder? Explain.

   As you take turns sharing your perceptions, be sure to provide reasons that support them. After all group members have shared, discuss connections among the ideas that were presented.

2. **List Your Rules** As a group, decide on the rules that you will follow as you work together. Two samples are provided. Add two more of your own. As you work together, you may add or revise rules based on your experience together.

   - Give everyone a chance to express and defend a position.
   - Allow group members to change their position if they feel that the evidence warrants it.

   - _____

   _____

   - _____

   _____

3. **Apply the Rules** Practice working as a group. Share what you have learned about place in American literature. Make sure each person in the group contributes. Take notes on and be prepared to share with the class one thing that you heard from another member of your group.

4. **Name Your Group** Choose a name that reflects the unit topic.

   Our group's name: _____

5. **Create a Communication Plan** Decide how you want to communicate with one another. For example, you might meet as a group after school, hold a video conference, text, or use email.

   Our group's decision: _____

   _____

Making a Schedule

First, find out the due dates for the Small-Group activities. Then, preview the texts and activities with your group, and make a schedule for completing the activities.

SELECTION	ACTIVITIES	DUE DATE
A Literature of Place		
American Regional Art		
from Dust Tracks on a Road		
Chicago Wilderness		
Sandburg's Chicago		
In the Longhouse, Oneida Museum Cloudy Day		
Introduction from The Way to Rainy Mountain		

Working on Group Projects

As your group works together, you'll find it more effective if each person has a specific role. Different projects require different roles. Before beginning a project, discuss the necessary roles, and choose one for each group member. Some possible roles are listed here. Add your ideas to the list.

Project Manager: monitors the schedule and keeps everyone on task

Researcher: organizes research activities

Recorder: takes notes during group meetings

_____

_____

_____

SCAN FOR MULTIMEDIA

A LITERATURE OF PLACE

Comparing Texts

In this lesson, you will read and compare the essay "A Literature of Place" with a gallery of American regional art. First, you will complete the first-read and close-read activities for "A Literature of Place." The work you do with your group on this title will help prepare you for the comparing task.

AMERICAN REGIONAL ART

About the Author

Barry Lopez (b. 1945) was born in Port Chester, New York, grew up in Southern California and New York City, and attended college in the Midwest before moving to Oregon, where he has lived since 1968. Lopez's many honors include the 1986 National Book Award for his book, *Arctic Dreams*. Lopez is also the author of eight works of fiction and two collections of essays. His works appear in many leading journals, are widely translated, and have been included in dozens of anthologies.

☷ STANDARDS

Reading Informational Text
By the end of grade 11, read and comprehend literary nonfiction in the grades 11–CCR text complexity band proficiently, with scaffolding as needed at the high end of the range.

Language
• Determine or clarify the meaning of unknown and multiple-meaning words and phrases based on *grades 11–12 reading and content*, choosing flexibly from a range of strategies.
• Use context as a clue to the meaning of a word or phrase.

A Literature of Place

Concept Vocabulary

As you perform your first read of "A Literature of Place," you will encounter these words.

| discern | temporal | spatial |

Context Clues If these words are unfamiliar to you, you may be able to determine their meanings by using **context clues**—words and phrases that appear in nearby text.

Example: This is a <u>huge</u>—therefore **unwieldy**—topic, and different writers approach it in vastly different ways.

Conclusion: When a topic is huge, it is difficult for writers to handle easily. *Unwieldy*, then, probably means something like "awkward" or "difficult to handle due to large size."

Apply your knowledge of context clues and other vocabulary strategies to determine the meanings of unfamiliar words you encounter during your first read.

First Read NONFICTION

Apply these strategies as you conduct your first read. You will have an opportunity to complete a close read after your first read.

NOTICE the general ideas of the text. *What* is it about? *Who* is involved?

ANNOTATE by marking vocabulary and key passages you want to revisit.

First Read

CONNECT ideas within the selection to what you already know and what you have already read.

RESPOND by completing the Comprehension Check and by writing a brief summary of the selection.

A Literature of Place

Barry Lopez

BACKGROUND

Nature writing, which Barry Lopez discusses in this essay, is literature written to describe the natural world and our relationship to it. This genre has a strong North American tradition. Possibly the most widely recognized American nature writer is Henry David Thoreau.

SCAN FOR MULTIMEDIA

1   In the United States in recent years, a kind of writing variously called "nature writing" or "landscape writing" has begun to receive critical attention, leading some to assume that this is a relatively new kind of work. In fact, writing that takes into account the impact nature and place have on culture is one of the oldest—and perhaps most singular—threads in American literature. Herman Melville in *Moby-Dick*, Henry David Thoreau, of course, and novelists such as Willa Cather, John Steinbeck and William Faulkner come quickly to mind, and more recently Peter Matthiessen, Wendell Berry, Wallace Stegner, and the poets W.S. Merwin, Amy Clampitt and Gary Snyder.

2   If there is anything different in this area of North American writing—and I believe there is—it is the hopeful tone it frequently strikes in an era of cynical detachment, and its explicitly dubious view of technological progress, even of capitalism.

3   The real topic of nature writing, I think, is not nature but the evolving structure of communities from which nature has been removed, often as a consequence of modern economic development. (A recent conference at the Library of Congress in Washington, "Watershed: Writers, Nature and Community," focused on this kind of writing. It was the largest literary conference ever held at the Library. Sponsors, in addition to the Library, were U.S. Poet

NOTES

Laureate Robert Hass and The Orion Society of Great Barrington, Massachusetts.) It is writing concerned, further, with the biological and spiritual fate of those communities. It also assumes that the fate of humanity and nature are inseparable. Nature writing in the United States merges here, I think, with other types of post-colonial writing, particularly in Commonwealth[1] countries. In numerous essays it addresses the problem of spiritual collapse in the West, and like those literatures it is in search of a modern human identity that lies beyond nationalism and material wealth.

4   This is a huge—not to say unwieldy—topic, and different writers approach it in vastly different ways. The classic struggle of writers to separate truth and illusion, to distinguish between roads to heaven and detours to hell, knows only continuance, not ending or solution. But I sense collectively now in writing in the United States the emergence of a concern for the world outside the self. It is as if someone had opened the door to a stuffy and too-much-studied room and shown us a great horizon where once there had been only walls.

5   I want to concentrate on a single aspect of this phenomenon— geography—but in doing so I hope to hew to a larger line of truth. I want to talk about geography as a shaping force, not a subject. Another way critics describe nature writing is to call it "the literature of place." A specific and particular setting for human experience and endeavor is, indeed, central to the work of many nature writers. I would say a sense of place is also critical to the development of a sense of morality and of human identity.

6   After setting out a few thoughts about place, I'd like to say something about myself as one writer who returns again and again to geography, as the writers of another generation once returned repeatedly to Freud and psychoanalysis.[2]

7   It is my belief that a human imagination is shaped by the architectures it encounters at an early age. The visual landscape, of course, or the depth, elevation and hues of a cityscape play a part here, as does the way sunlight everywhere etches lines to accentuate forms. But the way we imagine is also affected by streams of scent flowing faint or sharp in the larger oceans of air: by what the composer John Luther Adams calls the sonic landscape; and, say, by an awareness of how temperature and humidity rise and fall in a place over a year.

8   My imagination was shaped by the exotic nature of water in a dry California valley; by the sound of wind in the crowns of eucalyptus trees, by the tactile sensation of sheened earth, turned in furrows by a gang plow; by banks of saffron, mahogany, and scarlet cloud piled above a field of alfalfa at dusk; by encountering the musk from

---

1. **Commonwealth** association of independent nations, mostly former parts of the British Empire, united for purposes of mutual assistance.
2. **Freud and psychoanalysis** Sigmund Freud (1856–1939), Austrian physician and neurologist, is known as the founder of psychoanalysis, a method of analyzing and attempting to treat psychological disorders.

orange blossoms at the edge of an orchard; by the aftermath of a Pacific storm crashing a hot, flat beach.

9   Added to the nudge of these sensations were an awareness of the height and breadth of the sky, and of the geometry and force of the wind. Both perceptions grew directly out of my efforts to raise pigeons, and from the awe I felt before them as they maneuvered in the air. They gave me permanently a sense of the vertical component of life.

10   I became intimate with the elements of that particular universe. They fashioned me, and I return to them regularly in essays and stories in order to clarify or explain abstractions or to strike contrasts. I find the myriad relationships in that universe comforting, forming a "coherence" of which I once was a part.

11   If I were to try to explain the process of becoming a writer I could begin by saying that the comforting intimacy I knew in that California valley erected in me a kind of story I wanted to tell, a pattern I wanted to invoke—in countless ways. And I would add to this the two things that were most profoundly magical to me as a boy: animals and language. It's easy to see why animals might seem magical. Spiders and birds are bound differently than we are by gravity. Many wild creatures travel unerringly through the dark. And animals regularly respond to what we, even at our most attentive, cannot **discern**.

12   It's harder to say why language seemed magical, but I can be precise about this. The first book I read was *The Adventures of Tom Sawyer*. I still have the book. Underlined in it in pen are the first words I could recognize: *the, a, stop*, to *go*, to *see*. I can pick up the book today and recall my first feelings like a slow, silent detonation: words I heard people speak I was now able to perceive as marks on a page. I, myself, was learning to make these same marks on ruled paper. It seemed as glorious and mysterious as a swift flock of tumbler pigeons exploiting the invisible wind.

13   I can see my life prefigured in those two kinds of magic, the uncanny lives of creatures different from me (and, later, of cultures different from my own); and the twinned desires to go, to see. I became a writer who travels and one who focuses mostly, to be succinct, on what logical positivists sweep aside.

14   My travel is often to remote places—Antarctica, the Tanami Desert in central Australia, northern Kenya. In these places I depend on my own wits and resources, but heavily and just as often on the knowledge of interpreters—archaeologists, field scientists, anthropologists. Eminent among such helpers are indigenous[3] people, and I can quickly give you three reasons for my dependence on their insights. As a rule, indigenous people pay much closer attention to nuance in the physical world. They see more, and from a paucity of evidence, thoroughly observed, they can deduce more. Second, their

Mark context clues or indicate another strategy you used that helped you determine meaning.

discern (dih SURN) *v.*

MEANING:

---

3. **indigenous** (ihn DIHJ uh nuhs) *adj.* native.

NOTES

Mark context clues or indicate another strategy you used that helped you determine meaning.

temporal (TEHM puhr uhl) *adj.*

MEANING:

spatial (SPAY shuhl) *adj.*

MEANING:

history in a place, both tribal and personal, is typically deep. These histories create a **temporal** dimension in what is otherwise only a **spatial** landscape. Third, indigenous people tend to occupy the same moral universe as the landscape they sense.

15   Over time I have come to think of these three qualities—intimate attention; a *storied* relationship to place rather than a solely sensory awareness of it; and living in some sort of ethical unity with a place—I have come to think of these things as a fundamental human defense against loneliness. If you're intimate with a place, a place with whose history you're familiar, and you establish an ethical conversation with it, the implication that follows is this: the place knows you're there. It feels you. You will not be forgotten, cut off, abandoned.

16   As a writer I want to ask myself: How can you obtain this? How can you occupy a place and also have it occupy you? How can you find such a reciprocity?[4]

17   The key, I think, is to become vulnerable to a place. If you open yourself up you can build intimacy. Out of such intimacy will come a sense of belonging, a sense of not being isolated in the universe.

18   My question—how to secure this—is not idle. I want to be concrete about this, about how, actually, to enter a local geography. (We often daydream, I think, about entering childhood landscapes that dispel our anxiety. We court these feelings for a few moments in a park sometimes or during an afternoon in the woods.) Keeping this simple and practical, my first suggestion would be to be silent. Put aside the bird book, an analytic frame of mind, any compulsion to identify, and sit still. Concentrate instead on *feeling* a place, on using the sense of proprioception. Where in this volume of space are you situated? What is spread out behind you is as important as what you see before you. What lies beneath you is as relevant as what stands on the horizon. Actively use your ears to imagine the acoustical space you occupy. How does birdsong ramify[5] here? Through what air is it moving? Concentrate on smells in the belief that you *can* smell water and stone. Use your hands to get the heft and texture of a place— the tensile strength in a willow branch, the moisture in a pinch of soil, the different nap[6] of leaves. Open the vertical line of this place by consciously referring the color and form of the sky to what you see across the ground. Look *away* from what you want to scrutinize to gain a sense of its scale and proportion. Be wary of any obvious explanation for the existence of a color, a movement. Cultivate a sense of complexity, the sense that another landscape exists beyond the one you can subject to analysis.

19   The purpose of such attentiveness is to gain intimacy, to rid yourself of assumption. It should be like a conversation with someone you're attracted to, a person you don't want to send away by making too much of yourself. Such conversations, of course, can

---

4. **reciprocity** (rehs uh PROS uh tee) *n.* exchanging things with others for mutual benefit.
5. **ramify** (RAM uh fy) *v.* divide and spread.
6. **nap** *n.* soft, rough surface.

take place simultaneously on several levels. And they may easily be driven by more than simple curiosity. The compelling desire, as in human conversation, may be for a sustaining or informing relationship.

20   A succinct way to describe the frame of mind one should bring to a landscape is to say it rests on the distinction between imposing and proposing one's views. With a sincere proposal you hope to achieve an intimate, reciprocal relationship that will feed you in some way. To impose your views from the start is to truncate such a possibility, to preclude understanding.

21   Many of us, I think, long to become the companion of a place, not its authority, not its owner. And this brings me to a closing point. Perhaps you wonder, as I do, why over the last few decades people in Western countries have become so anxious about the fate of undeveloped land, and concerned about losing the intelligence of people who've kept intimate relationships with those places. I don't know where your thinking has led you, but I believe this curiosity about good relations with a particular stretch of land is directly related to speculation that it may be more important to human survival now to be in love than to be in a position of power. It may be more important now to enter into an ethical and reciprocal relationship with everything around us than to continue to work toward the sort of control of the physical world that, until recently, we aspired to.

22   The simple issue of our biological plausibility, our chance for biological survival, has become so precarious, so basic a question, that finding a way out of the predicament—if one is to be had—is imperative. It calls on our collective imaginations with an urgency we've never known before. We are in need not just of another kind of logic, another way of knowing, but of a radically different philosophical sensibility.

23   When I was a boy, running through orange groves in southern California, watching wind swirl in a grove of blue gum, and

swimming ecstatically in the foam of Pacific breakers, I had no such thoughts as these imperatives. I was content to watch a brace of pigeons fly across an azure sky, rotating on an axis that to this day I don't think I could draw. My comfort, my sense of inclusion in the small universe I inhabited, came from an appreciation of, a participation in, all that I saw, smelled, tasted and heard. That sense of inclusion not only assuaged my sense of loneliness as a child, it confirmed my imagination. And it is that single thing, the power of the human imagination to extrapolate from an odd handful of things—faint movement in a copse of trees, a wingbeat, the damp cold of field stones at night—to make from all this a pattern—the human ability to make a story, that fixed in me a sense of hope.

24   We keep each other alive with our stories. We need to share them as much as food. We also need good companions. One of the most extraordinary things about the land is that it knows this, and it compels language from some of us so that, as a community, we may actually speak of it. &

Comprehension Check

Complete the following items after you finish your first read. Review and clarify details with your group.

1. According to Barry Lopez, what is the fundamental topic of nature writing?

2. What two things were magical to Lopez when he was a boy?

3. According to Lopez, why are indigenous people good guides to remote places?

4. 📓 **Notebook** Write a summary of "A Literature of Place" in order to confirm your understanding of the essay.

- -

RESEARCH

Research to Explore Conduct research to find one or two photos that show the Southern California landscapes that Barry Lopez describes. You may want to share what you discover with your group.

Close Read the Text

With your group, revisit sections of the text you marked during your first read. **Annotate** details that you notice. What **questions** do you have? What can you **conclude**?

A LITERATURE OF PLACE

Analyze the Text

CITE TEXTUAL EVIDENCE support your answers.

📓 **Notebook** Complete the activities.

1. **Review and Clarify** With your group, reread paragraph 5 of the essay. What is the author's main idea in this paragraph? How does the main idea of this paragraph support the central idea of the essay as a whole?

2. **Present and Discuss** Now, work with your group to share passages from the selection that you found especially important. Take turns presenting your passages. Discuss what you noticed in the text, what questions you asked, and what conclusions you reached.

3. **Essential Question:** *What is the relationship between literature and place?* What has this essay taught you about the way that geography influences writing? Discuss with your group.

LANGUAGE DEVELOPMENT

Concept Vocabulary

discern	temporal	spatial

Why These Words? The three concept vocabulary words from the essay are related. With your group, determine what the words have in common. Write your ideas, and add another word that fits the category.

Practice

📓 **Notebook** Demonstrate your understanding of the concept vocabulary words by writing their meanings. Trade your definitions with a group member, and discuss any differences you notice.

Word Study

Latin Suffix: -al The concept vocabulary words *temporal* and *spatial* both end with the Latin suffix *-al*, which forms adjectives and means "of," "like," or "related to." Write definitions of *spatial* and *temporal* in which you demonstrate your understanding of the suffix *-al.* Then, find two other adjectives that end with this suffix. Write the words and their definitions.

📊 WORD NETWORK

Add words related to a sense of place from the text to your Word Network.

🗄 STANDARDS

Language
Identify and correctly use word patterns that indicate different meanings or parts of speech.

A LITERATURE OF PLACE

STANDARDS

Reading Informational Text
• Determine two or more central ideas of a text and analyze their development over the course of the text, including how they interact and build on one another to provide a complex analysis; provide an objective summary of the text.
• Analyze a complex set of ideas or sequence of events and explain how specific individuals, ideas, or events interact and develop over the course of the text.

Analyze Craft and Structure

Author's Choices: Central Ideas and Voice Students and other essay writers are often told to be objective and to avoid the use of personal statements in academic work. In "A Literature of Place," Lopez, who is a master writer and certainly knows this rule, ignores it. Instead, he injects himself directly into the essay, including many "I" statements and anecdotes from his own life. This creates several effects:

- It creates an intimate **voice**, or sense of the writer's personality captured in words.

- It adds clarity to the development of Lopez's **central,** or **main, ideas.** Lopez is able to share his thought process in an open, obvious way, thus leading readers through his thinking.

- Even though Lopez uses elevated language, the personal quality of the essay creates a conversational **tone,** or attitude, toward the topic and reader.

Practice

CITE TEXTUAL EVIDENCE to support your answers.

⊟ **Notebook** Work with your group to complete this reverse outline of Lopez's essay. Add notes about the central ideas and supporting details Lopez presents in each section. Then, answer the questions.

SECTION	CENTRAL IDEA	SUPPORTING DETAILS
I. Introduction: American Landscape Writing		
II. When and How People Develop a Sense of Geography		
III. Indigenous Understanding of Place		
IV. Proposing Views of New Landscapes Rather than Imposing Them		
V. How to Enter a Local Geography		
VI. Conclusion: Relationship Between Land and Community		

1. (a) In which sections of the essay does Lopez include personal opinions and anecdotes? (b) How does his use of personal information help readers understand abstract ideas? Cite at least two specific examples.

2. (a) How do his choices develop a connection between the writer and his readers? (b) How would the essay be affected if Lopez remained objective and impersonal throughout? Explain.

3. Describe Lopez's voice and tone. Cite specific examples from the essay that support your descriptions.

Conventions and Style

Punctuation Punctuation is much more than simple mechanics. It is an important tool for helping readers gain a clear and subtle sense of a writer's meaning. Consider, for example, how Lopez uses two punctuation marks in "A Literature of Place": the **dash (—)** and the **hyphen (-)**.

- **Dashes**, either singly or in pairs, have a variety of purposes. Dashes may be used for emphasis:

  If there is anything different in this area of North American writing—and I believe there is—it is the hopeful tone it frequently strikes. . . . (paragraph 2)

  A dash or pair of dashes may be used to add clarification:

  I want to concentrate on a single aspect of this phenomenon—geography—but in doing so I hope to hew to a larger line of truth. (paragraph 5)

  Finally, dashes may set off additional information, such as examples that deepen the main idea of a sentence.

  Use your hands to get the heft and texture of a place—the tensile strength in a willow branch. . . . (paragraph 18)

- **Hyphens** are shorter in length than dashes. Their main function is to join words together. Hyphens are often used to form compound adjectives. Compound adjectives are made up of two or more words that present a single idea to modify a noun.

full-page photograph	dust-covered furniture
first-aid kit	easy-to-follow directions

  In "A Literature of Place," Lopez uses hyphens to create his own unique compound adjective.

  It is as if someone had opened the door to a stuffy and too-much-studied room. . . . (paragraph 4)

Read It

1. With your group, locate the compound adjective *too-much-studied* in paragraph 4. Discuss what this adjective means and why you think Lopez chose to create his own compound adjective instead of using a more common modifier.

2. Reread paragraph 22, and consider the author's use of dashes. With your group, discuss the effect of these dashes and what the author suggests with this aside.

3. **Connect to Style** How does Lopez's liberal use of dashes affect the tone and mood of his essay? Explain your answer.

Write It

📓 **Notebook** In a paragraph, describe your own relationship to a specific place. As you discuss what this place is like and how it makes you feel, use dashes and hyphens to write precisely. Use a dash or pair of dashes to emphasize an idea, provide clarification, or give additional information. Use a hyphen or hyphens to create at least one compound adjective.

TIP

CLARIFICATION
Dashes are most effective when used sparingly. Too many dashes can be distracting or confusing. Dashes are best used to add a strong emphasis or when inserting a new sentence might interrupt the flow of ideas.

📝 **EVIDENCE LOG**

Before moving on to a new selection, go to your Evidence Log and record what you've learned from "A Literature of Place."

STANDARDS
Language
- Demonstrate command of the conventions of standard English capitalization, punctuation, and spelling when writing.
- Observe hyphenation conventions.

A LITERATURE OF PLACE

Comparing Text to Media

The works of art you are about to study are examples of American regional art. After completing the activities for this selection, you will compare how written and visual works communicate ideas.

AMERICAN REGIONAL ART

About the Artists

Edward Hopper
(1882–1967)

Guy A. Wiggins
(b. 1920)

Albert Bierstadt
(1830–1902)

Georgia O'Keeffe
(1887–1986)

Nell Choate Jones
(1879–1981)

Frederic Remington
(1861–1909)

American Regional Art

Media Vocabulary

These words will be useful to you as you analyze, discuss, and write about works of fine art.

Realism, Romanticism, and Impressionism: painting styles	• In Realism, a scene is depicted exactly as it appears. • In Romanticism, a scene is depicted with dramatic details, evoking an emotional response. • In Impressionism, a scene is suggested through brush strokes, the use of color and light, and the depiction of movement.
Palette: range of colors used in a particular work	• An artist has nearly infinite variations of color options from which to choose. • Color choices may help create an artwork's mood or atmosphere. For example, dark colors and shades of blue in a painting may suggest a somber or melancholy mood.
Perspective: method of giving a sense of depth on a flat or shallow surface	• Perspective indicates the vantage point from which a scene is viewed. • The subject may seem very far away, at a middle distance, or very close to viewers.

First Review MEDIA: ART AND PHOTOGRAPHY

Apply these strategies as you complete your first review. You will have an opportunity to complete a close review after your first review.

LOOK at each image and determine *whom* or *what* it portrays.

NOTE elements in each image that you find interesting and want to revisit.

CONNECT details in the images to other media you've experienced, texts you've read, or images you've seen.

RESPOND by completing the Comprehension Check.

First Review

LOOK NOTE CONNECT RESPOND

STANDARDS

Language
Acquire and use accurately general academic and domain-specific words and phrases, sufficient for reading, writing, speaking, and listening at the college and career readiness level; demonstrate independence in gathering vocabulary knowledge when considering a word or phrase important to comprehension or expression.

American Regional Art

BACKGROUND

Even though American art is influenced by the same developments in style that shape European art, it varies widely across the nation. Inspired by regional geography and culture, American painters and sculptors create works that depict an array of subjects in widely differing styles.

SCAN FOR MULTIMEDIA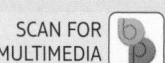

IMAGE 1: *The Lighthouse at Two Lights,*
Edward Hopper, Maine, 1929. A painter of Realist landscapes and cityscapes throughout America, Hopper has been described as a "pure painter," interested primarily in form, color, and the division of space.

NOTES

IMAGE 2: *Storm Lifting Over Wall Street*, **Guy A. Wiggins, New York, 2010.** A modern American artist who lives in New York City, Wiggins is a third-generation painter who inherited his Impressionist style from his father and grandfather.

NOTES

IMAGE 3: *Among the Sierra Nevada, California,* **Albert Bierstadt, California, 1868.** In creating his dramatic landscapes of the American West, Bierstadt used skills he gained through study in Germany and as a member of the Hudson River School in New York. He made many journeys west to gather material for his often enormous works.

NOTES

IMAGE 4: *Deer's Skull With Pedernal,* **Georgia O'Keeffe, New Mexico, 1936.** O'Keeffe is referred to as the "Mother of American Modernism," an experimental art movement that emerged primarily after World War I. She often painted the Pedernal, a mountain she could see from her New Mexico residence.

NOTES

IMAGE 5: *Georgia Red Clay,* **Nell Choate Jones, Georgia,1946.** In the 1920s, Jones was known for her European landscapes. After returning to the United States in 1936, she was inspired by the "picturesqueness" of her native rural Georgia. Her southern paintings are noted for their strong contours and use of color.

NOTES

IMAGE 6: *The Bronco Buster*, Frederic Remington, American West, 1895. Remington left his East Coast art school at the age of nineteen to travel to the West. His paintings and sculptures centered on horsemen and the landscapes of this frontier region.

NOTES

Comprehension Check

Complete the following items after you finish your first review. Review and clarify details with your group.

1. What structure dominates Image 1, the painting by Edward Hopper?

2. What kind of American place is depicted in Image 2, the painting by Guy A. Wiggins?

3. What does Image 4, the painting by Georgia O'Keeffe, depict?

RESEARCH

Research to Explore Chose an artist from this gallery who interests you, and formulate a research question about his or her life or work. Write your question here.

Close Review

With your group, revisit the artwork and your first-review notes. Record any new observations that seem important. What **questions** do you have? What can you **conclude**?

AMERICAN REGIONAL ART

Analyze the Media

Complete the activities.

1. **Present and Discuss** Choose the artwork you find most interesting or powerful. Share your choice with the group, and discuss why you chose it. Explain what you noticed in the artwork, what questions it raised for you, and what conclusions you reached.

2. **Review and Synthesize** With your group, review all the works of art. Do they do more than simply portray different geographical locales or regions? Explain.

3. 🔲 **Notebook Essential Question:** *What is the relationship between literature and place?* How do artists, like writers, establish connections to places? Support your response by identifying details from the works of art.

LANGUAGE DEVELOPMENT

Media Vocabulary

realism	impressionism	perspective
romanticism	palette	

Use the vocabulary words in your responses to the questions.

1. **(a)** In your view, which of the works of art most closely resembles real life? Explain your choice. **(b)** Which image portrays a scene with the greatest drama or sense of emotional intensity? Explain.

2. **(a)** In your view, which painting most clearly exaggerates elements of the scene? **(b)** What is the effect of this exaggeration? Explain.

3. Which image most clearly or dramatically conveys a sense of movement or action? Explain your choice.

🗏 STANDARDS

Language
Acquire and use accurately general academic and domain-specific words and phrases, sufficient for reading, writing, speaking, and listening at the college and career readiness level; demonstrate independence in gathering vocabulary knowledge when considering a word or phrase important to comprehension or expression.

American Regional Art **477**

A LITERATURE OF PLACE

AMERICAN REGIONAL ART

Writing to Compare

You have read the essay "A Literature of Place," by Barry Lopez, and viewed a gallery of American regional art. Now, deepen your understanding of both the text and the images by making connections between them and expressing your insights in writing.

Assignment

For Lopez, places give rise to stories. About his childhood, he writes: "The comforting intimacy of that California valley erected in me a kind of story I wanted to tell, a pattern I wanted to invoke—in countless ways."

- What "story" about place does Lopez tell in this essay? What kinds of details does he use to convey that story?

- What "story" about place do the artworks tell? What kinds of patterns and details do they use to "tell" those stories?

Write an **interpretive essay** in which you consider these questions. Think of the "story" as the main message or insight the work conveys. Work with your group to analyze the texts and complete the Prewriting activities. Then, write your own essay.

Prewriting

Analyze the Texts With your group, identify key ideas, details, and images in Lopez's essay. Then, select and analyze an image from the gallery and do the same. Decide what the writer and the artist are saying, in different ways, about place and our connection to it.

	KEY IDEAS, DETAILS, IMAGES, FEATURES	"STORY" BEING TOLD
Essay		
Artwork		

📓 **Notebook** Respond to these questions.

1. Why did your group choose the image you did?

2. How are the stories told by the image and the essay similar? How are they different?

📋 STANDARDS

Writing
• Write informative/explanatory texts to examine and convey complex ideas, concepts, and information clearly and accurately through the effective selection, organization, and analysis of content.
• Draw evidence from literary or informational texts to support analysis, reflection, and research.

Drafting

Tell Stories Before writing your essay, gather with your group for a "storytelling" session. Use your Prewriting notes to summarize aloud the story each selection tells or suggests about place and our connection to it. Take turns identifying key ideas, elements, and details in each work. Finally, decide how the two works express similar ideas and how they express different ones. Write your conclusions about the similarities and differences here:

SIMILAR IDEAS	DIFFERENT IDEAS

Choose an Organizational Structure Discuss various ways of organizing your essay.

- Will you first discuss Lopez's essay, then discuss the image, and then explain similarities and differences?

- Will you present a series of key ideas from the essay and show how the painting illustrates, extends, or departs from each one?

- Will you present the story told by the image and support the different parts of the story with quotations from Lopez's essay?

After your group discusses possible ways of structuring the essay, choose one and draft your essay independently.

Review, Revise, and Edit

Exchange drafts of your essay with your group members. Use one color to mark parts of your peer's essay that address Lopez's writing and a different color to mark parts of the essay that address the image. Offer suggestions for revising the essay to achieve greater balance. Then, use the feedback you receive to revise your essay. After you finalize your essay, read it aloud to the group. After the readings, discuss similarities and differences among your interpretations of the "stories" told by the works of art.

📝 EVIDENCE LOG

Before moving on to a new selection, go to your Evidence Log and record what you learned from "A Literature of Place" and the gallery of American regional art.

About the Author

Zora Neale Hurston
(1891–1960) grew up
in Florida. In 1925, she
moved to New York City,
where she soon established
herself as one of the bright
new talents of the Harlem
Renaissance. She returned
to the South for six years
to collect African American
folk tales. In 1935, she
published *Mules and Men*,
the first volume of black
American folklore compiled
by an African American. Her
work helped document the
African American connection
to the stories, songs, and
myths of Africa. Hurston
achieved critical and popular
success with the novels
Jonah's Gourd Vine (1934),
*Their Eyes Were Watching
God* (1937), *Moses, Man
of the Mountain* (1939),
and her prize-winning
autobiography, *Dust Tracks
on a Road* (1942).

from Dust Tracks on a Road

Concept Vocabulary

As you perform your first read of this excerpt from *Dust Tracks on a Road*,
you will encounter these words.

self-assurance	forward	brazenness

Base Words Words that seem unfamiliar may actually contain words you
know. Try looking for familiar base words within unfamiliar words. The word
irreplaceable, for example, contains the base word *replace*, which means
"to provide a substitute for." In this word, the prefix *ir-* means "not," and
the suffix *-able* means "capable of being." *Irreplaceable*, then, means "not
having the ability to be substituted for."

Note how the addition of prefixes or suffixes affects the meaning in
these words.

un**name**able	impossible to name
wreckage	pieces left after something is wrecked or destroyed
humorless	without a sense of humor
pre**exist**ing	existing at an earlier time

Apply your knowledge of base words and other vocabulary strategies to
determine the meanings of unfamiliar words you encounter during your
first read.

First Read NONFICTION

Apply these strategies as you conduct your first read. You will have an
opportunity to complete a close read after your first read.

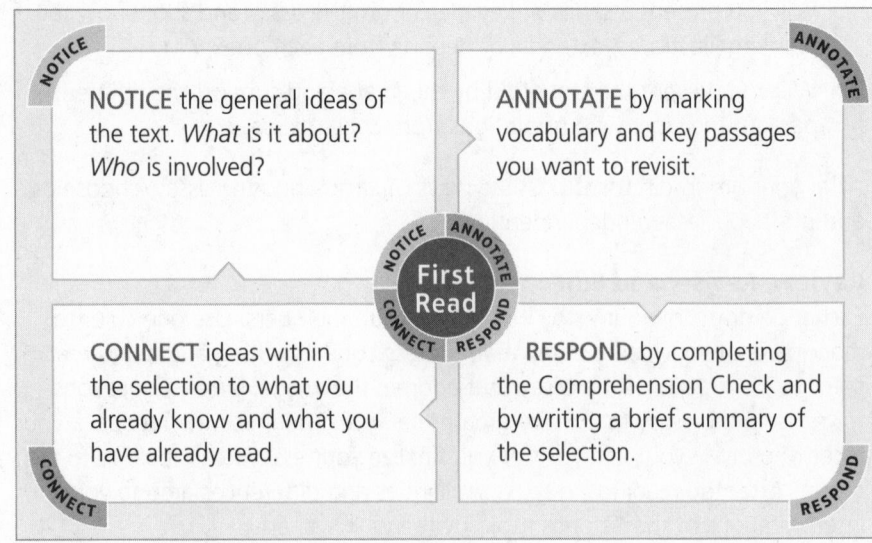

NOTICE the general ideas of the text. *What* is it about? *Who* is involved?

ANNOTATE by marking vocabulary and key passages you want to revisit.

CONNECT ideas within the selection to what you already know and what you have already read.

RESPOND by completing the Comprehension Check and by writing a brief summary of the selection.

⬛ STANDARDS

Reading Informational Text
By the end of grade 11, read and
comprehend literary nonfiction in
the grades 11–CCR text complexity
band proficiently, with scaffolding as
needed at the high end of the range.

Language
Identify and correctly use patterns of
word changes that indicate different
meanings or parts of speech.

from
Dust Tracks
on a **Road**

Zora Neale Hurston

BACKGROUND

In this excerpt from Zora Neale Hurston's autobiography, the young Zora experiences an event that opens her eyes to the world of literature and sets the stage for her career as a writer.

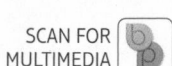

SCAN FOR
MULTIMEDIA

1   I used to take a seat on top of the gatepost and watch the world go by. One way to Orlando[1] ran past my house, so the carriages and cars would pass before me. The movement made me glad to see it. Often the white travelers would hail me, but more often I hailed them, and asked. "Don't you want me to go a piece of the way with you?"

2   They always did. I know now that I must have caused a great deal of amusement among them, but my **self-assurance** must have carried the point, for I was always invited to come along. I'd ride up the road

NOTES

Mark base words or indicate another strategy you used that helped you determine meaning.

self-assurance (sehlf uh SHUR uhns) *n.*

MEANING:

---

1. **Orlando** (awr LAN doh) city in central Florida, about five miles from Eatonville, Hurston's hometown.

Mark base words or indicate another strategy you used that helped you determine meaning.

forward (FAWR wuhrd) *adj.*

MEANING:

brazenness (BRAY zuhn nuhs) *n.*

MEANING:

for perhaps a half-mile, then walk back. I did not do this with the permission of my parents, nor with their foreknowledge.[2]

3   When they found out about it later, I usually got a whipping. My grandmother worried about my forward ways a great deal. She had known slavery and to her my brazenness was unthinkable.

4   "Git down offa dat gate-post! You li'l sow, you! Git down! Setting up dere looking dem white folks right in de face! They's gowine[3] to lynch you, yet. And don't stand in dat doorway gazing out at 'em neither. Youse too brazen to live long."[4]

5   Nevertheless. I kept right on gazing at them, and "going a piece of the way" whenever I could make it. The village seemed dull to me most of the time. If the village was singing a chorus, I must have missed the tune.

6   Perhaps a year before the old man[5] died, I came to know two other white people for myself. They were women.

7   It came about this way. The whites who came down from the North were often brought by their friends to visit the village school. A Negro school was something strange to them, and while they were always sympathetic and kind, curiosity must have been present, also. They came and went, came and went. Always, the room was hurriedly put in order, and we were threatened with a prompt and bloody death if we cut one caper while the visitors were present. We always sang a spiritual, led by Mr. Calhoun himself. Mrs. Calhoun always stood in the back, with a palmetto switch[6] in her hand as a squelcher. We were all little angels for the duration, because we'd better be. She would cut her eyes and give us a glare that meant trouble, then turn her face towards the visitors and beam as much as to say it was a great privilege and pleasure to teach lovely children like us. They couldn't see that palmetto hickory in her hand behind all those benches, but we knew where our angelic behavior was coming from.

8   Usually, the visitors gave warning a day ahead and we would be cautioned to put on shoes, comb our heads, and see to ears and fingernails. There was a close inspection of every one of us before we marched in that morning. Knotty heads, dirty ears and fingernails got hauled out of line, strapped and sent home to lick the calf over again.

9   This particular afternoon, the two young ladies just popped in. Mr. Calhoun was flustered, but he put on the best show he could. He dismissed the class that he was teaching up at the front of the room, then called the fifth grade in reading. That was my class.

10   So we took our readers and went up front. We stood up in the usual line, and opened to the lesson. It was the story of Pluto and

---

2. **foreknowledge** *n.* awareness of something before it happens or exists.
3. **gowine** "going."
4. **"Git down . . . live long"** Hurston's grandmother's fears reflect the fact of the times that it was often dangerous for African Americans to interact confidently with whites.
5. **the old man** white farmer who had developed a friendship with Hurston.
6. **palmetto** (pal MEHT oh) **switch** *n.* whip made from the fan-shaped leaves of the palmetto, a type of palm tree.

Persephone. It was new and hard to the class in general, and Mr. Calhoun was very uncomfortable as the readers stumbled along, spelling out words with their lips, and in mumbling undertones before they exposed them experimentally to the teacher's ears.

11   Then it came to me. I was fifth or sixth down the line. The story was not new to me, because I had read my reader through from lid to lid, the first week that Papa had bought it for me.

12   That is how it was that my eyes were not in the book, working out the paragraph which I knew would be mine by counting the children ahead of me. I was observing our visitors, who held a book between them, following the lesson. They had shiny hair, mostly brownish. One had a looping gold chain around her neck. The other one was dressed all over in black and white with a pretty finger ring on her left hand. But the thing that held my eyes were their fingers. They were long and thin, and very white, except up near the tips. There they were baby pink. I had never seen such hands. It was a fascinating discovery for me. I wondered how they felt. I would have given those hands more attention, but the child before me was almost through. My turn next, so I got on my mark, bringing my eyes back to the book and made sure of my place. Some of the stories I had reread several times, and this Greco-Roman myth was one of my favorites. I was exalted by it and that is the way I read my paragraph.

13   "Yes, Jupiter had seen her (Persephone). He had seen the maiden picking flowers in the field. He had seen the chariot of the dark monarch pause by the maiden's side. He had seen him when he seized Persephone. He had seen the black horses leap down Mount Aetna's fiery throat. Persephone was now in Pluto's dark realm and he had made her his wife."

14   The two women looked at each other and then back to me. Mr. Calhoun broke out with a proud smile beneath his bristly moustache, and instead of the next child taking up where I had ended, he nodded to me to go on. So I read the story to the end, where flying Mercury, the messenger of the Gods, brought Persephone back to the sunlit earth and restored her to the arms of Dame Ceres, her mother, that the world might have springtime and summer flowers, autumn and harvest. But because she had bitten the pomegranate[7] while in Pluto's kingdom, she must return to him for three months of each year, and be his queen. Then the world had winter, until she returned to earth.

15   The class was dismissed, and the visitors smiled us away and went into a low-voiced conversation with Mr. Calhoun for a few minutes. They glanced my way once or twice and I began to worry. Not only was I barefooted, but my feet and legs were dusty. My hair was more uncombed than usual, and my nails were not shiny clean. Oh, I'm going to catch it now. Those ladies saw me, too. Mr. Calhoun is promising to 'tend to me. So I thought.

---

7. **pomegranate** (POM uh gran iht) *n.* round, red-skinned fruit with many seeds.

16   Then Mr. Calhoun called me. I went up thinking how awful it was to get a whipping before company. Furthermore, I heard a snicker run over the room. Hennie Clark and Stell Brazzle did it out loud, so I would be sure to hear them. The smart-aleck was going to get it. I slipped one hand behind me and switched my dress tail at them, indicating scorn.

17   "Come here, Zora Neale," Mr. Calhoun cooed as I reached the desk. He put his hand on my shoulder and gave me little pats. The ladies smiled and held out those flower-looking fingers towards me. I seized the opportunity for a good look.

18   "Shake hands with the ladies, Zora Neale," Mr. Calhoun prompted and they took my hand one after the other and smiled. They asked if I loved school, and I lied that I did. There was *some* truth in it, because I liked geography and reading, and I liked to play at recess time. Who ever it was invented writing and arithmetic got no thanks from me. Neither did I like the arrangement where the teacher could sit up there with a palmetto stem and lick me whenever he saw fit. I hated things I couldn't do anything about. But I knew better than to bring that up right there, so I said yes, I *loved* school.

19   "I can tell you do," Brown Taffeta gleamed. She patted my head, and was lucky enough not to get sandspurs[8] in her hand. Children who roll and tumble in the grass in Florida are apt to get sandspurs in their hair. They shook hands with me again and I went back to my seat.

20   When school let out at three o'clock, Mr. Calhoun told me to wait. When everybody had gone, he told me I was to go to the Park House, that was the hotel in Maitland,[9] the next afternoon to call upon Mrs. Johnstone and Miss Hurd. I must tell Mama to see that I was clean

---

8. **sandspurs** *n.* spiny burrs that are the seeds of a grasslike weed.
9. **Maitland** (MAYT luhnd) city in Florida, close to Eatonville.

and brushed from head to feet, and I must wear shoes and stockings. The ladies liked me, he said, and I must be on my best behavior.

21   The next day I was let out of school an hour early, and went home to be stood up in a tub full of suds and be scrubbed and have my ears dug into. My sandy hair sported a red ribbon to match my red and white checked gingham dress, starched until it could stand alone. Mama saw to it that my shoes were on the right feet, since I was careless about left and right. Last thing, I was given a handkerchief to carry, warned again about my behavior, and sent off, with my big brother John to go as far as the hotel gate with me.

22   First thing, the ladies gave me strange things, like stuffed dates and preserved ginger, and encouraged me to eat all that I wanted. Then they showed me their Japanese dolls and just talked. I was then handed a copy of *Scribner's Magazine*,[10] and asked to read a place that was pointed out to me. After a paragraph or two, I was told with smiles, that that would do.

23   I was led out on the grounds and they took my picture under a palm tree. They handed me what was to me then a heavy cylinder done up in fancy paper, tied with a ribbon, and they told me goodbye, asking me not to open it until I got home.

24   My brother was waiting for me down by the lake, and we hurried home, eager to see what was in the thing. It was too heavy to be candy or anything like that. John insisted on toting it for me.

25   My mother made John give it back to me and let me open it. Perhaps, I shall never experience such joy again. The nearest thing to that moment was the telegram accepting my first book. One hundred goldy-new pennies rolled out of the cylinder. Their gleam lit up the world. It was not avarice[11] that moved me. It was the beauty of the thing. I stood on the mountain. Mama let me play with my pennies for a while, then put them away for me to keep.

26   That was only the beginning. The next day I received an Episcopal hymn-book bound in white leather with a golden cross stamped into the front cover, a copy of *The Swiss Family Robinson*, and a book of fairy tales.

27   I set about to commit the song words to memory. There was no music written there, just the words. But there was to my consciousness music in between them just the same. "When I Survey the Wondrous Cross" seemed the most beautiful to me, so I committed that to memory first of all. Some of them seemed dull and without life, and I pretended they were not there. If white people liked trashy singing like that, there must be something funny about them that I had not noticed before. I stuck to the pretty ones where the words marched to a throb I could feel.

28   A month or so after the young ladies returned to Minnesota, they sent me a huge box packed with clothes and books. The red coat with

---

10. ***Scribner's Magazine*** literary magazine, now no longer published.
11. **avarice** (AV uhr ihs) *n.* extreme desire for wealth; greed.

a wide circular collar and the red tam[12] pleased me more than any of the other things. My chums pretended not to like anything that I had, but even then I knew that they were jealous. Old Smarty had gotten by them again. The clothes were not new, but they were very good. I shone like the morning sun.

29   But the books gave me more pleasure than the clothes. I had never been too keen on dressing up. It called for hard scrubbings with Octagon soap suds getting in my eyes, and none too gentle fingers scrubbing my neck and gouging in my ears.

30   In that box were *Gulliver's Travels, Grimm's Fairy Tales, Dick Whittington, Greek and Roman Myths*, and best of all, *Norse Tales*. Why did the Norse tales strike so deeply into my soul? I do not know, but they did. I seemed to remember seeing Thor swing his mighty short-handled hammer as he sped across the sky in rumbling thunder, lightning flashing from the tread of his steeds and the wheels of his chariot. The great and good Odin, who went down to the well of knowledge to drink, and was told that the price of a drink from that fountain was an eye. Odin drank deeply, then plucked out one eye without a murmur and handed it to the grizzly keeper, and walked away. That held majesty for me.

31   Of the Greeks, Hercules moved me most. I followed him eagerly on his tasks. The story of the choice of Hercules as a boy when he met Pleasure and Duty, and put his hand in that of Duty and followed her steep way to the blue hills of fame and glory, which she pointed out at the end, moved me profoundly. I resolved to be like him. The tricks and turns of the other Gods and Goddesses left me cold. There were other thin books about this and that sweet and gentle little girl who gave up her heart to Christ and good works. Almost always they died from it, preaching as they passed. I was utterly indifferent to their deaths. In the first place I could not conceive of death, and in the next place they never had any funerals that amounted to a hill of beans, so I didn't care how soon they rolled up their big, soulful, blue eyes and kicked the bucket. They had no meat on their bones.

32   But I also met Hans Andersen and Robert Louis Stevenson. They seemed to know what I wanted to hear and said it in a way that tingled me. Just a little below these friends was Rudyard Kipling in his *Jungle Books*. I loved his talking snakes as much as I did the hero.

33   I came to start reading the Bible through my mother. She gave me a licking one afternoon for repeating something I had overheard a neighbor telling her. She locked me in her room after the whipping, and the Bible was the only thing in there for me to read. I happened to open to the place where David was doing some mighty smiting, and I got interested. David went here and he went there, and no matter where he went, he smote 'em hip and thigh. Then he sung songs to his harp awhile, and went out and smote some more. Not one time did David stop and preach about sins and other things. All

---

12. **tam** *n.* cap with a wide, round, flat top and sometimes a center pompom.

David wanted to know from God was who to kill and when. He took care of the other details himself. Never a quiet moment. I liked him a lot. So I read a great deal more in the Bible, hunting for some more active people like David. Except for the beautiful language of Luke and Paul, the New Testament still plays a poor second to the Old Testament for me. The Jews had a God who laid about Him when they needed Him. I could see no use waiting until Judgment Day to see a man who was just crying for a good killing, to be told to go and roast. My idea was to give him a good killing first, and then if he got roasted later on, so much the better. ❧

NOTES

Comprehension Check

Complete the following items after you finish your first read. Review and clarify details with your group.

1. Why is young Zora Neale scolded by her grandmother?

2. At school, what detail in the visitors' physical appearance holds Zora's attention?

3. What is in the huge box that Mrs. Johnstone and Miss Hurd send Zora from Minnesota?

4. Which ancient Greek hero does Zora decide to emulate?

5. Why does Zora enjoy reading about David in the Bible?

6. 🖥 **Notebook** Confirm your understanding of the text by writing a summary.

- -

RESEARCH

Research to Clarify Choose at least one unfamiliar detail from the text. Briefly research that detail. In what way does the information you learned shed light on an aspect of the autobiography?

Research to Explore Do research to learn how author Alice Walker brought the nearly forgotten writings of Zora Neale Hurston back into the mainstream of American literature. You may want to share what you discover with your group.

from DUST TRACKS ON A ROAD

Close Read the Text

With your group, revisit sections of the text you marked during your first read. **Annotate** details that you notice. What **questions** do you have? What can you **conclude**?

Analyze the Text

> **CITE TEXTUAL EVIDENCE** to support your answers.

 Notebook Complete the activities.

1. **Review and Clarify** With your group, reread paragraphs 1–5. What do these paragraphs suggest about the place where Hurston grew up? How do these details reveal Hurston's purpose and point of view?

2. **Present and Discuss** Now, work with your group to share the passages from the selection that you found especially important. Take turns presenting your passages. Discuss what you noticed in the selection, what questions you asked, and what conclusions you reached.

3. **Essential Question:** *What is the relationship between literature and place?* What have you learned about literature and place from reading this autobiography? Discuss with your group.

LANGUAGE DEVELOPMENT

Concept Vocabulary

self-assurance	forward	brazenness

Why These Words? The three concept vocabulary words from the text are related. With your group, determine what the words have in common. Write your ideas, and add another word that fits the category.

Practice

 Notebook Imagine a person who could be described using these words. Then, write sentences that explain how that person embodies the characteristics these words indicate.

Word Study

Multiple-Meaning Words Many words in English have more than one meaning. For example, the word *forward* can mean "at or toward the front," or it can mean "progressive" or "advanced." In the excerpt from Hurston' autobiography, it has a different meaning altogether. Find at least one other word in the text that has more than one meaning. Write the definition of the word as it is used in the text and any alternate definitions. Use a dictionary to confirm the word's multiple meanings.

Analyze Craft and Structure

Literary Nonfiction **Autobiography** is a nonfiction narrative account of a writer's life told in his or her own words. Because of their personal content, autobiographies often reveal **social context**—the attitudes, customs, and beliefs of the culture in which the writer lived. Hurston's autobiography provides a glimpse into the social context of her African American community in rural Florida during the early twentieth century. Hurston brings additional life to her narrative by using a variety of literary elements, notably dialogue and dialect:

- **Dialogue:** the conversations among people
- **Dialect:** the form of a language spoken by people of a particular region or group—usually, dialect does not follow the conventional rules the language's standard grammar or pronunciation.

Hurston's use of dialogue allows the people who were part of her early life to speak for themselves. Her use of dialect allows them to speak with authenticity. Both dialogue and dialect add nuance and depth to the reader's understanding of Hurston's experience.

Practice

CITE TEXTUAL EVIDENCE to support your answers.

Work with your group to analyze Hurston's use of literary elements in this excerpt. Use the chart to capture your analysis.

PASSAGE	LITERARY ELEMENT	WHAT THE ELEMENT REVEALS
Paragraph 3	Social context	
Paragraph 4	Dialogue, dialect	
Paragraph 8	Social context	
Paragraph 12	Social context.	
Paragraph 18	Dialogue	
Paragraph 22	Social context	

from DUST TRACKS ON A ROAD

Author's Style

Figurative Meanings One notable aspect of Hurston's writing style is her strong and often comic use of two types of figurative, or imaginative, language: overstatement and idioms.

- **Overstatement**, sometimes called **hyperbole**, is deliberate exaggeration for effect. For instance, Hurston writes in paragraph 7 that the students were "threatened with a prompt and bloody death" if they misbehaved while visitors were present at school. The deliberately exaggerated punishment adds humor and a mischievous spark to Hurston's recollection.

- **Idioms** are expressions that are peculiar to a given language, region, community, or class of people and that cannot be understood literally. For example, when Zora asks the travelers in paragraph 1 whether they want her to go a "piece of the way" with them, she means "go a short distance." She is not speaking about a literal piece or chunk of the road.

Read It

1. Work individually to locate each of these idioms in the excerpt. Use context clues to define each idiom. Then, restate each idiom in your own words.

   a. cut one caper (paragraph 7)

   b. from lid to lid (paragraph 11)

   c. I'm going to catch it now (paragraph 15)

2. **Connect to Style** Reread this passage from paragraph 31 of the excerpt. Mark one example of overstatement and two idioms. Then, with your group, discuss the ways these literary elements add to Hurston's portrayal of her younger self.

   > *I was utterly indifferent to their deaths. In the first place I could not conceive of death, and in the next place they never had any funerals that amounted to a hill of beans, so I didn't care how soon they rolled up their big, soulful, blue eyes and kicked the bucket. They had no meat on their bones.*

Write It

Write a paragraph describing a gift that you gave or received. In your paragraph, use at least one idiom and one example of overstatement.

TIP

CLARIFICATION

Like slang words and phrases, idioms often change over time. When you read texts from different eras, you may come across expressions that are seldom used today. Figure out the meanings of such unfamiliar expressions by analyzing context clues.

STANDARDS

Reading Informational Text
• Determine the meaning of words and phrases as they are used in a text, including figurative, connotative, and technical meanings; analyze how an author uses and refines the meaning of a key term or terms over the course of a text.
• Determine an author's point of view or purpose in a text in which the rhetoric is particularly effective, analyzing how style and content contribute to the power, persuasiveness, or beauty of the text.

Language
Interpret figures of speech in context and analyze their role in the text.

Speaking and Listening

Assignment

As a group, prepare and deliver an **oral presentation** based on events in the excerpt from Hurston's autobiography. Choose one of these three options.

☐ **Compare-and-Contrast Discussion** As a group, discuss the similarities and differences between the way young Zora sees herself and the way others (travelers, her family, the visitors, her classmates) see her.

☐ **Informative Talk** Present an informative speech about Hurston's childhood, summarizing and reenacting (if appropriate) the key events of the excerpt from her point of view.

☐ **Interview** Stage an interview between the adult Hurston and a journalist. One team member will play the reporter and ask questions about Hurston's childhood and influences. Another member will portray Hurston and use details from the excerpt to provide complete and accurate responses. Work together as a team to write questions and answers.

Project Plan Use the chart to assign tasks for each group member. For example, if you choose the compare-and-contrast discussion, choose a leader to moderate the discussion. Then, work together to compile a list of people in Hurston's text. Divide these people among group members, and take notes about their portrayals in the excerpt—how does Hurston believe each person perceived her?

Oral presentation option: _____

TASK	WHO IS RESPONSIBLE	NOTES

📝 EVIDENCE LOG

Before moving on to a new selection, go to your Evidence Log and record what you learned from the excerpt from *Dust Tracks on a Road*.

☰ STANDARDS
Speaking and Listening
Adapt speech to a variety of contexts and tasks, demonstrating a command of formal English when indicated or appropriate.

POETRY COLLECTION 1

Comparing Text to Media

In this lesson, you will read and compare poetry by Carl Sandburg with the photo gallery "Sandburg's Chicago." First, you will complete the first-read and close-read activities for the poems.

SANDBURG'S CHICAGO

POETRY COLLECTION 1

Chicago

Wilderness

Concept Vocabulary

As you perform your first read of "Chicago" and "Wilderness," you will encounter these words.

brawling	wanton	cunning

Context Clues If these words are unfamiliar to you, try using **context clues** to determine their meanings. There are various types of context clues that may help you as you read.

> **Definition:** The king regarded his chief minister with a **sneer**, his scorn clearly apparent in the curl in his upper lip.
>
> **Contrast of Ideas:** The coach praised her players after the game, even though she had **admonished** them beforehand.

Apply your knowledge of context clues and other vocabulary strategies to determine the meanings of unfamiliar words you encounter during your first read.

First Read POETRY

Apply these strategies as you conduct your first read. You will have an opportunity to complete a close read after your first read.

NOTICE who or what is "speaking" each poem and whether the poem tells a story or describes a single moment.

ANNOTATE by marking vocabulary and key passages you want to revisit.

First Read

CONNECT ideas within the selections to what you already know and what you have already read.

RESPOND by completing the Comprehension Check.

About the Poet
Carl Sandburg

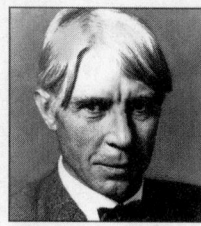

Carl Sandburg (1878–1967) was an optimist who believed in the power of ordinary people to fulfill their dreams. His poems were concrete and direct, capturing the energy and enthusiasm of industrial America. His vivid portraits of the working class made him one of the most popular poets of his day.

The son of Swedish immigrants, Sandburg left school after eighth grade to help support his family through work as a laborer. When he was nineteen, however, he set out to see the country, hitching rides on freight trains and taking odd jobs wherever he landed. He volunteered for military service during the Spanish-American War, though he did not fight. Later, he attended college for a brief period before hitting the road again.

The Bard of Chicago In 1912, Sandburg settled in the dynamic industrial city of Chicago. He worked as a newspaper reporter and began to publish his poetry in literary magazines. His first book, *Chicago Poems,* gained recognition for both Sandburg and Chicago. His second, *Cornhuskers,* won the Pulitzer Prize in 1918 and was followed by *Smoke and Steel* (1920) and *Slabs of the Sunburnt West* (1922).

While continuing to write poetry, Sandburg launched a career as a folksinger. His recitals included folk songs that he collected from cowboys, lumberjacks, factory workers, and hobos as he toured the country. His collection of this material, *The American Songbag,* appeared in 1927.

Winning Awards During his tours of the country, Sandburg also delivered lectures on Walt Whitman and Abraham Lincoln. His carefully researched, multivolume biography of Lincoln earned him a second Pulitzer Prize in 1940. In 1951, Sandburg received a third Pulitzer Prize for his *Complete Poems*. He was also awarded the United States Presidential Medal in 1964.

Sandburg offered a variety of definitions of poetry, among them these two: "Poetry is a search for syllables to shoot at the barriers of the unknown and the unknowable," and "Poetry is the opening and closing of a door, leaving those who look through to guess about what is seen during a moment."

Backgrounds

Chicago

This poem was published in *Poetry* magazine in 1914 and in book form in 1916. Sandburg described the poem as "a chant of defiance by Chicago" against other major cities in the United States and Europe.

Wilderness

Sandburg's poem "Wilderness" is an example of a prose poem, a poetic work written in prose that uses poetic techniques, such as imagery and figurative language. Sandburg's poem is organized in seven stanzas, each of which develops a single main idea.

Chicago

Carl Sandburg

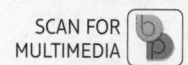

Hog Butcher for the World,
Tool Maker, Stacker of Wheat,
Player with Railroads and the Nation's Freight Handler;
Stormy, husky, **brawling**,
5 City of the Big Shoulders:

They tell me you are wicked and I believe them, for I have seen
your painted women under the gas lamps luring the farm boys.
And they tell me you are crooked and I answer: Yes, it is true I
have seen the gunman kill and go free to kill again.
And they tell me you are brutal and my reply is: On the faces of
women and children I have seen the marks of **wanton** hunger.
And having answered so I turn once more to those who sneer at
this my city, and I give them back the sneer and say to them:
10 Come and show me another city with lifted head singing so proud
to be alive and coarse and strong and **cunning**.
Flinging magnetic curses amid the toil of piling job on job, here is
a tall bold slugger set vivid against the little soft cities;
Fierce as a dog with tongue lapping for action, cunning as a
savage pitted against the wilderness,
              Bareheaded,
              Shoveling,
15   Wrecking,
              Planning,
              Building, breaking, rebuilding,
Under the smoke, dust all over his mouth, laughing with
white teeth,
Under the terrible burden of destiny laughing as a young man
laughs,
20 Laughing even as an ignorant fighter laughs who has never lost
a battle,
Bragging and laughing that under his wrist is the pulse, and
under his ribs the heart of the people,
                    Laughing!
Laughing the stormy, husky, brawling laughter of Youth, half-
naked, sweating, proud to be a Hog Butcher, Tool Maker,
Stacker of Wheat, Player with Railroads and Freight Handler
to the Nation.

NOTES

Mark context clues or indicate
another strategy you used that
helped you determine meaning.

brawling (BRAWL ihng) *adj.*

MEANING:

wanton (WON tuhn) *adj.*

MEANING:

cunning (KUHN ihng) *adj.*

MEANING:

Wilderness

Carl Sandburg

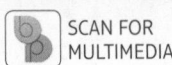

SCAN FOR
MULTIMEDIA

NOTES

1   There is a wolf in me . . . fangs pointed for tearing gashes . . . a red
tongue for raw meat . . . and the hot lapping of blood—I keep this
wolf because the wilderness gave it to me and the wilderness will not
let it go.

2   There is a fox in me . . . a silver-gray fox . . . I sniff and guess . . . I pick
things out of the wind and air . . . I nose in the dark night and take
sleepers and eat them and hide the feathers . . . I circle and loop and
double-cross.

3 There is a hog in me . . . a snout and a belly . . . a machinery for eating and grunting . . . a machinery for sleeping satisfied in the sun—I got this too from the wilderness and the wilderness will not let it go.

4 There is a fish in me . . . I know I came from salt-blue water-gates . . . I scurried with shoals of herring . . . I blew waterspouts with porpoises . . . before land was . . . before the water went down . . . before Noah . . . before the first chapter of Genesis.[1]

5 There is a baboon in me . . . clambering-clawed . . . dog-faced . . . yawping a galoot's[2] hunger . . . hairy under the armpits . . . here are the hawk-eyed hankering men . . . here are the blonde and blue-eyed women . . . here they hide curled asleep waiting . . . ready to snarl and kill . . . ready to sing and give milk . . . waiting—I keep the baboon because the wilderness says so.

6 There is an eagle in me and a mockingbird . . . and the eagle flies among the Rocky Mountains of my dreams and fights among the Sierra crags of what I want . . . and the mockingbird warbles in the early forenoon before the dew is gone, warbles in the underbrush of my Chattanoogas of hope, gushes over the blue Ozark foothills of my wishes—And I got the eagle and the mockingbird from the wilderness.

7 O, I got a zoo, I got a menagerie, inside my ribs, under my bony head, under my red-valve heart—and I got something else: it is a man-child heart, a woman-child heart: it is a father and mother and lover: it came from God-Knows-Where: it is going to God-Knows-Where— For I am the keeper of the zoo: I say yes and no: I sing and kill and work: I am a pal of the world: I came from the wilderness.

---

1. **before Noah . . . Genesis** In Genesis, the first book of the Bible, Noah builds an ark to save himself, his family, and some of the world's animals from a terrible flood.
2. **galoot** *n.* uncivilized person.

MEDIA CONNECTION

💬 **Discuss It** How does hearing "Wilderness" read by its author affect your understanding of the poem? For example, does the reading seem to limit the ideas in the poem only to the person who wrote it, or does the reading add life to the poem?

Write your response before sharing your ideas.

Carl Sandburg Reads "Wilderness"

SCAN FOR MULTIMEDIA

Comprehension Check

Complete the following items after you finish your first read. Review and clarify details with your group.

CHICAGO

1. In lines 6–8, what do "they" tell the speaker about Chicago?

2. According to the speaker, how does the city of Chicago laugh?

3. About what does the city of Chicago brag?

WILDERNESS

1. From where did the speaker get the wolf, the hog, the eagle, and the mockingbird?

2. Why does the speaker keep the baboon?

3. Who does the speaker claim to be in the last line of the poem?

RESEARCH

Research to Clarify Choose at least one unfamiliar detail from one of the poems. Briefly research that detail. In what way does the information you learned shed light on an aspect of the poem?

Research to Explore Do research to find some facts about the city of Chicago in the early twentieth century. Be prepared to discuss how your findings reinforce what Sandburg expresses poetically. You also may want to use the information as you discuss "Sandburg's Chicago," the photo gallery in this lesson.

POETRY COLLECTION 1

Close Read the Text

With your group, revisit sections of the text you marked during your first read. **Annotate** what you notice. What **questions** do you have? What can you **conclude**?

Analyze the Text

> **CITE TEXTUAL EVIDENCE**
> to support your answers.

 Notebook Complete the activities.

1. **Review and Clarify** With your group, reread lines 1–5 of "Chicago" and line 1 of "Wilderness." Compare and contrast the speakers in these poems, focusing on the images they use and on the values or characteristics suggested by these images.

2. **Present and Discuss** Now, work with your group to share passages from the poems that you found especially important. Take turns presenting your passages. Discuss what you noticed in the poems, what questions you asked, and what conclusions you reached.

3. **Essential Question:** *What is the relationship between literature and place?* What have you learned about literature and place from reading these poems?

> **TIP**
>
> **GROUP DISCUSSION**
> The sounds of poetry often contribute to the meanings of lines and images. Read aloud striking or confusing passages before you begin to discuss them as a group.

LANGUAGE DEVELOPMENT

Concept Vocabulary

> brawling   wanton   cunning

Why These Words? The three concept vocabulary words from these texts are related. With your group, determine what the words have in common. Write your ideas, and add another word that fits the category.

Practice

 Notebook Confirm your understanding of these words by writing synonyms and antonyms for them. Challenge yourself to come up with two synonyms and two antonyms for each. Then, trade lists with another group member. Discuss similarities and differences in your lists.

> **WORD NETWORK**
>
> Add words related to a sense of place from the text to your Word Network.

Word Study

Present Participle A **present participle** is a verb form that ends in *-ing* and can function as an adjective, by modifying a noun or a pronoun. For instance, the speaker in "Chicago" uses the adjective *brawling*, the present participle of the verb *brawl*, to describe the city.

Find three other examples of present participles in lines 12–23 of "Chicago," and list them by line number. Then, form three present participles of your own from verbs of your choice.

> **STANDARDS**
> **Language**
> Identify and correctly use patterns of word changes that indicate different meanings or parts of speech.

POETRY COLLECTION 1

Analyze Craft and Structure

Language and Meaning Poets use figurative language and other devices to break through the usual ways of seeing and describing the world. In "Chicago" and "Wilderness," Sandburg's notable devices include imagery, repetition, and personification.

- **Imagery** is descriptive or figurative language that appeals to the senses of sight, hearing, touch, taste, or smell. For example, the line "white petals on a rain-wet branch" is a concrete visual image.
- **Repetition** of words and phrases emphasizes important ideas, adds emotional intensity, and creates a musical quality. In "Wilderness," six of the seven lines begin with "There is . . . in me."
- **Personification** is a figure of speech in which a nonhuman subject is given human qualities. In "Chicago," the city is personified as a strong young man. In "Wilderness," personification takes a different form. In a reversal of the usual pattern, human attributes and emotions are given animal qualities.

Practice

CITE TEXTUAL EVIDENCE
to support your answers.

🖘 **Notebook** Work individually to answer these questions. Then, share and discuss your responses with your group.

1. In stanza 2 of "Wilderness," what imagery makes the description of the fox especially vivid? Explain.

2. (a) Identify the repeated elements in lines 6–8 of "Chicago." (b) What is the effect of this repetition?

3. **Apostrophe** is a figure of speech in which a speaker directly addresses a thing, concept, or person who is dead or absent. (a) In "Chicago," who or what is meant by "you" in lines 6–8? (b) Whom does the speaker address in line 10?

4. Use this chart to analyze instances of imagery, repetition, and personification in Sandburg's poems. Record two examples of each. Then, discuss the effect of each example with your group.

DEVICE	CHICAGO	WILDERNESS
Imagery		
Repetition		
Personification		

:≡ STANDARDS

Reading Literature
• Determine the meaning of words and phrases as they are used in the text, including figurative and connotative meanings; analyze the impact of specific word choices on meaning and tone, including words with multiple meanings or language that is particularly fresh, engaging, or beautiful.
• Analyze how an author's choices concerning how to structure specific parts of a text contribute to its overall structure and meaning as well as its aesthetic impact.

Language
Interpret figures of speech in context and analyze their role in the text.

Author's Style

Poetic Structures In "Chicago" and "Wilderness," Carl Sandburg uses two structures to create striking and powerful rhythms.

- **Line Lengths:** The individual lines of a poem may be long or short, and of the same or different lengths. They may be grouped into stanzas that look uniform and compact, or they may be strung out across the page. In "Chicago," Sandburg employs highly varied line lengths that are grouped in many different ways. Some lines contain a single word, whereas others include more than a dozen words. This dramatic variety reflects and reinforces the poet's portrayal of the city—Chicago is not a place that can be contained in the neat squares of equal line lengths and compact stanzas.

- **Ellipsis:** Ellipsis is the intentional omission of words or phrases signaled by a series of points (. . .). In line 1 of "Wilderness," for example, the first three images are set off by ellipses. The effect is to invite the reader to consider each surprising image and use his or her imagination to fill in the missing ideas.

Read It

1. Reread lines 13–22 of "Chicago." With your group, discuss the effects Sandburg achieves by varying the line lengths in this passage.

2. In stanza 4 of "Wilderness," what does the speaker's use of ellipsis suggest about human identity, memory, and history? Discuss with your group.

3. **Connect to Style** What is the overall effect of Sandburg's use of varied line lengths and ellipses in these poems? Support your answer with examples from the texts.

Write It

Write a short poem about a wild person, animal, or place. Vary your line lengths to create a specific tone or mood. Use at least one instance of ellipsis to draw attention to a particularly vivid detail or encourage your reader to consider missing information.

 TIP

CLARIFICATION

Poets use line length to create a specific mood or feeling. A series of choppy or uneven lines may create a hectic or uneasy feeling. On the other hand, a series of equal lines can create a sense of stability and order.

✎ EVIDENCE LOG

Before moving on to a new selection, go to your Evidence Log and record what you've learned from "The Poetry of Carl Sandburg."

POETRY COLLECTION 1

Comparing Text to Media

These photographs of Chicago were taken by various photographers. After studying the photo gallery, you will compare the ways in which poetry and photography can express ideas about the significance of place.

SANDBURG'S CHICAGO

Sandburg's Chicago

Media Vocabulary

These words will be useful to you as you analyze, discuss, and write about photography.

Focal Point: center of activity or attention in a photograph	• The focal point of an image is typically linked to the photographer's main idea. • The focal point is not necessarily in the middle of the image, or even in the foreground.
Depth of Field: distance between the closest and most distant objects that are in focus	• A very small area of focus is called a shallow depth of field; a very large one is called a deep depth of field. • Analyzing the depth of field helps viewers understand what the subject of the photograph is and what the photographer wants to say about that subject.
Foreground and Background: closer objects are in the foreground, while more distant objects are in the background	• Foreground and background are usually determined by perspective, or a photographer's vantage point. • Despite apparent differences in dimensions, foreground and background are often equally important in a photograph.

First Review MEDIA: ART AND PHOTOGRAPHY

Apply these strategies as you conduct your first review. You will have an opportunity to complete a close review after your first review.

STANDARDS

Reading Informational Text
By the end of grade 11, read and comprehend literary nonfiction in the grades 11–CCR text complexity band proficiently, with scaffolding as needed at the high end of the range.

Language
Acquire and use accurately general academic and domain-specific words and phrases, sufficient for reading, writing, speaking, and listening at the college and career readiness level; demonstrate independence in gathering vocabulary knowledge when considering a word or phrase important to comprehension or expression.

LOOK at each image and determine *whom* or *what* it portrays.

NOTE elements in each image that you find interesting and want to revisit.

CONNECT details in the images to other media you've experienced, texts you've read, or images you've seen.

RESPOND by completing the Comprehension Check.

First Review — LOOK · NOTE · CONNECT · RESPOND

Sandburg's Chicago

BACKGROUND

As a hub for travel and trade, Chicago has been vital to America's culture and economy for more than a century. Between 1890 and 1982, Chicago was the second-largest city in the United States and came to be considered the prototypical American city.

SCAN FOR
MULTIMEDIA

PHOTO 1: Chicago & Alton Railroad Shops at Bloomington, Illinois. Circa 1904. As the primary rail hub of the United States, immense volumes of freight passed through Chicago from cities, such as Bloomington, all over the country. The third line of Sandburg's "Chicago"—"Player with Railroads and the Nation's Freight Handler"—echoes this fact.

NOTES

PHOTO 2: State St., Chicago, Illinois (N. from Adams): Noonday Crowds on a Thoroughfare 18 Miles Long. Circa 1903. This picture shows bustling downtown Chicago at the turn of the twentieth century.

NOTES

PHOTO 3: Police Holding Two Men Related to the Alexandro Murder Case. Circa 1905. As Chicago's population grew, so did its reputation as a center for organized crime.

NOTES

PHOTO 4: An Instantaneous Flash Picture of the Chicago Board of Trade in Session.
Circa 1900. The Chicago Board of Trade, organized in 1848, was the first grain futures exchange in the United States. A futures exchange is a contract to buy specific amounts of a commodity, such as grain or lumber, at a specific price for delivery at a future time.

PHOTO 5: Italian Family in Chicago Tenement. Circa 1910. In the early twentieth century, Chicago became known for its large immigrant neighborhoods, many of which were densely packed and impoverished. The photographer, Lewis Wickes Hine, shot many photos of America's poor, and he is famous for his work to end child labor.

NOTES

Comprehension Check

Complete the following items after you finish your first review. Review and clarify details with your group.

1. What type of business in the Chicago area does Photo 1 depict?

2. Which details in Photo 2 show that Chicago was a densely populated, busy place?

3. In Photo 3, what is happening? Why has a crowd gathered?

4. In Photo 4, what group is in session?

5. Who are the people in Photo 5, and what are their living conditions like?

6. 🖹 **Notebook** Confirm your understanding of the photo gallery by writing a description of the settings, people, and events that the photographs portray.

Close Review

With your group, revisit the photographs and your first-review notes. Record any new observations that seem important. What **questions** do you have? What can you **conclude**?

SANDBURG'S CHICAGO

Analyze the Media

> **CITE TEXTUAL EVIDENCE**
> to support your answers.

Complete the activities.

1. **Present and Discuss** Choose the photograph you find most interesting or powerful. Share your choice with your group, and discuss why you chose it. Explain what you notice in the photograph, what questions it raises for you, and what conclusions you reach about it.

2. **Review and Synthesize** With your group, review all the photographs. Do they do more than simply present various aspects of a large American city? Explain.

3. 📓 **Notebook Essential Question:** *What is the relationship between literature and place?* Why might Carl Sandburg have felt that Chicago, with scenes like these, was a worthy topic for a poem? Refer to specific photographs in your response.

LANGUAGE DEVELOPMENT

Media Vocabulary

focal point	depth of field	foreground and background

Use the vocabulary words in your responses to the questions.

1. In Photo 2, to what detail is your eye drawn first? Why? How does that detail influence the way you see the rest of the photograph?

2. On what area in Photo 4 does the photographer focus? What kind of mood or atmosphere does this focus create?

3. In Photo 5, how does the child on the far right affect your impressions of the photograph?

STANDARDS

Language
Acquire and use accurately general academic and domain-specific words and phrases, sufficient for reading, writing, speaking, and listening at the college and career readiness level; demonstrate independence in gathering vocabulary knowledge when considering a word or phrase important to comprehension or expression.

POETRY COLLECTION 1

SANDBURG'S CHICAGO

Writing to Compare

Both "Chicago" by Carl Sandburg and the photo gallery "Sandburg's Chicago" provide information about early-twentieth-century Chicago. Now, analyze the texts and consider how the medium in which information is provided affects your understanding of the subject.

Assignment

Create a **multimedia presentation** about early-twentieth-century Chicago in which you weave together Sandburg's poem, images from the photo essay, and your own knowledge and ideas. Choose from these options:

☐ a **slide show** that presents the travel journal of someone visiting Chicago during the early twentieth century

☐ a plan for an informative **website** about early-twentieth-century Chicago

☐ a **museum exhibit guide** for a show featuring the photo essay

Either in your presentation or in a separate written text, explain how poetic words and photographic images bring early-twentieth-century Chicago to life for readers and viewers in different ways.

▤ STANDARDS

Reading Informational Text
Integrate and evaluate multiple sources of information presented in different media or formats as well as in words in order to address a question or solve a problem.

Speaking and Listening
Make strategic use of digital media in presentations to enhance understanding of findings, reasoning, and evidence and to add interest.

Analyze the Texts

Compare the Text and Photographs With your group, identify ways in which the poem and the photo essay convey information. Use the chart to capture your observations.

INFORMATION ABOUT CHICAGO	WHAT I LEARNED FROM "CHICAGO"	WHAT I LEARNED FROM "SANDBURG'S CHICAGO"	HOW TEXT COMPARES TO PHOTOGRAPHS
jobs and transportation			
what the city is like			
details about people			

⊟ **Notebook** Respond to these questions.

1. Do the photographs reveal dimensions of the city that the poem does not? Explain.

2. Does the poem conjure aspects of the city that the photographs do not? Explain.

Planning and Prewriting

Organize Tasks Make a list of tasks you will need to complete in order to create your multimedia presentation. Assign the tasks to individual group members. You may add to or modify this list as needed.

TASK LIST

Research and Choose Photographs: Decide whether you need additional photos of Chicago. If you do, research and choose those images.

Assigned to: _____.

Research and Choose Texts: Decide whether you need additional information about Chicago. If you do, research and select relevant information.

Assigned to: _____.

Write Text: Identify all the parts of your presentation that need to be written. For example, you may need captions for photos, text for the different parts of the web site or museum guide, or travel journal entries.

Assigned to: _____.

Locate Other Media: Find additional media—audio, video, or other visuals—to add interest and information. For example, you may want to include a map of Illinois or Chicago, recordings of portions of the poem, or voice-overs of travel journal entries.

Assigned to: _____.

Make a Rough Outline: Set a sequence for your content as well as any special sections you want to include. You may always revise the sequence later as your project takes shape.

Assigned to: _____.

Drafting

Inform Your Audience As you assemble the pieces of your presentation, work to answer basic questions such as these:

- What was Chicago known for in the early twentieth century?
- Who lived there? Where did they come from? Why were they drawn to Chicago?
- What did they do there? How did they make a living?

Include Comparisons of Texts to Photographs Use your Prewriting notes to explain how poetic words and photographic images bring early-twentieth-century Chicago to life for readers and viewers in different ways. Do this in your presentation or in a short written text that accompanies it.

Review, Revise, and Edit

Make sure all the images and other media you have chosen add value to the presentation. If necessary, cut content to make your presentation more focused and effective.

☑ EVIDENCE LOG

Before moving on to a new selection, go to your Evidence Log and record what you learned from the poem "Chicago" and the photo graphic "Sandburg's Chicago."

POETRY COLLECTION 2

Comparing Texts

In this lesson, you will compare two poems to an excerpt from a memoir. First, you will complete the first-read and close-read activities for the poems. The work you do with your group will help prepare you for the comparing task.

INTRODUCTION *from* THE WAY TO RAINY MOUNTAIN

POETRY COLLECTION 2

In the Longhouse, Oneida Museum

Cloudy Day

Concept Vocabulary

As you perform your first read, you will encounter these words.

> strife   sinister   vigilant

Context Clues If these words are unfamiliar to you, try using **context clues**—words and phrases that appear nearby in the text—to help you determine their meanings.

> **Example:** Luis is **gregarious**, unlike his shy and quiet brother.
>
> **Conclusion:** The word *unlike* indicates that *shy* and *quiet* are in opposition to *gregarious. Gregarious* may mean "outgoing and talkative."

Apply your knowledge of context clues and other vocabulary strategies to determine the meanings of unfamiliar words you encounter during your first read.

First Read POETRY

Apply these strategies as you conduct your first read. You will have an opportunity to complete a close read after your first read.

≔ STANDARDS

Reading Literature
By the end of grade 11, read and comprehend literature, including stories, dramas, and poems, in the grades 11–CCR text complexity band proficiently, with scaffolding as needed at the high end of the range.

Language
• Determine or clarify the meaning of unknown and multiple-meaning words and phrases based on *grades 11–12 reading and content,* choosing flexibly from a range of strategies.
• Use context as a clue to the meaning of a word or phrase.

NOTICE *who* or *what* is "speaking" each poem and whether the poem tells a story or describes a single moment.

ANNOTATE by marking vocabulary and key passages you want to revisit.

First Read

CONNECT ideas within the selections to what you already know and what you have already read.

RESPOND by completing the Comprehension Check.

About the Poets

Roberta Hill (b. 1947) was raised near Green Bay, Wisconsin, among the Oneida, one of the Iroquois nations. Her poetry often reflects feelings provoked by the legacy of forced migration and the dispossession of Oneida lands. The poems in her first collection, *Star Quilt* (1984), are organized according to six directions: north, south, east, west, skyward, and earthward.

In his poems, **Jimmy Santiago Baca** (b. 1952) celebrates the power of literature to change lives. Baca ran away from home at age 13 and then served a five-year prison sentence. While in jail, he learned to read and write, and discovered a deep passion for poetry. Following his literary heroes, the poets Pablo Neruda and Federico García Lorca, Baca devotes his life to writing and teaching. His workshops have helped many people improve their lives through writing and education.

Backgrounds

In the Longhouse, Oneida Museum

The Oneida Nation Museum in Green Bay, Wisconsin, presents displays and educational programming to help visitors understand Oneida and Iroquois history and culture. One of the museum's permanent exhibits shows a traditional Oneida longhouse, a large communal home constructed by covering a wooden frame with elm bark.

Cloudy Day

Baca wrote this poem while serving time in a maximum-security prison. "Cloudy Day" was included in *Immigrants in Our Own Land* (1979), Baca's first collection of poetry, published the same year the poet was released from prison.

In the
Longhouse,[1]
Oneida[2] Museum

Roberta Hill

House of five fires, you never raised me.
Those nights when the throat of the furnace
wheezed and rattled its regular death,
I wanted your wide door,

5 your mottled air of bark and working sunlight,
wanted your smokehole with its stars,
and your roof curving its singing mouth above me.
Here are the tiers once filled with sleepers,

and their low laughter measured harmony or **strife**.
10 Here I could wake amazed at winter,
my breath in the draft a chain of violets.
The house I left as a child now seems

a shell of sobs. Each year I dream it **sinister**
and dig in my heels to keep out the intruder
15 banging at the back door. My eyes burn
from cat urine under the basement stairs

and the hall reveals a nameless hunger,
as if without a history, I should always walk
the cluttered streets of this hapless continent.
20 Thinking it best I be wanderer,

I rode whatever river, ignoring every zigzag,
every spin. I've been a fragment, less than my name,
shaking in a solitary landscape,
like the last burnt leaf on an oak.

25 What autumn wind told me you'd be waiting?
House of five fires, they take you for a tomb,
but I know better. When desolation comes,
I'll hide your ridgepole[3] in my spine

and melt into crow call, reminding my children
30 that spiders near your door
joined all the reddening blades of grass
without oil, hasp[4] or uranium.

NOTES

Mark context clues or indicate another strategy you used that helped you determine meaning.

strife (stryf) n.
MEANING:

sinister (SIHN uh stuhr) adj.
MEANING:

1. **Longhouse** n. large, communal dwelling traditionally constructed by the Iroquois.
2. **Oneida** (oh NY duh) Native American people living originally near Oneida Lake in New York and now also in Wisconsin and Ontario.
3. **ridgepole** n. horizontal beam at the ridge of a roof, to which the upper ends of the rafters are attached.
4. **hasp** n. hinged metal fastening for a door.

Cloudy Day

Jimmy Santiago Baca

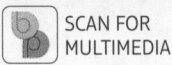 SCAN FOR MULTIMEDIA

NOTES

Mark context clues or identify another strategy you used that helped you determine meaning.

vigilant (VIHJ uh luhnt) *adj.*

MEANING:

It is windy today. A wall of wind crashes against,
windows clunk against, iron frames
as wind swings past broken glass
and seethes, like a frightened cat
5   in empty spaces of the cellblock.

In the exercise yard
we sat huddled in our prison jackets,
on our haunches against the fence,
and the wind carried our words
10 over the fences,
while the **vigilant** guard on the tower
held his cap at the sudden gust.

I could see the main tower from where I sat,
and the wind in my face
15 gave me the feeling I could grasp
the tower like a cornstalk,
and snap it from its roots of rock.

The wind plays it like a flute,
this hollow shoot of rock.
20 The brim girded with barbwire
with a guard sitting there also,
listening intently to the sounds
as clouds cover the sun.

I thought of the day I was coming to prison,
25 in the back seat of a police car,
hands and ankles chained, the policeman pointed,
    "See that big water tank? The big
    silver one out there, sticking up?
    That's the prison."

30 And here I am, I cannot believe it.
Sometimes it is such a dream, a dream,
where I stand up in the face of the wind,
like now, it blows at my jacket,
and my eyelids flick a little bit,
35 while I stare disbelieving. . . .

The third day of spring,
and four years later, I can tell you,
how a man can endure, how a man
can become so cruel, how he can die
40 or become so cold. I can tell you this,
I have seen it every day, every day,
and still I am strong enough to love you,
love myself and feel good;
even as the earth shakes and trembles,
45 and I have not a thing to my name,
I feel as if I have everything, everything.

By Jimmy Santiago Baca, from *Immigrants in Our Own Land*, copyright ©1979 by Jimmy Santiago Baca.
Reprinted by permission of New Directions Publishing

Comprehension Check

Complete the following items after you finish your first read. Review and clarify details with your group.

IN THE LONGHOUSE, ONEIDA MUSEUM

1. Name three parts of the longhouse that the speaker mentions in this poem.

2. What activity does the speaker's "nameless hunger" impel or motivate?

3. Near the end of the poem, what wrong understanding of the longhouse does the speaker say "they" hold?

CLOUDY DAY

1. Where is the speaker?

2. What memory does the speaker describe in the middle of the poem?

3. According to the final lines, what is the speaker still strong enough to do?

RESEARCH

Research to Clarify Choose at least one unfamiliar detail from one of the poems. Briefly research that detail. In what way does the information you learned shed light on an aspect of the poem?

Research to Explore Research the life and work of either Roberta Hill or Jimmy Santiago Baca.

Close Read the Text

With your group, revisit sections of the poems you marked during your first read. **Annotate** what you notice. What **questions** do you have? What can you **conclude**?

POETRY COLLECTION 2

Analyze the Text

CITE TEXTUAL EVIDENCE
to support your answers.

Complete the activities.

1. **Review and Clarify** With your group, reread lines 36–46 of "Cloudy Day." Identify and analyze one or more contrasts you find.

2. **Present and Discuss** Now, work with your group to share key passages from "In the Longhouse, Oneida Museum" and "Cloudy Day." Take turns presenting your passages. Discuss what you noticed in the poems, what questions you asked, and what conclusions you reached.

3. **Essential Question:** *What is the relationship between literature and place?* How do these poems link poetry and place? Discuss.

TIP

GROUP DISCUSSION
One group member can assume the role of note-taker and read notes to the group at the end of the discussion. This strategy can help all group members make sure they remember the same information.

LANGUAGE DEVELOPMENT

Concept Vocabulary

strife	sinister	vigilant

Why These Words? The three concept words from the poems are related. With your group, determine what the words have in common. How do these word choices add to the power of the poems?

Practice

Use the concept vocabulary words in a conversation with your group members. Each group member should use each word at least once.

 WORD NETWORK

Add words related to a sense of place from the texts to your Word Network.

Word Study

📓 **Notebook Etymology** A word's **etymology** is its history—including its language of origin and how its form and meaning have developed over time. Some words have a surprising etymology. For instance, the concept vocabulary word *sinister* comes from a Latin word meaning "left" or "on the left side." In the past, a number of cultures associated the left side with clumsiness, bad luck, or even evil.

Use a specialized reference, such as an etymological dictionary, to look up the etymology of the word *dexterity*. Write your findings, and discuss them with your group. Explain how the word's etymology is related to that of *sinister*.

STANDARDS

Language
Consult general and specialized reference materials, both print and digital, to find the pronunciation of a word or determine or clarify its precise meaning, its part of speech, its etymology, or its standard usage.

Analyze Craft and Structure

Poetic Devices Poets often use **figurative language**, or language that is used imaginatively rather than literally and includes one or more **figures of speech**, devices for making unexpected comparisons. Three common figures of speech are personification, simile, and metaphor.

- **Personification:** A nonhuman subject is presented as if it had human qualities. For example, a writer might describe a bridge as "groaning under the weight of the traffic it bears."

- **Simile:** Two dissimilar things are compared using *like, as, seems, than, as if*, or a similar connecting word. For example, an author describing a raucous sports fan might write, "The fan roared like a wild animal."

- **Metaphor:** Two dissimilar things are compared without a connecting word such as *like* or *as*. For example, in "The Highwayman," the poet Alfred Noyes uses a ship metaphor when he writes, "The moon was a ghostly galleon tossed upon cloudy seas."

STANDARDS

Reading Literature
- Analyze how an author's choices concerning how to structure specific parts of a text contribute to its overall structure and meaning as well as its aesthetic impact.

Language
Demonstrate understanding of figurative language, word relationships, and nuances in word meaning.

Practice

> **CITE TEXTUAL EVIDENCE**
> to support your answers.

As a group, complete the chart with examples of figurative language from both poems. Then, discuss the insight or emotion each example helps to convey.

EXAMPLE PASSAGE	TYPE OF FIGURATIVE LANGUAGE	EFFECT

Author's Style

Poetic Conventions Traditional structural elements used in verse, or **poetic conventions,** include **repetition, end-stopped lines, enjambment,** and **stanza breaks**. These techniques focus and direct the reader's attention.

POETIC CONVENTION	EXPLANATION	EXAMPLE
Repetition	Repetition reminds readers of an idea already expressed or emphasizes an important point.	*Sometimes it is such a dream, a dream …* (line 31, "Cloudy Day")
End-Stopped Lines	These are lines that complete a grammatical unit, usually with a punctuation mark at the end. End-stops highlight the structure of ideas.	*House of five fires, you never raised me.* (line 1, "In the Longhouse, Oneida Museum")
Enjambment	These are lines that do not end with a grammatical break and that do not make full sense without the line that follows. Enjambed lines create flow. Words at the ends of lines may receive a subtle emphasis.	*The house I left as a child now seems / a shell of sobs.* (lines 12–13, "In the Longhouse, Oneida Museum")
Stanza Breaks	The breaks in stanzas, or groups of lines, are similar to paragraphs in prose. They point to shifts in the speaker's thoughts and feelings.	*And here I am, I cannot believe it.* (line 30, "Cloudy Day")

Read It

1. Work individually. Identify the poetic conventions in each of these passages from the poems. Then, discuss with your group the effect the combination of conventions creates.

   a. lines 1–6 and 25–28, "In the Longhouse, Oneida Museum"

   b. lines 1–7, "Cloudy Day"

2. **Connect to Style** With your group, identify the poetic conventions in lines 40–43 of "Cloudy Day." Then, explain and evaluate their effect.

Write It

📓 **Notebook** Using the first nine lines of "In the Longhouse, Oneida Museum" as a model, write a short poem about a memory. Include at least three of the four poetic conventions: repetition, end-stopped lines, enjambment, and stanza breaks.

 TIP

CLARIFICATION
A poet's style reflects choices about both language and structure. Word choices include imagery and figurative language. Structure choices include line and stanza breaks.

📝 EVIDENCE LOG

Before moving on to a new selection, go to your Evidence Log and record what you've learned from the poems in "Poetry Collection 2."

Poetry Collection 2 **519**

POETRY COLLECTION 2

Comparing Texts

You will now read an excerpt from a memoir. Begin by completing the first-read and close-read activities. Then, compare the use of poetic elements in the Introduction from *The Way to Rainy Mountain* with the use of similar elements in the poems in Poetry Collection 2.

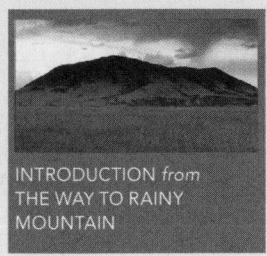

INTRODUCTION *from* THE WAY TO RAINY MOUNTAIN

About the Author

N. Scott Momaday (b. 1934) won the Pulitzer Prize for his first novel, *House Made of Dawn* (1969). A Native American from Oklahoma, much of his work draws on his Kiowa heritage, especially the Kiowa people's traditional tales and folklore. In addition to novels, Momaday has published poetry and nonfiction and painted his own illustrations for his work. He is the recipient of numerous awards and honors, including the National Medal of Arts in 2007.

Introduction *from* The Way to Rainy Mountain

Concept Vocabulary

As you perform your first read, you will encounter these words.

reverence	rites	deicide

Context Clues If these words are unfamiliar to you, try using **context clues** to help you determine their meanings.

> **Example:** Fans were **elated** when the hometown team won the state championship.
>
> **Conclusion:** The phrase "won the state championship" is a context clue. Winning an important game or an award is usually a happy occasion. *Elated,* then, must mean something like "very happy."

Apply your knowledge of context clues and other vocabulary strategies to determine the meanings of unfamiliar words you encounter during your first read.

First Read NONFICTION

Apply these strategies as you conduct your first read. You will have an opportunity to complete a close read after your first read.

:::icon::: **STANDARDS**

Reading Informational Text
By the end of grade 11, read and comprehend literary nonfiction in the grades 11–CCR text complexity band proficiently, with scaffolding as needed at the high end of the range.

Language
• Determine or clarify the meaning of unknown and multiple-meaning words and phrases based on *grades 11–12 reading and content,* choosing flexibly from a range of strategies.

• Use context as a clue to the meaning of a word or phrase.

NOTICE the general ideas of the text. *What* is it about? *Who* is involved?

ANNOTATE by marking vocabulary and key passages you want to revisit.

First Read

NOTICE · ANNOTATE · CONNECT · RESPOND

CONNECT ideas within the selection to what you already know and what you have already read.

RESPOND by completing the Comprehension Check and by writing a brief summary of the selection.

Introduction
from The Way to Rainy Mountain

N. Scott Momaday

BACKGROUND

Throughout the nineteenth century, the United States expanded across the continent, and Native American nations were forced from their traditional lands onto reservations. In this introduction from his memoir, N. Scott Momaday describes both history of his Kiowa ancestors who were forcibly resettled and their relationship with the land.

SCAN FOR MULTIMEDIA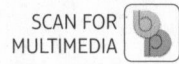

NOTES

1   A single knoll rises out of the plain in Oklahoma, north and west of the Wichita Range.[1] For my people, the Kiowas, it is an old landmark, and they gave it the name Rainy Mountain. The hardest weather in the world is there. Winter brings blizzards, hot tornadic winds arise in the spring, and in summer the prairie is an anvil's edge. The grass turns brittle and brown, and it cracks beneath your feet. There are green belts along the rivers and creeks, linear groves of hickory and pecan, willow and witch hazel. At a distance in July or August the steaming foliage seems almost to writhe in fire. Great green and yellow grasshoppers are everywhere in the tall grass, popping up like corn to sting the flesh, and tortoises crawl about on the red earth, going nowhere in the plenty of time. Loneliness is an aspect of the land. All things in the plain are isolate; there is no confusion of objects in the eye, but *one* hill or *one* tree or *one* man. To look upon that landscape in the early morning, with the sun at your back, is to lose the sense of proportion. Your imagination comes to life, and this, you think, is where Creation was begun.

2   I returned to Rainy Mountain in July. My grandmother had died in the spring, and I wanted to be at her grave. She had lived to be very old and at last infirm. Her only living daughter was with her when she died, and I was told that in death her face was that of a child.

3   I like to think of her as a child. When she was born, the Kiowas were living that last great moment of their history. For more than a hundred years they had controlled the open range from the Smoky Hill River to the Red, from the headwaters of the Canadian to the

---

1. **Wichita** (WIHCH uh taw) **Range** mountain range in southwestern Oklahoma.

fork of the Arkansas and Cimarron.[2] In alliance with the Comanches,[3] they had ruled the whole of the southern Plains. War was their sacred business, and they were among the finest horsemen the world has ever known. But warfare for the Kiowas was preeminently a matter of disposition rather than of survival, and they never understood the grim, unrelenting advance of the U.S. Cavalry. When at last, divided and ill-provisioned, they were driven onto the Staked Plains in the cold rains of autumn, they fell into panic. In Palo Duro Canyon they abandoned their crucial stores to pillage and had nothing then but their lives. In order to save themselves, they surrendered to the soldiers at Fort Sill[4] and were imprisoned in the old stone corral that now stands as a military museum. My grandmother was spared the humiliation of those high gray walls by eight or ten years, but she must have known from birth the affliction of defeat, the dark brooding of old warriors.

4   Her name was Aho, and she belonged to the last culture to evolve in North America. Her forebears came down from the high country in western Montana nearly three centuries ago. They were a mountain people, a mysterious tribe of hunters whose language has never been positively classified in any major group. In the late seventeenth century they began a long migration to the south and east. It was a journey toward the dawn, and it led to a golden age. Along the way the Kiowas were befriended by the Crows,[5] who gave them the culture and religion of the Plains. They acquired horses, and their ancient nomadic spirit was suddenly free of the ground. They acquired Tai-me, the sacred Sun Dance doll, from that moment the object and symbol of their worship, and so shared in the divinity of the sun. Not least, they acquired the sense of destiny, therefore courage and pride. When they entered upon the southern Plains they had been transformed. No longer were they slaves to the simple necessity of survival; they were a lordly and dangerous society of fighters and thieves, hunters and priests of the sun. According to their origin myth, they entered the world through a hollow log. From one point of view, their migration was the fruit of an old prophecy, for indeed they emerged from a sunless world.

5   Although my grandmother lived out her long life in the shadow of Rainy Mountain, the immense landscape of the continental interior lay like memory in her blood. She could tell of the Crows, whom she had never seen, and of the Black Hills,[6] where she had never been. I wanted to see in reality what she had seen more perfectly

---

2. **Smoky Hill . . . Cimarron** (SIHM uh ron) rivers that run through or near Oklahoma. The area Momaday is defining stretches from central Kansas south through Oklahoma and from the Texas panhandle east to Tulsa, Oklahoma.
3. **Comanches** (kuh MAN cheez) Native American people of the southern Great Plains.
4. **Fort Sill** fort established by the United States government in 1869 as a base of operations during U.S. Army battles with Native Americans of the southern Plains.
5. **Crows** members of a Native American tribe of the northern Plains.
6. **Black Hills** mountain range running from southwestern South Dakota to northeastern Wyoming.

in the mind's eye, and traveled fifteen hundred miles to begin my pilgrimage.

6   Yellowstone,[7] it seemed to me, was the top of the world, a region of deep lakes and dark timber, canyons and waterfalls. But, beautiful as it is, one might have the sense of confinement there. The skyline in all directions is close at hand, the high wall of the woods and deep cleavages of shade. There is a perfect freedom in the mountains, but it belongs to the eagle and the elk, the badger and the bear. The Kiowas reckoned their stature by the distance they could see, and they were bent and blind in the wilderness.

7   Descending eastward, the highland meadows are a stairway to the plain. In July the inland slope of the Rockies is luxuriant with flax and buckwheat, stonecrop and larkspur.[8] The earth unfolds and the limit of the land recedes. Clusters of trees, and animals growing far in the distance, cause the vision to reach away and wonder to build upon the mind. The sun follows a longer course in the day, and the sky is immense beyond all comparison. The great billowing clouds that sail upon it are shadows that move upon the grain like water, dividing light. Farther down, in the land of the Crows and Blackfeet,[9] the plain is yellow. Sweet clover takes hold of the hills and bends upon itself to cover and seal the soil. There the Kiowas paused on their way; they had come to the place where they must change their lives. The sun is at home on the plains. Precisely there does it have the certain character of a god. When the Kiowas came to the land of the Crows, they could see the dark lees of the hills at dawn across the Bighorn River, the profusion of light on the grain shelves, the oldest deity ranging after the solstices. Not yet would they veer southward to the caldron[10] of the land that lay below; they must wean their blood from the northern winter and hold the mountains a while longer in their view. They bore Tai-me in procession to the east.

8   A dark mist lay over the Black Hills, and the land was like iron. At the top of a ridge I caught sight of Devil's Tower upthrust against the gray sky as if in the birth of time the core of the earth had broken through its crust and the motion of the world was begun. There are things in nature that engender an awful quiet in the heart of man; Devil's Tower is one of them. Two centuries ago, because they could not do otherwise, the Kiowas made a legend at the base of the rock. My grandmother said:

9   Eight children were there at play, seven sisters and their brother. Suddenly the boy was struck dumb; he trembled and began to run upon his hands and feet. His fingers became claws, and his body was covered with fur. Directly there was a bear where the boy had been. The sisters were terrified; they ran, and the bear after them. They

---

7. **Yellowstone** Yellowstone National Park, located primarily in Wyoming but extending into southern Montana and eastern Idaho.
8. **flax . . . larkspur** various types of plants.
9. **Blackfeet** Native American people from the region that includes northern Montana and parts of southern Alberta, Canada.
10. **caldron** (KAWL druhn) *n.* pot for boiling liquids; large kettle.

came up to the stump of a great tree, and the tree spoke to them. It bade them climb upon it, and as they did so it began to rise into the air. The bear came to kill them, but they were just beyond its reach. It reared against the tree and scored the bark all around with its claws. The seven sisters were borne into the sky, and they became the stars of the Big Dipper.

10   From that moment, and so long as the legend lives, the Kiowas have kinsmen in the night sky. Whatever they were in the mountains, they could be no more. However tenuous their well-being, however much they had suffered and would suffer again, they had found a way out of the wilderness.

11   My grandmother had a **reverence** for the sun, a holy regard that now is all but gone out of mankind. There was a wariness in her, and an ancient awe. She was a Christian in her later years, but she had come a long way about, and she never forgot her birthright. As a child she had been to the Sun Dances; she had taken part in those annual **rites**, and by them she had learned the restoration of her people in the presence of Tai-me. She was about seven when the last Kiowa Sun Dance was held in 1887 on the Washita River above Rainy Mountain Creek. The buffalo were gone. In order to consummate the ancient sacrifice—to impale the head of a buffalo bull upon the medicine tree—a delegation of old men journeyed into Texas, there to beg and barter for an animal from the Goodnight herd. She was ten when the Kiowas came together for the last time as a living Sun Dance culture. They could find no buffalo; they had to hang an old hide from the sacred tree. Before the dance could begin, a company of soldiers rode out from Fort Sill under orders to disperse the tribe. Forbidden without cause the essential act of their faith, having seen the wild herds slaughtered and left to rot upon the ground, the Kiowas backed away forever from the medicine tree. That was July 20, 1890, at the great bend of the Washita. My grandmother was there. Without bitterness, and for as long as she lived, she bore a vision of **deicide**.

12   Now that l can have her only in memory, I see my grandmother in the several postures that were peculiar to her: standing at the wood stove on a winter morning and turning meat in a great iron skillet; sitting at the south window, bent above her beadwork, and afterwards, when her vision failed, looking down for a long time into the fold of her hands; going out upon a cane, very slowly as she did when the weight of age came upon her; praying. I remember her most often at prayer. She made long, rambling prayers out of suffering and hope, having seen many things. I was never sure that I had the right to hear, so exclusive were they of all mere custom and company. The last time I saw her she prayed standing by the side of her bed at night, naked to the waist, the light of a kerosene lamp moving upon her dark skin. Her long, black hair, always drawn and braided in the day, lay upon her shoulders and against her breasts like a shawl. I do not speak Kiowa, and I never understood her

prayers, but there was something inherently sad in the sound, some merest hesitation upon the syllables of sorrow. She began in a high and descending pitch, exhausting her breath to silence; then again and again—and always the same intensity of effort, of something that is, and is not, like urgency in the human voice. Transported so in the dancing light among the shadows of her room, she seemed beyond the reach of time. But that was illusion; I think I knew then that I should not see her again.

13   Houses are like sentinels in the plain, old keepers of the weather watch. There, in a very little while, wood takes on the appearance of great age. All colors wear soon away in the wind and rain, and then the wood is burned gray and the grain appears and the nails turn red with rust. The windowpanes are black and opaque; you imagine there is nothing within, and indeed there are many ghosts, bones given up to the land. They stand here and there against the sky, and you approach them for a longer time than you expect. They belong in the distance; it is their domain.

14   Once there was a lot of sound in my grandmother's house, a lot of coming and going, feasting and talk. The summers there were full of excitement and reunion. The Kiowas are a summer people; they abide the cold and keep to themselves, but when the season turns and the land becomes warm and vital they cannot hold still; an old love of going returns upon them. The aged visitors who came to my grandmother's house when I was a child were made of lean and leather, and they bore themselves upright. They wore great black hats and bright ample shirts that shook in the wind. They rubbed fat upon their hair and wound their braids with strips of colored cloth. Some of them painted their faces and carried the scars of old and cherished enmities. They were an old council of warlords, come to remind and be reminded of who they were. Their wives and daughters served them well. The women might indulge themselves; gossip was at once the mark and compensation of their servitude. They made loud and elaborate talk among themselves, full of jest and gesture, fright and false alarm. They went abroad in fringed and flowered shawls, bright beadwork and German silver. They were at home in the kitchen, and they prepared meals that were banquets.

15   There were frequent prayer meetings, and great nocturnal feasts. When I was a child I played with my cousins outside, where the lamplight fell upon the ground and the singing of the old people rose up around us and carried away into the darkness. There were a lot of good things to eat, a lot of laughter and surprise. And afterwards, when the quiet returned, I lay down with my grandmother and could hear the frogs away by the river and feel the motion of the air.

16   Now there is a funeral silence in the rooms, the endless wake of some final word. The walls have closed in upon my grandmother's house. When I returned to it in mourning, I saw for the first time in my life how small it was. It was late at night, and there was a white moon, nearly full. I sat for a long time on the stone steps by

the kitchen door. From there I could see out across the land; I could see the long row of trees by the creek, the low light upon the rolling plains, and the stars of the Big Dipper. Once I looked at the moon and caught sight of a strange thing. A cricket had perched upon the handrail, only a few inches away from me. My line of vision was such that the creature filled the moon like a fossil. It had gone there, I thought, to live and die, for there, of all places, was its small definition made whole and eternal. A warm wind rose up and purled like the longing within me.

17   The next morning I awoke at dawn and went out on the dirt road to Rainy Mountain. It was already hot, and the grasshoppers began to fill the air. Still, it was early in the morning, and the birds sang out of the shadows. The long yellow grass on the mountain shone in the bright light, and a scissortail hied above the land. There, where it ought to be, at the end of a long and legendary way, was my grandmother's grave. Here and there on the dark stones were ancestral names. Looking back once, I saw the mountain and came away. ❧

Comprehension Check

Complete the following items after you finish your first read. Review and clarify details with your group.

1. What reason does Momaday give for returning to Rainy Mountain in July?

2. What legend did the ancient Kiowas create about the origin of Devil's Tower?

3. Name three activities that Momaday recalls as he thinks about his grandmother's house.

4. 📓 **Notebook** Confirm your understanding by writing a summary of the selection.

- -

RESEARCH

Research to Explore Use online or library sources to find photographs of a place Momaday describes, such as Rainy Mountain or Devil's Tower.

526 UNIT 4 • GRIT AND GRANDEUR

Close Read the Text

With your group, revisit sections of the text you marked during your first read. **Annotate** what you notice. What **questions** do you have? What can you **conclude**?

Analyze the Text

CITE TEXTUAL EVIDENCE to support your answers.

Complete the activities.

1. **Review and Clarify** With your group, reread paragraph 3. Discuss how the lives of the Kiowa changed in the span of a century. How is North American geography important in light of the events that took place during that time?

2. **Present and Discuss** Now, work with your group to share passages from the selection that you found especially important. Take turns presenting your passages. Discuss what you noticed in the selection, what questions you asked, and what conclusions you reached.

3. **Essential Question:** *What is the relationship between literature and place?* What has this memoir taught you about the power of place in literature? Discuss with your group.

INTRODUCTION *from* THE WAY TO RAINY MOUNTAIN

TIP

GROUP DISCUSSION
Beware of "groupthink," which occurs when people change their opinions or beliefs to agree with others and avoid conflict. If you disagree with the direction the group is taking, state your own opinion and the reasons behind it.

LANGUAGE DEVELOPMENT

Concept Vocabulary

reverence	rites	deicide

Why These Words? The three concept vocabulary words are related. With your group, determine what the words have in common. How do these word choices enhance the impact of the memoir?

Practice

🔲 **Notebook** Confirm your understanding of the concept vocabulary words by using them in a brief explanatory paragraph. Be sure to use context clues that hint at each word's meaning.

Word Study

Latin Roots: *-dei-* and *-cid-* According to paragraph 11 of the Introduction from his memoir, Momaday's grandmother remembered the *deicide* that occurred when the soldiers disrupted the Sun Dance, an essential act of the Kiowa faith. The word *deicide* is formed from two Latin roots: *-dei-*, meaning "god," and *-cid-*, meaning "killing" or "cutting." Find and define another word with the root *-dei-* and another word with the root *-cid-*.

⊞ WORD NETWORK

Add words related to a sense of place from the text to your Word Network.

▤ STANDARDS

Language
Identify and correctly use patterns of word changes that indicate different meanings or parts of speech.

Introduction *from* The Way to Rainy Mountain **527**

INTRODUCTION *from* THE WAY
TO RAINY MOUNTAIN

:= **STANDARDS**

Reading Informational Text
• Determine the meaning of words
and phrases as they are used in a
text, including figurative, connotative,
and technical meanings; analyze
how an author uses and refines the
meaning of a key term or terms over
the course of a text.
• Determine an author's point
of view or purpose in a text in
which the rhetoric is particularly
effective, analyzing how style and
content contribute to the power,
persuasiveness, or beauty of the text.

Analyze Craft and Structure

Literary Nonfiction Prose writing that relates the stories of real people, places, or events, and includes literary elements we usually associate with poetry or fiction is called **literary nonfiction.** A writer of literary nonfiction might use description or imagery. Likewise, he or she might tell a story from a highly subjective, or personal, perspective. The level of subjectivity and objectivity—subjectivity's opposite—varies depending on the type of literary nonfiction.

- **Historical writing** relates fact-based events from the past and usually has an objective tone. The author is often a historian who did not experience events firsthand.

- **Reflective writing** explores a topic or event from the writer's life. Reflective writing, by definition, includes the writer's personal thoughts and emotions.

In his memoir, N. Scott Momaday combines these two genres. He weaves Kiowa history and descriptions of the natural world into a personal account of the death of his grandmother and his trip to her grave.

Practice

CITE TEXTUAL EVIDENCE
to support your answers.

Work independently to analyze how Momaday combines historical and reflective writing. Use the chart to record your observations. Then, share and discuss your responses with your group. An example has been done for you.

PARAGRAPH	HISTORICAL DETAIL	PERSONAL REFLECTION	INTERPRETATION
3	*In order to save themselves, they surrendered to the soldiers at Fort Sill and were imprisoned in the old stone corral. . . .*	*My grandmother was spared the humiliation of those high gray walls . . . but she must have known from birth the affliction of defeat. . . .*	Momaday feels his tribe's defeat and humiliation, even though he never experienced it.

Author's Style

Poetic Prose The Introduction from *The Way to Rainy Mountain* is prose, yet Momaday's style includes many strong poetic elements, such as **figurative language** and **imagery**. For example, he uses a vivid simile in paragraph 16 to describe a cricket perching on a handrail: "My line of vision was such that the creature filled the moon like a fossil."

POETIC ELEMENT	DEFINITION	EXAMPLES
figurative language	language that is used imaginatively rather than literally	Simile: *the steaming foliage seems almost to writhe in fire* Metaphor: *and in summer the prairie is an anvil's edge* Personification: *Sweet clover takes hold of the hills*
imagery	words and phrases that appeal to the senses and create word pictures in readers' minds	The grass turns brittle and brown, and it cracks beneath your feet. It reared against the tree and scored the bark all around with its claws.

Read It

1. Work individually to mark the figurative language or imagery in each line. With your group, discuss reasons Momaday uses each poetic element.

   a. Great green and yellow grasshoppers are everywhere in the tall grass, popping up like corn to sting the flesh. . . .

   b. In July the inland slope of the Rockies is luxuriant with flax and buckwheat, stonecrop and larkspur.

   c. From one point of view, their migration was the fruit of an old prophecy, for indeed they emerged from a sunless world.

   d. His fingers became claws, and his body was covered in fur.

2. **Connect to Style** Reread this sentence from paragraph 7 of the text. Identify the poetic elements that Momaday uses.

   > *The great billowing clouds that sail upon it are shadows that move upon the grain like water, dividing light.*

3. 📖 **Notebook** How do poetic elements contribute to the power or beauty of the memoir?

Write It

Write a brief description of an outdoor scene. Include figurative language and imagery to create a poetic impact with your prose.

≡ STANDARDS

Language
Demonstrate understanding of figurative language, word relationships, and nuances in word meanings.

POETRY COLLECTION 2

INTRODUCTION *from* THE WAY
TO RAINY MOUNTAIN

Writing to Compare

You have read and analyzed the poems "In the Longhouse, Oneida Museum" and "Cloudy Day," as well as the Introduction from *The Way to Rainy Mountain.* Now, deepen your understanding of these works by analyzing and comparing how the writers use poetic language.

Assignment

Poetic language is rich in imagery and detail. It conveys meaning through words, rhythms, and sounds that stir the emotions. In a single image, it can communicate a range of insights. Write an **informative essay** in which you examine the role and effects of poetic language in the two poems and the memoir excerpt. Consider the use of figurative language, imagery, and descriptive details in each work. In particular, explain how the writers use poetic language to develop a sense of place and a portrait of the people who have lived there. Work together to analyze the texts, but work on your own to write your essay.

Prewriting

Analyze the Texts As a group, choose passages from each selection that are especially evocative, or that offer insights into a place or its people. Identify within those passages details, images, comparisons, sounds, or other elements that stir the emotions or communicate important information. Use the chart to capture your notes.

LITERARY WORK	PASSAGE	ELEMENTS OF POETIC LANGUAGE	EFFECTS
In the Longhouse . . .			
Cloudy Day			
Introduction *from* The Way to Rainy Mountain			

📓 **Notebook** Respond to these questions.

1. Which portrait of a place and its people do you find most powerful? Why?

2. How is the poetic language of the poems different from the poetic language of the memoir?

Drafting

Identify Key Components Use your discussion and Prewriting notes to decide what you want to say in your essay. In a sentence or two, share your main idea with your group. Ask for feedback. Then, record a draft of your thesis here.

Thesis: _____

_____

_____

Choose a Structure Next, decide how you want to structure your essay. Will you discuss each text one by one, or will you address one point of comparison at a time—for example, how the poems create a sense of place, how the poems shed light on a people, or how the poems evoke deep emotion? Lay out your ideas using a simple organizer like this one.

Introduction	Thesis:
Body Section 1	Main Idea:
Body Section 2	Main Idea:
Body Section 3	Main Idea:
Conclusion	Closing Thought:

Choose Passages Decide which passages from each text best support your main ideas. Add them to your chart. Then, as you draft, integrate the quotations, following punctuation conventions. Make sure to use quotation marks to indicate where a quoted word or phrase begins and ends, and cite line or page numbers in parentheses after the close quotation marks.

> **Example:** In "Cloudy Day," Baca describes the prison tower as a "cornstalk" (16) and as a "hollow shoot of rock" (19). Both of these images create a dry, brittle, and desolate feeling.

Review, Revise, and Edit

When you are done drafting your essay, review and revise it. Make sure every body paragraph helps develop your thesis. If necessary, add quotations or other evidence to support your ideas. Once you are satisfied with the content of your essay, edit for word choice, sentence structure, and tone. Finally, proofread to eliminate errors in grammar, usage, spelling, and punctuation.

✒ EVIDENCE LOG

Before moving on to a new selection, go to your Evidence Log and record what you learned from "In the Longhouse, Oneida Museum," "Cloudy Day," and the Introduction from *The Way to Rainy Mountain*.

▤ STANDARDS

Writing
• Write informative/explanatory texts to examine and convey complex ideas, concepts, and information clearly and accurately through the effective selection, organization, and analysis of content.
• Draw evidence from literary or informational texts to support analysis, reflection, and research.

Give an Explanatory Talk

Assignment

In "A Literature of Place," Barry Lopez writes:

> It is my belief that a human imagination is shaped by the architectures it encounters at an early age.

Consider how Lopez's point applies to the texts in Small-Group Learning. Are they all inspired by a childhood sense of place, or are there other sources of inspiration? Work with your group to create and deliver an **oral presentation** in which you explain your understanding of the sense of place demonstrated in each of the texts in this section.

Plan With Your Group

Analyze the Prompt With your group, discuss the prompt. Begin by analyzing Lopez's quotation. What does he mean by "architectures"? Paraphrase the quotation to be sure your group shares a complete understanding of Lopez's point. Then, read the rest of the prompt, and discuss the outcome and requirements of the assignment.

Analyze the Texts As a group, develop a preliminary thesis that can incorporate evidence from each source text. Then, decide how to label the graphic organizer. On the bottom row, write the title of the text that you think most strongly illustrates Lopez's point. In the row above that, write the title that has the next-strongest connection and so on.

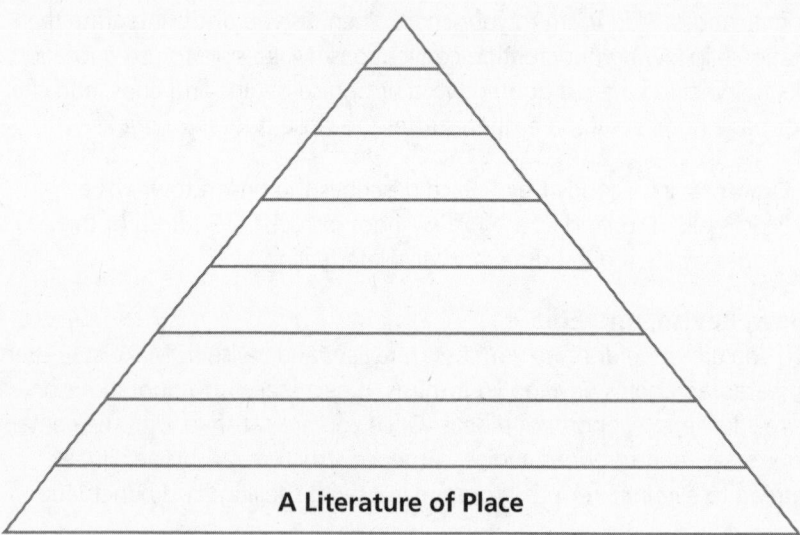

A Literature of Place

Gather Evidence Have each group member select one or more texts to analyze in detail. Then, discuss the texts as a group, noting evidence you might include in your oral presentation. One group member should be the note-taker, but all should offer suggestions.

☰ STANDARDS

Speaking and Listening
Work with peers to promote civil, democratic discussions and decision-making, set clear goals and deadlines, and establish individual roles as needed.

Organize Your Presentation Review your group's notes. Determine the order in which you will discuss the source texts. You might begin by discussing the texts that provide your strongest evidence. Alternatively, you might decide to hold one strong piece of evidence until the end of the presentation.

Rehearse With Your Group

Practice With Your Group Do a run-through of your talk, and use this checklist to evaluate your rehearsal and guide your revisions.

CONTENT	PRESENTATION TECHNIQUES
☐ Speakers respond to the prompt specifically and completely.	☐ Speakers use formal language.
☐ Examples from the text clearly support each speaker's explanation.	☐ Speakers maintain eye contact and speak clearly.
	☐ Speakers stay connected with the audience, even when referring to notes.
	☐ No single speaker dominates the presentation.

Fine-Tune the Content Check that your presentation includes a clear thesis statement that responds to Lopez's quotation. Also, ensure that all of the textual evidence clearly relates to the prompt.

Use academic vocabulary or domain-specific words as needed. For example, literary terms can help you name specific techniques and text structures authors use to create a strong sense of place. You might need geographic or architectural terminology to describe specific places. Consult reference materials to be sure your presentation uses technical terms correctly.

Polish Your Presentation Look for ways to improve your presentation by making it smoother, clearer, or more interesting. Prepare note cards with source quotations, and practice reading from notes while presenting. Consider adding music or sound effects to set a tone or emphasize key points.

Present and Evaluate

When your group presents your explanation, listen respectfully to the members of your group, and be ready to take your turn. As you listen to other groups, notice how their talks differ from yours, both in content and in presentation techniques.

☰ STANDARDS

Speaking and Listening
Present information, findings, and supporting evidence, conveying a clear and distinct perspective and a logical argument, such that listeners can follow the line of reasoning, alternative or opposing perspectives are addressed, and the organization, development, substance, and style are appropriate to purpose, audience, and a range of formal and informal tasks.

Language
Acquire and use accurately general academic and domain-specific words and phrases, sufficient for reading, writing, speaking, and listening at the college and career readiness level; demonstrate independence in gathering vocabulary knowledge when considering a word or phrase important to comprehension or expression.

ESSENTIAL QUESTION:

What is the relationship between literature and place?

The ways in which an author may be influenced by a particular place are as varied as literature itself. The physical setting, the events that took place there, the people who were involved, the author's view of the world—all of these elements affect how an author sees and writes about a landscape. In this section, you will complete your study of the importance of place in American literature by exploring an additional selection related to the topic. Then, you will share what you learn with classmates. To choose a text, follow these steps.

Look Back Think about the selections you have already studied. Which aspects of the concept of place do you wish to explore further? Which time period interests you the most?

Look Ahead Preview the texts by reading the descriptions. Which one seems most interesting and appealing to you?

Look Inside Take a few minutes to scan the text you chose. Choose a different one if this text doesn't meet your needs.

Independent Learning Strategies

Throughout your life, in school, in your community, and in your career, you will need to rely on yourself to learn and work on your own. Review these strategies and the actions you can take to practice them during Independent Learning. Add ideas of your own for each category.

STRATEGY	ACTION PLAN
Create a schedule	• Understand your goals and deadlines. • Make a plan for what to do each day. •
Practice what you have learned	• Use first-read and close-read strategies to deepen your understanding. • After you read, evaluate the usefulness of the evidence to help you understand the topic. • Consult reference sources for additional information that can help you clarify meaning. •
Take notes	• Record important ideas and information. • Review your notes before preparing to share with a group. •

SCAN FOR
MULTIMEDIA

CONTENTS

Choose one selection. Selections are available online only.

PERFORMANCE-BASED ASSESSMENT PREP

Review Evidence for an Explanatory Essay
Complete your Evidence Log for the unit by evaluating what you have learned and synthesizing the information you have recorded.

SCAN FOR
MULTIMEDIA

First-Read Guide

Use this page to record your first-read ideas.

Tool Kit
First-Read Guide and
Model Annotation

Selection Title: _____

NOTICE

NOTICE new information or ideas you learned about the unit topic as you first read this text.

ANNOTATE

ANNOTATE by marking vocabulary and key passages you want to revisit.

First Read

NOTICE · ANNOTATE · CONNECT · RESPOND

CONNECT

CONNECT ideas within the selection to other knowledge, the Essential Question, and the selections you have read. Use reliable reference material to clarify historical context.

RESPOND

RESPOND by writing a brief summary of the selection.

STANDARD

Reading Read and comprehend complex literary and informational texts independently and proficiently.

Close-Read Guide

Use this page to record your close-read ideas.

Selection Title: _____

Tool Kit
Close-Read Guide and
Model Annotation

Close Read the Text

Revisit sections of the text you marked during your first read. Read these sections closely and **annotate** what you notice. Ask yourself **questions** about the text. What can you **conclude**? Write down your ideas.

Analyze the Text

Think about the author's choices of patterns, structure, techniques, and ideas included in the text. Select one and record your thoughts about what this choice conveys.

QuickWrite

Pick a paragraph from the text that grabbed your interest. Explain the power of this passage.

_____
_____
_____
_____
_____
_____
_____
_____

:: STANDARD

Reading Read and comprehend complex literary and informational texts independently and proficiently.

Share Your Independent Learning

Prepare to Share

What is the relationship between literature and place?

Even when you read or learn something independently, you can continue to grow by sharing what you have learned with others. Reflect on the text you explored independently, and write notes about its connection to the unit. In your notes, consider why this text belongs in this unit.

Learn From Your Classmates

💬 Discuss It Share your ideas about the text you explored on your own. As you talk with your classmates, jot down ideas that you learn from them.

Reflect

Review your notes, and mark the most important insight you gained from these writing and discussion activities. Explain how this idea adds to your understanding of the importance of place in literature.

Review Evidence for an Explanatory Essay

At the beginning of this unit, you took a position on the following question:

What makes certain places live on in our memory?

✐ EVIDENCE LOG

Review your Evidence Log and your QuickWrite from the beginning of the unit. Have your ideas or thesis changed?

☐ YES	☐ NO
Identify at least three pieces of text evidence that convinced you to change your thesis.	Identify at least three pieces of evidence that reinforced your initial response.
1.	1.
2.	2.
3.	3.

State your thesis now: _____

_____

_____

Identify a possible alternate viewpoint: _____

_____

_____

Evaluate the Strength of Your Evidence Consider your explanation. Do you have enough evidence to support your thesis? Do you have enough evidence to show that your thesis is stronger than an alternate viewpoint? If not, make a plan.

☐ Do some research. ☐ Talk with my classmates

☐ Reread a selection. ☐ Speak with an expert.

☐ Other: _____

▤ STANDARDS

Writing
Introduce a topic; organize complex ideas, concepts, and information so that each new element builds on that which precedes it to create a unified whole; include formatting, graphics, and multimedia when useful to aiding comprehension.

SOURCES

• WHOLE-CLASS SELECTIONS

• SMALL-GROUP SELECTIONS

• INDEPENDENT-LEARNING SELECTION

PART 1
Writing to Sources: Explanatory Essay

In this unit, you read a variety of texts in which setting plays a critical role. In some cases, setting provides a framework for events. In others, setting points to the theme of the text.

Assignment

Write an **explanatory essay** in which you use examples from the texts in this unit and from your own life to answer this question:

> What makes certain places live on in our memory?

Analyze at least three texts from the unit to show how their authors address the question. Determine how and why a setting becomes essential rather than trivial to the meaning of a literary work. Cite examples from your chosen texts. Then, integrate one or more anecdotes from your own life into the essay. Show how and why certain places have especially affected you. Make the transition between examples from texts and anecdotes clear and smooth. Conclude with a section that ties your ideas together.

Reread the Assignment Review the assignment to be sure you fully understand it. The task may reference some of the academic words presented at the beginning of the unit. Be sure you understand each of the words given below in order to complete the assignment correctly.

Academic Vocabulary

analyze	literal	trivialize
subordinate	determine	

WORD NETWORK

As you write and revise your explanatory essay, use your Word Network to help vary your word choices.

Review the Elements of an Explanatory Essay Before you begin writing, read the Explanatory Essay Rubric. Once you have completed your first draft, check it against the rubric. If one or more of the elements are missing or not as strong as they could be, revise your essay to add or strengthen those components.

STANDARDS
Writing
• Write informative/explanatory texts to examine and convey complex ideas, concepts, and information clearly and accurately through the effective selection, organization, and analysis of content.
• Write routinely over extended time frames and shorter time frames for a range of tasks, purposes, and audiences.

Explanatory Essay Rubric

	Focus and Organization	Evidence and Elaboration	Language Conventions
4	The introduction is engaging and reveals the topic in a way that appeals to a reader. Examples progress logically, linked by transitional words and phrases. The conclusion leaves a strong impression on the reader.	Ideas are supported with specific and relevant textual evidence and anecdotes. The tone of the essay is formal and objective. Vocabulary is strategic and appropriate for the audience and purpose.	The essay effectively demonstrates standard English conventions of usage and mechanics.
3	The introduction is engaging and clearly reveals the topic. Examples progress logically, with frequent use of transitional words and phrases. The conclusion follows from the rest of the text.	Ideas are supported with specific textual evidence and anecdotes. The tone of the essay is mostly formal and objective. Vocabulary is mostly strategic and appropriate for the audience and purpose.	The essay demonstrates fluency in standard English conventions of usage and mechanics.
2	The introduction states the topic. Examples progress somewhat logically, with some use of transitional words and phrases. The conclusion restates the main ideas.	Many ideas are supported with textual evidence or anecdotes. The tone of the essay is occasionally formal and objective. Vocabulary is somewhat appropriate for the audience and purpose.	The essay demonstrates some grasp of standard English conventions of usage and mechanics.
1	The introduction does not clearly state the topic, or it is missing altogether. Examples do not progress logically. Sentences may seem disconnected. The conclusion does not follow from the ideas and analysis or it is missing altogether.	Most ideas are not supported with textual evidence or anecdotes or the examples are irrelevant or contradict the thesis. The tone of the essay is informal. Vocabulary is limited or ineffective.	The essay contains mistakes in standard English conventions of usage and mechanics.

PART 2
Speaking and Listening: Oral Presentation

> **Assignment**
> After completing the final draft of your explanatory essay, use it as the foundation for a three-to-five-minute **oral presentation**.

Do not simply read your text aloud. Instead, take the following steps to make your presentation lively and engaging.

- Go back to your text, and mark your thesis statement. Then, annotate the most important ideas and supporting details from each part of your essay.

- Emphasize the connections between your ideas and your textual evidence so that listeners can easily follow your line of thinking.

- Practice reading with expression any quotations from the texts that you have chosen, as well as any anecdotes that you have included.

- Refer to your annotated text to guide your presentation, keep it focused, and hold the audience's attention.

- Deliver your presentation with a formal but sincere tone.

Review the Rubric The criteria by which your presentation will be evaluated appear in this rubric. Review the criteria before presenting to ensure that you are prepared.

STANDARDS
Speaking and Listening
Present information, findings, and supporting evidence, conveying a clear and distinct perspective, such that listeners can follow the line of reasoning, alternative or opposing perspectives are addressed, and the organization, development, substance, and style are appropriate to purpose, audience, and a range of formal and informal tasks.

	Content	Presentation Techniques
3	The presentation is specifically geared to the target audience.	The speaker enunciates clearly and uses an appropriate volume.
	Key ideas are presented logically.	The speaker uses a formal but sincere tone overall, varying tone and pace to maintain the audience's interest.
	Examples from the chosen texts are introduced clearly and cited correctly.	The speaker maintains effective eye contact.
2	The presentation is mostly geared to the target audience.	The speaker enunciates clearly most of the time and usually uses an appropriate volume.
	Key ideas follow in a generally understandable way.	The speaker may be inconsistent in maintaining a formal but sincere tone overall or in varying tone and pace to maintain the audience's interest.
	Examples from the chosen texts are introduced but may not be cited specifically.	The speaker makes occasional eye contact.
1	The presentation is not clearly geared to the target audience.	The speaker mumbles occasionally, speaks too quickly, or does not speak loudly enough.
	Key ideas are hard to identify.	The speaker fails to vary tone or varies it in inappropriate ways.
	Examples from the chosen texts may not be appropriate or useful for the audience.	The speaker rarely or never makes eye contact.

Reflect on the Unit

Now that you've completed the unit, take a few moments to reflect on your learning. Use the questions below to think about where you succeeded, what skills and strategies helped you, and where you can continue to grow in the future.

Reflect on the Unit Goals

Look back at the goals at the beginning of the unit. Use a different colored pen to rate yourself again. Think about readings and activities that contributed the most to the growth of your understanding. Record your thoughts.

Reflect on the Learning Strategies

Discuss It Write a reflection on whether you were able to improve your learning based on your Action Plans. Think about what worked, what didn't, and what you might do to keep working on these strategies. Record your ideas before a class discussion.

Reflect on the Text

Choose a selection that you found challenging, and explain what made it difficult.

Describe something that surprised you about a text in the unit.

Which activity taught you the most about the relationship between literature and place? What did you learn?

☰ STANDARDS
Speaking and Listening
Present information, findings, and supporting evidence, conveying a clear and distinct perspective, such that listeners can follow the line of reasoning, alternative or opposing perspectives are addressed, and the organization, development, substance, and style are appropriate to purpose, audience, and a range of formal and informal tasks.

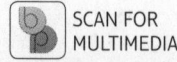 SCAN FOR MULTIMEDIA

Facing Our Fears

Victims and Victors

The Hollywood Blacklist

Discuss It How should we respond to those who hold different political views or values than we do?

Write your response before sharing your ideas.

 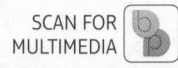

UNIT 5

UNIT INTRODUCTION

ESSENTIAL QUESTION: How do we respond when challenged by fear?

LAUNCH TEXT
ARGUMENT MODEL
Is It Foolish to Fear?

 WHOLE-CLASS LEARNING

HISTORICAL PERSPECTIVES

Focus Period: 1920–1960
Times of Trouble

ANCHOR TEXT: DRAMA

The Crucible
Arthur Miller

Act I

Act II

Act III

Act IV

MEDIA: AUDIO PERFORMANCE

The Crucible
L.A. Theatre Works

COMPARE

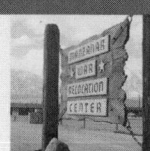 **SMALL-GROUP LEARNING**

AUTOBIOGRAPHY

from Farewell to Manzanar
Jeanne Wakatsuki Houston and James D. Houston

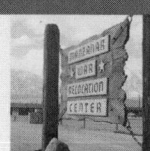

COMPARE

MEDIA: VIDEO

Interview With George Takei
Archive of American Television

SHORT STORY

Antojos
Julia Alvarez

 INDEPENDENT LEARNING

MAGAZINE ARTICLE

What You Don't Know Can Kill You
Jason Daley

RISK AHEAD

POETRY

Runagate Runagate
Robert Hayden

POETRY COLLECTION

1-800-FEAR
Jody Gladding

Bears at Raspberry Time
Hayden Carruth

For Black Women Who Are Afraid
Toi Derricotte

ESSAY

What Are You So Afraid Of?
Akiko Busch

PERFORMANCE TASK

WRITING FOCUS:
Write an Argument

PERFORMANCE TASK

SPEAKING AND LISTENING FOCUS:
Present an Argument

PERFORMANCE-BASED ASSESSMENT PREP

Review Evidence for an Argument

PERFORMANCE-BASED ASSESSMENT

Argument: Essay and Speech

PROMPT:

Is fear always a harmful emotion?

Unit Goals

Throughout this unit, you will deepen your perspective on the concept of fear by reading, writing, speaking, listening, and presenting. These goals will help you succeed on the Unit Performance-Based Assessment.

Rate how well you meet these goals right now. You will revisit your ratings later when you reflect on your growth during this unit.

SCALE	1 NOT AT ALL WELL	2 NOT VERY WELL	3 SOMEWHAT WELL	4 VERY WELL	5 EXTREMELY WELL

READING GOALS

	1	2	3	4	5
• Read a variety of texts to gain the knowledge and insight needed to write about fear.	○	○	○	○	○
• Expand your knowledge and use of academic and concept vocabulary.	○	○	○	○	○

WRITING AND RESEARCH GOALS

	1	2	3	4	5
• Write an argumentative essay that has a clear structure and that draws evidence from texts and background knowledge to support a claim.	○	○	○	○	○
• Conduct research projects of various lengths to explore a topic and clarify meaning.	○	○	○	○	○

LANGUAGE GOALS

	1	2	3	4	5
• Correctly use pronouns to add variety to your writing and presentations.	○	○	○	○	○
• Use irony to add a level of meaning to your writing and presentations.	○	○	○	○	○

SPEAKING AND LISTENING GOALS

	1	2	3	4	5
• Collaborate with your team to build on the ideas of others, develop consensus, and communicate.	○	○	○	○	○
• Integrate audio, visuals, and text to present information.	○	○	○	○	○

STANDARDS

Language
Acquire and use accurately general academic and domain-specific words and phrases, sufficient for reading, writing, speaking, and listening at the college and career readiness level; demonstrate independence in gathering vocabulary knowledge when considering a word or phrase important to comprehension or expression.

SCAN FOR MULTIMEDIA

Academic Vocabulary: Argument

Understanding and using academic terms can help you read, write, and speak with precision and clarity. Here are five academic words that will be useful to you in this unit as you analyze and write arguments.

Complete the chart.

1. Review each word, its root, and the mentor sentences.

2. Use the information and your own knowledge to predict the meaning of each word.

3. For each word, list at least two related words.

4. Refer to a dictionary or other resources if needed.

TIP

FOLLOW THROUGH
Study the words in this chart, and mark them or their forms wherever they appear in the unit.

WORD	MENTOR SENTENCES	PREDICT MEANING	RELATED WORDS
assert ROOT: **-ser-** "join"	1. You cannot simply *assert* a position; you must support it with convincing evidence. 2. In the debate, my opponent was too timid and did not *assert* his ideas clearly.		assertion; assertively
relevant ROOT: **-lev-** "raise"	1. That old-fashioned show is not *relevant* to most young viewers. 2. Chapter three may be *relevant* to your fascination with architecture.		
certify ROOT: **-cert-** "sure"	1. After an election, an outside party may be brought in to *certify* the results. 2. Before you quote an expert, you should *certify* her credentials.		
immutable ROOT: **-mut-** "move"	1. Some ideas are simply *immutable* and unchanging. 2. Shakespeare's characters are not *immutable*, because they can be interpreted in so many different ways.		
definitive ROOT: **-fin-** "end"	1. In my opinion, that is the *definitive* biography of Arthur Miller. 2. It is too early to reach any *definitive* conclusions about the issue.		

This selection is an example of an **argumentative text**, a type of writing in which the author presents a claim and organizes evidence and reasons to support that claim. This is the type of writing you will develop in the Performance-Based Assessment at the end of the unit.

As you read, notice how the writer uses relevant evidence to develop the claim. Mark the text to answer this question: What is the writer's position, and what evidence supports it?

Is It Foolish to Fear?

NOTES

1   Fear of falling, fear of flying, fear of snakes and spiders—sometimes it seems that we humans are controlled by our fears. Some of us may seek professional help to rid ourselves of fears. However, fear plays an important role in life. It is not foolish to fear—it is a matter of survival.

2   Fear may feel negative, because it is an emotion that can be painful. The physical responses we have to objects or situations that we fear are often grouped together and characterized as a "fight or flight" instinct. Something alarms you, and instantly your brain causes a number of chemicals to be released into your bloodstream. Those chemicals race through the body, causing your heart to race, your muscles to tense, and your breathing to quicken. Your pupils dilate, so bright light hurts, but you can see more clearly. Your surface veins constrict, making your skin feel cold.

3   Long ago, such responses made it easier for early humans to escape from predators. Dilated pupils meant that they could see better in dim light. Quick breathing and tense muscles allowed them to run faster or leap higher than they normally could. Their skin grew cold as blood flowed to the major muscles, letting arms and legs move more rapidly. The entire body became an instrument focused

SCAN FOR
MULTIMEDIA

NOTES

on surviving danger. If flight was possible, the person would run. If it was not, he or she would fight. Either way, fear stimulated the brain and primed the body for a response.

4 This response to fear was good for everyone who displayed it. The humans who felt and responded to fear most strongly were likely to be the ones who survived, whether the fear stimulus was a tiger, an earthquake, or a violent storm.

5 Today, our fear stimulus might be a dark alley, a swaying rope bridge, or a barking dog. We sense danger, and our bodies react. We may feel foolish when the alley proves to be empty, the bridge safe, and the dog friendly. Nevertheless, that initial rush of fear serves as our protector and should never be ignored.

6 Today, modern psychotherapies may include conditioning—a stimulus-response learning process—that helps people rid themselves of fears. After just a few sessions, nearly anyone can stop being afraid of speaking in public or driving through a tunnel. So why shouldn't we all condition ourselves to become braver?

7 First, there is a difference between fear and phobia. A phobia is an unnecessary fear of something that is unlikely to cause harm. For example, some people are afraid of clowns, but the odds of a clown's being harmful are small. Second, without fear, one would be in constant danger. It is important to be afraid of an oncoming car, a flying brick, or the rattling tail at the end of an unfamiliar snake. In such cases, fear is a matter of self-preservation.

8 Few of us enjoy being afraid. It is physically and mentally uncomfortable, and once any danger has passed, we may feel that our fears were unwarranted. It is worth remembering, however, that ever since you were a small child perched at the top of a staircase or toddling near a hot stove, a logical, sensible, inbred fear has protected you from harm. ❧

🗂 WORD NETWORK FOR FACING OUR FEARS

Vocabulary A Word Network is a collection of words related to a topic. As you read the unit selections, identify interesting words related to the idea of fear, and add them to your Word Network. For example, you might begin by adding words from the Launch Text, such as *alarms*. For each word you add, note a related word, such as a synonym or an antonym. Continue to add words as you complete this unit.

alarms | calms

FEAR

🔧 **Tool Kit**
Word Network Model

Summary

Write a summary of "Is It Foolish to Fear?" A **summary** is a concise, complete, and accurate overview of a text. It should not include a statement of your opinion or an analysis.

Launch Activity

Record "Popular" Fears As a class, brainstorm for a list of fears that you have read about or seen portrayed in movies or television shows. Have a volunteer write each fear along the bottom of the chalkboard, another display area in your classroom, or a large piece of paper. Try to develop a row of ten to twelve fears.

- Now, work together to construct a bar graph. Take three sticky notes, and write your name on each one.

- Take turns going to the board (or other display location). Place one note each above a fear that you think actually afflicts many people. Make sure to place your notes above any that are already there so that you build columns.

- When you have all finished placing your notes, stand back and look at the graph you have constructed.

- Based on the graph, draw a conclusion about the fears that are commonly portrayed in books and entertainment media. Do these fears accurately represent those of regular people in real life? Discuss these questions, and come to a consensus. Write your consensus at the top of your bar graph.

QuickWrite

Consider class discussions, the video, and the Launch Text as you think about the prompt. Record your first thoughts here.

PROMPT: **Is fear always a harmful emotion?**

Review your QuickWrite. Summarize your thoughts in one sentence to record in your Evidence Log. Then, record textual details or evidence from "Is It Foolish to Fear?" that supports your initial position.

Prepare for the Performance-Based Assessment at the end of the unit by completing the Evidence Log after each selection.

🔧 **Tool Kit**
Evidence Log Model

Title of Text: _____   Date: _____

CONNECTION TO PROMPT	TEXT EVIDENCE/DETAILS	ADDITIONAL NOTES/IDEAS

How does this text change or add to my thinking?   Date: _____

ESSENTIAL QUESTION:

How do we respond when challenged by fear?

As you read these selections, work with your whole class to explore the meaning and power of fear.

From Text to Topic One person's unreasonable fears can make his or her life very difficult. What might happen, then, when a shared fear afflicts a family, a whole town, or an entire country? Arthur Miller explores this prospect in *The Crucible,* one of his most famous plays. Using a carefully researched case of mass hysteria from America's colonial past, Miller draws attention to fears haunting American culture in the 1950s. The story that he presents is powerful in its own right, but it also encourages audiences to consider how unrestrained, unreasonable fear can damage a society. As you read *The Crucible,* consider what the narrative shows about the far-reaching influence of fear.

Whole-Class Learning Strategies

Throughout your life, in school, in your community, and in your career, you will continue to learn and work in large-group environments.

Review these strategies and the actions you can take to practice them as you work with your whole class. Add ideas of your own for each step. Get ready to use these strategies during Whole-Class Learning.

STRATEGY	ACTION PLAN
Listen actively	• Eliminate distractions. For example, put your cellphone away. • Record brief notes on main ideas and points of confusion. •
Clarify by asking questions	• If you're confused, other people probably are, too. Ask a question to help your whole class. • Ask follow-up questions as needed—for example, if you do not understand the clarification, or if you want to make an additional connection. •
Monitor understanding	• Notice what information you already know and be ready to build on it. • Ask for help if you are struggling. •
Interact and share ideas	• Share your ideas and answer questions, even if you are unsure. • Build on the ideas of others by adding details or making a connection. •

SCAN FOR
MULTIMEDIA

CONTENTS

Times of Trouble

Voices of the Period

"The only thing we have to fear is fear itself."

—Franklin Delano Roosevelt,
32nd president of the United States

"I have learned over the years that when one's mind is made up, this diminishes fear; knowing what must be done does away with fear."

—Rosa Parks,
political activist sometimes referred to
as "the first lady of civil rights"

"If you're not frightened that you might fail, you'll never do the job. If you're frightened, you'll work like crazy."

—César Chávez,
political activist and co-founder of the
National Farm Workers Association

"Neither a wise man nor a brave man lies down on the tracks of history to wait for the train of the future to run over him."

—Dwight D. Eisenhower,
34th president of the United States

History of the Period

The Roaring Twenties World War I ended in 1918, and in the decade that followed, the nation seemed to go on a binge of building, consumption, and speculation. The economy boomed, and skyscrapers rose. Prohibition made the sale of liquor illegal, which led to bootlegging and the rise of organized crime. Radio, jazz, and movies helped shape American culture. As people let go of prewar values, they let the "roar" of the Roaring Twenties drown out the sounds of war and the horror of death.

The Great Depression The boom, of course, could not last, and in October 1929 the stock market crashed, spurring what is known as the Great Depression. By mid-1932, about 12 million Americans—one-quarter of the country's workforce—were unemployed. Hungry and panicked people waited for food in bread lines and at soup kitchens. The government seemed unable to turn the economy around. Depression became more than an economic fact—it became a national state of mind.

The New Deal When elected president in 1932, Franklin Delano Roosevelt took action immediately, initiating a package of major economic reforms that came to be known as the New Deal. Many Americans soon found work on huge public projects, including building dams and bridges; conserving land; and recording the past and present in photographs, artwork, and writing. Roosevelt's leadership and policies helped end the Depression

TIMELINE

1925: F. Scott Fitzgerald's *The Great Gatsby* is published.

1927: Charles Lindbergh flies solo and nonstop from New York to Paris.

1920

1922: Egypt The tomb of King Tutankhamun is discovered.

1925: Louis Armstrong and his Hot Five become a headlining act on the radio.

Integration of Knowledge and Ideas

Notebook What does the information in the graphs help you understand about the differences between World War I and World War II in terms of military deaths? What factors likely affected the increase of military deaths in World War II?

Military Deaths in World War I

CENTRAL POWERS
Austria-Hungary
Germany

ALLIES
United States
British Empire
France
Russia

equals 250,000 military deaths

Military Deaths in World War II

AXIS POWERS
Germany
Italy
Japan

ALLIES
United States
USSR
British Empire

equals 500,000 military deaths

and earned him an unprecedented three reelections: in 1936, 1940, and 1944.

World War II Just twenty years after the end of World War I, Germany, under the rule of Adolf Hitler, ignited the Second World War with its invasion of neighboring countries. The dominant mood in the United States, however, was one of isolationism, with most Americans preferring to stay out of the conflict. This attitude changed dramatically when Japanese forces attacked the naval base at Pearl Harbor, Hawaii, on December 7, 1941. With more than 3,000 American casualties and the destruction of much of the American battleship fleet, neutrality and isolationism came to a swift end. The United States quickly declared war on the Axis Powers: Germany, Japan, and Italy. It took years of bitter fighting in Europe, North Africa, and the Pacific before the Allies—the United States, Great Britain, France, and the Soviet Union—defeated Italy, Germany, and then Japan. Japan surrendered only after the United States dropped an atomic bomb on the cities of Hiroshima and then Nagasaki. Peace—and the Atomic Age—had arrived.

Face-Off With Communism The threat of Communist infiltration and influence became a fixation in the United States after World War II.

1928: China Chiang Kai-shek becomes the leader of China's Nationalist government.

1933: Germany Adolf Hitler becomes Chancellor of Germany.

1939: Poland An invasion by German forces sets off World War II, which will extend across Europe and into Asia and North Africa.

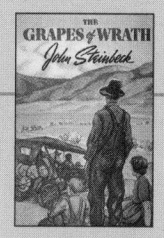

1940

1929: The stock market crashes in October, followed by the Great Depression of the 1930s.

1933: President Franklin D. Roosevelt closes banks; Congress passes New Deal laws.

1937: Zora Neale Hurston's *Their Eyes Were Watching God* is published.

1939: John Steinbeck's *The Grapes of Wrath* is published.

The United States battled against Communist China in Korea from 1950 to 1953. With the rise of the Soviet Union, the Cold War—competition between Eastern Bloc countries and the West—became intense. Fear of unchecked Soviet aggression marked the period. Espionage, economic sanctions, treaties, defense measures, and diplomatic conflicts were constantly in the news. By the mid-1950s, the country faced another Communist threat as conflict began in Vietnam.

Meanwhile, a "Red Scare," led by Senator Joseph McCarthy of Wisconsin, spread fear of Communist infiltration at home. Cold War anxiety was intensified by the existence of the atomic bomb, which created global fears as well as a new urgency surrounding the management of international conflict. In some ways, the postwar period could be characterized as an Age of Anxiety, as Americans seemed unable to stop thinking about terrible things that could or might happen. Schools regularly held air-raid drills, and Communists were hunted everywhere.

Postwar Boom The United States emerged from World War II as the most powerful nation on Earth. In the 1950s, despite the pressures of the Cold War, the nation enjoyed widespread prosperity, its suburbs expanded, and its consumer society flourished. Americans' incomes almost doubled in the 1950s, transforming American lives. By the mid-1950s, sixty percent of Americans were defined as being in the "middle class."

The Television Age The influence of television became especially powerful in the postwar era.

In 1946, the nation had six TV stations; ten years later, there were more than 400 stations; by 1960, there was a television in almost every American home.

Television spearheaded revolutions in consumerism and mass communication. Millions of Americans saw the same advertisements and the same entertainment. Many watched television news broadcasts to learn about the Soviet Union's launch of the first artificial satellite to orbit the Earth, which initiated the space race. Some 70 million Americans watched Richard Nixon lose the 1960 election debates to John F. Kennedy, forever changing the structure of political campaigns.

The American Dilemma Deep conflicts between American ideals and the reality of the treatment of African Americans continued into the postwar decades. However, the 1950s saw the foundations of significant change in desegregating American society, beginning with the 1954 landmark Supreme Court decision in *Brown* v. *Board of Education of Topeka, Kansas*, which overturned the earlier decision that "separate but equal" facilities were legal. From that moment on, a Civil Rights movement began to build force under the leadership of people such as Martin Luther King, Jr., and the participation of a growing number of protestors, from students in Arkansas to bus riders in Alabama.

TIMELINE

1941: Japanese forces bomb Pearl Harbor, bringing the United States into World War II.

1947: The Cold War between the United States and the Soviet Union begins.

1950–1953: Korea The Korean War is fought.

1940

1945: World War II ends; the United Nations charter is signed.

1949: Arthur Miller's *Death of a Salesman* is produced.

Literature Selections

Literature of the Focus Period A key selection in this unit was written during the Focus Period and pertains to fear and its effects:

The Crucible, Arthur Miller

Connections Across Time A consideration of fear preceded and followed the Focus Period. Indeed, the theme has shaped the work of writers and commentators in various time periods and locations.

from *Farewell to Manzanar,* Jeanne Wakatsuki Houston and James D. Houston

"Antojos," Julia Alvarez

"What You Don't Know Can Kill You," Jason Daley

"Runagate Runagate," Robert Hayden

"1-800-FEAR," Jody Gladding

"Bears at Raspberry Time," Hayden Carruth

"For Black Women Who Are Afraid," Toi Derricotte

"What Are You So Afraid Of?" Akiko Busch

ADDITIONAL FOCUS PERIOD LITERATURE

Student Edition

UNIT 1
"The Pedestrian," Ray Bradbury

UNIT 3
Brown v. Board of Education: Opinion of the Court, Earl Warren

The Poetry of Langston Hughes

UNIT 4
"The Rockpile," James Baldwin

UNIT 6
"The Jilting of Granny Weatherall," Katherine Anne Porter

1954: The Supreme Court rules public school segregation unconstitutional in *Brown v. Board of Education*.

1957: USSR The Soviet Union launches *Sputnik I,* the first space satellite.

1959: Alaska and Hawaii are admitted to the Union as the 49th and 50th states.

1950: Thousands are falsely accused of treason following Senator McCarthy's claims of Communist infiltration in the government.

1955: Rosa Parks is arrested, triggering the Montgomery Bus Boycott.

1960

1959: Lorraine Hansberry's *A Raisin in the Sun* is produced.

For much of the twentieth century, the theater was the center of American intellectual life. Great plays offered thrilling stories, crackling dialogue, and philosophical truth. As Arthur Miller wrote:

"Great drama is great questions or it is nothing but technique. I could not imagine a theater worth my time that did not want to change the world."

Dramatic literature shares many elements with prose, fiction, and poetry, but is written to be acted out on a stage before an audience rather than read quietly on your own. In a sense, when you read a play, you are not experiencing the work as it was meant to be experienced. You are reading a script, which is only part of the piece. However, you can help bring the drama to life and create the performance in your own imagination by applying the following strategies.

Picture the Action Reading a play without envisioning the action is like watching a movie with your eyes shut. Use the stage directions and other details to create the scene in your mind. Consider the situation, characters' motivations and feelings, and how staging or performance choices might convey those elements.

Refer to the Cast of Characters The details of characters' relationships are usually conveyed through dialogue, gestures, body language, and action rather than through direct statements. In addition, some plays feature numerous characters whose relationships to one another are complex. One way to keep things clear is to refer to the Cast of Characters list whenever a character joins—or re-joins—the action.

Summarize the Action Most plays are broken into smaller units called acts. Some plays are then broken into even smaller sections called scenes. These breaks give you an opportunity to review the action. Take the opportunities afforded by these separations to consider various questions: What conflicts are developing or intensifying? What decisions are characters making? Toward what outcome does the story seem to be heading?

Be an Actor Consider studying with a group and acting out scenes that you find difficult. When you inject appropriate emotion into the text, the meaning and nuances will often become clearer. You may also make connections among language, imagery, and character that you otherwise might not have noticed.

Close Read the Text

Annotating the text as you read can help you tackle the challenges of reading a play rather than watching it in performance. Here are two sample annotations of an excerpt from *The Crucible*, Act I. The setting is home of Reverend Samuel Parris, the minister of the church in the Puritan colony of Salem, Massachusetts, in 1692. Betty, Parris's young daughter, is suffering a mysterious ailment. Parris and Abigail Williams, Betty's cousin, are in the sick room when Susanna Walcott arrives with a message from the doctor.

ANNOTATE: This stage direction is very specific.

QUESTION: What does this stage direction suggest about the situation?

CONCLUDE: Susanna seems to regard Betty as an object of curiosity. Parris seems to be trying to protect Betty by physically blocking Susanna's view.

SUSANNA WALCOTT, *a little younger than Abigail, a nervous, hurried girl enters.*

Parris, *eagerly*: What does the doctor say, child?

Susanna, *craning around* PARRIS *to get a look at* BETTY: He bid me come and tell you, reverend sir, that he cannot discover no medicine for it in his books.

Parris: Then he must search on.

Susanna: Aye, sir, he have been searchin' his books since he left you, sir. But he bid me tell you, that you might look to unnatural things for the cause of it.

Parris, *his eyes going wide*: No—no. There be no unnatural cause here. Tell him I have sent for Reverend Hale of Beverly, and Mr. Hale will surely confirm that. Let him look to medicine and put out all thought of unnatural causes here. There be none.

Susanna: Aye, sir. He bid me tell you. *She turns to go.*

Abigail: Speak nothin' of it in the village, Susanna.

Parris: Go directly home and speak nothing of unnatural causes.

Susanna: Aye, sir. I pray for her. *She goes out.*

ANNOTATE: When Susanna mentions "unnatural things," Parris reacts physically and then repeats the phrase "unnatural causes" three times.

QUESTION: Why does the playwright present Parris's reaction in this way?

CONCLUDE: To the Puritans of Salem, "unnatural causes" means the presence of dark, supernatural forces. Parris is terrified for his daughter's health, but he may be even more afraid of gossip and accusations.

The Crucible, Act I

Concept Vocabulary

You will encounter the following words as you read Act I of *The Crucible.* Before reading, note how familiar you are with each word. Then, rank the words in order from most familiar (1) to least familiar (3).

WORD	YOUR RANKING
vindictive	
calumny	
defamation	

After completing the first read, come back to the concept vocabulary and review your rankings. Mark changes to your original rankings as needed.

First Read DRAMA

Apply these strategies as you conduct your first read. You will have an opportunity to complete the close-read notes after your first read.

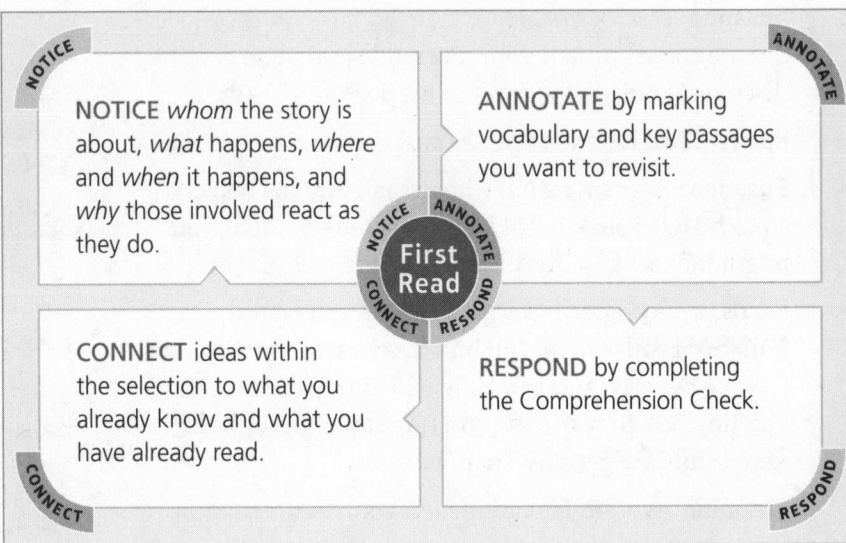

NOTICE *whom* the story is about, *what* happens, *where* and *when* it happens, and *why* those involved react as they do.

ANNOTATE by marking vocabulary and key passages you want to revisit.

CONNECT ideas within the selection to what you already know and what you have already read.

RESPOND by completing the Comprehension Check.

First Read

NOTICE · ANNOTATE · CONNECT · RESPOND

⚙ Tool Kit
First-Read Guide and Model Annotation

☷ STANDARDS

Reading Literature
By the end of grade 11, read and comprehend literature, including stories, dramas, and poems, in the grades 11–CCR text complexity band proficiently, with scaffolding as needed at the high end of the range.

About the Playwright
Arthur Miller (1915–2005)

Arthur Miller was born in New York City and grew up during the Great Depression. By the time he graduated from high school in 1932, his father's family business had gone bankrupt, and Miller was forced to take odd jobs to raise money for college tuition.

Major Talent Miller began writing plays during his college years at the University of Michigan. In 1947, his play *All My Sons* was performed on Broadway to immediate acclaim, establishing Miller as a bright new talent. Two years later, *Death of a Salesman* opened on Broadway, earning Miller a Pulitzer Prize and elevating him to the status of a premier American playwright. His next play, *The Crucible*, opened to mixed reviews in 1953, largely because of its controversial political content. *The Crucible* was clearly a comment on the "witch hunts" for Communists that were being carried out at the time by Wisconsin Senator Joseph McCarthy and by the House Un-American Activities Committee (HUAC).

In the Shadow of McCarthyism Miller's experience with the HUAC hearings parallels the situation he portrayed in *The Crucible*. Called before the committee in 1956, Miller, like his *Crucible* character John Proctor, admitted to his own socialist leanings but refused to "name names" about fellow celebrities in the theater and in Hollywood.

At the time of his House testimony, Miller was firmly established as a major literary figure and celebrity, a status that soon skyrocketed when he married Marilyn Monroe, the most famous Hollywood star of the 1950s. Miller's celebrity did not protect him from the committee, however, and the "Red Scare" period continued to haunt him for the rest of his life. "It was as though the whole country had been born anew," he wrote, "without a memory even of certain elemental decencies which a year or two earlier no one would have imagined could be altered, let alone forgotten." The very personal terror Miller felt as a result of his dealings with HUAC he claimed underlay "every word in *The Crucible*."

Voice of Conscience Today, Miller is regarded as one of the true giants of the American theater. His *Death of a Salesman* is often discussed as the greatest American play ever written. Playwright Edward Albee said of Miller, "Arthur never compromised. He never sold out." Miller was able to use art to make enormously important social and political points that still resonate today.

Background for
The Crucible

In 1692, the British colony of Massachusetts was convulsed by a witchcraft hysteria that resulted in the execution of 20 people and the jailing of more than 100 others. The incident, though unprecedented for New England, was not unique. During the sixteenth and seventeenth centuries, witch hunts swept through Europe, resulting in tens of thousands of executions.

For the New England colonies, the witchcraft episode was perhaps inevitable. Enduring harsh conditions and punishing hardship from day to day, many colonists attributed their misfortunes to the power of evil. In the small parish of Salem Village, many were quick to blame witchcraft when the minister's daughter and several other girls were afflicted by seizures and lapsed into unconsciousness.

A hunt to identify witches spread until some of the colony's most prominent citizens stood accused. Many historians have seen a pattern of social and economic animosity behind the accusations, but most scholars feel that mass hysteria—a strong, irrational fear that quickly spreads—was also a strong contributing factor.

A *crucible* is a heat-resistant container in which metals are melted or fused at very high temperatures. The word is used symbolically to suggest a severe trial or test. When *The Crucible* was first published, Arthur Miller added a note about the play's historical accuracy. He pointed out that he had fused many historical characters into one dramatic character, that he had raised Abigail's age, and that the characters of Hathorne and Danforth represented a composite of several historical judges. Miller then explained, "The fate of each character is exactly that of his historical model, and there is no one in the drama who did not play a similar—and in some cases exactly the same—role in history."

The Crucible

Act I

Arthur Miller

CHARACTERS

Reverend Parris	Martha Corey
Betty Parris	Reverend John Hale
Tituba	Elizabeth Proctor
Abigail Williams	Francis Nurse
Susanna Walcott	Ezekiel Cheever
Mrs. Ann Putnam	Marshal Herrick
Thomas Putnam	Judge Hathorne
Mercy Lewis	Deputy Governor Danforth
Mary Warren	Sarah Good
John Proctor	Hopkins
Rebecca Nurse	Giles Corey

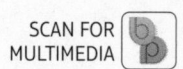
NOTES

(An Overture)

1 *A small upper bedroom in the home of* REVEREND SAMUEL PARRIS, *Salem, Massachusetts, in the spring of the year 1692.*

2 *There is a narrow window at the left. Through its leaded panes the morning sunlight streams. A candle still burns near the bed, which is at the right. A chest, a chair, and a small table are the other furnishings. At the back a door opens on the landing of the stairway to the ground floor. The room gives off an air of clean spareness. The roof rafters are exposed, and the wood colors are raw and unmellowed.*

3 *As the curtain rises,* REVEREND PARRIS *is discovered kneeling beside the bed, evidently in prayer. His daughter,* BETTY PARRIS, *aged ten, is lying on the bed, inert.*

⌘ ⌘ ⌘

4 At the time of these events Parris was in his middle forties. In history he cut a villainous path, and there is very little good to be said for him. He believed he was being persecuted wherever he went, despite his best efforts to win people and God to his side. In meeting, he felt insulted if someone rose to shut the door without first asking his permission. He was a widower with no interest in children, or talent with them. He regarded them as young adults, and until this strange crisis he, like the rest of Salem, never conceived that the children were anything but thankful for being permitted to walk straight, eyes slightly lowered, arms at the sides, and mouths shut until bidden to speak.

5 His house stood in the "town"—but we today would hardly call it a village. The meeting house was nearby, and from this point outward—toward the bay or inland—there were a few small-windowed, dark houses snuggling against the raw Massachusetts winter. Salem had been established hardly forty years before. To the European world the whole province was a barbaric frontier inhabited by a sect of fanatics who, nevertheless, were shipping out products of slowly increasing quantity and value.

6 No one can really know what their lives were like. They had no novelists—and would not have permitted anyone to read a novel if one were handy. Their creed forbade anything resembling a theater or "vain enjoyment." They did not celebrate Christmas, and a holiday from work meant only that they must concentrate even more upon prayer.

CLOSE READ

ANNOTATE: In paragraph 8, mark the phrase that is an informal twist on a familiar saying about not involving yourself in other people's personal lives.

QUESTION: Why does Miller use this casual phrase?

CONCLUDE: What is the effect of this language, especially when applied to a discussion of Puritans?

2. **New Jerusalem** in the Bible, the holy city of heaven.

7   Which is not to say that nothing broke into this strict and somber way of life. When a new farmhouse was built, friends assembled to "raise the roof," and there would be special foods cooked and probably some potent cider passed around. There was a good supply of ne'er-do-wells in Salem, who dallied at the shovelboard[1] in Bridget Bishop's tavern. Probably more than the creed, hard work kept the morals of the place from spoiling, for the people were forced to fight the land like heroes for every grain of corn, and no man had very much time for fooling around.

8   That there were some jokers, however, is indicated by the practice of appointing a two-man patrol whose duty was to "walk forth in the time of God's worship to take notice of such as either lye about the meeting house, without attending to the word and ordinances, or that lye at home or in the fields without giving good account thereof, and to take the names of such persons, and to present them to the magistrates, whereby they may be accordingly proceeded against." This predilection for minding other people's business was time-honored among the people of Salem, and it undoubtedly created many of the suspicions which were to feed the coming madness. It was also, in my opinion, one of the things that a John Proctor would rebel against, for the time of the armed camp had almost passed, and since the country was reasonably—although not wholly—safe, the old disciplines were beginning to rankle. But, as in all such matters, the issue was not clear-cut, for danger was still a possibility, and in unity still lay the best promise of safety.

9   The edge of the wilderness was close by. The American continent stretched endlessly west, and it was full of mystery for them. It stood, dark and threatening, over their shoulders night and day, for out of it Indian tribes marauded from time to time, and Reverend Parris had parishioners who had lost relatives to these heathen.

10   The parochial snobbery of these people was partly responsible for their failure to convert the Indians. Probably they also preferred to take land from heathens rather than from fellow Christians. At any rate, very few Indians were converted, and the Salem folk believed that the virgin forest was the Devil's last preserve, his home base and the citadel of his final stand. To the best of their knowledge the American forest was the last place on earth that was not paying homage to God.

11   For these reasons, among others, they carried about an air of innate resistance, even of persecution. Their fathers had, of course, been persecuted in England. So now they and their church found it necessary to deny any other sect its freedom, lest their New Jerusalem[2] be defiled and corrupted by wrong ways and deceitful ideas.

12   They believed, in short, that they held in their steady hands the candle that would light the world. We have inherited this belief, and it has helped and hurt us. It helped them with the discipline it gave them. They were a dedicated folk, by and large, and they had to be to survive the life they had chosen or been born into in this country.

13   The proof of their belief's value to them may be taken from the opposite character of the first Jamestown settlement, farther south, in Virginia. The Englishmen who landed there were motivated mainly by a hunt for profit. They had thought to pick off the wealth of the new country and then return rich to England. They were a band of individualists, and a much more ingratiating group than the Massachusetts men. But Virginia destroyed them. Massachusetts tried to kill off the Puritans, but they combined; they set up a communal society which, in the beginning, was little more than an armed camp with an autocratic and very devoted leadership. It was, however, an autocracy by consent, for they were united from top to bottom by a commonly held ideology whose perpetuation was the reason and justification for all their sufferings. So their self-denial, their purposefulness, their suspicion of all vain pursuits, their hard-handed justice, were altogether perfect instruments for the conquest of this space so antagonistic to man.

14   But the people of Salem in 1692 were not quite the dedicated folk that arrived on the *Mayflower*. A vast differentiation had taken place, and in their own time a revolution had unseated the royal government and substituted a junta[3] which was at this moment in power. The times, to their eyes, must have been out of joint, and to the common folk must have seemed as insoluble and complicated as do ours today. It is not hard to see how easily many could have been led to believe that the time of confusion had been brought upon them by deep and darkling forces. No hint of such speculation appears on the court record, but social disorder in any age breeds such mystical suspicions, and when, as in Salem, wonders are brought forth from below the social surface, it is too much to expect people to hold back very long from laying on the victims with all the force of their frustrations.

15   The Salem tragedy, which is about to begin in these pages, developed from a paradox. It is a paradox in whose grip we still live, and there is no prospect yet that we will discover its resolution. Simply, it was this: for good purposes, even high purposes, the people of Salem developed a theocracy, a combine of state and religious power whose function was to keep the community together, and to prevent any kind of disunity that might open it to destruction by material or ideological enemies. It was forged for a necessary purpose and accomplished that

3. junta (HOON tuh) *n.* assembly or council.

purpose. But all organization is and must be grounded on the idea of exclusion and prohibition, just as two objects cannot occupy the same space. Evidently the time came in New England when the repressions of order were heavier than seemed warranted by the dangers against which the order was organized. The witch-hunt was a perverse manifestation of the panic which set in among all classes when the balance began to turn toward greater individual freedom.

16 When one rises above the individual villainy displayed, one can only pity them all, just as we shall be pitied someday. It is still impossible for man to organize his social life without repressions, and the balance has yet to be struck between order and freedom.

17 The witch-hunt was not, however, a mere repression. It was also, and as importantly, a long overdue opportunity for everyone so inclined to express publicly his guilt and sins, under the cover of accusations against the victims. It suddenly became possible—and patriotic and holy—for a man to say that Martha Corey had come into his bedroom at night, and that, while his wife was sleeping at his side, Martha laid herself down on his chest and "nearly suffocated him." Of course it was her spirit only, but his satisfaction at confessing himself was no lighter than if it had been Martha herself. One could not ordinarily speak such things in public.

18 Long-held hatreds of neighbors could now be openly expressed, and vengeance taken, despite the Bible's charitable injunctions. Land-lust which had been expressed before by constant bickering over boundaries and deeds, could now be elevated to the arena of morality; one could cry witch against one's neighbor and feel perfectly justified in the bargain. Old scores could be settled on a plane of heavenly combat between Lucifer[4] and the Lord; suspicions and the envy of the miserable toward the happy could and did burst out in the general revenge.

19 REVEREND PARRIS *is praying now, and, though we cannot hear his words, a sense of his confusion hangs about him. He mumbles, then seems about to weep; then he weeps, then prays again; but his daughter does not stir on the bed.*

20 *The door opens, and his Negro slave enters.* TITUBA *is in her forties.* PARRIS *brought her with him from Barbados, where he spent some years as a merchant before entering the ministry. She enters as one does who can no longer bear to be barred from the sight of her beloved, but she is also very frightened because her slave sense has warned her that, as always, trouble in this house eventually lands on her back.*

21 **Tituba,** *already taking a step backward*: My Betty be hearty soon?

22 **Parris:** Out of here!

4. **Lucifer** (LOO suh fuhr) the Devil.

23 **Tituba,** *backing to the door:* My Betty not goin' die . . .

24 **Parris,** *scrambling to his feet in a fury:* Out of my sight! *She is gone.* Out of my—*He is overcome with sobs. He clamps his teeth against them and closes the door and leans against it, exhausted.* Oh, my God! God help me! *Quaking with fear, mumbling to himself through his sobs, he goes to the bed and gently takes* BETTY's *hand.* Betty. Child. Dear child. Will you wake, will you open up your eyes! Betty, little one . . .

25 *He is bending to kneel again when his niece,* ABIGAIL WILLIAMS, *seventeen, enters—a strikingly beautiful girl, an orphan, with an endless capacity for dissembling. Now she is all worry and apprehension and propriety.*

26 **Abigail:** Uncle? *He looks to her.* Susanna Walcott's here from Doctor Griggs.

27 **Parris:** Oh? Let her come, let her come.

28 **Abigail,** *leaning out the door to call to Susanna, who is down the hall a few steps:* Come in, Susanna.

29 SUSANNA WALCOTT, *a little younger than Abigail, a nervous, hurried girl enters.*

30 **Parris,** *eagerly:* What does the doctor say, child?

31 **Susanna,** *craning around* PARRIS *to get a look at* BETTY: He bid me come and tell you, reverend sir, that he cannot discover no medicine for it in his books.

32 **Parris:** Then he must search on.

33 **Susanna:** Aye, sir, he have been searchin' his books since he left you, sir. But he bid me tell you, that you might look to unnatural things for the cause of it.

34 **Parris,** *his eyes going wide:* No—no. There be no unnatural cause here. Tell him I have sent for Reverend Hale of Beverly, and Mr. Hale will surely confirm that. Let him look to medicine and put out all thought of unnatural causes here. There be none.

35 **Susanna:** Aye, sir. He bid me tell you. *She turns to go.*

36 **Abigail:** Speak nothin' of it in the village, Susanna.

37 **Parris:** Go directly home and speak nothing of unnatural causes.

38 **Susanna:** Aye, sir. I pray for her. *She goes out.*

39 **Abigail:** Uncle, the rumor of witchcraft is all about; I think you'd best go down and deny it yourself. The parlor's packed with people, sir. I'll sit with her.

40 **Parris,** *pressed, turns on her:* And what shall I say to them? That my daughter and my niece I discovered dancing like heathen in the forest?

41 **Abigail:** Uncle, we did dance; let you tell them I confessed it— and I'll be whipped if I must be. But they're speakin' of witchcraft. Betty's not witched.

CLOSE READ

ANNOTATE: In the stage directions in paragraph 24, mark details that suggest Parris's extreme emotions.

QUESTION: Why does Miller include these details?

CONCLUDE: How would these details affect the audience's perceptions of Parris in a performance?

42 **Parris:** Abigail, I cannot go before the congregation when I know you have not opened with me. What did you do with her in the forest?

43 **Abigail:** We did dance, uncle, and when you leaped out of the bush so suddenly, Betty was frightened and then she fainted. And there's the whole of it.

44 **Parris:** Child. Sit you down.

45 **Abigail,** *quavering, as she sits*: I would never hurt Betty. I love her dearly.

46 **Parris:** Now look you, child, your punishment will come in its time. But if you trafficked with spirits in the forest I must know it now, for surely my enemies will, and they will ruin me with it.

47 **Abigail:** But we never conjured spirits.

48 **Parris:** Then why can she not move herself since midnight? This child is desperate! *Abigail lowers her eyes.* It must come out—my enemies will bring it out. Let me know what you done there. Abigail, do you understand that I have many enemies?

49 **Abigail:** I have heard of it, uncle.

50 **Parris:** There is a faction that is sworn to drive me from my pulpit. Do you understand that?

51 **Abigail:** I think so, sir.

52 **Parris:** Now then, in the midst of such disruption, my own household is discovered to be the very center of some obscene practice. Abominations are done in the forest—

53 **Abigail:** It were sport, uncle!

54 **Parris,** *pointing at* BETTY: You call this sport? *She lowers her eyes. He pleads*: Abigail, if you know something that may help the doctor, for God's sake tell it to me. *She is silent.* I saw Tituba waving her arms over the fire when I came on you. Why was she doing that? And I heard a screeching and gibberish coming from her mouth. She were swaying like a dumb beast over that fire!

55 **Abigail:** She always sings her Barbados songs, and we dance.

56 **Parris:** I cannot blink what I saw, Abigail, for my enemies will not blink it. I saw a dress lying on the grass.

57 **Abigail,** *innocently*: A dress?

58 **Parris**—*it is very hard to say*: Aye, a dress. And I thought I saw—someone naked running through the trees!

59 **Abigail,** *in terror*: No one was naked! You mistake yourself, uncle!

60 **Parris,** *with anger*: I saw it! *He moves from her. Then, resolved*: Now tell me true, Abigail. And I pray you feel the weight of truth upon you, for now my ministry's at stake, my ministry and perhaps your cousin's life. Whatever abomination you have

done, give me all of it now, for I dare not be taken unaware when I go before them down there.

61 **Abigail:** There is nothin' more. I swear it, uncle.

62 **Parris,** *studies her, then nods, half convinced:* Abigail, I have fought here three long years to bend these stiff-necked people to me, and now, just now when some good respect is rising for me in the parish, you compromise my very character. I have given you a home, child. I have put clothes upon your back—now give me upright answer. Your name in the town—it is entirely white, is it not?

63 **Abigail,** *with an edge of resentment:* Why, I am sure it is, sir. There be no blush about my name.

64 **Parris,** *to the point:* Abigail, is there any other cause than you have told me, for your being discharged from Goody[5] Proctor's service? I have heard it said, and I tell you as I heard it, that she

5. Goody title used for a married woman; short for Goodwife.

In the 1996 film version of *The Crucible*, Winona Ryder portrays Abigail Williams.

CLOSE READ

ANNOTATE: In the dialogue between Parris and Abigail, paragraphs 65–69, mark details that suggest Abigail's reputation in Salem may be questionable.

QUESTION: Why does Miller include these details about Abigail at this point in the play?

CONCLUDE: What conflicts do these clues suggest are at work in Salem?

comes so rarely to the church this year for she will not sit so close to something soiled. What signified that remark?

65 **Abigail:** She hates me, uncle, she must, for I would not be her slave. It's a bitter woman, a lying, cold, sniveling woman, and I will not work for such a woman!

66 **Parris:** She may be. And yet it has troubled me that you are now seven month out of their house, and in all this time no other family has ever called for your service.

67 **Abigail:** They want slaves, not such as I. Let them send to Barbados for that. I will not black my face for any of them! *With ill-concealed resentment at him*: Do you begrudge my bed, uncle?

68 **Parris:** No—no.

69 **Abigail,** *in a temper*: My name is good in the village! I will not have it said my name is soiled! Goody Proctor is a gossiping liar!

70 *Enter* MRS. ANN PUTNAM. *She is a twisted soul of forty-five, a death-ridden woman, haunted by dreams.*

71 **Parris,** *as soon as the door begins to open*: No—no. I cannot have anyone. *He sees her, and a certain deference springs into him, although his worry remains.* Why, Goody Putnam, come in.

72 **Mrs. Putnam,** *full of breath, shiny-eyed*: It is a marvel. It is surely a stroke of hell upon you.

73 **Parris:** No, Goody Putnam. It is—

74 **Mrs. Putnam,** *glancing at* BETTY: How high did she fly, how high?

75 **Parris:** No, no, she never flew—

76 **Mrs. Putnam,** *very pleased with it*: Why, it's sure she did. Mr. Collins saw her goin' over Ingersoll's barn, and come down light as bird, he says!

77 **Parris:** Now, look you, Goody Putnam, she never— *Enter* THOMAS PUTNAM, *a well-to-do, hard-handed landowner, near fifty.* Oh, good morning, Mr. Putnam.

78 **Putnam:** It is a providence the thing is out now! It is a providence. *He goes directly to the bed.*

79 **Parris:** What's out, sir, what's—?

80 MRS. PUTNAM *goes to the bed.*

81 **Putnam,** *looking down at* BETTY: Why, *her* eyes is closed! Look you, Ann.

82 **Mrs. Putnam:** Why, that's strange. *To* PARRIS: Ours is open.

83 **Parris,** *shocked*: Your Ruth is sick?

84 **Mrs. Putnam,** *with vicious certainty*: I'd not call it sick; the Devil's touch is heavier than sick. It's death, y'know, it's death drivin' into them, forked and hoofed.

85 **Parris:** Oh, pray not! Why, how does Ruth ail?

86 **Mrs. Putnam:** She ails as she must—she never waked this morning, but her eyes open and she walks, and hears naught, sees naught, and cannot eat. Her soul is taken, surely.

87 PARRIS *is struck.*

88 **Putnam,** *as though for further details*: They say you've sent for Reverend Hale of Beverly?

89 **Parris,** *with dwindling conviction now*: A precaution only. He has much experience in all demonic arts, and I—

90 **Mrs. Putnam:** He has indeed; and found a witch in Beverly last year, and let you remember that.

91 **Parris:** Now, Goody Ann, they only thought that were a witch, and I am certain there be no element of witchcraft here.

92 **Putnam:** No witchcraft! Now look you, Mr. Parris—

93 **Parris:** Thomas, Thomas, I pray you, leap not to witchcraft. I know that you—you least of all, Thomas, would ever wish so disastrous a charge laid upon me. We cannot leap to witchcraft. They will howl me out of Salem for such corruption in my house.

94   A word about Thomas Putnam. He was a man with many grievances, at least one of which appears justified. Some time before, his wife's brother-in-law, James Bayley, had been turned down as minister at Salem. Bayley had all the qualifications, and a two-thirds vote into the bargain, but a faction stopped his acceptance, for reasons that are not clear.

95   Thomas Putnam was the eldest son of the richest man in the village. He had fought the Indians at Narragansett, and was deeply interested in parish affairs. He undoubtedly felt it poor payment that the village should so blatantly disregard his candidate for one of its more important offices, especially since he regarded himself as the intellectual superior of most of the people around him.

96   His **vindictive** nature was demonstrated long before the witchcraft began. Another former Salem minister, George Burroughs, had had to borrow money to pay for his wife's funeral, and, since the parish was remiss in his salary, he was soon bankrupt. Thomas and his brother John had Burroughs jailed for debts the man did not owe. The incident is important only in that Burroughs succeeded in becoming minister where Bayley, Thomas Putnam's brother-in-law, had been rejected; the motif of resentment is clear here. Thomas Putnam felt that his own name and the honor of his family had been smirched by the village, and he meant to right matters however he could.

97   Another reason to believe him a deeply embittered man was his attempt to break his father's will, which left a disproportionate amount to a stepbrother. As with every other public cause in which he tried to force his way, he failed in this.

NOTES

vindictve (vihn DIHK tihv) *adj.* characterized by an intense, unreasoning desire for revenge

So it is not surprising to find that so many accusations against people are in the handwriting of Thomas Putnam, or that his name is so often found as a witness corroborating the supernatural testimony, or that his daughter led the crying-out at the most opportune junctures of the trials, especially when—But we'll speak of that when we come to it.

98 **Putnam**—*at the moment he is intent upon getting* PARRIS. *for whom he has only contempt, to move toward the abyss:*[6] Mr. Parris, I have taken your part in all contention here, and I would continue; but I cannot if you hold back in this. There are hurtful, vengeful spirits layin' hands on these children.

99 **Parris:** But, Thomas, you cannot—

100 **Putnam:** Ann! Tell Mr. Parris what you have done.

101 **Mrs. Putnam:** Reverend Parris, I have laid seven babies unbaptized in the earth. Believe me, sir, you never saw more hearty babies born. And yet, each would wither in my arms the very night of their birth. I have spoke nothin', but my heart has clamored intimations. And now, this year, my Ruth, my only—I see her turning strange. A secret child she has become this year, and shrivels like a sucking mouth were pullin' on her life too. And so I thought to send her to your Tituba—

102 **Parris:** To Tituba! What may Tituba—?

103 **Mrs. Putnam:** Tituba knows how to speak to the dead, Mr. Parris.

104 **Parris:** Goody Ann, it is a formidable sin to conjure up the dead!

105 **Mrs. Putnam:** I take it on my soul, but who else may surely tell us what person murdered my babies?

106 **Parris,** *horrified*: Woman!

107 **Mrs. Putnam:** They were murdered, Mr. Parris! And mark this proof! Mark it! Last night my Ruth were ever so close to their little spirits; I know it, sir. For how else is she struck dumb now except some power of darkness would stop her mouth? It is a marvelous sign, Mr. Parris!

108 **Putnam:** Don't you understand it, sir? There is a murdering witch among us, bound to keep herself in the dark. PARRIS *turns to* BETTY, *a frantic terror rising in him*. Let your enemies make of it what they will, you cannot blink it more.

109 **Parris,** *to* ABIGAIL: Then you were conjuring spirits last night.

110 **Abigail,** *whispering*: Not I, sir—Tituba and Ruth.

111 **Parris** *turns now, with new fear, and goes to* BETTY, *looks down at her, and then, gazing off*: Oh, Abigail, what proper payment for my charity! Now I am undone.

112 **Putnam:** You are not undone! Let you take hold here. Wait for no one to charge you—declare it yourself. You have discovered witchcraft—

CLOSE READ

ANNOTATE: Mark details in Mrs. Putnam's speech in paragraph 101 that relate to things that are unexplainable or secret.

QUESTION: What do these details suggest about the ways in which Mrs. Putnam understands the world?

CONCLUDE: How do these details add to the growing sense of tension in the scene?

113 **Parris:** In my house? In my house, Thomas? They will topple me with this! They will make of it a—

114 *Enter* MERCY LEWIS, *the Putnams' servant, a fat, sly, merciless girl of eighteen.*

115 **Mercy:** Your pardons. I only thought to see how Betty is.

116 **Putnam:** Why aren't you home? Who's with Ruth?

117 **Mercy:** Her grandma come. She's improved a little, I think—she give a powerful sneeze before.

118 **Mrs. Putnam:** Ah, there's a sign of life!

119 **Mercy:** I'd fear no more, Goody Putnam. It were a grand sneeze; another like it will shake her wits together, I'm sure. *She goes to the bed to look.*

120 **Parris:** Will you leave me now, Thomas? I would pray a while alone.

121 **Abigail:** Uncle, you've prayed since midnight. Why do you not go down and—

122 **Parris:** No—no. *To* PUTNAM: I have no answer for that crowd. I'll wait till Mr. Hale arrives. *To get* MRS. PUTNAM *to leave*: If you will, Goody Ann . . .

123 **Putnam:** Now look you, sir. Let you strike out against the Devil, and the village will bless you for it! Come down, speak to them—pray with them. They're thirsting for your word, Mister! Surely you'll pray with them.

124 **Parris,** *swayed*: I'll lead them in a psalm, but let you say nothing of witchcraft yet. I will not discuss it. The cause is yet unknown. I have had enough contention since I came; I want no more.

125 **Mrs. Putnam:** Mercy, you go home to Ruth, d'y'hear?

126 **Mercy:** Aye, mum.

127 MRS. PUTNAM *goes out.*

128 **Parris,** *to* ABIGAIL: If she starts for the window, cry for me at once.

129 **Abigail:** I will, uncle.

130 **Parris,** *to* PUTNAM: There is a terrible power in her arms today. *He goes out with* PUTNAM.

131 **Abigail,** *with hushed trepidation*: How is Ruth sick?

132 **Mercy:** It's weirdish. I know not—she seems to walk like a dead one since last night.

133 **Abigail,** *turns at once and goes to* BETTY, *and now, with fear in her voice*: Betty? BETTY *doesn't move. She shakes her.* Now stop this! Betty! Sit up now!

134 BETTY *doesn't stir.* MERCY *comes over.*

135 **Mercy:** Have you tried beatin' her? I gave Ruth a good one and it waked her for a minute. Here, let me have her.

136 **Abigail,** *holding* MERCY *back*: No, he'll be comin' up. Listen, now: if they be questioning us, tell them we danced—I told him as much already.

137 **Mercy:** Aye. And what more?

138 **Abigail:** He knows Tituba conjured Ruth's sisters to come out of the grave.

139 **Mercy:** And what more?

140 **Abigail:** He saw you naked.

141 **Mercy:** *clapping her hands together with a frightened laugh*: Oh, Jesus!

142 *Enter* MARY WARREN, *breathless. She is seventeen, a subservient, naive, lonely girl.*

143 **Mary Warren:** What'll we do? The village is out! I just come from the farm; the whole country's talkin' witchcraft! They'll be callin' us witches, Abby!

144 **Mercy,** *pointing and looking at* MARY WARREN: She means to tell. I know it.

145 **Mary Warren:** Abby, we've got to tell. Witchery's a hangin' error, a hangin' like they done in Boston two year ago! We must

In this still from the 1996 film version of *The Crucible*, the other girls hold Betty Parris back as she attempts to fly.

tell the truth, Abby! You'll only be whipped for dancin', and the other things!

146 **Abigail:** Oh, *we'll* be whipped!

147 **Mary Warren:** I never done none of it, Abby. I only looked!

148 **Mercy,** *moving menacingly toward* MARY: Oh, you're a great one for lookin', aren't you, Mary Warren? What a grand peeping courage you have!

149 BETTY, *on the bed, whimpers.* ABIGAIL *turns to her at once.*

150 **Abigail:** Betty? *She goes to* BETTY. Now, Betty, dear, wake up now. It's Abigail. *She sits* BETTY *up and furiously shakes her.* I'll beat you, Betty! BETTY *whimpers.* My, you seem improving. I talked to your papa and I told him everything. So there's nothing to—

151 **Betty,** *darts off the bed, frightened of* ABIGAIL, *and flattens herself against the wall:* I want my mama!

152 **Abigail,** *with alarm, as she cautiously approaches* BETTY: What ails you, Betty? Your mama's dead and buried.

153 **Betty:** I'll fly to Mama. Let me fly! *She raises her arms as though to fly, and streaks for the window, gets one leg out.*

154 **Abigail,** *pulling her away from the window:* I told him everything, he knows now, he knows everything we—

155 **Betty:** You drank blood, Abby! You didn't tell him that!

156 **Abigail:** Betty, you never say that again! You will never—

157 **Betty:** You did, you did! You drank a charm to kill John Proctor's wife! You drank a charm to kill Goody Proctor!

158 **Abigail,** *smashes her across the face:* Shut it! Now shut it!

159 **Betty:** *collapsing on the bed:* Mama. Mama! *She dissolves into sobs.*

160 **Abigail:** Now look you. All of you. We danced. And Tituba conjured Ruth Putnam's dead sisters. And that is all. And mark this. Let either of you breathe a word, or the edge of a word, about the other things, and I will come to you in the black of some terrible night and I will bring a pointy reckoning that will shudder you. And you know I can do it; I saw Indians smash my dear parents' heads on the pillow next to mine, and I have seen some reddish work done at night, and I can make you wish you had never seen the sun go down! *She goes to* BETTY *and roughly sits her up.* Now, you—sit up and stop this!

161 *But* BETTY *collapses in her hands and lies inert on the bed.*

162 **Mary Warren,** *with hysterical fright:* What's got her? ABIGAIL *stares in fright at* BETTY. Abby, she's going to die! It's a sin to conjure, and we—

163 **Abigail,** *starting for* MARY: I say shut it, Mary Warren!

164 *Enter* JOHN PROCTOR. *On seeing him,* MARY WARREN *leaps in fright.*

CLOSE READ

ANNOTATE: In Abigail's speech in paragraph 160, mark the short sentences.

QUESTION: Why does Miller mix short and long sentences in this speech?

CONCLUDE: How do these short sentences add to the emotional intensity of Abigail's speech?

calumny (KAL uhm nee) *n.* the making of false statements with the intent to harm

165   Proctor was a farmer in his middle thirties. He need not have been a partisan of any faction in the town, but there is evidence to suggest that he had a sharp and biting way with hypocrites. He was the kind of man—powerful of body, even-tempered, and not easily led—who cannot refuse support to partisans without drawing their deepest resentment. In Proctor's presence a fool felt his foolishness instantly—and a Proctor is always marked for **calumny** therefore.

166   But as we shall see, the steady manner he displays does not spring from an untroubled soul. He is a sinner, a sinner not only against the moral fashion of the time, but against his own vision of decent conduct. These people had no ritual for the washing away of sins. It is another trait we inherited from them, and it has helped to discipline us as well as to breed hypocrisy among us. Proctor, respected and even feared in Salem, has come to regard himself as a kind of fraud. But no hint of this has yet appeared on the surface, and as he enters from the crowded parlor below it is a man in his prime we see, with a quiet confidence and an unexpressed, hidden force. Mary Warren, his servant, can barely speak for embarrassment and fear.

167   **Mary Warren:** Oh! I'm just going home, Mr. Proctor.

168   **Proctor:** Be you foolish, Mary Warren? Be you deaf? I forbid you leave the house, did I not? Why shall I pay you? I am looking for you more often than my cows!

169   **Mary Warren:** I only come to see the great doings in the world.

170   **Proctor:** I'll show you a great doin' on your arse one of these days. Now get you home; my wife is waitin' with your work! *Trying to retain a shred of dignity, she goes slowly out.*

171   **Mercy Lewis,** *both afraid of him and strangely titillated*: I'd best be off. I have my Ruth to watch. Good morning, Mr. Proctor.

172   Mercy *sidles out. Since* PROCTOR's *entrance,* ABIGAIL *has stood as though on tiptoe, absorbing his presence, wide-eyed. He glances at her, then goes to* BETTY *on the bed.*

173   **Abigail:** Gah! I'd almost forgot how strong you are, John Proctor!

174   **Proctor,** *looking at* ABIGAIL *now, the faintest suggestion of a knowing smile on his face*: What's this mischief here?

175   **Abigail,** *with a nervous laugh*: Oh, she's only gone silly somehow.

176   **Proctor:** The road past my house is a pilgrimage to Salem all morning. The town's mumbling witchcraft.

177   **Abigail:** Oh, posh! *Winningly she comes a little closer, with a confidential, wicked air.* We were dancin' in the woods last night, and my uncle leaped in on us. She took fright, is all.

178   **Proctor,** *his smile widening*: Ah, you're wicked yet, aren't y'! *A trill of expectant laughter escapes her, and she dares come closer, feverishly*

looking into his eyes. You'll be clapped in the stocks before you're twenty. *He takes a step to go, and she springs into his path.*

179 **Abigail:** Give me a word, John. A soft word. *Her concentrated desire destroys his smile.*

180 **Proctor:** No, no, Abby. That's done with.

181 **Abigail,** *tauntingly:* You come five mile to see a silly girl fly? I know you better.

182 **Proctor,** *setting her firmly out of his path:* I come to see what mischief your uncle's brewin' now. *With final emphasis:* Put it out of mind, Abby.

183 **Abigail,** *grasping his hand before he can release her:* John—I am waitin' for you every night.

184 **Proctor:** Abby, I never give you hope to wait for me.

185 **Abigail,** *now beginning to anger—she can't believe it:* I have something better than hope, I think!

186 **Proctor:** Abby, you'll put it out of mind. I'll not be comin' for you more.

187 **Abigail:** You're surely sportin' with me.

188 **Proctor:** You know me better.

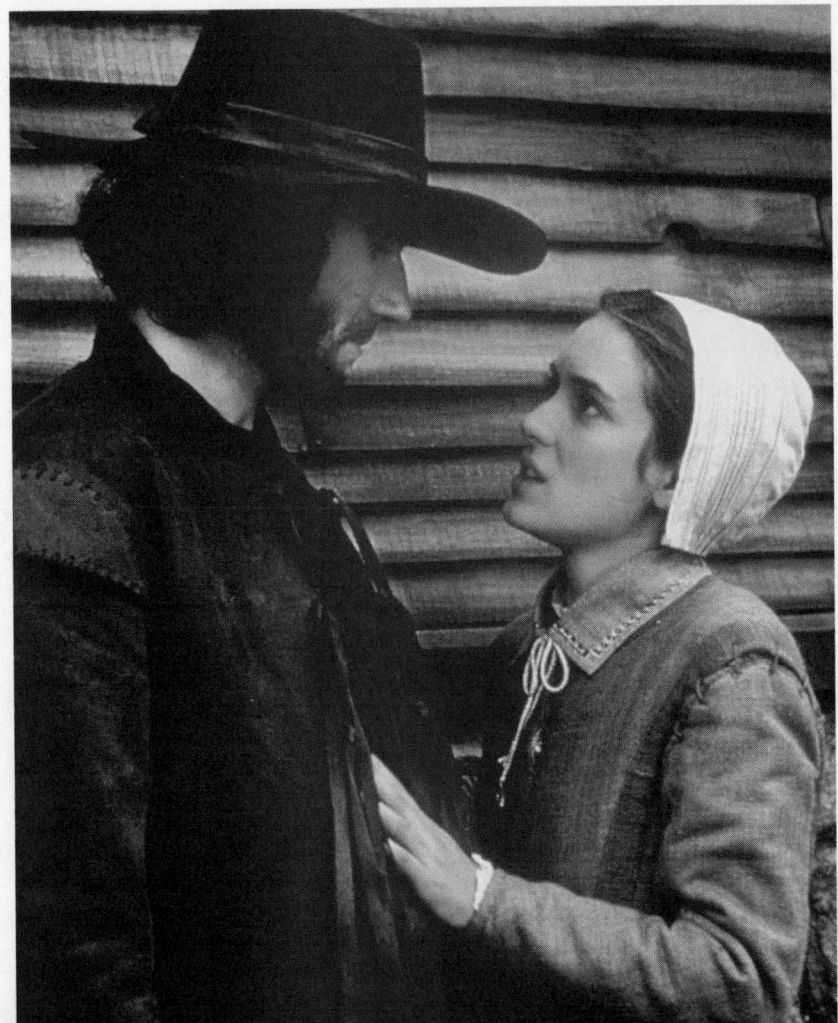

In the 1996 film version of *The Crucible*, Daniel Day-Lewis portrays John Proctor. Here, Abigail, played by Winona Ryder, pleads with Proctor.

189 **Abigail:** I know how you clutched my back behind your house and sweated like a stallion whenever I come near! Or did I dream that? It's she put me out, you cannot pretend it were you. I saw your face when she put me out, and you loved me then and you do now!

190 **Proctor:** Abby, that's a wild thing to say—

191 **Abigail:** A wild thing may say wild things. But not so wild, I think. I have seen you since she put me out; I have seen you nights.

192 **Proctor:** I have hardly stepped off my farm this seven month.

193 **Abigail:** I have a sense for heat, John, and yours has drawn me to my window, and I have seen you looking up, burning in your loneliness. Do you tell me you've never looked up at my window?

194 **Proctor:** I may have looked up.

195 **Abigail,** *now softening*: And you must. You are no wintry man. I know you, John. I *know* you. *She is weeping.* I cannot sleep for dreamin'; I cannot dream but I wake and walk about the house as though I'd find you comin' through some door. *She clutches him desperately.*

196 **Proctor,** *gently pressing her from him, with great sympathy but firmly*: Child—

197 **Abigail,** *with a flash of anger*: How do you call me child!

198 **Proctor:** Abby, I may think of you softly from time to time. But I will cut off my hand before I'll ever reach for you again. Wipe it out of mind. We never touched, Abby.

199 **Abigail:** Aye, but we did.

200 **Proctor:** Aye, but we did not.

201 **Abigail,** *with a bitter anger*: Oh, I marvel how such a strong man may let such a sickly wife be—

202 **Proctor,** *angered—at himself as well*: You'll speak nothin' of Elizabeth!

203 **Abigail:** She is blackening my name in the village! She is telling lies about me! She is a cold, sniveling woman, and you bend to her! Let her turn you like a—

204 **Proctor,** *shaking her*: Do you look for whippin'?

205 *A psalm is heard being sung below.*

206 **Abigail,** *in tears*: I look for John Proctor that took me from my sleep and put knowledge in my heart! I never knew what pretense Salem was, I never knew the lying lessons I was taught by all these Christian women and their covenanted men! And now you bid me tear the light out of my eyes? I will not, I cannot! You loved me, John Proctor, and whatever sin it is, you

love me yet! *He turns abruptly to go out. She rushes to him.*
John, pity me, pity me!

207 *The words "going up to Jesus" are heard in the psalm. and* BETTY *claps
her ears suddenly and whines loudly.*

208 **Abigail:** Betty? *She hurries to* BETTY, *who is now sitting up and
screaming.* PROCTOR *goes to* BETTY *as* ABIGAIL *is trying to pull her
hands down, calling "Betty!"*

209 **Proctor,** *growing unnerved*: What's she doing? Girl, what ails
you? Stop that wailing!

210 *The singing has stopped in the midst of this, and now* PARRIS *rushes in.*

211 **Parris:** What happened? What are you doing to her? Betty! *He
rushes to the bed, crying, "Betty, Betty!"* MRS. PUTNAM *enters, feverish
with curiosity, and with her* THOMAS PUTNAM *and* MERCY LEWIS. PARRIS,
at the bed, keeps lightly slapping BETTY's *face, while she moans and
tries to get up.*

212 **Abigail:** She heard you singin' and suddenly she's up and
screamin'.

213 **Mrs. Putnam:** The psalm! The psalm! She cannot bear to hear
the Lord's name!

214 **Parris:** No. God forbid. Mercy, run to the doctor! Tell him what's
happened here! MERCY LEWIS *rushes out.*

215 **Mrs. Putnam:** Mark it for a sign, mark it!

216 REBECCA NURSE, *seventy-two, enters. She is white-haired, leaning upon
her walking-stick.*

217 **Putnam,** *pointing at the whimpering* BETTY: That is a notorious sign
of witchcraft afoot, Goody Nurse, a prodigious sign!

218 **Mrs. Putnam:** My mother told me that! When they cannot bear
to hear the name of—

219 **Parris,** *trembling*: Rebecca, Rebecca, go to her, we're lost. She
suddenly cannot bear to hear the Lord's—

220 GILES COREY, *eighty-three, enters. He is knotted with muscle, canny,
inquisitive, and still powerful.*

221 **Rebecca:** There is hard sickness here, Giles Corey, so please to
keep the quiet.

222 **Giles:** I've not said a word. No one here can testify I've said a
word. Is she going to fly again? I hear she flies.

223 **Putnam:** Man, be quiet now!

224 *Everything is quiet.* REBECCA *walks across the room to the bed.
Gentleness exudes from her.* BETTY *is quietly whimpering, eyes shut.*
REBECCA *simply stands over the child, who gradually quiets.*

225 And while they are so absorbed, we may put a word in for
Rebecca. Rebecca was the wife of Francis Nurse, who, from all

accounts, was one of those men for whom both sides of the argument had to have respect. He was called upon to arbitrate disputes as though he were an unofficial judge, and Rebecca also enjoyed the high opinion most people had for him. By the time of the delusion, they had three hundred acres, and their children were settled in separate homesteads within the same estate. However, Francis had originally rented the land, and one theory has it that, as he gradually paid for it and raised his social status, there were those who resented his rise.

226   Another suggestion to explain the systematic campaign against Rebecca, and inferentially against Francis, is the land war he fought with his neighbors, one of whom was a Putnam. This squabble grew to the proportions of a battle in the woods between partisans of both sides, and it is said to have lasted for two days. As for Rebecca herself, the general opinion of her character was so high that to explain how anyone dared cry her out for a witch—and more, how adults could bring themselves to lay hands on her—we must look to the fields and boundaries of that time.

227   As we have seen. Thomas Putnam's man for the Salem ministry was Bayley. The Nurse clan had been in the faction that prevented Bayley's taking office. In addition, certain families allied to the Nurses by blood or friendship, and whose farms were contiguous with the Nurse farm or close to it, combined to break away from the Salem town authority and set up Topsfield, a new and independent entity whose existence was resented by old Salemites.

228   That the guiding hand behind the outcry was Putnam's is indicated by the fact that, as soon as it began, this Topsfield-Nurse faction absented themselves from church in protest and disbelief. It was Edward and Jonathan Putnam who signed the first complaint against Rebecca; and Thomas Putnam's little daughter was the one who fell into a fit at the hearing and pointed to Rebecca as her attacker. To top it all, Mrs. Putnam—who is now staring at the bewitched child on the bed—soon accused Rebecca's spirit of "tempting her to iniquity," a charge that had more truth in it than Mrs. Putnam could know.

229 **Mrs. Putnam,** *astonished*: What have you done?

230 REBECCA, *in thought, now leaves the bedside and sits.*

231 **Parris,** *wondrous and relieved*: What do you make of it. Rebecca?

232 **Putnam,** *eagerly*: Goody Nurse, will you go to my Ruth and see if you can wake her?

233 **Rebecca,** *sitting*: I think she'll wake in time. Pray calm yourselves. I have eleven children, and I am twenty-six times a grandma, and I have seen them all through their silly seasons, and when it come on them they will run the Devil bowlegged

keeping up with their mischief. I think she'll wake when she tires of it. A child's spirit is like a child, you can never catch it by running after it; you must stand still, and, for love, it will soon itself come back.

234 **Proctor:** Aye, that's the truth of it, Rebecca.

235 **Mrs. Putnam:** This is no silly season, Rebecca. My Ruth is bewildered, Rebecca; she cannot eat.

236 **Rebecca:** Perhaps she is not hungered yet. *To* PARRIS: I hope you are not decided to go in search of loose spirits, Mr. Parris. I've heard promise of that outside.

237 **Parris:** A wide opinion's running in the parish that the Devil may be among us, and I would satisfy them that they are wrong.

238 **Proctor:** Then let you come out and call them wrong. Did you consult the wardens before you called this minister to look for devils?

239 **Parris:** He is not coming to look for devils!

240 **Proctor:** Then what's he coming for?

241 **Putnam:** There be children dyin' in the village, Mister!

242 **Proctor:** I seen none dyin'. This society will not be a bag to swing around your head, Mr. Putnam. *To* PARRIS: Did you call a meeting before you—?

243 **Putnam:** I am sick of meetings; cannot the man turn his head without he have a meeting?

244 **Proctor:** He may turn his head, but not to Hell!

245 **Rebecca:** Pray, John, be calm. *Pause. He defers to her.* Mr. Parris, I think you'd best send Reverend Hale back as soon as he come. This will set us all to arguin' again in the society, and we thought to have peace this year. I think we ought rely on the doctor now, and good prayer.

246 **Mrs. Putnam:** Rebecca, the doctor's baffled!

247 **Rebecca:** If so he is, then let us go to God for the cause of it. There is prodigious danger in the seeking of loose spirits. I fear it, I fear it. Let us rather blame ourselves and—

248 **Putnam:** How may we blame ourselves? I am one of nine sons; the Putnam seed have peopled this province. And yet I have but one child left of eight—and now she shrivels!

249 **Rebecca:** I cannot fathom that.

250 **Mrs. Putnam,** *with a growing edge of sarcasm*: But I must! You think it God's work you should never lose a child, nor grandchild either, and I bury all but one? There are wheels within wheels in this village, and fires within fires!

251 **Putnam,** *to* PARRIS: When Reverend Hale comes, you will proceed to look for signs of witchcraft here.

NOTES

CLOSE READ

ANNOTATE: In paragraphs 261–271, mark details related to property, salaries, and other business matters.

QUESTION: Why does Miller include details about the business relationships among the characters?

CONCLUDE: What is the effect of these details, particularly in suggesting simmering conflicts?

252 **Proctor,** *to* PUTNAM: You cannot command Mr. Parris. We vote by name in this society, not by acreage.

253 **Putnam:** I never heard you worried so on this society, Mr. Proctor. I do not think I saw you at Sabbath meeting since snow flew.

254 **Proctor:** I have trouble enough without I come five mile to hear him preach only hellfire and bloody damnation. Take it to heart, Mr. Parris. There are many others who stay away from church these days because you hardly ever mention God any more.

255 **Parris,** *now aroused*: Why, that's a drastic charge!

256 **Rebecca:** It's somewhat true; there are many that quail to bring their children—

257 **Parris:** I do not preach for children, Rebecca. It is not the children who are unmindful of their obligations toward this ministry.

258 **Rebecca:** Are there really those unmindful?

259 **Parris:** I should say the better half of Salem village—

260 **Putnam:** And more than that!

261 **Parris:** Where is my wood? My contract provides I be supplied with all my firewood. I am waiting since November for a stick, and even in November I had to show my frostbitten hands like some London beggar!

262 **Giles:** You are allowed six pound a year to buy your wood, Mr. Parris.

263 **Parris:** I regard that six pound as part of my salary. I am paid little enough without I spend six pound on firewood.

264 **Proctor:** Sixty, plus six for firewood—

265 **Parris:** The salary is sixty-six pound, Mr. Proctor! I am not some preaching farmer with a book under my arm; I am a graduate of Harvard College.

266 **Giles:** Aye, and well instructed in arithmetic!

267 **Parris:** Mr. Corey, you will look far for a man of my kind at sixty pound a year! I am not used to this poverty; I left a thrifty business in the Barbados to serve the Lord. I do not fathom it, why am I persecuted here? I cannot offer one proposition but there be a howling riot of argument. I have often wondered if the Devil be in it somewhere; I cannot understand you people otherwise.

268 **Proctor:** Mr. Parris, you are the first minister ever did demand the deed to this house—

269 **Parris:** Man! Don't a minister deserve a house to live in?

270 **Proctor:** To live in, yes. But to ask ownership is like you shall own the meeting house itself; the last meeting I were at you

spoke so long on deeds and mortgages I thought it were an auction.

271 **Parris:** I want a mark of confidence, is all! I am your third preacher in seven years. I do not wish to be put out like the cat whenever some majority feels the whim. You people seem not to comprehend that a minister is the Lord's man in the parish; a minister is not to be so lightly crossed and contradicted—

272 **Putnam:** Aye!

273 **Parris:** There is either obedience or the church will burn like Hell is burning!

274 **Proctor:** Can you speak one minute without we land in Hell again? I am sick of Hell!

275 **Parris:** It is not for you to say what is good for you to hear!

276 **Proctor:** I may speak my heart, I think!

277 **Parris,** *in a fury*: What, are we Quakers?[7] We are not Quakers here yet, Mr. Proctor. And you may tell that to your followers!

278 **Proctor:** My followers!

279 **Parris—***now he's out with it*: There is a party in this church. I am not blind; there is a faction and a party.

280 **Proctor:** Against you?

281 **Putnam:** Against him and all authority!

282 **Proctor:** Why, then I must find it and join it.

283 *There is shock among the others.*

284 **Rebecca:** He does not mean that.

285 **Putnam:** He confessed it now!

286 **Proctor:** I mean it solemnly, Rebecca; I like not the smell of this "authority."

287 **Rebecca:** No, you cannot break charity with your minister. You are another kind, John. Clasp his hand, make your peace.

288 **Proctor:** I have a crop to sow and lumber to drag home. *He goes angrily to the door and turns to* COREY *with a smile*. What say you, Giles, let's find the party. He says there's a party.

289 **Giles:** I've changed my opinion of this man, John. Mr. Parris, I beg your pardon. I never thought you had so much iron in you.

290 **Parris,** *surprised*: Why, thank you, Giles!

291 **Giles:** It suggests to the mind what the trouble be among us all these years. *To all*: Think on it. Wherefore is everybody suing everybody else? Think on it now, it's a deep thing, and dark as a pit. I have been six time in court this year—

292 **Proctor,** *familiarly, with warmth, although he knows he is approaching the edge of Giles's tolerance with this*: Is it the Devil's fault that a man cannot say you good morning without you clap

7. **Quakers** members of the Society of Friends, a Christian religious sect that was founded in the mid-seventeenth century and that has no formal creed, rites, or priesthood. Unlike the Quakers, the Puritans had a rigid code of conduct and were expected to heed to the words of their ministers.

him for **defamation**? You're old, Giles, and you're not hearin' so well as you did.

293   **Giles**—*he cannot be crossed*: John Proctor, I have only last month collected four pound damages for you publicly sayin' I burned the roof off your house, and I—

294   **Proctor,** *laughing*: I never said no such thing, but I've paid you for it, so I hope I can call you deaf without charge. Now come along, Giles, and help me drag my lumber home.

295   **Putnam:** A moment, Mr. Proctor. What lumber is that you're draggin', if I may ask you?

296   **Proctor:** My lumber. From out my forest by the riverside.

297   **Putnam:** Why, we are surely gone wild this year. What anarchy is this? That tract is in my bounds, it's in my bounds, Mr. Proctor.

298   **Proctor:** In your bounds! *Indicating* REBECCA: I bought that tract from Goody Nurse's husband five months ago.

299   **Putnam:** He had no right to sell it. It stands clear in my grandfather's will that all the land between the river and—

300   **Proctor:** Your grandfather had a habit of willing land that never belonged to him, if I may say it plain.

301   **Giles:** That's God's truth; he nearly willed away my north pasture but he knew I'd break his fingers before he'd set his name to it. Let's get your lumber home, John. I feel a sudden will to work coming on.

302   **Putnam:** You load one oak of mine and you'll fight to drag it home!

303   **Giles:** Aye, and we'll win too, Putnam—this fool and I. Come on! *He turns to* PROCTOR *and* *starts out.*

304   **Putnam:** I'll have my men on you, Corey! I'll clap a writ on you!

305   *Enter* REVEREND JOHN HALE *of Beverly.*

306   Mr. Hale is nearing forty, a tight-skinned, eager-eyed intellectual. This is a beloved errand for him; on being called here to ascertain witchcraft he felt the pride of the specialist whose unique knowledge has at last been publicly called for. Like almost all men of learning, he spent a good deal of time pondering the invisible world, especially since he had himself encountered a witch in his parish not long before. That woman, however, turned into a mere pest under his searching scrutiny, and the child she had allegedly been afflicting recovered her normal behavior after Hale had given her his kindness and a few days of rest in his own house. However, that experience never raised a doubt in his mind as to the reality of the underworld or the existence of Lucifer's many-faced lieutenants. And his belief is not to his discredit. Better minds than Hale's

were—and still are—convinced that there is a society of spirits beyond our ken. One cannot help noting that one of his lines has never yet raised a laugh in any audience that has seen this play: it is his assurance that "We cannot look to superstition in this. The Devil is precise." Evidently we are not quite certain even now whether diabolism is holy and not to be scoffed at. And it is no accident that we should be so bemused.

307 Like Reverend Hale and the others on this stage, we conceive the Devil as a necessary part of a respectable view of cosmology. Ours is a divided empire in which certain ideas and emotions and actions are of God, and their opposites are of Lucifer. It is as impossible for most men to conceive of a morality without sin as of an earth without "sky." Since 1692 a great but superficial change has wiped out God's beard and the Devil's horns, but the world is still gripped between two diametrically opposed absolutes. The concept of unity, in which positive and negative are attributes of the same force, in which good and evil are relative, ever-changing, and always joined to the same phenomenon—such a concept is still reserved to the physical sciences and to the few who have grasped the history of ideas. When it is recalled that until the Christian era the underworld was never regarded as a hostile area, that all gods were useful and essentially friendly to man despite occasional lapses; when we see the steady and methodical inculcation into humanity of the idea of man's worthlessness—until redeemed—the necessity of the Devil may become evident as a weapon, a weapon designed and used time and time again in every age to whip men into a surrender to a particular church or church-state.

308 Our difficulty in believing the—for want of a better word— political inspiration of the Devil is due in great part to the fact that he is called up and damned not only by our social antagonists but by our own side, whatever it may be. The Catholic Church, through its Inquisition, is famous for cultivating Lucifer as the arch-fiend, but the Church's enemies relied no less upon the Old Boy to keep the human mind enthralled. Luther[8] was himself accused of alliance with Hell, and he in turn accused his enemies. To complicate matters further, he believed that he had had contact with the Devil and had argued theology with him. I am not surprised at this, for at my own university a professor of history—a Lutheran,[9] by the way—used to assemble his graduate students, draw the shades, and commune in the classroom with Erasmus.[10] He was never, to my knowledge, officially scoffed at for this, the reason being that the university officials, like most of us, are the children of a history which still sucks at the Devil's teats. At this writing, only England has held back before the temptations of contemporary diabolism. In the countries of the Communist ideology, all resistance of any import is linked to the totally malign capitalist

8. **Luther** Martin Luther (1483–1546), German theologian who led the Protestant Reformation.

9. **Lutheran** member of the Protestant denomination founded by Martin Luther.

10. **Erasmus** Desiderius Erasmus (1466?–1536), Dutch humanist, scholar, and theologian.

11. **succubi** (SUHK yuh by) *n.* female demons thought to lie on sleeping men.

12. **abrogation** (ab ruh GAY shuhn) *n.* abolishment.

13. **congerie** (KON juh ree) *n.* heap; pile.

succubi,[11] and in America any man who is not reactionary in his views is open to the charge of alliance with the Red hell. Political opposition, thereby, is given an inhumane overlay which then justifies the abrogation[12] of all normally applied customs of civilized intercourse. A political policy is equated with moral right, and opposition to it with diabolical malevolence. Once such an equation is effectively made, society becomes a congerie[13] of plots and counterplots, and the main role of government changes from that of the arbiter to that of the scourge of God.

309   The results of this process are no different now from what they ever were, except sometimes in the degree of cruelty inflicted, and not always even in that department. Normally, the actions and deeds of a man were all that society felt comfortable in judging. The secret intent of an action was left to the ministers, priests, and rabbis to deal with. When diabolism rises, however, actions are the least important manifests of the true nature of a man. The Devil, as Reverend Hale said, is a wily one, and, until an hour before he fell, even God thought him beautiful in Heaven.

310   The analogy, however, seems to falter when one considers that, while there were no witches then, there are Communists and capitalists now, and in each camp there is certain proof that spies of each side are at work undermining the other. But this is a snobbish objection and not at all warranted by the facts. I have no doubt that people *were* communing with, and even worshiping, the Devil in Salem, and if the whole truth could be known in this case, as it is in others, we should discover a regular and conventionalized propitiation of the dark spirit. One certain evidence of this is the confession of Tituba, the slave of Reverend Parris, and another is the behavior of the children who were known to have indulged in sorceries with her.

14. **klatches** *n.* informal gatherings.

15. **fetishes** *n.* objects believed to have magical power.

16. **Dionysiac** (dy uh NIHS ee ak) *adj.* characteristic of Dionysus, add part of speech Greek god of wine and revelry; thus, wild, frenzied, sensuous.

311   There are accounts of similar *klatches*[14] in Europe, where the daughters of the towns would assemble at night and, sometimes with fetishes,[15] sometimes with a selected young man, give themselves to love, with some bastardly results. The Church, sharp-eyed as it must be when gods long dead are brought to life, condemned these orgies as witchcraft and interpreted them, rightly, as a resurgence of the Dionysiac[16] forces it had crushed long before. Sex, sin, and the Devil were early linked, and so they continued to be in Salem, and are today. From all accounts there are no more puritanical mores in the world than those enforced by the Communists in Russia, where women's fashions, for instance, are as prudent and all-covering as any American Baptist would desire. The divorce laws lay a tremendous responsibility on the father for the care of his children. Even the laxity of divorce regulations in the early years

of the revolution was undoubtedly a revulsion from the nineteenth-century Victorian[17] immobility of marriage and the consequent hypocrisy that developed from it. If for no other reasons, a state so powerful, so jealous of the uniformity of its citizens, cannot long tolerate the atomization of the family. And yet, in American eyes at least, there remains the conviction that the Russian attitude toward women is lascivious. It is the Devil working again, just as he is working within the Slav who is shocked at the very idea of a woman's disrobing herself in a burlesque show. Our opposites are always robed in sexual sin, and it is from this unconscious conviction that demonology gains both its attractive sensuality and its capacity to infuriate and frighten.

312   Coming into Salem now, Reverend Hale conceives of himself much as a young doctor on his first call. His painfully acquired armory of symptoms, catchwords, and diagnostic procedures are now to be put to use at last. The road from Beverly is unusually busy this morning, and he has passed a hundred rumors that make him smile at the ignorance of the yeomanry in this most precise science. He feels himself allied with the best minds of Europe—kings, philosophers, scientists, and ecclesiasts of all churches. His goal is light, goodness and its preservation, and he knows the exaltation of the blessed whose intelligence, sharpened by minute examinations of enormous tracts, is finally called upon to face what may be a bloody fight with the Fiend himself.

313   *He appears loaded down with half a dozen heavy books.*

314   **Hale:** Pray you, someone take these!

315   **Parris,** *delighted*: Mr. Hale! Oh! it's good to see you again! *Taking some books*: My, they're heavy!

316   **Hale,** *setting down his books*: They must be; they are weighted with authority.

317   **Parris,** *a little scared*: Well, you do come prepared!

318   **Hale:** We shall need hard study if it comes to tracking down the Old Boy. *Noticing* REBECCA: You cannot be Rebecca Nurse?

319   **Rebecca:** I am, sir. Do you know me?

320   **Hale:** It's strange how I knew you, but I suppose you look as such a good soul should. We have all heard of your great charities in Beverly.

321   **Parris:** Do you know this gentleman? Mr. Thomas Putnam. And his good wife Ann.

322   **Hale:** Putnam! I had not expected such distinguished company, sir.

323   **Putnam,** *pleased*: It does not seem to help us today, Mr. Hale. We look to you to come to our house and save our child.

324   **Hale:** Your child ails too?

NOTES

17. **Victorian** characteristic of the time when Victoria was queen of England (1837–1901), an era associated with respectability, prudery, and hypocrisy.

CLOSE READ

ANNOTATE: Mark details in paragraph 312 that are reflected in the dialogue and action of paragraphs 313–318.

QUESTION: Why does Miller include these details?

CONCLUDE: What impression does Hale make on other characters, and on the audience or readers?

325 **Mrs. Putnam:** Her soul, her soul seems flown away. She sleeps and yet she walks . . .

326 **Putnam:** She cannot eat.

327 **Hale:** Cannot eat! *Thinks on it. Then, to* PROCTOR *and* GILES COREY: Do you men have afflicted children?

328 **Parris:** No, no, these are farmers. John Proctor—

329 **Giles Corey:** He don't believe in witches.

330 **Proctor,** *to* HALE: I never spoke on witches one way or the other. Will you come, Giles?

331 **Giles:** No—no, John, I think not. I have some few queer questions of my own to ask this fellow.

332 **Proctor:** I've heard you to be a sensible man, Mr. Hale. I hope you'll leave some of it in Salem.

333 PROCTOR *goes.* HALE *stands embarrassed for an instant.*

334 **Parris,** *quickly*: Will you look at my daughter, sir? *Leads* HALE *to the bed.* She has tried to leap out the window; we discovered her this morning on the highroad, waving her arms as though she'd fly.

335 **Hale,** *narrowing his eyes*: Tries to fly.

336 **Putnam:** She cannot bear to hear the Lord's name, Mr. Hale; that's a sure sign of witchcraft afloat.

337 **Hale,** *holding up his hands*: No, no. Now let me instruct you. We cannot look to superstition in this. The Devil is precise; the marks of his presence are definite as stone, and I must tell you all that I shall not proceed unless you are prepared to believe me if I should find no bruise of hell upon her.

338 **Parris:** It is agreed, sir—it is agreed—we will abide by your judgment.

339 **Hale:** Good then. *He goes to the bed, looks down at* BETTY. *To* PARRIS: Now, sir, what were your first warning of this strangeness?

340 **Parris:** Why, sir—I discovered her—*indicating* ABIGAIL—and my niece and ten or twelve of the other girls, dancing in the forest last night.

341 **Hale,** *surprised*: You permit dancing?

342 **Parris:** No, no, it were secret—

343 **Mrs. Putnam,** *unable to wait*: Mr. Parris's slave has knowledge of conjurin', sir.

344 **Parris,** *to* MRS. PUTNAM: We cannot be sure of that, Goody Ann—

345 **Mrs. Putnam,** *frightened, very softly*: I know it, sir. I sent my child—she should learn from Tituba who murdered her sisters.

346 **Rebecca,** *horrified*: Goody Ann! You sent a child to conjure up the dead?

CLOSE READ

ANNOTATE: In paragraphs 339–344, mark punctuation that reveals how characters respond to Hale.

QUESTION: Why does Miller use this punctuation?

CONCLUDE: How does this punctuation suggest the ways in which these lines should be delivered and the emotions they should convey?

347 **Mrs. Putnam:** Let God blame me, not you, not you, Rebecca! I'll not have you judging me any more! *To* HALE: Is it a natural work to lose seven children before they live a day?

348 **Parris:** Sssh!

349 REBECCA, *with great pain, turns her face away. There is a pause.*

350 **Hale:** Seven dead in childbirth.

351 **Mrs. Putnam,** *softly*: Aye. *Her voice breaks: she looks up at him. Silence.* HALE *is impressed.* PARRIS *looks to him. He goes to his books, opens one, turns pages, then reads. All wait, avidly.*

352 **Parris,** *hushed*: What book is that?

353 **Mrs. Putnam:** What's there, sir?

354 **Hale,** *with a tasty love of intellectual pursuit*: Here is all the invisible world, caught, defined, and calculated. In these books the Devil stands stripped of all his brute disguises. Here are all your familiar spirits—your incubi[18] and succubi, your witches that go by land, by air, and by sea; your wizards of the night and of the day. Have no fear now—we shall find him out if he has come among us, and I mean to crush him utterly if he has shown his face! *He starts for the bed.*

355 **Rebecca:** Will it hurt the child, sir?

356 **Hale:** I cannot tell. If she is truly in the Devil's grip we may have to rip and tear to get her free.

357 **Rebecca:** I think I'll go, then. I am too old for this. *She rises.*

358 **Parris,** *striving for conviction*: Why, Rebecca, we may open up the boil of all our troubles today!

359 **Rebecca:** Let us hope for that. I go to God for you, sir.

360 **Parris,** *with trepidation—and resentment*: I hope you do not mean we go to Satan here! *Slight pause.*

361 **Rebecca:** I wish I knew. *She goes out; they feel resentful of her note of moral superiority.*

362 **Putnam,** *abruptly*: Come, Mr. Hale, let's get on. Sit you here.

363 **Giles:** Mr. Hale, I have always wanted to ask a learned man— what signifies the readin' of strange books?

364 **Hale:** What books?

365 **Giles:** I cannot tell; she hides them.

366 **Hale:** Who does this?

367 **Giles:** Martha, my wife. I have waked at night many a time and found her in a corner, readin' of a book. Now what do you make of that?

368 **Hale:** Why, that's not necessarily—

18. incubi (IHN kyuh by) *n.* spirits or demons thought to lie on sleeping women.

369 **Giles:** It discomfits me! Last night—mark this—I tried and tried and could not say my prayers. And then she close her book and walks out of the house, and suddenly—mark this—I could pray again!

370   Old Giles must be spoken for, if only because his fate was to be so remarkable and so different from that of all the others. He was in his early eighties at this time, and was the most comical hero in the history. No man has ever been blamed for so much. If a cow was missed, the first thought was to look for her around Corey's house; a fire blazing up at night brought suspicion of arson to his door. He didn't give a hoot for public opinion, and only in his last years—after he had married Martha—did he bother much with the church. That she stopped his prayer is very probable, but he forgot to say that he'd only recently learned any prayers and it didn't take much to make him stumble over them. He was a crank and a nuisance, but withal a deeply innocent and brave man. In court, once, he was asked if it were true that he had been frightened by the strange behavior of a hog and had then said he knew it to be the Devil in an animal's shape. "What frighted you?" he was asked. He forgot everything but the word "frighted," and instantly replied, "I do not know that I ever spoke that word in my life."

371 **Hale:** Ah! The stoppage of prayer—that is strange. I'll speak further on that with you.

372 **Giles:** I'm not sayin' she's touched the Devil, now, but I'd admire to know what books she reads and why she hides them. She'll not answer me, y' see.

373 **Hale:** Aye, we'll discuss it. *To all*: Now mark me, if the Devil is in her you will witness some frightful wonders in this room, so please to keep your wits about you. Mr. Putnam, stand close in case she flies. Now, Betty, dear, will you sit up? PUTNAM *comes in closer, ready-handed.* HALE *sits* BETTY *up, but she hangs limp in his hands.* Hmmm. *He observes her carefully. The others watch breathlessly.* Can you hear me? I am John Hale, minister of Beverly. I have come to help you, dear. Do you remember my two little girls in Beverly? *She does not stir in his hands.*

374 **Parris,** *in fright*: How can it be the Devil? Why would he choose my house to strike? We have all manner of licentious people in the village!

375 **Hale:** What victory would the Devil have to win a soul already bad? It is the best the Devil wants, and who is better than the minister?

376 **Giles:** That's deep, Mr. Parris, deep, deep!

377 **Parris,** *with resolution now*: Betty! Answer Mr. Hale! Betty!

378 **Hale:** Does someone afflict you, child? It need not be a woman, mind you, or a man. Perhaps some bird invisible to others

comes to you—perhaps a pig, a mouse, or any beast at all. Is there some figure bids you fly? *The child remains limp in his hands. In silence he lays her back on the pillow. Now, holding out his hands toward her, he intones*: In nomine Domini Sabaoth sui filiique ite ad infernos.[19] *She does not stir. He turns to* ABIGAIL, *his eyes narrowing*. Abigail, what sort of dancing were you doing with her in the forest?

379 **Abigail:** Why—common dancing is all.

380 **Parris:** I think l ought to say that I—I saw a kettle in the grass where they were dancing.

381 **Abigail:** That were only soup.

382 **Hale:** What sort of soup were in this kettle, Abigail?

383 **Abigail:** Why, it were beans—and lentils, I think, and—

384 **Hale:** Mr. Parris, you did not notice, did you, any living thing in the kettle? A mouse, perhaps, a spider, a frog—?

385 **Parris,** *fearfully*: I—do believe there were some movement—in the soup.

386 **Abigail:** That jumped in, we never put it in!

387 **Hale,** *quickly*: What jumped in?

388 **Abigail:** Why, a very little frog jumped—

389 **Parris:** A frog, Abby!

390 **Hale,** *grasping* ABIGAIL: Abigail, it may be your cousin is dying. Did you call the Devil last night?

391 **Abigail:** I never called him! Tituba, Tituba . . .

392 **Parris,** *blanched*: She called the Devil?

393 **Hale:** I should like to speak with Tituba.

394 **Parris:** Goody Ann, will you bring her up? MRS. PUTNAM *exits*.

395 **Hale:** How did she call him?

396 **Abigail:** I know not—she spoke Barbados.

397 **Hale:** Did you feel any strangeness when she called him? A sudden cold wind, perhaps? A trembling below the ground?

398 **Abigail:** I didn't see no Devil! *Shaking* BETTY: Betty, wake up. Betty! Betty!

399 **Hale:** You cannot evade me, Abigail. Did your cousin drink any of the brew in that kettle?

400 **Abigail:** She never drank it!

401 **Hale:** Did you drink it?

402 **Abigail:** No, sir!

403 **Hale:** Did Tituba ask you to drink it?

404 **Abigail:** She tried, but I refused.

405 **Hale:** Why are you concealing? Have you sold yourself to Lucifer?

NOTES

19. **In nomine Domini Sabaoth sui filiique ite ad infernos** (ihn NOH mee nay DOH mee nee SAB ay oth SOO ee FEE lee ee kway EE tay ahd ihn FUR nohs) "In the name of the Lord of Hosts and his son, get thee to the lower world" (Latin).

406 **Abigail:** I never sold myself! I'm a good girl! I'm a proper girl!

407 MRS. PUTNAM *enters with* TITUBA, *and instantly* ABIGAIL *points at* TITUBA.

408 **Abigail:** She made me do it! She made Betty do it!

409 **Tituba,** *shocked and angry*: Abby!

410 **Abigail:** She makes me drink blood!

411 **Parris:** Blood!!

412 **Mrs. Putnam:** My baby's blood?

413 **Tituba:** No, no, chicken blood. I give she chicken blood!

414 **Hale:** Woman, have you enlisted these children for the Devil?

415 **Tituba:** No, no, sir, I don't truck with no Devil!

416 **Hale:** Why can she not wake? Are you silencing this child?

417 **Tituba:** I love me Betty!

418 **Hale:** You have sent your spirit out upon this child, have you not? Are you gathering souls for the Devil?

419 **Abigail:** She sends her spirit on me in church: she makes me laugh at prayer!

420 **Parris:** She have often laughed at prayer!

421 **Abigail:** She comes to me every night to go and drink blood!

422 **Tituba:** You beg *me* to conjure! She beg *me* make charm—

423 **Abigail:** Don't lie! *To* HALE: She comes to me while I sleep: she's always making me dream corruptions!

424 **Tituba:** Why you say that, Abby?

425 **Abigail:** Sometimes I wake and find myself standing in the open doorway and not a stitch on my body! I always hear her laughing in my sleep. I hear her singing her Barbados songs and tempting me with—

426 **Tituba:** Mister Reverend. I never—

427 **Hale,** *resolved now*: Tituba, I want you to wake this child.

428 **Tituba:** I have no power on this child, sir.

429 **Hale:** You most certainly do, and you will free her from it now! When did you compact with the Devil?

430 **Tituba:** I don't compact with no Devil!

431 **Parris:** You will confess yourself or I will take you out and whip you to your death, Tituba!

432 **Putnam:** This woman must be hanged! She must be taken and hanged!

433 **Tituba,** *terrified, falls to her knees*: No, no, don't hang Tituba! I tell him I don't desire to work for him, sir.

434 **Parris:** The Devil?

435 **Hale:** Then you saw him! TITUBA *weeps.* Now Tituba, I know that when we bind ourselves to Hell it is very hard to break with it. We are going to help you tear yourself free—

436 **Tituba,** *frightened by the coming process*: Mister Reverend, I do believe somebody else be witchin' these children.

437 **Hale:** Who?

438 **Tituba:** I don't know, sir, but the Devil got him numerous witches.

439 **Hale:** Does he! *It is a clue.* Tituba, look into my eyes. Come, look into me. *She raises her eyes to his fearfully.* You would be a good Christian woman, would you not, Tituba?

440 **Tituba:** Aye, sir, a good Christian woman.

441 **Hale:** And you love these little children?

442 **Tituba:** Oh, yes, sir, I don't desire to hurt little children.

443 **Hale:** And you love God, Tituba?

444 **Tituba:** I love God with all my bein'.

445 **Hale:** Now, in God's holy name—

446 **Tituba:** Bless Him. Bless Him. *She is rocking on her knees, sobbing in terror.*

Arthur Miller wrote the screenplay for the 1996 film version of *The Crucible* and was pleased at the film's ability to "open wide enough to contain a whole society and move in close enough to see into a girl's heart." One way in which the film "opened wide" was to show this scene of the girls dancing in the forest, which is merely described in dialogue in the play.

447 **Hale:** And to His glory—

448 **Tituba:** Eternal glory. Bless Him—bless God . . .

449 **Hale:** Open yourself, Tituba—open yourself and let God's holy light shine on you.

450 **Tituba:** Oh, bless the Lord.

451 **Hale:** When the Devil come to you does he ever come—with another person? *She stares up into his face.* Perhaps another person in the village? Someone you know.

452 **Parris:** Who came with him?

453 **Putnam:** Sarah Good? Did you ever see Sarah Good with him? Or Osburn?

454 **Parris:** Was it man or woman came with him?

455 **Tituba:** Man or woman. Was—was woman.

456 **Parris:** What woman? A woman, you said. What woman?

457 **Tituba:** It was black dark, and I—

458 **Parris:** You could see him, why could you not see her?

459 **Tituba:** Well, they was always talking; they was always runnin' round and carryin' on—

460 **Parris:** You mean out of Salem? Salem witches?

461 **Tituba:** I believe so, yes, sir.

462 *Now* HALE *takes her hand. She is surprised.*

463 **Hale:** Tituba. You must have no fear to tell us who they are, do you understand? We will protect you. The Devil can never overcome a minister. You know that, do you not?

464 **Tituba,** *kisses* HALE's *hand: Aye*, sir, oh, I do.

465 **Hale:** You have confessed yourself to witchcraft, and that speaks a wish to come to Heaven's side. And we will bless you, Tituba.

466 **Tituba,** *deeply relieved*: Oh, God bless you, Mr. Hale!

467 **Hale,** *with rising exaltation*: You are God's instrument put in our hands to discover the Devil's agent among us. You are selected, Tituba, you are chosen to help us cleanse our village. So speak utterly, Tituba, turn your back on him and face God—face God, Tituba, and God will protect you.

468 **Tituba,** *joining with him*: Oh, God, protect Tituba!

469 **Hale,** *kindly*: Who came to you with the Devil? Two? Three? Four? How many?

470 TITUBA *pants, and begins rocking back and forth again, staring ahead.*

471 **Tituba:** There was four. There was four.

472 **Parris,** *pressing in on her*: Who? Who? Their names, their names!

473 **Tituba,** *suddenly bursting out*: Oh, how many times he bid me kill you, Mr. Parris!

474 **Parris:** Kill me!

475 **Tituba,** *in a fury*: He say Mr. Parris must be kill! Mr. Parris no goodly man. Mr. Parris mean man and no gentle man, and he bid me rise out of my bed and cut your throat! *They gasp.* But I tell him "No! I don't hate that man. I don't want kill that man." But he say, "You work for me, Tituba, and I make you free! I give you pretty dress to wear, and put you way high up in the air, and you gone fly back to Barbados!" And I say, "You lie, Devil, you lie!" And then he come one stormy night to me, and he say, "Look! I have *white* people belong to me." And I look—and there was Goody Good.

476 **Parris:** Sarah Good!

477 **Tituba,** *rocking and weeping*: Aye, sir, and Goody Osburn.

478 **Mrs. Putnam:** I knew it! Goody Osburn were midwife to me three times. I begged you, Thomas, did I not? I begged him not to call Osburn because I feared her. My babies always shriveled in her hands!

479 **Hale:** Take courage, you must give us all their names. How can you bear to see this child suffering? Look at her, Tituba. *He is indicating* BETTY *on the bed.* Look at her God-given innocence; her soul is so tender; we must protect her, Tituba: the Devil is out and preying on her like a beast upon the flesh of the pure lamb. God will bless you for your help.

480 ABIGAIL *rises, staring as though inspired, and cries out.*

481 **Abigail:** I want to open myself! *They turn to her, startled. She is enraptured, as though in a pearly light.* I want the light of God. I want the sweet love of Jesus! I danced for the Devil; I saw him: I wrote in his book; I go back to Jesus; I kiss His hand. I saw Sarah Good with the Devil! I saw Goody Osburn with the Devil! I saw Bridget Bishop with the Devil!

482 *As she is speaking,* BETTY *is rising from the bed, a fever in her eyes, and picks up the chant.*

483 **Betty,** *staring too*: I saw George Jacobs with the Devil! I saw Goody Howe with the Devil!

484 **Parris:** She speaks! *He rushes to embrace* BETTY. She speaks!

485 **Hale:** Glory to God! It is broken, they are free!

486 **Betty,** *calling out hysterically and with great relief*: I saw Martha Bellows with the Devil!

487 **Abigail:** I saw Goody Sibber with the Devil! *It is rising to a great glee.*

488 **Putnam:** The marshal, I'll call the marshal!

489 PARRIS *is shouting a prayer of thanksgiving.*

490 **Betty:** I saw Alice Barrow with the Devil!

491 *The curtain begins to fall.*

CLOSE READ

ANNOTATE: In paragraphs 481–489, mark details that suggest the escalating emotional frenzy.

QUESTION: Why does Miller use this language?

CONCLUDE: What is the effect of this heightened language at the end of Act I?

492 **Hale,** *as* PUTNAM *goes out*: Let the marshal bring irons!

493 **Abigail:** I saw Goody Hawkins with the Devil!

494 **Betty:** I saw Goody Bibber with the Devil!

495 **Abigail:** I saw Goody Booth with the Devil!

496 *On their ecstatic cries—*

THE CURTAIN FALLS

Comprehension Check

Complete the following items after you finish your first read.

1. Why does Parris send for Reverend Hale?

2. What does Mrs. Putnam believe happened to her babies?

3. What conflict exists between Abigail and Proctor?

4. What is a source of disagreement between Proctor and Putnam?

5. To what does Tituba confess?

6. 🗒 **Notebook** Write a timeline of the key events in Act I of *The Crucible*. Include important events mentioned in the text that occur before the action of the play begins.

- -

RESEARCH

Research to Clarify Choose at least one unfamiliar detail from the text. Briefly research that detail. In what way does the information you learned shed light on an aspect of Act I?

Close Read the Text

Reread paragraphs 165–166 in which Miller introduces readers to John Proctor. Mark details that describe Proctor's character. How do Proctor's actions in the following scene with Abigail reflect key points made in this description?

ANNOTATE · QUESTION · Close Read · CONCLUDE

THE CRUCIBLE, ACT I

Analyze the Text

CITE TEXTUAL EVIDENCE
to support your answers.

📓 **Notebook** Respond to these questions.

1. (a) What is Betty's condition when the play opens? (b) What does Abigail say she and Betty were doing in the forest? (c) **Make Inferences** What seems to be the main reason for Reverend Parris's concern about the girls' behavior in the forest? Explain.

2. (a) What do Abigail, Betty, Mercy, and Mary discuss after Parris leaves his daughter's room? (b) **Predict** What events does this scene suggest may occur later in the play?

3. (a) Who is Reverend Hale? (b) **Evaluate** Do you think he is fair and impartial in his actions so far? Explain.

4. (a) **Connect** What evidence suggests that sharp divisions exist among the people of Salem? (b) **Apply** Name two other characters who may be accused of witchcraft by the end of the play. Explain your choices.

🔧 **Tool Kit**
Close-Read Guide and Model Annotation

LANGUAGE DEVELOPMENT

Concept Vocabulary

| vindictive | calumny | defamation |

Why These Words? The three concept vocabulary words are all used to describe speech or actions intended to harm others, particularly their reputations. What other words in Act I relate to this concept?

Practice

📓 **Notebook** Use each concept vocabulary word in a sentence that demonstrates its meaning.

🔗 WORD NETWORK

Add words related to fear from the text to your Word Network.

Word Study

📓 **Notebook** **Latin Root: -fama-** The Latin root -fama-, meaning "reputation," is found in many words that relate to the idea of public opinion. For example, *defamation* involves discrediting someone's reputation through untruthful statements. That idea is at the very heart of the action of *The Crucible*.

1. Use library or online resources to find the legal definition of "defamation of character." Explain how this meaning relates to the Latin root -fama-.

2. Explain how the root -fama- helps you determine the meanings of the words *famously*, *infamy*, and *euphemism*. Use a college-level dictionary to check your definitions.

📋 STANDARDS

Language
Demonstrate understanding of figurative language, word relationships, and nuances in word meanings.

THE CRUCIBLE, ACT I

Analyze Craft and Structure

Structural Elements of Drama Most plays are written to be performed, not read. When reading drama, it is important to identify the text structures that provide information about the setting, characters, and conflicts. Dramatic text structures include the following.

- **Dialogue** is the words actors speak—their lines.
- **Stage directions** are notes included in a play to indicate how the work is meant to be performed or staged. Stage directions may describe sets, costumes, lighting, sound, props, and—in some cases—the ways in which actors should move and deliver their lines. These instructions may be printed in italics, set in brackets, or otherwise visually differentiated from the dialogue. Reading stage directions can help you picture the action and imagine how characters might look and sound in performance.
- **Dramatic exposition** refers to the prose commentaries, or brief essays, inserted by the playwright to provide information about the characters or situation. Dramatic exposition is a common element in twentieth-century American drama.

STANDARDS

Reading Literature
• Analyze the impact of the author's choices regarding how to develop and relate elements of a story or drama.
• Analyze how an author's choices concerning how to structure specific parts of a text contribute to its overall structure and meaning as well as its aesthetic impact.

Practice

CITE TEXTUAL EVIDENCE to support your answers.

📝 **Notebook** Respond to these questions.

1. Give two examples of stage directions that are essential to understanding the action in Act I. Explain each choice.
2. Use the chart to examine how two specific events or characters described in the play's opening dramatic exposition are carried into the action of Act I.

EVENT/CHARACTER		DESCRIPTION		ACTION
	→		→	
	→		→	

3. (a) According to the opening dramatic exposition, how did most of the members of Salem feel about the vast forest that surrounded them? (b) How might these attitudes have affected the girls' actions in the forest as well as Parris's reaction to what he saw there?
4. In Act I, what seeds of conflict exist between Rebecca Nurse, Reverend Parris, and the Putnams? Explain, citing details from all three text structures—dialogue, stage directions, and dramatic exposition—that support your response.

Conventions and Style

Personal Pronouns A **pronoun** is a word that substitutes for a noun or noun phrase. **Personal pronouns** are those that reflect "person" in the grammatical sense of first person, second person, and so on. Such personal pronouns take different forms depending on gender, number, and **case,** or the word's function in a sentence.

- **Nominative Case:** The pronoun is the subject of the sentence.
- **Objective Case:** The pronoun is the object of a verb or preposition.
- **Possessive Case:** The pronoun expresses ownership.

The chart provides examples of personal pronouns according to case.

	NOMINATIVE	OBJECTIVE	POSSESSIVE
First-person pronouns refer to the person speaking.	I, we	me, us	mine, ours
Second-person pronouns refer to the person spoken to.	you	you	your, yours
Third-person pronouns refer to a person spoken about.	he, she, it, they	him, her, it, them	his, hers, its, theirs

The Crucible is set in 1692, when people commonly used pronoun forms such as *thee* and *thou* that are now archaic. However, Miller makes the stylistic choice to use modern personal pronouns. He also chooses to use nonstandard pronouns in Tituba's dialogue.

Read It

1. Mark the pronouns in each excerpt from the play. Label the case and person of each pronoun.

   a. **Parris:** Now look you, child, your punishment will come in its time. But if you trafficked with spirits in the forest I must know it now, for surely my enemies will, and they will ruin me with it.

   b. **Putnam,** *pleased:* It does not seem to help us today, Mr. Hale. We look to you to come to our house and save our child.

2. **Connect to Style** Reread the dialogue between Tituba and Hale in paragraphs 413–417. Identify and classify each pronoun. Note whether each example reflects standard usage.

Write It

📓 **Notebook** Rewrite each line of dialogue to sound more realistic by replacing repeated nouns with personal pronouns. Decide whether or not to reflect standard usage, and explain the reasons for your choices.

1. **Proctor** *to Abigail:* Abigail must change Abigail's behavior if Abigail hopes to regain Proctor's respect.

2. **Tituba:** Tituba loves Betty. Betty has always treated Tituba kindly.

3. **Hale:** The people of Salem must confess what the people of Salem have done if the people of Salem hope to receive the people of Salem's rightful forgiveness.

📝 EVIDENCE LOG

Before moving on to Act II, go to your Evidence Log and record what you learned from Act I of *The Crucible.*

STANDARDS

Language
- Demonstrate command of the conventions of standard English grammar and usage when writing or speaking.
- Apply the understanding that usage is a matter of convention, can change over time, and is sometimes contested.
- Apply knowledge of language to understand how language functions in different contexts, to make effective choices for meaning or style, and to comprehend more fully when reading or listening.

Playwright

Arthur Miller

The Crucible, Act II

Concept Vocabulary

You will encounter the following words as you read Act II of *The Crucible*. Before reading, note how familiar you are with each word. Then, rank the words in order from most familiar (1) to least familiar (3).

WORD	YOUR RANKING
condemnation	
magistrates	
proceedings	

After completing the first read, come back to the concept vocabulary and review your rankings. Mark changes to your original rankings as needed.

First Read DRAMA

Apply these strategies as you conduct your first read. You will have an opportunity to complete the close-read notes after your first read.

NOTICE whom the story is about, *what* happens, *where* and *when* it happens, and *why* those involved react as they do.

ANNOTATE by marking vocabulary and key passages you want to revisit.

First Read

CONNECT ideas within the selection to what you already know and what you have already read.

RESPOND by completing the Comprehension Check and by writing a brief summary of the selection.

▦ STANDARDS

Reading Literature
By the end of grade 11, read and comprehend literature, including stories, dramas, and poems, in the grades 11–CCR text complexity band proficiently, with scaffolding as needed at the high end of the range.

The **Crucible**

Act II

Arthur Miller

REVIEW AND ANTICIPATE

As Act I draws to a close, Salem is in the grip of mounting hysteria. What had begun as concern over the strange behavior of Betty—a reaction that may have stemmed from guilty feelings about her activities in the woods the night before—had swelled by the act's end to a mass hysteria, in which accusations of witchcraft were being made and accepted against a growing number of Salem's citizens. As you read, pay close attention to the nature of the accusations and the growing numbers of the accused.

SCAN FOR MULTIMEDIA

1 *The common room of* PROCTOR'S *house, eight days later.*

2 *At the right is a door opening on the fields outside.*

3 *A fireplace is at the left, and behind it a stairway leading upstairs. It is the low, dark, and rather long living room of the time. As the curtain rises, the room is empty. From above,* ELIZABETH *is heard softly singing to the children. Presently the door opens and* JOHN PROCTOR *enters, carrying his gun. He glances about the room as he comes toward the fireplace, then halts for an instant as he hears her singing. He continues on to the fireplace, leans the gun against the wall as he swings a pot out of the fire and smells it. Then he lifts out the ladle and tastes. He is not quite pleased. He reaches to a cupboard, takes a pinch of salt, and drops it into the pot. As he is tasting again, her footsteps*

NOTES

are heard on the stair. He swings the pot into the fireplace and goes to a basin and washes his hands and face. ELIZABETH *enters.*

4 **Elizabeth:** What keeps you so late? It's almost dark.

5 **Proctor:** I were planting far out to the forest edge.

6 **Elizabeth:** Oh, you're done then.

7 **Proctor:** Aye, the farm is seeded. The boys asleep?

8 **Elizabeth:** They will be soon. *And she goes to the fireplace, proceeds to ladle up stew in a dish.*

9 **Proctor:** Pray now for a fair summer.

10 **Elizabeth:** Aye.

11 **Proctor:** Are you well today?

12 **Elizabeth:** I am. *She brings the plate to the table, and, indicating the food:* It is a rabbit.

13 **Proctor,** *going to the table:* Oh, is it! In Jonathan's trap?

14 **Elizabeth:** No, she walked into the house this afternoon; I found her sittin' in the corner like she come to visit.

15 **Proctor:** Oh, that's a good sign walkin' in.

16 **Elizabeth:** Pray God. It hurt my heart to strip her, poor rabbit. *She sits and watches him taste it.*

17 **Proctor:** It's well seasoned.

18 **Elizabeth,** *blushing with pleasure:* I took great care. She's tender?

19 **Proctor:** Aye. *He eats. She watches him.* I think we'll see green fields soon. It's warm as blood beneath the clods.

20 **Elizabeth:** That's well.

21 PROCTOR *eats, then looks up.*

22 **Proctor:** If the crop is good I'll buy George Jacob's heifer. How would that please you?

23 **Elizabeth:** Aye, it would.

24 **Proctor,** *with a grin:* I mean to please you, Elizabeth.

25 **Elizabeth**—*it is hard to say:* I know it, John.

26 *He gets up, goes to her, kisses her. She receives it. With a certain disappointment, he returns to the table.*

27 **Proctor,** *as gently as he can:* Cider?

28 **Elizabeth,** *with a sense of reprimanding herself for having forgot:* Aye! *She gets up and goes and pours a glass for him. He now arches his back.*

29 **Proctor:** This farm's a continent when you go foot by foot droppin' seeds in it.

30 **Elizabeth,** *coming with the cider:* It must be.

31 **Proctor,** *drinks a long draught, then, putting the glass down:* You ought to bring some flowers in the house.

32 **Elizabeth:** Oh! I forgot! I will tomorrow.

33 **Proctor:** It's winter in here yet. On Sunday let you come with me, and we'll walk the farm together; I never see such a load of flowers on the earth. *With good feeling he goes and looks up at the sky through the open doorway.* Lilacs have a purple smell. Lilac is the smell of nightfall, I think. Massachusetts is a beauty in the spring!

34 **Elizabeth:** Aye, it is.

35 *There is a pause. She is watching him from the table as he stands there absorbing the night. It is as though she would speak but cannot. Instead, now, she takes up his plate and glass and fork and goes with them to the basin. Her back is turned to him. He turns to her and watches her. A sense of their separation rises.*

36 **Proctor:** I think you're sad again. Are you?

37 **Elizabeth—***she doesn't want friction, and yet she must:* You come so late I thought you'd gone to Salem this afternoon.

38 **Proctor:** Why? I have no business in Salem.

39 **Elizabeth:** You did speak of going, earlier this week.

40 **Proctor—***he knows what she means:* I thought better of it since.

41 **Elizabeth:** Mary Warren's there today.

42 **Proctor:** Why'd you let her? You heard me forbid her go to Salem any more!

43 **Elizabeth:** I couldn't stop her.

44 **Proctor,** *holding back a full* **condemnation** *of her:* It is a fault, it is a fault, Elizabeth—you're the mistress here, not Mary Warren.

condemnation (kon dehm NAY shuhn) *n.* very strong disapproval

45 **Elizabeth:** She frightened all my strength away.

46 **Proctor:** How may that mouse frighten you, Elizabeth? You—

47 **Elizabeth:** It is a mouse no more. I forbid her go, and she raises up her chin like the daughter of a prince and says to me, "I must go to Salem, Goody Proctor; I am an official of the court!"

48 **Proctor:** Court! What court?

49 **Elizabeth:** Aye, it is a proper court they have now. They've sent four judges out of Boston, she says, weighty **magistrates** of the General Court, and at the head sits the Deputy Governor of the Province.

magistrates (MAJ uh strayts) *n.* officials who have some of the powers of a judge

50 **Proctor,** *astonished:* Why, she's mad.

51 **Elizabeth:** I would to God she were. There be fourteen people in the jail now, she says. PROCTOR *simply looks at her, unable to grasp it.* And they'll be tried, and the court have power to hang them too, she says.

CLOSE READ

ANNOTATE: In paragraphs 55 through 66, mark details that relate to thought, belief, or conviction.

QUESTION: Why does Miller repeat these sorts of references?

CONCLUDE: What do these details suggest about the struggle the Proctors are experiencing?

52 **Proctor,** *scoffing but without conviction*: Ah, they'd never hang—

53 **Elizabeth:** The Deputy Governor promise hangin' if they'll not confess, John. The town's gone wild, I think. She speak of Abigail, and I thought she were a saint, to hear her. Abigail brings the other girls into the court, and where she walks the crowd will part like the sea for Israel.[1] And folks are brought before them, and if they scream and howl and fall to the floor— the person's clapped in the jail for bewitchin' them.

54 **Proctor,** *wide-eyed*: Oh, it is a black mischief.

55 **Elizabeth:** I think you must go to Salem, John. *He turns to her.* I think so. You must tell them it is a fraud.

56 **Proctor,** *thinking beyond this*: Aye, it is, it is surely.

57 **Elizabeth:** Let you go to Ezekiel Cheever—he knows you well. And tell him what she said to you last week in her uncle's house. She said it had naught to do with witchcraft, did she not?

58 **Proctor,** *in thought*: Aye, she did, she did. *Now, a pause.*

59 **Elizabeth,** *quietly, fearing to anger him by prodding*: God forbid you keep that from the court, John. I think they must be told.

60 **Proctor,** *quietly, struggling with his thought*: Aye, they must, they must. It is a wonder they do believe her.

61 **Elizabeth:** I would go to Salem now, John—let you go tonight.

62 **Proctor:** I'll think on it.

63 **Elizabeth,** *with her courage now*: You cannot keep it, John.

64 **Proctor,** *angering*: I know I cannot keep it. I say I will think on it!

65 **Elizabeth,** *hurt, and very coldly*: Good, then, let you think on it. *She stands and starts to walk out of the room.*

66 **Proctor:** I am only wondering how I may prove what she told me, Elizabeth. If the girl's a saint now, I think it is not easy to prove she's fraud, and the town gone so silly. She told it to me in a room alone—I have no proof for it.

67 **Elizabeth:** You were alone with her?

68 **Proctor,** *stubbornly*: For a moment alone, aye.

69 **Elizabeth:** Why, then, it is not as you told me.

70 **Proctor,** *his anger rising*: For a moment, I say. The others come in soon after.

71 **Elizabeth,** *quietly—she has suddenly lost all faith in him*: Do as you wish, then. *She starts to turn.*

72 **Proctor:** Woman. *She turns to him.* I'll not have your suspicion any more.

73 **Elizabeth,** *a little loftily*: I have no—

74 **Proctor:** I'll not have it!

75 **Elizabeth:** Then let you not earn it.

76 **Proctor,** *with a violent undertone*: You doubt me yet?

77 **Elizabeth,** *with a smile, to keep her dignity*: John, if it were not Abigail that you must go to hurt, would you falter now? I think not.

78 **Proctor:** Now look you—

79 **Elizabeth:** I see what I see, John.

80 **Proctor,** *with solemn warning*: You will not judge me more, Elizabeth. I have good reason to think before I charge fraud on Abigail, and I will think on it. Let you look to your own improvement before you go to judge your husband any more. I have forgot Abigail, and—

81 **Elizabeth:** And I.

82 **Proctor:** Spare me! You forget nothin' and forgive nothin'. Learn charity, woman. I have gone tiptoe in this house all seven month since she is gone. I have not moved from there to there without I think to please you, and still an everlasting funeral marches round your heart. I cannot speak but I am doubted, every moment judged for lies, as though I come into a court when I come into this house!

83 **Elizabeth:** John, you are not open with me. You saw her with a crowd, you said. Now you—

84 **Proctor:** I'll plead my honesty no more, Elizabeth.

85 **Elizabeth**—*now she would justify herself*: John. I am only—

86 **Proctor:** No more! I should have roared you down when first you told me your suspicion. But I wilted, and, like a Christian, I confessed. Confessed! Some dream I had must have mistaken you for God that day. But you're not, you're not, and let you remember it! Let you look sometimes for the goodness in me, and judge me not.

87 **Elizabeth:** I do not judge you. The magistrate sits in your heart that judges you. I never thought you but a good man, John— *with a smile*—only somewhat bewildered.

88 **Proctor,** *laughing bitterly*: Oh. Elizabeth, your justice would freeze beer! *He turns suddenly toward a sound outside. He starts for the door as* MARY WARREN *enters. As soon as he sees her, he goes directly to her and grabs her by the cloak, furious.* How do you go to Salem when I forbid it? Do you mock me? *Shaking her.* I'll whip you if you dare leave this house again!

Strangely, she doesn't resist him, but hangs limply by his grip.

89 **Mary Warren:** I am sick, I am sick, Mr. Proctor. Pray, pray, hurt me not. *Her strangeness throws him off, and her evident pallor and weakness. He frees her.* My insides are all shuddery; I am in the proceedings all day, sir.

proceedings (pruh SEE dihngz) *n.*
events in a court of law

2. poppet *n.* doll.

90 **Proctor,** *with draining anger—his curiosity is draining it*: And what of these **proceedings** here? When will you proceed to keep this house, as you are paid nine pound a year to do—and my wife not wholly well?

91 *As though to compensate,* MARY WARREN *goes to* ELIZABETH *with a small rag doll.*

92 **Mary Warren:** I made a gift for you today, Goody Proctor. I had to sit long hours in a chair, and passed the time with sewing.

93 **Elizabeth,** *perplexed, looking at the doll*: Why, thank you, it's a fair poppet.[2]

94 **Mary Warren,** *with a trembling, decayed voice*: We must all love each other now, Goody Proctor.

95 **Elizabeth,** *amazed at her strangeness*: Aye, indeed we must.

96 **Mary Warren,** *glancing at the room*: I'll get up early in the morning and clean the house. I must sleep now. *She turns and starts off.*

97 **Proctor:** Mary. *She halts.* Is it true? There be fourteen women arrested?

98 **Mary Warren:** No, sir. There be thirty-nine now—*She suddenly breaks off and sobs and sits down, exhausted.*

99 **Elizabeth:** Why, she's weepin'! What ails you, child?

100 **Mary Warren:** Goody Osburn—will hang!

101 *There is a shocked pause, while she sobs.*

102 **Proctor:** Hang! *He calls into her face.* Hang, y'say?

103 **Mary Warren,** *through her weeping*: Aye.

104 **Proctor:** The Deputy Governor will permit it?

105 **Mary Warren:** He sentenced her. He must. *To ameliorate it*: But not Sarah Good. For Sarah Good confessed, y'see.

106 **Proctor:** Confessed! To what?

107 **Mary Warren:** That she—*in horror at the memory*—she sometimes made a compact with Lucifer, and wrote her name in his black book—with her blood—and bound herself to torment Christians till God's thrown down—and we all must worship Hell forevermore.

108 *Pause.*

109 **Proctor:** But—surely you know what a jabberer she is. Did you tell them that?

110 **Mary Warren:** Mr. Proctor, in open court she near to choked us all to death.

111 **Proctor:** How, choked you?

112 **Mary Warren:** She sent her spirit out.

113 **Elizabeth:** Oh, Mary, Mary, surely you—

114 **Mary Warren,** *with an indignant edge*: She tried to kill me many times, Goody Proctor!

115 **Elizabeth:** Why, I never heard you mention that before.

116 **Mary Warren:** I never knew it before. I never knew anything before. When she come into the court I say to myself, I must not accuse this woman, for she sleep in ditches, and so very old and poor. But then—then she sit there, denying and denying, and I feel a misty coldness climbin' up my back, and the skin on my skull begin to creep, and I feel a clamp around my neck and I cannot breathe air; and then—*entranced*—I hear a voice, a screamin' voice, and it were my voice—and all at once I remembered everything she done to me!

117 **Proctor:** Why? What did she do to you?

118 **Mary Warren,** *like one awakened to a marvelous secret insight*: So many time, Mr. Proctor, she come to this very door, beggin' bread and a cup of cider—and mark this: whenever I turned her away empty, she *mumbled*.

119 **Elizabeth:** Mumbled! She may mumble if she's hungry.

120 **Mary Warren:** But *what* does she mumble? You must remember, Goody Proctor. Last month—a Monday, I think—she walked away, and I thought my guts would burst for two days after. Do you remember it?

121 **Elizabeth:** Why—I do, I think, but—

122 **Mary Warren:** And so I told that to Judge Hathorne, and he asks her so. "Goody Osburn," says he, "what curse do you mumble that this girl must fall sick after turning you away?" And then she replies—*mimicking an old crone*—"Why, your excellence, no curse at all. I only say my commandments; I hope I may say my commandments," says she!

123 **Elizabeth:** And that's an upright answer.

124 **Mary Warren:** Aye, but then Judge Hathorne say, "Recite for us your commandments!"—*leaning avidly toward them*—and of all the ten she could not say a single one. She never knew no commandments, and they had her in a flat lie!

125 **Proctor:** And so condemned her?

126 **Mary Warren,** *now a little strained, seeing his stubborn doubt*: Why, they must when she condemned herself.

CLOSE READ

ANNOTATE: In paragraphs 116–118, mark details that relate to new knowledge or awareness.

QUESTION: Why does Miller include these details?

CONCLUDE: What do these details suggest about the ways in which the characters and situation in Salem are changing?

127 **Proctor:** But the proof, the proof!

128 **Mary Warren,** *with greater impatience with him*: I told you the proof. It's hard proof, hard as rock, the judges said.

129 **Proctor,** *pauses an instant, then*: You will not go to court again, Mary Warren.

130 **Mary Warren:** I must tell you, sir, I will be gone every day now. I am amazed you do not see what weighty work we do.

131 **Proctor:** What work you do? It's strange work for a Christian girl to hang old women!

132 **Mary Warren:** But, Mr. Proctor, they will not hang them if they confess. Sarah Good will only sit in jail some time—*recalling*—and here's a wonder for you: think on this. Goody Good is pregnant!

133 **Elizabeth:** Pregnant! Are they mad? The woman's near to sixty!

134 **Mary Warren:** They had Doctor Griggs examine her, and she's full to the brim. And smokin' a pipe all these years, and no husband either! But she's safe, thank God, for they'll not hurt the innocent child. But be that not a marvel? You must see it, sir, it's God's work we do. So I'll be gone every day for some time. I'm—I am an official of the court, they say, and I—*She has been edging toward offstage.*

135 **Proctor:** I'll official you! *He strides to the mantel, takes down the whip hanging there.*

136 **Mary Warren,** *terrified, but coming erect, striving for her authority*: I'll not stand whipping any more!

137 **Elizabeth,** *hurriedly, as* PROCTOR *approaches*: Mary, promise now you'll stay at home—

138 **Mary Warren,** *backing from him, but keeping her erect posture, striving, striving for her way*: The Devil's loose in Salem, Mr. Proctor: we must discover where he's hiding!

139 **Proctor:** I'll whip the Devil out of you! *With whip raised he reaches out for her, and she streaks away and yells.*

140 **Mary Warren,** *pointing at* ELIZABETH: I saved her life today!

141 *Silence. His whip comes down.*

142 **Elizabeth,** *softly*: I am accused?

143 **Mary Warren,** *quaking*: Somewhat mentioned. But I said I never see no sign you ever sent your spirit out to hurt no one, and seeing I do live so closely with you, they dismissed it.

144 **Elizabeth:** Who accused me?

145 **Mary Warren:** I am bound by law, I cannot tell it. *To* PROCTOR: I only hope you'll not be so sarcastical no more. Four judges and

the King's deputy sat to dinner with us but an hour ago. I— I would have you speak civilly to me, from this out.

146 **Proctor,** *in horror, muttering in disgust at her*: Go to bed.

147 **Mary Warren,** *with a stamp of her foot*: I'll not be ordered to bed no more, Mr. Proctor! I am eighteen and a woman, however single!

148 **Proctor:** Do you wish to sit up? Then sit up.

149 **Mary Warren:** I wish to go to bed!

150 **Proctor,** *in anger*: Good night, then!

151 **Mary Warren:** Good night. *Dissatisfied, uncertain of herself, she goes out. Wide-eyed, both* PROCTOR *and* ELIZABETH *stand staring.*

152 **Elizabeth,** *quietly*: Oh, the noose, the noose is up!

153 **Proctor:** There'll be no noose.

154 **Elizabeth:** She wants me dead. I knew all week it would come to this!

155 **Proctor,** *without conviction*: They dismissed it. You heard her say—

156 **Elizabeth:** And what of tomorrow? She will cry me out until they take me!

157 **Proctor:** Sit you down.

158 **Elizabeth:** She wants me dead, John, you know it!

159 **Proctor:** I say sit down! *She sits, trembling. He speaks quietly, trying to keep his wits.* Now we must be wise, Elizabeth.

160 **Elizabeth,** *with sarcasm, and a sense of being lost*: Oh, indeed, indeed!

161 **Proctor:** Fear nothing. I'll find Ezekiel Cheever. I'll tell him she said it were all sport.

162 **Elizabeth:** John, with so many in the jail, more than Cheever's help is needed now, I think. Would you favor me with this? Go to Abigail.

163 **Proctor,** *his soul hardening as he senses . . .* : What have I to say to Abigail?

164 **Elizabeth,** *delicately*: John—grant me this. You have a faulty understanding of young girls. There is a promise made in any bed—

165 **Proctor,** *striving against his anger*: What promise!

166 **Elizabeth:** Spoke or silent, a promise is surely made. And she may dote on it now—I am sure she does—and thinks to kill me, then to take my place.

167 PROCTOR'S *anger is rising; he cannot speak.*

NOTES

CLOSE READ

ANNOTATE: In paragraphs 146–151, mark details in both dialogue and stage directions that relate to childish behavior, and others that relate to mature behavior.

QUESTION: Why does Miller include these details?

CONCLUDE: What is the effect of these details, particularly in characterizing Mary Warren and her motivations?

168 **Elizabeth:** It is her dearest hope, John, I know it. There be a thousand names: why does she call mine? There be a certain danger in calling such a name—I am no Goody Good that sleeps in ditches, nor Osburn, drunk and half-witted. She'd dare not call out such a farmer's wife but there be monstrous profit in it. She thinks to take my place, John.

169 **Proctor:** She cannot think it! *He knows it is true.*

170 **Elizabeth,** *"reasonably"*: John, have you ever shown her somewhat of contempt? She cannot pass you in the church but you will blush—

171 **Proctor:** I may blush for my sin.

172 **Elizabeth:** I think she sees another meaning in that blush.

173 **Proctor:** And what see you? What see you, Elizabeth?

174 **Elizabeth,** *"conceding"*: I think you be somewhat ashamed, for I am there, and she so close.

175 **Proctor:** When will you know me, woman? Were I stone I would have cracked for shame this seven month!

176 **Elizabeth:** Then go and tell her she's a whore. Whatever promise she may sense—break it. John, break it.

177 **Proctor,** *between his teeth*: Good, then. I'll go. *He starts for his rifle.*

178 **Elizabeth,** *trembling, fearfully*: Oh, how unwillingly!

179 **Proctor,** *turning on her, rifle in hand*: I will curse her hotter than the oldest cinder in hell. But pray, begrudge me not my anger!

180 **Elizabeth:** Your anger! I only ask you—

181 **Proctor:** Woman, am I so base? Do you truly think me base?

182 **Elizabeth:** I never called you base.

183 **Proctor:** Then how do you charge me with such a promise? The promise that a stallion gives a mare I gave that girl!

184 **Elizabeth:** Then why do you anger with me when I bid you break it?

185 **Proctor:** Because it speaks deceit, and I am honest! But I'll plead no more! I see now your spirit twists around the single error of my life, and I will never tear it free!

186 **Elizabeth,** *crying out*: You'll tear it free—when you come to know that I will be your only wife, or no wife at all! She has an arrow in you yet, John Proctor, and you know it well!

187 *Quite suddenly, as though from the air, a figure appears in the doorway. They start slightly. It is* MR. HALE. *He is different now— drawn a little, and there is a quality of deference, even of guilt, about his manner now.*

188 **Hale:** Good evening.

189 **Proctor,** *still in his shock*: Why, Mr. Hale! Good evening to you, sir. Come in, come in.

190 **Hale,** *to* Elizabeth: I hope I do not startle you.

191 **Elizabeth:** No, no, it's only that I heard no horse—

192 **Hale:** You are Goodwife Proctor.

193 **Proctor:** Aye, Elizabeth.

194 **Hale,** *nods, then*: I hope you're not off to bed yet.

195 **Proctor,** *setting down his gun*: No, no. HALE *comes further into the room. And* PROCTOR, *to explain his nervousness*: We are not used to visitors after dark, but you're welcome here. Will you sit you down, sir?

196 **Hale:** I will. *He sits.* Let you sit, Goodwife Proctor.

197 *She does, never letting him out of her sight. There is a pause as* HALE *looks about the room.*

198 **Proctor,** *to break the silence*: Will you drink cider, Mr. Hale?

In the 1996 film version of *The Crucible*, actor Rob Campbell portrays Reverend Hale.

199 **Hale:** No, it rebels my stomach; I have some further traveling yet tonight. Sit you down, sir. PROCTOR *sits*. I will not keep you long, but I have some business with you.

200 **Proctor:** Business of the court?

201 **Hale:** No—no, I come of my own, without the court's authority. Hear me. *He wets his lips*. I know not if you are aware, but your wife's name is—mentioned in the court.

202 **Proctor:** We know it, sir. Our Mary Warren told us. We are entirely amazed.

203 **Hale:** I am a stranger here, as you know. And in my ignorance I find it hard to draw a clear opinion of them that come accused before the court. And so this afternoon, and now tonight, I go from house to house—I come now from Rebecca Nurse's house and—

204 **Elizabeth,** *shocked*: Rebecca's charged!

205 **Hale:** God forbid such a one be charged. She is, however— mentioned somewhat.

206 **Elizabeth,** *with an attempt at a laugh*: You will never believe, I hope, that Rebecca trafficked with the Devil.

207 **Hale:** Woman, it is possible.

208 **Proctor,** *taken aback*: Surely you cannot think so.

209 **Hale:** This is a strange time, Mister. No man may longer doubt the powers of the dark are gathered in monstrous attack upon this village. There is too much evidence now to deny it. You will agree, sir?

210 **Proctor,** *evading*: I—have no knowledge in that line. But it's hard to think so pious a woman be secretly a Devil's bitch after seventy year of such good prayer.

211 **Hale:** Aye. But the Devil is a wily one, you cannot deny it. However, she is far from accused, and I know she will not be. *Pause*. I thought, sir, to put some questions as to the Christian character of this house, if you'll permit me.

212 **Proctor,** *coldly, resentful*: Why, we—have no fear of questions, sir.

213 **Hale:** Good, then. *He makes himself more comfortable*. In the book of record that Mr. Parris keeps, I note that you are rarely in the church on Sabbath Day.

214 **Proctor:** No, sir, you are mistaken.

215 **Hale:** Twenty-six time in seventeen month, sir. I must call that rare. Will you tell me why you are so absent?

216 **Proctor:** Mr. Hale, I never knew I must account to that man for I come to church or stay at home. My wife were sick this winter.

217 **Hale:** So I am told. But you, Mister, why could you not come alone?

218 **Proctor:** I surely did come when I could, and when I could not I prayed in this house.

219 **Hale:** Mr. Proctor, your house is not a church: your theology must tell you that.

220 **Proctor:** It does, sir, it does; and it tells me that a minister may pray to God without he have golden candlesticks upon the altar.

221 **Hale:** What golden candlesticks?

222 **Proctor:** Since we built the church there were pewter candlesticks upon the altar; Francis Nurse made them y'know, and a sweeter hand never touched the metal. But Parris came, and for twenty week he preach nothin' but golden candlesticks until he had them. I labor the earth from dawn of day to blink of night, and I tell you true, when I look to heaven and see my money glaring at his elbows—it hurt my prayer, sir, it hurt my prayer. I think, sometimes, the man dreams cathedrals, not clapboard meetin' houses.

223 **Hale,** *thinks, then*: And yet, Mister, a Christian on Sabbath Day must be in church. *Pause.* Tell me—you have three children?

224 **Proctor:** Aye. Boys.

225 **Hale:** How comes it that only two are baptized?

226 **Proctor,** *starts to speak, then stops, then, as though unable to restrain this*: I like it not that Mr. Parris should lay his hand upon my baby. I see no light of God in that man. I'll not conceal it.

227 **Hale:** I must say it, Mr. Proctor; that is not for you to decide. The man's ordained, therefore the light of God is in him.

228 **Proctor,** *flushed with resentment but trying to smile*: What's your suspicion, Mr. Hale?

229 **Hale:** No, no, I have no—

230 **Proctor:** I nailed the roof upon the church, I hung the door—

231 **Hale:** Oh, did you! That's a good sign, then.

232 **Proctor:** It may be I have been too quick to bring the man to book, but you cannot think we ever desired the destruction of religion. I think that's in your mind, is it not?

233 **Hale,** *not altogether giving way*: I—have—there is a softness in your record, sir, a softness.

234 **Elizabeth:** I think, maybe, we have been too hard with Mr. Parris. I think so. But sure we never loved the Devil here.

235 **Hale,** *nods, deliberating this. Then, with the voice of one administering a secret test*: Do you know your Commandments, Elizabeth?

236 **Elizabeth,** *without hesitation, even eagerly*: I surely do. There be no mark of blame upon my life, Mr. Hale. I am a covenanted Christian woman.

NOTES

CLOSE READ
ANNOTATE: In paragraphs 220–222, mark the name of the item that appears several times in the conversation between Hale and Proctor.

QUESTION: Why is this item important?

CONCLUDE: How do you think the audience feels about Parris after hearing this exchange?

237 **Hale:** And you, Mister?

238 **Proctor,** *a trifle unsteadily*: I—am sure I do, sir.

239 **Hale,** *glances at her open face, then at* JOHN, *then*: Let you repeat them, if you will.

240 **Proctor:** The Commandments.

241 **Hale:** Aye.

242 **Proctor,** *looking off, beginning to sweat*: Thou shalt not kill.

243 **Hale:** Aye.

244 **Proctor,** *counting on his fingers*: Thou shalt not steal. Thou shalt not covet thy neighbor's goods, nor make unto thee any graven image. Thou shalt not take the name of the Lord in vain; thou shalt have no other gods before me. *With some hesitation*: Thou shalt remember the Sabbath Day and keep it holy. *Pause. Then*: Thou shalt honor thy father and mother. Thou shalt not bear false witness. *He is stuck. He counts back on his fingers, knowing one is missing.* Thou shalt not make unto thee any graven image.

245 **Hale:** You have said that twice, sir.

246 **Proctor,** *lost*: Aye. *He is flailing for it.*

247 **Elizabeth,** *delicately*: Adultery, John.

248 **Proctor,** *as though a secret arrow had pained his heart*: Aye. *Trying to grin it away—to* HALE: You see, sir, between the two of us we do know them all. HALE *only looks at* PROCTOR, *deep in his attempt to define this man.* PROCTOR *grows more uneasy.* I think it be a small fault.

249 **Hale:** Theology, sir, is a fortress; no crack in a fortress may be accounted small. *He rises; he seems worried now. He paces a little, in deep thought.*

250 **Proctor:** There be no love for Satan in this house, Mister.

251 **Hale:** I pray it, I pray it dearly. *He looks to both of them, an attempt at a smile on his face, but his misgivings are clear.* Well, then—I'll bid you good night.

252 **Elizabeth,** *unable to restrain herself*: Mr. Hale. *He turns.* I do think you are suspecting me somewhat? Are you not?

253 **Hale,** *obviously disturbed—and evasive*: Goody Proctor, I do not judge you. My duty is to add what I may to the godly wisdom of the court. I pray you both good health and good fortune. *To* JOHN: Good night, sir. *He starts out.*

254 **Elizabeth,** *with a note of desperation*: I think you must tell him, John.

255 **Hale:** What's that?

256 **Elizabeth**, *restraining a call*: Will you tell him?

257 *Slight pause.* HALE *looks questioningly at* JOHN.

258 **Proctor,** *with difficulty*: I—I have no witness and cannot prove it, except my word be taken. But I know the children's sickness had naught to do with witchcraft.

259 **Hale,** *stopped, struck*: Naught to do—?

260 **Proctor:** Mr. Parris discovered them sportin' in the woods. They were startled and took sick.

261 *Pause.*

262 **Hale:** Who told you this?

263 **Proctor,** *hesitates, then*: Abigail Williams.

264 **Hale:** Abigail.

265 **Proctor:** Aye.

266 **Hale,** *his eyes wide*: Abigail Williams told you it had naught to do with witchcraft!

267 **Proctor:** She told me the day you came, sir.

268 **Hale,** *suspiciously*: Why—why did you keep this?

269 **Proctor:** I never knew until tonight that the world is gone daft with this nonsense.

270 **Hale:** Nonsense! Mister, I have myself examined Tituba, Sarah Good, and numerous others that have confessed to dealing with the Devil. They have *confessed* it.

271 **Proctor:** And why not, if they must hang for denyin' it? There are them that will swear to anything before they'll hang; have you never thought of that?

272 **Hale:** I have. I—I have indeed. *It is his own suspicion, but he resists it. He glances at* ELIZABETH, *then at* JOHN. And you—would you testify to this in court?

273 **Proctor:** I—had not reckoned with goin' into court. But if I must I will.

274 **Hale:** Do you falter here?

275 **Proctor:** I falter nothing, but I may wonder if my story will be credited in such a court. I do wonder on it, when such a steady-minded minister as you will suspicion such a woman that never lied, and cannot, and the world knows she cannot! I may falter somewhat, Mister; I am no fool.

276 **Hale,** *quietly—it has impressed him*: Proctor, let you open with me now, for I have a rumor that troubles me. It's said you hold no belief that there may even be witches in the world. Is that true, sir?

277 **Proctor—***he knows this is critical, and is striving against his disgust with* HALE *and with himself for even answering*: I know not what I have said, I may have said it. I have wondered if there be witches in the world—although I cannot believe they come among us now.

CLOSE READ

ANNOTATE: In paragraphs 268–274, mark questions and exclamations.

QUESTION: Why does Miller use exclamations and questions here?

CONCLUDE: What is the effect of these sentence types in this scene?

278 **Hale:** Then you do not believe—

279 **Proctor:** I have no knowledge of it; the Bible speaks of witches, and I will not deny them.

280 **Hale:** And you, woman?

281 **Elizabeth:** I—I cannot believe it.

282 **Hale,** *shocked*: You cannot!

283 **Proctor:** Elizabeth, you bewilder him!

284 **Elizabeth,** *to* HALE: I cannot think the Devil may own a woman's soul, Mr. Hale, when she keeps an upright way, as I have. I am a good woman, I know it; and if you believe I may do only good work in the world, and yet be secretly bound to Satan, then I must tell you, sir, I do not believe it.

285 **Hale:** But, woman, you do believe there are witches in—

286 **Elizabeth:** If you think that I am one, then I say there are none.

287 **Hale:** You surely do not fly against the Gospel, the Gospel—

288 **Proctor:** She believe in the Gospel, every word!

289 **Elizabeth:** Question Abigail Williams about the Gospel, not myself!

In the 1996 film adaptation of *The Crucible*, Joan Allen portrays Elizabeth Proctor.

290 HALE *stares at her*.

291 **Proctor:** She do not mean to doubt the Gospel, sir, you cannot think it. This be a Christian house, sir, a Christian house.

292 **Hale:** God keep you both; let the third child be quickly baptized, and go you without fail each Sunday to Sabbath prayer; and keep a solemn, quiet way among you. I think—

293 GILES COREY *appears in doorway*.

294 **Giles:** John!

295 **Proctor:** Giles! What's the matter?

296 **Giles:** They take my wife.

297 FRANCIS NURSE *enters*.

298 **Giles:** And his Rebecca!

299 **Proctor,** *to* FRANCIS: Rebecca's in the *jail*!

300 **Francis:** Aye, Cheever come and take her in his wagon. We've only now come from the jail, and they'll not even let us in to see them.

301 **Elizabeth:** They've surely gone wild now, Mr. Hale!

302 **Francis,** *going to* HALE: Reverend Hale! Can you not speak to the Deputy Governor? I'm sure he mistakes these people—

303 **Hale:** Pray calm yourself, Mr. Nurse.

304 **Francis:** My wife is the very brick and mortar of the church. Mr. Hale—*indicating* GILES—and Martha Corey, there cannot be a woman closer yet to God than Martha.

305 **Hale:** How is Rebecca charged, Mr. Nurse?

306 **Francis,** *with a mocking, half-hearted laugh*: For murder, she's charged! *Mockingly quoting the warrant*: "For the marvelous and supernatural murder of Goody Putnam's babies." What am I to do, Mr. Hale?

307 **Hale,** *turns from* FRANCIS, *deeply troubled, then*: Believe me, Mr. Nurse, if Rebecca Nurse be tainted, then nothing's left to stop the whole green world from burning. Let you rest upon the justice of the court; the court will send her home. I know it.

308 **Francis:** You cannot mean she will be tried in court!

309 **Hale,** *pleading*: Nurse, though our hearts break, we cannot flinch: these are new times, sir. There is a misty plot afoot so subtle we should be criminal to cling to old respects and ancient friendships. I have seen too many frightful proofs in court—the Devil is alive in Salem, and we dare not quail to follow wherever the accusing finger points!

310 **Proctor,** *angered*: How may such a woman murder children?

311 **Hale,** *in great pain*: Man, remember, until an hour before the Devil fell, God thought him beautiful in Heaven.

312 **Giles:** I never said my wife were a witch, Mr. Hale: I only said she were reading books!

313 **Hale:** Mr. Corey, exactly what complaint were made on your wife?

314 **Giles:** That bloody mongrel Walcott charge her. Y'see, he buy a pig of my wife four or five year ago, and the pig died soon after. So he come dancin' in for his money back. So my Martha, she says to him. "Walcott, if you haven't the wit to feed a pig properly, you'll not live to own many," she says. Now he goes to court and claims that from that day to this he cannot keep a pig alive for more than four weeks because my Martha bewitch them with her books!

315 *Enter* EZEKIEL CHEEVER. *A shocked silence.*

316 **Cheever:** Good evening to you, Proctor.

317 **Proctor:** Why, Mr. Cheever. Good evening.

318 **Cheever:** Good evening, all. Good evening, Mr. Hale.

319 **Proctor:** I hope you come not on business of the court.

320 **Cheever:** I do, Proctor, aye. I am clerk of the court now, y'know.

321 *Enter* MARSHAL HERRICK, *a man in his early thirties, who is somewhat shamefaced at the moment.*

322 **Giles:** It's a pity, Ezekiel, that an honest tailor might have gone to Heaven must burn in Hell. You'll burn for this, do you know it?

323 **Cheever:** You know yourself I must do as I'm told. You surely know that, Giles. And I'd as lief³ you'd not be sending me to Hell. I like not the sound of it, I tell you: I like not the sound of it. *He fears* PROCTOR, *but starts to reach inside his coat.* Now believe me, Proctor, how heavy be the law, all its tonnage I do carry on my back tonight. *He takes out a warrant.* I have a warrant for your wife.

324 **Proctor,** *to* Hale: You said she were not charged!

325 **Hale:** I know nothin' of it. *To* CHEEVER: When were she charged?

326 **Cheever:** I am given sixteen warrant tonight, sir, and she is one.

327 **Proctor:** Who charged her?

328 **Cheever:** Why, Abigail Williams charge her.

329 **Proctor:** On what proof, what proof?

330 **Cheever,** *looking about the room*: Mr. Proctor, I have little time. The court bid me search your house, but I like not to search a house. So will you hand me any poppets that your wife may keep here?

331 **Proctor:** Poppets?

332 **Elizabeth:** I never kept no poppets, not since I were a girl.

3. as lief (leef) *adv.* rather.

333 **Cheever,** *embarrassed, glancing toward the mantel where sits* MARY WARREN'S *poppet*: I spy a poppet, Goody Proctor.

334 **Elizabeth:** Oh! *Going for it*: Why, this is Mary's.

335 **Cheever,** *shyly*: Would you please to give it to me?

336 **Elizabeth**, *handing it to him, asks* HALE: Has the court discovered a text in poppets now?

337 **Cheever,** *carefully holding the poppet*: Do you keep any others in this house?

338 **Proctor:** No, nor this one either till tonight. What signifies a poppet?

339 **Cheever:** Why, a poppet—*he gingerly turns the poppet over*—a poppet may signify—Now, woman, will you please to come with me?

340 **Proctor:** She will not! *To* ELIZABETH: Fetch Mary here.

341 **Cheever,** *ineptly reaching toward* ELIZABETH: No, no, I am forbid to leave her from my sight.

342 **Proctor,** *pushing his arm away*: You'll leave her out of sight and out of mind, Mister. Fetch Mary, Elizabeth. ELIZABETH *goes upstairs.*

343 **Hale:** What signifies a poppet, Mr. Cheever?

344 **Cheever,** *turning the poppet over in his hands*: Why, they say it may signify that she—*he has lifted the poppet's skirt, and his eyes widen in astonished fear*. Why, this, this—

345 **Proctor,** *reaching for the poppet*: What's there?

346 **Cheever:** Why—*He draws out a long needle from the poppet*—it is a needle! Herrick, Herrick, it is a needle!

347 HERRICK *comes toward him.*

348 **Proctor,** *angrily, bewildered*: And what signifies a needle!

349 **Cheever,** *his hands shaking*: Why, this go hard with her, Proctor, this—I had my doubts, Proctor. I had my doubts, but here's calamity.

350 *To* HALE, *showing the needle*: You see it, sir, it is a needle!

351 **Hale:** Why? What meanin' has it?

352 **Cheever,** *wide-eyed, trembling*: The girl, the Williams girl, Abigail Williams, sir. She sat to dinner in Reverend Parris's house tonight, and without word nor warnin' she falls to the floor. Like a struck beast, he says, and screamed a scream that a bull would weep to hear. And he goes to save her, and, stuck two inches in the flesh of her belly, he draw a needle out. And demandin' of her how she come to be so stabbed, she—*to* PROCTOR *now*—testify it were your wife's familiar spirit pushed it in.

353 **Proctor:** Why, she done it herself! *To* HALE: I hope you're not takin' this for proof, Mister!

CLOSE READ

ANNOTATE: In paragraph 352, mark details that add vividness and drama to Cheever's account of the dinner scene.

QUESTION: Why does Miller give Cheever these strong, descriptive lines?

CONCLUDE: What is the effect of this description?

354 Hale, *struck by the proof, is silent.*

355 **Cheever:** 'Tis hard proof! *To* HALE: I find here a poppet Goody Proctor keeps. I have found it, sir. And in the belly of the poppet a needle's stuck. I tell you true, Proctor, I never warranted to see such proof of Hell, and I bid you obstruct me not, for I—

356 *Enter* ELIZABETH *with* MARY WARREN. PROCTOR, *seeing* MARY WARREN, *draws her by the arm to* HALE.

357 **Proctor:** Here now! Mary, how did this poppet come into my house?

358 **Mary Warren,** *frightened for herself, her voice very small*: What poppet's that, sir?

359 **Proctor,** *impatiently, points at the doll in* CHEEVER'S *hand*: This poppet, this poppet.

360 **Mary Warren,** *evasively, looking at it*: Why, I—I think it is mine.

361 **Proctor:** It is your poppet, is it not?

362 **Mary Warren,** *not understanding the direction of this*: It—is, sir.

363 **Proctor:** And how did it come into this house?

364 **Mary Warren,** *glancing about at the avid faces*: Why—I made it in the court, sir, and—give it to Goody Proctor tonight.

365 **Proctor,** *to* HALE: Now, sir—do you have it?

366 **Hale:** Mary Warren, a needle have been found inside this poppet.

367 **Mary Warren,** *bewildered*: Why, I meant no harm by it, sir.

368 **Proctor,** *quickly*: You stuck that needle in yourself?

369 **Mary Warren:** I—I believe I did, sir, I—

370 **Proctor,** *to* HALE: What say you now?

371 **Hale,** *watching* MARY WARREN *closely*: Child, you are certain this be your natural memory? May it be, perhaps that someone conjures you even now to say this?

372 **Mary Warren:** Conjures me? Why, no, sir, I am entirely myself, I think. Let you ask Susanna Walcott—she saw me sewin' it in court. *Or better still*: Ask Abby. Abby sat beside me when I made it.

373 **Proctor,** *to* HALE, *of* CHEEVER: Bid him begone. Your mind is surely settled now. Bid him out, Mr. Hale.

374 **Elizabeth:** What signifies a needle?

375 **Hale:** Mary—you charge a cold and cruel murder on Abigail.

376 **Mary Warren:** Murder! I charge no—

377 **Hale:** Abigail were stabbed tonight; a needle were found stuck into her belly—

378 **Elizabeth:** And she charges me?

379 **Hale:** Aye.

380 **Elizabeth,** *her breath knocked out*: Why—! The girl is murder! She must be ripped out of the world!

381 Cheever, *pointing at* ELIZABETH: You've heard that, sir! Ripped out of the world! Herrick, you heard it!

382 Proctor, *suddenly snatching the warrant out of* CHEEVER'S *hands*: Out with you.

383 Cheever: Proctor, you dare not touch the warrant.

384 Proctor, *ripping the warrant*: Out with you!

385 Cheever: You've ripped the Deputy Governor's warrant, man!

386 Proctor: Damn the Deputy Governor! Out of my house!

387 Hale: Now, Proctor, Proctor!

388 Proctor: Get y'gone with them! You are a broken minister.

389 Hale: Proctor, if she is innocent, the court—

390 Proctor: If *she* is innocent! Why do you never wonder if Parris be innocent, or Abigail? Is the accuser always holy now? Were they born this morning as clean as God's fingers? I'll tell you what's walking Salem—vengeance is walking Salem. We are what we always were in Salem, but now the little crazy children are jangling the keys of the kingdom, and common vengeance writes the law! This warrant's vengeance! I'll not give my wife to vengeance!

391 Elizabeth: I'll go, John—

392 Proctor: You will not go!

393 Herrick: I have nine men outside. You cannot keep her. The law binds me, John. I cannot budge.

394 Proctor, *to* HALE, *ready to break him*: Will you see her taken?

395 Hale: Proctor, the court is just—

396 Proctor: Pontius Pilate![4] God will not let you wash your hands of this!

397 Elizabeth: John—I think I must go with them. *He cannot bear to look at her*. Mary, there is bread enough for the morning; you will bake, in the afternoon. Help Mr. Proctor as you were his daughter—you owe me that, and much more. *She is fighting her weeping. To* PROCTOR: When the children wake, speak nothing of witchcraft—it will frighten them.

398 *She cannot go on.*

399 Proctor: I will bring you home. I will bring you soon.

400 Elizabeth: Oh, John, bring me soon!

401 Proctor: I will fall like an ocean on that court! Fear nothing, Elizabeth.

402 Elizabeth, *with great fear*: I will fear nothing. *She looks about the room, as though to fix it in her mind*. Tell the children I have gone to visit someone sick.

4. **Pontius Pilate** Roman governor who condemned Jesus to be crucified. Pilate washed his hands before the crowd to show that he refused to take responsibility for Jesus' death.

403 *She walks out the door.* HERRICK *and* CHEEVER *behind her. For a moment,* PROCTOR *watches from the doorway. The clank of chain is heard.*

404 **Proctor:** Herrick! Herrick, don't chain her! *He rushes out the door. From outside:* Damn you, man, you will not chain her! Off with them! I'll not have it! I will not have her chained!

405 *There are other men's voices against his.* HALE, *in a fever of guilt and uncertainty, turns from the door to avoid the sight:* MARY WARREN *bursts into tears and sits weeping.* GILES COREY *calls to* HALE.

406 **Giles:** And yet silent, minister? It is fraud, you know it is fraud! What keeps you, man?

407 PROCTOR *is half braced, half pushed into the room by two deputies and* HERRICK.

408 **Proctor:** I'll pay you, Herrick. I will surely pay you!

409 **Herrick,** *panting:* In God's name, John, I cannot help myself. I must chain them all. Now let you keep inside this house till I am gone! *He goes out with his deputies.*

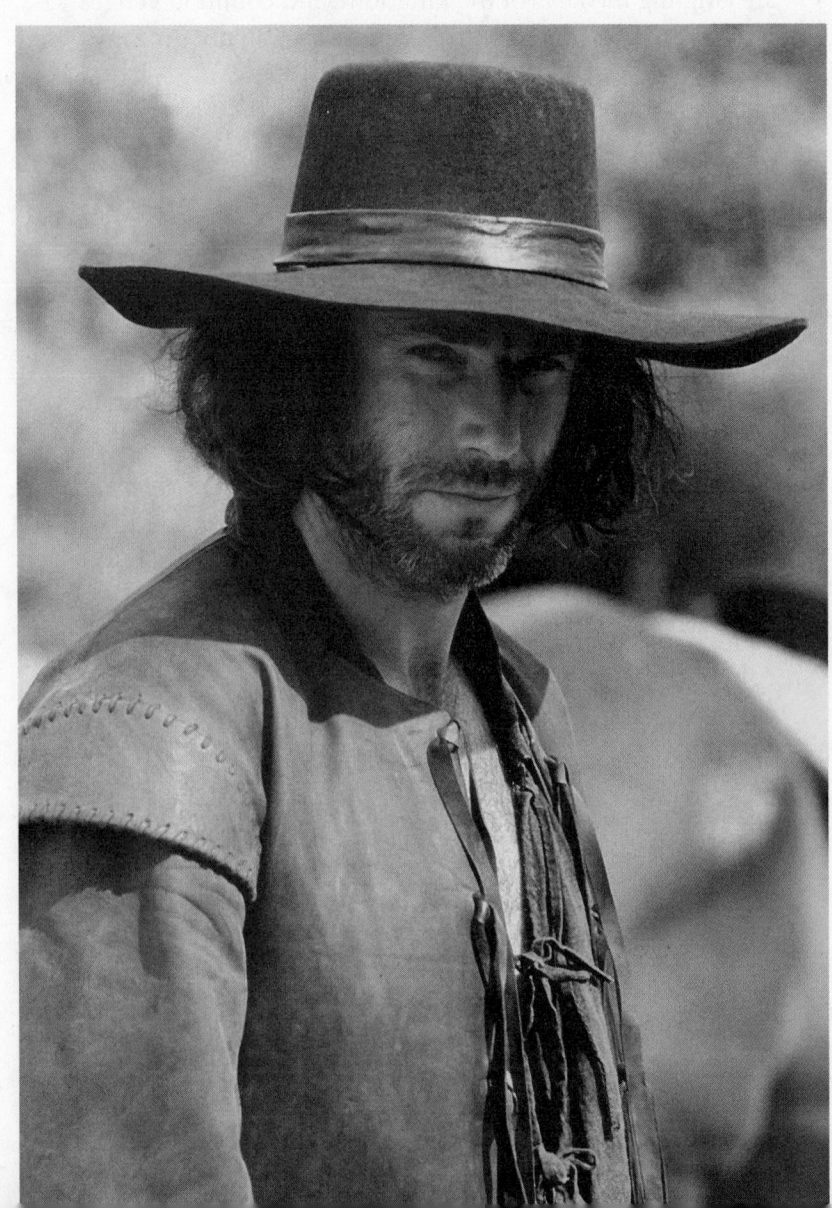

410 PROCTOR *stands there, gulping air. Horses and a wagon creaking are heard.*

411 **Hale,** *in great uncertainty*: Mr. Proctor—

412 **Proctor:** Out of my sight!

413 **Hale:** Charity, Proctor, charity. What I have heard in her favor, I will not fear to testify in court. God help me. I cannot judge her guilty or innocent—I know not. Only this consider: the world goes mad, and it profit nothing you should lay the cause to the vengeance of a little girl.

414 **Proctor:** You are a coward! Though you be ordained in God's own tears, you are a coward now!

415 **Hale:** Proctor, I cannot think God be provoked so grandly by such a petty cause. The jails are packed—our greatest judges sit in Salem now—and hangin's promised. Man, we must look to cause proportionate. Were there murder done, perhaps, and never brought to light? Abomination? Some secret blasphemy that stinks to Heaven? Think on cause, man, and let you help me to discover it. For there's your way, believe it, there is your only way, when such confusion strikes upon the world. *He goes to* GILES *and* FRANCIS. Let you counsel among yourselves; think on your village and what may have drawn from heaven such thundering wrath upon you all. I shall pray God open up our eyes.

416 HALE *goes out*.

417 **Francis,** *struck by* HALE'S *mood*: I never heard no murder done in Salem.

418 **Proctor—**he has been reached by HALE'S *words*: Leave me, Francis, leave me.

419 **Giles,** *shaken*: John—tell me, are we lost?

420 **Proctor:** Go home now, Giles. We'll speak on it tomorrow.

421 **Giles:** Let you think on it. We'll come early, eh?

422 **Proctor:** Aye. Go now, Giles.

423 **Giles:** Good night, then.

424 GILES COREY *goes out. After a moment*:

425 **Mary Warren,** *in a fearful squeak of a voice*: Mr. Proctor, very likely they'll let her come home once they're given proper evidence.

426 **Proctor:** You're coming to the court with me, Mary. You will tell it in the court.

427 **Mary Warren:** I cannot charge murder on Abigail.

428 **Proctor,** *moving menacingly toward her*: You will tell the court how that poppet come here and who stuck the needle in.

429 **Mary Warren:** She'll kill me for sayin' that! PROCTOR *continues toward her*. Abby'll charge lechery[5] on you, Mr. Proctor!

430 **Proctor,** *halting*: She's told you!

CLOSE READ
ANNOTATE: In paragraph 415, mark words and phrases that relate to causes and effects.

QUESTION: Why does Miller include this speech with this seeming expression of logic?

CONCLUDE: What is the effect of this speech?

5. **lechery** (LEHCH uhr ee) *n.* lust; adultery—a charge almost as serious as witchcraft in this Puritan community.

431 **Mary Warren:** I have known it, sir. She'll ruin you with it. I know she will.

432 **Proctor,** *hesitating, and with deep hatred of himself:* Good. Then her saintliness is done with. MARY *backs from him.* We will slide together into our pit; you will tell the court what you know.

433 **Mary Warren,** *in terror:* I cannot, they'll turn on me—

434 PROCTOR *strides and catches her, and she is repeating,* "I cannot. I cannot!"

435 **Proctor:** My wife will never die for me! I will bring your guts into your mouth but that goodness will not die for me!

436 **Mary Warren,** *struggling to escape him:* I cannot do it. I cannot!

437 **Proctor,** *grasping her by the throat as though he would strangle her:* Make your peace with it! Now Hell and Heaven grapple on our backs, and all our old pretense is ripped away—make your peace! *He throws her to the floor, where she sobs.* "I cannot. I cannot . . ." *And now, half to himself, staring, and turning to the open door:* Peace. It is a providence, and no great change; we are only what we always were, but naked now. *He walks as though toward a great horror, facing the open sky.* Aye, naked! And the wind, God's icy wind, will blow!

438 *And she is over and over again sobbing,* "I cannot, I cannot. I cannot" *as*

THE CURTAIN FALLS

Comprehension Check

Complete the following items after you finish your first read.

1. Why does Hale visit the Proctors' home?

2. What do some of the accused, such as Sarah Good, do to save themselves from hanging?

3. What evidence of Elizabeth's guilt does Cheever find?

4. 📓 **Notebook** Write a summary of Act II of *The Crucible*.

- -

RESEARCH

Research to Explore Conduct research on an aspect of the text you find interesting. For example, you may want to learn about the Court of Oyer and Terminer, established to try and convict Salem witches.

Close Read the Text

Reread paragraphs 334–339. Mark Cheever's answers to the question "What signifies a poppet?" What do his replies indicate about his knowledge of the significance of the poppet?

ANNOTATE QUESTION **Close Read** CONCLUDE

THE CRUCIBLE, ACT II

Analyze the Text

CITE TEXTUAL EVIDENCE to support your answers.

📓 **Notebook** Respond to these questions.

1. (a) **Interpret** How does news of the arrest of Rebecca Nurse affect the Proctors? (b) **Connect** What does this news suggest about Abigail Williams's changing status in Salem? Explain.

2. **Evaluate** Is Hale a good person? Why, or why not?

3. **Infer** Did Mary Warren know how the poppet she gave Elizabeth would be used? Explain.

4. **Predict** What does the dialogue of Cheever and Herrick suggest will happen to Elizabeth? What chance does she have to prove her innocence?

LANGUAGE DEVELOPMENT

Concept Vocabulary

| condemnation | magistrates | proceedings |

Why These Words? The three concept vocabulary words are all related to courts of law. What other words in Act II relate to this concept?

Practice

📓 **Notebook** Write a paragraph about a court case, real or imaginary, that uses all three concept vocabulary words. Make sure the context of the paragraph demonstrates each word's meaning.

Word Study

📓 **Notebook** **Technical Words** Most professions have specialized vocabulary—words that are particular to the field, or that have specific meanings when used in that context. In *The Crucible,* Arthur Miller uses legal terminology, such as *magistrates* and *proceedings*. *Magistrates* applies only to the field of law. However, *proceedings,* when used without the final *s,* has a general meaning in everyday speech. It is a form of the verb *proceed,* meaning "continue a course of action."

1. Find two more words in Act II that are examples of legal terminology. Write those words and their definitions.

2. Use a legal dictionary to locate three other words used in the field of law. Write those definitions. If any of the terms also have meanings in general speech, write those definitions as well.

 WORD NETWORK

Add words related to fear from the text to your Word Network.

⊞ STANDARDS

Language
• Consult general and specialized reference materials, both print and digital, to find the pronunciation of a word or determine or clarify its precise meaning, its part of speech, its etymology, or its standard usage.
• Acquire and use accurately general academic and domain-specific words and phrases, sufficient for reading, writing, speaking, and listening at the college and career readiness level; demonstrate independence in gathering vocabulary knowledge when considering a word or phrase important to comprehension or expression.

THE CRUCIBLE, ACT II

Analyze Craft and Structure

Literary Elements in Drama All narrative writing is driven by **conflict,** or a struggle between opposing forces. The conflict is introduced, developed, and resolved through the **plot,** or the story's sequence of related events. The plot unfolds over a series of stages, often referred to as the "dramatic arc." These stages include the rising action, climax, falling action, and resolution. There are two broad categories of conflict that are explored in literature. In a complex narrative like this play, there are often numerous conflicts, and most characters experience both types:

- **External conflict** occurs between a character and an outside force, such as another person, society as a whole, nature, or even fate.
- **Internal conflict** occurs within the mind of a character who is torn between conflicting values or desires.

In the rising action of a play, the central conflicts are introduced and begin to build. These conflicts then intensify, and they often lead to other conflicts. It is important to note that characters' internal conflicts can be just as crucial to the plot as the external conflicts.

Practice

CITE TEXTUAL EVIDENCE
to support your answers.

Answer these questions.

1. (a) What external conflict confronts the people who are charged with witchcraft? (b) Describe the internal conflict that the accused face.

2. (a) What conflicts do Elizabeth and John Proctor struggle with in their marriage? (b) Which of these conflicts are internal and which are external? Explain.

3. Proctor knows that Abigail Williams is a fraud. What conflicts cause him to hesitate about revealing this knowledge?

4. What profound conflict does Proctor note when he confronts Hale with these words?
"I'll tell you what's walking Salem—vengeance is walking Salem. We are what we always were …but now the little crazy children are jangling the keys of the kingdom …"

STANDARDS
Reading Literature
• Analyze the impact of the author's choices regarding how to develop and relate elements of a story or drama.
• Analyze how an author's choices concerning how to structure specific parts of a text contribute to its overall structure and meaning as well as its aesthetic impact.

Speaking and Listening

Assignment

Participate in a **whole-class discussion** about whether Mary Warren will defend or condemn Elizabeth Proctor in court. Refresh your memory by reviewing Act II. Then, follow these steps to prepare for the discussion.

1. **Consider the Situation** Review your notes from Act II. Jot down your thoughts about the situation in Salem on the evening of Elizabeth's arrest. Think about how these circumstances might affect Mary.

2. **Analyze Mary Warren's Character** Scan Acts I and II to find details about Mary's character. Use the chart to note reasons she may lie in court and reasons she may tell the truth. For each reason you list, jot down reminders of textual evidence you might refer to during the discussion.

REASONS MARY MAY LIE IN COURT	REASONS MARY MAY TELL THE TRUTH

3. **Prepare for the Discussion** Review your notes. Decide which is stronger—the evidence that suggests Mary will tell the truth or the evidence that suggests she will lie. Make a prediction as to what she will do and why.

4. **Participate in the Discussion** During the discussion, listen carefully to your classmates. Remember you can change your viewpoint of Mary when presented with evidence you had not previously considered. Use the evaluation guide to consider the quality of the discussion.

EVALUATION GUIDE

Rate each statement on a scale of 1 (not demonstrated) to 5 (demonstrated).

☐ Students presented a clear prediction about Mary Warren.

☐ Students supported predictions with evidence from Acts I and II.

☐ Students spoke clearly and expressively.

☐ Students who were not speaking listened respectfully and responded with relevant information.

✎ EVIDENCE LOG

Before moving on to Act III, go to your Evidence Log and record what you learned from Act II of *The Crucible.*

▦ STANDARDS

Speaking and Listening
Come to discussions prepared, having read and researched material under study; explicitly draw on that preparation by referring to evidence from texts and other research on the topic or issue to stimulate a thoughtful, well-reasoned exchange of ideas.

Playwright

Arthur Miller

The Crucible, Act III

Concept Vocabulary

You will encounter the following words as you read Act III of *The Crucible*. Before reading, note how familiar you are with each word. Then, rank the words in order from most familiar (1) to least familiar (3).

WORD	YOUR RANKING
remorseless	
effrontery	
callously	

After completing the first read, come back to the concept vocabulary and review your rankings. Mark changes to your original rankings as needed.

First Read DRAMA

Apply these strategies as you conduct your first read. You will have an opportunity to complete the close-read notes after your first read.

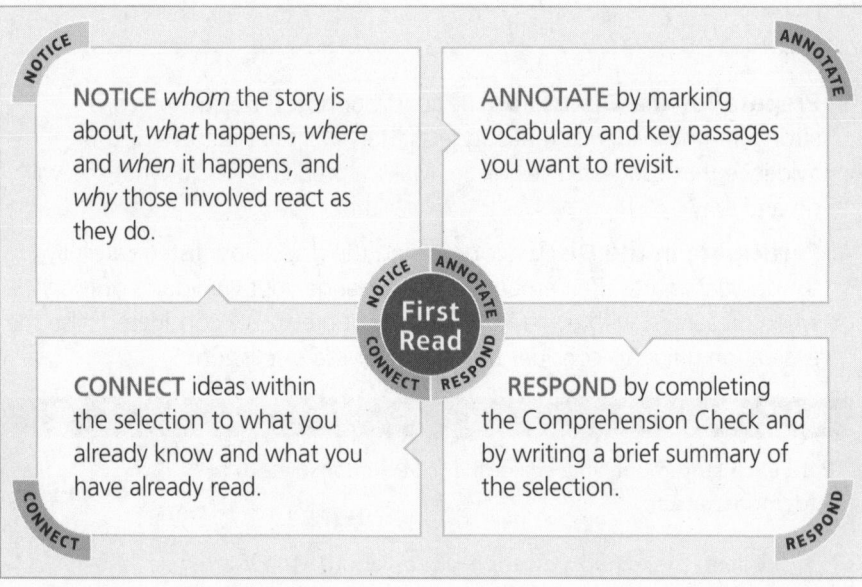

NOTICE *whom* the story is about, *what* happens, *where* and *when* it happens, and *why* those involved react as they do.

ANNOTATE by marking vocabulary and key passages you want to revisit.

CONNECT ideas within the selection to what you already know and what you have already read.

RESPOND by completing the Comprehension Check and by writing a brief summary of the selection.

First Read

≡ STANDARDS

Reading Literature
By the end of grade 11, read and comprehend literature, including stories, dramas, and poems, in the grades 11–CCR text complexity band proficiently, with scaffolding as needed at the high end of the range.

The **Crucible**
Act III

Arthur Miller

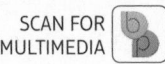

SCAN FOR
MULTIMEDIA

REVIEW AND ANTICIPATE

Act II ends as Elizabeth Proctor is accused of witchcraft and carted off to jail as a result of the scheming of Abigail Williams. John Proctor demands that Mary Warren tell the court the truth; Mary, though aware of Abigail's ploys, is terrified of exposing her. Find out how Mary handles this tricky and dangerous situation as you continue reading.

1 *The vestry room of the Salem meeting house, now serving as the anteroom of the General Court.*

2 *As the curtain rises, the room is empty, but for sunlight pouring through two high windows in the back wall. The room is solemn, even forbidding. Heavy beams jut out, boards of random widths make up the walls. At the right are two doors leading into the meeting house proper, where the court is being held. At the left another door leads outside.*

3 *There is a plain bench at the left, and another at the right. In the center a rather long meeting table, with stools and a considerable armchair snugged up to it.*

4 *Through the partitioning wall at the right we hear a prosecutor's voice,* JUDGE HATHORNE'S *, asking a question; then a woman's voice,* MARTHA COREY'S, *replying.*

NOTES

5 **Hathorne's Voice:** Now, Martha Corey, there is abundant evidence in our hands to show that you have given yourself to the reading of fortunes. Do you deny it?

6 **Martha Corey's Voice:** I am innocent to a witch. I know not what a witch is.

7 **Hathorne's Voice:** How do you know, then, that you are not a witch?

8 **Martha Corey's Voice:** If I were, I would know it.

9 **Hathorne's Voice:** Why do you hurt these children?

10 **Martha Corey's Voice:** I do not hurt them. I scorn it!

11 **Giles's Voice,** *roaring*: I have evidence for the court!

12 *Voices of townspeople rise in excitement.*

13 **Danforth's Voice:** You will keep your seat!

14 **Giles's Voice:** Thomas Putnam is reaching out for land!

15 **Danforth's Voice:** Remove that man, Marshal!

16 **Giles's Voice:** You're hearing lies, lies!

17 *A roaring goes up from the people.*

18 **Hathorne's Voice:** Arrest him, excellency!

19 **Giles's Voice:** I have evidence. Why will you not hear my evidence?

20 *The door opens and* GILES *is half carried into the vestry room by* HERRICK.

21 **Giles:** Hands off, damn you, let me go!

22 **Herrick:** Giles, Giles!

23 **Giles:** Out of my way, Herrick! I bring evidence—

24 **Herrick:** You cannot go in there, Giles; it's a court!

25 *Enter* HALE *from the court.*

26 **Hale:** Pray be calm a moment.

27 **Giles:** You, Mr. Hale, go in there and demand I speak.

28 **Hale:** A moment, sir, a moment.

29 **Giles:** They'll be hangin' my wife!

remorseless (re MAWRS lihs) *adj.* relentless; cruel

30 JUDGE HATHORNE *enters. He is in his sixties, a bitter,* **remorseless** *Salem judge.*

31 **Hathorne:** How do you dare come roarin' into this court! Are you gone daft, Corey?

32 **Giles:** You're not a Boston judge yet, Hathorne. You'll not call me daft!

33 *Enter* DEPUTY GOVERNOR DANFORTH *and, behind him,* EZEKIEL CHEEVER *and* PARRIS. *On his appearance, silence falls.* DANFORTH *is a grave man in his sixties, of some humor and sophistication that does not, however,*

interfere with an exact loyalty to his position and his cause. He comes down to GILES, *who awaits his wrath.*

34 **Danforth,** *looking directly at* GILES: Who is this man?

35 **Parris:** Giles Corey, sir, and a more contentious—

36 **Giles,** *to* PARRIS: I am asked the question, and I am old enough to answer it! *To* DANFORTH, *who impresses him and to whom he smiles through his strain*: My name is Corey, sir, Giles Corey. I have six hundred acres, and timber in addition. It is my wife you be condemning now. *He indicates the courtroom.*

37 **Danforth:** And how do you imagine to help her cause with such contemptuous riot? Now be gone. Your old age alone keeps you out of jail for this.

38 **Giles,** *beginning to plead*: They be tellin' lies about my wife, sir, I—

39 **Danforth:** Do you take it upon yourself to determine what this court shall believe and what it shall set aside?

40 **Giles:** Your Excellency, we mean no disrespect for—

41 **Danforth:** Disrespect indeed! It is disruption, Mister. This is the highest court of the supreme government of this province, do you know it?

42 **Giles,** *beginning to weep*: Your Excellency, I only said she were readin' books, sir, and they come and take her out of my house for—

43 **Danforth,** *mystified*: Books! What books?

44 **Giles,** *through helpless sobs*: It is my third wife, sir: I never had no wife that be so taken with books, and I thought to find the cause of it, d'y'see, but it were no witch I blamed her for. *He is openly weeping.* I have broke charity with the woman, I have broke charity with her. *He covers his face, ashamed.* DANFORTH *is respectfully silent.*

45 **Hale:** Excellency, he claims hard evidence for his wife's defense. I think that in all justice you must—

46 **Danforth:** Then let him submit his evidence in proper affidavit.[1] You are certainly aware of our procedure here, Mr. Hale. *To* HERRICK: Clear this room.

47 **Herrick:** Come now, Giles. *He gently pushes* COREY *out.*

48 **Francis:** We are desperate, sir; we come here three days now and cannot be heard.

49 **Danforth:** Who is this man?

50 **Francis:** Francis Nurse, Your Excellency.

51 **Hale:** His wife's Rebecca that were condemned this morning.

CLOSE READ

ANNOTATE: In paragraphs 42–46, mark examples of nonstandard English.

QUESTION: Why does Miller use this type of language here?

CONCLUDE: What is the effect of this language, particularly on the audience's understanding of Giles Corey?

1. **affidavit** (af uh DAY viht) *n.* written statement made under oath.

52 **Danforth:** Indeed! I am amazed to find you in such uproar. I have only good report of your character, Mr. Nurse.

53 **Hathorne:** I think they must both be arrested in contempt, sir.

54 **Danforth,** *to* FRANCIS: Let you write your plea, and in due time I will—

55 **Francis:** Excellency, we have proof for your eyes: God forbid you shut them to it. The girls, sir, the girls are frauds.

56 **Danforth:** What's that?

57 **Francis:** We have proof of it, sir. They are all deceiving you.

58 DANFORTH *is shocked, but studying* FRANCIS.

59 **Hathorne:** This is contempt, sir, contempt!

60 **Danforth:** Peace, Judge Hathorne. Do you know who I am, Mr. Nurse?

61 **Francis:** I surely do, sir, and I think you must be a wise judge to be what you are.

62 **Danforth:** And do you know that near to four hundred are in the jails from Marblehead to Lynn, and upon my signature?

63 **Francis:** I—

64 **Danforth:** And seventy-two condemned to hang by that signature?

65 **Francis:** Excellency, I never thought to say it to such a weighty judge, but you are deceived.

66 *Enter* GILES COREY *from left. All tum to see as he beckons in* MARY WARREN *with* PROCTOR. MARY *is keeping her eyes to the ground;* PROCTOR *has her elbow as though she were near collapse.*

67 **Parris,** *on seeing her, in shock*: Mary Warren! *He goes directly to bend close to her face.* What are you about here?

68 **Proctor,** *pressing* PARRIS *away from her with a gentle but firm motion of protectiveness*: She would speak with the Deputy Governor.

69 **Danforth,** *shocked by this, turns to* HERRICK: Did you not tell me Mary Warren were sick in bed?

70 **Herrick:** She were, Your Honor. When I go to fetch her to the court last week, she said she were sick.

71 **Giles:** She has been strivin' with her soul all week. Your Honor; she comes now to tell the truth of this to you.

72 **Danforth:** Who is this?

73 **Proctor:** John Proctor, sir. Elizabeth Proctor is my wife.

74 **Parris:** Beware this man, Your Excellency, this man is mischief.

75 **Hale,** *excitedly*: I think you must hear the girl, sir, she—

76 **Danforth,** *who has become very interested in* MARY WARREN *and only raises a hand toward* HALE: Peace. What would you tell us, Mary Warren?

77 Proctor *looks at her, but she cannot speak.*

78 **Proctor:** She never saw no spirits, sir.

79 **Danforth,** *with great alarm and surprise, to* MARY: Never saw no spirits!

80 **Giles,** *eagerly:* Never.

81 **Proctor,** *reaching into his jacket:* She has signed a deposition, sir—

82 **Danforth,** *instantly:* No, no. I accept no depositions. *He is rapidly calculating this; he turns from her to* PROCTOR. Tell me, Mr. Proctor, have you given out this story in the village?

83 **Proctor:** We have not.

84 **Parris:** They've come to overthrow the court, sir! This man is—

85 **Danforth:** I pray you, Mr. Parris. Do you know, Mr. Proctor, that the entire contention of the state in these trials is that the voice of Heaven is speaking through the children?

86 **Proctor:** I know that, sir.

87 **Danforth,** *thinks, staring at* PROCTOR, *then turns to* MARY WARREN: And you, Mary Warren, how come you to cry out people for sending their spirits, against you?

88 **Mary Warren:** It were pretense, sir.

89 **Danforth:** I cannot hear you.

90 **Proctor:** It were pretense, she says.

91 **Danforth:** Ah? And the other girls? Susanna Walcott, and—the others? They are also pretending?

92 **Mary Warren:** Aye, sir.

93 **Danforth,** *wide-eyed:* Indeed. *Pause. He is baffled by this. He turns to study* PROCTOR'*s face.*

94 **Parris,** *in a sweat:* Excellency, you surely cannot think to let so vile a lie be spread in open court!

95 **Danforth:** Indeed not, but it strike hard upon me that she will dare come here with such a tale. Now, Mr. Proctor, before I decide whether I shall hear you or not, it is my duty to tell you this. We burn a hot fire here; it melts down all concealment.

96 **Proctor:** I know that, sir.

97 **Danforth:** Let me continue. I understand well, a husband's tenderness may drive him to extravagance in defense of a wife. Are you certain in your conscience, Mister, that your evidence is the truth?

98 **Proctor:** It is. And you will surely know it.

99 **Danforth:** And you thought to declare this revelation in the open court before the public?

100 **Proctor:** I thought I would, aye—with your permission.

101 **Danforth,** *his eyes narrowing*: Now, sir, what is your purpose in so doing?

102 **Proctor:** Why, I—I would free my wife, sir.

103 **Danforth:** There lurks nowhere in your heart, nor hidden in your spirit, any desire to undermine this court?

104 **Proctor,** *with the faintest faltering*: Why, no, sir.

105 **Cheever,** *clears his throat, awakening*: I—Your Excellency.

106 **Danforth:** Mr. Cheever.

107 **Cheever:** I think it be my duty, sir—*Kindly, to* PROCTOR: You'll not deny it, John. *To* DANFORTH: When we come to take his wife, he damned the court and ripped your warrant.

108 **Parris:** Now you have it!

109 **Danforth:** He did that, Mr. Hale?

110 **Hale,** *takes a breath*: Aye, he did.

111 **Proctor:** It were a temper, sir. I knew not what I did.

112 **Danforth,** *studying him*: Mr. Proctor.

113 **Proctor:** Aye, sir.

114 **Danforth,** *straight into his eyes*: Have you ever seen the Devil?

115 **Proctor:** No, sir.

116 **Danforth:** You are in all respects a Gospel Christian?

117 **Proctor:** I am, sir.

118 **Parris:** Such a Christian that will not come to church but once in a month!

119 **Danforth,** *restrained—he is curious*: Not come to church?

120 **Proctor:** I—I have no love for Mr. Parris. It is no secret. But God I surely love.

121 **Cheever:** He plow on Sunday, sir.

122 **Danforth:** Plow on Sunday!

123 **Cheever,** *apologetically*: I think it be evidence, John. I am an official of the court, I cannot keep it.

124 **Proctor:** I—I have once or twice plowed on Sunday. I have three children, sir, and until last year my land give little.

125 **Giles:** You'll find other Christians that do plow on Sunday if the truth be known.

126 **Hale:** Your Honor, I cannot think you may judge the man on such evidence.

127 **Danforth:** I judge nothing. *Pause. He keeps watching* PROCTOR, *who tries to meet his gaze.* I tell you straight, Mister—I have seen marvels in this court. I have seen people choked before my eyes by spirits; I have seen them stuck by pins and slashed by daggers. I have until this moment not the slightest reason to suspect that the children may be deceiving me. Do you understand my meaning?

128 **Proctor:** Excellency, does it not strike upon you that so many of these women have lived so long with such upright reputation, and—

129 **Parris:** Do you read the Gospel, Mr. Proctor?

130 **Proctor:** I read the Gospel.

131 **Parris:** I think not, or you should surely know that Cain were an upright man, and yet he did kill Abel.[2]

132 **Proctor:** Aye, God tells us that. *To* DANFORTH: But who tells us Rebecca Nurse murdered seven babies by sending out her spirit on them? It is the children only, and this one will swear she lied to you.

133 DANFORTH *considers, then beckons* HATHORNE *to him.* HATHORNE *leans in, and he speaks in his ear.* HATHORNE *nods.*

134 **Hathorne:** Aye, she's the one.

135 **Danforth:** Mr. Proctor, this morning, your wife send me a claim in which she states that she is pregnant now.

136 **Proctor:** My wife pregnant!

137 **Danforth:** There be no sign of it—we have examined her body.

138 **Proctor:** But if she say she is pregnant, then she must be! That woman will never lie, Mr. Danforth.

139 **Danforth:** She will not?

140 **Proctor:** Never, sir, never.

141 **Danforth:** We have thought it too convenient to be credited. However, if I should tell you now that I will let her be kept another month; and if she begin to show her natural signs, you shall have her living yet another year until she is delivered—what say you to that? JOHN PROCTOR *is struck silent.* Come now. You say your only purpose is to save your wife. Good, then, she is saved at least this year, and a year is long. What say you, sir? It is done now. *In conflict,* PROCTOR *glances at* FRANCIS *and* GILES. Will you drop this charge?

142 **Proctor:** I—I think I cannot.

143 **Danforth,** *now an almost imperceptible hardness in his voice*: Then your purpose is somewhat larger.

144 **Parris:** He's come to overthrow this court, Your Honor!

145 **Proctor:** These are my friends. Their wives are also accused—

2. **Cain . . . Abel** In the Bible, Cain, the oldest son of Adam and Eve, killed his brother Abel.

CLOSE READ

ANNOTATE: In the stage directions in paragraph 143, mark the adverb and the adjective in the description of Danforth's voice.

QUESTION: Why does Miller use these modifiers?

CONCLUDE: How do these modifiers add to the portrayal of Danforth's character?

146 **Danforth,** *with a sudden briskness of manner*: I judge you not, sir. I am ready to hear your evidence.

147 **Proctor:** I come not to hurt the court: I only—

148 **Danforth,** *cutting him off*: Marshal, go into the court and bid Judge Stoughton and Judge Sewall declare recess for one hour. And let them go to the tavern, if they will. All witnesses and prisoners are to be kept in the building.

149 **Herrick:** Aye, sir. *Very deferentially*: If I may say it, sir. I know this man all my life. It is a good man, sir.

150 **Danforth—***it is the reflection on himself he resents*: I am sure of it, Marshal. HERRICK *nods, then goes out*. Now, what deposition do you have for us, Mr. Proctor? And I beg you be clear, open as the sky, and honest.

151 **Proctor**, *as he takes out several papers*: I am no lawyer, so I'll—

152 **Danforth:** The pure in heart need no lawyers. Proceed as you will.

153 **Proctor,** *handing* DANFORTH *a paper*: Will you read this first, sir? It's a sort of testament. The people signing it declare their good opinion of Rebecca, and my wife, and Martha Corey.

154 DANFORTH *looks down at the paper.*

155 **Parris,** *to enlist* DANFORTH's *sarcasm*: Their good opinion! But DANFORTH *goes on reading, and* PROCTOR *is heartened.*

156 **Proctor:** These are all landholding farmers, members of the church. *Delicately, trying to point out a paragraph*: If you'll notice, sir—they've known the women many years and never saw no sign they had dealings with the Devil.

157 PARRIS *nervously moves over and reads over* DANFORTH's *shoulder.*

158 **Danforth,** *glancing down a long list*: How many names are here?

159 **Francis:** Ninety-one, Your Excellency.

160 **Parris,** *sweating*: These people should be summoned. DANFORTH *looks up at him questioningly*. For questioning.

161 **Francis,** *trembling with anger*: Mr. Danforth, I gave them all my word no harm would come to them for signing this.

162 **Parris:** This is a clear attack upon the court!

163 **Hale,** *to* PARRIS, *trying to contain himself*: Is every defense an attack upon the court? Can no one—?

164 **Parris:** All innocent and Christian people are happy for the courts in Salem! These people are gloomy for it. *To* DANFORTH *directly*: And I think you will want to know, from each and every one of them, what discontents them with you!

165 **Hathorne:** I think they ought to be examined, sir.

166 **Danforth:** It is not necessarily an attack, I think. Yet—

167 **Francis:** These are all covenanted Christians, sir.

168 **Danforth:** Then I am sure they may have nothing to fear. *Hands* CHEEVER *the paper*. Mr. Cheever, have warrants drawn for all of these—arrest for examination. *To* PROCTOR: Now, Mister, what other information do you have for us? FRANCIS *is still standing, horrified*. You may sit, Mr. Nurse.

169 **Francis:** I have brought trouble on these people; I have—

170 **Danforth:** No, old man, you have not hurt these people if they are of good conscience. But you must understand, sir, that a person is either with this court or he must be counted against it, there be no road between. This is a sharp time, now, a precise time—we live no longer in the dusky afternoon when evil mixed itself with good and befuddled the world. Now, by God's grace, the shining sun is up, and them that fear not light will surely praise it. I hope you will be one of those. MARY WARREN *suddenly sobs*. She's not hearty, I see.

171 **Proctor:** No, she's not, sir. *To* MARY, *bending to her, holding her hand, quietly*: Now remember what the angel Raphael said to the boy Tobias.[3] Remember it.

172 **Mary Warren,** *hardly audible*: Aye.

173 **Proctor:** "Do that which is good, and no harm shall come to thee."

174 **Mary Warren:** Aye.

175 **Danforth:** Come, man, we wait you.

176 MARSHAL HERRICK *returns, and takes his post at the door.*

177 **Giles:** John, my deposition, give him mine.

178 **Proctor:** Aye. *He hands* DANFORTH *another paper*. This is Mr. Corey's deposition.

179 **Danforth:** Oh? *He looks down at it. Now* HATHORNE *comes behind him and reads with him.*

180 **Hathorne,** *suspiciously*: What lawyer drew this, Corey?

181 **Giles:** You know I never hired a lawyer in my life, Hathorne.

182 **Danforth,** *finishing the reading*: It is very well phrased. My compliments. Mr. Parris, if Mr. Putnam is in the court, will you bring him in? HATHORNE *takes the deposition, and walks to the window with it*. PARRIS *goes into the court*. You have no legal training, Mr. Corey?

183 **Giles,** *very pleased*: I have the best, sir—I am thirty-three time in court in my life. And always plaintiff, too.

184 **Danforth:** Oh, then you're much put-upon.

185 **Giles:** I am never put-upon: I know my rights, sir, and I will have them. You know, your father tried a case of mine—might be thirty-five year ago, I think.

3. **Raphael . . . Tobias** In the Bible, Tobias is guided by the archangel Raphael to save two people who have prayed to die. One of the two is Tobias's father, Tobit, who is despondent because he has lost his sight. The other is Sara, a woman who is afflicted by a demon that has killed each of her seven husbands on their wedding days. With Raphael's aid, Tobias exorcises the devil from Sara and cures his father of blindness.

186 **Danforth:** Indeed.

187 **Giles:** He never spoke to you of it?

188 **Danforth:** No. I cannot recall it.

189 **Giles:** That's strange, he gave me nine pound damages. He were a fair judge, your father. Y'see, I had a white mare that time, and this fellow come to borrow the mare—*Enter* PARRIS *with* THOMAS PUTNAM. *When he sees* PUTNAM, GILES'S *ease goes; he is hard.* Aye, there he is.

190 **Danforth:** Mr. Putnam, I have here an accusation by Mr. Corey against you. He states that you coldly prompted your daughter to cry witchery upon George Jacobs that is now in jail.

191 **Putnam:** It is a lie.

192 **Danforth,** *turning to* GILES: Mr. Putnam states your charge is a lie. What say you to that?

193 **Giles,** *furious, his fists clenched*: A fart on Thomas Putnam, that is what I say to that!

194 **Danforth:** What proof do you submit for your charge, sir?

195 **Giles:** My proof is there! *Pointing to the paper.* If Jacobs hangs for a witch he forfeit up his property—that's law! And there is none but Putnam with the coin to buy so great a piece. This man is killing his neighbors for their land!

196 **Danforth:** But proof, sir, proof.

197 **Giles,** *pointing at his deposition*: The proof is there! I have it from an honest man who heard Putnam say it! The day his daughter cried out on Jacobs, he said she'd given him a fair gift of land.

198 **Hathorne:** And the name of this man?

199 **Giles,** *taken aback*: What name?

200 **Hathorne:** The man that give you this information.

201 **Giles,** *hesitates, then*: Why, I—I cannot give you his name.

202 **Hathorne:** And why not?

203 **Giles,** *hesitates, then bursts out*: You know well why not! He'll lay in jail if I give his name!

204 **Hathorne:** This is contempt of the court, Mr. Danforth!

205 **Danforth,** *to avoid that*: You will surely tell us the name.

206 **Giles:** I will not give you no name. I mentioned my wife's name once and I'll burn in hell long enough for that. I stand mute.

207 **Danforth:** In that case, I have no choice but to arrest you for contempt of this court, do you know that?

208 **Giles:** This is a hearing; you cannot clap me for contempt of a hearing.

209 **Danforth:** Oh, it is a proper lawyer! Do you wish me to declare the court in full session here? Or will you give me good reply?

210 **Giles,** *faltering*: I cannot give you no name, sir, I cannot.

211 **Danforth:** You are a foolish old man. Mr. Cheever, begin the record. The court is now in session. I ask you, Mr. Corey—

212 **Proctor,** *breaking in*: Your Honor—he has the story in confidence, sir, and he—

213 **Parris:** The Devil lives on such confidences! *To* DANFORTH: Without confidences there could be no conspiracy, Your Honor!

214 **Hathorne:** I think it must be broken, sir.

215 **Danforth,** *to* GILES: Old man, if your informant tells the truth let him come here openly like a decent man. But if he hide in anonymity I must know why. Now sir, the government and central church demand of you the name of him who reported Mr. Thomas Putnam a common murderer.

216 **Hale:** Excellency—

217 **Danforth:** Mr. Hale.

218 **Hale:** We cannot blink it more. There is a prodigious fear of this court in the country—

219 **Danforth:** Then there is a prodigious guilt in the country. Are you afraid to be questioned here?

220 **Hale:** I may only fear the Lord, sir, but there is fear in the country nevertheless.

221 **Danforth,** *angered now*: Reproach me not with the fear in the country; there is fear in the country because there is a moving plot to topple Christ in the country!

222 **Hale:** But it does not follow that everyone accused is part of it.

223 **Danforth:** No uncorrupted man may fear this court. Mr. Hale! None! *To* GILES: You are under arrest in contempt of this court. Now sit you down and take counsel with yourself, or you will be set in the jail until you decide to answer all questions.

224 GILES COREY *makes a rush for* PUTNAM. PROCTOR *lunges and holds him.*

225 **Proctor:** No, Giles!

226 **Giles,** *over* PROCTOR's *shoulder at* PUTNAM: I'll cut your throat, Putnam. I'll kill you yet!

227 **Proctor,** *forcing him into a chair*: Peace, Giles, peace. *Releasing him.* We'll prove ourselves. Now we will. *He starts to turn to* DANFORTH.

228 **Giles:** Say nothin' more, John. *Pointing at* DANFORTH: He's only playin' you! He means to hang us all!

229 MARY WARREN *bursts into sobs.*

CLOSE READ

ANNOTATE: In paragraphs 218–222, mark references to fear.

QUESTION: Why does Miller repeat the word *fear* so many times?

CONCLUDE: How do Hale's and Danforth's reactions to this word capture their central disagreement?

effrontery (ih FRUHN tuh ree)
n. shameless boldness

230 **Danforth:** This is a court of law, Mister. I'll have no **effrontery** here!

231 **Proctor:** Forgive him, sir, for his old age. Peace, Giles, we'll prove it all now. *He lifts up* MARY's *chin.* You cannot weep, Mary. Remember the angel, what he say to the boy. Hold to it, now; there is your rock. MARY *quiets. He takes out a paper, and turns to* DANFORTH. This is Mary Warren's deposition. I—I would ask you remember, sir, while you read it, that until two week ago she were no different than the other children are today. *He is speaking reasonably, restraining all his fears, his anger, his anxiety.* You saw her scream, she howled, she swore familiar spirits choked her; she even testified that Satan, in the form of women now in jail, tried to win her soul away, and then when she refused—

232 **Danforth:** We know all this.

233 **Proctor:** Aye, sir. She swears now that she never saw Satan; nor any spirit, vague or clear, that Satan may have sent to hurt her. And she declares her friends are lying now.

234 PROCTOR *starts to hand* DANFORTH *the deposition, and* HALE *comes up to* DANFORTH *in a trembling state.*

235 **Hale:** Excellency, a moment. I think this goes to the heart of the matter.

236 **Danforth,** *with deep misgivings*: It surely does.

237 **Hale:** I cannot say he is an honest man; I know him little. But in all justice, sir, a claim so weighty cannot be argued by a farmer. In God's name, sir, stop here; send him home and let him come again with a lawyer—

238 **Danforth,** *patiently*: Now look you, Mr. Hale—

239 **Hale:** Excellency, I have signed seventy-two death warrants; I am a minister of the Lord, and I dare not take a life without there be a proof so immaculate no slightest qualm of conscience may doubt it.

240 **Danforth:** Mr. Hale, you surely do not doubt my justice.

241 **Hale:** I have this morning signed away the soul of Rebecca Nurse, Your Honor. I'll not conceal it, my hand shakes yet as with a wound! I pray you, sir, *this* argument let lawyers present to you.

242 **Danforth:** Mr. Hale, believe me: for a man of such terrible learning you are most bewildered—I hope you will forgive me. I have been thirty-two year at the bar, sir, and I should be confounded were I called upon to defend these people. Let you consider, now—*To* PROCTOR *and the others*: And I bid you all do likewise. In an ordinary crime, how does one defend the accused? One calls up witnesses to prove his innocence. But

witchcraft is *ipso facto*,[4] on its face and by its nature, an invisible crime, is it not? Therefore, who may possibly be witness to it? The witch and the victim. None other. Now we cannot hope the witch will accuse herself: granted? Therefore, we must rely upon her victims—and they do testify, the children certainly do testify. As for the witches, none will deny that we are most eager for all their confessions. Therefore, what is left for a lawyer to bring out? I think I have made my point. Have I not?

243 **Hale:** But this child claims the girls are not truthful, and if they are not—

244 **Danforth:** That is precisely what I am about to consider, sir. What more may you ask of me? Unless you doubt my probity?[5]

245 **Hale,** *defeated*: I surely do not, sir. Let you consider it, then.

246 **Danforth:** And let you put your heart to rest. Her deposition, Mr. Proctor.

247 PROCTOR *hands it to him.* HATHORNE *rises, goes beside* DANFORTH *and starts reading.* PARRIS *comes to his other side.* DANFORTH *looks at* JOHN PROCTOR, *then proceeds to read.* HALE *gets up, finds position near the judge, reads too.* PROCTOR *glances at* GILES. FRANCIS *prays silently, hands pressed together.* CHEEVER *waits placidly, the sublime official, dutiful.* MARY WARREN *sobs once.* JOHN PROCTOR *touches her head reassuringly. Presently* DANFORTH *lifts his eyes, stands up, takes out a kerchief and blows his nose. The others stand aside as he moves in thought toward the window.*

248 **Parris,** *hardly able to contain his anger and fear*: I should like to question—

249 **Danforth**—*his first real outburst, in which his contempt for* PARRIS *is clear*: Mr. Parris, I bid you be silent! *He stands in silence, looking out the window. Now, having established that he will set the gait*: Mr. Cheever, will you go into the court and bring the children here?* CHEEVER *gets up and goes out upstage.* DANFORTH *now turns to* MARY. Mary Warren, how came you to this turnabout? Has Mr. Proctor threatened you for this deposition?

250 **Mary Warren:** No, sir.

251 **Danforth:** Has he ever threatened you?

252 **Mary Warren,** *weaker*: No, sir.

253 **Danforth,** *sensing a weakening*: Has he threatened you?

254 **Mary Warren:** No, sir.

255 **Danforth:** Then you tell me that you sat in my court, **callously** lying, when you knew that people would hang by your evidence? *She does not answer.* Answer me!

256 **Mary Warren,** *almost inaudibly*: I did, sir.

---

4. *ipso facto* (ihp soh FAK toh) "by that very fact"; "therefore" (Latin).

5. probity (PROH buh tee) *n.* complete honesty; integrity.

callously (KAL uhs lee) *adv.* without sympathy; coldly

257 **Danforth:** How were you instructed in your life? Do you not know that God damns all liars? *She cannot speak.* Or is it now that you lie?

258 **Mary Warren:** No, sir—I am with God now.

259 **Danforth:** You are with God now.

260 **Mary Warren:** Aye, sir.

261 **Danforth,** *containing himself:* I will tell you this—you are either lying now, or you were lying in the court, and in either case you have committed perjury and you will go to jail for it. You cannot lightly say you lied, Mary. Do you know that?

262 **Mary Warren:** I cannot lie no more. I am with God. I am with God.

263 *But she breaks into sobs at the thought of it, and the right door opens, and enter* SUSANNA WALCOTT, MERCY LEWIS, BETTY PARRIS, *and finally* ABIGAIL. CHEEVER *comes to* DANFORTH.

264 **Cheever:** Ruth Putnam's not in the court, sir, nor the other children.

265 **Danforth:** These will be sufficient. Sit you down, children. *Silently they sit.* Your friend, Mary Warren, has given us a deposition. In which she swears that she never saw familiar spirits, apparitions, nor any manifest of the Devil. She claims as well that none of you have seen these things either. *Slight pause.* Now, children, this is a court of law. The law, based upon the Bible, and the Bible, writ by Almighty God, forbid the practice of witchcraft, and describe death as the penalty thereof. But likewise, children, the law and Bible damn all bearers of false witness. *Slight pause.* Now then. It does not escape me that this deposition may be devised to blind us; it may well be that Mary Warren has been conquered by Satan, who sends her here to distract our sacred purpose. If so, her neck will break for it. But if she speak true, I bid you now drop your guile and confess your pretense, for a quick confession will go easier with you. *Pause.* Abigail Williams, rise. ABIGAIL *slowly rises.* Is there any truth in this?

266 **Abigail:** No, sir.

267 **Danforth,** *thinks, glances at* MARY *then back to* ABIGAIL: Children, a very augur bit[6] will now be turned into your souls until your honesty is proved. Will either of you change your positions now, or do you force me to hard questioning?

268 **Abigail:** I have naught to change, sir. She lies.

269 **Danforth,** *to* MARY: You would still go on with this?

270 **Mary Warren,** *faintly:* Aye, sir.

6. augur (AW guhr) bit sharp point of an augur, a tool used for boring holes.

271 **Danforth,** *turning to* ABIGAIL: A poppet were discovered in Mr. Proctor's house, stabbed by a needle. Mary Warren claims that you sat beside her in the court when she made it, and that you saw her make it and witnessed how she herself stuck her needle into it for safe-keeping. What say you to that?

272 **Abigail,** *with a slight note of indignation*: It is a lie, sir.

273 **Danforth,** *after a slight pause*: While you worked for Mr. Proctor, did you see poppets in that house?

274 **Abigail:** Goody Proctor always kept poppets.

275 **Proctor:** Your Honor, my wife never kept no poppets. Mary Warren confesses it was her poppet.

276 **Cheever:** Your Excellency.

277 **Danforth:** Mr. Cheever.

278 **Cheever:** When I spoke with Goody Proctor in that house, she said she never kept no poppets. But she said she did keep poppets when she were a girl.

279 **Proctor:** She has not been a girl these fifteen years, Your Honor.

280 **Hathorne:** But a poppet will keep fifteen years, will it not?

281 **Proctor:** It will keep if it is kept, but Mary Warren swears she never saw no poppets in my house, nor anyone else.

282 **Parris:** Why could there not have been poppets hid where no one ever saw them?

283 **Proctor,** *furious*: There might also be a dragon with five legs in my house, but no one has ever seen it.

284 **Parris:** We are here, Your Honor, precisely to discover what no one has ever seen.

285 **Proctor:** Mr. Danforth, what profit this girl to turn herself about? What may Mary Warren gain but hard questioning and worse?

286 **Danforth:** You are charging Abigail Williams with a marvelous cool plot to murder, do you understand that?

287 **Proctor:** I do, sir. I believe she means to murder.

288 **Danforth,** *pointing at* ABIGAIL, *incredulously*: This child would murder your wife?

289 **Proctor:** It is not a child. Now hear me, sir. In the sight of the congregation she were twice this year put out of this meetin' house for laughter during prayer.

290 **Danforth,** *shocked, turning to* ABIGAIL: What's this? Laughter during—!

291 **Parris:** Excellency, she were under Tituba's power at that time, but she is solemn now.

292 **Giles:** Aye, now she is solemn and goes to hang people!

CLOSE READ
ANNOTATE: Mark the pronoun Proctor uses to refer to Abigail in the first sentence of paragraph 289.

QUESTION: Why does Miller have Proctor refer to Abigail in this way?

CONCLUDE: What is the effect of this use of language?

CLOSE READ

ANNOTATE: In paragraphs 297 to 304, mark the punctuation that indicates characters are not fully stating their thoughts.

QUESTION: What does this punctuation suggest is happening in the scene?

CONCLUDE: What is the effect of these abbreviated bits of dialogue?

293 **Danforth:** Quiet, man.

294 **Hathorne:** Surely it have no bearing on the question, sir. He charges contemplation of murder.

295 **Danforth:** Aye. *He studies* ABIGAIL *for a moment, then*: Continue, Mr. Proctor.

296 **Proctor:** Mary. Now tell the Governor how you danced in the woods.

297 **Parris,** *instantly*: Excellency, since I come to Salem this man is blackening my name. He—

298 **Danforth:** In a moment, sir. *To* MARY WARREN, *sternly, and surprised*. What is this dancing?

299 **Mary Warren:** I—*She glances at* ABIGAIL, *who is staring down at her remorselessly. Then, appealing to* PROCTOR: Mr. Proctor—

300 **Proctor,** *taking it right up*: Abigail leads the girls to the woods. Your Honor, and they have danced there naked—

301 **Parris:** Your Honor, this—

302 **Proctor,** *at once*: Mr. Parris discovered them himself in the dead of night! There's the "child" she is!

303 **Danforth**—*it is growing into a nightmare, and he turns, astonished, to* PARRIS: Mr. Parris—

304 **Parris:** I can only say, sir, that I never found any of them naked, and this man is—

305 **Danforth:** But you discovered them dancing in the woods? *Eyes on* PARRIS, *he points at* ABIGAIL. Abigail?

306 **Hale:** Excellency, when I first arrived from Beverly, Mr. Parris told me that.

307 **Danforth:** Do you deny it, Mr. Parris?

308 **Parris:** I do not, sir, but I never saw any of them naked.

309 **Danforth:** But she have danced?

310 **Parris,** *unwillingly*: Aye, sir.

311 **Danforth,** *as though with new eyes, looks at* ABIGAIL.

312 **Hathorne:** Excellency, will you permit me? *He points at* MARY WARREN.

313 **Danforth,** *with great worry*: Pray, proceed.

314 **Hathorne:** You say you never saw no spirits, Mary, were never threatened or afflicted by any manifest of the Devil or the Devil's agents.

315 **Mary Warren,** *very faintly*: No, sir.

316 **Hathorne,** *with a gleam of victory*: And yet, when people accused of witchery confronted you in court, you would faint, saying their spirits came out of their bodies and choked you—

317 **Mary Warren**: That were pretense, sir.

318 **Danforth**: I cannot hear you.

319 **Mary Warren**: Pretense, sir.

320 **Parris**: But you did turn cold, did you not? I myself picked you up many times, and your skin were icy. Mr. Danforth, you—

321 **Danforth**: I saw that many times.

322 **Proctor**: She only pretended to faint, Your Excellency. They're all marvelous pretenders.

323 **Hathorne**: Then can she pretend to faint now?

324 **Proctor**: Now?

325 **Parris**: Why not? Now there are no spirits attacking her, for none in this room is accused of witchcraft. So let her turn herself cold now, let her pretend she is attacked now, let her faint. *He turns to* MARY WARREN. Faint!

326 **Mary Warren**: Faint?

327 **Parris**: Aye, faint. Prove to us how you pretended in the court so many times.

328 **Mary Warren,** *looking to* PROCTOR: I—cannot faint now, sir.

329 **Proctor,** *alarmed, quietly*: Can you not pretend it?

330 **Mary Warren**: I—*She looks about as though searching for the passion to faint.* I—have no sense of it now, I—

331 **Danforth**: Why? What is lacking now?

332 **Mary Warren**: I—cannot tell, sir, I—

333 **Danforth**: Might it be that here we have no afflicting spirit loose, but in the court there were some?

334 **Mary Warren**: I never saw no spirits.

335 **Parris**: Then see no spirits now, and prove to us that you can faint by your own will, as you claim.

336 **Mary Warren,** *stares, searching for the emotion of it, and then shakes her head*: I—cannot do it.

337 **Parris**: Then you will confess, will you not? It were attacking spirits made you faint!

338 **Mary Warren**: No, sir. I—

339 **Parris**: Your Excellency, this is a trick to blind the court!

340 **Mary Warren**: It's not a trick! *She stands.* I—I used to faint because I—I thought I saw spirits.

341 **Danforth**: *Thought* you saw them!

342 **Mary Warren**: But I did not, Your Honor.

343 **Hathorne**: How could you think you saw them unless you saw them?

344 **Mary Warren:** I—I cannot tell how, but I did. I—I heard the other girls screaming, and you, Your Honor, you seemed to believe them, and I—It were only sport in the beginning, sir, but then the whole world cried spirits, spirits, and I—I promise you, Mr. Danforth, I only thought I saw them but I did not.

345 DANFORTH *peers at her.*

346 **Parris,** *smiling, but nervous because* DANFORTH *seems to be struck by* MARY WARREN'*s story*: Surely Your Excellency is not taken by this simple lie.

347 **Danforth,** *turning worriedly to* ABIGAIL: Abigail. I bid you now search your heart and tell me this—and beware of it, child, to God every soul is precious and His vengeance is terrible on them that take life without cause. Is it possible, child, that the spirits you have seen are illusion only, some deception that may cross your mind when—

348 **Abigail:** Why, this—this—is a base question, sir.

349 **Danforth:** Child, I would have you consider it—

350 **Abigail:** I have been hurt, Mr. Danforth; I have seen my blood runnin' out! I have been near to murdered every day because I done my duty pointing out the Devil's people—and this is my reward? To be mistrusted, denied, questioned like a—

351 **Danforth,** *weakening*: Child, I do not mistrust you—

352 **Abigail,** *in an open threat*: Let *you* beware, Mr. Danforth. Think you to be so mighty that the power of Hell may not turn your wits? Beware of it! There is—*Suddenly from an accusatory attitude, her face turns, looking into the air above—it is truly frightened.*

353 **Danforth,** *apprehensively*: What is it, child?

354 **Abigail,** *looking about in the air, clasping her arms about her as though cold*: I—I know not. A wind, a cold wind, has come. *Her eyes fall on* MARY WARREN.

355 **Mary Warren,** *terrified, pleading*: Abby!

356 **Mercy Lewis,** *shivering*: Your Honor, I freeze!

357 **Proctor:** They're pretending!

358 **Hathorne,** *touching* ABIGAIL'*s hand*: She is cold, Your Honor, touch her!

359 **Mercy Lewis,** *through chattering teeth*: Mary, do you send this shadow on me?

360 **Mary Warren:** Lord, save me!

361 **Susanna Walcott:** I freeze, I freeze!

362 **Abigail,** *shivering, visibly*: It is a wind, a wind!

363 **Mary Warren:** Abby, don't do that!

364 **Danforth,** *himself engaged and entered by* ABIGAIL: Mary Warren, do you witch her? I say to you, do you send your spirit out?

365 *With a hysterical cry* MARY WARREN *starts to run.* PROCTOR *catches her.*

366 **Mary Warren,** *almost collapsing*: Let me go, Mr. Proctor, I cannot, I cannot—

367 **Abigail,** *crying to Heaven*: Oh, Heavenly Father, take away this shadow!

368 *Without warning or hesitation,* PROCTOR *leaps at* ABIGAIL *and, grabbing her by the hair, pulls her to her feet. She screams in pain.* DANFORTH, *astonished, cries,* "What are you about?" *and* HATHORNE *and* PARRIS *call.* "Take your hands off her!" *and out of it all comes* PROCTOR's *roaring voice.*

369 **Proctor:** How do you call Heaven! Whore! Whore!

370 HERRICK *breaks* PROCTOR *from her.*

371 **Herrick:** John!

The girls react to a possible "bewitchment" by Mary Warren.

372 **Danforth:** Man! Man, what do you—

373 **Proctor,** *breathless and in agony:* It is a whore!

374 **Danforth,** *dumfounded:* You charge—?

375 **Abigail:** Mr. Danforth, he is lying!

376 **Proctor:** Mark her! Now she'll suck a scream to stab me with, but—

377 **Danforth:** You will prove this! This will not pass!

378 **Proctor,** *trembling, his life collapsing about him:* I have known her, sir. I have known her.

379 **Danforth:** You—you are a lecher?

380 **Francis,** *horrified:* John, you cannot say such a—

381 **Proctor:** Oh. Francis, I wish you had some evil in you that you might know me! *To* DANFORTH: A man will not cast away his good name. You surely know that.

382 **Danforth,** *dumfounded:* In—in what time? In what place?

383 **Proctor,** *his voice about to break, and his shame great:* In the proper place—where my beasts are bedded. On the last night of my joy, some eight months past. She used to serve me in my house, sir. *He has to clamp his jaw to keep from weeping.* A man may think God sleeps, but God sees everything, I know it now. I beg you, sir, I beg you—see her what she is. My wife, my dear good wife, took this girl soon after, sir, and put her out on the highroad. And being what she is, a lump of vanity, sir—*He is being overcome.* Excellency, forgive me, forgive me. *Angrily against himself, he turns away from the* GOVERNOR *for a moment. Then, as though to cry out is his only means of speech left:* She thinks to dance with me on my wife's grave! And well she might, for I thought of her softly. God help me, I lusted, and there *is* a promise in such sweat. But it is a whore's vengeance, and you must see it; I set myself entirely in your hands. I know you must see it now.

384 **Danforth,** *blanched, in horror, turning to* ABIGAIL: You deny every scrap and tittle of this?

385 **Abigail:** If I must answer that, I will leave and I will not come back again!

386 DANFORTH *seems unsteady.*

387 **Proctor:** I have made a bell of my honor! I have rung the doom of my good name—you will believe me, Mr. Danforth! My wife is innocent, except she knew a whore when she saw one!

388 **Abigail,** *stepping up to* DANFORTH: What look do you give me? DANFORTH *cannot speak.* I'll not have such looks! *She turns and starts for the door.*

389 **Danforth:** You will remain where you are! HERRICK *steps into her path. She comes up short, fire in her eyes.* Mr. Parris, go into the court and bring Goodwife Proctor out.

390 **Parris,** *objecting*: Your Honor, this is all a—

391 **Danforth,** *sharply to* PARRIS: Bring her out! And tell her not one word of what's been spoken here. And let you knock before you enter. PARRIS *goes out.* Now we shall touch the bottom of this swamp. *To* PROCTOR: Your wife, you say, is an honest woman.

392 **Proctor:** In her life, sir, she have never lied. There are them that cannot sing, and them that cannot weep—my wife cannot lie. I have paid much to learn it, sir.

393 **Danforth:** And when she put this girl out of your house, she put her out for a harlot?

394 **Proctor:** Aye, sir.

395 **Danforth:** And knew her for a harlot?

396 **Proctor:** Aye, sir, she knew her for a harlot.

397 **Danforth:** Good then. *To* ABIGAIL: And if she tell me, child, it were for harlotry, may God spread His mercy on you! *There is a knock. He calls to the door.* Hold! *To* ABIGAIL: Turn your back. Turn your back. *To* PROCTOR: Do likewise. *Both turn their backs—*ABIGAIL *with indignant slowness.* Now let neither of you turn to face Goody Proctor. No one in this room is to speak one word, or raise a gesture aye or nay. *He turns toward the door, calls*: Enter! The door opens. ELIZABETH *enters with* PARRIS. PARRIS *leaves her. She stands alone, her eyes looking for* PROCTOR. Mr. Cheever, report this testimony in all exactness. Are you ready?

398 **Cheever:** Ready, sir.

399 **Danforth:** Come here, woman. ELIZABETH *comes to him, glancing at* PROCTOR's *back.* Look at me only, not at your husband. In my eyes only.

400 **Elizabeth,** *faintly*: Good, sir.

401 **Danforth:** We are given to understand that at one time you dismissed your servant, Abigail Williams.

402 **Elizabeth:** That is true, sir.

403 **Danforth:** For what cause did you dismiss her? *Slight pause. Then* ELIZABETH *tries to glance at* PROCTOR. You will look in my eyes only and not at your husband. The answer is in your memory and you need no help to give it to me. Why did you dismiss Abigail Williams?

404 **Elizabeth,** *not knowing what to say, sensing a situation, wetting her lips to stall for time*: She—dissatisfied me. *Pause.* And my husband.

Elizabeth Proctor is brought in for questioning.

NOTES

405 **Danforth:** In what way dissatisfied you?

406 **Elizabeth:** She were—*She glances at* PROCTOR *for a cue.*

407 **Danforth:** Woman, look at me? ELIZABETH *does.* Were she slovenly? Lazy? What disturbance did she cause?

408 **Elizabeth:** Your Honor, I—in that time I were sick. And I—My husband is a good and righteous man. He is never drunk as some are, nor wastin' his time at the shovelboard, but always at his work. But in my sickness—you see, sir, I were a long time sick after my last baby, and I thought I saw my husband somewhat turning from me. And this girl—*She turns to* ABIGAIL.

409 **Danforth:** Look at me.

410 **Elizabeth:** Aye, sir. Abigail Williams—*She breaks off.*

411 **Danforth:** What of Abigail Williams?

412 **Elizabeth:** I came to think he fancied her. And so one night I lost my wits, I think, and put her out on the highroad.

413 **Danforth:** Your husband—did he indeed turn from you?

414 **Elizabeth,** *in agony*: My husband—is a goodly man, sir.

415 **Danforth:** Then he did not turn from you.

416 **Elizabeth,** *starting to glance at* PROCTOR: He—

417 **Danforth**, *reaches out and holds her face, then*: Look at me! To your own knowledge, has John Proctor ever committed the crime of lechery? *In a crisis of indecision she cannot speak.* Answer my question! Is your husband a lecher!

418 **Elizabeth,** *faintly*: No, sir.

419 **Danforth:** Remove her, Marshal.

420 **Proctor:** Elizabeth, tell the truth!

421 **Danforth:** She has spoken. Remove her!

422 **Proctor,** *crying out*: Elizabeth, I have confessed it!

423 **Elizabeth:** Oh, God! *The door closes behind her.*

424 **Proctor:** She only thought to save my name!

425 **Hale:** Excellency, it is a natural lie to tell; I beg you, stop now before another is condemned! I may shut my conscience to it no more—private vengeance is working through this testimony! From the beginning this man has struck me true. By my oath to Heaven, I believe him now, and I pray you call back his wife before we—

426 **Danforth:** She spoke nothing of lechery, and this man has lied!

427 **Hale:** I believe him! *Pointing at* ABIGAIL: This girl has always struck me false! She has—

428 ABIGAIL, *with a weird, wild, chilling cry, screams up to the ceiling.*

429 **Abigail:** You will not! Begone! Begone, I say!

430 **Danforth:** What is it, child? *But* ABIGAIL, *pointing with fear, is now raising up her frightened eyes, her awed face, toward the ceiling—the girls are doing the same—and now* HATHORNE, HALE, PUTNAM, CHEEVER, HERRICK, *and* DANFORTH *do the same.* What's there? *He lowers his eyes from the ceiling, and now he is frightened; there is real tension in his voice.* Child! *She is transfixed—with all the girls, she is whimpering, open-mouthed, agape at the ceiling.* Girls! Why do you—?

431 **Mercy Lewis,** *pointing*: It's on the beam! Behind the rafter!

432 **Danforth,** *looking up*: Where!

433 **Abigail:** Why—? *She gulps.* Why do you come, yellow bird?

434 **Proctor:** Where's a bird? I see no bird!

435 **Abigail,** *to the ceiling*: My face? My face?

436 **Proctor:** Mr. Hale—

437 **Danforth:** Be quiet!

438 **Proctor,** *to* HALE: Do you see a bird?

439 **Danforth:** Be quiet!

440 **Abigail,** *to the ceiling, in a genuine conversation with the "bird," as though trying to talk it out of attacking her*: But God made my face; you cannot want to tear my face. Envy is a deadly sin, Mary.

441 **Mary Warren,** *on her feet with a spring, and horrified, pleading*: Abby!

442 **Abigail,** *unperturbed, continuing to the "bird"*: Oh, Mary, this is a black art to change your shape. No, I cannot, I cannot stop my mouth; it's God's work I do.

443 **Mary Warren:** Abby, I'm *here!*

444 **Proctor,** *frantically*: They're pretending, Mr. Danforth!

445 **Abigail**—*now she takes a backward step, as though in fear the bird will swoop down momentarily*: Oh, please, Mary! Don't come down.

446 **Susanna Walcott:** Her claws, she's stretching her claws!

447 **Proctor:** Lies, lies.

448 **Abigail,** *backing further, eyes still fixed above*: Mary, please don't hurt me!

449 **Mary Warren,** *to* DANFORTH: I'm not hurting her!

450 **Danforth,** *to* MARY WARREN: Why does she see this vision?

451 **Mary Warren:** She sees nothin'!

452 **Abigail,** *now staring full front as though hypnotized, and mimicking the exact tone of* MARY WARREN'*s cry*: She sees nothin'!

453 **Mary Warren,** *pleading*: Abby, you mustn't!

454 **Abigail and All the Girls,** *all transfixed*: Abby, you mustn't!

455 **Mary Warren,** *to all the girls*: I'm here, I'm here!

456 **Girls:** I'm here, I'm here!

457 **Danforth,** *horrified*: Mary Warren! Draw back your spirit out of them!

458 **Mary Warren:** Mr. Danforth!

459 **Girls,** *cutting her off*: Mr. Danforth!

460 **Danforth:** Have you compacted with the Devil? Have you?

461 **Mary Warren:** Never, never!

462 **Girls:** Never, never!

463 **Danforth,** *growing hysterical*: Why can they only repeat you?

464 **Proctor:** Give me a whip—I'll stop it!

465 **Mary Warren:** They're sporting. They—!

466 **Girls:** They're sporting!

467 **Mary Warren,** *turning on them all hysterically and stamping her feet*: Abby, stop it!

468 **Girls,** *stamping their feet*: Abby, stop it!

469 **Mary Warren:** Stop it!

470 **Girls:** Stop it!

471 **Mary Warren,** *screaming it out at the top of her lungs, and raising her fists*: Stop it!!

472 **Girls,** *raising their fists*: Stop it!!

473 MARY WARREN, *utterly confounded, and becoming overwhelmed by* ABIGAIL's—*and the* GIRLS'—*utter conviction, starts to whimper, hands half raised, powerless, and all the girls begin whimpering exactly as she does.*

474 **Danforth:** A little while ago you were afflicted. Now it seems you afflict others; where did you find this power?

475 **Mary Warren,** *staring at* ABIGAIL: I—have no power.

476 **Girls:** I have no power.

477 **Proctor:** They're gulling[7] you, Mister!

478 **Danforth:** Why did you turn about this past two weeks? You have seen the Devil, have you not?

479 **Hale,** *indicating* ABIGAIL *and the* GIRLS: You cannot believe them!

480 **Mary Warren:** I—

481 **Proctor,** *sensing her weakening*: Mary, God damns all liars!

482 **Danforth,** *pounding it into her*: You have seen the Devil, you have made compact with Lucifer, have you not?

NOTES

CLOSE READ
ANNOTATE: In paragraphs 471–481, mark details in both stage directions and dialogue that relate to power and powerlessness.

QUESTION: Why does Miller highlight these concepts in this scene?

CONCLUDE: What change in the courtroom do these details emphasize?

7. **gulling** *v.* fooling.

Abigail "sees" the yellow bird she claims is Mary Warren's spirit.

The Crucible, Act III **653**

483 **Proctor:** God damns liars, Mary!

484 MARY *utters something unintelligible, staring at* ABIGAIL, *who keeps watching the "bird" above.*

485 **Danforth:** I cannot hear you. What do you say? MARY *utters again unintelligibly.* You will confess yourself or you will hang! *He turns her roughly to face him.* Do you know who I am? I say you will hang if you do not open with me!

486 **Proctor:** Mary, remember the angel Raphael—do that which is good and—

487 **Abigail,** *pointing upward*: The wings! Her wings are spreading! Mary, please, don't, don't—!

488 **Hale:** I see nothing, Your Honor!

489 **Danforth:** Do you confess this power! *He is an inch from her face.* Speak!

490 **Abigail:** She's going to come down! She's walking the beam!

491 **Danforth:** Will you speak!

492 **Mary Warren,** *staring in horror*: I cannot!

493 **Girls:** I cannot!

494 **Parris:** Cast the Devil out! Look him in the face! Trample him! We'll save you, Mary, only stand fast against him and—

495 **Abigail,** *looking up*: Look out! She's coming down!

496 *She and all the girls run to one wall, shielding their eyes. And now, as though cornered, they let out a gigantic scream, and* MARY, *as though infected, opens her mouth and screams with them. Gradually* ABIGAIL *and the girls leave off, until only* MARY *is left there, staring up at the "bird," screaming madly. All watch her, horrified by this evident fit.* PROCTOR *strides to her.*

497 **Proctor:** Mary, tell the Governor what they—*He has hardly got a word out, when, seeing him coming for her, she rushes out of his reach, screaming in horror.*

498 **Mary Warren:** Don't touch me—don't touch me! *At which the girls halt at the door.*

499 **Proctor,** *astonished*: Mary!

500 **Mary Warren,** *pointing at* PROCTOR: You're the Devil's man!

He is stopped in his tracks.

501 **Parris:** Praise God!

502 **Girls:** Praise God!

503 **Proctor,** *numbed*: Mary, how—?

504 **Mary Warren:** I'll not hang with you! I love God. I love God.

505 **Danforth,** *to* MARY: He bid you do the Devil's work?

506 Mary Warren, *hysterically, indicating* PROCTOR: He come at me by night and every day to sign, to sign, to—

507 Danforth: Sign what?

508 Parris: The Devil's book? He come with a book?

509 Mary Warren, *hysterically, pointing at* PROCTOR, *fearful of him*: My name, he want my name. "I'll murder you," he says, "if my wife hangs! We must go and overthrow the court," he says!

510 DANFORTH's *head jerks toward* PROCTOR, *shock and horror in his face.*

511 Proctor, *turning, appealing to* HALE: Mr. Hale!

512 Mary Warren, *her sobs beginning*: He wake me every night, his eyes were like coals and his fingers claw my neck, and I sign, I sign . . .

513 Hale: Excellency, this child's gone wild!

514 Proctor, *as* DANFORTH's *wide eyes pour on him*: Mary, Mary!

515 Mary Warren, *screaming at him*: No, I love God; I go your way no more. I love God. I bless God. *Sobbing, she rushes to* ABIGAIL. Abby, Abby, I'll never hurt you more! *They all watch, as* ABIGAIL, *out of her infinite charity, reaches out and draws the sobbing* MARY *to her, and then looks up to* DANFORTH.

516 Danforth, *to* PROCTOR: What are you? PROCTOR *is beyond speech in his anger.* You are combined with anti-Christ,[8] are you not? I have seen your power; you will not deny it! What say you, Mister?

517 Hale: Excellency—

518 Danforth: I will have nothing from you, Mr. Hale! *To* PROCTOR: Will you confess yourself befouled with Hell, or do you keep that black allegiance yet? What say you?

519 Proctor, *his mind wild, breathless*: I say—I say—God is dead!

520 Parris: Hear it, hear it!

521 Proctor, *laughs insanely, then*: A fire, a fire is burning! I hear the boot of Lucifer. I see his filthy face! And it is my face, and yours, Danforth! For them that quail to bring men out of ignorance, as I have quailed, and as you quail now when you know in all your black hearts that this be fraud—God damns our kind especially, and we will burn, we will burn together.

522 Danforth: Marshal! Take him and Corey with him to the jail!

523 Hale, *staring across to the door*: I denounce these proceedings!

524 Proctor: You are pulling Heaven down and raising up a whore!

525 Hale: I denounce these proceedings, I quit this court! *He slams the door to the outside behind him.*

526 Danforth, *calling to him in a fury*: Mr. Hale! Mr. Hale!

THE CURTAIN FALLS

NOTES

CLOSE READ
ANNOTATE: Mark the repeated sentence in paragraphs 504 and 515.

QUESTION: Why does Miller repeat this sentence?

CONCLUDE: What is the effect of this repetition?

8. **anti-Christ** In the Bible, a spirit of opposition to Christianity, to be embodied someday in a person who will spread universal evil.

Comprehension Check

Complete the following items after you finish your first read.

1. Where does the action of Act III take place?

2. At the beginning of Act III, what "hard evidence" do Giles and Francis provide that the girls are frauds?

3. What appears to happen to Abigail and the others girls after they are accused by Mary Warren of pretending?

4. Why is Elizabeth Proctor brought into the Court?

5. 📖 **Notebook** Write a summary of Act III of *The Crucible*.

- -

RESEARCH

Research to Explore Conduct research on an aspect of the text you find interesting. For example, you may want to learn the possible medical reasons for the behavior of Abigail and the other accusers.

Close Read the Text

Reread paragraph 368, and mark the text in quotations. Why does Miller present the action in this way? What effect would this create for an audience?

THE CRUCIBLE, ACT III

Analyze the Text

> **CITE TEXTUAL EVIDENCE** to support your answers.

Notebook Respond to these questions.

1. (a) **Draw Conclusions** How does Danforth react to the news that Proctor has a deposition from Mary? (b) **Analyze** Why do you think Danforth asks whether Proctor has told the story to the village? Explain.

2. **Make Inferences** Why do you think Hale is so insistent that lawyers be brought in to argue Proctor's case?

3. (a) **Interpret** Why does Proctor confess to the affair with Abigail? (b) **Analyze** What does his confession reveal about his character?

4. (a) What term does Danforth use to describe Abigail and the girls? (b) **Analyze** What does his use of this term show about his views of the accusers?

LANGUAGE DEVELOPMENT

Concept Vocabulary

remorseless	effrontery	callously

Why These Words? The concept vocabulary words refer to different kinds of disregard for others. What other words in Act III relate to this concept?

Practice

Notebook Use each concept vocabulary word in a sentence that demonstrates the word's meaning.

Word Study

Notebook **Connotation** The **connotation** of a word refers to emotional connections that add meaning beyond its literal definition. Words can have similar connotations that vary mainly in degree, or intensity. For example, both *remorseless* and *callously* have similar negative connotations, but *remorseless* is a more extreme word. It suggests a harshness that goes beyond mere callousness. *Unfeeling*, on the other hand, has a less intense connotation.

1. Write two synonyms for each of these words: *denounce, eager, fraud, coldly.*

2. For each trio of words from item 1, indicate which has the most intense connotation and which has the least intense connotation.

WORD NETWORK

Add words related to fear from the text to your Word Network.

STANDARDS

Language
• Demonstrate understanding of figurative language, word relationships, and nuances in word meanings.
• Analyze nuances in the meaning of words with similar denotations.

The Crucible, Act III **657**

THE CRUCIBLE, ACT III

Analyze Craft and Structure

Character Development The term **characterization** refers to the ways in which a writer reveals a character's personality. There are two types of characterization. In **direct characterization,** the author simply tells readers what a character is like. A playwright might use direct characterization in stage directions, but most dramatic literature requires **indirect characterization,** in which characters' traits are revealed through various types of details:

- the character's words, actions, and appearance
- other characters' comments
- other characters' reactions

Understanding characters through characterization is the key to unlocking their **motivations**—the reasons they feel, think, and behave as they do. Like people in real life, characters in plays are not always what they seem. Fear, greed, guilt, love, loyalty, pride, and revenge are some of the forces that drive human behavior, but they may be masked or hidden.

Practice

CITE TEXTUAL EVIDENCE to support your answers.

📓 **Notebook** Respond to these questions.

1. (a) Identify two examples of direct characterization of Giles Corey in stage directions. (b) Identify two examples of indirect characterization—in dialogue or in action—that amplify the examples of direct characterization. Explain your choices.

2. (a) Identify three examples of indirect characterization that reveal Mary Warren's personality. (b) For each example, explain what readers learn about her.

3. (a) What is Elizabeth's motivation for evading Danforth's questions about Abigail's dismissal from the Proctor household? (b) Considering Elizabeth's belief that lying is a sin, what does her evasion suggest about her character, her feelings for her husband, and her understanding of the court proceedings?

4. (a) What motivates Hale to denounce the proceedings and quit the court? (b) How does Hale's character change from the beginning to the end of Act III?

📊 STANDARDS

Reading Literature
• Analyze the impact of the author's choices regarding how to develop and relate elements of a story or drama.
• Analyze a case in which grasping point of view requires distinguishing what is directly stated in a text from what is really meant.

Author's Style

Author's Choices: Literary Devices Like characters, situations are also not always what they seem. When there is a contrast between expectation and reality, or between words and meaning, **irony** is at work. Playwrights often use irony to build suspense and create tension. Two types of irony are dramatic irony and verbal irony.

- **Dramatic irony** is the discrepancy between what a character believes or understands and what the audience knows to be true.

  EXAMPLE: In Shakespeare's *Romeo and Juliet*, the Capulets believe Juliet to be dead. The audience knows that she has taken a potion that mimics death, but that she is alive and will awaken.

- **Verbal irony** occurs when a character says one thing but means another.

  EXAMPLE: In Act III, Scene ii, of Shakespeare's *Julius Caesar*, Mark Antony refers to Brutus and the rest of Caesar's murderers as "honourable men." He does not really mean this.

Read It

Complete this chart by recording two examples of dramatic irony and two examples of verbal irony in Act III. For examples of dramatic irony, describe what the audience understands or knows that the characters themselves do not. For examples of verbal irony, write what each speaker really means. For all examples, analyze the effect of the discrepancy.

EXAMPLE	TYPE OF IRONY	ANALYSIS

EVIDENCE LOG

Before moving on to Act IV, go to your Evidence Log and record what you learned from Act III of *The Crucible*.

Write It

Notebook In what ways is Elizabeth Proctor's testimony ironic?

Playwright

Arthur Miller

The Crucible, Act IV

Concept Vocabulary

You will encounter the following words as you read Act IV of *The Crucible*. Before reading, note how familiar you are with each word. Then, rank the words in order from most familiar (1) to least familiar (3).

WORD	YOUR RANKING
conciliatory	
adamant	
disputation	

After completing the first read, come back to the concept vocabulary and review your rankings. Mark changes to your original rankings as needed.

First Read DRAMA

Apply these strategies as you conduct your first read. You will have an opportunity to complete the close-read notes after your first read.

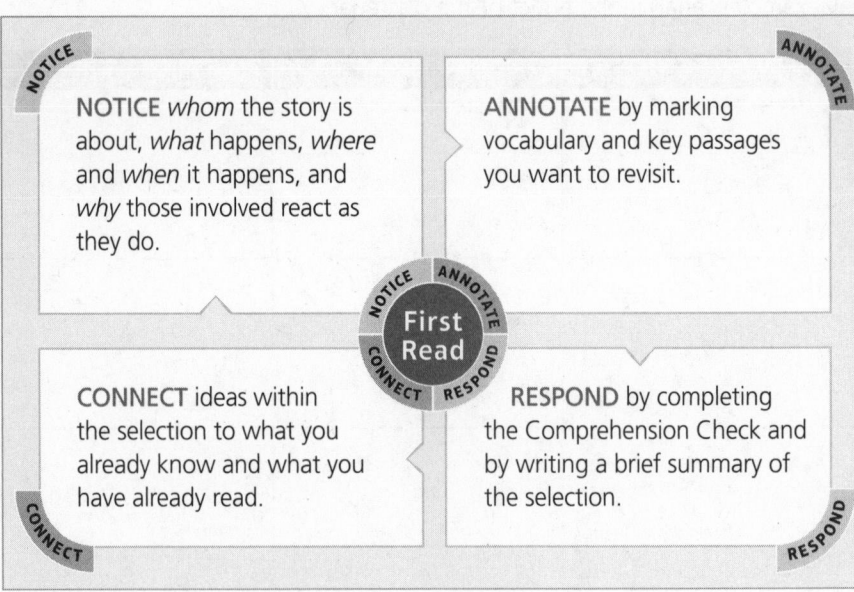

NOTICE *whom* the story is about, *what* happens, *where* and *when* it happens, and *why* those involved react as they do.

ANNOTATE by marking vocabulary and key passages you want to revisit.

CONNECT ideas within the selection to what you already know and what you have already read.

RESPOND by completing the Comprehension Check and by writing a brief summary of the selection.

:≡ STANDARDS

Reading Literature
By the end of grade 11, read and comprehend literature, including stories, dramas, and poems, in the grades 11–CCR text complexity band proficiently, with scaffolding as needed at the high end of the range.

The Crucible
Act IV
Arthur Miller

SCAN FOR MULTIMEDIA

REVIEW AND ANTICIPATE

"Is every defense an attack upon the court?" Hale asks in Act III. Danforth observes, "A person is either with this court or he must be counted against it." Such remarks stress the powerlessness of people like John Proctor and Giles Corey against the mounting injustices in Salem. In pursuing justice, their efforts backfire, and their own names join the list of those accused. What do you think the final outcome will be? Who will survive, and who will perish? Read the final act to see if your predictions are correct.

1 *A cell in Salem jail, that fall.*

2 *At the back is a high barred window; near it, a great, heavy door. Along the walls are two benches.*

3 *The place is in darkness but for the moonlight seeping through the bars. It appears empty. Presently footsteps are heard coming down a corridor beyond the wall, keys rattle, and the door swings open.* MARSHAL HERRICK *enters with a lantern.*

4 *He is nearly drunk, and heavy-footed. He goes to a bench and nudges a bundle of rags lying on it.*

5 **Herrick:** Sarah, wake up! Sarah Good! *He then crosses to the other benches.*

NOTES

The Crucible, Act IV **661**

6 **Sarah Good,** *rising in her rags*: Oh, Majesty! Comin', comin'! Tituba, he's here, His Majesty's come!

7 **Herrick:** Go to the north cell; this place is wanted now. *He hangs his lantern on the wall.* TITUBA *sits up.*

8 **Tituba:** That don't look to me like His Majesty; look to me like the marshal.

9 **Herrick,** *taking out a flask*: Get along with you now, clear this place. *He drinks, and* SARAH GOOD *comes and peers up into his face.*

10 **Sarah Good:** Oh, is it you, Marshal! I thought sure you be the devil comin' for us. Could I have a sip of cider for me goin' away?

11 **Herrick,** *handing her the flask*: And where are you off to, Sarah?

12 **Tituba,** *as* SARAH *drinks*: We goin' to Barbados, soon the Devil gits here with the feathers and the wings.

13 **Herrick:** Oh? A happy voyage to you.

14 **Sarah Good:** A pair of bluebirds wingin' southerly, the two of us! Oh, it be a grand transformation, Marshal. *She raises the flask to drink again.*

15 **Herrick,** *taking the flask from her lips*: You'd best give me that or you'll never rise off the ground. Come along now.

16 **Tituba:** I'll speak to him for you, if you desires to come along, Marshal.

17 **Herrick:** I'd not refuse it, Tituba; it's the proper morning to fly into Hell.

18 **Tituba:** Oh, it be no Hell in Barbados. Devil, him be pleasure man in Barbados, him be singin' and dancin' in Barbados. It's you folks—you riles him up 'round here; it be too cold 'round here for that Old Boy. He freeze his soul in Massachusetts, but in Barbados he just as sweet and—*A bellowing cow is heard, and* TITUBA *leaps up and calls to the window*: Aye, sir! That's him, Sarah!

19 **Sarah Good:** I'm here, Majesty! *They hurriedly pick up their rags as* HOPKINS, *a guard, enters.*

20 **Hopkins:** The Deputy Governor's arrived.

21 **Herrick,** *grabbing* TITUBA: Come along, come along.

22 **Tituba,** *resisting him*: No, he comin' for me. I goin' home!

23 **Herrick,** *pulling her to the door*: That's not Satan, just a poor old cow with a hatful of milk. Come along now, out with you!

24 **Tituba,** *calling to the window*: Take me home, Devil! Take me home!

25 **Sarah Good,** *following the shouting* TITUBA *out*: Tell him I'm goin', Tituba! Now you tell him Sarah Good is goin' too!

CLOSE READ

ANNOTATE: In paragraphs 18–24, mark each reference to the Devil.

QUESTION: Why does Miller have Sarah Good and Tituba refer to the Devil by various names?

CONCLUDE: What is the effect of these details?

26 *In the corridor outside* TITUBA *calls on—"Take me home. Devil; Devil take me home!" and* HOPKINS'S *voice orders her to move on.* HERRICK *returns and begins to push old rags and straw into a corner. Hearing footsteps, he turns, and enter* DANFORTH *and* JUDGE HATHORNE. *They are in greatcoats and wear hats against the bitter cold. They are followed in by* CHEEVER, *who carries a dispatch case and a flat wooden box containing his writing materials.*

27 **Herrick:** Good morning, Excellency.

28 **Danforth:** Where is Mr. Parris?

29 **Herrick**: I'll fetch him. *He starts for the door.*

30 **Danforth:** Marshal. HERRICK *stops.* When did Reverend Hale arrive?

31 **Herrick:** It were toward midnight, I think.

32 **Danforth,** *suspiciously*: What is he about here?

33 **Herrick:** He goes among them that will hang, sir. And he prays with them. He sits with Goody Nurse now. And Mr. Parris with him.

34 **Danforth:** Indeed. That man have no authority to enter here, Marshal. Why have you let him in?

35 **Herrick:** Why, Mr. Parris command me, sir. I cannot deny him.

36 **Danforth:** Are you drunk, Marshal?

37 **Herrick:** No, sir; it is a bitter night, and I have no fire here.

38 **Danforth,** *containing his anger*: Fetch Mr. Parris.

39 **Herrick:** Aye, sir.

40 **Danforth:** There is a prodigious stench in this place.

41 **Herrick:** I have only now cleared the people out for you.

42 **Danforth:** Beware hard drink, Marshal.

43 **Herrick:** Aye, sir. *He waits an instant for further orders. But* DANFORTH, *in dissatisfaction, turns his back on him, and* HERRICK *goes out. There is a pause.* DANFORTH *stands in thought.*

44 **Hathorne:** Let you question Hale, Excellency; I should not be surprised he have been preaching in Andover[1] lately.

45 **Danforth:** We'll come to that; speak nothing of Andover. Parris prays with him. That's strange. *He blows on his hands, moves toward the window, and looks out.*

46 **Hathorne:** Excellency, I wonder if it be wise to let Mr. Parris so continuously with the prisoners. DANFORTH *turns to him, interested.* I think, sometimes, the man has a mad look these days.

47 **Danforth:** Mad?

1. **Andover** During the height of the terror in Salem Village, a similar hysteria broke out in the nearby town of Andover. There, many respected people were accused of practicing witchcraft and confessed to escape death. However, the people of Andover soon began questioning the reality of the situation, and the hysteria quickly subsided.

CLOSE READ

ANNOTATE: In paragraph 52, mark the word that Cheever repeats as he describes a conflict that is going on in the community.

QUESTION: Why does Miller have Cheever repeat this word?

CONCLUDE: How does this repeated word add to the effect of this dialogue?

48 **Hathorne:** I met him yesterday coming out of his house, and I bid him good morning—and he wept and went his way. I think it is not well the village sees him so unsteady.

49 **Danforth:** Perhaps he have some sorrow.

50 **Cheever,** *stamping his feet against the cold*: I think it be the cows, sir.

51 **Danforth:** Cows?

52 **Cheever:** There be so many cows wanderin' the highroads, now their masters are in the jails, and much disagreement who they will belong to now. I know Mr. Parris be arguin' with farmers all yesterday—there is great contention, sir, about the cows. Contention make him weep, sir; it were always a man that weep for contention. *He turns, as do* HATHORNE *and* DANFORTH *hearing someone coming up the corridor.* DANFORTH *raises his head as* PARRIS *enters. He is gaunt, frightened, and sweating in his greatcoat.*

53 **Parris,** *to* DANFORTH, *instantly*: Oh, good morning, sir, thank you for coming. I beg your pardon wakin' you so early. Good morning, Judge Hathorne.

54 **Danforth:** Reverend Hale have no right to enter this—

55 **Parris:** Excellency, a moment. *He hurries back and shuts the door.*

56 **Hathorne:** Do you leave him alone with the prisoners?

57 **Danforth:** What's his business here?

58 **Parris,** *prayerfully holding up his hands*: Excellency, hear me. It is a providence. Reverend Hale has returned to bring Rebecca Nurse to God.

59 **Danforth,** *surprised*: He bids her confess?

60 **Parris,** *sitting*: Hear me. Rebecca have not given me a word this three month since she came. Now she sits with him, and her sister and Martha Corey and two or three others, and he pleads with them, confess their crimes and save their lives.

61 **Danforth:** Why—this is indeed a providence. And they soften, they soften?

62 **Parris:** Not yet, not yet. But I thought to summon you, sir, that we might think on whether it be not wise, to—*He dares not say it.* I had thought to put a question, sir, and I hope you will not—

63 **Danforth:** Mr. Parris, be plain, what troubles you?

64 **Parris:** There is news, sir, that the court—the court must reckon with. My niece, sir, my niece—I believe she has vanished.

65 **Danforth:** Vanished!

66 **Parris:** I had thought to advise you of it earlier in the week, but—

67 **Danforth:** Why? How long is she gone?

68 **Parris:** This be the third night. You see, sir, she told me she would stay a night with Mercy Lewis. And next day, when she does not return, I send to Mr. Lewis to inquire. Mercy told him she would sleep in *my* house for a night.

69 **Danforth:** They are both gone?!

70 **Parris,** *in fear of him*: They are, sir.

71 **Danforth,** *alarmed*: I will send a party for them. Where may they be?

72 **Parris:** Excellency. I think they be aboard a ship. DANFORTH *stands agape*. My daughter tells me how she heard them speaking of ships last week, and tonight I discover my—my strongbox is broke into. *He presses his fingers against his eyes to keep back tears.*

73 **Hathorne,** *astonished*: She have robbed you?

74 **Parris:** Thirty-one pound is gone. I am penniless. *He covers his face and sobs.*

75 **Danforth:** Mr. Parris, you are a brainless man! *He walks in thought, deeply worried.*

76 **Parris:** Excellency, it profit nothing you should blame me. I cannot think they would run off except they fear to keep in Salem any more. *He is pleading.* Mark it, sir. Abigail had close knowledge of the town, and since the news of Andover has broken here—

77 **Danforth:** Andover is remedied. The court returns there on Friday, and will resume examinations.

78 **Parris:** I am sure of it, sir. But the rumor here speaks rebellion in Andover, and it—

79 **Danforth:** There is no rebellion in Andover!

80 **Parris:** I tell you what is said here, sir. Andover have thrown out the court, they say, and will have no part of witchcraft. There be a faction here, feeding on that news, and I tell you true, sir, I fear there will be riot here.

81 **Hathorne:** Riot! Why at every execution I have seen naught but high satisfaction in the town.

82 **Parris:** Judge Hathorne—it were another sort that hanged till now. Rebecca Nurse is no Bridget that lived three year with Bishop before she married him. John Proctor is not Isaac Ward that drank his family to ruin. *To* DANFORTH: I would to God it were not so, Excellency, but these people have great weight yet in the town. Let Rebecca stand upon the gibbet[2] and send up some righteous prayer, and I fear she'll wake a vengeance on you.

2. **gibbet** (JIHB iht) *n.* gallows.

83 **Hathorne:** Excellency, she is condemned a witch. The court have—

84 **Danforth,** *in deep concern, raising a hand to* HATHORNE: Pray you. *To* PARRIS: How do you propose, then?

85 **Parris:** Excellency, I would postpone these hangin's for a time.

86 **Danforth:** There will be no postponement.

87 **Parris:** Now Mr. Hale's returned, there is hope, I think—for if he bring even one of these to God, that confession surely damns the others in the public eye, and none may doubt more that they are all linked to Hell. This way, unconfessed and claiming innocence, doubts are multiplied, many honest people will weep for them, and our good purpose is lost in their tears.

88 **Danforth,** *after thinking a moment, then going to* CHEEVER: Give me the list.

89 CHEEVER *opens the dispatch case, searches.*

90 **Parris:** It cannot be forgot, sir, that when I summoned the congregation for John Proctor's excommunication there were hardly thirty people come to hear it. That speak a discontent, I think, and—

91 **Danforth,** *studying the list*: There will be no postponement.

Parris: Excellency—

92 **Danforth:** Now, sir—which of these in your opinion may be brought to God? I will myself strive with him till dawn. *He hands the list to* PARRIS, *who merely glances at it.*

93 **Parris:** There is not sufficient time till dawn.

94 **Danforth:** I shall do my utmost. Which of them do you have hope for?

95 **Parris,** *not even glancing at the list now, and in a quavering voice, quietly*: Excellency—a dagger—*He chokes up.*

96 **Danforth:** What do you say?

97 **Parris:** Tonight, when I open my door to leave my house—a dagger clattered to the ground. *Silence.* DANFORTH *absorbs this. Now* PARRIS *cries out*: You cannot hang this sort. There is danger for me. I dare not step outside at night!

98 REVEREND HALE *enters. They look at him for an instant in silence. He is steeped in sorrow, exhausted, and more direct than he ever was.*

99 **Danforth:** Accept my congratulations. Reverend Hale; we are gladdened to see you returned to your good work.

100 **Hale,** *coming to* DANFORTH *now*: You must pardon them. They will not budge.

HERRICK *enters, waits.*

101 **Danforth,** *conciliatory*: You misunderstand, sir; I cannot pardon these when twelve are already hanged for the same crime. It is not just.

conciliatory (kuhn SIHL ee uh tawr ee) *adj.* in a manner intended to make peace and bring about agreement

102 **Parris,** *with failing heart*: Rebecca will not confess?

103 **Hale:** The sun will rise in a few minutes. Excellency, I must have more time.

104 **Danforth:** Now hear me, and beguile yourselves no more. I will not receive a single plea for pardon or postponement. Them that will not confess will hang. Twelve are already executed: the names of these seven are given out, and the village expects to see them die this morning. Postponement now speaks a floundering on my part; reprieve or pardon must cast doubt upon the guilt of them that died till now. While I speak God's law, I will not crack its voice with whimpering. If retaliation is your fear, know this—I should hang ten thousand that dared to rise against the law, and an ocean of salt tears could not melt the resolution of the statutes. Now draw yourselves up like men and help me, as you are bound by Heaven to do. Have you spoken with them all, Mr. Hale?

105 **Hale:** All but Proctor. He is in the dungeon.

106 **Danforth,** *to* HERRICK: What's Proctor's way now?

107 **Herrick:** He sits like some great bird: you'd not know he lived except he will take food from time to time.

108 **Danforth,** *after thinking a moment*: His wife—his wife must be well on with child now.

109 **Herrick:** She is, sir.

110 **Danforth:** What think you, Mr. Parris? You have closer knowledge of this man; might her presence soften him?

111 **Parris:** It is possible, sir. He have not laid eyes on her these three months. I should summon her.

112 **Danforth,** *to* HERRICK: Is he yet **adamant**? Has he struck at you again?

113 **Herrick:** He cannot, sir, he is chained to the wall now.

114 **Danforth,** *after thinking on it*: Fetch Goody Proctor to me. Then let you bring him up.

115 **Herrick:** Aye, sir. HERRICK *goes. There is silence.*

116 **Hale:** Excellency, if you postpone a week and publish to the town that you are striving for their confessions, that speak mercy on your part, not faltering.

117 **Danforth:** Mr. Hale, as God have not empowered me like Joshua to stop this sun from rising,[3] so I cannot withhold from them the perfection of their punishment.

118 **Hale,** *harder now*: If you think God wills you to raise rebellion, Mr. Danforth, you are mistaken!

119 **Danforth,** *instantly*: You have heard rebellion spoken in the town?

adamant (AD uh muhnt) *adj.* unrelenting; refusing to be persuaded

3. **Joshua . . . rising** In the Bible, Joshua, leader of the Israelites after the death of Moses, asks God to make the sun and the moon stand still during a battle, and his request is granted.

120 **Hale:** Excellency, there are orphans wandering from house to house; abandoned cattle bellow on the highroads, the stink of rotting crops hangs everywhere, and no man knows when the harlot's cry will end his life—and you wonder yet if rebellion's spoke? Better you should marvel how they do not burn your province!

121 **Danforth:** Mr. Hale, have you preached in Andover this month?

122 **Hale:** Thank God they have no need of me in Andover.

123 **Danforth:** You baffle me, sir. Why have you returned here?

124 **Hale:** Why, it is all simple. I come to do the Devil's work. I come to counsel Christians they should belie themselves. *His sarcasm collapses.* There is blood on my head! Can you not see the blood on my head!!

125 **Parris:** Hush! *For he has heard footsteps. They all face the door.* HERRICK *enters with* ELIZABETH. *Her wrists are linked by heavy chain, which* HERRICK *now removes. Her clothes are dirty; her face is pale and gaunt.* HERRICK *goes out.*

126 **Danforth,** *very politely*: Goody Proctor. *She is silent.* I hope you are hearty?

127 **Elizabeth,** *as a warning reminder*: I am yet six month before my time.

128 **Danforth:** Pray be at your ease, we come not for your life. We—*uncertain how to plead, for he is not accustomed to it.* Mr. Hale, will you speak with the woman?

129 **Hale:** Goody Proctor, your husband is marked to hang this morning. *Pause.*

130 **Elizabeth,** *quietly*: I have heard it.

131 **Hale:** You know, do you not, that I have no connection with the court? *She seems to doubt it.* I come of my own, Goody Proctor. I would save your husband's life, for if he is taken I count myself his murderer. Do you understand me?

132 **Elizabeth:** What do you want of me?

133 **Hale:** Goody Proctor, I have gone this three month like our Lord into the wilderness. I have sought a Christian way, for damnation's doubled on a minister who counsels men to lie.

134 **Hathorne:** It is no lie, you cannot speak of lies.

135 **Hale:** It is a lie! They are innocent!

136 **Danforth:** I'll hear no more of that!

137 **Hale,** *continuing to* ELIZABETH: Let you not mistake your duty as I mistook my own. I came into this village like a bridegroom to his beloved, bearing gifts of high religion; the very crowns of holy law I brought, and what I touched with my bright confidence, it died; and where I turned the eye of my great faith,

blood flowed up. Beware, Goody Proctor—cleave to no faith when faith brings blood. It is mistaken law that leads you to sacrifice. Life, woman, life is God's most precious gift; no principle, however glorious, may justify the taking of it. I beg you, woman, prevail upon your husband to confess. Let him give his lie. Quail not before God's judgment in this, for it may well be God damns a liar less than he that throws his life away for pride. Will you plead with him? I cannot think he will listen to another.

138 **Elizabeth,** *quietly*: I think that be the Devil's argument.

139 **Hale,** *with a climactic desperation*: Woman, before the laws of God we are as swine! We cannot read His will!

140 **Elizabeth:** I cannot dispute with you, sir; I lack learning for it.

141 **Danforth,** *going to her*: Goody Proctor, you are not summoned here for **disputation**. Be there no wifely tenderness within you? He will die with the sunrise. Your husband. Do you understand it? *She only looks at him.* What say you? Will you contend with him? *She is silent.* Are you stone? I tell you true, woman, had I no other proof of your unnatural life, your dry eyes now would be sufficient evidence that you delivered up your soul to Hell! A very ape would weep at such calamity! Have the devil dried up any tear of pity in you? *She is silent.* Take her out. It profit nothing she should speak to him!

disputation (dihs pyu TAY shuhn) *n.* debate or argument

142 **Elizabeth,** *quietly*: Let me speak with him, Excellency.

143 **Parris,** *with hope*: You'll strive with him? *She hesitates.*

144 **Danforth:** Will you plead for his confession or will you not?

145 **Elizabeth:** I promise nothing. Let me speak with him.

146 *A sound—the sibilance of dragging feet on stone. They turn. A pause.* HERRICK *enters with* JOHN PROCTOR. *His wrists are chained. He is another man, bearded, filthy, his eyes misty as though webs had overgrown them. He halts inside the doorway, his eyes caught by the sight of* ELIZABETH. *The emotion flowing between them prevents anyone from speaking for an instant. Now* HALE, *visibly affected, goes to* DANFORTH *and speaks quietly.*

147 **Hale:** Pray, leave them Excellency.

148 **Danforth,** *pressing* HALE *impatiently aside*: Mr. Proctor, you have been notified, have you not? PROCTOR *is silent, staring at* ELIZABETH. I see light in the sky, Mister; let you counsel with your wife, and may God help you turn your back on Hell. PROCTOR *is silent, staring at* ELIZABETH.

149 **Hale,** *quietly*: Excellency, let—

150 **Danforth** *brushes past* HALE *and walks out.* HALE *follows.* CHEEVER *stands and follows.* HATHORNE *behind.* HERRICK *goes.* PARRIS, *from a safe distance, offers*:

ANNOTATE: In paragraph 152, mark each action that actors playing John and Elizabeth Proctor are told to do.

QUESTION: Why does Miller provide such a specific description of the characters' actions?

CONCLUDE: What is the effect of this description?

151 **Parris:** If you desire a cup of cider, Mr. Proctor, I am sure I— PROCTOR *turns an icy stare at him, and he breaks off.* PARRIS *raises his palms toward* PROCTOR. God lead you now. PARRIS *goes out.*

152 *Alone,* PROCTOR *walks to her, halts. It is as though they stood in a spinning world. It is beyond sorrow, above it. He reaches out his hand as though toward an embodiment not quite real, and as he touches her, a strange soft sound, half laughter, half amazement, comes from his throat. He pats her hand. She covers his hand with hers. And then, weak, he sits. Then she sits, facing him.*

153 **Proctor:** The child?

154 **Elizabeth:** It grows.

155 **Proctor:** There is no word of the boys?

156 **Elizabeth:** They're well. Rebecca's Samuel keeps them.

157 **Proctor:** You have not seen them?

158 **Elizabeth:** I have not. *She catches a weakening in herself and downs it.*

159 **Proctor:** You are a—marvel, Elizabeth.

160 **Elizabeth:** You—have been tortured?

161 **Proctor:** Aye. *Pause. She will not let herself be drowned in the sea that threatens her.* They come for my life now.

162 **Elizabeth:** I know it.

163 *Pause.*

164 **Proctor:** None—have yet confessed?

165 **Elizabeth:** There be many confessed.

166 **Proctor:** Who are they?

167 **Elizabeth:** There be a hundred or more, they say. Goody Ballard is one; Isaiah Goodkind is one. There be many.

168 **Proctor:** Rebecca?

169 **Elizabeth:** Not Rebecca. She is one foot in Heaven now; naught may hurt her more.

170 **Proctor:** And Giles?

171 **Elizabeth:** You have not heard of it?

172 **Proctor:** I hear nothin', where I am kept.

173 **Elizabeth:** Giles is dead.

174 *He looks at her incredulously.*

175 **Proctor:** When were he hanged?

176 **Elizabeth,** *quietly, factually*: He were not hanged. He would not answer aye or nay to his indictment; for if he denied the charge they'd hang him surely, and auction out his property. So he stand mute, and died Christian under the law. And so his sons

will have his farm. It is the law, for he could not be condemned a wizard without he answer the indictment, aye or nay.

177 **Proctor:** Then how does he die?

178 **Elizabeth,** *gently*: They press him, John.

179 **Proctor:** Press?

180 **Elizabeth:** Great stones they lay upon his chest until he plead aye or nay. *With a tender smile for the old man*: They say he give them but two words. "More weight," he says. And died.

181 **Proctor,** *numbed—a thread to weave into his agony*: "More weight."

182 **Elizabeth:** Aye. It were a fearsome man, Giles Corey.

183 *Pause.*

184 **Proctor,** *with great force of will, but not quite looking at her*: I have been thinking I would confess to them, Elizabeth. *She shows nothing.* What say you? If I give them that?

185 **Elizabeth:** I cannot judge you, John.

186 *Pause.*

187 **Proctor,** *simply—a pure question*: What would you have me do?

188 **Elizabeth:** As you will, I would have it. *Slight pause*: I want you living, John. That's sure.

189 **Proctor,** *pauses, then with a flailing of hope*: Giles's wife? Have she confessed?

As the play reaches its climax, John and Elizabeth Proctor discuss whether he should confess to save his life.

CLOSE READ

ANNOTATE: In paragraph 199, mark the adjective that modifies John Proctor's "longing."

QUESTION: Why does Miller use this word?

CONCLUDE: What is the effect of this word, and how might it guide the performance of an actor playing John Proctor?

190 **Elizabeth:** She will not.

191 *Pause.*

192 **Proctor:** It is a pretense, Elizabeth.

193 **Elizabeth:** What is?

194 **Proctor:** I cannot mount the gibbet like a saint. It is a fraud. I am not that man. *She is silent.* My honesty is broke, Elizabeth; I am no good man. Nothing's spoiled by giving them this lie that were not rotten long before.

195 **Elizabeth:** And yet you've not confessed till now. That speak goodness in you.

196 **Proctor:** Spite only keeps me silent. It is hard to give a lie to dogs. *Pause, for the first time he turns directly to her.* I would have your forgiveness, Elizabeth.

197 **Elizabeth:** It is not for me to give, John, I am—

198 **Proctor:** I'd have you see some honesty in it. Let them that never lied die now to keep their souls. It is pretense for me, a vanity that will not blind God nor keep my children out of the wind. *Pause.* What say you?

199 **Elizabeth,** *upon a heaving sob that always threatens:* John, it come to naught that I should forgive you, if you'll not forgive yourself. *Now he turns away a little, in great agony.* It is not my soul, John, it is yours. *He stands, as though in physical pain, slowly rising to his feet with a great immortal longing to find his answer. It is difficult to say, and she is on the verge of tears.* Only be sure of this, for I know it now: Whatever you will do, it is a good man does it. *He turns his doubting, searching gaze upon her.* I have read my heart this three month, John. *Pause.* I have sins of my own to count. It needs a cold wife to prompt lechery.

200 **Proctor,** *in great pain:* Enough, enough—

201 **Elizabeth,** *now pouring out her heart:* Better you should know me!

202 **Proctor:** I will not hear it! I know you!

203 **Elizabeth:** You take my sins upon you, John—

204 **Proctor,** *in agony:* No. I take my own, my own!

205 **Elizabeth:** John, I counted myself so plain, so poorly made, no honest love could come to me! Suspicion kissed you when I did; I never knew how I should say my love. It were a cold house I kept! *In fright, she swerves, as* HATHORNE *enters.*

206 **Hathorne:** What say you, Proctor? The sun is soon up.

207 **Proctor,** *his chest heaving, stares, turns to* ELIZABETH. *She comes to him as though to plead, her voice quaking.*

208 **Elizabeth:** Do what you will. But let none be your judge. There be no higher judge under Heaven than Proctor is! Forgive me,

forgive me, John—I never knew such goodness in the world! *She covers her face, weeping.*

209 PROCTOR *turns from her to* HATHORNE; *he is off the earth, his voice hollow.*

210 **Proctor:** I want my life.

211 **Hathorne** *electrified, surprised*: You'll confess yourself?

212 **Proctor:** I will have my life.

213 **Hathorne,** *with a mystical tone*: God be praised! It is a providence! *He rushes out the door, and his voice is heard calling down the corridor*: He will confess! Proctor will confess!

214 **Proctor,** *with a cry, as he strides to the door*: Why do you cry it? *In great pain he turns back to her.* It is evil, is it not? It is evil.

215 **Elizabeth,** in *terror, weeping*: I cannot judge you, John. I cannot!

216 **Proctor:** Then who will judge me? *Suddenly clasping his hands*: God in Heaven, what is John Proctor, what is John Proctor? *He moves as an animal, and a fury is riding in him, a tantalized search.* I think it is honest, I think so; I am no saint. *As though she had denied this he calls angrily at her*: Let Rebecca go like a saint; for me it is fraud! *Voices are heard in the hall, speaking together in suppressed excitement.*

217 **Elizabeth:** I am not your judge, I cannot be. *As though giving him release*: Do as you will, do as you will!

218 **Proctor:** Would you give them such a lie? Say it. Would you ever give them this? *She cannot answer.* You would not; if tongs of fire were singeing you you would not! It is evil. Good, then— it is evil, and I do it!

219 HATHORNE *enters with* DANFORTH, *and, with them,* CHEEVER, PARRIS, *and* HALE. *It is a businesslike, rapid entrance, as though the ice had been broken.*

220 **Danforth,** *with great relief and gratitude*: Praise to God, man, praise to God; you shall be blessed in Heaven for this. CHEEVER *has hurried to the bench with pen, ink, and paper.* PROCTOR *watches him.* Now then, let us have it. Are you ready, Mr. Cheever?

221 **Proctor,** *with a cold, cold horror at their efficiency*: Why must it be written?

222 **Danforth:** Why, for the good instruction of the village. Mister; this we shall post upon the church door! *To* PARRIS, *urgently*: Where is the marshal?

223 **Parris,** *runs to the door and calls down the corridor*: Marshal! Hurry!

224 **Danforth:** Now, then, Mister, will you speak slowly, and directly to the point, for Mr. Cheever's sake. *He is on record now, and is really dictating to* CHEEVER, *who writes.* Mr. Proctor, have you seen

the Devil in your life? PROCTOR's *jaws lock.* Come, man, there is light in the sky; the town waits at the scaffold; I would give out this news. Did you see the Devil?

225 **Proctor:** I did.

226 **Parris:** Praise God!

227 **Danforth:** And when he come to you, what were his demand? PROCTOR *is silent.* DANFORTH *helps.* Did he bid you to do his work upon the earth?

228 **Proctor:** He did.

229 **Danforth:** And you bound yourself to his service? DANFORTH *turns, as* REBECCA NURSE *enters, with* HERRICK *helping to support her. She is barely able to walk.* Come in, come in, woman!

230 **Rebecca,** *brightening as she sees* PROCTOR: Ah, John! You are well, then, eh?

231 PROCTOR *turns his face to the wall.*

232 **Danforth:** Courage, man, courage—let her witness your good example that she may come to God herself. Now hear it, Goody Nurse! Say on, Mr. Proctor. Did you bind yourself to the Devil's service?

233 **Rebecca,** *astonished*: Why, John!

234 **Proctor,** *through his teeth, his face turned from* REBECCA: I did.

235 **Danforth:** Now, woman, you surely see it profit nothin' to keep this conspiracy any further. Will you confess yourself with him?

236 **Rebecca:** Oh, John—God send his mercy on you!

237 **Danforth:** I say, will you confess yourself. Goody Nurse?

238 **Rebecca:** Why, it is a lie, it is a lie; how may I damn myself? I cannot, I cannot.

239 **Danforth:** Mr. Proctor. When the Devil came to you did you see Rebecca Nurse in his company? PROCTOR *is silent.* Come, man, take courage—did you ever see her with the Devil?

240 **Proctor,** *almost inaudibly*: No.

241 DANFORTH, *now sensing trouble, glances at* JOHN *and goes to the table, and picks up a sheet—the list of condemned.*

242 **Danforth:** Did you ever see her sister, Mary Easty, with the Devil?

243 **Proctor:** No, I did not.

244 **Danforth,** *his eyes narrow on* PROCTOR: Did you ever see Martha Corey with the Devil?

245 **Proctor:** I did not.

246 **Danforth,** *realizing, slowly putting the sheet down*: Did you ever see anyone with the Devil?

CLOSE READ

ANNOTATE: In the stage directions in paragraphs 231–240, mark the actions that John Proctor takes after Rebecca Nurse enters the room.

QUESTION: Why does Miller include these stage directions?

CONCLUDE: What is the effect of these details?

247 **Proctor:** I did not.

248 **Danforth:** Proctor, you mistake me. I am not empowered to trade your life for a lie. You have most certainly seen some person with the Devil. PROCTOR *is silent.* Mr. Proctor, a score of people have already testified they saw this woman with the Devil.

249 **Proctor:** Then it is proved. Why must I say it?

250 **Danforth:** Why "must" you say it! Why, you should rejoice to say it if your soul is truly purged of any love for Hell!

251 **Proctor:** They think to go like saints. I like not to spoil their names.

252 **Danforth,** *inquiring, incredulous*: Mr. Proctor, do you think they go like saints?

253 **Proctor,** *evading*: This woman never thought she done the Devil's work.

254 **Danforth:** Look you, sir. I think you mistake your duty here. It matter nothing what she thought—she is convicted of the unnatural murder of children, and you for sending your spirit out upon Mary Warren. Your soul alone is the issue here, Mister, and you will prove its whiteness or you cannot live in a

John Proctor makes his final defense.

Christian country. Will you tell me now what persons conspired with you in the Devil's company? PROCTOR *is silent.* To your knowledge was Rebecca Nurse ever—

255 **Proctor:** I speak my own sins: I cannot judge another. *Crying out, with hatred*: I have no tongue for it.

256 **Hale,** *quickly to* DANFORTH: Excellency. It is enough he confess himself. Let him sign it, let him sign it.

257 **Parris,** *feverishly*: It is a great service, sir. It is a weighty name; it will strike the village that Proctor confess. I beg you, let him sign it. The sun is up, Excellency!

258 **Danforth,** *considers; then with dissatisfaction*: Come, then, sign your testimony. *To* CHEEVER: Give it to him. CHEEVER *goes to* PROCTOR, *the confession and a pen in hand.* PROCTOR *does not look at it.* Come, man, sign it.

259 **Proctor,** *after glancing at the confession*: You have all witnessed it—it is enough.

260 **Danforth:** You will not sign it?

261 **Proctor:** You have all witnessed it; what more is needed?

262 **Danforth:** Do you sport with me? You will sign your name or it is no confession, Mister! *His breast heaving with agonized breathing,* PROCTOR *now lays the paper down and signs his name.*

263 **Parris:** Praise be to the Lord!

264 PROCTOR *has just finished signing when* DANFORTH *reaches for the paper. But* PROCTOR *snatches it up, and now a wild terror is rising in him, and a boundless anger.*

265 **Danforth,** *perplexed, but politely extending his hand*: If you please, sir.

266 **Proctor:** No.

267 **Danforth,** *as though* PROCTOR *did not understand*: Mr. Proctor, I must have—

268 **Proctor:** No, no. I have signed it. You have seen me. It is done! You have no need for this.

269 **Parris:** Proctor, the village must have proof that—

270 **Proctor:** Damn the village! I confess to God, and God has seen my name on this! It is enough!

271 **Danforth:** No, sir, it is—

272 **Proctor:** You came to save my soul, did you not? Here! I have confessed myself: it is enough!

273 **Danforth:** You have not con—

274 **Proctor:** I have confessed myself! Is there no good penitence but it be public? God does not need my name nailed upon the church! God sees my name; God knows how black my sins are! It is enough!

275 **Danforth:** Mr. Proctor—

276 **Proctor:** You will not use me! I am no Sarah Good or Tituba. I am John Proctor! You will not use me! It is no part of salvation that you should use me!

277 **Danforth:** I do not wish to—

278 **Proctor:** I have three children—how may I teach them to walk like men in the world, and I sold my friends?

279 **Danforth:** You have not sold your friends—

280 **Proctor:** Beguile me not! I blacken all of them when this is nailed to the church the very day they hang for silence!

281 **Danforth:** Mr. Proctor, I must have good and legal proof that you—

282 **Proctor:** You are the high court, your word is good enough! Tell them I confessed myself; say Proctor broke his knees and wept like a woman; say what you will, but my name cannot—

283 **Danforth,** *with suspicion*: It is the same, is it not? If I report it or you sign to it?

284 **Proctor—***he knows it is insane*: No, it is not the same! What others say and what I sign to is not the same!

285 **Danforth:** Why? Do you mean to deny this confession when you are free?

286 **Proctor:** I mean to deny nothing!

287 **Danforth:** Then explain to me. Mr. Proctor, why you will not let—

288 **Proctor,** *with a cry of his whole soul*: Because it is my name! Because I cannot have another in my life! Because I lie and sign myself to lies! Because I am not worth the dust on the feet of them that hang! How may I live without my name? I have given you my soul; leave me my name!

289 **Danforth,** *pointing at the confession in* PROCTOR's *hand*: Is that document a lie? If it is a lie I will not accept it! What say you? I will not deal in lies, Mister! PROCTOR *is motionless.* You will give me your honest confession in my hand, or I cannot keep you from the rope. PROCTOR *does not reply.* What way do you go, Mister?

290 *His breast heaving, his eyes staring,* PROCTOR *tears the paper and crumples it, and he is weeping in fury, but erect.*

291 **Danforth:** Marshal!

292 **Parris,** *hysterically, as though the tearing paper were his life*: Proctor, Proctor!

293 **Hale:** Man, you will hang! You cannot!

294 **Proctor,** *his eyes full of tears*: I can. And there's your first marvel, that I can. You have made your magic now, for now I do think

CLOSE READ
ANNOTATE: In paragraph 288, mark the repeated words.

QUESTION: Why do you think Miller has Proctor repeat these words?

CONCLUDE: What is the effect of this repetition?

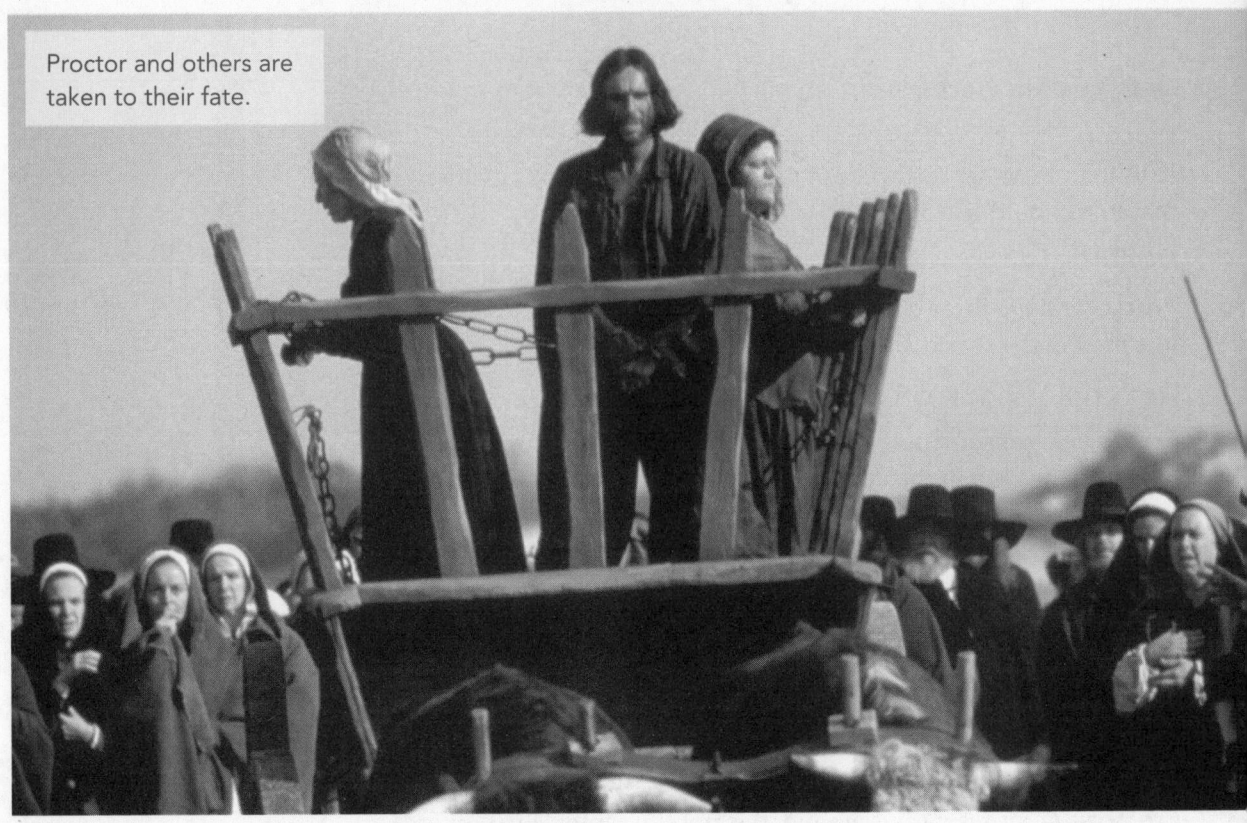

Proctor and others are taken to their fate.

NOTES

I see some shred of goodness in John Proctor. Not enough to weave a banner with, but white enough to keep it from such dogs. ELIZABETH, *in a burst of terror, rushes to him and weeps against his hand.* Give them no tear! Tears pleasure them! Show honor now, show a stony heart and sink them with it! *He has lifted her, and kisses her now with great passion.*

295 **Rebecca:** Let you fear nothing! Another judgment waits us all!

296 **Danforth:** Hang them high over the town! Who weeps for these, weeps for corruption! *He sweeps out past them.* HERRICK *starts to lead* REBECCA, *who almost collapses, but* PROCTOR *catches her, and she glances up at him apologetically.*

297 **Rebecca:** I've had no breakfast.

298 **Herrick:** Come, man.

299 HERRICK *escorts them out,* HATHORNE *and* CHEEVER *behind them.* ELIZABETH *stands staring at the empty doorway.*

300 **Parris,** *in deadly fear, to* ELIZABETH: Go to him, Goody Proctor! There is yet time!

301 *From outside a drumroll strikes the air.* PARRIS *is startled.* ELIZABETH *jerks about toward the window.*

302 **Parris:** Go to him! *He rushes out the door, as though to hold back his fate.* Proctor! Proctor!

303 *Again, a short burst of drums.*

304 **Hale:** Woman, plead with him! *He starts to rush out the door, and then goes back to her.* Woman! It is pride, it is vanity. *She avoids his*

eyes, and moves to the window. He drops to his knees. Be his helper!—What profit him to bleed? Shall the dust praise him? Shall the worms declare his truth? Go to him, take his shame away!

305 **Elizabeth**, *supporting herself against collapse, grips the bars of the window, and with a cry*: He have his goodness now. God forbid I take it from him!

306 *The final drumroll crashes, then heightens violently.* HALE *weeps in frantic prayer, and the new sun is pouring in upon her face, and the drums rattle like bones in the morning air.*

THE CURTAIN FALLS

Comprehension Check

Complete the following items after you finish your first read.

1. As Act IV opens, what is to take place at daybreak?

2. Why has Reverend Hale returned to Salem?

3. What does Parris say Abigail has recently done?

4. What does Danforth want John Proctor to do?

5. 🖻 **Notebook** Write a summary of Act IV of *The Crucible*.

- -

RESEARCH

Research to Clarify Choose at least one unfamiliar detail from the text. Briefly research that detail. In what way does the information you learned shed light on an aspect of the play?

Research to Explore Conduct research on an aspect of the text you find interesting. For example, you may want to learn more about the play's reception during the McCarthy era.

Close Read the Text

Reread Parris's remarks about the executions, beginning with paragraph 82. Mark references to the "sort" who were hanged previously. What does Miller want his audience to infer about the people who are about to die?

ANNOTATE · QUESTION · Close Read · CONCLUDE

Analyze the Text

CITE TEXTUAL EVIDENCE to support your answers.

(📝) **Notebook** Respond to these questions.

1. (a) When Hale urges Danforth to pardon the prisoners, why does Danforth refuse? (b) **Analyze** What does Danforth's attitude reveal about his sense of justice and the legitimacy of the executions?

2. (a) When urged by Hale to persuade her husband to confess, how does Elizabeth Proctor characterize Hale's argument? (b) **Interpret** What does Elizabeth mean by characterizing Hale's argument in this way?

3. **Interpret** Why does Proctor confess and then retract his confession?

4. **Essential Question:** *How do we respond when challenged by fear?* What have you learned about how people respond to fear from reading this play?

LANGUAGE DEVELOPMENT

Concept Vocabulary

conciliatory	adamant	disputation

Why These Words? The concept vocabulary words relate to arguments and people's attitudes when engaged in them. What other words in Act IV relate to this concept?

Practice

(📝) **Notebook** Write a one-paragraph summary of Act IV that uses all three concept vocabulary words.

Word Study

(📝) **Notebook Etymology** The origin and development of a word is its **etymology**. The word *adamant* comes from the Greek word *adamas*, which refers to the hardest metal in the world. It is also the name of a character from Greek mythology. In contemporary English usage, *adamant* is most often used in a figurative sense.

1. Write a definition of *adamant* based on your understanding of its etymology. Check your answer in a college-level dictionary.

2. Use an etymological dictionary to research the Greek origins of the words *tantalize* and *cereal*. Explain your findings.

Analyze Craft and Structure

Author's Choices: Literary Forms An **allegory** is a narrative that works on two levels of meaning: a literal meaning and one or more symbolic meanings.

- The **literal meaning** presents the characters and conflicts at face value. The literal story is complete and can be understood without reference to other stories or situations.

- The **symbolic meaning** interprets the characters and conflicts at a representative level—a deeper meaning that readers must infer. Characters may be symbols for real people, and the conflicts may focus readers on events or ideas that are not part of the literal narrative. Understanding an allegory's symbolic meaning can reveal the **theme**—the work's message or insight.

The Crucible is an allegory that Arthur Miller wrote to comment on the way that the 1950s "Red Scare" encouraged and preyed upon Americans' fears. At that time, Senator Joseph McCarthy and the separate House Un-American Activities Committee (HUAC) accused many Americans of being Communists, intent on overthrowing the United States government. Those targeted by HUAC investigation were often blacklisted and lost their jobs. After many life-ruining accusations, the public turned against the Communist hunts.

Practice

CITE TEXTUAL EVIDENCE to support your answers.

📓 **Notebook** Respond to these questions.

1. Use the chart to cite specific passages from the play and explain their importance to both the literal story and Miller's allegory. Begin with the twisted logic of Danforth's speech in paragraph 104 of Act IV.

PASSAGE	LITERAL MEANING	ALLEGORICAL MEANING
Danforth's speech in Act IV, paragraph 104		

2. (a) At the end of the play, John Proctor, Rebecca Nurse, and others make the noble decision. Is it the right decision? Explain. (b) What is Miller saying about those who stood fast against HUAC?

3. Miller has written about similarities between the Salem trials and the HUAC investigations: "Three hundred years apart, both prosecutors were alleging membership in a secret disloyal group; should the accused confess, his honesty could be proved only in precisely the same way—by naming former confederates." Explain how these ideas are developed in each act of *The Crucible*.

THE CRUCIBLE, ACT IV

Analyze Craft and Structure

Biblical Allusions Some of the conflicts in *The Crucible* arise out of the religious worldview that dominates the Salem community. That worldview is revealed, in part, through the characters' actions and the descriptions of their way of life. It is also revealed through **Biblical allusions**—passing or unexplained references to people, places, or events from the Bible.

Biblical allusions remind characters—and the audience—of the religious beliefs on which the Puritan community is based. Allusions also help to portray individual characters. For example, in Act IV, paragraph 117, Danforth says, "Mr. Hale, as God have not empowered me like Joshua to stop this sun from rising, so I cannot withhold from them the perfection of their punishment." A note in the text identifies the source of this allusion, and the context makes its meaning clear: Just as Joshua could not delay the sun's movement, so Danforth cannot (or will not) delay his quest to obtain confessions from the condemned. The Biblical allusion reinforces the idea that Danforth sees his work as a mission from God.

Practice

CITE TEXTUAL EVIDENCE
to support your answers.

Some of the allusions Miller uses in *The Crucible* appear in the chart.
Determine what each allusion means. Then, explain what it reveals about the characters or situation.

BIBLICAL ALLUSION	MEANING IN CONTEXT
Act II, paragraph 53: "Abigail brings the other girls into the court, and where she walks the crowd will part like the sea for Israel." (Source: Exodus 14:21–22)	
Act II, paragraph 396: "Pontius Pilate! God will not let you wash your hands of this!" (Source: Matthew 27:22–26)	
Act III, paragraph 131: "I think not, or you should surely know that Cain were an upright man, and yet he did kill Abel." (Source: Genesis 4:1–8)	
Act IV, paragraph 133: "Goody Proctor, I have gone this three month like our Lord into the wilderness." (Source: Luke 4:1)	

Author's Style

Realism In visual art and literature, **Realism** is the presentation of the details of everyday life, showing them as they actually are (or were) seen and experienced. All the elements of a realistic drama—including the setting, plot, and dialogue—are presented in ways that mirror real life.

- The **setting**, or place and time in which the drama unfolds, is like a place in the real world. It may be an actual location or historical place and time. This setting may be represented on stage with historically accurate props, backdrops, and costumes that are recognizable as objects, places, and clothing from real life.

- The playwright bases the **plot**, or action of the play, on events that either did happen or could happen in real life. Characters' reactions to these events are authentic and plausible.

- The **dialogue**, or conversation between and among characters, reflects the ways in which people actually speak or did speak in a past era. Characters may use slang, regionalisms, dialect, or formal language. These choices reflect their circumstances and personalities.

Read It

Review the opening scene of Act IV. Identify and describe one example of each dramatic element that is presented in a realistic way. Explain which textual details create or emphasize the realistic quality.

ELEMENT	EXAMPLE	HOW MILLER MAKES IT SEEM REAL
Setting		
Plot Event		
Dialogue		

Write It

⬡ **Notebook** In a paragraph, explain why you think Miller chose to tell the story of *The Crucible* in a realistic way. Why might realism be especially valuable in a play based on actual historical events?

THE CRUCIBLE, ACT IV

Writing to Sources

When you write an argument, you take a position and then present reasons and evidence that develop and support it.

Assignment

Identify a theme from *The Crucible* that is relevant to today's world. Then, write an **argumentative essay** in which you make a claim as to why this theme still matters, or—perhaps—matters even more than it once did. Support your claim and your chosen theme with evidence from the text. Include these elements in your essay:

- a clear explanation of a theme expressed in *The Crucible*
- a clear claim about the relevance of the theme to today's world
- reasons that support the claim
- textual evidence from the play that supports your reasons

Vocabulary Connection In your essay, consider including some of the concept vocabulary words.

conciliatory	adamant	disputation

Reflect on Your Writing

After you have written your argumentative essay, answer these questions.

1. In what ways did writing your essay increase your understanding and appreciation of *The Crucible?*

2. Which reasons and forms of evidence do you see as the most persuasive in your essay? How did these items help you build your argument?

3. **Why These Words?** The words you choose make a difference in your writing. Which words did you use to make your essay more persuasive?

STANDARDS

Writing
• Write arguments to support claims in an analysis of substantive topics or texts, using valid reasoning and relevant and sufficient evidence.
• Apply *grades 11–12 Reading standards* to literature.

Speaking and Listening
Present information, findings, and supporting evidence, conveying a clear and distinct perspective, such that listeners can follow the line of reasoning, alternative or opposing perspectives are addressed, and the organization, development, substance, and style are appropriate to purpose, audience, and a range of formal and informal tasks.

Speaking and Listening

Assignment

Prepare a **thematic analysis** in which you choose one theme from *The Crucible*, introduce it, and illustrate it with a dramatic reading of three sections of dialogue from the play. Follow these steps to complete the assignment.

1. **Identify a Theme** Review your notes on the play, and choose one theme that you think might be effectively illustrated with dialogue.

2. **Locate Examples** Once you have chosen a theme, scan the play to locate three pieces of dialogue that clearly illustrate that theme. Consider these questions:

   - Is it possible to find examples of dialogue from three different characters? The variety can strengthen your main idea and make your presentation more interesting.

   - Is it possible to find examples from three different sections or acts of the play? Connecting ideas across the whole play may help your listeners understand why the theme you chose is central to an understanding of Miller's text.

3. **Craft an Introduction** Decide how you will introduce the theme you chose, and how you will transition from your explanation to the dramatic readings.

4. **Prepare Your Delivery** Practice your presentation in front of a mirror or present it to a friend or family member. Keep these suggestions in mind:

   - Vary your intonation (tone and pitch) to reflect each character you portray. Speak naturally, but with attention to your enunciation and volume, when delivering your introduction.

   - Use facial expressions and gestures to help convey characters' emotions and meaning.

5. **Evaluate Analyses** As your classmates deliver their analyses, listen carefully. Use an evaluation guide like the one shown to assess their presentations.

EVALUATION GUIDE
Rate each statement on a scale of 1 (not demonstrated) to 5 (demonstrated).
☐ The speaker clearly introduced the theme.
☐ The speaker chose three examples from the play that illustrated the theme well.
☐ The speaker used a variety of vocal tones and pitches.
☐ The speaker used effective gestures and facial expressions.

✐ **EVIDENCE LOG**

Before moving on to a new selection, go to your Evidence Log and record what you learned from *The Crucible,* Act IV.

THE CRUCIBLE

Comparing Text to Media

Now that you have read the text of *The Crucible*, listen to an audio performance of Act I. As you listen, consider the choices the actors make in their portrayals. You will then analyze the ways in which the theatrical production interprets the written text and compare the audio and written versions.

THE CRUCIBLE (audio)

About the Theater Company

L.A. Theatre Works is a nonprofit organization dedicated to recording live performances of classic and contemporary plays. Founded in 1974 in Los Angeles, California, the organization has more than 250 plays in its Audio Theatre Collection, featuring many of Hollywood's best-known actors. Those recordings can be downloaded, streamed, or borrowed from libraries across the country. LATW also airs performances in weekly public radio programs and presents live performances as well.

The Crucible (audio)

Media Vocabulary

These words will be useful to you as you analyze, discuss, and write about audio performances.

audio play: theatrical performance of a drama produced for radio, podcast, or another non-visual and non-print recorded form	• Before the arrival of television, audio plays were popular on the radio. • Audio plays may incorporate sound effects to add information, or music to suggest mood.
inflection: the rise and fall of pitch and tone in a person's voice	• The pitch of a voice is how high or low it is, and tone refers to the quality of the sound produced, such as a whisper or a growl. • Inflection conveys emotion, and is part of an actor's interpretation of a character.
expression: tone of voice that indicates specific emotion	• The expression in a voice may hint at a character's unspoken thoughts or feelings.

First Review MEDIA: AUDIO

Apply these strategies as you listen to the audio performance of Act I of *The Crucible*.

LISTEN and note *who* is speaking, *what* they're saying, and *how* they're saying it.

NOTE elements that you find interesting and want to revisit.

CONNECT ideas in the audio to other media you've experienced, texts you've read, or images you've seen.

RESPOND by completing the Comprehension Check.

≣ STANDARDS

Reading Literature
By the end of grade 11, read and comprehend literature, including stories, dramas, and poems, in the grades 11–CCR text complexity band proficiently, with scaffolding as needed at the high end of the range.

The Crucible

L.A. Theatre Works

BACKGROUND

As part of the L.A. Theatre Works series, Martin Jenkins directed a radio play adaptation of *The Crucible* in 1988. You will listen to Act I. The cast features Richard Dreyfuss as Reverend Hale and Stacy Keach as John Proctor.

SCAN FOR MULTIMEDIA

NOTES

Comprehension Check

Complete the following items after you finish your first review.

1. As the play opens, what is wrong with Reverend Parris's daughter Betty?

2. Why has Parris called for Reverend Hale?

3. What story does Abigail insist the other girls tell about their activities in the woods?

4. How does Tituba's story change as she is questioned?

5. What specific accusations end this excerpt of the audio performance?

- -

Research to Clarify Choose at least one unfamiliar detail from the text. Briefly research that detail. In what way does the information you learned shed light on an aspect of the audio performance of *The Crucible?*

Research to Explore Conduct research on an aspect of the text you find interesting. For example, you may want to learn about the practice of midwifery, the profession of helping to deliver babies, as it was practiced in colonial America.

Close Review

Listen to the audio performance again. Write down any new observations that seem important. What **questions** do you have? What can you **conclude**?

REVIEW · QUESTION · CONCLUDE
Close Review

THE CRUCIBLE (audio)

Analyze the Media

📓 **Notebook** Respond to these questions.

1. (a) What does Abigail try to convince the other girls to say?
   (b) **Make Inferences** Why do the others seem willing to follow Abigail's wishes? Explain.

2. (a) What does Reverend Hale carry when he enters the scene?
   (b) **Analyze** How are the objects he carries symbols that help audiences understand his character and social position?

3. (a) What circumstances lead to Tituba's confession?
   (b) **Draw Conclusions** Is Tituba's confession likely to be trustworthy? Why or why not?

4. (a) **Interpret** What is each character in Act I afraid of?
   (b) **Evaluate** Which character feels the deepest fear? Explain the reasons for your choice.

5. **Essential Question:** *How do we respond when challenged by fear?* What have you learned about the nature of fear from listening to this audio performance?

Media Vocabulary

audio play	inflection	expression

1. (a) What are the first and last sounds the audience hears at the beginning and end of Act I of this radio play? (b) What theme is emphasized by the director's choice to highlight these sounds? Explain.

2. (a) What choices do the actors make that emphasize the emotional intensity of the situation in Act I? Cite specific examples. (b) What production techniques add to the intense atmosphere? Cite specific choices.

3. What acting choices do the performers make in this radio play to help audiences distinguish characters?

⚏ STANDARDS
Reading Literature
Cite strong and thorough textual evidence to support analysis of what the text says explicitly as well as inferences drawn from the text, including determining where the text leaves matters uncertain.

THE CRUCIBLE

THE CRUCIBLE (audio)

Writing to Compare

You have read *The Crucible*, and you have listened to a performance of Act I. The performance of a play is not simply a reading of the text. Instead, actors and directors make choices that reveal their interpretations. If you have read a play, you are in a good position to evaluate those choices.

Assignment

Write a **critical review** of the L.A. Theatre Works production of Act I of *The Crucible*. In your review, consider these questions.

- How does the performance present the setting, characters, and events? How does it establish a mood?
- Is the interpretation effective and insightful, or does it misinterpret the play?

In your conclusion, state whether you would or would not recommend the L.A. Theatre Works production to students studying the play or to general audiences.

Prewriting

Analyze the Texts To conduct a comparison of the text and the performance, follow these steps. Use the chart to capture your observations.

- Find portions of the audio performance that follow the text exactly.
- Find other portions that depart from the text. For example, dialogue may be cut or added. Consider reasons for these changes.
- Consider why the director or actors made certain choices and what each choice communicates.

STANDARDS

Reading Literature
Analyze multiple interpretations of a story, drama, or poem, evaluating how each version interprets the source text.

Writing
Apply grades 11–12 Reading standards to literature.

ELEMENT	NOTEWORTHY CHOICES	EFFECTIVENESS OF CHOICES
Portrayal of Characters		
Presentation of Setting		
Creation of Mood		
Portrayal of Action		

Notebook Does the performance bring out elements of the text that surprised you? If so, are these good surprises or disappointing ones?

Drafting

Develop Your Ideas Before you begin writing, go over your Prewriting notes. Decide which of your insights are most compelling and can be best supported with evidence. Mark or highlight those notes, and then develop each one separately. To do so, express each note in a complete sentence. Then, record quotations, passages, or paraphrases that support it.

Organize Ideas Use the outline to organize your ideas and supporting evidence. Note that a critical review often begins with a summary of the work being reviewed as well as a brief statement of the reviewer's opinion.

 EVIDENCE LOG

Before moving on to a new selection, go to your Evidence Log and record what you learned from the L.A. Theatre Works audio performance of Act I of *The Crucible.*

Outline for Critical Review

Introduction: • State the title of the work and the production being reviewed. • State the main idea—your opinion of the performance.	
Body: Paragraph Develop main idea with supporting reason and evidence	
Body: Paragraph Develop main idea with supporting reason and evidence	
Body: Paragraph Develop main idea with supporting reason and evidence	
Conclusion • Restate main idea • End with a memorable image or insight	

Review, Revise, and Edit

When you have finished drafting, revise your work. Mark ideas that need more support, and then return to your notes, the original play, or the performance to find useful evidence. Check for logical transitions between paragraphs and major sections. Edit your work to eliminate errors in grammar, sentence structure, and word choice. Finally, proofread your review to correct any lingering spelling and punctuation errors.

Write an Argument

You have just read a play about mass hysteria and a community's response to it. You have also listened to an audio performance of Act I of that play, which brought the characters and their collective fears to life.

Assignment

In *The Crucible,* rumors spread across Salem and the result is mass hysteria in the community. Use your knowledge of *The Crucible* to write a brief **argumentative essay** in which you state and defend your position on this question:

> **Could any of the characters in *The Crucible* have done more to end the hysteria in Salem?**

As you prepare to write your essay, first choose a position and state a claim. Then, develop and support that claim with quotations and examples from the text, as well as information about mass hysteria from secondary sources.

🔊 Tool Kit

Student Model of an Argument

Elements of an Argument

An **argument** is a logical way of presenting a viewpoint, belief, or stand on an issue. One form of argument is the response to literature, a deep analysis of a text that leads to a conclusion or claim. This analysis may involve the text as a whole, an element of the text, or ideas that extend beyond the text to embrace other writings, human behavior, or world events. A well-written argumentative essay about literature may change readers' understanding of a text and its meaning or importance.

An effective argumentative essay contains these elements:

- a precise claim
- consideration of counterclaims, or opposing positions, and a discussion of their strengths and weaknesses
- logical organization that makes clear connections among claim, counterclaim, reasons, and evidence
- valid reasoning and relevant and sufficient evidence
- a concluding statement or section that logically completes the argument
- formal and objective language and tone
- error-free grammar, including correct use of indefinite pronouns

Model Argument For a model of a well-crafted argument, see the Launch Text, "Is It Foolish to Fear?" Challenge yourself to find all of the elements of an effective argument in the text. You will have an opportunity to review these elements as you prepare to write your own argument.

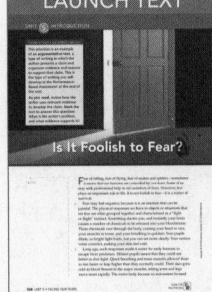

LAUNCH TEXT

Is It Foolish to Fear?

Prewriting / Planning

Ask Questions One way to start writing an argument is to ask and answer questions about the topic. Your answers to the questions will help you focus your response. Use the following questions as a starting point for your own inquiry.

1. How might someone put an end to mass hysteria in a situation like the one that unfolds in *The Crucible*?

_____

_____

2. Which character or characters in *The Crucible* would be most capable of ending the hysteria? Why?

_____

_____

Now, write a **claim**, or the position you will argue in your essay, based on your answers to these questions.

_____

_____

Gather Evidence In an argument about a work of literature, most of your evidence will derive from the text itself. However, the prompt asks you to do some research on the topic to support your claim. In the Launch Text, the writer uses researched facts to underscore ideas about fear.

> *Something alarms you, and instantly your brain causes a number of chemicals to be released into your bloodstream. Those chemicals race through the body, causing your heart to race, your muscles to tense, and your breathing to quicken. Your pupils dilate, so bright light hurts, but you can see more clearly. Your surface veins constrict, making your skin feel cold.*
>
> —"Is It Foolish to Fear?"

Make a list of the types of sources you might use to find information about the topic of mass hysteria. Note your ideas here.

✐ EVIDENCE LOG

Review your Evidence Log and identify key details you may want to cite in your argument.

▤ STANDARDS

Writing
Introduce precise, knowledgeable claim(s), establish the significance of the claim(s), distinguish the claim(s) from alternate or opposing claims, and create an organization that logically sequences claim(s), counterclaims, reasons, and evidence.

ENRICHING WRITING WITH RESEARCH

Using Research Argumentative or explanatory writing can almost always be strengthened by research. Use the library or credible online resources to locate specific information that supports your claim.

Read It

This excerpt from the Launch Text provides an example of evidence found during research. In this case, the writer located an interesting fact about fear that could be used as part of a counterclaim—if there is a way to rid ourselves of fear, why shouldn't we use it?

> **LAUNCH TEXT EXCERPT**
>
> Today, <u>modern psychotherapies may include conditioning—stimulus-response learning process—that helps people rid themselves of fears.</u> After just a few sessions, nearly anyone can stop being afraid of speaking in public or driving through a tunnel. So why shouldn't we all condition ourselves to become braver?

Notice that the definition of *conditioning* and the description of its use are broad enough that the writer does not need to cite a particular source.

Evaluating Sources for Research As you locate sources of information, examine them carefully. Not every resource is trustworthy. Consider these questions before using a source.

- Is the author an expert in the field? Look up his or her name to find out. You may also look up the publication to ensure that it is a solid resource with a reputation for reliability and credibility.
- Is the article objective—neutral and unbiased—or does it represent one person's opinion? If it is a statement of opinion, is that opinion thoughtfully considered and supported?
- Is the article up to date? Check the date on all sources to make sure that they are current.
- Is information in the article supported by convincing facts and details?

If you are consulting a website, consider its domain. Domains such as .edu or .gov indicate sites that are affiliated with colleges or government agencies. You are likely to find reliable facts and figures on sites with those domains. Other websites may be affiliated with respected magazines and journals, and the information there is likely to be credible. Look for a date on the page to ensure that you are reading up-to-date information.

Always use more than one source as you research your topic. Doing so will allow you to cross-check information to be sure that you are using dependable evidence.

▤ STANDARDS
Writing
• Develop claim(s) and counterclaims fairly and thoroughly, supplying the most relevant evidence for each while pointing out the strengths and limitations of both in a manner that anticipates the audience's knowledge level, concerns, values, and possible biases.
• Gather relevant information from multiple authoritative print and digital sources, using advanced searches effectively; assess the strengths and limitations of each source in terms of the task, purpose, and audience; integrate information into the text selectively to maintain the flow of ideas, avoiding plagiarism and overreliance on any one source and following a standard format for citation.

Write It

Effective writers seamlessly integrate different kinds of information into an argument. Consider these sentences from the Launch Text.

> LAUNCH TEXT EXCERPT
>
> First, there is a difference between fear and phobia.
>
> A phobia is an unnecessary fear of something that is unlikely to cause harm.
>
> For example, some people are afraid of clowns, but the odds of a clown's being harmful are small.

The writer presents the first of two rebuttals of the counterargument.

The writer gives a definition from research.

The writer offers an example.

In this example, the first and last sentences state the writer's own reason and example, but the sentence in between is a researched definition. The sentences are sequenced to form a complete idea. When crafting your argument, work to sequence sentences logically, integrating your own ideas with researched evidence.

Use Information From Sources As you gather information from research, decide where it might fit into your writing. Ask yourself these questions:

- Is there a term that I should define for my reader?
- Can I introduce a fact from history that will help to support my claim?
- Did I find a fact or detail that addresses a possible counterclaim?

Record Information As you complete your research, use this chart to organize your findings.

TIP

CONVENTIONS
Use punctuation correctly when citing sources.

- Underline or italicize the titles of books, newspapers, magazines, journals, or websites.
- Use quotation marks around titles of articles, chapters, or essays.

RESEARCH THAT DEFINES TERMS	RESEARCH THAT SUPPORTS MY CLAIM	RESEARCH THAT ADDRESSES A COUNTERCLAIM

Drafting

Present Your Reasoning You may use **deductive** or **inductive** reasoning to present a strong case for your claim.

TYPE OF REASONING	DEFINITION	EXAMPLE
deductive reasoning	a general conclusion applied to a specific instance or situation	Helmet laws have been shown to reduce accidents. If we had a stronger helmet law, Alicia Martinez would not have been injured last month.
inductive reasoning	specific facts used to lead to a general conclusion	Bicycle injury rates in Oaktown decreased when a helmet law was passed. Therefore, a helmet law will help our community prevent bicycle injuries.

In the Launch Text, the writer uses inductive reasoning to present a claim based on a series of facts. Facts about the human response to fear lead to and support a claim about the usefulness of fear for survival.

Use one of these patterns to draft your argument.

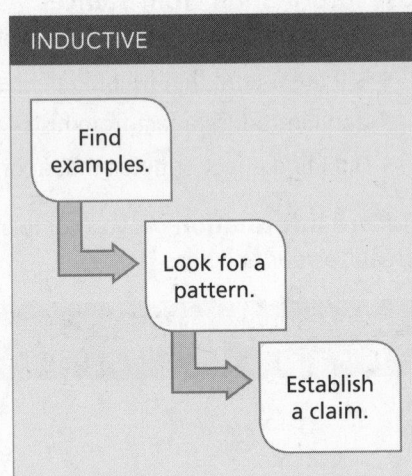

Write a First Draft Use inductive or deductive reasoning to write your first draft. Make sure to include a precise claim and to address counterclaims where possible. Use formal language and an objective tone to communicate your points clearly and effectively. Blend evidence from the text and audio performance of the play with evidence from your research on mass hysteria. Write a conclusion that follows logically from your argument, supports your claim, and adds interest to your writing.

STANDARDS

Writing
• Introduce precise, knowledgeable claim(s), establish the significance of the claim(s), distinguish the claim(s) from alternate or opposing claims, and create an organization that logically sequences claim(s), counterclaims, reasons, and evidence.
• Provide a concluding statement or section that follows from and supports the argument presented.

LANGUAGE DEVELOPMENT: CONVENTIONS

Make Effective Choices: Indefinite Pronouns

An **indefinite pronoun,** like any pronoun, is a word that takes the place of a noun, a noun phrase, or another pronoun. However, an indefinite pronoun does not refer to a specific person, place, thing, or idea. Indefinite pronouns may be singular or plural.

Read It

These sentences from the Launch Text use indefinite pronouns to refer to people or things that are unspecified, general, or universal.

- *__Some__ of us may seek professional help to rid ourselves of fears.* **(an unspecified number)**

- *__Something__ alarms you, and instantly your brain causes a number of chemicals to be released. . . .* **(an unspecified thing)**

- *This response to fear was good for __everyone__ who displayed it.* **(all people)**

- *After just a few sessions, nearly __anyone__ can stop being afraid of speaking in public. . . .* **(any unspecified person)**

- *__Few__ of us enjoy being afraid.* **(an unspecified small number)**

Write It

As you draft your argument, be sure to observe proper subject-verb agreement when you use indefinite pronouns.

SINGULAR INDEFINITE PRONOUNS	PLURAL INDEFINITE PRONOUNS
another, other	both
anybody, anyone, anything	few
each	many
either, neither	others
everybody, everyone, everything	several
little, much	
nobody, no one, nothing	
one	
somebody, someone, something	

A few indefinite pronouns may be singular or plural, depending on their **antecedents,** the words that they replace. These include *all, any, more, most, none,* and *some.*

 TIP

USAGE
Certain indefinite pronouns may also be used as adjectives. Be sure you know which part of speech you are using. Study these examples.

- *Neither* plans to attend the party. (pronoun)

- *Neither* student plans to attend the party. (adjective)

≡ STANDARDS
Language
Demonstrate command of the conventions of standard English grammar and usage when writing or speaking.

Revising

Evaluating Your Draft

Use this checklist to evaluate the effectiveness of your first draft. Then, use your evaluation and the instruction on this page to guide your revision.

FOCUS AND ORGANIZATION	EVIDENCE AND ELABORATION	CONVENTIONS
☐ Provides an introduction that establishes a precise claim.	☐ Develops the claim by using facts and details that provide relevant evidence and reasons.	☐ Attends to the norms and conventions of the discipline, especially in the use of indefinite pronouns.
☐ Distinguishes the claim from opposing claims.	☐ Provides adequate examples for each major idea.	
☐ Provides a conclusion that follows from the argument.	☐ Uses vocabulary and word choices that are appropriate for the audience and purpose.	
☐ Establishes a logical organization and develops a progression throughout the argument.	☐ Establishes and maintains a formal style and objective tone.	
☐ Uses words, phrases, and clauses to clarify the relationships between and among ideas.		

WORD NETWORK

Include interesting words from your Word Network in your argument.

Revising for Focus and Organization

Clarifying Relationships Be sure to provide clear connections among claim, counterclaim, reasons, and evidence. Could you add transitional words or phrases like these to clarify the relationships between ideas?

for example	in addition	nevertheless	because
instead of	however	furthermore	consequently
similarly	for this reason	especially	meanwhile

Revising for Evidence and Elaboration

Vocabulary and Tone When you write an argument about a literary text, consider using vocabulary specific to the study of literature. Words such as *character, setting, scene, conflict, dialogue, antagonist,* and so on may be appropriate to your task and may add to the formal tone of your essay.

Use of Source Material Reread your essay as though you were seeing it for the first time. Ask yourself these questions:

- Does every point that I make have supporting examples?
- Do I correctly cite examples from the play and other sources?
- Does my evidence from research blend well with my examples from the play?

STANDARDS

Writing
- Use words, phrases, and clauses as well as varied syntax to link the major sections of the text, create cohesion, and clarify the relationships between claim(s) and reasons, between reasons and evidence, and between claim(s) and counterclaims.
- Establish and maintain a formal style and objective tone while attending to the norms and conventions of the discipline in which they are writing.

PEER REVIEW

Exchange essays with a classmate. Use the checklist to evaluate your classmate's argument and provide supportive feedback.

1. Does the writer state a clear claim?

☐ yes ☐ no If no, explain what confused you.

2. Does the writer offer ample evidence from the play?

☐ yes ☐ no If no, tell what you think might be missing.

3. Are elements from research woven into the essay? Are the citations clear?

☐ yes ☐ no If no, suggest what your classmate might add.

4. What is the strongest part of your classmate's essay? Why?

_____

_____

_____

_____

Editing and Proofreading

Edit for Conventions Reread your draft for accuracy and consistency. Correct errors in grammar and word usage. Look for correct use of indefinite pronouns.

Proofread for Accuracy Read your draft carefully, looking for errors in spelling and punctuation. Make sure to underline or italicize the name of the play and to capitalize and spell characters' names correctly as you cite examples.

Publishing and Presenting

Create a final draft, print it, and place it in a folder in the classroom library. Attach an index card to the folder so that classmates can read your work and make constructive comments. Try to read and comment on at least three of your classmates' essays.

Reflecting

Reflect on what you learned by writing your argumentative essay. Was it difficult to weave evidence from research into the evidence you found from the play? If you had to start this assignment over again, what might you do differently?

STANDARDS

Writing
Develop and strengthen writing as needed by planning, revising, editing, rewriting, or trying a new approach, focusing on addressing what is most significant for a specific purpose and audience.

ESSENTIAL QUESTION:

How do we respond when challenged by fear?

As you read these selections, work with your group to explore the meaning and power of fear.

From Text to Topic In the middle of the twentieth century, fear was a powerful force in America—fear of economic hardship, fear of war, fear of other forms of government, and even the fear of total annihilation. Still, fear was not, and is not, unique to a particular country and a particular time. As you read the selections in this section, consider what other ideas cause people to fear—and what people's reactions reveal about themselves and the times in which they live.

Small-Group Learning Strategies

Throughout your life, in school, in your community, and in your career, you will continue to learn and work with others.

Review these strategies and the actions you can take to practice them as you work in teams. Add ideas of your own for each step. Use these strategies during Small-Group Learning.

STRATEGY	ACTION PLAN
Prepare	• Complete your assignments so that you are prepared for group work. • Organize your thinking so you can contribute to your group's discussions. •
Participate fully	• Make eye contact to signal that you are listening and taking in what is being said. • Use text evidence when making a point. •
Support others	• Build on ideas from others in your group. • Invite others who have not yet spoken to do so. •
Clarify	• Paraphrase the ideas of others to ensure that your understanding is correct. • Ask follow-up questions. •

SCAN FOR
MULTIMEDIA

CONTENTS

COMPARE

PERFORMANCE TASK

SPEAKING AND LISTENING FOCUS
Present an Argument

The Small-Group readings explore unreasonable fear from two different
perspectives. In a story, a woman is swept away by her fear of others; in a real-life
experience, a community—including its smallest children—becomes the focus of
a nation's fears. After reading, your group will create and present a debate about
what we can learn from fearful encounters.

Working as a Team

1. **Take a Position** In your group, discuss the following question:

   Which do you think creates the most frightening situation: a danger that you know about, a danger that you suspect may come to pass, or the feeling that danger is a possibility? Explain.

   As you take turns sharing your positions, provide reasons for your choice. After all group members have shared, discuss some of the criteria by which you have evaluated these fears.

2. **List Your Rules** As a group, decide on the rules that you will follow as you work together. Samples are provided; add two more of your own. You may add or revise rules based on your experience together.

   - Encourage everyone to give examples in defense of his or her position.
   - Remind everyone to listen respectfully and offer helpful comments.

   - _____

     _____

   - _____

     _____

3. **Apply the Rules** Practice working as a group. Share what you have learned about fear. Make sure each person in the group contributes. Take notes on and be prepared to share with the class one thing that you heard from another member of your group.

4. **Name Your Group** Choose a name that reflects the unit topic.

   Our group's name: _____

5. **Create a Communication Plan** Decide how you want to communicate with one another. For example, you might discuss the topic during lunch, use online collaboration tools, or schedule a set of video chats.

   Our group's decision: _____

   _____

Making a Schedule

First, find out the due dates for the small-group activities. Then, preview the texts and activities with your group, and make a schedule for completing the tasks.

SELECTION	ACTIVITIES	DUE DATE
from Farewell to Manzanar		
Interview With George Takei		
Antojos		

Working on Group Projects

As your group works together, you'll find it more effective if each person has a specific role. Different projects require different roles. Before beginning a project, discuss the necessary roles, and choose one for each group member. Here are some possible roles; add your own ideas.

Project Manager: monitors the schedule and keeps everyone on task

Researcher: organizes research activities

Recorder: takes notes during group meetings

_____

_____

_____

_____

_____

_____

from FAREWELL TO MANZANAR

Comparing Text to Media

In this lesson, you will compare an excerpt from the autobiography *Farewell to Manzanar* and a video interview with the actor George Takei. First, you will complete the first-read and close-read activities for the excerpt from *Farewell to Manzanar*. The work you do with your group on this title will help prepare you for the comparing task.

INTERVIEW WITH GEORGE TAKEI

About the Authors
Jeanne Wakatsuki Houston (b. 1934) and **James D. Houston** (1933–2009) co-wrote not only this autobiography, but also a collection of related essays. Each author has also written several works independently.

from Farewell to Manzanar

Concept Vocabulary

As you perform your first read of the excerpt from *Farewell to Manzanar*, you will encounter these words.

collaborator	conspirators	espionage

Base Words If these words are unfamiliar to you, analyze each one to see whether it contains a base word you know. Then, use your knowledge of the "inside" word, along with context, to identify the meaning of the unfamiliar word. Study this example.

> **Context:** By 1775, many American colonists considered the taxes and other burdensome restrictions imposed by the British to be **insupportable**.
>
> **Familiar "Inside" Word:** *support*, meaning "bear" or "carry"
>
> **Conclusion:** The taxes and restrictions are said to be burdensome, so *insupportable* might mean "unbearable" or "intolerable."

Apply your knowledge of base words and other vocabulary strategies to determine the meanings of unfamiliar words you encounter during your first read.

First Read NONFICTION

Apply these strategies as you conduct your first read. You will have an opportunity to conduct a close read after your first read.

STANDARDS

Reading Informational Text
By the end of grade 11, read and comprehend literary nonfiction in the grades 11–CCR text complexity band proficiently, with scaffolding as needed at the high end of the range.

Language
• Determine or clarify the meaning of unknown and multiple-meaning words and phrases based on *grades 11–12 reading and content*, choosing flexibly from a range of strategies.
• Identify and correctly use patterns of word changes that indicate different meanings or parts of speech.

NOTICE the general ideas of the text. *What* is it about? *Who* is involved?

ANNOTATE by marking vocabulary and key passages you want to revisit.

First Read

CONNECT ideas within the selection to what you already know and what you have already read.

RESPOND by completing the Comprehension Check and by writing a brief summary of the selection.

from Farewell to Manzanar

Jeanne Wakatsuki Houston
and James D. Houston

BACKGROUND

During World War II, the United States fought the Axis powers, which included Japan. Afraid of Japanese sympathizers, and driven by racial prejudices, the federal government ordered about 120,000 Japanese Americans to leave their homes and live in facilities known as internment camps. As this excerpt opens, Jeanne Wakatsuki's father arrives at Manzanar, one such internment camp, after his detention on false charges of having aided the enemy.

SCAN FOR MULTIMEDIA

Inu

NOTES

1   With Papa back our cubicle was filled to overflowing. Woody brought in another army bunk and tick mattress, up next to Mama's. But that was not what crowded the room. It was Papa himself, his dark, bitter, brooding presence. Once moved in, it seemed he didn't go outside for months. He sat in there, or paced, alone a great deal of the time, and Mama had to bring his meals from the mess hall.

2   He made her bring him extra portions of rice, or cans of the syrupy fruit they served. He would save this up and concoct brews in a homemade still he kept behind the door, brews that smelled so bad

Mama was ashamed to let in any visitors. Day after day he would sip his rice wine or his apricot brandy, sip till he was blind drunk and passed out. In the morning he would wake up groaning like the demon in a kabuki[1] drama; he would vomit and then start sipping again. He terrified all of us, lurching around the tiny room, cursing in Japanese and swinging his bottles wildly. No one could pacify him. Mama got nothing but threats and abuse for her attempts to comfort him.

3   I turned eight that fall. I remember telling myself that he never went out and never associated with others because he thought he was better than they were and was angry at being forced to live so close to them for the first time in his life. I told myself they whispered about him because he brewed his own foul-smelling wine in our barracks.

4   All of this was partly true. But there were deeper, uglier reasons for his isolation. I first sensed it one night when Mama and I went to the latrine together. By this time the stalls were partitioned. Two Terminal Island[2] women about Mama's age were leaving just as we walked in. They lingered by the doorway, and from inside my stall I could hear them whispering about Papa, deliberately, just loud enough for us to hear. They kept using the word "inu." I knew it meant "dog," and I thought at the time they were backbiting him because he never socialized.

5   Spoken Japanese is full of disrespectful insult words that can be much more cutting than mere vulgarity. They have to do with bad manners, or worse, breaches of faith and loyalty. Years later I learned that *inu* also meant **collaborator** or informer. Members of the Japanese American Citizens League were being called *inu* for having helped the army arrange a peaceful and orderly evacuation. Men who cooperated with camp authorities in any way could be labeled *inu,* as well as those genuine informers inside the camp who relayed information to the War Department and to the FBI.

6   For the women in the late-night latrine Papa was an *inu* because he had been released from Fort Lincoln earlier than most of the Issei[3] men, many of whom had to remain up there separated from their families throughout the war. After investigating his record, the Justice Department found no reason to detain him any longer. But the rumor was that, as an interpreter, he had access to information from fellow Isseis that he later used to buy his release.

7   This whispered charge, added to the shame of everything that had happened to him, was simply more than he could bear. He did not yet have the strength to resist it. He exiled himself, like a leper,[4] and he drank.

❅ ❅ ❅

Mark base words or indicate another strategy you used that helped you determine meaning.

collaborator (kuh LAB uh ray tuhr) *n.*

MEANING:

---

1. **kabuki** (kuh BOO kee) *n.* stylized form of classical Japanese theater.
2. **Terminal Island** Japanese American community in Los Angeles that was entirely destroyed after the inhabitants were interned.
3. **Issei** (EE say) first-generation Japanese Americans, who have emigrated from Japan.
4. **like a leper** Historically, individuals with the disease leprosy were isolated from society, out of fear of contagion.

Yes Yes No No

27. Are you willing to serve in the Armed Forces of the United States on combat duty, wherever ordered?

(yes)   (no)

28. Will you swear unqualified allegiance to the United States of America and faithfully defend the United States from any or all attack by foreign or domestic forces, and forswear any form of allegiance or obedience to the Japanese emperor, or any other foreign government, power, or organization?

(yes)   (no)

—from the *War Relocation Authority Application for Leave Clearance, 1943*

8   Later in December the administration gave each family a Christmas tree hauled in from the Sierras. A new director had been appointed and this was his gesture of apology for all the difficulties that had led up to the riot, a promise of better treatment and better times to come.

9   It was an honest gesture, but it wasn't much of a Christmas that year. The presents were makeshift, the wind was roaring, Papa was drunk. Better times were a long way off, and the difficulties, it seemed, had just begun. Early in February the government's Loyalty Oath appeared. Everyone seventeen and over was required to fill it out. This soon became the most divisive issue of all. It cut deeper than the riot, because no one could avoid it. Not even Papa. After five months of self-imposed isolation, this debate was what finally forced him out of the barracks and into circulation again.

10   At the time, I was too young to understand the problem. I only knew there was no peace in our cubicle for weeks. Block organizers would come to talk to Papa and my brothers. They would huddle over the table awhile, muttering like **conspirators**, sipping tea or one of his concoctions. Their voices gradually would rise to shouts and threats. Mama would try to calm the men down. Papa would tell her to shut up, then Granny would interrupt and order him to quit disgracing Mama all the time. Once he just shoved Granny across the room, up against the far wall and back into her chair, and where she sat sniffling while the arguments went on.

11   If the organizers weren't there, Papa would argue with Woody. Or rather, Woody would listen to Papa lecture him on *true* loyalty, pacing from bunk to bunk, waving his cane.

12   "Listen to me, Woodrow. When a soldier goes into war he must go believing he is never coming back. This is why the Japanese are such courageous warriors. They are prepared to die. They expect nothing else. But to do that, you must *believe* in what you're fighting for. If you do not believe, you will not be willing to die. If you are not willing to die, you won't fight well. And if you don't fight well you will

Mark base words or indicate another strategy you used that helped you determine meaning.

conspirators (kuhn SPIHR uh tuhrz) *n.*

MEANING:

probably be killed stupidly, for the wrong reason, and unheroically. So tell me, how can you think of going off to fight?"

13 Woody always answered softly, respectfully, with a boyish and submissive smile.

14 "I will fight well, Papa."

15 "In this war? How is it possible?"

16 "I am an American citizen. America is at war."

17 "But look where they have put us!"

18 "The more of us who go into the army, the sooner the war will be over, the sooner you and Mama will be out of here."

19 "Do you think I would risk losing a son for that?"

20 "You want me to answer NO NO, Papa?"

21 "Do you think that is what I'm telling you? Of course you cannot answer NO NO. If you say NO NO; you will be shipped back to Japan with all those other *bakatare*!"

22 "But if I answer YES YES I will be drafted anyway, no matter how I feel about it. That is why they are giving us the oath to sign."

23 "No! That is not true! They are looking for volunteers. And only a fool would volunteer."

24 Papa stared hard at Woody, making this a challenge. Woody shrugged, still smiling his boyish smile, and did not argue. He knew that when the time came he would join the army, and he knew it was pointless to begin the argument again. It was a circle. His duty as a son was to sit and listen to Papa thrash his way around it and around it and around it.

25 A circle, or you might have called it a corral, like Manzanar itself, with no exit save via three narrow gates. The first led into the infantry, the second back across the Pacific. The third, called *relocation*, was just opening up: Interned citizens who could find a job and a sponsor somewhere inland, away from the west coast, were beginning to trickle out of camp. But the program was bogged down in paperwork. It was taking months to process applications and security clearances. A loyalty statement required of everyone, it was hoped, might save some time and a lot of red tape. This, together with the search for "loyal" soldiers, had given rise to the ill-fated "oath."

26 Two weeks before the December Riot, JACL[5] leaders met in Salt Lake City and passed a resolution pledging Nisei[6] to volunteer out of the camps for military service. In January the government announced its plan to form an all-Nisei combat regiment. While recruiting for this unit and speeding up the relocation program, the government figured it could simultaneously weed out the "disloyal" and thus get a clearer idea of exactly how many agents and Japanese sympathizers it actually had to deal with. This part of it would have been comical if

---

5. **JACL** Japanese American Citizens League.
6. **Nisei** (NEE say) second-generation Japanese Americans, who were born in the United States.

the results were not so grotesque. No self-respecting **espionage** agent would willingly admit he was disloyal. Yet the very idea of the oath itself—appearing at the end of that first chaotic year—became the final goad that prodded many once-loyal citizens to turn militantly anti-American.

27   From the beginning Papa knew his own answer would be YES YES. He agreed with Woody on this much, even though it meant swearing allegiance to the government that had sent him to Fort Lincoln and denying his connections with the one country in the world where he might still have the rights of a citizen. The alternative was worse. If he said NO NO, he could be sent to Tule Lake camp in northern California where all the "disloyal" were to be assembled for what most people believed would be eventual repatriation to Japan. Papa had no reason to return to Japan. He was too old to start over. He believed America would win the war, and he knew, even after all he'd endured, that if he had a future it still lay in this country. What's more, a move to Tule Lake could mean a further splitting up of our family.

28   This was a hard choice to make, and even harder to hold to. Anti-American feeling in camp ran stronger than ever. Pro-Japan forces were trying to organize a NO NO vote by blocks, in massive resistance. Others wanted to boycott the oath altogether in a show of noncooperation or through the mistaken fear that *anyone* who accepted the form would be shipped out of camp: the NO NOs back to Japan, the YES YESs into an American society full of wartime hostility and racial hate.

29   A meeting to debate the matter was called in our mess hall. Papa knew that merely showing his face would draw stares and muttered comments. YES YES was just what they expected of an *inu*. But he had to speak his mind before the NO NO contingent carried the block. Saying NO NO as an individual was one thing, bullying the entire camp into it was quite another. At the very least he didn't want to be sucked into such a decision without having his own opinion heard.

30   Woody wanted to go with him, but Papa said it was a meeting for "heads of households" only and he insisted on going alone. From the time he heard about it he purposely drank nothing stronger than tea. He shaved and trimmed his mustache and put on a silk tie. His limp was nearly gone now, but he carried his cane and went staggering off down the narrow walkway between the barracks, punching at the packed earth in front of him.

31   About four o'clock I was playing hopscotch in the firebreak with three other girls. It was winter, the sun had already dropped behind Mount Whitney. Now a wind was rising, the kind of biting, steady wind that could bring an ocean of sand into camp at any moment with almost no warning. I was hurrying back to the barracks when I heard a great commotion inside the mess hall, men shouting wildly, as if a fire had broken out. The loudest voice was Papa's, cursing.

32   "*Eta!* (trash) *Eta! Bakayaro! Bakayaro!*"

NOTES

Mark base words or indicate another strategy you used that helped you determine meaning.

espionage (EHS pee uh nozh) *n.*

MEANING:

33   The door of the mess hall flew open and a short, beefy man came tearing out. He jumped off the porch, running as his feet hit the ground. He didn't get far. Papa came through the doorway right behind him, in a flying leap, bellowing like a warrior, "Yaaaaaah!" He let go of his cane as he landed on the man's back, and they both tumbled into the dirt. The wind was rising. Half the sky was dark with a tide of sand pouring toward us. The dust billowed and spun as they kicked and pummeled and thrashed each other.

34   At the meeting, when Papa stood up to defend the YES YES position, murmurs of "*Inu, inu*" began to circulate around the mess hall. This man then jumped up at the speaker's table and made the charge aloud. Papa went for him. Now, outside in the dirt, Papa had him by the throat and would have strangled him, but some other men pulled them apart. I had never seen him so livid, yelling and out of his head with rage. While they pinned his arms, he kicked at the sand, sending windblown bursts of it toward the knot of men dragging his opponent out of reach.

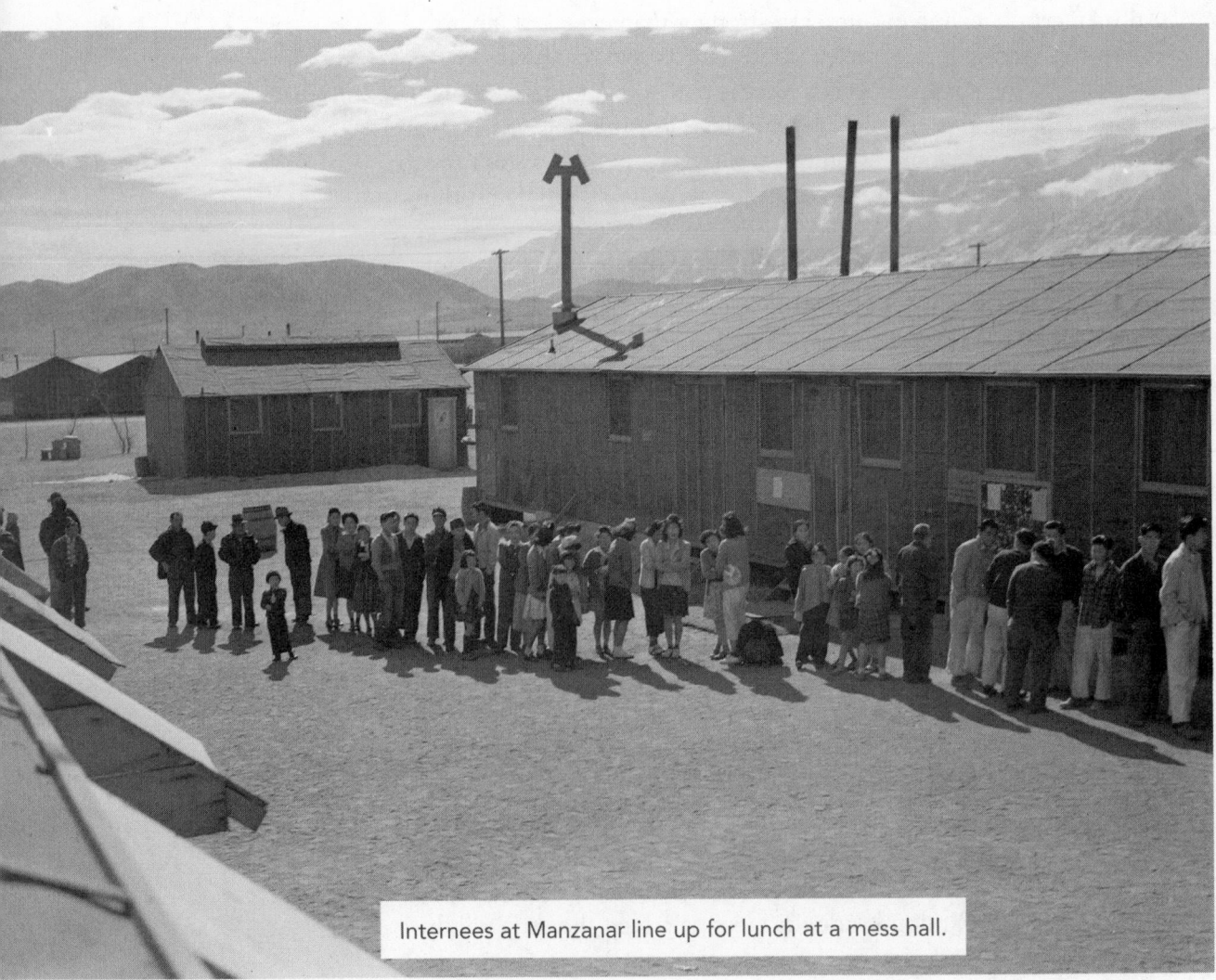

Internees at Manzanar line up for lunch at a mess hall.

35   A few moments later the sandstorm hit. The sky turned black as night. Everyone ran for cover. Two men hustled Papa to our barracks. The fighting against the wind and sand to get there calmed him down some.

36   Back inside he sat by the stove holding his teacup and didn't speak for a long time. One cheekbone was raw where it had been mashed into the sand. Mama kept pouring him little trickles of tea. We listened to the wind howl. When the sand died down, the sky outside stayed black. The storm had knocked out the electricity all over the camp. It was a cold, lonely night, and we huddled around our oil stove while Mama and Woody and Chizu began to talk about the day.

37   A young woman came in, a friend of Chizu's, who lived across the way. She had studied in Japan for several years. About the time I went to bed she and Papa began to sing songs in Japanese, warming their hands on either side of the stove, facing each other in its glow. After a while Papa sang the first line of the Japanese national anthem, *Kimi ga yo*. Woody, Chizu, and Mama knew the tune, so they hummed along while Papa and the other woman sang the words. It can be a hearty or a plaintive tune, depending on your mood. From Papa, that night, it was a deep-throated lament. Almost invisible in the stove's small glow, tears began running down his face.

38   I had seen him cry a few times before. It only happened when he was singing or when someone else sang a song that moved him. He played the three-stringed *samisen*, which Kiyo and I called his "pinko-pinko." We would laugh together when we heard him plucking it and whining out old Japanese melodies. We would hold our ears and giggle. It was always a great joke between us, except for those rare times when Papa began to weep at the lyrics. Then we would just stare quietly—as I did that night—from some hidden corner of the room. This was always mysterious and incomprehensible.

39   The national anthem, I later learned, is what he had sung every morning as a schoolboy in Japan. They still sing it there, the way American kids pledge allegiance to the flag. It is not a martial song, or a victory song, the way many national anthems are. It is really a poem, whose words go back to the ninth century:

> *Kimi ga yo wa chiyoni*
> *yachiyoni sa-za-re i-shi no i-wa-o to*
> *na-ri-te ko-ke no musu made.*

> May thy peaceful reign last long.
> May it last for thousands of years,
> Until this tiny stone will grow
> Into a massive rock, and the moss
> Will cover it deep and thick.

40 It is a patriotic song that can also be read as a proverb, as a personal credo for endurance. The stone can be the kingdom or it can be a man's life. The moss is the greenery that, in time, will spring even from a rock. In Japan, before the turn of the century, outside my father's house there stood one of those stone lanterns, with four stubby legs and a small pagoda-like roof. Each morning someone in the household would pour a bucketful of water over his lantern, and after several years a skin of living vegetation began to show on the stone. As a boy he was taught that the last line of the anthem refers to a certain type of mossy lichen with exquisitely tiny white flowers sprinkled in amongst the green. ❧

Comprehension Check

Complete the following items after you finish your first read. Review and clarify details with your group.

1. Identify two meanings for the Japanese word *inu*.

2. According to Jeanne Wakatsuki Houston, what is the most divisive issue among the internees?

3. Why doesn't Woody argue with Papa?

4. On what type of occasion does Papa cry, according to Jeanne Wakatsuki Houston?

5. 📓 **Notebook** Confirm your understanding of the text by writing a summary.

- -

RESEARCH

Research to Clarify Choose at least one unfamiliar detail from the text. Briefly research that detail. In what way does the information you learned shed light on an aspect of the text?

Close Read the Text

With your group, revisit sections of the text you marked during your first read. **Annotate** what you notice. What **questions** do you have? What can you **conclude?**

(Close Read — ANNOTATE · QUESTION · CONCLUDE)

from FAREWELL TO MANZANAR

Analyze the Text

> **CITE TEXTUAL EVIDENCE**
> to support your answers.

Notebook Complete the activities.

1. **Review and Clarify** With your group, reread paragraphs 4 and 5 of the excerpt from *Farewell to Manzanar.* What do the authors suggest about the obstacles and challenges confronting Papa?

2. **Present and Discuss** Now, work with your group to share the passages from the text that you found especially important. Take turns presenting your passages. Discuss what you noticed in the selections, what questions you asked, and what conclusions you reached.

3. **Essential Question:** *How do we respond when challenged by fear?* What has this text taught you about people's responses to fear? Discuss with your group.

LANGUAGE DEVELOPMENT

Concept Vocabulary

> collaborator   conspirators   espionage

Why These Words? The three concept vocabulary words from the text are related. With your group, determine what the words have in common. Write your ideas, and add another word that fits the category.

Practice

Notebook Confirm your understanding of these words by looking up their definitions in a dictionary. Then, use the words to write a short narrative paragraph. Include context clues that hint at each word's meaning.

Word Study

Latin Suffix: -or The suffix -*or* can be used to form nouns from verbs. For example, the words *collaborator* and *conspirators* are formed from *collaborate* and *conspire*, respectively. Reread paragraphs 2 and 8 of the selection. In each paragraph, find one noun formed from the suffix -*or*. Write the nouns and their meanings; then, list the verb used to form each noun.

WORD NETWORK

Add words related to fear from the text to your Word Network.

STANDARDS

Language
• Identify and correctly use patterns of word changes that indicate different meanings of parts or speech.
• Verify the preliminary determination of the meaning of a word or phrase.

from FAREWELL TO MANZANAR

Analyze Craft and Structure

Development of Complex Ideas Fiction writers use the tools of **characterization** to show what imaginary characters are like. Narrative nonfiction writers use the same tools to describe real people. There are two types of characterization: direct and indirect.

- With **direct characterization**, a writer explicitly states what a person is like—for example, "It was Papa himself, his dark, bitter, brooding presence." Here, Jeanne Wakatsuki Houston simply tells readers that her father was unhappy and sullen.

- With **indirect characterization**, writers provide details that allow readers to infer what people are like. A writer might describe a person's physical appearance and behavior, quote his or her statements, or report what other people say about him or her. For instance, when Houston recalls that other people called her father "inu," readers can infer that her father was neither liked nor respected.

To fully understand the people and their motivations in works of narrative nonfiction, compare and contrast descriptive details, statements, facts, and opinions presented in the text.

Practice

CITE TEXTUAL EVIDENCE
to support your answers.

📝 **Notebook** Work independently to answer the questions and complete the chart. Then, share your responses with your group.

1. (a) Why do the other Japanese Americans in the camp view Papa as a traitor? (b) How do their opinions affect Houston's perceptions of her father?

2. (a) What does Papa's YES YES position reveal about him? (b) How does his stance on this issue give readers insight about his values and priorities?

3. Use the chart to record details about Papa's behavior during important episodes in the text. Then, use those details to make inferences about his feelings.

EPISODE	PAPA'S BEHAVIOR	INFERENCE
Return to Manzanar (paragraphs 1–10)		
Meeting at the mess hall (paragraphs 29–35)		
Papa singing songs (paragraphs 36–40)		

Author's Style

Author's Point of View *Farewell to Manzanar* is an autobiographical account in which the author looks back on events she experienced as a young girl. The use of **first-person point of view**, signaled by pronouns such as *I, me,* and *my,* tells readers that the author is relating her own story. However, because the author is recalling these events years after they happened, the narrative unfolds on at least two levels. At times, Jeanne Wakatsuki Houston relates events from the perspective of a young child. At other times, she offers insights and reflections from an adult perspective. Sometimes, Houston signals a narrative shift with clues such as "at the time" and "years later I learned." At other points, though, the narrative shift is implied.

Read It

1. Use this chart to compile your notes on shifting perspectives in the selection. Reread each passage identified in the left-hand column. Then, write a comment on the narrative perspective or shift in the right-hand column.

PASSAGE	COMMENT(S) ON NARRATIVE PERSPECTIVE/SHIFT
paragraphs 9–10	
paragraphs 28–29	
paragraphs 39–40	

2. 📓 **Notebook Connect to Style** What is the overall effect of narrative shifts in the selection? Do such shifts clarify Houston's principal issues and conflicts? Explain your answer.

Write It

📓 **Notebook** Write a short narrative account of an event from your childhood. Use first-person point of view to tell your story, but shift perspectives to highlight the differences between how you experienced the event as a child and how you understand it now.

⋮☰ STANDARDS

Reading Informational Text
• Cite strong and thorough textual evidence to support analysis of what the text says explicitly as well as inferences drawn from the text, including determining where the text leaves matters uncertain.
• Analyze a complex set of ideas or sequence of events and explain how specific individuals, ideas, or events interact and develop over the course of the text.
• Determine an author's point of view or purpose in a text in which the rhetoric is particularly effective, analyzing how style and content contribute to the power, persuasiveness, or beauty of the text.

from FAREWELL TO MANZANAR

Comparing Text to Media

This interview with George Takei, which focuses on the actor's internment experience during World War II, was drawn from the Archive of American Television. Watch and listen to the interview. Then, compare and contrast the points of view of two people who experienced similar hardships.

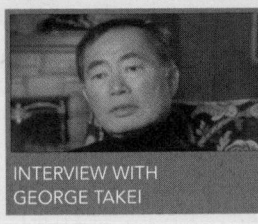

INTERVIEW WITH GEORGE TAKEI

About the Interviewee

George Takei (b. 1937) was born into a Japanese American family in Los Angeles. In college, he became interested in theater and made acting his career. Best known for portraying Hikaru Sulu in the original *Star Trek*, Takei has participated in dozens of films and television programs. He also has appeared in *Allegiance*, a musical inspired by his internment experience.

Interview With George Takei

Media Vocabulary

These words will be useful to you as you analyze, discuss, and write about video interviews.

Documentary: program or film that provides a factual record or report of real events	• Documentaries may consist largely of interviews with people who are uniquely qualified to report on certain events or topics. • Interviews may take place in a variety of formats and allow different types of interactions between the interviewer and the interviewee.
Eyewitness Account: description given by someone who was present at an event	• Eyewitness testimony is valuable for its immediacy and presumed credibility. • Eyewitnesses, however, may be biased and only partially trustworthy.
Framing: composing a visual so that an enclosing border surrounds the image in the foreground	• Framing may offer a counterpoint or contrast between foreground and background images. • Framing may alternate with close-up views, in which no background is visible.

First Review MEDIA: VIDEO

Apply these strategies as you perform your first review. You will have an opportunity to complete a close review after your first review.

WATCH *who* speaks, *what* they say, and *how* they say it.

NOTE elements that you find interesting and want to revisit.

CONNECT ideas in the video to other media you've experienced, texts you've read, or images you've seen.

RESPOND by completing the Comprehension Check.

First Review — WATCH NOTE CONNECT RESPOND

≣ STANDARDS

Reading Informational Text
By the end of grade 11, read and comprehend literary nonfiction in the grades 11–CCR text complexity band proficiently, with scaffolding as needed at the high end of the range.

Language
Acquire and use accurately general academic and domain-specific words and phrases, sufficient for reading, writing, speaking, and listening at the college and career readiness level; demonstrate independence in gathering vocabulary knowledge when considering a word or phrase important to comprehension or expression.

Interview With George Takei

BACKGROUND

The internment of Japanese Americans lasted from March 1942 to March 1946. However, Executive Order 9066, which established the policy of internment, was only officially repealed and apologized for in 1976. In this interview, George Takei describes how he and his family were forced from their home in Los Angeles and interned at two different camps—one in Arkansas and one in northern California— during World War II.

SCAN FOR MULTIMEDIA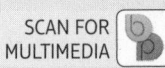

NOTES

Comprehension Check

Complete the following items after you finish your first review. Review and clarify details with your group.

1. How old was Takei at the time of the attack on Pearl Harbor?

2. What does Takei remember about the day that he and his family were ordered out of their home?

3. As a young child, how did Takei feel about the internment camps?

4. What were the two key questions posed by the government's loyalty questionnaire?

5. How did Takei's parents respond to the key questions? What reasons did they give?

6. Why were Takei and his family transferred from a camp in Arkansas to Tule Lake in northern California?

7. 🖹 **Notebook** Confirm your understanding of the interview by summarizing Takei's comments about the significance of the loyalty questionnaire.

Close Review

With your group, revisit the video interview and your first-review notes. Record any new observations that seem important. What **questions** do you have? What can you **conclude**?

INTERVIEW WITH GEORGE TAKEI

Analyze the Media

▣ **Notebook** Complete the activities.

1. **Present and Discuss** Choose the interview segment you find most interesting or powerful. Share your choice with the group, and discuss why you chose it. Explain what you noticed in the segment, what questions it raised for you, and what conclusions you reached about it.

2. **Review and Synthesize** How does Takei reveal his perspective on the treatment of Japanese Americans during the war? Consider his tone of voice and facial expressions in addition to the details he shares.

3. **Essential Question:** *How do we respond when challenged by fear?* What have you learned about people's responses to fear from watching this interview?

LANGUAGE DEVELOPMENT

Media Vocabulary

| documentary | eyewitness account | framing |

Use the vocabulary words in your responses to the questions.

1. Why is George Takei qualified to present a factual report on the internment camp experience?

2. **(a)** How does Takei's perspective offer a different way of seeing America's involvement in World War II? **(b)** What is the value of considering alternative perspectives on historic events?

3. What effect is created by having Takei talk in the foreground of a scene set in a comfortably furnished room?

▤ STANDARDS

Speaking and Listening
Evaluate a speaker's point of view, reasoning, and use of evidence and rhetoric, assessing the stance, premises, links among ideas, word choice, points of emphasis, and tone used.

Language
Acquire and use accurately general academic and domain-specific words and phrases, sufficient for reading, writing, speaking, and listening at the college and career readiness level; demonstrate independence in gathering vocabulary knowledge when considering a word or phrase important to comprehension or expression.

from FAREWELL TO MANZANAR

INTERVIEW WITH GEORGE TAKEI

Writing to Compare

Both the excerpt from *Farewell to Manzanar* and the interview with George Takei provide primary-source information about the experiences of interned Japanese Americans during World War II. Deepen your understanding of both sources by comparing the two accounts and the perspectives they express.

Assignment

Choose one of these three prompts, and respond to it in a **compare-and-contrast essay**.

☐ How are Papa's and Woody's understandings of the Loyalty Oath and its implications in *Farewell to Manzanar* similar to and different from Takei's parents' position on the same topic?

☐ Consider Houston's and Takei's reactions to their parents' decisions. How are they alike and different?

☐ What events do Houston and Takei emphasize in their respective accounts? How are their treatments of those events similar and different? Consider the details on which they focus, their word choices, and their tones.

Prewriting

Analyze the Texts Before you choose a prompt to address, discuss the two texts with your group. Consider the following questions.

- How does each selection describe the Loyalty Oath and peoples' responses to it? What arguments are used to support both "yes" and "no" responses? What consequences follow each decision?

- What similar and different information and insights about the experiences of interned Japanese do the two texts present?

📓 **Notebook** Record your ideas during the group discussion.

FAREWELL TO MANZANAR	INTERVIEW WITH GEORGE TAKEI

📓 **Notebook** Respond to these questions.

1. How do the points of view differ, in general?

2. What do these two texts suggest about the universal experience of Japanese Americans during World War II?

▦ STANDARDS

Reading Informational Text
Integrate and evaluate multiple sources of information presented in different media or formats as well as in words in order to address a question or solve a problem.

Writing
- Apply *grades 11–12 Reading standards* to literary nonfiction.
- Write informative/explanatory texts to examine and convey complex ideas, concepts, and information clearly and accurately through the effective selection, organization, and analysis of content.

Drafting

Choose a Question Work independently to plan and write your essay. First, review your Prewriting notes.

- Which aspect of the autobiography or interview do you find most interesting or important?
- What strikes you as the most powerful difference between the two?

Your answers to these questions should help you choose a topic. Place a checkmark in the box next to your choice.

Write a Thesis Statement Your thesis statement should respond to your chosen prompt in one or two sentences. Write a first version of your thesis statement here. You may adjust or even change it altogether as you draft and refine your ideas.

Thesis Statement: _____

_____

_____

Select Evidence Share your thesis statements other group members who are working from the same prompt. Then, work together to discuss and choose evidence from both the autobiography and the interview that will support each person's thesis. Use the chart to list the evidence you plan to use in your essay.

EVIDENCE FROM AUTOBIOGRAPHY	EVIDENCE FROM INTERVIEW

Write a First Draft Begin your essay with a thesis statement that offers a one- or two-sentence response to the prompt. Then, in the body of the essay, develop your thesis with details, quotations, or other support from the selections. Decide whether you will write about one selection first and then about the other one, or whether you will discuss the two texts' similarities and then their differences. Make a short outline to set up a structure to follow. Then, draft your essay.

Review, Revise, and Edit

Read your draft aloud to your group. Ask for feedback, take notes, and then use your peers' suggestions and your own ideas to revise your draft. Make sure your treatment of the two selections is balanced. Then, check for logical transitions as you shift attention from one selection to the other. After revising, edit to improve grammar, word choice, and sentence structure. Proofread to eliminate errors in spelling and punctuation.

📝 EVIDENCE LOG

Before moving on to a new selection, go to your Evidence Log and record what you've learned from the excerpt from *Farewell to Manzanar* and the interview with George Takei.

About the Author

Julia Alvarez (b. 1950) was born in New York City but spent much of her childhood in the Dominican Republic. She and her family returned to the United States when her father's participation in a plot to overthrow the dictator Rafael Trujillo was discovered—a move that she considers foundational to her decision to be a writer. Calling writing "a way to understand yourself," Alvarez often draws upon her personal experiences and her Caribbean heritage for inspiration.

Antojos

Concept Vocabulary

As you perform your first read of "Antojos," you will encounter the following words.

cantina	cabana	machetes

Context Clues If these words are unfamiliar to you, try using **context clues**—other words and phrases that appear in the surrounding text—to help you determine their meanings. Here is an example of how to apply the strategy.

> **Unfamiliar Word:** *replete*
>
> **Context:** Although the story lacks action, it is replete with interesting characters.
>
> **Conclusion:** The word *Although* indicates that the words *lacks action* are in contrast or opposition to the word *replete*. *Replete,* then, must mean something opposite to "lacking"—perhaps "filled."

Apply your knowledge of context clues and other vocabulary strategies to determine the meanings of unfamiliar words you encounter during your first read.

First Read FICTION

Apply these strategies as you conduct your first read. You will have an opportunity to complete a close read after your first read.

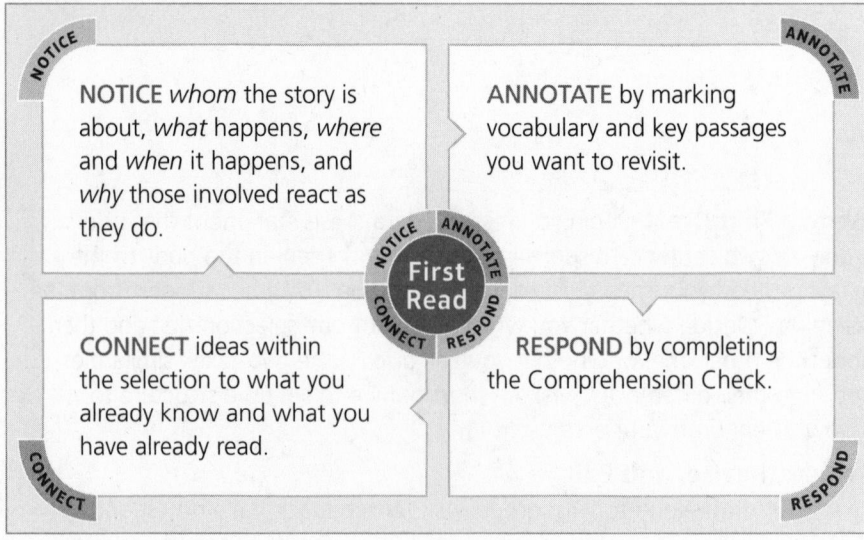

NOTICE *whom* the story is about, *what* happens, *where* and *when* it happens, and *why* those involved react as they do.

ANNOTATE by marking vocabulary and key passages you want to revisit.

CONNECT ideas within the selection to what you already know and what you have already read.

RESPOND by completing the Comprehension Check.

First Read

☷ STANDARDS

Reading Literature
By the end of grade 11, read and comprehend literature, including stories, dramas, and poems, in the grades 11–CCR text complexity band proficiently, with scaffolding as needed at the high end of the range.

Language
• Determine or clarify the meaning of unknown and multiple-meaning words and phrases based on *grades 11–12 reading and content*, choosing flexibly from a range of strategies.
• Use context as a clue to the meaning of a word or phrase.

Antojos

Julia Alvarez

BACKGROUND

Alvarez's homeland, the Dominican Republic, won independence in 1844 after a successful rebellion against Haitian rule. In the century that followed, however, the country suffered through several dictatorships and frequent foreign domination. One of the most ruthless dictators was Rafael Trujillo, who ruled the country with the support of the military and his secret police from 1930 until he was assassinated in 1961. Despite his death, the climate of fear created by Trujillo persisted into the 1980s, flavoring the setting of "Antojos."

SCAN FOR MULTIMEDIA

1 For the first time since Yolanda had reached the hills, there was a shoulder on the left side of the narrow road. She pulled the car over out of a sense of homecoming: Every other visit she had stayed with her family in the capital.

2 Once her own engine was off, she heard the sound of another motor, approaching, a pained roar as if the engine were falling apart. She made out an undertow of men's voices. Quickly, she got back into the car, locked the door, and pulled off the shoulder, hugging her right side of the road.

NOTES

3   —Just in time too. A bus came lurching around the curve, obscuring her view with a belching of exhaust, the driver saluting or warning with a series of blasts on his horn. It was an old army bus, the official name brushed over with paint that didn't quite match the regulation gray. The passengers saw her only at the last moment, and all up and down her side of the bus, men poked out of the windows, hooting and yelling, waving purple party flags, holding out bottles and beckoning to her. She speeded up and left them behind, the small compact climbing easily up the snakey highway, its well-oiled hum a gratifying sound after the hullabaloo of the bus.

4   She tried the radio again, but all she could tune to was static even here on the summit hills. She would have to wait until she got to the coast to hear news of the hunger march in the capital. Her family had been worried that trouble would break out, for the march had been scheduled on the anniversary of the failed revolution nineteen years ago today. A huge turnout was expected. She bet that bus she had just passed had been delayed by breakdowns on its way to the capital. In fact, earlier on the road when she had first set out, Yolanda had passed buses and truckloads of men, drinking and shouting slogans. It crossed her mind that her family had finally agreed to loan her a car because they knew she'd be far safer on the north coast than in the capital city where revolutions always broke out.

5   The hills began to plane out into a high plateau, the road widening. Left and right, roadside stands began appearing. Yolanda slowed down and kept an eye out for guavas, supposedly in season this far north. Piled high on wooden stands were fruits she hadn't seen in so many years: pinkish-yellow mangoes, and tamarind pods oozing their rich sap, and small cashew fruits strung on a rope to keep them from bruising each other. There were little brown packets of roasted cashews and bars of milk fudge wrapped in waxed paper and tied with a string, the color of which told what filling was inside the bar. Strips of meat, buzzing with flies, hung from the windows of butcher stalls. An occasional display of straw hats and baskets and hammocks told that tourists sometimes did pass by here. Looking at the stores spread before her, it was hard to believe the poverty the organizers of the march kept discussing on the radio. There seemed to be plenty here to eat—except for guavas.

6   In the capital, her aunts had plied her with what she most craved after so many years away. "Any little *antojo*,[1] you must tell us!" They wanted to spoil her, so she'd stay on in her nativeland before she forgot where she had come from. "What exactly does it mean, *antojo*?" Yolanda asked. Her aunts were proven right: After so many years away, their niece was losing her Spanish.

7   "An *antojo*—" The aunts exchanged quizzical looks. "How to put it? An *antojo* is like a craving for something you have to eat."

8   A cousin blew out her cheeks. "Calories."

---

1. **antojo** (ahn TOH hoh) "craving" (Spanish). The story explores additional connotations of the word.

9   An *antojo*, one of the older aunts continued, was a very old Spanish word from before "your United States was thought of," she added tartly. In the countryside some *campesinos*[2] still used the word to mean possession by an island spirit demanding its due.

10   Her island spirit certainly was a patient soul, Yolanda joked. She hadn't had her favorite *antojo*, guavas, since her last trip seven years ago. Well, on this trip, her aunts promised, Yoyo could eat guavas to her heart's content. But when the gardener was summoned, he wasn't so sure. Guavas were no longer in season, at least not in the hotter lowlands of the south. Maybe up north, the chauffeur could pick her up some on his way back from some errand. Yolanda took this opportunity to inform her aunts of her plans: She could pick the guavas herself when she went up north in a few days.

11   —She was going up north? By herself? A woman alone on the road! "This is not the States." Her old aunts had tried to dissuade her. "Anything can happen." When Yolanda challenged them, "What?" they came up with boogeymen stories that made her feel as if she were talking to china dolls.[3] Haitian hougans[4] and Communist kidnappers. "And Martians?" Yolanda wanted to tease them. They had led such sheltered lives, riding from one safe place to another in their air-conditioned cars.

12   She had left the fruit stands behind her and was approaching a compound very much like her family's in the capital. The underbrush stopped abruptly at a high concrete wall, topped with broken bottle glass. Parked at the door was a chocolate-brown Mercedes. Perhaps the owners had come up to their country home for the weekend to avoid the troubles in the capital?

13   Just beyond the estate, Yolanda came upon a small village— ALTAMIRA in rippling letters on the corrugated tin roof of the first house. It was a little cluster of houses on either side of the road, a good place to stretch her legs before what she'd heard was a steep and slightly (her aunts had warned "very") dangerous descent to the coast. Yolanda pulled up at a **cantina**, the thatched roof held up by several posts. Instead of a menu, there was a yellowing, grimy poster for Palmolive soap tacked on one of the posts with a picture of a blonde woman under a spraying shower, her head thrown back in seeming ecstasy, her mouth opened in a wordless cry. ("Palmolive?" Yolanda wondered.) She felt even thirstier and grimier looking at this lathered beauty after her hot day on the road.

14   An old woman emerged at last from a shack behind the **cabana**, buttoning up a torn housedress, and followed closely by a little boy, who kept ducking behind her whenever Yolanda smiled at him. Asking him his name just drove him further into the folds of the old woman's skirt.

Mark context clues or indicate another strategy you used that helped you determine meaning.

cantina (kan TEE nuh) *n.*

MEANING:

cabana (kuh BAN uh) *n.*

MEANING:

---

2. ***campesinos*** (kahm pay SEE nohs) "poor farmers; simple rural dwellers" (Spanish).
3. **china dolls** old-fashioned, delicate dolls made of fragile, high-quality porcelain or ceramic ware.
4. **Haitian hougans** (oo GAHNZ) voodoo priests or cult leaders.

15   "You must excuse him, doña,"[5] she apologized. "He's not used to being among people." But Yolanda knew the old woman meant, not the people in the village, but the people with money who drove through Altamira to the beaches on the coast. "Your name," the old woman repeated, as if Yolanda hadn't asked him in Spanish. The little boy mumbled at the ground. "Speak up!" the old woman scolded, but her voice betrayed pride when she spoke up for him. "This little know-nothing is José Duarte Sánchez y Mella García."

16   Yolanda laughed. Not only were those a lot of names for such a little boy, but they certainly were momentous: the surnames of the three liberators of the country!

17   "Can I serve the doña in any way?" the woman asked. Yolanda gave the tree line beyond the woman's shack a glance. "You think you might have some guavas around?"

18   The old woman's face scrunched up. "Guavas?" she murmured and thought to herself a second. "Why, they're all around, doña. But I can't say as I've seen any."

19   "With your permission—" José Duarte had joined a group of little boys who had come out of nowhere and were milling around the car, boasting how many automobiles they had ridden in. At Yolanda's mention of guavas, he sprung forward, pointing across the road towards the summit of the western hills. "I know where there's a whole grove of them." Behind him, his little companions nodded.

20   "Go on, then!" His grandmother stamped her foot as if she were scatting a little animal. "Get the doña some."

21   A few boys dashed across the road and disappeared up a steep path on the hillside, but before José could follow, Yolanda called him back. She wanted to go along too. The little boy looked towards his grandmother, unsure of what to think. The old woman shook her head. The doña would get hot, her nice clothes would get all dirty. José would get the doña as many guavas as she was wanting.

22   "But they taste so much better when you've picked them yourself." Yolanda's voice had an edge, for suddenly, it was as if the woman had turned into the long arm of her family, keeping her away from seeing her country on her own.

23   The few boys who had stayed behind with José had congregated around the car. Each one claimed to be guarding it for the doña. It occurred to Yolanda that there was a way to make this a treat all the way around. "What do you say we take the car?"

24   "*Sí, Sí, Sí*,"[6] the boys screamed in a riot of excitement.

25   The old woman hushed them but agreed that was not a bad idea if the doña insisted on going. There was a dirt road up ahead she could follow a ways and then cross over onto the road that was paved all the way to the coffee barns. The woman pointed south in the direction of the big house. Many workers took that short cut to work.

---

5. **doña** (DOH nyah) "madam" (Spanish).
6. *Sí, Sí, Sí* (see) "Yes, Yes, Yes" (Spanish).

26   They piled into the car, half a dozen boys in the back, and José as co-pilot in the passenger seat beside Yolanda. They turned onto a bumpy road off the highway, which got bumpier and bumpier, and climbed up into wilder, more desolate country. Branches scraped the sides and pebbles pelted the underside of the car. Yolanda wanted to turn back, but there was no room to maneuver the car around. Finally, with a great snapping of twigs and thrashing of branches across the windshield, as if the countryside were loath to release them, the car burst forth onto smooth pavement and the light of day. On either side of the road were groves of guava trees. Among them, the boys who had gone ahead on foot were already pulling down branches and shaking loose a rain of guavas. The fruit was definitely in season.

27   For the next hour or so, Yolanda and her crew scavenged the grove, the best of the pick going into the beach basket Yolanda had gotten out of the trunk, with the exception of the ones she ate right on the spot, relishing the slightly bumpy feel of the skin in her hand, devouring the crunchy, sweet white meat. The boys watched her, surprised by her odd hunger.

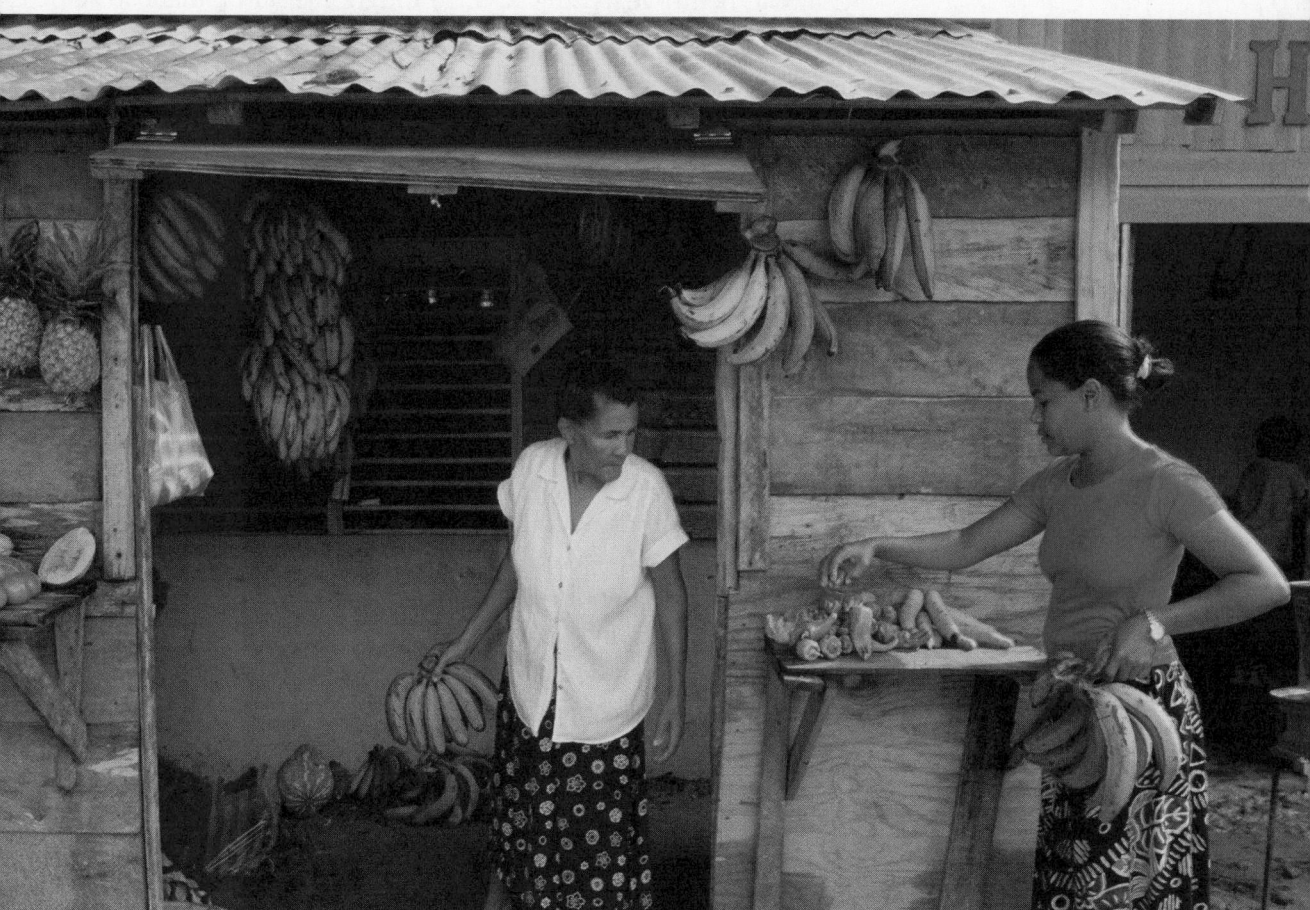

28   Yolanda and José, partners, wandered far from the path that cut through the grove. Soon they were bent double to avoid getting entangled in the thick canopy of branches overhead. Each addition to the basket caused a spill from the stash already piled high above the brim. Finally, it was a case of abandoning the treasure in order to cart some of it home. With José hugging the basket to himself and Yolanda parting the wayward branches in front of them, they headed back toward the car.

29   When they cleared the thicket of guava branches, the sun was low on the western horizon. There was no sign of the other boys. "They must have gone to round up the goats," José observed.

30   Yolanda glanced at her watch: It was past six o'clock. She'd never make the north coast by nightfall, but at least she could get off the dangerous mountain roads while it was still light. She hurried José back to the car, where they found a heap of guavas the other boys had left behind on the shoulder of the road. Enough guavas to appease even the greediest island spirit for life!

31   They packed the guavas in the trunk quickly and climbed in, but the car had not gone a foot before it lurched forward with a horrible hobble. Yolanda closed her eyes and laid her head down on the wheel, then glanced over at José. The way his eyes were searching the inside of the car for a clue as to what could have happened, she could tell he didn't know how to change a flat tire either.

32   It was no use regretting having brought the car up that bad stretch of road. The thing to do now was to act quickly. Soon the sun would set and night would fall swiftly, no lingering dusk as in the States. She explained to José that they had a flat tire and had to hike back to town and send for help down the road to the big house. Whoever tended to the brown Mercedes would know how to change the tire on her car.

33   "With your permission," José offered meekly. He pointed down the paved road. "This goes directly to the big house." The doña could just wait in the car and he would be back in no time with someone from the Miranda place.

34   She did not like the idea of staying behind in the car, but José could probably go and come back much quicker without her. "All right," she said to the boy. "I'll tell you what." She pointed to her watch. It was almost six thirty. "If you're back by the time this hand is over here, I'll give you"—she held up one finger—"a dollar." The boy's mouth fell open. In no time, he had shot out of his side of the car and was headed at a run toward the Miranda place. Yolanda climbed out as well and walked down a pace, until the boy had disappeared in one of the turnings of the road.

35   Suddenly, the countryside was so very quiet. She looked up at the purple sky. A breeze was blowing through the grove, rustling the leaves, so they whispered like voices, something indistinct. Here and there a light flickered on the hills, a *campesino* living out his solitary life. This was what she had been missing without really knowing

that she was missing it all these years. She had never felt at home in the States, never, though she knew she was lucky to have a job, so she could afford her own life and not be run by her family. But independence didn't have to be exile. She could come home, home to places like these very hills, and live here on her own terms.

36   Heading back to the car, Yolanda stopped. She had heard footsteps in the grove. Could José be back already? Branches were being thrust aside, twigs snapped. Suddenly, a short, dark man, and then a slender, light-skinned man emerged from a footpath on the opposite side of the grove from the one she and José had scavenged. They wore ragged work clothes stained with patches of sweat; their faces were drawn and tired. Yolanda's glance fell on the machetes that hung from their belts.

37   The men's faces snapped awake from their stupor at the sight of her. They looked beyond her at the car. "Yours?" the darker man spoke first. It struck her, even then, as an absurd question. Who else's would it be here in the middle of nowhere?

38   "Is there some problem?" the darker man spoke up again. The taller one was looking her up and down with interest. They were now both in front of her on the road, blocking her escape. Both—she had looked them up and down as well—were strong and quite capable of catching her if she made a run for the Mirandas'. Not that she could have moved, for her legs seemed suddenly to have been hammered into the ground beneath her. She thought of explaining that she was just out for a drive before dinner at the big house, so that these men would think someone knew where she was, someone would come looking for her if they tried to carry her off. But she found she could not speak. Her tongue felt as if it'd been stuffed in her mouth like a rag to keep her quiet.

39   The men exchanged a look—it seemed to Yolanda of collusion. Then the shorter, darker one spoke up again. "Señorita,[7] are you all right?" He peered at her. The darkness of his complexion in the growing darkness of the evening made it difficult to distinguish an expression. He was no taller than Yolanda, but he gave the impression of being quite large, for he was broad and solid, like something not yet completely carved out of a piece of wood. His companion was tall and of a rich honey-brown color that matched his honey-brown eyes. Anywhere else, Yolanda would have found him extremely attractive, but here on a lonely road, with the sky growing darker by seconds, his good looks seemed dangerous, a lure to catch her off her guard.

40   "Can we help you?" the shorter man repeated.

41   The handsome one smiled knowingly. Two long, deep dimples appeared like gashes on either side of his mouth. "*Americana*,"

NOTES

Mark context clues or indicate another strategy you used that helped you determine meaning.

machetes (muh SHEHT eez) *n.*

MEANING:

> They were now both in front of her on the road, blocking her escape.

---

7. **Señorita** (say nyoh REE tah) "Miss" (Spanish).

he said to the other in Spanish, pointing to the car. "She doesn't understand."

42   The darker man narrowed his eyes and studied Yolanda a moment. "*Americana?*" he asked her as if not quite sure what to make of her.

43   She had been too frightened to carry out any strategy, but now a road was opening before her. She laid her hand on her chest—she could feel her pounding heart—and nodded. Then, as if the admission itself loosened her tongue, she explained in English how it came that she was on a back road by herself, her craving for guavas, her never having learned to change a flat. The two men stared at her, uncomprehendingly, rendered docile by her gibberish. Strangely enough, it soothed her to hear herself speaking something they could not understand. She thought of something her teacher used to say to her when as a young immigrant girl she was learning English, "Language is power." It was her only defense now.

44   Yolanda made the motions of pumping. The darker man looked at the other, who had shown better luck at understanding the foreign lady. But his companion shrugged, baffled as well. "I'll show you." Yolanda waved for them to follow her. And suddenly, as if after pulling and pulling at roots, she had finally managed to yank them free of the soil they had clung to, she found she could move her own feet forward to the car.

45   The small group stood staring at the sagging tire a moment, the two men kicking at it as if punishing it for having failed the señorita. They squatted by the passenger's side, conversing in low tones. Yolanda led them to the rear of the car, where the men lifted the spare out of its sunken nest—then set to work, fitting the interlocking pieces of the jack, unpacking the tools from the deeper hollows of the trunk. They laid their machetes down on the side of the road, out of the way. Yolanda turned on the headlights to help them see in the growing darkness. Above the small group, the sky was purple with twilight.

46   There was a problem with the jack. It squeaked and labored, but the car would not rise. The shorter man squirmed his way underneath and placed the mechanism deeper under the bowels of the car. There, he pumped vigorously, his friend bracing him by holding him down by the ankles. Slowly, the car rose until the wheel hung suspended. When the man came out from under the car, his hand was bloody where his knuckles had scraped against the pavement.

47   Yolanda pointed to the man's hand. She had been sure that if any blood were going to be spilled tonight, it would be hers. She offered him the towel she kept draped on her car seat to absorb her perspiration. But he waved it away and sucked his knuckles to make the bleeding stop.

48   Once the flat had been replaced with the spare, the two men lifted the deflated tire into the trunk and put away the tools. They handed Yolanda her keys. There was still no sign of José and the Mirandas. Yolanda was relieved. As she had waited, watching the two men hard

at work, she had begun to dread the boy's return with help. The two men would realize she spoke Spanish. It was too late to admit that she had tricked them, to explain she had done so only because she thought her survival was on the line. The least she could do now was to try and repay them, handsomely, for their trouble.

49   "I'd like to give you something." She began reaching for the purse she'd retrieved from the trunk. The English words sounded hollow on her tongue. She rolled up a couple of American bills and offered them to the men. The shorter man held up his hand. Yolanda could see where the blood had dried dark streaks on his palm. *"No, no, señorita. Nuestro placer."*[8] Our pleasure.

50   Yolanda turned to the other man, who had struck her as more pliant than his sterner companion. "Please," she urged the bills on him. But he too looked down at the ground with the bashfulness she had observed in José of country people not wanting to offend. She felt the poverty of her response and stuffed the bills quickly into his pocket.

51   The two men picked up their machetes and raised them to their shoulders like soldiers their guns. The tall man motioned towards the big house. *"Directo, directo."*[9] He enunciated the words carefully. Yolanda looked in the direction of his hand. In the faint light of what was left of day, she could barely make out the road ahead. It was as if the guava grove had overgrown into the road and woven its mat of branches so securely and tightly in all directions, she would not be able to escape.

52   But finally, she was off! While the two men waited a moment on the shoulder to see if the tire would hold, Yolanda drove a few yards, poking her head out the window before speeding up. *"Gracias!"*[10] she called, and they waved, appreciatively, at the foreign lady making an effort in their native tongue. When she looked for them in her rear-view mirror, they had disappeared into the darkness of the guava grove.

53   Just ahead, her lights described the figure of a small boy: José was walking alone, listlessly, as if he did not particularly want to get to where he was going.

54   Yolanda leaned over and opened the door for him. The small overhead light came on; she saw that the boy's face was streaked with tears.

55   "Why, what's wrong, José?"

56   The boy swallowed hard. "They would not come. They didn't believe me." He took little breaths between words to keep his tears at bay. He had lost his chance at a whole dollar. "And the guard, he said if I didn't stop telling stories, he was going to whip me."

57   "What did you tell him, José?"

---

8. ***Nuestro placer*** (noo AYS troh plah SAYR) "Our pleasure" (Spanish).
9. ***Directo, directo*** (dee REHK toh) "Straight, straight" (Spanish).
10. ***Gracias*** (GRAH see ahs) "Thank you" (Spanish).

Antojos   **731**

58   "I told him you had broken your car and you needed help fixing it."

59   She should have gone along with José to the Mirandas'. Given all the trouble in the country, they would be suspicious of a boy coming to their door at nightfall with some story about a lady on a back road with a broken car. "Don't you worry, José." Yolanda patted the boy. She could feel the bony shoulder through the thin fabric of his worn shirt. "You can still have your dollar. You did your part."

60   But the shame of being suspected of lying seemed to have obscured any immediate pleasure he might feel in her offer. Yolanda tried to distract him by asking what he would buy with his money, what he most craved, thinking that on a subsequent trip, she might bring him his little *antojo*. But José Duarte Sánchez y Mella said nothing, except a bashful thank you when she left him off at the cantina with his promised dollar. In the glow of the headlights, Yolanda made out the figure of the old woman in the black square of her doorway, waving goodbye. Above the picnic table on a near post, the Palmolive woman's skin shone; her head was thrown back, her mouth opened as if she were calling someone over a great distance. ⤬

Comprehension Check

Complete these items after you finish your first read. Review and clarify details with your group.

1. What political event is taking place in the city as Yolanda drives into the hills?

2. Whom does Yolanda meet at a roadside cantina?

3. What are *antojos*?

4. As Yolanda and José start to leave the guava grove, what happens to the car?

5. What does Yolanda pretend when she is approached by the two men?

6. **⬛ Notebook** Confirm your understanding of the text by creating a storyboard of key events.

RESEARCH

Research to Clarify Choose at least one unfamiliar detail from the text. Briefly research that detail. In what way does the information you learned shed light on an aspect of the story?

Research to Explore Conduct research on an aspect of the text you find interesting. For example, you may want to learn about the history and culture of the Dominican Republic.

ANTOJOS

Close Read the Text

With your group, revisit sections of the text you marked during your first read. **Annotate** what you notice. What **questions** do you have? What can you **conclude?**

Analyze the Text

CITE TEXTUAL EVIDENCE to support your answers.

Notebook Complete the activities.

1. **Review and Clarify** With your group, reread paragraphs 1–4 of "Antojos." What do these paragraphs suggest about the country's political situation and the economic issues that shape the story?

2. **Present and Discuss** Now, work with your group to share the passages from the selection that you found especially important. Take turns presenting your passages. Discuss what you noticed in the selection, what questions you asked, and what conclusions you reached.

3. **Essential Question:** *How do we respond when challenged by fear?* What have you learned about people's responses to fear from reading this story? Discuss with your group.

Concept Vocabulary

cantina	cabana	machetes

Why These Words? The three concept vocabulary words are related. With your group, determine what the words have in common. How do these word choices enhance the impact of the text?

Practice

Notebook Confirm your understanding of the concept vocabulary words by using them in sentences. Include context clues that hint at each word's meaning.

Word Study

Notebook **Loanwords** A **loanword** is a word that one language borrows from another language and makes its own. The English language is rich with loanwords; for instance, *cantina*, *cabana*, and *machetes* are all borrowed from Spanish. Use a dictionary to look up these loanwords from paragraph 5 of "Antojos": *plateau*, *mango*, *hammock*. For each word, write down its meaning and the language from which it is borrowed.

Analyze Craft and Structure

Author's Choices: Narrative Structure Many stories begin at the start of a series of events and continue in a straightforward time sequence known as **chronological order**. However, some writers use a variety of different plot devices that play with the order of events, thus helping to build interest and suspense.

- *In medias res:* This term is Latin for "in the middle of things." When a story begins *in medias res*, the reader is dropped directly into the action. Introductory segments, or exposition, that tell the reader who characters are and what has already happened are omitted.

- **Flashback:** A flashback is a scene from the past that interrupts the present action of a story. A writer may present a flashback as a character's memory, a story told by a character, or a dream or daydream.

- **Foreshadowing:** Foreshadowing is the placing of textual clues to suggest events that have yet to occur. Foreshadowing often seeds details that contribute to a particular mood or atmosphere.

Alvarez uses all of these plot devices to provide background information, heighten suspense, and add interest and excitement to this story.

Practice

> **CITE TEXTUAL EVIDENCE** to support your answers.

Analyze Alvarez's use of plot devices in this story. Work together as a group to complete the chart.

PASSAGE	PLOT DEVICE	SIGNIFICANT DETAILS	EFFECT
paragraphs 1–3			
paragraphs 6–11			
paragraph 26			

ANTOJOS

Conventions and Style

Pronouns and Antecedents A **pronoun** is a word that stands for a noun, a noun phrase, or another pronoun—known as the pronoun's **antecedent**. A pronoun and its antecedent must agree in number (singular or plural), person (first, second, or third), and gender (feminine, masculine, or neuter).

Pronouns are useful because they allow speakers and writers to avoid the repetition of nouns and noun phrases, which may be awkward or cumbersome. However, a pronoun should be used only when its antecedent is clear to the listener or reader. Consider these sentences:

*Maya sent Gloria an email during **her** trip to Italy.*

*Kirk told Malik that **he** would be elected team captain.*

In each sentence, the antecedent of the pronoun is unclear. Who was traveling in Italy: Maya or Gloria? Who would be elected captain: Kirk or Malik?

When you notice an ambiguous pronoun in your writing, try restructuring the sentence so that the pronoun and antecedent are closer together. Alternatively, try repeating the antecedent for clarity. Notice that the antecedents are clear in these revised sentences:

*During Maya's trip to Italy, **she** sent Gloria an email.*

*Kirk told Malik that **he**, Kirk, would be elected team captain.*

Read It

1. Reread paragraph 38 of "Antojos," and note the multiple switches of pronouns and antecedents. Mark three pronouns in the paragraph, and identify their antecedents.

2. **Connect to Style** Reread paragraphs 44–46. Mark the personal pronouns, and identify their antecedents. As a group, compare your annotations. Then, working individually, explain in a few sentences how the careful use of pronouns helps make the events of this story clear.

Write It

Write a paragraph describing a trip or voyage you've taken with a friend or family member. Use at least five personal pronouns in your paragraph. Make sure that the antecedent for each pronoun is clear.

STANDARDS

Language
Demonstrate command of the conventions of standard English grammar and usage when writing or speaking.

Research

Assignment

Choose one of the following **research project** options.

☐ **Timeline** Create a timeline of the key events of the dictatorship of Rafael Trujillo in the Dominican Republic, covering the years 1930–1961. Events that you may want to include are the Parsley Massacre, Hurricane San Zenón, the Batista imprisonment, the Betancourt assassination attempt, and Trujillo's assassination.

☐ **Map** Create a map of the Dominican Republic indicating the route Yolanda may have traveled to get from Santo Domingo through the mountains to Altamira, together with a description of that route.

☐ **Field-Guide Entry** Create a field-guide entry for the guava plant, *Psidium guajava*, including facts and diagrams about how and where it grows.

In your report, include a section in which you explain how the information you researched contributes to your understanding of the characters, setting, and conflicts depicted in "Antojos" by Julia Alvarez.

Research Plan Use the chart to record the tasks you will need to accomplish as your group progresses through the assignment. With your group, decide how you will divide up the research and writing tasks necessary to complete the work.

📝 EVIDENCE LOG

Before moving on to a new selection, go to your Evidence Log and record what you learned from "Antojos."

STANDARDS
Writing
Conduct short as well as more sustained research projects to answer a question or solve a problem; narrow or broaden the inquiry when appropriate; synthesize multiple sources on the subject, demonstrating understanding of the subject under investigation.

INFORMATION NEEDED	IMAGES OR MEDIA NEEDED	SOURCES TO USE	WRITING TASKS TO COMPLETE

Present an Argument

Assignment

You have read an autobiography, watched an interview, and read a short story about people who are either affected by other people's fears or face their own. Work with your group to plan and present a **debate** on this question:

Do people usually learn from their fear?

Divide into teams on opposite sides of the argument. Find examples from the texts that you can cite to support your ideas. Then, conduct your debate for the class.

Plan With Your Group

Analyze the Prompt Divide into two subgroups. One will support the "yes" response to the question, and the other will support the "no" response. With your subgroup, discuss how the people and characters in the selections respond to their fears. Consider both the actions of the people telling the stories and those of the people or characters they describe. Decide which details and examples from the texts provide the most relevant support for your side of the debate.

TITLE	WHO EXPERIENCES FEAR?	HOW DO THEY RESPOND?
from Farewell to Manzanar		
Interview With George Takei		
Antojos		

The most logical examples in support of our side are:

STANDARDS

Speaking and Listening
Propel conversations by posing and responding to questions that probe reasoning and evidence; ensure a hearing for a full range of positions on a topic or issue; clarify, verify, or challenge ideas and conclusions; and promote divergent and creative perspectives.

Gather Evidence and Media Examples Find details from the texts and interview that you will cite in support of your side of the debate. Note that your personal opinion may not the be the same as the one you will argue. Choose the evidence that best supports your assigned position. If they are relevant and you are comfortable sharing, you may also refer to personal experiences or anecdotes from your own life. Make sure all members of your subgroup make suggestions and contribute to the discussion.

Organize Your Debate Work together to come up with a list of main points in support of your group's claim, as well as a list of details, examples, and other evidence to support each point. Divide these points and corresponding evidence evenly among group members. Brainstorm some counterarguments that the other side may use to refute your points. Decide how you might respond to each counterargument.

Rehearse With Your Group

Practice With Your Group As you prepare to participate in the debate, use this checklist to evaluate the effectiveness of your group's practice sessions. Then, use your evaluation and the instructions here to guide improvements.

CONTENT	EFFECTIVENESS	PRESENTATION TECHNIQUES
☐ The speakers present and defend a claim. ☐ The main ideas are supported with evidence from the texts in Small-Group Learning.	☐ The language used is well chosen and appropriate for the audience and purpose. ☐ The speakers acknowledge and refute counterarguments.	☐ The speakers enunciate clearly and respond to one another respectfully. ☐ The speakers use vocal tone, eye contact, and body language to emphasize key points.

Fine-Tune the Content Does each speaker from your side have sufficient evidence to support his or her claim? If not, work with your subgroup to locate more evidence.

Improve Your Debate Form Keep your language formal and objective as you debate the topic. Refute counterarguments clearly and respectfully. If needed, return to the texts and look for more details and examples to support your points.

Brush Up on Your Presentation Techniques A key part of a debate is responding to the opposition's ideas. Remember to listen carefully to what the other team says and respond thoughtfully.

Present and Evaluate

As you present your debate, work as a group. Support your teammates and build on each other's points to support your claim and refute counterclaims. As you watch other groups debate, think about how well they meet the requirements on the checklist.

▤ STANDARDS
Speaking and Listening
Present information, findings, and supporting evidence, conveying a clear and distinct perspective and a logical argument, such that listeners can follow the line of reasoning, alternative or opposing perspectives are addressed, and the organization, development, substance, and style are appropriate to purpose, audience, and a range of formal and informal tasks.

ESSENTIAL QUESTION:

How do we respond when challenged by fear?

Is the way in which we respond to fear an essential part of each of our identities as individuals? Is it a key part of a communal or national identity? In this section, you will complete your study of responses to fear by exploring an additional selection related to the topic. You'll then share what you learn with classmates. To choose a text, follow these steps.

Look Back Think about the selections you have already studied. What more do you want to know about the topic of fear?

Look Ahead Preview the texts by reading the descriptions. Which one seems most interesting and appealing to you?

Look Inside Take a few minutes to scan the text you chose. Choose a different one if this text doesn't meet your needs.

Independent Learning Strategies

Throughout your life, in school, in your community, and in your career, you will need to rely on yourself to learn and work on your own. Review these strategies and the actions you can take to practice them during Independent Learning. Add ideas of your own to each category.

STRATEGY	ACTION PLAN
Create a schedule	• Understand your goals and deadlines. • Make a plan for what to do each day. •
Practice what you have learned	• Use first-read and close-read strategies to deepen your understanding. • After you read, evaluate the usefulness of the evidence to help you understand the topic. • Consult reference sources for additional information that can help you clarify meaning. •
Take notes	• Record important ideas and information. • Review your notes before preparing to share with a group. •

SCAN FOR
MULTIMEDIA

CONTENTS

Choose one selection. Selections are available online only.

First-Read Guide

Use this page to record your first-read ideas.

Selection Title: _____

Tool Kit
First-Read Guide and
Model Annotation

NOTICE new information or ideas you learned about the unit topic as you first read this text.

ANNOTATE by marking vocabulary and key passages you want to revisit.

First Read

NOTICE · ANNOTATE · CONNECT · RESPOND

CONNECT ideas within the selection to other knowledge and the selections you have read.

RESPOND by writing a brief summary of the selection.

STANDARD
Reading Read and comprehend complex literary and informational texts independently and proficiently.

Close-Read Guide

Use this page to record your close-read ideas.

🔧 **Tool Kit**
Close-Read Guide and
Model Annotation

Selection Title: _____

Close Read the Text

Revisit sections of the text you marked during your first read. Read these sections closely and **annotate** what you notice. Ask yourself **questions** about the text. What can you **conclude?** Write down your ideas.

Analyze the Text

Think about the author's choices of patterns, structure, techniques, and ideas included in the text. Select one and record your thoughts about what this choice conveys.

QuickWrite

Pick a paragraph from the text that grabbed your interest. Explain the power of this passage.

_____
_____
_____
_____
_____
_____
_____
_____
_____

📇 STANDARD
Reading Read and comprehend complex literary and informational texts independently and proficiently.

Go to your Evidence Log and record what you learned from the text you read.

Share Your Independent Learning

Prepare to Share

Is fear always a harmful emotion?

Even when you read something independently, your understanding continues to grow when you share what you have learned with others. Reflect on the text you explored independently, and write notes about its connection to the unit. In your notes, consider why this text belongs in this unit.

Learn from Your Classmates

Discuss It Share your ideas about the text you explored on your own. As you talk with your classmates, jot down ideas that you learn from them.

Reflect

Review your notes, and mark the most important insight you gained from these writing and discussion activities. Explain how this idea adds to your understanding of the topic of fear.

☷ STANDARDS

Speaking and Listening
Initiate and participate effectively in a range of collaborative discussions with diverse partners on *grades 11–12 topics, texts, and issues,* building on others' ideas and expressing their own clearly and persuasively.

Review Evidence for an Argument

At the beginning of this unit, you took a position on the following question:

Is fear always a harmful emotion?

✐ EVIDENCE LOG

Review your Evidence Log and your QuickWrite from the beginning of the unit. Has your position changed?

☐ YES	☐ NO
Identify at least three pieces of evidence that convinced you to change your mind.	Identify at least three pieces of evidence that reinforced your original position.
1.	1.
2.	2.
3.	3.

State your position now: _____

_____

_____

Identify a possible counterclaim: _____

_____

_____

Evaluate the Strength of Your Evidence Consider your argument. Do you have enough evidence to support your claim? Do you have enough evidence to refute a counterclaim? If not, make a plan.

☐ Do more research   ☐ Talk with my classmates

☐ Reread a selection   ☐ Ask an expert

☐ Other:_____

≡ STANDARDS

Writing
Introduce precise, knowledgeable claim(s), establish the significance of the claim(s), distinguish the claim(s) from alternate or opposing claims, and create an organization that logically sequences claim(s), counterclaims, reasons, and evidence.

SOURCES

- WHOLE-CLASS SELECTIONS
- SMALL-GROUP SELECTIONS
- INDEPENDENT-LEARNING SELECTION

PART 1
Writing to Sources: Argument

In this unit, you read about characters and real people who experience fear and react to it. In these texts, fear moves beyond a personal emotion, leading readers to question the role fear plays on a larger level in communities and between groups of people.

Assignment

Write an **argumentative essay** that responds to this question:

> Is fear always a harmful emotion?

Begin by asserting a claim. Cite relevant evidence from at least three texts from this unit, as well as from your own experience, to support that claim. Organize your evidence in a logical way that helps you structure your argument clearly and definitively. Use formal language and an objective tone, and end your argument with a conclusion that flows naturally from your claim and the evidence you presented.

Reread the Assignment Review the assignment to be sure you fully understand it. The task may reference some of the academic words presented at the beginning of the unit. Be sure you understand each of the words here in order to complete the assignment correctly.

Academic Vocabulary

assert	certify	definitive
relevant	immutable	

WORD NETWORK

As you write and revise your essay, use your Word Network to help vary your word choices.

Review the Elements of Effective Argument Before you begin writing, read the Argument Rubric. Once you have completed your first draft, check it against the rubric. If one or more of the elements is missing or not as strong as it could be, revise your essay to add or strengthen that component.

STANDARDS

Writing
- Write arguments to support claims in an analysis of substantive topics or texts, using valid reasoning and relevant and sufficient evidence.
- Write routinely over extended time frames and shorter time frames for a range of tasks, purposes, and audiences.

Argument Rubric

	Focus and Organization	Evidence and Elaboration	Language Conventions
4	The introduction clearly and effectively states a precise, logical claim. The essay clearly acknowledges counterclaims and uses sufficient reasons and evidence to refute them. Writing always follows a logical organizational structure and makes clear connections among ideas. The argument includes a conclusion that follows from and supports the claim.	Body paragraphs always use valid reasoning and include relevant and sufficient evidence. The tone of the argument is always formal and objective. The argument always uses language that is appropriate for the purpose and audience.	The argument consistently and accurately follows the conventions of standard English usage and mechanics. Writing always uses indefinite pronouns correctly and effectively.
3	The introduction clearly states a precise claim. The essay acknowledges counterclaims and uses reasons and evidence to refute them. Writing mostly follows a logical organizational structure and makes clear connections among ideas. The argument includes a conclusion that mostly follows from and supports the claim.	Body paragraphs mostly use valid reasoning and include relevant and sufficient evidence. The tone of the argument is mostly formal and objective. The argument mostly uses language that is appropriate for the purpose and audience.	The argument mostly follows the conventions of standard English usage and mechanics. Writing mostly uses indefinite pronouns correctly.
2	The introduction states a claim. The essay acknowledges counterclaims. Writing follows a somewhat logical organizational structure and makes connections among ideas. The argument includes a conclusion that somewhat follows from and supports the claim.	Body paragraphs sometimes use valid reasoning and relevant evidence. The tone of the argument is sometimes formal and objective. The argument occasionally uses language that is inappropriate for the purpose and audience.	The argument sometimes follows the conventions of standard English usage and mechanics. Writing sometimes uses indefinite pronouns correctly.
1	The introduction does not state a claim. The essay does not acknowledge counterclaims. Writing does not follow a logical organizational structure or make clear connections among ideas. The argument does not include a conclusion, or it includes a conclusion that does not follow from or support the claim.	Body paragraphs do not use valid reasoning or evidence to support claims. The tone of the argument is informal or inappropriate. The argument uses language that is not appropriate for the purpose and audience.	The argument does not follow the conventions of standard English usage and mechanics. Writing does not use indefinite pronouns correctly.

PART 2
Speaking and Listening: Speech

Assignment

After completing a final draft of your essay, prepare a **speech** in which you present your argument. Use your voice, facial expressions, and gestures to effectively communicate your ideas to your audience.

Follow these steps to make your speech dynamic and interesting.

- Review your argument, and mark the ideas and evidence you want to emphasize.
- Practice reading your essay aloud several times. Consider revising wording to make your text more effective as a speech. For example, you may want to begin or end with more dramatic language. As you read, remember to look up from your paper occassionally. Making eye contact with your audience will help them feel more engaged.
- When you deliver your speech, use pauses effectively, speak slowly and clearly, and vary your volume to add drama.

Review the Rubric The criteria by which your speech will be evaluated appear in this rubric. Review these criteria before presenting to ensure that you are prepared.

☷ **STANDARDS**
Speaking and Listening
Present information, findings, and supporting evidence, conveying a clear and distinct perspective, such that listeners can follow the line of reasoning, alternative or opposing perspectives are addressed, and the organization, development, substance, and style are appropriate to purpose, audience, and a range of formal and informal tasks.

	Content	Effectiveness	Presentation Techniques
3	The speaker presents a clear and effective claim.	Language is always appropriate for the audience and task.	The speaker always uses tone of voice and body language effectively.
	The speaker always uses well-chosen evidence to support his or her ideas.	The speaker emphasizes all of his or her key points.	The speaker maintains effective eye contact.
2	The speaker presents a claim.	Language is mostly appropriate for the audience and task.	The speaker mostly uses tone of voice and body language effectively.
	The speaker uses some well-chosen evidence to support his or her ideas.	The speaker emphasizes most of his or her key points.	The speaker mostly maintains effective eye contact.
1	The speaker does not present a clear claim.	Language is not appropriate for the audience and task.	The speaker does not use tone of voice or body language effectively.
	The speaker does not use well-chosen evidence to support his or her ideas.	The speaker does not emphasize his or her key points.	The speaker does not make eye contact with the audience.

Reflect on the Unit

Now that you've completed the unit, take a few moments to reflect on your learning. Use the questions below to think about where you succeeded, what skills and strategies helped you, and where you can continue to grow in the future.

Reflect on the Unit Goals

Look back at the goals at the beginning of the unit. Use a different colored pen to rate yourself again. Think about readings and activities that contributed the most to the growth of your understanding. Record your thoughts.

Reflect on the Learning Strategies

Discuss It Write a reflection on whether you were able to improve your learning based on your Action Plans. Think about what worked, what didn't, and what you might do to keep working on these strategies. Record your ideas before joining a class discussion.

Reflect on the Text

Choose a selection that you found challenging, and explain what made it difficult.

Explain something that surprised you about a text in the unit.

Which activity taught you the most about responding to fear? What did you learn?

▓▓ STANDARDS

Speaking and Listening
Come to discussions prepared, having read and researched material under study; explicitly draw on that preparation by referring to evidence from texts and other research on the topic or issue to stimulate a thoughtful, well-reasoned exchange of ideas.

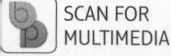
SCAN FOR
MULTIMEDIA

Ordinary Lives, Extraordinary Tales

The American Short Story

Why Do Stories Matter? That's Like
Asking Why You Should Eat

💬 **Discuss It** Which of the thoughts expressed in this video
are most similar to your own thoughts about stories?

Write your response before sharing your ideas.

SCAN FOR
MULTIMEDIA

UNIT 6

ESSENTIAL QUESTION: What do stories reveal about the human condition?

LAUNCH TEXT
NARRATIVE MODEL
Old Man at the Bridge
Ernest Hemingway

 WHOLE-CLASS LEARNING

HISTORICAL PERSPECTIVES

Focus Period: 1950–Present
A Fast-Changing Society

ANCHOR TEXT: SHORT STORY

Everyday Use
Alice Walker

MEDIA CONNECTION:
Alice Walker's "Everyday Use"

ANCHOR TEXT: SHORT STORY

Everything Stuck to Him
Raymond Carver

ANCHOR TEXT: SHORT STORY

The Leap
Louise Erdrich

 SMALL-GROUP LEARNING

LITERARY HISTORY

A Brief History of the Short Story
D. F. McCourt

COMPARE

SHORT STORY

An Occurrence at Owl Creek Bridge
Ambrose Bierce

SHORT STORY

The Jilting of Granny Weatherall
Katherine Anne Porter

INDEPENDENT LEARNING

SHORT STORY

The Tell-Tale Heart
Edgar Allan Poe

SHORT STORY

The Man to Send Rain Clouds
Leslie Marmon Silko

SHORT STORY

Ambush
Tim O'Brien

SHORT STORY

Housepainting
Lan Samantha Chang

PERFORMANCE TASK

WRITING FOCUS:
Write a Narrative

PERFORMANCE TASK

SPEAKING AND LISTENING FOCUS:
Present a Narrative

PERFORMANCE-BASED ASSESSMENT PREP

Review Notes for a Narrative

PERFORMANCE-BASED ASSESSMENT

Narrative: Short Story and Storytelling Session

PROMPT:
How does a fictional character or characters respond to life-changing news?

Unit Goals

Throughout this unit, you will deepen your perspective on how stories explore the human condition by reading, writing, speaking, listening, and presenting. These goals will help you succeed on the Unit Performance-Based Assessment.

Rate how well you meet these goals right now. You will revisit your ratings later when you reflect on your growth during this unit.

SCALE	1	2	3	4	5
	NOT AT ALL WELL	NOT VERY WELL	SOMEWHAT WELL	VERY WELL	EXTREMELY WELL

READING GOALS   1   2   3   4   5

- Analyze narratives to understand how authors order the action, introduce and develop characters, and introduce and develop multiple themes.

- Expand your knowledge and use of academic and concept vocabulary.

WRITING AND RESEARCH GOALS   1   2   3   4   5

- Write a narrative text that uses effective narrative techniques to develop fictional experiences, events, and characters.

- Conduct research projects of various lengths to explore topics and clarify meaning.

LANGUAGE GOALS   1   2   3   4   5

- Make effective style choices regarding figurative language and dialect.

- Demonstrate an understanding of frequently confused words, passive voice, and sentence fragments.

SPEAKING AND LISTENING GOALS   1   2   3   4   5

- Collaborate with your team to build on the ideas of others, develop consensus, and communicate.

- Integrate audio, visuals, and text to present information.

▦ STANDARDS

Language
Acquire and use accurately general academic and domain-specific words and phrases, sufficient for reading, writing, speaking, and listening at the college and career readiness level; demonstrate independence in gathering vocabulary knowledge when considering a word or phrase important to comprehension or expression.

SCAN FOR MULTIMEDIA

Academic Vocabulary: Narrative Text

Understanding and using academic terms can help you read, write, and speak with precision and clarity. Here are five academic words that will be useful to you in this unit as you analyze and write fictional narratives.

Complete the chart.

1. Review each word, its root, and the mentor sentences.

2. Use the information and your own knowledge to predict the meaning of each word.

3. For each word, list at least two related words.

4. Refer to a dictionary or other resources if needed.

TIP

FOLLOW THROUGH
Study the words in this chart, and mark them or their forms wherever they appear in the unit.

WORD	MENTOR SENTENCES	PREDICT MEANING	RELATED WORDS
colloquial ROOT: **-loqu-** "speak"; "say"	1. When I was studying Spanish, I learned formal terms more easily than *colloquial* expressions. 2. I love how the poet combines cultured diction with *colloquial* language.		colloquially; colloquialism
protagonist ROOT: **-agon-** "contest"	1. Is the *protagonist* of the story really a talking dog? 2. In this movie, the *protagonist* must defeat a politician who has a sinister goal.		
tension ROOT: **-tens-** "stretch"	1. News of an important announcement increased the level of *tension* at school. 2. What *tension* I felt as my turn to speak drew close!		
resolution ROOT: **-solv-** "loosen"	1. In the play's *resolution*, the thief is caught and taken to jail. 2. The two sides in the dispute reached a surprising and imaginative *resolution*.		
epiphany ROOT: **-phan-/-phen-** "show"	1. That *epiphany* changed my life because it made my career choice clear. 2. At the end of the story, Julia has an *epiphany*, but we aren't sure if she will act on that insight.		

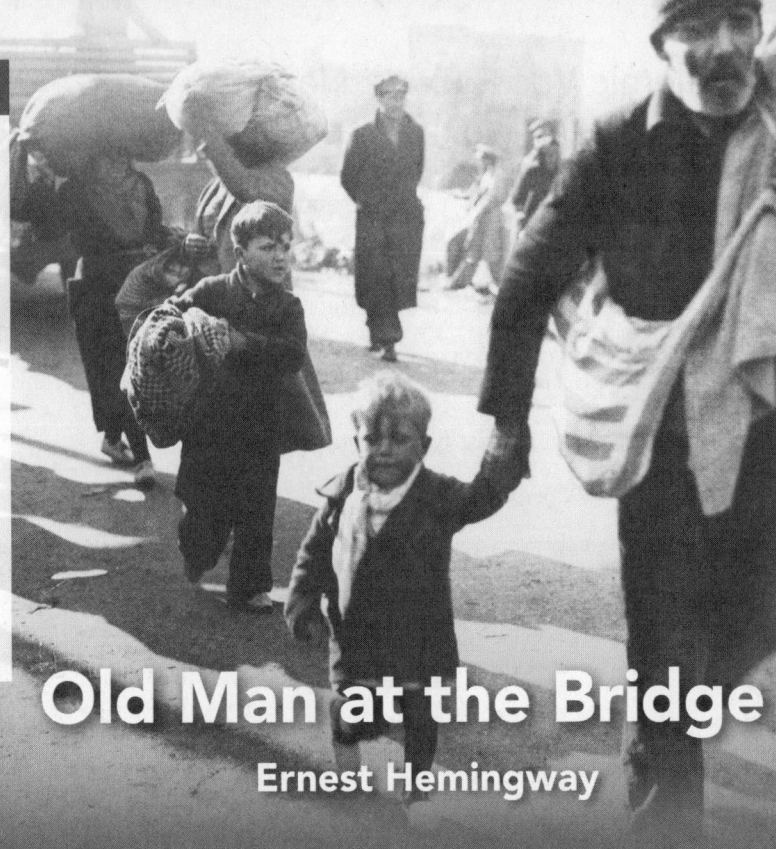

LAUNCH TEXT | NARRATIVE MODEL

This selection is an example of a **narrative text**. It is a **fictional narrative** because it is narrated by a character and describes events that did not actually happen. This is the type of writing you will develop in the Performance-Based Assessment at the end of the unit.

As you read, look closely at the author's use of details and dialogue. Mark words and phrases that suggest the personalities of the narrator and the old man, as well as the tension of the situation in which they meet.

Old Man at the Bridge
Ernest Hemingway

1 An old man with steel rimmed spectacles and very dusty clothes sat by the side of the road. There was a pontoon bridge across the river and carts, trucks, and men, women and children were crossing it. The mule-drawn carts staggered up the steep bank from the bridge with soldiers helping push against the spokes of the wheels. The trucks ground up and away heading out of it all and the peasants plodded along in the ankle deep dust. But the old man sat there without moving. He was too tired to go any farther.

2 It was my business to cross the bridge, explore the bridgehead beyond and find out to what point the enemy had advanced. I did this and returned over the bridge. There were not so many carts now and very few people on foot, but the old man was still there.

3 "Where do you come from?" I asked him.

4 "From San Carlos," he said, and smiled.

5 That was his native town and so it gave him pleasure to mention it and he smiled.

6 "I was taking care of animals," he explained.

7 "Oh," I said, not quite understanding.

8 "Yes," he said, "I stayed, you see, taking care of animals. I was the last one to leave the town of San Carlos."

9 He did not look like a shepherd nor a herdsman and I looked at his black dusty clothes and his gray dusty face and his steel rimmed spectacles and said, "What animals were they?"

10 "Various animals," he said, and shook his head. "I had to leave them."

11 I was watching the bridge and the African looking country of the Ebro Delta and wondering how long now it would be before we would see the enemy, and listening all the while for the first noises that would signal that ever mysterious event called contact, and the old man still sat there.

12 "What animals were they?" I asked.

13 "There were three animals altogether," he explained. "There were two goats and a cat and then there were four pairs of pigeons."

14 "And you had to leave them?" I asked.

15 "Yes. Because of the artillery. The captain told me to go because of the artillery."

SCAN FOR MULTIMEDIA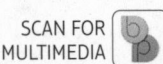

16   "And you have no family?" I asked, watching the far end of the bridge where a few last carts were hurrying down the slope of the bank.

17   "No," he said, "only the animals I stated. The cat, of course, will be all right. A cat can look out for itself, but I cannot think what will become of the others."

18   "What politics have you?" I asked.

19   "I am without politics," he said. "I am seventy-six years old. I have come twelve kilometers now and I think now I can go no further."

20   "This is not a good place to stop," I said. "If you can make it, there are trucks up the road where it forks for Tortosa."

21   "I will wait a while," he said, "and then I will go. Where do the trucks go?"

22   "Towards Barcelona," I told him.

23   "I know no one in that direction," he said, "but thank you very much. Thank you again very much."

24   He looked at me very blankly and tiredly, then said, having to share his worry with some one, "The cat will be all right, I am sure. There is no need to be unquiet about the cat. But the others. Now what do you think about the others?"

25   "Why they'll probably come through it all right."

26   "You think so?"

27   "Why not," I said, watching the far bank where now there were no carts.

28   "But what will they do under the artillery when I was told to leave because of the artillery?"

29   "Did you leave the dove cage unlocked?" I asked.

30   "Yes."

31   "Then they'll fly."

32   "Yes, certainly they'll fly. But the others. It's better not to think about the others," he said.

33   "If you are rested I would go," I urged. "Get up and try to walk now."

34   "Thank you," he said and got to his feet, swayed from side to side and then sat down backwards in the dust.

35   "I was taking care of animals," he said dully, but no longer to me. "I was only taking care of animals."

36   There was nothing to do about him. It was Easter Sunday and the Fascists were advancing toward the Ebro. It was a gray overcast day with a low ceiling so their planes were not up. That and the fact that cats know how to look after themselves was all the good luck that old man would ever have. &

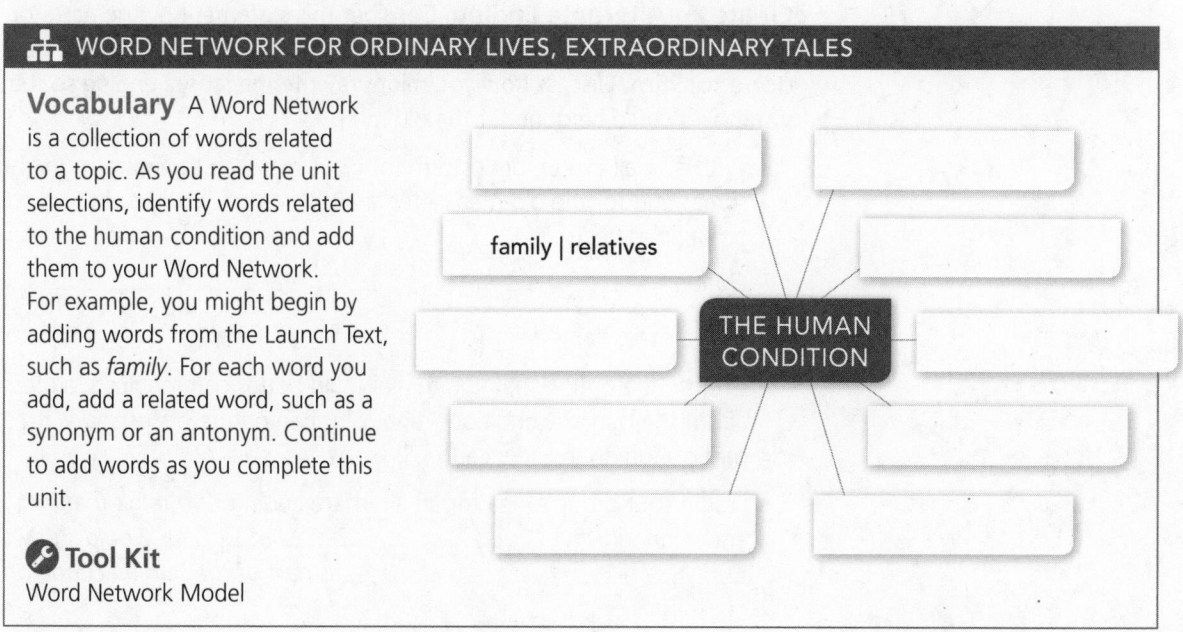

WORD NETWORK FOR ORDINARY LIVES, EXTRAORDINARY TALES

Vocabulary A Word Network is a collection of words related to a topic. As you read the unit selections, identify words related to the human condition and add them to your Word Network. For example, you might begin by adding words from the Launch Text, such as *family*. For each word you add, add a related word, such as a synonym or an antonym. Continue to add words as you complete this unit.

family | relatives

THE HUMAN CONDITION

🔧 **Tool Kit**
Word Network Model

Summary

Write a summary of "Old Man at the Bridge." Remember that a **summary** is a concise, complete, and accurate overview of a text. It should not include a statement of your opinion or an analysis.

Launch Activity

Create an Alternate Ending Consider this statement by the narrator near the end of "Old Man at the Bridge": **There was nothing to be done for him.** Discuss how you might rewrite the story's ending so that something *could* be done for the old man.

- With a small group, brainstorm for ways in which the narrator might do something for the old man, after all. Record the two options that your group likes best.

    Option 1: _____

    Option 2: _____

- Choose the option that you think would better communicate a message about the human condition—about human nature or situations that are part of human experience.

- Frame your group's idea for an alternate ending: *We think that an ending in which* _____ *would show that* _____ *is part of the human condition.*

QuickWrite

Consider class discussions, the video, and the Launch Text as you think about the prompt. Record your first thoughts here.

PROMPT: **How does a fictional character or characters respond to life-changing news?**

EVIDENCE LOG FOR THE HUMAN CONDITION

Review your QuickWrite. Summarize your initial idea in one sentence to record in your Evidence Log. Then, record details from "Old Man at the Bridge" that connect to your idea.

Prepare for the Performance-Based Assessment at the end of the unit by completing the Evidence Log after each selection.

🔧 **Tool Kit**
Evidence Log Model

Title of Text: _____ Date: _____

CONNECTION TO PROMPT	TEXT EVIDENCE/DETAILS	ADDITIONAL NOTES/IDEAS

How does this text change or add to my thinking? Date: _____

SCAN FOR MULTIMEDIA

ESSENTIAL QUESTION:

What do stories reveal about the human condition?

As you read these selections, work with your whole class to explore how short stories provide insights into what it means to be human.

From Text to Topic For one family, conflict over an heirloom highlights individual strengths and weaknesses, and suggests different ways of valuing the past. For one father and daughter, a present moment opens a window to a poignant memory. For one woman, a series of anecdotes reveals her mother's extraordinary character. As you read these stories, consider the understanding of human nature that informs each one—how it reveals qualities that we equate with the human condition, regardless of time or place.

Whole-Class Learning Strategies

Throughout your life, in school, in your community, and in your career, you will continue to learn and work in large-group environments.

Review these strategies and the actions you can take to practice them as you work with your whole class. Add ideas of your own for each step. Get ready to use these strategies during Whole-Class Learning.

STRATEGY	ACTION PLAN
Listen actively	• Eliminate distractions. For example, put your cellphone away. • Record brief notes on main ideas and points of confusion. •
Clarify by asking questions	• If you're confused, other people probably are, too. Ask a question to help your whole class. • Ask follow-up questions as needed. •
Monitor understanding	• Notice what information you already know, and be ready to build on it. • Ask for help if you are struggling. •
Interact and share ideas	• Share your ideas and offer answers, even if you are unsure. • Build on the ideas of others by adding details or making a connection. •

SCAN FOR MULTIMEDIA

CONTENTS

A Fast-Changing Society

Voices of the Period

"*There is more recognition now that things are changing, but not because there is a political move to do it. It is simply a result of the information being there. Our survival won't depend on political or economic systems. It's going to depend on the courage of the individual to speak the truth, and to speak it lovingly and not destructively.*"

—Buckminster Fuller, architect and inventor

"*[E]xperience has taught me that you cannot value dreams according to the odds of their coming true. Their real value is in stirring within us the will to aspire.*"

—Sonia Sotomayor, Supreme Court Justice

"*Beyond work and love, I would add two other ingredients that give meaning to life. First, to fulfill whatever talents we are born with. However blessed we are by fate with different abilities and strengths, we should try to develop them to the fullest. . . . Second, we should try to leave the world a better place than when we entered it.*"

—Michio Kaku, futurist, theoretical physicist, and author

History of the Period

Chasing the American Dream By the 1950s, postwar America was "on top of the world" with pride and confidence in its position as a world power. The nation had a booming economy and a booming population. As a result of a strong job market and the availability of federal loans to returning soldiers and other service personnel, Americans purchased houses in record numbers. More than eighty percent of new homes were in suburbs, which became the new lifestyle norm—a change made possible by the rise of "car culture."

The Age of Aquarius Elected president in 1960, John F. Kennedy spearheaded new domestic and foreign programs, known collectively as the New Frontier. Among these initiatives was the goal of landing an American on the moon and the establishment of the Peace Corps, an overseas volunteer program. A national spirit of optimism turned to grief, however, when Kennedy was assassinated in 1963.

The escalating and increasingly unpopular war in Vietnam elicited waves of protest, with idealistic but strident demands for an end to the conflict, as well as changes in society. As the 1960s wore on, more and more Americans made strong assertions of their individuality. This new spirit of independence energized passions for justice and equality. Some Americans expressed idealistic values that called for an "Age of Aquarius"—an era of universal peace and love. At the same time, some Americans created a counterculture, seeking lifestyles that challenged the prevailing

TIMELINE

1950

1952: The U.S. detonates the first hydrogen bomb.

1957: Jack Kerouac's *On the Road* is published.

1957: President Eisenhower sends troops to Little Rock, Arkansas, to enforce high school integration.

1963: President John F. Kennedy is assassinated.

1965: Congress passes the Voting Rights Act.

norms in music, art, literature, occupations, speech, and dress.

Protest and Progress Although there were times of crisis and confrontation, the 1960s also was an era of genuine progress, especially in the continuing struggle for civil rights and racial equality. Civil rights leaders and other Americans, both black and white, protested segregation and racism. Violence and unrest spread as protestors faced resistance in places such as Birmingham and Selma, Alabama. The nation made momentous progress when, under the leadership of President Lyndon B. Johnson, Congress passed key legislation in 1964 and 1965 to counter racism. A century after constitutional amendments guaranteed rights to African Americans, the struggle to claim them continued.

Changing Roles Throughout the 1960s, American women struggled for greater economic and social power, changing the workforce and the political landscape in the process. In 1970, thousands of women marched to honor the fiftieth anniversary of women's suffrage. The women's movement continued to gain strength in the 1970s, with various groups forming to protest gender discrimination.

Following the lead of the civil rights and women's movements, other groups from a variety of backgrounds, ranging from Native Americans to migrant workers to gays and lesbians, organized to demand their rights. Over time, most Americans have come to appreciate the variety of perspectives that diversity can bring. Today, virtually every societal group has entered into the mainstream of American political, business, and artistic life.

Leadership and Conflict Voters sent Ronald Reagan, the Republican governor of California, to the White House in 1980 and again in 1984. George H. W. Bush, Reagan's vice president, was elected president in 1988 and sought reelection in 1992, but was defeated by to Democrats Bill Clinton and his running mate, Al Gore—the youngest ticket in American history—who were reelected in 1996. In 2000, Vice President Al Gore lost his presidential bid to George Bush's son, George W. Bush. Bush was reelected in 2004. The contests of 2008 and 2012 resulted in historic victories, with the election and reelection of Barack Obama, the nation's first African American president.

9/11: A World Transformed The terrorist attacks of September 11, 2001, had an enormous impact on the American consciousness. In addition to the tragic loss of thousands of lives, the threat of terrorism brought profound changes to the sense of security and openness that Americans had long enjoyed. The 9/11 attacks also precipitated controversial military action in Afghanistan and later in Iraq. Today, the continued rise of global terrorism continues to challenge the world's safety.

Planet Earth In 1962, Rachel Carson's book *Silent Spring* exposed the sometimes catastrophic effect of human actions on the natural world. In 1972, American astronauts took a photograph of Earth that became famously known as "the big blue marble." Over the years, Americans have become increasingly aware of the importance of caring for the planet's health. In recent years, human-induced climate change—long a concern of scientists—has emerged as a significant issue in the public's consciousness and actions to slow its impact are widely discussed and argued about in the media and in government.

1968: Civil rights leader Martin Luther King, Jr., is assassinated.

1969: Astronaut Neil Armstrong becomes the first person to set foot on the moon.

1972: Congress passes the Equal Rights Amendment, but it fails to achieve ratification.

1973: The last U.S. combat troops leave Vietnam, where war has been waged since 1955.

1974: President Richard Nixon resigns after the Watergate crisis.

1980

Integration of Knowledge and Ideas

Notebook According to this survey, what total percentage of teenagers go online at least once a day? What do the graph and table suggest about entertainment among today's teens?

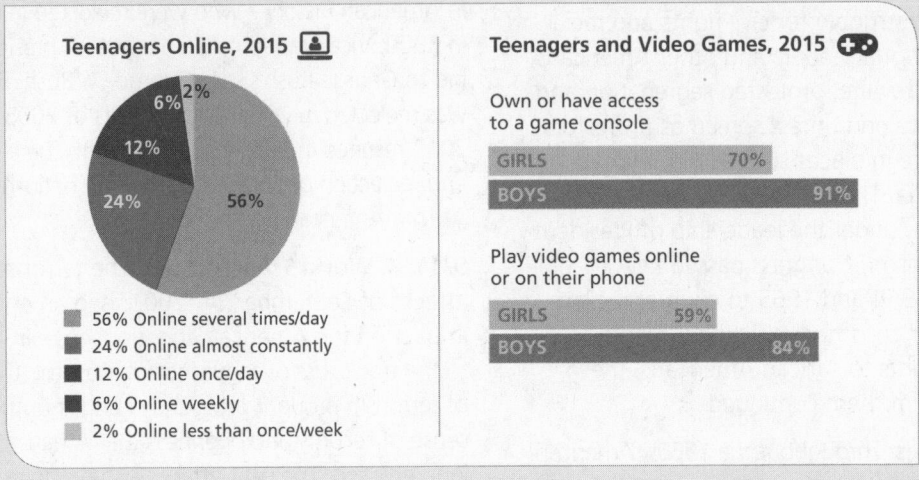

Teenagers Online, 2015

- 2%
- 6%
- 12%
- 24%
- 56%

- 56% Online several times/day
- 24% Online almost constantly
- 12% Online once/day
- 6% Online weekly
- 2% Online less than once/week

Teenagers and Video Games, 2015

Own or have access to a game console

| GIRLS | 70% |
| BOYS | 91% |

Play video games online or on their phone

| GIRLS | 59% |
| BOYS | 84% |

Source: Pew Research Center's Teens Relationship Survey 2014, 2015

A Technological Revolution With the introduction of the microprocessor in the 1970s, life shifted dramatically. In a breathtakingly short time, computers—which began as military and business tools—transformed industry and became personal companions for many Americans. Ever smaller, faster, and easier to use, technology—via the Internet—can now electronically connect anyone with everyone, raising complex questions about privacy and personal relations.

The New Millennium Despite technological advances, traditional issues still dominate human affairs. How do—and how should—human beings relate to the natural world? How can people of different cultures live together peacefully? How can people build a better future? One thing is certain: Although the world will continue to change as the new millennium moves forward, Americans will continue to explore new aspects and applications of the principles of life, liberty, and the pursuit of happiness.

TIMELINE

1982: Alice Walker's *The Color Purple* is published.

1991: South Africa Apartheid, the system of racial segregation, is repealed.

1980

1981: IBM releases its first personal computer.

1989: Germany The Berlin Wall, constructed in 1961, comes down.

1991: USSR The Soviet Union is dissolved, resulting in the formation of fifteen independent nations.

Literature Selections

Literature of the Focus Period Some of the selections in this unit were written during the Focus Period and pertain to an exploration of the human condition:

"Everyday Use," Alice Walker

"Everything Stuck to Him," Raymond Carver

"The Leap," Louise Erdrich

"A Brief History of the Short Story," D. F. McCourt

"The Man to Send Rain Clouds," Leslie Marmon Silko

"Ambush," Tim O'Brien

"Housepainting," Lan Samantha Chang

Connections Across Time Literary works that consider aspects of the human condition are not confined to the Focus Period, of course. They have been a topic of interest in every era of literature in every culture since ancient times. These American short stories are from a period that precedes the Focus Period by several decades:

"An Occurrence at Owl Creek Bridge," Ambrose Bierce

"The Jilting of Granny Weatherall," Katherine Anne Porter

"The Tell-Tale Heart," Edgar Allan Poe

ADDITIONAL FOCUS PERIOD LITERATURE

Student Edition

UNIT 1
"Speech to the Young
Speech to the Progress-Toward,"
Gwendolyn Brooks

"The Pedestrian," Ray Bradbury

UNIT 2
"Sweet Land of . . . Conformity?"
Claude Fischer

"Hamadi," Naomi Shihab Nye

UNIT 3
from *The Warmth of Other Suns*, Isabel Wilkerson

"Books as Bombs," Louis Menand

UNIT 4
"In the Longhouse, Oneida Museum,"
Roberta Hill

"Cloudy Day," Jimmy Santiago Baca

"The Rockpile," James Baldwin

UNIT 5
The Crucible, Arthur Miller

from *Farewell to Manzanar*, Jeanne Wakatsuki Houston and James D. Houston

"What You Don't Know Can Kill You,"
Jason Daley

"Runagate Runagate," Robert Hayden

"For Black Women Who Are Afraid,"
Toi Derricote

"What Are You So Afraid Of?" Akiko Busch

1993: Toni Morrison wins the Nobel Prize for Literature.

1996: Scotland "Dolly" the sheep becomes the first mammal to be cloned from an adult cell.

2001: Terrorists use commercial planes to attack the United States on 9/11, killing some 3,000 people.

2008: Barack Obama is elected the first African American president of the United States.

— Present —

2010: The population of the United States reaches 308.7 million.

About the Author

When **Alice Walker**
(b. 1944) was eight, she
suffered an injury that
blinded her in one eye
and left her scarred. For
comfort, she turned to
reading and writing poetry.
Later, she became a highly
successful writer with many
bestsellers—among them
the novel *The Color Purple*,
a 1983 Pulitzer Prize winner.
Her writing is renowned for
its keen observations about
relationships and for its
strong personal voice. Walker
has also published numerous
short-story collections and
many volumes of poetry.

 Tool Kit

First-Read Guide and
Model Annotation

Everyday Use

Concept Vocabulary

You will encounter the following words as you read "Everyday Use." Before
reading, note how familiar you are with each word. Then, rank the words in
order from most familiar (1) to least familiar (6).

WORD	YOUR RANKING
sidle	
shuffle	
furtive	
cowering	
awkward	
hangdog	

After completing the first read, come back to the concept vocabulary and
review your rankings. Mark changes to your original rankings as needed.

First Read FICTION

Apply these strategies as you conduct your first read. You will have an
opportunity to complete the close-read notes after your first read.

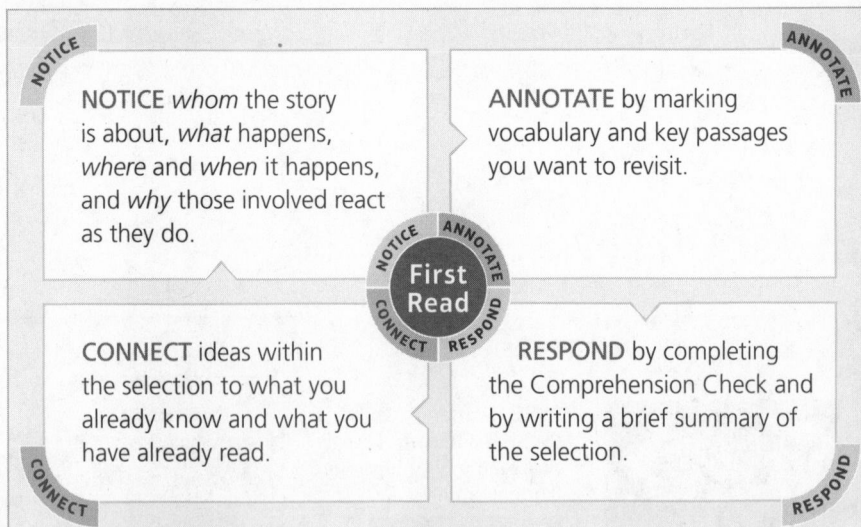

NOTICE *whom* the story is about, *what* happens, *where* and *when* it happens, and *why* those involved react as they do.

ANNOTATE by marking vocabulary and key passages you want to revisit.

CONNECT ideas within the selection to what you already know and what you have already read.

RESPOND by completing the Comprehension Check and by writing a brief summary of the selection.

First Read

STANDARDS
Reading Literature
By the end of grade 11, read and
comprehend literature, including
stories, dramas, and poems, in the
grades 11–CCR text complexity
band proficiently, with scaffolding as
needed at the high end of the range.

Everyday Use

Alice Walker

BACKGROUND

Quilts play an important part in this story. Quilting, in which layers of
fabric and padding are sewn together, dates back to the Middle Ages
and perhaps even to ancient Egypt. Today, quilts serve both practical and
aesthetic purposes: keeping people warm, recycling old clothing, providing
focal points for social gatherings, preserving precious bits of family history,
and adding color and beauty to a home. Pay attention to how these
purposes relate to the tension that arises among the characters you meet in
this story.

SCAN FOR
MULTIMEDIA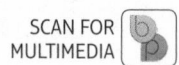

1   I will wait for her in the yard that Maggie and I made so clean and
wavy yesterday afternoon. A yard like this is more comfortable
than most people know. It is not just a yard. It is like an extended
living room. When the hard clay is swept clean as a floor and the fine
sand around the edges lined with tiny, irregular grooves, anyone can
come and sit and look up into the elm tree and wait for the breezes
that never come inside the house.

2   Maggie will be nervous until after her sister goes: she will stand
hopelessly in corners, homely and ashamed of the burn scars down
her arms and legs, eyeing her sister with a mixture of envy and awe.
She thinks her sister has held life always in the palm of one hand, that
"no" is a word the world never learned to say to her.

NOTES

CLOSE READ
ANNOTATE: In paragraph 2,
mark the adjectives that
describe Maggie.

QUESTION: Why does
the author choose these
adjectives?

CONCLUDE: What portrait
of Maggie do these
adjectives help paint?

3   You've no doubt seen those TV shows where the child who has "made it" is confronted, as a surprise, by her own mother and father, tottering in weakly from backstage. (A pleasant surprise, of course: What would they do if parent and child came on the show only to curse out and insult each other?) On TV mother and child embrace and smile into each other's faces. Sometimes the mother and father weep, the child wraps them in her arms and leans across the table to tell how she would not have made it without their help. I have seen these programs.

4   Sometimes I dream a dream in which Dee and I are suddenly brought together on a TV program of this sort. Out of a dark and soft-seated limousine I am ushered into a bright room filled with many people. There I meet a smiling, gray, sporty man like Johnny Carson who shakes my hand and tells me what a fine girl I have. Then we are on the stage and Dee is embracing me with tears in her eyes. She pins on my dress a large orchid, even though she has told me once that she thinks orchids are tacky flowers.

5   In real life I am a large, big-boned woman with rough, man-working hands. In the winter I wear flannel nightgowns to bed and overalls during the day. I can kill and clean a hog as mercilessly as a man. My fat keeps me hot in zero weather. I can work outside all day, breaking ice to get water for washing; I can eat pork liver cooked over the open fire minutes after it comes steaming from the hog. One winter I knocked a bull calf straight in the brain between the eyes with a sledge hammer and had the meat hung up to chill before nightfall. But of course all of this does not show on television. I am the way my daughter would want me to be: a hundred pounds lighter, my skin like an uncooked barley pancake. My hair glistens in the hot bright lights. Johnny Carson has much to do to keep up with my quick and witty tongue.

6   But that is a mistake. I know even before I wake up. Who ever knew a Johnson with a quick tongue? Who can even imagine me looking a strange white man in the eye? It seems to me I have talked to them always with one foot raised in flight, with my head turned in whichever way is farthest from them. Dee, though. She would always look anyone in the eye. Hesitation was no part of her nature.

7   "How do I look, Mama?" Maggie says, showing just enough of her thin body enveloped in pink skirt and red blouse for me to know she's there, almost hidden by the door.

8   "Come out into the yard," I say.

9   Have you ever seen a lame animal, perhaps a dog run over by some careless person rich enough to own a car, sidle up to someone who is ignorant enough to be kind to him? That is the way my Maggie walks. She has been like this, chin on chest, eyes on ground, feet in shuffle, ever since the fire that burned the other house to the ground.

sidle (SY duhl) v. move sideways, as in an unobtrusive, stealthy, or shy manner

shuffle (SHUHF uhl) n. dragging movement of the feet over the ground or floor without lifting them

10   Dee is lighter than Maggie, with nicer hair and a fuller figure. She's a woman now, though sometimes I forget. How long ago was it that the other house burned? Ten, twelve years? Sometimes I can still hear the flames and feel Maggie's arms sticking to me, her hair smoking and her dress falling off her in little black papery flakes. Her eyes seemed stretched open, blazed open by the flames reflected in them. And Dee. I see her standing off under the sweet gum tree she used to dig gum out of; a look of concentration on her face as she watched the last dingy gray board of the house fall in toward the red-hot brick chimney. Why don't you do a dance around the ashes? I'd want to ask her. She had hated the house that much.

11   I used to think she hated Maggie, too. But that was before we raised the money, the church and me, to send her to Augusta to school. She used to read to us without pity; forcing words, lies, other folks' habits, whole lives upon us two, sitting trapped and ignorant underneath her voice. She washed us in a river of make-believe, burned us with a lot of knowledge we didn't necessarily need to know. Pressed us to her with the serious way she read, to shove us away at just the moment, like dimwits, we seemed about to understand.

12   Dee wanted nice things. A yellow organdy dress to wear to her graduation from high school; black pumps to match a green suit she'd made from an old suit somebody gave me. She was determined to stare down any disaster in her efforts. Her eyelids would not flicker for minutes at a time. Often I fought off the temptation to shake her. At sixteen she had a style of her own, and knew what style was.

13   I never had an education myself. After second grade the school was closed down. Don't ask me why: in 1927 colored asked fewer questions than they do now. Sometimes Maggie reads to me. She stumbles along good-naturedly but can't see well. She knows she is not bright. Like good looks and money, quickness passed her by. She will marry John Thomas (who has mossy teeth in an earnest face) and then I'll be free to sit here and I guess just sing church songs to myself. Although I never was a good singer. Never could carry a tune. I was always better at a man's job. I used to love to milk till I was hooved in the side in '49. Cows are soothing and slow and don't bother you, unless you try to milk them the wrong way.

14   I have deliberately turned my back on the house. It is three rooms, just like the one that burned, except the roof is tin; they don't make shingle roofs any more. There are no real windows, just some holes cut in the sides, like the portholes in a ship, but not round and not square, with rawhide holding the shutters up on the outside. This house is in a pasture, too, like the other one. No doubt when Dee sees it she will want to tear it down. She wrote me once that no matter where we "choose" to live, she will manage to come see us. But she will never bring her friends. Maggie and I thought about this and Maggie asked me, "Mama, when did Dee ever *have* any friends?"

CLOSE READ

ANNOTATE: In paragraph 14, mark Maggie's response to Dee's declaration about never bringing friends to Mama's house.

QUESTION: What is surprising about this response?

CONCLUDE: What might this response signal to readers?

furtive (FUHR tihv) *adj.*
done or acting in a stealthy manner to avoid being noticed; secret

15 She had a few. **Furtive** boys in pink shirts hanging about on washday after school. Nervous girls who never laughed. Impressed with her they worshiped the well-turned phrase, the cute shape, the scalding humor that erupted like bubbles in lye.[1] She read to them.

16 When she was courting Jimmy T she didn't have much time to pay to us, but turned all her faultfinding power on him. He *flew* to marry a cheap city girl from a family of ignorant flashy people. She hardly had time to recompose herself.

17 When she comes I will meet—but there they are!

18 Maggie attempts to make a dash for the house, in her shuffling way, but I stay her with my hand. "Come back here," I say. And she stops and tries to dig a well in the sand with her toe.

19 It is hard to see them clearly through the strong sun. But even the first glimpse of leg out of the car tells me it is Dee. Her feet were always neat-looking, as if God himself had shaped them with a certain style. From the other side of the car comes a short, stocky man. Hair is all over his head a foot long and hanging from his chin like a kinky mule tail. I hear Maggie suck in her breath. "Uhnnnh," is what it sounds like. Like when you see the wriggling end of a snake just in front of your foot on the road. "Uhnnnh."

20 Dee next. A dress down to the ground, in this hot weather. A dress so loud it hurts my eyes. There are yellows and oranges enough to throw back the light of the sun. I feel my whole face warming from the heat waves it throws out. Earrings gold, too, and hanging down to her shoulders. Bracelets dangling and making noises when she moves her arm up to shake the folds of the dress out of her armpits. The dress is loose and flows, and as she walks closer, I like it. I hear Maggie go "Uhnnnh" again. It is her sister's hair. It stands straight up like the wool on a sheep. It is black as night and around the edges are two long pigtails that rope about like small lizards disappearing behind her ears.

21 "Wa-su-zo-Tean-o!"[2] she says, coming on in that gliding way the dress makes her move. The short stocky fellow with the hair to his navel is all grinning and he follows up with "Asalamalakim,[3] my mother and sister!" He moves to hug Maggie but she falls back, right up against the back of my chair. I feel her trembling there and when I look up I see the perspiration falling off her chin.

22 "Don't get up," says Dee. Since I am stout it takes something of a push. You can see me trying to move a second or two before I make it. She turns, showing white heels through her sandals, and goes back to the car. Out she peeks next with a Polaroid. She stoops down quickly and lines up picture after picture of me sitting there in front

CLOSE READ

ANNOTATE: In paragraph 20, mark sentence fragments—groups of words punctuated as sentences that do not contain both a subject and a verb.

QUESTION: Why does the author use fragments in this description?

CONCLUDE: How does the use of fragments add to the drama or tension of the moment?

---

1. **lye** (ly) *n.* strong alkaline solution used in cleaning and making soap.
2. **Wa-su-zo-Tean-o** (wah soo zoh TEEN oh) "Good morning" in Lugandan, a language spoken in the African country of Uganda.
3. **Asalamalakim** *Salaam aleikhim* (suh LAHM ah LY keem) Arabic greeting meaning "Peace be with you" that is commonly used by Muslims.

of the house with Maggie **cowering** behind me. She never takes a shot without making sure the house is included. When a cow comes nibbling around the edge of the yard she snaps it and me and Maggie and the house. Then she puts the Polaroid in the back seat of the car, and comes up and kisses me on the forehead.

23   Meanwhile Asalamalakim is going through motions with Maggie's hand. Maggie's hand is as limp as a fish, and probably as cold, despite the sweat, and she keeps trying to pull it back. It looks like Asalamalakim wants to shake hands but wants to do it fancy. Or maybe he don't know how people shake hands. Anyhow, he soon gives up on Maggie.

24   "Well," I say. "Dee."

25   "No, Mama," she says. "Not 'Dee,' Wangero Leewanika Kemanjo!"

26   "What happened to 'Dee'?" I wanted to know.

27   "She's dead." Wangero said. "I couldn't bear it any longer, being named after the people who oppress me."

28   "You know as well as me you was named after your aunt Dicie," I said. Dicie is my sister. She named Dee. We called her "Big Dee" after Dee was born.

29   "But who was *she* named after?" asked Wangero.

30   "I guess after Grandma Dee," I said.

31   "And who was she named after?" asked Wangero.

32   "Her mother," I said, and saw Wangero was getting tired. "That's about as far back as I can trace it," I said. Though, in fact, I probably could have carried it back beyond the Civil War through the branches.

33   "Well," said Asalamalakim, "there you are."

34   "Uhnnnh," I heard Maggie say.

35   "There I was not," I said, "before 'Dicie' cropped up in our family, so why should I try to trace it that far back?"

36   He just stood there grinning, looking down on me like somebody inspecting a Model A car. Every once in a while he and Wangero sent eye signals over my head.

37   "How do you pronounce this name?" I asked.

38   "You don't have to call me by it if you don't want to," said Wangero.

39   "Why shouldn't I?" I asked. "If that's what you want us to call you, we'll call you."

40   "I know it might sound **awkward** at first," said Wangero.

41   "I'll get used to it," I said. "Ream it out again."

42   Well, soon we got the name out of the way. Asalamalakim had a name twice as long and three times as hard. After I tripped over it two or three times he told me to just call him Hakim-a-barber. I wanted to ask him was he a barber, but I didn't really think he was, so I didn't ask.

43   "You must belong to those beef-cattle people down the road," I said. They said "Asalamalakim" when they met you, too, but they didn't shake hands. Always too busy: feeding the cattle, fixing the fences,

cowering (KOW uhr ihng) *adj.* crouching or drawing back in fear or shame

"I couldn't bear it any longer, being named after the people who oppress me."

awkward (AWK wuhrd) *adj.* not graceful or skillful in movement or shape; clumsy putting up salt-lick shelters, throwing down hay. When the white folks poisoned some of the herd the men stayed up all night with rifles in their hands. I walked a mile and a half just to see the sight.

44   Hakim-a-barber said, "I accept some of their doctrines, but farming and raising cattle is not my style." (They didn't tell me, and I didn't ask, whether Wangero (Dee) had really gone and married him.)

45   We sat down to eat and right away he said he didn't eat collards[4] and pork was unclean. Wangero, though, went on through the chitlins[5] and corn bread, the greens and everything else. She talked a blue streak over the sweet potatoes. Everything delighted her. Even the fact that we still used the benches her daddy made for the table when we couldn't afford to buy chairs.

46   "Oh, Mama!" she cried. Then turned to Hakim-a-barber. "I never knew how lovely these benches are. You can feel the rump prints," she said, running her hands underneath her and along the bench. Then she gave a sigh and her hand closed over Grandma Dee's butter dish. "That's it!" she said. "I knew there was something I wanted to ask you if I could have." She jumped up from the table and went over in the corner where the churn stood, the milk in it clabber by now. She looked at the churn and looked at it.

47   "This churn top is what I need," she said. "Didn't Uncle Buddy whittle it out of a tree you all used to have?"

48   "Yes," I said.

49   "Uh huh," she said happily. "And I want the dasher, too."

50   "Uncle Buddy whittle that, too?" asked the barber.

51   Dee (Wangero) looked up at me.

52   "Aunt Dee's first husband whittled the dash," said Maggie so low you almost couldn't hear her. "His name was Henry, but they called him Stash."

53   "Maggie's brain is like an elephant's," Wangero said, laughing. "I can use the churn top as a centerpiece for the alcove table," she said, sliding a plate over the churn, "and I'll think of something artistic to do with the dasher."

54   When she finished wrapping the dasher the handle stuck out. I took it for a moment in my hands. You didn't even have to look close to see where hands pushing the dasher up and down to make butter had left a kind of sink in the wood. In fact, there were a lot of small sinks; you could see where thumbs and fingers had sunk into the wood. It was beautiful light yellow wood, from a tree that grew in the yard where Big Dee and Stash had lived.

55   After dinner Dee (Wangero) went to the trunk at the foot of my bed and started rifling through it. Maggie hung back in the kitchen over the dishpan. Out came Wangero with two quilts. They had been pieced by Grandma Dee and then Big Dee and me had hung them on the quilt frames on the front porch and quilted them. One was in the Lone Star pattern. The other was Walk Around the Mountain. In both of them

---

4. **collards** *n.* leaves of the collard plant, often referred to as "collard greens."
5. **chitlins** *n.* chitterlings, a pork dish popular among southern African Americans.

were scraps of dresses Grandma Dee had worn fifty and more years ago. Bits and pieces of Grandpa Jarrell's Paisley shirts. And one teeny faded blue piece, about the size of a penny matchbox, that was from Great Grandpa Ezra's uniform that he wore in the Civil War.

56   "Mama," Wangero said sweet as a bird. "Can I have these old quilts?"

57   I heard something fall in the kitchen, and a minute later the kitchen door slammed.

58   "Why don't you take one or two of the others?" I asked. "These old things was just done by me and Big Dee from some tops your grandma pieced before she died."

59   "No," said Wangero. "I don't want those. They are stitched around the borders by machine."

60   "That'll make them last better," I said.

61   "That's not the point," said Wangero. "These are all pieces of dresses Grandma used to wear. She did all this stitching by hand. Imagine!" She held the quilts securely in her arms, stroking them.

62   "Some of the pieces, like those lavender ones, come from old clothes her mother handed down to her," I said, moving up to touch the quilts. Dee (Wangero) moved back just enough so that I couldn't reach the quilts. They already belonged to her.

63   "Imagine!" she breathed again, clutching them closely to her bosom.

64   "The truth is," I said, "I promised to give them quilts to Maggie, for when she marries John Thomas."

65   She gasped like a bee had stung her.

66   "Maggie can't appreciate these quilts!" she said. "She'd probably be backward enough to put them to everyday use."

67   "I reckon she would," I said. "God knows I been saving 'em for long enough with nobody using 'em. I hope she will!" I didn't want to bring up how I had offered Dee (Wangero) a quilt when she went away to college. Then she had told me they were old-fashioned, out of style.

68   "But they're *priceless*!" she was saying now, furiously; for she has a temper. "Maggie would put them on the bed and in five years they'd be in rags. Less than that!"

69   "She can always make some more," I said. "Maggie knows how to quilt."

70   Dee (Wangero) looked at me with hatred. "You just will not understand. The point is these quilts, *these quilts*!"

71   "Well," I said, stumped. "What would *you* do with them?"

72   "Hang them," she said. As if that was the only thing you *could* do with quilts.

73   Maggie by now was standing in the door. I could almost hear the sound her feet made as they scraped over each other.

74   "She can have them, Mama," she said, like somebody used to never winning anything, or having anything reserved for her.

NOTES

CLOSE READ
ANNOTATE: In paragraph 55, mark details that describe the fabrics used in the quilts.

QUESTION: Why does the author include this information?

CONCLUDE: How does this information affect readers' sympathies?

hangdog (HANG DAWG) *adj.*
sad; ashamed; guilty

CLOSE READ

ANNOTATE: In paragraph 76, mark the sentences in which Mama expresses Maggie's feelings and thoughts.

QUESTION: Why does the author choose to have Mama express Maggie's feelings?

CONCLUDE: How does this choice emphasize differences in Mama's relationships with her two daughters?

75   "I can 'member Grandma Dee without the quilts."

76   I looked at her hard. She had filled her bottom lip with checkerberry snuff and it gave her face a kind of dopey, hangdog look. It was Grandma Dee and Big Dee who taught her how to quilt herself. She stood there with her scarred hands hidden in the folds of her skirt. She looked at her sister with something like fear but she wasn't mad at her. This was Maggie's portion. This was the way she knew God to work.

77   When I looked at her like that something hit me in the top of my head and ran down to the soles of my feet. Just like when I'm in church and the spirit of God touches me and I get happy and shout. I did something I never had done before: hugged Maggie to me, then dragged her on into the room, snatched the quilts out of Miss Wangero's hands and dumped them into Maggie's lap. Maggie just sat there on my bed with her mouth open.

78   "Take one or two of the others," I said to Dee.

79   But she turned without a word and went out to Hakim-a-barber.

80   "You just don't understand,'" she said, as Maggie and I came out to the car.

81   "What don't I understand?" I wanted to know.

82   "Your heritage," she said. And then she turned to Maggie, kissed her, and said, "You ought to try to make something of yourself, too, Maggie. It's really a new day for us. But from the way you and Mama still live you'd never know it."

83   She put on some sunglasses that hid everything above the tip of her nose and her chin.

84   Maggie smiled; maybe at the sunglasses. But a real smile, not scared. After we watched the car dust settle I asked Maggie to bring me a dip of snuff. And then the two of us sat there just enjoying, until it was time to go in the house and go to bed. 🥄

MEDIA CONNECTION

Alice Walker's "Everyday Use"

💬 **Discuss It** How does listening to someone tell this story help you understand Mama and the tensions among the characters?

Write your response before sharing your ideas.

SCAN FOR MULTIMEDIA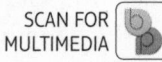

Comprehension Check

Complete the following items after you finish your first read.

1. Early in the story, how does Mama describe herself?

2. According to Mama, how did Dee treat her and Maggie when she came home from college?

3. Who arrives with Dee/Wangero on this visit?

4. Why has Dee changed her name to Wangero?

5. What household objects does Dee/Wangero want? Which ones does Mama give her?

6. 🖥 **Notebook** To confirm your understanding, write a summary of "Everyday Use."

- -

RESEARCH

Research to Clarify Choose at least one unfamiliar detail from the text. Briefly research that detail. In what way does the information you learned shed light on an aspect of the story?

Research to Explore Conduct research on an aspect of the text you find interesting. For example, you may want to learn about the Black Power movement of the 1970s that led to the cultural nationalism Dee/Wangero and Asalamalakim find appealing.

EVERYDAY USE

Close Read the Text

1. This model, from paragraph 10 of the text, shows two sample annotations, along with questions and conclusions. Close read the passage, and find another detail to annotate. Then, write a question and your conclusion.

> **ANNOTATE:** These details contrast the two daughters' reactions to the fire.
>
> **QUESTION:** Why does the author include these details?
>
> **CONCLUDE:** The details emphasize Maggie's involvement and Dee's distance.

Close Read
ANNOTATE · QUESTION · CONCLUDE

Sometimes I can still . . . feel Maggie's arms sticking to me, her hair smoking and her dress falling off her in little black papery flakes. . . . And Dee. I see her standing off under the sweet gum tree. . . . Why don't you do a dance around the ashes? I'd want to ask her.

> **ANNOTATE:** This question is sarcastic and funny.
>
> **QUESTION:** What does this detail reveal about Mama?
>
> **CONCLUDE:** Mama is not naive; she has good insight about her daughters.

🔧 **Tool Kit**

Close-Read Guide and Model Annotation

2. For more practice, go back into the text and complete the close-read notes.

3. Revisit a section of the text you found important during your first read. Read this section closely, and **annotate** what you notice. Ask yourself **questions** such as "Why did the author make this choice?" What can you **conclude**?

Analyze the Text

CITE TEXTUAL EVIDENCE to support your answers.

📓 **Notebook** Respond to these questions.

1. **Make Inferences** What does Mama's dream of being on Johnny Carson's show illustrate about her relationship to Dee/Wangero?

2. (a) **Interpret** What do the quilts symbolize, or represent?
   (b) **Compare and Contrast** In what ways do the quilts hold different meanings for Dee/Wangero and for Maggie?

3. (a) What does Dee/Wangero plan to do with the items that she requests?
   (b) **Evaluate** What is ironic about her request for these objects and her professed interest in her heritage?

4. **Historical Perspectives** How do Dee/Wangero's and her companion's clothing and overall appearances reflect a change in African American culture in the 1960s?

5. **Essential Question:** *What do stories reveal about the human condition?* What has reading this story taught you about family relationships?

Analyze Craft and Structure

Literary Elements: Character Writers reveal key messages or themes in stories through **characterization**—what characters say, what they do, and how they interact with other characters.

Short stories often feature a main character as a first-person narrator. It is through this character's eyes that readers learn about events and perceive the other characters. This first-person narrator serves as a guide through the world of the story, presenting his or her thoughts, feelings, observations, and perceptions. Inevitably, every narrator comes with biases, or leanings, so readers have to decide how much they trust the narrator's interpretation of events. The perspective the first-person narrator brings to the story is a key element that leads readers to the story's **themes,** or insights about life.

Practice

CITE TEXTUAL EVIDENCE
to support your answers.

Notebook **Respond to these questions.**

1. (a) Who is the narrator of "Everyday Use"? (b) Identify three thoughts and feelings that the narrator shares with readers. (c) Do you trust this narrator's account of people and events? Explain.
2. In the chart, record details about Mama and Dee/Wangero related to their appearances, life experiences, relationships, and values. Then, identify a possible theme that Walker develops by setting up contrasts between these two characters.

MAMA	DEE (WANGERO)

THEME:

3. Think about the words and actions of Hakim-a-barber. How does the inclusion of this character help develop other characters in the story?

EVERYDAY USE

Concept Vocabulary

sidle	furtive	awkward
shuffle	cowering	hangdog

Why These Words? These concept vocabulary words help reveal the tentative way Maggie acts in the story. Mama describes Maggie as *cowering* behind her and as moving her feet in a *shuffle*. These words describe a person who wants to be invisible.

1. How do the concept vocabulary words help you understand why Mama and Dee/Wangero have different attitudes toward Maggie?

2. What other words in the selection connect to this concept?

Practice

🖙 **Notebook** The concept vocabulary words appear in "Everyday Use."

1. Write three sentences, using two of the concept words in each sentence, to demonstrate your understanding of the words' meanings.

2. Choose an antonym—a word with an opposite meaning—for each concept vocabulary word. How would the story be different if these words were used to describe Maggie?

Word Study

Exocentric Compounds Most compound words contain at least one word part that connects directly to what is being named or described. For example, the compound word *sunflower* names a type of flower. Some compound words, however, connect two words of which neither names the thing or person described. These **exocentric compound** words are often used to name or describe people—for example, *tattletale*, *birdbrain*, and *pickpocket*. In "Everyday Use," the narrator describes Maggie as having "a dopey, hangdog look." *Hangdog* means "guilty" or "ashamed."

1. Use a dictionary to find five examples of exocentric compounds. Record them here.

2. Use each of your choices in a sentence. Be sure to include context clues that hint at each word's meaning.

🖧 WORD NETWORK

Add words related to the human condition from the text to your Word Network.

🔢 STANDARDS

Language
• Apply the understanding that usage is a matter of convention, can change over time, and is sometimes contested.
• Resolve issues of complex or contested usage, consulting references as needed.
• Vary syntax for effect, consulting references for guidance as needed; apply an understanding of syntax to the study of complex texts when reading.

Conventions and Style

Dialect Writers may use dialect and regionalisms to add depth to characters and settings.

- **Dialect** is a way of using English that is specific to a certain area or group of people.
- **A regionalism** is an expression common to a specific place.

These nonstandard forms of language can make characters more realistic by reflecting culture, customs, and educational levels.

Read It

1. Study the examples of dialogue in this chart. Then, use formal English to rewrite each sentence. One example has been done for you.

FROM "EVERYDAY USE"	FORMAL ENGLISH
"You know as well as me you was named after your aunt Dicie." (paragraph 28)	"You know as well as I do that you were named after your aunt Dicie."
"I'll get used to it. . . . Ream it out again." (paragraph 41)	
"The truth is . . . I promised to give them quilts to Maggie, for when she marries John Thomas." (paragraph 64)	
"I reckon she would. . . . God knows I been saving 'em for long enough with nobody using 'em." (paragraph 67)	

2. **Connect to Style** Find one other example of dialect or regionalism in "Everyday Use." Explain how the example develops a character or the setting.

Write It

📓 **Notebook** Use examples from "Everyday Use" to describe what would be lost if Alice Walker had chosen to write dialogue using the same style that she uses for description.

EVERYDAY USE

Writing to Sources

Narrative writing would be dull if it only reported basic events. However, vivid descriptive details about setting and characters can bring a narrative to life and engage readers. For example, recall how the narrator in "Everyday Use" describes Maggie: "Have you ever seen a lame animal, perhaps a dog run over by some careless person rich enough to own a car, sidle up to someone who is ignorant enough to be kind to him?" This description helps readers picture precisely how Maggie moves and acts around other people.

Assignment

Write a short **narrative** of 500 words or less in which you retell an event from "Everyday Use" from the perspective of a character other than Mama. You may choose to describe Dee's visit or an event from the past. Make sure your narrative is consistent with the characters and setting created by Walker. Include descriptive details that illustrate the character's thoughts and engage the reader.

Include these elements in your narrative:

- a narrator other than Mama from "Everyday Use"
- a clear description of the event, including how the narrator feels about it
- dialect or regionalisms in dialogue or narration, as appropriate

Vocabulary Connection Consider including a few of the concept vocabulary words in your narrative.

sidle	furtive	awkward
shuffle	cowering	hangdog

Reflect on Your Writing

After you have written your short narrative, answer these questions.

1. How did writing your narrative strengthen your understanding of Walker's story?

2. What part of writing this narrative was most challenging, and how did you handle it?

3. **Why These Words?** The words you choose make a difference in your writing. Which words did you choose to create vivid descriptive details?

STANDARDS

Writing
Write narratives to develop real or imagined experiences or events using effective technique, well-chosen details, and well-structured event sequences.

Speaking and Listening
• Initiate and participate effectively in a range of collaborative discussions with diverse partners on *grades 11–12 topics, texts, and issues,* building on others' ideas and expressing their own clearly and persuasively.
• Come to discussions prepared, having read and researched material under study; explicitly draw on that preparation by referring to evidence from texts and other research on the topic or issue to stimulate a thoughtful, well-reasoned exchange of ideas.

Speaking and Listening

Assignment

Have a **partner discussion** about what factors lead a person to embrace, reject, or feel neutral about his or her heritage. Before working with your partner, think about the two daughters' perspectives on heritage, and take notes about how the text inspires your own thoughts on the subject. As you discuss, build on one another's ideas, asking respectful questions, listening politely, and adding your own insights. At the end of your discussion, create an extended definition of *heritage*. Follow these steps to complete the assignment.

1. **Focus on the Text** Choose examples from the story.

   - Consider ways the author indirectly describes characters.

   - Compare and contrast the three women's attitudes toward objects in the house.

   - Discuss what the story's resolution says about heritage.

2. **Share Personal Experiences** Share your own experiences with heritage and traditions in your family. Consider questions such as the following:

   - What are some objects in your home or family that are part of a heritage or tradition?

   - How and when are these objects used? Every day? Only on holidays?

   - Does everyone recognize the objects as special?

3. **Craft an Extended Definition** To create an extended definition of *heritage*, come to a consensus about the most important ideas to include.

   - Summarize your notes in three main points.

   - Summarize your personal experiences with heritage.

   - Draft and refine an extended definition that includes all of your most important thoughts.

4. **Evaluate the Activity** When you have finished, use the evaluation guide to analyze the way that you and your partner worked together to discuss a topic and create an extended definition.

EVALUATION GUIDE

Rate each statement on a scale of 1 (not demonstrated) to 5 (demonstrated).

☐ Both partners contributed equally to the discussion.

☐ Partners commented upon the text and also shared personal experiences.

☐ Partners were attentive to and respectful of the thoughts presented.

☐ Partners worked collaboratively to create an extended definition of *heritage*.

✎ EVIDENCE LOG

Before moving on to a new selection, go to your Evidence Log and record what you learned from "Everyday Use."

About the Author

Born in a small Oregon logging town to a mill worker and a waitress, **Raymond Carver** (1938–1988) drew heavily from his life in his stories about the hardships of the working poor. By age twenty, Carver had two children and was struggling to support his family, taking on a series of jobs as a janitor, a sawmill worker, and a gas-station attendant. In 1958, he took a creative writing class, and soon he began to work nights and study writing during the day. His earliest acclaim was for his 1967 story "Will You Please Be Quiet, Please?" In 1971, he began a decade-long partnership with the editor Gordon Lish, who encouraged a "less-is-more" writing approach. Carver's writing became lean and sparse, earning him a reputation as an expert minimalist and one of the greatest storytellers of his time.

Everything Stuck to Him

Concept Vocabulary

You will encounter the following words as you read "Everything Stuck to Him." Before reading, note how familiar you are with each word. Then, rank the words in order from most familiar (1) to least familiar (4).

WORD	YOUR RANKING
waterfowl	
letterhead	
overcast	
shotgun	

After completing the first read, come back to the concept vocabulary and review your rankings. Mark changes to your original rankings as needed.

First Read FICTION

Apply these strategies as you conduct your first read. You will have an opportunity to complete the close-read notes after your first read.

NOTICE *whom* the story is about, *what* happens, *where* and *when* it happens, and *why* those involved react as they do.

ANNOTATE by marking vocabulary and key passages you want to revisit.

First Read

CONNECT ideas within the selection to what you already know and what you have already read.

RESPOND by completing the Comprehension Check and by writing a brief summary of the selection.

STANDARDS

Reading Literature
By the end of grade 11, read and comprehend literature, including stories, dramas, and poems, in the grades 11–CCR text complexity band proficiently, with scaffolding as needed at the high end of the range.

Everything
Stuck to Him

Raymond Carver

BACKGROUND

This is a frame story, or a story within a story. There are many frame narratives in world literature, including the *Arabian Nights* and *The Canterbury Tales*. "The Notorious Jumping Frog of Calaveras County," by Mark Twain (in Unit 4), is an American example. In frame narratives, the introductory story is typically of secondary importance to the internal one. Consider whether this is true of Carver's tale.

SCAN FOR
MULTIMEDIA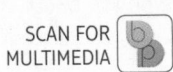

NOTES

1   She's in Milan for Christmas and wants to know what it was like when she was a kid.

2   Tell me, she says. Tell me what it was like when I was a kid. She sips Strega,[1] waits, eyes him closely.

3   She is a cool, slim, attractive girl, a survivor from top to bottom.

4   That was a long time ago. That was twenty years ago, he says.

5   You can remember, she says. Go on.

6   What do you want to hear? he says. What else can I tell you? I could tell you about something that happened when you were a baby. It involves you, he says. But only in a minor way.

---

1. **Strega** Italian herbal liqueur.

waterfowl (WAWT uhr fowl)
n. birds that live in or near water

letterhead (LEHT uhr hehd)
n. personalized stationery

7   Tell me, she says. But first fix us another so you won't have to stop in the middle.

8   He comes back from the kitchen with drinks, settles into his chair, begins.

9   They were kids themselves, but they were crazy in love, this eighteen-year-old boy and this seventeen-year-old girl when they married. Not all that long afterwards they had a daughter.

10 The baby came along in late November during a cold spell that just happened to coincide with the peak of the **waterfowl** season. The boy loved to hunt, you see. That's part of it.

11 The boy and girl, husband and wife, father and mother, they lived in a little apartment under a dentist's office. Each night they cleaned the dentist's place upstairs in exchange for rent and utilities. In summer they were expected to maintain the lawn and the flowers. In winter the boy shoveled snow and spread rock salt on the walks. Are you still with me? Are you getting the picture?

12 I am, she says.

13 That's good, he says. So one day the dentist finds out they were using his **letterhead** for their personal correspondence. But that's another story.

14 He gets up from his chair and looks out the window. He sees the tile rooftops and the snow that is falling steadily on them.

15 Tell the story, she says.

16 The two kids were very much in love. On top of this they had great ambitions. They were always talking about the things they were going to do and the places they were going to go.

17 Now the boy and girl slept in the bedroom, and the baby slept in the living room. Let's say the baby was about three months old and had only just begun to sleep through the night.

18 On this one Saturday night after finishing his work upstairs, the boy stayed in the dentist's office and called an old hunting friend of his father's.

19 Carl, he said when the man picked up the receiver, believe it or not, I'm a father.

20 Congratulations, Carl said. How is the wife?

21 She's fine, Carl. Everybody's fine.

22 That's good, Carl said, I'm glad to hear it. But if you called about going hunting, I'll tell you something. The geese are flying to beat the band. I don't think I've ever seen so many. Got five today. Going back in the morning, so come along if you want to.

23 I want to, the boy said.

24 The boy hung up the telephone and went downstairs to tell the girl. She watched while he laid out his things. Hunting coat, shell bag, boots, socks, hunting cap, long underwear, pump gun.

25 What time will you be back? the girl said.

26 Probably around noon, the boy said. But maybe as late as six o'clock. Would that be too late?

27 It's fine, she said. The baby and I will get along fine. You go and have some fun. When you get back, we'll dress the baby up and go visit Sally.

28 The boy said, Sounds like a good idea.

29 Sally was the girl's sister. She was striking. I don't know if you've seen pictures of her. The boy was a little in love with Sally, just as he

CLOSE READ

ANNOTATE: In paragraphs 18–24, mark the phrases that the author uses to refer to the two protagonists of the remembered (internal) story.

QUESTION: Why does the author name Carl, a minor character, but leave the two protagonists unnamed?

CONCLUDE: What effect does this choice have on the way that readers perceive the characters?

was a little in love with Betsy, who was another sister the girl had. The boy used to say to the girl, If we weren't married, I could go for Sally.

30 What about Betsy? the girl used to say. I hate to admit it, but I truly feel she's better looking than Sally and me. What about Betsy?

31 Betsy too, the boy used to say.

32 After dinner he turned up the furnace and helped her bathe the baby. He marveled again at the infant who had half his features and half the girl's. He powdered the tiny body. He powdered between fingers and toes.

33 He emptied the bath into the sink and went upstairs to check the air. It was **overcast** and cold. The grass, what there was of it, looked like canvas, stiff and gray under the street light.

34 Snow lay in piles beside the walk. A car went by. He heard sand under the tires. He let himself imagine what it might be like tomorrow, geese beating the air over his head, **shotgun** plunging against his shoulder.

35 Then he locked the door and went downstairs.

36 In bed they tried to read. But both of them fell asleep, she first, letting the magazine sink to the quilt.

37 It was the baby's cries that woke him up.

38 The light was on out there, and the girl was standing next to the crib rocking the baby in her arms. She put the baby down, turned out the light, and came back to the bed.

39 He heard the baby cry. This time the girl stayed where she was. The baby cried fitfully and stopped. The boy listened, then dozed. But the baby's cries woke him again. The living room light was burning. He sat up and turned on the lamp.

40 I don't know what's wrong, the girl said, walking back and forth with the baby. I've changed her and fed her, but she keeps on crying. I'm so tired I'm afraid I might drop her.

41 You come back to bed, the boy said. I'll hold her for a while.

42 He got up and took the baby, and the girl went to lie down again.

43 Just rock her for a few minutes, the girl said from the bedroom. Maybe she'll go back to sleep.

44 The boy sat on the sofa and held the baby. He jiggled it in his lap until he got its eyes to close, his own eyes closing right along. He rose carefully and put the baby back in the crib.

45 It was a quarter to four, which gave him forty-five minutes. He crawled into bed and dropped off. But a few minutes later the baby was crying again, and this time they both got up.

46 The boy did a terrible thing. He swore.

47 For God's sake, what's the matter with you? the girl said to the boy. Maybe she's sick or something. Maybe we shouldn't have given her the bath.

48 The boy picked up the baby. The baby kicked its feet and smiled.

49   Look, the boy said, I really don't think there's anything wrong with her.

50   How do you know that? the girl said. Here, let me have her. I know I ought to give her something, but I don't know what it's supposed to be.

51   The girl put the baby down again. The boy and the girl looked at the baby, and the baby began to cry.

52   The girl took the baby. Baby, baby, the girl said with tears in her eyes.

53   Probably it's something on her stomach, the boy said.

54   The girl didn't answer. She went on rocking the baby, paying no attention to the boy.

55   The boy waited. He went to the kitchen and put on water for coffee. He drew his woolen underwear on over his shorts and T-shirt, buttoned up, then got into his clothes.

56   What are you doing? the girl said.

57   Going hunting, the boy said.

58   I don't think you should, she said. I don't want to be left alone with her like this.

59   Carl's planning on me going, the boy said. We've planned it.

60   I don't care about what you and Carl planned, she said. And I don't care about Carl, either. I don't even know Carl.

61   You've met Carl before. You know him, the boy said. What do you mean you don't know him?

62   That's not the point and you know it, the girl said.

63   What is the point? the boy said. The point is we planned it.

64   The girl said, I'm your wife. This is your baby. She's sick or something. Look at her. Why else is she crying?

65   I know you're my wife, the boy said.

66   The girl began to cry. She put the baby back in the crib. But the baby started up again. The girl dried her eyes on the sleeve of her nightgown and picked the baby up.

67   The boy laced up his boots. He put on his shirt, his sweater, his coat. The kettle whistled on the stove in the kitchen.

68   You're going to have to choose, the girl said. Carl or us. I mean it.

69   What do you mean? the boy said.

70   You heard what I said, the girl said. If you want a family, you're going to have to choose.

71   They stared at each other. Then the boy took up his hunting gear and went outside. He started the car. He went around to the car windows and, making a job of it, scraped away the ice.

72   He turned off the motor and sat awhile. And then he got out and went back inside.

> If you want a family, you're going to have to choose.

CLOSE READ

ANNOTATE: In paragraphs 74–84, mark the main parts of speech—nouns, verbs, and any adjectives or adverbs.

QUESTION: Why does the author omit most modifiers?

CONCLUDE: What is the effect of the author's choice to limit the types of words used in this scene?

73   The living-room light was on. The girl was asleep on the bed. The baby was asleep beside her.

74   The boy took off his boots. Then he took off everything else. In his socks and his long underwear, he sat on the sofa and read the Sunday paper.

75   The girl and the baby slept on. After a while, the boy went to the kitchen and started frying bacon.

76   The girl came out in her robe and put her arms around the boy.

77   Hey, the boy said.

78   I'm sorry, the girl said.

79   It's all right, the boy said.

80   I didn't mean to snap like that.

81   It was my fault, he said.

82   You sit down, the girl said. How does a waffle sound with bacon?

83   Sounds great, the boy said.

84   She took the bacon out of the pan and made waffle batter. He sat at the table and watched her move around the kitchen.

85   She put a plate in front of him with bacon, a waffle. He spread butter and poured syrup. But when he started to cut, he turned the plate into his lap.

86   I don't believe it, he said, jumping up from the table.

87   If you could see yourself, the girl said.

88   The boy looked down at himself, at everything stuck to his underwear.

89   I was starved, he said, shaking his head.

90   You were starved, she said, laughing.

91   He peeled off the woolen underwear and threw it at the bathroom door. Then he opened his arms and the girl moved into them.

92   We won't fight anymore, she said.

93   The boy said, We won't.

94   He gets up from his chair and refills their glasses.

95   That's it, he says. End of story. I admit it's not much of a story.

96   I was interested, she says.

97   He shrugs and carries his drink over to the window. It's dark now but still snowing.

98   Things change, he says. I don't know how they do. But they do without your realizing it or wanting them to.

99   Yes, that's true, only—But she does not finish what she started.

100 She drops the subject. In the window's reflection he sees her study her nails. Then she raises her head. Speaking brightly, she asks if he is going to show her the city, after all.

101 He says, Put your boots on and let's go.

102 But he stays by the window, remembering. They had laughed. They had leaned on each other and laughed until the tears had come, while everything else—the cold, and where he'd go in it—was outside, for a while anyway. ❧

Comprehension Check

Complete the following items after you finish your first read.

1. Where and at what time of year does the introductory story take place?

2. How old are the boy and girl in the internal story?

3. What does the boy want to do on Sunday?

4. What causes the quarrel between the young husband and wife?

5. What event at breakfast explains the story's title?

6. 📓 **Notebook** Write a summary of "Everything Stuck to Him" to confirm your understanding of the text.

- -

RESEARCH

Research to Clarify Choose at least one unfamiliar detail from the story. Briefly research that detail. In what way does the information you learned shed light on an aspect of the story?

Research to Explore Conduct research on an aspect of the text you find interesting. Think about ways in which your research helped deepen your understanding of the story.

Close Read the Text

1. This model, from paragraph 11 of the text, shows two sample annotations, along with questions and conclusions. Close read the passage, and find another detail to annotate. Then, write a question and your conclusion.

> ANNOTATE: The narrator uses third-person pronouns.
>
> QUESTION: Why does the narrator use this point of view?
>
> CONCLUDE: The narrator may be trying to distance himself from the person he was.

ANNOTATE: The narrator asks two questions.

QUESTION: Why do these questions appear here?

CONCLUDE: The narrator is pausing to check his daughter's understanding of the story thus far.

> Each night they cleaned the dentist's place upstairs in exchange for rent and utilities. In summer they were expected to maintain the lawn and the flowers. In winter the boy shoveled snow and spread rock salt on the walks. Are you still with me? Are you getting the picture?

Close Read
ANNOTATE · QUESTION · CONCLUDE

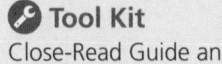

Tool Kit
Close-Read Guide and Model Annotation

2. For more practice, go back into the text, and complete the close-read notes.

3. Revisit a section of the text you found important during your first read. Read this section closely, and **annotate** what you notice. Ask yourself **questions** such as "Why did the author make this choice?" What can you **conclude**?

Analyze the Text

CITE TEXTUAL EVIDENCE
to support your answers.

Notebook Respond to these questions.

1. **Make Inferences** What does the daughter's request suggest about her relationship to her father?

2. (a) **Interpret** Why might the boy have been so eager to go hunting with Carl? (b) **Support** What details in the text support your interpretation?

3. **Make a Judgment** Was the girl right to insist that the boy stay home? Explain your answer.

4. **Historical Perspectives** Could this story have taken place in any historical period, or do you see evidence that the tale is specifically anchored in the mid-twentieth century? Explain.

5. **Essential Question:** *What do stories reveal about the human condition?* What have you learned about relationships and youth by reading this text?

STANDARDS

Reading Literature
• Cite strong and thorough textual evidence to support analysis of what the text says explicitly as well as inferences drawn from the text, including determining where the text leaves matters uncertain.
• Analyze how an author's choices concerning how to structure specific parts of a text contribute to its overall structure and meaning as well as its aesthetic impact.

Analyze Craft and Structure

Narrative Structure A **frame story** is a narrative that consists of two parts: an introductory story and an internal story. The narrative begins and ends with the **introductory story**, which frames the **internal story** like bookends.

- In this narrative structure, the internal story, or story-within-a-story, is typically the more important tale.
- The internal story usually takes place in another time and place.
- The narrator of the introductory story may or may not be a character in the internal story.

Practice

CITE TEXTUAL EVIDENCE to support your answers.

📓 **Notebook** **Respond to these questions.**

1. In which paragraph does the internal story begin? How do you know?

2. Use this chart to record notes about the internal story in "Everything Stuck to Him."

ELEMENTS	DETAILS AND IMAGES
Setting	
Characters	
Conflict	
Climax	
Resolution	

3. Suppose that the internal story had a first-person narrator. How do you think the story's emotional impact would be different? Explain.

4. Reread paragraphs 93–99, when the narrative returns to the introductory story.
   (a) What do you think the father may mean when he says, "Things change"?
   (b) Why do you think the adult daughter "does not finish what she started"?

EVERYTHING STUCK TO HIM

Concept Vocabulary

| waterfowl | letterhead | overcast | shotgun |

Why These Words? The concept vocabulary words are all compound words. They help create a sense of the internal story's setting and action. For example, the sky was *overcast*, and the boy planned to hunt *waterfowl*.

1. How does the concept vocabulary clarify the reader's understanding of the internal story's setting and action?

2. What other compound words in the selection can you identify?

Practice

🔲 **Notebook** The concept vocabulary words appear in "Everything Stuck to Him."

1. Use each word in a sentence that demonstrates your understanding of the word's meaning.

2. Challenge yourself to replace each concept vocabulary word in the sentences you wrote with one or two related words. How does each word change affect the meaning of your original sentence?

Word Study

Endocentric Compounds A compound word is made up of two or more individual words. An **endocentric compound** combines one word that conveys the basic meaning and a modifier that restricts or specifies the meaning of the word. For example, the compound word *waterfowl* combines the words *water* and *fowl*. The modifier *water* describes the type of fowl, or bird.

1. Find five examples of endocentric compounds, and record them.

2. For each word, note the base word and the modifier. Finally, provide a definition of each word.

🔧 **WORD NETWORK**

Add words related to the human condition from the text to your Word Network.

STANDARDS

Language
• Demonstrate command of the conventions of standard English grammar and usage when writing or speaking.
• Apply knowledge of language to understand how language functions in different contexts, to make effective choices for meaning or style, and to comprehend more fully when reading or listening.

Conventions and Style

Pronouns and Antecedents An experienced writer may stretch or break the rules and conventions of standard English in order to achieve an effect, create a personal style, or capture the reader's attention.

Carver purposely breaks English conventions in "Everything Stuck to Him." For example, he does not enclose dialogue with quotation marks. He also leaves the subjects of some sentences deliberately ambiguous, or unclear. This is especially true when the subjects of his sentences are **pronouns,** words that stand for a person, place, or thing, without a clear **antecedent,** what the pronoun refers to.

TIP

FOLLOW THROUGH
Refer to the Grammar Handbook to learn more about these terms.

> EXAMPLE
>
> **"She's** in Milan for Christmas and wants to know what it was like when she was a kid."
>
> The pronoun *she* does not have a clear antecedent. Readers need to gather details over the next few paragraphs before concluding that "She" is the narrator's adult daughter.

Read It

1. Analyze examples of pronouns in Carver's story that lack a clear antecedent. In the right-hand column, rewrite the example so that the meaning is clear.

PASSAGE	REWRITE
The boy loved to hunt, you see. That's part of it. (paragraph 10)	When he was younger, the narrator loved to hunt. His love of hunting will be an important part of the story.
He gets up from his chair and looks out the window. (paragraph 14)	
It's fine, she said. (paragraph 27)	
That's not the point and you know it, the girl said. (paragraph 62)	
It was my fault, he said. (paragraph 81)	

2. **Connect to Style** Reread paragraphs 94–95 of "Everything Stuck to Him." Mark the pronouns, and identify their antecedents. Then, write a possible explanation of why Carver leaves pronoun-antecedent relationships unclear. What effect does this ambiguity have on readers?

Write It

Notebook Choose a short passage from "Everything Stuck to Him" that contains unclear antecedents, and rewrite it to be unambiguous. Then, explain how the rewrite changes the impact of the passage.

EVERYTHING STUCK TO HIM

Writing to Sources

Narrative writing often contains factual details that make the plot and setting seem realistic, even when the story is fictional.

Assignment

Colic is a condition in which an otherwise healthy baby cries for extended periods of time. Conduct research on colic and its effects on newborns and parents. Then, integrate the information you find into a realistic **narrative scene** that shows how the boy and the girl in "Everything Stuck to Him" might have reacted if they had known what colic is and whether or not their baby had it.

Your narrative should include:

- information about colic and its effects
- details from "Everything Stuck to Him," used as background to develop events and dialogue
- a minimalist style consistent with Carver's

Vocabulary and Conventions Connection In your narrative, consider including several of the concept vocabulary words. Consider whether ambiguous pronouns will help you create an effective narrative.

waterfowl	letterhead	overcast	shotgun

Reflect on Your Writing

After you have written your narrative, answer the following questions.

1. How did your effort to imitate Carver's style influence your understanding of his story and writing style?

2. What details about colic or characteristics of the boy and the girl characters did you use in your writing? How did they help support your narrative?

3. **Why These Words?** The words you choose make a difference in your writing. Which words helped you to convey important ideas precisely?

≡ STANDARDS

Reading Literature
Analyze the impact of the author's choices regarding how to develop and relate elements of a story or drama.

Writing
Write narratives to develop real or imagined experiences or events using effective technique, well-chosen details, and well-structured event sequences.

Speaking and Listening
Adapt speech to a variety of contexts and tasks, demonstrating a command of formal English when indicated or appropriate.

Speaking and Listening

Assignment

With a partner, improvise a **dialogue** between the father and his daughter that continues the conversation they were having at the end of "Everything Stuck to Him." Once you have polished and rehearsed your dialogue, present it to the class. After your presentation, lead a whole-class discussion about how the dialogue connected to the story and continued its themes. Follow these steps to complete the assignment.

1. **Analyze the Characters** With your partner, discuss the relationship between the father and his daughter. Decide what the daughter was starting to say at the end of the story before she changed the subject. Draw a conclusion about what happened to the mother. Make sure your decisions are consistent with information in the story.

2. **Plan Your Dialogue** As you develop your dialogue, focus on each character's motivations. Why is the daughter bringing this topic up now? Is there anything the father has been wanting to say to his daughter? Do the characters want to reach an understanding or resolution before their dialogue is over?

3. **Prepare Your Delivery** Practice your dialogue with your partner. Pay attention to nonverbal methods of communication, such as tone, pitch, volume, pacing, facial expressions, and body language.

4. **Evaluate Dialogues** As your classmates deliver their dialogues, listen carefully. Use an evaluation guide like the one shown to analyze their dialogues.

EVALUATION GUIDE

Rate each statement on a scale of 1 (not demonstrated) to 4 (demonstrated).

☐ Partners clearly enacted the characters and the situation.

☐ Partners crafted a dialogue consistent with the story.

☐ Partners communicated clearly and expressively.

☐ Partners used a variety of speaking tones and pitches.

☐ Partners used gestures and other body language effectively.

📝 EVIDENCE LOG

Before moving on to a new selection, go to your Evidence Log and record what you learned from "Everything Stuck to Him."

About the Author

Award-winning novelist, poet, and short-story writer **Louise Erdrich** (b.1954) was born to a German American father and a mother who was half Chippewa. In a popular series of interrelated novels, including *Love Medicine* (1984) and *The Beet Queen* (1986), Erdrich describes the lives of three families living in a fictional North Dakota town. Native American traditions and lore have greatly influenced Erdrich's writing, which often merges local history with current issues and employs multiple narrators to reflect a complex variety of perspectives. Her 2012 novel *The Round House* won the National Book Award.

The Leap

Concept Vocabulary

You will encounter the following words as you read "The Leap." Before reading, note how familiar you are with each word. Then, rank the words in order from most familiar (1) to least familiar (6).

WORD	YOUR RANKING
encroaching	
instantaneously	
anticipation	
constricting	
perpetually	
superannuated	

After completing the first read, come back to the concept vocabulary and review your rankings. Mark changes to your original rankings as needed.

First Read FICTION

Apply these strategies as you conduct your first read. You will have an opportunity to complete the close-read notes after your first read.

NOTICE *whom* the story is about, *what* happens, *where* and *when* it happens, and *why* those involved react as they do.

ANNOTATE by marking vocabulary and key passages you want to revisit.

First Read

CONNECT ideas within the selection to what you already know and what you have already read.

RESPOND by completing the Comprehension Check.

The Leap

Louise Erdrich

BACKGROUND

Traveling circuses first came to the United States from Great Britain in 1793 and quickly established themselves as a part of American popular culture. Showcasing a variety of performers—including clowns, animal trainers, and trapeze artists—circuses would draw and thrill crowds in large cities and small towns alike.

SCAN FOR
MULTIMEDIA

1   **M**y mother is the surviving half of a blindfold trapeze act, not a fact I think about much even now that she is sightless, the result of **encroaching** and stubborn cataracts. She walks slowly through her house here in New Hampshire, lightly touching her way along walls and running her hands over knickknacks, books, the drift of a grown child's belongings and castoffs. She has never upset an object or as much as brushed a magazine onto the floor. She has never lost her balance or bumped into a closet door left carelessly open.

2   It has occurred to me that the catlike precision of her movements in old age might be the result of her early training, but she shows so little of the drama or flair one might expect from a performer that I tend to forget the Flying Avalons. She has kept no sequined costume, no photographs, no fliers or posters from that part of her youth. I would, in fact, tend to think that all memory of double somersaults and heart-stopping catches had left her arms and legs were it not for the fact that sometimes, as I sit sewing in the room of the rebuilt house in which I slept as a child, I hear the crackle, catch a whiff of smoke from the stove downstairs, and suddenly the room goes dark, the stitches burn beneath my fingers, and I am sewing with a needle of hot silver, a thread of fire.

NOTES

encroaching (ehn KROHCH ihng) *adj.* intruding; steadily advancing

CLOSE READ

ANNOTATE: In paragraph 2, mark descriptive words and phrases in the final sentence.

QUESTION: Why might the author have chosen to craft such a long, almost poetic, sentence to follow two ordinary sentences?

CONCLUDE: What overall effect does this sentence create?

3   I owe her my existence three times. The first was when she saved herself. In the town square a replica tent pole, cracked and splintered, now stands cast in concrete. It commemorates the disaster that put our town smack on the front page of the Boston and New York tabloids. It is from those old newspapers, now historical records, that I get my information. Not from my mother, Anna of the Flying Avalons, nor from any of her in-laws, nor certainly from the other half of her particular act, Harold Avalon, her first husband. In one news account it says, "The day was mildly overcast, but nothing in the air or temperature gave any hint of the sudden force with which the deadly gale would strike."

4   I have lived in the West, where you can see the weather coming for miles, and it is true that out here we are at something of a disadvantage. When extremes of temperature collide, a hot and cold front, winds generate **instantaneously** behind a hill and crash upon you without warning. That, I think, was the likely situation on that day in June. People probably commented on the pleasant air, grateful that no hot sun beat upon the striped tent that stretched over the entire center green. They bought their tickets and surrendered them in **anticipation**. They sat. They ate caramelized popcorn and roasted peanuts. There was time, before the storm, for three acts. The White Arabians[1] of Ali-Khazar rose on their hind legs and waltzed. The Mysterious Bernie folded himself into a painted cracker tin, and the Lady of the Mists made herself appear and disappear in surprising places. As the clouds gathered outside, unnoticed, the ringmaster cracked his whip, shouted his introduction, and pointed to the ceiling of the tent, where the Flying Avalons were perched.

5   They loved to drop gracefully from nowhere, like two sparkling birds, and blow kisses as they threw off their plumed helmets and high-collared capes. They laughed and flirted openly as they beat their way up again on the trapeze bars. In the final vignette of their act, they actually would kiss in midair, pausing, almost hovering as they swooped past one another. On the ground, between bows, Harry Avalon would skip quickly to the front rows and point out the smear of my mother's lipstick, just off the edge of his mouth. They made a romantic pair all right, especially in the blindfold sequence.

6   That afternoon, as the anticipation increased, as Mr. and Mrs. Avalon tied sparkling strips of cloth onto each other's face and as they puckered their lips in mock kisses, lips destined "never again to meet," as one long breathless article put it, the wind rose, miles off, wrapped itself into a cone, and howled. There came a rumble of electrical energy, drowned out by the sudden roll of drums. One detail not mentioned by the press, perhaps unknown—Anna was pregnant at the time, seven months and hardly showing, her stomach muscles were that strong. It seems incredible that she would work high above the ground when any fall could be so dangerous, but the

instantaneously (ihn stuhn TAY nee uhs lee) *adv.* immediately

anticipation (an tihs uh PAY shuhn) *n.* eager expectation

---

1. **Arabians** horses of the Arabian breed.

explanation—I know from watching her go blind—is that my mother lives comfortably in extreme elements. She is one with the constant dark now, just as the air was her home, familiar to her, safe, before the storm that afternoon.

7   From opposite ends of the tent they waved, blind and smiling, to the crowd below. The ringmaster removed his hat and called for silence, so that the two above could concentrate. They rubbed their hands in chalky powder, then Harry launched himself and swung, once, twice, in huge calibrated beats across space. He hung from his knees and on the third swing stretched wide his arms, held his hands out to receive his pregnant wife as she dove from her shining bar.

8   It was while the two were in midair, their hands about to meet, that lightning struck the main pole and sizzled down the guy wires, filling the air with a blue radiance that Harry Avalon must certainly have seen through the cloth of his blindfold as the tent buckled and the edifice[2] toppled him forward, the swing continuing and not returning in its sweep, and Harry going down, down into the crowd with his last thought, perhaps, just a prickle of surprise at his empty hands.

9   My mother once said that I'd be amazed at how many things a person can do within the act of falling. Perhaps, at the time, she was teaching me to dive off a board at the town pool, for I associate the idea with midair somersaults. But I also think she meant that even in that awful doomed second one could think, for she certainly did. When her hands did not meet her husband's, my mother tore her blindfold away. As he swept past her on the wrong side, she could have grasped his ankle, the toe-end of his tights, and gone down clutching him. Instead, she changed direction. Her body twisted toward a heavy wire and she managed to hang on to the braided metal, still hot from the lightning strike. Her palms were burned so terribly that once healed they bore no lines, only the blank scar tissue of a quieter future. She was lowered, gently, to the sawdust ring just underneath the dome of the canvas roof, which did not entirely settle but was held up on one end and jabbed through, torn, and still on fire in places from the giant spark, though rain and men's jackets soon put that out.

10   Three people died, but except for her hands my mother was not seriously harmed until an overeager rescuer broke her arm in extricating her and also, in the process, collapsed a portion of the tent bearing a huge buckle that knocked her unconscious. She was taken to the town hospital, and there she must have hemorrhaged,[3] for they kept her, confined to her bed, a month and a half before her baby was born without life.

11   Harry Avalon had wanted to be buried in the circus cemetery next to the original Avalon, his uncle, so she sent him back with his brothers. The child, however, is buried around the corner, beyond

NOTES

CLOSE READ

ANNOTATE: Mark the section of paragraph 9 that interrupts the story the narrator is telling about her mother's feat at the circus years earlier.

QUESTION: Why does the narrator interrupt her story?

CONCLUDE: How does this interruption affect the reader's understanding of both the mother and the narrator?

---

2. **edifice** (EHD uh fihs) *n.* large structure or building.
3. **hemorrhaged** (HEHM uh rihjd) *v.* bled heavily.

CLOSE READ

ANNOTATE: In paragraph 12, mark words and phrases that describe increasing size or clarity.

QUESTION: For the narrator, what types of things are becoming larger or more clearly defined?

CONCLUDE: What does this passage suggest about the narrator's perspective on life?

this house and just down the highway. Sometimes I used to walk there just to sit. She was a girl, but I rarely thought of her as a sister or even as a separate person really. I suppose you could call it the egocentrism[4] of a child, of all young children, but I considered her a less finished version of myself.

12   When the snow falls, throwing shadows among the stones, I can easily pick hers out from the road, for it is bigger than the others and in the shape of a lamb at rest, its legs curled beneath. The carved lamb looms larger as the years pass, though it is probably only my eyes, the vision shifting, as what is close to me blurs and distances sharpen. In odd moments, I think it is the edge drawing near, the edge of everything, the unseen horizon we do not really speak of in the eastern woods. And it also seems to me, although this is probably an idle fantasy, that the statue is growing more sharply etched, as if, instead of weathering itself into a porous mass, it is hardening on the hillside with each snowfall, perfecting itself.

13   It was during her confinement in the hospital that my mother met my father. He was called in to look at the set of her arm, which was complicated. He stayed, sitting at her bedside, for he was something of an armchair traveler and had spent his war quietly, at an air force training grounds, where he became a specialist in arms and legs broken during parachute training exercises. Anna Avalon had been to many of the places he longed to visit—Venice, Rome, Mexico, all through France and Spain. She had no family of her own and was taken in by the Avalons, trained to perform from a very young age. They toured Europe before the war, then based themselves in New York. She was illiterate.

14   It was in the hospital that she finally learned to read and write, as a way of overcoming the boredom and depression of those weeks, and it was my father who insisted on teaching her. In return for stories of her adventures, he graded her first exercises. He bought her her first book, and over her bold letters, which the pale guides of the penmanship pads could not contain, they fell in love.

15   I wonder if my father calculated the exchange he offered: one form of flight for another. For after that, and for as long as I can remember, my mother has never been without a book. Until now, that is, and it remains the greatest difficulty of her blindness. Since my father's recent death, there is no one to read to her, which is why I returned, in fact, from my failed life where the land is flat. I came home to read to my mother, to read out loud, to read long into the dark if I must, to read all night.

16   Once my father and mother married, they moved onto the old farm he had inherited but didn't care much for. Though he'd been thinking of moving to a larger city, he settled down and broadened his practice in this valley. It still seems odd to me, when they could have gone anywhere else, that they chose to stay in the town where

4. **egocentrism** (ee goh SEHN trihz uhm) *n.* self-centeredness; inability to distinguish one's own needs and interests from those of others.

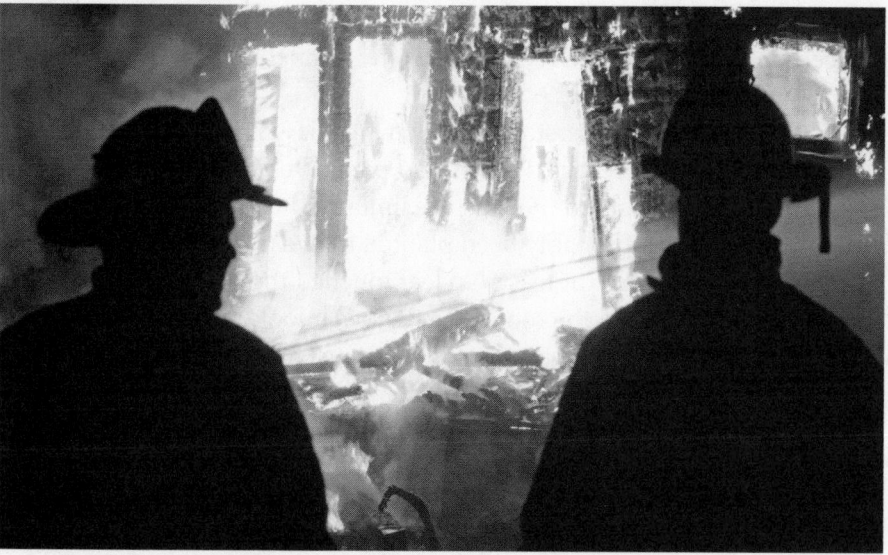

the disaster had occurred, and which my father in the first place had found so constricting. It was my mother who insisted upon it, after her child did not survive. And then, too, she loved the sagging farmhouse with its scrap of what was left of a vast acreage of woods and hidden hay fields that stretched to the game park.

17   I owe my existence, the second time then, to the two of them and the hospital that brought them together. That is the debt we take for granted since none of us asks for life. It is only once we have it that we hang on so dearly.

18   I was seven the year the house caught fire, probably from standing ash. It can rekindle, and my father, forgetful around the house and perpetually exhausted from night hours on call, often emptied what he thought were ashes from cold stoves into wooden or cardboard containers. The fire could have started from a flaming box, or perhaps a buildup of creosote inside the chimney was the culprit. It started right around the stove, and the heart of the house was gutted. The baby-sitter, fallen asleep in my father's den on the first floor, woke to find the stairway to my upstairs room cut off by flames. She used the phone, then ran outside to stand beneath my window.

19   When my parents arrived, the town volunteers had drawn water from the fire pond and were spraying the outside of the house, preparing to go inside after me, not knowing at the time that there was only one staircase and that it was lost. On the other side of the house, the superannuated extension ladder broke in half. Perhaps the clatter of it falling against the walls woke me, for I'd been asleep up to that point.

20   As soon as I awakened, in the small room that I now use for sewing, I smelled the smoke. I followed things by the letter then, was good at memorizing instructions, and so I did exactly what was taught in the second-grade home fire drill. I got up. I touched the back of my door before opening it. Finding it hot, I left it closed and

constricting (kuhn STRIHKT ihng) *adj.* limiting; tightening

perpetually (puhr PEHCH oo uhl lee) *adv.* happening all the time

superannuated (soo puhr AN yu ayt ihd) *adj.* too old to be usable; obsolete

The Leap **799**

stuffed my rolled-up rug beneath the crack. I did not hide under my bed or crawl into my closet. I put on my flannel robe, and then I sat down to wait.

21   Outside, my mother stood below my dark window and saw clearly that there was no rescue. Flames had pierced one side wall, and the glare of the fire lighted the massive limbs and trunk of the vigorous old elm that had probably been planted the year the house was built, a hundred years ago at least. No leaf touched the wall, and just one thin branch scraped the roof. From below, it looked as though even a squirrel would have had trouble jumping from the tree onto the house, for the breadth of that small branch was no bigger than my mother's wrist.

22   Standing there, beside Father, who was preparing to rush back around to the front of the house, my mother asked him to unzip her dress. When he wouldn't be bothered, she made him understand. He couldn't make his hands work, so she finally tore it off and stood there in her pearls and stockings. She directed one of the men to lean the broken half of the extension ladder up against the trunk of the tree. In surprise, he complied. She ascended. She vanished. Then she could be seen among the leafless branches of late November as she made her way up and, along her stomach, inched the length of a bough that curved above the branch that brushed the roof.

23   Once there, swaying, she stood and balanced. There were plenty of people in the crowd and many who still remember, or think they do, my mother's leap through the ice-dark air toward that thinnest extension, and how she broke the branch falling so that it cracked in her hands, cracked louder than the flames as she vaulted with it toward the edge of the roof, and how it hurtled down end over end without her, and their eyes went up, again, to see where she had flown.

24   I didn't see her leap through air, only heard the sudden thump and looked out my window. She was hanging by the backs of her heels from the new gutter we had put in that year, and she was smiling. I was not surprised to see her, she was so matter-of-fact. She tapped on the window. I remember how she did it, too. It was the friendliest tap, a bit tentative, as if she was afraid she had arrived too early at a friend's house. Then she gestured at the latch, and when I opened the window she told me to raise it wider and prop it up with the stick so it wouldn't crush her fingers. She swung down, caught the ledge, and crawled through the opening. Once she was in my room, I realized she had on only underclothing, a bra of the heavy stitched cotton women used to wear and step-in, lace-trimmed drawers. I remember feeling light-headed, of course, terribly relieved, and then embarrassed for her to be seen by the crowd undressed.

25   I was still embarrassed as we flew out the window, toward earth, me in her lap, her toes pointed as we skimmed toward the painted target of the fire fighter's net.

CLOSE READ

ANNOTATE: In paragraph 24, mark words and phrases that describe the mother's manner as she rescues her daughter.

QUESTION: What aspect of the mother's character does the author emphasize with these details?

CONCLUDE: What is the effect of the contrast between the mother's actions and her attitude?

I know that she's right. I knew it even then. As you fall there is time to think. Curled as I was, against her stomach, I was not startled by the cries of the crowd or the looming faces. The wind roared and beat its hot breath at our back, the flames whistled. I slowly wondered what would happen if we missed the circle or bounced out of it. Then I wrapped my hands around my mother's hands. I felt the brush of her lips and heard the beat of her heart in my ears, loud as thunder, long as the roll of drums. ❧

Comprehension Check

Complete the following items after you finish your first read.

1. What happened when lightning hit the circus tent while the Avalons were performing?

2. What did Anna's second husband teach Anna to do?

3. Why has the narrator returned from the West to live with her mother?

4. How did Anna Avalon save the narrator when the narrator was seven years old?

5. 📓 **Notebook** To confirm your understanding, create a timeline of key events in "The Leap."

RESEARCH

Research to Clarify Choose at least one unfamiliar detail from the text. Briefly research that detail. In what way does the information you learned shed light on an aspect of the story?

THE LEAP

Close Read the Text

1. This model, from paragraph 9 of the text, shows two sample annotations, along with questions and conclusions. Close read the passage, and find another detail to annotate. Then, write a question and your conclusion.

Close Read
ANNOTATE · QUESTION · CONCLUDE

> ANNOTATE: This sentence describes Anna's actions as she falls.
>
> QUESTION: What do these actions suggest about Anna?
>
> CONCLUDE: She is brave and quick thinking.

Her body twisted toward a heavy wire and she managed to hang on to the braided metal, still hot from the lightning strike. Her palms were burned so terribly that once healed they bore no lines, only the blank scar tissue of a quieter future.

> ANNOTATE: This phrase seems to have a deeper meaning for Anna's future.
>
> QUESTION: What later decision does this phrase suggest?
>
> CONCLUDE: Anna will leave her circus life behind.

2. For more practice, go back into the text and complete the close-read notes.

3. Revisit a section of the text you found important during your first read. Read this section closely and **annotate** what you notice. Ask yourself **questions** such as "Why did the author make this choice?" What can you **conclude**?

Tool Kit
Close-Read Guide and Model Annotation

Analyze the Text

CITE TEXTUAL EVIDENCE to support your answers.

📓 **Notebook** Respond to these questions.

1. (a) What is the source for the narrator's account of the tent pole disaster? (b) **Interpret** What does this explanation suggest about the impact of the disaster on Anna? Explain.

2. **Analyze** What does the narrator's return from the West to her mother's house suggest about her feelings toward her mother? Does she feel obligated, or does she feel something deeper?

3. **Historical Perspectives** What connections can you make between Anna's life changes and the United States before and after World War II?

4. **Essential Question Connection:** *What do stories reveal about the human condition?* What have you learned about human bravery and sacrifice by reading this story?

STANDARDS

Reading Literature
• Cite strong and thorough textual evidence to support analysis of what the text says explicitly as well as inferences drawn from the text, including determining where the text leaves matters uncertain.
• Analyze the impact of the author's choices regarding how to develop and relate elements of a story or drama.

Analyze Craft and Structure

Narrative Structure In literary works, **suspense** is the feeling of growing curiosity, tension, or anxiety the reader feels about the outcome of events. Writers create suspense by raising questions in the minds of their readers. Suspense reaches its peak at the climax of a plot. In "The Leap," Erdrich skillfully uses two techniques to build suspense.

- **Foreshadowing** is the use of clues to suggest events that have not yet happened. For example, at the end of paragraph 2, details such as "I hear the crackle," "the stitches burn," and "a thread of fire" hint at the impact of the powerful fire that the narrator will describe in the climax of the short story.

- **Pacing** is the speed or rhythm of writing. Writers may deliberately speed up or slow down pacing in order to create suspense. For example, in paragraph 4, the narrator delays her account of the tent pole disaster by describing the setting and the circus acts. These digressions increase readers' feelings of tension and anticipation.

Practice

CITE TEXTUAL EVIDENCE to support your answers.

📓 **Notebook** Respond to these questions.

1. Reread paragraph 7 and identify three details that contribute to suspense.

2. Reread paragraphs 18–19. Describe how the story is paced in these paragraphs. What effect does this pacing create?

3. Use this chart to record notes about Erdrich's use of suspense, foreshadowing, and pacing.

PARAGRAPH(S)	NOTES ON SUSPENSE, FORESHADOWING, OR PACING
3	
6–9	
15	
24	

4. Describe the overall effect of pacing and foreshadowing in the story. How do these elements affect the reader's understanding of events, characters, and themes?

THE LEAP

Concept Vocabulary

| encroaching | anticipation | perpetually |
| instantaneously | constricting | superannuated |

Why These Words? These concept vocabulary words all suggest distance or closeness, especially in relation to time. For example, *instantaneously* means "in an instant," or "immediately." Something that happens *perpetually* is continuous or endless. A *superannuated* tool or object is so old-fashioned or worn out that it is no longer useful.

1. How does the concept vocabulary clarify the reader's understanding of the story?

2. What other words in the selection connect to this concept?

Practice

📓 **Notebook** Respond to these questions.

1. Use each concept vocabulary word in a sentence that demonstrates your understanding of the word's meaning.

2. Challenge yourself to replace each concept vocabulary word in your sentences with a synonym. How does changing the words affect the meanings of your sentences? Which word choices are more effective?

🔲 **WORD NETWORK**

Add words related to the human condition from the text to your Word Network.

📋 **STANDARDS**

Reading Literature
Determine the meaning of words and phrases as they are used in the text, including figurative and connotative meanings; analyze the impact of specific word choices on meaning and tone, including words with multiple meanings or language that is particularly fresh, engaging, or beautiful.

Language
Identify and correctly use patterns of word changes that indicate different meanings or parts of speech.

Word Study

Latin Root: *-strict-* The Latin root *-strict-* means "to bind" or "to compress." In paragraph 16, the narrator's father finds his hometown *constricting*, or limiting. The word *constrict* also has a medical meaning. It is used to describe a part of the body that narrows, closes, or compresses. For example, when you step out in bright sunlight, your pupils *constrict*, or get smaller, to take in less light.

1. Find four words that contain the root *-strict-*. Challenge yourself to come up with one word that has a medical meaning.

2. For each word you choose, record the word, its part of speech, and its meaning. Use a print or online college-level dictionary as needed.

Author's Style

Motif A **motif** is an important recurring, or repeating, element in literature, mythology, or other type of artistic expression. In "The Leap," Erdrich uses recurring motifs to highlight symbols and develop themes.

- A **symbol** is a person, place, object, or idea that represents not only itself but also something beyond or outside itself.
- A **theme** in a work is an underlying central insight about human life or behavior.

The first step in interpreting motifs is to recognize when they are present. While reading, be alert to repetition in events, imagery, description, or dialogue. For example, you might notice the repetition of Anna's three "leaps." Once you have identified a possible motif, consider what this repetition may represent and how it connects to the story's themes.

Read It

1. Use the chart to analyze motifs in "The Leap." Consider how the meanings and associations of each motif change with each appearance.

MOTIF	WHERE IT APPEARS	ANALYSIS
"roll of drums"	paragraph 6	
	paragraph 26	
arms/limbs	paragraph 10	
	paragraph 13	
	paragraph 21	

2. Explain how Anna's three leaps are both literal and symbolic.

3. **Connect to Style** How does Erdrich use recurring images to develop the story's most important themes?

Write It

📝 **Notebook** Another motif in the story is the idea of the narrator's debt to her mother for her existence. This motif first occurs in paragraph 3: "I owe her my existence three times." In a paragraph, explain what this motif contributes to the story. What would be lost if this motif were omitted?

THE LEAP

Writing to Sources

An anecdote is a brief story about an interesting, amusing, or strange event. An anecdote is told to entertain or to make a point. The person telling an anecdote may include a brief opinion or argument to underscore a moral or lesson. For example, in paragraph 17 of "The Leap" the narrator provides this commentary:

> I owe my existence, the second time then, to the two of them and the hospital that brought them together. That is the debt we take for granted since none of us asks for life. It is once we have it that we hang on so dearly.

Assignment

Write a short, entertaining **anecdote** about an event in your or your family's past. Tell about a time when a parent, teacher, or coach intervened in a situation in a way that made you feel grateful. Include an opinion that highlights an important lesson. Conclude your anecdote with a paragraph that explains how your experience compares to that of the narrator in "The Leap."

Vocabulary and Conventions Connection You may want to use some of the concept vocabulary words in your anecdote. Consider varying your pacing or adding foreshadowing to increase suspense.

encroaching	anticipation	perpetually
instantaneously	constricting	superannuated

- -

Reflect on Your Writing

After completing your anecdote, answer the following questions.

1. How did writing an anecdote improve your understanding of Erdrich's style?

2. What literary elements did you use to make your anecdote more entertaining or effective? Were they successful? Explain.

3. **Why These Words?** The words you choose make a difference in your writing. Which words helped you convey important details or ideas?

STANDARDS

Writing
Write narratives to develop real or imagined experiences or events using effective technique, well-chosen details, and well-structured event sequences.

Speaking and Listening
Present information, findings, and supporting evidence, conveying a clear and distinct perspective, such that listeners can follow the line of reasoning, alternative or opposing perspectives are addressed, and the organization, development, substance, and style are appropriate to purpose, audience, and a range of formal and informal tasks.

Speaking and Listening

Assignment

Choose one of the following quotations, and explain in a brief **oral response to literature** how it connects to the plot and themes of "The Leap." Present your response to the class, and lead the class in a discussion of your ideas.

- Love is the chain whereby to bind a child to its parents.

  — Abraham Lincoln

- Courage is grace under pressure.

  — Ernest Hemingway

- What do we owe to those we love?

  — Ellen McLaughlin

1. **Analyze the Quotations** Carefully consider each quotation—both its meaning and its associations. Paraphrase each quotation and think about its purpose. Lincoln's statement, for example, focuses on children, parents, and love; Hemingway provides a concise definition of courage. Choose the quotation that you think is the best match with "The Leap."

2. **Connect to Plot and Theme** Review the major plot events in the story. Check that you understand the chronology of events, as well as their causes and effects. Then, state one important theme the events bring out, and explain how that theme relates to the quotation you selected.

3. **Prepare Your Delivery** As you practice, be sure to pay attention to nonverbal methods of communication, such as volume, tone, pitch, pacing, posture, gestures, eye contact, and facial expressions.

4. **Evaluate Responses** As your classmates deliver their oral responses, listen carefully. Use an evaluation guide like the one shown to analyze their responses.

EVALUATION GUIDE

Rate each statement on a scale of 1 (not demonstrated) to 4 (demonstrated).

☐ The speaker clearly identified the quotation being discussed.

☐ The speaker identified specific and persuasive links between the meaning of the quotation and the story's plot and theme.

☐ The speaker used a variety of inflections and tones when speaking.

☐ The speaker used appropriate pacing, posture, gestures, and facial expressions.

✐ EVIDENCE LOG

Before moving on to a new selection, go to your Evidence Log and record what you learned from "The Leap."

WRITING TO SOURCES

• EVERYDAY USE

• EVERYTHING STUCK TO HIM

• THE LEAP

Write a Narrative

You have read three short stories that employ flashbacks or framing devices to tell stories. Now you will use your understanding of those texts to create a narrative that explores a question related to the human condition in a fresh way.

Assignment

Write a **fictional narrative** addressing this question:

> ### How do stressful situations often reveal the best and worst in people?

Begin by creating a fictional scenario that is dramatic and stressful enough to trigger widely different responses from characters. Then, think about how you might develop characters whose reactions will give readers insight into the issues raised by the prompt. Finally, reflect on the structure of the stories you read in this unit. Use plot devices similar to the ones in those texts, such as frame stories or flashbacks, to add interest to your narrative and provide additional insight into characters and events.

Elements of a Fictional Narrative

A **fictional narrative** is a story about an imagined experience. The elements of such narratives are invented by their authors. A fictional narrative may feature a narrator who is part of the story or a narrator who is a detached observer of the action.

A well-written fictional narrative usually contains these elements:

- a clear and consistent point of view
- well-developed characters
- a smooth sequence of events or experiences, which may include flashbacks, subplots, or frame stories
- effective use of dialogue, description, and/or reflection to develop the story
- sensory language and precise, descriptive details to clarify experiences
- a conclusion that brings the story to a satisfying close

Model Narrative Text For a model of a well-crafted fictional narrative, see the Launch Text, "Old Man at the Bridge."

Challenge yourself to find all of the elements of an effective fictional narrative in the text. You will have an opportunity to review these elements as you prepare to write your own fictional narrative.

LAUNCH TEXT

Old Man at the Bridge

🔧 Tool Kit
Student Model of
a Fictional Narrative

STANDARDS

Writing
• Write narratives to develop real or imagined experiences or events using effective technique, well-chosen details, and well-structured event sequences.
• Write routinely over extended time frames and shorter time frames for a range of tasks, purposes, and audiences.

Prewriting / Planning

Focus on a Conflict The stories that you, like all writers, tell are influenced by your own life. Make a list of conflicts you have experienced, witnessed, or studied. Choose a conflict from your list, and think about ways you can turn that conflict into a fictional story that reveals characters at their best and worst.

 EVIDENCE LOG

Review your Evidence Log and identify key details you may want to use in your narrative.

Create a Story Chart Make a story chart, like the one shown, to plan the stages of your narrative. Events from "Old Man at the Bridge" have been filled in so that you can trace the narrative arc in the Launch Text.

STORY CHART			
Exposition: Establish the setting and characters, and set up the conflict.	**Rising Action:** Describe the events that increase the conflict and tension.	**Climax:** Identify the point of greatest tension.	**Resolution:** Tell how the conflict is or is not resolved.
During the Spanish Civil War, an old man sits by a bridge while others evacuate. The narrator stops to talk to him.	*The narrator wants to get the old man out of danger, but the old man is too tired to move.*	*The old man tries to get up and move, but he sits back down. He can't get up. He is worried about animals he left behind.*	*The conflict doesn't resolve: The old man gives up; the narrator leaves him to face the advancing enemy alone.*

Develop Your Characters Once you have selected the characters who will appear in your narrative, start to develop them using a chart like this one.

	MAIN CHARACTER
Appearance	
Attitude/Personal Characteristics	
Motivations	

Connect to Texts After you have identified the basic plot events and characters, decide how you can use *plot devices* to add interest to your story. Review the use of the *frame story* in "Everything Stuck to Him" and "The Leap." Determine if a similar framing device might work for your story. Also, consider Erdrich's use of *foreshadowing* in "The Leap." Just as she dropped hints about the fire, you could hint at later events in your story.

One final device to consider is the **flashback,** in which the action suddenly reverts back to a past event that was important to the main character's development or to the present action of the story.

≡ STANDARDS
Writing
• Engage and orient the reader by setting out a problem, situation, or observation and its significance, establishing one or multiple point(s) of view, and introducing a narrator and/or characters; create a smooth progression of experiences or events.
• Use a variety of techniques to sequence events so that they build on one another to create a coherent whole and build toward a particular tone and outcome.

Drafting

Establish a Point of View The point of view you choose helps set the tone for your story. Are you going to be a neutral observer, reporting on events rather than participating in them? Then, you will use a third-person narrator. Are you going to interpret events directly through the eyes of a narrator who participates in the events of the story? Then, you will write using a first-person point of view. Notice how the choice of point of view affects the examples in this chart.

NARRATOR	DESCRIPTION	EXAMPLE
First-person	The narrator is a character in the story.	*I knew what I had to do. I had to tell Shana the truth.*
Third-person omniscient	The narrator is outside the story and knows everything that happens.	*Julia was finally ready to tell Shana the truth, but Shana didn't want to hear it.*
Third-person limited	The narrator is outside the story and knows only what one character does and thinks.	*Julia was finally ready to tell Shana the truth. But would Shana listen?*

Begin the Story Memorably You can draw from a variety of strategies to engage your readers right from the start. Remember to select a strategy that sets a proper tone for your story, whether you intend your story to be serious or humorous, thoughtful or lighthearted. Here are a few ideas to grab the attention of your audience:

- *Start off with a simple declarative statement:* It was not my most heroic moment.
- *Start off with a question:* What makes us do the right thing in the worst possible situations?
- *Start in the middle of the action:* As I looked down at the 200-foot drop I said to myself, "What am I doing here?"

Highlight the Conflict When you are setting up the exposition, rising action, and climax of the story, be sure to emphasize the main conflict. The prompt asks you to explore how people react in times of stress. This lends itself naturally to describing characters and their responses to events in a way that builds tension throughout the story until the climax.

End in a Satisfying Way Make sure that your ending flows naturally from the events of the story. Above all, though, end it in a way that will be satisfying and memorable, and that reinforces the main point of the story—people under stress behave both their best and their worst. Keep in mind that it can be just as effective to end a story with some elements unresolved as it is to tie all the loose ends up neatly.

STANDARDS

Writing
- Engage and orient the reader by setting out a problem, situation, or observation and its significance, establishing one or multiple point(s) of view, and introducing a narrator and/or characters; create a smooth progression of experiences or events.
- Use a variety of techniques to sequence events so that they build on one another to create a coherent whole and build toward a particular tone and outcome.
- Provide a conclusion that follows from and reflects on what is experienced, observed, or resolved over the course of the narrative.

LANGUAGE DEVELOPMENT: STYLE

Add Variety: Dialogue

Dialogue The conversations between and among people in a story are called **dialogue**. This narrative technique can serve several purposes:

- exposing conflict between characters
- revealing personality traits
- providing explanation or advancing the plot
- showing what characters think and value
- indicating what characters understand and how they communicate

Read It

These sentences from the Launch Text use dialogue to establish a connection between the two characters and to reveal their feelings and traits.

- *"Where do you come from?" I asked him.* (The narrator expresses his interest mainly through questions directed to the old man.)
- *"I am without politics," he said. "I am seventy-six years old. I have come twelve kilometers now and I think now I can go no further."* (The old man states his problem and reveals his innocence in his own words.)
- *"Why not," I said, watching the far bank where now there were no carts.* (The narrator's curt response suggests that the old man's problems are not his main concern.)
- *"I was taking care of animals," he said dully, but no longer to me. "I was only taking care of animals."* (The old man talks to himself, expressing his confusion and sorrow.)

Write It

As you draft your narrative, look for ways to incorporate dialogue. Start a new paragraph each time the speaker changes. There are a variety of ways in which to write dialogue. Notice in these examples how the words being spoken are set apart from their tags, such as *he said* or *I urged.*

PLACEMENT OF DIALOGUE	EXAMPLE
before a tag	*"Where do you come from?" I asked him.*
after a tag	*. . . I looked at his black dusty clothes and his gray dusty face and his steel rimmed spectacles and said, "What animals were they?"*
splitting a single sentence	*"I know no one in that direction," he said, "but thank you very much."*
splitting multiple sentences	*"If you are rested I would go," I urged. "Get up and try to walk now."*

PUNCTUATION
Punctuate dialogue correctly.

- Use quotation marks before and after a character's spoken words.
- Use a comma to set off the speaker's tag from the speaker's words.
- Use quotation marks around each part of a divided quotation.
- If end punctuation, such as a question mark or an exclamation point, is part of the quotation, keep it inside the quotation marks.

MAKING WRITING SOPHISTICATED

Integrating Sensory Language Vivid, detailed description makes characters and settings come alive for readers. An important part of such description is **sensory language**, which features details that appeal to one of the five senses. Writers use sensory language to describe how things look, sound, taste, feel, or smell. Vivid sensory adjectives, adverbs, and verbs can combine to create an overall impression of a scene or event. Notice how each of these examples affects you as you read it.

	ADJECTIVE	ADVERB	VERB
Sight	scarlet	garishly	soar
Hearing (Sound)	piercing	softly	creak
Taste	bitter	juicily	savor
Touch	slippery	roughly	tap
Smell	rancid	fragrantly	reek

Read It

These examples from the Launch Text show how the writer uses sensory language to establish a sense of place

LAUNCH TEXT EXCERPT

The initial description sets the scene. Readers can envision the old man and can both "see" and "hear" the peasants, carts, and trucks.

An old man with steel rimmed spectacles and very dusty clothes sat by the side of the road. There was a pontoon bridge across the river and carts, trucks, and men, women and children were crossing it. The mule-drawn carts staggered up the steep bank from the bridge with soldiers helping push against the spokes of the wheels. The trucks ground up and away heading out of it all and the peasants plodded along in the ankle deep dust. But the old man sat there without moving. He was too tired to go any farther.

…

The comparison in this paragraph shows the dryness of the Spanish countryside and points to the silence and the strain on the narrator as he listens for the enemy's approach.

I was watching the bridge and the African looking country of the Ebro Delta and wondering how long now it would be before we would see the enemy, and listening all the while for the first noises that would signal that ever mysterious event called contact, and the old man still sat there.

Write It

Think of sensory words and phrases that can clarify a reader's impression of your characters and the situations in which you place them. Start by completing this chart with specific details. Then, go back to your draft to determine how to incorporate those details into your narrative.

SENSE	CHARACTER 1	CHARACTER 2	SETTING
Sight			
Hearing (Sound)			
Taste			
Touch			
Smell			

Use a Thesaurus to Find Precise Words Even the most experienced writers sometimes refer to a thesaurus to find the words that best express what they want to say. A thesaurus can be a valuable resource when it comes to finding sensory language that fits your needs. Here are thesaurus lists of synonyms for the first three examples from the chart of sensory words. Note that not every synonym is appropriate in every case; you must choose the word that works best in context.

    SCARLET *syn.* crimson, red, ruby, cherry, garnet

    GARISHLY *syn.* brashly, gaudily, brightly, vulgarly, flamboyantly

    SOAR *syn.* fly, ascend, rocket, circle, arise, climb

▤ STANDARDS

Writing
Use precise words and phrases, telling details, and sensory language to convey a vivid picture of the experiences, events, setting, and/or characters.

Language
Consult general and specialized reference materials, both print and digital, to find the pronunciation of a word or determine or clarify its precise meaning, its part of speech, its etymology, or its standard usage.

Revising

Evaluating Your Draft

Use the following checklist to evaluate the effectiveness of your first draft. Then, use your evaluation and the instruction on this page to guide your revision.

FOCUS AND ORGANIZATION	EVIDENCE AND ELABORATION	CONVENTIONS
☐ Provides an introduction that sets the scene and introduces characters and conflict.	☐ Uses techniques such as dialogue, description, and reflection to develop the experience being narrated.	☐ Attends to the norms and conventions of the discipline, especially the correct punctuation of dialogue.
☐ Establishes a sequence of events that unfolds smoothly and logically.	☐ Uses sensory language and precise details to clarify events for the reader.	
☐ Incorporates plot devices, such as foreshadowing, flashback, and frame stories, to add interest to the story.	☐ Uses vocabulary and word choices that are appropriate for the audience and purpose.	
☐ Provides a conclusion that resolves the narrative in a satisfying way.		

Revising for Focus and Organization

Sequence of Events Maintaining a consistent point of view will help you present a realistic perspective on setting, characters, and events. Would a reader be puzzled about what happened first, next, and last in your narrative? Consider adding time words and phrases that clarify the sequence. Some examples are given here.

after a while	at that point	before	by then
eventually	initially	just then	later
meanwhile	previously	soon afterward	ultimately

Conclusion Remember that your conclusion should settle or resolve the conflict and provide a satisfying ending for the reader. Is your conclusion too abrupt? Should you add more detail to the falling action in the plot to make your conclusion seem more plausible?

Revising for Evidence and Elaboration

Dialogue The effectiveness of your narrative depends on how well you establish a believable conversation between the characters. Have you captured the "sound" of each character? Would each character be likely to say the words you have given him or her? If not, make some changes to your dialogue to improve its authenticity.

⛓ **WORD NETWORK**

Include interesting words from your Word Network in your narrative.

☰ STANDARDS

Writing
• Use narrative techniques, such as dialogue, pacing, description, reflection, and multiple plot lines, to develop experiences, events, and/or characters.
• Provide a conclusion that follows from and reflects on what is experienced, observed, or resolved over the course of the narrative.

PEER REVIEW

Exchange drafts with a classmate. Use the checklist to evaluate your classmate's narrative, and provide supportive feedback.

1. Does the dialogue advance the plot or serve some other important purpose, such as building tension?

☐ yes ☐ no   If no, suggest what you might change.

2. Does the introduction clearly set a scene and introduce the conflict?

☐ yes ☐ no   If no, tell what you think should be added.

3. Is the ending satisfying, believable, and understandable?

☐ yes ☐ no   If no, tell what you found confusing.

4. What is the strongest part of your classmate's narrative? Why?

_____

_____

_____

Editing and Proofreading

Edit for Conventions Reread your draft for accuracy and consistency. Correct errors in grammar and word usage. Make sure that you have used sensory language correctly in context.

Proofread for Accuracy Read your draft carefully, correcting errors in spelling and punctuation. Punctuate dialogue correctly, using quotation marks and commas or end marks as needed.

Publishing and Presenting

Work with a partner to present your narrative as a dramatic dialogue. Each of you should take the part of one of your characters and read the dialogue as though you were actors in a play. If you wish, one of you may read the narration as well. Practice together and then present your dialogue to the class.

Reflecting

Reflect on what you learned by writing your narrative. Are you happy with the characters you chose? Were you able to incorporate them into a unified narrative? What was difficult about incorporating a narrative technique, such as flashback or foreshadowing, into your narrative?

⁝≣ STANDARDS
Writing
Develop and strengthen writing as needed by planning, revising, editing, rewriting, or trying a new approach, focusing on addressing what is most significant for a specific purpose and audience.

SCAN FOR
MULTIMEDIA

ESSENTIAL QUESTION:

What do stories reveal about the human condition?

As you read these selections, work with your group to explore how short stories allow us to see life from vastly different perspectives.

From Text to Topic Perhaps the word *change* best characterizes the past few decades of American life. In a time of rapid change, Americans have embraced new technologies, new social rules, and new ways of interacting with the rest of the world. As you read the selections in this section, consider how they address enduring human traits and what it means to live in a civil society.

Small-Group Learning Strategies

Throughout your life, in school, in your community, and in your career, you will continue to develop strategies when you work in teams. Use these strategies during Small-Group Learning. Add ideas of your own at each step.

STRATEGY	ACTION PLAN
Prepare	• Complete your assignments so that you are prepared for group work. • Organize your thinking so you can contribute to your group's discussions. •
Participate fully	• Make eye contact to signal that you are listening and taking in what is being said. • Use text evidence when making a point. •
Support others	• Build on ideas from others in your group. • Invite others who have not yet spoken to join the discussion. •
Clarify	• Paraphrase the ideas of others to ensure that your understanding is correct. • Ask follow-up questions. •

CONTENTS

COMPARE

PERFORMANCE TASK

SPEAKING AND LISTENING FOCUS
Present a Narrative

The Small-Group readings focus on "last moments"—of characters' lives and possibly even for short stories as a genre. After reading, your group will write and present a narrative.

Working as a Team

1. **Take a Position** In your group, discuss the following question:

   > What life experiences or situations are universal—true for all people in all times and places?

   As you take turns sharing your positions, be sure to provide reasons for your response. After all group members have shared, discuss how people deal with these experiences or situations differently and what their responses reveal about their personalities.

2. **List Your Rules** As a group, decide on the rules that you will follow as you work together. Two samples are provided. Add two more of your own. As you work together, you may add or revise rules based on your experience together.

   - Encourage a variety of ideas before you look for common features.
   - Give group members the chance to comment further on their ideas as discussion continues.

   - _____
     _____

   - _____
     _____

3. **Apply the Rules** Practice working as a group. Share what you have learned about the ways in which stories reveal truths about the human condition. Make sure each person in the group contributes. Take notes on and be prepared to share with the class one insight that you heard from another member of your group.

4. **Name Your Group** Choose a name that reflects the unit topic.

   Our group's name: _____

5. **Create a Communication Plan** Decide how you want to communicate with one another. For example, you might use online collaboration tools, email, or instant messaging.

   Our group's decision: _____

   _____

Making a Schedule

First, find out the due dates for the small-group activities. Then, preview the texts and activities with your group, and make a schedule for completing the tasks.

SELECTION	ACTIVITIES	DUE DATE
A Brief History of the Short Story		
An Occurrence at Owl Creek Bridge		
The Jilting of Granny Weatherall		

Working on Group Projects

As your group works together, you'll find it more effective if each person has a specific role. Different projects require different roles. Before beginning a project, discuss the necessary roles, and choose one for each group member. Some possible roles are listed here. Add your ideas to the list.

Project Manager: monitors the schedule and keeps everyone on task

Researcher: organizes research activities

Recorder: takes notes during group meetings

_____

_____

_____

_____

_____

_____

_____

_____

SCAN FOR
MULTIMEDIA

About the Author

As a child, **D. F. ("Duff") McCourt**, a freelance writer and the co-founder and editor of *AE—The Canadian Science Fiction Review*, developed a great love for books and magazines. That passion continued into his adult life. A writer of published short stories and novellas himself, he is interested in the history of both forms. He believes firmly that the strength of magazines as a medium is essential to the continued vitality of science fiction and other genres.

A Brief History of the Short Story

Concept Vocabulary

As you perform your first read of "A Brief History of the Short Story," you will encounter these words.

| supplanted | ascendant | renaissance |

Context Clues If these words are unfamiliar to you, try using **context clues**—words and phrases that appear in nearby text—to help you determine their meanings. There are various types of context clues that you may encounter as you read.

Restatement, or Synonyms: That **diminutive** child is so <u>tiny</u> that she can't reach the first step.

Definition: Studies show that the vocabulary children learn when they are very young is **formative**, or <u>fundamental to their development</u>.

Contrast of Ideas: That social movement could have **soldiered on**. Instead, it <u>died out</u>.

Apply your knowledge of context clues and other vocabulary strategies to determine the meanings of unfamiliar words you encounter during your first read.

First Read NONFICTION

Apply these strategies as you conduct your first read. You will have an opportunity to complete a close read after your first read.

NOTICE the general ideas of the text. *What* is it about? *Who* is involved?

ANNOTATE by marking vocabulary and key passages you want to revisit.

First Read

CONNECT ideas within the selection to what you already know and what you have already read.

RESPOND by completing the Comprehension Check and by writing a brief summary of the selection.

STANDARDS

Reading Informational Text
By the end of grade 11, read and comprehend literary nonfiction in the grades 11–CCR text complexity band proficiently, with scaffolding as needed at the high end of the range.

Language
Use context as a clue to the meaning of a word or phrase.

A Brief History of the Short Story

D. F. McCourt

BACKGROUND

Electronic books, or e-books, are digital files that can display on various devices, such as computers and cellphones, in a way similar to printed books. Though e-books first emerged in the late 1990s, they failed to gain popularity until the mid-2000s, when dedicated electronic reading devices improved the quality of the reading experience. This new medium has allowed more writers to publish a wider variety of work, including short stories. It has also lowered the costs that writers and publishers previously faced when bringing new work to appreciative audiences.

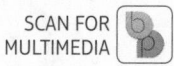

SCAN FOR MULTIMEDIA

NOTES

1　There's something you should know. The short story was very nearly drowned in the tub as an infant. As literary forms go, the short story is very young. Certainly its roots go back centuries— we can see it gestating in *The Canterbury Tales*,[1] in fairy tales, and in poems of a middling length. Arguably, even the conversational traditions of the anecdote, the joke, and the parable can be seen as precursors of the form. But the short story as we know it sprang into full-fledged existence as recently as the 1820s. It appeared, unheralded, to fill a sudden need created by the invention of the "gift book."

2　Gift books were annual collections of poems, artwork, and literary criticism, aimed primarily at an audience of upper-class women in England and North America. Seeking additional ways to fill the pages of these popular publications, editors began soliciting submissions of short pieces of prose to accompany artwork already purchased (rather the opposite of the way it is usually done these days). In so doing, they created the first paying market for short fiction. All modern literary magazines can trace their pedigree back to these gift books. In 1837, Nathaniel Hawthorne collected a number of stories that he had written for the gift book market and published them to great critical acclaim as *Twice Told Tales*. And with that, short stories had arrived.

---

1. **The Canterbury Tales** collection of stories written by Geoffrey Chaucer in the fourteenth century.

3   Two hundred years may seem quite a long time, but consider that the novel dates back to at least 1605 (the year Miguel de Cervantes's *Don Quixote* was published) and you get a better idea of the short story's relative youth. Over its entire lifetime, the fate of the form has been inextricably tied to that of magazines. In the early twentieth century, literacy in the United States and Canada became near universal for the first time and, as a direct result, magazine sales boomed. On the erudite[2] front, there were publications like *The English Review* and *The Southwest Review*, but there were also the decidedly lower brow *Argosy* and *Adventure*. This was the era of the pulp magazine and it brought with it the birth of genre literature.

4   Horror stories, detective stories, and most especially science fiction evolved in short stories, cut their teeth in the magazines. It is no surprise that the beginning of the Golden Age of Science Fiction is identified most strongly not with a novel but with the publication of a magazine (the July 1939 issue of *Astounding Science Fiction*, to be precise). Most of the formative novels of early- and mid-twentieth-century science fiction were more like grown-up short stories in form than like other contemporary novels. In fact, some of the most famous science fiction novels—including Isaac Asimov's *Foundation*, A. E. Van Vogt's *The Silkie*, Robert A. Heinlein's *Orphans of the Sky*, and Ray Bradbury's *The Martian Chronicles*—were fix-ups (a term for a novel created by stitching a series of previously published short stories together). It wasn't until quite recently, around the 1984 publication of William Gibson's *Neuromancer* and the 1985 publication of Margaret Atwood's *The Handmaid's Tale*, that the two parallel traditions of the science fiction novel and the modern literary novel began to collide.

5   And yet, despite the fact that in its brief history the short story had brought into existence entire genres and traditions of literature, it came perilously close to death. In the 1950s, owning a television suddenly became within reach of the average North American family. The half-an-hour-less-commercials format of shows like *I Love Lucy*, *Dragnet*, and *The Honeymooners* targeted the same entertainment niche as the magazine. Over the decades that followed, the circulation numbers of almost all magazines that ran short fiction saw a steady decline. The novel soldiered on, but the state of the short story became so dire that in 2007 Stephen King[3] opened his piece "What Ails the Short Story" for the *New York Times Book Review* thus:

> *The American short story is alive and well. Do you like the sound of that? Me too. I only wish it were actually true.*

6   So much can happen in four years. 2007 was the year that e-book readers burst onto the scene and, while the rise of the online magazine was already underway, it has stepped up considerably in the years since. More importantly, in 2007 television was still clinging to its cultural sovereignty, but it has since been firmly **supplanted**

Mark context clues or indicate another strategy you used that helped you determine meaning.

supplanted (suh PLANT ihd) *v.*

MEANING:

---

2. **erudite** (EHR oo dyt) *adj.* characterized by great knowledge; learned or scholarly.
3. **Stephen King** (b. 1947) American author of horror novels and short stories.

by the Internet. At the turn of the millennium, there was much ink spilled over the decline in the amount of reading people were doing, but the truth is that many of us are reading more than ever, we just aren't doing it on paper. When reading on a screen rather than the page, there are new considerations. A narrative of a few thousand words can be easily read, enjoyed, and digested while sitting before a monitor; a novella, far less so. This is an environment practically designed for the literary form Edgar Allan Poe defined as a tale that "can be read in one sitting." Further, e-book readers are allowing publishers to easily make shorter works available at a reasonable price, without having to worry that a book's spine be thick enough to hold its own on a bookstore shelf.

7   Video, of course, is quite at home online, but the real meat of the Internet has always been text. Preferably text that limits itself to a screen or two in length. As long as the Internet holds its throne as the defining medium of our time, the short story will be **ascendant**. It is true however that the form is undoubtedly being influenced and changed by the demands of its new homes. Personally, I'm thrilled to be taking part in that continued evolution, thrilled just to be present for the **renaissance** of the form that shaped science fiction, thrilled to be able to say unequivocally: "The short story is alive and well." ❧

Comprehension Check

Complete the following items after you finish your first read. Review and clarify details with your group.

1. According to the author, what significant event happened in 1837?

2. According to the author, what three genres owe their origins to the short story?

3. Why did the short story nearly die in the 1950s? What developments made it strong again?

4. 🖴 **Notebook** Confirm your understanding of the text by writing a summary.

- -

RESEARCH

Research to Explore Conduct research on an aspect of the text you find interesting. For example, you may want to learn more about one of the short-story magazines the author mentions: *The English Review, The Southwest Review, Argosy, Adventure,* or *Astounding Science Fiction.* Share your discoveries with your group.

A BRIEF HISTORY OF THE
SHORT STORY

TIP

GROUP DISCUSSION
Almost everyone has
personal preferences
regarding short fiction.
Encourage group members
to relate the author's
information and insights
to their own reading
experiences.

Close Read the Text

With your group, revisit sections of the text you marked
during your first read. **Annotate** details that you notice.
What **questions** do you have? What can you **conclude**?

Analyze the Text

CITE TEXTUAL EVIDENCE
to support your answers.

Complete the activities.

1. **Review and Clarify** With your group, reread paragraphs 1–2. How did
   the gift book give rise to the short story and to literary magazines?

2. **Present and Discuss** Now, work with your group to share the passages
   from the selection that you found especially important. Take turns
   presenting your passages. Discuss what you noticed in the selection,
   what questions you asked, and what conclusions you reached.

3. **Essential Question:** *What do stories reveal about the human
   condition?* How does this literary history shed light on the short story's
   ability to address the human condition? Discuss with your group.

LANGUAGE DEVELOPMENT

Concept Vocabulary

supplanted	ascendant	renaissance

Why These Words? The three concept vocabulary words from the text are
related. With your group, determine what the words have in common. Write
your ideas and add another word that fits the category.

Practice

 Notebook Confirm your understanding of these words from the text by
using them in sentences. Be sure to use context clues that hint at each word's
meaning.

Word Study

Latin Root: -scend- Many words in English use the Latin root -*scend*-,
which means "climb." For example, *ascendant* is an adjective that combines
the root -*scend*- with the prefix *ad-*, meaning "to" or "toward." *Ascendant*,
then, means "climbing toward" or "rising." Find several other words that
have this same root. Use a reliable print or digital dictionary to verify your
choices. Record the words and their meanings.

 WORD NETWORK

Add words related to the
human condition from the
text to your Word Network.

 STANDARDS

Reading Informational Text
• Analyze a complex set of ideas or
sequence of events and explain how
specific individuals, ideas, or events
interact and develop over the course
of the text.
• Analyze and evaluate the
effectiveness of the structure an
author uses in his or her exposition
or argument, including whether
the structure makes points clear,
convincing, and engaging.

Language
Identify and correctly use patterns of
word changes that indicate different
meanings or parts of speech.

Analyze Craft and Structure

Sequence of Events Authors often use **chronological order**, or the order in which things happened, to structure nonfiction pieces that describe historical events or explain a change over time. When you read a text that describes a sequence of events, look at how specific people, ideas, or events are connected. Consider the details the author chooses to include about each time period and why those details might be significant or important.

GROUP DISCUSSION
As members of your group discuss their charts, you may find it helpful to plot out key events on a timeline.

Practice

CITE TEXTUAL EVIDENCE
to support your answers.

Use the chart below to analyze how McCourt structures events in "A Brief History of the Short Story." Then, share your chart with your group, and discuss how McCourt uses this organization to emphasize his main ideas about the short story.

PARAGRAPH	TIME FRAME	EVENT	SIGNIFICANCE
1	• 14th century • 1820s	• *Canterbury Tales* published • "gift books" invented	• first use of short story form • created need for short stories
2			
3			
4			
5–6			
7–8			

A BRIEF HISTORY OF THE
SHORT STORY

TIP

CLARIFICATION

Some grammar handbooks
or style guides may advise
against using passive voice.
However, it is a stylistic
choice that may give clarity
or provide emphasis. For
example, "The reactor was
shut down" emphasizes the
event, whereas "The head
engineer shut the reactor
down" gives more emphasis
to the person performing the
action.

Conventions and Style

Active and Passive Voice In grammar, **voice** reveals the relationship
between the subject of a sentence and the action described in that sentence.
Voice may be either active or passive.

- In active voice, the subject of the sentence *performs* the action.

  Isabel reads science fiction novels.

  A high-speed elevator carried passengers to the Observation Deck.

- In **passive voice,** the subject of the sentence *receives* the action. Passive
  voice often uses or implies a form of the verb "be," such as *am, is, are,
  was,* or *were.*

  Science fiction novels are read by Isabel.

  The passengers were carried to the Observation Deck by a high-speed
  elevator.

Active voice helps the writer create strong, clear writing. Active voice also
keeps writing concise because it uses fewer words than passive voice does
to describe an action. However, the passive voice may be useful in scientific
writing or other explanations because it removes names or pronouns and
instead focuses on describing facts or concepts. Passive voice can also be useful
when the writer does not know—or does not want to name—the person or
thing performing the action, or when that person or thing is unimportant.

  The lost toddler was found in the mall's food court.

  The rumors that are being spread have no basis in fact.

Read It

1. Label each of these sentences from the text as active or passive.

  a. The short story was very nearly drowned in the tub as an infant.

  b. All modern literary magazines can trace their pedigree back to these
     gift books.

  c. But the short story . . . sprang into full-fledged existence as recently as
     the 1820s.

  d. A narrative of a few thousand words can be easily read, enjoyed, and
     digested while sitting before a monitor. . . .

Connect to Style With your group, discuss why the author's use of
the active voice is effective, as well as why he uses the passive voice when
he does.

Write It

📓 **Notebook** Write a paragraph to express your thoughts about a short
story you found particularly exciting or moving. Experiment with using both
the active and the passive voice in your writing.

STANDARDS
Writing
Conduct short as well as more
sustained research projects to
answer a question or solve a
problem; narrow or broaden the
inquiry when appropriate; synthesize
multiple sources on the subject,
demonstrating understanding of the
subject under investigation.

Language
Apply the understanding that usage
is a matter of convention, can
change over time, and is sometimes
contested.

Research

Assignment

As a group, create a **research report** that relates to "A Brief History of the Short Story" to share with the class. Choose one of these options:

- [ ] an **extended definition** of the term *short story* that shows how its meaning has developed over time

- [ ] a **graph** that shows how e-book sales compare with print book sales over time, along with a summary of what you learned about publishing trends and people's reading habits

- [ ] an **analytical paper** that presents and compares what a variety of famous American authors have said about the short story genre

Project Plan Have each group member review "A Brief History of the Short Story" and do some general reading about the subject you have chosen, to get an idea of the information you need. Then, as a group, list these kinds of information. Assign individual group members to research different aspects of the topic. Finally, determine how you will present the text and what images will accompany it.

Conduct Research Use this chart to keep track of the types of information you are researching and the group member assigned to each type. Also, record the sources each person consults and the details needed for proper citation.

 EVIDENCE LOG

Before moving on to a new selection, go to your Evidence Log and record what you learned from "A Brief History of the Short Story."

KIND OF INFORMATION	WHO IS RESPONSIBLE	SOURCE INFORMATION FOR CITATION

AN OCCURRENCE AT
OWL CREEK BRIDGE

Comparing Texts

In this lesson, you will read and compare "An Occurrence at Owl Creek Bridge" and "The Jilting of Granny Weatherall." The work you do with your group on "An Occurrence at Owl Creek Bridge" will help prepare you for the comparing task.

THE JILTING OF GRANNY
WEATHERALL

About the Author

Ambrose Bierce
(1842–1914?) was born in Ohio and raised on a farm in Indiana. The poverty in which he was raised helped foster Bierce's unsentimental outlook. His writing and worldview were further shaped by his career as a Union officer in the Civil War. The brutality he saw during the war cemented his cynicism. Bierce explored themes of cruelty and death in his writing, earning himself the nickname "Bitter Bierce."

An Occurrence at Owl Creek Bridge

Concept Vocabulary

As you perform your first read of "An Occurrence at Owl Creek Bridge," you will encounter these words.

> etiquette   deference   dictum

Context Clues If these words are unfamiliar to you, try using **context clues** such as these to help you determine their meanings.

> **Elaborating Details:** The former officer was **abject** when he was reduced in rank from captain to corporal.
>
> **Restatement, or Synonyms:** The general was a **paragon** of leadership, the standard against which other officers were judged.

Apply your knowledge of context clues and other vocabulary strategies to determine the meanings of unfamiliar words you encounter during your first read.

First Read FICTION

Apply these strategies as you conduct your first read. You will have an opportunity to complete a close read after your first read.

NOTICE *whom* the story is about, *what* happens, *where* and *when* it happens, and *why* those involved react as they do.

ANNOTATE by marking vocabulary and key passages you want to revisit.

First Read

CONNECT ideas within the selection to what you already know and what you have already read.

RESPOND by completing the Comprehension Check and by writing a brief summary of the selection.

☰ STANDARDS

Reading Literature
By the end of grade 11, read and comprehend literature, including stories, dramas, and poems, in the grades 11–CCR text complexity band proficiently, with scaffolding as needed at the high end of the range.

Language
Use context as a clue to the meaning of a word or phrase.

An Occurrence at Owl Creek Bridge

Ambrose Bierce

SCAN FOR
MULTIMEDIA

BACKGROUND

The senseless violence, death, and destruction Ambrose Bierce witnessed during the American Civil War (1861–1865) convinced him that war was terrible and futile. He set much of his best fiction, including this story, against the backdrop of this divisive war, in which the agricultural South, whose economy was based on slavery, battled the more industrialized North. Fought mostly in the South, the war caused hundreds of thousands of casualties on both sides.

I

1   A man stood upon a railroad bridge in northern Alabama, looking down into the swift water twenty feet below. The man's hands were behind his back, the wrists bound with a cord. A rope closely encircled his neck. It was attached to a stout cross timber above his head and the slack fell to the level of his knees. Some loose boards laid upon the sleepers supporting the metals of the railway supplied a footing for him and his executioners—two private soldiers of the Federal army, directed by a sergeant who in civil life may have been a deputy sheriff. At a short remove upon the same temporary platform was an officer in the uniform of his rank, armed. He was a captain. A sentinel at each end of the bridge stood with his rifle in

NOTES

the position known as "support," that is to say, vertical in front of the left shoulder, the hammer resting on the forearm thrown straight across the chest—a formal and unnatural position, enforcing an erect carriage of the body. It did not appear to be the duty of these two men to know what was occurring at the center of the bridge; they merely blockaded the two ends of the foot planking that traversed it.

2 Beyond one of the sentinels nobody was in sight: the railroad ran straight away into a forest for a hundred yards, then, curving, was lost to view. Doubtless there was an out-post farther along. The other bank of the stream was open ground—a gentle acclivity[1] topped with a stockade of vertical tree trunks, loopholed for rifles, with a single embrasure through which protruded the muzzle of a brass cannon commanding the bridge. Midway of the slope between bridge and fort were the spectators—a single company of infantry in line, at "parade rest," the butts of the rifles on the ground, the barrels inclining slightly backward against the right shoulder, the hands crossed upon the stock. A lieutenant stood at the right of the line, the point of his sword upon the ground, his left hand resting upon his right. Excepting the group of four at the center of the bridge, not a man moved. The company faced the bridge, staring stonily, motionless. The sentinels, facing the banks of the stream, might have been statues to adorn the bridge. The captain stood with folded arms, silent, observing the work of his subordinates, but making no sign. Death is a dignitary who when he comes announced is to be received with formal manifestations of respect, even by those most familiar with him. In the code of military **etiquette** silence and fixity are forms of **deference**.

3 The man who was engaged in being hanged was apparently about thirty-five years of age. He was a civilian, if one might judge from his habit, which was that of a planter. His features were good—a straight nose, firm mouth, broad forehead, from which his long, dark hair was combed straight back, falling behind his ears to the collar of his well-fitting frock coat. He wore a mustache and pointed beard, but no whiskers; his eyes were large and dark gray, and had a kindly expression which one would hardly have expected in one whose neck was in the hemp. Evidently this was no vulgar assassin. The liberal military code makes provision for hanging many kinds of persons, and gentlemen are not excluded.

4 The preparations being complete, the two private soldiers stepped aside and each drew away the plank upon which he had been standing. The sergeant turned to the captain, saluted and placed himself immediately behind that officer, who in turn moved apart one pace. These movements left the condemned man and the sergeant standing on the two ends of the same plank, which spanned three of the crossties of the bridge. The end upon which the civilian stood almost, but not quite, reached a fourth. This plank had been held in place by the weight of the captain; it was now held by that of

Mark context clues or indicate another strategy you used that helped you determine meaning.

etiquette (EHT ih kiht) *n.*

MEANING:

deference (DEHF uhr uhns) *n.*

MEANING:

---

1. **acclivity** (uh KLIHV uh tee) *n.* upward slope.

the sergeant. At a signal from the former the latter would step aside, the plank would tilt and the condemned man go down between two ties. The arrangement commended itself to his judgment as simple and effective. His face had not been covered nor his eyes bandaged. He looked a moment at his "unsteadfast footing," then let his gaze wander to the swirling water of the stream racing madly beneath his feet. A piece of dancing driftwood caught his attention and his eyes followed it down the current. How slowly it appeared to move! What a sluggish stream!

5   He closed his eyes in order to fix his last thoughts upon his wife and children. The water, touched to gold by the early sun, the brooding mists under the banks at some distance down the stream, the fort, the soldiers, the piece of drift—all had distracted him. And now he became conscious of a new disturbance. Striking through the thought of his dear ones was a sound which he could neither ignore nor understand, a sharp, distinct, metallic percussion like the stroke of a blacksmith's hammer upon the anvil; it had the same ringing quality. He wondered what it was, and whether immeasurably distant or near by—it seemed both. Its recurrence was regular, but as slow as the tolling of a death knell. He awaited each stroke with impatience and—he knew not why—apprehension. The intervals of silence grew progressively longer; the delays became maddening. With their greater infrequency the sounds increased in strength and sharpness. They hurt his ear like the thrust of a knife; he feared he would shriek. What he heard was the ticking of his watch.

6   He unclosed his eyes and saw again the water below him. "If I could free my hands," he thought, "I might throw off the noose and spring into the stream. By diving I could evade the bullets and, swimming vigorously, reach the bank, take to the woods and get away home. My home, thank God, is as yet outside their lines; my wife and little ones are still beyond the invader's farthest advance."

7   As these thoughts, which have here to be set down in words, were flashed into the doomed man's brain rather than evolved from it the captain nodded to the sergeant. The sergeant stepped aside.

II

8   Peyton Farquhar was a well-to-do planter, of an old and highly respected Alabama family. Being a slave owner and like other slave owners a politician he was naturally an original secessionist and ardently devoted to the Southern cause. Circumstances of an imperious nature, which it is unnecessary to relate here, had prevented him from taking service with the gallant army that had fought the disastrous campaigns ending with the fall of Corinth,[2] and he chafed under the inglorious restraint, longing for the release of his energies, the larger life of the soldier, the opportunity for distinction.

2. **Corinth** Mississippi town that was the site of an 1862 Civil War battle.

Mark context clues or indicate another strategy you used that helped you determine meaning.

dictum (DIHK tuhm) *n.*

MEANING:

That opportunity, he felt, would come, as it comes to all in war time. Meanwhile he did what he could. No service was too humble for him to perform in aid of the South, no adventure too perilous for him to undertake if consistent with the character of a civilian who was at heart a soldier, and who in good faith and without too much qualification assented to at least a part of the frankly villainous **dictum** that all is fair in love and war.

9   One evening while Farquhar and his wife were sitting on a rustic bench near the entrance to his grounds, a gray-clad soldier rode up to the gate and asked for a drink of water. Mrs. Farquhar was only too happy to serve him with her own white hands. While she was fetching the water her husband approached the dusty horseman and inquired eagerly for news from the front.

10   "The Yanks are repairing the railroads," said the man, "and are getting ready for another advance. They have reached the Owl Creek bridge, put it in order and built a stockade on the north bank. The commandant has issued an order, which is posted everywhere, declaring that any civilian caught interfering with the railroad, its bridges, tunnels or trains will be summarily hanged. I saw the order."

11   "How far is it to the Owl Creek bridge?" Farquhar asked.

12   "About thirty miles."

13   "Is there no force on this side the creek?"

14   "Only a picket post[3] half a mile out, on the railroad, and a single sentinel at this end of the bridge."

15   "Suppose a man—a civilian and student of hanging—should elude the picket post and perhaps get the better of the sentinel," said Farquhar, smiling, "what could he accomplish?"

16   The soldier reflected. "I was there a month ago," he replied. "I observed that the flood of last winter had lodged a great quantity of

---

3. **picket post** troops sent ahead with news of a surprise attack.

driftwood against the wooden pier at this end of the bridge. It is now dry and would burn like tow."[4]

17   The lady had now brought the water, which the soldier drank. He thanked her ceremoniously, bowed to her husband and rode away. An hour later, after nightfall, he repassed the plantation, going northward in the direction from which he had come. He was a Federal scout.

III

18   As Peyton Farquhar fell straight downward through the bridge he lost consciousness and was as one already dead. From this state he was awakened—ages later, it seemed to him—by the pain of a sharp pressure upon his throat, followed by a sense of suffocation. Keen, poignant agonies seemed to shoot from his neck downward through every fiber of his body and limbs. These pains appeared to flash along well-defined lines of ramification[5] and to beat with an inconceivably rapid periodicity. They seemed like streams of pulsating fire heating him to an intolerable temperature. As to his head, he was conscious of nothing but a feeling of fullness—of congestion. These sensations were unaccompanied by thought. The intellectual part of his nature was already effaced: he had power only to feel, and feeling was torment. He was conscious of motion. Encompassed in a luminous cloud, of which he was now merely the fiery heart, without material substance, he swung through unthinkable arcs of oscillation, like a vast pendulum. Then all at once, with terrible suddenness, the light about him shot upward with the noise of a loud plash; a frightful roaring was in his ears, and all was cold and dark. The power of thought was restored; he knew that the rope had broken and he had fallen into the stream. There was no additional strangulation; the noose about his neck was already suffocating him and kept the water from his lungs. To die of hanging at the bottom of a river!—the idea seemed to him ludicrous. He opened his eyes in the darkness and saw above him a gleam of light, but how distant, how inaccessible! He was still sinking, for the light became fainter and fainter until it was a mere glimmer. Then it began to grow and brighten, and he knew that he was rising toward the surface—knew it with reluctance, for he was now very comfortable. "To be hanged and drowned," he thought, "that is not so bad; but I do not wish to be shot. No; I will not be shot; that is not fair."

19   He was not conscious of an effort, but a sharp pain in his wrist apprised him that he was trying to free his hands. He gave the struggle his attention, as an idler might observe the feat of a juggler, without interest in the outcome. What splendid effort!— what magnificent, what superhuman strength! Ah, that was a fine endeavor!

---

4. **tow** (toh) *n.* coarse, broken fibers of hemp or flax before spinning.
5. **flash along well-defined lines of ramification** spread out quickly along branches from a central point.

Bravo! The cord fell away; his arms parted and floated upward, the hands dimly seen on each side in the growing light. He watched them with a new interest as first one and then the other pounced upon the noose at his neck. They tore it away and thrust it fiercely aside, its undulations resembling those of a water-snake. "Put it back, put it back!" He thought he shouted these words to his hands, for the undoing of the noose had been succeeded by the direst pang that he had yet experienced. His neck ached horribly; his brain was on fire; his heart, which had been fluttering faintly, gave a great leap, trying to force itself out at his mouth. His whole body was racked and wrenched with an insupportable anguish! But his disobedient hands gave no heed to the command. They beat the water vigorously with quick, downward strokes, forcing him to the surface. He felt his head emerge: his eyes were blinded by the sunlight; his chest expanded convulsively, and with a supreme and crowning agony his lungs engulfed a great draft of air, which instantly he expelled in a shriek!

20   He was now in full possession of his physical senses. They were, indeed, preternaturally[6] keen and alert. Something in the awful disturbance of his organic system had so exalted and refined them that they made record of things never before perceived. He felt the ripples upon his face and heard their separate sounds as they struck. He looked at the forest on the bank of the stream, saw the individual trees, the leaves and the veining of each leaf—saw the very insects upon them: the locusts, the brilliant-bodied flies, the gray spiders stretching their webs from twig to twig. He noted the prismatic colors in all the dewdrops upon a million blades of grass. The humming of the gnats that danced above the eddies of the stream, the beating of the dragonflies' wings, the strokes of the water spiders' legs, like oars which had lifted their boat— all these made audible music. A fish slid along beneath his eyes and he heard the rush of its body parting the water.

21   He had come to the surface facing down the stream: in a moment the visible world seemed to wheel slowly round, himself the pivotal point, and he saw the bridge, the fort, the soldiers upon the bridge, the captain, the sergeant, the two privates, his executioners. They were in silhouette against the blue sky. They shouted and gesticulated, pointing at him. The captain had drawn his pistol, but did not fire; the others were unarmed. Their movements were grotesque and horrible, their forms gigantic.

22   Suddenly he heard a sharp report and something struck the water smartly within a few inches of his head, spattering his face with spray. He heard a second report, and saw one of the sentinels with his rifle at his shoulder, a light cloud of blue smoke rising from the muzzle. The man in the water saw the eye of the man on the bridge gazing into his own through the sights of the rifle. He observed that it was a gray eye and remembered having read that gray eyes were keenest, and that all famous marksmen had them. Nevertheless, this one had missed.

---

6. **preternaturally** (pree tuhr NACH uhr uh lee) *adv.* abnormally; extraordinarily.

23   A counterswirl had caught Farquhar and turned him half round; he was again looking into the forest on the bank opposite the fort. The sound of a clear, high voice in a monotonous singsong now rang out behind him and came across the water with a distinctness that pierced and subdued all other sounds, even the beating of the ripples in his ears. Although no soldier, he had frequented camps enough to know the dread significance of that deliberate, drawling, aspirated chant; the lieutenant on shore was taking a part in the morning's work. How coldly and pitilessly—with what an even, calm intonation, presaging,[7] and enforcing tranquility in the men—with what accurately measured intervals fell those cruel words:

24   "Attention, company! . . . Shoulder arms! . . . Ready! . . . Aim! . . . Fire!"

25   Farquhar dived—dived as deeply as he could. The water roared in his ears like the voice of Niagara, yet he heard the dulled thunder of the volley and, rising again toward the surface, met shining bits of metal, singularly flattened, oscillating slowly downward. Some of them touched him on the face and hands, then fell away, continuing their descent. One lodged between his collar and neck; it was uncomfortably warm and he snatched it out.

26   As he rose to the surface, gasping for breath, he saw that he had been a long time under water; he was perceptibly farther down stream—nearer to safety. The soldiers had almost finished reloading; the metal ramrods flashed all at once in the sunshine as they were drawn from the barrels, turned in the air, and thrust

---

7. **presaging** (prih SAY jihng) *v.* predicting; warning.

into their sockets. The two sentinels fired again, independently and ineffectually.

27 The hunted man saw all this over his shoulder; he was now swimming vigorously with the current. His brain was as energetic as his arms and legs: he thought with the rapidity of lightning.

28 "The officer," he reasoned, "will not make that martinet's[8] error a second time. It is as easy to dodge a volley as a single shot. He has probably already given the command to fire at will. God help me, I cannot dodge them all!"

29 An appalling plash within two yards of him was followed by a loud, rushing sound, *diminuendo*,[9] which seemed to travel back through the air to the fort and died in an explosion which stirred the very river to its deeps! A rising sheet of water curved over him, fell down upon him, blinded him, strangled him! The cannon had taken a hand in the game. As he shook his head free from the commotion of the smitten water he heard the deflected shot humming through the air ahead, and in an instant it was cracking and smashing the branches in the forest beyond.

30 "They will not do that again," he thought; "the next time they will use a charge of grape.[10] I must keep my eye upon the gun; the smoke will apprise me—the report arrives too late; it lags behind the missile. That is a good gun."

31 Suddenly he felt himself whirled round and round—spinning like a top. The water, the banks, the forests, the now distant bridge, fort and men—all were commingled and blurred. Objects were represented by their colors only; circular horizontal streaks of color—that was all he saw. He had been caught in a vortex and was being whirled on with a velocity of advance and gyration that made him giddy and sick. In a few moments he was flung upon the gravel at the foot of the left bank of the stream—the southern bank—and behind a projecting point which concealed him from his enemies. The sudden arrest of his motion, the abrasion of one of his hands on the gravel, restored him, and he wept with delight. He dug his fingers into the sand, threw it over himself in handfuls and audibly blessed it. It looked like diamonds, rubies, emeralds; he could think of nothing beautiful which it did not resemble. The trees upon the bank were giant garden plants; he noted a definite order in their arrangement, inhaled the fragrance of their blooms. A strange, roseate[11] light shone through the spaces among their trunks and the wind made in their branches the music of aeolian harps.[12] He had no wish to perfect his escape—was content to remain in that enchanting spot until retaken.

---

8. **martinet** (mahr tuh NEHT) *n.* strict military disciplinarian.
9. **diminuendo** (duh mihn yoo EHN doh) musical term used to describe a gradual reduction in volume.
10. **charge of grape** cluster of small iron balls—"grape shot"—that disperse once fired from a cannon.
11. **roseate** (ROH zee iht) *adj.* rose-colored.
12. **aeolian** (ee OH lee uhn) **harps** stringed instruments that produce music when played by the wind. In Greek mythology, Aeolus is the god of the winds.

32 A whiz and rattle of grapeshot among the branches high above his head roused him from his dream. The baffled cannoneer had fired him a random farewell. He sprang to his feet, rushed up the sloping bank, and plunged into the forest.

33 All that day he traveled, laying his course by the rounding sun. The forest seemed interminable; nowhere did he discover a break in it, not even a woodman's road. He had not known that he lived in so wild a region. There was something uncanny in the revelation.

34 By night fall he was fatigued, footsore, famishing. The thought of his wife and children urged him on. At last he found a road which led him in what he knew to be the right direction. It was as wide and straight as a city street, yet it seemed untraveled. No fields bordered it, no dwelling anywhere. Not so much as the barking of a dog suggested human habitation. The black bodies of the trees formed a straight wall on both sides, terminating on the horizon in a point, like a diagram in a lesson in perspective. Overhead, as he looked up through this rift in the wood, shone great golden stars looking unfamiliar and grouped in strange constellations. He was sure they were arranged in some order which had a secret and malign significance. The wood on either side was full of singular noises, among which—once, twice, and again, he distinctly heard whispers in an unknown tongue.

35 His neck was in pain and lifting his hand to it he found it horribly swollen. He knew that it had a circle of black where the rope had bruised it. His eyes felt congested: he could no longer close them. His tongue was swollen with thirst; he relieved its fever by thrusting it forward from between his teeth into the cold air. How softly the turf had carpeted the untraveled avenue—he could no longer feel the roadway beneath his feet!

36 Doubtless, despite his suffering, he had fallen asleep while walking, for now he sees another scene—perhaps he has merely recovered from a delirium. He stands at the gate of his own home. All is as he left it, and all bright and beautiful in the morning sunshine. He must have traveled the entire night. As he pushes open the gate and passes up the wide white walk, he sees a flutter of female garments; his wife, looking fresh and cool and sweet, steps down from the veranda to meet him. At the bottom of the steps she stands waiting, with a smile of ineffable joy, an attitude of matchless grace and dignity. Ah, how beautiful she is! He springs forward with extended arms. As he is about to clasp her he feels a stunning blow upon the back of the neck; a blinding white light blazes all about him with a sound like the shock of a cannon—then all is darkness and silence!

37 Peyton Farquhar was dead; his body, with a broken neck, swung gently from side to side beneath the timbers of the Owl Creek bridge. ❧

Comprehension Check

Complete the following items after you finish your first read. Review and clarify details with your group.

1. As the story begins, what event is about to take place on the bridge?

2. In the war that divides the nation, which side does Farquhar support?

3. Why has Farquhar been sentenced to die?

4. What surprising event happens after Farquhar first loses consciousness?

5. How do the soldiers try to stop Farquhar after he drops into the water?

6. 🗐 **Notebook** Confirm your understanding of the story by writing a summary.

- -

RESEARCH

Research to Clarify Choose at least one unfamiliar detail from the story. Briefly research that detail. In what way does the information you learned shed light on an aspect of the story?

Research to Explore Conduct research on an aspect of the story you find interesting. For example, you may want to learn about the Battle of Shiloh, which took place in part along Owl Creek.

Close Read the Text

With your group, revisit sections of the text you marked during your first read. **Annotate** details that you notice. What **questions** do you have? What can you **conclude**?

AN OCCURRENCE AT
OWL CREEK BRIDGE

Analyze the Text

CITE TEXTUAL EVIDENCE
to support your answers.

Complete the activities.

1. **Review and Clarify** With your group, reread paragraphs 36–37 of the selection. Do the details in the story prepare readers for that ending, or does it come as a complete surprise? What does the ending suggest about the nature of reality?

2. **Present and Discuss** Now, work with your group to share the passages from the text that you found especially important. Take turns presenting your passages. Discuss what you noticed in the selection, what questions you asked, and what conclusions you reached.

3. **Essential Question:** *What do stories reveal about the human condition?* What has this narrative taught you about the human condition? Discuss with your group.

LANGUAGE DEVELOPMENT

Concept Vocabulary

| etiquette | deference | dictum |

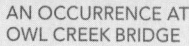

Why These Words? The concept vocabulary words from the text are related. With your group, determine what the words have in common. Write your ideas, and add another word that fits the category.

WORD NETWORK

Add words related to the human condition from the text to your Word Network.

Practice

Notebook Confirm your understanding of these words from the text by using them in a short narrative paragraph. Then, trade papers with another group member and challenge him or her to underline the context clues that reveal the meaning of each word.

Word Study

Latin Suffix: -um In "An Occurrence at Owl Creek Bridge," the author uses the word *dictum*, which is the singular form of the Latin noun *dicta*. The Latin suffix *-um* is used to form the singular of many Latin nouns, including *bacteria*, *curricula*, and *media*. Use a dictionary or online source to find three other words that feature this suffix. Record the words and their meanings.

STANDARDS

Language
• Determine or clarify the meaning of unknown and multiple-meaning words and phrases based on *grades 11–12 reading and content,* choosing flexibly from a range of strategies.
• Identify and correctly use patterns of word changes that indicate different meanings or parts of speech.

AN OCCURRENCE AT
OWL CREEK BRIDGE

Analyze Craft and Structure

Author's Choices: Structure Ambrose Bierce chose to structure this story in three sections, each representing a shift in time and perspective. The shift in perspective is amplified by Bierce's choice of point of view, which affects every aspect of the story. Different points of view convey different types of information to the reader.

- In stories told from an **omnisicient third-person point of view,** the narrator is an observer who can describe everything that happens, as well as the private thoughts and feelings of all the characters.

- In stories told from a **limited third-person point of view,** readers' information is limited to what a single character feels, thinks, and observes.

The point of view in this story shifts. As it shifts, so do the emotional tone and sense of time. To emphasize this change, Bierce introduces yet another narrative approach. He uses **stream of consciousness,** a technique in which a character's thoughts are presented as the mind experiences them—in short bursts without obvious logic.

TIP

COLLABORATION
You may want to have individual group members complete the activity and questions first, and then work as a group to share and agree on responses.

Practice

CITE TEXTUAL EVIDENCE
to support your answers.

📓 **Notebook** Complete the activity and questions.

1. Working with your group, reread the story to find examples of the two different points of view Bierce uses. Then, use a chart like this one to analyze the effect of these choices.

THIRD-PERSON POINT OF VIEW	
Limited or Omniscient?	Effect

2. **(a)** What do you learn in Section II about the main character's home life, political loyalties, and motivations? **(b)** How does this detailed information shed light on the scene described in Section I?

3. **(a)** What point of view does Bierce use in Section III? **(b)** Explain why this choice of point of view is essential to the story's overall impact. **(c)** What is the effect of the shift in point of view in the last paragraph of the story?

4. **(a)** Which details in the second paragraph of Section III are revealed through the use of stream of consciousness? **(b)** What is the "sharp pain" that sparks Farquhar's thoughts? **(c)** In what way does this passage mimic the natural, jumbled flow of thought?

📋 **STANDARDS**

Reading Literature
Analyze how an author's choices concerning how to structure specific parts of a text contribute to its overall structure and meaning as well as its aesthetic impact.

Conventions and Style

Varying Syntax for Effect Writers often vary their **syntax**, or the structures of their sentences, to achieve particular effects. In doing so, they may even choose to deviate from the conventions of standard English grammar. Ambrose Bierce, for example, employs a device known as **asyndeton**—the omission of a coordinating conjunction, such as *and* or *or*, where one would normally appear—to reinforce the stream-of-consciousness feel of Section III of "An Occurrence at Owl Creek Bridge."

Consider this excerpt from the story:

> He looked at the forest on the bank of the stream, saw the individual trees, the leaves and the veining of each leaf—saw the very insects upon them: the locusts, the brilliant-bodied flies, <u>the</u> gray spiders stretching their webs from twig to twig. (paragraph 20)

Typically, the coordinating conjunction *and* would precede the underlined word. Bierce's choice to employ asyndeton, however, speeds up the rhythm of the passage. The reader gets the sense that the narrator is listing each creature just as it catches Farquhar's eye—that the reader is experiencing Farquhar's world at the very moment that he is.

Read It

1. Work individually. Read these examples of Bierce's use of asyndeton in "An Occurrence at Owl Creek Bridge." In each sentence, mark where Bierce has chosen to omit a coordinating conjunction.

   a. The humming of the gnats that danced above the eddies of the stream, the beating of the dragonflies' wings, the strokes of the water spiders' legs, like oars which had lifted their boat—all these made audible music.

   b. A rising sheet of water curved over him, fell down upon him, blinded him, strangled him!

   c. It looked like diamonds, rubies, emeralds; he could think of nothing beautiful which it did not resemble.

   d. The trees upon the bank were giant garden plants; he noted a definite order in their arrangement, inhaled the fragrance of their blooms.

2. Connect to Style Reread paragraph 21 of "An Occurrence at Owl Creek Bridge," and identify the sentence in which Bierce employs asyndeton. Then, discuss with your group how the syntax of this sentence contributes to Bierce's stream-of-consciousness narration.

Write It

📓 **Notebook** Write a one-paragraph stream-of-consciousness narrative. Use asyndeton in at least one of your sentences. Indicate where you have omitted any coordinating conjunctions.

☰ STANDARDS

Language
• Apply the understanding that usage is a matter of convention, can change over time, and is sometimes contested.
• Vary syntax for effect, consulting references for guidance as needed; apply an understanding of syntax to the study of complex texts when reading.

AN OCCURRENCE AT OWL CREEK BRIDGE

Comparing Texts

You will now read "The Jilting of Granny Weatherall." First, complete the first-read and close-read activities. Then, compare the narrative structures in "The Jilting of Granny Weatherall" and "An Occurrence at Owl Creek Bridge."

THE JILTING OF GRANNY WEATHERALL

About the Author

The life of **Katherine Anne Porter** (1890–1980) spanned World War I, the Great Depression, World War II, and the rise of the nuclear age. For Porter, her fiction was an "effort to grasp the meaning of those threats, to trace them to their sources, and to understand the logic of this majestic and terrible failure of the life of man in the Western world." Her stories often feature characters at pivotal moments, who face dramatic change, the constricting bonds of family, and the weight of the past.

☰ STANDARDS

Reading Literature
By the end of grade 11, read and literature, including stories, dramas, and poems, nonfiction in the grades 11–CCR text complexity band proficiently, with scaffolding as needed at the high end of the range.

Language
Identify and correctly use patterns of word changes that indicate different meanings or parts of speech.

The Jilting of Granny Weatherall

Concept Vocabulary

As you perform your first read of "The Jilting of Granny Weatherall," you will encounter these words.

> clammy   hypodermic   dyspepsia

Familiar Word Parts Separating an unfamiliar word into its parts—roots, prefixes, or suffixes—can often help you determine its meaning.

> **Example:** The root -circ- means "ring" or "circle." Thus, something that is *circular* has a ringlike shape, and something that *circulates* moves in a ringlike path. When you come across an unfamiliar word that contains the root -circ-, such as *circuitous,* you know that it has properties that relate to a circle. Even if you cannot identify a word's exact definition, you can approximate the meaning well enough to keep reading. *Circuitous* is an adjective that means "roundabout; indirect."

Apply your knowledge of familiar word parts and other vocabulary strategies to determine the meanings of unfamiliar words you encounter during your first read.

First Read FICTION

Apply these strategies as you conduct your first read. You will have an opportunity to complete a close read after your first read.

NOTICE *whom* the story is about, *what* happens, *where* and *when* it happens, and why those involved react as they do.

ANNOTATE by marking vocabulary and key passages you want to revisit

First Read

CONNECT ideas within the selection to what you already know and what you have already read.

RESPOND by completing the Comprehension Check and by writing a brief summary of the selection.

The Jilting of Granny Weatherall

Katherine Anne Porter

BACKGROUND

Katherine Anne Porter's view of life and the fiction she wrote were shaped by a sense of disillusionment resulting from World War I, the despair of the Great Depression, and the World War II horrors of Nazism and nuclear warfare. Sometimes, as in the novel *Ship of Fools*, Porter focuses on political issues such as Nazism. In contrast, works such as "The Jilting of Granny Weatherall" pinpoint the dissolving families and communities of the modern age.

SCAN FOR
MULTIMEDIA

NOTES

1   She flicked her wrist neatly out of Doctor Harry's pudgy careful fingers and pulled the sheet up to her chin. The brat ought to be in knee breeches. Doctoring around the country with spectacles on his nose! "Get along now, take your schoolbooks and go. There's nothing wrong with me."

2   Doctor Harry spread a warm paw like a cushion on her forehead where the forked green vein danced and made her eyelids twitch. "Now, now, be a good girl, and we'll have you up in no time."

3   "That's no way to speak to a woman nearly eighty years old just because she's down. I'd have you respect your elders, young man."

4   "Well, Missy, excuse me," Doctor Harry patted her cheek. "But I've got to warn you, haven't I? You're a marvel, but you must be careful or you're going to be good and sorry."

5   "Don't tell me what I'm going to be. I'm on my feet now, morally speaking. It's Cornelia. I had to go to bed to get rid of her."

6   Her bones felt loose, and floated around in her skin, and Doctor Harry floated like a balloon around the foot of the bed. He floated and pulled down his waistcoat and swung his glasses on a cord. "Well, stay where you are, it certainly can't hurt you."

7   "Get along and doctor your sick," said Granny Weatherall. "Leave a well woman alone. I'll call for you when I want you . . . Where were you forty years ago when I pulled through milk leg[1] and double pneumonia? You weren't even born. Don't let Cornelia lead you on," she shouted, because Doctor Harry appeared to float up to the ceiling and out. "I pay my own bills, and I don't throw my money away on nonsense!"

8   She meant to wave good-bye, but it was too much trouble. Her eyes closed of themselves, it was like a dark curtain drawn around the bed. The pillow rose and floated under her, pleasant as a hammock in a light wind. She listened to the leaves rustling outside the window. No, somebody was swishing newspapers: no, Cornelia and Doctor Harry were whispering together. She leaped broad awake, thinking they whispered in her ear.

9   "She was never like this, never like this!" "Well, what can we expect?" "Yes, eighty years old. . . ."

10   Well, and what if she was? She still had ears. It was like Cornelia to whisper around doors. She always kept things secret in such a public way. She was always being tactful and kind. Cornelia was dutiful; that was the trouble with her. Dutiful and good: "So good and dutiful," said Granny, "that I'd like to spank her." She saw herself spanking Cornelia and making a fine job of it.

11   "What'd you say, Mother?"

12   Granny felt her face tying up in hard knots.

13   "Can't a body think, I'd like to know?"

14   "I thought you might want something."

15   "I do. I want a lot of things. First off, go away and don't whisper."

16   She lay and drowsed, hoping in her sleep that the children would keep out and let her rest a minute. It had been a long day. Not that she was tired. It was always pleasant to snatch a minute now and then. There was always so much to be done, let me see: tomorrow.

17   Tomorrow was far away and there was nothing to trouble about. Things were finished somehow when the time came; thank God there was always a little margin over for peace: then a person could spread out the plan of life and tuck in the edges orderly. It was good to have everything clean and folded away, with the hair brushes and tonic bottles sitting straight on the white embroidered linen: the day started without fuss and the pantry shelves laid out with rows of jelly glasses and brown jugs and white stone-china jars with blue whirligigs and words painted on them: coffee, tea, sugar, ginger,

---

1. **milk leg** painful swelling of the leg.

cinnamon, allspice: and the bronze clock with the lion on top nicely dusted off. The dust that lion could collect in twenty-four hours! The box in the attic with all those letters tied up, well, she'd have to go through that tomorrow. All those letters—George's letters and John's letters and her letters to them both—lying around for the children to find afterwards made her uneasy. Yes, that would be tomorrow's business. No use to let them know how silly she had been once.

18   While she was rummaging around she found death in her mind and it felt **clammy** and unfamiliar. She had spent so much time preparing for death there was no need for bringing it up again. Let it take care of itself now. When she was sixty she had felt very old, finished, and went around making farewell trips to see her children and grandchildren, with a secret in her mind: This is the very last of your mother, children! Then she made her will and came down with a long fever. That was all just a notion like a lot of other things, but it was lucky too, for she had once for all got over the idea of dying for a long time. Now she couldn't be worried. She hoped she had better sense now. Her father had lived to be one hundred and two years old and had drunk a noggin of strong hot toddy on his last birthday. He told the reporters it was his daily habit, and he owed his long life to that. He had made quite a scandal and was very pleased about it. She believed she'd just plague Cornelia a little.

19   "Cornelia! Cornelia!" No footsteps, but a sudden hand on her cheek. "Bless you, where have you been?"

20   "Here, mother."

21   "Well, Cornelia, I want a noggin of hot toddy."

22   "Are you cold, darling?"

23   "I'm chilly, Cornelia. Lying in bed stops the circulation. I must have told you that a thousand times."

24   Well, she could just hear Cornelia telling her husband that Mother was getting a little childish and they'd have to humor her. The thing that most annoyed her was that Cornelia thought she was deaf, dumb, and blind. Little hasty glances and tiny gestures tossed around her and over her head saying, "Don't cross her, let her have her way, she's eighty years old," and she sitting there as if she lived in a thin glass cage. Sometimes Granny almost made up her mind to pack up and move back to her own house where nobody could remind her every minute that she was old. Wait, wait, Cornelia, till your own children whisper behind your back!

25   In her day she had kept a better house and had got more work done. She wasn't too old yet for Lydia to be driving eighty miles for advice when one of the children jumped the track, and Jimmy still dropped in and talked things over: "Now, Mammy, you've a good business head, I want to know what you think of this? . . ." Old. Cornelia couldn't change the furniture around without asking. Little things, little things! They had been so sweet when they were little. Granny wished the old days were back again with the children young and everything to be done over. It had been a hard pull, but not too

NOTES

Mark familiar word parts or indicate another strategy you used that helped you determine meaning.

clammy (KLAM ee) *adj.*

MEANING:

much for her. When she thought of all the food she had cooked, and all the clothes she had cut and sewed, and all the gardens she had made—well, the children showed it. There they were, made out of her, and they couldn't get away from that. Sometimes she wanted to see John again and point to them and say, Well, I didn't do so badly, did I? But that would have to wait. That was for tomorrow. She used to think of him as a man, but now all the children were older than their father, and he would be a child beside her if she saw him now. It seemed strange and there was something wrong in the idea. Why, he couldn't possibly recognize her. She had fenced in a hundred acres once, digging the post holes herself and clamping the wires with just a negro boy to help. That changed a woman. John would be looking for a young woman with the peaked Spanish comb in her hair and the painted fan. Digging post holes changed a woman. Riding country roads in the winter when women had their babies was another thing: sitting up nights with sick horses and sick children and hardly ever losing one. John, I hardly ever lost one of them! John would see that in a minute, that would be something he could understand, she wouldn't have to explain anything!

26   It made her feel like rolling up her sleeves and putting the whole place to rights again. No matter if Cornelia was determined to be everywhere at once, there were a great many things left undone on this place. She would start tomorrow and do them. It was good to be strong enough for everything, even if all you made melted and changed and slipped under your hands, so that by the time you finished you almost forgot what you were working for. What was it I set out to do? she asked herself intently, but she could not remember. A fog rose over the valley, she saw it marching across the creek swallowing the trees and moving up the hill like an army of ghosts. Soon it would be at the near edge of the orchard, and then it was time to go in and light the lamps. Come in, children, don't stay out in the night air.

27   Lighting the lamps had been beautiful. The children huddled up to her and breathed like little calves waiting at the bars in the twilight. Their eyes followed the match and watched the flame rise and settle in a blue curve, then they moved away from her. The lamp was lit, they didn't have to be scared and hang on to mother any more. Never, never, never more. God, for all my life I thank Thee. Without Thee, my God, I could never have done it. Hail Mary, full of grace.

28   I want you to pick all the fruit this year and see that nothing is wasted. There's always someone who can use it. Don't let good things rot for want of using. You waste life when you waste good food. Don't let things get lost. It's bitter to lose things. Now, don't let me get to thinking, not when I am tired and taking a little nap before supper. . . .

29   The pillow rose about her shoulders and pressed against her heart and the memory was being squeezed out of it: oh, push down the pillow, somebody: it would smother her if she tried to hold it. Such a

fresh breeze blowing and such a green day with no threats in it. But he had not come, just the same. What does a woman do when she has put on the white veil and set out the white cake for a man and he doesn't come? She tried to remember. No, I swear he never harmed me but in that. He never harmed me but in that . . . and what if he did? There was the day, the day, but a whirl of dark smoke rose and covered it, crept up and over into the bright field where everything was planted so carefully in orderly rows. That was hell, she knew hell when she saw it. For sixty years she had prayed against remembering him and against losing her soul in the deep pit of hell, and now the two things were mingled in one and the thought of him was a smoky cloud from hell that moved and crept in her head when she had just got rid of Doctor Harry and was trying to rest a minute. Wounded vanity, Ellen, said a sharp voice in the top of her mind. Don't let your wounded vanity get the upper hand of you. Plenty of girls get jilted. You were jilted, weren't you? Then stand up to it. Her eyelids wavered and let in streamers of blue-gray light like tissue paper over her eyes. She must get up and pull the shades down or she'd never sleep. She was in bed again and the shades were not down. How could that happen? Better turn over, hide from the light, sleeping in the light gave you nightmares. "Mother, how do you feel now?" and a stinging wetness on her forehead. But I don't like having my face washed in cold water!

30   Hapsy? George? Lydia? Jimmy? No, Cornelia, and her features were swollen and full of little puddles. "They're coming, darling, they'll all be here soon." Go wash your face, child, you look funny.

31   Instead of obeying, Cornelia knelt down and put her head on the pillow. She seemed to be talking but there was no sound. "Well, are you tongue-tied? Whose birthday is it? Are you going to give a party?"

32   Cornelia's mouth moved urgently in strange shapes. "Don't do that, you bother me, daughter."

33   "Oh, no, Mother. Oh, no. . . ."

34   Nonsense. It was strange about children. They disputed your every word. "No what, Cornelia?"

35   "Here's Doctor Harry."

36   "I won't see that boy again. He just left five minutes ago."

37   "That was this morning, Mother. It's night now. Here's the nurse."

38   "This is Doctor Harry, Mrs. Weatherall. I never saw you look so young and happy!"

39   "Ah, I'll never be young again—but I'd be happy if they'd let me lie in peace and get rested."

40   She thought she spoke up loudly, but no one answered. A warm weight on her forehead, a warm bracelet on her wrist, and a breeze went on whispering, trying to tell her something. A shuffle of leaves in the everlasting hand of God, He blew on them and they danced and rattled. "Mother, don't mind, we're going to give you a little **hypodermic**." "Look here, daughter, how do ants get in this bed? I saw sugar ants yesterday." Did you send for Hapsy too?

41   It was Hapsy she really wanted. She had to go a long way back through a great many rooms to find Hapsy standing with a baby on her arm. She seemed to herself to be Hapsy also, and the baby on Hapsy's arm was Hapsy and himself and herself, all at once, and there was no surprise in the meeting. Then Hapsy melted from within and turned flimsy as gray gauze and the baby was a gauzy shadow, and Hapsy came up close and said, "I thought you'd never come," and looked at her very searchingly and said, "You haven't changed a bit!" They leaned forward to kiss, when Cornelia began whispering from a long way off, "Oh, is there anything you want to tell me? Is there anything I can do for you?"

42   Yes, she had changed her mind after sixty years and she would like to see George. I want you to find George. Find him and be sure to tell him I forgot him. I want him to know I had my husband just the same and my children and my house like any other woman. A good house too and a good husband that I loved and fine children out of him.

Mark familiar word parts or indicate another strategy you used that helped you determine meaning.

hypodermic (hy puh DUR mihk) *n.*

MEANING:

Better than I hoped for even. Tell him I was given back everything he took away and more. Oh, no, oh, God, no, there was something else besides the house and the man and the children. Oh, surely they were not all? What was it? Something not given back. . . . Her breath crowded down under her ribs and grew into a monstrous frightening shape with cutting edges; it bored up into her head, and the agony was unbelievable: Yes, John, get the Doctor now, no more talk, my time has come.

43 When this one was born it should be the last. The last. It should have been born first, for it was the one she had truly wanted. Everything came in good time. Nothing left out, left over. She was strong, in three days she would be as well as ever. Better. A woman needed milk in her to have her full health.

44 "Mother, do you hear me?"

45 "I've been telling you—"

46 "Mother, Father Connolly's here."

47 "I went to Holy Communion only last week. Tell him I'm not so sinful as all that."

48 "Father just wants to speak to you."

49 He could speak as much as he pleased. It was like him to drop in and inquire about her soul as if it were a teething baby, and then stay on for a cup of tea and a round of cards and gossip. He always had a funny story of some sort, usually about an Irishman who made his little mistakes and confessed them, and the point lay in some absurd thing he would blurt out in the confessional showing his struggles between native piety and original sin. Granny felt easy about her soul. Cornelia, where are your manners? Give Father Connolly a chair. She had her secret comfortable understanding with a few favorite saints who cleared a straight road to God for her. All as surely signed and sealed as the papers for the new Forty Acres. Forever . . . heirs and assigns[2] forever. Since the day the wedding cake was not cut, but thrown out and wasted. The whole bottom dropped out of the world, and there she was blind and sweating with nothing under her feet and the walls falling away. His hand had caught her under the breast, she had not fallen, there was the freshly polished floor with the green rug on it, just as before. He had cursed like a sailor's parrot and said, "I'll kill him for you." Don't lay a hand on him, for my sake leave something to God. "Now, Ellen, you must believe what I tell you. . . ."

50 So there was nothing, nothing to worry about any more, except sometimes in the night one of the children screamed in a nightmare, and they both hustled out shaking and hunting for the matches and calling, "There, wait a minute, here we are!" John, get the doctor now, Hapsy's time has come. But there was Hapsy standing by the bed in a white cap. "Cornelia, tell Hapsy to take off her cap. I can't see her plain."

NOTES

---

2. **assigns** *n.* people to whom property is transferred.

51   Her eyes opened very wide and the room stood out like a picture she had seen somewhere. Dark colors with the shadows rising towards the ceiling in long angles. The tall black dresser gleamed with nothing on it but John's picture, enlarged from a little one, with John's eyes very black when they should have been blue. You never saw him, so how do you know how he looked? But the man insisted the copy was perfect, it was very rich and handsome. For a picture, yes, but it's not my husband. The table by the bed had a linen cover and a candle and a crucifix. The light was blue from Cornelia's silk lampshades. No sort of light at all, just frippery. You had to live forty years with kerosene lamps to appreciate honest electricity. She felt very strong and she saw Doctor Harry with a rosy nimbus around him.

52   "You look like a saint, Doctor Harry, and I vow that's as near as you'll ever come to it."

53   "She's saying something."

54   "I heard you, Cornelia. What's all this carrying on?"

55   "Father Connolly's saying—"

56   Cornelia's voice staggered and bumped like a cart in a bad road. It rounded corners and turned back again and arrived nowhere. Granny stepped up in the cart very lightly and reached for the reins, but a man sat beside her and she knew him by his hands, driving

the cart. She did not look in his face, for she knew without seeing, but looked instead down the road where the trees leaned over and bowed to each other and a thousand birds were singing a Mass. She felt like singing too, but she put her hand in the bosom of her dress and pulled out a rosary, and Father Connolly murmured Latin in a very solemn voice and tickled her feet.[3] My God, will you stop that nonsense? I'm a married woman. What if he did run away and leave me to face the priest by myself? I found another a whole world better. I wouldn't have exchanged my husband for anybody except St. Michael[4] himself, and you may tell him that for me with a thank you in the bargain.

57   Light flashed on her closed eyelids, and a deep roaring shook her. Cornelia, is that lightning? I hear thunder. There's going to be a storm. Close all the windows. Call the children in. . . . "Mother, here we are, all of us." "Is that you, Hapsy?" "Oh, no. I'm Lydia. We drove as fast as we could." Their faces drifted above her, drifted away. The rosary fell out of her hands and Lydia put it back. Jimmy tried to help, their hands fumbled together, and Granny closed two fingers around Jimmy's thumb. Beads wouldn't do, it must be something alive. She was so amazed her thoughts ran round and round. So, my dear Lord, this is my death and I wasn't even thinking about it. My children have come to see me die. But I can't, it's not time. Oh, I always hated surprises. I wanted to give Cornelia the amethyst set—Cornelia, you're to have the amethyst set, but Hapsy's to wear it when she wants, and, Doctor Harry, do shut up. Nobody sent for you. Oh, my dear Lord, do wait a minute. I meant to do something about the Forty Acres, Jimmy doesn't need it and Lydia will later on, with that worthless husband of hers. I meant to finish the altar cloth and send six bottles of wine to Sister Borgia for her **dyspepsia**. I want to send six bottles of wine to Sister Borgia, Father Connolly, now don't let me forget.

58   Cornelia's voice made short turns and tilted over and crashed. "Oh, Mother, oh, Mother, oh Mother. . . ."

59   "I'm not going, Cornelia. I'm taken by surprise. I can't go."

60   You'll see Hapsy again. What about her? "I thought you'd never come." Granny made a long journey outward, looking for Hapsy. What if I don't find her? What then? Her heart sank down and down, there was no bottom to death, she couldn't come to the end of it. The blue light from Cornelia's lampshade drew into a tiny point in the center of her brain, it flickered and winked like an eye, quietly it fluttered and dwindled. Granny lay curled down within herself, amazed and watchful, staring at the point of light that was herself; her body was now only a deeper mass of shadow in an endless darkness and this darkness would curl around the light and swallow it up. God, give a sign!

Mark familiar word parts or indicate another strategy you used that helped you determine meaning.

dyspepsia (dihs PEHP see uh) n.

MEANING:

---

3. **murmured . . . feet** administered the last rites of the Catholic Church.
4. **St. Michael** one of the archangels.

61 For the second time there was no sign. Again no bridegroom and the priest in the house. She could not remember any other sorrow because this grief wiped them all away. Oh, no, there's nothing more cruel than this—I'll never forgive it. She stretched herself with a deep breath and blew out the light. ❧

Comprehension Check

Complete the following items after you finish your first read. Review and clarify details with your group.

1. Where is Granny Weatherall as she speaks to the doctor?

2. Who is taking care of Granny Weatherall as she is dying?

3. What journey did Granny Weatherall take when she was sixty years old?

4. What happened to Granny Weatherall sixty years earlier?

5. What does Granny Weatherall want George to know?

6. 🗒 **Notebook** Confirm your understanding of the text by writing a summary.

- -

RESEARCH

Research to Clarify Choose at least one unfamiliar detail from the text. Briefly research that detail. In what way does the information you learned shed light on an aspect of the story?

Research to Explore Conduct research on an aspect of the text you find interesting. For example, you may want to learn about doctors' house calls—why they once were a widespread practice, why they are less common today, and whether they might again become popular. Share your findings with your group.

Close Read the Text

With your group, revisit sections of the text you marked during your first read. **Annotate** details that you notice. What **questions** do you have? What can you **conclude**?

THE JILTING OF
GRANNY WEATHERALL

Analyze the Text

> **CITE TEXTUAL EVIDENCE**
> to support your answers.

Complete the activities.

1. **Review and Clarify** With your group, reread the sections of the story that describe Hapsy (paragraphs 41, 50, and 57–60). Discuss her role in Granny Weatherall's thoughts. Why do you think Hapsy is such an important figure for Granny Weatherall?

2. **Present and Discuss** Now, work with your group to share the passages from the selection that you found especially important. Take turns presenting your passages. Discuss what you noticed in the story, what questions you asked, and what conclusions you reached.

3. **Essential Question:** *What do stories reveal about the human condition?* What has this story taught you about life and loss? Discuss with your group.

> **TIP**
>
> **GROUP DISCUSSION**
> Granny Weatherall's jumbled thoughts concern the past and the present. As you discuss the story, cite textual evidence to support your interpretation of when the events are taking place.

LANGUAGE DEVELOPMENT

Concept Vocabulary

hypodermic	clammy	dyspepsia

Why These Words? The three concept vocabulary words from the text are related. With your group, determine what the words have in common. Write your ideas, and add another word that fits the category.

Practice

Confirm your understanding of the concept vocabulary words by using them in a short conversation with your group members. If you are unsure about the exact meaning of a word, look it up in a print or online college-level dictionary before you begin.

Word Study

Greek Prefix: *dys-* In "The Jilting of Granny Weatherall," Granny Weatherall thinks about Sister Borgia's *dyspepsia*. This word includes the Greek prefix *dys-*, meaning "bad" or "difficult." This prefix often appears in scientific terms involving medical or psychological diagnoses. Use a dictionary or online resource to identify three other words that have this prefix. Write the words and their meanings. Explain how the meaning of the prefix contributes to the meaning of each word.

> **WORD NETWORK**
> Add words related to the human condition from the text to your Word Network.

> **STANDARDS**
> **Language**
> Identify and correctly use patterns of word changes that indicate different meanings or parts of speech.

THE JILTING OF
GRANNY WEATHERALL

Analyze Craft and Structure

Author's Choices: Narrative Structure People's thoughts do not flow in neat patterns. Instead, they move unpredictably among perceptions, memories, and ideas. During the early 1900s, some writers began using a literary device called **stream of consciousness** to try to re-create a sense of the disjointed, natural flow of thought. Stream-of-consciousness narratives feature the following qualities:

- They present sequences of thought as if they were coming directly from a character's mind. The thoughts may or may not be complete or relate to one another.

- They tend to omit punctuation and transitions that appear in more traditional prose.

Stream-of-consciousness narratives often involve the use of **flashback,** a scene from the past that interrupts the present action of a story. A flashback may take the form of a memory, a story, a dream or daydream, or a switch by the narrator to a time in the past. Stream-of-consciousness stories may also involve shifts in the **narrative point of view,** or the perspective from which events are told. In this story, Porter's third-person narrator essentially disappears into Granny Weatherall's first-person narration.

Practice

📓 **Notebook** Work with your group to answer the questions.

1. Use the chart to identify two points at which Granny's thoughts shift from one subject to another without an obvious transition. What associations might connect her thoughts in each of these examples?

THOUGHT OR MEMORY	TRIGGERING DETAIL	NEXT THOUGHT OR MEMORY

2. **(a)** What details trigger Granny's flashback to lighting the lamps when the children were young? **(b)** What is the connection between the flashback and her experience in the present?

3. Analyze two other flashbacks in the story. **(a)** Identify the form the flashback takes (i.e., dream, memory, etc.). **(b)** Explain what you learn from each flashback about Granny's life.

4. **(a)** What qualities does the use of stream-of-consciousness narration, flashback, and shifting narrative point of view lend to the story? **(b)** Overall, do you think these techniques are effective for the telling of this particular tale? Explain.

📋 **STANDARDS**

Reading Literature
Analyze how an author's choices concerning how to structure specific parts of a text contribute to its overall structure and meaning as well as its aesthetic impact.

Author's Style

Author's Choices: Figurative Language Literary works almost always contain two broad types of language—literal and figurative. Literal language means what it says, conveying information, ideas, and feelings in a direct way. **Figurative language,** by contrast, is language that is used imaginatively and expresses more than its literal meanings. Two common types of figurative language are metaphors and similes.

- A **metaphor** is a direct comparison between two apparently unlike things.

  Example: *Doctor Harry spread a warm* paw . . . *on her forehead. . . .* (paragraph 2)

- A **simile** is a comparison between two apparently unlike things made using an explicit comparison word such as *like, as, than,* or *resembles.*

  Example: *The pillow rose and floated under her, pleasant as a hammock in a light wind.* (paragraph 8)

Porter uses these devices to show how Granny Weatherall makes connections in her mind as she begins to lose her connection to reality.

STANDARDS

Reading Literature
Determine the meaning of words and phrases as they are used in the text, including figurative and connotative meanings; analyze the impact of specific word choices on meaning and tone, including words with multiple meanings or language that is particularly fresh, engaging, or beautiful.

Language
Demonstrate understanding of figurative language, word relationships, and nuances in word meanings.

Read It

1. Work individually. Use this chart to identify the simile or metaphor in each passage from "The Jilting of Granny Weatherall."

PASSAGE	METAPHOR OR SIMILE	EFFECT
Her bones felt loose, and floated around in her skin, and Doctor Harry floated like a balloon around the foot of the bed. (paragraph 6)		
Cornelia's voice staggered and bumped like a cart in a bad road. (paragraph 56)		
Things were finished somehow when the time came; thank God there was always a little margin over for peace: then a person could spread out the plan of life and tuck in the edges orderly. (paragraph 17)		

2. **Connect to Style** With your group, discuss how the author's use of simile and metaphor affects what you envision as you read each of the passages in the chart.

Write It

Notebook Write a paragraph in which you describe what you learned about the human condition from "The Jilting of Granny Weatherall." Use at least one simile and one metaphor to make your language more vivid and interesting.

AN OCCURRENCE AT
OWL CREEK BRIDGE

THE JILTING OF
GRANNY WEATHERALL

Writing to Compare

You have read two classic American stories that employ nonlinear narrative techniques: "An Occurrence at Owl Creek Bridge" and "The Jilting of Granny Weatherall." Now, deepen your understanding of both stories by comparing them and sharing your analysis in a group presentation.

Assignment

Prepare and deliver an **oral presentation** in which you compare and contrast how stream-of-consciousness narration works in the two stories you have studied. During your presentation, include dramatic readings of relevant passages to highlight important features of the stream-of-consciousness technique. End your presentation by drawing conclusions about the strengths and limitations of this literary device. Then, hold a brief question-and-answer session with your audience.

Planning

Define the Term Work with your group to craft a definition of stream of consciousness. Complete this sentence.

Stream of consciousness is _____

_____

_____

Analyze the Texts Review the stories individually, looking for passages that illustrate specific features of stream-of-consciousness narration. Use the chart to gather your ideas. Then, work together as a group to select examples that best reveal similarities and differences between the two stories. Aim to include at least two passages from each story.

	PROPOSED PASSAGE	QUALITY OR EFFECT IT SHOWS
An Occurrence at Owl Creek Bridge		
The Jilting of Granny Weatherall		

Organize the Presentation

Outline the Content Your presentation should include these elements:

- a formal introduction in which you define stream of consciousness
- explanations of at least two effects of stream-of-consciousness narration
- dramatic readings from the stories that provide strong examples of each effect and reveal similarities and differences between the two works
- a memorable conclusion
- a lively question-and-answer session

With your group, follow this outline frame to plan an effective sequence. Decide how you will transition from explanations to examples.

> **Outline Frame**
>
> 1. **Introduction:** Define stream-of-consciousness narration.
>
> 2 **Present Point 1:** Explain one effect of stream-of-consciousness narration. *Deliver readings:* Read passages from each story that show similarities and differences in how this quality appears in the two stories.
>
> 3. **Present Point 2:** Explain a second effect of stream-of-consciousness narration. *Deliver readings:* Read passages from each story that show similarities and differences in how this quality appears in the two stories.
>
> 4. **Conclusion:** Explain what makes stream-of-consciousness narration effective in the two stories under discussion.
>
> 5. **Question & Answer Session**

Assign Tasks and Write Some of the sections of your presentation need to be written ahead of time, whereas others simply need preparation. Decide whether you will work together to draft or prepare for each section, or whether you will assign the different tasks to individual group members.

Annotate Passages and Rehearse An annotated reading script will help you deliver dramatic readings with power and expression. Copy the passages exactly and practice reading them aloud several times, trying different approaches. The following annotations can help you remember the best choices.

/ = brief pause	// = longer pause
underscore = emphasis	double underscore = strong emphasis
!!! = speed up	XXX = slow down

Deliver the Presentation

Keep the following points in mind as you give your oral presentation:

- Do not keep your eyes glued to the page during the dramatic readings. Instead, look up to make a connection with your audience.
- Speak clearly and avoid either rushing or speaking too slowly.

During the final question-and-answer session, share the responsibility of answering. If your audience is reluctant to speak, pose and answer questions that they might find interesting.

📝 EVIDENCE LOG

Before moving on to a new selection, go to your Evidence Log and record what you learned from "An Occurrence at Owl Creek Bridge" and "The Jilting of Granny Weatherall."

SOURCES

- A BRIEF HISTORY OF THE SHORT STORY

- AN OCCURRENCE AT OWL CREEK BRIDGE

- THE JILTING OF GRANNY WEATHERALL

Present a Narrative

Assignment

You have read a history of the short story, and you have read and compared two short stories that feature stream-of-consciousness narration. Review how the technique is used in short stories. Then, work with your group to plan, present, and video-record a **stream-of-consciousness narrative** that responds to this statement:

> **The day felt as if it would never end.**

Form teams and work together to find examples from the texts to help you write. Then, present your video narrative for the class.

Plan With Your Group

Analyze the Text Divide into two subgroups. One will analyze stream-of-consciousness techniques within one of the selections; the other group will analyze the other selection. Decide which techniques your group will use in your narrative.

TITLE	WHICH CHARACTERS ARE REVEALED THROUGH STREAM OF CONSCIOUSNESS? HOW?
An Occurrence at Owl Creek Bridge	
The Jilting of Granny Weatherall	

The best examples of the techniques are:

Draft Your Narrative With your group, plan your narrative, roughing out the plot and characters. Identify the main conflict, and decide how it will be resolved. Then, work on incorporating stream-of-consciousness techniques into the story.

Plan Use of Media Consider how to make the best use of the digital media available to you. With your group, discuss graphics, audio, or visual elements you will use to help viewers better understand your stream-of-consciousness video.

STANDARDS

Speaking and Listening
Propel conversations by posing and responding to questions that probe reasoning and evidence; ensure a hearing for a full range of positions on a topic or issue; clarify, verify, or challenge ideas and conclusions; and promote divergent and creative perspectives.

Organize Your Presentation Decide how your group will convert your story into a script and then a video. Create a detailed storyboard. Make sure that your stream-of-consciousness techniques are visually represented. Make a plan for presenting your narrative by answering questions such as these: How many different characters are in your video? How will you divide the technical tasks? Use this chart to organize tasks.

Rehearse With Your Group

Practice With Your Group As you act out your narrative, use this checklist to evaluate the effectiveness of your group's first run-through. Then, use your evaluation and the instructions here to guide your revision.

CONTENT	USE OF MEDIA	PRESENTATION TECHNIQUES
☐ The narrative relates to the prompt.	☐ Digital media is used effectively to aid understanding and create interest.	☐ Actors speak clearly, with appropriate emotion.
☐ Stream-of-consciousness techniques are used in the narrative.		☐ Actors seem well prepared.

Film the Narrative When you are satisfied with your narrative, find a quiet place to film it using a recorder or smart phone. Depending on your equipment, you may want to film several versions before deciding on the one you want to share. If desired, you may want to use digital effects to enhance the presentation.

Present and Evaluate

Present your video to the class, and invite feedback. As you watch other groups' videos, evaluate how well they meet the requirements on the checklist.

⠿ STANDARDS
Writing
• Write narratives to develop real or imagined experiences or events using well-chosen details, and well-structured event sequences.
• Use narrative techniques, such as dialogue, pacing, description, reflection, and multiple plot lines, to develop experiences, events, and/or characters.

ESSENTIAL QUESTION:

What do stories reveal about the human condition?

Some situations are shaped by changes in society, but many aspects of human life are timeless. In this section, you will complete your study of short stories and the human condition by exploring an additional selection related to the topic. You'll then share what you learn with classmates. To choose a text, follow these steps.

Look Back Think about the selections you have already studied. What more do you want to know about short stories and the insights they provide?

Look Ahead Preview the texts by reading the descriptions. Which one seems most interesting and appealing to you?

Look Inside Take a few minutes to scan the text you chose. Choose a different one if this text doesn't meet your needs.

Independent Learning Strategies

Throughout your life, in school, in your community, and in your career, you will need to rely on yourself to learn and work on your own. Review these strategies and the actions you can take to practice them during Independent Learning. Add ideas of your own for each category.

STRATEGY	ACTION PLAN
Create a schedule	• Understand your goals and deadlines. • Make a plan for what to do each day. •
Practice what you have learned	• Use first-read and close-read strategies to deepen your understanding. • After you read, evaluate the usefulness of the evidence to help you understand the topic. • Consider the quality and reliability of the source. •
Take notes	• Record important ideas and information. • Review your notes before preparing to share with a group. •

SCAN FOR
MULTIMEDIA

CONTENTS

Choose one selection. Selections are available online only.

PERFORMANCE-BASED ASSESSMENT PREP

Review Notes for a Narrative

Complete your Evidence Log for the unit by evaluating what you have learned and synthesizing the information you have recorded.

SCAN FOR MULTIMEDIA

First-Read Guide

Use this page to record your first-read ideas.

Selection Title: _____

🔧 Tool Kit
First-Read Guide and
Model Annotation

NOTICE new information or ideas you learn about the unit topic as you first read this text.

ANNOTATE by marking vocabulary and key passages you want to revisit.

First Read

CONNECT ideas within the selection to other knowledge and the selections you have read.

RESPOND by writing a brief summary of the selection.

⊞ STANDARD
Reading Read and comprehend complex literary and informational texts independently and proficiently.

Close-Read Guide

Use this page to record your close-read ideas.

Selection Title: _____

 Tool Kit
Close-Read Guide and
Model Annotation

Close Read the Text

Revisit sections of the text you marked during your first read. Read these sections closely and **annotate** what you notice. Ask yourself **questions** about the text. What can you **conclude**? Write down your ideas.

Analyze the Text

Think about the author's choices of patterns, structure, techniques, and ideas included in the text. Select one and record your thoughts about what this choice conveys.

QuickWrite

Pick a paragraph from the text that grabbed your interest. Explain the power of this passage.

_____

_____

_____

_____

_____

_____

_____

▦ STANDARD
Reading Read and comprehend complex literary and informational texts independently and proficiently.

Share Your Independent Learning

Prepare to Share

What do stories reveal about the human condition?

Even when you read something independently, you can continue to grow by sharing what you have learned with others. Reflect on the text you explored independently, and write notes about its connection to the unit. In your notes, consider why this text belongs in this unit.

Learn From Your Classmates

Discuss It Share your ideas about the text you explored on your own. As you talk with your classmates, jot down ideas that you learn from them.

Reflect

Review your notes, and mark the most important insight you gained from these writing and discussion activities. Explain how this idea adds to your understanding of the importance of stories as they reveal the human condition.

Review Notes for a Narrative

At the beginning of this unit, you expressed a point of view about the following question:

> **How does a fictional character or characters respond to life-changing news?**

✎ EVIDENCE LOG

Review your Evidence Log and your QuickWrite from the beginning of the unit. Have your ideas changed?

☐ YES	☐ NO
Identify at least three textual details that caused you to alter your ideas.	Identify at least three textual details that reinforced your original ideas.
1.	**1.**
2.	**2.**
3.	**3.**

Give one example of life-changing news that might affect someone strongly:

_____

_____

Give one example of a way in which someone might react to that news:

_____

_____

Evaluate the Strength of Your Content Do you have enough content to write your narrative? Do you have enough details to develop multiple characters? If not, make a plan.

☐ Do research about short stories ☐ Talk with my classmates

☐ Reread a selection ☐ Ask a fiction writer

☐ Other:_____

SOURCES

- WHOLE-CLASS SELECTIONS
- SMALL-GROUP SELECTIONS
- INDEPENDENT-LEARNING SELECTION

PART 1
Writing to Sources: Narrative

In this unit, you read a variety of texts in which ordinary lives prove to contain extraordinary moments. You met characters who encounter stressful, unexpected, or life-changing situations. In each case, characters' responses reveal their strengths and weaknesses, as well as their hopes and fears. By reading stories about fictional characters, you may have learned something useful about what it means to be human.

Assignment

Write a **short story** in which you introduce and develop a protagonist, and set up a problem or conflict the character must face. Use the third-person point of view. Before you write, think about your answer to this question:

> ### How does a fictional character or characters respond to life-changing news?

As your character faces conflicts, how does he or she respond? Will your character's response be instructive to readers? If so, how? If not, why not? What will your character learn, and in what ways will he or she change? Bring your character's story to a resolution or epiphany that demonstrates a truth about the human condition.

Reread the Assignment Review the assignment to be sure you fully understand it. The task may reference some of the academic words presented at the beginning of the unit. Be sure you understand each of the words given below in order to complete the assignment correctly.

Academic Vocabulary

colloquial	tension	epiphany
protagonist	resolution	

Review the Elements of a Narrative Before you begin writing, read the Narrative Rubric. Once you have completed your first draft, check it against the rubric. If one or more of the elements is missing or not as strong as it could be, revise your narrative to add or strengthen that component.

WORD NETWORK

As you write and revise your narrative, use your Word Network to help vary your word choices.

STANDARDS

Writing
• Write narratives to develop real or imagined experiences or events using effective technique, well-chosen details, and well-structured event sequences.
• Write routinely over extended time frames and shorter time frames for a range of tasks, purposes, and audiences.

Narrative Rubric

	Focus and Organization	Technique and Development	Language Conventions
4	The introduction engages the reader and introduces original characters and conflict. The narrative establishes an engrossing sequence of events that unfolds smoothly and logically. The conclusion follows from and resolves the narrative in a satisfying way.	The narrative adeptly incorporates dialogue and description. Precise details and sensory language give the reader a clear picture of events.	The narrative consistently uses conventions of standard English usage and mechanics.
3	The introduction is somewhat engaging and introduces characters and conflict. The narrative establishes a sequence of events that unfolds smoothly and logically. The conclusion follows from and resolves the narrative.	Dialogue and description move the narrative forward. Some precise details and sensory language give the reader a picture of events.	The narrative demonstrates accuracy in conventions of standard English usage and mechanics.
2	The introduction introduces characters and conflict. Events are mostly in sequence, but some events may not belong or may be omitted. The conclusion follows from the narrative.	Some dialogue or description may appear. Some details give the reader a general picture of events.	The narrative demonstrates some accuracy in conventions of standard English usage and mechanics.
1	The introduction fails to introduce characters and conflict, or there is no introduction. Events are not in a clear sequence, and some events may be omitted. The conclusion does not follow from the narrative, or there is no conclusion.	Dialogue and description do not appear or are minimal and seem to appear as afterthoughts. Few details are included, or details fail to give the reader a picture of events.	The narrative contains mistakes in conventions of standard English usage and mechanics.

PART 2

Speaking and Listening: Storytelling Session

Assignment

After completing your narrative, conduct a **storytelling session** for your class. Memorize the key plot points, character descriptions, and most important lines of dialogue from your story. You may refer to some notes as you tell your story, but do not read aloud. When you address your audience, remember to use appropriate eye contact, adequate volume, and clear pronunciation.

Select digital audio to add interest and enhance the mood of your story. Consider using sound effects, background music, or an instrumental musical score to accompany your story.

To be an effective storyteller, consider the following:

- Keep it simple. What can you cut from your written narrative while retaining the gist of the story?
- Pump up the emotion. How can music and sound cues affect your audience and improve their listening experience?

Review the Rubric Before you tell your story, check your plans against this rubric. If one or more of the elements is missing or not as strong as it could be, revise your presentation.

STANDARDS

Speaking and Listening
Make strategic use of digital media in presentations to enhance understanding of findings, reasoning, and evidence and to add interest.

	Content	Use of Media	Presentation Techniques
3	The storyteller engages the audience by describing original characters, conflict, and resolution.	Included media have a positive impact on listener experience.	The speaker's word choice, volume, pitch, and eye contact reflect the story's content and are appropriate to the audience.
2	The storyteller describes characters, conflict, and resolution.	Included media neither improve nor detract from listener experience.	The speaker's word choice, volume, pitch, and eye contact somewhat reflect the story's content and are appropriate to the audience.
1	The storyteller's presentation is flat and dull, or the sequence of events is hard to follow.	Included media are distracting or otherwise detract from listener experience.	The speaker's word choice, volume, pitch, and eye contact do not reflect the story's content and are not appropriate to the audience.

Reflect on the Unit

Now that you've completed the unit, take a few moments to reflect on your learning. Use the questions below to think about where you succeeded, what skills and strategies helped you, and where you can continue to grow in the future.

Reflect on the Unit Goals

Look back at the goals at the beginning of the unit. Use a different colored pen to rate yourself again. Think about readings and activities that contributed the most to the growth of your understanding. Record your thoughts.

Reflect on the Learning Strategies

Discuss It Write a reflection on whether you were able to improve your learning based on your Action Plans. Think about what worked, what didn't, and what you might do to keep working on these strategies. Record your ideas before joining a class discussion.

Reflect on the Text

Choose a selection that you found challenging, and explain what made it difficult.

Explain something that surprised you about a text in the unit.

Which activity taught you the most about how stories reveal the human condition? What did you learn?

STANDARDS

Speaking and Listening
Come to discussions prepared, having read and researched material under study; explicitly draw on that preparation by referring to evidence from texts and other research on the topic or issue to stimulate a thoughtful, well-reasoned exchange of ideas.

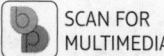
SCAN FOR MULTIMEDIA

RESOURCES

CONTENTS

Marking the Text: Strategies and Tips for Annotation

When you close read a text, you read for comprehension and then reread to unlock layers of meaning and to analyze a writer's style and techniques. Marking a text as you read it enables you to participate more fully in the close-reading process.

Following are some strategies for text mark-ups, along with samples of how the strategies can be applied. These mark-ups are suggestions; you and your teacher may want to use other mark-up strategies.

✱	Key Idea
!	I love it!
?	I have questions
◯	Unfamiliar or important word
----	Context Clues

Suggested Mark-Up Notations

WHAT I NOTICE	HOW TO MARK UP	QUESTIONS TO ASK
Key Ideas and Details	• Highlight key ideas or claims. • Underline supporting details or evidence.	• What does the text say? What does it leave unsaid? • What inferences do you need to make? • What details lead you to make your inferences?
Word Choice	• Circle unfamiliar words. • Put a dotted line under context clues, if any exist. • Put an exclamation point beside especially rich or poetic passages.	• What inferences about word meaning can you make? • What tone and mood are created by word choice? • What alternate word choices might the author have made?
Text Structure	• Highlight passages that show key details supporting the main idea. • Use arrows to indicate how sentences and paragraphs work together to build ideas. • Use a right-facing arrow to indicate foreshadowing. • Use a left-facing arrow to indicate flashback.	• Is the text logically structured? • What emotional impact do the structural choices create?
Author's Craft	• Circle or highlight instances of repetition, either of words, phrases, consonants, or vowel sounds. • Mark rhythmic beats in poetry using checkmarks and slashes. • Underline instances of symbolism or figurative language.	• Does the author's style enrich or detract from the reading experience? • What levels of meaning are created by the author's techniques?

TOOL KIT: CLOSE READING

CLOSE READING

First Read

* Key Idea
! I love it!
? I have questions
◯ Unfamiliar or important word
---- Context Clues

NOTES

In a first read, work to get a sense of the main idea of a text. Look for key details and ideas that help you understand what the author conveys to you. Mark passages which prompt a strong response from you.

Here is how one reader marked up this text.

MODEL

INFORMATIONAL TEXT

from Classifying the Stars

Cecilia H. Payne

1   *   Sunlight and starlight are composed of waves of various lengths, which the eye, even aided by a telescope, is unable to separate. We must use more than a telescope. In order to sort out the **?** component colors, the light must be dispersed by a prism, or split up by some other means. For instance, sunbeams passing through rain drops, are transformed into the myriad-tinted rainbow. **!** The familiar rainbow spanning the sky is Nature's most glorious demonstration that light is composed of many colors.

2   *   The very beginning of our knowledge of the nature of a star dates back to 1672, when Isaac Newton gave to the world the results of his experiments on passing sunlight through a prism. To describe the beautiful band of rainbow tints, produced when sunlight was dispersed by his three-cornered piece of glass, he took from the Latin the word *spectrum*, meaning an appearance. The rainbow is the spectrum of the Sun. . . .

3   *   In 1814, more than a century after Newton, the spectrum of the Sun was obtained in such purity that an amazing detail was seen and studied by the German optician, Fraunhofer. He saw that the multiple spectral tints, ranging from delicate violet to deep red, were crossed by hundreds of fine dark lines. In other words, there were narrow gaps in the spectrum where certain shades were wholly blotted out. We must remember that the word spectrum is applied not only to sunlight, but also to the light of any glowing substance when its rays are sorted out by a prism or a grating.

MODEL

First-Read Guide

Use this page to record your first-read ideas.

You may want to use a guide like this to organize your thoughts after you read. Here is how a reader completed a First-Read Guide.

Selection Title: _____Classifying the Stars_____

NOTICE

NOTICE new information or ideas you learned about the unit topic as you first read this text.

Light = different waves of colors. (Spectrum)

Newton - the first person to observe these waves using a prism.

Faunhofer saw gaps in the spectrum.

ANNOTATE

ANNOTATE by marking vocabulary and key passages you want to revisit.

Vocabulary
   myriad
   grating
   component colors

Different light types = different lengths

Isaac Newton also worked theories of gravity.

<u>Multiple spectral tints?</u> "colors of various appearance"

Key Passage:
Paragraph 3 shows that Fraunhofer discovered more about the nature of light spectrums: he saw the spaces in between the tints.

First Read

CONNECT

CONNECT ideas within the selection to other knowledge and the selections you have read.

I remember learning about prisms in science class.

Double rainbows! My favorite. How are they made?

RESPOND

RESPOND by writing a brief summary of the selection.

Science allows us to see things not visible to the naked eye. What we see as sunlight is really a spectrum of colors. By using tools, such as prisms, we can see the components of sunlight and other light. They appear as single colors or as multiple colors separated by gaps of no color. White light contains a rainbow of colors.

TOOL KIT: CLOSE READING

CLOSE READING

* Key Idea
! I love it!
? I have questions
◯ Unfamiliar or important word
---- Context Clues

In a close read, go back into the text to study it in greater detail. Take the time to analyze not only the author's ideas but the way that those ideas are conveyed. Consider the genre of the text, the author's word choice, the writer's unique style, and the message of the text.

Here is how one reader close read this text.

MODEL

INFORMATIONAL TEXT

from Classifying the Stars

Cecilia H. Payne

NOTES

explanation of sunlight and starlight

1 Sunlight and starlight are composed of waves of various lengths, which the eye, even aided by a telescope, is unable to separate. We must use more than a telescope. In order to sort out the component colors, the light must be dispersed by a prism, or split up by some other means. For instance, sunbeams passing through rain drops, are transformed into the myriad-tinted rainbow. The familiar rainbow spanning the sky is Nature's most glorious demonstration that light is composed of many colors.

What is light and where do the colors come from?

This paragraph is about Newton and the prism.

2 The very beginning of our knowledge of the nature of a star dates back to 1672, when Isaac Newton gave to the world the results of his experiments on passing sunlight through a prism. To describe the beautiful band of rainbow tints, produced when sunlight was dispersed by his three-cornered piece of glass, he took from the Latin the word *spectrum*, meaning an appearance. The rainbow is the spectrum of the Sun. . . .

What discoveries helped us understand light?

Fraunhofer and gaps in spectrum

3 In 1814, more than a century after Newton, the spectrum of the Sun was obtained in such purity that an amazing detail was seen and studied by the German optician, Fraunhofer. He saw that the multiple spectral tints, ranging from delicate violet to deep red, were crossed by hundreds of fine dark lines. In other words, there were narrow gaps in the spectrum where certain shades were wholly blotted out. We must remember that the word spectrum is applied not only to sunlight, but also to the light of any glowing substance when its rays are sorted out by a prism or a grating.

Close-Read Guide

Use this page to record your close-read ideas.

Selection Title: _Classifying the Stars_

You can use the Close-Read Guide to help you dig deeper into the text. Here is how a reader completed a Close-Read Guide.

Close Read the Text

Revisit sections of the text you marked during your first read. Read these sections closely and **annotate** what you notice. Ask yourself **questions** about the text. What can you **conclude?** Write down your ideas.

Paragraph 3: Light is composed of waves of various lengths. Prisms let us see different colors in light. This is called the spectrum. Fraunhofer proved that there are gaps in the spectrum, where certain shades are blotted out.

More than one researcher studied this and each built off the ideas that were already discovered.

Analyze the Text

Think about the author's choices of patterns, structure, techniques, and ideas included in the text. Select one, and record your thoughts about what this choice conveys.

The author showed the development of human knowledge of the spectrum chronologically. Helped me see how ideas were built upon earlier understandings. Used dates and "more than a century after Newton" to show time.

QuickWrite

Pick a paragraph from the text that grabbed your interest. Explain the power of this passage.

The first paragraph grabbed my attention, specifically the sentence "The familiar rainbow spanning the sky is Nature's most glorious demonstration that light is composed of many colors." The paragraph began as a straightforward scientific explanation. When I read the word "glorious," I had to stop and deeply consider what was being said. It is a word loaded with personal feelings. With that one word, the author let the reader know what was important to her.

TOOL KIT: CLOSE READING

CLOSE READING

Analyzing Legal Meanings and Reasoning

Reading historical and legal texts requires careful analysis of both the vocabulary and the logical flow of ideas that support a conclusion.

NOTES

Understanding Legal Meanings

The language of historical and legal documents is formal, precise, and technical. Many words in these texts have specific meanings that you need to understand in order to follow the flow of ideas. For example, the second amendment to the U.S. Constitution states that "A well regulated Militia being necessary to the security of a free State, the right of the people to keep and bear Arms shall not be infringed." To understand this amendment, it is important to know that in this context *militia* means "armed forces," *bear* means "carry," and *infringed* means "denied." To understand legal meanings:

- Use your knowledge of word roots to help you understand unfamiliar words. Many legal terms use familiar Greek or Latin roots, prefixes, or suffixes.

- Do not assume that you know a word's legal meaning: Use a dictionary to check the meanings of key words to be certain that you are applying the correct meaning.

- Paraphrase the text to aid comprehension. Replace difficult words with synonyms to make sure you follow the logic of the argument.

Delineating Legal Reasoning

Works of public advocacy, such as court decisions, political proclamations, proposed laws, or constitutional amendments, use careful reasoning to support conclusions. These strategies can help you understand the legal reasoning in an argument:

- State the **purpose** of the document in your own words to help you focus on the writer's primary goal.

- Look for the line of reasoning that supports the **arguments** presented. To be valid and persuasive, key arguments should be backed up by clearly stated logical analysis. Be aware of persuasive techniques, such as citing facts and statistics, referring to expert testimonials, and using emotional language with strong connotations.

- Identify the **premises,** or evidence, upon which a decision rests. In legal texts, premises often include **precedents,** which are earlier examples that must be followed or specifically overturned. Legal reasoning is usually based on the decisions of earlier trials. Be sure you understand precedents in order to identify how the court arrived at the current decision.

Note the strategies used to evaluate legal meanings and reasoning in this Supreme Court decision from 1954 regarding the legality of segregated, "separate but equal" schools for students of different races.

LEGAL TEXT

from *Brown v. Board of Education of Topeka*, Opinion of the Supreme Court by Chief Justice Earl Warren

We come then to the question presented: Does segregation of children in public schools solely on the basis of race, even though the physical facilities and other "tangible" factors may be equal, deprive the children of the minority group of equal educational opportunities? We believe that it does.

In *Sweatt v. Painter*, in finding that a segregated law school for Negroes could not provide them equal educational opportunities, this Court relied in large part on "those qualities which are incapable of objective measurement but which make for greatness in a law school." In *McLaurin v. Oklahoma State Regents*, the Court, in requiring that a Negro admitted to a white graduate school be treated like all other students, again resorted to intangible considerations: ". . . his ability to study, to engage in discussions and exchange views with other students, and, in general, to learn his profession." Such considerations apply with added force to children in grade and high schools. To separate them from others of similar age and qualifications solely because of their race generates a feeling of inferiority as to their status in the community that may affect their hearts and minds in a way unlikely ever to be undone. The effect of this separation on their educational opportunities was well stated by a finding in the Kansas case by a court which nevertheless felt compelled to rule against the Negro plaintiffs: Segregation of white and colored children in public schools has a detrimental effect upon the colored children. The impact is greater when it has the sanction of the law, for the policy of separating the races is usually interpreted as denoting the inferiority of the negro group. A sense of inferiority affects the motivation of a child to learn. Segregation with the sanction of law, therefore, has a tendency to [retard] the educational and mental development of negro children and to deprive them of some of the benefits they would receive in a racially integrated school system. Whatever may have been the extent of psychological knowledge at the time of *Plessy v. Ferguson*, this finding is amply supported by modern authority. Any language in *Plessy v. Ferguson* contrary to this finding is rejected.

We conclude that, in the field of public education, the doctrine of "separate but equal" has no place. Separate educational facilities are inherently unequal.

Use Word Roots The word *tangible* comes from the Latin root meaning "to touch." In this decision, the court contrasts tangible, measurable features with intangible features that are difficult to measure.

Identify the Premises The court cites two precedents: earlier cases relating to unequal education opportunities for black students.

Paraphrase the Text Here's one way you might break down the ideas in this sentence when you paraphrase: Segregating students just because of their race makes them feel as if they are less valued by our society. This separation can have a permanent negative influence on their character.

Line of Reasoning The conclusion makes the **purpose** of the decision clear: to overturn the precedent established by *Plessy v. Ferguson*. The **argument** describes the reasons the Court no longer considers the reasoning in that earlier case to be valid.

TOOL KIT: CLOSE READING

WRITING

Argument

When you think of the word *argument*, you might think of a disagreement between two people, but an argument is more than that. An argument is a logical way of presenting a belief, conclusion, or stance. A good argument is supported with reasoning and evidence.

Argument writing can be used for many purposes, such as to change a reader's point of view or opinion or to bring about an action or a response from a reader.

Elements of an Argumentative Text

An **argument** is a logical way of presenting a viewpoint, belief, or stand on an issue. A well-written argument may convince the reader, change the reader's mind, or motivate the reader to take a certain action.

An effective argument contains these elements:

- a precise claim
- consideration of counterclaims, or opposing positions, and a discussion of their strengths and weaknesses
- logical organization that makes clear connections among claim, counterclaim, reasons, and evidence
- valid reasoning and evidence
- a concluding statement or section that logically completes the argument
- formal and objective language and tone
- error-free grammar, including accurate use of transitions

ARGUMENT: SCORE 1

Community Service Should be a Requirement for High School Graduation

Volunteering is a great idea for high school students. Those who don't volunteer are missing out.

You can learn a lot at your volunteer job. It might not seem like a big deal at the time, but the things you learn and do can be useful. You might volunteer somewhere with a spreadsheet. Everyone needs to know how to use a spreadsheet! That's going to be a useful again really soon.

Their lots of reasons to get involved. One of them is to become a better student in school. Also, to feel better about yourself and not act out so much.

So, volunteering helps you learn and get better at lots of things, not just what you are doing at your volunteer job. It's good not just to learn reading and writing and math and science all the time—the usual stuff we study in school. That's how volunteering can help you out.

Students today are really busy and they can't add anything more to they're busy schedules. But I think they can add a little more if it doesn't take too much time. Especially if it is important like volunteering.

High school students who volunteer get involved with the real world outside school, and that means a lot. They have a chance to do something that can make a difference in the world. This helps them learn things that maybe they can't learn in school, like, how to be kind and jenerous and care about making the world a better place.

Volunteering in high school is a great idea. Everybody should do it. There are lots of different ways to volunteer. You can even do it on weekends with your friends.

| The claim is not clearly stated in the introduction. |

| The argument contains mistakes in standard English conventions of usage and mechanics. |

| The vocabulary used is limited and ineffective, and the tone is informal. |

| The writer does not acknowledge counterclaims. |

TOOL KIT: WRITING

WRITING

MODEL

ARGUMENT: SCORE 2

Community Service Should be a Requirement for High School Graduation

High school students should have to volunteer before they can graduate. It makes sense because it is helpful to them and others. Some students would volunteer anyway even if it wasn't required, but some wouldn't. If they have to do it for graduation then they won't miss out.

Their lots of reasons to get involved. One is to be a better student in school. Researchers have done studies to see the connection between community service and doing well in school. One study showed that most schools with programs said grades went up most of the time for kids that volunteered. Another study said elementary and middle school kids got better at problem-solving and were more interested in school. One study said students showed more responsibility. Another researcher discovered that kids who been volunteering have better self-esteem. They also have fewer problems.

Volunteering helps you learn and improve at lots of things, not just what you are doing at your volunteer job. One thing you might get better at is being a nicer person, like having more patience and listening well to others. Because you might need those skills when you are volunteering at a senior center or a preschool.

Some people say that volunteering in high school should NOT be required for graduation. They say students already have too much to do and they can't add anything more to they're schedules. But they can add a little more if it doesn't take too much time. Especially if it is important like volunteering.

Why should students be forced to do something, even if it is good? Well, that's just the way it is. When you force students to do something that is good, you are doing them a favor. Like forcing them to eat their vegetables or do their homework. The kids might not like it at first but what do you want to bet they are happy about it later on. That's the point.

Volunteering should be required for all high school students before they graduate. That's not just because they can do a lot of good in the world, but also because doing community service will help them in lots of ways.

> The introduction establishes the claim.

> The tone of the argument is occasionally formal and objective.

> The writer briefly acknowledges and refutes counterclaims

> The writers relies too much on weak anecdotal evidence.

> The conclusion offers some insight into the claim and restates some information.

ARGUMENT: SCORE 3

Community Service Should be a Requirement for High School Graduation

Requiring community service for high school graduation is an excellent idea that offers benefits not only to the community but to the student as well. Making it a requirement ensures that all students will be able to get in on the act.

The claim is established in the introduction but is not as clear as it could be.

Volunteering is a great way to build skills. It might not seem like a big deal at the time, but the experience you gain is very likely to be useful in the future. For example, while tracking, sorting, and distributing donations at an afterschool program, a volunteer might learn how to use a spreadsheet. That's going to come in handy very quickly, both in and out of school.

Participating in service learning can help you do better in school. ("Service learning" is when community service is part of a class curriculum.) For example, one study found that most schools with service learning programs reported grade point averages of participating students improved 76 percent of the time. Another study showed improved problem-solving skills and increased interest in academics among elementary and middle school students.

The tone of the argument is mostly formal and objective.

A study showed that middle and high school students who participated in quality service learning projects showed more personal and social responsibility. Another study found that students were more likely to help each other and be kind to each other, and care about doing their best. Studies also show better self-esteem and fewer behavioral problems in students who have been involved with service learning.

The writer does not transition very well into new topics.

Despite all this, many people say that volunteering in high school should NOT be a requirement for graduation. They point out that students today are already over-stressed and over-scheduled. There simply isn't room for anything more.

The writer uses some transitional phrases.

True! But community service doesn't have to take up a lot of time. It might be possible for a group of time-stressed students to use class-time to organize a fundraiser, or to squeeze their service into a single "marathon" weekend. It's all a question of priorities.

The writer gives a reason for the counterclaim, but does not provide firm examples.

In short, volunteering is a great way for students to help others, and reap benefits for themselves as well. Making it a requirement ensures that all students have the chance to grow through involvement with their communities. Volunteering opens doors and offers life-long benefits, and high school is the perfect time to get started!

The conclusion restates the claim and provides additional detail.

TOOL KIT: WRITING

MODEL

ARGUMENT: SCORE 4

Community Service Should be a Requirement for High School Graduation

Every high school student should be required to do community service in order to graduate. Volunteering offers life-long benefits that will prepare all students for adulthood.

First and foremost, studies show that participating in service learning —when community service is part of a class curriculum—often helps students do better in school. For example, a study conducted by Leeward County found that 83 percent of schools with service learning programs reported grade point averages of participating students improved 76 percent of the time. Another study, conducted by Hilliard Research, showed improved problem-solving skills and increased interest in academics among elementary and middle school students who participated in service learning.

But it's not just academic performance that can improve through volunteering: There are social and psychological benefits as well. For example, a student survey showed that students who participated in quality service learning projects showed more personal and social responsibility. Another survey found that students involved in service learning were more likely to be kind to each other, and care about doing their best. Studies also show better self-esteem and fewer behavioral problems in students who have been involved with service learning.

Despite all this, there are still many who say that volunteering in high school should NOT be a requirement for graduation. They point out that students today are already over-stressed and over-scheduled. What's more, requiring community service for graduation would be particularly hard on athletes and low-income students who work after school to help their families make ends meet.

Good points, but community service does not have to take up vast quantities of time. It might be possible for a group of time-stressed students to use class-time to organize a fundraiser, or to compress their service into a single "marathon" weekend. Showing students that helping others is something to make time for is an important lesson.

In short, volunteering encourages engagement: It shows students that their actions matter, and that they have the power—and responsibility—to make the world a better place. What could be a more important lesson than that?

The introduction establishes the writer claim in a clear and compelling way.

The writer uses a variety of sentence transitions.

Sources of evidence are comprehensive and contain relevant information.

Counterclaims are clearly acknowledged and refuted.

The conclusion offers fresh insight into the claim.

TOOL KIT: WRITING

Argument Rubric

	Focus and Organization	Evidence and Elaboration	Conventions
4	The introduction engages the reader and establishes a claim in a compelling way. The argument includes valid reasons and evidence that address and support the claim while clearly acknowledging counterclaims. The ideas progress logically, and transitions make connections among ideas clear. The conclusion offers fresh insight into the claim.	The sources of evidence are comprehensive and specific and contain relevant information. The tone of the argument is always formal and objective. The vocabulary is always appropriate for the audience and purpose.	The argument intentionally uses standard English conventions of usage and mechanics.
3	The introduction engages the reader and establishes the claim. The argument includes reasons and evidence that address and support my claim while acknowledging counterclaims. The ideas progress logically, and some transitions are used to help make connections among ideas clear. The conclusion restates the claim and important information.	The sources of evidence contain relevant information. The tone of the argument is mostly formal and objective. The vocabulary is generally appropriate for the audience and purpose.	The argument demonstrates general accuracy in standard English conventions of usage and mechanics.
2	The introduction establishes a claim. The argument includes some reasons and evidence that address and support the claim while briefly acknowledging counterclaims. The ideas progress somewhat logically. A few sentence transitions are used that connect readers to the argument. The conclusion offers some insight into the claim and restates information.	The sources of evidence contain some relevant information. The tone of the argument is occasionally formal and objective. The vocabulary is somewhat appropriate for the audience and purpose.	The argument demonstrates some accuracy in standard English conventions of usage and mechanics.
1	The introduction does not clearly state the claim. The argument does not include reasons or evidence for the claim. No counterclaims are acknowledged. The ideas do not progress logically. Transitions are not included to connect ideas. The conclusion does not restate any information that is important.	Reliable and relevant evidence is not included. The vocabulary used is limited or ineffective. The tone of the argument is not objective or formal.	The argument contains mistakes in standard English conventions of usage and mechanics.

WRITING

Informative/Explanatory Texts

Informative and explanatory writing should rely on facts to inform or explain. Informative writing serves several purposes: to increase readers' knowledge of a subject, to help readers better understand a procedure or process, or to provide readers with an enhanced comprehension of a concept. It should also feature a clear introduction, body, and conclusion.

Elements of Informative/Explanatory Texts

Informative/explanatory texts present facts, details, data, and other kinds of evidence to give information about a topic. Readers turn to informational and explanatory texts when they wish to learn about a specific idea, concept, or subject area, or if they want to learn how to do something.

An effective informative/explanatory text contains these elements:

- a topic sentence or thesis statement that introduces the concept or subject
- relevant facts, examples, and details that expand upon a topic
- definitions, quotations, and/or graphics that support the information given
- headings (if desired) to separate sections of the essay
- a structure that presents information in a direct, clear manner
- clear transitions that link sections of the essay
- precise words and technical vocabulary where appropriate
- formal and object language and tone
- a conclusion that supports the information given and provides fresh insights

INFORMATIVE: SCORE 1

How Technology is Changing the Way We Work

Lot's of people work on computers. So, technology is everywhere. If you feel comfortable using computers and all kinds of other technology, your going to be a head at work, for sure.

They're new Devices and Apps out there every day. Each different job has its own gadgets and programs and apps that you have to learn. Every day their more new apps and devices, they can do all kinds of things.

In the past, people only worked at the office. They didn't get to work at home. Now, if you have a smart phone, you can check your email wherever. You can work at home on a computer. You can work in cafés or wherever. Also on a tablet. If you wanted to, you can be working all the time. But that will be a drag!

Technology is now an important part of almost every job. You also have to have a website. You have to have a social media page. Maybe if your business is doing really well you could afford to hire someone to take care of all that stuff—but it would be better if you knew how to do it yourself.

Technology brings people together and helps them work. It could be someone next to you or someone even on the other side of the world. You can connect with them using email. You can send a text. You could have a conference or video call.

Working from home is cheaper for the worker and boss. They can get stuff done during the day like going to the post office or the library, or picking up their kids at school. This is all thanks to technology.

Lots of jobs today are in technology. Way more than before! That's why it's a good idea to take classes and learn about something in technology, because then you will be able to find a job.

There are apps to find houses for sale, find restaurants, learn new recipes, keep track of how much you exercise, and all kinds of other things, like playing games and tuning your guitar. And there are apps to help you work. It's hard to imagine how people would manage to work now without this kind of technology to help them.

The writer's opening statement does not adequately introduce the thesis, and there are numerous spelling mistakes.

The writer's word choice often does not support the proper tone the essay ought to have.

The essay's sentences are often not purposeful, varied, or well-controlled.

The writer does not include a concluding statement.

TOOL KIT: WRITING

WRITING

MODEL

INFORMATIVE: SCORE 2

How Technology is Changing the Way We Work

Technology affects the way we work, in every kind of job and industry. Each different job has its own gadgets and programs and apps that you have to learn. Every day there are more new apps and devices that can do all kinds of things.

> The writer's opening does not clearly introduce the thesis.

In the past, people went to the office to work. That's not always true today. Now if you have a smart phone, you can check your email wherever you are. You can work at home on a desktop computer. You can work on a laptop in a café or wherever. Or a tablet. Technology makes it so people can work all the time.

It doesn't matter whether the person is on the other side of the world—technology brings you together. Theirs email. Theirs text messaging. You have conference calls. You've got video calling. All these things let people work together wherever they are. And don't forget, today people can access files from the cloud. That helps them work from whatever device they want. More than one person can work on the same file.

> The essay is somewhat lacking in organizational structure.

Different kinds of work places and schedules are becoming more common and normal. Working from home has benefits businesses. It means cost savings. It means higher productivity. It means higher job satisfaction. They can get stuff done during the day like going to the post office or the bank, or picking up their kids at school. That is very convenient.

> The essay has many interesting details, bu some do not relate specifically to the topic.

It's also true that lots and lots of jobs today are in technology, or related to technology in some way. Way more than before! That's why it's a good idea to get a degree or take classes and learn about something in technology, because it seems like that's where all the new jobs are. Software designers make a really good salary, and so do other tech-related jobs.

> The writer's word choice is overly informal.

Technology is now an important part of almost every job. It's no longer enough to be just a photographer or whatever. You have to get a social media page. You have to be able to use the latest tech gadgets. You can't just take pictures.

> The writer's sentence are disjointed and ineffective.

In todays world, technology is changing how we work. You have to be able to feel comfortable with technology in order to survive at work. Even if you really don't like technology, you don't really have a choice. So, get used to it!

> The conclusion follow logically but is not mature and is overly informal.

INFORMATIVE: SCORE 3

How Technology Is Changing the Way We Work

Technology has been changing how we work for a long time, but the pace of change has gotten dramatically faster. No industry or job is exempt. Powerful computing technology and Internet connectivity affects all sectors of the economy. It doesn't matter what job you're talking about: Technology is transforming the way people work. It's an exciting time to be entering the workforce!

The Office Is Everywhere

Technology is rapidly changing not just *how* but *where, when,* and *with whom* we work. It used to be that work was something that happened only at the office. All kinds of different work places and schedules are becoming much more common and normal. According to a study, telecommuting (working from home) rose 79 percent between 2005 and 2012. Working from home has benefits for both the employee and employer. It means cost savings for both, increased productivity, and higher job satisfaction.

The Cloud

Cloud and other data storage and sharing options mean that workers have access to information whenever they want, wherever they are. Whether it's one person who wants the convenience of being able to work on a file from several devices (and locations), or several people who are working on something together, the ability to store data in the cloud and access it from anywhere is a huge change in the way we work. It's almost like all being in the same office, working on the same computer.

Tech Industries and Jobs

Technology is changing the way we work in part by making technology itself such an important element in almost every profession. Therefore, you can see it's no longer good enough to be just a photographer or contractor. You have to know something about technology to do your job, market yourself, and track your performance. No matter what jobs someone does they have to be tech-savvy to be able to use their devices to connect and interact with each other across the globe.

Conclusion

In todays world, technology is quickly and continuously changing how we work, what we do, where and when we do it. In order to do well and thrive, everyone has to be a little bit of a tech geek. So, get used to technology being a part of your work life. And get used to change. Because, in a constantly changing technological world, change is going to be one of the few things that stays the same!

The thesis is introduced but is buried in the introduction.

The writer uses headings to help make the organization of ideas clear.

Statistics support the writer's claim.

The writer uses some transitions and sentence connections, but more would be helpful.

There are a few errors in spelling and punctuation but they do not detract from the effectiveness of the essay.

The conclusion sums up the main ideas of the essay and links to the opening statements.

TOOL KIT: WRITING

WRITING

MODEL

INFORMATIVE: SCORE 4

How Technology Is Changing the Way We Work

While advances in technology have been changing how we work for hundreds of years, the pace of change has accelerated dramatically in the past two decades. With powerful computing technology and Internet connectivity affecting all sectors of the economy, no industry or profession is exempt. It doesn't matter whether you're talking about financial advisors, architects, or farmers: Technology is transforming the way people work.

The Office Is Everywhere

Technology is rapidly revolutionizing not just *how* but *where, when,* and *with whom* we work. It used to be that work was something that happened strictly at the office. In fact, non-traditional work places are becoming much more common. According to one study, telecommuting rose 79 percent between 2005 and 2012. Working from home has proven benefits for both the employee and employer, including cost savings for both, increased productivity, and job satisfaction.

Working with the Cloud

Another important technological advancement that is impacting how we work is the development of cloud computing. Whether it's one person who wants the convenience of being able to work from several devices, or several people who are working together from different locations, the ability to store data in the cloud and access it from anywhere is a huge change in the way we work. Over long distances, coworkers can not only *communicate* with each other, they can *collaborate*, in real time, by sharing and accessing files through the. Only five years ago, this kind of instant access was impossible.

Tech Industries and Jobs

Technology is changing the way we work is by making technology itself an important element in almost every job. It's no longer good enough to be just a photographer or contractor: you have to know something about technology to perform, market, and track your work. No matter what job someone is doing, he or she has to be tech-savvy to be able to use their devices to connect and interact.

Conclusion

In today's world, technology is quickly and continuously changing what work we do, and how, where, when, and with whom we do it. Comfort with new technology—and with rapid technological change—is a prerequisite for success, no matter where your interests lie, or what kind of job you are looking to find. It's a brave new technological world of work, and it's changing every day!

The opening paragraph ends with a thesis, which is strong and clear.

The writer makes an effort to be thoughtful and engage the reader.

Headings help ensure that the organizing structure of the essay is clear and effective.

The sentences in the essay are purposeful and varied.

The progression of ideas in the essay is logical and well-controlled.

The writer's word choice contributes to the clarity of the essay and shows awareness of the essay's purpose and tone.

Informative/Explanatory Rubric

	Focus and Organization	Evidence and Elaboration	Conventions
4	The introduction engages the reader and states a thesis in a compelling way. The essay includes a clear introduction, body, and conclusion. The conclusion summarizes ideas and offers fresh insight into the thesis.	The essay includes specific reasons, details, facts, and quotations from selections and outside resources to support the thesis. The tone of the essay is always formal and objective. The language is always precise and appropriate for the audience and purpose.	The essay uses standard English conventions of usage and mechanics. The essay contains no spelling errors.
3	The introduction engages the reader and sets forth the thesis. The essay includes an introduction, body, and conclusion. The conclusion summarizes ideas and supports the thesis.	The essay includes some specific reasons, details, facts, and quotations from selections and outside resources to support the thesis. The tone of the essay is mostly formal and objective. The language is generally precise and appropriate for the audience and purpose.	The essay demonstrates general accuracy in standard English conventions of usage and mechanics. The essay contains few spelling errors.
2	The introduction sets forth the thesis. The essay includes an introduction, body, and conclusion, but one or more parts are weak. The conclusion partially summarizes ideas but may not provide strong support of the thesis.	The essay includes a few reasons, details, facts, and quotations from selections and outside resources to support the thesis. The tone of the essay is occasionally formal and objective. The language is somewhat precise and appropriate for the audience and purpose.	The essay demonstrates some accuracy in standard English conventions of usage and mechanics. The essay contains some spelling errors.
1	The introduction does not state the thesis clearly. The essay does not include an introduction, body, and conclusion. The conclusion does not summarize ideas and may not relate to the thesis.	Reliable and relevant evidence is not included. The tone of the essay is not objective or formal. The language used is imprecise and not appropriate for the audience and purpose.	The essay contains mistakes in standard English conventions of usage and mechanics. The essay contains many spelling errors.

TOOL KIT: WRITING

WRITING

Narration

Narrative writing conveys experience, either real or imaginary, and uses time to provide structure. It can be used to inform, instruct, persuade, or entertain. Whenever writers tell a story, they are using narrative writing. Most types of narrative writing share certain elements, such as characters, setting, a sequence of events, and, often, a theme.

Elements of a Narrative Text

A **narrative** is any type of writing that tells a story, whether it is fiction, nonfiction, poetry, or drama.

An effective nonfiction narrative usually contains these elements:

- an engaging beginning in which characters and setting are established
- characters who participate in the story events
- a well-structured, logical sequence of events
- details that show time and place
- effective story elements such as dialogue, description, and reflection
- the narrator's thoughts, feelings, or views about the significance of events
- use of language that brings the characters and setting to life

An effective fictional narrative usually contains these elements:

- an engaging beginning in which characters, setting, or a main conflict is introduced
- a main character and supporting characters who participate in the story events
- a narrator who relates the events of the plot from a particular point of view
- details that show time and place
- conflict that is resolved in the course of the narrative
- narrative techniques such as dialogue, description, and suspense
- use of language that vividly brings to life characters and events

NARRATIVE: SCORE 1

Getting Away With It

That night, Luanne made two mistakes.

She ran in the house.

The McTweedys were rich and had a huge place and there was an expensive rug.

She was sad in her room remembering what happened:

She was carrying a tray of glasses back to the kitchen and spilled on the carpet. She tried to put furniture over it. Then she ran in the rain.

Luanne should have come clean. She would of said I'm sorry, Mrs. Mc Tweedy, I spilled punch on ur carpet.

She knew getting away with it felt crummy for some reason. it was wrong and she also didn't want to get in trouble.

The phone rings.

"Oh, hello?"

"It's Mrs. Tweedy's!" said her mom. "You forgot to get paid!"

Luanne felt relieve. She was going to do the right thing.

> The introduction is interesting but is not built upon.

> The chronology and situation are unclear.

> The narrative contains mistakes in standard English conventions of usage and mechanics.

> The name of the character does not remain consistent.

> The conclusion reveals what will happen but is not interesting.

TOOL KIT: WRITING

► WRITING

Getting Away With It

That night, Luanne made two fatal mistakes: ruining a rug, and thinking she could get away with it.

She ran in the house.

The McTweedys hired her to be a waiter at their party. They were rich and had a huge place and there was an expensive rug.

She was sad in her room remembering what happened:

Luanne was wearing black pants and a white shirt. She was carrying a tray of glasses back to the kitchen. One spilled on the carpet. She tried to put furniture to cover up the stain. She ran away in the rain.

Luanne should have come clean right away. But what would she have said? I'm sorry, Mrs. McTweedy, but I spilled punch all over your expensive carpet.

Luanne imagined getting away with it. But getting away with it felt crummy for some reason. She knew it was wrong somehow, but she also didn't want to get in trouble.

The phone rang.

"Oh, hello, how was the party?"

Luanne felt like throwing up.

"Mrs. McTweedy's on the phone!" her mom sang out. "She said you forgot your check!"

Luanne felt relieved. But she already made up her mind to do the right thing.

The introduction establishes a clear context.

The writer has made some mistakes in spelling, grammar, and punctuation.

The chronology is sometimes unclear.

Narrative techniques such as the use of dialogue, are used at times.

The conclusion tells what will happen but not interesting.

R22 RESOURCES: TOOL KIT

Getting Away With It

That night, Luanne made two fatal mistakes: (1) ruining a priceless Persian rug, and (2) thinking she could get away with it.

She bursted in the front door breathless.

"How was it?" called her mom.

The McTweedys had hired her to serve drinks at their fundraiser. Henry and Estelle McTweedy loved having parties. They were rich and had a huge apartment filled with rare books, art, and tapestries from all over the world.

"Luanne? Are you alright?"

"Just tired, Mom."

Actually she was face-planted on her bed, replaying the scene over and over just in case she could change it.

It was like a movie: A girl in black trousers and a crisp white shirt carrying a tray of empty glasses back to the kitchen. Then the girl's horrified expression as she realizes that one of the glasses was not quite as empty as she'd thought and was dripping onto the carpet. The girl frantically moving furniture to cover up the stain. The girl running out of the apartment into the hard rain.

Luanne kicked herself. She should have come clean right away. But what would she have said? I'm sorry, Mrs. McTweedy, but I spilled punch all over your expensive carpet.

Luanne imagined getting away with it. But getting away with it felt crummy for some reason. She knew it was wrong somehow, but she also didn't want to get in trouble.

The phone was ringing. Luanne froze.

"Oh, hello there, Mrs. McTweedy! How was the party?"

Luanne felt felt like throwing up.

"Mrs. McTweedy's on the phone!" her mom sang out. "She said you forgot your check!"

Luanne felt relief. It was nothing at all! Although she'd already made up her mind to come clean. Because she had to do the right thing.

She walked into the kitchen. And then she explained the whole thing to both her mom and Mrs. McTweedy.

The story's introduction establishes a clear context and point of view.

Descriptive details, sensory language, and precise words and phrases help to bring the narrative to life.

The writer mostly attends to the norms and conventions of usage and punctuation, but sometimes makes mistakes.

The writer has effectively used dialogue in her story.

The conclusion follows logically but is not memorable.

MODEL

NARRATIVE: SCORE 4

Getting Away With It

That night, Luanne made two fatal mistakes: (1) ruining a priceless Persian rug, and (2) thinking she could get away with it.

She'd burst in the front door breathless.

"How was it?" called her mother from the kitchen.

The McTweedys had hired Luanne to serve drinks at their fundraiser. Henry and Estelle McTweedy loved entertaining. They loved traveling, and the opera, and the finer things in life. They had a huge apartment filled with rare books, art, and tapestries from all over the world.

"Luanne? Are you alright?"

"Just tired, Mom."

Actually she was face-down on her bed, replaying the humiliating scene over and over just in case she could make it come out differently.

It was like a movie: A girl in black trousers and a crisp white shirt carrying a tray of empty glasses back to the kitchen. Cut to the girl's horrified expression as she realizes that one of the glasses —not quite as empty as she'd thought—was dripping its lurid contents onto the carpet. Close in on the girl's frantic attempts to move furniture over the stain. Montage of images showing the girl running out of the apartment into the pounding rain. Fade to Black.

Luanne could kick herself. She should have come clean right away. But what would she have said? *I'm sorry, Mrs. McTweedy, but I spilled punch all over your irreplaceable carpet.*

Luanne imagined getting away with it. If she got away with it, she'd be a person who got away with things. For the rest of her life, no matter what, she'd be a person who got away with things. And if something good happened to her, she'd feel like she didn't deserve it.

Somewhere in the house, a phone was ringing. Luanne froze and listened in.

"Oh, hello there, Estelle! How was the party?" Luanne felt cold, then hot. Her skin prickled. She was sweating. She felt like throwing up.

"Mrs. McTweedy's on the phone!" Luanne's mother sang out. "She wants to tell you that you forgot your check!"

Luanne felt a surge a relief wash over her—it was nothing, nothing at all!—but she'd already made up her mind to come clean. Not because owning up to it was so Right, but because getting away with it was so wrong. Which made it right.

Luanne padded into the kitchen. "Don't hang up," she told her mother.

The writer provides an introduction that establishes a clear context and point of view.

The writer has used descriptive details, sensory language, and precise words and phrases.

The writer's use of movie terminology is clever and memorable.

The narrative presents a clear chronological sequence of events.

The writer effectively uses narrative techniques, such as dialogue.

The story's conclusion is abrupt but fitting. It reveals a critical decision that resolves the conflict.

Narrative Rubric

	Focus and Organization	Development of Ideas/Elaboration	Conventions
4	The introduction establishes a clear context and point of view. Events are presented in a clear sequence, building to a climax, then moving toward the conclusion. The conclusion follows from and reflects on the events and experiences in the narrative.	Narrative techniques such as dialogue, pacing, and description are used effectively to develop characters, events, and setting. Descriptive details, sensory language, and precise words and phrases are used to convey the experiences in the narrative and to help the reader imagine the characters and setting. Voice is established through word choice, sentence structure, and tone.	The narrative uses standard English conventions of usage and mechanics. Deviations from standard English are intentional and serve the purpose of the narrative. Rules of spelling and punctuation are followed.
3	The introduction gives the reader some context and sets the point of view. Events are presented logically, though there are some jumps in time. The conclusion logically ends the story, but provides only some reflection on the experiences related in the story.	Narrative techniques such as dialogue, pacing, and description are used occasionally. Descriptive details, sensory language, and precise words and phrases are used occasionally. Voice is established through word choice, sentence structure, and tone occasionally, though not evenly.	The narrative mostly uses standard English conventions of usage and mechanics, though there are some errors. There are few errors in spelling and punctuation.
2	The introduction provides some description of a place. The point of view can be unclear at times. Transitions between events are occasionally unclear. The conclusion comes abruptly and provides only a small amount of reflection on the experiences related in the narrative.	Narrative techniques such as dialogue, pacing, and description are used sparingly. The story contains few examples of descriptive details and sensory language. Voice is not established for characters, so that it becomes difficult to determine who is speaking.	The narrative contains some errors in standard English conventions of usage and mechanics. There are many errors in spelling and punctuation.
1	The introduction fails to set a scene or is omitted altogether. The point of view is not always clear. The events are not in a clear sequence, and events that would clarify the narrative may not appear. The conclusion does not follow from the narrative or is omitted altogether.	Narrative techniques such as dialogue, pacing, and description are not used. Descriptive details are vague or missing. No sensory language is included. Voice has not been developed.	The text contains mistakes in standard English conventions of usage and mechanics. Rules of spelling and punctuation have not been followed.

RESEARCH

Conducting Research

We are lucky to live in an age when information is accessible and plentiful. However, not all information is equally useful, or even accurate. Strong research skills will help you locate and evaluate information.

Narrowing or Broadening a Topic

The first step of any research project is determining your topic. Consider the scope of your project and choose a topic that is narrow enough to address completely and effectively. If you can name your topic in just one or two words, it is probably too broad. Topics such as Shakespeare, jazz, or science fiction are too broad to cover in a single report. Narrow a broad topic into smaller subcategories.

When you begin to research a topic, pay attention to the amount of information available. If you feel overwhelmed by the number of relevant sources, you may need to narrow your topic further.

If there isn't enough information available as your research, you might need to broaden your topic. A topic is too narrow when it can be thoroughly presented in less space than the required size of your assignment. It might also be too narrow if you can find little or no information in library and media sources, so consider broadening your topic to include other related ideas.

Generating Research Questions

Use research questions to focus your research. Specific questions can help you avoid time-wasting digressions. For example, instead of simply hunting for information about Mark Twain, you might ask, "What jobs did Mark Twain have, other than being a writer?" or "Which of Twain's books was most popular during his lifetime?"

In a research report, your research question often becomes your thesis statement, or may lead up to it. The question will also help you focus your research into a comprehensive but flexible search plan, as well as prevent you from gathering unnecessary details. As your research teaches you more about your topic, you may find it necessary to refocus your original question.

Consulting Print and Digital Sources

Effective research combines information from several sources, and does not rely too heavily on a single source. The creativity and originality of your research depends on how you combine ideas from multiple sources. Plan to consult a variety of resources, such as the following:

- **Primary and Secondary Sources:** To get a thorough view of your topic, use primary sources (firsthand or original accounts, such as interview transcripts, eyewitness reports, and newspaper articles) and secondary sources (accounts, created after an event occurred, such as encyclopedia entries).

- **Print and Digital Resources:** The Internet allows fast access to data, but print resources are often edited more carefully. Use both print and digital resources in order to guarantee the accuracy of your findings.

- **Media Resources:** You can find valuable information in media resources such as documentaries, television programs, podcasts, and museum exhibitions. Consider attending public lectures given by experts to gain an even more in-depth view of your topic.

- **Original Research:** Depending on your topic, you may wish to conduct original research to include among your sources. For example, you might interview experts or eyewitnesses, or conduct a survey of people in your community.

Using Online Encyclopedias

Online encyclopedias are often written by anonymous contributors who are not required to fact-check information. These sites can be very useful as a launching point for research, but should not be considered accurate. Look for footnotes, endnotes, or hyperlinks that support facts with reliable sources that have been carefully checked by editors.

Evaluating Sources It is important to evaluate the credibility, validity, and accuracy of any information you find, as well as its appropriateness for your purpose and audience. You may find the information you need to answer your research question in specialized and authoritative sources, such as almanacs (for social, cultural, and natural statistics), government publications (for law, government programs, and subjects such as agriculture), and information services. Also, consider consumer, workplace, and public documents.

Ask yourself questions such as these to evaluate these additional sources:

- **Authority:** Is the author well known? What are the author's credentials? Does the source include references to other reliable sources? Does the author's tone win your confidence? Why or why not?

- **Bias:** Does the author have any obvious biases? What is the author's purpose for writing? Who is the target audience?

- **Currency:** When was the work created? Has it been revised? Is there more current information available?

RESEARCH

Using Search Terms

Finding information on the Internet can be both easy and challenging. Type a word or phrase into a general search engine and you will probably get hundreds—or thousands—of results. However, those results are not guaranteed to be relevant or accurate.

These strategies can help you find information from the Internet:

- Create a list of keywords that apply to your topic before you begin using a search engine. Consult a thesaurus to expand your list.
- Enter six to eight keywords.
- Choose precise nouns. Most search engines ignore articles and prepositions. Verbs may be used in multiple contexts, leading to sources that are not relevant. Use modifiers, such as adjectives, when necessary to specify a category.
- Use quotation marks to focus a search. Place a phrase in quotation marks to find pages that include exactly that phrase. Add several phrases in quotation marks to narrow your results.
- Spell carefully. Many search engines autocorrect spelling, but they cannot produce accurate results for all spelling errors.
- Scan search results before you click them. The first result isn't always the most relevant. Read the text and consider the domain before make a choice.
- Utilize more than one search engine.

Evaluating Internet Domains

Not everything you read on the Internet is true, so you have to evaluate sources carefully. The last three letters of an Internet URL identify the Website's domain, which can help you evaluate the information of the site.

- **.gov**—Government sites are sponsored by a branch of the United States federal government, such as the Census Bureau, Supreme Court, or Congress. These sites are considered reliable.
- **.edu**—Education domains include schools from kindergartens to universities. Information from an educational research center or department is likely to be carefully checked. However, education domains can also include student pages that are not edited or monitored.
- **.org**—Organizations are nonprofit groups and usually maintain a high level of credibility. Keep in mind that some organizations may express strong biases.
- **.com** and **.net**—Commercial sites exist to make a profit. Information may be biased to show a product or service in a good light. The company may be providing information to encourage sales or promote a positive image.

Taking Notes

Take notes as you locate and connect useful information from multiple sources, and keep a reference list of every source you use. This will help you make distinctions between the relative value and significance of specific data, facts, and ideas.

For long-term research projects, create source cards and notecards to keep track of information gathered from multiple resources.

Source Cards

Create a card that identifies each source.

- For print materials, list the author, title, publisher, date of publication, and relevant page numbers.
- For Internet sources, record the name and Web address of the site, and the date you accessed the information.
- For media sources, list the title, person, or group credited with creating the media, and the year of production.

Notecards

Create a separate notecard for each item of information.

- Include the fact or idea, the letter of the related source card, and the specific page(s) on which the fact or idea appears.
- Use quotation marks around words and phrases taken directly from print or media resources.
- Mark particularly useful or relevant details using your own annotation method, such as stars, underlining, or colored highlighting.

Source Card	[A]

Marsh, Peter. *Eye to Eye: How People Interact.* Salem House Publishers, 1988.

Notecard

Gestures vary from culture to culture. The American "OK" symbol (thumb and forefinger) is considered insulting in Greece and Turkey.

Source Card: A, p. 54.

Quote Accurately Responsible research begins with the first note you take. Be sure to quote and paraphrase your sources accurately so you can identify these sources later. In your notes, circle all quotations and paraphrases to distinguish them from your own comments. When photocopying from a source, include the copyright information. When printing out information from an online source, include the Web address.

Reviewing Research Findings

While conducting research, you will need to review your findings, checking that you have collected enough accurate and appropriate information.

Considering Audience and Purpose

Always keep your audience in mind as you gather information, since different audiences may have very different needs. For example, if you are writing an in-depth analysis of a text that your entire class has read together and you are writing for your audience, you will not need to gather background information that has been thoroughly discussed in class. However, if you are writing the same analysis for a national student magazine, you cannot assume that all of your readers have the same background information. You will need to provide facts from reliable sources to help orient these readers to your subject. When considering whether or not your research will satisfy your audience, ask yourself:

- Who am I writing for?
- Have I collected enough information to explain my topic to this audience?
- Are there details in my research that I can omit because they are already familiar to my audience?

Your purpose for writing will also influence your review of research. If you are researching a question to satisfy your own curiosity, you can stop researching when you feel you understand the answer completely. If you are writing a research report that will be graded, you need to consider the criteria of the assignment. When considering whether or not you have enough information, ask yourself:

- What is my purpose for writing?
- Will the information I have gathered be enough to achieve my purpose?
- If I need more information, where might I find it?

Synthesizing Sources

Effective research writing does not merely present facts and details; it synthesizes—gathers, orders, and interprets—them. These strategies will help you synthesize information effectively:

- Review your notes and look for connections and patterns among the details you have collected.
- Arrange notes or notecards in different ways to help you decide how to best combine related details and present them in a logical way.
- Pay close attention to details that support one other, emphasizing the same main idea.
- Also look for details that challenge each other, highlighting ideas about which there is no single, or consensus, opinion. You might decide to conduct additional research to help you decide which side of the issue has more support.

Types of Evidence

When reviewing your research, also consider the kinds of evidence you have collected. The strongest writing contains a variety of evidence effectively. This chart describes three of the most common types of evidence: statistical, testimonial, and anecdotal.

TYPE OF EVIDENCE	DESCRIPTION	EXAMPLE
Statistical evidence includes facts and other numerical data used to support a claim or explain a topic.	Examples of statistical evidence include historical dates and information, quantitative analyses, poll results, and quantitative descriptions.	"Although it went on to become a hugely popular novel, the first edition of William Goldman's book sold fewer than 3,000 copies."
Testimonial evidence includes any ideas or opinions presented by others, especially experts in a field.	Firsthand testimonies present ideas from eyewitnesses to events or subjects being discussed.	"The ground rose and fell like an ocean at ebb tide." —Fred J. Hewitt, eyewitness to the 1906 San Francisco earthquake
	Secondary testimonies include commentaries on events by people who were not involved. You might quote a well-known literary critic when discussing a writer's most famous novel, or a prominent historian when discussing the effects of an important event	Gladys Hansen insists that "there was plenty of water in hydrants throughout [San Francisco] . . . The problem was this fire got away."
Anecdotal evidence presents one person's view of the world, often by describing specific events or incidents.	Compelling research should not rely solely on this form of evidence, but it can be very useful for adding personal insights and refuting inaccurate generalizations. An individual's experience can be used with other forms of evidence to present complete and persuasive support.	Although many critics claim the novel is universally beloved, at least one reader "threw the book against a wall because it made me so angry."

Incorporating Research Into Writing

Avoiding Plagiarism

Plagiarism is the unethical presentation of someone else's ideas as your own. You must cite sources for direct quotations, paraphrased information, or facts that are specific to a single source. When you are drafting and revising, circle any words or ideas that are not your own. Follow the instructions on pages R34 and R35 to correctly cite those passages.

Review for Plagiarism Always take time to review your writing for unintentional plagiarism. Read what you have written and take note of any phrases or sentences that do not have your personal writing voice. Compare those passages with your resource materials. You might have copied them without remembering the exact source. Add a correct citation to give credit to the original author. If you cannot find the questionable phrase in your notes, revise it to ensure that your final report reflects your own thinking and not someone else's work.

- - -

Quoting and Paraphrasing

When including ideas from research into your writing, you will decide to quote directly or paraphrase.

Direct Quotation Use the author's exact words when they are interesting or persuasive. You might decide to include direct quotations for these reasons:

- to share an especially clear and relevant statement
- to reference a historically significant passage
- to show that an expert agrees with your position
- to present an argument that you will counter in your writing.

Include complete quotations, without deleting or changing words. If you need to omit words for space or clarity, use ellipsis points to indicate the omission. Enclose direct quotations in quotation marks and indicate the author's name.

Paraphrase A paraphrase restates an author's ideas in your own words. Be careful to paraphrase accurately. Beware of making sweeping generalizations in a paraphrase that were not made by the original author. You may use some words from the original source, but a legitimate paraphrase does more than simply rearrange an author's phrases, or replace a few words with synonyms.

Original Text	"*The Tempest* was written as a farewell to art and the artist's life, just before the completion of his forty-ninth year, and everything in the play bespeaks the touch of autumn." Brandes, Georg. "Analogies Between *The Tempest* and *A Midsummer Night's Dream*." *The Tempest*, by William Shakespeare, William Heinemann, 1904, p. 668.
Patchwork Plagiarism phrases from the original are rearranged, but too closely follows the original text.	A farewell to art, Shakespeare's play, *The Tempest*, was finished just before the completion of his forty-ninth year. The artist's life was to end within three years. The touch of autumn is apparent in nearly everything in the play.
Good Paraphrase	Images of autumn occur throughout *The Tempest*, which Shakespeare wrote as a way of saying goodbye to both his craft and his own life.

Maintaining the Flow of Ideas

Effective research writing is much more that just a list of facts. Be sure to maintain the flow of ideas by connecting research information to your own ideas. Instead of simply stating a piece of evidence, use transition words and phrases to explain the connection between information you found from outside resources and your own ideas and purpose for writing. The following transitions can be used to introduce, compare, contrast, and clarify.

Useful Transitions

When providing examples:

for example   for instance   to illustrate   in [name of resource], [author]

When comparing and contrasting ideas or information:

in the same way   similarly   however   on the other hand

When clarifying ideas or opinions:

in other words   that is   to explain   to put it another way

Choosing an effective organizational structure for your writing will help you create a logical flow of ideas. Once you have established a clear organizational structure, insert facts and details from your research in appropriate places to provide evidence and support for your writing.

ORGANIZATIONAL STRUCTURE	USES
Chronological order presents information in the sequence in which it happens.	historical topics; science experiments; analysis of narratives
Part-to-whole order examines how several categories affect a larger subject.	analysis of social issues; historical topics
Order of importance presents information in order of increasing or decreasing importance.	persuasive arguments; supporting a bold or challenging thesis
Comparison-and-contrast organization outlines the similarities and differences of a given topic.	addressing two or more subjects

RESEARCH

Formats for Citing Sources

In research writing, cite your sources. In the body of your paper, provide a footnote, an endnote, or a parenthetical citation, identifying the sources of facts, opinions, or quotations. At the end of your paper, provide a bibliography or a Works Cited list, a list of all the sources referred to in your research. Follow an established format, such as Modern Language Association (MLA) style.

Parenthetical Citations (MLA Style)

A parenthetical citation briefly identifies the source from which you have taken a specific quotation, factual claim, or opinion. It refers readers to one of the entries on your Works Cited list. A parenthetical citation has the following features:

- It appears in parentheses.
- It identifies the source by the last name of the author, editor, or translator, or by the title (for a lengthy title, list the first word only).
- It provides a page reference, the page(s) of the source on which the information cited can be found.

A parenthetical citation generally falls outside a closing quotation mark but within the final punctuation of a clause or sentence. For a long quotation set off from the rest of your text, place the citation at the end of the excerpt without any punctuation following.

Sample Parenthetical Citations

It makes sense that baleen whales such as the blue whale, the bowhead whale, the humpback whale, and the sei whale (to name just a few) grow to immense sizes (Carwardine et al. 19–21). The blue whale has grooves running from under its chin to partway along the length of its underbelly. As in some other whales, these grooves expand and allow even more food and water to be taken in (Ellis 18–21).

Authors' last names

Page numbers where information can be found

Works Cited List (MLA Style)

A Works Cited list must contain accurate information to enable a reader to locate each source you cite. The basic components of an entry are as follows:

- name of the author, editor, translator, and/or group responsible for the work
- title of the work
- publisher
- date of publication

For print materials, the information for a citation generally appears on the copyright and title pages. For the format of a Works Cited list, consult the examples on this page and in the MLA Style for Listing Sources chart.

Sample Works Cited List (MLA 8th Edition)

Carwardine, Mark, et al. *The Nature Company Guides: Whales, Dolphins, and Porpoises.* Time-Life, 1998.

"Discovering Whales." *Whales on the Net.* Whales in Danger, 1998, www.whales.org.au/ discover/index.html. Accessed 11 Apr. 2017.

Neruda, Pablo. "Ode to Spring." *Odes to Opposite*, translated by Ken Krabbenhoft, edited and illustrated by Ferris Cook, Little, 1995, p. 16.

The Saga of the Volsungs. Translated by Jesse L. Byock, Penguin, 1990.

List an anonymous work by title.

List both the title of the work and the collection in which it is found.

Works Cited List or Bibliography?

A Works Cited list includes only those sources you paraphrased or quoted directly in your research paper. By contrast, a bibliography lists all the sources you consulted during research— even those you did not cite.

MLA (8th Edition) Style for Listing Sources

Book with one author	Pyles, Thomas. *The Origins and Development of the English Language.* 2nd ed., Harcourt Brace Jovanovich, 1971. [Indicate the edition or version number when relevant.]
Book with two authors	Pyles, Thomas, and John Algeo. *The Origins and Development of the English Language.* 5th ed., Cengage Learning, 2004.
Book with three or more authors	Donald, Robert B., et al. *Writing Clear Essays.* Prentice Hall, 1983.
Book with an editor	Truth, Sojourner. *Narrative of Sojourner Truth.* Edited by Margaret Washington, Vintage Books, 1993.
Introduction to a work in a published edition	Washington, Margaret. Introduction. *Narrative of Sojourner Truth,* by Sojourner Truth, edited by Washington, Vintage Books, 1993, pp. v–xi.
Single work in an anthology	Hawthorne, Nathaniel. "Young Goodman Brown." *Literature: An Introduction to Reading and Writing,* edited by Edgar V. Roberts and Henry E. Jacobs, 5th ed., Prentice Hall, 1998, pp. 376–385. [Indicate pages for the entire selection.]
Signed article from an encyclopedia	Askeland, Donald R. "Welding." *World Book Encyclopedia,* vol. 21, World Book, 1991, p. 58.
Signed article in a weekly magazine	Wallace, Charles. "A Vodacious Deal." *Time,* 14 Feb. 2000, p. 63.
Signed article in a monthly magazine	Gustaitis, Joseph. "The Sticky History of Chewing Gum." *American History,* Oct. 1998, pp. 30–38.
Newspaper article	Thurow, Roger. "South Africans Who Fought for Sanctions Now Scrap for Investors." *Wall Street Journal,* 11 Feb. 2000, pp. A1+. [For a multipage article that does not appear on consecutive pages, write only the first page number on which it appears, followed by the plus sign.]
Unsigned editorial or story	"Selective Silence." Editorial. *Wall Street Journal,* 11 Feb. 2000, p. A14. [If the editorial or story is signed, begin with the author's name.]
Signed pamphlet or brochure	[Treat the pamphlet as though it were a book.]
Work from a library subscription service	Ertman, Earl L. "Nefertiti's Eyes." *Archaeology,* Mar.–Apr. 2008, pp. 28–32. *Kids Search,* EBSCO, New York Public Library. Accessed 7 Jan. 2017. [Indicating the date you accessed the information is optional but recommended.]
Filmstrips, slide programs, videocassettes, DVDs, and other audiovisual media	*The Diary of Anne Frank.* 1959. Directed by George Stevens, performances by Millie Perkins, Shelley Winters, Joseph Schildkraut, Lou Jacobi, and Richard Beymer, Twentieth Century Fox, 2004. [Indicating the original release date after the title is optional but recommended.]
CD-ROM (with multiple publishers)	Simms, James, editor. *Romeo and Juliet.* By William Shakespeare, Attica Cybernetics / BBC Education / Harper, 1995.
Radio or television program transcript	"Washington's Crossing of the Delaware." *Weekend Edition Sunday,* National Public Radio, 23 Dec. 2013. Transcript.
Web page	"Fun Facts About Gum." ICGA, 2005–2017, www.gumassociation.org/index.cfm/facts-figures/fun-facts-about-gum. Accessed 19 Feb. 2017. [Indicating the date you accessed the information is optional but recommended.]
Personal interview	Smith, Jane. Personal interview, 10 Feb. 2017.

All examples follow the style given in the MLA Handbook, 8th edition, published in 2016.

MODEL

Evidence Log

Unit Title: _Discovery_

Perfomance-Based Assessment Prompt:
Do all discoveries benefit humanity?

My initial thoughts:
Yes - all knowledge moves us forward.

As you read multiple texts about a topic, your thinking may change. Use an Evidence Log like this one to record your thoughts, to track details you might use in later writing or discussion, and to make further connections.

Here is a sample to show how one reader's ideas deepened as she read two texts.

Title of Text: _Classifying the Stars_   Date: _Sept. 17_

CONNECTION TO THE PROMPT	TEXT EVIDENCE/DETAILS	ADDITIONAL NOTES/IDEAS
Newton shared his discoveries and then other scientists built on his discoveries.	Paragraph 2: "Isaac Newton gave to the world the results of his experiments on passing sunlight through a prism." Paragraph 3: "In 1814 . . . the German optician, Fraunhofer . . . saw that the multiple spectral tints . . . were crossed by hundreds of fine dark lines."	It's not always clear how a discovery might benefit humanity in the future.

How does this text change or add to my thinking? _This confirms what I think._   Date: _Sept. 20_

Title of Text: _Cell Phone Mania_   Date: _Sept. 21_

CONNECTION TO THE PROMPT	TEXT EVIDENCE/DETAILS	ADDITIONAL NOTES/IDEAS
Cell phones have made some forms of communication easier, but people don't talk to each other as much as they did in the past.	Paragraph 7: "Over 80% of young adults state that texting is their primary method of communicating with friends. This contrasts with older adults who state that they prefer a phone call."	Is it good that we don't talk to each other as much? Look for article about social media to learn more about this question.

How does this text change or add to my thinking?   Date: _Sept. 25_
Maybe there are some downsides to discoveries. I still think that knowledge moves us forward, but there are sometimes unintended negative effects.

Word Network

A word network is a collection of words related to a topic. As you read the selections in a unit, identify interesting theme-related words and build your vocabulary by adding them to your Word Network.

Use your Word Network as a resource for your discussions and writings. Here is an example:

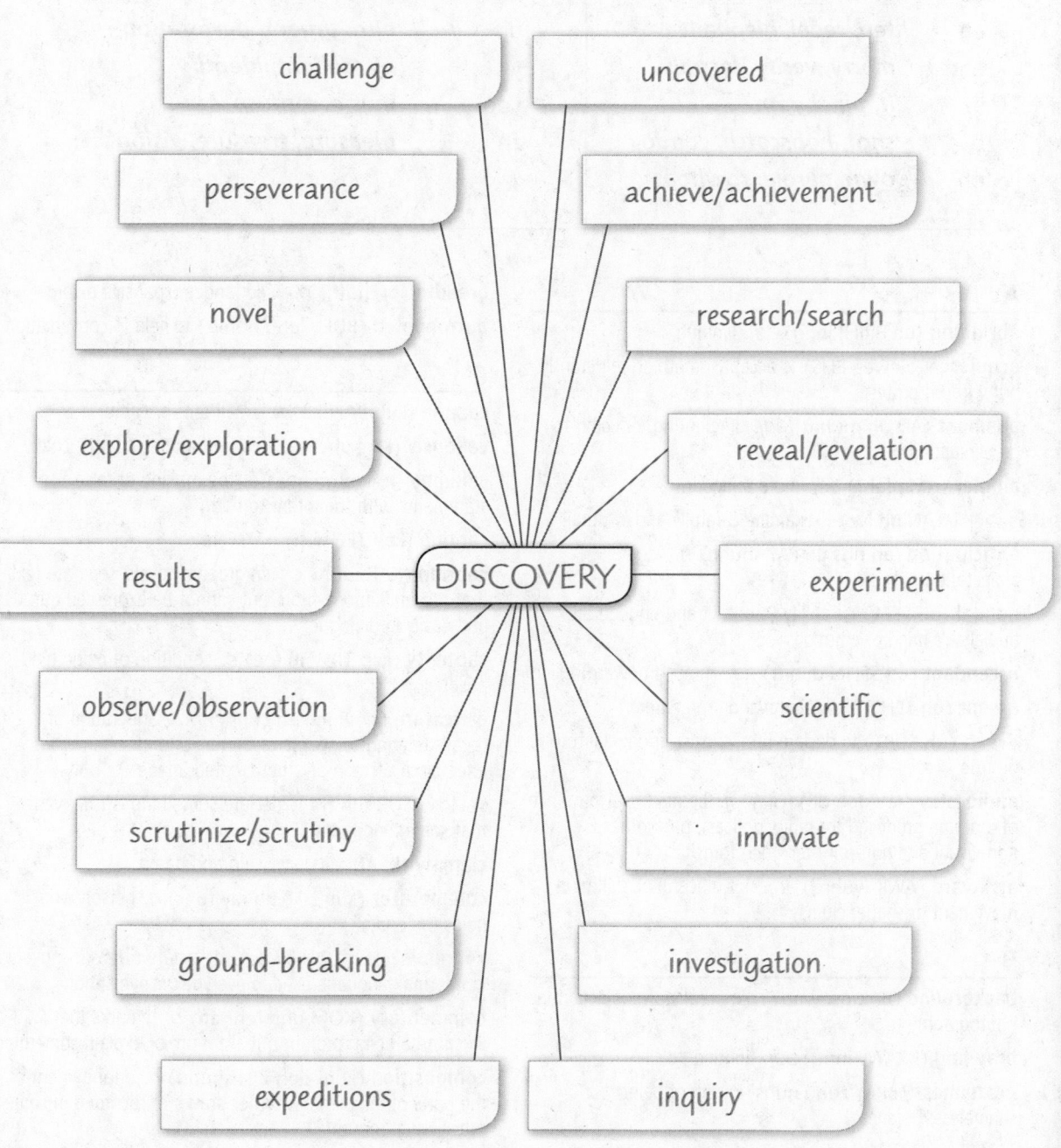

ACADEMIC / CONCEPT VOCABULARY

Academic vocabulary appears in **blue type**.

Pronunciation Key

Symbol	Sample Words	Symbol	Sample Words
a	*at, catapult, Alabama*	oo	*boot, soup, crucial*
ah	*father, charms, argue*	ow	*now, stout, flounder*
ai	*care, various, hair*	oy	*boy, toil, oyster*
aw	*law, maraud, caution*	s	*say, nice, press*
awr	*pour, organism, forewarn*	sh	*she, abolition, motion*
ay	*ape, sails, implication*	u	*full, put, book*
ee	*even, teeth, really*	uh	*ago, focus, contemplation*
eh	*ten, repel, elephant*	ur	*bird, urgent. perforation*
ehr	*merry, verify, terribly*	y	*by, delight, identify*
ih	*it, pin, hymn*	yoo	*music, confuse, few*
o	*shot, hopscotch, condo*	zh	*pleasure, treasure, vision*
oh	*own, parole, rowboat*		

A

abridging (uh BRIHJ ihng) *adj.* limiting

acquiesce (ak wee EHS) *v.* accept something reluctantly but without protest

adamant (AD uh muhnt) *adj.* unrelenting; refusing to be persuaded

ampler (AM pluhr) *adj.* more abundant

analyze (AN uh lyz) *v.* examine carefully and in detail

anticipation (an tihs uh PAY shuhn) *n.* eager expectation

appeal (uh PEEL) *n.* ability to attract and engage an audience's mind or emotions

ascendant (uh SEHN duhnt) *adj.* moving upward; rising

assent (uh SEHNT) *n.* approval or agreement

assert (uh SURT) *v.* declare firmly; insist upon; claim to be true

audio play (AW dee oh) (play) *n.* theatrical performance of a drama produced for radio, podcast, or another non-visual and non-print recorded form

awkward (AWK wuhrd) *adj.* not graceful or skillful in movement or shape; clumsy

B

background (BAK grownd) *n.* more distant objects in a photograph

brawling (BRAWL ihng) *adj.* fighting noisily

brazenness (BRAY zuhn nuhs) *n.* act of being shameless; boldness

breadth (brehdth) *n.* wide range; expansive extent

buttonholed (BUHT uhn hohld) *v.* held in conversation

C

cabana (kuh BAN uh) *n.* small tent or cabin

callously (KAL uhs lee) *adv.* without sympathy; coldly

calumny (KAL uhm nee) *n.* the making of false statements with the intent to harm

cantina (kan TEE nuh) *n.* tavern

caption (KAP shuhn) *n.* in graphic novels, separate text that presents information that cannot be expressed quickly and easily in dialogue

captivity (kap TIHV ih tee) *n.* condition of being held prisoner

caricature (KAIR ih kuh chuhr) *n.* exaggeration of details relating to people or events, often for humorous effect, in a cartoon or other created image

certify (SUR tuh fy) *v.* declare something is true; verify that something is true

clammy (KLAM ee) *adj.* cold and damp

collaborator (kuh LAB uh ray tuhr) *n.* person who helps the enemy

colloquial (kuh LOH kwee uhl) *adj.* written or spoken in informal language used in everyday conversation

commentary (KOM uhn tehr ee) *n.* remarks that illustrate a point, prompt a realization, or explain something

composition (kom puh ZIH shuhn) *n.* arrangement of the parts of an image, whether drawn or recorded in some other visual format

conceded (kuhn SEED ihd) *v.* admitted

conciliatory (kuhn SIHL ee uh tawr ee) *adj.* in a manner intended to make peace and bring about agreement

conclave (KON klayv) *n.* private meeting

condemnation (kon dehm NAY shuhn) *n.* very strong disapproval

confirm (kuhn FURM) *v.* prove the truth of; verify

consecrate (KON sih krayt) *v.* set apart as holy; dedicate

conspirators (kuhn SPIHR uh tuhrz) *n.* people who join in a secret plan

constrains (kuhn STRAYNZ) *v.* requires or forces

constricting (kuhn STRIHKT ihng) *adj.* limiting; tightening

conviction (kuhn VIHK shuhn) *n.* strong belief; certainty

corrupted (kuh RUHPT ihd) *adj.* dishonest

cowering (KOW uhr ihng) *adj.* crouching or drawing back in fear or shame

cross-section (KRAWS sehk shuhn) *n.* view of a three-dimensional object that shows the interior as if a cut has been made across the object

cunning (KUHN ihng) *adj.* done with skill or cleverness

D

dedicated (DEHD uh kayt ihd) *adj.* committed; devoted

deduction (dih DUHK shuhn) *n.* the process of using reason or logic to come to a conclusion or form an opinion

defamation (dehf uh MAY shuhn) *n.* unjust injury to someone's good reputation through the making of false statements

deference (DEHF uhr uhns) *n.* great respect

definitive (dih FIHN uh tihv) *adj.* deciding or settling a question; final

degraded (dih GRAYD ihd) *adj.* reduced in respectablility; disgraced

deicide (DEE uh syd) *n.* killing of a god

dejected (dee JEHK tihd) *adj.* depressed; sad

demonstrate (DEHM uhn strayt) *v.* show how to do something

denounce (dih NOWNS) *v.* criticize harshly

depth of field (dehpth) (uhv) (feeld) n. distance between the closest and most distant objects that are in focus

despotism (DEHS puh tihz uhm) *n.* absolute rule; tyranny

determine (dih TUR muhn) *v.* decide; find out, as the exact cause or reason

dictum (DIHK tuhm) *n.* short statement that expresses a general truth; saying or proverb

digress (dih GREHS) *v.* go off topic in speaking or writing

dilatory (dihl uh TAWR ee) *adj.* inclined to delay; slow

discern (dih SURN) *v.* recognize as different

disparity (dihs PAR uh tee) *n.* great difference or inequality

disposition (DIHS puh ZIHSH uhn) *n.* act of settling a case or argument; decision

disputation (dihs pyu TAY shuhn) *n.* debate or argument

dissented (dih SENT ihd) *v.* rejected an official opinion; disagreed

documentary (dok yuh MEHN tuhr ee) *n.* program or film that provides a factual record or report of real events

dyspepsia (dihs PEHP see uh) *n.* indigestion

E

effrontery (ih FRUHN tuh ree) *n.* shameless boldness

eminence (EHM uh nuhns) *n.* position of great importance or superiority

eminent (EHM uh nuhnt) *adj.* distinguished; famous; noteworthy

emperor (EHM puhr uhr) *n.* ruler of highest rank and authority, especially of an empire

encroaching (ehn KROHCH ihng) *adj.* intruding; steadily advancing

epiphany (ih PIHF uh nee) *n.* flash of insight and understanding

equivocate (ih KWIHV uh kayt) *v.* use unclear language to avoid committing oneself to something

espionage (EHS pee uh nozh) *n.* use of spies to obtain secret information

establish (ehs TAB lihsh) *v.* set up; prove; demonstrate

etiquette (EHT uh kiht) *n.* proper manners

exalted (ehg ZAWLT ihd) *adj.* of high rank

exasperating (ehg ZAS puh rayt ihng) *adj.* annoying

exercise (EHK suhr syz) *n.* implementation; state of putting something into action

expression (ehk SPREHSH uhn) *n.* tone of voice that indicates specific emotion

eyewitness account (Y WIHT nihs) (uh KOWNT) n. description given by someone who was present at an event

F

figure (FIHG yuhr) *n.* one of a set of drawings or illustrations

fix (fihks) *n.* difficult or awkward situation

focal point (FOH kuhl) (poynt) *n.* center of activity or attention in a photograph

foment (foh MEHNT) *v.* stir up; agitate

foreground (FAWR grownd) *n.* nearer or closer objects in a photograph

forward (FAWR wuhrd) *adj.* bold; brazen; shameless

frame (fraym) *n.* main spoken narrative of a production

framing (FRAYM ihng) *n.* composing a visual so that an enclosing border surrounds the image in the foreground

furtive (FUR tihv) *adj.* done or acting in a stealthy way to avoid being noticed; secret

G

garrulous (GAR uh luhs) *adj.* very talkative

gilded (GIHLD ihd) *adj.* covered with a thin layer of gold

grandeur (GRAN juhr) *n.* state of being impressive; magnificence

H

hallow (HAL oh) *v.* make sacred; consecrate

hangdog (HANG dawg) *adj.* sad; ashamed; guilty

hermitage (HUR muh tihj) *n.* secluded retreat

hospitality (hos puh TAL uh tee) *n.* warm, welcoming attitude toward guests

host (hohst) *n.* master of ceremonies, moderator, or interviewer on a broadcast

hypodermic (hy puh DUR mihk) *n.* injection of medicine

I

immutable (ih MYOO tuh buhl) *adj.* never changing; not changeable

impact (IHM pakt) *n.* collision; powerful or lasting effect

imperial (ihm PEER ee uhl) *adj.* like something associated with an empire; magnificent or majestic

imploring (ihm PLAWR ihng) *v.* asking or begging someone for something

importunities (ihm pawr TOO nuh teez) *n.* annoyingly urgent requests

impressionism (ihm PREHSH uh nihz uhm) *n.* style of art where mood, color, and light matter more than details

incident (IHN suh duhnt) *n.* event; occurrence

indecisions (ihn dih SIHZH uhnz) *n.* things not decided or finalized

infallibility (ihn fal uh BIHL uh tee) *n.* inability to be in error

inflection (ihn FLEHK shuhn) *n.* rise and fall of pitch and tone in a person's voice

informational (ihn fuhr MAY shuh nuhl) *adj.* giving knowledge and facts

infringed (ihn FRIHNJD) *v.* violated

inquire (ihn KWYR) *v.* ask for information

instantaneously (ihn stuhn TAY nee uhs lee) *adv.* immediately

insurgent (ihn SUR juhnt) *adj.* rebellious or in revolt against a government in power

integrity (in TEHG rih tee) *n.* virtue of following moral or ethical principles

interminable (ihn TUR muh nuh buhl) *adj.* seemingly unending

interview (IHN tuhr vyoo) *n.* conversation in which a host asks questions of one or more guests

J

jurisdiction (juhr ihs DIHK shuhn) *n.* legal power to hear and decide cases

L

labeling and **captions** (LAY buhl ihng) (KAP shuhnz) *n.* written labels and other text that often accompany politically charged images to clarify their meanings

layout (LAY owt) *n.* overall design and look of a graphic presentation

legacy (LEHG uh see) *n.* anything handed down from someone

letterhead (LEHT uhr hehd) *n.* personalized stationery

literal (LIHT uhr uhl) *adj.* true to fact; not exaggerated

loathsome (LOHTH suhm) *adj.* causing disgust

loitered (LOY tuhrd) *v.* lingered; moved slowly

M

machetes (muh SHEHT eez) *n.* knives

magistrates (MAJ uh strayts) *n.* officials who have some of the powers of a judge

malice (MAL ihs) *n.* desire to harm or inflict injury

mission (MIHSH uhn) *n.* goal or ambition

monotonous (muh NOT uh nuhs) *adj.* boring due to a lack of variety

motifs (moh TEEFS) *n.* major themes, features, or elements

multitudes (MUHL tuh toodz) *n.* large number of people or things; masses

O

obdurate (OB duhr iht) *adj.* resistant to persuasion

obliged (uh BLYJD) *adj.* grateful

oppressed (uh PREHST) *v.* deprived of rights or power

ornamented (AWR nuh mehnt ihd) *adj.* decorated; adorned

overcast (OH vuhr kast) *adj.* covered with clouds, as a gray sky

overture (OH vuhr chuhr) *n.* musical introduction to an opera or symphony

P

palette (PAL iht) *n.* range of colors used in a particular work

perish (PEH rihsh) *v.* die

perpetually (puhr PEHCH oo uh lee) *adv.* happening all the time

persistence (puhr SIHS tuhns) *n.* act of not giving up

perspective (puhr SPEHK tihv) *n.* method of giving a sense of depth on a flat or shallow surface

petition (puh TIHSH uhn) *v.* formally request; seek help from

picturesquely (pihk chuh REHSK lee) *adv.* in a way that resembles a picture; in a way that is striking or interesting

plaintiffs (PLAYN tihfs) *n.* people who bring a lawsuit to court

policy (POL uh see) *n.* particular course of action by a person, government, organization

populist (POP yuh lihst) *adj.* related to serving the needs of common people

prejudices (PREHJ uh dihs ihz) *n.* unfavorable opinions or feelings formed beforehand or without factual support

prelude (PRAY lood) *n.* introduction to a musical work; overture

prescribed (prih SKRYBD) *v.* stated in writing; set down as a rule

proceedings (pruh SEE dihngz) *n.* events in a court of law

prolific (pruh LIHF ihk) *adj.* fruitful; abundant

propaganda (prop uh GAN duh) *n.* information, ideas, or rumors spread widely and deliberately to help or harm a person, group, movement, cause, or nation

protagonist (proh TAG uh nihst) *n.* main character in a play, story, or novel

Q

quaint (kwaynt) *adj.* unusual; curious; singular

R

racket (RAK iht) *n.* noisy confusion; uproar

realism (REE uh lihz uhm) *n.* style of art closely resembling reality

rectitude (REHK tuh tood) *n.* morally correct behavior or thinking; uprightness

redeemers (rih DEE muhrz) *n.* people who pay for the wrongdoing of others

redress (rih DREHS) *n.* correction; setting right of some wrong

relevant (REHL uh vuhnt) *adj.* puposeful; meaningful

remorseless (rih MAWRS lihs) *adj.* relentless; cruel

renaissance (REHN uh sons) *n.* revival; period of cultural importance

rend (rehnd) *v.* tear apart with violent force

resolution (rehz uh LOO shuhn) *n.* act of coming to a decision; the part of a story in which the plot is made clear

reverence (REHV uhr uhns) *n.* feeling of deep respect

rites (ryts) *n.* ceremonies

romanticism (roh MAN tuh sihz uhm) *n.* style of art evoking emotion by idealizing subjects

S

salutary (SAL yuh tehr ee) *adj.* beneficial; promoting a positive purpose

sanctity (SANGK tuh tee) *n.* fact of being sacred; holiness

scourge (skurj) *n.* cause of serious trouble or suffering

self-assurance (sehlf uh SHUR uhns) *n.* self-confidence

sequence (SEE kwuhns) *n.* particular order

shotgun (SHOT guhn) *n.* gun with a long, smooth barrel, that is often used to fire "shot," or small, pellet-like ammunition

shuffle (SHUHF uhl) *n.* dragging movement of the feet over the ground or floor without lifting them

sidle (SY duhl) *v.* move sideways, as in an unobtrusive, stealthy, or shy manner

significant (sihg NIHF uh kuhnt) *adj.* full of meaning; important

sinister (SIHN uh stuhr) *adj.* evil; threatening

sovereign (SOV ruhn) *n.* monarch or ruler

spatial (SPAY shuhl) *adj.* existing in space

special elements (SPEHSH uhl) (EHL uh muhnts) *n.* features that provide points of emphasis in a production

specific (spih SIHF ihk) *adj.* definite; precise; particular

specifications (spehs uh fuh KAY shuhnz) *n.* section of a patent application in which the inventor fully describes the invention

speech balloon (speech) (buh LOON) *n.* shape used in graphic novels and comic books to show what a character says

squalor (SKWOL uhr) *n.* filth; wretchedness

stolid (STOL ihd) *adj.* feeling little or no emotion

strife (stryf) *n.* act of fighting

subordinate (suh BAWR duh niht) *adj.* having less importance

sufficed (suh FYST) *v.* was adequate

superannuated (soo puhr AN yu ayt uhd) *adj.* too old to be usable; obsolete

superfluous (suh PUR floo uhs) *adj.* more than is needed or wanted; unnecessary

supplanted (suh PLANT ihd) *v.* took the place of; removed

supplement (SUHP luh muhnt) *n.* something added; *v.* add to

symbolism (SIHM buh lihz uhm) *n.* use of images or objects to represent ideas or qualities

T

tedious (TEE dee uhs) *adj.* boring; dull

teeming (TEE mihng) *adj.* full

temporal (TEHM puhr uhl) *adj.* not eternal; limited by time

tension (TEHN shuhn) *n.* mental or nervous stress; uneasiness; state of strained relations

tone (tohn) *n.* production's attitude toward a subject or audience

transcendent (tran SEHN duhnt) *adj.* beyond the limits of possible experience

treason (TREE zuhn) *n.* betrayal of trust or faith, especially against one's country

trivialize (TRIHV ee uhl yz) *v.* treat as not important; make trivial

tyranny (TIHR uh nee) *n.* oppressive power

U

unalienable (un AYL yuh nuh buhl) *adj.* impossible to take away or give up

unique (yoo NEEK) *adj.* being the only one of its kind

unrequited (uhn rih KWY tihd) *adj.* not repaid or avenged

V

vassals (VAS uhlz) *n.* subjects of a kingdom; servants

vast (vast) *adj.* very great in size

verbatim (vuhr BAY tihm) *adv.* in exactly the same words; *adj.* repeating the original word for word

vigilant (VIHJ uh luhnt) *adj.* on the alert; watchful

vindictive (vihn DIHK tihv) *adj.* characterized by an intense, unreasoning desire for revenge

vital (VY tuhl) *adj.* necessary or important

W

wanton (WON tuhn) *adj.* unrestrained; wild

waterfowl (WAWT uhr fowl) *n.* birds that live in or near water

wretched (REHCH ihd) *adj.* very unhappy; miserable

VOCABULARIO ACADÉMICO/ VOCABULARIO DE CONCEPTOS

abridging: abreviar *v.* limitar

acquiesce: consentir *v.* aceptar algo con pocas ganas pero sin protestar

adamant: terco/a *adj.* que no se deja convencer; inflexible

ampler: más copioso/a *adj.* más abundante

analyze: analizar *v.* examinar detalladamente y en profundidad

anticipation: anticipación *s.* expectación; espera ansiosa

appeal: cautivar *v.* capacidad de atraer e involucrar al público, sus pensamientos o emociones

ascendant: ascendente *adj.* que se mueve hacia arriba; que se eleva

assent: consentimiento *s.* aprobación o acuerdo

assert: aseverar *v.* afirmar; insistir

audio play: radioteatro *s.* obra de teatro producida para la radio, para un *podcast* o para otro tipo de grabación no visual ni impresa

awkward: torpe *adj.* desmañado/a; sin gracia, patoso

B

backdrop: fondo *s.* escena o decorado detrás de fotografías y retratos

background: fondo *s.* objetos lejanos en una fotografía

brawling: pendenciero/a *adj.* que se pelea ruidosamente; alborotador/a

brazenness: descaro *s.* no tener vergüenza; atrevimiento

breadth: anchura *s.* amplitud

buttonholed: acorraló *v.* detuvo a alguien en una conversación

C

cabana: cabaña *s.* tienda pequeña, choza

callously: despiadadamente *adv.* sin compasión; fríamente

calumny: calumnia *s.* afirmación falsa que intenta herir o dañar

cantina: cantina *s.* taberna

caption: leyenda *s.* en las novelas gráficas, texto en un recuadro que presenta información que no puede expresarse rápida y fácilmente en el diálogo

captivity: cautividad *s.* estado de privación de libertad; ser prisionero

caricature: caricatura *s.* exageración, generalmente con efecto humorístico, de detalles relacionados con personas o sucesos en una tira cómica u otra imagen creada

certify: certificar *v.* declarar que algo es cierto

clammy: sudado/a *adj.* frío y húmedo

collaborator: colaboracionista *s.* persona que colabora con o ayuda al enemigo

colloquial: coloquial *adj.* lenguaje informal que se usa en las conversaciones diarias

commentary: comentario *s.* observación o ejemplo que ilustra una idea, una opinión o explica algo

composition: composición *s.* disposición de las partes de una imagen, ya sea de un dibujo o de cualquier otro formato visual

conceded: concedió *v.* admitió

conciliatory: conciliador/a *adj.* que tiene la intención de hacer las paces y llegar a un acuerdo

conclave: cónclave *s.* reunión privada

condemnation: condena *s.* fuerte desaprobación; repulsa

confirm: confirmar *v.* probar la certeza de algo; verificar

consecrate: consagrar *v.* declarar algo como sagrado; dedicar

conspirators: conspiradores *s.* personas que se unen a un plan secreto

constrains: constriñe *v.* requiere, obliga

constricting: estrecho/a *adj.* limitado/a

conviction: condena *s.* acto de dar a alguien un veredicto de culpabilidad

conviction: convicción *s.* creencia firme

correlate: correlacionar *v.* mostrar la conexión entre dos elementos

corrupted: corrupto/a *adj.* deshonesto/a

cowering: achicarse *v.* encogerse de miedo

cross-section: sección transversal *s.* imagen de un objeto tridimensional que muestra su interior como si se hubiera hecho un corte transversal del objeto

cunning: astuto/a *adj.* con ingenio y astucia

D

dedicate: dedicar *v.* apartar para un objetivo especial

deduction: deducción *s.* el proceso de usar la razón o la lógica para llegar a una conclusión o formar una opinion

defamation: difamación *s.* dañar la reputación de alguien injustamente mediante afirmaciones falsas

deference: deferencia *s.* gran respeto

defining: definir *v.* aclarar el significado; explicar

definitive: definitivo *adj.* que decide y resuelve una cuestión

degraded: degradado *adj.* con respetabilidad reducida; desgraciado

deicide: deicidio *s.* matar a un dios

dejected: abatido/a *adj.* deprimido/a; triste

demonstrate: demostrar *v.* enseñar cómo hacer algo

denounce: denunciar *v.* criticar duramente

depth of field: profundidad de campo *s.* la distancia entre los objetos más cercanos y los más lejanos que enfoca una cámara

despotism: despotismo *s.* ejercicio de autoridad absoluta

determine: determinar *v.* decidir; buscar la causa o la razón exacta

dictum: dicho *s.* un enunciado corto que expresa una verdad general; un refrán o proverbio

digress: divagar *v.* desviarse del tema al hablar o escribir

dilatory: dilatorio/a *adj.* inclinado a retrasarse; lento/a

discern: discernir *v.* reconocer como diferente

disparity: disparidad *s.* gran diferencia o desigualdad

disposition: disposición *s.* el acto de llegar a un acuerdo en un caso o discusión; predisposición

disputation: disputa *s.* debate o discusión

dissented: disintió *v.* rechazó una opinion oficial; estuvo en desacuerdo

documentary: documental *s.* programa o película que ofrece datos o un informe sobre hechos reales

dyspepsia: dispepsia *s.* indigestión

E

effrontery: desfachatez *s.* descaro; desvergüenza

eminence: eminencia *s.* persona con un cargo de gran importancia o superioridad

eminent: eminente *adj.* distinguido; famoso; notorio

emperor: emperador *s.* gobernante supremo de un imperio

encroaching: traspasar *v.* infringir; meterse; avanzar continuamente

epiphany: epifanía *s.* sensación súbita de comprensión o entendimiento

equivocate: usar equívocos *v.* usar un lenguaje ambiguo para evitar comprometerse a algo

espionage: espionaje *s.* uso de espías para obtener información secreta

establish: establecer *v.* instituir, crear, montar

etiquette: etiqueta *s.* buenos modales

exalted: elevado/a *adj.* de alto rango

exasperating: exasperante *adj.* molesto

exercise: ejercicio *s.* implementación; puesta en práctica

expression: expresión *s.* tono de voz que indica una emoción específica

eyewitness account: declaración de un testigo *s.* descripción hecha por alguien que estuvo presente en un suceso

F

faultfinder: criticón/a *adj.* persona que critica con frecuencia; un quejica

figure: figura *s.* grupo de dibujos o ilustraciones

fix: momento difícil *s.* una situación complicada

focal point: punto de enfoque *s.* el centro de actividad o de atención de una fotografía

foment: fomentar *v.* suscitar, promover; agitar

foreground: primer plano *s.* objetos más cercanos en una fotografía

forward: atrevido/a *adj.* audaz; descarado/a

frame: prototipo *s.* la narrativa oral principal de una producción

framing: composición *s.* creación visual de forma que el marco rodee la imagen del primer plano

furtive: furtivo/a *adj.* hecho de forma sigilosa, a escondidas, para evitar ser descubierto: secreto/a

G

garrulous: charlatán/a *adj.* que habla mucho; parlanchín/a

gilded: bañado en oro *adj.* cubierto con una capa fina de oro

grandeur: esplendor *s.* magnificencia; grandeza; majestuosidad

H

hallow: santificar *v.* hacer sagrado; consagrar

hangdog: abatido/a *adj.* avergonzado/a; triste; culpable

heedless: ignorando *adj.* sin escuchar el consejo; imprudente

hermitage: retiro *s.* lugar apartado, solitario

hospitality: hospitalidad *s.* actitud cálida de bienvenida hacia los invitados

host: anfitrión *s.* maestro de ceremonia, moderador o presentador de un programa

hypodermic: inyección hipodérmica *s.* inyección de un medicamento

I

immutable: inmutable *adj.* que no cambia nunca

impact: colisión *s.* choque; *v.* colisionar, chocar

imperial: imperial *adj.* de calidad superior

imploring: implorar *v.* pedir algo a alguien o suplicar

importunities: importunidades *s.* peticiones urgentes molestas

impressionism: impresionismo *s.* estilo artístico en el que el estado de ánimo, el color y la luz importan más que los detalles

incident: incidente *s.* suceso

indecisions: indecisiones *s.* cosas que no están decididas o finalizadas

infallibility: infalibilidad *s.* imposibilidad de equivocarse

inflection: inflexión *s.* subidas y bajadas en el tono de voz de una persona

informational: informativo/a *adj.* que proporciona conocimientos y hechos

infringed: infringió *v.* violó la ley

instantaneously: instantáneamente *adv.* inmediatamente

insurgent: insurgente *adj.* rebelde o que se rebela contra el gobierno en el poder

integrity: integridad *s.* la virtud de seguir principios morales o éticos

interminable: interminable *adj.* que parece que no tiene fin

interview: entrevista *s.* conversación en la que un presentador hace preguntas a uno o más invitados

inquire: inquirir *v.* solicitar información; indagar

investigate: investigar *v.* indagar a fondo

J

jurisdiction: jurisdicción *s.* poder legal para escuchar una causa y dictar sentencia

L

labeling and **captions: rótulos** y **leyendas** *s.* etiquetas y texto que suelen acompañar las imágenes de contenido político para clarificar su significado

layout: diseño *s.* la disposición gráfica de una presentación

legacy: legado *s.* algo heredado, que se traspasa

letterhead: membrete *s.* papelería personalizada

literal: literal *adj.* acorde a los hechos; sin exagerar

loathsome: repugnante *adj.* que causa gran desagrado

loitered: deambuló *v.* holgazaneó; que se movió despacio

M

machetes: machetes *s.* cuchillos

magistrates: magistrados *s.* cargos públicos que tienen el poder de un juez

majority: mayoría *s.* más de la mitad

malice: malicia *s.* deseo de herir a alguien

mission: misión *s.* objetivo o ambición

monotonous: monótono/a *adj.* aburrido/a debido a la falta de variación

motifs: motivos *s.* temas, características o elementos principales

multitudes: multitudes *s.* gran número de personas

O

obdurate: obstinado/a *adj.* resistente a la persuasión

obliged: agradecido/a *adj.* que da las gracias

oppressed: oprimidos/as *s.* personas cuyo derechos son pisoteados por otros

ornamented: ornamentado *adj.* decorado; adornado

overcast: nublado *adj.* cubierto de nubes

overture: obertura *s.* introducción musical de un ópera o sinfonía

P

palette: paleta *s.* rango de colores usados en una obra determinada

perish: perecer *v.* morir; ser matado

perpetually: perpetuamente *adv.* que sucede todo el tiempo

persistence: persistencia *s.* acción de no darse por vencido

perspective: perspectiva *s.* método mediante el cual se le da sentido de profundidad a una superficie plana

petition: petición *s.* hacer una solicitud formal; buscar la ayuda de alguien

picturesquely: de modo pintoresco *adv.* de manera que parece un cuadro; de manera sorprendente o interesante

plaintiffs: demandantes *s.* las personas que interponen una demanda en un juicio

policy: política *s.* acciones específicas de una persona, gobierno u organización

populist: populista *adj.* persona que cree servir las necesidades del pueblo

prejudices: prejuicios *s.* sentimientos u opiniones desfavorables formados con anterioridad o sin apoyarse en los hechos

prelude: preludio *s.* introducción de una obra musical; obertura

prescribed: prescrito *v.* manifestado por escrito; mandado

proceedings: pleito *s.* proceso judicial, los sucesos de un juzgado

prolific: prolífico *adj.* fructífero

propaganda: propaganda *s.* información, ideas o rumores que se divulgan amplia y deliberadamente para hacerle daño a una persona, grupo, movimiento, causa o nación

protagonist: protagonista *s.* el personaje principal de una obra de teatro, cuento o novela

Q

quaint: singular *adj.* inusual; curioso

R

racket: barullo *s.* confusión ruidosa; jaleo

realism: realismo *s.* estilo artístico que se parece mucho a la realidad

rectitude: rectitud *s.* comportamiento o pensamiento moralmente correcto; integridad

redeemers: redentores *s.* personas que pagan por las malas acciones de otros

redress: rectificación *s.* corrección reparación de un daño

relevant: relevante *adj.* pertinente

remorseless: despiadado/a *adj.* que no tiene remordimientos; cruel

renaissance: renacimiento *s.* resurgimiento; periodo de importancia cultural

rend: rasgar *v.* hacer pedazos con fuerza

resolution: resolución *s.* acción de resolver o decidir; expresión formal de una opinión

reverence: reverencia *s.* sentimiento de profundo respeto

rites: ritos *s.* ceremonias

romanticism: romanticismo *s.* estilo artístico que evoca la emoción idealizando los sujetos

S

salutary: saludable *adj.* beneficioso/a

sanctity: santidad *s.* hecho de ser sagrado

scourge: azote *s.* causa de serios problemas o sufrimiento

self-assurance: autoconfianza *s.* seguridad en uno mismo

sequence: secuencia *s.* en un orden particular; *v.* (secuenciar) poner en orden

sequence photography: secuencia fotográfica *n.* una serie de imágenes en las que se ve el sujeto en instantes sucesivos

shotgun: escopeta *s.* arma de cañón largo, con frecuencia usada para disparar perdigones

shuffle: arrastrar los pies *v.* caminar sin levantar los pies

sidle: caminar de lado *v.* moverse de costado furtiva o tímidamente

significant: significativo/a *adj.* lleno/a de significado; importante

sinister: siniestro *adj.* malvado; amenazador

sovereign: soberano *s.* un monarca o gobernante

spatial: espacial *adj.* que existe en el espacio

special elements: elementos especiales *s.* características que dan puntos de énfasis en una producción

specific: específico/a *adj.* definido/a; preciso/a; particular

specifications: especificaciones *s.* apartado de una patente en que el inventor describe con detalle el invento

speech balloon: bocadillo *s.* el modo en que se representa lo que dice cada personaje en las novelas gráficas

squalor: mugre *s.* suciedad; estado lamentable

stolid: impasible *adj.* imperturbable; que no siente emoción alguna

strife: lucha *s.* acción de luchar; conflicto

subordinate: subordinado/a *adj.* que tiene menos importancia

subordinate: subordinado/a *s.* una persona de menor rango o clase

superannuated: viejo/a *adj.* demasiado viejo/a para usarse; obsoleto/a

superfluous: superfluo/a *adj.* más de lo necesario o deseado; innecesario/a

supplanted: suplantó *v.* tomó el lugar de; quitó a

supplement: suplemento *s.* algo añadido

surrealism: surrealismo *s.* uso intencional de detalles imaginativos y hasta extraños en el arte

symbolism: simbolismo *s.* uso de imágenes u objetos para representar ideas o cualidades

T

tedious: tedioso/a *adj.* aburrido/a, soso/a

teeming: repleto/a *adj.* lleno/a

temporal: temporal *adj.* no eterno, limitado por el tiempo

tension: tensión *s.* estrés causado al tirar

tone: tono *s.* la actitud de una producción hacia un tema o el público

transcendent: trascendente *adj.* más allá de los límites de la experiencia posible

treason: traición *s.* deslealtad hacia la confianza o la fe

trivialize: trivializar *v.* quitar importancia; hacer trivial

tyranny: tiranía *s.* poder opresivo

U

unalienable: inalienable *adj.* imposible de quitar o de abandonar

unique: único/a *adj.* que es el único de su especie o tipo

unrequited: no correspondido *adj.* que no se ha liquidado o vengado

V

vassals: vasallos *s.* sujetos de un reino; siervos

vast: vasto/a *adj.* de gran tamaño

verbatim: textualmente *adv.* palabra por palabra

vigilant: vigilante *adj.* en alerta, atento/a

vindictive: vengativo/a *adj.* lleno/a de un deseo intenso e irracional de venganza

W

wanton: excesivo/a *adj.* descontrolado/a; sin ley

waterfowl: ave acuática *s.* relativo a las aves acuáticas

wretched: desdichado/a *adj.* muy infeliz; desgraciado/a

LITERARY TERMS HANDBOOK

ALLEGORY An *allegory* is a story or tale with two or more levels of meaning—a literal level and one or more symbolic levels. The events, setting, and characters in an allegory are symbols for ideas and qualities.

ALLUSION An *allusion* is a reference to a well-known person, place, event, literary work, or work of art. Writers often make allusions to stories from the Bible, to Greek and Roman myths, to plays by Shakespeare, to political and historical events, and to other materials with which they can expect their readers to be familiar.

ANALOGY An *analogy* is an extended comparison of relationships. It is based on the idea that the relationship between one pair of things is like the relationship between another pair. Unlike a metaphor, an analogy involves an explicit comparison, often using the words *like* or *as*.

ANAPHORA Anaphora is a type of parallel structure in which a word or phrase is repeated at the beginning of successive clauses for emphasis.

ANECDOTE An *anecdote* is a brief story about an interesting, amusing, or strange event. An anecdote is told to entertain or to make a point.

APPEAL An *appeal* is a rhetorical device used in argumentative writing to persuade an audience.

An appeal to ethics (Ethos) shows that an argument is just or fair.

An appeal to logic (Logos) shows that an argument is well reasoned.

An appeal to authority shows that a higher power supports the ideas.

An appeal to emotion (Pathos) is designed to influence readers' feelings.

ARGUMENT An *argument* is writing or speech that attempts to convince a reader to think or act in a particular way. An argument is a logical way of presenting a belief, conclusion, or stance. A good argument is supported with reasoning and evidence.

AUTOBIOGRAPHY An *autobiography* is a form of nonfiction in which a person tells his or her own life story. *Memoirs*, first-person accounts of personally or historically significant events in which the writer was a participant or an eyewitness, are a form of autobiographical writing.

BIOGRAPHY A *biography* is a form of nonfiction in which a writer tells the life story of another person.

CATALOGUE A *catalogue* in poetry is a list of people, objects, or situations, used to evoke a range of experience and/or emotion.

CHARACTER A *character* is a person or an animal that takes part in the action of a literary work. The following are some terms used to describe various types of characters:

The *main character* in a literary work is the one on whom the work focuses. *Major characters* in a literary work include the main character and any other characters who play significant roles. A *minor character* is one who does not play a significant role. A *round character* is one who is complex and multifaceted, like a real person. A *flat character* is one who is one-dimensional. A *dynamic character* is one who changes in the course of a work. A *static character* is one who does not change in the course of a work.

CHARACTERIZATION *Characterization* is the act of creating and developing a character. In **direct characterization,** a writer simply states a character's traits. In *indirect characterization,* character is revealed through one of the following means:

1. words, thoughts, or actions of the character
2. descriptions of the character's appearance or background
3. what other characters say about the character
4. the ways in which other characters react to the character

CLAIM A *claim* is a particular belief, conclusion, or point of view that a writer presents in an *argument.*

CONCESSION *Concession* is a rhetorical device that acknowledges the opposition's arguments.

CONFLICT A *conflict* is a struggle between opposing forces. Sometimes this struggle is internal, or within a character. At other times, this struggle is external, or between a character and an outside force. Conflict is one of the primary elements of narrative literature because most plots develop from conflicts.

CONNOTATION The *connotation* is an association that a word calls to mind in addition to the dictionary meaning of the word. Many words that are similar in their dictionary meanings, or denotations, are quite different in their connotations. Poets and other writers choose their words carefully so that the connotations of those words will be appropriate.

COUNTERCLAIM A *counterclaim* is an objection or challenge to the *claim*—or particular belief, conclusion, or point of view—that a writer presents in an *argument.* Counterclaims are often brought up by the writer of the argument in anticipation of challenges.

DENOTATION The *denotation* of a word is its objective meaning, independent of other associations that the word brings to mind.

DESCRIPTION A *description* is a portrayal, in words, of something that can be perceived by the senses. Writers create descriptions by using images.

DIALECT A *dialect* is the form of a language spoken by people in a particular region or group. Writers often use dialect to make their characters seem realistic and to create local color.

DIALOGUE A *dialogue* is a conversation between characters. Writers use dialogue to reveal character, to present events, to add variety to narratives, and to arouse their readers' interest.

DICTION *Diction* is a writer's or speaker's word choice. Diction is part of a writer's style and may be described as formal or informal, plain or ornate, common or technical, abstract or concrete.

DRAMA A *drama* is a story written to be performed by actors. The playwright supplies dialogue for the characters to speak, as well as *stage directions* that give information about costumes, lighting, scenery, properties, the setting, and the characters' movements and ways of speaking. Dramatic conventions include soliloquies, asides, or the passage of time between acts or scenes. *Dramatic exposition* is a brief essay, or prose commentary, inserted by the writer to help readers and producers understand the characters and past conflicts. *Background knowledge* includes information about the period during which the action takes place.

DRAMATIC MONOLOGUE A *dramatic monologue* is a poem or speech in which an imaginary character speaks to a silent listener.

DRAMATIC POEM A *dramatic poem* is one that makes use of the conventions of drama. Such poems may be monologues or dialogues or may present the speech of many characters. Robert Frost's "The Death of the Hired Man" is a famous example of a dramatic poem.

See also *Dramatic Monologue*.

EPIC THEME An *epic theme* is an underlying message that all people of all times are connected by their shared experiences.

EDITORIAL An *editorial* is a form of persuasive writing or argument. Editorials must have a clear position, be supported by reasons, and include an appeal to ethics, logic, authority, and/or emotion.

ELLIPTICAL PHRASING *Elliptical phrasing* is a style of poetry in which the poet omits words that are expected to be understood by the reader.

ENUMERATION *Enumeration* is a document style in which the major ideas are listed in numerical order.

ESSAY An *essay* is a short nonfiction work about a particular subject. Essays can be classified as *formal* or *informal, personal,* or *impersonal*. They can also be classified according to purpose, such as *cause-and-effect, satirical,* or *reflective.* Modes of discourse, such as *expository*, *descriptive*, *persuasive*, or *narrative*, are other means of classifying essays.

EXPLANATORY ESSAY An *explanatory essay* describes and summarizes information gathered from a number of sources on a concept.

FICTION *Fiction* is prose writing that tells about imaginary characters and events. Short stories and novels are works of fiction.

FIGURATIVE LANGUAGE *Figurative language* is writing or speech not meant to be taken literally. Writers use figurative language to express ideas in vivid and imaginative ways.

FIGURE OF SPEECH A *figure of speech* is an expression or a word used imaginatively rather than literally.

FLASHBACK A *flashback* is a section of a literary work that interrupts the chronological presentation of events to relate an event from an earlier time. A writer may present a flashback as a character's memory or recollection, as part of an account or story told by a character, as a dream or a daydream, or simply by having the narrator switch to a time in the past.

FORESHADOWING *Foreshadowing* in a literary work is the use of clues to suggest events that have yet to occur.

FRAME STORY A *frame story* is a story that brackets—or frames—another story or group of stories. This device creates a story-within-a-story narrative structure.

FREE VERSE *Free verse* is poetry that lacks a regular rhythmical pattern, or meter. A writer of free verse is at liberty to use any rhythms that are appropriate to what he or she is saying.

GENRE A *genre* is a division, or type, of literature. Literature is commonly divided into three major genres: poetry, prose, and drama. Each major genre can in turn be divided into smaller genres. Poetry can be divided into lyric, concrete, dramatic, narrative, and epic poetry. Prose can be divided into fiction and nonfiction. Drama can be divided into serious drama, tragedy, comic drama, melodrama, and farce.

HUMOR *Humor*, used in an argument, can be an effective rhetorical device. Humorous language and details make characters and situations seem funny.

HYPERBOLE A *hyperbole* is a deliberate exaggeration or overstatement, often used for comic effect.

IDIOMATIC EXPRESSION *Idiomatic expressions* are figures of speech that cannot be understood literally. For example, a rainstorm might be described as "raining cats and dogs."

IN MEDIA RES *In media res*, which is Latin for "in the middle of things," is a plot device writers use to grab reader's attention.

IMAGE An *image* is a word or phrase that appeals to one or more of the five senses—sight, hearing, touch, taste, or smell.

IMAGERY *Imagery* is the descriptive or figurative language used in literature to create word pictures for the reader. These pictures, or images, are created by details of sight, sound, taste, touch, smell, or movement.

INCONGRUITY *Incongruity* is a technique writers use to create humor and occurs when two or more ideas relate to one another in a way that is contrary to the readers' expectations.

IRONY *Irony* is a contrast between what is stated and what is meant, or between what is expected to happen and what actually happens. In *verbal irony*, a word or a phrase is used to suggest the opposite of its usual meaning. In *dramatic irony*, there is a contradiction between what a character thinks and what the reader or audience knows. In *irony of situation*, an event occurs that contradicts the expectations of the characters, of the reader, or of the audience.

LETTER A *letter* is a written message or communication addressed to a reader or readers and is generally sent by mail. Letters may be *private* or *public*, depending on their intended audience. A public letter, also called a *literary letter* or *epistle*, is a work of literature written in the form of a personal letter but created for publication.

MEMOIR A *memoir* is a type of nonfiction autobiographical writing that tells about a person's own life, usually focusing on the writer's involvement in historically or culturally significant events—either as a participant or an eyewitness.

METAPHOR A *metaphor* is a figure of speech in which one thing is spoken of as though it were something else. The identification suggests a comparison between the two things that are identified, as in "death is a long sleep."

A *mixed metaphor* occurs when two metaphors are jumbled together. For example, thorns and rain are illogically mixed in "the thorns of life rained down on him." A *dead metaphor* is one that has been overused and has become a common expression, such as "the arm of the chair" or "nightfall."

MONOLOGUE A *monologue* is a speech delivered entirely by one person or character.

MOTIF A *motif* is a recurrent, or repeated, object or idea in a literary work.

NARRATION *Narration* is writing that tells a story. The act of telling a story is also called *narration*. The *narrative*, or story, is told by a storyteller called the *narrator*. A story is usually told chronologically, in the order in which events take place in time, though it may include flashbacks and foreshadowing. Narratives may be true or fictional. Narration is one of the forms of discourse and is used in novels, short stories, plays, narrative poems, anecdotes, autobiographies, biographies, and reports.

NARRATIVE A *narrative* is a story told in fiction, nonfiction, poetry, or drama. Narratives are often classified by their content or purpose. An *exploration narrative* is a firsthand account of an explorer's travels in a new land. "The Interesting Narrative of the Life of Olaudah Equiano" is a *slave narrative*, an account of the experiences of an enslaved person. A *historical narrative* is a narrative account of significant historical events.

A *personal narrative* is a first-person story about a real-life experience. In a *reflective narrative* the author describes describes his or her feelings about a scene, incident, memory, or event. A *nonlinear narrative* does not follow chronological order. It may contain flashbacks, dream sequences, or other devices that interrupt the chronological order of events.

NARRATOR A *narrator* is a speaker or character who tells a story. A story or novel may be narrated by a main character, by a minor character, or by someone uninvolved in the story. The narrator may speak in the first person or in the third person. An *omniscient narrator* is all-knowing, while a limited narrator knows only what one character does.

NONFICTION *Nonfiction* is prose writing that presents and explains ideas or that tells about real people, places, objects, or events. Two of the main types of literary nonfiction are historical writing and reflective writing. Essays, biographies, autobiographies, journals, and reports are all examples of nonfiction.

NOVEL A *novel* is a long work of fiction. A novel often has a complicated plot, many major and minor characters, a significant theme, and several varied settings. Novels can be classified in many ways, based on the historical periods in which they are written, the subjects and themes that they treat, the techniques that are used in them, and the literary movements that inspired them. A *novella* is not as long as a novel but is longer than a short story.

ONOMATOPOEIA *Onomatopoeia* is the use of words that imitate sounds. Examples of such words are *buzz, hiss, murmur,* and *rustle*.

ORATORY *Oratory* is public speaking that is formal, persuasive, and emotionally appealing. Patrick Henry's "Speech in the Virginia Convention" (p. 100) is an example of oratory.

OXYMORON An *oxymoron* is a figure of speech that combines two opposing or contradictory ideas. An oxymoron, such as "freezing fire," suggests a paradox in just a few words.

PACING *Pacing* is the speed or rhythm of writing. Writers use different paces to achieve different effects, such as suspense.

PARADOX A *paradox* is a statement that seems to be contradictory but that actually presents a truth.

PARALLELISM *Parallelism* is the presentation of similar ideas, in sequence, using the same grammatical structure.

PARALLEL STRUCTURE In a list, each item should use *parallel structure* in which the part of speech and grammatical phrasing is the same for all items.

PERSONIFICATION *Personification* is a form of figurative language in which a nonhuman subject is given human characteristics. Effective personification of things or ideas makes them seem vital and alive, as if they were human.

PHILOSOPHICAL ASSUMPTIONS Beliefs that are taken for granted are *philosophical assumptions*. Some assumptions are *explicit*, or directly stated. Other assumptions are *implicit*, meaning the reader must make inferences to understand.

PLOT *Plot* is the sequence of events in a literary work. In most fiction, the plot involves both characters and a central conflict. The plot usually begins with an *exposition* that introduces the setting, the characters, and the basic situation. This is followed by the *inciting incident,* which introduces the central conflict. The conflict then increases during the *development* until it reaches a high point of interest or suspense, the *climax*. The climax is followed by the end, or resolution, of the central conflict. Any events that occur after the *resolution* make up the *denouement*. The events that lead up to the climax make up the *rising action*. The events that follow the climax make up the *falling action*.

POETRY *Poetry* is one of the three major types of literature. In poetry, form and content are closely connected, like the two faces of a single coin. Poems are often divided into lines and stanzas and often employ regular rhythmical patterns, or meters. Most poems use highly concise, musical, and emotionally charged language. Many also make use of imagery, figurative language, and special devices such as rhyme.

POETIC STRUCTURE The basic structures of poetry are lines and stanzas. A *line* is a group of words arranged in a row. A line of poetry may break, or end, in different ways. Varied *line lengths* can create unpredictable rhythms.

An *end-stopped line* is one in which both the grammatical structure and sense are complete at the end of the line.

A *run-on, or enjambed*, line is one in which both the grammatical structure and sense continue past the end of the line.

POINT OF VIEW *Point of view* is the perspective, or vantage point, from which a story is told. Three commonly used points of view are first person, omniscient third person, and limited third person.

In the *first-person point of view*, the narrator is a character in the story and refers to himself or herself with the first-person pronoun "I."

The two kinds of third-person point of view, limited and omniscient, are called "third person" because the narrator uses third-person pronouns such as "he" and "she" to refer to the characters. There is no "I" telling the story.

In stories told from the omniscient third-person point of view, the narrator knows and tells about what each character feels and thinks.

In stories told from the *limited third-person point of view,* the narrator relates the inner thoughts and feelings of only one character, and everything is viewed from this character's perspective.

PREAMBLE A *preamble* is a statement that explains who is issuing the document and for what purpose.

PRIMARY SOURCE A *primary source* is one created by someone who directly participated in or observed the event being described.

PROSE *Prose* is the ordinary form of written language. Most writing that is not poetry, drama, or song is considered prose. Prose is one of the major genres of literature. It occurs in two forms: fiction and nonfiction.

PROTAGONIST The protagonist is the main character in a literary work.

REFRAIN A *refrain* is a repeated line or group of lines in a poem or song. Most refrains end stanzas. Although some refrains are nonsense lines, many increase suspense or emphasize character and theme.

REGIONALISM *Regionalism* in literature is the tendency among certain authors to write about specific geographical areas. Regional writers present the distinct culture of an area, including its speech, customs, beliefs, and history.

RHETORICAL DEVICES Rhetorical devices are special patterns of words and ideas that create emphasis and stir emotion, especially in speeches or other oral presentations. *Parallelism*, for example, is the repetition of a grammatical structure in order to create a rhythm and make words more memorable. Other common rhetorical devices include: *analogy, drawing comparisons between two unlike things; charged language,* words that appeal to the emotions; *concession*, an acknowledgement of the opposition's argument; *humor*, using language and details that make characters or situations funny; *paradox*, statements that seem to contradict but present a truth *restatement,* expressing the same idea in different words

rhetorical questions, questions with obvious answers, **tone, the author's attitude toward the audience**

RHYME *Rhyme* is the repetition of sounds at the ends of words. Rhyming words have identical vowel sounds in their final accented syllables. The consonants before the vowels may be different, but any consonants occurring after these vowels are the same, as in *frog* and *bog* or *willow* and *pillow*. **End rhyme** occurs when rhyming words are repeated at the ends of lines. **Internal rhyme** occurs when rhyming words fall within a line. **Approximate,** or **slant, rhyme** occurs when the rhyming sounds are similar, but not exact, as in *prove* and *glove*.

REPETITION *Repetition* of words and phrases is a literary device used in prose and poetry to emphasize important ideas.

RHYTHM *Rhythm* is the pattern of beats, or stresses, in spoken or written language. Prose and free verse are written in the irregular rhythmical patterns of everyday speech.

RHETORICAL QUESTIONS Rhetorical questions call attention to an issue by implying obvious answers.

ROMANTICISM *Romanticism* was a literary and artistic movement of the nineteenth century that arose in reaction to eighteenth-century Neoclassicism and placed a premium on imagination, emotion, nature, individuality, and exotica. Romanticism is particularly evident in the works of the Transcendentalists.

SECONDARY SOURCE A *secondary source* is one created by someone with indirect knowledge of the event being described. Secondary sources rely on **primary sources,** or firsthand descriptions.

SENSORY LANGUAGE *Sensory language* is writing or speech that appeals to one or more of the five senses.

SEQUENCE OF EVENTS Authors often use **sequence of events**, or the order in which things happened, to structure nonfiction pieces that describe historical events or explain a change over time. Authors frequently describe important events in **chronological order,** or time order.

SETTING The *setting* of a literary work is the time and place of the action. A setting may serve any of a number of functions. It may provide a background for the action. It may be a crucial element in the plot or central conflict. It may also create a certain emotional atmosphere, or mood.

SHORT STORY A *short story* is a brief work of fiction. The short story resembles the novel but generally has a simpler plot and setting. In addition, the short story tends to reveal character at a crucial moment rather than developing it through many incidents. For example, Thomas Wolfe's "The Far and the Near" concentrates on what happens to a train engineer when he visits people who had waved to him every day.

SERIAL COMMA A *serial comma* is a comma placed after each item in a list except for the final item.

SIMILE A *simile* is a figure of speech that makes a direct comparison between two subjects, using either *like* or as.

SLANT RHYME In *slant rhyme,* the final sounds in two lines of a poem are similar, but not identical.

SOCIAL COMMENTARY In works of *social commentary,* an author seeks to highlight, usually in a critical way, an aspect of society.

SPEAKER The *speaker* is the voice of a poem. Although the speaker is often the poet, the speaker may also be a fictional character or even an inanimate object or another type of nonhuman entity. Interpreting a poem often depends upon recognizing who the speaker is, whom the speaker is addressing, and what the speaker's attitude, or tone, is.

STANZA A *stanza* is a group of lines in a poem that are considered to be a unit. Many poems are divided into stanzas that are separated by spaces. Stanzas often function just like paragraphs in prose. Each stanza states and develops a single main idea.

Stanzas are commonly named according to the number of lines found in them, as follows:

1. Couplet: a two-line stanza
2. Tercet: a three-line stanza
3. Quatrain: a four-line stanza
4. Cinquain: a five-line stanza
5. Sestet: a six-line stanza
6. Heptastich: a seven-line stanza
7. Octave: an eight-line stanza

STREAM OF CONSCIOUSNESS *Stream of consciousness* is a narrative technique that presents thoughts as if they were coming directly from a character's mind. Instead of being arranged in chronological order, the events are presented from the character's point of view, mixed in with the character's thoughts just as they might spontaneously occur.

STYLE A writer's *style* includes word choice, tone, degree of formality, figurative language, rhythm, grammatical structure, sentence length, organization—in short, every feature of a writer's use of language.

SUSPENSE *Suspense* is a feeling of growing uncertainty about the outcome of events. Writers create suspense by raising questions in the minds of their readers. Suspense builds until the climax of the plot, at which point the suspense reaches its peak.

SYMBOL A *symbol* is anything that stands for or represents something else. A **conventional symbol** is one that is widely known and accepted, such as a voyage symbolizing life or a skull symbolizing death. A **personal**

symbol is one developed for a particular work by a particular author.

SYMBOLISM *Symbolism* refers to an author's use of people, places, or objects to represent abstract qualities or ideas.

SYNTAX *Syntax* is the structure of sentences.

THEME A *theme* is a central message or insight into life revealed by a literary work. In most works of fiction, the theme is only indirectly stated: A story, poem, or play most often has an *implied theme*.

TONE The tone of a literary work is the writer's attitude toward his or her subject, characters, or audience. A writer's tone may be formal or informal, friendly or distant, personal or pompous. The tone of a work can also be described as technical, conversational, or colloquial.

TRANSCENDENTALISM *Transcendentalism* was an American literary and philosophical movement of the nineteenth century. The Transcendentalists, who were based in New England, believed that intuition and the individual conscience "transcend" experience and thus are better guides to truth than the senses and logical reason. Influenced by Romanticism, the Transcendentalists respected the individual spirit and the natural world, believing that divinity was present everywhere, in nature and in each person.

USAGE *Usage* is the way in which a word or phrase is used. The meaning, pronunciation, and spelling of some words have changed over time.

VOICE A writer's voice is the way in which the writer's personality is revealed in his or her writing. Elements that influence a writer's style are diction, the types of words used, syntax, the types of sentences used, and tone, the writer's attitude toward the topic or audience.

LITERARY TERMS HANDBOOK

ALLEGORY / ALEGORÍA Una *alegoría* es un relato o cuento con dos niveles de significado: un nivel literal y uno o más niveles simbólicos. Los hechos, ambientación y personajes de una alegoría son símbolos de ideas o cualidades.

ALLUSION / ALUSIÓN Una *alusión* es una referencia a una persona, lugar, hecho, obra literaria u obra de arte muy conocida. Los escritores a menudo hacen alusiones a relatos de la Biblia, a los mitos griegos y romanos, a las obras de Shakespeare, a hechos políticos e históricos y a otros materiales con los que suponen que sus lectores estén familiarizados.

ANALOGY / ANALOGÍA Una *analogía* establece una comparación extensa de relaciones. Se basa en la idea de que la relación entre un par de cosas es como la relación entre otro par. A diferencia de la metáfora, una analogía requiere una comparación explícita, a menudo usando las palabras *como* o *semejante*.

ANAPHORA / ANÁFORA Una *anáfora* es un tipo de estructura paralela en la que una palabra o frase se repite al principio de cláusulas consecutivas para dar énfasis.

ANECDOTE / ANÉCDOTA Una *anécdota* es un relato breve sobre un hecho interesante, divertido o extraño, que se narra con el fin de entretener o decir algo importante.

APPEAL / APELACIÓN Una *apelación* es un recurso retórico que se usa en los escritos de argumentación para persuadir al público.

Una apelación a la ética (Ethos) muestra que un argumento es justo.

Una apelación a la lógica (Logos) muestra que un argumento está bien razonado.

Una apelación a la autoridad muestra que alguien importante respalda las ideas.

Una apelación a las emociones (Pathos) tiene como fin influenciar los sentimientos de los lectores.

ARGUMENT / ARGUMENTO Un *argumento* es un escrito o discurso que trata de convencer al lector para que siga una acción o adopte una opinión en particular. Un argumento es una manera lógica de presentar una creencia, una conclusión o una postura. Un buen argumento se respalda con razonamientos y pruebas.

AUTOBIOGRAPHY / AUTOBIOGRAFÍA Una *autobiografía* es una forma de no-ficción en la que una persona narra su propia vida. Las *memorias* son relatos en primera persona de hechos personal o históricamente significativos en los que el escritor participó o de los cuales fue testigo directo. Las memorias son una forma de escrito autobiográfico.

BIOGRAPHY / BIOGRAFÍA Una *biografía* es una forma de no-ficción en la que un escritor cuenta la vida de otra persona.

CATALOGUE / CATÁLOGO Un *catálogo* en poesía es una lista de gente, objetos o situaciones que se usan para evocar un abanico de experiencias o emociones.

CHARACTER / PERSONAJE Un *personaje* es una persona o animal que participa de la acción en una obra literaria. A continuación hay algunos términos que se usan para describir varios tipos de personajes:

El *protagonista*, o *personaje principal*, en una obra literaria es aquel en el que se centra la obra. Los *personajes importantes* en una obra literaria incluyen el personaje principal y otros personajes que tienen papeles significativos. Un *personaje menor* es aquel que no tiene un papel importante. Un *personaje complejo* es aquel que muestra muchos rasgos diferentes. Un *personaje plano* muestra solo un rasgo. Un *personaje dinámico* se desarrolla y crece en el curso del relato. Un *personaje estático* no cambia a lo largo de la obra.

CHARACTERIZATION / CARACTERIZACIÓN La *caracterización* es el acto de crear y desarrollar un personaje. En una *caracterización directa*, el autor expresa explícitamente los rasgos de un personaje. En una *caracterización indirecta*, el personaje se revela a partir de una de estas maneras:

1. palabras, pensamientos o acciones del personaje
2. descripciones de la apariencia física del personaje o de su procedencia
3. lo que otros personajes dicen sobre el personaje
4. la forma en la que otros personajes reaccionan al personaje

CLAIM / AFIRMACIÓN Una *afirmación* es una opinión, conclusión o punto de vista determinado que el escritor presenta mediante un *argumento*.

CONCESSION / CONCESIÓN La *concesión* es un recurso retórico que reconoce los argumentos de la oposición.

CONFLICT / CONFLICTO Un *conflicto* es una lucha entre fuerzas opuestas. A veces la lucha es interna, o dentro de un personaje. Otras veces la lucha es externa, o entre un personaje y una fuerza exterior. El conflicto es uno de los elementos principales de la literatura narrativa porque la mayoría de tramas se desarrollan a partir de conflictos.

CONNOTATION / CONNOTACIÓN La *connotación* es la asociación que una palabra trae a la mente, además de su definición del diccionario. Muchas palabras que son similares en sus significados del diccionario, o denotaciones, son muy diferentes en sus connotaciones. Los poetas y otros escritores escogen sus palabras cuidadosamente para que las connotaciones de esas palabras sean apropiadas.

COUNTERCLAIM / CONTRAARGUMENTO

Un **contraargumento** es una objeción o desafío a la **afirmación**—u opinión, conclusión o punto de vista determinado—que el escritor presenta en un **argumento**. El escritor suele incluir contraargumentos para anticiparse a los desafíos.

DENOTATION / DENOTACIÓN

La **denotación** de una palabra es su significado objetivo, independientemente de otras asociaciones que esa palabra traiga a la mente.

DESCRIPTION / DESCRIPCIÓN

Una **descripción** es un retrato en palabras de algo que se puede percibir con los sentidos. Los escritores crean descripciones usando imágenes.

DIALECT / DIALECTO

El **dialecto** es la forma de un lenguaje hablado por la gente en una región o grupo particular. Los escritores a menudo usan dialecto para hacer que sus personajes parezcan más reales y para reflejar el habla de una zona determinada.

DIALOGUE / DIÁLOGO

Un **diálogo** es una conversación entre personajes. Los escritores usan el diálogo para revelar personajes, para presentar hechos, para añadir variedad a la narración o para despertar el interés de los lectores.

DICTION / DICCIÓN

La **dicción** comprende la elección de palabras que hace un autor o hablante. La dicción es parte del estilo de un escritor y se puede describir como formal o informal, sencilla u ornamentada, común o técnica, abstracta o concreta.

DRAMA / DRAMA

Un **drama** es una historia escrita para ser representada por actores. El guión de un drama proporciona el diálogo para que los personajes hablen, así como las **acotaciones** que dan información sobre el vestuario, la iluminación, la ambientación, los objetos y la manera en la que los personajes se mueven o hablan. Las convenciones dramáticas incluyen soliloquios, apartes, o el paso del tiempo entre actos o escenas. La **exposición dramática** es un ensayo breve o comentario en prosa del escritor y que tiene como objetivo que los lectores y productores entiendan a los personajes y sus conflictos. El **conocimiento previo** incluye información sobre el período en el cual tiene lugar la acción.

DRAMATIC MONOLOGUE / MONÓLOGO DRAMÁTICO

Un **monólogo dramático** es un poema o discurso en el que un personaje imaginario le habla a un oyente silencioso.

DRAMATIC POEM / POEMA DRAMÁTICO

Un **poema dramático** es aquel que usa las reglas del drama. Estos poemas pueden ser monólogos o diálogos o pueden presentar el parlamento de varios personajes. "The Death of the Hired Man" de Robert Frost es un ejemplo muy famoso de poema dramático.

Ver también **monólogo dramático**.

EPIC THEME / TEMA ÉPICO

Un **tema épico** es el mensaje subyacente de que todas las personas de todas las épocas están conectadas por experiencias compartidas.

EDITORIAL / EDITORIAL

Un **editorial** es una forma de escritura persuasiva o argumento. Los editoriales deben tener una postura clara, respaldarse con razonamientos e incluir una apelación a la ética, a la lógica, a la autoridad o a la emoción.

ELLIPTICAL PHRASING / FRASEO ELÍPTICO

El **fraseo elíptico** es un estilo de poesía en el que el poeta omite palabras que se espera que sean comprendidas por el lector.

ENUMERATION / ENUMERACIÓN

Una **enumeración** es un estilo de documento en el que las ideas principales se listan en orden numérico.

ESSAY / ENSAYO

Un **ensayo** es una obra breve de no-ficción sobre un tema en particular. Los ensayos pueden clasificarse como **formal** o **informal**, **personal** o **impersonal**. También se pueden clasificar de acuerdo a su propósito, como por ejemplo **de causa y efecto**, **satírico** o **reflexivo**. Otras maneras de clasificar ensayos es por el modo de discurso, como por ejemplo **expositivo**, **descriptivo**, **persuasivo** o **narrativo**.

EXPLANATORY ESSAY / ENSAYO EXPLICATIVO

Un **ensayo explicativo** describe y resume información sobre un concepto recogida a partir de varias fuentes.

FICTION / FICCIÓN

La **ficción** es un escrito en prosa que cuenta algo sobre personajes y hechos imaginarios. Los cuentos y las novelas son obras de ficción.

FIGURATIVE LANGUAGE / LENGUAJE FIGURADO

El **lenguaje figurado** es un escrito o discurso que no se debe interpretar literalmente. Los escritores usan lenguaje figurado para expresar ideas de forma vívida e imaginativa.

FIGURE OF SPEECH / FIGURA RETÓRICA

Una **figura retória** es una expresión o palabra usada de forma imaginativa en vez de literal.

FLASHBACK / FLASHBACK

Un **flashback** o **escena retrospectiva** es una sección de una obra literaria que interrumple la presentación cronológica de los hechos para relatar un hecho de un tiempo anterior. Un escritor puede presentar un flashback como el recuerdo de un personaje, como parte de lo que cuenta un personaje, como un sueño o simplemente haciendo que el narrador cambie a un tiempo en el pasado.

FORESHADOWING / PREFIGURACIÓN

La **prefiguración** es el uso, en una obra literaria, de claves que sugieren hechos que van a suceder.

FRAME STORY / CUENTO DE ENMARQUE

Un **cuento de enmarque** es un relato dentro del cual se incluye otro relato o relatos. Este recurso permite crear una estructura narrativa del tipo "cuento dentro del cuento".

FREE VERSE / VERSO LIBRE

El **verso libre** es una forma poética en la que no se sigue un patrón regular de metro ni de rima. Un escritor de verso libre tiene la libertad de usar cualquier ritmo que sea apropiado a lo que está diciendo.

GENRE / GÉNERO

Un **género** es una categoría o tipo de literatura. La literatura se divide por lo general en tres géneros principales: poesía, prosa y drama. Cada uno de estos géneros principales se dividen a su vez en géneros más pequeños. La poesía se puede dividir en lírica, concreta, dramática, narrativa y épica. La prosa se puede dividir en ficción y no ficción. El drama se puede dividir en drama serio, tragedia, drama cómico, melodrama y farsa.

HUMOR / HUMOR El *humor*, usado en un argumento, puede ser un recurso retórico efectivo. El lenguaje y los detalles humorísticos pueden hacer que los personajes y las situaciones parezcan divertidos.

HYPERBOLE / HIPÉRBOLE Una *hipérbole* es una exageración o magnificación deliberada que a menudo se usa para producir un efecto cómico.

IDIOMATIC EXPRESSION / EXPRESIÓN IDIOMÁTICA Las *expresiones idiomáticas* son figuras retóricas que no se pueden entender literalmente. Por ejemplo, una tormenta se puede describir como "llover a cántaros".

IMAGE / IMAGEN Una *imagen* es una palabra o frase que apela a uno o más de los cinco sentidos: la vista, el oído, el tacto, el gusto o el olfato.

IMAGERY / IMÁGENES Las *imágenes* son el lenguaje figurado o descriptivo que se usa en la literatura para crear una descripción verbal para los lectores. Estas descripciones verbales, o imágenes, se crean incluyendo detalles visuales, auditivos, gustativos, táctiles, olfativos o de movimiento.

IN MEDIA RES / IN MEDIA RES *In media res*, que quiere decir "en el medio de las cosas" en latín, es un resurso que usan los escritores para captar la atención del lector.

INCONGRUITY / INCONGRUENCIA La *incongruencia* es una técnica que usan los escritores para crear humor y ocurre cuando dos o más ideas se relacionan entre sí de una manera que no es de la esperada por el lector.

IRONY / IRONÍA *Ironía* es un contraste entre lo que se dice y lo que se quiere decir, o entre lo que se espera que ocurra y lo que pasa en realidad. En una *ironía verbal*, las palabras se usan para sugerir lo opuesto a lo que se dice. En la *ironía dramática* hay una contradicción entre lo que el personaje piensa y lo que el lector o la audiencia sabe que es verdad. En una *ironía situacional*, ocurre un suceso que contradice directamente las expectativas de los personajes, del lector o de la audiencia.

LETTER / CARTA Una *carta* es un mensaje escrito dirigido a un lector o lectores y generalmente se envía por correo. Las cartas pueden ser *privadas* o *públicas*, dependiendo de la audiencia a la que van dirigidas. Una *carta pública*, también llamada *carta literaria* o *epístola*, es una obra literara escrita en forma de carta personal pero creada para ser publicada.

MEMOIR / MEMORIAS Unas **memorias** son un tipo de escrito de no ficción autobiográfica en el que el autor cuenta algo de su propia vida, generalmente centrándose

en la participación del autor en hechos significativos históricos o culturales, ya sea como participante directo o como testigo.

METAPHOR / METÁFORA Una **metáfora** es una figura literaria en la que algo se describe como si fuera otra cosa. La identificación sugiere una comparación entre las dos cosas que se identifican, como "la muerte es un largo sueño".

Una *metáfora mixta* ocurre cuando dos metáforas se unen. Por ejemplo, las espinas y la lluvia se mezclan ilógicamente en "le llovieron encima las espinas de la vida". Una *metáfora muerta* es aquella que se ha sobreutilizado mucho y se ha convertido en una expresión común, como "el brazo del sillón" o "la noche que cae".

MONOLOGUE / MONÓLOGO Un *monólogo* es un discurso narrado por completo por una sola persona o personaje.

MOTIF / MOTIVO El *motivo* es un objeto o idea que se repite de forma recurrente en una obra literaria.

NARRATION / NARRACIÓN Una *narración* es un escrito que cuenta una historia. El acto de contar una historia de forma oral también se llama *narración*. La *narrativa*, o relato, la cuenta el *narrador.* Un relato generalmente se cuenta en orden cronológico, en el orden en el que suceden los hechos, aunque puede incluir flashbacks y prefiguración. Las narrativas pueden ser verdaderas o inventadas. La narración es una de las muchas formas de discurso que existen y se usa en novelas, cuentos, obras de teatro, poemas narrativos, anécdotas, autobiografías, biografías e informes.

NARRATIVE / RELATO Se llama *relato* a la historia que se narra en una obra de ficción, de no-ficción, en un poema o en un drama. Los relatos a menudo se clasifican por su contenido o propósito. Un *relato de exploración* es una narración en primera persona de los viajes de un explorador en una tierra desconocida. "The Interesting Narrative of the Life of Olaudah Equiano" es un *relato de esclavos*, la narración de las experiencias de una persona esclavizada. Un *relato histórico* es la narración de hechos históricos significativos. Un *relato personal* es una narración en primera persona sobre una experiencia real. En un *relato de reflexión* el autor describe sus sentimientos sobre una escena, incidente, recuerdo o hecho. Un *relato no lineal* no sigue el orden cronológico. Puede contener flashbacks, secuencias de sueño u otros recursos que interrumpen el orden cronológico de los hechos.

NARRATOR / NARRADOR Un *narrador* es el hablante o el personaje que cuenta una historia. El cuento o novela lo puede narrar un personaje principal, un personaje menor o alguien que no está involucrado en la trama. El narrador puede hablar en primera persona o en tercera persona. Un *narrador omnisciente* lo sabe todo, mientras que un *narrador limitado* sólo sabe lo que hace un personaje.

NONFICTION / NO-FICCIÓN La *no-ficción* es un escrito en prosa que presenta y explica ideas o cuenta algo acerca de personas, lugares, ideas o hechos reales. Dos de los tipos principales de literatura de no-ficción son los escritos históricos y los escritos de reflexión. Los ensayos, las biografías, las autobiografías, los diarios y los reportajes son todos ejemplos de no-ficción.

NOVEL / NOVELA Una *novela* es una obra extensa de ficción. A menudo tiene una trama complicada, con personajes principales y secundarios, con un tema significativo y una ambientación variada. Las novelas pueden clasificarse de muchas maneras, basadas en los periodos históricos en los que se escribieron, en los temas que tratan, en las técnicas que se usan en ellas y en los movimientos literarios que las inspiraron. Una *novela corta* no es tan extensa como una novela, pero es más larga que un cuento.

ONOMATOPOEIA / ONOMATOPEYA La *onomatopeya* es el uso de palabras que imitan sonidos, tales como *zum*, *pío-pío*, *tic-tac* o *susurro*.

ORATORY / ORATORIA La *oratoria* es hablar en público de manera formal, persuasiva y emocionalmente atractiva. El "Discurso en la Convención de Virginia" es un ejemplo de oratoria.

OXYMORON / OXÍMORON Un *oxímoron* es una figura literaria que combina dos ideas opuestas o contradictorias. Un oxímoron, como "fuego helado", sugiere una paradoja en solo unas palabras.

PACING / RITMO LITERARIO El *ritmo literario* es la velocidad o el paso de la escritura. Los escritores usan diferentes ritmos literarios para lograr distintos efectos, como el suspenso.

PARADOX / PARADOJA Una *paradoja* es un enunciado que parece contradictorio pero que sin embargo presenta una verdad.

PARALLELISM / PARALELISMO El *paralelismo* es la presentación de ideas similares, en secuencia, usando la misma estructura gramatical.

PARALLEL STRUCTURE / ESTRUCTURA PARALELA En una lista, cada objeto listado debe usar *estructura paralela* en la cual la morfología y frase gramatical sea igual para todos los objetos.

PERSONIFICATION / PERSONIFICACIÓN La *personificación* es una forma de lenguaje figurado en la que se da rasgos y actitudes humanas a un sujeto no humano. La personificación efectiva de cosas o ideas hace que se vean llenas de vida, como si fueran humanas.

PHILOSOPHICAL ASSUMPTIONS / SUPOSICIONES FILOSÓFICAS Las creencias que se dan por sentadas son *suposiciones filosóficas*. Algunas suposiciones son *explícitas*, o enunciadas directamente. Otras suposiciones son *implícitas*, que quiere decir que el lector debe hacer inferencias para comprenderlas.

PLOT / TRAMA o ARGUMENTO La *trama* o *argumento* es la secuencia de los eventos que suceden en una obra literaria. En la mayoría de las obras de ficción, la trama implica tanto a los personajes como al conflicto central. La trama por lo general empieza con una *exposición* que introduce la ambientación, los personajes y la situación básica. A ello le sigue el *suceso desencadenante*, que introduce el conflicto central. Este conflicto aumenta durante el *desarrollo* hasta que alcanza el punto más alto de interés o suspenso, llamado *clímax*. Al clímax le sigue el final o resolución del conflicto central. Todos los hechos que ocurren después de la *resolución*, forman el *desenlace*. Todos los sucesos que conducen al clímax constituyen la *acción dramática creciente*. Los sucesos que siguen al clímax forman la *acción dramática decreciente*.

POETIC STRUCTURE / ESTRUCTURA POÉTICA Las *estructuras poéticas* básicas son los versos y las estrofas. Un *verso* es un grupo de palabras ordenadas en un mismo renglón. Un verso puede terminar, o cortarse, de distintas maneras. La variedad en la *extensión de los versos* crea ritmos inesperados.

En un *verso no encabalgado* la estructura gramatical y el sentido se completan al final de esa línea.

En un *verso encabalgado* tanto la estructura gramatical como el sentido de una línea continúa en el verso que sigue.

POETRY / POESÍA La *poesía* es uno de los tres géneros literarios más importantes. En poesía, la forma y el contenido están íntimamente relacionados, como dos caras de la misma moneda. Los poemas a menudo se dividen en versos y estrofas y emplean patrones rítmicos regulares, llamados metros. La mayoría de los poemas están escritos en un lenguaje altamente conciso, musical y emocionalmente rico. Muchos también hacen uso de imágenes, de figuras retóricas y de sonoros, tales como la rima.

POINT OF VIEW / PUNTO DE VISTA El *punto de vista* es la perspectiva desde la cual se narran o describen los hechos de un relato. Tres puntos de vista que se usan frecuentemente son: primera persona, tercera persona omnisciente y tercera persona limitada.

En el *punto de vista de primera persona*, el narrador es un personaje del relato y se refiere a sí mismo con el pronombre de primera persona "yo".

Los dos tipos de punto de vista de tercera persona, limitado y omnisciente, se llaman "tercera persona" porque el narrador usa pronombres de tercera persona como "él o "ella" para referirse a los personajes. No hay "yo" que narre la historia.

En los relatos contados desde el *punto de vista de tercera persona omnisciente*, el narrador conoce y cuenta cosas sobre lo que cada personaje piensa y siente.

En los relatos contados desde el *punto de vista de tercera persona limitada*, el narrador relata los pensamientos internos y sentimientos de sólo un personaje y todo se ve desde el punto de vista de ese personaje.

PREAMBLE / PREÁMBULO El *preámbulo* es un enunciado que explica quién expide un documento y con qué propósito.

PRIMARY SOURCE / FUENTE PRIMARIA Una *fuente primaria* es la que ha sido creada por alguien que participó u observó directamente el suceso que se describe.

PROSE / PROSA La *prosa* es la forma común del lenguaje escrito. La mayoría de los escritos que no son poesía, ni drama, ni canciones, se consideran prosa. La prosa es uno de los géneros literarios más importantes y puede ser de dos formas: de ficción y de no-ficción.

PROTAGONIST / PROTAGONISTA El o la *protagonista* es el personaje principal de una obra literaria.

REFRAIN / REFRÁN Un *refrán* es un verso o grupo de versos que se repite en un poema o canción. Muchos refranes terminan estrofas. Si bien es cierto que algunos refranes no tienen sentido, la mayoría sirve para aumentar el suspenso o para realzar un personaje o enfatizar un tema.

REGIONALISM / REGIONALISMO El *regionalismo* en literatura es la tendencia entre ciertos autores a escribir sobre áreas geográficas específicas. Los escritores regionales presentan la cultura específica de un área, incluyendo su dialecto, costumbres, creencias e historia.

REPETITION / REPETICIÓN La *repetición* de palabras y frases es un recurso literario que se usa en prosa y poesía para dar énfasis a ideas importantes.

RHETORICAL DEVICES / FIGURAS RETÓRICAS Las *figuras retóricas* son patrones especiales de palabras e ideas que dan énfasis y producen emoción, especialmente en discursos y otras presentaciones orales. El *paralelismo*, por ejemplo, es la repetición de una estructura gramatical con el propósito de crear un ritmo y hacer que las palabras resulten más memorables.

Otras figuras retóricas muy frecuentes son: la *analogía*, que establece una comparación entre dos cosas diferentes; el *lenguaje emocionalmente cargado*, en el que las palabras apelan a las emociones; la *concesión*, mediante la que se acepta el argumento del oponente; el *humor*, que usa el lenguaje y los detalles para hacer que los personajes o las situaciones resulten cómicas; la *paradoja*, enunciados que parecen contradecirse pero que presentan una verdad; la *reafirmación*, en la que se expresa la misma idea con distintas palabras; las *preguntas retóricas*, que son interrogaciones cuyas respuestas son obvias; el *tono*, la actitud del autor hacia la audiencia.

RHETORICAL QUESTIONS / PREGUNTAS RETÓRICAS Las *preguntas retóricas* llaman la atención a un hecho al insinuar respuestas obvias.

RIMA La *rima* es la repetición de los sonidos finales de las palabras. Las palabras que riman tienen sonidos vocálicos iguales en las sílabas finales acentuadas. Las consonantes que están antes de esas vocales acentuadas pueden ser diferentes, pero las consonantes que estén después de esas vocales deben ser iguales, como en *frog* y *bog* o en *willow* y *pillow*. La *rima de final de verso* tiene lugar cuando se repiten las palabras que riman al final de dos o más versos. La *rima interna* se produce cuando las palabras que riman están en el mismo verso. La *rima aproximada* tiene lugar cuando los sonidos son parecidos pero no exactos, como en *prove* y *glove*.

RITMO El *ritmo* es el patrón de cadencia o acentuación en la lengua hablada o escrita. La prosa y el verso libre se escriben en los patrones rítmicos irregulares del lenguaje hablado cotidiano.

ROMANTICISM / ROMANTICISMO El *romanticismo* fue un movimiento literario y artístico del siglo. XIX que surgió como reacción contra el neoclasicismo del siglo. XVII y que daba énfasis a la imaginación, la emoción, la naturaleza, la individualidad y lo exótico. El romanticismo es particularmente evidente en las obras de los transcendentalistas.

SECONDARY SOURCE / FUENTE SECUNDARIA Una *fuente secundaria* es la que ha sido creada por alguien con información indirecta del suceso que se describe. Las fuentes secundarias dependen de las *fuentes primarias*, o descripciones de primera mano.

SENSORY LANGUAGE / LENGUAJE SENSORIAL El *lenguaje sensorial* es un escrito o discurso que incluye detalles que apelan a uno o más de los sentidos.

SEQUENCE OF EVENTS / SECUENCIA DE SUCESOS Los autores a menudo usan la *secuencia de sucesos*, o el orden en que sucenden las cosas, para estructurar piezas de no ficción que describen hechos históricos o que explican cambios a lo largo del tiempo. Los autores frecuentemente describen hechos importantes en *orden cronológico,* u orden de tiempo.

SETTING / AMBIENTACIÓN La *ambientación* de una obra literaria es la época y el lugar en el que se desarrolla la acción. La ambientación puede servir varias funciones. Puede proporcionar el telón de fondo para la acción. Puede ser un elemento crucial en la trama o conflicto central. También puede crear una atmósfera emotiva.

SHORT STORY / CUENTO Un *cuento* es una obra breve de ficción. El cuento se parece a la novela, pero suele tener una trama y ambientación más sencillas. Además, el cuento tiende a revelar el carácter de los personajes en un momento particular en lugar de irlo desarrollando a lo largo de numerosos acontecimientos. Por ejemplo, el cuento "The Far and the Near" de Thomas Wolfe se centra en lo que le sucede a un maquinista cuando visita a la gente que lo ha saludado diariamente.

SERIAL COMMA / COMA EN SERIE En inglés, se pone una *coma en serie* después de cada objeto en una lista, excepto en el objeto final.

SIMILE / SÍMIL Un *símil* es una figura retórica en la que se usa la palabra *como* para establecer una comparación directa entre dos cosas.

SLANT RHYME / RIMA ASONANTE En una *rima asonante* los sonidos finales de dos versos del poema son similares, pero no idénticos.

SOCIAL COMMENTARY / COMENTARIO SOCIAL En obras de *comentario social,* el autor tiene como objetivo resaltar, de forma crítica, un aspecto de la sociedad.

SPEAKER / HABLANTE El *hablante* es la voz de un poema. Aunque a menudo el hablante es el poeta, el hablante puede ser también un personaje imaginario o incluso un objeto inanimado o cualquier otro tipo de sujeto no humano. Interpretar un poema a menudo depende de reconocer quién es el hablante, a quién se dirige el hablante y cuál es la actitud o tono del hablante.

STANZA / ESTROFA Una *estrofa* es un grupo de versos en un poema que se consideran una unidad. Muchos poemas se dividen en estrofas que están separadas por espacios. Las estrofas a menudo funcionan como los párrafos en la prosa. Cada estrofa enuncia y desarrolla una sola idea principal.

Las estrofas a menudo reciben su nombre del número de versos que las componen, como siguen:

1. Pareado o dístico: estrofa de dos versos
2. terceta: estrofa de tres versos
3. cuarteta: estrofa de cuatro versos
4. quintilla: estrofa de cinco versos
5. sextilla: estrofa de seis versos
6. septeto: estrofa de siete versos
7. octavilla: estrofa de ocho versos

STREAM OF CONSCIOUSNESS / MONÓLOGO INTERIOR El *monólogo interior* es una técnica narrativa que presenta los pensamientos como si vinieran directamente de la mente de un personaje. En vez de ordenarse cronológicamente, los hechos se presentan desde el punto de vista del personaje, mezclados con los pensamientos como si ocurrieran espontáneamente.

STYLE / ESTILO El *estilo* de un escritor incluye su dicción, tono, grado de formalidad, lenguaje figurado, ritmo, estructura gramatical, tamaño de las oraciones, organización, etc. En resumen, cada rasgo del uso del lenguaje de un escritor.

SUSPENSE / SUSPENSO El *suspenso* es la sensación creciente de incertidumbre sobre el resultado de los hechos.

Los escritores crean suspenso poniendo preguntas en la mente de sus lectores. El suspenso crece hasta el clímax de la trama, punto en el que alcanza su momento álgido.

SYMBOL / SÍMBOLO Un *símbolo* es algo que representa otra cosa. Un *símbolo convencional* es uno ampliamente conocido y aceptado, como un viaje como símbolo de la vida o una calavera como símbolo de la muerte. Un *símbolo personal* es el que desarrolla un autor en concreto para una obra en particular.

SYMBOLISM / SIMBOLISMO El *simbolismo* hace referencia al uso de personas, lugares u objetos que usa un autor para representar cualidades o ideas abstractas.

SYNTAX / SINTAXIS La *sintaxis* es la estructura de las oraciones.

THEME / TEMA Un *tema* es el mensaje central o la concepción de la vida que revela una obra literaria. El tema de un ensayo a menudo se menciona directamente en la tesis. En la mayoría de obras de ficción el tema se enuncia sólo indirectamente: un cuento, poema u obra de teatro a menudo tienen un *tema implícito*.

TONE / TONO El *tono* de una obra literaria es la actitud del escritor hacia su tema, sus personajes o su audiencia. El tono de un escritor puede ser formal o informal, amistoso o distante, personal o pretencioso. El tono de una obra también se puede describir como técnico, conversacional o coloquial.

TRANSCENDENTALISM /TRANSCENDENTALISMO El *transcendentalismo* fue un movimiento estadounidense literario y filosófico del siglo. XIX. Los transcendentalistas, que estaban radicados en Nueva Inglaterra, creían que la intuición y consciencia individual "transcendían" la experiencia y por tanto eran mejores guías a la verdad que los sentidos y la razón lógica. Influidos por el Romanticismo, los transcendentalistas respetaban el espíritu individual y el mundo natural, creyendo que lo divino estaba presente en todas partes, en la naturaleza y en cada persona.

USAGE / USO El *uso* es la manera en la que una palabra o frase se usa. El significado, pronunciación y ortografía de algunas de las palabras ha cambiado con el tiempo.

VOICE / VOZ La *voz* es el "sonido" distintivo de un escritor, o la manera en que "habla" en la página. Se relaciona a elementos tales como la dicción, los tipos de palabras, la sintaxis, el tipo de oraciones empleadas y el tono, que es la actitud del autor hacia el tema o la audiencia.

PARTS OF SPEECH

Every English word, depending on its meaning and its use in a sentence, can be identified as one of the eight parts of speech. These are nouns, pronouns, verbs, adjectives, adverbs, prepositions, conjunctions, and interjections. Understanding the parts of speech will help you learn the rules of English grammar and usage.

Nouns A **noun** names a person, place, or thing. A **common noun** names any one of a class of persons, places, or things. A **proper noun** names a specific person, place, or thing.

Common Noun	Proper Noun
writer, country, novel	Charles Dickens, Great Britain, *Hard Times*

Pronouns A **pronoun** is a word that stands for one or more nouns. The word to which a pronoun refers (whose place it takes) is the **antecedent** of the pronoun.

A **personal pronoun** refers to the person speaking (first person); the person spoken to (second person); or the person, place, or thing spoken about (third person).

	Singular	Plural
First Person	I, me, my, mine	we, us, our, ours
Second Person	you, your, yours	you, your, yours
Third Person	he, him, his, she, her, hers, it, its	they, them, their, theirs

A **reflexive pronoun** reflects the action of a verb back on its subject. It indicates that the person or thing performing the action also is receiving the action.

I keep *myself* fit by taking a walk every day.

An **intensive pronoun** adds emphasis to a noun or pronoun.

It took the work of the president *himself* to pass the law.

A **demonstrative** pronoun points out a specific person(s), place(s), or thing(s).

this, that, these, those

A **relative pronoun** begins a subordinate clause and connects it to another idea in the sentence.

that, which, who, whom, whose

An **interrogative pronoun** begins a question.

what, which, who, whom, whose

An **indefinite pronoun** refers to a person, place, or thing that may or may not be specifically named.

all, another, any, both, each, everyone, few, most, none, no one, somebody

Verbs A **verb** expresses action or the existence of a state or condition.

An **action verb** tells what action someone or something is performing.

gather, read, work, jump, imagine, analyze, conclude

A **linking verb** connects the subject with another word that identifies or describes the subject. The most common linking verb is *be*.

appear, be, become, feel, look, remain, seem, smell, sound, stay, taste

A **helping verb,** or **auxiliary verb,** is added to a main verb to make a verb phrase.

be, do, have, should, can, could, may, might, must, will, would

Adjectives An **adjective** modifies a noun or pronoun by describing it or giving it a more specific meaning. An adjective answers the questions:

What kind?	*purple* hat, *happy* face, *loud* sound
Which one?	*this* bowl
How many?	*three* cars
How much?	*enough* food

The articles *the, a,* and *an* are adjectives.

A **proper adjective** is an adjective derived from a proper noun.

French, Shakespearean

Adverbs An **adverb** modifies a verb, an adjective, or another adverb by telling *where, when, how,* or *to what extent*.

will answer *soon, extremely* sad, calls *more* often

Prepositions A **preposition** relates a noun or pronoun that appears with it to another word in the sentence.

Dad made a meal *for* us. We talked *till* dusk. Bo missed school *because of* his illness.

Conjunctions A **conjunction** connects words or groups of words. A **coordinating conjunction** joins words or groups of words of equal rank.

bread *and* cheese, brief *but* powerful

Correlative conjunctions are used in pairs to connect words or groups of words of equal importance.

both Luis *and* Rosa, *neither* you *nor* I

Subordinating conjunctions indicate the connection between two ideas by placing one below the other in rank or importance. A subordinating conjunction introduces a subordinate, or dependent, clause.

> We will miss her *if* she leaves. Hank shrieked *when* he slipped on the ice.

Interjections An **interjection** expresses feeling or emotion. It is not related to other words in the sentence.

> ah, hey, ouch, well, yippee

PHRASES AND CLAUSES

Phrases A **phrase** is a group of words that does not have both a subject and a verb and that functions as one part of speech. A phrase expresses an idea but cannot stand alone.

Prepositional Phrases A **prepositional phrase** is a group of words that begins with a preposition and ends with a noun or pronoun that is the **object of the preposition.**

> before dawn   as a result of the rain

An **adjective phrase** is a prepositional phrase that modifies a noun or pronoun.

> Eliza appreciates the beauty **of a well-crafted poem.**

An **adverb phrase** is a prepositional phrase that modifies a verb, an adjective, or an adverb.

> She reads Spenser's sonnets **with great pleasure.**

Appositive Phrases An **appositive** is a noun or pronoun placed next to another noun or pronoun to add information about it. An **appositive phrase** consists of an appositive and its modifiers.

> Mr. Roth, **my music teacher**, is sick.

Verbal Phrases A **verbal** is a verb form that functions as a different part of speech (not as a verb) in a sentence. **Participles, gerunds,** and **infinitives** are verbals.

A **verbal phrase** includes a verbal and any modifiers or complements it may have. Verbal phrases may function as nouns, as adjectives, or as adverbs.

A **participle** is a verb form that can act as an adjective. Present participles end in *-ing;* past participles of regular verbs end in *-ed.*

A **participial phrase** consists of a participle and its modifiers or complements. The entire phrase acts as an adjective.

> Jenna's backpack, **loaded with equipment,** was heavy.
> **Barking incessantly,** the dogs chased the squirrels out of sight.

A **gerund** is a verb form that ends in *-ing* and is used as a noun.

A **gerund phrase** consists of a gerund with any modifiers or complements, all acting together as a noun.

> **Taking photographs of wildlife** is her main hobby. [acts as subject]
> We always enjoy **listening to live music.** [acts as object]

An **infinitive** is a verb form, usually preceded by *to,* that can act as a noun, an adjective, or an adverb.

An **infinitive phrase** consists of an infinitive and its modifiers or complements, and sometimes its subject, all acting together as a single part of speech.

> She tries **to get out into the wilderness often.** [acts as a noun; direct object of *tries*]
> The Tigers are the team **to beat.** [acts as an adjective; describes *team*]
> I drove twenty miles **to witness the event.** [acts as an adverb; tells why I drove]

Clauses A **clause** is a group of words with its own subject and verb.

Independent Clauses An independent clause can stand by itself as a complete sentence.

> George Orwell wrote with extraordinary insight.

Subordinate Clauses A subordinate clause, also called a dependent clause, cannot stand by itself as a complete sentence. Subordinate clauses always appear connected in some way with one or more independent clauses.

> George Orwell, **who wrote with extraordinary insight,** produced many politically relevant works.

An **adjective clause** is a subordinate clause that acts as an adjective. It modifies a noun or a pronoun by telling *what kind* or *which one.* Also called relative clauses, adjective clauses usually begin with a **relative pronoun:** *who, which, that, whom,* or *whose.*

> "The Lamb" is the poem **that I memorized for class.**

An **adverb clause** is a subordinate clause that, like an adverb, modifies a verb, an adjective, or an adverb. An adverb clause tells *where, when, in what way, to what extent, under what condition,* or *why.*

The students will read another poetry collection **if their schedule allows.**
When I recited the poem, Mr. Lopez was impressed.

A **noun clause** is a subordinate clause that acts as a noun.

William Blake survived on **whatever he made as an engraver.**

SENTENCE STRUCTURE

Subject and Predicate A **sentence** is a group of words that expresses a complete thought. A sentence has two main parts: a *subject* and a *predicate*.

A **fragment** is a group of words that does not express a complete thought. It lacks an independent clause.

The **subject** tells *whom* or *what* the sentence is about. The **predicate** tells what the subject of the sentence does or is.

A subject or a predicate can consist of a single word or of many words. All the words in the subject make up the **complete subject.** All the words in the predicate make up the **complete predicate.**

Complete Subject	Complete Predicate
Both of those girls	have already read *Macbeth*.

The **simple subject** is the essential noun, pronoun, or group of words acting as a noun that cannot be left out of the complete subject. The **simple predicate** is the essential verb or verb phrase that cannot be left out of the complete predicate.

Both of those girls | **have** already **read** *Macbeth*. [Simple subject: *Both;* simple predicate: *have read*]

A **compound subject** is two or more subjects that have the same verb and are joined by a conjunction.

Neither the horse nor the driver looked tired.

A **compound predicate** is two or more verbs that have the same subject and are joined by a conjunction.

She **sneezed and coughed** throughout the trip.

Complements A **complement** is a word or word group that completes the meaning of the subject or verb in a sentence. There are four kinds of complements: *direct objects, indirect objects, objective complements,* and *subject complements.*

A **direct object** is a noun, a pronoun, or a group of words acting as a noun that receives the action of a transitive verb.

We watched the **liftoff**.
She drove **Zach** to the launch site.

An **indirect object** is a noun or pronoun that appears with a direct object and names the person or thing to which or for which something is done.

He sold the **family** a mirror. [The direct object is *mirror.*]

An **objective complement** is an adjective or noun that appears with a direct object and describes or renames it.

The decision made her **unhappy**.
[The direct object is *her.*]
Many consider Shakespeare the greatest **playwright.** [The direct object is *Shakespeare.*]

A **subject complement** follows a linking verb and tells something about the subject. There are two kinds: *predicate nominatives* and *predicate adjectives.*

A **predicate nominative** is a noun or pronoun that follows a linking verb and identifies or renames the subject.

"A Modest Proposal" is a **pamphlet.**

A **predicate adjective** is an adjective that follows a linking verb and describes the subject of the sentence.

"A Modest Proposal" is **satirical.**

Classifying Sentences by Structure

Sentences can be classified according to the kind and number of clauses they contain. The four basic sentence structures are *simple, compound, complex,* and *compound-complex.*

A **simple sentence** consists of one independent clause.
Terrence enjoys modern British literature.

A **compound sentence** consists of two or more independent clauses. The clauses are joined by a conjunction or a semicolon.
Terrence enjoys modern British literature, but his brother prefers the classics.

A **complex sentence** consists of one independent clause and one or more subordinate clauses.
Terrence, who reads voraciously, enjoys modern British literature.

A **compound-complex sentence** consists of two or more independent clauses and one or more subordinate clauses.
Terrence, who reads voraciously, enjoys modern British literature, but his brother prefers the classics.

Classifying Sentences by Function

Sentences can be classified according to their function or purpose. The four types are *declarative, interrogative, imperative,* and *exclamatory.*

A **declarative sentence** states an idea and ends with a period.

An **interrogative sentence** asks a question and ends with a question mark.

An **imperative sentence** gives an order or a direction and ends with either a period or an exclamation mark.

An **exclamatory sentence** conveys a strong emotion and ends with an exclamation mark.

PARAGRAPH STRUCTURE

An effective paragraph is organized around one **main idea,** which is often stated in a **topic sentence.** The other sentences support the main idea. To give the paragraph **unity,** make sure the connection between each sentence and the main idea is clear.

Unnecessary Shift in Person

Do not change needlessly from one grammatical person to another. Keep the person consistent in your sentences.

> **Max** went to the bakery, but **you** can't buy mints there. [shift from third person to second person]

Max went to the bakery, but **he** can't buy mints there. [consistent]

Unnecessary Shift in Voice

Do not change needlessly from active voice to passive voice in your use of verbs.

> Elena and I **searched** the trail for evidence, but no clues **were found.** [shift from active voice to passive voice]

> Elena and I **searched** the trail for evidence, but we **found** no clues. [consistent]

AGREEMENT

Subject and Verb Agreement

A singular subject must have a singular verb. A plural subject must have a plural verb.

> **Dr. Boone uses** a telescope to view the night sky.
> The **students use** a telescope to view the night sky.

A verb always agrees with its subject, not its object.

> *Incorrect:* The best part of the show were the jugglers.
> *Correct:* The best part of the show was the jugglers.

A phrase or clause that comes between a subject and verb does not affect subject-verb agreement.

> His **theory,** as well as his claims, **lacks** support.

Two subjects joined by *and* usually take a plural verb.

> The **dog** and the **cat are** healthy.

Two singular subjects joined by *or* or *nor* take a singular verb.

> The **dog** or the **cat is** hiding.

Two plural subjects joined by *or* or *nor* take a plural verb.

> The **dogs** or the **cats are** coming home with us.

When a singular and a plural subject are joined by *or* or *nor,* the verb agrees with the closer subject.

> Either the **dogs** or the **cat is** behind the door.
> Either the **cat** or the **dogs are** behind the door.

Pronoun and Antecedent Agreement

Pronouns must agree with their antecedents in number and gender. Use singular pronouns with singular antecedents and plural pronouns with plural antecedents.

> **Doris Lessing** uses **her** writing to challenge ideas about women's roles.
> **Writers** often use **their** skills to promote social change.

Use a singular pronoun when the antecedent is a singular indefinite pronoun such as *anybody, each, either, everybody, neither, no one, one, or someone.*

> Judge **each** of the articles on **its** merits.

Use a plural pronoun when the antecedent is a plural indefinite pronoun such as *both, few, many, or several.*

> **Both** of the articles have **their** flaws.

The indefinite pronouns *all, any, more, most, none,* and *some* can be singular or plural depending on the number of the word to which they refer.

> **Most** of the *books* are in **their** proper places.
> **Most** of the *book* has been torn from **its** binding.

USING VERBS

Principal Parts of Regular and Irregular Verbs

A verb has four principal parts:

Present	Present Participle	Past	Past Participle
learn	learning	learned	learned
discuss	discussing	discussed	discussed
stand	standing	stood	stood
begin	beginning	began	begun

Regular verbs such as *learn* and *discuss* form the past and past participle by adding *-ed* to the present form. **Irregular verbs** such as *stand* and *begin* form the past and past participle in other ways. If you are in doubt about the principal parts of an irregular verb, check a dictionary.

The Tenses of Verbs

The different tenses of verbs indicate the time an action or condition occurs.

The **present tense** expresses an action that happens regularly or states a current condition or a general truth.

> Tourists **flock** to the site yearly.

Daily exercise **is** good for your health.

The **past tense** expresses a completed action or a condition that is no longer true.

> The squirrel **dropped** the nut and **ran** up the tree.
> I **was** very tired last night by 9:00.

The **future tense** indicates an action that will happen in the future or a condition that will be true.

> The Glazers **will visit** us tomorrow.
> They **will be** glad to arrive from their long journey.

The **present perfect tense** expresses an action that happened at an indefinite time in the past or an action that began in the past and continues into the present.

> Someone **has cleaned** the trash from the park.
> The puppy **has been** under the bed all day.

The **past perfect tense** shows an action that was completed before another action in the past.

> Gerard **had revised** his essay before he turned it in.

The **future perfect tense** indicates an action that will have been completed before another action takes place.

> Mimi **will have painted** the kitchen by the time we finish the shutters.

USING MODIFIERS

Degrees of Comparison

Adjectives and adverbs take different forms to show the three degrees of comparison: the *positive*, the *comparative*, and the *superlative*.

Positive	Comparative	Superlative
fast	faster	fastest
crafty	craftier	craftiest
abruptly	more abruptly	most abruptly
badly	worse	worst

Using Comparative and Superlative Adjectives and Adverbs

Use comparative adjectives and adverbs to compare two things. Use superlative adjectives and adverbs to compare three or more things.

> This season's weather was **drier** than last year's.
> This season has been one of the **driest** on record.
> Jake practices **more often** than Jamal.
> Of everyone in the band, Jake practices **most often.**

USING PRONOUNS

Pronoun Case

The **case** of a pronoun is the form it takes to show its function in a sentence. There are three pronoun cases: *nominative*, *objective*, and *possessive*.

Nominative	Objective	Possessive
I, you, he, she, it, we, you, they	me, you, him, her, it, us, you, them	my, your, yours, his, her, hers, its, our, ours, their, theirs

Use the **nominative case** when a pronoun functions as a *subject* or as a *predicate nominative.*

> **They** are going to the movies. [subject]
> The biggest movie fan is **she.** [predicate nominative]

Use the **objective case** for a pronoun acting as a *direct object*, an *indirect object*, or the *object of a preposition.*

> The ending of the play surprised **me.** [direct object]
> Mary gave **us** two tickets to the play. [indirect object]
> The audience cheered for **him.** [object of preposition]

Use the **possessive case** to show ownership.

> The red suitcase is **hers.**

Diction The words you choose contribute to the overall effectiveness of your writing. **Diction** refers to word choice and to the clearness and correctness of those words. You can improve one aspect of your diction by choosing carefully between commonly confused words, such as the pairs listed below.

accept, except

Accept is a verb that means "to receive" or "to agree to." *Except* is a preposition that means "other than" or "leaving out."

> Please **accept** my offer to buy you lunch this weekend.
>
> He is busy every day **except** the weekends.

affect, effect

Affect is normally a verb meaning "to influence" or "to bring about a change in." *Effect* is usually a noun meaning "result."

> The distractions outside **affect** Steven's ability to concentrate.
>
> The teacher's remedies had a positive **effect** on Steven's ability to concentrate.

among, between

Among is usually used with three or more items, and it emphasizes collective relationships or indicates distribution. *Between* is generally used with only two items, but it can be used with more than two if the emphasis is on individual (one-to-one) relationships within the group.

> I had to choose a snack **among** the various vegetables.
>
> He handed out the booklets **among** the conference participants.
>
> Our school is **between** a park and an old barn.
>
> The tournament included matches **between** France, Spain, Mexico, and the United States.

amount, number

Amount refers to overall quantity and is mainly used with mass nouns (those that can't be counted). *Number* refers to individual items that can be counted.

> The **amount** of attention that great writers have paid to Shakespeare is remarkable.
>
> A **number** of important English writers have been fascinated by the legend of King Arthur.

assure, ensure, insure

Assure means "to convince [someone of something]; to guarantee." *Ensure* means "to make certain [that something happens]." *Insure* means "to arrange for payment in case of loss."

> The attorney **assured** us we'd win the case.
>
> The rules **ensure** that no one gets treated unfairly.
>
> Many professional musicians **insure** their valuable instruments.

bad, badly

Use the adjective *bad* before a noun or after linking verbs such as *feel, look,* and *seem*. Use *badly* whenever an adverb is required.

> The situation may seem **bad**, but it will improve over time.
>
> Though our team played **badly** today, we will focus on practicing for the next match.

beside, besides

Beside means "at the side of" or "close to." *Besides* means "in addition to."

> The stapler sits **beside** the pencil sharpener in our classroom.
>
> **Besides** being very clean, the classroom is also very organized.

can, may

The helping verb *can* generally refers to the ability to do something. The helping verb *may* generally refers to permission to do something.

> I **can** run one mile in six minutes.
>
> **May** we have a race during recess?

complement, compliment

The verb *complement* means "to enhance"; the verb *compliment* means "to praise."

> Online exercises **complement** the textbook lessons.
>
> Ms. Lewis **complimented** our team on our excellent debate.

compose, comprise

Compose means "to make up; constitute." *Comprise* means "to include or contain." Remember that the whole comprises its parts or is composed of its parts, and the parts compose the whole.

> The assignment **comprises** three different tasks.
>
> The assignment is **composed** of three different tasks.
>
> Three different tasks **compose** the assignment.

different from, different than

Different from is generally preferred over *different than,* but *different than* can be used before a clause. Always use *different from* before a noun or pronoun.

> Your point of view is so **different from** mine.
>
> His idea was so **different from** [or **different than**] what we had expected.

farther, further

Use *farther* to refer to distance. Use *further* to mean "to a greater degree or extent" or "additional."

> Chiang has traveled **farther** than anybody else in the class.
>
> If I want **further** details about his travels, I can read his blog.

fewer, less

Use *fewer* for things that can be counted. Use *less* for amounts or quantities that cannot be counted. *Fewer* must be followed by a plural noun.

Fewer students drive to school since the weather improved.

There is **less** noise outside in the mornings.

good, well

Use the adjective *good* before a noun or after a linking verb. Use *well* whenever an adverb is required, such as when modifying a verb.

I feel **good** after sleeping for eight hours.

I did **well** on my test, and my soccer team played **well** in that afternoon's game. It was a **good** day!

its, it's

The word *its* with no apostrophe is a possessive pronoun. The word *it's* is a contraction of "it is."

Angelica will try to fix the computer and **its** keyboard.

It's a difficult job, but she can do it.

lay, lie

Lay is a transitive verb meaning "to set or put something down." Its principal parts are *lay, laying, laid, laid. Lie* is an intransitive verb meaning "to recline" or "to exist in a certain place." Its principal parts are *lie, lying, lay, lain.*

Please **lay** that box down and help me with the sofa.

When we are done moving, I am going to **lie** down.

My hometown **lies** sixty miles north of here.

like, as

Like is a preposition that usually means "similar to" and precedes a noun or pronoun. The conjunction *as* means "in the way that" and usually precedes a clause.

Like the other students, I was prepared for a quiz.

As I said yesterday, we expect to finish before noon.

Use **such as,** not **like,** before a series of examples.

Foods **such as** apples, nuts, and pretzels make good snacks.

of, have

Do not use *of* in place of *have* after auxiliary verbs such as *would, could, should, may, might,* or *must.* The contraction of *have* is formed by adding *-ve* after these verbs.

I **would have** stayed after school today, but I had to help cook at home.

Mom **must've** called while I was still in the gym.

principal, principle

Principal can be an adjective meaning "main; most important." It can also be a noun meaning "chief officer of a school." *Principle* is a noun meaning "moral rule" or "fundamental truth."

His strange behavior was the **principal** reason for our concern.

Democratic **principles** form the basis of our country's laws.

raise, rise

Raise is a transitive verb that usually takes a direct object. *Rise* is intransitive and never takes a direct object.

Iliana and Josef **raise** the flag every morning.

They **rise** from their seats and volunteer immediately whenever help is needed.

than, then

The conjunction *than* is used to connect the two parts of a comparison. The adverb *then* usually refers to time.

My backpack is heavier **than** hers.

I will finish my homework and **then** meet my friends at the park.

that, which, who

Use the relative pronoun *that* to refer to things or people. Use *which* only for things and *who* only for people.

That introduces a restrictive phrase or clause, that is, one that is essential to the meaning of the sentence. *Which* introduces a nonrestrictive phrase or clause—one that adds information but could be deleted from the sentence—and is preceded by a comma.

Ben ran to the park **that** just reopened.

The park, **which** just reopened, has many attractions.

The man **who** built the park loves to see people smiling.

when, where, why

Do not use *when, where,* or *why* directly after a linking verb, such as *is.* Reword the sentence.

Incorrect: The morning is when he left for the beach.

Correct: He left for the beach in the morning.

who, whom

In formal writing, use *who* only as a subject in clauses and sentences. Use *whom* only as the object of a verb or of a preposition.

Who paid for the tickets?

Whom should I pay for the tickets?

I can't recall to **whom** I gave the money for the tickets.

your, you're

Your is a possessive pronoun expressing ownership. *You're* is the contraction of "you are."

Have you finished writing **your** informative essay?

You're supposed to turn it in tomorrow. If **you're** late, **your** grade will be affected.

Capitalization

First Words

Capitalize the first word of a sentence.

Stories about knights and their deeds interest me.

Capitalize the first word of direct speech.

Sharon asked, "Do you like stories about knights?"

Capitalize the first word of a quotation that is a complete sentence.

Einstein said, "Anyone who has never made a mistake has never tried anything new."

Proper Nouns and Proper Adjectives

Capitalize all proper nouns, including geographical names, historical events and periods, and names of organizations.

| Thames River | John Keats | the Renaissance |
| United Nations | World War II | Sierra Nevada |

Capitalize all proper adjectives.

| Shakespearean play | British invasion |
| American citizen | Latin American literature |

Academic Course Names

Capitalize course names only if they are language courses, are followed by a number, or are preceded by a proper noun or adjective.

| Spanish | Honors Chemistry | History 101 |
| geology | algebra | social studies |

Titles

Capitalize personal titles when followed by the person's name.

Ms. Hughes   Dr. Perez   King George

Capitalize titles showing family relationships when they are followed by a specific person's name, unless they are preceded by a possessive noun or pronoun.

Uncle Oscar   Mangan's sister   his aunt Tessa

Capitalize the first word and all other key words in the titles of books, stories, songs, and other works of art.

Frankenstein   "Shooting an Elephant"

Punctuation

End Marks

Use a **period** to end a declarative sentence or an imperative sentence.

We are studying the structure of sonnets.
Read the biography of Mary Shelley.

Use periods with initials and abbreviations.

| D. H. Lawrence | Mrs. Browning |
| Mt. Everest | Maple St. |

Use a **question mark** to end an interrogative sentence.

What is Macbeth's fatal flaw?

Use an **exclamation mark** after an exclamatory sentence or a forceful imperative sentence.

That's a beautiful painting!   Let me go now!

Commas

Use a **comma** before a coordinating conjunction to separate two independent clauses in a compound sentence.

The game was very close, but we were victorious.

Use commas to separate three or more words, phrases, or clauses in a series.

William Blake was a writer, artist, and printer.

Use commas to separate coordinate adjectives.

It was a witty, amusing novel.

Use a comma after an introductory word, phrase, or clause.

When the novelist finished his book, he celebrated with his family.

Use commas to set off nonessential expressions.

Old English, of course, requires translation.

Use commas with places and dates.

Coventry, England   September 1, 1939

Semicolons

Use a **semicolon** to join closely related independent clauses that are not already joined by a conjunction.

Tanya likes to write poetry; Heather prefers prose.

Use semicolons to avoid confusion when items in a series contain commas.

They traveled to London, England; Madrid, Spain; and Rome, Italy.

Colons

Use a **colon** before a list of items following an independent clause.

Notable Victorian poets include the following: Tennyson, Arnold, Housman, and Hopkins.

Use a colon to introduce information that summarizes or explains the independent clause before it.

She just wanted to do one thing: rest.

Malcolm loves volunteering: He reads to sick children every Saturday afternoon.

Quotation Marks

Use **quotation marks** to enclose a direct quotation.

"Short stories," Ms. Hildebrand said, "should have rich, well-developed characters."

An **indirect quotation** does not require quotation marks.

Ms. Hildebrand said that short stories should have well-developed characters.

Use quotation marks around the titles of short written works, episodes in a series, songs, and works mentioned as parts of collections.

"The Lagoon"   "Boswell Meets Johnson"

Italics

Italicize the titles of long written works, movies, television and radio shows, lengthy works of music, paintings, and sculptures.

Howards End   *60 Minutes*   *Guernica*

For handwritten material, you can use underlining instead of italics.

<u>The Princess Bride</u>   <u>Mona Lisa</u>

Dashes

Use **dashes** to indicate an abrupt change of thought, a dramatic interrupting idea, or a summary statement.

> I read the entire first act of *Macbeth*—you won't believe what happens next.
>
> The director—what's her name again?—attended the movie premiere.

Hyphens

Use a **hyphen** with certain numbers, after certain prefixes, with two or more words used as one word, and with a compound modifier that comes before a noun.

> seventy-two
>
> self-esteem
>
> president-elect
>
> five-year contract

Parentheses

Use **parentheses** to set off asides and explanations when the material is not essential or when it consists of one or more sentences. When the sentence in parentheses interrupts the larger sentence, it does not have a capital letter or a period.

> He listened intently (it was too dark to see who was speaking) to try to identify the voices.

When a sentence in parentheses falls between two other complete sentences, it should start with a capital letter and end with a period.

> The quarterback threw three touchdown passes. (We knew he could do it.) Our team won the game by two points.

Apostrophes

Add an **apostrophe** and an *s* to show the possessive case of most singular nouns and of plural nouns that do not end in *-s* or *-es*.

> Blake's poems   the mice's whiskers

Names ending in *s* form their possessives in the same way, except for classical and biblical names, which add only an apostrophe to form the possessive.

> Dickens's   Hercules'

Add an apostrophe to show the possessive case of plural nouns ending in *-s* and *-es*.

> the girls' songs   the Ortizes' car

Use an apostrophe in a contraction to indicate the position of the missing letter or letters.

> She's never read a Coleridge poem she didn't like.

Brackets

Use **brackets** to enclose clarifying information inserted within a quotation.

> Columbus's journal entry from October 21, 1492, begins as follows: "At 10 o'clock, we arrived at a cape of the island [San Salvador], and anchored, the other vessels in company."

Ellipses

Use three ellipsis points, also known as an **ellipsis,** to indicate where you have omitted words from quoted material.

> Wollestonecraft wrote, "The education of women has of late been more attended to than formerly; yet they are still . . . ridiculed or pitied. . . ."

In the example above, the four dots at the end of the sentence are the three ellipsis points plus the period from the original sentence.

Use an ellipsis to indicate a pause or interruption in speech.

> "When he told me the news," said the coach, "I was . . . I was shocked . . . completely shocked."

Spelling

Spelling Rules

Learning the rules of English spelling will help you make **generalizations** about how to spell words.

Word Parts

The three word parts that can combine to form a word are roots, prefixes, and suffixes. Many of these word parts come from the Greek, Latin, and Anglo-Saxon languages.

The **root word** carries a word's basic meaning.

Root and Origin	Meaning	Examples
-leg- (-log-) [Gr.]	to say, speak	*legal, logic*
-pon- (-pos-) [L.]	to put, place	*postpone, deposit*

A **prefix** is one or more syllables added to the beginning of a word that alter the meaning of the root.

Prefix and Origin	Meaning	Example
anti- [Gr.]	against	*antipathy*
inter- [L.]	between	*international*
mis- [A.S.]	wrong	*misplace*

A **suffix** is a letter or group of letters added to the end of a root word that changes the word's meaning or part of speech.

Suffix and Origin	Meaning and Example	Part of Speech
-ful [A.S.]	full of: *scornful*	adjective
-ity [L.]	state of being: *adversity*	noun
-ize (-ise) [Gr.]	to make: *idolize*	verb
-ly [A.S.]	in a manner: *calmly*	adverb

Rules for Adding Suffixes to Root Words

When adding a suffix to a root word ending in *y* preceded by a consonant, change *y* to *i* unless the suffix begins with *i*.

   ply + -able = pliable   happy + -ness = happiness

   defy + -ing = defying   cry + -ing = crying

For a root word ending in *e*, drop the *e* when adding a suffix beginning with a vowel.

   drive + -ing = driving   move + -able = movable

   SOME EXCEPTIONS: traceable, seeing, dyeing

For root words ending with a consonant + vowel + consonant in a stressed syllable, double the final consonant when adding a suffix that begins with a vowel.

   mud + -y = muddy   submit + -ed = submitted

   SOME EXCEPTIONS: mixing, fixed

Rules for Adding Prefixes to Root Words

When a prefix is added to a root word, the spelling of the root remains the same.

   un- + certain = uncertain   mis- + spell = misspell

With some prefixes, the spelling of the prefix changes when joined to the root to make the pronunciation easier.

   in- + mortal = immortal   ad- + vert = avert

Orthographic Patterns

Certain letter combinations in English make certain sounds. For instance, *ph* sounds like *f*, *eigh* usually makes a long *a* sound, and the *k* before an *n* is often silent.

   pharmacy   n**eigh**bor   **k**nowledge

Understanding **orthographic patterns** such as these can help you improve your spelling.

Forming Plurals

The plural form of most nouns is formed by adding *-s* to the singular.

   computer**s**   gadget**s**   Washington**s**

For words ending in *s, ss, x, z, sh,* or *ch,* add *-es*.

   circus**es**   tax**es**   wish**es**   bench**es**

For words ending in *y* or *o* preceded by a vowel, add *-s*.

   key**s**   patio**s**

For words ending in *y* preceded by a consonant, change the *y* to an *i* and add *-es*.

   cit**ies**   enem**ies**   troph**ies**

For most words ending in *o* preceded by a consonant, add *-es*.

   echo**es**   tomato**es**

Some words form the plural in irregular ways.

   women   oxen   children   teeth   deer

Foreign Words Used in English

Some words used in English are actually foreign words that have been adopted. Learning to spell these words requires memorization. When in doubt, check a dictionary.

   sushi   enchilada   au pair   fiancé

   laissez faire   croissant

INDEX OF SKILLS

Assessment

INDEX OF AUTHORS AND TITLES

The following authors and titles appear in the print and online versions of *my*Perspectives.

ADDITIONAL SELECTIONS: AUTHOR AND TITLE INDEX

The following authors and titles appear in the Online Literature Library.

INDEX OF AUTHORS AND TITLES

Acknowledgments

The following selections appear in Grade 11 of *my*Perspectives. Some selections appear online only.

Arte Publico Press. "The Latin Deli" from *America's Review* by Judith Ortiz Cofer (©1992 Arte Publico Press—University of Houston).

Audible Inc. "How to Tell a True War Story" from *The Things They Carried* by Tim O'Brien. Copyright ©1990 by Tim O'Brien.

BBC Worldwide Americas, Inc. Boston Tea Party ©BBC Worldwide Learning; The U. S. Constitution ©BBC Worldwide Learning; Great Lives: Emily Dickinson—BBC Worldwide Learning; Civil Rights Marches ©BBC Worldwide Learning; CBS Sunday Morning segment "Mark Twain and Tom Sawyer" ©BBC Worldwide Learning.

Bloomsbury Publishing Plc. "Antojos," Copyright ©1991 by Julia Alvarez. Later published in slightly different form in *How the Garcia Girls Lost Their Accents*. Used with permission of Bloomsbury Publishing Plc.

Brooks Permissions. "Speech to the Young, Speech to the Progress-Toward," reprinted By Consent of Brooks Permissions.

Browning, Sarah. "The Fifth Fact," from *Whisky in the Garden of Eden* (The Word Words, Washington, DC, 2007). Used with permission.

Chopin, Kate. "The Story of An Hour" by Kate Chopin, originally appeared in *Vogue*, 1894.

CNN. The Hollywood Blacklist: 1947–1960 ©CNN.

Contently. Why Do Stories Matter? That's Like Asking Why You Should Eat ©Contently 2015

Copper Canyon Press. Hayden Carruth, "Bears at Raspberry Time" from *Collected Shorter Poems* 1946–1991. Copyright ©1983 by Hayden Carruth. Reprinted with the permission of The Permissions Company, Inc., on behalf of Copper Canyon Press, www.coppercanyonpress.org.

Daily Signal. "Rugged Individualism Fades from National Character" by Marion Smith, from *Daily Signal*, June 11, 2012; http://dailysignal.com/print/?post_id=99695. Used with permission.

Don Congdon Associates. "The Pedestrian," reprinted by permission of Don Congdon Associates, Inc. Copyright ©1951 by the Fortnightly Publishing Company, renewed 1979 by Ray Bradbury.

Douglass, Frederick. "What to the Slave is the 4th of July?" by Frederick Douglass (1818–1895).

Dunbar, Paul Laurence. "Douglass" by Paul Laurence Dunbar (1872–1906).

Espada, Martin. "Who Burns for the Perfection of Paper," from *city of coughing and dead radiators* by Martin Espada. Copyright ©1993 by Martin Espada. Used by permission of the author.

Estate of Galway Kinnell. "Reckless Genius" by Galway Kinnell, from Salon.com. Used with permission of the Estate of Galway Kinnell.

Faber & Faber, Ltd. (UK). "The Love Song of J. Alfred Prufrock" from *Collected Poems*, 1909–1062 by T.S. Eliot. Reprinted by permission of the publisher, Faber and Faber, Ltd.

Farrar, Straus and Giroux. Jacket design and excerpts from *The United States Constitution: A Graphic Adaptation* by Jonathan Hennessey, artwork by Aaron McConnell. Text copyright ©2008 by Jonathan Hennessey. Artwork Copyright ©2008 by Aaron McConnell. Reprinted by permission of Hill and Wang, a division of Farrar, Straus and Giroux, LLC.; "The Fish" from *The Complete Poems* 1927–1979 by Elizabeth Bishop. Copyright ©1979, 1983 by Alice Helen Methfessel. Reprinted by permission of Farrar, Straus and Giroux, LLC.

Fischer, Claude. "Sweet Land of...Conformity?," *Boston Globe*, June 6, 2010, as adapted from the blog, Made in America.

Harold Ober Associates. "Dream Variations," reprinted by permission of Harold Ober Associates Incorporated. Copyright ©1994 by The Estate Of Langston Hughes; "I, Too," reprinted by permission of Harold Ober Associates Incorporated. Copyright ©1994 by The Estate Of Langston Hughes; "The Negro Speaks of Rivers," reprinted by permission of Harold Ober Associates Incorporated. Copyright ©1994 by The Estate Of Langston Hughes; "Refugee in America," reprinted by permission of Harold Ober Associates Incorporated. Copyright ©1994 by The Estate Of Langston Hughes.

Harper's Magazine. "The Leap," Copyright ©1990 Harper's Magazine. All rights reserved. Reproduced from the March issue by special permission.

HarperCollins Publishers. Pages 33–40 from *Dust Tracks on a Road* by Zora Neale Hurston. Copyright 1942 by Zora Neale Hurston; renewed ©1970 by John C. Hurston. Reprinted by permission of HarperCollins Publishers; "Untying the Knot" from *Pilgrim at Tinker Creek* by Annie Dillard. Copyright ©1974 by Annie Dillard. Reprinted by permission of HarperCollins Publishers.

HarperCollins Publishers Ltd. (UK). "Storyteller," "How to Tell a True War Story" from *The Things They Carried* by Tim O'Brien. Copyright ©1990 by Tim O'Brien. Reprinted by permission of HarperCollins Publishers Ltd.

Harvard Law Review. "Reflections on the Bicentennial of the United States Constitution," republished with permission of *Harvard Law Review*, from Harvard Law Review, 101, November 1987; permission conveyed through Copyright Clearance Center, Inc.

Harvard University Press. "They shut me up in Prose," *The Poems of Emily Dickinson: Reading Edition*, edited by Ralph W. Franklin, Cambridge, Mass.: The Belknap Press of Harvard University Press, Copyright ©1998, 1999 by the President and Fellows of Harvard College. Copyright ©1951, 1955 by the President and Fellows of Harvard College. Copyright © renewed 1979, 1983 by the President and Fellows of Harvard College. Copyright ©1914, 1918, 1919, 1924, 1929, 1930, 1932, 1935, 1937, 1942 by Martha Dickinson Bianchi. Copyright ©1952, 1957, 1958, 1963, 1965 by Mary L. Hampson; "I'm Nobody," *The Poems of Emily Dickinson*, edited by Thomas H. Johnson, Cambridge, Mass.: The Belknap Press of Harvard University Press, Copyright ©1951, 1955 by the President and Fellows of Harvard College. Copyright ©renewed 1979, 1983 by the President and Fellows of Harvard College. Copyright ©1914, 1918, 1919, 1924, 1929, 1930, 1932, 1935, 1937, 1942 by Martha Dickinson Bianchi. Copyright ©1952, 1957, 1958, 1963, 1965 by Mary L. Hampson.

Henry Holt & Co. "A Balance Between Nature and Nurture" by Gloria Steinem. Copyright ©2005 by Gloria Steinem. From the audio book collection THIS I BELIEVE: The Personal Philosophies of Remarkable Men and Women edited by Jay Allison and Dan Gediman. Copyright ©2006 by This I Believe, Inc. Used by permission of Henry Holt and Company, LLC. All rights reserved; "A Balance Between

Credits

Photo locators denoted as follows Top (T), Center (C), Bottom (B), Left (L), Right (R), Background (Bkgd)

Cover ©niroworld/Fotolia, (Bkgd) Brandon Bourdages/ 123RF GB Ltd.

vi (C) David Smart/Shutterstock, (Bkgd) Ja-images/Shutterstock; **viii** Hidesy/Shutterstock; **x** Corbis; **xii** Spaces Images/Blend Images/Getty Images; **xiv** Fred de Noyelle/Godong/Corbis; **xvi** Sergey Nivens/Fotolia; **2** (C) David Smart/Shutterstock, (Bkgd) Ja-images/Shutterstock; **3** (B) Ken Schulze/Shutterstock, (BCL) Fine Art Premium/Corbis, (BCR) Zack Frank/Shutterstock, (BL) Prints & Photographs Division, Library of Congress, LC-USZC4-5315.,(BR) Louis S. Glanzman/National Geographic/Getty Images, (C) DEA/G. Dagli Orti/Getty Images, (CBR) Ramn Cami/EyeEm/Getty Images, (CL) 2/Craig Brewer/Ocean/Corbis, (CR) Jacek Chabraszewski/Shuterstock, (CT) Sergign/Shutterstock, (T) LDDesign/Shutterstock, (TCL) GL Archive/Alamy, (TCR) J. Helgason/Shutterstock, (TL) SuperStock/Glow Images, (TR) Rawpixel/Shutterstock; **6** LDDesign/Shutterstock; **11** (B) Prints & Photographs Division, Library of Congress, LC-USZC4-5315., (BR) Fine Art Premium/Corbis, (C) 2/Craig Brewer/Ocean/Corbis, (T) SuperStock/Glow Images, (TR) GL Archive/ Alamy; **12** (L) World History Archive/Alamy, (R) SuperStock/Glow Images; **13** (C) Lvy Close Images/Alamy, (L) The Gallery Collection/ Corbis, (R) Larryhw/123RF; **14** North Wind Picture Archives/Alamy; **15** (C) People and Politics/Alamy, (L) Bettmann/Corbis, (R) Dbimages/Alamy; **16, 18, 24, 26, 28** GL Archive/Alamy; **17** Painting/Alamy; **21** Susan Law Cain/Shutterstock; **23** Hank Walker/The LIFE Picture Collection/Getty Images; **30** (B) People and Politics/Alamy, (T) Everett Historical/ Shutterstock; **31, 34, 36, 38** 2/Craig Brewer/Ocean/Corbis; **40, 42, 46, 48, 50** Fine Art Premium/Corbis; **41** Akademie/Alamy; **50** Fine Art Premium/Corbis; **53** Prints & Photographs Division, Library of Congress, LC-USZC4-5315.; **54** North Wind Picture Archives/Alamy; **55** Prints and Photographs Division, Library of Congress, cph.3a13536.; **56** (B) Fotosearch/Stringer/Getty,(T) Universal Images Group Limited/Alamy; **57** (BL) Universal Images Group Limited/Alamy, (C) Prints and Photographs Division, Library of Congress, cph.3a13536.; **57** (T) Prints & Photographs Division, Library of Congress, LC-USZC4-5315.; (TL) North Wind Picture Archives/Alamy; **58** Prints & Photographs Division, Library of Congress, LC-USZC4-5315.; **60** LDDesign/Shutterstock; **69** (B) Ken Schulze/ Shutterstock, (C) DEA/G. Dagli Orti/Getty Images, (T) Sergign/ Shutterstock; **72** (BL) Akhil Reed Amar,(TL) Sergign/Shutterstock; **73, 79, 80** Sergign/Shutterstock; **82** (BL) David Shoenfelt, (TL) Sergign/ Shutterstock; **90** Sergign/Shutterstock; **92** World History Archive/Alamy; **93, 98** DEA/G. Dagli Orti/Getty Images; **95** ClassicStock/Alamy; **103, 119** Everett Historical/Shutterstock; **110** Glasshouse Images/Alamy; **118, 120, 122, 124** Ken Schulze/Shutterstock; **129** (T): Rawpixel/ Shutterstock, (TC): J. Helgason/Shutterstock, (B): Louis S. Glanzman/ National Geographic/Getty Images, (BC): Zack Frank/Shutterstock, (C): Jacek Chabraszewski/Shuterstock, (CB): Ramn Cami/EyeEm/Getty Images; **138** Hidesy/Shutterstock; **139** (BC) Nebraska State Historical Society, [Digital ID, e.g., nbhips 12036], (BCR) Babayuka/Shutterstock, (BR) Denis Belitsky/Shutterstock, (C) Mansell/The LIFE Picture Collection/ Getty Images, (BC) Eugene Ivanov/Shutterstock, (B(CL)) Atomic/Alamy, (BCR) adoc-photos/Corbis, (CL) Win Nondakowit/123RF, (CR) Pictorial Press Ltd/Alamy, (TC) Zack Frank/Shutterstock, (T) Everett Historical/ Shutterstock, (TC) Richard Cavalleri/Shutterstock, (CL) Solarseven/ Shutterstock, (TL) Ralf Hettler/Getty Images, (TR) Pogonici/Shutterstock; **142** Everett Historical/Shutterstock; **147** (B) Atomic/Alamy, (BL) Win Nondakowit/123RF, (T) Ralf Hettler/Getty Images, (TL) Solarseven/ Shutterstock; **148** (L) DEA/G. DAGLI ORTI/Getty Images, (R) Bettmann/ Corbis; **149** (L) Bettmann/Corbis, (R) Ralf Hettler/Getty Images; **150** (L) Everett Historical/Shutterstock, (R) De Agostini Picture Library/ Getty Images; **151** Joe_Potato/Getty Images; **152,154,164, 166,168** Solarseven/Shutterstock; **153** History Archives/Alamy; **156** (B) Pictorial Press Ltd/Alamy, (T) Ase/Shutterstock; **160** Strelka/Shutterstock; **161** Sarun T/Shutterstock; **162** Alex Pix/ Shutterstock; **170, 172, 180, 182, 184** Win Nondakowit/123RF; **171** Atomic/Alamy; **173** Victor Tongdee/Shutterstock; **174** Liveshot/ Shutterstock; **176** Poprotskiy Alexey/Shutterstock; **177** Edward Bruns/ Shutterstock; **178** GlebStock/Shutterstock; **186** (TL) Win Nondakowit/123RF, (TR) Atomic/Alamy; **187** Atomic/Alamy; **189** (B)

Atomic/Alamy, (T) Win Nondakowit/123RF; **190** (B) Atomic/Alamy, (T) Win Nondakowit/123RF; **192** Everett Historical/Shutterstock; **201** (B) Solomon D. Butcher/Nebraska State Historical Society, (BR) Eugene Ivanov/Shutterstock, (C) Mansell/The LIFE Picture Collection/Getty Images, (T) Richard Cavalleri/Shutterstock, (TR) Zack Frank/Shutterstock; **204** Everett Historical/Shutterstock; **205 ,201 ,212** Richard Cavalleri/ Shutterstock; **207** W2 Photography/Corbis; **214** Everett Collection/ Alamy; **215, 226, 228** Zack Frank/Shutterstock; **220** Nelson Sirlin/ Shutterstock; **223** Nobeastsofierce/Shutterstock; **231** Mansell/The LIFE Picture Collection/Getty Images; **232** The National Archives Records of the Patent and Trademark Office, 1836–1978; **234** Mansell/The LIFE Picture Collection/Getty Images; **236, 238, 244, 246** Eugene Ivanov/ Shutterstock; **237** Lebrecht Music and Arts Photo Library/Alamy; **248** E.O. Hoppe/Corbis; **249, 258, 260** Solomon D. Butcher/Nebraska State Historical Society; **254** Erich Lessing/Art Resource, New York; **265** (T): Pogonici/Shutterstock, (B): Denis Belitsky/Shutterstock, (BR): Babayuka/ Shutterstock, (C): adoc-photos/Corbis, (TR): Pictorial Press Ltd/Alamy; **274** (C) Corbis, (Bkgd) BBC Worldwide Learning; **275** (B) National Archives/Getty Images, (BC) fstockfoto/Shutterstock, (BCR) Harold M. Lambert/Lambert/Getty Images, (BL) National Photo Company Collection/Library of Congress, (BR) Bettmann/Corbis, (C) Library of Congress Prints and Photographs Division [LC-USZ62-75334], (BC) Heritage Image Partnership Ltd/Alamy, (CBL) Corbis, (CBR) Three Lions/ Getty Images, (CT) GL Archive/Alamy, (CTR) Jack Delano Farm Security Administration/Office of War Information Black-and-White Negatives collection, Prints & Photographs Division, Library of Congress, LC-USF34-040837-D, (T) Hill Street Studios/Getty Images, (TC) Corbis, (TCL) Kutay Tanir/Digital Vision/Getty Images, (TCR) Bettmann/Corbis, (TL) Everett Historical/Shutterstock, (TR) Herber W. Pelton/Corbis; **278** Hill Street Studios/Getty Images; **283** (B) Corbis, (BC) National Photo Company Collection/Library of Congress, (T) Everett Historical/ Shutterstock, (TC) Kutay Tanir/Digital Vision/Getty Images; **284** Everett Historical/Shutterstock; **285** (L) Bob Pardue-SC/Alamy, (R) Randy Raszler/ Fotolia; **286** (C) World History Archive/Alamy, (L, R) Everett Historical/ Shutterstock; **287** (L) Everett Historical/Shutterstock, (R) Jorisvo/ Shutterstock; **288** Library of Congress Prints and Photographs Division [LC-3a18122u]; 289,294,296,298 Kutay Tanir/Digital Vision/Getty Images; **300** Library of Congress Prints and Photographs Division [LC-3a32145u]; **301, 304, 306, 308** National Photo Company Collection/Library of Congress; **311, 312, 314, 316** Corbis; **313** (B) Corbis, (T) Everett Collection/AGE Fotostock; **315** Corbis, (BC) Everett Collection/AGE Fotostock; **327** (B) National Archives/Getty Images, (BC) fstockfoto/Shutterstock, (C) Library of Congress Prints and Photographs Division [LC-USZ62-75334]; **327** (BC) Heritage Image Partnership Ltd/ Alamy, (T) Corbis, (TC) GL Archive/Alamy; **330** Library of Congress Prints and Photographs Division [LC-3c19343u]; **331, 334, 336** Corbis; **338** (CL) Everett Collection Historical/Alamy, (TL) GL Archive/Alamy; **338** (TR) Library of Congress Prints and Photographs Division [LC-USZ62-75334]; **339, 343, 345** GL Archive/Alamy; **346** (CL) Sandra Sleight Brennan; **346, 350** (TL) GL Archive/Alamy; **346** (TR), **347, 349, 350** (CL) Library of Congress Prints and Photographs Division [LC-USZ62-75334]; **352** Missouri History Museum, St. Louis.; **3**53, 356, 358 Heritage Image Partnership Ltd/Alamy; **360** (CL) New York Times Co/Getty Images, (TL) fstockfoto/Shutterstock, (TR) National Archives/Getty Images; **361, 367, 369** fstockfoto/Shutterstock; **370** (CL) Jackie Mader/The Hechinger Report, (TL) fstockfoto/Shutterstock, (TR) National Archives/Getty Images; **379** Young Soldier: Separate Study of a Soldier Giving Water to a Wounded Companion, (detail) 1861, Winslow Homer, Oil, gouache, black crayon on canvas, 36 x 17.5 cm., United States, 1836–1910, Cooper-Hewitt, National Museum of Design; **383** (T) Herber W. Pelton/ Corbis; **383** (B) Bettmann/Corbis; 383 (BC) Harold M. Lambert/Lambert/ Getty Images; **383** (C): Jack Delano Farm Security Administration/Office of War Information Black-and-White Negatives collection, Prints & Photographs Division, Library of Congress, LC-USF34-040837-D, (BC): Three Lions/Getty Images, (TC): Bettmann/Corbis, **392** Spaces Images/ Blend Images/Getty Images; **393** (B) George Burba/123RF, (BC) Marilyn Angel Wynn/Nativestock/Getty Images, (BCL) Pictorial Press Ltd/Alamy, (BCR) Ekaterina Fribus/Fotolia, (BL) Herbert Kratky/123RF, (BR) Anna Baburkina/Shutterstock, (T) Library of Congress, (C) Lake County